PRAISE FOR *THE LINUX PROGRAMMING INTERFACE*

"If I had to choose a single book to sit next to my machine when writing software for Linux, this would be it."
—MARTIN LANDERS, SOFTWARE ENGINEER, GOOGLE

"Michael Kerrisk's new book [is] a thing of beauty. A book you're proud to just have on the shelf, but too useful to stay there."
—SERGE HALLYN, LINUX KERNEL DEVELOPER

"I found *The Linux Programming Interface* to be extremely useful and expect to return to it frequently. Anyone who has an interest in programming for Linux will likely feel the same way."
—JAKE EDGE, LWN.NET

"This book, with its detailed descriptions and examples, contains everything you need to understand the details and nuances of the low-level programming APIs in Linux . . . no matter what the level of reader, there will be something to be learnt from this book."
—MEL GORMAN, AUTHOR OF *Understanding the Linux Virtual Memory Manager*

"Michael's inexhaustible determination to get his information right, and to express it clearly and concisely, has resulted in a strong reference source for programmers. While this work is targeted at Linux programmers, it will be of value to any programmer working in the UNIX/POSIX ecosystem."
—DAVID BUTENHOF, AUTHOR OF *Programming with POSIX Threads* AND CONTRIBUTOR TO THE POSIX AND UNIX STANDARDS

"Simply the best Linux programming book since Steven's Unix programming books."
—CHRIS BARBER, CB1, INC.

"... encyclopedic in the breadth and depth of its coverage, and textbook-like in its wealth of worked examples and exercises. Each topic is clearly and comprehensively covered, from theory to hands-on working code. Professionals, students, educators, this is the Linux/UNIX reference that you have been waiting for."
—ANTHONY ROBINS, ASSOCIATE PROFESSOR OF COMPUTER SCIENCE, THE UNIVERSITY OF OTAGO

"... a very thorough—yet easy to read—explanation of UNIX system and network programming, with an emphasis on Linux systems. It's certainly a book I'd recommend to anybody wanting to get into UNIX programming (in general) or to experienced UNIX programmers wanting to know what's new in the popular GNU/Linux system."
—FERNANDO GONT, NETWORK SECURITY RESEARCHER, IETF PARTICIPANT, AND RFC AUTHOR

"If you think you don't need this book since you know everything already, that's what I thought too, and I was wrong."
—BERT HUBERT, NETHERLABS COMPUTER CONSULTING

'Michael's book is a different kind of beast . . . *everything* relating to the subject that I could reasonably think of is in the book, in a very thorough and maniacally complete yet enjoyably readable way."
—FEDERICO LUCIFREDI, SLASHDOT.ORG

"... an essential resource for the serious or professional Linux and UNIX systems programmer. Michael Kerrisk covers the use of all the key APIs across both the Linux and UNIX system interfaces with clear descriptions and tutorial examples and stresses the importance and benefits of following standards such as the Single UNIX Specification and POSIX 1003.1."
—ANDREW JOSEY, DIRECTOR, STANDARDS, THE OPEN GROUP, AND CHAIR OF THE POSIX 1003.1 WORKING GROUP

"What could be better than an encyclopedic reference to the Linux system, from the standpoint of the system programmer, written by none other than the maintainer of the man pages himself? *The Linux Programming Interface* is comprehensive and detailed. I firmly expect it to become an indispensable addition to my programming bookshelf."
—BILL GALLMEISTER, AUTHOR OF *POSIX.4 Programmer's Guide: Programming for the Real World*

THE LINUX PROGRAMMING INTERFACE

A Linux and UNIX® System Programming Handbook

MICHAEL KERRISK

no starch press

San Francisco

Thirteenth printing

24 23 22 21   13 14 15 16

ISBN-10: 1-59327-220-0
ISBN-13: 978-1-59327-220-3

Publisher: William Pollock
Production Editor: Riley Hoffman
Cover Design: Octopod Studios
Front Cover Photo: Rob Suisted
Back Cover Photo: Lynley Cook
Copyeditor: Marilyn Smith
Compositor: Susan Glinert Stevens
Proofreader: Linda Seifert
For technical reviewers, please refer to the author's acknowledgements

For information on distribution, translations, or bulk sales, please contact No Starch Press, Inc. directly:

No Starch Press, Inc.
245 8th Street, San Francisco, CA 94103
phone: 1.415.863.9900; info@nostarch.com; www.nostarch.com

Library of Congress Cataloging-in-Publication Data

```
Kerrisk, Michael, 1961-
  The Linux programming interface : a Linux and UNIX system programming handbook / by Michael Kerrisk.
      p. cm.
  Includes bibliographical references and index.
  ISBN-13: 978-1-59327-220-3 (hardcover)
  ISBN-10: 1-59327-220-0 (hardcover)
 1.  Linux. 2.  UNIX (Computer file) 3.  Operating systems (Computers)  I. Title.
  QA76.76.063K496 2010
  005.4'32--dc22
                                             2010001947
```

[S]

For Cecilia, who lights up my world.

BRIEF CONTENTS

CONTENTS IN DETAIL

23 TIMERS AND SLEEPING   479

24 PROCESS CREATION   513

25 PROCESS TERMINATION   531

PREFACE

Subject

In this book, I describe the Linux programming interface—the system calls, library functions, and other low-level interfaces provided by Linux, a free implementation of the UNIX operating system. These interfaces are used, directly or indirectly, by every program that runs on Linux. They allow applications to perform tasks such as file I/O, creating and deleting files and directories, creating new processes, executing programs, setting timers, communicating between processes and threads on the same computer, and communicating between processes residing on different computers connected via a network. This set of low-level interfaces is sometimes also known as the *system programming* interface.

Although I focus on Linux, I give careful attention to standards and portability issues, and clearly distinguish the discussion of Linux-specific details from the discussion of features that are common to most UNIX implementations and standardized by POSIX and the Single UNIX Specification. Thus, this book also provides a comprehensive description of the UNIX/POSIX programming interface and can be used by programmers writing applications targeted at other UNIX systems or intended to be portable across multiple systems.

Intended audience

This book is aimed primarily at the following audience:

- programmers and software designers building applications for Linux, other UNIX systems, or other POSIX-conformant systems;
- programmers porting applications between Linux and other UNIX implementations or between Linux and other operating systems;
- instructors and advanced students teaching or learning Linux or UNIX system programming; and
- system managers and "power users" wishing to gain a greater understanding of the Linux/UNIX programming interface and of how various pieces of system software are implemented.

I assume you have some prior programming experience, but no previous system programming experience is required. I also assume you have a reading knowledge of the C programming language, and know how to use the shell and common Linux or UNIX commands. If you are new to Linux or UNIX, you will find it helpful to read the programmer-oriented review of fundamental concepts of Linux and UNIX systems in Chapter 2.

> The standard tutorial reference for C is [Kernighan & Ritchie, 1988]. [Harbison & Steele, 2002] goes into even more detail on C, and includes coverage of changes introduced with the C99 standard. [van der Linden, 1994] is an alternative look at C that is both highly amusing and instructive. [Peek et al., 2001] provides a good, brief introduction to using a UNIX system.
>
> Throughout this book, indented small-font paragraphs like these are used for asides containing rationale, implementation details, background information, historical notes, and other topics that are ancillary to the main text.

Linux and UNIX

This book could have been purely about standard UNIX (that is, POSIX) system programming because most features found on other UNIX implementations are also present on Linux and vice versa. However, while writing portable applications is a worthy goal, it is also important to describe Linux extensions to the standard UNIX programming interface. One reason for this is the popularity of Linux. Another is that the use of nonstandard extensions is sometimes essential, either for performance reasons or to access functionality that is unavailable in the standard UNIX programming interface. (All UNIX implementations provide nonstandard extensions for these reasons.)

Therefore, while I've designed this book to be useful to programmers working with all UNIX implementations, I also provide full coverage of programming features that are specific to Linux. These features include:

- *epoll*, a mechanism for obtaining notification of file I/O events;
- *inotify*, a mechanism for monitoring changes in files and directories;
- capabilities, a mechanism for granting a process a subset of the powers of the superuser;

- extended attributes;
- i-node flags;
- the *clone()* system call;
- the /proc file system; and
- Linux-specific details of the implementation of file I/O, signals, timers, threads, shared libraries, interprocess communication, and sockets.

Usage and organization

You can use this book in at least two ways:

- As a tutorial introduction to the Linux/UNIX programming interface. You can read the book linearly. Later chapters build on material presented in earlier chapters, with forward references minimized as far as possible.
- As a comprehensive reference to the Linux/UNIX programming interface. An extensive index and frequent cross-references allow topics to be read in random order.

I've grouped the chapters of this book into the following parts:

1. *Background and concepts*: history of UNIX, C, and Linux and overview of UNIX standards (Chapter 1); a programmer-oriented introduction to Linux and UNIX concepts (Chapter 2); and fundamental concepts for system programming on Linux and UNIX (Chapter 3).

2. *Fundamental features of the system programming interface*: file I/O (Chapter 4 and Chapter 5); processes (Chapter 6); memory allocation (Chapter 7); users and groups (Chapter 8); process credentials (Chapter 9); time (Chapter 10); system limits and options (Chapter 11); and retrieving system and process information (Chapter 12).

3. *More advanced features of the system programming interface*: file I/O buffering (Chapter 13); file systems (Chapter 14); file attributes (Chapter 15); extended attributes (Chapter 16); access control lists (Chapter 17); directories and links (Chapter 18); monitoring file events (Chapter 19); signals (Chapter 20 to Chapter 22); and timers (Chapter 23).

4. *Processes, programs, and threads*: process creation, process termination, monitoring child processes, and executing programs (Chapter 24 to Chapter 28); and POSIX threads (Chapter 29 to Chapter 33).

5. *Advanced process and program topics*: process groups, sessions, and job control (Chapter 34); process priorities and scheduling (Chapter 35); process resources (Chapter 36); daemons (Chapter 37); writing secure privileged programs (Chapter 38); capabilities (Chapter 39); login accounting (Chapter 40); and shared libraries (Chapter 41 and Chapter 42).

6. *Interprocess communication (IPC)*: IPC overview (Chapter 43); pipes and FIFOs (Chapter 44); System V IPC—message queues, semaphores, and shared memory (Chapter 45 to Chapter 48); memory mappings (Chapter 49); virtual memory operations (Chapter 50); POSIX IPC—message queues, semaphores, and shared memory (Chapter 51 to Chapter 54); and file locking (Chapter 55).

7. *Sockets and network programming*: IPC and network programming with sockets (Chapter 56 to Chapter 61).

8. *Advanced I/O topics*: terminals (Chapter 62); alternative I/O models (Chapter 63); and pseudoterminals (Chapter 64).

Example programs

I illustrate the use of most of the interfaces described in this book with short, complete programs, many of which are designed to allow you to easily experiment from the command line to see just how various system calls and library functions work. Consequently, this book contains a lot of example code—around 15,000 lines of C source code and shell session logs.

Although reading and experimenting with the example programs is a useful starting point, the most effective way to consolidate the concepts discussed in this book is to write code, either modifying the example programs to try out your own ideas or writing new programs.

All of the source code in this book is available for download from the book's web site. The source code distribution also includes many additional programs that don't appear in the book. The purpose and details of these programs are described in comments in the source code. *Makefiles* are provided for building the programs, and an accompanying README file gives further details about the programs.

The source code is freely redistributable and modifiable under the terms of the GNU Affero General Public License (Affero GPL) version 3, a copy of which is provided in the source code distribution.

Exercises

Most chapters conclude with a set of exercises, some of which are suggestions for various experiments using the provided example programs. Other exercises are questions relating to concepts discussed in the chapter, and still others are suggestions for programs you might write in order to consolidate your understanding of the material. You'll find solutions to selected exercises in Appendix F.

Standards and portability

Throughout this book, I've taken special care to consider portability issues. You'll find frequent references to relevant standards, especially the combined POSIX.1-2001 and Single UNIX Specification version 3 (SUSv3) standard. You'll also find details about changes in the recent revision of that standard, the combined POSIX.1-2008 and SUSv4 standard. (Because SUSv3 was a much larger revision, and it is the UNIX standard that is in most widespread effect at the time of writing, discussions of standards in the book are generally framed in terms of SUSv3, with notes on the differences in SUSv4. However, you can assume that, except where noted, statements about specifications in SUSv3 also hold true in SUSv4.)

For features that are not standardized, I indicate the range of differences on other UNIX implementations. I also highlight those major features of Linux that are implementation-specific, as well as minor differences between the implementation of system calls and library functions on Linux and other UNIX implementations. Where a feature is not indicated as being Linux-specific, you can normally assume that it is a standard feature that appears on most or all UNIX implementations.

I've tested most of the example programs presented in this book (other than those that exploit features that are noted as being Linux-specific) on some or all of Solaris, FreeBSD, Mac OS X, Tru64 UNIX, and HP-UX. To improve portability to some of these systems, the web site for this book provides alternative versions of certain example programs with extra code that doesn't appear in the book.

Linux kernel and C library versions

The primary focus of this book is on Linux 2.6.*x*, the kernel version in widest use at the time of writing. Details for Linux 2.4 are also covered, and I've indicated where features differ between Linux 2.4 and 2.6. Where new features appear in the Linux 2.6.*x* series, the exact kernel version number of their appearance (e.g., 2.6.34) is noted.

With respect to the C library, the main focus is on the GNU C library (*glibc*) version 2. Where relevant, differences across *glibc* 2.*x* versions are noted.

As this book was heading to press, Linux kernel version 2.6.35 had just been released, and *glibc* version 2.12 had been recently released. This book is current with respect to both of these software versions. Changes that occur in the Linux and *glibc* interfaces after publication of this book will be noted on the book's web site.

Using the programming interface from other languages

Although the example programs are written in C, you can use the interfaces described in this book from other programming languages—for example, compiled languages such as C++, Pascal, Modula, Ada, FORTRAN, and D, and scripting languages such as Perl, Python, and Ruby. (Java requires a different approach; see, for example, [Rochkind, 2004].) Different techniques will be required to obtain the necessary constant definitions and function declarations (except in the case of C++), and some extra work may be needed to pass function arguments in the manner required by C linkage conventions. Notwithstanding these differences, the essential concepts are the same, and you'll find the information in this book is applicable even if you are working in another programming language.

About the author

I started using UNIX and C in 1987, when I spent several weeks sitting in front of an HP Bobcat workstation with a copy of the first edition of Marc Rochkind's *Advanced UNIX Programming* and what ultimately became a very dog-eared printed copy of the C shell manual page. My approach then was one that I still try to follow today, and that I recommend to anyone approaching a new software technology: take the time to read the documentation (if it exists) and write small (but increasingly large) test programs until you become confident of your understanding of the software. I've found that, in the long run, this kind of self-training more than pays for itself in terms of saved time. Many of the programming examples in this book are constructed in ways that encourage this learning approach.

I've primarily been a software engineer and designer. However, I'm also a passionate teacher, and have spent several years teaching in both academic and commercial environments. I've run many week-long courses teaching UNIX system programming, and that experience informs the writing of this book.

I've been using Linux for about half as long as I've been using UNIX, and, over that time, my interest has increasingly centered on the boundary between the kernel and user space: the Linux programming interface. This interest has drawn me into a number of interrelated activities. I intermittently provide input and bug reports for the POSIX/SUS standard; I carry out tests and design reviews of new user-space interfaces added to the Linux kernel (and have helped find and fix many code and design bugs in those interfaces); I've been a regular speaker at conferences on topics related to interfaces and their documentation; and I've been invited on a number of occasions to the annual Linux Kernel Developers Summit. The common thread tying all of these activities together is my most visible contribution in the Linux world: my work on the *man-pages* project (*http://www.kernel.org/doc/man-pages/*).

The *man-pages* project provides pages in sections 2, 3, 4, 5, and 7 of the Linux manual pages. These are the manual pages describing the programming interfaces provided by the Linux kernel and the GNU C library—the same topic area as this book. I've been involved with *man-pages* for more than a decade. Since 2004, I've been the project maintainer, a task that involves, in roughly equal measure, writing documentation, reading kernel and library source code, and writing programs to verify the details for documentation. (Documenting an interface is a great way to find bugs in that interface.) I've also been the biggest contributor to *man-pages*—of the approximately 900 pages in *man-pages*, I am the author of 140, and the coauthor of another 125. So, even before you picked up this book, it's quite likely you've read some of my published work. I hope that you've found that work useful, and that you'll find this book even more so.

Acknowledgements

Without the support of a good many people, this book would have been far less than it is. It is a great pleasure to thank them.

A large team of technical reviewers around the world read drafts, found errors, pointed out confusing explanations, suggested rewordings and diagrams, tested programs, proposed exercises, identified aspects of the behavior of Linux and other UNIX implementations that I was not aware of, and offered support and encouragement. Many reviewers generously supplied insights and comments that I was able to incorporate into the book, at times making me look more knowledgeable than I am. Any mistakes that remain are, of course, my own.

Thanks especially to the following reviewers (listed alphabetically by surname), who either commented on large sections of the manuscript, commented extensively on smaller sections of the manuscript, or (magnificently) commented extensively on large sections of the manuscript:

- Christophe Blaess is a consulting software engineer and professional trainer who specializes in industrial (realtime and embedded) applications of Linux. Christophe is the author of *Programmation système en C sous Linux*, a fine French book covering many of the same topics as this book. He generously read and commented on many chapters of my book.

- David Butenhof (Hewlett-Packard) was a member of the original working group for POSIX threads and for the Single UNIX Specification threads extensions, and is the author of *Programming with POSIX Threads*. He wrote the original DCE Threads reference implementation for the Open Software Foundation, and was lead architect of the threads implementation for OpenVMS and Digital UNIX. David reviewed the threads chapters, suggested many improvements, and patiently corrected several details of my understanding of the POSIX threads API.

- Geoff Clare works at The Open Group on their UNIX conformance test suites, has been involved with UNIX standardization for more than 20 years, and is one of half a dozen key participants in the Austin Group, which develops the joint standard that forms POSIX.1 and the base volumes of the Single UNIX Specification. Geoff provided detailed review of parts of the manuscript related to standard UNIX interfaces, patiently and politely suggested numerous fixes and improvements, spotted many obscure bugs, and provided much assistance in focusing on the importance of standards for portable programming.

- Loïc Domaigné (then at German Air Traffic Control) is a software systems engineer working on the design and development of distributed, concurrent, and fault-tolerant embedded systems with hard realtime requirements. He provided review input for the threads specification in SUSv3, and is an enthusiastic educator and knowledgeable contributor in various online technical forums. Loïc carried out a detailed review of the threads chapters, as well as many other parts of the book. He also implemented a number of clever programs to verify details of the Linux threads implementation, provided a great deal of enthusiasm and encouragement, and proposed numerous ideas to improve the overall presentation of the material.

- Gert Döring programmed *mgetty* and *sendfax*, a pair of programs that together are one of the most widely used open source fax packages for UNIX and Linux. These days, he works mainly on building and operating large IPv4-based and IPv6-based networks, a task that includes working with colleagues across Europe to define the operational policies that ensure the smooth operation of the infrastructure of the Internet. Gert provided extensive and useful feedback on the chapters covering terminals, login accounting, process groups, sessions, and job control.

- Wolfram Gloger is an IT consultant who has worked on a range of Free and Open Source Software (FOSS) projects in the past decade and a half. Among other things, Wolfram is the implementer of the *malloc* package used in the GNU C library. Currently, he works on web services development, with a particular focus on E-learning, although he still does occasional work on the kernel and system libraries. Wolfram reviewed a number of chapters, especially helping with my discussion of memory-related topics.

- Fernando Gont is a member of the Centro de Estudios de Informática (CEDI) at the Universidad Tecnológica Nacional, Argentina. He focuses on Internet engineering, with active participation in the Internet Engineering Task Force (IETF), where he has authored a number of *Request for Comments* (RFC) documents. Fernando also works on security assessment of communications protocols for the UK Centre for the Protection of National Infrastructure (CPNI), and has produced the first thorough security assessment of the TCP and IP protocols. Fernando provided a very thorough review of the network programming chapters, explained many details of TCP/IP, and suggested a multitude of improvements to the material.

- Andreas Grünbacher (SUSE Labs) is a kernel hacker and author of the Linux implementation of extended attributes and POSIX access control lists. Andreas provided thorough review of many chapters, much encouragement, and the single comment that probably most changed the structure of the book.

- Christoph Hellwig is a Linux storage and file-systems consultant and a well-known kernel hacker who has worked on many parts of the Linux kernel. Christoph kindly took time out from writing and reviewing Linux kernel patches to review several chapters of this book, suggesting many useful corrections and improvements.

- Andreas Jaeger led the development of the Linux port to the x86-64 architecture. As a GNU C Library developer, he ported the library to x86-64, and helped make the library standards-conformant in several areas, especially in the math library. He is currently Program Manager for openSUSE at Novell. Andreas reviewed far more chapters than I could possibly have hoped, suggested a multitude of improvements, and warmly encouraged the ongoing work on the book.

- Rick Jones, also known as "Mr. Netperf" (Networked Systems Performance Curmudgeon at Hewlett-Packard), provided valuable review of the network programming chapters.

- Andi Kleen (then at SUSE Labs) is a well-known and long-term kernel hacker who has worked on many and diverse areas of the Linux kernel, including networking, error handling, scalability, and low-level architecture code. Andi did an extensive review of the material on network programming, expanded my knowledge of many details of the Linux TCP/IP implementation, and suggested many ways to improve my presentation of the subject.

- Martin Landers (Google) was still a student when I had the good fortune to meet him as a colleague. Since then, he has managed to pack rather a lot into a short time, having worked variously as software architect, IT trainer, and professional hacker. I was fortunate indeed to have Martin as a reviewer. He contributed numerous incisive comments and corrections that greatly improved many chapters of the book.

- Jamie Lokier is a well-known kernel hacker who has been contributing to Linux development for 15 years. He nowadays describes himself as "a consultant in solving difficult problems that often have embedded Linux somewhere." Jamie provided an extraordinarily thorough review of the chapters on memory mappings, POSIX shared memory, and virtual memory operations. His comments corrected many details of my understanding of these topics and greatly improved the structure of the chapters.

- Barry Margolin has been a system programmer, system administrator, and support engineer throughout his 25-year career. He is currently a Senior Performance Engineer at Akamai Technologies. He is a frequent, well-respected contributor in various online forums discussing UNIX and Internet topics, and has reviewed a number of books on these topics. Barry reviewed a number of chapters of this book, suggesting many improvements.

- Paul Pluzhnikov (Google) was formerly the technical lead and a key developer of the *Insure++* memory-debugging tool. He is also a sometime *gdb* hacker, and a frequent responder in online forums answering questions on debugging, memory allocation, shared libraries, and run-time environments. Paul reviewed a wide range of chapters, suggesting many valuable improvements.

- John Reiser (with Tom London) carried out one of the earliest ports of UNIX to a 32-bit architecture: the VAX-11/780. He is also the creator of the *mmap()* system call. John reviewed many chapters (including, obviously, the chapter on *mmap()*), providing a multitude of historical insights and crystal-clear technical explanations that greatly improved the chapters.

- Anthony Robins (Associate Professor of Computer Science, University of Otago, New Zealand), a close friend of more than three decades, was the first reader of the drafts of several chapters, and offered valuable early comments and ongoing encouragement as the project evolved.

- Michael Schröder (Novell) is one of the main authors of the GNU *screen* program, a task that has imbued him with a thorough knowledge of the subtleties and differences in terminal-driver implementations. Michael reviewed the chapters covering terminals and pseudoterminals, and the chapter on process groups, sessions, and job control, providing much useful feedback.

- Manfred Spraul, who worked on the IPC code (among other things) in the Linux kernel, generously reviewed several of the chapters on IPC and suggested many improvements.

- Tom Swigg, a former UNIX training colleague at Digital, was an early reviewer who supplied important feedback on several chapters. A software engineer and IT trainer for more than 25 years, Tom currently works at London South Bank University, programming and supporting Linux in a VMware environment.

- Jens Thoms Törring is part of a fine tradition of physicists turned programmers, and has produced a variety of open source device drivers and other software. Jens read a surprisingly diverse collection of chapters, providing unique and valuable insight on how each could be improved.

Many other technical reviewers also read various parts of the book and made valuable comments. In alphabetical order by surname, thank you to George Anzinger (MontaVista Software), Stefan Becher, Krzysztof Benedyczak, Daniel Brahneborg, Andries Brouwer, Annabel Church, Dragan Cvetkovic, Floyd L. Davidson, Stuart Davidson (Hewlett-Packard Consulting), Kasper Dupont, Peter Fellinger (jambit GmbH), Mel Gorman (IBM), Niels Göllesch, Claus Gratzl, Serge Hallyn (IBM), Markus Hartinger (jambit GmbH), Richard Henderson (Red Hat), Andrew Josey (The Open Group), Dan Kegel (Google), Davide Libenzi, Robert Love (Google), H.J. Lu (Intel Corporation), Paul Marshall, Chris Mason, Michael Matz (SUSE), Trond Myklebust, James Peach, Mark Phillips (Automated Test Systems), Nick Piggin (SUSE Labs, Novell), Kay Johannes Potthoff, Florian Rampp, Stephen Rothwell (Linux Technology Centre, IBM), Markus Schwaiger, Stephen Tweedie (Red Hat), Britta Vargas, Chris Wright, Michal Wronski, and Umberto Zamuner.

Aside from technical review, I received many other kinds of help from various people and organizations.

Thanks to the following people for answering technical questions: Jan Kara, Dave Kleikamp, and Jon Snader. Thanks to Claus Gratzl and Paul Marshall for system management assistance.

Thanks to the Linux Foundation (LF), which, during 2008, funded me as a Fellow to work full time on the *man-pages* project and on testing and design review of the Linux programming interface. Although the Fellowship provided no direct financial support for working on this book, it did keep me and my family fed, and the ability to focus full time on documenting and testing the Linux programming interface was a boon to my "private" project. At a more individual level, thanks to Jim Zemlin for being my "interface" while working at the LF, and to the members of the LF Technical Advisory Board, who supported my application for the Fellowship.

Thanks to Alejandro Forero Cuervo for suggesting the title of the book!

More than 25 years ago, Robert Biddle intrigued me during my first degree with tales of UNIX, C, and Ratfor; thank you. Thanks to the following people, who, although not directly connected with this project, encouraged me on the path of writing during my second degree at the University of Canterbury, New Zealand: Michael Howard, Jonathan Mane-Wheoki, Ken Strongman, Garth Fletcher, Jim Pollard, and Brian Haig.

The late Richard Stevens wrote several superb books on UNIX programming and TCP/IP, which I, like a multitude of programmers, have found to be a wonderful source of technical information over the years. Readers of those books will note several visual aspects that are similar between my book and those of Richard Stevens. This is no accident. As I considered how to design my book, and looked around more generally at book designs, time and again, the approach employed by Richard Stevens seemed the best solution, and where this was so, I have employed the same visual approach.

Thanks to the following people and organizations for providing UNIX systems that enabled me to run test programs and verify details on other UNIX implementations: Anthony Robins and Cathy Chandra, for test systems at the University of Otago, New Zealand; Martin Landers, Ralf Ebner, and Klaus Tilk, for test systems at the Technische Universität in Munich, Germany; Hewlett-Packard, for making their *testdrive* systems freely available on the Internet; and Paul de Weerd for providing OpenBSD access.

Heartfelt thanks to two Munich companies, and their owners, who, in addition to providing me with flexible employment and enjoyable colleagues, were extraordinarily generous in allowing me to use their offices while writing this book. Thanks to Thomas Kahabka and Thomas Gmelch of exolution GmbH, and, especially, to Peter Fellinger and Markus Hartinger of jambit GmbH.

Thanks for various kinds of help to the following people: Dan Randow, Karen Korrel, Claudio Scalmazzi, Michael Schüpbach, and Liz Wright. Thanks to Rob Suisted and Lynley Cook for the photographs used on the front and back covers.

Thanks to the following people who encouraged and supported me in various ways on this project: Deborah Church, Doris Church, and Annie Currie.

Thanks to the team at No Starch Press for all sorts of help on an enormous project. Thanks to Bill Pollock for being straight-talking from the start, having rock-solid faith in the project, and patiently keeping an eye on the project. Thanks to my initial production editor, Megan Dunchak. Thanks to my copyeditor, Marilyn Smith, who, despite my best efforts at clarity and consistency, still found many things to fix. Riley Hoffman had overall responsibility for layout and design of the book, and also took up the reins as production editor as we came into the home straight. Riley graciously bore with my many requests to achieve the right layout and produced a superb final result. Thank you.

I now know the truth of the cliché that a writer's family also pays the price of the writer's work. Thanks to Britta and Cecilia for their support, and for putting up with the many hours that I had to be away from family as I finished the book.

Permissions

The Institute of Electrical and Electronics Engineers and The Open Group have kindly given permission to quote portions of text from IEEE Std 1003.1, 2004 Edition, Standard for Information Technology—Portable Operating System Interface (POSIX), The Open Group Base Specifications Issue 6. The complete standard can be consulted online at *http://www.unix.org/version3/online.html*.

Web site and source code of example programs

You can find further information about this book, including errata and source code for the example programs, at *http://man7.org/tlpi/*.

Training courses

I teach courses on system programming, based on the content of this book, as well as a number of other related topics, including network programming. For details, see *http://man7.org/training/*.

Feedback

I welcome bug reports, suggestions for code improvements, and fixes to further improve code portability. Book bugs and general suggestions about how the explanations in the book can be improved are also welcome. (A current list of errata can be found at *http://man7.org/tlpi/errata/*.) Since changes in the Linux programming interface are varied and sometimes too frequent for one person to keep up with, I would be happy to receive suggestions about new and changed features that should be covered in a future edition of this book.

Michael Timothy Kerrisk
Munich, Germany and Christchurch, New Zealand
August 2010

mtk@man7.org

1

HISTORY AND STANDARDS

Linux is a member of the UNIX family of operating systems. In computing terms, UNIX has a long history. The first part of this chapter provides a brief outline of that history. We begin with a description of the origins of the UNIX system and the C programming language, and then consider the two key currents that led to the Linux system as it exists today: the GNU project and the development of the Linux kernel.

One of the notable features of the UNIX system is that its development was not controlled by a single vendor or organization. Rather, many groups, both commercial and noncommercial, contributed to its evolution. This history resulted in many innovative features being added to UNIX, but also had the negative consequence that UNIX implementations diverged over time, so that writing applications that worked on all UNIX implementations became increasingly difficult. This led to a drive for standardization of UNIX implementations, which we discuss in the second part of this chapter.

> Two definitions of the term UNIX are in common use. One of these denotes operating systems that have passed the official conformance tests for the Single UNIX Specification and thus are officially granted the right to be branded as "UNIX" by The Open Group (the holders of the UNIX trademark). At the time of writing, none of the free UNIX implementations (e.g., Linux and FreeBSD) has obtained this branding.

The other common meaning attached to the term UNIX denotes those systems that look and behave like classical UNIX systems (i.e., the original Bell Laboratories UNIX and its later principal offshoots, System V and BSD). By this definition, Linux is generally considered to be a UNIX system (as are the modern BSDs). Although we give close attention to the Single UNIX Specification in this book, we'll follow this second definition of UNIX, so that we'll often say things such as "Linux, like other UNIX implementations. . . ."

1.1 A Brief History of UNIX and C

The first UNIX implementation was developed in 1969 (the same year that Linus Torvalds was born) by Ken Thompson at Bell Laboratories, a division of the telephone corporation, AT&T. It was written in assembler for a Digital PDP-7 minicomputer. The name UNIX was a pun on MULTICS (*Multiplexed Information and Computing Service*), the name of an earlier operating system project in which AT&T collaborated with Massachusetts Institute of Technology (MIT) and General Electric. (AT&T had by this time withdrawn from the project in frustration at its initial failure to develop an economically useful system.) Thompson drew several ideas for his new operating system from MULTICS, including a tree-structured file system, a separate program for interpreting commands (the shell), and the notion of files as unstructured streams of bytes.

In 1970, UNIX was rewritten in assembly language for a newly acquired Digital PDP-11 minicomputer, then a new and powerful machine. Vestiges of this PDP-11 heritage can be found in various names still used on most UNIX implementations, including Linux.

A short time later, Dennis Ritchie, one of Thompson's colleagues at Bell Laboratories and an early collaborator on UNIX, designed and implemented the C programming language. This was an evolutionary process; C followed an earlier interpreted language, B. B was initially implemented by Thompson and drew many of its ideas from a still earlier programming language named BCPL. By 1973, C had matured to a point where the UNIX kernel could be almost entirely rewritten in the new language. UNIX thus became one of the earliest operating systems to be written in a high-level language, a fact that made subsequent porting to other hardware architectures possible.

The genesis of C explains why it, and its descendant C++, have come to be used so widely as system programming languages today. Previous widely used languages were designed with other purposes in mind: FORTRAN for mathematical tasks performed by engineers and scientists; COBOL for commercial systems processing streams of record-oriented data. C filled a hitherto empty niche, and unlike FORTRAN and COBOL (which were designed by large committees), the design of C arose from the ideas and needs of a few individuals working toward a single goal: developing a high-level language for implementing the UNIX kernel and associated software. Like the UNIX operating system itself, C was designed by professional programmers for their own use. The resulting language was small, efficient, powerful, terse, modular, pragmatic, and coherent in its design.

UNIX First through Sixth editions

Between 1969 and 1979, UNIX went through a number of releases, known as *editions*. Essentially, these releases were snapshots of the evolving development version at AT&T. [Salus, 1994] notes the following dates for the first six editions of UNIX:

- First Edition, November 1971: By this time, UNIX was running on the PDP-11 and already had a FORTRAN compiler and versions of many programs still used today, including *ar, cat, chmod, chown, cp, dc, ed, find, ln, ls, mail, mkdir, mv, rm, sh, su*, and *who*.

- Second Edition, June 1972: By this time, UNIX was installed on ten machines within AT&T.

- Third Edition, February 1973: This edition included a C compiler and the first implementation of pipes.

- Fourth Edition, November 1973: This was the first version to be almost totally written in C.

- Fifth Edition, June 1974: By this time, UNIX was installed on more than 50 systems.

- Sixth Edition, May 1975: This was the first edition to be widely used outside AT&T.

Over the period of these releases, the use and reputation of UNIX began to spread, first within AT&T, and then beyond. An important contribution to this growing awareness was the publication of a paper on UNIX in the widely read journal *Communications of the ACM* ([Ritchie & Thompson, 1974]).

At this time, AT&T held a government-sanctioned monopoly on the US telephone system. The terms of AT&T's agreement with the US government prevented it from selling software, which meant that it could not sell UNIX as a product. Instead, beginning in 1974 with Fifth Edition, and especially with Sixth Edition, AT&T licensed UNIX for use in universities for a nominal distribution fee. The university distributions included documentation and the kernel source code (about 10,000 lines at the time).

AT&T's release of UNIX into universities greatly contributed to the popularity and use of the operating system, and by 1977, UNIX was running at some 500 sites, including 125 universities in the United States and several other countries. UNIX offered universities an interactive multiuser operating system that was cheap yet powerful, at a time when commercial operating systems were very expensive. It also gave university computer science departments the source code of a real operating system, which they could modify and offer to their students to learn from and experiment with. Some of these students, armed with UNIX knowledge, became UNIX evangelists. Others went on to found or join the multitude of startup companies selling inexpensive computer workstations running the easily ported UNIX operating system.

The birth of BSD and System V

January 1979 saw the release of Seventh Edition UNIX, which improved the reliability of the system and provided an enhanced file system. This release also contained a number of new tools, including *awk, make, sed, tar, uucp*, the Bourne shell, and a FORTRAN 77 compiler. The release of Seventh Edition is also significant because, from this point, UNIX diverged into two important variants: BSD and System V, whose origins we now briefly describe.

Thompson spent the 1975/1976 academic year as a visiting professor at the University of California at Berkeley, the university from which had graduated. There, he worked with several graduate students, adding many new features to UNIX. (One of these students, Bill Joy, subsequently went on to cofound Sun Microsystems, an early entry in the UNIX workstation market.) Over time, many new tools and features were developed at Berkeley, including the *C shell*, the *vi* editor, an improved file system (the *Berkeley Fast File System*), *sendmail*, a Pascal compiler, and virtual memory management on the new Digital VAX architecture.

Under the name Berkeley Software Distribution (BSD), this version of UNIX, including its source code, came to be widely distributed. The first full distribution was 3BSD in December 1979. (Earlier releases from Berkeley—BSD and 2BSD— were distributions of new tools produced at Berkeley, rather than complete UNIX distributions.)

In 1983, the *Computer Systems Research Group* at the University of California at Berkeley released 4.2BSD. This release was significant because it contained a complete TCP/IP implementation, including the sockets application programming interface (API) and a variety of networking tools. 4.2BSD and its predecessor 4.1BSD became widely distributed within universities around the world. They also formed the basis for SunOS (first released in 1983), the UNIX variant sold by Sun. Other significant BSD releases were 4.3BSD, in 1986, and the final release, 4.4BSD, in 1993.

> The very first ports of the UNIX system to hardware other than the PDP-11 occurred during 1977 and 1978, when Dennis Ritchie and Steve Johnson ported it to the Interdata 8/32 and Richard Miller at the University of Wollongong in Australia simultaneously ported it to the Interdata 7/32. The Berkeley Digital VAX port was based on an earlier (1978) port by John Reiser and Tom London. Known as 32V, this port was essentially the same as Seventh Edition for the PDP-11, except for the larger address space and wider data types.

In the meantime, US antitrust legislation forced the breakup of AT&T (legal maneuvers began in the mid-1970s, and the breakup became effective in 1982), with the consequence that, since it no longer held a monopoly on the telephone system, the company was permitted to market UNIX. This resulted in the release of System III (three) in 1981. System III was produced by AT&T's UNIX Support Group (USG), which employed many hundreds of developers to enhance UNIX and develop UNIX applications (notably, document preparation packages and software development tools). The first release of System V (five) followed in 1983, and a series of releases led to the definitive System V Release 4 (SVR4) in 1989, by which time System V had incorporated many features from BSD, including networking facilities. System V was licensed to a variety of commercial vendors, who used it as the basis of their UNIX implementations.

Thus, in addition to the various BSD distributions spreading through academia, by the late 1980s, UNIX was available in a range of commercial implementations on various hardware. These implementations included Sun's SunOS and later Solaris, Digital's Ultrix and OSF/1 (nowadays, after a series of renamings and acquisitions, HP Tru64 UNIX), IBM's AIX, Hewlett-Packard's (HP's) HP-UX, NeXT's NeXTStep, A/UX for the Apple Macintosh, and Microsoft and SCO's XENIX for the Intel x86-32 architecture. (Throughout this book, the Linux implementation for x86-32 is referred to as Linux/x86-32.) This situation was in sharp contrast to the typical proprietary hardware/operating system scenarios of the time, where each vendor produced one, or at most a few, proprietary computer chip architectures, on which they sold their own proprietary operating system(s). The proprietary nature of most vendor systems meant that purchasers were locked into one vendor. Switching to another proprietary operating system and hardware platform could become very expensive because of the need to port existing applications and retrain staff. This factor, coupled with the appearance of cheap single-user UNIX workstations from a variety of vendors, made the portable UNIX system increasingly attractive from a commercial perspective.

1.2   A Brief History of Linux

The term *Linux* is commonly used to refer to the entire UNIX-like operating system of which the Linux kernel forms a part. However, this is something of a misnomer, since many of the key components contained within a typical commercial Linux distribution actually originate from a project that predates the inception of Linux by several years.

1.2.1   The GNU Project

In 1984, Richard Stallman, an exceptionally talented programmer who had been working at MIT, set to work on creating a "free" UNIX implementation. Stallman's outlook was a moral one, and *free* was defined in a legal sense, rather than a financial sense (see *http://www.gnu.org/philosophy/free-sw.html*). Nevertheless, the legal freedom that Stallman described carried with it the implicit consequence that software such as operating systems would be available at no or very low cost.

Stallman militated against the legal restrictions placed on proprietary operating systems by computer vendors. These restrictions meant that purchasers of computer software in general could not see the source code of the software they were buying, and they certainly could not copy, change, or redistribute it. He pointed out that such a framework encouraged programmers to compete with each other and hoard their work, rather than to cooperate and share it.

In response, Stallman started the GNU project (a recursively defined acronym for "GNU's not UNIX") to develop an entire, freely available, UNIX-like system, consisting of a kernel and all associated software packages, and encouraged others to join him. In 1985, Stallman founded the Free Software Foundation (FSF), a non-profit organization to support the GNU project as well as the development of free software in general.

> When the GNU project was started, BSD was not free in the sense that Stallman meant. Use of BSD still required a license from AT&T, and users could not freely modify and redistribute the AT&T code that formed part of BSD.

One of the important results of the GNU project was the development of the GNU *General Public License* (GPL), the legal embodiment of Stallman's notion of free software. Much of the software in a Linux distribution, including the kernel, is licensed under the GPL or one of a number of similar licenses. Software licensed under the GPL must be made available in source code form, and must be freely redistributable under the terms of the GPL. Modifications to GPL-licensed software are freely permitted, but any distribution of such modified software must also be under the terms of the GPL. If the modified software is distributed in executable form, the author must also allow any recipients the option of obtaining the modified source for no more than the cost of distribution. The first version of the GPL was released in 1989. The current version of the license, version 3, was released in 2007. Version 2 of the license, released in 1991, remains in wide use, and is the license used for the Linux kernel. (Discussions of various free software licenses can be found in [St. Laurent, 2004] and [Rosen, 2005].)

The GNU project did not initially produce a working UNIX kernel, but did produce a wide range of other programs. Since these programs were designed to run on a UNIX-like operating system, they could be, and were, used on existing UNIX implementations and, in some cases, even ported to other operating systems. Among the more well-known programs produced by the GNU project are the *Emacs* text editor, *GCC* (originally the GNU C compiler, but now renamed the GNU compiler collection, comprising compilers for C, C++, and other languages), the *bash* shell, and *glibc* (the GNU C library).

By the early 1990s, the GNU project had produced a system that was virtually complete, except for one important component: a working UNIX kernel. The GNU project had started work on an ambitious kernel design, known as the GNU/HURD, based on the Mach microkernel. However, the HURD was far from being in a form that could be released. (At the time of writing, work continues on the HURD, which currently runs only on the x86-32 architecture.)

> Because a significant part of the program code that constitutes what is commonly known as the Linux system actually derives from the GNU project, Stallman prefers to use the term *GNU/Linux* to refer to the entire system. The question of naming (Linux versus GNU/Linux) is the source of some debate in the free software community. Since this book is primarily concerned with the API of the Linux kernel, we'll generally use the term *Linux*.

The stage was set. All that was required was a working kernel to go with the otherwise complete UNIX system already produced by the GNU project.

1.2.2 The Linux Kernel

In 1991, Linus Torvalds, a Finnish student at the University of Helsinki, was inspired to write an operating system for his Intel 80386 PC. In the course of his studies, Torvalds had come into contact with Minix, a small UNIX-like operating system kernel developed in the mid-1980s by Andrew Tanenbaum, a university professor in Holland. Tanenbaum made Minix, complete with source code, available as a tool for teaching operating system design in university courses. The Minix kernel could be built and run on a 386 system. However, since its primary purpose was as a teaching tool, it was designed to be largely independent of the hardware architecture, and it did not take full advantage of the 386 processor's capabilities.

Torvalds therefore started on a project to create an efficient, full-featured UNIX kernel to run on the 386. Over a few months, Torvalds developed a basic kernel that allowed him to compile and run various GNU programs. Then, on October 5, 1991, Torvalds requested the help of other programmers, making the following now much-quoted announcement of version 0.02 of his kernel in the *comp.os.minix* Usenet newsgroup:

> Do you pine for the nice days of Minix-1.1, when men were men and wrote their own device drivers? Are you without a nice project and just dying to cut your teeth on a OS you can try to modify for your needs? Are you finding it frustrating when everything works on Minix? No more all-nighters to get a nifty program working? Then this post might be just for you. As I mentioned a month ago, I'm working on a free version of a Minix-look-alike for AT-386 computers. It has finally reached the stage where it's even usable (though may not be depending on what you want), and I am willing to put out the sources for wider distribution. It is just version 0.02 . . . but I've successfully run bash, gcc, gnu-make, gnu-sed, compress, etc. under it.

Following a time-honored tradition of giving UNIX clones names ending with the letter *X*, the kernel was (eventually) baptized Linux. Initially, Linux was placed under a more restrictive license, but Torvalds soon made it available under the GNU GPL.

The call for support proved effective. Other programmers joined Torvalds in the development of Linux, adding various features, such as an improved file system, networking support, device drivers, and multiprocessor support. By March 1994, the developers were able to release version 1.0. Linux 1.2 appeared in March 1995, Linux 2.0 in June 1996, Linux 2.2 in January 1999, and Linux 2.4 in January 2001. Work on the 2.5 development kernel began in November 2001, and led to the release of Linux 2.6 in December 2003.

An aside: the BSDs

It is worth noting that another free UNIX was already available for the x86-32 during the early 1990s. Bill and Lynne Jolitz had developed a port of the already mature BSD system for the x86-32, known as 386/BSD. This port was based on the BSD Net/2 release (June 1991), a version of the 4.3BSD source code in which all remaining proprietary AT&T source code had either been replaced or, in the case of six source code files that could not be trivially rewritten, removed. The Jolitzes ported the Net/2 code to x86-32, rewrote the missing source files, and made the first release (version 0.0) of 386/BSD in February 1992.

After an initial wave of success and popularity, work on 386/BSD lagged for various reasons. In the face of an increasingly large backlog of patches, two alternative development groups soon appeared, creating their own releases based on 386/BSD: NetBSD, which emphasizes portability to a wide range of hardware platforms, and FreeBSD, which emphasizes performance and is the most widespread of the modern BSDs. The first NetBSD release was 0.8, in April 1993. The first FreeBSD CD-ROM (version 1.0) appeared in December 1993. Another BSD, OpenBSD, appeared in 1996 (as an initial version numbered 2.0) after forking from the NetBSD project. OpenBSD emphasizes security. In mid-2003, a new BSD,

DragonFly BSD, appeared after a split from FreeBSD 4.*x*. DragonFly BSD takes a different approach from FreeBSD 5.*x* with respect to design for symmetric multi-processing (SMP) architectures.

Probably no discussion of the BSDs in the early 1990s is complete without mention of the lawsuits between UNIX System Laboratories (USL, the AT&T subsidiary spun off to develop and market UNIX) and Berkeley. In early 1992, the company Berkeley Software Design, Incorporated (BSDi, nowadays part of Wind River) began distributing a commercially supported BSD UNIX, BSD/OS, based on the Net/2 release and the Jolitzes' 386/BSD additions. BSDi distributed binaries and source code for $995 (US dollars), and advised potential customers to use their telephone number 1-800-ITS-UNIX.

In April 1992, USL filed suit against BSDi in an attempt to prevent BSDi from selling a product that USL claimed was still encumbered by proprietary USL source code and trade secrets. USL also demanded that BSDi cease using the deceptive telephone number. The suit was eventually widened to include a claim against the University of California. The court ultimately dismissed all but two of USL's claims, and a countersuit by the University of California against USL ensued, in which the university claimed that USL had not given due credit for the use of BSD code in System V.

While these suits were pending, USL was acquired by Novell, whose CEO, the late Ray Noorda, stated publicly that he would prefer to compete in the market-place rather than in the court. Settlement was finally reached in January 1994, with the University of California being required to remove 3 of the 18,000 files in the Net/2 release, make some minor changes to a few other files, and add USL copy-right notices to around 70 other files, which the university nevertheless could continue to distribute freely. This modified system was released as 4.4BSD-Lite in June 1994. (The last release from the university was 4.4BSD-Lite, Release 2 in June 1995.) At this point, the terms of the legal settlement required BSDi, FreeBSD, and NetBSD to replace their Net/2 base with the modified 4.4BSD-Lite source code. As [McKusick et al., 1996] notes, although this caused some delay in the development of the BSD derivatives, it also had the positive effect that these systems resynchronized with the three years of development work done by the uni-versity's Computer Systems Research Group since the release of Net/2.

Linux kernel version numbers

Like most free software projects, Linux follows a release-early, release-often model, so that new kernel revisions appear frequently (sometimes even daily). As the Linux user base increased, the release model was adapted to decrease disruption to existing users. Specifically, following the release of Linux 1.0, the kernel developers adopted a kernel version numbering scheme with each release numbered *x.y.z*: *x* representing a major version, *y* a minor version within that major version, and *z* a revision of the minor version (minor improvements and bug fixes).

Under this model, two kernel versions were always under development: a *stable* branch for use on production systems, which had an even minor version number, and a more volatile *development* branch, which carried the next higher odd minor version number. The theory—not always followed strictly in practice—was that all new features should be added in the current development kernel series, while new revisions in the stable kernel series should be restricted to minor improvements and bug fixes. When the current development branch was deemed suitable for release, it became the new stable branch and was assigned an even minor version number. For example, the 2.3.z development kernel branch resulted in the 2.4 stable kernel branch.

Following the 2.6 kernel release, the development model was changed. The main motivation for this change arose from problems and frustrations caused by the long intervals between stable kernel releases. (Nearly three years passed between the release of Linux 2.4.0 and 2.6.0.) There have periodically been discussions about fine-tuning this model, but the essential details have remained as follows:

- There is no longer a separation between stable and development kernels. Each new 2.6.z release can contain new features, and goes through a life cycle that begins with the addition of new features, which are then stabilized over the course of a number of candidate release versions. When a candidate version is deemed sufficiently stable, it is released as kernel 2.6.z. Release cycles are typically about three months long.

- Sometimes, a stable 2.6.z release may require minor patches to fix bugs or security problems. If these fixes have a sufficiently high priority, and the patches are deemed simple enough to be "obviously" correct, then, rather than waiting for the next 2.6.z release, they are applied to create a release with a number of the form 2.6.z.r, where r is a sequential number for a minor revision of this 2.6.z kernel.

- Additional responsibility is shifted onto distribution vendors to ensure the stability of the kernel provided with a distribution.

Later chapters will sometimes note the kernel version in which a particular API change (i.e., new or modified system call) occurred. Although, prior to the 2.6.z series, most kernel changes occurred in the odd-numbered development branches, we'll generally refer to the following stable kernel version in which the change appeared, since most application developers would normally be using a stable kernel, rather than one of the development kernels. In many cases, the manual pages note the precise development kernel in which a particular feature appeared or changed.

For changes that appear in the 2.6.z kernel series, we note the precise kernel version. When we say that a feature is new in kernel 2.6, without a z revision number, we mean a feature that was implemented in the 2.5 development kernel series and first appeared in the stable kernel at version 2.6.0.

> At the time of writing, the 2.4 stable Linux kernel is still supported by maintainers who incorporate essential patches and bug fixes, and periodically release new revisions. This allows installed systems to continue to use 2.4 kernels, rather than being forced to upgrade to a new kernel series (which may entail significant work in some cases).

Ports to other hardware architectures

During the initial development of Linux, efficient implementation on the Intel 80386 was the primary goal, rather than portability to other processor architectures. However, with the increasing popularity of Linux, ports to other processor architectures began to appear, starting with an early port to the Digital Alpha chip. The list of hardware architectures to which Linux has been ported continues to grow and includes x86-64, Motorola/IBM PowerPC and PowerPC64, Sun SPARC and SPARC64 (UltraSPARC), MIPS, ARM (Acorn), IBM zSeries (formerly System/390), Intel IA-64 (Itanium; see [Mosberger & Eranian, 2002]), Hitachi SuperH, HP PA-RISC, and Motorola 68000.

Linux distributions

Precisely speaking, the term *Linux* refers just to the kernel developed by Linus Torvalds and others. However, the term *Linux* is commonly used to mean the kernel, plus a wide range of other software (tools and libraries) that together make a complete operating system. In the very early days of Linux, the user was required to assemble all of this software, create a file system, and correctly place and configure all of the software on that file system. This demanded considerable time and expertise. As a result, a market opened for Linux distributors, who created packages (*distributions*) to automate most of the installation process, creating a file system and installing the kernel and other required software.

The earliest distributions appeared in 1992, and included MCC Interim Linux (Manchester Computing Centre, UK), TAMU (Texas A&M University), and SLS (SoftLanding Linux System). The oldest surviving commercial distribution, Slackware, appeared in 1993. The noncommercial Debian distribution appeared at around the same time, and SUSE and Red Hat soon followed. The currently very popular Ubuntu distribution first appeared in 2004. Nowadays, many distribution companies also employ programmers who actively contribute to existing free software projects or initiate new projects.

1.3   Standardization

By the late 1980s, the wide variety of available UNIX implementations also had its drawbacks. Some UNIX implementations were based on BSD, others were based on System V, and some drew features from both variants. Furthermore, each commercial vendor had added extra features to its own implementation. The consequence was that moving software and people from one UNIX implementation to another became steadily more difficult. This situation created strong pressure for standardization of the C programming language and the UNIX system, so that applications could more easily be ported from one system to another. We now look at the resulting standards.

1.3.1   The C Programming Language

By the early 1980s, C had been in existence for ten years, and was implemented on a wide variety of UNIX systems and on other operating systems. Minor differences had arisen between the various implementations, in part because certain aspects of how the language should function were not detailed in the existing de facto standard for C, Kernighan and Ritchie's 1978 book, *The C Programming Language*. (The older C syntax described in that book is sometimes called *traditional C* or *K&R C*.) Furthermore, the appearance of C++ in 1985 highlighted certain improvements and additions that could be made to C without breaking existing programs, notably function prototypes, structure assignment, type qualifiers (*const* and *volatile*), enumeration types, and the *void* keyword.

These factors created a drive for C standardization that culminated in 1989 with the approval of the American National Standards Institute (ANSI) C standard (X3.159-1989), which was subsequently adopted in 1990 as an International Organization for Standardization (ISO) standard (ISO/IEC 9899:1990). As well as defining the syntax and semantics of C, this standard described the operation of the standard C library, which includes the *stdio* functions, string-handling functions, math functions, various header files, and so on. This version of C is usually known as *C89* or (less commonly) *ISO C90*, and is fully described in the second (1988) edition of Kernighan and Ritchie's *The C Programming Language*.

A revision of the C standard was adopted by ISO in 1999 (ISO/IEC 9899:1999; see *http://www.open-std.org/jtc1/sc22/wg14/www/standards*). This standard is usually referred to as C99, and includes a range of changes to the language and its standard library. These changes include the addition of *long long* and Boolean data types, C++-style (//) comments, restricted pointers, and variable-length arrays. (At the time of writing, work is in progress on a further revision of the C standard, informally named C1X. The new standard is expected to be ratified in 2011.)

The C standards are independent of the details of any operating system; that is, they are not tied to the UNIX system. This means that C programs written using only the standard C library should be portable to any computer and operating system providing a C implementation.

> Historically, C89 was often called *ANSI C*, and this term is sometimes still used with that meaning. For example, *gcc* employs that meaning; its *−ansi* qualifier means "support all ISO C90 programs." However, we avoid this term because it is now somewhat ambiguous. Since the ANSI committee adopted the C99 revision, properly speaking, ANSI C is now C99.

1.3.2   The First POSIX Standards

The term POSIX (an abbreviation of *Portable Operating System Interface*) refers to a group of standards developed under the auspices of the Institute of Electrical and Electronic Engineers (IEEE), specifically its Portable Application Standards Committee (PASC, *http://www.pasc.org/*). The goal of the PASC standards is to promote application portability at the source code level.

> The name POSIX was suggested by Richard Stallman. The final *X* appears because the names of most UNIX variants end in *X*. The standard notes that the name should be pronounced "pahz-icks," like "positive."

The most interesting of the POSIX standards for our purposes are the first POSIX standard, referred to as POSIX.1 (or, more fully, POSIX 1003.1), and the subsequent POSIX.2 standard.

POSIX.1 and POSIX.2

POSIX.1 became an IEEE standard in 1988 and, with minor revisions, was adopted as an ISO standard in 1990 (ISO/IEC 9945-1:1990). (The original POSIX standards are not available online, but can be purchased from the IEEE at *http://www.ieee.org/*.)

POSIX.1 was initially based on an earlier (1984) unofficial standard produced by an association of UNIX vendors called */usr/group*.

POSIX.1 documents an API for a set of services that should be made available to a program by a conforming operating system. An operating system that does this can be certified as *POSIX.1 conformant*.

POSIX.1 is based on the UNIX system call and the C library function API, but it doesn't require any particular implementation to be associated with this interface. This means that the interface can be implemented by any operating system, not specifically a UNIX operating system. In fact, some vendors have added APIs to their proprietary operating systems that make them POSIX.1 conformant, while at the same time leaving the underlying operating system largely unchanged.

A number of extensions to the original POSIX.1 standard were also important. IEEE POSIX 1003.1b (POSIX.1b, formerly called POSIX.4 or POSIX 1003.4), ratified in 1993, contains a range of realtime extensions to the base POSIX standard. IEEE POSIX 1003.1c (POSIX.1c), ratified in 1995, is the definition of POSIX threads. In 1996, a revised version of the POSIX.1 standard (ISO/IEC 9945-1:1996) was produced, leaving the core text unchanged, but incorporating the realtime and threads extensions. IEEE POSIX 1003.1g (POSIX.1g) defined the networking APIs, including sockets. IEEE POSIX 1003.1d (POSIX.1d), ratified in 1999, and POSIX.1j, ratified in 2000, defined additional realtime extensions to the POSIX base standard.

> The POSIX.1b realtime extensions include file synchronization; asynchronous I/O; process scheduling; high-precision clocks and timers; and interprocess communication using semaphores, shared memory, and message queues. The prefix *POSIX* is often applied to the three interprocess communication methods to distinguish them from the similar, but older, System V semaphores, shared memory, and message queues.

A related standard, POSIX.2 (1992, ISO/IEC 9945-2:1993), standardized the shell and various UNIX utilities, including the command-line interface of the C compiler.

FIPS 151-1 and FIPS 151-2

FIPS is an abbreviation for Federal Information Processing Standard, the name of a set of standards specified by the US government for the purchase of its computer systems. In 1989, FIPS 151-1 was published. This standard was based on the 1988 IEEE POSIX.1 standard and the draft ANSI C standard. The main difference between FIPS 151-1 and POSIX.1 (1988) was that the FIPS standard required some features that POSIX.1 left as optional. Because the US government is a major purchaser of computer systems, most computer vendors ensured that their UNIX systems conformed to the FIPS 151-1 version of POSIX.1.

FIPS 151-2 aligned with the 1990 ISO edition of POSIX.1, but was otherwise unchanged. The now outdated FIPS 151-2 was withdrawn as a standard in February 2000.

1.3.3 X/Open Company and The Open Group

X/Open Company was a consortium formed by an international group of computer vendors to adopt and adapt existing standards in order to produce a comprehensive, consistent set of open systems standards. It produced the *X/Open Portability Guide*, a series of portability guides based on the POSIX standards. The first important release of this guide was Issue 3 (XPG3) in 1989, followed by XPG4 in 1992. XPG4 was revised in 1994, which resulted in XPG4 version 2, a standard that also incorporated important parts of AT&T's System V Interface Definition Issue 3, described in Section 1.3.7. This revision was also known as *Spec 1170*, with 1170 referring to the number of *interfaces*—functions, header files, and commands—defined by the standard.

When Novell, which acquired the UNIX systems business from AT&T in early 1993, later divested itself of that business, it transferred the rights to the UNIX trademark to X/Open. (The plan to make this transfer was announced in 1993, but legal requirements delayed the transfer until early 1994.) XPG4 version 2 was subsequently repackaged as the *Single UNIX Specification* (SUS, or sometimes SUSv1), and is also known as *UNIX 95*. This repackaging included XPG4 version 2, the X/Open Curses Issue 4 version 2 specification, and the X/Open Networking Services (XNS) Issue 4 specification. Version 2 of the Single UNIX Specification (SUSv2, *http://www.unix.org/version2/online.html*) appeared in 1997, and UNIX implementations certified against this specification can call themselves *UNIX 98*. (This standard is occasionally also referred to as XPG5.)

In 1996, X/Open merged with the *Open Software Foundation* (OSF) to form *The Open Group*. Nearly every company or organization involved with the UNIX system is now a member of The Open Group, which continues to develop API standards.

> OSF was one of two vendor consortia formed during the UNIX wars of the late 1980s. Among others, OSF included Digital, IBM, HP, Apollo, Bull, Nixdorf, and Siemens. OSF was formed primarily in response to the threat created by a business alliance between AT&T (the originators of UNIX) and Sun (the most powerful player in the UNIX workstation market). Consequently, AT&T, Sun, and other companies formed the rival *UNIX International* consortium.

1.3.4 SUSv3 and POSIX.1-2001

Beginning in 1999, the IEEE, The Open Group, and the ISO/IEC Joint Technical Committee 1 collaborated in the *Austin Common Standards Revision Group* (CSRG, *http://www.opengroup.org/austin/*) with the aim of revising and consolidating the POSIX standards and the Single UNIX Specification. (The Austin Group is so named because its inaugural meeting was in Austin, Texas in September 1998.) This resulted in the ratification of POSIX 1003.1-2001, sometimes just called POSIX.1-2001, in December 2001 (subsequently approved as an ISO standard, ISO/IEC 9945:2002).

POSIX 1003.1-2001 replaces SUSv2, POSIX.1, POSIX.2, and a raft of other earlier POSIX standards. This standard is also known as the Single UNIX Specification Version 3, and we'll generally refer to it in the remainder of this book as *SUSv3*.

The SUSv3 base specifications consists of around 3700 pages, divided into the following four parts:

- *Base Definitions* (XBD): This part contains definitions, terms, concepts, and specifications of the contents of header files. A total of 84 header file specifications are provided.

- *System Interfaces* (XSH): This part begins with various useful background information. Its bulk consists of the specification of various functions (which are implemented as either system calls or library functions on specific UNIX implementations). A total of 1123 system interfaces are included in this part.

- *Shell and Utilities* (XCU): This specifies the operation of the shell and various UNIX commands. A total of 160 utilities are specified in this part.

- *Rationale* (XRAT): This part includes informative text and justifications relating to the earlier parts.

In addition, SUSv3 includes the *X/Open CURSES Issue 4 Version 2* (XCURSES) specification, which specifies 372 functions and 3 header files for the *curses* screen-handling API.

In all, 1742 interfaces are specified in SUSv3. By contrast, POSIX.1-1990 (with FIPS 151-2) specified 199 interfaces, and POSIX.2-1992 specified 130 utilities.

SUSv3 is available online at *http://www.unix.org/version3/online.html*. UNIX implementations certified against SUSv3 can call themselves *UNIX 03*.

There have been various minor fixes and improvements for problems discovered since the ratification of the original SUSv3 text. These have resulted in the appearance of *Technical Corrigendum Number 1*, whose improvements were incorporated in a 2003 revision of SUSv3, and *Technical Corrigendum Number 2*, whose improvements were incorporated in a 2004 revision.

POSIX conformance, XSI conformance, and the XSI extension

Historically, the SUS (and XPG) standards deferred to the corresponding POSIX standards and were structured as functional supersets of POSIX. As well as specifying additional interfaces, the SUS standards made mandatory many of the interfaces and behaviors that were deemed optional in POSIX.

This distinction survives somewhat more subtly in POSIX 1003.1-2001, which is both an IEEE standard and an Open Group Technical Standard (i.e., as noted already, it is a consolidation of earlier POSIX and SUS standards). This document defines two levels of conformance:

- *POSIX conformance*: This defines a baseline of interfaces that a conforming implementation must provide. It permits the implementation to provide other optional interfaces.

- *X/Open System Interface* (XSI) *conformance*: To be XSI conformant, an implementation must meet all of the requirements of POSIX conformance and also must provide a number of interfaces and behaviors that are only optionally required for POSIX conformance. An implementation must reach this level of conformance in order to obtain the *UNIX 03* branding from The Open Group.

The additional interfaces and behaviors required for XSI conformance are collectively known as the *XSI extension*. They include support for features such as threads, *mmap()* and *munmap()*, the *dlopen* API, resource limits, pseudoterminals, System V IPC, the *syslog* API, *poll()*, and login accounting.

In later chapters, when we talk about SUSv3 conformance, we mean XSI conformance.

> Because POSIX and SUSv3 are now part of the same document, the additional interfaces and the selection of mandatory options required for SUSv3 are indicated via the use of shading and margin markings within the document text.

Unspecified and weakly specified

Occasionally, we refer to an interface as being "unspecified" or "weakly specified" within SUSv3.

By an *unspecified interface*, we mean one that is not defined at all in the formal standard, although in a few cases there are background notes or rationale text that mention the interface.

Saying that an interface is *weakly specified* is shorthand for saying that, while the interface is included in the standard, important details are left unspecified (commonly because the committee members could not reach an agreement due to differences in existing implementations).

When using interfaces that are unspecified or weakly specified, we have few guarantees when porting applications to other UNIX implementations, and portable applications should avoid relying on the behavior of a specific implementation. Nevertheless, in a few cases, such an interface is quite consistent across implementations, and where this is so, we generally note it as such.

LEGACY features

Sometimes, we note that SUSv3 marks a specified feature as *LEGACY*. This term denotes a feature that is retained for compatibility with older applications, but whose limitations mean that its use should be avoided in new applications. In many cases, some other API exists that provides equivalent functionality.

1.3.5 SUSv4 and POSIX.1-2008

In 2008, the Austin group completed a revision of the combined POSIX.1 and Single UNIX Specification. As with the preceding version of the standard, it consists of a base specification coupled with an XSI extension. We'll refer to this revision as SUSv4.

The changes in SUSv4 are less wide-ranging than those that occurred for SUSv3. The most significant changes are as follows:

- SUSv4 adds new specifications for a range of functions. Among the newly specified functions that we mention in this book are *dirfd()*, *fdopendir()*, *fexecve()*, *futimens()*, *mkdtemp()*, *psignal()*, *strsignal()*, and *utimensat()*. Another range of new file-related functions (e.g., *openat()*, described in Section 18.11) are analogs of existing functions (e.g., *open()*), but differ in that they interpret relative pathnames with respect to the directory referred to by an open file descriptor, rather than relative to the process's current working directory.

- Some functions specified as options in SUSv3 become a mandatory part of the base standard in SUSv4. For example, a number of functions that were part of the XSI extension in SUSv3 become part of the base standard in SUSv4. Among the functions that become mandatory in SUSv4 are those in the *dlopen* API (Section 42.1), the realtime signals API (Section 22.8), the POSIX semaphore API (Chapter 53), and the POSIX timers API (Section 23.6).

- Some functions in SUSv3 are marked as obsolete in SUSv4. These include *asctime()*, *ctime()*, *ftw()*, *gettimeofday()*, *getitimer()*, *setitimer()*, and *siginterrupt()*.

- Specifications of some functions that were marked as obsolete in SUSv3 are removed in SUSv4. These functions include *gethostbyname()*, *gethostbyaddr()*, and *vfork()*.

- Various details of existing specifications in SUSv3 are changed in SUSv4. For example, various functions are added to the list of functions that are required to be async-signal-safe (Table 21-1 on page 426).

In the remainder of this book, we note changes in SUSv4 where they are relevant to the topic being discussed.

1.3.6 UNIX Standards Timeline

Figure 1-1 summarizes the relationships between the various standards described in the preceding sections, and places the standards in chronological order. In this diagram, the solid lines indicate direct descent between standards, and the dashed arrows indicate cases where one standard influenced another standard, was incorporated as part of another standard, or simply deferred to another standard.

The situation with networking standards is somewhat complex. Standardization efforts in this area began in the late 1980s with the formation of the POSIX 1003.12 committee to standardize the sockets API, the X/Open Transport Interface (XTI) API (an alternative network programming API based on System V's Transport Layer Interface), and various associated APIs. The gestation of this standard occurred over several years, during which time POSIX 1003.12 was renamed POSIX 1003.1g. It was ratified in 2000.

In parallel with the development of POSIX 1003.1g, X/Open was also developing its X/Open Networking Specification (XNS). The first version of this specification, XNS Issue 4, was part of the first version of the Single UNIX Specification. It was succeeded by XNS Issue 5, which formed part of SUSv2. XNS Issue 5 was essentially the same as the then current (6.6) draft of POSIX.1g. This was followed by XNS Issue 5.2, which differed from XNS Issue 5 and the ratified POSIX.1g standard in marking the XTI API as obsolete and in including coverage of Internet Protocol version 6 (IPv6), which was being designed in the mid-1990s. XNS Issue 5.2 formed the basis for the networking material included in SUSv3, and is thus now superseded. For similar reasons, POSIX.1g was withdrawn as a standard soon after it was ratified.

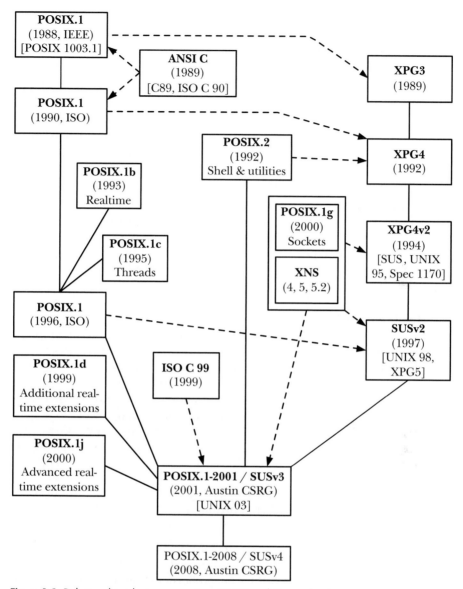

Figure 1-1: Relationships between various UNIX and C standards

1.3.7 Implementation Standards

In addition to the standards produced by independent or multiparty groups, reference is sometimes made to the two implementation standards defined by the final BSD release (4.4BSD) and AT&T's System V Release 4 (SVR4). The latter implementation standard was formalized by AT&T's publication of the System V Interface Definition (SVID). In 1989, AT&T published Issue 3 of the SVID, which defined the interface that a UNIX implementation must provide in order to be able to call itself System V Release 4. (The SVID is available online at *http://www.sco.com/developers/devspecs/*.)

> Because the behavior of some system calls and library functions varies between SVR4 and BSD, many UNIX implementations provide compatibility libraries and conditional-compilation facilities that emulate the behavior of whichever UNIX flavor is not used as the base for that particular implementation (see Section 3.6.1). This eases the burden of porting an application from another UNIX implementation.

1.3.8 Linux, Standards, and the Linux Standard Base

As a general goal, Linux (i.e., kernel, *glibc*, and tool) development aims to conform to the various UNIX standards, especially POSIX and the Single UNIX Specification. However, at the time of writing, no Linux distributions are branded as "UNIX" by The Open Group. The problems are time and expense. Each vendor distribution would need to undergo conformance testing to obtain this branding, and it would need to repeat this testing with each new distribution release. Nevertheless, it is the de facto near-conformance to various standards that has enabled Linux to be so successful in the UNIX market.

With most commercial UNIX implementations, the same company both develops and distributes the operating system. With Linux, things are different, in that implementation is separate from distribution, and multiple organizations—both commercial and noncommercial—handle Linux distribution.

Linus Torvalds doesn't contribute to or endorse a particular Linux distribution. However, in terms of other individuals carrying out Linux development, the situation is more complex. Many developers working on the Linux kernel and on other free software projects are employed by various Linux distribution companies or work for companies (such as IBM and HP) with a strong interest in Linux. While these companies can influence the direction in which Linux moves by allocating programmer hours to certain projects, none of them controls Linux as such. And, of course, many of the other contributors to the Linux kernel and GNU projects work voluntarily.

> At the time of writing, Torvalds is employed as a fellow at the Linux Foundation (*http://www.linux-foundation.org/*; formerly the Open Source Development Laboratory, OSDL), a nonprofit consortium of commercial and noncommercial organizations chartered to foster the growth of Linux.

Because there are multiple Linux distributors and because the kernel implementers don't control the contents of distributions, there is no "standard" commercial Linux as such. Each Linux distributor's kernel offering is typically based on a snapshot of the mainline (i.e., the Torvalds) kernel at a particular point in time, with a number of patches applied.

These patches typically provide features that, to a greater or lesser extent, are deemed commercially desirable, and thus able to provide competitive differentiation in the marketplace. In some cases, these patches are later accepted into the mainline kernel. In fact, some new kernel features were initially developed by a distribution company, and appeared in their distribution before eventually being integrated into the mainline. For example, version 3 of the *Reiserfs* journaling file system was part of some Linux distributions long before it was accepted into the mainline 2.4 kernel.

The upshot of the preceding points is that there are (mostly minor) differences in the systems offered by the various Linux distribution companies. On a much smaller scale, this is reminiscent of the splits in implementations that occurred in the early years of UNIX. The Linux Standard Base (LSB) is an effort to ensure compatibility among the various Linux distributions. To do this, the LSB (*http:// www.linux-foundation.org/en/LSB*) develops and promotes a set of standards for Linux systems with the aim of ensuring that binary applications (i.e., compiled programs) can run on any LSB-conformant system.

> The binary portability promoted by the LSB contrasts with the source code portability promoted by POSIX. Source code portability means that we can write a C program and then successfully compile and run it on any POSIX-conformant system. Binary compatibility is much more demanding and is generally not feasible across different hardware platforms. It allows us to compile a program once for a given hardware platform, and then run that compiled program on any conformant implementation running on that hardware platform. Binary portability is an essential requirement for the commercial viability of independent software vendor (ISV) applications built for Linux.

1.4 Summary

The UNIX system was first implemented in 1969 on a Digital PDP-7 minicomputer by Ken Thompson at Bell Laboratories (part of AT&T). The operating system drew many ideas, as well as its punned name, from the earlier MULTICS system. By 1973, UNIX had been moved to the PDP-11 mini-computer and rewritten in C, a programming language designed and implemented at Bell Laboratories by Dennis Ritchie. Legally prevented from selling UNIX, AT&T instead distributed the complete system to universities for a nominal charge. This distribution included source code, and became very popular within universities, since it provided a cheap operating system whose code could be studied and modified by computer science academics and students.

The University of California at Berkeley played a key role in the development of the UNIX system. There, Ken Thompson and a number of graduate students extended the operating system. By 1979, the University was producing its own UNIX distribution, BSD. This distribution became widespread in academia and formed the basis for several commercial implementations.

Meanwhile, the breakup of the AT&T monopoly permitted the company to sell the UNIX system. This resulted in the other major variant of UNIX, System V, which also formed the basis for several commercial implementations.

Two different currents led to the development of (GNU/) Linux. One of these was the GNU project, founded by Richard Stallman. By the late 1980s, the GNU project had produced an almost complete, freely distributable UNIX implementation. The one part lacking was a working kernel. In 1991, inspired by the Minix kernel written by Andrew Tanenbaum, Linus Torvalds produced a working UNIX kernel for the Intel x86-32 architecture. Torvalds invited other programmers to join him in improving the kernel. Many programmers did so, and, over time, Linux was extended and ported to a wide variety of hardware architectures.

The portability problems that arose from the variations in UNIX and C implementations that existed by the late 1980s created a strong pressure for standardization. The C language was standardized in 1989 (C89), and a revised standard was produced in 1999 (C99). The first attempt to standardize the operating system interface yielded POSIX.1, ratified as an IEEE standard in 1988, and as an ISO standard in 1990. During the 1990s, further standards were drafted, including various versions of the Single UNIX Specification. In 2001, the combined POSIX 1003.1-2001 and SUSv3 standard was ratified. This standard consolidates and extends various earlier POSIX standards and earlier versions of the Single UNIX Specification. In 2008, a less wide-ranging revision of the standard was completed, yielding the combined POSIX 1003.1-2008 and SUSv4 standard.

Unlike most commercial UNIX implementations, Linux separates implementation from distribution. Consequently, there is no single "official" Linux distribution. Each Linux distributor's offering consists of a snapshot of the current stable kernel, with various patches applied. The LSB develops and promotes a set of standards for Linux systems with the aim of ensuring binary application compatibility across Linux distributions, so that compiled applications should be able to run on any LSB-conformant system running on the same hardware.

Further information

Further information about UNIX history and standards can be found in [Ritchie, 1984], [McKusick et al., 1996], [McKusick & Neville-Neil, 2005], [Libes & Ressler, 1989], [Garfinkel et al., 2003], [Stevens & Rago, 2005], [Stevens, 1999], [Quartermann & Wilhelm, 1993], [Goodheart & Cox, 1994], and [McKusick, 1999].

[Salus, 1994] is a detailed history of UNIX, from which much of the information at the beginning of this chapter was drawn. [Salus, 2008] provides a short history of Linux and other free software projects. Many details of the history of UNIX can also be found in the online book *History of UNIX*, written by Ronda Hauben. This book is available at *http://www.dei.isep.ipp.pt/~acc/docs/unix.html*. An extremely detailed timeline showing the releases of various UNIX implementations can be found at *http://www.levenez.com/unix/*.

[Josey, 2004] provides an overview of the history of the UNIX system and the development of SUSv3, guidance on how to use the specification, summary tables of the interfaces in SUSv3, and migration guides for the transitions from SUSv2 to SUSv3 and C89 to C99.

As well as providing software and documentation, the GNU web site (*http://www.gnu.org/*) contains a number of philosophical papers on the subject of free software. [Williams, 2002] is a biography of Richard Stallman.

Torvalds provides his own account of the development of Linux in [Torvalds & Diamond, 2001].

2

FUNDAMENTAL CONCEPTS

This chapter introduces a range of concepts related to Linux system programming. It is intended for readers who have worked primarily with other operating systems, or who have only limited experience with Linux or another UNIX implementation.

2.1 The Core Operating System: The Kernel

The term *operating system* is commonly used with two different meanings:

- To denote the entire package consisting of the central software managing a computer's resources and all of the accompanying standard software tools, such as command-line interpreters, graphical user interfaces, file utilities, and editors.

- More narrowly, to refer to the central software that manages and allocates computer resources (i.e., the CPU, RAM, and devices).

The term *kernel* is often used as a synonym for the second meaning, and it is with this meaning of the term *operating system* that we are concerned in this book.

Although it is possible to run programs on a computer without a kernel, the presence of a kernel greatly simplifies the writing and use of other programs, and increases the power and flexibility available to programmers. The kernel does this by providing a software layer to manage the limited resources of a computer.

The Linux kernel executable typically resides at the pathname `/boot/vmlinuz`, or something similar. The derivation of this filename is historical. On early UNIX implementations, the kernel was called `unix`. Later UNIX implementations, which implemented virtual memory, renamed the kernel as `vmunix`. On Linux, the filename mirrors the system name, with the *z* replacing the final *x* to signify that the kernel is a compressed executable.

Tasks performed by the kernel

Among other things, the kernel performs the following tasks:

- *Process scheduling*: A computer has one or more central processing units (CPUs), which execute the instructions of programs. Like other UNIX systems, Linux is a *preemptive multitasking* operating system, *Multitasking* means that multiple processes (i.e., running programs) can simultaneously reside in memory and each may receive use of the CPU(s). *Preemptive* means that the rules governing which processes receive use of the CPU and for how long are determined by the kernel process scheduler (rather than by the processes themselves).

- *Memory management*: While computer memories are enormous by the standards of a decade or two ago, the size of software has also correspondingly grown, so that physical memory (RAM) remains a limited resource that the kernel must share among processes in an equitable and efficient fashion. Like most modern operating systems, Linux employs virtual memory management (Section 6.4), a technique that confers two main advantages:
  - Processes are isolated from one another and from the kernel, so that one process can't read or modify the memory of another process or the kernel.
  - Only part of a process needs to be kept in memory, thereby lowering the memory requirements of each process and allowing more processes to be held in RAM simultaneously. This leads to better CPU utilization, since it increases the likelihood that, at any moment in time, there is at least one process that the CPU(s) can execute.

- *Provision of a file system*: The kernel provides a file system on disk, allowing files to be created, retrieved, updated, deleted, and so on.

- *Creation and termination of processes*: The kernel can load a new program into memory, providing it with the resources (e.g., CPU, memory, and access to files) that it needs in order to run. Such an instance of a running program is termed a *process*. Once a process has completed execution, the kernel ensures that the resources it uses are freed for subsequent reuse by later programs.

- *Access to devices*: The devices (mice, monitors, keyboards, disk and tape drives, and so on) attached to a computer allow communication of information between the computer and the outside world, permitting input, output, or both. The kernel provides programs with an interface that standardizes and simplifies access to devices, while at the same time arbitrating access by multiple processes to each device.

- *Networking*: The kernel transmits and receives network messages (packets) on behalf of user processes. This task includes routing of network packets to the target system.

- *Provision of a system call application programming interface (API)*: Processes can request the kernel to perform various tasks using kernel entry points known as *system calls*. The Linux system call API is the primary topic of this book. Section 3.1 details the steps that occur when a process performs a system call.

In addition to the above features, multiuser operating systems such as Linux generally provide users with the abstraction of a *virtual private computer*; that is, each user can log on to the system and operate largely independently of other users. For example, each user has their own disk storage space (home directory). In addition, users can run programs, each of which gets a share of the CPU and operates in its own virtual address space, and these programs can independently access devices and transfer information over the network. The kernel resolves potential conflicts in accessing hardware resources, so users and processes are generally unaware of the conflicts.

Kernel mode and user mode

Modern processor architectures typically allow the CPU to operate in at least two different modes: *user mode* and *kernel mode* (sometimes also referred to as *supervisor mode*). Hardware instructions allow switching from one mode to the other. Correspondingly, areas of virtual memory can be marked as being part of *user space* or *kernel space*. When running in user mode, the CPU can access only memory that is marked as being in user space; attempts to access memory in kernel space result in a hardware exception. When running in kernel mode, the CPU can access both user and kernel memory space.

Certain operations can be performed only while the processor is operating in kernel mode. Examples include executing the halt instruction to stop the system, accessing the memory-management hardware, and initiating device I/O operations. By taking advantage of this hardware design to place the operating system in kernel space, operating system implementers can ensure that user processes are not able to access the instructions and data structures of the kernel, or to perform operations that would adversely affect the operation of the system.

Process versus kernel views of the system

In many everyday programming tasks, we are accustomed to thinking about programming in a process-oriented way. However, when considering various topics covered later in this book, it can be useful to reorient our perspective to consider things from the kernel's point of view. To make the contrast clear, we now consider how things look first from a process viewpoint and then from a kernel viewpoint.

A running system typically has numerous processes. For a process, many things happen asynchronously. An executing process doesn't know when it will next time out, which other processes will then be scheduled for the CPU (and in what order), or when it will next be scheduled. The delivery of signals and the occurrence of interprocess communication events are mediated by the kernel, and can occur at any time for a process. Many things happen transparently for a process. A process doesn't know where it is located in RAM or, in general, whether a particular part of its memory space is currently resident in memory or held in the swap area (a reserved area of disk space used to supplement the computer's RAM). Similarly, a process doesn't know where on the disk drive the files it accesses are being held; it simply refers to the files by name. A process operates in isolation; it can't directly communicate with another process. A process can't itself create a new process or even end its own existence. Finally, a process can't communicate directly with the input and output devices attached to the computer.

By contrast, a running system has one kernel that knows and controls everything. The kernel facilitates the running of all processes on the system. The kernel decides which process will next obtain access to the CPU, when it will do so, and for how long. The kernel maintains data structures containing information about all running processes and updates these structures as processes are created, change state, and terminate. The kernel maintains all of the low-level data structures that enable the filenames used by programs to be translated into physical locations on the disk. The kernel also maintains data structures that map the virtual memory of each process into the physical memory of the computer and the swap area(s) on disk. All communication between processes is done via mechanisms provided by the kernel. In response to requests from processes, the kernel creates new processes and terminates existing processes. Lastly, the kernel (in particular, device drivers) performs all direct communication with input and output devices, transferring information to and from user processes as required.

Later in this book we'll say things such as "a process can create another process," "a process can create a pipe," "a process can write data to a file," and "a process can terminate by calling *exit()*." Remember, however, that the kernel mediates all such actions, and these statements are just shorthand for "a process can *request that the kernel* create another process," and so on.

Further information

Modern texts covering operating systems concepts and design, with particular reference to UNIX systems, include [Tanenbaum, 2007], [Tanenbaum & Woodhull, 2006], and [Vahalia, 1996], the last of these containing much detail on virtual memory architectures. [Goodheart & Cox, 1994] provide details on System V Release 4. [Maxwell, 1999] provides an annotated listing of selected parts of the Linux 2.2.5 kernel. [Lions, 1996] is a detailed exposition of the Sixth Edition UNIX source code that remains a useful introduction to UNIX operating system internals. [Bovet & Cesati, 2005] describes the implementation of the Linux 2.6 kernel.

2.2 The Shell

A *shell* is a special-purpose program designed to read commands typed by a user and execute appropriate programs in response to those commands. Such a program is sometimes known as a *command interpreter*.

The term *login shell* is used to denote the process that is created to run a shell when the user first logs in.

Whereas on some operating systems the command interpreter is an integral part of the kernel, on UNIX systems, the shell is a user process. Many different shells exist, and different users (or, for that matter, a single user) on the same computer can simultaneously use different shells. A number of important shells have appeared over time:

- *Bourne shell (sh)*: This is the oldest of the widely used shells, and was written by Steve Bourne. It was the standard shell for Seventh Edition UNIX. The Bourne shell contains many of the features familiar in all shells: I/O redirection, pipelines, filename generation (globbing), variables, manipulation of environment variables, command substitution, background command execution, and functions. All later UNIX implementations include the Bourne shell in addition to any other shells they might provide.

- *C shell (csh)*: This shell was written by Bill Joy at the University of California at Berkeley. The name derives from the resemblance of many of the flow-control constructs of this shell to those of the C programming language. The C shell provided several useful interactive features unavailable in the Bourne shell, including command history, command-line editing, job control, and aliases. The C shell was not backward compatible with the Bourne shell. Although the standard interactive shell on BSD was the C shell, shell scripts (described in a moment) were usually written for the Bourne shell, so as to be portable across all UNIX implementations.

- *Korn shell (ksh)*: This shell was written as the successor to the Bourne shell by David Korn at AT&T Bell Laboratories. While maintaining backward compatibility with the Bourne shell, it also incorporated interactive features similar to those provided by the C shell.

- *Bourne again shell (bash)*: This shell is the GNU project's reimplementation of the Bourne shell. It supplies interactive features similar to those available in the C and Korn shells. The principal authors of *bash* are Brian Fox and Chet Ramey. Bash is probably the most widely used shell on Linux. (On Linux, the Bourne shell, *sh*, is typically provided by *bash* emulating *sh* as closely as possible.)

> POSIX.2-1992 specified a standard for the shell that was based on the then current version of the Korn shell. Nowadays, the Korn shell and *bash* both conform to POSIX, but provide a number of extensions to the standard, and many of these extensions differ between the two shells.

The shells are designed not merely for interactive use, but also for the interpretation of *shell scripts*, which are text files containing shell commands. For this purpose, each of the shells has the facilities typically associated with programming languages: variables, loop and conditional statements, I/O commands, and functions.

Each of the shells performs similar tasks, albeit with variations in syntax. Unless referring to the operation of a specific shell, we typically refer to "the shell," with the understanding that all shells operate in the manner described. Most of the examples in this book that require a shell use *bash*, but, unless otherwise noted, the reader can assume these examples work the same way in other Bourne-type shells.

2.3   Users and Groups

Each user on the system is uniquely identified, and users may belong to groups.

Users

Every user of the system has a unique *login name* (username) and a corresponding numeric *user ID* (UID). For each user, these are defined by a line in the system *password file*, /etc/passwd, which includes the following additional information:

- *Group ID*: the numeric group ID of the first of the groups of which the user is a member.
- *Home directory*: the initial directory into which the user is placed after logging in.
- *Login shell*: the name of the program to be executed to interpret user commands.

The password record may also include the user's password, in encrypted form. However, for security reasons, the password is often stored in the separate *shadow password file*, which is readable only by privileged users.

Groups

For administrative purposes—in particular, for controlling access to files and other system resources—it is useful to organize users into *groups*. For example, the people in a team working on a single project, and thus sharing a common set of files, might all be made members of the same group. In early UNIX implementations, a user could be a member of only one group. BSD allowed a user to simultaneously belong to multiple groups, an idea that was taken up by other UNIX implementations and the POSIX.1-1990 standard. Each group is identified by a single line in the system *group file*, /etc/group, which includes the following information:

- *Group name*: the (unique) name of the group.
- *Group ID* (GID): the numeric ID associated with this group.
- *User list*: a comma-separated list of login names of users who are members of this group (and who are not otherwise identified as members of the group by virtue of the group ID field of their password file record).

Superuser

One user, known as the *superuser*, has special privileges within the system. The superuser account has user ID 0, and normally has the login name *root*. On typical UNIX systems, the superuser bypasses all permission checks in the system. Thus, for example, the superuser can access any file in the system, regardless of the permissions on that file, and can send signals to any user process in the system. The system administrator uses the superuser account to perform various administrative tasks on the system.

2.4 Single Directory Hierarchy, Directories, Links, and Files

The kernel maintains a single hierarchical directory structure to organize all files in the system. (This contrasts with operating systems such as Microsoft Windows, where each disk device has its own directory hierarchy.) At the base of this hierarchy is the *root directory*, named / (slash). All files and directories are children or further removed descendants of the root directory. Figure 2-1 shows an example of this hierarchical file structure.

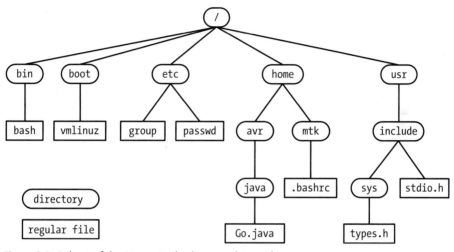

Figure 2-1: Subset of the Linux single directory hierarchy

File types

Within the file system, each file is marked with a *type*, indicating what kind of file it is. One of these file types denotes ordinary data files, which are usually called *regular* or *plain* files to distinguish them from other file types. These other file types include devices, pipes, sockets, directories, and symbolic links.

The term *file* is commonly used to denote a file of any type, not just a regular file.

Directories and links

A *directory* is a special file whose contents take the form of a table of filenames coupled with references to the corresponding files. This filename-plus-reference association is called a *link*, and files may have multiple links, and thus multiple names, in the same or in different directories.

Directories may contain links both to files and to other directories. The links between directories establish the directory hierarchy shown in Figure 2-1.

Every directory contains at least two entries: . (dot), which is a link to the directory itself, and .. (dot-dot), which is a link to its *parent directory*, the directory above it in the hierarchy. Every directory, except the root directory, has a parent. For the root directory, the dot-dot entry is a link to the root directory itself (thus, /.. equates to /).

Symbolic links

Like a normal link, a *symbolic link* provides an alternative name for a file. But whereas a normal link is a filename-plus-pointer entry in a directory list, a symbolic link is a specially marked file containing the name of another file. (In other words, a symbolic link has a filename-plus-pointer entry in a directory, and the file referred to by the pointer contains a string that names another file.) This latter file is often called the *target* of the symbolic link, and it is common to say that the symbolic link "points" or "refers" to the target file. When a pathname is specified in a system call, in most circumstances, the kernel automatically *dereferences* (or synonymously, *follows*) each symbolic link in the pathname, replacing it with the filename to which it points. This process may happen recursively if the target of a symbolic link is itself a symbolic link. (The kernel imposes limits on the number of dereferences to handle the possibility of circular chains of symbolic links.) If a symbolic link refers to a file that doesn't exist, it is said to be a *dangling link*.

Often *hard link* and *soft link* are used as alternative terms for normal and symbolic links. The reasons for having two different types of links are explained in Chapter 18.

Filenames

On most Linux file systems, filenames can be up to 255 characters long. Filenames may contain any characters except slashes (/) and null characters (\0). However, it is advisable to employ only letters and digits, and the . (period), _ (underscore), and - (hyphen) characters. This 65-character set, [-._a-zA-Z0-9], is referred to in SUSv3 as the *portable filename character set*.

We should avoid the use of characters in filenames that are not in the portable filename character set because those characters may have special meanings within the shell, within regular expressions, or in other contexts. If a filename containing characters with special meanings appears in such contexts, then these characters must be *escaped*; that is, specially marked—typically with a preceding backslash (\)—to indicate that they should not be interpreted with those special meanings. In contexts where no escape mechanism is available, the filename is not usable.

We should also avoid filenames beginning with a hyphen (-), since such filenames may be mistaken for options when specified in a shell command.

Pathnames

A *pathname* is a string consisting of an optional initial slash (/) followed by a series of filenames separated by slashes. All but the last of these component filenames identifies a directory (or a symbolic link that resolves to a directory). The last component of a pathname may identify any type of file, including a directory. The series of component filenames preceding the final slash is sometimes referred to as the *directory* part of a pathname, while the name following the final slash is sometimes referred to as the file or *base* part of the pathname.

A pathname is read from left to right; each filename resides in the directory specified by the preceding part of the pathname. The string .. can be used anywhere in a pathname to refer to the parent of the location so far specified in the pathname.

A pathname describes the location of a file within the single directory hierarchy, and is either absolute or relative:

- An *absolute pathname* begins with a slash (/) and specifies the location of a file with respect to the root directory. Examples of absolute pathnames for files in Figure 2-1 are /home/mtk/.bashrc, /usr/include, and / (the pathname of the root directory).

- A *relative pathname* specifies the location of a file relative to a process's current working directory (see below), and is distinguished from an absolute pathname by the absence of an initial slash. In Figure 2-1, from the directory usr, the file types.h could be referenced using the relative pathname include/sys/types.h, while from the directory avr, the file .bashrc could be accessed using the relative pathname ../mtk/.bashrc.

Current working directory

Each process has a *current working directory* (sometimes just referred to as the process's *working directory* or *current directory*). This is the process's "current location" within the single directory hierarchy, and it is from this directory that relative pathnames are interpreted for the process.

A process inherits its current working directory from its parent process. A login shell has its initial current working directory set to the location named in the home directory field of the user's password file entry. The shell's current working directory can be changed with the *cd* command.

File ownership and permissions

Each file has an associated user ID and group ID that define the owner of the file and the group to which it belongs. The ownership of a file is used to determine the access rights available to users of the file.

For the purpose of accessing a file, the system divides users into three categories: the *owner* of the file (sometimes termed the *user* of the file), users who are members of the group matching the file's group ID (*group*), and the rest of the world (*other*). Three permission bits may be set for each of these categories of user (making a total of nine permission bits): *read* permission allows the contents of the file to be read; *write* permission allows modification of the contents of the file; and *execute* permission allows execution of the file, which is either a program or a script to be processed by some interpreter (usually, but not always, one of the shells).

These permissions may also be set on directories, although their meanings are slightly different: *read* permission allows the contents of (i.e., the filenames in) the directory to be listed; *write* permission allows the contents of the directory to be changed (i.e., filenames can be added, removed, and changed); and *execute* (sometimes called *search*) permission allows access to files within the directory (subject to the permissions on the files themselves).

2.5   File I/O Model

One of the distinguishing features of the I/O model on UNIX systems is the concept of *universality of I/O*. This means that the same system calls (*open()*, *read()*, write(), close(), and so on) are used to perform I/O on all types of files, including devices. (The kernel translates the application's I/O requests into appropriate file-system or device-driver operations that perform I/O on the target file or device.) Thus, a program employing these system calls will work on any type of file.

The kernel essentially provides one file type: a sequential stream of bytes, which, in the case of disk files, disks, and tape devices, can be randomly accessed using the *lseek()* system call.

Many applications and libraries interpret the *newline* character (ASCII code 10 decimal, sometimes also known as *linefeed*) as terminating one line of text and commencing another. UNIX systems have no *end-of-file* character; the end of a file is detected by a read that returns no data.

File descriptors

The I/O system calls refer to open files using a *file descriptor*, a (usually small) non-negative integer. A file descriptor is typically obtained by a call to *open()*, which takes a pathname argument specifying a file upon which I/O is to be performed.

Normally, a process inherits three open file descriptors when it is started by the shell: descriptor 0 is *standard input*, the file from which the process takes its input; descriptor 1 is *standard output*, the file to which the process writes its output; and descriptor 2 is *standard error*, the file to which the process writes error messages and notification of exceptional or abnormal conditions. In an interactive shell or program, these three descriptors are normally connected to the terminal. In the *stdio* library, these descriptors correspond to the file streams *stdin*, *stdout*, and *stderr*.

The *stdio* library

To perform file I/O, C programs typically employ I/O functions contained in the standard C library. This set of functions, referred to as the *stdio* library, includes *fopen()*, *fclose()*, *scanf()*, *printf()*, *fgets()*, *fputs()*, and so on. The *stdio* functions are layered on top of the I/O system calls (*open()*, *close()*, *read()*, *write()*, and so on).

> We assume that the reader is already familiar with the C standard I/O (*stdio*) functions, and don't cover them in this book. Further information on the *stdio* library can be found in [Kernighan & Ritchie, 1988], [Harbison & Steele, 2002], [Plauger, 1992], and [Stevens & Rago, 2005].

2.6 Programs

Programs normally exist in two forms. The first form is *source code*, human-readable text consisting of a series of statements written in a programming language such as C. To be executed, source code must be converted to the second form: binary machine-language instructions that the computer can understand. (This contrasts with a *script*, which is a text file containing commands to be directly processed by a program such as a shell or other command interpreter.) The two meanings of the term *program* are normally considered synonymous, since the step of compiling and linking converts source code into semantically equivalent binary machine code.

Filters

A *filter* is the name often applied to a program that reads its input from *stdin*, performs some transformation of that input, and writes the transformed data to *stdout*. Examples of filters include *cat*, *grep*, *tr*, *sort*, *wc*, *sed*, and *awk*.

Command-line arguments

In C, programs can access the *command-line arguments*, the words that are supplied on the command line when the program is run. To access the command-line arguments, the *main()* function of the program is declared as follows:

```
int main(int argc, char *argv[])
```

The *argc* variable contains the total number of command-line arguments, and the individual arguments are available as strings pointed to by members of the array *argv*. The first of these strings, *argv[0]*, identifies the name of the program itself.

2.7 Processes

Put most simply, a *process* is an instance of an executing program. When a program is executed, the kernel loads the code of the program into virtual memory, allocates space for program variables, and sets up kernel bookkeeping data structures to record various information (such as process ID, termination status, user IDs, and group IDs) about the process.

From a kernel point of view, processes are the entities among which the kernel must share the various resources of the computer. For resources that are limited, such as memory, the kernel initially allocates some amount of the resource to the process, and adjusts this allocation over the lifetime of the process in response to the demands of the process and the overall system demand for that resource. When the process terminates, all such resources are released for reuse by other processes. Other resources, such as the CPU and network bandwidth, are renewable, but must be shared equitably among all processes.

Process memory layout

A process is logically divided into the following parts, known as *segments*:

- *Text*: the instructions of the program.
- *Data*: the static variables used by the program.
- *Heap*: an area from which programs can dynamically allocate extra memory.
- *Stack*: a piece of memory that grows and shrinks as functions are called and return and that is used to allocate storage for local variables and function call linkage information.

Process creation and program execution

A process can create a new process using the *fork()* system call. The process that calls *fork()* is referred to as the *parent process*, and the new process is referred to as the *child process*. The kernel creates the child process by making a duplicate of the parent process. The child inherits copies of the parent's data, stack, and heap segments, which it may then modify independently of the parent's copies. (The program text, which is placed in memory marked as read-only, is shared by the two processes.)

The child process goes on either to execute a different set of functions in the same code as the parent, or, frequently, to use the *execve()* system call to load and execute an entirely new program. An *execve()* call destroys the existing text, data, stack, and heap segments, replacing them with new segments based on the code of the new program.

Several related C library functions are layered on top of *execve()*, each providing a slightly different interface to the same functionality. All of these functions have names starting with the string *exec*, and where the differences don't matter, we'll use the notation *exec()* to refer generally to these functions. Be aware, however, that there is no actual function with the name *exec()*.

Commonly, we'll use the verb *to exec* to describe the operation performed by *execve()* and the library functions layered on top of it.

Process ID and parent process ID

Each process has a unique integer *process identifier* (PID). Each process also has a *parent process identifier* (PPID) attribute, which identifies the process that requested the kernel to create this process.

Process termination and termination status

A process can terminate in one of two ways: by requesting its own termination using the *_exit()* system call (or the related *exit()* library function), or by being killed by the delivery of a signal. In either case, the process yields a *termination status*, a small nonnegative integer value that is available for inspection by the parent process using the *wait()* system call. In the case of a call to *_exit()*, the process explicitly specifies its own termination status. If a process is killed by a signal, the termination status is set according to the type of signal that caused the death of the process. (Sometimes, we'll refer to the argument passed to *_exit()* as the *exit status* of the process, as distinct from the termination status, which is either the value passed to *_exit()* or an indication of the signal that killed the process.)

By convention, a termination status of 0 indicates that the process succeeded, and a nonzero status indicates that some error occurred. Most shells make the termination status of the last executed program available via a shell variable named *$?*.

Process user and group identifiers (credentials)

Each process has a number of associated user IDs (UIDs) and group IDs (GIDs). These include:

- *Real user ID* and *real group ID*: These identify the user and group to which the process belongs. A new process inherits these IDs from its parent. A login shell gets its real user ID and real group ID from the corresponding fields in the system password file.

- *Effective user ID* and *effective group ID*: These two IDs (in conjunction with the supplementary group IDs discussed in a moment) are used in determining the permissions that the process has when accessing protected resources such as files and interprocess communication objects. Typically, the process's effective IDs have the same values as the corresponding real IDs. Changing the effective IDs is a mechanism that allows a process to assume the privileges of another user or group, as described in a moment.
- *Supplementary group IDs*: These IDs identify additional groups to which a process belongs. A new process inherits its supplementary group IDs from its parent. A login shell gets its supplementary group IDs from the system group file.

Privileged processes

Traditionally, on UNIX systems, a *privileged process* is one whose *effective* user ID is 0 (superuser). Such a process bypasses the permission restrictions normally applied by the kernel. By contrast, the term *unprivileged* (or *nonprivileged*) is applied to processes run by other users. Such processes have a nonzero effective user ID and must abide by the permission rules enforced by the kernel.

A process may be privileged because it was created by another privileged process—for example, by a login shell started by *root* (superuser). Another way a process may become privileged is via the set-user-ID mechanism, which allows a process to assume an effective user ID that is the same as the user ID of the program file that it is executing.

Capabilities

Since kernel 2.2, Linux divides the privileges traditionally accorded to the superuser into a set of distinct units called *capabilities*. Each privileged operation is associated with a particular capability, and a process can perform an operation only if it has the corresponding capability. A traditional superuser process (effective user ID of 0) corresponds to a process with all capabilities enabled.

Granting a subset of capabilities to a process allows it to perform some of the operations normally permitted to the superuser, while preventing it from performing others.

Capabilities are described in detail in Chapter 39. In the remainder of the book, when noting that a particular operation can be performed only by a privileged process, we'll usually identify the specific capability in parentheses. Capability names begin with the prefix CAP_, as in CAP_KILL.

The *init* process

When booting the system, the kernel creates a special process called *init*, the "parent of all processes," which is derived from the program file /sbin/init. All processes on the system are created (using *fork()*) either by *init* or by one of its descendants. The *init* process always has the process ID 1 and runs with superuser privileges. The *init* process can't be killed (not even by the superuser), and it terminates only when the system is shut down. The main task of *init* is to create and monitor a range of processes required by a running system. (For details, see the *init(8)* manual page.)

Daemon processes

A *daemon* is a special-purpose process that is created and handled by the system in the same way as other processes, but which is distinguished by the following characteristics:

- It is long-lived. A daemon process is often started at system boot and remains in existence until the system is shut down.
- It runs in the background, and has no controlling terminal from which it can read input or to which it can write output.

Examples of daemon processes include *syslogd*, which records messages in the system log, and *httpd*, which serves web pages via the Hypertext Transfer Protocol (HTTP).

Environment list

Each process has an *environment list*, which is a set of *environment variables* that are maintained within the user-space memory of the process. Each element of this list consists of a name and an associated value. When a new process is created via *fork()*, it inherits a copy of its parent's environment. Thus, the environment provides a mechanism for a parent process to communicate information to a child process. When a process replaces the program that it is running using *exec()*, the new program either inherits the environment used by the old program or receives a new environment specified as part of the *exec()* call.

Environment variables are created with the *export* command in most shells (or the *setenv* command in the C shell), as in the following example:

```
$ export MYVAR='Hello world'
```

> Whenever we present a shell session log showing interactive input and output, the input text is always boldfaced. Sometimes, we include commentary in the log in italic text, adding notes about the commands entered or the output produced.

C programs can access the environment using an external variable (*char **environ*), and various library functions allow a process to retrieve and modify values in its environment.

Environment variables are used for a variety of purposes. For example, the shell defines and uses a range of variables that can be accessed by scripts and programs executed from the shell. These include the variable HOME, which specifies the pathname of the user's login directory, and the variable PATH, which specifies a list of directories that the shell should search when looking for programs corresponding to commands entered by the user.

Resource limits

Each process consumes resources, such as open files, memory, and CPU time. Using the *setrlimit()* system call, a process can establish upper limits on its consumption of various resources. Each such *resource limit* has two associated values: a *soft limit*, which limits the amount of the resource that the process may consume; and a *hard limit*, which is a ceiling on the value to which the soft limit may be adjusted. An unprivileged process may change its soft limit for a particular resource to any value in the range from zero up to the corresponding hard limit, but can only lower its hard limit.

When a new process is created with *fork()*, it inherits copies of its parent's resource limit settings.

The resource limits of the shell can be adjusted using the *ulimit* command (*limit* in the C shell). These limit settings are inherited by the child processes that the shell creates to execute commands.

2.8 Memory Mappings

The *mmap()* system call creates a new *memory mapping* in the calling process's virtual address space.

Mappings fall into two categories:

- A *file mapping* maps a region of a file into the calling process's virtual memory. Once mapped, the file's contents can be accessed by operations on the bytes in the corresponding memory region. The pages of the mapping are automatically loaded from the file as required.

- By contrast, an *anonymous mapping* doesn't have a corresponding file. Instead, the pages of the mapping are initialized to 0.

The memory in one process's mapping may be shared with mappings in other processes. This can occur either because two processes map the same region of a file or because a child process created by *fork()* inherits a mapping from its parent.

When two or more processes share the same pages, each process may see the changes made by other processes to the contents of the pages, depending on whether the mapping is created as private or shared. When a mapping is *private*, modifications to the contents of the mapping are not visible to other processes and are not carried through to the underlying file. When a mapping is *shared*, modifications to the contents of the mapping are visible to other processes sharing the same mapping and are carried through to the underlying file.

Memory mappings serve a variety of purposes, including initialization of a process's text segment from the corresponding segment of an executable file, allocation of new (zero-filled) memory, file I/O (memory-mapped I/O), and interprocess communication (via a shared mapping).

2.9 Static and Shared Libraries

An *object library* is a file containing the compiled object code for a (usually logically related) set of functions that may be called from application programs. Placing code for a set of functions in a single object library eases the tasks of program creation and maintenance. Modern UNIX systems provide two types of object libraries: *static libraries* and *shared libraries*.

Static libraries

Static libraries (sometimes also known as *archives*) were the only type of library on early UNIX systems. A static library is essentially a structured bundle of compiled object modules. To use functions from a static library, we specify that library in the link command used to build a program. After resolving the various function references from the main program to the modules in the static library, the linker extracts copies of the required object modules from the library and copies these into the resulting executable file. We say that such a program is *statically linked*.

The fact that each statically linked program includes its own copy of the object modules required from the library creates a number of disadvantages. One is that the duplication of object code in different executable files wastes disk space. A corresponding waste of memory occurs when statically linked programs using the same library function are executed at the same time; each program requires its own copy of the function to reside in memory. Additionally, if a library function requires modification, then, after recompiling that function and adding it to the static library, all applications that need to use the updated function must be relinked against the library.

Shared libraries

Shared libraries were designed to address the problems with static libraries.

If a program is linked against a shared library, then, instead of copying object modules from the library into the executable, the linker just writes a record into the executable to indicate that at run time the executable needs to use that shared library. When the executable is loaded into memory at run time, a program called the *dynamic linker* ensures that the shared libraries required by the executable are found and loaded into memory, and performs run-time linking to resolve the function calls in the executable to the corresponding definitions in the shared libraries. At run time, only a single copy of the code of the shared library needs to be resident in memory; all running programs can use that copy.

The fact that a shared library contains the sole compiled version of a function saves disk space. It also greatly eases the job of ensuring that programs employ the newest version of a function. Simply rebuilding the shared library with the new function definition causes existing programs to automatically use the new definition when they are next executed.

2.10 Interprocess Communication and Synchronization

A running Linux system consists of numerous processes, many of which operate independently of each other. Some processes, however, cooperate to achieve their intended purposes, and these processes need methods of communicating with one another and synchronizing their actions.

One way for processes to communicate is by reading and writing information in disk files. However, for many applications, this is too slow and inflexible.

Therefore, Linux, like all modern UNIX implementations, provides a rich set of mechanisms for *interprocess communication* (IPC), including the following:

- *signals*, which are used to indicate that an event has occurred;
- *pipes* (familiar to shell users as the | operator) and *FIFOs*, which can be used to transfer data between processes;
- *sockets*, which can be used to transfer data from one process to another, either on the same host computer or on different hosts connected by a network;
- *file locking*, which allows a process to lock regions of a file in order to prevent other processes from reading or updating the file contents;
- *message queues*, which are used to exchange messages (packets of data) between processes;
- *semaphores*, which are used to synchronize the actions of processes; and
- *shared memory*, which allows two or more processes to share a piece of memory. When one process changes the contents of the shared memory, all of the other processes can immediately see the changes.

The wide variety of IPC mechanisms on UNIX systems, with sometimes overlapping functionality, is in part due to their evolution under different variants of the UNIX system and the requirements of various standards. For example, FIFOs and UNIX domain sockets essentially perform the same function of allowing unrelated processes on the same system to exchange data. Both exist in modern UNIX systems because FIFOs came from System V, while sockets came from BSD.

2.11 Signals

Although we listed them as a method of IPC in the previous section, signals are more usually employed in a wide range of other contexts, and so deserve a longer discussion.

Signals are often described as "software interrupts." The arrival of a signal informs a process that some event or exceptional condition has occurred. There are various types of signals, each of which identifies a different event or condition. Each signal type is identified by a different integer, defined with symbolic names of the form SIGxxxx.

Signals are sent to a process by the kernel, by another process (with suitable permissions), or by the process itself. For example, the kernel may send a signal to a process when one of the following occurs:

- the user typed the *interrupt* character (usually *Control-C*) on the keyboard;
- one of the process's children has terminated;
- a timer (alarm clock) set by the process has expired; or
- the process attempted to access an invalid memory address.

Within the shell, the *kill* command can be used to send a signal to a process. The *kill()* system call provides the same facility within programs.

When a process receives a signal, it takes one of the following actions, depending on the signal:

- it ignores the signal;
- it is killed by the signal; or
- it is suspended until later being resumed by receipt of a special-purpose signal.

For most signal types, instead of accepting the default signal action, a program can choose to ignore the signal (useful if the default action for the signal is something other than being ignored), or to establish a *signal handler*. A signal handler is a programmer-defined function that is automatically invoked when the signal is delivered to the process. This function performs some action appropriate to the condition that generated the signal.

In the interval between the time it is generated and the time it is delivered, a signal is said to be *pending* for a process. Normally, a pending signal is delivered as soon as the receiving process is next scheduled to run, or immediately if the process is already running. However, it is also possible to *block* a signal by adding it to the process's *signal mask*. If a signal is generated while it is blocked, it remains pending until it is later unblocked (i.e., removed from the signal mask).

2.12 Threads

In modern UNIX implementations, each process can have multiple *threads* of execution. One way of envisaging threads is as a set of processes that share the same virtual memory, as well as a range of other attributes. Each thread is executing the same program code and shares the same data area and heap. However, each thread has its own stack containing local variables and function call linkage information.

Threads can communicate with each other via the global variables that they share. The threading API provides *condition variables* and *mutexes*, which are primitives that enable the threads of a process to communicate and synchronize their actions, in particular, their use of shared variables. Threads can also communicate with one another using the IPC and synchronization mechanisms described in Section 2.10.

The primary advantages of using threads are that they make it easy to share data (via global variables) between cooperating threads and that some algorithms transpose more naturally to a multithreaded implementation than to a multiprocess implementation. Furthermore, a multithreaded application can transparently take advantage of the possibilities for parallel processing on multiprocessor hardware.

2.13 Process Groups and Shell Job Control

Each program executed by the shell is started in a new process. For example, the shell creates three processes to execute the following pipeline of commands (which displays a list of files in the current working directory sorted by file size):

```
$ ls -l | sort -k5n | less
```

All major shells, except the Bourne shell, provide an interactive feature called *job control*, which allows the user to simultaneously execute and manipulate multiple commands or pipelines. In job-control shells, all of the processes in a pipeline are placed in a new *process group* or *job*. (In the simple case of a shell command line containing a single command, a new process group containing just a single process is created.) Each process in a process group has the same integer *process group identifier*, which is the same as the process ID of one of the processes in the group, termed the *process group leader*.

The kernel allows for various actions, notably the delivery of signals, to be performed on all members of a process group. Job-control shells use this feature to allow the user to suspend or resume all of the processes in a pipeline, as described in the next section.

2.14 Sessions, Controlling Terminals, and Controlling Processes

A *session* is a collection of process groups (jobs). All of the processes in a session have the same *session identifier*. A *session leader* is the process that created the session, and its process ID becomes the session ID.

Sessions are used mainly by job-control shells. All of the process groups created by a job-control shell belong to the same session as the shell, which is the session leader.

Sessions usually have an associated *controlling terminal*. The controlling terminal is established when the session leader process first opens a terminal device. For a session created by an interactive shell, this is the terminal at which the user logged in. A terminal may be the controlling terminal of at most one session.

As a consequence of opening the controlling terminal, the session leader becomes the *controlling process* for the terminal. The controlling process receives a SIGHUP signal if a terminal disconnect occurs (e.g., if the terminal window is closed).

At any point in time, one process group in a session is the *foreground process group* (*foreground job*), which may read input from the terminal and send output to it. If the user types the *interrupt* character (usually *Control-C*) or the *suspend* character (usually *Control-Z*) on the controlling terminal, then the terminal driver sends a signal that kills or suspends (i.e., stops) the foreground process group. A session can have any number of *background process groups* (*background jobs*), which are created by terminating a command with the ampersand (&) character.

Job-control shells provide commands for listing all jobs, sending signals to jobs, and moving jobs between the foreground and background.

2.15 Pseudoterminals

A *pseudoterminal* is a pair of connected virtual devices, known as the *master* and *slave*. This device pair provides an IPC channel allowing data to be transferred in both directions between the two devices.

The key point about a pseudoterminal is that the slave device provides an interface that behaves like a terminal, which makes it possible to connect a terminal-oriented program to the slave device and then use another program connected to the master device to drive the terminal-oriented program. Output written by the driver program undergoes the usual input processing performed by the terminal driver (for example, in the default mode, a carriage return is mapped to a newline) and is then passed as input to the terminal-oriented program connected to the slave. Anything that the terminal-oriented program writes to the slave is passed (after performing all of the usual terminal output processing) as input to the driver program. In other words, the driver program is performing the function normally performed by the user at a conventional terminal.

Pseudoterminals are used in a variety of applications, most notably in the implementation of terminal windows provided under an X Window System login and in applications providing network login services, such as *telnet* and *ssh*.

2.16 Date and Time

Two types of time are of interest to a process:

- *Real time* is measured either from some standard point (*calendar* time) or from some fixed point, typically the start, in the life of a process (*elapsed* or *wall clock* time). On UNIX systems, calendar time is measured in seconds since midnight on the morning of January 1, 1970, Universal Coordinated Time (usually abbreviated UTC), and coordinated on the base point for timezones defined by the longitudinal line passing through Greenwich, England. This date, which is close to the birth of the UNIX system, is referred to as the *Epoch*.

- *Process time*, also called *CPU time*, is the total amount of CPU time that a process has used since starting. CPU time is further divided into *system CPU time*, the time spent executing code in *kernel mode* (i.e., executing system calls and performing other kernel services on behalf of the process), and *user CPU time*, the time spent executing code in *user mode* (i.e., executing normal program code).

The *time* command displays the real time, the system CPU time, and user CPU time taken to execute the processes in a pipeline.

2.17 Client-Server Architecture

At various points in this book, we discuss the design and implementation of client-server applications.

A *client-server application* is one that is broken into two component processes:

- a *client*, which asks the server to carry out some *service* by sending it a request message; and

- a *server*, which examines the client's request, performs appropriate actions, and then sends a response message back to the client.

Sometimes, the client and server may engage in an extended dialogue of requests and responses.

Typically, the client application interacts with a user, while the server application provides access to some shared resource. Commonly, there are multiple instances of client processes communicating with one or a few instances of the server process.

The client and server may reside on the same host computer or on separate hosts connected via a network. To communicate with one another, the client and server use the IPC mechanisms discussed in Section 2.10.

Servers may implement a variety of services, such as:

- providing access to a database or other shared information resource;
- providing access to a remote file across a network;
- encapsulating some business logic;
- providing access to a shared hardware resource (e.g., a printer); or
- serving web pages.

Encapsulating a service within a single server is useful for a number of reasons, such as the following:

- *Efficiency*: It may be cheaper to provide one instance of a resource (e.g., a printer) that is managed by a server than to provide the same resource locally on every computer.
- *Control, coordination, and security*: By holding a resource (especially an information resource) at a single location, the server can coordinate access to the resource (e.g., so that two clients don't simultaneously update the same piece of information) or secure it so that it is made available to only selected clients.
- *Operation in a heterogeneous environment*: In a network, the various clients, and the server, can be running on different hardware and operating system platforms.

2.18 Realtime

Realtime applications are those that need to respond in a timely fashion to input. Frequently, such input comes from an external sensor or a specialized input device, and output takes the form of controlling some external hardware. Examples of applications with realtime response requirements include automated assembly lines, bank ATMs, and aircraft navigation systems.

Although many realtime applications require rapid responses to input, the defining factor is that the response is guaranteed to be delivered within a certain deadline time after the triggering event.

The provision of realtime responsiveness, especially where short response times are demanded, requires support from the underlying operating system. Most operating systems don't natively provide such support because the requirements of realtime responsiveness can conflict with the requirements of multiuser time-sharing operating systems. Traditional UNIX implementations are not realtime operating systems, although realtime variants have been devised. Realtime variants of Linux have also been created, and recent Linux kernels are moving toward full native support for realtime applications.

POSIX.1b defined a number of extensions to POSIX.1 for the support of real-time applications. These include asynchronous I/O, shared memory, memory-mapped files, memory locking, realtime clocks and timers, alternative scheduling policies, realtime signals, message queues, and semaphores. Even though they don't strictly qualify as realtime, most UNIX implementations now support some or all of these extensions. (During the course of this book, we describe those features of POSIX.1b that are supported by Linux.)

> In this book, we use the term *real time* to refer to the concept of calendar or elapsed time, and the term *realtime* to denote an operating system or application providing the type of responsiveness described in this section.

2.19 The /proc File System

Like several other UNIX implementations, Linux provides a /proc file system, which consists of a set of directories and files mounted under the /proc directory.

The /proc file system is a virtual file system that provides an interface to kernel data structures in a form that looks like files and directories on a file system. This provides an easy mechanism for viewing and changing various system attributes. In addition, a set of directories with names of the form /proc/*PID*, where *PID* is a process ID, allows us to view information about each process running on the system.

The contents of /proc files are generally in human-readable text form and can be parsed by shell scripts. A program can simply open and read from, or write to, the desired file. In most cases, a process must be privileged to modify the contents of files in the /proc directory.

As we describe various parts of the Linux programming interface, we'll also describe the relevant /proc files. Section 12.1 provides further general information on this file system. The /proc file system is not specified by any standards, and the details that we describe are Linux-specific.

2.20 Summary

In this chapter, we surveyed a range of fundamental concepts related to Linux system programming. An understanding of these concepts should provide readers with limited experience on Linux or UNIX with enough background to begin learning system programming.

3

SYSTEM PROGRAMMING CONCEPTS

This chapter covers various topics that are prerequisites for system programming. We begin by introducing system calls and detailing the steps that occur during their execution. We then consider library functions and how they differ from system calls, and couple this with a description of the (GNU) C library.

Whenever we make a system call or call a library function, we should always check the return status of the call in order to determine if it was successful. We describe how to perform such checks, and present a set of functions that are used in most of the example programs in this book to diagnose errors from system calls and library functions.

We conclude by looking at various issues related to portable programming, specifically the use of feature test macros and the standard system data types defined by SUSv3.

3.1 System Calls

A *system call* is a controlled entry point into the kernel, allowing a process to request that the kernel perform some action on the process's behalf. The kernel makes a range of services accessible to programs via the system call application programming interface (API). These services include, for example, creating a new process, performing I/O, and creating a pipe for interprocess communication. (The *syscalls(2)* manual page lists the Linux system calls.)

Before going into the details of how a system call works, we note some general points:

- A system call changes the processor state from user mode to kernel mode, so that the CPU can access protected kernel memory.
- The set of system calls is fixed. Each system call is identified by a unique number. (This numbering scheme is not normally visible to programs, which identify system calls by name.)
- Each system call may have a set of arguments that specify information to be transferred from user space (i.e., the process's virtual address space) to kernel space and vice versa.

From a programming point of view, invoking a system call looks much like calling a C function. However, behind the scenes, many steps occur during the execution of a system call. To illustrate this, we consider the steps in the order that they occur on a specific hardware implementation, the x86-32. The steps are as follows:

1. The application program makes a system call by invoking a wrapper function in the C library.

2. The wrapper function must make all of the system call arguments available to the system call trap-handling routine (described shortly). These arguments are passed to the wrapper via the stack, but the kernel expects them in specific registers. The wrapper function copies the arguments to these registers.

3. Since all system calls enter the kernel in the same way, the kernel needs some method of identifying the system call. To permit this, the wrapper function copies the system call number into a specific CPU register (%eax).

4. The wrapper function executes a *trap* machine instruction (int 0x80), which causes the processor to switch from user mode to kernel mode and execute code pointed to by location 0x80 (128 decimal) of the system's trap vector.

   > More recent x86-32 architectures implement the sysenter instruction, which provides a faster method of entering kernel mode than the conventional int 0x80 trap instruction. The use of sysenter is supported in the 2.6 kernel and from *glibc* 2.3.2 onward.

5. In response to the trap to location 0x80, the kernel invokes its *system_call()* routine (located in the assembler file arch/x86/kernel/entry.S) to handle the trap. This handler:

   a) Saves register values onto the kernel stack (Section 6.5).

   b) Checks the validity of the system call number.

   c) Invokes the appropriate system call service routine, which is found by using the system call number to index a table of all system call service routines (the kernel variable *sys_call_table*). If the system call service routine has any arguments, it first checks their validity; for example, it checks that addresses point to valid locations in user memory. Then the service routine performs the required task, which may involve modifying values at addresses specified in the given arguments and transferring data between user memory and kernel memory (e.g., in I/O operations). Finally, the service routine returns a result status to the *system_call()* routine.

d) Restores register values from the kernel stack and places the system call return value on the stack.

e) Returns to the wrapper function, simultaneously returning the processor to user mode.

6. If the return value of the system call service routine indicated an error, the wrapper function sets the global variable *errno* (see Section 3.4) using this value. The wrapper function then returns to the caller, providing an integer return value indicating the success or failure of the system call.

> On Linux, system call service routines follow a convention of returning a nonnegative value to indicate success. In case of an error, the routine returns a negative number, which is the negated value of one of the *errno* constants. When a negative value is returned, the C library wrapper function negates it (to make it positive), copies the result into *errno*, and returns −1 as the function result of the wrapper to indicate an error to the calling program.
>
> This convention relies on the assumption that system call service routines don't return negative values on success. However, for a few of these routines, this assumption doesn't hold. Normally, this is not a problem, since the range of negated *errno* values doesn't overlap with valid negative return values. However, this convention does cause a problem in one case: the F_GETOWN operation of the *fcntl()* system call, which we describe in Section 63.3.

Figure 3-1 illustrates the above sequence using the example of the *execve()* system call. On Linux/x86-32, *execve()* is system call number 11 (__NR_execve). Thus, in the *sys_call_table* vector, entry 11 contains the address of *sys_execve()*, the service routine for this system call. (On Linux, system call service routines typically have names of the form *sys_xyz()*, where *xyz()* is the system call in question.)

The information given in the preceding paragraphs is more than we'll usually need to know for the remainder of this book. However, it illustrates the important point that, even for a simple system call, quite a bit of work must be done, and thus system calls have a small but appreciable overhead.

> As an example of the overhead of making a system call, consider the *getppid()* system call, which simply returns the process ID of the parent of the calling process. On one of the author's x86-32 systems running Linux 2.6.25, 10 million calls to *getppid()* required approximately 2.2 seconds to complete. This amounts to around 0.3 microseconds per call. By comparison, on the same system, 10 million calls to a C function that simply returns an integer required 0.11 seconds, or around one-twentieth of the time required for calls to *getppid()*. Of course, most system calls have significantly more overhead than *getppid()*.

Since, from the point of view of a C program, calling the C library wrapper function is synonymous with invoking the corresponding system call service routine, in the remainder of this book, we use wording such as "invoking the system call *xyz()*" to mean "calling the wrapper function that invokes the system call *xyz()*."

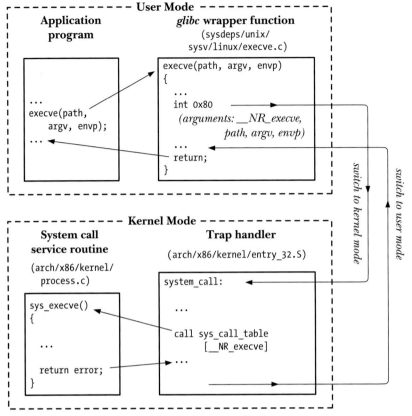

Figure 3-1: Steps in the execution of a system call

Appendix A describes the *strace* command, which can be used to trace the system calls made by a program, either for debugging purposes or simply to investigate what a program is doing.

More information about the Linux system call mechanism can be found in [Love, 2010], [Bovet & Cesati, 2005], and [Maxwell, 1999].

3.2 Library Functions

A *library function* is simply one of the multitude of functions that constitutes the standard C library. (For brevity, when talking about a specific function in the rest of the book we'll often just write *function* rather than *library function*.) The purposes of these functions are very diverse, including such tasks as opening a file, converting a time to a human-readable format, and comparing two character strings.

Many library functions don't make any use of system calls (e.g., the string-manipulation functions). On the other hand, some library functions are layered on top of system calls. For example, the *fopen()* library function uses the *open()* system call to actually open a file. Often, library functions are designed to provide a more caller-friendly interface than the underlying system call. For example, the *printf()* function provides output formatting and data buffering, whereas the *write()* system call just outputs a block of bytes. Similarly, the *malloc()* and *free()* functions perform various bookkeeping tasks that make them a much easier way to allocate and free memory than the underlying *brk()* system call.

3.3 The Standard C Library; The GNU C Library (*glibc*)

There are different implementations of the standard C library on the various UNIX implementations. The most commonly used implementation on Linux is the GNU C library (*glibc*, *http://www.gnu.org/software/libc/*).

> The principal developer and maintainer of the GNU C library was initially Roland McGrath. Nowadays, this task is carried out by Ulrich Drepper.
>
> Various other C libraries are available for Linux, including libraries with smaller memory requirements for use in embedded device applications. Examples include *uClibc* (*http://www.uclibc.org/*) and *diet libc* (*http://www.fefe.de/dietlibc/*). In this book, we confine the discussion to *glibc*, since that is the C library used by most applications developed on Linux.

Determining the version of *glibc* on the system

Sometimes, we need to determine the version of *glibc* on a system. From the shell, we can do this by running the *glibc* shared library file as though it were an executable program. When we run the library as an executable, it displays various text, including its version number:

```
$ /lib/libc.so.6
GNU C Library stable release version 2.10.1, by Roland McGrath et al.
Copyright (C) 2009 Free Software Foundation, Inc.
This is free software; see the source for copying conditions.
There is NO warranty; not even for MERCHANTABILITY or FITNESS FOR A
PARTICULAR PURPOSE.
Compiled by GNU CC version 4.4.0 20090506 (Red Hat 4.4.0-4).
Compiled on a Linux >>2.6.18-128.4.1.el5<< system on 2009-08-19.
Available extensions:
        The C stubs add-on version 2.1.2.
        crypt add-on version 2.1 by Michael Glad and others
        GNU Libidn by Simon Josefsson
        Native POSIX Threads Library by Ulrich Drepper et al
        BIND-8.2.3-T5B
        RT using linux kernel aio
For bug reporting instructions, please see:
<http://www.gnu.org/software/libc/bugs.html>.
```

In some Linux distributions, the GNU C library resides at a pathname other than /lib/libc.so.6. One way of determining the location of the library is to run the *ldd* (list dynamic dependencies) program against an executable linked dynamically against *glibc* (most executables are linked in this manner). We can then inspect the resulting library dependency list to find the location of the *glibc* shared library:

```
$ ldd myprog | grep libc
        libc.so.6 => /lib/tls/libc.so.6 (0x4004b000)
```

There are two means by which an application program can determine the version of the GNU C library present on the system: by testing constants or by calling a library function. From version 2.0 onward, *glibc* defines two constants, __GLIBC__ and _GLIBC_MINOR__, that can be tested at compile time (in #if statements). On a system with *glibc* 2.12 installed, these constants would have the values 2 and 12. However, these constants are of limited use in a program that is compiled on one system but run on another system with a different *glibc*. To handle this possibility, a program can call the *gnu_get_libc_version()* function to determine the version of *glibc* available at run time.

```
#include <gnu/libc-version.h>

const char *gnu_get_libc_version(void);
```
                    Returns pointer to null-terminated, statically allocated string
                                      containing GNU C library version number

The *gnu_get_libc_version()* function returns a pointer to a string, such as *2.12*.

> We can also obtain version information by using the *confstr()* function to retrieve the value of the (*glibc*-specific) _CS_GNU_LIBC_VERSION configuration variable. This call returns a string such as *glibc 2.12*.

3.4 Handling Errors from System Calls and Library Functions

Almost every system call and library function returns some type of status value indicating whether the call succeeded or failed. This status value should *always* be checked to see whether the call succeeded. If it did not, then appropriate action should be taken—at the very least, the program should display an error message warning that something unexpected occurred.

Although it is tempting to save typing time by excluding these checks (especially after seeing examples of UNIX and Linux programs where status values are not checked), it is a false economy. Many hours of debugging time can be wasted because a check was not made on the status return of a system call or library function that "couldn't possibly fail."

> A few system calls never fail. For example, *getpid()* always successfully returns the ID of a process, and *_exit()* always terminates a process. It is not necessary to check the return values from such system calls.

Handling system call errors

The manual page for each system call documents the possible return values of the call, showing which value(s) indicate an error. Usually, an error is indicated by a return of −1. Thus, a system call can be checked with code such as the following:

```
fd = open(pathname, flags, mode);        /* system call to open a file */
if (fd == -1) {
    /* Code to handle the error */
}
...
```

```
if (close(fd) == -1) {
    /* Code to handle the error */
}
```

When a system call fails, it sets the global integer variable *errno* to a positive value that identifies the specific error. Including the <errno.h> header file provides a declaration of *errno*, as well as a set of constants for the various error numbers. All of these symbolic names commence with E. The section headed ERRORS in each manual page provides a list of possible *errno* values that can be returned by each system call. Here is a simple example of the use of *errno* to diagnose a system call error:

```
cnt = read(fd, buf, numbytes);
if (cnt == -1) {
    if (errno == EINTR)
        fprintf(stderr, "read was interrupted by a signal\n");
    else {
        /* Some other error occurred */
    }
}
```

Successful system calls and library functions never reset *errno* to 0, so this variable may have a nonzero value as a consequence of an error from a previous call. Furthermore, SUSv3 permits a successful function call to set *errno* to a nonzero value (although few functions do this). Therefore, when checking for an error, we should always first check if the function return value indicates an error, and only then examine *errno* to determine the cause of the error.

A few system calls (e.g., *getpriority()*) can legitimately return −1 on success. To determine whether an error occurs in such calls, we set *errno* to 0 before the call, and then check it afterward. If the call returns −1 and *errno* is nonzero, an error occurred. (A similar statement also applies to a few library functions.)

A common course of action after a failed system call is to print an error message based on the *errno* value. The *perror()* and *strerror()* library functions are provided for this purpose.

The *perror()* function prints the string pointed to by its *msg* argument, followed by a message corresponding to the current value of *errno*.

```
#include <stdio.h>

void perror(const char *msg);
```

A simple way of handling errors from system calls would be as follows:

```
fd = open(pathname, flags, mode);
if (fd == -1) {
    perror("open");
    exit(EXIT_FAILURE);
}
```

The *strerror()* function returns the error string corresponding to the error number given in its *errnum* argument.

```
#include <string.h>

char *strerror(int errnum);
```
> Returns pointer to error string corresponding to *errnum*

The string returned by *strerror()* may be statically allocated, which means that it could be overwritten by subsequent calls to *strerror()*.

If *errnum* specifies an unrecognized error number, *strerror()* returns a string of the form *Unknown error nnn*. On some other implementations, *strerror()* instead returns NULL in this case.

Because *perror()* and *strerror()* functions are locale-sensitive (Section 10.4), error descriptions are displayed in the local language.

Handling errors from library functions

The various library functions return different data types and different values to indicate failure. (Check the manual page for each function.) For our purposes, library functions can be divided into the following categories:

- Some library functions return error information in exactly the same way as system calls: a −1 return value, with *errno* indicating the specific error. An example of such a function is *remove()*, which removes a file (using the *unlink()* system call) or a directory (using the *rmdir()* system call). Errors from these functions can be diagnosed in the same way as errors from system calls.

- Some library functions return a value other than −1 on error, but nevertheless set *errno* to indicate the specific error condition. For example, *fopen()* returns a NULL pointer on error, and the setting of *errno* depends on which underlying system call failed. The *perror()* and *strerror()* functions can be used to diagnose these errors.

- Other library functions don't use *errno* at all. The method for determining the existence and cause of errors depends on the particular function and is documented in the function's manual page. For these functions, it is a mistake to use *errno*, *perror()*, or *strerror()* to diagnose errors.

3.5 Notes on the Example Programs in This Book

In this section, we describe various conventions and features commonly employed by the example programs presented in this book.

3.5.1 Command-Line Options and Arguments

Many of the example programs in this book rely on command-line options and arguments to determine their behavior.

Traditional UNIX command-line options consist of an initial hyphen, a letter that identifies the option, and an optional argument. (GNU utilities provide an extended option syntax consisting of two initial hyphens, followed by a string identifying the option and an optional argument.) To parse these options, we use the standard *getopt()* library function (described in Appendix B).

le programs that has a nontrivial command-line syntax pro-
ility for the user: if invoked with the *--help* option, the pro-
message that indicates the syntax for command-line options

3.5.2 Common Functions and Header Files

Most of the example programs include a header file containing commonly required definitions, and they also use a set of common functions. We discuss the header file and functions in this section.

Common header file

Listing 3-1 is the header file used by nearly every program in this book. This header file includes various other header files used by many of the example programs, defines a *Boolean* data type, and defines macros for calculating the minimum and maximum of two numeric values. Using this header file allows us to make the example programs a bit shorter.

Listing 3-1: Header file used by most example programs

——————————————————————————————— `lib/tlpi_hdr.h`

```
#ifndef TLPI_HDR_H
#define TLPI_HDR_H        /* Prevent accidental double inclusion */

#include <sys/types.h>  /* Type definitions used by many programs */
#include <stdio.h>      /* Standard I/O functions */
#include <stdlib.h>     /* Prototypes of commonly used library functions,
                           plus EXIT_SUCCESS and EXIT_FAILURE constants */
#include <unistd.h>     /* Prototypes for many system calls */
#include <errno.h>      /* Declares errno and defines error constants */
#include <string.h>     /* Commonly used string-handling functions */

#include "get_num.h"    /* Declares our functions for handling numeric
                           arguments (getInt(), getLong()) */

#include "error_functions.h"  /* Declares our error-handling functions */

typedef enum { FALSE, TRUE } Boolean;

#define min(m,n) ((m) < (n) ? (m) : (n))
#define max(m,n) ((m) > (n) ? (m) : (n))

#endif
```

——————————————————————————————— `lib/tlpi_hdr.h`

Error-diagnostic functions

To simplify error handling in our example programs, we use the error-diagnostic functions whose declarations are shown in Listing 3-2.

Listing 3-2: Declarations for common error-handling functions

—————————————————————————————————————— `lib/error_functions.h`

```
#ifndef ERROR_FUNCTIONS_H
#define ERROR_FUNCTIONS_H

void errMsg(const char *format, ...);

#ifdef __GNUC__

    /* This macro stops 'gcc -Wall' complaining that "control reaches
       end of non-void function" if we use the following functions to
       terminate main() or some other non-void function. */

#define NORETURN __attribute__ ((__noreturn__))
#else
#define NORETURN
#endif

void errExit(const char *format, ...) NORETURN ;

void err_exit(const char *format, ...) NORETURN ;

void errExitEN(int errnum, const char *format, ...) NORETURN ;

void fatal(const char *format, ...) NORETURN ;

void usageErr(const char *format, ...) NORETURN ;

void cmdLineErr(const char *format, ...) NORETURN ;

#endif
```

—————————————————————————————————————— `lib/error_functions.h`

To diagnose errors from system calls and library functions, we use *errMsg()*,
errExit(), *err_exit()*, and *errExitEN()*.

```
#include "tlpi_hdr.h"

void errMsg(const char *format, ...);
void errExit(const char *format, ...);
void err_exit(const char *format, ...);
void errExitEN(int errnum, const char *format, ...);
```

The *errMsg()* function prints a message on standard error. Its argument list is the
same as for *printf()*, except that a terminating newline character is automatically
appended to the output string. The *errMsg()* function prints the error text corresponding to the current value of *errno*—this consists of the error name, such as
EPERM, plus the error description as returned by *strerror()*—followed by the formatted
output specified in the argument list.

The *errExit()* function operates like *errMsg()*, but also terminates the program,
either by calling *exit()* or, if the environment variable EF_DUMPCORE is defined with a

nonempty string value, by calling *abort()* to produce a core dump file for use with the debugger. (We explain core dump files in Section 22.1.)

The *err_exit()* function is similar to *errExit()*, but differs in two respects:

- It doesn't flush standard output before printing the error message.
- It terminates the process by calling *_exit()* instead of *exit()*. This causes the process to terminate without flushing *stdio* buffers or invoking exit handlers.

The details of these differences in the operation of *err_exit()* will become clearer in Chapter 25, where we describe the differences between *_exit()* and *exit()*, and consider the treatment of *stdio* buffers and exit handlers in a child created by *fork()*. For now, we simply note that *err_exit()* is especially useful if we write a library function that creates a child process that needs to terminate because of an error. This termination should occur without flushing the child's copy of the parent's (i.e., the calling process's) *stdio* buffers and without invoking exit handlers established by the parent.

The *errExitEN()* function is the same as *errExit()*, except that instead of printing the error text corresponding to the current value of *errno*, it prints the text corresponding to the error number (thus, the *EN* suffix) given in the argument *errnum*.

Mainly, we use *errExitEN()* in programs that employ the POSIX threads API. Unlike traditional UNIX system calls, which return –1 on error, the POSIX threads functions diagnose an error by returning an error number (i.e., a positive number of the type normally placed in *errno*) as their function result. (The POSIX threads functions return 0 on success.)

We could diagnose errors from the POSIX threads functions using code such as the following:

```
errno = pthread_create(&thread, NULL, func, &arg);
if (errno != 0)
    errExit("pthread_create");
```

However, this approach is inefficient because *errno* is defined in threaded programs as a macro that expands into a function call that returns a modifiable lvalue. Thus, each use of *errno* results in a function call. The *errExitEN()* function allows us to write a more efficient equivalent of the above code:

```
int s;

s = pthread_create(&thread, NULL, func, &arg);
if (s != 0)
    errExitEN(s, "pthread_create");
```

> In C terminology, an *lvalue* is an expression referring to a region of storage. The most common example of an lvalue is an identifier for a variable. Some operators also yield lvalues. For example, if *p* is a pointer to a storage area, then **p* is an lvalue. Under the POSIX threads API, *errno* is redefined to be a function that returns a pointer to a thread-specific storage area (see Section 31.3).

To diagnose other types of errors, we use *fatal()*, *usageErr()*, and *cmdLineErr()*.

```
#include "tlpi_hdr.h"

void fatal(const char *format, ...);
void usageErr(const char *format, ...);
void cmdLineErr(const char *format, ...);
```

The *fatal()* function is used to diagnose general errors, including errors from library functions that don't set *errno*. Its argument list is the same as for *printf()*, except that a terminating newline character is automatically appended to the out-put string. It prints the formatted output on standard error and then terminates the program as with *errExit()*.

The *usageErr()* function is used to diagnose errors in command-line argument usage. It takes an argument list in the style of *printf()* and prints the string *Usage:* followed by the formatted output on standard error, and then terminates the pro-gram by calling *exit()*. (Some of the example programs in this book provide their own extended version of the *usageErr()* function, under the name *usageError()*.)

The *cmdLineErr()* function is similar to *usageErr()*, but is intended for diagnosing errors in the command-line arguments specified to a program.

The implementations of our error-diagnostic functions are shown in Listing 3-3.

Listing 3-3: Error-handling functions used by all programs

—— **lib/**

```
error_functions.c #include <stdarg.h>
#include "error_functions.h"
#include "tlpi_hdr.h"
#include "ename.c.inc"            /* Defines ename and MAX_ENAME */

NORETURN
static void
terminate(Boolean useExit3)
{
    char *s;

    /* Dump core if EF_DUMPCORE environment variable is defined and
       is a nonempty string; otherwise call exit(3) or _exit(2),
       depending on the value of 'useExit3'. */

    s = getenv("EF_DUMPCORE");

    if (s != NULL && *s != '\0')
        abort();
    else if (useExit3)
        exit(EXIT_FAILURE);
    else
        _exit(EXIT_FAILURE);
}
```

```c
static void
outputError(Boolean useErr, int err, Boolean flushStdout,
        const char *format, va_list ap)
{
#define BUF_SIZE 500
    char buf[BUF_SIZE], userMsg[BUF_SIZE], errText[BUF_SIZE];

    vsnprintf(userMsg, BUF_SIZE, format, ap);

    if (useErr)
        snprintf(errText, BUF_SIZE, " [%s %s]",
                (err > 0 && err <= MAX_ENAME) ?
                ename[err] : "?UNKNOWN?", strerror(err));
    else
        snprintf(errText, BUF_SIZE, ":");

    snprintf(buf, BUF_SIZE, "ERROR%s %s\n", errText, userMsg);

    if (flushStdout)
        fflush(stdout);         /* Flush any pending stdout */
    fputs(buf, stderr);
    fflush(stderr);             /* In case stderr is not line-buffered */
}

void
errMsg(const char *format, ...)
{
    va_list argList;
    int savedErrno;

    savedErrno = errno;         /* In case we change it here */

    va_start(argList, format);
    outputError(TRUE, errno, TRUE, format, argList);
    va_end(argList);

    errno = savedErrno;
}

void
errExit(const char *format, ...)
{
    va_list argList;

    va_start(argList, format);
    outputError(TRUE, errno, TRUE, format, argList);
    va_end(argList);

    terminate(TRUE);
}
```

```c
void
err_exit(const char *format, ...)
{
    va_list argList;

    va_start(argList, format);
    outputError(TRUE, errno, FALSE, format, argList);
    va_end(argList);

    terminate(FALSE);
}

void
errExitEN(int errnum, const char *format, ...)
{
    va_list argList;

    va_start(argList, format);
    outputError(TRUE, errnum, TRUE, format, argList);
    va_end(argList);

    terminate(TRUE);
}

void
fatal(const char *format, ...)
{
    va_list argList;

    va_start(argList, format);
    outputError(FALSE, 0, TRUE, format, argList);
    va_end(argList);

    terminate(TRUE);
}

void
usageErr(const char *format, ...)
{
    va_list argList;

    fflush(stdout);             /* Flush any pending stdout */

    fprintf(stderr, "Usage: ");
    va_start(argList, format);
    vfprintf(stderr, format, argList);
    va_end(argList);

    fflush(stderr);             /* In case stderr is not line-buffered */
    exit(EXIT_FAILURE);
}
```

```
void
cmdLineErr(const char *format, ...)
{
    va_list argList;

    fflush(stdout);             /* Flush any pending stdout */

    fprintf(stderr, "Command-line usage error: ");
    va_start(argList, format);
    vfprintf(stderr, format, argList);
    va_end(argList);

    fflush(stderr);             /* In case stderr is not line-buffered */
    exit(EXIT_FAILURE);
}
```

―――――――――――――――――――――――――――――――― **lib/error_functions.c**

The file ename.c.inc included by Listing 3-3 is shown in Listing 3-4. This file defines an array of strings, *ename*, that are the symbolic names corresponding to each of the possible *errno* values. Our error-handling functions use this array to print out the symbolic name corresponding to a particular error number. This is a workaround to deal with the facts that, on the one hand, the string returned by *strerror()* doesn't identify the symbolic constant corresponding to its error message, while, on the other hand, the manual pages describe errors using their symbolic names. Printing out the symbolic name gives us an easy way of looking up the cause of an error in the manual pages.

> The content of the ename.c.inc file is architecture-specific, because *errno* values vary somewhat from one Linux hardware architecture to another. The version shown in Listing 3-4 is for a Linux 2.6/x86-32 system. This file was built using a script (lib/Build_ename.sh) included in the source code distribution for this book. This script can be used to build a version of ename.c.inc that should be suitable for a specific hardware platform and kernel version.

Note that some of the strings in the *ename* array are empty. These correspond to unused error values. Furthermore, some of the strings in *ename* consist of two error names separated by a slash. These strings correspond to cases where two symbolic error names have the same numeric value.

> From the ename.c.inc file, we can see that the EAGAIN and EWOULDBLOCK errors have the same value. (SUSv3 explicitly permits this, and the values of these constants are the same on most, but not all, other UNIX systems.) These errors are returned by a system call in circumstances in which it would normally block (i.e., be forced to wait before completing), but the caller requested that the system call return an error instead of blocking. EAGAIN originated on System V, and it was the error returned for system calls performing I/O, semaphore operations, message queue operations, and file locking (*fcntl()*). EWOULDBLOCK originated on BSD, and it was returned by file locking (*flock()*) and socket-related system calls.
>
> Within SUSv3, EWOULDBLOCK is mentioned only in the specifications of various interfaces related to sockets. For these interfaces, SUSv3 permits either EAGAIN or EWOULDBLOCK to be returned by nonblocking calls. For all other non-blocking calls, only the error EAGAIN is specified in SUSv3.

Listing 3-4: Linux error names (x86-32 version)

———————————————————————————————————— lib/ename.c.inc

```
static char *ename[] = {
    /*   0 */ "",
    /*   1 */ "EPERM", "ENOENT", "ESRCH", "EINTR", "EIO", "ENXIO", "E2BIG",
    /*   8 */ "ENOEXEC", "EBADF", "ECHILD", "EAGAIN/EWOULDBLOCK", "ENOMEM",
    /*  13 */ "EACCES", "EFAULT", "ENOTBLK", "EBUSY", "EEXIST", "EXDEV",
    /*  19 */ "ENODEV", "ENOTDIR", "EISDIR", "EINVAL", "ENFILE", "EMFILE",
    /*  25 */ "ENOTTY", "ETXTBSY", "EFBIG", "ENOSPC", "ESPIPE", "EROFS",
    /*  31 */ "EMLINK", "EPIPE", "EDOM", "ERANGE", "EDEADLK/EDEADLOCK",
    /*  36 */ "ENAMETOOLONG", "ENOLCK", "ENOSYS", "ENOTEMPTY", "ELOOP", "",
    /*  42 */ "ENOMSG", "EIDRM", "ECHRNG", "EL2NSYNC", "EL3HLT", "EL3RST",
    /*  48 */ "ELNRNG", "EUNATCH", "ENOCSI", "EL2HLT", "EBADE", "EBADR",
    /*  54 */ "EXFULL", "ENOANO", "EBADRQC", "EBADSLT", "", "EBFONT", "ENOSTR",
    /*  61 */ "ENODATA", "ETIME", "ENOSR", "ENONET", "ENOPKG", "EREMOTE",
    /*  67 */ "ENOLINK", "EADV", "ESRMNT", "ECOMM", "EPROTO", "EMULTIHOP",
    /*  73 */ "EDOTDOT", "EBADMSG", "EOVERFLOW", "ENOTUNIQ", "EBADFD",
    /*  78 */ "EREMCHG", "ELIBACC", "ELIBBAD", "ELIBSCN", "ELIBMAX",
    /*  83 */ "ELIBEXEC", "EILSEQ", "ERESTART", "ESTRPIPE", "EUSERS",
    /*  88 */ "ENOTSOCK", "EDESTADDRREQ", "EMSGSIZE", "EPROTOTYPE",
    /*  92 */ "ENOPROTOOPT", "EPROTONOSUPPORT", "ESOCKTNOSUPPORT",
    /*  95 */ "EOPNOTSUPP/ENOTSUP", "EPFNOSUPPORT", "EAFNOSUPPORT",
    /*  98 */ "EADDRINUSE", "EADDRNOTAVAIL", "ENETDOWN", "ENETUNREACH",
    /* 102 */ "ENETRESET", "ECONNABORTED", "ECONNRESET", "ENOBUFS", "EISCONN",
    /* 107 */ "ENOTCONN", "ESHUTDOWN", "ETOOMANYREFS", "ETIMEDOUT",
    /* 111 */ "ECONNREFUSED", "EHOSTDOWN", "EHOSTUNREACH", "EALREADY",
    /* 115 */ "EINPROGRESS", "ESTALE", "EUCLEAN", "ENOTNAM", "ENAVAIL",
    /* 120 */ "EISNAM", "EREMOTEIO", "EDQUOT", "ENOMEDIUM", "EMEDIUMTYPE",
    /* 125 */ "ECANCELED", "ENOKEY", "EKEYEXPIRED", "EKEYREVOKED",
    /* 129 */ "EKEYREJECTED", "EOWNERDEAD", "ENOTRECOVERABLE", "ERFKILL"
};

#define MAX_ENAME 132
```

———————————————————————————————————— lib/ename.c.inc

Functions for parsing numeric command-line arguments

The header file in Listing 3-5 provides the declaration of two functions that we frequently use for parsing integer command-line arguments: *getInt()* and *getLong()*. The primary advantage of using these functions instead of *atoi()*, *atol()*, and *strtol()* is that they provide some basic validity checking of numeric arguments.

```
#include "tlpi_hdr.h"

int getInt(const char *arg, int flags, const char *name);
long getLong(const char *arg, int flags, const char *name);
                              Both return arg converted to numeric form
```

The *getInt()* and *getLong()* functions convert the string pointed to by *arg* to an *int* or a *long*, respectively. If *arg* doesn't contain a valid integer string (i.e., only digits and the characters + and -), then these functions print an error message and terminate the program.

If the *name* argument is non-NULL, it should contain a string identifying the argument in *arg*. This string is included as part of any error message displayed by these functions.

The *flags* argument provides some control over the operation of the *getInt()* and *getLong()* functions. By default, these functions expect strings containing signed decimal integers. By ORing (|) one or more of the GN_* constants defined in Listing 3-5 into *flags*, we can select alternative bases for conversion and restrict the range of the number to being nonnegative or greater than 0.

The implementations of the *getInt()* and *getLong()* functions are provided in Listing 3-6.

> Although the *flags* argument allows us to enforce the range checks described in the main text, in some cases, we don't request such checks in our example programs, even though it might seem logical to do so. For example, in Listing 47-1, we don't check the *init-value* argument. This means that the user could specify a negative number as the initial value for a semaphore, which would result in an error (ERANGE) in the subsequent *semctl()* system call, because a semaphore can't have a negative value. Omitting range checks in such cases allows us to experiment not just with the correct use of system calls and library functions, but also to see what happens when invalid arguments are supplied. Real-world applications would usually impose stronger checks on their command-line arguments.

Listing 3-5: Header file for get_num.c

――――――――――――――――――――――――――――――――――――――― lib/get_num.h
```
#ifndef GET_NUM_H
#define GET_NUM_H

#define GN_NONNEG      01      /* Value must be >= 0 */
#define GN_GT_0        02      /* Value must be > 0 */

                              /* By default, integers are decimal */
#define GN_ANY_BASE    0100    /* Can use any base - like strtol(3) */
#define GN_BASE_8      0200    /* Value is expressed in octal */
#define GN_BASE_16     0400    /* Value is expressed in hexadecimal */

long getLong(const char *arg, int flags, const char *name);

int getInt(const char *arg, int flags, const char *name);

#endif
```
――――――――――――――――――――――――――――――――――――――― lib/get_num.h

Listing 3-6: Functions for parsing numeric command-line arguments

――――――――――――――――――――――――――――――――――――――― lib/get_num.c
```
#include <stdio.h>
#include <stdlib.h>
#include <string.h>
#include <limits.h>
#include <errno.h>
#include "get_num.h"
```

```
static void
gnFail(const char *fname, const char *msg, const char *arg, const char *name)
{
    fprintf(stderr, "%s error", fname);
    if (name != NULL)
        fprintf(stderr, " (in %s)", name);
    fprintf(stderr, ": %s\n", msg);
    if (arg != NULL && *arg != '\0')
        fprintf(stderr, "        offending text: %s\n", arg);

    exit(EXIT_FAILURE);
}

static long
getNum(const char *fname, const char *arg, int flags, const char *name)
{
    long res;
    char *endptr;
    int base;

    if (arg == NULL || *arg == '\0')
        gnFail(fname, "null or empty string", arg, name);

    base = (flags & GN_ANY_BASE) ? 0 : (flags & GN_BASE_8) ? 8 :
                        (flags & GN_BASE_16) ? 16 : 10;

    errno = 0;
    res = strtol(arg, &endptr, base);
    if (errno != 0)
        gnFail(fname, "strtol() failed", arg, name);

    if (*endptr != '\0')
        gnFail(fname, "nonnumeric characters", arg, name);

    if ((flags & GN_NONNEG) && res < 0)
        gnFail(fname, "negative value not allowed", arg, name);

    if ((flags & GN_GT_0) && res <= 0)
        gnFail(fname, "value must be > 0", arg, name);

    return res;
}

long
getLong(const char *arg, int flags, const char *name)
{
    return getNum("getLong", arg, flags, name);
}

int
getInt(const char *arg, int flags, const char *name)
{
    long res;

    res = getNum("getInt", arg, flags, name);
```

```
    if (res > INT_MAX || res < INT_MIN)
        gnFail("getInt", "integer out of range", arg, name);

    return res;
}
```
─── lib/get_num.c

3.6 Portability Issues

In this section, we consider the topic of writing portable system programs. We introduce feature test macros and the standard system data types defined by SUSv3, and then look at some other portability issues.

3.6.1 Feature Test Macros

Various standards govern the behavior of the system call and library function APIs (see Section 1.3). Some of these standards are defined by standards bodies such as The Open Group (Single UNIX Specification), while others are defined by the two historically important UNIX implementations: BSD and System V Release 4 (and the associated System V Interface Definition).

Sometimes, when writing a portable application, we may want the various header files to expose only the definitions (constants, function prototypes, and so on) that follow a particular standard. To do this, we define one or more of the *feature test macros* listed below when compiling a program. One way that we can do this is by defining the macro in the program source code before including any header files:

```
#define _BSD_SOURCE 1
```

Alternatively, we can use the *–D* option to the C compiler:

```
$ cc -D_BSD_SOURCE prog.c
```

> The term *feature test macro* may seem confusing, but it makes sense if we look at things from the perspective of the implementation. The implementation decides which of the *features* available in each header it should make visible, by *testing* (with #if) which values the application has defined for these *macros*.

The following feature test macros are specified by the relevant standards, and consequently their usage is portable to all systems that support these standards:

_POSIX_SOURCE
> If defined (with any value), expose definitions conforming to POSIX.1-1990 and ISO C (1990). This macro is superseded by _POSIX_C_SOURCE.

_POSIX_C_SOURCE
> If defined with the value 1, this has the same effect as _POSIX_SOURCE. If defined with a value greater than or equal to 199309, also expose definitions for POSIX.1b (realtime). If defined with a value greater than or equal to 199506, also expose definitions for POSIX.1c (threads). If defined with the value 200112, also expose definitions for the POSIX.1-2001 base specification (i.e., the XSI extension is excluded). (Prior to version 2.3.3, the

glibc headers don't interpret the value 200112 for _POSIX_C_SOURCE.) If defined with the value 200809, also expose definitions for the POSIX.1-2008 base specification. (Prior to version 2.10, the *glibc* headers don't interpret the value 200809 for _POSIX_C_SOURCE.)

_XOPEN_SOURCE

If defined (with any value), expose POSIX.1, POSIX.2, and X/Open (XPG4) definitions. If defined with the value 500 or greater, also expose SUSv2 (UNIX 98 and XPG5) extensions. Setting to 600 or greater additionally exposes SUSv3 XSI (UNIX 03) extensions and C99 extensions. (Prior to version 2.2, the *glibc* headers don't interpret the value 600 for _XOPEN_SOURCE.) Setting to 700 or greater also exposes SUSv4 XSI extensions. (Prior to version 2.10, the *glibc* headers don't interpret the value 700 for _XOPEN_SOURCE.) The values 500, 600, and 700 for _XOPEN_SOURCE were chosen because SUSv2, SUSv3, and SUSv4 are Issues 5, 6, and 7, respectively, of the X/Open specifications.

The following feature test macros listed are *glibc*-specific:

_BSD_SOURCE

If defined (with any value), expose BSD definitions. Explicitly setting just this macro causes BSD definitions to be favored in a few cases where standards conflict.

_SVID_SOURCE

If defined (with any value), expose System V Interface Definition (SVID) definitions.

_GNU_SOURCE

If defined (with any value), expose all of the definitions provided by setting all of the preceding macros, as well as various GNU extensions.

When the GNU C compiler is invoked without special options, _POSIX_SOURCE, _POSIX_C_SOURCE=200809 (200112 with *glibc* versions 2.5 to 2.9, or 199506 with *glibc* versions earlier than 2.4), _BSD_SOURCE, and _SVID_SOURCE are defined by default.

If individual macros are defined, or the compiler is invoked in one of its standard modes (e.g., *cc –ansi* or *cc –std=c99*), then only the requested definitions are supplied. There is one exception: if _POSIX_C_SOURCE is not otherwise defined, and the compiler is not invoked in one of its standard modes, then _POSIX_C_SOURCE is defined with the value 200809 (200112 with *glibc* versions 2.4 to 2.9, or 199506 with *glibc* versions earlier than 2.4).

Defining multiple macros is additive, so that we could, for example, use the following *cc* command to explicitly select the same macro settings as are provided by default:

```
$ cc -D_POSIX_SOURCE -D_POSIX_C_SOURCE=199506 \
            -D_BSD_SOURCE -D_SVID_SOURCE prog.c
```

The <features.h> header file and the *feature_test_macros(7)* manual page provide further information on precisely what values are assigned to each of the feature test macros.

_POSIX_C_SOURCE, _XOPEN_SOURCE, and POSIX.1/SUS

Only the _POSIX_C_SOURCE and _XOPEN_SOURCE feature test macros are specified in POSIX.1-2001/SUSv3, which requires that these macros be defined with the values 200112 and 600, respectively, in conforming applications. Defining _POSIX_C_SOURCE as 200112 provides conformance to the POSIX.1-2001 base specification (i.e., *POSIX conformance*, excluding the XSI extension). Defining _XOPEN_SOURCE as 600 provides conformance to SUSv3 (i.e., *XSI conformance*, the base specification plus the XSI extension). Analogous statements apply for POSIX.1-2008/SUSv4, which require that the two macros be defined with the values 200809 and 700.

SUSv3 specifies that setting _XOPEN_SOURCE to 600 should supply all of the features that are enabled if _POSIX_C_SOURCE is set to 200112. Thus, an application needs to define only _XOPEN_SOURCE for SUSv3 (i.e., XSI) conformance. SUSv4 makes an analogous specification that setting _XOPEN_SOURCE to 700 should supply all of the features that are enabled if _POSIX_C_SOURCE is set to 200809.

Feature test macros in function prototypes and source code examples

The manual pages describe which feature test macro(s) must be defined in order to make a particular constant definition or function declaration visible from a header file.

All of the source code examples in this book are written so that they will compile using either the default GNU C compiler options or the following options:

```
$ cc -std=c99 -D_XOPEN_SOURCE=600
```

The prototype of each function shown in this book indicates any feature test macro(s) that must be defined in order to employ that function in a program compiled with either the default compiler options or the options in the *cc* command just shown. The manual pages provide more precise descriptions of the feature test macro(s) required to expose the declaration of each function.

3.6.2 System Data Types

Various implementation data types are represented using standard C types, for example, process IDs, user IDs, and file offsets. Although it would be possible to use the C fundamental types such as *int* and *long* to declare variables storing such information, this reduces portability across UNIX systems, for the following reasons:

- The sizes of these fundamental types vary across UNIX implementations (e.g., a *long* may be 4 bytes on one system and 8 bytes on another), or sometimes even in different compilation environments on the same implementation. Furthermore, different implementations may use different types to represent the same information. For example, a process ID might be an *int* on one system but a *long* on another.

- Even on a single UNIX implementation, the types used to represent information may differ between releases of the implementation. Notable examples on Linux are user and group IDs. On Linux 2.2 and earlier, these values were represented in 16 bits. On Linux 2.4 and later, they are 32-bit values.

To avoid such portability problems, SUSv3 specifies various standard system data types, and requires an implementation to define and use these types appropriately.

Each of these types is defined using the C typedef feature. For example, the *pid_t* data type is intended for representing process IDs, and on Linux/x86-32 this type is defined as follows:

```
typedef int pid_t;
```

Most of the standard system data types have names ending in *_t*. Many of them are declared in the header file <sys/types.h>, although a few are defined in other header files.

An application should employ these type definitions to portably declare the variables it uses. For example, the following declaration would allow an application to correctly represent process IDs on any SUSv3-conformant system:

```
pid_t mypid;
```

Table 3-1 lists some of the system data types we'll encounter in this book. For certain types in this table, SUSv3 requires that the type be implemented as an *arithmetic type*. This means that the implementation may choose the underlying type as either an integer or a floating-point (real or complex) type.

Table 3-1: Selected system data types

Data type	SUSv3 type requirement	Description
blkcnt_t	signed integer	File block count (Section 15.1)
blksize_t	signed integer	File block size (Section 15.1)
cc_t	unsigned integer	Terminal special character (Section 62.4)
clock_t	integer or real-floating	System time in clock ticks (Section 10.7)
clockid_t	an arithmetic type	Clock identifier for POSIX.1b clock and timer functions (Section 23.6)
comp_t	not in SUSv3	Compressed clock ticks (Section 28.1)
dev_t	integer	Device number, consisting of major and minor numbers (Section 15.1)
DIR	no type requirement	Directory stream (Section 18.8)
fd_set	structure type	File descriptor set for *select()* (Section 63.2.1)
fsblkcnt_t	unsigned integer	File-system block count (Section 14.11)
fsfilcnt_t	unsigned integer	File count (Section 14.11)
gid_t	integer	Numeric group identifier (Section 8.3)
id_t	integer	A generic type for holding identifiers; large enough to hold at least *pid_t*, *uid_t*, and *gid_t*
in_addr_t	32-bit unsigned integer	IPv4 address (Section 59.4)
in_port_t	16-bit unsigned integer	IP port number (Section 59.4)
ino_t	unsigned integer	File i-node number (Section 15.1)
key_t	an arithmetic type	System V IPC key (Section 45.2)
mode_t	integer	File permissions and type (Section 15.1)
mqd_t	no type requirement, but shall not be an array type	POSIX message queue descriptor
msglen_t	unsigned integer	Number of bytes allowed in System V message queue (Section 46.4)

Table 3-1: Selected system data types (continued)

Data type	SUSv3 type requirement	Description
msgqnum_t	unsigned integer	Counts of messages in System V message queue (Section 46.4)
nfds_t	unsigned integer	Number of file descriptors for *poll()* (Section 63.2.2)
nlink_t	integer	Count of (hard) links to a file (Section 15.1)
off_t	signed integer	File offset or size (Sections 4.7 and 15.1)
pid_t	signed integer	Process ID, process group ID, or session ID (Sections 6.2, 34.2, and 34.3)
ptrdiff_t	signed integer	Difference between two pointer values, as a signed integer
rlim_t	unsigned integer	Resource limit (Section 36.2)
sa_family_t	unsigned integer	Socket address family (Section 56.4)
shmatt_t	unsigned integer	Count of attached processes for a System V shared memory segment (Section 48.8)
sig_atomic_t	integer	Data type that can be atomically accessed (Section 21.1.3)
siginfo_t	structure type	Information about the origin of a signal (Section 21.4)
sigset_t	integer or structure type	Signal set (Section 20.9)
size_t	unsigned integer	Size of an object in bytes
socklen_t	integer type of at least 32 bits	Size of a socket address structure in bytes (Section 56.3)
speed_t	unsigned integer	Terminal line speed (Section 62.7)
ssize_t	signed integer	Byte count or (negative) error indication
stack_t	structure type	Description of an alternate signal stack (Section 21.3)
suseconds_t	signed integer allowing range [−1, 1000000]	Microsecond time interval (Section 10.1)
tcflag_t	unsigned integer	Terminal mode flag bit mask (Section 62.2)
time_t	integer	Calendar time in seconds since the Epoch (Section 10.1)
timer_t	an arithmetic type	Timer identifier for POSIX.1b interval timer functions (Section 23.6)
uid_t	integer	Numeric user identifier (Section 8.1)

When discussing the data types in Table 3-1 in later chapters, we'll often make statements that some type "is an integer type [specified by SUSv3]." This means that SUSv3 requires the type to be defined as an integer, but doesn't require that a particular native integer type (e.g., *short*, *int*, or *long*) be used. (Often, we won't say which particular native data type is actually used to represent each of the system data types in Linux, because a portable application should be written so that it doesn't care which data type is used.)

Printing system data type values

When printing values of one of the numeric system data types shown in Table 3-1 (e.g., *pid_t* and *uid_t*), we must be careful not to include a representation dependency in the *printf()* call. A representation dependency can occur because C's argument promotion rules convert values of type *short* to *int*, but leave values of type *int* and *long* unchanged. This means that, depending on the definition of the system data type, either an *int* or a *long* is passed in the *printf()* call. However, because *printf()* has no way to determine the types of its arguments at run time, the caller must explicitly provide this information using the %d or %ld format specifier. The problem is that simply coding one of these specifiers within the *printf()* call creates an implementation dependency. The usual solution is to use the %ld specifier and always cast the corresponding value to *long*, like so:

```
pid_t mypid;

mypid = getpid();            /* Returns process ID of calling process */
printf("My PID is %ld\n", (long) mypid);
```

We make one exception to the above technique. Because the *off_t* data type is the size of *long long* in some compilation environments, we cast *off_t* values to this type and use the %lld specifier, as described in Section 5.10.

> The C99 standard defines the z length modifier for *printf()*, to indicate that the following integer conversion corresponds to a *size_t* or *ssize_t* type. Thus, we could write %zd instead of using %ld plus a cast for *ssize_t*, and analogously %zu for *size_t*. Although this specifier is available in *glibc*, we avoid it because it is not available on all UNIX implementations.
>
> The C99 standard also defines the j length modifier, which specifies that the corresponding argument is of type *intmax_t* (or *uintmax_t*), an integer type that is guaranteed to be large enough to be able to represent an integer of any type. Ultimately, the use of an *(intmax_t)* cast plus the %jd specifier should replace the *(long)* cast plus the %ld specifier as the best way of printing numeric system data type values, since the former approach also handles *long long* values and any extended integer types such as *int128_t*. However, (again) we avoid this technique since it is not possible on all UNIX implementations.

3.6.3   Miscellaneous Portability Issues

In this section, we consider a few other portability issues that we may encounter when writing system programs.

Initializing and using structures

Each UNIX implementation specifies a range of standard structures that are used in various system calls and library functions. As an example, consider the *sembuf* structure, which is used to represent a semaphore operation to be performed by the *semop()* system call:

```
struct sembuf {
    unsigned short sem_num;     /* Semaphore number */
    short          sem_op;      /* Operation to be performed */
    short          sem_flg;     /* Operation flags */
};
```

Although SUSv3 specifies structures such as *sembuf*, it is important to realize the following:

- In general, the order of field definitions within such structures is not specified.
- In some cases, extra implementation-specific fields may be included in such structures.

Consequently, it is not portable to use a structure initializer such as the following:

```
struct sembuf s = { 3, -1, SEM_UNDO };
```

Although this initializer will work on Linux, it won't work on another implementation where the fields in the *sembuf* structure are defined in a different order. To portably initialize such structures, we must use explicit assignment statements, as in the following:

```
struct sembuf s;

s.sem_num = 3;
s.sem_op  = -1;
s.sem_flg = SEM_UNDO;
```

If we are using C99, then we can employ that language's new syntax for structure initializers to write an equivalent initialization:

```
struct sembuf s = { .sem_num = 3, .sem_op = -1, .sem_flg = SEM_UNDO };
```

Considerations about the order of the members of standard structures also apply if we want to write the contents of a standard structure to a file. To do this portably, we can't simply do a binary write of the structure. Instead, the structure fields must be written individually (probably in text form) in a specified order.

Using macros that may not be present on all implementations

In some cases, a macro may not be defined on all UNIX implementations. For example, the WCOREDUMP() macro (which checks whether a child process produced a core dump file) is widely available, but it is not specified in SUSv3. Therefore, this macro might not be present on some UNIX implementations. In order to portably handle such possibilities, we can use the C preprocessor #ifdef directive, as in the following example:

```
#ifdef WCOREDUMP
    /* Use WCOREDUMP() macro */
#endif
```

Variation in required header files across implementations

In some cases, the header files required to prototype various system calls and library functions vary across UNIX implementations. In this book, we show the requirements on Linux and note any variations from SUSv3.

Some of the function synopses in this book show a particular header file with the accompanying comment */* For portability */*. This indicates that the header file is not required on Linux or by SUSv3, but because some other (especially older) implementations may require it, we should include it in portable programs.

> For many of the functions that it specified, POSIX.1-1990 required that the header <sys/types.h> be included before any other headers associated with the function. However, this requirement was redundant, because most contemporary UNIX implementations did not require applications to include this header for these functions. Consequently, SUSv1 removed this requirement. Nevertheless, when writing portable programs, it is wise to make this one of the first header files included. (However, we omit this header from our example programs because it is not required on Linux and omitting it allows us to make the example programs one line shorter.)

3.7 Summary

System calls allow processes to request services from the kernel. Even the simplest system calls have a significant overhead by comparison with a user-space function call, since the system must temporarily switch to kernel mode to execute the system call, and the kernel must verify system call arguments and transfer data between user memory and kernel memory.

The standard C library provides a multitude of library functions that perform a wide range of tasks. Some library functions employ system calls to do their work; others perform tasks entirely within user space. On Linux, the usual standard C library implementation that is used is *glibc*.

Most system calls and library functions return a status indicating whether a call has succeeded or failed. Such status returns should always be checked.

We introduced a number of functions that we have implemented for use in the example programs in this book. The tasks performed by these functions include diagnosing errors and parsing command-line arguments.

We discussed various guidelines and techniques that can help us write portable system programs that run on any standards-conformant system.

When compiling an application, we can define various feature test macros that control the definitions exposed by header files. This is useful if we want to ensure that a program conforms to some formal or implementation-defined standard(s).

We can improve the portability of system programs by using the system data types defined in various standards, rather than native C types. SUSv3 specifies a wide range of system data types that an implementation should support and that an application should employ.

3.8 Exercise

3-1. When using the Linux-specific *reboot()* system call to reboot the system, the second argument, *magic2*, must be specified as one of a set of magic numbers (e.g., LINUX_REBOOT_MAGIC2). What is the significance of these numbers? (Converting them to hexadecimal provides a clue.)

4

FILE I/O: THE UNIVERSAL
I/O MODEL

We now start to look in earnest at the system call API. Files are a good place to start, since they are central to the UNIX philosophy. The focus of this chapter is the system calls used for performing file input and output.

We introduce the concept of a file descriptor, and then look at the system calls that constitute the so-called universal I/O model. These are the system calls that open and close a file, and read and write data.

We focus on I/O on disk files. However, much of the material covered here is relevant for later chapters, since the same system calls are used for performing I/O on all types of files, such as pipes and terminals.

Chapter 5 extends the discussion in this chapter with further details on file I/O. One other aspect of file I/O, buffering, is complex enough to deserve its own chapter. Chapter 13 covers I/O buffering in the kernel and in the *stdio* library.

4.1 Overview

All system calls for performing I/O refer to open files using a *file descriptor*, a (usually small) nonnegative integer. File descriptors are used to refer to all types of open files, including pipes, FIFOs, sockets, terminals, devices, and regular files. Each process has its own set of file descriptors.

By convention, most programs expect to be able to use the three standard file descriptors listed in Table 4-1. These three descriptors are opened on the program's behalf by the shell, before the program is started. Or, more precisely, the program inherits copies of the shell's file descriptors, and the shell normally operates with these three file descriptors always open. (In an interactive shell, these three file descriptors normally refer to the terminal under which the shell is running.) If I/O redirections are specified on a command line, then the shell ensures that the file descriptors are suitably modified before starting the program.

Table 4-1: Standard file descriptors

File descriptor	Purpose	POSIX name	*stdio* stream
0	standard input	STDIN_FILENO	*stdin*
1	standard output	STDOUT_FILENO	*stdout*
2	standard error	STDERR_FILENO	*stderr*

When referring to these file descriptors in a program, we can use either the numbers (0, 1, or 2) or, preferably, the POSIX standard names defined in <unistd.h>.

> Although the variables *stdin*, *stdout*, and *stderr* initially refer to the process's standard input, output, and error, they can be changed to refer to any file by using the *freopen()* library function. As part of its operation, *freopen()* may change the file descriptor underlying the reopened stream. In other words, after an *freopen()* on *stdout*, for example, it is no longer safe to assume that the underlying file descriptor is still 1.

The following are the four key system calls for performing file I/O (programming languages and software packages typically employ these calls only indirectly, via I/O libraries):

- *fd = open(pathname, flags, mode)* opens the file identified by *pathname*, returning a file descriptor used to refer to the open file in subsequent calls. If the file doesn't exist, *open()* may create it, depending on the settings of the *flags* bitmask argument. The *flags* argument also specifies whether the file is to be opened for reading, writing, or both. The *mode* argument specifies the permissions to be placed on the file if it is created by this call. If the *open()* call is not being used to create a file, this argument is ignored and can be omitted.

- *numread = read(fd, buffer, count)* reads at most *count* bytes from the open file referred to by *fd* and stores them in *buffer*. The *read()* call returns the number of bytes actually read. If no further bytes could be read (i.e., end-of-file was encountered), *read()* returns 0.

- *numwritten = write(fd, buffer, count)* writes up to *count* bytes from *buffer* to the open file referred to by *fd*. The *write()* call returns the number of bytes actually written, which may be less than *count*.

- *status = close(fd)* is called after all I/O has been completed, in order to release the file descriptor *fd* and its associated kernel resources.

Before we launch into the details of these system calls, we provide a short demonstration of their use in Listing 4-1. This program is a simple version of the *cp(1)* command. It copies the contents of the existing file named in its first command-line argument to the new file named in its second command-line argument.

We can use the program in Listing 4-1 as follows:

```
$ ./copy oldfile newfile
```

Listing 4-1: Using I/O system calls

── fileio/copy.c
```c
#include <sys/stat.h>
#include <fcntl.h>
#include "tlpi_hdr.h"

#ifndef BUF_SIZE        /* Allow "cc -D" to override definition */
#define BUF_SIZE 1024
#endif

int
main(int argc, char *argv[])
{
    int inputFd, outputFd, openFlags;
    mode_t filePerms;
    ssize_t numRead;
    char buf[BUF_SIZE];

    if (argc != 3 || strcmp(argv[1], "--help") == 0)
        usageErr("%s old-file new-file\n", argv[0]);

    /* Open input and output files */

    inputFd = open(argv[1], O_RDONLY);
    if (inputFd == -1)
        errExit("opening file %s", argv[1]);

    openFlags = O_CREAT | O_WRONLY | O_TRUNC;
    filePerms = S_IRUSR | S_IWUSR | S_IRGRP | S_IWGRP |
                S_IROTH | S_IWOTH;        /* rw-rw-rw- */
    outputFd = open(argv[2], openFlags, filePerms);
    if (outputFd == -1)
        errExit("opening file %s", argv[2]);

    /* Transfer data until we encounter end of input or an error */

    while ((numRead = read(inputFd, buf, BUF_SIZE)) > 0)
        if (write(outputFd, buf, numRead) != numRead)
            fatal("write() returned error or partial write occurred");
    if (numRead == -1)
        errExit("read");

    if (close(inputFd) == -1)
        errExit("close input");
    if (close(outputFd) == -1)
        errExit("close output");

    exit(EXIT_SUCCESS);
}
```
── fileio/copy.c

4.2   Universality of I/O

One of the distinguishing features of the UNIX I/O model is the concept of *universality of I/O*. This means that the same four system calls—*open()*, *read()*, *write()*, and *close()*—are used to perform I/O on all types of files, including devices such as terminals. Consequently, if we write a program using only these system calls, that program will work on any type of file. For example, the following are all valid uses of the program in Listing 4-1:

```
$ ./copy test test.old        Copy a regular file
$ ./copy a.txt /dev/tty        Copy a regular file to this terminal
$ ./copy /dev/tty b.txt        Copy input from this terminal to a regular file
$ ./copy /dev/pts/16 /dev/tty  Copy input from another terminal
```

Universality of I/O is achieved by ensuring that each file system and device driver implements the same set of I/O system calls. Because details specific to the file system or device are handled within the kernel, we can generally ignore device-specific factors when writing application programs. When access to specific features of a file system or device is required, a program can use the catchall *ioctl()* system call (Section 4.8), which provides an interface to features that fall outside the universal I/O model.

4.3   Opening a File: *open()*

The *open()* system call either opens an existing file or creates and opens a new file.

```
#include <sys/stat.h>
#include <fcntl.h>

int open(const char *pathname, int flags, ... /* mode_t mode */);
```
                          Returns file descriptor on success, or –1 on error

The file to be opened is identified by the *pathname* argument. If *pathname* is a symbolic link, it is dereferenced. On success, *open()* returns a file descriptor that is used to refer to the file in subsequent system calls. If an error occurs, *open()* returns –1 and *errno* is set accordingly.

The *flags* argument is a bit mask that specifies the *access mode* for the file, using one of the constants shown in Table 4-2.

> Early UNIX implementations used the numbers 0, 1, and 2 instead of the names shown in Table 4-2. Most modern UNIX implementations define these constants to have those values. Thus, we can see that O_RDWR is not equivalent to O_RDONLY | O_WRONLY; the latter combination is a logical error.

When *open()* is used to create a new file, the *mode* bit-mask argument specifies the permissions to be placed on the file. (The *mode_t* data type used to type *mode* is an integer type specified in SUSv3.) If the *open()* call doesn't specify O_CREAT, *mode* can be omitted.

Table 4-2: File access modes

Access mode	Description
O_RDONLY	Open the file for reading only
O_WRONLY	Open the file for writing only
O_RDWR	Open the file for both reading and writing

We describe file permissions in detail in Section 15.4. Later, we'll see that the permissions actually placed on a new file depend not just on the *mode* argument, but also on the process umask (Section 15.4.6) and the (optionally present) default access control list (Section 17.6) of the parent directory. In the meantime, we'll just note that the *mode* argument can be specified as a number (typically in octal) or, preferably, by ORing (|) together zero or more of the bit-mask constants listed in Table 15-4, on page 295.

Listing 4-2 shows examples of the use of *open()*, some of which employ additional *flags* bits that we describe shortly.

Listing 4-2: Examples of the use of *open()*

```
/* Open existing file for reading */

fd = open("startup", O_RDONLY);
if (fd == -1)
    errExit("open");

/* Open new or existing file for reading and writing, truncating to zero
   bytes; file permissions read+write for owner, nothing for all others */

fd = open("myfile", O_RDWR | O_CREAT | O_TRUNC, S_IRUSR | S_IWUSR);
if (fd == -1)
    errExit("open");

/* Open new or existing file for writing; writes should always
   append to end of file */

fd = open("w.log", O_WRONLY | O_CREAT | O_APPEND,
                S_IRUSR | S_IWUSR);
if (fd == -1)
    errExit("open");
```

File descriptor number returned by *open()*

SUSv3 specifies that if *open()* succeeds, it is guaranteed to use the lowest-numbered unused file descriptor for the process. We can use this feature to ensure that a file is opened using a particular file descriptor. For example, the following sequence ensures that a file is opened using standard input (file descriptor 0).

```
    if (close(STDIN_FILENO) == -1)        /* Close file descriptor 0 */
        errExit("close");

    fd = open(pathname, O_RDONLY);
    if (fd == -1)
        errExit("open");
```

Since file descriptor 0 is unused, *open()* is guaranteed to open the file using that descriptor. In Section 5.5, we look at the use of *dup2()* and *fcntl()* to achieve a similar result, but with more flexible control over the file descriptor used. In that section, we also show an example of why it can be useful to control the file descriptor on which a file is opened.

4.3.1 The *open() flags* Argument

In some of the example *open()* calls shown in Listing 4-2, we included other bits (O_CREAT, O_TRUNC, and O_APPEND) in *flags* in addition to the file access mode. We now consider the *flags* argument in more detail. Table 4-3 summarizes the full set of constants that can be bit-wise ORed (|) in *flags*. The final column indicates which of these constants are standardized in SUSv3 or SUSv4.

Table 4-3: Values for the *flags* argument of *open()*

Flag	Purpose	SUS?
O_RDONLY	Open for reading only	v3
O_WRONLY	Open for writing only	v3
O_RDWR	Open for reading and writing	v3
O_CLOEXEC	Set the close-on-exec flag (since Linux 2.6.23)	v4
O_CREAT	Create file if it doesn't already exist	v3
O_DIRECTORY	Fail if *pathname* is not a directory	v4
O_EXCL	With O_CREAT: create file exclusively	v3
O_LARGEFILE	Used on 32-bit systems to open large files	
O_NOCTTY	Don't let *pathname* become the controlling terminal	v3
O_NOFOLLOW	Don't dereference symbolic links	v4
O_TRUNC	Truncate existing file to zero length	v3
O_APPEND	Writes are always appended to end of file	v3
O_ASYNC	Generate a signal when I/O is possible	
O_DIRECT	File I/O bypasses buffer cache	
O_DSYNC	Provide synchronized I/O data integrity (since Linux 2.6.33)	v3
O_NOATIME	Don't update file last access time on *read()* (since Linux 2.6.8)	
O_NONBLOCK	Open in nonblocking mode	v3
O_SYNC	Make file writes synchronous	v3

The constants in Table 4-3 are divided into the following groups:

- *File access mode flags*: These are the O_RDONLY, O_WRONLY, and O_RDWR flags described earlier. Only one of these values should be specified in *flags*. The access mode can be retrieved using the *fcntl()* F_GETFL operation (Section 5.3).

- *File creation flags*: These are the flags shown in the second part of Table 4-3. They control various aspects of the behavior of the *open()* call itself. These flags can't be retrieved or changed.

- *Open file status flags*: These are the remaining flags in Table 4-3. They affect the semantics of subsequent I/O system calls and can be retrieved and modified using the *fcntl()* F_GETFL and F_SETFL operations (Section 5.3). These flags are sometimes simply called the *file status flags*.

> Since kernel 2.6.22, the Linux-specific files in the directory /proc/*PID*/fdinfo can be read to obtain information about the file descriptors of any process on the system. There is one file in this directory for each of the process's open file descriptors, with a name that matches the number of the descriptor. The *pos* field in this file shows the current file offset (Section 4.7). The *flags* field is an octal number that shows the file access mode flags and open file status flags. (To decode this number, we need to look at the numeric values of these flags in the C library header files.)

Details for the *flags* constants are as follows:

O_APPEND
> Writes are always appended to the end of the file. We discuss the significance of this flag in Section 5.1.

O_ASYNC
> Generate a signal when I/O becomes possible on the file descriptor returned by *open()*. This feature, termed *signal-driven I/O*, is available only for certain file types, such as terminals, FIFOs, and sockets. (The O_ASYNC flag is not specified in SUSv3; however, it, or the older synonym, FASYNC, is found on most UNIX implementations.) On Linux, specifying the O_ASYNC flag when calling *open()* has no effect. To enable signal-driven I/O, we must instead set this flag using the *fcntl()* F_SETFL operation (Section 5.3). (Several other UNIX implementations behave similarly.) Refer to Section 63.3 for more information about the O_ASYNC flag.

O_CLOEXEC (since Linux 2.6.23)
> Enable the close-on-exec flag (FD_CLOEXEC) for the new file descriptor. We describe the FD_CLOEXEC flag in Section 27.4. Using the O_CLOEXEC flag allows a program to avoid additional *fcntl()* F_GETFD and F_SETFD operations to set the close-on-exec flag. It is also necessary in multithreaded programs to avoid the race conditions that could occur using the latter technique. These races can occur when one thread opens a file descriptor and then tries to mark it close-on-exec at the same time as another thread does a *fork()* and then an *exec()* of an arbitrary program. (Suppose that the second thread manages to both *fork()* and *exec()* between the time the first thread opens the file descriptor and uses *fcntl()* to set the close-on-exec flag.) Such races

could result in open file descriptors being unintentionally passed to unsafe programs. (We say more about race conditions in Section 5.1.)

O_CREAT

If the file doesn't already exist, it is created as a new, empty file. This flag is effective even if the file is being opened only for reading. If we specify O_CREAT, then we must supply a *mode* argument in the *open()* call; otherwise, the permissions of the new file will be set to some random value from the stack.

O_DIRECT

Allow file I/O to bypass the buffer cache. This feature is described in Section 13.6. The _GNU_SOURCE feature test macro must be defined in order to make this constant definition available from <fcntl.h>.

O_DIRECTORY

Return an error (*errno* equals ENOTDIR) if *pathname* is not a directory. This flag is an extension designed specifically for implementing *opendir()* (Section 18.8). The _GNU_SOURCE feature test macro must be defined in order to make this constant definition available from <fcntl.h>.

O_DSYNC (since Linux 2.6.33)

Perform file writes according to the requirements of synchronized I/O data integrity completion. See the discussion of kernel I/O buffering in Section 13.3.

O_EXCL

This flag is used in conjunction with O_CREAT to indicate that if the file already exists, it should not be opened; instead, *open()* should fail, with *errno* set to EEXIST. In other words, this flag allows the caller to ensure that it is the process creating the file. The check for existence and the creation of the file are performed *atomically*. We discuss the concept of atomicity in Section 5.1. When both O_CREAT and O_EXCL are specified in *flags*, *open()* fails (with the error EEXIST) if *pathname* is a symbolic link. SUSv3 requires this behavior so that a privileged application can create a file in a known location without there being a possibility that a symbolic link would cause the file to be created in a different location (e.g., a system directory), which would have security implications.

O_LARGEFILE

Open the file with large file support. This flag is used on 32-bit systems in order to work with large files. Although it is not specified in SUSv3, the O_LARGEFILE flag is found on several other UNIX implementations. On 64-bit Linux implementations such as Alpha and IA-64, this flag has no effect. See Section 5.10 for more information.

O_NOATIME (since Linux 2.6.8)

Don't update the file last access time (the *st_atime* field described in Section 15.1) when reading from this file. To use this flag, the effective user ID of the calling process must match the owner of the file, or the process must be privileged (CAP_FOWNER); otherwise, *open()* fails with the error EPERM.

(In reality, for an unprivileged process, it is the process's file-system user ID, rather than its effective user ID, that must match the user ID of the file when opening a file with the O_NOATIME flag, as described in Section 9.5.) This flag is a nonstandard Linux extension. To expose its definition from <fcntl.h>, we must define the _GNU_SOURCE feature test macro. The O_NOATIME flag is intended for use by indexing and backup programs. Its use can significantly reduce the amount of disk activity, because repeated disk seeks back and forth across the disk are not required to read the contents of a file and to update the last access time in the file's i-node (Section 14.4). Functionality similar to O_NOATIME is available using the MS_NOATIME *mount()* flag (Section 14.8.1) and the FS_NOATIME_FL flag (Section 15.5).

O_NOCTTY

If the file being opened is a terminal device, prevent it from becoming the controlling terminal. Controlling terminals are discussed in Section 34.4. If the file being opened is not a terminal, this flag has no effect.

O_NOFOLLOW

Normally, *open()* dereferences *pathname* if it is a symbolic link. However, if the O_NOFOLLOW flag is specified, then *open()* fails (with *errno* set to ELOOP) if *pathname* is a symbolic link. This flag is useful, especially in privileged programs, for ensuring that *open()* doesn't dereference a symbolic link. To expose the definition of this flag from <fcntl.h>, we must define the _GNU_SOURCE feature test macro.

O_NONBLOCK

Open the file in nonblocking mode. See Section 5.9.

O_SYNC

Open the file for synchronous I/O. See the discussion of kernel I/O buffering in Section 13.3.

O_TRUNC

If the file already exists and is a regular file, then truncate it to zero length, destroying any existing data. On Linux, truncation occurs whether the file is being opened for reading or writing (in both cases, we must have write permission on the file). SUSv3 leaves the combination of O_RDONLY and O_TRUNC unspecified, but most other UNIX implementations behave in the same way as Linux.

4.3.2 Errors from *open()*

If an error occurs while trying to open the file, *open()* returns –1, and *errno* identifies the cause of the error. The following are some possible errors that can occur (in addition to those already noted when describing the *flags* argument above):

EACCES

The file permissions don't allow the calling process to open the file in the mode specified by *flags*. Alternatively, because of directory permissions, the file could not be accessed, or the file did not exist and could not be created.

EISDIR

The specified file is a directory, and the caller attempted to open it for writing. This isn't allowed. (On the other hand, there are occasions when it can be useful to open a directory for reading. We consider an example in Section 18.11.)

EMFILE

The process resource limit on the number of open file descriptors has been reached (RLIMIT_NOFILE, described in Section 36.3).

ENFILE

The system-wide limit on the number of open files has been reached.

ENOENT

The specified file doesn't exist, and O_CREAT was not specified, or O_CREAT was specified, and one of the directories in *pathname* doesn't exist or is a symbolic link pointing to a nonexistent pathname (a dangling link).

EROFS

The specified file is on a read-only file system and the caller tried to open it for writing.

ETXTBSY

The specified file is an executable file (a program) that is currently executing. It is not permitted to modify (i.e., open for writing) the executable file associated with a running program. (We must first terminate the program in order to be able to modify the executable file.)

When we later describe other system calls or library functions, we generally won't list the range of possible errors that may occur in the above fashion. (Such a list can be found in the corresponding manual page for each system call or library function.) We do so here for two reasons. One of these is that *open()* is the first system call that we describe in detail, and the above list illustrates that a system call or library function may fail for any of a number of reasons. Second, the specific reasons why *open()* may fail make an interesting list in themselves, illustrating a number of factors and checks that come into play when a file is accessed. (The above list is incomplete: see the *open(2)* manual page for more reasons why *open()* may fail.)

4.3.3 The *creat()* System Call

In early UNIX implementations, *open()* had only two arguments and could not be used to create a new file. Instead, the *creat()* system call was used to create and open a new file.

```
#include <fcntl.h>

int creat(const char *pathname, mode_t mode);
                                        Returns file descriptor, or –1 on error
```

The *creat()* system call creates and opens a new file with the given *pathname*, or if the file already exists, opens the file and truncates it to zero length. As its function result, *creat()* returns a file descriptor that can be used in subsequent system calls. Calling *creat()* is equivalent to the following *open()* call:

```
fd = open(pathname, O_WRONLY | O_CREAT | O_TRUNC, mode);
```

Because the *open() flags* argument provides greater control over how the file is opened (e.g., we can specify O_RDWR instead of O_WRONLY), *creat()* is now obsolete, although it may still be seen in older programs.

4.4   Reading from a File: *read()*

The *read()* system call reads data from the open file referred to by the descriptor *fd*.

```
#include <unistd.h>

ssize_t read(int fd, void *buffer, size_t count);
```
                           Returns number of bytes read, 0 on EOF, or −1 on error

The *count* argument specifies the maximum number of bytes to read. (The *size_t* data type is an unsigned integer type.) The *buffer* argument supplies the address of the memory buffer into which the input data is to be placed. This buffer must be at least *count* bytes long.

> System calls don't allocate memory for buffers that are used to return informa-tion to the caller. Instead, we must pass a pointer to a previously allocated memory buffer of the correct size. This contrasts with several library functions that *do* allocate memory buffers in order to return information to the caller.

A successful call to *read()* returns the number of bytes actually read, or 0 if end-of-file is encountered. On error, the usual −1 is returned. The *ssize_t* data type is a signed integer type used to hold a byte count or a −1 error indication.

A call to *read()* may read less than the requested number of bytes. For a regular file, the probable reason for this is that we were close to the end of the file.

When *read()* is applied to other types of files—such as pipes, FIFOs, sockets, or terminals—there are also various circumstances where it may read fewer bytes than requested. For example, by default, a *read()* from a terminal reads characters only up to the next newline (\n) character. We consider these cases when we cover other file types in subsequent chapters.

Using *read()* to input a series of characters from, say, a terminal, we might expect the following code to work:

```
#define MAX_READ 20
char buffer[MAX_READ];

if (read(STDIN_FILENO, buffer, MAX_READ) == -1)
    errExit("read");
printf("The input data was: %s\n", buffer);
```

The output from this piece of code is likely to be strange, since it will probably include characters in addition to the string actually entered. This is because *read()*

doesn't place a terminating null byte at the end of the string that *printf()* is being asked to print. A moment's reflection leads us to realize that this must be so, since *read()* can be used to read any sequence of bytes from a file. In some cases, this input might be text, but in other cases, the input might be binary integers or C structures in binary form. There is no way for *read()* to tell the difference, and so it can't attend to the C convention of null terminating character strings. If a terminating null byte is required at the end of the input buffer, we must put it there explicitly:

```
char buffer[MAX_READ + 1];
ssize_t numRead;

numRead = read(STDIN_FILENO, buffer, MAX_READ);
if (numRead == -1)
    errExit("read");

buffer[numRead] = '\0';
printf("The input data was: %s\n", buffer);
```

Because the terminating null byte requires a byte of memory, the size of *buffer* must be at least one greater than the largest string we expect to read.

4.5 Writing to a File: *write()*

The *write()* system call writes data to an open file.

```
#include <unistd.h>

ssize_t write(int fd, const void *buffer, size_t count);
```
                                    Returns number of bytes written, or –1 on error

The arguments to *write()* are similar to those for *read()*: *buffer* is the address of the data to be written; *count* is the number of bytes to write from *buffer*; and *fd* is a file descriptor referring to the file to which data is to be written.

On success, *write()* returns the number of bytes actually written; this may be less than *count*. For a disk file, possible reasons for such a *partial write* are that the disk was filled or that the process resource limit on file sizes was reached. (The relevant limit is RLIMIT_FSIZE, described in Section 36.3.)

When performing I/O on a disk file, a successful return from *write()* doesn't guarantee that the data has been transferred to disk, because the kernel performs buffering of disk I/O in order to reduce disk activity and expedite *write()* calls. We consider the details in Chapter 13.

4.6 Closing a File: *close()*

The *close()* system call closes an open file descriptor, freeing it for subsequent reuse by the process. When a process terminates, all of its open file descriptors are automatically closed.

```
#include <unistd.h>

int close(int fd);
```
                                    Returns 0 on success, or −1 on error

It is usually good practice to close unneeded file descriptors explicitly, since this makes our code more readable and reliable in the face of subsequent modifications. Furthermore, file descriptors are a consumable resource, so failure to close a file descriptor could result in a process running out of descriptors. This is a particularly important issue when writing long-lived programs that deal with multiple files, such as shells or network servers.

Just like every other system call, a call to *close()* should be bracketed with error-checking code, such as the following:

```
if (close(fd) == -1)
    errExit("close");
```

This catches errors such as attempting to close an unopened file descriptor or close the same file descriptor twice, and catches error conditions that a specific file system may diagnose during a close operation.

> NFS (Network File System) provides an example of an error that is specific to a file system. If an NFS commit failure occurs, meaning that the data did not reach the remote disk, then this error is propagated to the application as a failure in the *close()* call.

4.7   Changing the File Offset: *lseek()*

For each open file, the kernel records a *file offset*, sometimes also called the *read-write offset* or *pointer*. This is the location in the file at which the next *read()* or *write()* will commence. The file offset is expressed as an ordinal byte position relative to the start of the file. The first byte of the file is at offset 0.

The file offset is set to point to the start of the file when the file is opened and is automatically adjusted by each subsequent call to *read()* or *write()* so that it points to the next byte of the file after the byte(s) just read or written. Thus, successive *read()* and *write()* calls progress sequentially through a file.

The *lseek()* system call adjusts the file offset of the open file referred to by the file descriptor *fd*, according to the values specified in *offset* and *whence*.

```
#include <unistd.h>

off_t lseek(int fd, off_t offset, int whence);
```
                            Returns new file offset if successful, or −1 on error

The *offset* argument specifies a value in bytes. (The *off_t* data type is a signed integer type specified by SUSv3.) The *whence* argument indicates the base point from which *offset* is to be interpreted, and is one of the following values:

SEEK_SET
> The file offset is set *offset* bytes from the beginning of the file.

SEEK_CUR
> The file offset is adjusted by *offset* bytes relative to the current file offset.

SEEK_END
> The file offset is set to the size of the file plus *offset*. In other words, *offset* is interpreted with respect to the next byte after the last byte of the file.

Figure 4-1 shows how the *whence* argument is interpreted.

> In earlier UNIX implementations, the integers 0, 1, and 2 were used, rather than the SEEK_* constants shown in the main text. Older versions of BSD used different names for these values: L_SET, L_INCR, and L_XTND.

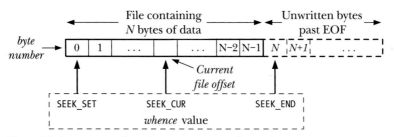

Figure 4-1: Interpreting the *whence* argument of *lseek()*

If *whence* is SEEK_CUR or SEEK_END, *offset* may be negative or positive; for SEEK_SET, *offset* must be nonnegative.

The return value from a successful *lseek()* is the new file offset. The following call retrieves the current location of the file offset without changing it:

```
curr = lseek(fd, 0, SEEK_CUR);
```

> Some UNIX implementations (but not Linux) have the nonstandard *tell(fd)* function, which serves the same purpose as the above *lseek()* call.

Here are some other examples of *lseek()* calls, along with comments indicating where the file offset is moved to:

```
lseek(fd, 0, SEEK_SET);        /* Start of file */
lseek(fd, 0, SEEK_END);        /* Next byte after the end of the file */
lseek(fd, -1, SEEK_END);       /* Last byte of file */
lseek(fd, -10, SEEK_CUR);      /* Ten bytes prior to current location */
lseek(fd, 10000, SEEK_END);    /* 10001 bytes past last byte of file */
```

Calling *lseek()* simply adjusts the kernel's record of the file offset associated with a file descriptor. It does not cause any physical device access.

We describe some further details of the relationship between file offsets, file descriptors, and open files in Section 5.4.

We can't apply *lseek()* to all types of files. Applying *lseek()* to a pipe, FIFO, socket, or terminal is not permitted; *lseek()* fails, with *errno* set to ESPIPE. On the other hand, it is possible to apply *lseek()* to devices where it is sensible to do so. For example, it is possible to seek to a specified location on a disk or tape device.

> The *l* in the name *lseek()* derives from the fact that the *offset* argument and the return value were both originally typed as *long*. Early UNIX implementations provided a *seek()* system call, which typed these values as *int*.

File holes

What happens if a program seeks past the end of a file, and then performs I/O? A call to *read()* will return 0, indicating end-of-file. Somewhat surprisingly, it is possible to write bytes at an arbitrary point past the end of the file.

The space in between the previous end of the file and the newly written bytes is referred to as a *file hole*. From a programming point of view, the bytes in a hole exist, and reading from the hole returns a buffer of bytes containing 0 (null bytes).

File holes don't, however, take up any disk space. The file system doesn't allocate any disk blocks for a hole until, at some later point, data is written into it. The main advantage of file holes is that a sparsely populated file consumes less disk space than would otherwise be required if the null bytes actually needed to be allocated in disk blocks. Core dump files (Section 22.1) are common examples of files that contain large holes.

> The statement that file holes don't consume disk space needs to be qualified slightly. On most file systems, file space is allocated in units of blocks (Section 14.3). The size of a block depends on the file system, but is typically something like 1024, 2048, or 4096 bytes. If the edge of a hole falls within a block, rather than on a block boundary, then a complete block is allocated to store the data in the other part of the block, and the part corresponding to the hole is filled with null bytes.

Most native UNIX file systems support the concept of file holes, but many nonnative file systems (e.g., Microsoft's VFAT) do not. On a file system that doesn't support holes, explicit null bytes are written to the file.

The existence of holes means that a file's nominal size may be larger than the amount of disk storage it utilizes (in some cases, considerably larger). Writing bytes into the middle of the file hole will decrease the amount of free disk space as the kernel allocates blocks to fill the hole, even though the file's size doesn't change. Such a scenario is uncommon, but nevertheless one to be aware of.

> SUSv3 specifies a function, *posix_fallocate(fd, offset, len)*, that ensures that space is allocated on disk for the byte range specified by *offset* and *len* for the disk file referred to by the descriptor *fd*. This allows an application to be sure that a later *write()* to the file won't fail because disk space is exhausted (which could otherwise occur if a hole in the file was filled in, or some other application consumed space on the disk before the full extent of the file was written). Historically, the *glibc* implementation of this function achieved the desired result by writing a 0 byte into each block in the specified range. Since version 2.6.23, Linux provides an *fallocate()* system call, which provides a more efficient way of ensuring that the necessary space is allocated, and the *glibc posix_fallocate()* implementation makes use of this system call when it is available.

Section 14.4 describes how holes are represented in a file, and Section 15.1 describes the *stat()* system call, which can tell us the current size of a file, as well as the number of blocks actually allocated to the file.

Example program

Listing 4-3 demonstrates the use of *lseek()* in conjunction with *read()* and *write()*. The first command-line argument to this program is the name of a file to be opened. The remaining arguments specify I/O operations to be performed on the file. Each of these operations consists of a letter followed by an associated value (with no separating space):

- *soffset*: Seek to byte *offset* from the start of the file.
- *rlength*: Read *length* bytes from the file, starting at the current file offset, and display them in text form.
- *Rlength*: Read *length* bytes from the file, starting at the current file offset, and display them in hexadecimal.
- *wstr*: Write the string of characters specified in *str* at the current file offset.

Listing 4-3: Demonstration of *read()*, *write()*, and *lseek()*

── `fileio/seek_io.c`

```c
#include <sys/stat.h>
#include <fcntl.h>
#include <ctype.h>
#include "tlpi_hdr.h"

int
main(int argc, char *argv[])
{
    size_t len;
    off_t offset;
    int fd, ap, j;
    unsigned char *buf;
    ssize_t numRead, numWritten;

    if (argc < 3 || strcmp(argv[1], "--help") == 0)
        usageErr("%s file {r<length>|R<length>|w<string>|s<offset>}...\n",
                argv[0]);

    fd = open(argv[1], O_RDWR | O_CREAT,
                S_IRUSR | S_IWUSR | S_IRGRP | S_IWGRP |
                S_IROTH | S_IWOTH);                      /* rw-rw-rw- */
    if (fd == -1)
        errExit("open");

    for (ap = 2; ap < argc; ap++) {
        switch (argv[ap][0]) {
        case 'r':   /* Display bytes at current offset, as text */
        case 'R':   /* Display bytes at current offset, in hex */
            len = getLong(&argv[ap][1], GN_ANY_BASE, argv[ap]);
```

```
        buf = malloc(len);
        if (buf == NULL)
            errExit("malloc");

        numRead = read(fd, buf, len);
        if (numRead == -1)
            errExit("read");

        if (numRead == 0) {
            printf("%s: end-of-file\n", argv[ap]);
        } else {
            printf("%s: ", argv[ap]);
            for (j = 0; j < numRead; j++) {
                if (argv[ap][0] == 'r')
                    printf("%c", isprint(buf[j]) ? buf[j] : '?');
                else
                    printf("%02x ", buf[j]);
            }
            printf("\n");
        }

        free(buf);
        break;

    case 'w':  /* Write string at current offset */
        numWritten = write(fd, &argv[ap][1], strlen(&argv[ap][1]));
        if (numWritten == -1)
            errExit("write");
        printf("%s: wrote %ld bytes\n", argv[ap], (long) numWritten);
        break;

    case 's':  /* Change file offset */
        offset = getLong(&argv[ap][1], GN_ANY_BASE, argv[ap]);
        if (lseek(fd, offset, SEEK_SET) == -1)
            errExit("lseek");
        printf("%s: seek succeeded\n", argv[ap]);
        break;

    default:
        cmdLineErr("Argument must start with [rRws]: %s\n", argv[ap]);
    }
}

exit(EXIT_SUCCESS);
}
```
—— `fileio/seek_io.c`

The following shell session log demonstrates the use of the program in Listing 4-3,
showing what happens when we attempt to read bytes from a file hole:

```
$ touch tfile                     Create new, empty file
$ ./seek_io tfile s100000 wabc    Seek to offset 100,000, write "abc"
s100000: seek succeeded
wabc: wrote 3 bytes
```

```
$ ls -l tfile                                Check size of file
-rw-r--r--    1 mtk      users   100003 Feb 10 10:35 tfile
$ ./seek_io tfile s10000 R5                  Seek to offset 10,000, read 5 bytes from hole
s10000: seek succeeded
R5: 00 00 00 00 00                           Bytes in the hole contain 0
```

4.8 Operations Outside the Universal I/O Model: *ioctl()*

The *ioctl()* system call is a general-purpose mechanism for performing file and device operations that fall outside the universal I/O model described earlier in this chapter.

```
#include <sys/ioctl.h>

int ioctl(int fd, int request, ... /* argp */);
```
                     Value returned on success depends on *request*, or −1 on error

The *fd* argument is an open file descriptor for the device or file upon which the control operation specified by *request* is to be performed. Device-specific header files define constants that can be passed in the *request* argument.

As indicated by the standard C ellipsis (...) notation, the third argument to *ioctl()*, which we label *argp*, can be of any type. The value of the *request* argument enables *ioctl()* to determine what type of value to expect in *argp*. Typically, *argp* is a pointer to either an integer or a structure; in some cases, it is unused.

We'll see a number of uses for *ioctl()* in later chapters (see, for example, Section 15.5).

> The only specification that SUSv3 makes for *ioctl()* is for operations to control STREAMS devices. (The STREAMS facility is a System V feature that is not supported by the mainline Linux kernel, although a few add-on implementations have been developed.) None of the other *ioctl()* operations described in this book is specified in SUSv3. However, the *ioctl()* call has been part of the UNIX system since early versions, and consequently several of the *ioctl()* operations that we describe are provided on many other UNIX implementations. As we describe each *ioctl()* operation, we note portability issues.

4.9 Summary

In order to perform I/O on a regular file, we must first obtain a file descriptor using *open()*. I/O is then performed using *read()* and *write()*. After performing all I/O, we should free the file descriptor and its associated resources using *close()*. These system calls can be used to perform I/O on all types of files.

The fact that all file types and device drivers implement the same I/O interface allows for universality of I/O, meaning that a program can typically be used with any type of file without requiring code that is specific to the file type.

For each open file, the kernel maintains a file offset, which determines the location at which the next read or write will occur. The file offset is implicitly updated by reads and writes. Using *lseek()*, we can explicitly reposition the file offset to any location within the file or past the end of the file. Writing data at a position beyond the previous end of the file creates a hole in the file. Reads from a file hole return bytes containing zeros.

The *ioctl()* system call is a catchall for device and file operations that don't fit into the standard file I/O model.

4.10 Exercises

4-1. The *tee* command reads its standard input until end-of-file, writing a copy of the input to standard output and to the file named in its command-line argument. (We show an example of the use of this command when we discuss FIFOs in Section 44.7.) Implement *tee* using I/O system calls. By default, *tee* overwrites any existing file with the given name. Implement the *-a* command-line option (*tee -a file*), which causes *tee* to append text to the end of a file if it already exists. (Refer to Appendix B for a description of the *getopt()* function, which can be used to parse command-line options.)

4-2. Write a program like *cp* that, when used to copy a regular file that contains holes (sequences of null bytes), also creates corresponding holes in the target file.

5

FILE I/O: FURTHER DETAILS

In this chapter, we extend the discussion of file I/O that we started in the previous chapter.

In continuing the discussion of the *open()* system call, we explain the concept of *atomicity*—the notion that the actions performed by a system call are executed as a single uninterruptible step. This is a necessary requirement for the correct operation of many system calls.

We introduce another file-related system call, the multipurpose *fcntl()*, and show one of its uses: fetching and setting open file status flags.

Next, we look at the kernel data structures used to represent file descriptors and open files. Understanding the relationship between these structures clarifies some of the subtleties of file I/O discussed in subsequent chapters. Building on this model, we then explain how to duplicate file descriptors.

We then consider some system calls that provide, extended read and write functionality. These system calls allow us to perform I/O at a specific location in a file without changing the file offset, and to transfer data to and from multiple buffers in a program.

We briefly introduce the concept of nonblocking I/O, and describe some extensions provided to support I/O on very large files.

Since temporary files are used by many system programs, we'll also look at some library functions that allow us to create and use temporary files with randomly generated unique names.

5.1 Atomicity and Race Conditions

Atomicity is a concept that we'll encounter repeatedly when discussing the operation of system calls. Various system call operations are executed atomically. By this, we mean that the kernel guarantees that all of the steps in the operation are completed without being interrupted by another process or thread.

Atomicity is essential to the successful completion of some operations. In particular, it allows us to avoid *race conditions* (sometimes known as *race hazards*). A race condition is a situation where the result produced by two processes (or threads) operating on shared resources depends in an unexpected way on the relative order in which the processes gain access to the CPU(s).

In the next few pages, we look at two situations involving file I/O where race conditions occur, and show how these conditions are eliminated through the use of *open()* flags that guarantee the atomicity of the relevant file operations.

We revisit the topic of race conditions when we describe *sigsuspend()* in Section 22.9 and *fork()* in Section 24.4.

Creating a file exclusively

In Section 4.3.1, we noted that specifying O_EXCL in conjunction with O_CREAT causes *open()* to return an error if the file already exists. This provides a way for a process to ensure that it is the creator of a file. The check on the prior existence of the file and the creation of the file are performed atomically. To see why this is important, consider the code shown in Listing 5-1, which we might resort to in the absence of the O_EXCL flag. (In this code, we display the process ID returned by the *getpid()* system call, which enables us to distinguish the output of two different runs of this program.)

Listing 5-1: Incorrect code to exclusively open a file

—— *from* `fileio/bad_exclusive_open.c`

```
fd = open(argv[1], O_WRONLY);    /* Open 1: check if file exists */
if (fd != -1) {                  /* Open succeeded */
    printf("[PID %ld] File \"%s\" already exists\n",
            (long) getpid(), argv[1]);
    close(fd);
} else {
    if (errno != ENOENT) {          /* Failed for unexpected reason */
        errExit("open");
    } else {
        /* WINDOW FOR FAILURE */
        fd = open(argv[1], O_WRONLY | O_CREAT, S_IRUSR | S_IWUSR);
        if (fd == -1)
            errExit("open");

        printf("[PID %ld] Created file \"%s\" exclusively\n",
                (long) getpid(), argv[1]);           /* MAY NOT BE TRUE! */
    }
}
```

—— *from* `fileio/bad_exclusive_open.c`

Aside from the long-winded use of two calls to *open()*, the code in Listing 5-1 also contains a bug. Suppose that when our process first called *open()*, the file did not exist, but by the time of the second *open()*, some other process had created the file. This could happen if the kernel scheduler decided that the process's time slice had expired and gave control to another process, as shown in Figure 5-1, or if the two processes were running at the same time on a multiprocessor system. Figure 5-1 portrays the case where two processes are both executing the code shown in Listing 5-1. In this scenario, process A would wrongly conclude that it had created the file, since the second *open()* succeeds whether or not the file exists.

While the chance of the process wrongly believing it was the creator of the file is relatively small, the possibility that it may occur nevertheless renders this code unreliable. The fact that the outcome of these operations depends on the order of scheduling of the two processes means that this is a race condition.

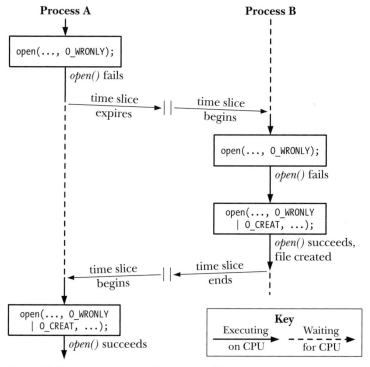

Figure 5-1: Failing to exclusively create a file

To demonstrate that there is indeed a problem with this code, we could replace the commented line WINDOW FOR FAILURE in Listing 5-1 with a piece of code that creates an artificially long delay between the check for file existence and the creation of the file:

```
printf("[PID %ld] File \"%s\" doesn't exist yet\n", (long) getpid(), argv[1]);
if (argc > 2) {                    /* Delay between check and create */
    sleep(5);                      /* Suspend execution for 5 seconds */
    printf("[PID %ld] Done sleeping\n", (long) getpid());
}
```

The *sleep()* library function suspends the execution of a process for a specified number of seconds. We discuss this function in Section 23.4.

If we run two simultaneous instances of the program in Listing 5-1, we see that they both claim to have exclusively created the file:

```
$ ./bad_exclusive_open tfile sleep &
[PID 3317] File "tfile" doesn't exist yet
[1] 3317
$ ./bad_exclusive_open tfile
[PID 3318] File "tfile" doesn't exist yet
[PID 3318] Created file "tfile" exclusively
$ [PID 3317] Done sleeping
[PID 3317] Created file "tfile" exclusively        Not true
```

> In the penultimate line of the above output, we see the shell prompt mixed with output from the first instance of the test program.

Both processes claim to have created the file because the code of the first process was interrupted between the existence check and the creation of the file. Using a single *open()* call that specifies the O_CREAT and O_EXCL flags prevents this possibility by guaranteeing that the check and creation steps are carried out as a single atomic (i.e., uninterruptible) operation.

Appending data to a file

A second example of the need for atomicity is when we have multiple processes appending data to the same file (e.g., a global log file). For this purpose, we might consider using a piece of code such as the following in each of our writers:

```
if (lseek(fd, 0, SEEK_END) == -1)
    errExit("lseek");
if (write(fd, buf, len) != len)
    fatal("Partial/failed write");
```

However, this code suffers the same defect as the previous example. If the first process executing the code is interrupted between the *lseek()* and *write()* calls by a second process doing the same thing, then both processes will set their file offset to the same location before writing, and when the first process is rescheduled, it will overwrite the data already written by the second process. Again, this is a race condition because the results depend on the order of scheduling of the two processes.

Avoiding this problem requires that the seek to the next byte past the end of the file and the write operation happen atomically. This is what opening a file with the O_APPEND flag guarantees.

> Some file systems (e.g., NFS) don't support O_APPEND. In this case, the kernel reverts to the nonatomic sequence of calls shown above, with the consequent possibility of file corruption as just described.

5.2   File Control Operations: *fcntl()*

The *fcntl()* system call performs a range of control operations on an open file descriptor.

```
#include <fcntl.h>

int fcntl(int fd, int cmd, ...);
                        Return value on success depends on cmd; returns -1 on error
```

The *cmd* argument can specify a wide range of operations. We examine some of
them in the following sections, and delay examination of others until later chapters.

As indicated by the ellipsis, the third argument to *fcntl()* can be of different
types, or it can be omitted. The kernel uses the value of the *cmd* argument to determine the data type (if any) to expect for this argument.

5.3 Open File Status Flags

One use of *fcntl()* is to retrieve or modify the access mode and open file status flags
of an open file. (These are the values set by the *flags* argument specified in the call
to *open()*.) To retrieve these settings, we specify *cmd* as F_GETFL:

```
int flags, accessMode;

flags = fcntl(fd, F_GETFL);          /* Third argument is not required */
if (flags == -1)
    errExit("fcntl");
```

After the above piece of code, we could test if the file was opened for synchronized
writes as follows:

```
if (flags & O_SYNC)
    printf("writes are synchronized\n");
```

> SUSv3 requires that only status flags that were specified during an *open()* or a
> later *fcntl()* F_SETFL should be set on an open file. However, Linux deviates
> from this in one respect: if an application was compiled using one of the tech-
> niques described in Section 5.10 for opening large files, then O_LARGEFILE will
> always be set in the flags retrieved by F_GETFL.

Checking the access mode of the file is slightly more complex, since the O_RDONLY (0),
O_WRONLY (1), and O_RDWR (2) constants don't correspond to single bits in the open file
status flags. Therefore, to make this check, we mask the *flags* value with the constant O_ACCMODE, and then test for equality with one of the constants:

```
accessMode = flags & O_ACCMODE;
if (accessMode == O_WRONLY || accessMode == O_RDWR)
    printf("file is writable\n");
```

We can use the *fcntl()* F_SETFL command to modify some of the open file status flags.
The flags that can be modified are O_APPEND, O_NONBLOCK, O_NOATIME, O_ASYNC, and
O_DIRECT. Attempts to modify other flags are ignored. (Some other UNIX imple-
mentations allow *fcntl()* to modify other flags, such as O_SYNC.)

Using *fcntl()* to modify open file status flags is particularly useful in the following cases:

- The file was not opened by the calling program, so that it had no control over the flags used in the *open()* call (e.g., the file may be one of the three standard descriptors that are opened before the program is started).

- The file descriptor was obtained from a system call other than *open()*. Examples of such system calls are *pipe()*, which creates a pipe and returns two file descriptors referring to either end of the pipe, and *socket()*, which creates a socket and returns a file descriptor referring to the socket.

To modify the open file status flags, we use *fcntl()* to retrieve a copy of the existing flags, then modify the bits we wish to change, and finally make a further call to *fcntl()* to update the flags. Thus, to enable the O_APPEND flag, we would write the following:

```
int flags;

flags = fcntl(fd, F_GETFL);
if (flags == -1)
    errExit("fcntl");
flags |= O_APPEND;
if (fcntl(fd, F_SETFL, flags) == -1)
    errExit("fcntl");
```

5.4 Relationship Between File Descriptors and Open Files

Up until now, it may have appeared that there is a one-to-one correspondence between a file descriptor and an open file. However, this is not the case. It is possible—and useful—to have multiple descriptors referring to the same open file. These file descriptors may be open in the same process or in different processes.

To understand what is going on, we need to examine three data structures maintained by the kernel:

- the per-process file descriptor table;
- the system-wide table of open file descriptions; and
- the file system i-node table.

For each process, the kernel maintains a table of *open file descriptors*. Each entry in this table records information about a single file descriptor, including:

- a set of flags controlling the operation of the file descriptor (there is just one such flag, the close-on-exec flag, which we describe in Section 27.4); and
- a reference to the open file description.

The kernel maintains a system-wide table of all *open file descriptions*. (This table is sometimes referred to as the *open file table*, and its entries are sometimes called *open file handles*.) An open file description stores all information relating to an open file, including:

- the current file offset (as updated by *read()* and *write()*, or explicitly modified using *lseek()*);

- status flags specified when opening the file (i.e., the *flags* argument to *open()*);
- the file access mode (read-only, write-only, or read-write, as specified in *open()*);
- settings relating to signal-driven I/O (Section 63.3); and
- a reference to the *i-node* object for this file.

Each file system has a table of *i-nodes* for all files residing in the file system. The i-node structure, and file systems in general, are discussed in more detail in Chapter 14. For now, we note that the i-node for each file includes the following information:

- file type (e.g., regular file, socket, or FIFO) and permissions;
- a pointer to a list of locks held on this file; and
- various properties of the file, including its size and timestamps relating to different types of file operations.

> Here, we are overlooking the distinction between on-disk and in-memory representations of an i-node. The on-disk i-node records the persistent attributes of a file, such as its type, permissions, and timestamps. When a file is accessed, an in-memory copy of the i-node is created, and this version of the i-node records a count of the open file descriptions referring to the i-node and the major and minor IDs of the device from which the i-node was copied. The in-memory i-node also records various ephemeral attributes that are associated with a file while it is open, such as file locks.

Figure 5-2 illustrates the relationship between file descriptors, open file descriptions, and i-nodes. In this diagram, two processes have a number of open file descriptors.

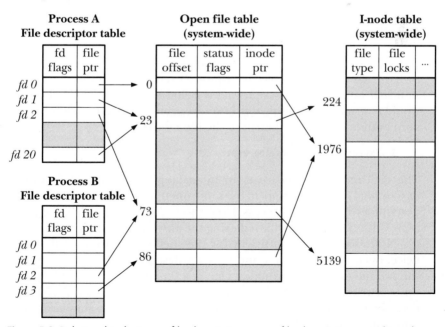

Figure 5-2: Relationship between file descriptors, open file descriptions, and i-nodes

In process A, descriptors 1 and 20 both refer to the same open file description (labeled 23). This situation may arise as a result of a call to *dup()*, *dup2()*, or *fcntl()* (see Section 5.5).

Descriptor 2 of process A and descriptor 2 of process B refer to a single open file description (73). This scenario could occur after a call to *fork()* (i.e., process A is the parent of process B, or vice versa), or if one process passed an open descriptor to another process using a UNIX domain socket (Section 61.13.3).

Finally, we see that descriptor 0 of process A and descriptor 3 of process B refer to different open file descriptions, but that these descriptions refer to the same i-node table entry (1976)—in other words, to the same file. This occurs because each process independently called *open()* for the same file. A similar situation could occur if a single process opened the same file twice.

We can draw a number of implications from the preceding discussion:

- Two different file descriptors that refer to the same open file description share a file offset value. Therefore, if the file offset is changed via one file descriptor (as a consequence of calls to *read()*, *write()*, or *lseek()*), this change is visible through the other file descriptor. This applies both when the two file descriptors belong to the same process and when they belong to different processes.

- Similar scope rules apply when retrieving and changing the open file status flags (e.g., O_APPEND, O_NONBLOCK, and O_ASYNC) using the *fcntl()* F_GETFL and F_SETFL operations.

- By contrast, the file descriptor flags (i.e., the close-on-exec flag) are private to the process and file descriptor. Modifying these flags does not affect other file descriptors in the same process or a different process.

5.5 Duplicating File Descriptors

Using the (Bourne shell) I/O redirection syntax 2>&1 informs the shell that we wish to have standard error (file descriptor 2) redirected to the same place to which standard output (file descriptor 1) is being sent. Thus, the following command would (since the shell evaluates I/O directions from left to right) send both standard output and standard error to the file results.log:

```
$ ./myscript > results.log 2>&1
```

The shell redirects standard error by making file descriptor 2 a duplicate of file descriptor 1, so that it refers to the same open file description (in the same way that descriptors 1 and 20 of process A refer to the same open file description in Figure 5-2). This effect can be achieved using the *dup()* and *dup2()* system calls.

Note that it is not sufficient for the shell simply to open the results.log file twice: once on descriptor 1 and once on descriptor 2. One reason for this is that the two file descriptors would not share a file offset pointer, and hence could end up overwriting each other's output. Another reason is that the file may not be a disk file. Consider the following command, which sends standard error down the same pipe as standard output:

```
$ ./myscript 2>&1 | less
```

The *dup()* call takes *oldfd*, an open file descriptor, and returns a new descriptor that refers to the same open file description. The new descriptor is guaranteed to be the lowest unused file descriptor.

```
#include <unistd.h>

int dup(int oldfd);
```
                          Returns (new) file descriptor on success, or –1 on error

Suppose we make the following call:

```
newfd = dup(1);
```

Assuming the normal situation where the shell has opened file descriptors 0, 1, and 2 on the program's behalf, and no other descriptors are in use, *dup()* will create the duplicate of descriptor 1 using descriptor 3.

If we wanted the duplicate to be descriptor 2, we could use the following technique:

```
close(2);              /* Frees file descriptor 2 */
newfd = dup(1);        /* Should reuse file descriptor 2 */
```

This code works only if descriptor 0 was open. To make the above code simpler, and to ensure we always get the file descriptor we want, we can use *dup2()*.

```
#include <unistd.h>

int dup2(int oldfd, int newfd);
```
                          Returns (new) file descriptor on success, or –1 on error

The *dup2()* system call makes a duplicate of the file descriptor given in *oldfd* using the descriptor number supplied in *newfd*. If the file descriptor specified in *newfd* is already open, *dup2()* closes it first. (Any error that occurs during this close is silently ignored.) The closing and reuse of *newfd* are performed atomically, which avoids the possibility that *newfd* is reused between the two steps in a signal handler or a parallel thread that allocates a file descriptor.

We could simplify the preceding calls to *close()* and *dup()* to the following:

```
dup2(1, 2);
```

A successful *dup2()* call returns the number of the duplicate descriptor (i.e., the value passed in *newfd*).

If *oldfd* is not a valid file descriptor, then *dup2()* fails with the error EBADF and *newfd* is not closed. If *oldfd* is a valid file descriptor, and *oldfd* and *newfd* have the same value, then *dup2()* does nothing—*newfd* is not closed, and *dup2()* returns the *newfd* as its function result.

A further interface that provides some extra flexibility for duplicating file descriptors is the *fcntl()* F_DUPFD operation:

```
newfd = fcntl(oldfd, F_DUPFD, startfd);
```

This call makes a duplicate of *oldfd* by using the lowest unused file descriptor greater than or equal to *startfd*. This is useful if we want a guarantee that the new descriptor (*newfd*) falls in a certain range of values. Calls to *dup()* and *dup2()* can always be recoded as calls to *close()* and *fcntl()*, although the former calls are more concise. (Note also that some of the *errno* error codes returned by *dup2()* and *fcntl()* differ, as described in the manual pages.)

From Figure 5-2, we can see that duplicate file descriptors share the same file offset value and status flags in their shared open file description. However, the new file descriptor has its own set of file descriptor flags, and its close-on-exec flag (FD_CLOEXEC) is always turned off. The interfaces that we describe next allow explicit control of the new file descriptor's close-on-exec flag.

The *dup3()* system call performs the same task as *dup2()*, but adds an additional argument, *flags*, that is a bit mask that modifies the behavior of the system call.

```
#define _GNU_SOURCE
#include <unistd.h>

int dup3(int oldfd, int newfd, int flags);
```
                    Returns (new) file descriptor on success, or –1 on error

Currently, *dup3()* supports one flag, O_CLOEXEC, which causes the kernel to enable the close-on-exec flag (FD_CLOEXEC) for the new file descriptor. This flag is useful for the same reasons as the *open()* O_CLOEXEC flag described in Section 4.3.1.

The *dup3()* system call is new in Linux 2.6.27, and is Linux-specific.

Since Linux 2.6.24, Linux also supports an additional *fcntl()* operation for duplicating file descriptors: F_DUPFD_CLOEXEC. This flag does the same thing as F_DUPFD, but additionally sets the close-on-exec flag (FD_CLOEXEC) for the new file descriptor. Again, this operation is useful for the same reasons as the *open()* O_CLOEXEC flag. F_DUPFD_CLOEXEC is not specified in SUSv3, but is specified in SUSv4.

5.6   File I/O at a Specified Offset: *pread()* and *pwrite()*

The *pread()* and *pwrite()* system calls operate just like *read()* and *write()*, except that the file I/O is performed at the location specified by *offset*, rather than at the current file offset. The file offset is left unchanged by these calls.

```
#include <unistd.h>

ssize_t pread(int fd, void *buf, size_t count, off_t offset);
```
                    Returns number of bytes read, 0 on EOF, or –1 on error
```
ssize_t pwrite(int fd, const void *buf, size_t count, off_t offset);
```
                    Returns number of bytes written, or –1 on error

Calling *pread()* is equivalent to *atomically* performing the following calls:

```
off_t orig;

orig = lseek(fd, 0, SEEK_CUR);      /* Save current offset */
lseek(fd, offset, SEEK_SET);
s = read(fd, buf, len);
lseek(fd, orig, SEEK_SET);          /* Restore original file offset */
```

For both *pread()* and *pwrite()*, the file referred to by *fd* must be seekable (i.e., a file descriptor on which it is permissible to call *lseek()*).

These system calls can be particularly useful in multithreaded applications. As we'll see in Chapter 29, all of the threads in a process share the same file descriptor table. This means that the file offset for each open file is global to all threads. Using *pread()* or *pwrite()*, multiple threads can simultaneously perform I/O on the same file descriptor without being affected by changes made to the file offset by other threads. If we attempted to use *lseek()* plus *read()* (or *write()*) instead, then we would create a race condition similar to the one that we described when discussing the O_APPEND flag in Section 5.1. (The *pread()* and *pwrite()* system calls can similarly be useful for avoiding race conditions in applications where multiple processes have file descriptors referring to the same open file description.)

> If we are repeatedly performing *lseek()* calls followed by file I/O, then the *pread()* and *pwrite()* system calls can also offer a performance advantage in some cases. This is because the cost of a single *pread()* (or *pwrite()*) system call is less than the cost of two system calls: *lseek()* and *read()* (or *write()*). However, the cost of system calls is usually dwarfed by the time required to actually perform I/O.

5.7 Scatter-Gather I/O: *readv()* and *writev()*

The *readv()* and *writev()* system calls perform scatter-gather I/O.

```
#include <sys/uio.h>

ssize_t readv(int fd, const struct iovec *iov, int iovcnt);
```
                    Returns number of bytes read, 0 on EOF, or –1 on error
```
ssize_t writev(int fd, const struct iovec *iov, int iovcnt);
```
                    Returns number of bytes written, or –1 on error

Instead of accepting a single buffer of data to be read or written, these functions transfer multiple buffers of data in a single system call. The set of buffers to be transferred is defined by the array *iov*. The integer *iovcnt* specifies the number of elements in *iov*. Each element of *iov* is a structure of the following form:

```
struct iovec {
    void  *iov_base;        /* Start address of buffer */
    size_t iov_len;         /* Number of bytes to transfer to/from buffer */
};
```

SUSv3 allows an implementation to place a limit on the number of elements in *iov*. An implementation can advertise its limit by defining IOV_MAX in <limits.h> or at run time via the return from the call *sysconf(_SC_IOV_MAX)*. (We describe *sysconf()* in Section 11.2.) SUSv3 requires that this limit be at least 16. On Linux, IOV_MAX is defined as 1024, which corresponds to the kernel's limit on the size of this vector (defined by the kernel constant UIO_MAXIOV).

However, the *glibc* wrapper functions for *readv()* and *writev()* silently do some extra work. If the system call fails because *iovcnt* is too large, then the wrapper function temporarily allocates a single buffer large enough to hold all of the items described by *iov* and performs a *read()* or *write()* call (see the discussion below of how *writev()* could be implemented in terms of *write()*).

Figure 5-3 shows an example of the relationship between the *iov* and *iovcnt* arguments, and the buffers to which they refer.

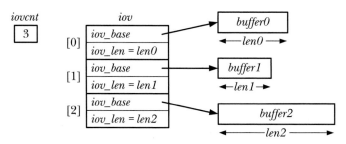

Figure 5-3: Example of an *iovec* array and associated buffers

Scatter input

The *readv()* system call performs *scatter input*: it reads a contiguous sequence of bytes from the file referred to by the file descriptor *fd* and places ("scatters") these bytes into the buffers specified by *iov*. Each of the buffers, starting with the one defined by *iov[0]*, is completely filled before *readv()* proceeds to the next buffer.

An important property of *readv()* is that it completes atomically; that is, from the point of view of the calling process, the kernel performs a single data transfer between the file referred to by *fd* and user memory. This means, for example, that when reading from a file, we can be sure that the range of bytes read is contiguous, even if another process (or thread) sharing the same file offset attempts to manipulate the offset at the same time as the *readv()* call.

On successful completion, *readv()* returns the number of bytes read, or 0 if end-of-file was encountered. The caller must examine this count to verify whether all requested bytes were read. If insufficient data was available, then only some of the buffers may have been filled, and the last of these may be only partially filled.

Listing 5-2 demonstrates the use of *readv()*.

> Using the prefix t_ followed by a function name as the name of an example program (e.g., t_readv.c in Listing 5-2) is our way of indicating that the program primarily demonstrates the use of a single system call or library function.

Listing 5-2: Performing scatter input with *readv( )*

———————————————————————— **fileio/t_readv.c**

```c
#include <sys/stat.h>
#include <sys/uio.h>
#include <fcntl.h>
#include "tlpi_hdr.h"

int
main(int argc, char *argv[])
{
    int fd;
    struct iovec iov[3];
    struct stat myStruct;       /* First buffer */
    int x;                      /* Second buffer */
#define STR_SIZE 100
    char str[STR_SIZE];         /* Third buffer */
    ssize_t numRead, totRequired;

    if (argc != 2 || strcmp(argv[1], "--help") == 0)
        usageErr("%s file\n", argv[0]);

    fd = open(argv[1], O_RDONLY);
    if (fd == -1)
        errExit("open");

    totRequired = 0;

    iov[0].iov_base = &myStruct;
    iov[0].iov_len = sizeof(struct stat);
    totRequired += iov[0].iov_len;

    iov[1].iov_base = &x;
    iov[1].iov_len = sizeof(x);
    totRequired += iov[1].iov_len;

    iov[2].iov_base = str;
    iov[2].iov_len = STR_SIZE;
    totRequired += iov[2].iov_len;

    numRead = readv(fd, iov, 3);
    if (numRead == -1)
        errExit("readv");

    if (numRead < totRequired)
        printf("Read fewer bytes than requested\n");

    printf("total bytes requested: %ld; bytes read: %ld\n",
            (long) totRequired, (long) numRead);
    exit(EXIT_SUCCESS);
}
```

———————————————————————— **fileio/t_readv.c**

Gather output

The *writev()* system call performs *gather output*. It concatenates ("gathers") data from all of the buffers specified by *iov* and writes them as a sequence of contiguous bytes to the file referred to by the file descriptor *fd*. The buffers are gathered in array order, starting with the buffer defined by *iov[0]*.

Like *readv()*, *writev()* completes atomically, with all data being transferred in a single operation from user memory to the file referred to by *fd*. Thus, when writing to a regular file, we can be sure that all of the requested data is written contiguously to the file, rather than being interspersed with writes by other processes (or threads).

As with *write()*, a partial write is possible. Therefore, we must check the return value from *writev()* to see if all requested bytes were written.

The primary advantages of *readv()* and *writev()* are convenience and speed. For example, we could replace a call to *writev()* by either:

* code that allocates a single large buffer, copies the data to be written from other locations in the process's address space into that buffer, and then calls *write()* to output the buffer; or

* a series of *write()* calls that output the buffers individually.

The first of these options, while semantically equivalent to using *writev()*, leaves us with the inconvenience (and inefficiency) of allocating buffers and copying data in user space.

The second option is not semantically equivalent to a single call to *writev()*, since the *write()* calls are not performed atomically. Furthermore, performing a single *writev()* system call is cheaper than performing multiple *write()* calls (refer to the discussion of system calls in Section 3.1).

Performing scatter-gather I/O at a specified offset

Linux 2.6.30 adds two new system calls that combine scatter-gather I/O functionality with the ability to perform the I/O at a specified offset: *preadv()* and *pwritev()*. These system calls are nonstandard, but are also available on the modern BSDs.

```
#define _BSD_SOURCE
#include <sys/uio.h>

ssize_t preadv(int fd, const struct iovec *iov, int iovcnt, off_t offset);
```
                          Returns number of bytes read, 0 on EOF, or −1 on error
```
ssize_t pwritev(int fd, const struct iovec *iov, int iovcnt, off_t offset);
```
                          Returns number of bytes written, or −1 on error

The *preadv()* and *pwritev()* system calls perform the same task as *readv()* and *writev()*, but perform the I/O at the file location specified by *offset* (like *pread()* and *pwrite()*). These system calls don't change the file offset.

These system calls are useful for applications (e.g., multithreaded applications) that want to combine the benefits of scatter-gather I/O with the ability to perform I/O at a location that is independent of the current file offset.

5.8 Truncating a File: *truncate()* **and** *ftruncate()*

The *truncate()* and *ftruncate()* system calls set the size of a file to the value specified by *length*.

```
#include <unistd.h>

int truncate(const char *pathname, off_t length);
int ftruncate(int fd, off_t length);
```
                                        Both return 0 on success, or −1 on error

If the file is longer than *length*, the excess data is lost. If the file is currently shorter than *length*, it is extended by padding with a sequence of null bytes or a hole.

The difference between the two system calls lies in how the file is specified. With *truncate()*, the file, which must be accessible and writable, is specified as a pathname string. If *pathname* is a symbolic link, it is dereferenced. The *ftruncate()* system call takes a descriptor for a file that has been opened for writing. It doesn't change the file offset for the file.

If the *length* argument to *ftruncate()* exceeds the current file size, SUSv3 allows two possible behaviors: either the file is extended (as on Linux) or the system call returns an error. XSI-conformant systems must adopt the former behavior. SUSv3 requires that *truncate()* always extend the file if *length* is greater than the current file size.

> The *truncate()* system call is unique in being the only system call that can change the contents of a file without first obtaining a descriptor for the file via *open()* (or by some other means).

5.9 Nonblocking I/O

Specifying the O_NONBLOCK flag when opening a file serves two purposes:

- If the file can't be opened immediately, then *open()* returns an error instead of blocking. One case where *open()* can block is with FIFOs (Section 44.7).

- After a successful *open()*, subsequent I/O operations are also nonblocking. If an I/O system call can't complete immediately, then either a partial data transfer is performed or the system call fails with one of the errors EAGAIN or EWOULDBLOCK. Which error is returned depends on the system call. On Linux, as on many UNIX implementations, these two error constants are synonymous.

Nonblocking mode can be used with devices (e.g., terminals and pseudoterminals), pipes, FIFOs, and sockets. (Because file descriptors for pipes and sockets are not obtained using *open()*, we must enable this flag using the *fcntl()* F_SETFL operation described in Section 5.3.)

O_NONBLOCK is generally ignored for regular files, because the kernel buffer cache ensures that I/O on regular files does not block, as described in Section 13.1. However, O_NONBLOCK does have an effect for regular files when mandatory file locking is employed (Section 55.4).

We say more about nonblocking I/O in Section 44.9 and in Chapter 63.

> Historically, System V–derived implementations provided the O_NDELAY flag, with similar semantics to O_NONBLOCK. The main difference was that a nonblocking *write()* on System V returned 0 if a *write()* could not be completed and a nonblocking *read()* returned 0 if no input was available. This behavior was problematic for *read()* because it was indistinguishable from an end-of-file condition, and so the first POSIX.1 standard introduced O_NONBLOCK. Some UNIX implementations continue to provide the O_NDELAY flag with the old semantics. On Linux, the O_NDELAY constant is defined, but it is synonymous with O_NONBLOCK.

5.10 I/O on Large Files

The *off_t* data type used to hold a file offset is typically implemented as a signed long integer. (A signed data type is required because the value −1 is used for representing error conditions.) On 32-bit architectures (such as x86-32) this would limit the size of files to $2^{31}-1$ bytes (i.e., 2 GB).

However, the capacity of disk drives long ago exceeded this limit, and thus the need arose for 32-bit UNIX implementations to handle files larger than this size. Since this is a problem common to many implementations, a consortium of UNIX vendors cooperated on the *Large File Summit* (LFS), to enhance the SUSv2 specification with the extra functionality required to access large files. We outline the LFS enhancements in this section. (The complete LFS specification, finalized in 1996, can be found at *http://opengroup.org/platform/lfs.html*.)

Linux has provided LFS support on 32-bit systems since kernel 2.4 (*glibc* 2.2 or later is also required). In addition, the corresponding file system must also support large files. Most native Linux file systems provide this support, but some nonnative file systems do not (notable examples are Microsoft's VFAT and NFSv2, both of which impose hard limits of 2 GB, regardless of whether the LFS extensions are employed).

> Because long integers use 64 bits on 64-bit architectures (e.g., x86-64, Alpha, and IA-64), these architectures generally don't suffer the limitations that the LFS enhancements were designed to address. Nevertheless, the implementation details of some native Linux file systems mean that the theoretical maximum size of a file may be less than $2^{63}-1$, even on 64-bit systems. In most cases, these limits are much higher than current disk sizes, so they don't impose a practical limitation on file sizes.

We can write applications requiring LFS functionality in one of two ways:

- Use an alternative API that supports large files. This API was designed by the LFS as a "transitional extension" to the Single UNIX Specification. Thus, this API is not required to be present on systems conforming to SUSv2 or SUSv3, but many conforming systems do provide it. This approach is now obsolete.

- Define the _FILE_OFFSET_BITS macro with the value 64 when compiling our programs. This is the preferred approach, because it allows conforming applications to obtain LFS functionality without making any source code changes.

The transitional LFS API

To use the transitional LFS API, we must define the `_LARGEFILE64_SOURCE` feature test macro when compiling our program, either on the command line, or within the source file before including any header files. This API provides functions capable of handling 64-bit file sizes and offsets. These functions have the same names as their 32-bit counterparts, but have the suffix *64* appended to the function name. Among these functions are *fopen64()*, *open64()*, *lseek64()*, *truncate64()*, *stat64()*, *mmap64()*, and *setrlimit64()*. (We've already described some of the 32-bit counterparts of these functions; others are described in later chapters.)

In order to access a large file, we simply use the 64-bit version of the function. For example, to open a large file, we could write the following:

```
fd = open64(name, O_CREAT | O_RDWR, mode);
if (fd == -1)
    errExit("open");
```

> Calling *open64()* is equivalent to specifying the `O_LARGEFILE` flag when calling *open()*. Attempts to open a file larger than 2 GB by calling *open()* without this flag return an error.

In addition to the aforementioned functions, the transitional LFS API adds some new data types, including:

- *struct stat64*: an analog of the *stat* structure (Section 15.1) allowing for large file sizes.
- *off64_t*: a 64-bit type for representing file offsets.

The *off64_t* data type is used with (among others) the *lseek64()* function, as shown in Listing 5-3. This program takes two command-line arguments: the name of a file to be opened and an integer value specifying a file offset. The program opens the specified file, seeks to the given file offset, and then writes a string. The following shell session demonstrates the use of the program to seek to a very large offset in the file (greater than 10 GB) and then write some bytes:

```
$ ./large_file x 10111222333
$ ls -l x                              Check size of resulting file
-rw-------   1 mtk     users    10111222337 Mar  4 13:34 x
```

Listing 5-3: Accessing large files

――――――――――――――――――――――――――――――――――――― **fileio/large_file.c**

```c
#define _LARGEFILE64_SOURCE
#include <sys/stat.h>
#include <fcntl.h>
#include "tlpi_hdr.h"

int
main(int argc, char *argv[])
{
    int fd;
    off64_t off;
```

```
    if (argc != 3 || strcmp(argv[1], "--help") == 0)
        usageErr("%s pathname offset\n", argv[0]);

    fd = open64(argv[1], O_RDWR | O_CREAT, S_IRUSR | S_IWUSR);
    if (fd == -1)
        errExit("open64");

    off = atoll(argv[2]);
    if (lseek64(fd, off, SEEK_SET) == -1)
        errExit("lseek64");

    if (write(fd, "test", 4) == -1)
        errExit("write");
    exit(EXIT_SUCCESS);
}
```

—— `fileio/large_file.c`

The `_FILE_OFFSET_BITS` macro

The recommended method of obtaining LFS functionality is to define the macro
`_FILE_OFFSET_BITS` with the value 64 when compiling a program. One way to do this
is via a command-line option to the C compiler:

```
$ cc -D_FILE_OFFSET_BITS=64 prog.c
```

Alternatively, we can define this macro in the C source before including any header
files:

```
#define _FILE_OFFSET_BITS 64
```

This automatically converts all of the relevant 32-bit functions and data types into
their 64-bit counterparts. Thus, for example, calls to *open()* are actually converted
into calls to *open64()*, and the *off_t* data type is defined to be 64 bits long. In other
words, we can recompile an existing program to handle large files without needing
to make any changes to the source code.

Using `_FILE_OFFSET_BITS` is clearly simpler than using the transitional LFS API,
but this approach relies on applications being cleanly written (e.g., correctly using
off_t to declare variables holding file offsets, rather than using a native C integer
type).

The `_FILE_OFFSET_BITS` macro is not required by the LFS specification, which
merely mentions this macro as an optional method of specifying the size of the *off_t*
data type. Some UNIX implementations use a different feature test macro to
obtain this functionality.

> If we attempt to access a large file using 32-bit functions (i.e., from a program
> compiled without setting `_FILE_OFFSET_BITS` to 64), then we may encounter the
> error EOVERFLOW. For example, this error can occur if we attempt to use the 32-bit
> version of *stat()* (Section 15.1) to retrieve information about a file whose size
> exceeds 2 GB.

Passing *off_t* **values to** *printf()*

One problem that the LFS extensions don't solve for us is how to pass *off_t* values to *printf()* calls. In Section 3.6.2, we noted that the portable method of displaying values of one of the predefined system data types (e.g., *pid_t* or *uid_t*) was to cast that value to *long*, and use the %ld *printf()* specifier. However, if we are employing the LFS extensions, then this is often not sufficient for the *off_t* data type, because it may be defined as a type larger than *long*, typically *long long*. Therefore, to display a value of type *off_t*, we cast it to *long long* and use the %lld *printf()* specifier, as in the following:

```
#define _FILE_OFFSET_BITS 64

off_t offset;          /* Will be 64 bits, the size of 'long long' */

/* Other code assigning a value to 'offset' */

printf("offset=%lld\n", (long long) offset);
```

Similar remarks also apply for the related *blkcnt_t* data type, which is employed in the *stat* structure (described in Section 15.1).

> If we are passing function arguments of the types *off_t* or *stat* between separately compiled modules, then we need to ensure that both modules use the same sizes for these types (i.e., either both were compiled with _FILE_OFFSET_BITS set to 64 or both were compiled without this setting).

5.11 The /dev/fd **Directory**

For each process, the kernel provides the special virtual directory /dev/fd. This directory contains filenames of the form /dev/fd/*n*, where *n* is a number corresponding to one of the open file descriptors for the process. Thus, for example, /dev/fd/0 is standard input for the process. (The /dev/fd feature is not specified by SUSv3, but several other UNIX implementations provide this feature.)

On some systems (but not Linux), opening one of the files in the /dev/fd directory is equivalent to duplicating the corresponding file descriptor. Thus, the following statements are equivalent:

```
fd = open("/dev/fd/1", O_WRONLY);
fd = dup(1);                       /* Duplicate standard output */
```

The *flags* argument of the *open()* call *is* interpreted, so that we should take care to specify the same access mode as was used by the original descriptor. Specifying other flags, such as O_CREAT, is meaningless (and ignored) in this context.

On Linux, opening one of the files in /dev/fd is equivalent to reopening the original file; that is, the new file descriptor is associated with a new open file description (and thus has distinct file status flags and file offset).

> /dev/fd is actually a symbolic link to the Linux-specific /proc/self/fd directory. The latter directory is a special case of the Linux-specific /proc/*PID*/fd directories, each of which contains symbolic links corresponding to all of the files held open by a process.

The files in the /dev/fd directory are rarely used within programs. Their most common use is in the shell. Many user-level commands take filename arguments, and sometimes we would like to put them in a pipeline and have one of the arguments be standard input or output instead. For this purpose, some programs (e.g., *diff*, *ed*, *tar*, and *comm*) have evolved the hack of using an argument consisting of a single hyphen (-) to mean "use standard input or output (as appropriate) for this filename argument." Thus, to compare a file list from *ls* against a previously built file list, we might write the following:

```
$ ls | diff - oldfilelist
```

This approach has various problems. First, it requires specific interpretation of the hyphen character on the part of each program, and many programs don't perform such interpretation; they are written to work only with filename arguments, and they have no means of specifying standard input or output as the files with which they are to work. Second, some programs instead interpret a single hyphen as a delimiter marking the end of command-line options.

Using /dev/fd eliminates these difficulties, allowing the specification of standard input, output, and error as filename arguments to any program requiring them. Thus, we can write the previous shell command as follows:

```
$ ls | diff /dev/fd/0 oldfilelist
```

As a convenience, the names /dev/stdin, /dev/stdout, and /dev/stderr are provided as symbolic links to, respectively, /proc/self/fd/0, /proc/self/fd/1, and /proc/self/fd/2 (equivalent to /dev/fd/0, /dev/fd/1, and /dev/fd/2).

5.12 Creating Temporary Files

Some programs need to create temporary files that are used only while the program is running, and these files should be removed when the program terminates. For example, many compilers create temporary files during the compilation process. The GNU C library provides a range of library functions for this purpose. (The variety is, in part, a consequence of inheritance from various other UNIX implementations.) Here, we describe two of these functions: *mkstemp()* and *tmpfile()*.

The *mkstemp()* function generates a unique filename based on a template supplied by the caller and opens the file, returning a file descriptor that can be used with I/O system calls.

```
#include <stdlib.h>

int mkstemp(char *template);
```
                                Returns file descriptor on success, or −1 on error

The *template* argument takes the form of a pathname in which the last 6 characters must be XXXXXX. These 6 characters are replaced with a string that makes the filename unique, and this modified string is returned via the *template* argument. Because *template* is modified, it must be specified as a character array, rather than as a string constant.

The *mkstemp()* function creates the file with read and write permissions for the file owner (and no permissions for other users), and opens it with the O_EXCL flag, guaranteeing that the caller has exclusive access to the file.

Typically, a temporary file is unlinked (deleted) soon after it is opened, using the *unlink()* system call (Section 18.3). Thus, we could employ *mkstemp()* as follows:

```
int fd;
char template[] = "/tmp/somestringXXXXXX";

fd = mkstemp(template);
if (fd == -1)
    errExit("mkstemp");
printf("Generated filename was: %s\n", template);
unlink(template);       /* Name disappears immediately, but the file
                           is removed only after close() */

/* Use file I/O system calls - read(), write(), and so on */

if (close(fd) == -1)
    errExit("close");
```

> The *tmpnam()*, *tempnam()*, and *mktemp()* functions can also be used to generate unique filenames. However, these functions should be avoided because they can create security holes in an application. See the manual pages for further details on these functions.

The *tmpfile()* function creates a uniquely named temporary file that is opened for reading and writing. (The file is opened with the O_EXCL flag to guard against the unlikely possibility that another process has already created a file with the same name.)

```
#include <stdio.h>

FILE *tmpfile(void);
```
                                            Returns file pointer on success, or NULL on error

On success, *tmpfile()* returns a file stream that can be used with the *stdio* library functions. The temporary file is automatically deleted when it is closed. To do this, *tmpfile()* makes an internal call to *unlink()* to remove the filename immediately after opening the file.

5.13 Summary

In the course of this chapter, we introduced the concept of atomicity, which is crucial to the correct operation of some system calls. In particular, the *open()* O_EXCL flag allows the caller to ensure that it is the creator of a file, and the *open()* O_APPEND flag ensures that multiple processes appending data to the same file don't overwrite each other's output.

The *fcntl()* system call performs a variety of file control operations, including changing open file status flags and duplicating file descriptors. Duplicating file descriptors is also possible using *dup()* and *dup2()*.

We looked at the relationship between file descriptors, open file descriptions, and file i-nodes, and noted that different information is associated with each of these three objects. Duplicate file descriptors refer to the same open file description, and thus share open file status flags and the file offset.

We described a number of system calls that extend the functionality of the conventional *read()* and *write()* system calls. The *pread()* and *pwrite()* system calls perform I/O at a specified file location without changing the file offset. The *readv()* and *writev()* calls perform scatter-gather I/O. The *preadv()* and *pwritev()* calls combine scatter-gather I/O functionality with the ability to perform I/O at a specified file location.

The *truncate()* and *ftruncate()* system calls can be used to decrease the size of a file, discarding the excess bytes, or to increase the size, padding with a zero-filled file hole.

We briefly introduced the concept of nonblocking I/O, and we'll return to it in later chapters.

The LFS specification defines a set of extensions that allow processes running on 32-bit systems to perform operations on files whose size is too large to be represented in 32 bits.

The numbered files in the /dev/fd virtual directory allow a process to access its own open files via file descriptor numbers, which can be particularly useful in shell commands.

The *mkstemp()* and *tmpfile()* functions allow an application to create temporary files.

5.14 Exercises

5-1. If you have access to a 32-bit Linux system, modify the program in Listing 5-3 to use standard file I/O system calls (*open()* and *lseek()*) and the *off_t* data type. Compile the program with the _FILE_OFFSET_BITS macro set to 64, and test it to show that a large file can be successfully created.

5-2. Write a program that opens an existing file for writing with the O_APPEND flag, and then seeks to the beginning of the file before writing some data. Where does the data appear in the file? Why?

5-3. This exercise is designed to demonstrate why the atomicity guaranteed by opening a file with the O_APPEND flag is necessary. Write a program that takes up to three command-line arguments:

> $ `atomic_append` *filename num-bytes* [*x*]

This program should open the specified filename (creating it if necessary) and append *num-bytes* bytes to the file by using *write()* to write a byte at a time. By default, the program should open the file with the O_APPEND flag, but if a third command-line argument (*x*) is supplied, then the O_APPEND flag should be omitted, and instead the program should perform an *lseek(fd, 0, SEEK_END)* call before each *write()*. Run two instances of this program at the same time without the *x* argument to write 1 million bytes to the same file:

```
$ atomic_append f1 1000000 & atomic_append f1 1000000
```

Repeat the same steps, writing to a different file, but this time specifying the *x* argument:

```
$ atomic_append f2 1000000 x & atomic_append f2 1000000 x
```

List the sizes of the files f1 and f2 using *ls −l* and explain the difference.

5-4. Implement *dup()* and *dup2()* using *fcntl()* and, where necessary, *close()*. (You may ignore the fact that *dup2()* and *fcntl()* return different *errno* values for some error cases.) For *dup2()*, remember to handle the special case where *oldfd* equals *newfd*. In this case, you should check whether *oldfd* is valid, which can be done by, for example, checking if *fcntl(oldfd, F_GETFL)* succeeds. If *oldfd* is not valid, then the function should return −1 with *errno* set to EBADF.

5-5. Write a program to verify that duplicated file descriptors share a file offset value and open file status flags.

5-6. After each of the calls to *write()* in the following code, explain what the content of the output file would be, and why:

```
fd1 = open(file, O_RDWR | O_CREAT | O_TRUNC, S_IRUSR | S_IWUSR);
fd2 = dup(fd1);
fd3 = open(file, O_RDWR);
write(fd1, "Hello,", 6);
write(fd2, " world", 6);
lseek(fd2, 0, SEEK_SET);
write(fd1, "HELLO,", 6);
write(fd3, "Gidday", 6);
```

5-7. Implement *readv()* and *writev()* using *read()*, *write()*, and suitable functions from the *malloc* package (Section 7.1.2).

6

PROCESSES

In this chapter, we look at the structure of a process, paying particular attention to the layout and contents of a process's virtual memory. We also examine some of the attributes of a process. In later chapters, we examine further process attributes (for example, process credentials in Chapter 9, and process priorities and scheduling in Chapter 35). In Chapters 24 to 27, we look at how processes are created, how they terminate, and how they can be made to execute new programs.

6.1   Processes and Programs

A *process* is an instance of an executing program. In this section, we elaborate on this definition and clarify the distinction between a program and a process.

A *program* is a file containing a range of information that describes how to construct a process at run time. This information includes the following:

- *Binary format identification*: Each program file includes metainformation describing the format of the executable file. This enables the kernel to interpret the remaining information in the file. Historically, two widely used formats for UNIX executable files were the original *a.out* ("assembler output") format and the later, more sophisticated *COFF* (Common Object File Format). Nowadays, most UNIX implementations (including Linux) employ the Executable and Linking Format (ELF), which provides a number of advantages over the older formats.

- *Machine-language instructions*: These encode the algorithm of the program.

- *Program entry-point address*: This identifies the location of the instruction at which execution of the program should commence.

- *Data*: The program file contains values used to initialize variables and also literal constants used by the program (e.g., strings).

- *Symbol and relocation tables*: These describe the locations and names of functions and variables within the program. These tables are used for a variety of purposes, including debugging and run-time symbol resolution (dynamic linking).

- *Shared-library and dynamic-linking information*: The program file includes fields listing the shared libraries that the program needs to use at run time and the pathname of the dynamic linker that should be used to load these libraries.

- *Other information*: The program file contains various other information that describes how to construct a process.

One program may be used to construct many processes, or, put conversely, many processes may be running the same program.

We can recast the definition of a process given at the start of this section as follows: a process is an abstract entity, defined by the kernel, to which system resources are allocated in order to execute a program.

From the kernel's point of view, a process consists of user-space memory containing program code and variables used by that code, and a range of kernel data structures that maintain information about the state of the process. The information recorded in the kernel data structures includes various identifier numbers (IDs) associated with the process, virtual memory tables, the table of open file descriptors, information relating to signal delivery and handling, process resource usages and limits, the current working directory, and a host of other information.

6.2 Process ID and Parent Process ID

Each process has a process ID (PID), a positive integer that uniquely identifies the process on the system. Process IDs are used and returned by a variety of system calls. For example, the *kill()* system call (Section 20.5) allows the caller to send a signal to a process with a specific process ID. The process ID is also useful if we need to build an identifier that is unique to a process. A common example of this is the use of the process ID as part of a process-unique filename.

The *getpid()* system call returns the process ID of the calling process.

```
#include <unistd.h>

pid_t getpid(void);
```
                                              Always successfully returns process ID of caller

The *pid_t* data type used for the return value of *getpid()* is an integer type specified by SUSv3 for the purpose of storing process IDs.

With the exception of a few system processes such as *init* (process ID 1), there is no fixed relationship between a program and the process ID of the process that is created to run that program.

The Linux kernel limits process IDs to being less than or equal to 32,767. When a new process is created, it is assigned the next sequentially available process ID. Each time the limit of 32,767 is reached, the kernel resets its process ID counter so that process IDs are assigned starting from low integer values.

> Once it has reached 32,767, the process ID counter is reset to 300, rather than 1. This is done because many low-numbered process IDs are in permanent use by system processes and daemons, and thus time would be wasted searching for an unused process ID in this range.
>
> In Linux 2.4 and earlier, the process ID limit of 32,767 is defined by the kernel constant PID_MAX. With Linux 2.6, things change. While the default upper limit for process IDs remains 32,767, this limit is adjustable via the value in the Linux-specific /proc/sys/kernel/pid_max file (which is one greater than the maximum process ID). On 32-bit platforms, the maximum value for this file is 32,768, but on 64-bit platforms, it can be adjusted to any value up to 2^{22} (approximately 4 million), making it possible to accommodate very large numbers of processes.

Each process has a parent—the process that created it. A process can find out the process ID of its parent using the *getppid()* system call.

```
#include <unistd.h>

pid_t getppid(void);
```
                        Always successfully returns process ID of parent of caller

In effect, the parent process ID attribute of each process represents the tree-like relationship of all processes on the system. The parent of each process has its own parent, and so on, going all the way back to process 1, *init*, the ancestor of all processes. (This "family tree" can be viewed using the *pstree(1)* command.)

If a child process becomes orphaned because its "birth" parent terminates, then the child is adopted by the *init* process, and subsequent calls to *getppid()* in the child return 1 (see Section 26.2).

The parent of any process can be found by looking at the PPid field provided in the Linux-specific /proc/*PID*/status file.

6.3 Memory Layout of a Process

The memory allocated to each process is composed of a number of parts, usually referred to as *segments*. These segments are as follows:

- The *text segment* contains the machine-language instructions of the program run by the process. The text segment is made read-only so that a process doesn't accidentally modify its own instructions via a bad pointer value. Since many processes may be running the same program, the text segment is made sharable so that a single copy of the program code can be mapped into the virtual address space of all of the processes.

- The *initialized data segment* contains global and static variables that are explicitly initialized. The values of these variables are read from the executable file when the program is loaded into memory.

- The *uninitialized data segment* contains global and static variables that are not explicitly initialized. Before starting the program, the system initializes all memory in this segment to 0. For historical reasons, this is often called the *bss* segment, a name derived from an old assembler mnemonic for "block started by symbol." The main reason for placing global and static variables that are initialized into a separate segment from those that are uninitialized is that, when a program is stored on disk, it is not necessary to allocate space for the uninitialized data. Instead, the executable merely needs to record the location and size required for the uninitialized data segment, and this space is allocated by the program loader at run time.

- The *stack* is a dynamically growing and shrinking segment containing stack frames. One stack frame is allocated for each currently called function. A frame stores the function's local variables (so-called automatic variables), arguments, and return value. Stack frames are discussed in more detail in Section 6.5.

- The *heap* is an area from which memory (for variables) can be dynamically allocated at run time. The top end of the heap is called the *program break*.

Less commonly used, but more descriptive labels for the initialized and uninitialized data segments are *user-initialized data segment* and *zero-initialized data segment*.

The *size(1)* command displays the size of the text, initialized data, and uninitialized data (*bss*) segments of a binary executable.

> The term *segment* as used in the main text should not be confused with the hardware segmentation used on some hardware architectures such as x86-32. Rather, segments are logical divisions of a process's virtual memory on UNIX systems.
>
> In many places in this book, we note that a library function returns a pointer to statically allocated memory. By this, we mean that the memory is allocated in either the initialized or the uninitialized data segment. (In some cases, the library function may instead do a one-time dynamic allocation of the memory on the heap; however, this implementation detail is irrelevant to the semantic point we describe here.) It is important to be aware of cases where a library function returns information via statically allocated memory, since that memory has an existence that is independent of the function invocation, and the memory may be overwritten by subsequent calls to the same function (or in some cases, by subsequent calls to related functions). The effect of using statically allocated memory is to render a function nonreentrant. We say more about reentrancy in Sections 21.1.2 and 31.1.

Listing 6-1 shows various types of C variables along with comments indicating in which segment each variable is located. These comments assume a nonoptimizing compiler and an application binary interface in which all arguments are passed on the stack. In practice, an optimizing compiler may allocate frequently used variables in registers, or optimize a variable out of existence altogether. Furthermore, some ABIs require function arguments and the function result to be passed via registers, rather than on the stack. Nevertheless, this example serves to demonstrate the mapping between C variables and the segments of a process.

Listing 6-1: Locations of program variables in process memory segments

—— *proc/mem_segments.c*

```
#include <stdio.h>
#include <stdlib.h>

char globBuf[65536];         /* Uninitialized data segment */
int primes[] = { 2, 3, 5, 7 };  /* Initialized data segment */

static int
square(int x)                /* Allocated in frame for square() */
{
    int result;              /* Allocated in frame for square() */

    result = x * x;
    return result;           /* Return value passed via register */
}

static void
doCalc(int val)              /* Allocated in frame for doCalc() */
{
    printf("The square of %d is %d\n", val, square(val));

    if (val < 1000) {
        int t;               /* Allocated in frame for doCalc() */

        t = val * val * val;
        printf("The cube of %d is %d\n", val, t);
    }
}

int
main(int argc, char *argv[])    /* Allocated in frame for main() */
{
    static int key = 9973;      /* Initialized data segment */
    static char mbuf[10240000]; /* Uninitialized data segment */
    char *p;                    /* Allocated in frame for main() */

    p = malloc(1024);           /* Points to memory in heap segment */

    doCalc(key);

    exit(EXIT_SUCCESS);
}
```

—— *proc/mem_segments.c*

An *application binary interface* (ABI) is a set of rules specifying how a binary executable should exchange information with some service (e.g., the kernel or a library) at run time. Among other things, an ABI specifies which registers and stack locations are used to exchange this information, and what meaning is attached to the exchanged values. Once compiled for a particular ABI, a binary executable should be able to run on any system presenting the same ABI. This contrasts with a standardized API (such as SUSv3), which guarantees portability only for applications compiled from source code.

Although not specified in SUSv3, the C program environment on most UNIX implementations (including Linux) provides three global symbols: *etext*, *edata*, and *end*. These symbols can be used from within a program to obtain the addresses of the next byte past, respectively, the end of the program text, the end of the initialized data segment, and the end of the uninitialized data segment. To make use of these symbols, we must explicitly declare them, as follows:

```
extern char etext, edata, end;
            /* For example, &etext gives the address of the next byte past
               the end of the program text / start of initialized data */
```

Figure 6-1 shows the arrangement of the various memory segments on the x86-32 architecture. The space labeled *argv, environ* at the top of this diagram holds the program command-line arguments (available in C via the *argv* argument of the *main()* function) and the process environment list (which we discuss shortly). The hexadecimal addresses shown in the diagram may vary, depending on kernel configuration and program linking options. The grayed-out areas represent invalid ranges in the process's virtual address space; that is, areas for which page tables have not been created (see the following discussion of virtual memory management).

We revisit the topic of process memory layout in a little more detail in Section 48.5, where we consider where shared memory and shared libraries are placed in a process's virtual memory.

6.4 Virtual Memory Management

The previous discussion of the memory layout of a process glossed over the fact that we were talking about the layout in *virtual memory*. Since an understanding of virtual memory is useful later on when we look at topics such as the *fork()* system call, shared memory, and mapped files, we now consider some of the details.

Like most modern kernels, Linux employs a technique known as *virtual memory management*. The aim of this technique is to make efficient use of both the CPU and RAM (physical memory) by exploiting a property that is typical of most programs: *locality of reference*. Most programs demonstrate two kinds of locality:

- *Spatial locality* is the tendency of a program to reference memory addresses that are near those that were recently accessed (because of sequential processing of instructions, and, sometimes, sequential processing of data structures).

- *Temporal locality* is the tendency of a program to access the same memory addresses in the near future that it accessed in the recent past (because of loops).

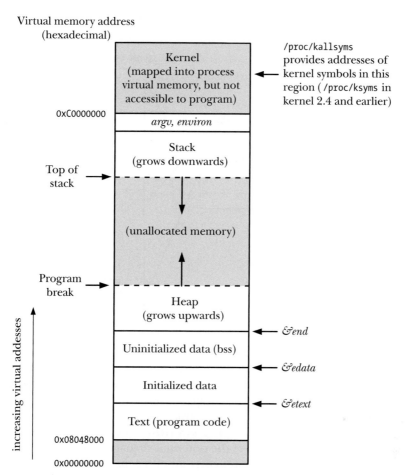

Virtual memory address
(hexadecimal)

Kernel
(mapped into process
virtual memory, but not
accessible to program)

/proc/kallsyms
provides addresses of
kernel symbols in this
region (/proc/ksyms in
kernel 2.4 and earlier)

0xC0000000

argv, environ

Stack
(grows downwards)

Top of
stack

(unallocated memory)

Program
break

Heap
(grows upwards)

&*end*

Uninitialized data (bss)

&*edata*

Initialized data

&*etext*

Text (program code)

0x08048000

0x00000000

increasing virtual addesses

Figure 6-1: Typical memory layout of a process on Linux/x86-32

The upshot of locality of reference is that it is possible to execute a program while maintaining only part of its address space in RAM.

A virtual memory scheme splits the memory used by each program into small, fixed-size units called *pages*. Correspondingly, RAM is divided into a series of *page frames* of the same size. At any one time, only some of the pages of a program need to be resident in physical memory page frames; these pages form the so-called *resident set*. Copies of the unused pages of a program are maintained in the *swap area*—a reserved area of disk space used to supplement the computer's RAM—and loaded into physical memory only as required. When a process references a page that is not currently resident in physical memory, a *page fault* occurs, at which point the kernel suspends execution of the process while the page is loaded from disk into memory.

> On x86-32, pages are 4096 bytes in size. Some other Linux implementations use larger page sizes. For example, Alpha uses a page size of 8192 bytes, and IA-64 has a variable page size, with the usual default being 16,384 bytes. A program can determine the system virtual memory page size using the call *sysconf(_SC_PAGESIZE)*, as described in Section 11.2.

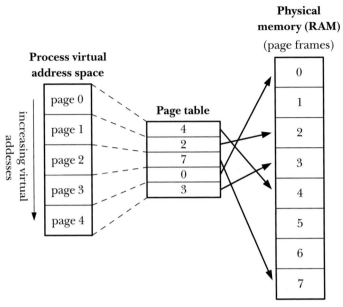

Figure 6-2: Overview of virtual memory

In order to support this organization, the kernel maintains a *page table* for each process (Figure 6-2). The page table describes the location of each page in the process's *virtual address space* (the set of all virtual memory pages available to the process). Each entry in the page table either indicates the location of a virtual page in RAM or indicates that it currently resides on disk.

Not all address ranges in the process's virtual address space require page-table entries. Typically, large ranges of the potential virtual address space are unused, so that it isn't necessary to maintain corresponding page-table entries. If a process tries to access an address for which there is no corresponding page-table entry, it receives a SIGSEGV signal.

A process's range of valid virtual addresses can change over its lifetime, as the kernel allocates and deallocates pages (and page-table entries) for the process. This can happen in the following circumstances:

- as the stack grows downward beyond limits previously reached;
- when memory is allocated or deallocated on the heap, by raising the program break using *brk()*, *sbrk()*, or the *malloc* family of functions (Chapter 7);
- when System V shared memory regions are attached using *shmat()* and detached using *shmdt()* (Chapter 48); and
- when memory mappings are created using *mmap()* and unmapped using *munmap()* (Chapter 49).

> The implementation of virtual memory requires hardware support in the form of a *paged memory management unit* (PMMU). The PMMU translates each virtual memory address reference into the corresponding physical memory address and advises the kernel of a page fault when a particular virtual memory address corresponds to a page that is not resident in RAM.

Virtual memory management separates the virtual address space of a process from the physical address space of RAM. This provides many advantages:

- Processes are isolated from one another and from the kernel, so that one process can't read or modify the memory of another process or the kernel. This is accomplished by having the page-table entries for each process point to distinct sets of physical pages in RAM (or in the swap area).

- Where appropriate, two or more processes can share memory. The kernel makes this possible by having page-table entries in different processes refer to the same pages of RAM. Memory sharing occurs in two common circumstances:

    - Multiple processes executing the same program can share a single (read-only) copy of the program code. This type of sharing is performed implicitly when multiple programs execute the same program file (or load the same shared library).

    - Processes can use the *shmget()* and *mmap()* system calls to explicitly request sharing of memory regions with other processes. This is done for the purpose of interprocess communication.

- The implementation of memory protection schemes is facilitated; that is, page-table entries can be marked to indicate that the contents of the corresponding page are readable, writable, executable, or some combination of these protections. Where multiple processes share pages of RAM, it is possible to specify that each process has different protections on the memory; for example, one process might have read-only access to a page, while another has read-write access.

- Programmers, and tools such as the compiler and linker, don't need to be concerned with the physical layout of the program in RAM.

- Because only a part of a program needs to reside in memory, the program loads and runs faster. Furthermore, the memory footprint (i.e., virtual size) of a process can exceed the capacity of RAM.

One final advantage of virtual memory management is that since each process uses less RAM, more processes can simultaneously be held in RAM. This typically leads to better CPU utilization, since it increases the likelihood that, at any moment in time, there is at least one process that the CPU can execute.

6.5 The Stack and Stack Frames

The stack grows and shrinks linearly as functions are called and return. For Linux on the x86-32 architecture (and on most other Linux and UNIX implementations), the stack resides at the high end of memory and grows downward (toward the heap). A special-purpose register, the *stack pointer*, tracks the current top of the stack. Each time a function is called, an additional frame is allocated on the stack, and this frame is removed when the function returns.

> Even though the stack grows downward, we still call the growing end of the stack the *top*, since, in abstract terms, that is what it is. The actual direction of stack growth is a (hardware) implementation detail. One Linux implementation, the HP PA-RISC, does use an upwardly growing stack.

In virtual memory terms, the stack segment increases in size as stack frames are allocated, but on most implementations, it won't decrease in size after these frames are deallocated (the memory is simply reused when new stack frames are allocated). When we talk about the stack segment growing and shrinking, we are considering things from the logical perspective of frames being added to and removed from the stack.

Sometimes, the term *user stack* is used to distinguish the stack we describe here from the *kernel stack*. The kernel stack is a per-process memory region maintained in kernel memory that is used as the stack for execution of the functions called internally during the execution of a system call. (The kernel can't employ the user stack for this purpose since it resides in unprotected user memory.)

Each (user) stack frame contains the following information:

- *Function arguments and local variables*: In C these are referred to as *automatic* variables, since they are automatically created when a function is called. These variables also automatically disappear when the function returns (since the stack frame disappears), and this forms the primary semantic distinction between automatic and static (and global) variables: the latter have a permanent existence independent of the execution of functions.

- *Call linkage information*: Each function uses certain CPU registers, such as the program counter, which points to the next machine-language instruction to be executed. Each time one function calls another, a copy of these registers is saved in the called function's stack frame so that when the function returns, the appropriate register values can be restored for the calling function.

Since functions can call one another, there may be multiple frames on the stack. (If a function calls itself recursively, there will be multiple frames on the stack for that function.) Referring to Listing 6-1, during the execution of the function *square()*, the stack will contain frames as shown in Figure 6-3.

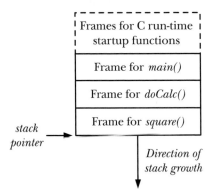

Figure 6-3: Example of a process stack

6.6 Command-Line Arguments (*argc, argv*)

Every C program must have a function called *main()*, which is the point where execution of the program starts. When the program is executed, the command-line arguments (the separate words parsed by the shell) are made available via two arguments to the function *main()*. The first argument, *int argc*, indicates how many command-line arguments there are. The second argument, *char *argv[]*, is an array of pointers to the command-line arguments, each of which is a null-terminated character string. The first of these strings, in *argv[0]*, is (conventionally) the name of the program itself. The list of pointers in *argv* is terminated by a NULL pointer (i.e., *argv[argc]* is NULL).

The fact that *argv[0]* contains the name used to invoke the program can be employed to perform a useful trick. We can create multiple links to (i.e., names for) the same program, and then have the program look at *argv[0]* and take different actions depending on the name used to invoke it. An example of this technique is provided by the *gzip(1)*, *gunzip(1)*, and *zcat(1)* commands: on some distributions, these are all links to the same executable file. (If we employ this technique, we must be careful to handle the possibility that the user might invoke the program via a link with a name other than any of those that we expect.)

Figure 6-4 shows an example of the data structures associated with *argc* and *argv* when executing the program in Listing 6-2. In this diagram, we show the terminating null bytes at the end of each string using the C notation \0.

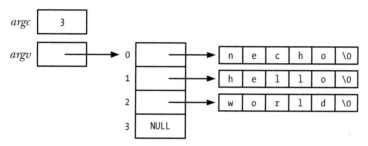

Figure 6-4: Values of *argc* and *argv* for the command *necho hello world*

The program in Listing 6-2 echoes its command-line arguments, one per line of output, preceded by a string showing which element of *argv* is being displayed.

Listing 6-2: Echoing command-line arguments

───proc/necho.c
```
#include "tlpi_hdr.h"

int
main(int argc, char *argv[])
{
    int j;

    for (j = 0; j < argc; j++)
        printf("argv[%d] = %s\n", j, argv[j]);

    exit(EXIT_SUCCESS);
}
```
───proc/necho.c

Since the *argv* list is terminated by a NULL value, we could alternatively code the body of the program in Listing 6-2 as follows, to output just the command-line arguments one per line:

```
char **p;

for (p = argv; *p != NULL; p++)
    puts(*p);
```

One limitation of the *argc/argv* mechanism is that these variables are available only as arguments to *main()*. To portably make the command-line arguments available in other functions, we must either pass *argv* as an argument to those functions or set a global variable pointing to *argv*.

There are a couple of nonportable methods of accessing part or all of this information from anywhere in a program:

- The command-line arguments of any process can be read via the Linux-specific /proc/*PID*/cmdline file, with each argument being terminated by a null byte. (A program can access its own command-line arguments via /proc/self/cmdline.)
- The GNU C library provides two global variables that may be used anywhere in a program in order to obtain the name used to invoke the program (i.e., the first command-line argument). The first of these, *program_invocation_name*, provides the complete pathname used to invoke the program. The second, *program_invocation_short_name*, provides a version of this name with any directory prefix stripped off (i.e., the basename component of the pathname). Declarations for these two variables can be obtained from <errno.h> by defining the macro _GNU_SOURCE.

As shown in Figure 6-1, the *argv* and *environ* arrays, as well as the strings they initially point to, reside in a single contiguous area of memory just above the process stack. (We describe *environ*, which holds the program's environment list, in the next section.) There is an upper limit on the total number of bytes that can be stored in this area. SUSv3 prescribes the use of the ARG_MAX constant (defined in <limits.h>) or the call *sysconf(_SC_ARG_MAX)* to determine this limit. (We describe *sysconf()* in Section 11.2.) SUSv3 requires ARG_MAX to be at least _POSIX_ARG_MAX (4096) bytes. Most UNIX implementations allow a considerably higher limit than this. SUSv3 leaves it unspecified whether an implementation counts overhead bytes (for terminating null bytes, alignment bytes, and the *argv* and *environ* arrays of pointers) against the ARG_MAX limit.

> On Linux, ARG_MAX was historically fixed at 32 pages (i.e., 131,072 bytes on Linux/x86-32), and included the space for overhead bytes. Starting with kernel 2.6.23, the limit on the total space used for *argv* and *environ* can be controlled via the RLIMIT_STACK resource limit, and a much larger limit is permitted for *argv* and *environ*. The limit is calculated as one-quarter of the soft RLIMIT_STACK resource limit that was in force at the time of the *execve()* call. For further details, see the *execve(2)* man page.

Many programs (including several of the examples in this book) parse command-line options (i.e., arguments beginning with a hyphen) using the *getopt()* library function. We describe *getopt()* in Appendix B.

6.7 Environment List

Each process has an associated array of strings called the *environment list*, or simply the *environment*. Each of these strings is a definition of the form *name=value*. Thus, the environment represents a set of name-value pairs that can be used to hold arbitrary information. The names in the list are referred to as *environment variables*.

When a new process is created, it inherits a copy of its parent's environment. This is a primitive but frequently used form of interprocess communication—the environment provides a way to transfer information from a parent process to its child(ren). Since the child gets a copy of its parent's environment at the time it is created, this transfer of information is one-way and once-only. After the child process has been created, either process may change its own environment, and these changes are not seen by the other process.

A common use of environment variables is in the shell. By placing values in its own environment, the shell can ensure that these values are passed to the processes that it creates to execute user commands. For example, the environment variable SHELL is set to be the pathname of the shell program itself. Many programs interpret this variable as the name of the shell that should be executed if the program needs to execute a shell.

Some library functions allow their behavior to be modified by setting environment variables. This allows the user to control the behavior of an application using the function without needing to change the code of the application or relink it against the corresponding library. An example of this technique is provided by the *getopt()* function (Appendix B), whose behavior can be modified by setting the POSIXLY_CORRECT environment variable.

In most shells, a value can be added to the environment using the *export* command:

```
$ SHELL=/bin/bash          Create a shell variable
$ export SHELL             Put variable into shell process's environment
```

In *bash* and the Korn shell, this can be abbreviated to:

```
$ export SHELL=/bin/bash
```

In the C shell, the *setenv* command is used instead:

```
% setenv SHELL /bin/bash
```

The above commands permanently add a value to the shell's environment, and this environment is then inherited by all child processes that the shell creates. At any point, an environment variable can be removed with the *unset* command (*unsetenv* in the C shell).

In the Bourne shell and its descendants (e.g., *bash* and the Korn shell), the following syntax can be used to add values to the environment used to execute a single program, without affecting the parent shell (and subsequent commands):

```
$ NAME=value program
```

This adds a definition to the environment of just the child process executing the named program. If desired, multiple assignments (delimited by white space) can precede the program name.

The *env* command runs a program using a modified copy of the shell's environment list. The environment list can be modified to both add and remove definitions from the list copied from the shell. See the *env(1)* manual page for further details.

The *printenv* command displays the current environment list. Here is an example of its output:

```
$ printenv
LOGNAME=mtk
SHELL=/bin/bash
HOME=/home/mtk
PATH=/usr/local/bin:/usr/bin:/bin:.
TERM=xterm
```

We describe the purpose of most of the above environment variables at appropriate points in later chapters (see also the *environ(7)* manual page).

From the above output, we can see that the environment list is not sorted; the order of the strings in the list is simply the arrangement that is most convenient for the implementation. In general, this is not a problem, since we normally want to access individual variables in the environment, rather than some ordered sequence of them.

The environment list of any process can be examined via the Linux-specific /proc/*PID*/environ file, with each *NAME=value* pair being terminated by a null byte.

Accessing the environment from a program

Within a C program, the environment list can be accessed using the global variable *char **environ*. (The C run-time startup code defines this variable and assigns the location of the environment list to it.) Like *argv*, *environ* points to a NULL-terminated list of pointers to null-terminated strings. Figure 6-5 shows the environment list data structures as they would appear for the environment displayed by the *printenv* command above.

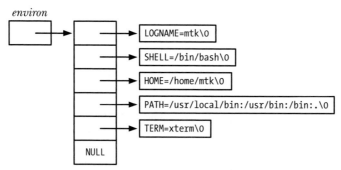

Figure 6-5: Example of process environment list data structures

The program in Listing 6-3 accesses *environ* in order to list all of the values in the process environment. This program yields the same output as the *printenv* command. The loop in this program relies on the use of pointers to walk through *environ*. While it would be possible to treat *environ* as an array (as we use *argv* in Listing 6-2), this is less natural, since the items in the environment list are in no particular order and there is no variable (corresponding to *argc*) that specifies the size of the environment list. (For similar reasons, we don't number the elements of the *environ* array in Figure 6-5.)

Listing 6-3: Displaying the process environment

─── proc/display_env.c
```
#include "tlpi_hdr.h"

extern char **environ;

int
main(int argc, char *argv[])
{
    char **ep;

    for (ep = environ; *ep != NULL; ep++)
        puts(*ep);

    exit(EXIT_SUCCESS);
}
```
─── proc/display_env.c

An alternative method of accessing the environment list is to declare a third argument to the *main()* function:

```
int main(int argc, char *argv[], char *envp[])
```

This argument can then be treated in the same way as *environ*, with the difference that its scope is local to *main()*. Although this feature is widely implemented on UNIX systems, its use should be avoided since, in addition to the scope limitation, it is not specified in SUSv3.

The *getenv()* function retrieves individual values from the process environment.

```
#include <stdlib.h>

char *getenv(const char *name);
```
                    Returns pointer to (value) string, or NULL if no such variable

Given the name of an environment variable, *getenv()* returns a pointer to the corresponding value string. Thus, in the case of our example environment shown earlier, */bin/bash* would be returned if SHELL was specified as the *name* argument. If no environment variable with the specified name exists, then *getenv()* returns NULL.

Note the following portability considerations when using *getenv()*:

• SUSv3 stipulates that an application should not modify the string returned by *getenv()*. This is because (in most implementations) this string is actually part of the environment (i.e., the *value* part of the *name=value* string). If we need to change the value of an environment variable, then we can use the *setenv()* or *putenv()* functions (described below).

- SUSv3 permits an implementation of *getenv()* to return its result using a statically allocated buffer that may be overwritten by subsequent calls to *getenv()*, *setenv()*, *putenv()*, or *unsetenv()*. Although the *glibc* implementation of *getenv()* doesn't use a static buffer in this way, a portable program that needs to preserve the string returned by a call to *getenv()* should copy it to a different location before making a subsequent call to one of these functions.

Modifying the environment

Sometimes, it is useful for a process to modify its environment. One reason is to make a change that is visible in all child processes subsequently created by that process. Another possibility is that we want to set a variable that is visible to a new program to be loaded into the memory of this process ("execed"). In this sense, the environment is not just a form of interprocess communication, but also a method of interprogram communication. (This point will become clearer in Chapter 27, where we explain how the *exec()* functions permit a program to replace itself by a new program within the same process.)

The *putenv()* function adds a new variable to the calling process's environment or modifies the value of an existing variable.

```
#include <stdlib.h>

int putenv(char *string);
```
Returns 0 on success, or nonzero on error

The *string* argument is a pointer to a string of the form *name=value*. After the *putenv()* call, this string is part of the environment. In other words, rather than duplicating the string pointed to by *string*, one of the elements of *environ* will be set to point to the same location as *string*. Therefore, if we subsequently modify the bytes pointed to by *string*, that change will affect the process environment. For this reason, *string* should not be an automatic variable (i.e., a character array allocated on the stack), since this memory area may be overwritten once the function in which the variable is defined returns.

Note that *putenv()* returns a nonzero value on error, rather than –1.

The *glibc* implementation of *putenv()* provides a nonstandard extension. If *string* doesn't contain an equal sign (=), then the environment variable identified by *string* is removed from the environment list.

The *setenv()* function is an alternative to *putenv()* for adding a variable to the environment.

```
#include <stdlib.h>

int setenv(const char *name, const char *value, int overwrite);
```
Returns 0 on success, or –1 on error

The *setenv()* function creates a new environment variable by allocating a memory buffer for a string of the form *name=value*, and copying the strings pointed to by *name* and *value* into that buffer. Note that we don't need to (in fact, must not) supply an equal sign at the end of *name* or the start of *value*, because *setenv()* adds this character when it adds the new definition to the environment.

The *setenv()* function doesn't change the environment if the variable identified by *name* already exists and *overwrite* has the value 0. If *overwrite* is nonzero, the environment is always changed.

The fact that *setenv()* copies its arguments means that, unlike with *putenv()*, we can subsequently modify the contents of the strings pointed to by *name* and *value* without affecting the environment. It also means that using automatic variables as arguments to *setenv()* doesn't cause any problems.

The *unsetenv()* function removes the variable identified by *name* from the environment.

```
#include <stdlib.h>

int unsetenv(const char *name);
```
Returns 0 on success, or −1 on error

As with *setenv()*, *name* should not include an equal sign.

Both *setenv()* and *unsetenv()* derive from BSD, and are less widespread than *putenv()*. Although not defined in the original POSIX.1 standard or in SUSv2, they are included in SUSv3.

> In versions of *glibc* before 2.2.2, *unsetenv()* was prototyped as returning *void*. This was how *unsetenv()* was prototyped in the original BSD implementation, and some UNIX implementations still follow the BSD prototype.

On occasion, it is useful to erase the entire environment, and then rebuild it with selected values. For example, we might do this in order to execute set-user-ID programs in a secure manner (Section 38.8). We can erase the environment by assigning NULL to *environ*:

```
environ = NULL;
```

This is exactly the step performed by the *clearenv()* library function.

```
#define _BSD_SOURCE        /* Or: #define _SVID_SOURCE */
#include <stdlib.h>

int clearenv(void)
```
Returns 0 on success, or a nonzero on error

In some circumstances, the use of *setenv()* and *clearenv()* can lead to memory leaks in a program. We noted above that *setenv()* allocates a memory buffer that is then made part of the environment. When we call *clearenv()*, it doesn't free this buffer (it can't, since it doesn't know of the buffer's existence). A program that repeatedly employed these two functions would steadily leak memory. In practice, this is unlikely to be a problem, because a program typically calls *clearenv()* just once on startup, in order to remove all entries from the environment that it inherited from its predecessor (i.e., the program that called *exec()* to start this program).

> Many UNIX implementations provide *clearenv()*, but it is not specified in SUSv3. SUSv3 specifies that if an application directly modifies *environ*, as is done by *clearenv()*, then the behavior of *setenv()*, *unsetenv()*, and *getenv()* is undefined. (The rationale behind this is that preventing a conforming application from directly modifying the environment allows the implementation full control over the data structures that it uses to implement environment variables.) The only way that SUSv3 permits an application to clear its environment is to obtain a list of all environment variables (by getting the names from *environ*), and then using *unsetenv()* to remove each of these names.

Example program

Listing 6-4 demonstrates the use of all of the functions discussed in this section. After first clearing the environment, this program adds any environment definitions provided as command-line arguments. It then: adds a definition for a variable called GREET, if one doesn't already exist in the environment; removes any definition for a variable named BYE; and, finally, prints the current environment list. Here is an example of the output produced when the program is run:

```
$ ./modify_env "GREET=Guten Tag" SHELL=/bin/bash BYE=Ciao
GREET=Guten Tag
SHELL=/bin/bash
$ ./modify_env SHELL=/bin/sh BYE=byebye
SHELL=/bin/sh
GREET=Hello world
```

If we assign NULL to *environ* (as is done by the call to *clearenv()* in Listing 6-4), then we would expect that a loop of the following form (as used in the program) would fail, since **environ* is invalid:

```
for (ep = environ; *ep != NULL; ep++)
    puts(*ep);
```

However, if *setenv()* and *putenv()* find that *environ* is NULL, they create a new environment list and set *environ* pointing to it, with the result that the above loop operates correctly.

Listing 6-4: Modifying the process environment

```
#define _GNU_SOURCE     /* To get various declarations from <stdlib.h> */
#include <stdlib.h>
#include "tlpi_hdr.h"

extern char **environ;

int
main(int argc, char *argv[])
{
    int j;
    char **ep;

    clearenv();         /* Erase entire environment */

    for (j = 1; j < argc; j++)
        if (putenv(argv[j]) != 0)
            errExit("putenv: %s", argv[j]);

    if (setenv("GREET", "Hello world", 0) == -1)
        errExit("setenv");

    unsetenv("BYE");

    for (ep = environ; *ep != NULL; ep++)
        puts(*ep);

    exit(EXIT_SUCCESS);
}
```

6.8 Performing a Nonlocal Goto: *setjmp()* and *longjmp()*

The *setjmp()* and *longjmp()* library functions are used to perform a *nonlocal goto*. The term *nonlocal* refers to the fact that the target of the goto is a location somewhere outside the currently executing function.

Like many programming languages, C includes the goto statement, which is open to endless abuse in making programs difficult to read and maintain, and is occasionally useful to make a program simpler, faster, or both.

One restriction of C's goto is that it is not possible to jump out of the current function into another function. However, such functionality can occasionally be useful. Consider the following common scenario in error handling: during a deeply nested function call, we encounter an error that should be handled by abandoning the current task, returning through multiple function calls, and then continuing execution in some much higher function (perhaps even *main()*). To do this, we could have each function return a status value that is checked and appropriately handled by its caller. This is perfectly valid, and, in many cases, the desirable method for handling this kind of scenario. However, in some cases, coding would be simpler if we could jump from the middle of the nested function call back to one of the functions that called it (the immediate caller, or the caller of the caller, and so on). This is the functionality that *setjmp()* and *longjmp()* provide.

> The restriction that a goto can't be used to jump between functions in C exists because all C functions reside at the same scope level (i.e., there is no nesting of function declarations in standard C, although *gcc* does permit this as an extension). Thus, given two functions, X and Y, the compiler has no way of knowing whether a stack frame for function X might be on the stack at the time Y is invoked, and thus whether a goto from function Y to function X would be possible. In languages such as Pascal, where function declarations can be nested, and a goto from a nested function to a function that encloses it is permitted, the static scope of a function allows the compiler to determine some information about the dynamic scope of the function. Thus, if function Y is lexically nested within function X, then the compiler knows that a stack frame for X must already be on the stack at the time Y is invoked, and can generate code for a goto from function Y to somewhere within function X.

```
#include <setjmp.h>

int setjmp(jmp_buf env);

                    Returns 0 on initial call, nonzero on return via longjmp()

void longjmp(jmp_buf env, int val);
```

Calling *setjmp()* establishes a target for a later jump performed by *longjmp()*. This target is exactly the point in the program where the *setjmp()* call occurred. From a programming point of view, after the *longjmp()*, it looks exactly as though we have just returned from the *setjmp()* call for a second time. The way in which we distinguish the second "return" from the initial return is by the integer value returned by *setjmp()*. The initial *setjmp()* returns 0, while the later "faked" return supplies whatever value is specified in the *val* argument of the *longjmp()* call. By using different values for the *val* argument, we can distinguish jumps to the same target from different points in the program.

Specifying the *val* argument to *longjmp()* as 0 would, if unchecked, cause the faked return from *setjmp()* to look as though it were the initial return. For this reason, if *val* is specified as 0, *longjmp()* actually uses the value 1.

The *env* argument used by both functions supplies the glue enabling the jump to be accomplished. The *setjmp()* call saves various information about the current process environment into *env*. This allows the *longjmp()* call, which must specify the same *env* variable, to perform the fake return. Since the *setjmp()* and *longjmp()* calls are in different functions (otherwise, we could use a simple goto), *env* is declared globally or, less commonly, passed as a function argument.

Along with other information, *env* stores a copy of the *program counter* register (which points to the currently executing machine-language instruction) and the *stack pointer* register (which marks the top of the stack) at the time of the call to *setjmp()*. This information enables the subsequent *longjmp()* call to accomplish two key steps:

- Strip off the stack frames for all of the intervening functions on the stack between the function calling *longjmp()* and the function that previously called *setjmp()*. This procedure is sometimes called "unwinding the stack," and is accomplished by resetting the stack pointer register to the value saved in the *env* argument.

- Reset the program counter register so that the program continues execution from the location of the initial *setjmp()* call. Again, this is accomplished using the value saved in *env*.

Example program

Listing 6-5 demonstrates the use of *setjmp()* and *longjmp()*. This program sets up a jump target with an initial call to *setjmp()*. The subsequent switch (on the value returned by *setjmp()*) is the means of detecting whether we have just completed the initial return from *setjmp()* or whether we have arrived back after a *longjmp()*. In the case of a 0 return—meaning we have just done the initial *setjmp()*—we call *f1()*, which either immediately calls *longjmp()* or goes on to call *f2()*, depending on the value of *argc* (i.e., the number of command-line arguments). If *f2()* is reached, it does an immediate *longjmp()*. A *longjmp()* from either function takes us back to the point of the *setjmp()* call. We use different *val* arguments in the two *longjmp()* calls, so that the switch statement in *main()* can determine the function from which the jump occurred and print a suitable message.

When we run the program in Listing 6-5 without any command-line arguments, this is what we see:

```
$ ./longjmp
Calling f1() after initial setjmp()
We jumped back from f1()
```

Specifying a command-line argument causes the jump to occur from *f2()*:

```
$ ./longjmp x
Calling f1() after initial setjmp()
We jumped back from f2()
```

Listing 6-5: Demonstrate the use of *setjmp()* and *longjmp()*

—— proc/longjmp.c

```c
#include <setjmp.h>
#include "tlpi_hdr.h"

static jmp_buf env;

static void
f2(void)
{
    longjmp(env, 2);
}

static void
f1(int argc)
{
    if (argc == 1)
        longjmp(env, 1);
    f2();
}

int
main(int argc, char *argv[])
{
    switch (setjmp(env)) {
    case 0:     /* This is the return after the initial setjmp() */
        printf("Calling f1() after initial setjmp()\n");
        f1(argc);               /* Never returns... */
        break;                  /* ... but this is good form */

    case 1:
        printf("We jumped back from f1()\n");
        break;

    case 2:
        printf("We jumped back from f2()\n");
        break;
    }

    exit(EXIT_SUCCESS);
}
```

—— proc/longjmp.c

Restrictions on the use of *setjmp()*

SUSv3 and C99 specify that a call to *setjmp()* may appear only in the following contexts:

- as the entire controlling expression of a selection or iteration statement (if, switch, while, and so on);

- as the operand of a unary ! (*not*) operator, where the resulting expression is the entire controlling expression of a selection or iteration statement;

- as part of a comparison operation (==, !=, <, and so on), where the other operand is an integer constant expression and the resulting expression is the entire controlling expression of a selection or iteration statement; or
- as a free-standing function call that is not embedded inside some larger expression.

Note that the C assignment statement doesn't figure in the list above. A statement of the following form is not standards-conformant:

```
s = setjmp(env);                    /* WRONG! */
```

These restrictions are specified because an implementation of *setjmp()* as a conventional function can't be guaranteed to have enough information to be able to save the values of all registers and temporary stack locations used in an enclosing expression so that they could then be correctly restored after a *longjmp()*. Thus, it is permitted to call *setjmp()* only inside expressions simple enough not to require temporary storage.

Abusing *longjmp()*

If the *env* buffer is declared global to all functions (which is typical), then it is possible to execute the following sequence of steps:

1. Call a function *x()* that uses *setjmp()* to establish a jump target in the global variable *env*.

2. Return from function *x()*.

3. Call a function *y()* that does a *longjmp()* using *env*.

This is a serious error. We can't do a *longjmp()* into a function that has already returned. Considering what *longjmp()* tries to do to the stack—it attempts to unwind the stack back to a frame that no longer exists—leads us to realize that chaos will result. If we are lucky, our program will simply crash. However, depending on the state of the stack, other possibilities include infinite call-return loops and the program behaving as though it really did return from a function that was not currently executing. (In a multithreaded program, a similar abuse is to call *longjmp()* in a different thread from that in which *setjmp()* was called.)

> SUSv3 says that if *longjmp()* is called from within a nested signal handler (i.e., a handler that was invoked while the handler for another signal was executing), then the program behavior is undefined.

Problems with optimizing compilers

Optimizing compilers may rearrange the order of instructions in a program and store certain variables in CPU registers, rather than RAM. Such optimizations generally rely on the run-time flow of control reflecting the lexical structure of the program. Since jump operations performed via *setjmp()* and *longjmp()* are established and executed at run time, and are not reflected in the lexical structure of the program, a compiler optimizer is unable to take them into account when performing its task. Furthermore, the semantics of some ABI implementations require *longjmp()* to restore copies of the CPU registers saved by the earlier *setjmp()* call.

This means that optimized variables may end up with incorrect values as a consequence of a *longjmp()* operation. We can see an example of this by examining the behavior of the program in Listing 6-6.

Listing 6-6: A demonstration of the interaction of compiler optimization and *longjmp()*

── proc/setjmp_vars.c

```
#include <stdio.h>
#include <stdlib.h>
#include <setjmp.h>

static jmp_buf env;

static void
doJump(int nvar, int rvar, int vvar)
{
    printf("Inside doJump(): nvar=%d rvar=%d vvar=%d\n", nvar, rvar, vvar);
    longjmp(env, 1);
}

int
main(int argc, char *argv[])
{
    int nvar;
    register int rvar;          /* Allocated in register if possible */
    volatile int vvar;          /* See text */

    nvar = 111;
    rvar = 222;
    vvar = 333;

    if (setjmp(env) == 0) {     /* Code executed after setjmp() */
        nvar = 777;
        rvar = 888;
        vvar = 999;
        doJump(nvar, rvar, vvar);

    } else {                    /* Code executed after longjmp() */

        printf("After longjmp(): nvar=%d rvar=%d vvar=%d\n", nvar, rvar, vvar);
    }

    exit(EXIT_SUCCESS);
}
```

── proc/setjmp_vars.c

When we compile the program in Listing 6-6 without optimization, we see the expected output:

```
$ cc -o setjmp_vars setjmp_vars.c
$ ./setjmp_vars
Inside doJump(): nvar=777 rvar=888 vvar=999
After longjmp(): nvar=777 rvar=888 vvar=999
```

However, when we compile with optimization, we get the following unexpected results:

```
$ cc -O -o setjmp_vars setjmp_vars.c
$ ./setjmp_vars
Inside doJump(): nvar=777 rvar=888 vvar=999
After longjmp(): nvar=111 rvar=222 vvar=999
```

Here, we see that after the *longjmp()*, *nvar* and *rvar* have been reset to their values at the time of the *setjmp()* call. This has occurred because the code reorganization performed by the optimizer has been confused as a consequence of the *longjmp()*. Any local variables that are candidates for optimization may be subject to this sort of problem; this generally means pointer variables and variables of any of the simple types *char*, *int*, *float*, and *long*.

We can prevent such code reorganization by declaring variables as volatile, which tells the optimizer not to optimize them. In the preceding program output, we see that the variable *vvar*, which was declared volatile, was correctly handled, even when we compiled with optimization.

Since different compilers do different types of optimizations, portable programs should employ the volatile keyword with all of the local variables of the aforementioned types in the function that calls *setjmp()*.

If we specify the *−Wextra (extra warnings)* option to the GNU C compiler, it produces the following helpful warning for the setjmp_vars.c program:

```
$ cc -Wall -Wextra -O -o setjmp_vars setjmp_vars.c
setjmp_vars.c: In function `main':
setjmp_vars.c:17: warning: variable `nvar' might be clobbered by `longjmp' or
`vfork'
setjmp_vars.c:18: warning: variable `rvar' might be clobbered by `longjmp' or
`vfork'
```

> It is instructive to look at the assembler output produced when compiling the setjmp_vars.c program both with and without optimization. The *cc −S* command produces a file with the extension *.s* containing the generated assembler code for a program.

Avoid *setjmp()* and *longjmp()* where possible

If goto statements are capable of rendering a program difficult to read, then nonlocal gotos can make things an order of magnitude worse, since they can transfer control between any two functions in a program. For this reason, *setjmp()* and *longjmp()* should be used sparingly. It is often worth the extra work in design and coding to come up with a program that avoids their use, because the program will be more readable and possibly more portable. Having said that, we revisit variants of these functions (*sigsetjmp()* and *siglongjmp()*, described in Section 21.2.1) when we discuss signals, since they are occasionally useful when writing signal handlers.

6.9 Summary

Each process has a unique process ID and maintains a record of its parent's process ID.

The virtual memory of a process is logically divided into a number of segments: text, (initialized and uninitialized) data, stack, and heap.

The stack consists of a series of frames, with a new frame being added as a function is invoked and removed when the function returns. Each frame contains the local variables, function arguments, and call linkage information for a single function invocation.

The command-line arguments supplied when a program is invoked are made available via the *argc* and *argv* arguments to *main()*. By convention, *argv[0]* contains the name used to invoke the program.

Each process receives a copy of its parent's environment list, a set of name-value pairs. The global variable *environ* and various library functions allow a process to access and modify the variables in its environment list.

The *setjmp()* and *longjmp()* functions provide a way to perform a nonlocal goto from one function to another (unwinding the stack). In order to avoid problems with compiler optimization, we may need to declare variables with the `volatile` modifier when making use of these functions. Nonlocal gotos can render a program difficult to read and maintain, and should be avoided whenever possible.

Further information

[Tanenbaum, 2007] and [Vahalia, 1996] describe virtual memory management in detail. The Linux kernel memory management algorithms and code are described in detail in [Gorman, 2004].

6.10 Exercises

6-1. Compile the program in Listing 6-1 (`mem_segments.c`), and list its size using *ls −l*. Although the program contains an array (*mbuf*) that is around 10 MB in size, the executable file is much smaller than this. Why is this?

6-2. Write a program to see what happens if we try to *longjmp()* into a function that has already returned.

6-3. Implement *setenv()* and *unsetenv()* using *getenv()*, *putenv()*, and, where necessary, code that directly modifies *environ*. Your version of *unsetenv()* should check to see whether there are multiple definitions of an environment variable, and remove them all (which is what the *glibc* version of *unsetenv()* does).

7

MEMORY ALLOCATION

Many system programs need to be able to allocate extra memory for dynamic data structures (e.g., linked lists and binary trees), whose size depends on information that is available only at run time. This chapter describes the functions that are used to allocate memory on the heap or the stack.

7.1 Allocating Memory on the Heap

A process can allocate memory by increasing the size of the heap, a variable-size segment of contiguous virtual memory that begins just after the uninitialized data segment of a process and grows and shrinks as memory is allocated and freed (see Figure 6-1 on page 119). The current limit of the heap is referred to as the *program break*.

To allocate memory, C programs normally use the *malloc* family of functions, which we describe shortly. However, we begin with a description of *brk()* and *sbrk()*, upon which the *malloc* functions are based.

7.1.1 Adjusting the Program Break: *brk()* and *sbrk()*

Resizing the heap (i.e., allocating or deallocating memory) is actually as simple as telling the kernel to adjust its idea of where the process's program break is. Initially, the program break lies just past the end of the uninitialized data segment (i.e., the same location as *&end*, shown in Figure 6-1).

After the program break is increased, the program may access any address in the newly allocated area, but no physical memory pages are allocated yet. The kernel automatically allocates new physical pages on the first attempt by the process to access addresses in those pages.

Traditionally, the UNIX system has provided two system calls for manipulating the program break, and these are both available on Linux: *brk()* and *sbrk()*. Although these system calls are seldom used directly in programs, understanding them helps clarify how memory allocation works.

```
#define _BSD_SOURCE               /* Or: #define _SVID_SOURCE */
#include <unistd.h>

int brk(void *end_data_segment);
```
                                      Returns 0 on success, or –1 on error
```
void *sbrk(intptr_t increment);
```
          Returns previous program break on success, or *(void *)* –1 on error

The *brk()* system call sets the program break to the location specified by *end_data_segment*. Since virtual memory is allocated in units of pages, *end_data_segment* is effectively rounded up to the next page boundary.

Attempts to set the program break below its initial value (i.e., below *&end*) are likely to result in unexpected behavior, such as a segmentation fault (the SIGSEGV signal, described in Section 20.2) when trying to access data in now nonexistent parts of the initialized or uninitialized data segments. The precise upper limit on where the program break can be set depends on a range of factors, including: the process resource limit for the size of the data segment (RLIMIT_DATA, described in Section 36.3); and the location of memory mappings, shared memory segments, and shared libraries.

A call to *sbrk()* adjusts the program break by adding *increment* to it. (On Linux, *sbrk()* is a library function implemented on top of *brk()*.) The *intptr_t* type used to declare *increment* is an integer data type. On success, *sbrk()* returns the previous address of the program break. In other words, if we have increased the program break, the return value points to the start of the newly allocated block of memory.

The call *sbrk(0)* returns the current setting of the program break without changing it. This can be useful if we want to track the size of the heap, perhaps in order to monitor the behavior of a memory allocation package.

> SUSv2 specified *brk()* and *sbrk()* (marking them LEGACY). SUSv3 removed their specifications.

7.1.2 Allocating Memory on the Heap: *malloc()* and *free()*

In general, C programs use the *malloc* family of functions to allocate and deallocate memory on the heap. These functions offer several advantages over *brk()* and *sbrk()*. In particular, they:

- are standardized as part of the C language;
- are easier to use in threaded programs;

- provide a simple interface that allows memory to be allocated in small units; and

- allow us to arbitrarily deallocate blocks of memory, which are maintained on a free list and recycled in future calls to allocate memory.

The *malloc()* function allocates *size* bytes from the heap and returns a pointer to the start of the newly allocated block of memory. The allocated memory is not initialized.

```
#include <stdlib.h>

void *malloc(size_t size);
```
                    Returns pointer to allocated memory on success, or NULL on error

Because *malloc()* returns *void **, we can assign it to any type of C pointer. The block of memory returned by *malloc()* is always aligned on a byte boundary suitable for efficient access to any type of C data structure. In practice, this means that it is allocated on an 8-byte or 16-byte boundary on most architectures.

> SUSv3 specifies that the call *malloc(0)* may return either NULL or a pointer to a small piece of memory that can (and should) be freed with *free()*. On Linux, *malloc(0)* follows the latter behavior.

If memory could not be allocated (perhaps because we reached the limit to which the program break could be raised), then *malloc()* returns NULL and sets *errno* to indicate the error. Although the possibility of failure in allocating memory is small, all calls to *malloc()*, and the related functions that we describe later, should check for this error return.

The *free()* function deallocates the block of memory pointed to by its *ptr* argument, which should be an address previously returned by *malloc()* or one of the other heap memory allocation functions that we describe later in this chapter.

```
#include <stdlib.h>

void free(void *ptr);
```

In general, *free()* doesn't lower the program break, but instead adds the block of memory to a list of free blocks that are recycled by future calls to *malloc()*. This is done for several reasons:

- The block of memory being freed is typically somewhere in the middle of the heap, rather than at the end, so that lowering the program break is not possible.

- It minimizes the number of *sbrk()* calls that the program must perform. (As noted in Section 3.1, system calls have a small but significant overhead.)

- In many cases, lowering the break would not help programs that allocate large amounts of memory, since they typically tend to hold on to allocated memory or repeatedly release and reallocate memory, rather than release it all and then continue to run for an extended period of time.

If the argument given to *free()* is a NULL pointer, then the call does nothing. (In other words, it is not an error to give a NULL pointer to *free()*.)

Making any use of *ptr* after the call to *free()*—for example, passing it to *free()* a second time—is an error that can lead to unpredictable results.

Example program

The program in Listing 7-1 can be used to illustrate the effect of *free()* on the program break. This program allocates multiple blocks of memory and then frees some or all of them, depending on its (optional) command-line arguments.

The first two command-line arguments specify the number and size of blocks to allocate. The third command-line argument specifies the loop step unit to be used when freeing memory blocks. If we specify 1 here (which is also the default if this argument is omitted), then the program frees every memory block; if 2, then every second allocated block; and so on. The fourth and fifth command-line arguments specify the range of blocks that we wish to free. If these arguments are omitted, then all allocated blocks (in steps given by the third command-line argument) are freed.

Listing 7-1: Demonstrate what happens to the program break when memory is freed

──memalloc/free_and_sbrk.c
```
#define _BSD_SOURCE
#include "tlpi_hdr.h"

#define MAX_ALLOCS 1000000

int
main(int argc, char *argv[])
{
    char *ptr[MAX_ALLOCS];
    int freeStep, freeMin, freeMax, blockSize, numAllocs, j;

    printf("\n");

    if (argc < 3 || strcmp(argv[1], "--help") == 0)
        usageErr("%s num-allocs block-size [step [min [max]]]\n", argv[0]);

    numAllocs = getInt(argv[1], GN_GT_0, "num-allocs");
    if (numAllocs > MAX_ALLOCS)
        cmdLineErr("num-allocs > %d\n", MAX_ALLOCS);

    blockSize = getInt(argv[2], GN_GT_0 | GN_ANY_BASE, "block-size");

    freeStep = (argc > 3) ? getInt(argv[3], GN_GT_0, "step") : 1;
    freeMin =  (argc > 4) ? getInt(argv[4], GN_GT_0, "min") : 1;
    freeMax =  (argc > 5) ? getInt(argv[5], GN_GT_0, "max") : numAllocs;

    if (freeMax > numAllocs)
        cmdLineErr("free-max > num-allocs\n");

    printf("Initial program break:          %10p\n", sbrk(0));

    printf("Allocating %d*%d bytes\n", numAllocs, blockSize);
```

```
    for (j = 0; j < numAllocs; j++) {
        ptr[j] = malloc(blockSize);
        if (ptr[j] == NULL)
            errExit("malloc");
    }

    printf("Program break is now:          %10p\n", sbrk(0));

    printf("Freeing blocks from %d to %d in steps of %d\n",
            freeMin, freeMax, freeStep);
    for (j = freeMin - 1; j < freeMax; j += freeStep)
        free(ptr[j]);

    printf("After free(), program break is: %10p\n", sbrk(0));

    exit(EXIT_SUCCESS);
}
```

———memalloc/free_and_sbrk.c

Running the program in Listing 7-1 with the following command line causes the
program to allocate 1000 blocks of memory and then free every second block:

```
$ ./free_and_sbrk 1000 10240 2
```

The output shows that after these blocks have been freed, the program break is left
unchanged from the level it reached when all memory blocks were allocated:

```
Initial program break:        0x804a6bc
Allocating 1000*10240 bytes
Program break is now:         0x8a13000
Freeing blocks from 1 to 1000 in steps of 2
After free(), program break is:  0x8a13000
```

The following command line specifies that all but the last of the allocated blocks
should be freed. Again, the program break remains at its "high-water mark."

```
$ ./free_and_sbrk 1000 10240 1 1 999
Initial program break:        0x804a6bc
Allocating 1000*10240 bytes
Program break is now:         0x8a13000
Freeing blocks from 1 to 999 in steps of 1
After free(), program break is:  0x8a13000
```

If, however, we free a complete set of blocks at the top end of the heap, we see that
the program break decreases from its peak value, indicating that *free()* has used
sbrk() to lower the program break. Here, we free the last 500 blocks of allocated
memory:

```
$ ./free_and_sbrk 1000 10240 1 500 1000
Initial program break:        0x804a6bc
Allocating 1000*10240 bytes
Program break is now:         0x8a13000
Freeing blocks from 500 to 1000 in steps of 1
After free(), program break is:  0x852b000
```

In this case, the (*glibc*) *free()* function is able to recognize that an entire region at the top end of the heap is free, since, when releasing blocks, it coalesces neighboring free blocks into a single larger block. (Such coalescing is done to avoid having a large number of small fragments on the free list, all of which may be too small to satisfy subsequent *malloc()* requests.)

> The *glibc free()* function calls *sbrk()* to lower the program break only when the free block at the top end is "sufficiently" large, where "sufficient" is determined by parameters controlling the operation of the *malloc* package (128 kB is a typical value). This reduces the number of *sbrk()* calls (i.e., the number of *brk()* system calls) that must be made.

To *free()* or not to *free()*?

When a process terminates, all of its memory is returned to the system, including heap memory allocated by functions in the *malloc* package. In programs that allocate memory and continue using it until program termination, it is common to omit calls to *free()*, relying on this behavior to automatically free the memory. This can be especially useful in programs that allocate many blocks of memory, since adding multiple calls to *free()* could be expensive in terms of CPU time, as well as perhaps being complicated to code.

Although relying on process termination to automatically free memory is acceptable for many programs, there are a couple of reasons why it can be desirable to explicitly free all allocated memory:

- Explicitly calling *free()* may make the program more readable and maintainable in the face of future modifications.

- If we are using a *malloc* debugging library (described below) to find memory leaks in a program, then any memory that is not explicitly freed will be reported as a memory leak. This can complicate the task of finding real memory leaks.

7.1.3 Implementation of *malloc()* and *free()*

Although *malloc()* and *free()* provide an interface for allocating memory that is much easier to use than *brk()* and *sbrk()*, it is still possible to make various programming errors when using them. Understanding how *malloc()* and *free()* are implemented provides us with insights into the causes of these errors and how we can avoid them.

The implementation of *malloc()* is straightforward. It first scans the list of memory blocks previously released by *free()* in order to find one whose size is larger than or equal to its requirements. (Different strategies may be employed for this scan, depending on the implementation; for example, *first-fit* or *best-fit*.) If the block is exactly the right size, then it is returned to the caller. If it is larger, then it is split, so that a block of the correct size is returned to the caller and a smaller free block is left on the free list.

If no block on the free list is large enough, then *malloc()* calls *sbrk()* to allocate more memory. To reduce the number of calls to *sbrk()*, rather than allocating exactly the number of bytes required, *malloc()* increases the program break in larger units (some multiple of the virtual memory page size), putting the excess memory onto the free list.

Looking at the implementation of *free()*, things start to become more interesting. When *free()* places a block of memory onto the free list, how does it know what size that block is? This is done via a trick. When *malloc()* allocates the block, it allocates extra bytes to hold an integer containing the size of the block. This integer is located at the beginning of the block; the address actually returned to the caller points to the location just past this length value, as shown in Figure 7-1.

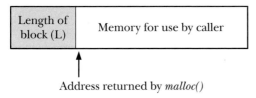

Figure 7-1: Memory block returned by *malloc()*

When a block is placed on the (doubly linked) free list, *free()* uses the bytes of the block itself in order to add the block to the list, as shown in Figure 7-2.

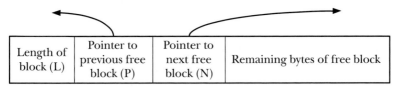

Figure 7-2: A block on the free list

As blocks are deallocated and reallocated over time, the blocks of the free list will become intermingled with blocks of allocated, in-use memory, as shown in Figure 7-3.

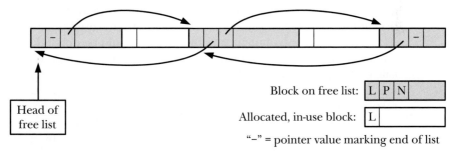

Figure 7-3: Heap containing allocated blocks and a free list

Now consider the fact that C allows us to create pointers to any location in the heap, and modify the locations they point to, including the *length, previous free block,* and *next free block* pointers maintained by *free()* and *malloc()*. Add this to the preceding description, and we have a fairly combustible mix when it comes to creating obscure programming bugs. For example, if, via a misdirected pointer, we accidentally increase one of the length values preceding an allocated block of memory, and subsequently deallocate that block, then *free()* will record the wrong size block of memory on the free list. Subsequently, *malloc()* may reallocate this block, leading to a scenario where the program has pointers to two blocks of allocated memory that it understands to be distinct, but which actually overlap. Numerous other pictures of what could go wrong can be drawn.

To avoid these types of errors, we should observe the following rules:

- After we allocate a block of memory, we should be careful not to touch any bytes outside the range of that block. This could occur, for example, as a result of faulty pointer arithmetic or off-by-one errors in loops updating the contents of a block.

- It is an error to free the same piece of allocated memory more than once. With *glibc* on Linux, we often get a segmentation violation (SIGSEGV signal). This is good, because it alerts us that we've made a programming error. However, more generally, freeing the same memory twice leads to unpredictable behavior.

- We should never call *free()* with a pointer value that wasn't obtained by a call to one of the functions in the *malloc* package.

- If we are writing a long-running program (e.g., a shell or a network daemon process) that repeatedly allocates memory for various purposes, then we should ensure that we deallocate any memory after we have finished using it. Failure to do so means that the heap will steadily grow until we reach the limits of available virtual memory, at which point further attempts to allocate memory fail. Such a condition is known as a *memory leak*.

Tools and libraries for *malloc* debugging

Failure to observe the rules listed above can lead to the creation of bugs that are obscure and difficult to reproduce. The task of finding such bugs can be eased considerably by using the *malloc* debugging tools provided by *glibc* or one of a number of *malloc* debugging libraries that are designed for this purpose.

Among the *malloc* debugging tools provided by *glibc* are the following:

- The *mtrace()* and *muntrace()* functions allow a program to turn tracing of memory allocation calls on and off. These functions are used in conjunction with the MALLOC_TRACE environment variable, which should be defined to contain the name of a file to which tracing information should be written. When *mtrace()* is called, it checks to see whether this file is defined and can be opened for writing; if so, then all calls to functions in the *malloc* package are traced and recorded in the file. Since the resulting file is not easily human-readable, a script—also called *mtrace*—is provided to analyze the file and produce a readable summary. For security reasons, calls to *mtrace()* are ignored by set-user-ID and set-group-ID programs.

- The *mcheck()* and *mprobe()* functions allow a program to perform consistency checks on blocks of allocated memory; for example, catching errors such as attempting to write to a location past the end of a block of allocated memory. These functions provide functionality that somewhat overlaps with the *malloc* debugging libraries described below. Programs that employ these functions must be linked with the *mcheck* library using the *cc −lmcheck* option.

- The MALLOC_CHECK_ environment variable (note the trailing underscore) serves a similar purpose to *mcheck()* and *mprobe()*. (One notable difference between the two techniques is that using MALLOC_CHECK_ doesn't require modification and recompilation of the program.) By setting this variable to different integer values, we can control how a program responds to memory allocation errors. Possible settings are: 0, meaning ignore errors; 1, meaning print diagnostic errors on *stderr*; and 2, meaning call *abort()* to terminate the program. Not all memory allocation and deallocation errors are detected via the use of `MALLOC_CHECK_`; it finds just the common ones. However, this technique is fast, easy to use, and has low run-time overhead compared with the use of *malloc* debugging libraries. For security reasons, the setting of `MALLOC_CHECK_` is ignored by set-user-ID and set-group-ID programs.

Further information about all of the above features can be found in the *glibc* manual.

A *malloc* debugging library offers the same API as the standard *malloc* package, but does extra work to catch memory allocation bugs. In order to use such a library, we link our application against that library instead of the *malloc* package in the standard C library. Because these libraries typically operate at the cost of slower run-time operation, increased memory consumption, or both, we should use them only for debugging purposes, and then return to linking with the standard *malloc* package for the production version of an application. Among such libraries are *Electric Fence* (*http://www.perens.com/FreeSoftware/*), *dmalloc* (*http://dmalloc.com/*), *Valgrind* (*http://valgrind.org/*), and *Insure++* (*http://www.parasoft.com/*).

> Both *Valgrind* and *Insure++* are capable of detecting many other kinds of bugs aside from those associated with heap allocation. See their respective web sites for details.

Controlling and monitoring the *malloc* package

The *glibc* manual describes a range of nonstandard functions that can be used to monitor and control the allocation of memory by functions in the *malloc* package, including the following:

- The *mallopt()* function modifies various parameters that control the algorithm used by *malloc()*. For example, one such parameter specifies the minimum amount of releasable space that must exist at the end of the free list before *sbrk()* is used to shrink the heap. Another parameter specifies an upper limit for the size of blocks that will be allocated from the heap; blocks larger than this are allocated using the *mmap()* system call (refer to Section 49.7).

- The *mallinfo()* function returns a structure containing various statistics about the memory allocated by *malloc()*.

Many UNIX implementations provide versions of *mallopt()* and *mallinfo()*. However, the interfaces offered by these functions vary across implementations, so they are not portable.

7.1.4 Other Methods of Allocating Memory on the Heap

As well as *malloc()*, the C library provides a range of other functions for allocating memory on the heap, and we describe those functions here.

Allocating memory with *calloc()* and *realloc()*

The *calloc()* function allocates memory for an array of identical items.

```
#include <stdlib.h>

void *calloc(size_t numitems, size_t size);
                Returns pointer to allocated memory on success, or NULL on error
```

The *numitems* argument specifies how many items to allocate, and *size* specifies their size. After allocating a block of memory of the appropriate size, *calloc()* returns a pointer to the start of the block (or NULL if the memory could not be allocated). Unlike *malloc()*, *calloc()* initializes the allocated memory to 0.

Here is an example of the use of *calloc()*:

```
struct myStruct { /* Some field definitions */ };
struct myStruct *p;

p = calloc(1000, sizeof(struct myStruct));
if (p == NULL)
    errExit("calloc");
```

The *realloc()* function is used to resize (usually enlarge) a block of memory previously allocated by one of the functions in the *malloc* package.

```
#include <stdlib.h>

void *realloc(void *ptr, size_t size);
                Returns pointer to allocated memory on success, or NULL on error
```

The *ptr* argument is a pointer to the block of memory that is to be resized. The *size* argument specifies the desired new size of the block.

On success, *realloc()* returns a pointer to the location of the resized block. This may be different from its location before the call. On error, *realloc()* returns NULL and leaves the block pointed to by *ptr* untouched (SUSv3 requires this).

When *realloc()* increases the size of a block of allocated memory, it doesn't initialize the additionally allocated bytes.

Memory allocated using *calloc()* or *realloc()* should be deallocated with *free()*.

> The call *realloc(ptr, 0)* is equivalent to calling *free(ptr)* followed by *malloc(0)*. If *ptr* is specified as NULL, then *realloc()* is equivalent to calling *malloc(size)*.

For the usual case, where we are increasing the size of the block of memory, *realloc()* attempts to coalesce the block with an immediately following block of memory on the free list, if one exists and is large enough. If the block lies at the end of the heap, then *realloc()* expands the heap. If the block of memory lies in the middle of the heap, and there is insufficient free space immediately following it, *realloc()* allocates a new block of memory and copies all existing data from the old block to the new block. This last case is common and CPU-intensive. In general, it is advisable to minimize the use of *realloc()*.

Since *realloc()* may relocate the block of memory, we must use the returned pointer from *realloc()* for future references to the memory block. We can employ *realloc()* to reallocate a block pointed to by the variable *ptr* as follows:

```
nptr = realloc(ptr, newsize);
if (nptr == NULL) {
    /* Handle error */
} else {                      /* realloc() succeeded */
    ptr = nptr;
}
```

In this example, we didn't assign the return value of *realloc()* directly to *ptr* because, if *realloc()* had failed, then *ptr* would have been set to NULL, making the existing block inaccessible.

Because *realloc()* may move the block of memory, any pointers that referred to locations inside the block before the *realloc()* call may no longer be valid after the call. The only type of reference to a location within the block that is guaranteed to remain valid is one formed by adding an offset to the pointer to the start of the block. We discuss this point in more detail in Section 48.6.

Allocating aligned memory: *memalign()* and *posix_memalign()*

The *memalign()* and *posix_memalign()* functions are designed to allocate memory starting at an address aligned at a specified power-of-two boundary, a feature that is useful for some applications (see, for example, Listing 13-1, on page 247).

```
#include <malloc.h>

void *memalign(size_t boundary, size_t size);
```
Returns pointer to allocated memory on success, or NULL on error

The *memalign()* function allocates *size* bytes starting at an address aligned to a multiple of *boundary*, which must be a power of two. The address of the allocated memory is returned as the function result.

The *memalign()* function is not present on all UNIX implementations. Most other UNIX implementations that provide *memalign()* require the inclusion of <stdlib.h> instead of <malloc.h> in order to obtain the function declaration.

SUSv3 doesn't specify *memalign()*, but instead specifies a similar function, named *posix_memalign()*. This function is a recent creation of the standards committees, and appears on only a few UNIX implementations.

```
#include <stdlib.h>

int posix_memalign(void **memptr, size_t alignment, size_t size);
```
Returns 0 on success, or a positive error number on error

The *posix_memalign()* function differs from *memalign()* in two respects:

- The address of the allocated memory is returned in *memptr*.
- The memory is aligned to a multiple of *alignment*, which must be a power-of-two multiple of *sizeof(void *)* (4 or 8 bytes on most hardware architectures).

Note also the unusual return value of this function—rather than returning −1 on error, it returns an error number (i.e., a positive integer of the type normally returned in *errno*).

If *sizeof(void *)* is 4, then we can use *posix_memalign()* to allocate 65,536 bytes of memory aligned on a 4096-byte boundary as follows:

```
int s;
void *memptr;

s = posix_memalign(&memptr, 1024 * sizeof(void *), 65536);
if (s != 0)
    /* Handle error */
```

Blocks of memory allocated using *memalign()* or *posix_memalign()* should be deallocated with *free()*.

> On some UNIX implementations, it is not possible to call *free()* on a block of memory allocated via *memalign()*, because the *memalign()* implementation uses *malloc()* to allocate a block of memory, and then returns a pointer to an address with a suitable alignment in that block. The *glibc* implementation of *memalign()* doesn't suffer this limitation.

7.2   Allocating Memory on the Stack: *alloca()*

Like the functions in the *malloc* package, *alloca()* allocates memory dynamically. However, instead of obtaining memory from the heap, *alloca()* obtains memory from the stack by increasing the size of the stack frame. This is possible because the calling function is the one whose stack frame is, by definition, on the top of the stack. Therefore, there is space above the frame for expansion, which can be accomplished by simply modifying the value of the stack pointer.

```
#include <alloca.h>

void *alloca(size_t size);
```
                              Returns pointer to allocated block of memory

The *size* argument specifies the number of bytes to allocate on the stack. The *alloca()* function returns a pointer to the allocated memory as its function result.

We need not—indeed, must not—call *free()* to deallocate memory allocated with *alloca()*. Likewise, it is not possible to use *realloc()* to resize a block of memory allocated by *alloca()*.

Although *alloca()* is not part of SUSv3, it is provided on most UNIX implementations and is thus reasonably portable.

Older versions of *glibc*, and some other UNIX implementations (mainly BSD derivatives), require the inclusion of <stdlib.h> instead of <alloca.h> to obtain the declaration of *alloca()*.

If the stack overflows as a consequence of calling *alloca()*, then program behavior is unpredictable. In particular, we don't get a NULL return to inform us of the error. (In fact, in this circumstance, we may receive a SIGSEGV signal. Refer to Section 21.3 for further details.)

Note that we can't use *alloca()* within a function argument list, as in this example:

```
func(x, alloca(size), z);          /* WRONG! */
```

This is because the stack space allocated by *alloca()* would appear in the middle of the space for the function arguments (which are placed at fixed locations within the stack frame). Instead, we must use code such as this:

```
void *y;

y = alloca(size);
func(x, y, z);
```

Using *alloca()* to allocate memory has a few advantages over *malloc()*. One of these is that allocating blocks of memory is faster with *alloca()* than with *malloc()*, because *alloca()* is implemented by the compiler as inline code that directly adjusts the stack pointer. Furthermore, *alloca()* doesn't need to maintain a list of free blocks.

Another advantage of *alloca()* is that the memory that it allocates is automatically freed when the stack frame is removed; that is, when the function that called *alloca()* returns. This is so because the code executed during function return resets the value of the stack pointer register to the end of the previous frame (i.e., assuming a downwardly growing stack, to the address just above the start of the current frame). Since we don't need to do the work of ensuring that allocated memory is freed on all return paths from a function, coding of some functions becomes much simpler.

Using *alloca()* can be especially useful if we employ *longjmp()* (Section 6.8) or *siglongjmp()* (Section 21.2.1) to perform a nonlocal goto from a signal handler. In this case, it is difficult or even impossible to avoid memory leaks if we allocated memory in the jumped-over functions using *malloc()*. By contrast, *alloca()* avoids this problem completely, since, as the stack is unwound by these calls, the allocated memory is automatically freed.

7.3 Summary

Using the *malloc* family of functions, a process can dynamically allocate and release memory on the heap. In considering the implementation of these functions, we saw that various things can go wrong in a program that mishandles the blocks of allocated memory, and we noted that a number of debugging tools are available to help locate the source of such errors.

The *alloca()* function allocates memory on the stack. This memory is automatically deallocated when the function that calls *alloca()* returns.

7.4   Exercises

7-1.   Modify the program in Listing 7-1 (free_and_sbrk.c) to print out the current value of the program break after each execution of *malloc()*. Run the program specifying a small allocation block size. This will demonstrate that *malloc()* doesn't employ *sbrk()* to adjust the program break on each call, but instead periodically allocates larger chunks of memory from which it passes back small pieces to the caller.

7-2.   (Advanced) Implement *malloc()* and *free()*.

8

USERS AND GROUPS

Every user has a unique login name and an associated numeric user identifier (UID). Users can belong to one or more groups. Each group also has a unique name and a group identifier (GID).

The primary purpose of user and group IDs is to determine ownership of various system resources and to control the permissions granted to processes accessing those resources. For example, each file belongs to a particular user and group, and each process has a number of user and group IDs that determine who owns the process and what permissions it has when accessing a file (see Chapter 9 for details).

In this chapter, we look at the system files that are used to define the users and groups on the system, and then describe the library functions used to retrieve information from these files. We conclude with a discussion of the *crypt()* function, which is used to encrypt and authenticate login passwords.

8.1 The Password File: /etc/passwd

The system *password file*, /etc/passwd, contains one line for each user account on the system. Each line is composed of seven fields separated by colons (:), as in the following example:

```
mtk:x:1000:100:Michael Kerrisk:/home/mtk:/bin/bash
```

In order, these fields are as follows:

- *Login name*: This is the unique name that the user must enter in order to log in. Often, this is also called the username. We can also consider the login name to be the human-readable (symbolic) identifier corresponding to the numeric user identifier (described in a moment). Programs such as *ls(1)* display this name, rather than the numeric user ID associated with the file, when asked to show the ownership of a file (as in *ls –l*).

- *Encrypted password*: This field contains a 13-character encrypted password, which we describe in more detail in Section 8.5. If the password field contains any other string—in particular, a string of other than 13 characters—then logins to this account are disabled, since such a string can't represent a valid encrypted password. Note, however, that this field is ignored if shadow passwords have been enabled (which is typical). In this case, the password field in /etc/passwd contains the letter *x*, and the encrypted password is instead stored in the shadow password file (Section 8.2). If the password field in /etc/passwd is empty, then no password is required to log in to this account (this is true even if shadow passwords are enabled).

  > Here, we assume that passwords are encrypted using Data Encryption Standard (DES), the historical and still widely used UNIX password-encryption scheme. It is possible to replace DES with other schemes, such as MD5, which produces a 128-bit *message digest* (a kind of hash) of its input. This value is stored as a 34-character string in the password (or shadow password) file.

- *User ID* (UID): This is the numeric ID for this user. If this field has the value 0, then this account has superuser privileges. There is normally one such account, with the login name *root*. On Linux 2.2 and earlier, user IDs are maintained as 16-bit values, allowing the range 0 through to 65,535; on Linux 2.4 and later, they are stored using 32 bits, allowing a much larger range.

  > It is possible (but unusual) to have more than one record in the password file with the same user ID, thus permitting multiple login names for the same user ID. This allows multiple users to access the same resources (e.g., files) using different passwords. The different login names can be associated with different sets of group IDs.

- *Group ID* (GID): This is the numeric ID of the first of the groups of which this user is a member. Further group memberships for this user are defined in the system group file.

- *Comment*: This field holds text about the user. This text is displayed by various programs, such as *finger(1)*.

- *Home directory*: This is the initial directory into which the user is placed after logging in. This field becomes the value of the HOME environment variable.

- *Login shell*: This is the program to which control is transferred once the user is logged in. Usually, this is one of the shells, such as *bash*, but it can be any program. If this field is empty, then the login shell defaults to /bin/sh, the Bourne shell. This field becomes the value of the SHELL environment variable.

On a stand-alone system, all the password information resides in the file /etc/passwd. However, if we are using a system such as Network Information System (NIS) or Lightweight Directory Access Protocol (LDAP) to distribute passwords in a network environment, part or all of this information resides on a remote system. As long as programs accessing password information employ the functions described later in this chapter (*getpwnam()*, *getpwuid()*, and so on), the use of NIS or LDAP is transparent to applications. Similar comments apply regarding the shadow password and group files discussed in the following sections.

8.2 The Shadow Password File: /etc/shadow

Historically, UNIX systems maintained all user information, including the encrypted password, in /etc/passwd. This presented a security problem. Since various unprivileged system utilities needed to have read access to other information in the password file, it had to be made readable to all users. This opened the door for password-cracking programs, which try encrypting large lists of likely passwords (e.g., standard dictionary words or people's names) to see if they match the encrypted password of a user. The *shadow password file*, /etc/shadow, was devised as a method of preventing such attacks. The idea is that all of the nonsensitive user information resides in the publicly readable password file, while encrypted passwords are maintained in the shadow password file, which is readable only by privileged programs.

In addition to the login name, which provides the match to the corresponding record in the password file, and the encrypted password, the shadow password file also contains a number of other security-related fields. Further details on these fields can be found in the *shadow(5)* manual page. We'll concern ourselves mainly with the encrypted password field, which we discuss in greater detail when looking at the *crypt()* library function later in Section 8.5.

SUSv3 doesn't specify shadow passwords. Not all UNIX implementations provide this feature, and on implementations where it is provided the details of the file locations and APIs vary.

8.3 The Group File: /etc/group

For various administrative purposes, in particular, controlling access to files and other system resources, it is useful to organize users into *groups*.

The set of groups to which a user belongs is defined by the combination of the group ID field in the user's password entry and the groups under which the user is listed in the group file. This strange split of information across two files is historical in origin. In early UNIX implementations, a user could be a member of only one group at a time. A user's initial group membership at login was determined by the group ID field of the password file and could be changed thereafter using the *newgrp(1)* command, which required the user to supply the group password (if the group was password protected). 4.2BSD introduced the concept of multiple simultaneous group memberships, which was later standardized in POSIX.1-1990. Under this scheme, the group file listed the extra group memberships of each user. (The *groups(1)* command displays the groups of which the shell process is a member, or, if one or more usernames are supplied as command-line arguments, then the group memberships of those users.)

The *group file*, /etc/group, contains one line for each group in the system. Each line consists of four colon-separated fields, as in the following examples:

```
users:x:100:
jambit:x:106:claus,felli,frank,harti,markus,martin,mtk,paul
```

In order, these fields are as follows:

- *Group name*: This is the name of the group. Like the login name in the password file, we can consider this to be the human-readable (symbolic) identifier corresponding to the numeric group identifier.

- *Encrypted password*: This field contains an optional password for the group. With the advent of multiple group memberships, group passwords are nowadays rarely used on UNIX systems. Nevertheless, it is possible to place a password on a group (a privileged user can do this using the *gpasswd* command). If a user is not a member of the group, *newgrp(1)* requests this password before starting a new shell whose group memberships include that group. If password shadowing is enabled, then this field is ignored (in this case, conventionally it contains just the letter *x*, but any string, including an empty string, may appear) and the encrypted passwords are actually kept in the *shadow group file*, /etc/gshadow, which can be accessed only by privileged users and programs. Group passwords are encrypted in a similar fashion to user passwords (Section 8.5).

- *Group ID* (GID): This is the numeric ID for this group. There is normally one group defined with the group ID 0, named *root* (like the /etc/passwd record with user ID of 0, but unlike the user ID 0, this group has no special privileges). On Linux 2.2 and earlier, group IDs are maintained as 16-bit values, allowing the range 0 through to 65,535; on Linux 2.4 and later, they are stored using 32 bits.

- *User list*: This is a comma-separated list of names of users who are members of this group. (This list consists of usernames rather than user IDs, since, as noted earlier, user IDs are not necessarily unique in the password file.)

To record that the user *avr* is a member of the groups *users*, *staff*, and *teach*, we would see the following record in the password file:

```
avr:x:1001:100:Anthony Robins:/home/avr:/bin/bash
```

And the following records would appear in the group file:

```
users:x:100:
staff:x:101:mtk,avr,martinl
teach:x:104:avr,rlb,alc
```

The fourth field of the password record, containing the group ID 100, specifies membership of the group *users*. The remaining group memberships are indicated by listing *avr* once in each of the relevant records in the group file.

8.4 Retrieving User and Group Information

In this section, we look at library functions that permit us to retrieve individual records from the password, shadow password, and group files, and to scan all of the records in each of these files.

Retrieving records from the password file

The *getpwnam()* and *getpwuid()* functions retrieve records from the password file.

```
#include <pwd.h>

struct passwd *getpwnam(const char *name);
struct passwd *getpwuid(uid_t uid);
```

Both return a pointer on success, or NULL on error;
see main text for description of the "not found" case

Given a login name in *name*, the *getpwnam()* function returns a pointer to a structure of the following type, containing the corresponding information from the password record:

```
struct passwd {
    char *pw_name;      /* Login name (username) */
    char *pw_passwd;    /* Encrypted password */
    uid_t pw_uid;       /* User ID */
    gid_t pw_gid;       /* Group ID */
    char *pw_gecos;     /* Comment (user information) */
    char *pw_dir;       /* Initial working (home) directory */
    char *pw_shell;     /* Login shell */
};
```

The *pw_gecos* and *pw_passwd* fields of the *passwd* structure are not defined in SUSv3, but are available on all UNIX implementations. The *pw_passwd* field contains valid information only if password shadowing is not enabled. (Programmatically, the simplest way to determine whether password shadowing is enabled is to follow a successful *getpwnam()* call with a call to *getspnam()*, described shortly, to see if it returns a shadow password record for the same username.) Some other implementations provide additional, nonstandard fields in this structure.

> The *pw_gecos* field derives its name from early UNIX implementations, where this field contained information that was used for communicating with a machine running the General Electric Comprehensive Operating System (GECOS). Although this usage has long since become obsolete, the field name has survived, and the field is used for recording information about the user.

The *getpwuid()* function returns exactly the same information as *getpwnam()*, but does a lookup using the numeric user ID supplied in the argument *uid*.

Both *getpwnam()* and *getpwuid()* return a pointer to a statically allocated structure. This structure is overwritten on each call to either of these functions (or to the *getpwent()* function described below).

Because they return a pointer to statically allocated memory, *getpwnam()* and *getpwuid()* are not reentrant. In fact, the situation is even more complex, since the returned *passwd* structure contains pointers to other information (e.g., the *pw_name* field) that is also statically allocated. (We explain reentrancy in Section 21.1.2.) Similar statements apply to the *getgrnam()* and *getgrgid()* functions (described shortly).

SUSv3 specifies an equivalent set of reentrant functions—*getpwnam_r()*, *getpwuid_r()*, *getgrnam_r()*, and *getgrgid_r()*—that include as arguments both a *passwd* (or *group*) structure and a buffer area to hold the other structures to which the fields of the *passwd* (*group*) structure point. The number of bytes required for this additional buffer can be obtained using the call *sysconf(_SC_GETPW_R_SIZE_MAX)* (or *sysconf(_SC_GETGR_R_SIZE_MAX)* in the case of the group-related functions). See the manual pages for details of these functions.

According to SUSv3, if a matching *passwd* record can't be found, then *getpwnam()* and *getpwuid()* should return NULL and leave *errno* unchanged. This means that we should be able to distinguish the error and the "not found" cases using code such as the following:

```
struct passwd *pwd;

errno = 0;
pwd = getpwnam(name);
if (pwd == NULL) {
    if (errno == 0)
        /* Not found */;
    else
        /* Error */;
}
```

However, a number of UNIX implementations don't conform to SUSv3 on this point. If a matching *passwd* record is not found, then these functions return NULL and set *errno* to a nonzero value, such as ENOENT or ESRCH. Before version 2.7, *glibc* produced the error ENOENT for this case, but since version 2.7, *glibc* conforms to the SUSv3 requirements. This variation across implementations arises in part because POSIX.1-1990 did not require these functions to set *errno* on error and allowed them to set *errno* for the "not found" case. The upshot of all of this is that it isn't really possible to portably distinguish the error and "not found" cases when using these functions.

Retrieving records from the group file

The *getgrnam()* and *getgrgid()* functions retrieve records from the group file.

```
#include <grp.h>

struct group *getgrnam(const char *name);
struct group *getgrgid(gid_t gid);
```
                      Both return a pointer on success, or NULL on error;
                      see main text for description of the "not found" case

The *getgrnam()* function looks up group information by group name, and the *getgrgid()* function performs lookups by group ID. Both functions return a pointer to a structure of the following type:

```
struct group {
    char *gr_name;        /* Group name */
    char *gr_passwd;      /* Encrypted password (if not password shadowing) */
    gid_t gr_gid;         /* Group ID */
    char **gr_mem;        /* NULL-terminated array of pointers to names
                             of members listed in /etc/group */
};
```

> The *gr_passwd* field of the *group* structure is not specified in SUSv3, but is available on most UNIX implementations.

As with the corresponding password functions described above, this structure is overwritten on each call to one of these functions.

If these functions can't find a matching *group* record, then they show the same variations in behavior that we described for *getpwnam()* and *getpwuid()*.

Example program

One common use of the functions that we have already described in this section is to convert symbolic user and group names into numeric IDs and vice versa. Listing 8-1 demonstrates these conversions, in the form of four functions: *userNameFromId()*, *userIdFromName()*, *groupNameFromId()*, and *groupIdFromName()*. As a convenience to the caller, *userIdFromName()* and *groupIdFromName()* also allow the *name* argument to be a (purely) numeric string; in that case, the string is converted directly to a number and returned to the caller. We employ these functions in some example programs later in this book.

Listing 8-1: Functions to convert user and group IDs to and from user and group names

```
───────────────────────────────────── users_groups/ugid_functions.c
#include <pwd.h>
#include <grp.h>
#include <ctype.h>
#include "ugid_functions.h"    /* Declares functions defined here */

char *          /* Return name corresponding to 'uid', or NULL on error */
userNameFromId(uid_t uid)
{
    struct passwd *pwd;

    pwd = getpwuid(uid);
    return (pwd == NULL) ? NULL : pwd->pw_name;
}

uid_t           /* Return UID corresponding to 'name', or -1 on error */
userIdFromName(const char *name)
{
    struct passwd *pwd;
    uid_t u;
    char *endptr;
```

```
    if (name == NULL || *name == '\0')  /* On NULL or empty string */
        return -1;                      /* return an error */

    u = strtol(name, &endptr, 10);      /* As a convenience to caller */
    if (*endptr == '\0')                /* allow a numeric string */
        return u;

    pwd = getpwnam(name);
    if (pwd == NULL)
        return -1;

    return pwd->pw_uid;
}

char *           /* Return name corresponding to 'gid', or NULL on error */
groupNameFromId(gid_t gid)
{
    struct group *grp;

    grp = getgrgid(gid);
    return (grp == NULL) ? NULL : grp->gr_name;
}

gid_t            /* Return GID corresponding to 'name', or -1 on error */
groupIdFromName(const char *name)
{
    struct group *grp;
    gid_t g;
    char *endptr;

    if (name == NULL || *name == '\0')  /* On NULL or empty string */
        return -1;                      /* return an error */

    g = strtol(name, &endptr, 10);      /* As a convenience to caller */
    if (*endptr == '\0')                /* allow a numeric string */
        return g;

    grp = getgrnam(name);
    if (grp == NULL)
        return -1;

    return grp->gr_gid;
}
```

———————————————————————————————————— **users_groups/ugid_functions.c**

Scanning all records in the password and group files

The *setpwent()*, *getpwent()*, and *endpwent()* functions are used to perform sequential scans of the records in the password file.

```
#include <pwd.h>

struct passwd *getpwent(void);
```

                    Returns pointer on success, or NULL on end of stream or error

```
void setpwent(void);
void endpwent(void);
```

The *getpwent()* function returns records from the password file one by one, returning NULL when there are no more records (or an error occurs). On the first call,
getpwent() automatically opens the password file. When we have finished with the
file, we call *endpwent()* to close it.

We can walk through the entire password file printing login names and user
IDs with the following code:

```
struct passwd *pwd;

while ((pwd = getpwent()) != NULL)
    printf("%-8s %5ld\n", pwd->pw_name, (long) pwd->pw_uid);

endpwent();
```

The *endpwent()* call is necessary so that any subsequent *getpwent()* call (perhaps in
some other part of our program or in some library function that we call) will
reopen the password file and start from the beginning. On the other hand, if we
are part-way through the file, we can use the *setpwent()* function to restart from the
beginning.

The *getgrent()*, *setgrent()*, and *endgrent()* functions perform analogous tasks for
the group file. We omit the prototypes for these functions because they are similar
to those of the password file functions described above; see the manual pages for
details.

Retrieving records from the shadow password file

The following functions are used to retrieve individual records from the shadow
password file and to scan all records in that file.

```
#include <shadow.h>

struct spwd *getspnam(const char *name);
```

                    Returns pointer on success, or NULL on not found or error

```
struct spwd *getspent(void);
```

                    Returns pointer on success, or NULL on end of stream or error

```
void setspent(void);
void endspent(void);
```

We won't describe these functions in detail, since their operation is similar to the corresponding password file functions. (These functions aren't specified in SUSv3, and aren't present on all UNIX implementations.)

The *getspnam()* and *getspent()* functions return pointers to a structure of type *spwd*. This structure has the following form:

```
struct spwd {
    char *sp_namp;          /* Login name (username) */
    char *sp_pwdp;          /* Encrypted password */

    /* Remaining fields support "password aging", an optional
       feature that forces users to regularly change their
       passwords, so that even if an attacker manages to obtain
       a password, it will eventually cease to be usable. */

    long sp_lstchg;         /* Time of last password change
                               (days since 1 Jan 1970) */
    long sp_min;            /* Min. number of days between password changes */
    long sp_max;            /* Max. number of days before change required */
    long sp_warn;           /* Number of days beforehand that user is
                               warned of upcoming password expiration */
    long sp_inact;          /* Number of days after expiration that account
                               is considered inactive and locked */
    long sp_expire;         /* Date when account expires
                               (days since 1 Jan 1970) */
    unsigned long sp_flag;  /* Reserved for future use */
};
```

We demonstrate the use of *getspnam()* in Listing 8-2.

8.5 Password Encryption and User Authentication

Some applications require that users authenticate themselves. Authentication typically takes the form of a username (login name) and password. An application may maintain its own database of usernames and passwords for this purpose. Sometimes, however, it is necessary or convenient to allow users to enter their standard username and password as defined in /etc/passwd and /etc/shadow. (For the remainder of this section, we assume a system where password shadowing is enabled, and thus that the encrypted password is stored in /etc/shadow.) Network applications that provide some form of login to a remote system, such as *ssh* and *ftp*, are typical examples of such programs. These applications must validate a username and password in the same way that the standard *login* program does.

For security reasons, UNIX systems encrypt passwords using a *one-way encryption* algorithm, which means that there is no method of re-creating the original password from its encrypted form. Therefore, the only way of validating a candidate password is to encrypt it using the same method and see if the encrypted result matches the value stored in /etc/shadow. The encryption algorithm is encapsulated in the *crypt()* function.

```
#define _XOPEN_SOURCE
#include <unistd.h>

char *crypt(const char *key, const char *salt);
```

> Returns pointer to statically allocated string containing
> encrypted password on success, or NULL on error

The *crypt()* algorithm takes a *key* (i.e., a password) of up to 8 characters, and applies a variation of the Data Encryption Standard (DES) algorithm to it. The *salt* argument is a 2-character string whose value is used to perturb (vary) the algorithm, a technique designed to make it more difficult to crack the encrypted password. The function returns a pointer to a statically allocated 13-character string that is the encrypted password.

> Details of DES can be found at *http://www.itl.nist.gov/fipspubs/fip46-2.htm*. As noted earlier, other algorithms may be used instead of DES. For example, MD5 yields a 34-character string starting with a dollar sign ($), which allows *crypt()* to distinguish DES-encrypted passwords from MD5-encrypted passwords.
>
> In our discussion of password encryption, we are using the word "encryption" somewhat loosely. Accurately, DES uses the given password string as an encryption key to encode a fixed bit string, while MD5 is a complex type of hashing function. The result in both cases is the same: an undecipherable and irreversible transformation of the input password.

Both the *salt* argument and the encrypted password are composed of characters selected from the 64-character set [a-zA-Z0-9/.]. Thus, the 2-character *salt* argument can cause the encryption algorithm to vary in any of 64 * 64 = 4096 different ways. This means that instead of preencrypting an entire dictionary and checking the encrypted password against all words in the dictionary, a cracker would need to check the password against 4096 encrypted versions of the dictionary.

The encrypted password returned by *crypt()* contains a copy of the original *salt* value as its first two characters. This means that when encrypting a candidate password, we can obtain the appropriate *salt* value from the encrypted password value already stored in /etc/shadow. (Programs such as *passwd(1)* generate a random *salt* value when encrypting a new password.) In fact, the *crypt()* function ignores any characters in the *salt* string beyond the first two. Therefore, we can specify the encrypted password itself as the *salt* argument.

In order to use *crypt()* on Linux, we must compile programs with the *–lcrypt* option, so that they are linked against the *crypt* library.

Example program

Listing 8-2 demonstrates how to use *crypt()* to authenticate a user. This program first reads a username and then retrieves the corresponding password record and (if it exists) shadow password record. The program prints an error message and exits if no password record is found, or if the program doesn't have permission to read from the shadow password file (this requires either superuser privilege or membership of the *shadow* group). The program then reads the user's password, using the *getpass()* function.

```
#define _BSD_SOURCE
#include <unistd.h>

char *getpass(const char *prompt);
```

> Returns pointer to statically allocated input password string
> on success, or NULL on error

The *getpass()* function first disables echoing and all processing of terminal special characters (such as the *interrupt* character, normally *Control-C*). (We explain how to change these terminal settings in Chapter 62.) It then prints the string pointed to by *prompt*, and reads a line of input, returning the null-terminated input string with the trailing newline stripped, as its function result. (This string is statically allocated, and so will be overwritten on a subsequent call to *getpass()*.) Before returning, *getpass()* restores the terminal settings to their original states.

Having read a password with *getpass()*, the program in Listing 8-2 then validates that password by using *crypt()* to encrypt it and checking that the resulting string matches the encrypted password recorded in the shadow password file. If the password matches, then the ID of the user is displayed, as in the following example:

```
$ su                            Need privilege to read shadow password file
Password:
# ./check_password
Username: mtk
Password:                       We type in password, which is not echoed
Successfully authenticated: UID=1000
```

The program in Listing 8-2 sizes the character array holding a username using the value returned by *sysconf(_SC_LOGIN_NAME_MAX)*, which yields the maximum size of a username on the host system. We explain the use of *sysconf()* in Section 11.2.

Listing 8-2: Authenticating a user against the shadow password file

―――――――――――――――――――――――――――――――――― *users_groups/check_password.c*
```
#define _BSD_SOURCE     /* Get getpass() declaration from <unistd.h> */
#define _XOPEN_SOURCE   /* Get crypt() declaration from <unistd.h> */
#include <unistd.h>
#include <limits.h>
#include <pwd.h>
#include <shadow.h>
#include "tlpi_hdr.h"

int
main(int argc, char *argv[])
{
    char *username, *password, *encrypted, *p;
    struct passwd *pwd;
    struct spwd *spwd;
    Boolean authOk;
    size_t len;
    long lnmax;
```

```
    lnmax = sysconf(_SC_LOGIN_NAME_MAX);
    if (lnmax == -1)                    /* If limit is indeterminate */
        lnmax = 256;                    /* make a guess */

    username = malloc(lnmax);
    if (username == NULL)
        errExit("malloc");

    printf("Username: ");
    fflush(stdout);
    if (fgets(username, lnmax, stdin) == NULL)
        exit(EXIT_FAILURE);             /* Exit on EOF */

    len = strlen(username);
    if (username[len - 1] == '\n')
        username[len - 1] = '\0';       /* Remove trailing '\n' */

    pwd = getpwnam(username);
    if (pwd == NULL)
        fatal("couldn't get password record");
    spwd = getspnam(username);
    if (spwd == NULL && errno == EACCES)
        fatal("no permission to read shadow password file");

    if (spwd != NULL)           /* If there is a shadow password record */
        pwd->pw_passwd = spwd->sp_pwdp;     /* Use the shadow password */

    password = getpass("Password: ");

    /* Encrypt password and erase cleartext version immediately */

    encrypted = crypt(password, pwd->pw_passwd);
    for (p = password; *p != '\0'; )
        *p++ = '\0';

    if (encrypted == NULL)
        errExit("crypt");

    authOk = strcmp(encrypted, pwd->pw_passwd) == 0;
    if (!authOk) {
        printf("Incorrect password\n");
        exit(EXIT_FAILURE);
    }

    printf("Successfully authenticated: UID=%ld\n", (long) pwd->pw_uid);

    /* Now do authenticated work... */

    exit(EXIT_SUCCESS);
}
```

―――――――――――――――――――――――――――――――――――――― users_groups/check_password.c

Listing 8-2 illustrates an important security point. Programs that read a password
should immediately encrypt that password and erase the unencrypted version from

memory. This minimizes the possibility of a program crash producing a core dump file that could be read to discover the password.

There are other possible ways in which the unencrypted password could be exposed. For example, the password could be read from the swap file by a privileged program if the virtual memory page containing the password is swapped out. Alternatively, a process with sufficient privilege could read /dev/mem (a virtual device that presents the physical memory of a computer as a sequential stream of bytes) in an attempt to discover the password.

The *getpass()* function appeared in SUSv2, which marked it LEGACY, noting that the name was misleading and the function provided functionality that was in any case easy to implement. The specification of *getpass()* was removed in SUSv3. It nevertheless appears on most UNIX implementations.

8.6 Summary

Each user has a unique login name and an associated numeric user ID. Users can belong to one or more groups, each of which also has a unique name and an associated numeric identifier. The primary purpose of these identifiers is to establish ownership of various system resources (e.g., files) and permissions for accessing them.

A user's name and ID are defined in the /etc/passwd file, which also contains other information about the user. A user's group memberships are defined by fields in the /etc/passwd and /etc/group files. A further file, /etc/shadow, which can be read only by privileged processes, is used to separate the sensitive password information from the publicly available user information in /etc/passwd. Various library functions are provided for retrieving information from each of these files.

The *crypt()* function encrypts a password in the same manner as the standard *login* program, which is useful for programs that need to authenticate users.

8.7 Exercises

8-1. When we execute the following code, which attempts to display the usernames for two different user IDs, we find that it displays the same username twice. Why is this?

```
printf("%s %s\n", getpwuid(uid1)->pw_name,
                  getpwuid(uid2)->pw_name);
```

8-2. Implement *getpwnam()* using *setpwent()*, *getpwent()*, and *endpwent()*.

9

PROCESS CREDENTIALS

Every process has a set of associated numeric user identifiers (UIDs) and group identifiers (GIDs). Sometimes, these are referred to as process credentials. These identifiers are as follows:

- real user ID and group ID;
- effective user ID and group ID;
- saved set-user-ID and saved set-group-ID;
- file-system user ID and group ID (Linux-specific); and
- supplementary group IDs.

In this chapter, we look in detail at the purpose of these process identifiers and describe the system calls and library functions that can be used to retrieve and change them. We also discuss the notion of privileged and unprivileged processes, and the use of the set-user-ID and set-group-ID mechanisms, which allow the creation of programs that run with the privileges of a specified user or group.

9.1 Real User ID and Real Group ID

The real user ID and group ID identify the user and group to which the process belongs. As part of the login process, a login shell gets its real user and group IDs from the third and fourth fields of the user's password record in the /etc/passwd file

(Section 8.1). When a new process is created (e.g., when the shell executes a program), it inherits these identifiers from its parent.

9.2 Effective User ID and Effective Group ID

On most UNIX implementations (Linux is a little different, as explained in Section 9.5), the effective user ID and group ID, in conjunction with the supplementary group IDs, are used to determine the permissions granted to a process when it tries to perform various operations (i.e., system calls). For example, these identifiers determine the permissions granted to a process when it accesses resources such as files and System V interprocess communication (IPC) objects, which themselves have associated user and group IDs determining to whom they belong. As we'll see in Section 20.5, the effective user ID is also used by the kernel to determine whether one process can send a signal to another.

A process whose effective user ID is 0 (the user ID of *root*) has all of the privileges of the superuser. Such a process is referred to as a *privileged process*. Certain system calls can be executed only by privileged processes.

> In Chapter 39, we describe Linux's implementation of capabilities, a scheme that divides the privileges granted to the superuser into a number of distinct units that can be independently enabled and disabled.

Normally, the effective user and group IDs have the same values as the corresponding real IDs, but there are two ways in which the effective IDs can assume different values. One way is through the use of system calls that we discuss in Section 9.7. The second way is through the execution of set-user-ID and set-group-ID programs.

9.3 Set-User-ID and Set-Group-ID Programs

A set-user-ID program allows a process to gain privileges it would not normally have, by setting the process's effective user ID to the same value as the user ID (owner) of the executable file. A set-group-ID program performs the analogous task for the process's effective group ID. (The terms *set-user-ID program* and *set-group-ID* program are sometimes abbreviated as *set-UID program* and *set-GID program*.)

Like any other file, an executable program file has an associated user ID and group ID that define the ownership of the file. In addition, an executable file has two special permission bits: the set-user-ID and set-group-ID bits. (In fact, every file has these two permission bits, but it is their use with executable files that interests us here.) These permission bits are set using the *chmod* command. An unprivileged user can set these bits for files that they own. A privileged user (CAP_FOWNER) can set these bits for any file. Here's an example:

```
$ su
Password:
# ls -l prog
-rwxr-xr-x    1 root     root       302585 Jun 26 15:05 prog
# chmod u+s prog                              Turn on set-user-ID permission bit
# chmod g+s prog                              Turn on set-group-ID permission bit
```

As shown in this example, it is possible for a program to have both of these bits set, although this is uncommon. When *ls –l* is used to list the permissions for a program that has the set-user-ID or set-group-ID permission bit set, then the *x* that is normally used to indicate that execute permission is set is replaced by an *s*:

```
# ls -l prog
-rwsr-sr-x   1 root     root        302585 Jun 26 15:05 prog
```

When a set-user-ID program is run (i.e., loaded into a process's memory by an *exec()*), the kernel sets the effective user ID of the process to be the same as the user ID of the executable file. Running a set-group-ID program has an analogous effect for the effective group ID of the process. Changing the effective user or group ID in this way gives a process (in other words, the user executing the program) privileges it would not normally have. For example, if an executable file is owned by *root* (superuser) and has the set-user-ID permission bit enabled, then the process gains superuser privileges when that program is run.

Set-user-ID and set-group-ID programs can also be designed to change the effective IDs of a process to something other than *root*. For example, to provide access to a protected file (or other system resource), it may suffice to create a special-purpose user (group) ID that has the privileges required to access the file, and create a set-user-ID (set-group-ID) program that changes the effective user (group) ID of a process to that ID. This permits the program to access the file without allowing it all of the privileges of the superuser.

Sometimes, we'll use the term set-user-ID-*root* to distinguish a set-user-ID program that is owned by *root* from one owned by another user, which merely gives a process the privileges accorded to that user.

> We have now started using the term *privileged* in two different senses. One is the sense defined earlier: a process with an effective user ID of 0, which has all of the privileges accorded to *root*. However, when we are talking about a set-user-ID program owned by a user other than *root*, we'll sometimes refer to a process as gaining the privileges accorded to the user ID of the set-user-ID program. Which sense of the term *privileged* we mean in each case should be clear from the context.
>
> For reasons that we explain in Section 38.3, the set-user-ID and set-group-ID permission bits don't have any effect for shell scripts on Linux.

Examples of commonly used set-user-ID programs on Linux include: *passwd(1)*, which changes a user's password; *mount(8)* and *umount(8)*, which mount and unmount file systems; and *su(1)*, which allows a user to run a shell under a different user ID. An example of a set-group-ID program is *wall(1)*, which writes a message to all terminals owned by the *tty* group (normally, every terminal is owned by this group).

In Section 8.5, we noted that the program in Listing 8-2 needed to be run from a *root* login so that it could access the /etc/shadow file. We could make this program runnable by any user by making it a set-user-ID-*root* program, as follows:

```
$ su
Password:
# chown root check_password          Make this program owned by root
# chmod u+s check_password           With the set-user-ID bit enabled
```

```
# ls -l check_password
-rwsr-xr-x    1 root    users    18150 Oct 28 10:49 check_password
# exit
$ whoami                             This is an unprivileged login
mtk
$ ./check_password                   But we can now access the shadow
Username: avr                        password file using this program
Password:
Successfully authenticated: UID=1001
```

The set-user-ID/set-group-ID technique is a useful and powerful tool, but one that can result in security breaches in applications that are poorly designed. In Chapter 38, we list a set of good practices that should be observed when writing set-user-ID and set-group-ID programs.

9.4 Saved Set-User-ID and Saved Set-Group-ID

The saved set-user-ID and saved set-group-ID are designed for use with set-user-ID and set-group-ID programs. When a program is executed, the following steps (among many others) occur:

1. If the set-user-ID (set-group-ID) permission bit is enabled on the executable, then the effective user (group) ID of the process is made the same as the owner of the executable. If the set-user-ID (set-group-ID) bit is not set, then no change is made to the effective user (group) ID of the process.

2. The values for the saved set-user-ID and saved set-group-ID are copied from the corresponding effective IDs. This copying occurs regardless of whether the set-user-ID or set-group-ID bit is set on the file being executed.

As an example of the effect of the above steps, suppose that a process whose real user ID, effective user ID, and saved set-user-ID are all 1000 execs a set-user-ID program owned by *root* (user ID 0). After the exec, the user IDs of the process will be changed as follows:

```
real=1000 effective=0 saved=0
```

Various system calls allow a set-user-ID program to switch its effective user ID between the values of the real user ID and the saved set-user-ID. Analogous system calls allow a set-group-ID program to modify its effective group ID. In this manner, the program can temporarily drop and regain whatever privileges are associated with the user (group) ID of the execed file. (In other words, the program can move between the states of potentially being privileged and actually operating with privilege.) As we'll elaborate in Section 38.2, it is secure programming practice for set-user-ID and set-group-ID programs to operate under the unprivileged (i.e., real) ID whenever the program doesn't actually need to perform any operations associated with the privileged (i.e., saved set) ID.

> The saved set-user-ID and saved set-group-ID are sometimes synonymously referred to as the *saved user ID* and *saved group ID*.

The saved set IDs are a System V invention adopted by POSIX. They were not provided on releases of BSD prior to 4.4. The initial POSIX.1 standard made support for these IDs optional, but later standards (starting with FIPS 151-1 in 1988) made support mandatory.

9.5   File-System User ID and File-System Group ID

On Linux, it is the file-system user and group IDs, rather than the effective user and group IDs, that are used (in conjunction with the supplementary group IDs) to determine permissions when performing file-system operations such as opening files, changing file ownership, and modifying file permissions. (The effective IDs are still used, as on other UNIX implementations, for the other purposes described earlier.)

Normally, the file-system user and group IDs have the same values as the corresponding effective IDs (and thus typically are the same as the corresponding real IDs). Furthermore, whenever the effective user or group ID is changed, either by a system call or by execution of a set-user-ID or set-group-ID program, the corresponding file-system ID is also changed to the same value. Since the file-system IDs follow the effective IDs in this way, this means that Linux effectively behaves just like any other UNIX implementation when privileges and permissions are being checked. The file-system IDs differ from the corresponding effective IDs, and hence Linux differs from other UNIX implementations, only when we use two Linux-specific system calls, *setfsuid()* and *setfsgid()*, to explicitly make them different.

Why does Linux provide the file-system IDs and in what circumstances would we want the effective and file-system IDs to differ? The reasons are primarily historical. The file-system IDs first appeared in Linux 1.2. In that kernel version, one process could send a signal to another if the effective user ID of the sender matched the real or effective user ID of the target process. This affected certain programs such as the Linux NFS (Network File System) server program, which needed to be able to access files as though it had the effective IDs of the corresponding client process. However, if the NFS server changed its effective user ID, it would be vulnerable to signals from unprivileged user processes. To prevent this possibility, the separate file-system user and group IDs were devised. By leaving its effective IDs unchanged, but changing its file-system IDs, the NFS server could masquerade as another user for the purpose of accessing files without being vulnerable to signals from user processes.

From kernel 2.0 onward, Linux adopted the SUSv3-mandated rules regarding permission for sending signals, and these rules don't involve the effective user ID of the target process (refer to Section 20.5). Thus, the file-system ID feature is no longer strictly necessary (a process can nowadays achieve the desired results by making judicious use of the system calls described later in this chapter to change the value of the effective user ID to and from an unprivileged value, as required), but it remains for compatibility with existing software.

Since the file-system IDs are something of an oddity, and they normally have the same values as the corresponding effective IDs, in the remainder of this book, we'll generally describe various file permission checks, as well as the setting of the ownership of new files, in terms of the effective IDs of a process. Even though the process's file-system IDs are really used for these purposes on Linux, in practice, their presence seldom makes an effective difference.

9.6 Supplementary Group IDs

The supplementary group IDs are a set of additional groups to which a process belongs. A new process inherits these IDs from its parent. A login shell obtains its supplementary group IDs from the system group file. As noted above, these IDs are used in conjunction with the effective and file-system IDs to determine permissions for accessing files, System V IPC objects, and other system resources.

9.7 Retrieving and Modifying Process Credentials

Linux provides a range of system calls and library functions for retrieving and changing the various user and group IDs that we have described in this chapter. Only some of these APIs are specified in SUSv3. Of the remainder, several are widely available on other UNIX implementations and a few are Linux-specific. We note portability issues as we describe each interface. Toward the end of this chapter, Table 9-1 summarizes the operation of all of the interfaces used to change process credentials.

As an alternative to using the system calls described in the following pages, the credentials of any process can be found by examining the Uid, Gid, and Groups lines provided in the Linux-specific /proc/*PID*/status file. The Uid and Gid lines list the identifiers in the order real, effective, saved set, and file system.

In the following sections, we use the traditional definition of a privileged process as one whose effective user ID is 0. However, Linux divides the notion of superuser privileges into distinct capabilities, as described in Chapter 39. Two capabilities are relevant for our discussion of all of the system calls used to change process user and group IDs:

- The CAP_SETUID capability allows a process to make arbitrary changes to its user IDs.
- The CAP_SETGID capability allows a process to make arbitrary changes to its group IDs.

9.7.1 Retrieving and Modifying Real, Effective, and Saved Set IDs

In the following paragraphs, we describe the system calls that retrieve and modify the real, effective, and saved set IDs. There are several system calls that perform these tasks, and in some cases their functionality overlaps, reflecting the fact that the various system calls originated on different UNIX implementations.

Retrieving real and effective IDs

The *getuid()* and *getgid()* system calls return, respectively, the real user ID and real group ID of the calling process. The *geteuid()* and *getegid()* system calls perform the corresponding tasks for the effective IDs. These system calls are always successful.

```
#include <unistd.h>

uid_t getuid(void);
                                    Returns real user ID of calling process
uid_t geteuid(void);
                                Returns effective user ID of calling process
gid_t getgid(void);
                                   Returns real group ID of calling process
gid_t getegid(void);
                               Returns effective group ID of calling process
```

Modifying effective IDs

The *setuid()* system call changes the effective user ID—and possibly the real user ID and the saved set-user-ID—of the calling process to the value given by the *uid* argument. The *setgid()* system call performs the analogous task for the corresponding group IDs.

```
#include <unistd.h>

int setuid(uid_t uid);
int setgid(gid_t gid);
                                   Both return 0 on success, or −1 on error
```

The rules about what changes a process can make to its credentials using *setuid()* and *setgid()* depend on whether the process is privileged (i.e., has an effective user ID equal to 0). The following rules apply to *setuid()*:

1. When an unprivileged process calls *setuid()*, only the effective user ID of the process is changed. Furthermore, it can be changed only to the same value as either the real user ID or saved set-user-ID. (Attempts to violate this constraint yield the error EPERM.) This means that, for unprivileged users, this call is useful only when executing a set-user-ID program, since, for the execution of normal programs, the process's real user ID, effective user ID, and saved set-user-ID all have the same value. On some BSD-derived implementations, calls to *setuid()* or *setgid()* by an unprivileged process have different semantics from other UNIX implementations: the calls change the real, effective, and saved set IDs (to the value of the current real or effective ID).

2. When a privileged process executes *setuid()* with a nonzero argument, then the real user ID, effective user ID, and saved set-user-ID are all set to the value specified in the *uid* argument. This is a one-way trip, in that once a privileged process has changed its identifiers in this way, it loses all privileges and therefore can't subsequently use *setuid()* to reset the identifiers back to 0. If this is not desired, then either *seteuid()* or *setreuid()*, which we describe shortly, should be used instead of *setuid()*.

The rules governing the changes that may be made to group IDs using *setgid()* are similar, but with *setgid()* substituted for *setuid()* and *group* for *user*. With these changes, rule 1 applies exactly as stated. In rule 2, since changing the group IDs doesn't cause a process to lose privileges (which are determined by the effective *user* ID), privileged programs can use *setgid()* to freely change the group IDs to any desired values.

The following call is the preferred method for a set-user-ID-*root* program whose effective user ID is currently 0 to irrevocably drop all privileges (by setting both the effective user ID and saved set-user-ID to the same value as the real user ID):

```
if (setuid(getuid()) == -1)
    errExit("setuid");
```

A set-user-ID program owned by a user other than *root* can use *setuid()* to switch the effective user ID between the values of the real user ID and saved set-user-ID for the security reasons described in Section 9.4. However, *seteuid()* is preferable for this purpose, since it has the same effect, regardless of whether the set-user-ID program is owned by *root*.

A process can use *seteuid()* to change its effective user ID (to the value specified by *euid*), and *setegid()* to change its effective group ID (to the value specified by *egid*).

```
#include <unistd.h>

int seteuid(uid_t euid);
int setegid(gid_t egid);
```
                                        Both return 0 on success, or −1 on error

The following rules govern the changes that a process may make to its effective IDs using *seteuid()* and *setegid()*:

1. An unprivileged process can change an effective ID only to the same value as the corresponding real or saved set ID. (In other words, for an unprivileged process, *seteuid()* and *setegid()* have the same effect as *setuid()* and *setgid()*, respectively, except for the BSD portability issues noted earlier.)

2. A privileged process can change an effective ID to any value. If a privileged process uses *seteuid()* to change its effective user ID to a nonzero value, then it ceases to be privileged (but may be able to regain privilege via the previous rule).

Using *seteuid()* is the preferred method for set-user-ID and set-group-ID programs to temporarily drop and later regain privileges. Here's an example:

```
euid = geteuid();              /* Save initial effective user ID (which
                                  is same as saved set-user-ID) */
if (seteuid(getuid()) == -1)   /* Drop privileges */
    errExit("seteuid");
if (seteuid(euid) == -1)       /* Regain privileges */
    errExit("seteuid");
```

Originally derived from BSD, *seteuid()* and *setegid()* are now specified in SUSv3 and appear on most UNIX implementations.

In older versions of the GNU C library (*glibc* 2.0 and earlier), *seteuid(euid)* is implemented as *setreuid(-1, euid)*. In modern versions of *glibc, seteuid(euid)* is implemented as *setresuid(-1, euid, -1)*. (We describe *setreuid(), setresuid(),* and their group analogs shortly.) Both implementations permit us to specify *euid* as the same value as the current effective user ID (i.e., no change). However, SUSv3 doesn't specify this behavior for *seteuid()*, and it is not possible on some other UNIX implementations. Generally, this potential variation across implementations is not apparent, since, in normal circumstances, the effective user ID has the same value as either the real user ID or the saved set-user-ID. (The only way in which we can make the effective user ID differ from both the real user ID and the saved set-user-ID on Linux is via the use of the nonstandard *setresuid()* system call.)

Analogous remarks apply for the *glibc* implementation of *setegid(egid)*, except that the switch in implementation from *setregid(-1, egid)* to *setresgid(-1, egid, -1)* occurred in *glibc* 2.2 or 2.3 (the precise version depends on the hardware architecture).

Modifying real and effective IDs

The *setreuid()* system call allows the calling process to independently change the values of its real and effective user IDs. The *setregid()* system call performs the analogous task for the real and effective group IDs.

```
#include <unistd.h>

int setreuid(uid_t ruid, uid_t euid);
int setregid(gid_t rgid, gid_t egid);
```
                                        Both return 0 on success, or -1 on error

The first argument to each of these system calls is the new real ID. The second argument is the new effective ID. If we want to change only one of the identifiers, then we can specify -1 for the other argument.

Originally derived from BSD, *setreuid()* and *setregid()* are now specified in SUSv3 and are available on most UNIX implementations.

As with the other system calls described in this section, rules govern the changes that we can make using *setreuid()* and *setregid()*. We describe these rules from the point of view of *setreuid()*, with the understanding that *setregid()* is similar, except as noted:

1. An unprivileged process can set the real user ID only to the current value of the real (i.e., no change) or effective user ID. The effective user ID can be set only to the current value of the real user ID, effective user ID (i.e., no change), or saved set-user-ID.

    > SUSv3 says that it is unspecified whether an unprivileged process can use *setreuid()* to change the value of the real user ID to the current value of the real user ID, effective user ID, or saved set-user-ID, and the details of precisely what changes can be made to the real user ID vary across implementations.

SUSv3 describes slightly different behavior for *setregid()*: an unprivileged process can set the real group ID to the current value of the saved set-group-ID or set the effective group ID to the current value of either the real group ID or the saved set-group-ID. Again, the details of precisely what changes can be made vary across implementations.

2. A privileged process can make any changes to the IDs.

3. For both privileged and unprivileged processes, the saved set-user-ID is also set to the same value as the (new) effective user ID if either of the following is true:

   a) *ruid* is not −1 (i.e., the real user ID is being set, even to the same value it already had), or

   b) the effective user ID is being set to a value other than the value of the real user ID prior to the call.

   Put conversely, if a process uses *setreuid()* only to change the effective user ID to the same value as the current real user ID, then the saved set-user-ID is left unchanged, and a later call to *setreuid()* (or *seteuid()*) can restore the effective user ID to the saved set-user-ID value. (SUSv3 doesn't specify the effect of *setreuid()* and *setregid()* on the saved set IDs, but SUSv4 specifies the behavior described here.)

The third rule provides a way for a set-user-ID program to permanently drop its privilege, using a call such as the following:

```
setreuid(getuid(), getuid());
```

A set-user-ID-*root* process that wants to change both its user and group credentials to arbitrary values should first call *setregid()* and then call *setreuid()*. If the calls are made in the opposite order, then the *setregid()* call will fail, because the program will no longer be privileged after the call to *setreuid()*. Similar remarks apply if we are using *setresuid()* and *setresgid()* (described below) for this purpose.

> BSD releases up to and including 4.3BSD did not have the saved set-user-ID and saved set-group-ID (which are nowadays mandated by SUSv3). Instead, on BSD, *setreuid()* and *setregid()* permitted a process to drop and regain privilege by swapping the values of the real and effective IDs back and forth. This had the undesirable side effect of changing the real user ID in order to change the effective user ID.

Retrieving real, effective, and saved set IDs

On most UNIX implementations, a process can't directly retrieve (or update) its saved set-user-ID and saved set-group-ID. However, Linux provides two (nonstandard) system calls allowing us to do just that: *getresuid()* and *getresgid()*.

```
#define _GNU_SOURCE
#include <unistd.h>

int getresuid(uid_t *ruid, uid_t *euid, uid_t *suid);
int getresgid(gid_t *rgid, gid_t *egid, gid_t *sgid);
```
                                        Both return 0 on success, or −1 on error

The *getresuid()* system call returns the current values of the calling process's real user ID, effective user ID, and saved set-user-ID in the locations pointed by its three arguments. The *getresgid()* system call does the same for the corresponding group IDs.

Modifying real, effective, and saved set IDs

The *setresuid()* system call allows the calling process to independently change the values of all three of its user IDs. The new values for each of the user IDs are specified by the three arguments to the system call. The *setresgid()* system call performs the analogous task for the group IDs.

```
#define _GNU_SOURCE
#include <unistd.h>

int setresuid(uid_t ruid, uid_t euid, uid_t suid);
int setresgid(gid_t rgid, gid_t egid, gid_t sgid);
```
                            Both return 0 on success, or –1 on error

If we don't want to change all of the identifiers, then specifying –1 for an argument leaves the corresponding identifier unchanged. For example, the following call is equivalent to *seteuid(x)*:

```
setresuid(-1, x, -1);
```

The rules about what changes may be made by *setresuid()* (*setresgid()* is similar) are as follows:

1. An unprivileged process can set any of its real user ID, effective user ID, and saved set-user-ID to any of the values currently in its current real user ID, effective user ID, or saved set-user-ID.
2. A privileged process can make arbitrary changes to its real user ID, effective user ID, and saved set-user-ID.
3. Regardless of whether the call makes any changes to other IDs, the file-system user ID is always set to the same value as the (possibly new) effective user ID.

Calls to *setresuid()* and *setresgid()* have an all-or-nothing effect. Either all of the requested identifiers are successfully changed or none are changed. (The same comment applies with respect to the other system calls described in this chapter that change multiple identifiers.)

Although *setresuid()* and *setresgid()* provide the most straightforward API for changing process credentials, we can't portably employ them in applications; they are not specified in SUSv3 and are available on only a few other UNIX implementations.

9.7.2   Retrieving and Modifying File-System IDs

All of the previously described system calls that change the process's effective user or group ID also always change the corresponding file-system ID. To change the file-system IDs independently of the effective IDs, we must employ two Linux-specific system calls: *setfsuid()* and *setfsgid()*.

```
#include <sys/fsuid.h>

int setfsuid(uid_t fsuid);
```

                              Always returns the previous file-system user ID

```
int setfsgid(gid_t fsgid);
```

                             Always returns the previous file-system group ID

The *setfsuid()* system call changes the file-system user ID of a process to the value
specified by *fsuid*. The *setfsgid()* system call changes the file system group ID to the
value specified by *fsgid*.

Again, there are rules about the kind of changes that can be made. The rules
for *setfsgid()* are similar to the rules for *setfsuid()*, which are as follows:

1. An unprivileged process can set the file-system user ID to the current value of
    the real user ID, effective user ID, file-system user ID (i.e., no change), or saved
    set-user-ID.

2. A privileged process can set the file-system user ID to any value.

The implementation of these calls is somewhat unpolished. To begin with, there
are no corresponding system calls that retrieve the current value of the file-system
IDs. In addition, the system calls do no error checking; if an unprivileged process
attempts to set its file-system ID to an unacceptable value, the attempt is silently
ignored. The return value from each of these system calls is the previous value of
the corresponding file-system ID, *whether the call succeeds or fails*. Thus, we do have a
way of finding out the current values of the file-system IDs, but only at the same
time as we try (either successfully or unsuccessfully) to change them.

Use of the *setfsuid()* and *setfsgid()* system calls is no longer necessary on Linux
and should be avoided in applications designed to be ported to other UNIX
implementations.

9.7.3   Retrieving and Modifying Supplementary Group IDs

The *getgroups()* system call returns the set of groups of which the calling process is
currently a member, in the array pointed to by *grouplist*.

```
#include <unistd.h>

int getgroups(int gidsetsize, gid_t grouplist[]);
```

      Returns number of group IDs placed in *grouplist* on success, or −1 on error

On Linux, as on most UNIX implementations, *getgroups()* simply returns the calling
process's supplementary group IDs. However, SUSv3 also allows an implementation to include the calling process's effective group ID in the returned *grouplist*.

The calling program must allocate the *grouplist* array and specify its length in the argument *gidsetsize*. On successful completion, *getgroups()* returns the number of group IDs placed in *grouplist*.

If the number of groups of which a process is a member exceeds *gidsetsize*, *getgroups()* returns an error (EINVAL). To avoid this possibility, we can size the *grouplist* array to be one greater (to portably allow for the possible inclusion of the effective group ID) than the constant NGROUPS_MAX (defined in <limits.h>), which defines the maximum number of supplementary groups of which a process may be a member. Thus, we could declare *grouplist* as follows:

```
gid_t grouplist[NGROUPS_MAX + 1];
```

In Linux kernels prior to 2.6.4, NGROUPS_MAX has the value 32. From kernel 2.6.4 onward, NGROUPS_MAX has the value 65,536.

An application can also determine the NGROUPS_MAX limit at run time in the following ways:

- Call *sysconf(_SC_NGROUPS_MAX)*. (We explain the use of *sysconf()* in Section 11.2.)
- Read the limit from the read-only, Linux-specific /proc/sys/kernel/ngroups_max file. This file is provided since kernel 2.6.4.

Alternatively, an application can make a call to *getgroups()* specifying *gidsetsize* as 0. In this case, *grouplist* is not modified, but the return value of the call gives the number of groups of which the process is a member.

The value obtained by any of these run-time techniques can then be used to dynamically allocate a *grouplist* array for a future *getgroups()* call.

A privileged process can use *setgroups()* and *initgroups()* to change its set of supplementary group IDs.

```
#define _BSD_SOURCE
#include <grp.h>

int setgroups(size_t gidsetsize, const gid_t *grouplist);
int initgroups(const char *user, gid_t group);
```
                                    Both return 0 on success, or −1 on error

The *setgroups()* system call replaces the calling process's supplementary group IDs with the set given in the array *grouplist*. The *gidsetsize* argument specifies the number of group IDs in the array argument *grouplist*.

The *initgroups()* function initializes the calling process's supplementary group IDs by scanning /etc/group and building a list of all groups of which the named *user* is a member. In addition, the group ID specified in *group* is also added to the process's set of supplementary group IDs.

The primary users of *initgroups()* are programs that create login sessions—for example, *login(1)*, which sets various process attributes prior to executing the user's login shell. Such programs typically obtain the value to be used for the *group* argument by reading the group ID field from the user's record in the password file. This is slightly confusing, since the group ID from the password file is not really a supplementary group, Instead, it defines the initial real group ID, effective group ID, and saved set-group-ID of the login shell. Nevertheless, this is how *initgroups()* is usually employed.

Although not part of SUSv3, *setgroups()* and *initgroups()* are available on all UNIX implementations.

9.7.4 Summary of Calls for Modifying Process Credentials

Table 9-1 summarizes the effects of the various system calls and library functions used to change process credentials.

Figure 9-1 provides a graphical overview of the same information given in Table 9-1. This diagram shows things from the perspective of the calls that change the user IDs, but the rules for changes to the group IDs are similar.

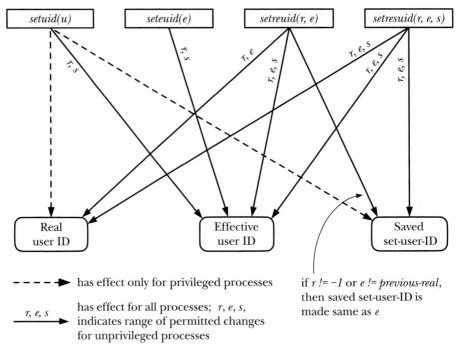

Figure 9-1: Effect of credential-changing functions on process user IDs

Table 9-1: Summary of interfaces used to change process credentials

Interface	Purpose and effect within:		Portability
	unprivileged process	**privileged process**	
setuid(u) *setgid(g)*	Change effective ID to the same value as current real or saved set ID	Change real, effective, and saved set IDs to any (single) value	Specified in SUSv3; BSD derivatives have different semantics
seteuid(e) *setegid(e)*	Change effective ID to the same value as current real or saved set ID	Change effective ID to any value	Specified in SUSv3
setreuid(r, e) *setregid(r, e)*	(Independently) change real ID to same value as current real or effective ID, and effective ID to same value as current real, effective, or saved set ID	(Independently) change real and effective IDs to any values	Specified in SUSv3, but operation varies across implementations
setresuid(r, e, s) *setresgid(r, e, s)*	(Independently) change real, effective, and saved set IDs to same value as current real, effective, or saved set ID	(Independently) change real, effective, and saved set IDs to any values	Not in SUSv3 and present on few other UNIX implementations
setfsuid(u) *setfsgid(u)*	Change file-system ID to same value as current real, effective, file system, or saved set ID	Change file-system ID to any value	Linux-specific
setgroups(n, l)	Can't be called from an unprivileged process	Set supplementary group IDs to any values	Not in SUSv3, but available on all UNIX implementations

Note the following supplementary information to Table 9-1:

- The *glibc* implementations of *seteuid()* and *setegid()* also allow the effective ID to be set to the same value it already has, but this is not specified in SUSv3.
- For calls to *setreuid()* and *setregid()* by both privileged and unprivileged processes, if *r* is not −1, or *e* is specified as a value different from the real ID prior to the call, then the saved set-user-ID or saved set-group-ID is also set to the same value as the (new) effective ID. (SUSv3 doesn't specify that *setreuid()* and *setregid()* make changes to the saved set IDs.)
- Whenever the effective user (group) ID is changed, the Linux-specific file-system user (group) ID is changed to the same value.
- Calls to *setresuid()* always modify the file-system user ID to have the same value as the effective user ID, regardless of whether the effective user ID is changed by the call. Calls to *setresgid()* have an analogous effect on the file-system group ID.

9.7.5 Example: Displaying Process Credentials

The program in Listing 9-1 uses the system calls and library functions described in the preceding pages to retrieve all of the process's user and group IDs, and then displays them.

Listing 9-1: Display all process user and group IDs

proccred/idshow.c

```c
#define _GNU_SOURCE
#include <unistd.h>
#include <sys/fsuid.h>
#include <limits.h>
#include "ugid_functions.h"   /* userNameFromId() & groupNameFromId() */
#include "tlpi_hdr.h"

#define SG_SIZE (NGROUPS_MAX + 1)

int
main(int argc, char *argv[])
{
    uid_t ruid, euid, suid, fsuid;
    gid_t rgid, egid, sgid, fsgid;
    gid_t suppGroups[SG_SIZE];
    int numGroups, j;
    char *p;

    if (getresuid(&ruid, &euid, &suid) == -1)
        errExit("getresuid");
    if (getresgid(&rgid, &egid, &sgid) == -1)
        errExit("getresgid");

    /* Attempts to change the file-system IDs are always ignored
       for unprivileged processes, but even so, the following
       calls return the current file-system IDs */

    fsuid = setfsuid(0);
    fsgid = setfsgid(0);

    printf("UID: ");
    p = userNameFromId(ruid);
    printf("real=%s (%ld); ", (p == NULL) ? "???" : p, (long) ruid);
    p = userNameFromId(euid);
    printf("eff=%s (%ld); ", (p == NULL) ? "???" : p, (long) euid);
    p = userNameFromId(suid);
    printf("saved=%s (%ld); ", (p == NULL) ? "???" : p, (long) suid);
    p = userNameFromId(fsuid);
    printf("fs=%s (%ld); ", (p == NULL) ? "???" : p, (long) fsuid);
    printf("\n");

    printf("GID: ");
    p = groupNameFromId(rgid);
    printf("real=%s (%ld); ", (p == NULL) ? "???" : p, (long) rgid);
```

```
        p = groupNameFromId(egid);
        printf("eff=%s (%ld); ", (p == NULL) ? "???" : p, (long) egid);
        p = groupNameFromId(sgid);
        printf("saved=%s (%ld); ", (p == NULL) ? "???" : p, (long) sgid);
        p = groupNameFromId(fsgid);
        printf("fs=%s (%ld); ", (p == NULL) ? "???" : p, (long) fsgid);
        printf("\n");

        numGroups = getgroups(SG_SIZE, suppGroups);
        if (numGroups == -1)
            errExit("getgroups");

        printf("Supplementary groups (%d): ", numGroups);
        for (j = 0; j < numGroups; j++) {
            p = groupNameFromId(suppGroups[j]);
            printf("%s (%ld) ", (p == NULL) ? "???" : p, (long) suppGroups[j]);
        }
        printf("\n");

        exit(EXIT_SUCCESS);
    }
```

——**proccred/idshow.c**

9.8   Summary

Each process has a number of associated user and group IDs (credentials). The real
IDs define the ownership of the process. On most UNIX implementations, the
effective IDs are used to determine a process's permissions when accessing
resources such as files. On Linux, however, the file-system IDs are used for determining permissions for accessing files, while the effective IDs are used for other
permission checks. (Because the file-system IDs normally have the same values as
the corresponding effective IDs, Linux behaves in the same way as other UNIX
implementations when checking file permissions.) A process's supplementary
group IDs are a further set of groups of which the process is considered to be a
member for the purpose of permission checking. Various system calls and library
functions allow a process to retrieve and change its user and group IDs.

When a set-user-ID program is run, the effective user ID of the process is set to
that of the owner of the file. This mechanism allows a user to assume the identity,
and thus the privileges, of another user while running a particular program. Correspondingly, set-group-ID programs change the effective group ID of the process
running a program. The saved set-user-ID and saved set-group-ID allow set-user-ID
and set-group-ID programs to temporarily drop and then later reassume privileges.

The user ID 0 is special. Normally, a single user account, named *root*, has this
user ID. Processes with an effective user ID of 0 are privileged—that is, they are
exempt from many of the permission checks normally performed when a process
makes various system calls (such as those used to arbitrarily change the various
process user and group IDs).

9.9 Exercises

9-1. Assume in each of the following cases that the initial set of process user IDs is *real=1000 effective=0 saved=0 file-system=0*. What would be the state of the user IDs after the following calls?

    a) *setuid(2000);*
    b) *setreuid(−1, 2000);*
    c) *seteuid(2000);*
    d) *setfsuid(2000);*
    e) *setresuid(−1, 2000, 3000);*

9-2. Is a process with the following user IDs privileged? Explain your answer.

```
real=0 effective=1000 saved=1000 file-system=1000
```

9-3. Implement *initgroups()* using *setgroups()* and library functions for retrieving information from the password and group files (Section 8.4). Remember that a process must be privileged in order to be able to call *setgroups()*.

9-4. If a process whose user IDs all have the value *X* executes a set-user-ID program whose user ID, *Y*, is nonzero, then the process credentials are set as follows:

```
real=X effective=Y saved=Y
```

(We ignore the file-system user ID, since it tracks the effective user ID.) Show the *setuid()*, *seteuid()*, *setreuid()*, and *setresuid()* calls, respectively, that would be used to perform the following operations:

    a) Suspend and resume the set-user-ID identity (i.e., switch the effective user ID to the value of the real user ID and then back to the saved set-user-ID).
    b) Permanently drop the set-user-ID identity (i.e., ensure that the effective user ID and the saved set-user-ID are set to the value of the real user ID).

(This exercise also requires the use of *getuid()* and *geteuid()* to retrieve the process's real and effective user IDs.) Note that for certain of the system calls listed above, some of these operations can't be performed.

9-5. Repeat the previous exercise for a process executing a set-user-ID-*root* program, which has the following initial set of process credentials:

```
real=X effective=0 saved=0
```

10

TIME

Within a program, we may be interested in two kinds of time:

- *Real time*: This is the time as measured either from some standard point (*calendar* time) or from some fixed point (typically the start) in the life of a process (*elapsed* or *wall clock* time). Obtaining the calendar time is useful to programs that, for example, timestamp database records or files. Measuring elapsed time is useful for a program that takes periodic actions or makes regular measurements from some external input device.

- *Process time*: This is the amount of CPU time used by a process. Measuring process time is useful for checking or optimizing the performance of a program or algorithm.

Most computer architectures have a built-in hardware clock that enables the kernel to measure real and process time. In this chapter, we look at system calls for dealing with both sorts of time, and library functions for converting between human-readable and internal representations of time. Since human-readable representations of time are dependent on the geographical location and on linguistic and cultural conventions, discussion of these representations leads us into an investigation of timezones and locales.

10.1 Calendar Time

Regardless of geographic location, UNIX systems represent time internally as a measure of seconds since the Epoch; that is, since midnight on the morning of 1 January 1970, Universal Coordinated Time (UTC, previously known as Greenwich Mean Time, or GMT). This is approximately the date when the UNIX system came into being. Calendar time is stored in variables of type *time_t*, an integer type specified by SUSv3.

> On 32-bit Linux systems, *time_t*, which is a signed integer, can represent dates in the range 13 December 1901 20:45:52 to 19 January 2038 03:14:07. (SUSv3 leaves the meaning of negative *time_t* values unspecified.) Thus, many current 32-bit UNIX systems face a theoretical *Year 2038* problem, which they may encounter before 2038, if they do calculations based on dates in the future. This problem will be significantly alleviated by the fact that by 2038, probably all UNIX systems will have long become 64-bit and beyond. However, 32-bit embedded systems, which typically have a much longer lifespan than desktop hardware, may still be afflicted by the problem. Furthermore, the problem will remain for any legacy data and applications that maintain time in a 32-bit *time_t* format.

The *gettimeofday()* system call returns the calendar time in the buffer pointed to by *tv*.

```
#include <sys/time.h>

int gettimeofday(struct timeval *tv, struct timezone *tz);
```
                                       Returns 0 on success, or −1 on error

The *tv* argument is a pointer to a structure of the following form:

```
struct timeval {
    time_t      tv_sec;     /* Seconds since 00:00:00, 1 Jan 1970 UTC */
    suseconds_t tv_usec;    /* Additional microseconds (long int) */
};
```

Although the *tv_usec* field affords microsecond precision, the accuracy of the value it returns is determined by the architecture-dependent implementation. (The *u* in *tv_usec* derives from the resemblance to the Greek letter μ ("mu") used in the metric system to denote one-millionth.) On modern x86-32 systems (i.e., Pentium systems with a Timestamp Counter register that is incremented once at each CPU clock cycle), *gettimeofday()* does provide microsecond accuracy.

The *tz* argument to *gettimeofday()* is a historical artifact. In older UNIX implementations, it was used to retrieve timezone information for the system. This argument is now obsolete and should always be specified as NULL. (SUSv4 marks *gettimeofday()* obsolete, presumably in favor of the POSIX clocks API described in Section 23.5.)

If the *tz* argument is supplied, then it returns a *timezone* structure whose fields contain whatever values were specified in the (obsolete) *tz* argument in a previous call to *settimeofday()*. This structure contains two fields: *tz_minuteswest* and *tz_dsttime*. The *tz_minuteswest* field indicates the number of minutes that must be added to times in this zone to match UTC, with a negative value indicating that an adjustment of minutes to the east of UTC (e.g., for Central European Time, one hour ahead of UTC, this field would contain the value –60). The *tz_dsttime* field contains a constant that was designed to represent the daylight saving time (DST) regime in force in this timezone. It is because the DST regime can't be represented using a simple algorithm that the *tz* argument is obsolete. (This field has never been supported on Linux.) See the *gettimeofday(2)* manual page for further details.

The *time()* system call returns the number of seconds since the Epoch (i.e., the same value that *gettimeofday()* returns in the *tv_sec* field of its *tv* argument).

```
#include <time.h>

time_t time(time_t *timep);
```
> Returns number of seconds since the Epoch, or *(time_t)* –1 on error

If the *timep* argument is not NULL, the number of seconds since the Epoch is also placed in the location to which *timep* points.

Since *time()* returns the same value in two ways, and the only possible error that can occur when using *time()* is to give an invalid address in the *timep* argument (EFAULT), we often simply use the following call (without error checking):

```
t = time(NULL);
```

> The reason for the existence of two system calls (*time()* and *gettimeofday()*) with essentially the same purpose is historical. Early UNIX implementations provided *time()*. 4.2BSD added the more precise *gettimeofday()* system call. The existence of *time()* as a system call is now redundant; it could be implemented as a library function that calls *gettimeofday()*.

10.2 Time-Conversion Functions

Figure 10-1 shows the functions used to convert between *time_t* values and other time formats, including printable representations. These functions shield us from the complexity brought to such conversions by timezones, daylight saving time (DST) regimes, and localization issues. (We describe timezones in Section 10.3 and locales in Section 10.4.)

> SUSv4 marks *ctime()* and *asctime()* obsolete, because they do not return localized strings (and they are nonreentrant).

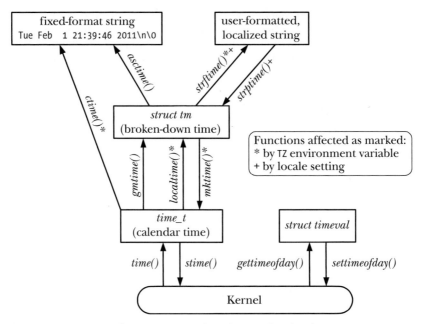

Figure 10-1: Functions for retrieving and working with calendar time

10.2.1 Converting *time_t* to Printable Form

The *ctime()* function provides a simple method of converting a *time_t* value into printable form.

```
#include <time.h>

char *ctime(const time_t *timep);
```

> Returns pointer to statically allocated string terminated
> by newline and \0 on success, or NULL on error

Given a pointer to a *time_t* value in *timep*, *ctime()* returns a 26-byte string containing the date and time in a standard format, as illustrated by the following example:

```
Wed Jun  8 14:22:34 2011
```

The string includes a terminating newline character and a terminating null byte. The *ctime()* function automatically accounts for local timezone and DST settings when performing the conversion. (We explain how these settings are determined in Section 10.3.) The returned string is statically allocated; future calls to *ctime()* will overwrite it.

SUSv3 states that calls to any of the functions *ctime()*, *gmtime()*, *localtime()*, or *asctime()* may overwrite the statically allocated structure that is returned by any of the other functions. In other words, these functions may share single copies of the returned character array and *tm* structure, and this is done in some versions of *glibc*. If we need to maintain the returned information across multiple calls to these functions, we must save local copies.

A reentrant version of *ctime()* is provided in the form of *ctime_r()*. (We explain reentrancy in Section 21.1.2.) This function permits the caller to specify an additional argument that is a pointer to a (caller-supplied) buffer that is used to return the time string. Other reentrant versions of functions mentioned in this chapter operate similarly.

10.2.2   Converting Between *time_t* and Broken-Down Time

The *gmtime()* and *localtime()* functions convert a *time_t* value into a so-called *broken-down time*. The broken-down time is placed in a statically allocated structure whose address is returned as the function result.

```
#include <time.h>

struct tm *gmtime(const time_t *timep);
struct tm *localtime(const time_t *timep);
```
                    Both return a pointer to a statically allocated broken-down
                              time structure on success, or NULL on error

The *gmtime()* function converts a calendar time into a broken-down time corresponding to UTC. (The letters *gm* derive from Greenwich Mean Time.) By contrast, *localtime()* takes into account timezone and DST settings to return a broken-down time corresponding to the system's local time.

> Reentrant versions of these functions are provided as *gmtime_r()* and *localtime_r()*.

The *tm* structure returned by these functions contains the date and time fields broken into individual parts. This structure has the following form:

```
struct tm {
    int tm_sec;        /* Seconds (0-60) */
    int tm_min;        /* Minutes (0-59) */
    int tm_hour;       /* Hours (0-23) */
    int tm_mday;       /* Day of the month (1-31) */
    int tm_mon;        /* Month (0-11) */
    int tm_year;       /* Year since 1900 */
    int tm_wday;       /* Day of the week (Sunday = 0)*/
    int tm_yday;       /* Day in the year (0-365; 1 Jan = 0)*/
    int tm_isdst;      /* Daylight saving time flag
                           > 0: DST is in effect;
                           = 0: DST is not effect;
                           < 0: DST information not available */
};
```

The *tm_sec* field can be up to 60 (rather than 59) to account for the leap seconds that are occasionally applied to adjust human calendars to the astronomically exact (the so-called *tropical*) year.

If the _BSD_SOURCE feature test macro is defined, then the *glibc* definition of the *tm* structure also includes two additional fields containing further information about the represented time. The first of these, *long int tm_gmtoff*, contains the number of seconds that the represented time falls east of UTC. The second field, *const char *tm_zone*, is the abbreviated timezone name (e.g., *CEST* for Central European Summer Time). SUSv3 doesn't specify either of these fields, and they appear on only a few other UNIX implementations (mainly BSD derivatives).

The *mktime()* function translates a broken-down time, expressed as local time, into a *time_t* value, which is returned as the function result. The caller supplies the broken-down time in a *tm* structure pointed to by *timeptr*. During this translation, the *tm_wday* and *tm_yday* fields of the input *tm* structure are ignored.

```
#include <time.h>

time_t mktime(struct tm *timeptr);
```
                    Returns seconds since the Epoch corresponding to *timeptr*
                    on success, or *(time_t)* −1 on error

The *mktime()* function may modify the structure pointed to by *timeptr*. At a minimum, it ensures that the *tm_wday* and *tm_yday* fields are set to values that correspond appropriately to the values of the other input fields.

In addition, *mktime()* doesn't require the other fields of the *tm* structure to be restricted to the ranges described earlier. For each field whose value is out of range, *mktime()* adjusts that field's value so that it is in range and makes suitable adjustments to the other fields. All of these adjustments are performed before *mktime()* updates the *tm_wday* and *tm_yday* fields and calculates the returned *time_t* value.

For example, if the input *tm_sec* field were 123, then on return, the value of this field would be 3, and the value of the *tm_min* field would have 2 added to whatever value it previously had. (And if that addition caused *tm_min* to overflow, then the *tm_min* value would be adjusted and the *tm_hour* field would be incremented, and so on.) These adjustments even apply for negative field values. For example, specifying −1 for *tm_sec* means the 59th second of the previous minute. This feature is useful since it allows us to perform date and time arithmetic on a broken-down time value.

The timezone setting is used by *mktime()* when performing the translation. In addition, the DST setting may or may not be used, depending on the value of the input *tm_isdst* field:

- If *tm_isdst* is 0, treat this time as standard time (i.e., ignore DST, even if it would be in effect at this time of year).

- If *tm_isdst* is greater than 0, treat this time as DST (i.e., behave as though DST is in effect, even if it would not normally be so at this time of year).

- If *tm_isdst* is less than 0, attempt to determine if DST would be in effect at this time of the year. This is typically the setting we want.

On completion (and regardless of the initial setting of *tm_isdst*), *mktime()* sets the *tm_isdst* field to a positive value if DST is in effect at the given date, or to 0 if DST is not in effect.

10.2.3 Converting Between Broken-Down Time and Printable Form

In this section, we describe functions that convert a broken-down time to printable form, and vice versa.

Converting from broken-down time to printable form

Given a pointer to a broken-down time structure in the argument *tm*, *asctime()* returns a pointer to a statically allocated string containing the time in the same form as *ctime()*.

```
#include <time.h>

char *asctime(const struct tm *timeptr);
```
> Returns pointer to statically allocated string terminated by
> newline and \0 on success, or NULL on error

By contrast with *ctime()*, local timezone settings have no effect on *asctime()*, since it is converting a broken-down time that is typically either already localized via *localtime()* or in UTC as returned by *gmtime()*.

As with *ctime()*, we have no control over the format of the string produced by *asctime()*.

> A reentrant version of *asctime()* is provided in the form of *asctime_r()*.

Listing 10-1 demonstrates the use of *asctime()*, as well as all of the time-conversion functions described so far in this chapter. This program retrieves the current calendar time, and then uses various time-conversion functions and displays their results. Here is an example of what we see when running this program in Munich, Germany, which (in winter) is on Central European Time, one hour ahead of UTC:

```
$ date
Tue Dec 28 16:01:51 CET 2010
$ ./calendar_time
Seconds since the Epoch (1 Jan 1970): 1293548517 (about 40.991 years)
  gettimeofday() returned 1293548517 secs, 715616 microsecs
Broken down by gmtime():
  year=110 mon=11 mday=28 hour=15 min=1 sec=57 wday=2 yday=361 isdst=0
Broken down by localtime():
  year=110 mon=11 mday=28 hour=16 min=1 sec=57 wday=2 yday=361 isdst=0

asctime() formats the gmtime() value as: Tue Dec 28 15:01:57 2010
ctime() formats the time() value as:     Tue Dec 28 16:01:57 2010
mktime() of gmtime() value:    1293544917 secs
mktime() of localtime() value: 1293548517 secs       3600 secs ahead of UTC
```

Listing 10-1: Retrieving and converting calendar times

––– time/calendar_time.c
```
#include <locale.h>
#include <time.h>
#include <sys/time.h>
#include "tlpi_hdr.h"
```

```c
#define SECONDS_IN_TROPICAL_YEAR (365.24219 * 24 * 60 * 60)

int
main(int argc, char *argv[])
{
    time_t t;
    struct tm *gmp, *locp;
    struct tm gm, loc;
    struct timeval tv;

    t = time(NULL);
    printf("Seconds since the Epoch (1 Jan 1970): %ld", (long) t);
    printf(" (about %6.3f years)\n", t / SECONDS_IN_TROPICAL_YEAR);

    if (gettimeofday(&tv, NULL) == -1)
        errExit("gettimeofday");
    printf("  gettimeofday() returned %ld secs, %ld microsecs\n",
            (long) tv.tv_sec, (long) tv.tv_usec);

    gmp = gmtime(&t);
    if (gmp == NULL)
        errExit("gmtime");

    gm = *gmp;          /* Save local copy, since *gmp may be modified
                           by asctime() or gmtime() */
    printf("Broken down by gmtime():\n");
    printf("  year=%d mon=%d mday=%d hour=%d min=%d sec=%d ", gm.tm_year,
            gm.tm_mon, gm.tm_mday, gm.tm_hour, gm.tm_min, gm.tm_sec);
    printf("wday=%d yday=%d isdst=%d\n", gm.tm_wday, gm.tm_yday, gm.tm_isdst);

    locp = localtime(&t);
    if (locp == NULL)
        errExit("localtime");

    loc = *locp;        /* Save local copy */

    printf("Broken down by localtime():\n");
    printf("  year=%d mon=%d mday=%d hour=%d min=%d sec=%d ",
            loc.tm_year, loc.tm_mon, loc.tm_mday,
            loc.tm_hour, loc.tm_min, loc.tm_sec);
    printf("wday=%d yday=%d isdst=%d\n\n",
            loc.tm_wday, loc.tm_yday, loc.tm_isdst);

    printf("asctime() formats the gmtime() value as: %s", asctime(&gm));
    printf("ctime() formats the time() value as:     %s", ctime(&t));

    printf("mktime() of gmtime() value:    %ld secs\n", (long) mktime(&gm));
    printf("mktime() of localtime() value: %ld secs\n", (long) mktime(&loc));

    exit(EXIT_SUCCESS);
}
```
———————————————————————————————————— **time/calendar_time.c**

The *strftime()* function provides us with more precise control when converting a broken-down time into printable form. Given a broken-down time pointed to by *timeptr*, *strftime()* places a corresponding null-terminated, date-plus-time string in the buffer pointed to by *outstr*.

```
#include <time.h>

size_t strftime(char *outstr, size_t maxsize, const char *format,
                const struct tm *timeptr);
```
                        Returns number of bytes placed in *outstr* (excluding
                            terminating null byte) on success, or 0 on error

The string returned in *outstr* is formatted according to the specification in *format*. The *maxsize* argument specifies the maximum space available in *outstr*. Unlike *ctime()* and *asctime()*, *strftime()* doesn't include a newline character at the end of the string (unless one is included in *format*).

On success, *strftime()* returns the number of bytes placed in *outstr*, excluding the terminating null byte. If the total length of the resulting string, including the terminating null byte, would exceed *maxsize* bytes, then *strftime()* returns 0 to indicate an error, and the contents of *outstr* are indeterminate.

The *format* argument to *strftime()* is a string akin to that given to *printf()*. Sequences beginning with a percent character (%) are conversion specifications, which are replaced by various components of the date and time according to the specifier character following the percent character. A rich set of conversion specifiers is provided, a subset of which is listed in Table 10-1. (For a complete list, see the *strftime(3)* manual page.) Except as otherwise noted, all of these conversion specifiers are standardized in SUSv3.

The %U and %W specifiers both produce a week number in the year. The %U week numbers are calculated such that the first week containing a Sunday is numbered 1, and the partial week preceding that is numbered 0. If Sunday happens to fall as the first day of the year, then there is no week 0, and the last day of the year falls in week 53. The %W week numbers work in the same way, but with Monday rather than Sunday.

Often, we want to display the current time in various demonstration programs in this book. For this purpose we provide the function *currTime()*, which returns a string containing the current time as formatted by *strftime()* when given the argument *format*.

```
#include "curr_time.h"

char *currTime(const char *format);
```
                Returns pointer to statically allocated string, or NULL on error

The *currTime()* function implementation is shown in Listing 10-2.

Table 10-1: Selected conversion specifiers for *strftime()*

Specifier	Description	Example
%%	A % character	%
%a	Abbreviated weekday name	Tue
%A	Full weekday name	Tuesday
%b, %h	Abbreviated month name	Feb
%B	Full month name	February
%c	Date and time	Tue Feb 1 21:39:46 2011
%d	Day of month (2 digits, 01 to 31)	01
%D	American date (same as %m/%d/%y)	02/01/11
%e	Day of month (2 characters)	1
%F	ISO date (same as %Y-%m-%d)	2011-02-01
%H	Hour (24-hour clock, 2 digits)	21
%I	Hour (12-hour clock, 2 digits)	09
%j	Day of year (3 digits, 001 to 366)	032
%m	Decimal month (2 digits, 01 to 12)	02
%M	Minute (2 digits)	39
%p	AM/PM	PM
%P	am/pm (GNU extension)	pm
%R	24-hour time (same as %H:%M)	21:39
%S	Second (00 to 60)	46
%T	Time (same as %H:%M:%S)	21:39:46
%u	Weekday number (1 to 7, Monday = 1)	2
%U	Sunday week number (00 to 53)	05
%w	Weekday number (0 to 6, Sunday = 0)	2
%W	Monday week number (00 to 53)	05
%x	Date (localized)	02/01/11
%X	Time (localized)	21:39:46
%y	2-digit year	11
%Y	4-digit year	2011
%Z	Timezone name	CET

Listing 10-2: A function that returns a string containing the current time

———time/curr_time.c

```
#include <time.h>
#include "curr_time.h"          /* Declares function defined here */

#define BUF_SIZE 1000

/* Return a string containing the current time formatted according to
   the specification in 'format' (see strftime(3) for specifiers).
   If 'format' is NULL, we use "%c" as a specifier (which gives the
   date and time as for ctime(3), but without the trailing newline).
   Returns NULL on error. */
```

```
char *
currTime(const char *format)
{
    static char buf[BUF_SIZE];   /* Nonreentrant */
    time_t t;
    size_t s;
    struct tm *tm;

    t = time(NULL);
    tm = localtime(&t);
    if (tm == NULL)
        return NULL;

    s = strftime(buf, BUF_SIZE, (format != NULL) ? format : "%c", tm);

    return (s == 0) ? NULL : buf;
}
```

Converting from printable form to broken-down time

The *strptime()* function is the converse of *strftime()*. It converts a date-plus-time string to a broken-down time.

```
#define _XOPEN_SOURCE
#include <time.h>

char *strptime(const char *str, const char *format, struct tm *timeptr);
                            Returns pointer to next unprocessed character in
                                       str on success, or NULL on error
```

The *strptime()* function uses the specification given in *format* to parse the date-plus-time string given in *str*, and places the converted broken-down time in the structure pointed to by *timeptr*.

On success, *strptime()* returns a pointer to the next unprocessed character in *str*. (This is useful if the string contains further information to be processed by the calling program.) If the complete format string could not be matched, *strptime()* returns NULL to indicate the error.

The format specification given to *strptime()* is akin to that given to *scanf(3)*. It contains the following types of characters:

- conversion specifications beginning with a percent character (%);

- white-space characters, which match zero or more white spaces in the input string; and

- non-white-space characters (other than %), which must match exactly the same characters in the input string.

The conversion specifications are similar to those given to *strftime()* (Table 10-1). The major difference is that the specifiers are more general. For example, both %a and %A can accept a weekday name in either full or abbreviated form, and %d or %e can be used to read a day of the month with or without a leading 0 in the case of single-digit days. In addition, case is ignored; for example, *May* and *MAY* are equivalent month names. The string %% is used to match a percent character in the input string. The *strptime(3)* manual page provides more details.

The *glibc* implementation of *strptime()* doesn't modify those fields of the *tm* structure that are not initialized by specifiers in *format*. This means that we can employ a series of *strptime()* calls to construct a single *tm* structure from information in multiple strings, such as a date string and a time string. While SUSv3 permits this behavior, it doesn't require it, and so we can't rely on it on other UNIX implementations. In a portable application, we must ensure that *str* and *format* contain input that will set all fields of the resulting *tm* structure, or make sure that the *tm* structure is suitably initialized before calling *strptime()*. In most cases, it would be sufficient to zero out the entire structure using *memset()*, but be aware that a value of 0 in the *tm_mday* field corresponds to the last day of the previous month in *glibc* and many other implementations of the time-conversion functions. Finally, note that *strptime()* never sets the value of the *tm_isdst* field of the *tm* structure.

> The GNU C library also provides two other functions that serve a similar purpose to *strptime()*: *getdate()* (specified in SUSv3 and widely available) and its reentrant analog *getdate_r()* (not specified in SUSv3 and available on only a few other UNIX implementations). We don't describe these functions here, because they employ an external file (identified by the environment variable DATEMSK) to specify the format used for scanning the date, which makes them somewhat awkward to use and also creates security vulnerabilities in set-user-ID programs.

Listing 10-3 demonstrates the use of *strptime()* and *strftime()*. This program takes a command-line argument containing a date and time, converts this to a broken-down time using *strptime()*, and then displays the result of performing the reverse conversion using *strftime()*. The program takes up to three arguments, of which the first two are required. The first argument is the string containing a date and time. The second argument is the format specification to be used by *strptime()* to parse the first argument. The optional third argument is the format string to be used by *strftime()* for the reverse conversion. If this argument is omitted, a default format string is used. (We describe the *setlocale()* function used in this program in Section 10.4.) The following shell session log shows some examples of the use of this program:

```
$ ./strtime "9:39:46pm 1 Feb 2011" "%I:%M:%S%p %d %b %Y"
calendar time (seconds since Epoch): 1296592786
strftime() yields: 21:39:46 Tuesday, 01 February 2011 CET
```

The following usage is similar, but this time we explicitly specify a format for *strftime()*:

```
$ ./strtime "9:39:46pm 1 Feb 2011" "%I:%M:%S%p %d %b %Y" "%F %T"
calendar time (seconds since Epoch): 1296592786
strftime() yields: 2011-02-01 21:39:46
```

Listing 10-3: Retrieving and converting calendar times

── time/strtime.c
```
#define _XOPEN_SOURCE
#include <time.h>
#include <locale.h>
#include "tlpi_hdr.h"

#define SBUF_SIZE 1000

int
main(int argc, char *argv[])
{
    struct tm tm;
    char sbuf[SBUF_SIZE];
    char *ofmt;

    if (argc < 3 || strcmp(argv[1], "--help") == 0)
        usageErr("%s input-date-time in-format [out-format]\n", argv[0]);

    if (setlocale(LC_ALL, "") == NULL)
        errExit("setlocale");    /* Use locale settings in conversions */

    memset(&tm, 0, sizeof(struct tm));          /* Initialize 'tm' */
    if (strptime(argv[1], argv[2], &tm) == NULL)
        fatal("strptime");

    tm.tm_isdst = -1;          /* Not set by strptime(); tells mktime()
                                  to determine if DST is in effect */
    printf("calendar time (seconds since Epoch): %ld\n", (long) mktime(&tm));

    ofmt = (argc > 3) ? argv[3] : "%H:%M:%S %A, %d %B %Y %Z";
    if (strftime(sbuf, SBUF_SIZE, ofmt, &tm) == 0)
        fatal("strftime returned 0");
    printf("strftime() yields: %s\n", sbuf);

    exit(EXIT_SUCCESS);
}
```
── time/strtime.c

10.3 Timezones

Different countries (and sometimes even different regions within a single country) operate on different timezones and DST regimes. Programs that input and output times must take into account the timezone and DST regime of the system on which they are run. Fortunately, all of the details are handled by the C library.

Timezone definitions

Timezone information tends to be both voluminous and volatile. For this reason, rather than encoding it directly into programs or libraries, the system maintains this information in files in standard formats.

These files reside in the directory /usr/share/zoneinfo. Each file in this directory contains information about the timezone regime in a particular country or region. These files are named according to the timezone they describe, so we may find files with names such as EST (US Eastern Standard Time), CET (Central European Time), UTC, Turkey, and Iran. In addition, subdirectories can be used to hierarchically group related timezones. Under a directory such as Pacific, we may find the files Auckland, Port_Moresby, and Galapagos. When we specify a timezone for use by a program, in effect, we are specifying a relative pathname for one of the timezone files in this directory.

The local time for the system is defined by the timezone file /etc/localtime, which is often linked to one of the files in /usr/share/zoneinfo.

> The format of timezone files is documented in the *tzfile(5)* manual page. Timezone files are built using *zic(8)*, the *zone information compiler*. The *zdump(8)* command can be used to display the time as it would be currently according to the timezone in a specified timezone file.

Specifying the timezone for a program

To specify a timezone when running a program, we set the TZ environment variable to a string consisting of a colon (:) followed by one of the timezone names defined in /usr/share/zoneinfo. Setting the timezone automatically influences the functions *ctime()*, *localtime()*, *mktime()*, and *strftime()*.

To obtain the current timezone setting, each of these functions uses *tzset(3)*, which initializes three global variables:

```
char *tzname[2];    /* Name of timezone and alternate (DST) timezone */
int daylight;       /* Nonzero if there is an alternate (DST) timezone */
long timezone;      /* Seconds difference between UTC and local
                       standard time */
```

The *tzset()* function first checks the TZ environment variable. If this variable is not set, then the timezone is initialized to the default defined in the timezone file /etc/localtime. If the TZ environment variable is defined with a value that can't be matched to a timezone file, or it is an empty string, then UTC is used. The TZDIR environment variable (a nonstandard GNU-extension) can be set to the name of a directory in which timezone information should be sought instead of in the default /usr/share/zoneinfo.

We can see the effect of the TZ variable by running the program in Listing 10-4. In the first run, we see the output corresponding to the system's default timezone (Central European Time, CET). In the second run, we specify the timezone for New Zealand, which at this time of year is on daylight saving time, 12 hours ahead of CET.

```
$ ./show_time
ctime() of time() value is:  Tue Feb  1 10:25:56 2011
asctime() of local time is:  Tue Feb  1 10:25:56 2011
strftime() of local time is: Tuesday, 01 Feb 2011, 10:25:56 CET
$ TZ=":Pacific/Auckland" ./show_time
ctime() of time() value is:  Tue Feb  1 22:26:19 2011
asctime() of local time is:  Tue Feb  1 22:26:19 2011
strftime() of local time is: Tuesday, 01 February 2011, 22:26:19 NZDT
```

Listing 10-4: Demonstrate the effect of timezones and locales

—————————————————————————————— `time/show_time.c`

```c
#include <time.h>
#include <locale.h>
#include "tlpi_hdr.h"

#define BUF_SIZE 200

int
main(int argc, char *argv[])
{
    time_t t;
    struct tm *loc;
    char buf[BUF_SIZE];

    if (setlocale(LC_ALL, "") == NULL)
        errExit("setlocale");    /* Use locale settings in conversions */

    t = time(NULL);

    printf("ctime() of time() value is:  %s", ctime(&t));

    loc = localtime(&t);
    if (loc == NULL)
        errExit("localtime");

    printf("asctime() of local time is:  %s", asctime(loc));

    if (strftime(buf, BUF_SIZE, "%A, %d %B %Y, %H:%M:%S %Z", loc) == 0)
        fatal("strftime returned 0");
    printf("strftime() of local time is: %s\n", buf);

    exit(EXIT_SUCCESS);
}
```

—————————————————————————————— `time/show_time.c`

SUSv3 defines two general ways in which the TZ environment variable can be set. As just described, TZ can be set to a character sequence consisting of a colon plus a string that identifies the timezone in an implementation-specific manner, typically as a pathname for a timezone description file. (Linux and some other UNIX implementations permit the colon to be omitted when using this form, but SUSv3 doesn't specify this; for portability, we should always include the colon.)

The other method of setting TZ is fully specified in SUSv3. In this method, we assign a string of the following form to TZ:

———
std offset [*dst* [*offset*][, *start-date* [*/time*] , *end-date* [*/time*]]]
———

Spaces are included in the line above for clarity, but none should appear in the TZ value. The brackets ([]) are used to indicate optional components.

The *std* and *dst* components are strings that define names for the standard and DST timezones; for example, *CET* and *CEST* for Central European Time and Central European Summer Time. The *offset* in each case specifies the positive or negative adjustment to add to the local time to convert it to UTC. The final four components provide a rule describing when the change from standard time to DST occurs.

The dates can be specified in a variety of forms, one of which is Mm.n.d. This notation means day d (0 = Sunday, 6 = Saturday) of week n (1 to 5, where 5 always means the last d day) of month m (1 to 12). If the *time* is omitted, it defaults to 02:00:00 (2 AM) in each case.

Here is how we could define TZ for Central Europe, where standard time is one hour ahead of UTC, and DST—running from the last Sunday in March to the last Sunday in October—is 2 hours ahead of UTC:

```
TZ="CET-1:00:00CEST-2:00:00,M3.5.0,M10.5.0"
```

We omitted the specification of the time for the DST changeover, since it occurs at the default of 02:00:00. Of course, the preceding form is less readable than the near equivalent:

```
TZ=":Europe/Berlin"
```

10.4 Locales

Several thousand languages are spoken across the world, of which a significant percentage are regularly used on computer systems. Furthermore, different countries use different conventions for displaying information such as numbers, currency amounts, dates, and times. For example, in most European countries, a comma, rather than a decimal point, is used to separate the integer and fractional parts of (real) numbers, and most countries use formats for writing dates that are different from the *MM/DD/YY* format used in the United States. SUSv3 defines a *locale* as the "subset of a user's environment that depends on language and cultural conventions."

Ideally, all programs designed to run in more than one location should deal with locales in order to display and input information in the user's preferred language and format. This constitutes the complex subject of *internationalization*. In the ideal world, we would write a program once, and then, wherever it was run, it would automatically do the right things when performing I/O; that is, it would perform the task of *localization*. Internationalizing programs is a somewhat time-consuming job, although various tools are available to ease the task. Program libraries such as *glibc* also provide facilities to help with internationalization.

> The term *internationalization* is often written as *I18N*, for *I* plus 18 letters plus *N*. As well as being quicker to write, this term has the advantage of avoiding the difference in the spelling of the term itself in British and American English.

Locale definitions

Like timezone information, locale information tends to be both voluminous and volatile. For this reason, rather than requiring each program and library to store locale information, the system maintains this information in files in standard formats.

Locale information is maintained in a directory hierarchy under /usr/share/locale (or /usr/lib/locale in some distributions). Each subdirectory under this directory contains information about a particular locale. These directories are named using the following convention:

---

language[_*territory*[.*codeset*]][@*modifier*]

The *language* is a two-letter ISO language code, and the *territory* is a two-letter ISO country code. The *codeset* designates a character-encoding set. The *modifier* provides a means of distinguishing multiple locale directories whose language, territory, and codeset are the same. An example of a complete locale directory name is de_DE.utf-8@euro, as the locale for: German language, Germany, UTF-8 character encoding, employing the euro as the monetary unit.

As indicated by the brackets shown in the directory naming format, various parts of the name of a locale directory can be omitted. Often the name consists of just a language and a territory. Thus, the directory en_US is the locale directory for the (English-speaking) United States, and fr_CH is the locale directory for the French-speaking region of Switzerland.

> The *CH* stands for *Confoederatio Helvetica*, the Latin (and thus locally language-neutral) name for Switzerland. With four official national languages, Switzerland is an example of a locale analog of a country with multiple timezones.

When we specify a locale to be used within a program, we are, in effect, specifying the name of one of the subdirectories under /usr/share/locale. If the locale specified to the program doesn't match a locale directory name exactly, then the C library searches for a match by stripping components from the specified locale in the following order:

1. codeset
2. normalized codeset
3. territory
4. modifier

The normalized codeset is a version of the codeset name in which all nonalphanumeric characters are removed, all letters are converted to lowercase, and the resulting string is preprended with the characters iso. The aim of normalizing is to handle variations in the capitalization and punctuation (e.g., extra hyphens) of codeset names.

As an example of this stripping process, if the locale for a program is specified as fr_CH.utf-8, but no locale directory by that name exists, then the fr_CH locale directory will be matched if it exists. If the fr_CH directory doesn't exist, then the fr locale directory will be used. In the unlikely event that the fr directory doesn't exist, then the *setlocale()* function, described shortly, will report an error.

> The file /usr/share/locale/locale.alias defines alternative ways of specifying locales to a program. See the *locale.aliases(5)* manual page for details.

Under each locale subdirectory is a standard set of files that specify the conventions for this locale, as shown in Table 10-2. Note the following further points concerning the information in this table:

- The LC_COLLATE file defines a set of rules describing how the characters in a character set are ordered (i.e., the "alphabetical" order for the character set). These rules determine the operation of the *strcoll(3)* and *strxfrm(3)* functions. Even languages using Latin-based scripts don't follow the same ordering rules. For example, several European languages have additional letters that, in some cases, sort after the letter *Z*. Other special cases include the Spanish two-letter sequence *ll*, which sorts as a single letter after *l*, and the German umlauted characters such as *ä*, which corresponds to *ae* and sorts as those two letters.

- The LC_MESSAGES directory is one step toward internationalizing the messages displayed by a program. More extensive internationalization of program messages can be accomplished through the use of either message catalogs (see the *catopen(3)* and *catgets(3)* manual pages) or the GNU *gettext* API (available at *http://www.gnu.org/*).

  Version 2.2.2 of *glibc* introduced a number of new, nonstandard locale categories. LC_ADDRESS defines rules for the locale-specific representation of a postal address. LC_IDENTIFICATION specifies information identifying the locale. LC_MEASUREMENT defines the measurement system for the locale (e.g., metric versus imperial). LC_NAME defines the locale-specific rules for representation of a person's names and title. LC_PAPER defines the standard paper size for the locale (e.g., US letter versus the A4 format used in most other countries). LC_TELEPHONE defines the rules for locale-specific representation of domestic and international telephone numbers, as well as the international country prefix and international dial-out prefix.

Table 10-2: Contents of locale-specific subdirectories

Filename	Purpose
LC_CTYPE	A file containing character classifications (see *isalpha(3)*) and rules for case conversion
LC_COLLATE	A file containing the collation rules for a character set
LC_MONETARY	A file containing formatting rules for monetary values (see *localeconv(3)* and `<locale.h>`)
LC_NUMERIC	A file containing formatting rules for numbers other than monetary values (see *localeconv(3)* and `<locale.h>`)
LC_TIME	A file containing formatting rules for dates and times
LC_MESSAGES	A directory containing files specifying formats and values used for affirmative and negative (yes/no) responses

The actual locales that are defined on a system can vary. SUSv3 doesn't make any requirements about this, except that a standard locale called *POSIX* (and synonymously, *C*, a name that exists for historical reasons) must be defined. This locale mirrors the historical behavior of UNIX systems. Thus, it is based on an ASCII character set, and uses English for names of days and months, and for yes/no responses. The monetary and numeric components of this locale are undefined.

> The *locale* command displays information about the current locale environment (within the shell). The command *locale -a* lists the full set of locales defined on the system.

Specifying the locale for a program

The *setlocale()* function is used to both set and query a program's current locale.

```
#include <locale.h>

char *setlocale(int category, const char *locale);
```
> Returns pointer to a (usually statically allocated) string identifying the new or current locale on success, or NULL on error

The *category* argument selects which part of the locale to set or query, and is specified as one of a set of constants whose names are the same as the locale categories listed in Table 10-2. Thus, for example, it is possible to set the locale for time displays to be Germany, while setting the locale for monetary displays to US dollars. Alternatively, and more commonly, we can use the value LC_ALL to specify that we want to set all aspects of the locale.

There are two different methods of setting the locale using *setlocale()*. The *locale* argument may be a string specifying one of the locales defined on the system (i.e., the name of one of the subdirectories under /usr/lib/locale), such as de_DE or en_US. Alternatively, *locale* may be specified as an empty string, meaning that locale settings should be taken from environment variables:

```
setlocale(LC_ALL, "");
```

We must make this call in order for a program to be cognizant of the locale environment variables. If the call is omitted, these environment variables will have no effect on the program.

When running a program that makes a *setlocale(LC_ALL, "")* call, we can control various aspects of the locale using a set of environment variables whose names again correspond to the categories listed in Table 10-2: LC_CTYPE, LC_COLLATE, LC_MONETARY, LC_NUMERIC, LC_TIME, and LC_MESSAGES. Alternatively, we can use the LC_ALL or the LANG environment variable to specify the setting of the entire locale. If more than one of the preceding variables is set, then LC_ALL has precedence over all of the other LC_* environment variables, and LANG has lowest precedence. Thus, it is possible to use LANG to set a default locale for all categories, and then use individual LC_* variables to set aspects of the locale to something other than this default.

As its result, *setlocale()* returns a pointer to a (usually statically allocated) string that identifies the locale setting for this category. If we are interested only in discovering the current locale setting, without changing it, then we can specify the *locale* argument as NULL.

Locale settings control the operation of a wide range of GNU/Linux utilities, as well as many functions in *glibc*. Among these are the functions *strftime()* and *strptime()* (Section 10.2.3), as shown by the results from *strftime()* when we run the program in Listing 10-4 in a number of different locales:

```
$ LANG=de_DE ./show_time                        German locale
ctime() of time() value is:  Tue Feb  1 12:23:39 2011
asctime() of local time is:  Tue Feb  1 12:23:39 2011
strftime() of local time is: Dienstag, 01 Februar 2011, 12:23:39 CET
```

The next run demonstrates that the LC_TIME has precedence over LANG:

```
$ LANG=de_DE LC_TIME=it_IT ./show_time          German and Italian locales
ctime() of time() value is:  Tue Feb  1 12:24:03 2011
asctime() of local time is:  Tue Feb  1 12:24:03 2011
strftime() of local time is: martedì, 01 febbraio 2011, 12:24:03 CET
```

And this run demonstrates that LC_ALL has precedence over LC_TIME:

```
$ LC_ALL=fr_FR LC_TIME=en_US ./show_time        French and US locales
ctime() of time() value is:  Tue Feb  1 12:25:38 2011
asctime() of local time is:  Tue Feb  1 12:25:38 2011
strftime() of local time is: mardi, 01 février 2011, 12:25:38 CET
```

10.5 Updating the System Clock

We now look at two interfaces that update the system clock: *settimeofday()* and *adjtime()*. These interfaces are rarely used by application programs (since the system time is usually maintained by tools such as the *Network Time Protocol* daemon), and they require that the caller be privileged (CAP_SYS_TIME).

The *settimeofday()* system call performs the converse of *gettimeofday()* (which we described in Section 10.1): it sets the system's calendar time to the number of seconds and microseconds specified in the *timeval* structure pointed to by *tv*.

```
#define _BSD_SOURCE
#include <sys/time.h>

int settimeofday(const struct timeval *tv, const struct timezone *tz);
```
                                          Returns 0 on success, or −1 on error

As with *gettimeofday()*, the use of the *tz* argument is obsolete, and this argument should always be specified as NULL.

The microsecond precision of the *tv.tv_usec* field doesn't mean that we have microsecond accuracy in controlling the system clock, since the clock's granularity may be larger than one microsecond.

Although *settimeofday()* is not specified in SUSv3, it is widely available on other UNIX implementations.

> Linux also provides the *stime()* system call for setting the system clock. The difference between *settimeofday()* and *stime()* is that the latter call allows the new calendar time to be expressed with a precision of only 1 second. As with *time()* and *gettimeofday()*, the reason for the existence of both *stime()* and *settimeofday()* is historical: the latter, more precise call was added by 4.2BSD.

Abrupt changes in the system time of the sort caused by calls to *settimeofday()* can have deleterious effects on applications (e.g., *make(1)*, a database system using timestamps, or time-stamped log files) that depend on a monotonically increasing system clock. For this reason, when making small changes to the time (of the order of a few seconds), it is usually preferable to use the *adjtime()* library function, which causes the system clock to gradually adjust to the desired value.

```
#define _BSD_SOURCE
#include <sys/time.h>

int adjtime(struct timeval *delta, struct timeval *olddelta);
```
                                        Returns 0 on success, or –1 on error

The *delta* argument points to a *timeval* structure that specifies the number of seconds and microseconds by which to change the time. If this value is positive, then a small amount of additional time is added to the system clock each second, until the desired amount of time has been added. If the *delta* value is negative, the clock is slowed down in a similar fashion.

> The rate of clock adjustment on Linux/x86-32 amounts to 1 second per 2000 seconds (or 43.2 seconds per day).

It may be that an incomplete clock adjustment was in progress at the time of the *adjtime()* call. In this case, the amount of remaining, unadjusted time is returned in the *timeval* structure pointed to by *olddelta*. If we are not interested in this value, we can specify *olddelta* as NULL. Conversely, if we are interested only in knowing the currently outstanding time correction to be made, and don't want to change the value, we can specify the *delta* argument as NULL.

Although not specified in SUSv3, *adjtime()* is available on most UNIX implementations.

> On Linux, *adjtime()* is implemented on top of a more general (and complex) Linux-specific system call, *adjtimex()*. This system call is employed by the *Network Time Protocol* (NTP) daemon. For further information, refer to the Linux source code, the Linux *adjtimex(2)* manual page, and the NTP specification ([Mills, 1992]).

10.6 The Software Clock (Jiffies)

The accuracy of various time-related system calls described in this book is limited to the resolution of the system *software clock*, which measures time in units called *jiffies*. The size of a jiffy is defined by the constant HZ within the kernel source code. This is the unit in which the kernel allocates the CPU to processes under the round-robin time-sharing scheduling algorithm (Section 35.1).

On Linux/x86-32 in kernel versions up to and including 2.4, the rate of the software clock was 100 hertz; that is, a jiffy is 10 milliseconds.

Because CPU speeds have greatly increased since Linux was first implemented, in kernel 2.6.0, the rate of the software clock was raised to 1000 hertz on Linux/x86-32. The advantages of a higher software clock rate are that timers can operate with greater accuracy and time measurements can be made with greater precision. However, it isn't desirable to set the clock rate to arbitrarily high values, because each clock interrupt consumes a small amount of CPU time, which is time that the CPU can't spend executing processes.

Debate among kernel developers eventually resulted in the software clock rate becoming a configurable kernel option (under *Processor type and features, Timer frequency*). Since kernel 2.6.13, the clock rate can be set to 100, 250 (the default), or 1000 hertz, giving jiffy values of 10, 4, and 1 milliseconds, respectively. Since kernel 2.6.20, a further frequency is available: 300 hertz, a number that divides evenly for two common video frame rates: 25 frames per second (PAL) and 30 frames per second (NTSC).

10.7 Process Time

Process time is the amount of CPU time used by a process since it was created. For recording purposes, the kernel separates CPU time into the following two components:

- *User CPU time* is the amount of time spent executing in user mode. Sometimes referred to as *virtual time*, this is the time that it appears to the program that it has access to the CPU.

- *System CPU time* is amount of time spent executing in kernel mode. This is the time that the kernel spends executing system calls or performing other tasks on behalf of the program (e.g., servicing page faults).

Sometimes, we refer to process time as the *total CPU time* consumed by the process.

When we run a program from the shell, we can use the *time(1)* command to obtain both process time values, as well as the real time required to run the program:

```
$ time ./myprog
real    0m4.84s
user    0m1.030s
sys     0m3.43s
```

The *times()* system call retrieves process time information, returning it in the structure pointed to by *buf*.

```
#include <sys/times.h>

clock_t times(struct tms *buf);
```
>   Returns number of clock ticks (*sysconf(_SC_CLK_TCK)*) since
>   "arbitrary" time in past on success, or *(clock_t)* −1 on error

This *tms* structure pointed to by *buf* has the following form:

```
struct tms {
    clock_t tms_utime;    /* User CPU time used by caller */
    clock_t tms_stime;    /* System CPU time used by caller */
```

```
    clock_t tms_cutime;  /* User CPU time of all (waited for) children */
    clock_t tms_cstime;  /* System CPU time of all (waited for) children */
};
```

The first two fields of the *tms* structure return the user and system components of CPU time used so far by the calling process. The last two fields return information about the CPU time used by all child processes that have terminated and for which the parent (i.e., the caller of *times()*) has done a *wait()* system call.

The *clock_t* data type used to type the four fields of the *tms* structure is an integer type that measures time in units called *clock ticks*. We can call *sysconf(_SC_CLK_TCK)* to obtain the number of clock ticks per second, and then divide a *clock_t* value by this number to convert to seconds. (We describe *sysconf()* in Section 11.2.)

> On most Linux hardware architectures, *sysconf(_SC_CLK_TCK)* returns the number 100. This corresponds to the kernel constant USER_HZ. However, USER_HZ can be defined with a value other than 100 on a few architectures, such as Alpha and IA-64.

On success, *times()* returns the elapsed (real) time in clock ticks since some arbitrary point in the past. SUSv3 deliberately does not specify what this point is, merely stating that it will be constant during the life of the calling process. Therefore, the only portable use of this return value is to measure elapsed time in the execution of the process by calculating the difference in the value returned by pairs of *times()* calls. However, even for this use, the return value of *times()* is unreliable, since it can overflow the range of *clock_t*, at which point the value would cycle to start again at 0 (i.e., a later *times()* call could return a number that is lower than an earlier *times()* call). The reliable way to measure the passage of elapsed time is to use *gettimeofday()* (described in Section 10.1).

On Linux, we can specify *buf* as NULL; in this case, *times()* simply returns a function result. However, this is not portable. The use of NULL for *buf* is not specified in SUSv3, and many other UNIX implementations require a non-NULL value for this argument.

The *clock()* function provides a simpler interface for retrieving the process time. It returns a single value that measures the total (i.e., user plus system) CPU time used by the calling process.

```
#include <time.h>

clock_t clock(void);
```
                    Returns total CPU time used by calling process measured in
                              CLOCKS_PER_SEC, or *(clock_t)* −1 on error

---

The value returned by *clock()* is measured in units of CLOCKS_PER_SEC, so we must divide by this value to arrive at the number of seconds of CPU time used by the process. CLOCKS_PER_SEC is fixed at 1 million by POSIX.1, regardless of the resolution of the underlying software clock (Section 10.6). The accuracy of *clock()* is nevertheless limited to the resolution of the software clock.

Although the *clock_t* return type of *clock()* is the same data type that is used in the *times()* call, the units of measurement employed by these two interfaces are different. This is the result of historically conflicting definitions of *clock_t* in POSIX.1 and the C programming language standard.

Even though `CLOCKS_PER_SEC` is fixed at 1 million, SUSv3 notes that this constant could be an integer variable on non-XSI-conformant systems, so that we can't portably treat it as a compile-time constant (i.e., we can't use it in #ifdef preprocessor expressions). Because it may be defined as a long integer (i.e., 1000000L), we always cast this constant to *long* so that we can portably print it with *printf()* (see Section 3.6.2).

SUSv3 states that *clock()* should return "the processor time used by the process." This is open to different interpretations. On some UNIX implementations, the time returned by *clock()* includes the CPU time used by all waited-for children. On Linux, it does not.

Example program

The program in Listing 10-5 demonstrates the use of the functions described in this section. The *displayProcessTimes()* function prints the message supplied by the caller, and then uses *clock()* and *times()* to retrieve and display process times. The main program makes an initial call to *displayProcessTimes()*, and then executes a loop that consumes some CPU time by repeatedly calling *getppid()*, before again calling *displayProcessTimes()* once more to see how much CPU time has been consumed within the loop. When we use this program to call *getppid()* 10 million times, this is what we see:

```
$ ./process_time 10000000
CLOCKS_PER_SEC=1000000  sysconf(_SC_CLK_TCK)=100

At program start:
        clock() returns: 0 clocks-per-sec (0.00 secs)
        times() yields: user CPU=0.00; system CPU: 0.00
After getppid() loop:
        clock() returns: 2960000 clocks-per-sec (2.96 secs)
        times() yields: user CPU=1.09; system CPU: 1.87
```

Listing 10-5: Retrieving process CPU times

——time/process_time.c
```c
#include <sys/times.h>
#include <time.h>
#include "tlpi_hdr.h"

static void              /* Display 'msg' and process times */
displayProcessTimes(const char *msg)
{
    struct tms t;
    clock_t clockTime;
    static long clockTicks = 0;

    if (msg != NULL)
        printf("%s", msg);
```

```
    if (clockTicks == 0) {        /* Fetch clock ticks on first call */
        clockTicks = sysconf(_SC_CLK_TCK);
        if (clockTicks == -1)
            errExit("sysconf");
    }

    clockTime = clock();
    if (clockTime == -1)
        errExit("clock");

    printf("        clock() returns: %ld clocks-per-sec (%.2f secs)\n",
            (long) clockTime, (double) clockTime / CLOCKS_PER_SEC);

    if (times(&t) == -1)
        errExit("times");
    printf("        times() yields: user CPU=%.2f; system CPU: %.2f\n",
            (double) t.tms_utime / clockTicks,
            (double) t.tms_stime / clockTicks);
}

int
main(int argc, char *argv[])
{
    int numCalls, j;

    printf("CLOCKS_PER_SEC=%ld  sysconf(_SC_CLK_TCK)=%ld\n\n",
            (long) CLOCKS_PER_SEC, sysconf(_SC_CLK_TCK));

    displayProcessTimes("At program start:\n");

    numCalls = (argc > 1) ? getInt(argv[1], GN_GT_0, "num-calls") : 100000000;
    for (j = 0; j < numCalls; j++)
        (void) getppid();

    displayProcessTimes("After getppid() loop:\n");

    exit(EXIT_SUCCESS);
}
```
—— time/process_time.c

10.8 Summary

Real time corresponds to the everyday definition of time. When real time is measured from some standard point, we refer to it as calendar time, by contrast with elapsed time, which is measured from some point (usually the start) in the life of a process.

Process time is the amount of CPU time used by a process, and is divided into user and system components.

Various system calls enable us to get and set the system clock value (i.e., calendar time, as measured in seconds since the Epoch), and a range of library functions allow conversions between calendar time and other time formats, including broken-down time and human-readable character strings. Describing such conversions took us into a discussion of locales and internationalization.

Using and displaying times and dates is an important part of many applications, and we'll make frequent use of the functions described in this chapter in later parts of this book. We also say a little more about the measurement of time in Chapter 23.

Further information

Details of how the Linux kernel measures time can be found in [Love, 2010].

An extensive discussion of timezones and internationalization can be found in the GNU C library manual (online at *http://www.gnu.org/*). The SUSv3 documents also cover locales in detail.

10.9 Exercise

10-1. Assume a system where the value returned by the call *sysconf(_SC_CLK_TCK)* is 100. Assuming that the *clock_t* value returned by *times()* is a signed 32-bit integer, how long will it take before this value cycles so that it restarts at 0? Perform the same calculation for the CLOCKS_PER_SEC value returned by *clock()*.

11

SYSTEM LIMITS AND OPTIONS

Each UNIX implementation sets limits on various system features and resources, and provides—or chooses not to provide—options defined in various standards. Examples include the following:

- How many files can a process hold open at one time?
- Does the system support realtime signals?
- What is the largest value that can be stored in a variable of type *int*?
- How big an argument list can a program have?
- What is the maximum length of a pathname?

While we could hard-code assumed limits and options into an application, this reduces portability, since limits and options may vary:

- *Across UNIX implementations*: Although limits and options may be fixed on an individual implementation, they can vary from one UNIX implementation to another. The maximum value that can be stored in an *int* is an example of such a limit.
- *At run time on a particular implementation*: The kernel may have been reconfigured to change a limit, for example. Alternatively, the application may have been compiled on one system, but run on another system with different limits and options.

- *From one file system to another*: For example, traditional System V file systems allow a filename to be up to 14 bytes, while traditional BSD file systems and most native Linux file systems allow filenames of up to 255 bytes.

Since system limits and options affect what an application may do, a portable application needs ways of determining limit values and whether options are supported. The C programming language standards and SUSv3 provide two principal avenues for an application to obtain such information:

- Some limits and options can be determined at compile time. For example, the maximum value of an *int* is determined by the hardware architecture and compiler design choices. Such limits can be recorded in header files.
- Other limits and options may vary at run time. For such cases, SUSv3 defines three functions—*sysconf()*, *pathconf()*, and *fpathconf()*—that an application can call to check these implementation limits and options.

SUSv3 specifies a range of limits that a conforming implementation may enforce, as well as a set of options, each of which may or may not be provided by a particular system. We describe a few of these limits and options in this chapter, and describe others at relevant points in later chapters.

11.1 System Limits

For each limit that it specifies, SUSv3 requires that all implementations support a *minimum value* for the limit. In most cases, this minimum value is defined as a constant in <limits.h> with a name prefixed by the string _POSIX_, and (usually) containing the string _MAX; thus, the form of the name is _POSIX_XXX_MAX.

If an application restricts itself to the minimum values that SUSv3 requires for each limit, then it will be portable to all implementations of the standard. However, doing so prevents an application from taking advantage of implementations that provide higher limits. For this reason, it is usually preferable to determine the limit on a particular system using <limits.h>, *sysconf()*, or *pathconf()*.

> The use of the string _MAX in the limit names defined by SUSv3 can appear confusing, given their description as *minimum* values. The rationale for the names becomes clear when we consider that each of these constants defines an upper limit on some resource or feature, and the standards are saying that this upper limit must have a certain minimum value.
>
> In some cases, *maximum values* are provided for a limit, and these values have names containing the string _MIN. For these constants, the converse holds true: they represent a lower limit on some resource, and the standards are saying that, on a conforming implementation, this lower limit can be no greater than a certain value. For example, the FLT_MIN limit (1E-37) defines the largest value that an implementation may set for the smallest floating-point number that may be represented, and all conforming implementations will be able to represent floating-point numbers at least this small.

Each limit has a *name*, which corresponds to the *minimum value name* described above, but lacks the _POSIX_ prefix. An implementation *may* define a constant with this name in <limits.h> to indicate the corresponding limit for this implementation.

If defined, this limit will always be at least the size of the minimum value described above (i.e., XXX_MAX >= _POSIX_XXX_MAX).

SUSv3 divides the limits that it specifies into three categories: *runtime invariant values*, *pathname variable values*, and *runtime increasable values*. In the following paragraphs, we describe these categories and provide some examples.

Runtime invariant values (possibly indeterminate)

A runtime invariant value is a limit whose value, if defined in <limits.h>, is fixed for the implementation. However, the value may be indeterminate (perhaps because it depends on available memory space), and hence omitted from <limits.h>. In this case (and even if the limit is also defined in <limits.h>), an application can use *sysconf()* to determine the value at run time.

The MQ_PRIO_MAX limit is an example of a runtime invariant value. As noted in Section 52.5.1, there is a limit on the priority for messages in POSIX message queues. SUSv3 defines the constant _POSIX_MQ_PRIO_MAX, with the value 32, as the minimum value that all conforming implementations must provide for this limit. This means that we can be sure that all conforming implementations will allow priorities from 0 up to at least 31 for message priorities. A UNIX implementation can set a higher limit than this, defining the constant MQ_PRIO_MAX in <limits.h> with the value of its limit. For example, on Linux, MQ_PRIO_MAX is defined with the value 32,768. This value can also be determined at run time using the following call:

```
lim = sysconf(_SC_MQ_PRIO_MAX);
```

Pathname variable values

Pathname variable values are limits that relate to pathnames (files, directories, terminals, and so on). Each limit may be constant for the implementation or may vary from one file system to another. In cases where a limit can vary depending on the pathname, an application can determine its value using *pathconf()* or *fpathconf()*.

The NAME_MAX limit is an example of a pathname variable value. This limit defines the maximum size for a filename on a particular file system. SUSv3 defines the constant _POSIX_NAME_MAX, with the value 14 (the old System V file-system limit), as the minimum value that an implementation must allow. An implementation may define NAME_MAX with a limit higher than this and/or make information about a specific file system available via a call of the following form:

```
lim = pathconf(directory_path, _PC_NAME_MAX)
```

The *directory_path* is a pathname for a directory on the file system of interest.

Runtime increasable values

A runtime increasable value is a limit that has a fixed minimum value for a particular implementation, and all systems running the implementation will provide at least this minimum value. However, a specific system may increase this limit at run time, and an application can find the actual value supported on the system using *sysconf()*.

An example of a runtime increasable value is NGROUPS_MAX, which defines the maximum number of simultaneous supplementary group IDs for a process

(Section 9.6). SUSv3 defines the corresponding minimum value, _POSIX_NGROUPS_MAX, with the value 8. At run time, an application can retrieve the limit using the call *sysconf(_SC_NGROUPS_MAX)*.

Summary of selected SUSv3 limits

Table 11-1 lists a few of the SUSv3-defined limits that are relevant to this book (other limits are introduced in later chapters).

Table 11-1: Selected SUSv3 limits

Name of limit (`<limits.h>`)	Min. value	sysconf() / pathconf() name (`<unistd.h>`)	Description
ARG_MAX	4096	_SC_ARG_MAX	Maximum bytes for arguments (*argv*) plus environment (*environ*) that can be supplied to an *exec()* (Sections 6.7 and 27.2.3)
none	none	_SC_CLK_TCK	Unit of measurement for *times()*
LOGIN_NAME_MAX	9	_SC_LOGIN_NAME_MAX	Maximum size of a login name (including terminating null byte)
OPEN_MAX	20	_SC_OPEN_MAX	Maximum number of file descriptors that a process can have open at one time, and one greater than maximum usable descriptor number (Section 36.2)
NGROUPS_MAX	8	_SC_NGROUPS_MAX	Maximum number of supplementary groups of which a process can be a member (Section 9.7.3)
none	1	_SC_PAGESIZE	Size of a virtual memory page (_SC_PAGE_SIZE is a synonym)
RTSIG_MAX	8	_SC_RTSIG_MAX	Maximum number of distinct realtime signals (Section 22.8)
SIGQUEUE_MAX	32	_SC_SIGQUEUE_MAX	Maximum number of queued realtime signals (Section 22.8)
STREAM_MAX	8	_SC_STREAM_MAX	Maximum number of *stdio* streams that can be open at one time
NAME_MAX	14	_PC_NAME_MAX	Maximum number of bytes in a filename, *excluding* terminating null byte
PATH_MAX	256	_PC_PATH_MAX	Maximum number of bytes in a pathname, *including* terminating null byte
PIPE_BUF	512	_PC_PIPE_BUF	Maximum number of bytes that can be written atomically to a pipe or FIFO (Section 44.1)

The first column of Table 11-1 gives the name of the limit, which may be defined as a constant in `<limits.h>` to indicate the limit for a particular implementation. The second column is the SUSv3-defined minimum for the limit (also defined in `<limits.h>`). In most cases, each of the minimum values is defined as a constant prefixed with the string _POSIX_. For example, the constant _POSIX_RTSIG_MAX (defined with the value 8) specifies the SUSv3-required minimum corresponding to the RTSIG_MAX implementation constant. The third column specifies the constant name that can be given at run time to *sysconf()* or *pathconf()* in order to retrieve the implementation limit. The constants beginning with _SC_ are for use with *sysconf()*; those beginning with _PC_ are for use with *pathconf()* and *fpathconf()*.

Note the following information supplementary to that shown in Table 11-1:

- The *getdtablesize()* function is an obsolete alternative for determining the process file descriptor limit (OPEN_MAX). This function was specified in SUSv2 (marked LEGACY), but was removed in SUSv3.
- The *getpagesize()* function is an obsolete alternative for determining the system page size (_SC_PAGESIZE). This function was specified in SUSv2 (marked LEGACY), but was removed in SUSv3.
- The constant FOPEN_MAX, defined in <stdio.h>, is synonymous with STREAM_MAX.
- NAME_MAX excludes the terminating null byte, while PATH_MAX includes it. This inconsistency repairs an earlier inconsistency in the POSIX.1 standard that left it unclear whether PATH_MAX included the terminating null byte. Defining PATH_MAX to include the terminator means that applications that allocated just PATH_MAX bytes for a pathname will still conform to the standard.

Determining limits and options from the shell: *getconf*

From the shell, we can use the *getconf* command to obtain the limits and options implemented by a particular UNIX implementation. The general form of this command is as follows:

```
$ getconf variable-name [ pathname ]
```

The *variable-name* identifies the limit of interest and is one of the SUSV3 standard limit names, such as ARG_MAX or NAME_MAX. Where the limit relates to a pathname, we must specify a pathname as the second argument to the command, as in the second of the following examples.

```
$ getconf ARG_MAX
131072
$ getconf NAME_MAX /boot
255
```

11.2   Retrieving System Limits (and Options) at Run Time

The *sysconf()* function allows an application to obtain the values of system limits at run time.

```
#include <unistd.h>

long sysconf(int name);
```

Returns value of limit specified by *name*,
or −1 if limit is indeterminate or an error occurred

The *name* argument is one of the _SC_* constants defined in <unistd.h>, some of which are listed in Table 11-1. The value of the limit is returned as the function result.

If a limit can't be determined, *sysconf()* returns −1. It may also return −1 if an error occurred. (The only specified error is EINVAL, indicating that *name* is not valid.) To distinguish the case of an indeterminate limit from an error, we must set *errno* to 0 before the call; if the call returns −1 and *errno* is set after the call, then an error occurred.

> The limit values returned by *sysconf()* (as well as *pathconf()* and *fpathconf()*) are always (*long*) integers. In the rationale text for *sysconf()*, SUSv3 notes that strings were considered as possible return values, but were rejected because of the complexity of implementation and use.

Listing 11-1 demonstrates the use of *sysconf()* to display various system limits. Running this program on one Linux 2.6.31/x86-32 system yields the following:

```
$ ./t_sysconf
_SC_ARG_MAX:            2097152
_SC_LOGIN_NAME_MAX:     256
_SC_OPEN_MAX:           1024
_SC_NGROUPS_MAX:        65536
_SC_PAGESIZE:           4096
_SC_RTSIG_MAX:          32
```

Listing 11-1: Using *sysconf()*

───syslim/t_sysconf.c
```c
#include "tlpi_hdr.h"

static void             /* Print 'msg' plus sysconf() value for 'name' */
sysconfPrint(const char *msg, int name)
{
    long lim;

    errno = 0;
    lim = sysconf(name);
    if (lim != -1) {        /* Call succeeded, limit determinate */
        printf("%s %ld\n", msg, lim);
    } else {
        if (errno == 0)     /* Call succeeded, limit indeterminate */
            printf("%s (indeterminate)\n", msg);
        else                /* Call failed */
            errExit("sysconf %s", msg);
    }
}

int
main(int argc, char *argv[])
{
    sysconfPrint("_SC_ARG_MAX:        ", _SC_ARG_MAX);
    sysconfPrint("_SC_LOGIN_NAME_MAX: ", _SC_LOGIN_NAME_MAX);
```

```
    sysconfPrint("_SC_OPEN_MAX:       ", _SC_OPEN_MAX);
    sysconfPrint("_SC_NGROUPS_MAX:    ", _SC_NGROUPS_MAX);
    sysconfPrint("_SC_PAGESIZE:       ", _SC_PAGESIZE);
    sysconfPrint("_SC_RTSIG_MAX:      ", _SC_RTSIG_MAX);
    exit(EXIT_SUCCESS);
}
```

——**syslim/t_sysconf.c**

SUSv3 requires that the value returned by *sysconf()* for a particular limit be constant for the lifetime of the calling process. For example, we can assume that the value returned for _SC_PAGESIZE won't change while a process is running.

> On Linux, there are some (sensible) exceptions to the statement that limit values are constant for the life of a process. A process can use *setrlimit()* (Section 36.2) to change various process resource limits that affect limit values reported by *sysconf()*: RLIMIT_NOFILE, which determines the number of files the process may open (_SC_OPEN_MAX); RLIMIT_NPROC (a resource limit not actually specified in SUSv3), which is the per-user limit on the number of processes that may be created by this process (_SC_CHILD_MAX); and RLIMIT_STACK, which, since Linux 2.6.23, determines the limit on the space allowed for the process's command-line arguments and environment (_SC_ARG_MAX; see the *execve(2)* manual page for details).

11.3 Retrieving File-Related Limits (and Options) at Run Time

The *pathconf()* and *fpathconf()* functions allow an application to obtain the values of file-related limits at run time.

```
#include <unistd.h>

long pathconf(const char *pathname, int name);
long fpathconf(int fd, int name);
```
                        Both return value of limit specified by *name*,
              or –1 if limit is indeterminate or an error occurred

The only difference between *pathconf()* and *fpathconf()* is the manner in which a file or directory is specified. For *pathconf()*, specification is by pathname; for *fpathconf()*, specification is via a (previously opened) file descriptor.

The *name* argument is one of the _PC_* constants defined in <unistd.h>, some of which are listed in Table 11-1. Table 11-2 provides some further details about the _PC_* constants that were shown in Table 11-1.

The value of the limit is returned as the function result. We can distinguish between an indeterminate return and an error return in the same manner as for *sysconf()*.

Unlike *sysconf()*, SUSv3 doesn't require that the values returned by *pathconf()* and *fpathconf()* remain constant over the lifetime of a process, since, for example, a file system may be dismounted and remounted with different characteristics while a process is running.

Table 11-2: Details of selected *pathconf()* _PC_* names

Constant	Notes
_PC_NAME_MAX	For a directory, this yields a value for files in the directory. Behavior for other file types is unspecified.
_PC_PATH_MAX	For a directory, this yields the maximum length for a relative pathname from this directory. Behavior for other file types is unspecified.
_PC_PIPE_BUF	For a FIFO or a pipe, this yields a value that applies to the referenced file. For a directory, the value applies to a FIFO created in that directory. Behavior for other file types is unspecified.

Listing 11-2 shows the use of *fpathconf()* to retrieve various limits for the file referred to by its standard input. When we run this program specifying standard input as a directory on an *ext2* file system, we see the following:

```
$ ./t_fpathconf < .
_PC_NAME_MAX:  255
_PC_PATH_MAX:  4096
_PC_PIPE_BUF:  4096
```

Listing 11-2: Using *fpathconf()*

─── **syslim/t_fpathconf.c**
```c
#include "tlpi_hdr.h"

static void              /* Print 'msg' plus value of fpathconf(fd, name) */
fpathconfPrint(const char *msg, int fd, int name)
{
    long lim;

    errno = 0;
    lim = fpathconf(fd, name);
    if (lim != -1) {        /* Call succeeded, limit determinate */
        printf("%s %ld\n", msg, lim);
    } else {
        if (errno == 0)     /* Call succeeded, limit indeterminate */
            printf("%s (indeterminate)\n", msg);
        else                /* Call failed */
            errExit("fpathconf %s", msg);
    }
}

int
main(int argc, char *argv[])
{
    fpathconfPrint("_PC_NAME_MAX: ", STDIN_FILENO, _PC_NAME_MAX);
    fpathconfPrint("_PC_PATH_MAX: ", STDIN_FILENO, _PC_PATH_MAX);
    fpathconfPrint("_PC_PIPE_BUF: ", STDIN_FILENO, _PC_PIPE_BUF);
    exit(EXIT_SUCCESS);
}
```
─── **syslim/t_fpathconf.c**

11.4 Indeterminate Limits

On occasion, we may find that some system limit is not defined by an implementation limit constant (e.g., PATH_MAX), and that *sysconf()* or *pathconf()* informs us that the limit (e.g., _PC_PATH_MAX) is indeterminate. In this case, we can employ one of the following strategies:

- When writing an application to be portable across multiple UNIX implementations, we could elect to use the minimum limit value specified by SUSv3. These are the constants with names of the form _POSIX_*_MAX, described in Section 11.1. Sometimes, this approach may not be viable because the limit is unrealistically low, as in the cases of _POSIX_PATH_MAX and _POSIX_OPEN_MAX.

- In some cases, a practical solution may be to ignore the checking of limits, and instead perform the relevant system or library function call. (Similar arguments can also apply with respect to some of the SUSv3 options described in Section 11.5.) If the call fails and *errno* indicates that the error occurred because some system limit was exceeded, then we can try again, modifying the application behavior as necessary. For example, most UNIX implementations impose a limit on the number of realtime signals that can be queued to a process. Once this limit is reached, attempts to send further signals (using *sigqueue()*) fail with the error EAGAIN. In this case, the sending process could simply retry, perhaps after some delay interval. Similarly, attempting to open a file whose name is too long yields the error ENAMETOOLONG, and an application could deal with this by trying again with a shorter name.

- We can write our own program or function to either deduce or estimate the limit. In each case, the relevant *sysconf()* or *pathconf()* call is made, and if this limit is indeterminate, the function returns a "good guess" value. While not perfect, such a solution is often viable in practice.

- We can employ a tool such as GNU *Autoconf*, an extensible tool that can determine the existence and settings of various system features and limits. The Autoconf program produces header files based on the information it determines, and these files can then be included in C programs. Further information about Autoconf can be found at *http://www.gnu.org/software/autoconf/*.

11.5 System Options

As well as specifying limits for various system resources, SUSv3 also specifies various options that a UNIX implementation may support. These include support for features such as realtime signals, POSIX shared memory, job control, and POSIX threads. With a few exceptions, implementations are not required to support these options. Instead, SUSv3 allows an implementation to advise—at both compile time and run time—whether it supports a particular feature.

An implementation can advertise support for a particular SUSv3 option at compile time by defining a corresponding constant in <unistd.h>. Each such constant starts with a prefix that indicates the standard from which it originates (e.g., _POSIX_ or _XOPEN_).

Each option constant, if defined, has one of the following values:

- A value of −1 means that *the option is not supported*. In this case, header files, data types, and function interfaces associated with the option need not be defined by the implementation. We may need to handle this possibility by conditional compilation using #if preprocessor directives.

- A value of 0 means that *the option may be supported*. An application must check at run time to see whether the option is supported.

- A value greater than 0 means that *the option is supported*. All header files, data types, and function interfaces associated with this option are defined and behave as specified. In many cases, SUSv3 requires that this positive value be 200112L, a constant corresponding to the year and month number in which SUSv3 was approved as a standard. (The analogous value for SUSv4 is 200809L.)

Where a constant is defined with the value 0, an application can use the *sysconf()* and *pathconf()* (or *fpathconf()*) functions to check at run time whether the option is supported. The *name* arguments passed to these functions generally have the same form as the corresponding compile-time constants, but with the prefix replaced by _SC_ or _PC_. The implementation must provide at least the header files, constants, and function interfaces necessary to perform the run-time check.

> SUSv3 is unclear on whether an undefined option constant has the same meaning as defining the constant with the value 0 ("the option may be supported") or with the value −1 ("the option is not supported"). The standards committee subsequently resolved that this case should mean the same as defining the constant with the value −1, and SUSv4 states this explicitly.

Table 11-3 lists some of the options specified in SUSv3. The first column of the table gives the name of the associated compile-time constant for the option (defined in <unistd.h>), as well as the corresponding *sysconf()* (_SC_*) or *pathconf()* (_PC_*) *name* argument. Note the following points regarding specific options:

- Certain options are required by SUSv3; that is, the compile-time constant always evaluates to a value greater than 0. Historically, these options were truly optional, but nowadays they are not. These options are marked with the character + in the *Notes* column. (In SUSv4, a range of options that were optional in SUSv3 become mandatory.)

> Although such options are required by SUSv3, some UNIX systems may nevertheless be installed in a nonconforming configuration. Thus, for portable applications, it may be worth checking whether an option that affects the application is supported, regardless of whether the standard requires that option.

- For certain options, the compile-time constant must have a value other than −1. In other words, either the option must be supported or support at run time must be checkable. These options are marked with the character * in the *Notes* column.

Table 11-3: Selected SUSv3 options

Option (constant) name (*sysconf()* / *pathconf()* name)	Description	Notes
_POSIX_ASYNCHRONOUS_IO (_SC_ASYNCHRONOUS_IO)	*Asynchronous I/O*	
_POSIX_CHOWN_RESTRICTED (_PC_CHOWN_RESTRICTED)	Only privileged processes can use *chown()* and *fchown()* to change the user ID and group ID of a file to arbitrary values (Section 15.3.2)	*
_POSIX_JOB_CONTROL (_SC_JOB_CONTROL)	*Job Control* (Section 34.7)	+
_POSIX_MESSAGE_PASSING (_SC_MESSAGE_PASSING)	*POSIX Message Queues* (Chapter 52)	
_POSIX_PRIORITY_SCHEDULING (_SC_PRIORITY_SCHEDULING)	*Process Scheduling* (Section 35.3)	
_POSIX_REALTIME_SIGNALS (_SC_REALTIME_SIGNALS)	*Realtime Signals Extension* (Section 22.8)	
_POSIX_SAVED_IDS (none)	Processes have saved set-user-IDs and saved set-group-IDs (Section 9.4)	+
_POSIX_SEMAPHORES (_SC_SEMAPHORES)	*POSIX Semaphores* (Chapter 53)	
_POSIX_SHARED_MEMORY_OBJECTS (_SC_SHARED_MEMORY_OBJECTS)	*POSIX Shared Memory Objects* (Chapter 54)	
_POSIX_THREADS (_SC_THREADS)	*POSIX Threads*	
_XOPEN_UNIX (_SC_XOPEN_UNIX)	The XSI extension is supported (Section 1.3.4)	

11.6 Summary

SUSv3 specifies limits that an implementation may enforce and system options that an implementation may support.

Often, it is desirable not to hard-code assumptions about system limits and options into a program, since these may vary across implementations and also on a single implementation, either at run time or across file systems. Therefore, SUSv3 specifies methods by which an implementation can advertise the limits and options it supports. For most limits, SUSv3 specifies a minimum value that all implementations must support. Additionally, each implementation can advertise its implementation-specific limits and options at compile time (via a constant definition in <limits.h> or <unistd.h>) and/or run time (via a call to *sysconf()*, *pathconf()*, or *fpathconf()*). These techniques may similarly be used to find out which SUSv3 options an implementation supports. In some cases, it may not be possible to determine a particular limit using either of these methods. For such indeterminate limits, we must resort to ad hoc techniques to determine the limit to which an application should adhere.

Further information

Chapter 2 of [Stevens & Rago, 2005] and Chapter 2 of [Gallmeister, 1995] cover similar ground to this chapter. [Lewine, 1991] also provides much useful (although now slightly outdated) background. Some information about POSIX options with notes on *glibc* and Linux details can be found at *http://people.redhat.com/drepper/ posix-option-groups.html*. The following Linux manual pages are also relevant: *sysconf(3)*, *pathconf(3)*, *feature_test_macros(7)*, *posixoptions(7)*, and *standards(7)*.

The best sources of information (though sometimes difficult reading) are the relevant parts of SUSv3, particularly Chapter 2 from the Base Definitions (XBD), and the specifications for *<unistd.h>*, *<limits.h>*, *sysconf()*, and *fpathconf()*. [Josey, 2004] provides guidance on the use of SUSv3.

11.7 Exercises

11-1. Try running the program in Listing 11-1 on other UNIX implementations if you have access to them.

11-2. Try running the program in Listing 11-2 on other file systems.

12

SYSTEM AND PROCESS INFORMATION

In this chapter, we look at ways of accessing a variety of system and process information. The primary focus of the chapter is a discussion of the /proc file system. We also describe the *uname()* system call, which is used to retrieve various system identifiers.

12.1 The /proc File System

In older UNIX implementations, there was typically no easy way to introspectively analyze (or change) attributes of the kernel, to answer questions such as the following:

- How many processes are running on the system and who owns them?
- What files does a process have open?
- What files are currently locked, and which processes hold the locks?
- What sockets are being used on the system?

Some older UNIX implementations solved this problem by allowing privileged programs to delve into data structures in kernel memory. However, this approach suffered various problems. In particular, it required specialized knowledge of the kernel data structures, and these structures might change from one kernel version to the next, requiring programs that depended on them to be rewritten.

In order to provide easier access to kernel information, many modern UNIX implementations provide a /proc virtual file system. This file system resides under the /proc directory and contains various files that expose kernel information, allowing processes to conveniently read that information, and change it in some cases, using normal file I/O system calls. The /proc file system is said to be virtual because the files and subdirectories that it contains don't reside on a disk. Instead, the kernel creates them "on the fly" as processes access them.

In this section, we present an overview of the /proc file system. In later chapters, we describe specific /proc files, as they relate to the topics of each chapter. Although many UNIX implementations provide a /proc file system, SUSv3 doesn't specify this file system; the details described in this book are Linux-specific.

12.1.1 Obtaining Information About a Process: /proc/*PID*

For each process on the system, the kernel provides a corresponding directory named /proc/*PID*, where *PID* is the ID of the process. Within this directory are various files and subdirectories containing information about that process. For example, we can obtain information about the *init* process, which always has the process ID 1, by looking at files under the directory /proc/1.

Among the files in each /proc/*PID* directory is one named status, which provides a range of information about the process:

```
$ cat /proc/1/status
Name:    init                         Name of command run by this process
State:   S (sleeping)                 State of this process
Tgid:    1                            Thread group ID (traditional PID, getpid())
Pid:     1                            Actually, thread ID (gettid())
PPid:    0                            Parent process ID
TracerPid:      0                     PID of tracing process (0 if not traced)
Uid:     0      0      0      0       Real, effective, saved set, and FS UIDs
Gid:     0      0      0      0       Real, effective, saved set, and FS GIDs
FDSize: 256                           # of file descriptor slots currently allocated
Groups:                               Supplementary group IDs
VmPeak:      852 kB                   Peak virtual memory size
VmSize:      724 kB                   Current virtual memory size
VmLck:         0 kB                   Locked memory
VmHWM:       288 kB                   Peak resident set size
VmRSS:       288 kB                   Current resident set size
VmData:      148 kB                   Data segment size
VmStk:        88 kB                   Stack size
VmExe:       484 kB                   Text (executable code) size
VmLib:         0 kB                   Shared library code size
VmPTE:        12 kB                   Size of page table (since 2.6.10)
Threads:        1                     # of threads in this thread's thread group
SigQ:    0/3067                       Current/max. queued signals (since 2.6.12)
SigPnd: 0000000000000000              Signals pending for thread
ShdPnd: 0000000000000000              Signals pending for process (since 2.6)
SigBlk: 0000000000000000              Blocked signals
SigIgn: fffffffe5770d8fc             Ignored signals
SigCgt: 00000000280b2603             Caught signals
CapInh: 0000000000000000              Inheritable capabilities
CapPrm: 00000000ffffffff             Permitted capabilities
```

```
CapEff: 00000000ffffffeff          Effective capabilities
CapBnd: 00000000ffffffff           Capability bounding set (since 2.6.26)
Cpus_allowed:    1                 CPUs allowed, mask (since 2.6.24)
Cpus_allowed_list:       0         Same as above, list format (since 2.6.26)
Mems_allowed:    1                 Memory nodes allowed, mask (since 2.6.24)
Mems_allowed_list:       0         Same as above, list format (since 2.6.26)
voluntary_ctxt_switches:      6998     Voluntary context switches (since 2.6.23)
nonvoluntary_ctxt_switches:   107     Involuntary context switches (since 2.6.23)
Stack usage:      8 kB             Stack usage high-water mark (since 2.6.32)
```

The above output is taken from kernel 2.6.32. As indicated by the *since* comments accompanying the file output, the format of this file has evolved over time, with new fields added (and in a few cases, removed) in various kernel versions. (Aside from the Linux 2.6 changes noted above, Linux 2.4 added the *Tgid*, *TracerPid*, *FDSize*, and *Threads* fields.)

The fact that the contents of this file have changed over time raises a general point about the use of /proc files: when these files consist of multiple entries, we should parse them defensively—in this case, looking for a match on a line containing a particular string (e.g., *PPid:*), rather than processing the file by (logical) line number.

Table 12-1 lists some of the other files found in each /proc/*PID* directory.

Table 12-1: Selected files in each /proc/*PID* directory

File	Description (process attribute)
cmdline	Command-line arguments delimited by \0
cwd	Symbolic link to current working directory
environ	Environment list *NAME=value* pairs, delimited by \0
exe	Symbolic link to file being executed
fd	Directory containing symbolic links to files opened by this process
maps	Memory mappings
mem	Process virtual memory (must *lseek()* to valid offset before I/O)
mounts	Mount points for this process
root	Symbolic link to root directory
status	Various information (e.g., process IDs, credentials, memory usage, signals)
task	Contains one subdirectory for each thread in process (Linux 2.6)

The /proc/*PID*/fd directory

The /proc/*PID*/fd directory contains one symbolic link for each file descriptor that the process has open. Each of these symbolic links has a name that matches the descriptor number; for example, /proc/1968/fd/1 is a symbolic link to the standard output of process 1968. Refer to Section 5.11 for further information.

As a convenience, any process can access its own /proc/*PID* directory using the symbolic link /proc/self.

Threads: the /proc/*PID*/task directory

Linux 2.4 added the notion of thread groups to properly support the POSIX threading model. Since some attributes are distinct for the threads in a thread group, Linux 2.4 added a task subdirectory under the /proc/*PID* directory. For each thread in this process, the kernel provides a subdirectory named /proc/*PID*/task/*TID*, where *TID* is the thread ID of the thread. (This is the same number as would be returned by a call to *gettid()* in the thread.)

Under each /proc/*PID*/task/*TID* subdirectory is a set of files and directories exactly like those that are found under /proc/*PID*. Since threads share many attributes, much of the information in these files is the same for each of the threads in the process. However, where it makes sense, these files show distinct information for each thread. For example, in the /proc/*PID*/task/*TID*/status files for a thread group, *State*, *Pid*, *SigPnd*, *SigBlk*, *CapInh*, *CapPrm*, *CapEff*, and *CapBnd* are some of the fields that may be distinct for each thread.

12.1.2 System Information Under /proc

Various files and subdirectories under /proc provide access to system-wide information. A few of these are shown in Figure 12-1.

Many of the files shown in Figure 12-1 are described elsewhere in this book. Table 12-2 summarizes the general purpose of the /proc subdirectories shown in Figure 12-1.

Table 12-2: Purpose of selected /proc subdirectories

Directory	Information exposed by files in this directory
/proc	Various system information
/proc/net	Status information about networking and sockets
/proc/sys/fs	Settings related to file systems
/proc/sys/kernel	Various general kernel settings
/proc/sys/net	Networking and sockets settings
/proc/sys/vm	Memory-management settings
/proc/sysvipc	Information about System V IPC objects

12.1.3 Accessing /proc Files

Files under /proc are often accessed using shell scripts (most /proc files that contain multiple values can be easily parsed with a scripting language such as Python or Perl). For example, we can modify and view the contents of a /proc file using shell commands as follows:

```
# echo 100000 > /proc/sys/kernel/pid_max
# cat /proc/sys/kernel/pid_max
100000
```

/proc files can also be accessed from a program using normal file I/O system calls. Some restrictions apply when accessing these files:

- Some /proc files are read-only; that is, they exist only to display kernel information and can't be used to modify that information. This applies to most files under the /proc/*PID* directories.

- Some /proc files can be read only by the file owner (or by a privileged process). For example, all files under /proc/*PID* are owned by the user who owns the corresponding process, and on some of these files (e.g., /proc/*PID*/environ), read permission is granted only to the file owner.

- Other than the files in the /proc/*PID* subdirectories, most files under /proc are owned by *root*, and the files that are modifiable can be modified only by *root*.

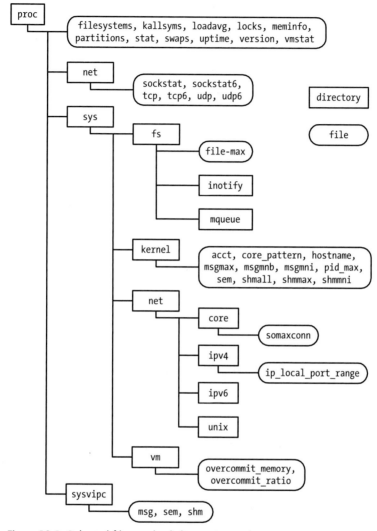

Figure 12-1: Selected files and subdirectories under /proc

Accessing files in /proc/*PID*

The /proc/*PID* directories are volatile. Each of these directories comes into existence when a process with the corresponding process ID is created and disappears when that process terminates. This means that if we determine that a particular /proc/*PID* directory exists, then we need to cleanly handle the possibility that the process has terminated, and the corresponding /proc/*PID* directory has been deleted, by the time we try to open a file in that directory.

Example program

Listing 12-1 demonstrates how to read and modify a /proc file. This program reads and displays the contents of /proc/sys/kernel/pid_max. If a command-line argument is supplied, the program updates the file using that value. This file (which is new in Linux 2.6) specifies an upper limit for process IDs (Section 6.2). Here is an example of the use of this program:

```
$ su                              Privilege is required to update pid_max file
Password:
# ./procfs_pidmax 10000
Old value: 32768
/proc/sys/kernel/pid_max now contains 10000
```

Listing 12-1: Accessing /proc/sys/kernel/pid_max

──sysinfo/procfs_pidmax.c
```c
#include <fcntl.h>
#include "tlpi_hdr.h"

#define MAX_LINE 100

int
main(int argc, char *argv[])
{
    int fd;
    char line[MAX_LINE];
    ssize_t n;

    fd = open("/proc/sys/kernel/pid_max", (argc > 1) ? O_RDWR : O_RDONLY);
    if (fd == -1)
        errExit("open");

    n = read(fd, line, MAX_LINE);
    if (n == -1)
        errExit("read");

    if (argc > 1)
        printf("Old value: ");
    printf("%.*s", (int) n, line);

    if (argc > 1) {
        if (lseek (fd, 0, SEEK_SET) == -1)
            errExit("lseek");

        if (write(fd, argv[1], strlen(argv[1])) != strlen(argv[1]))
            fatal("write() failed");

        system("echo /proc/sys/kernel/pid_max now contains "
                "`cat /proc/sys/kernel/pid_max`");
    }

    exit(EXIT_SUCCESS);
}
```
──sysinfo/procfs_pidmax.c

12.2 System Identification: *uname()*

The *uname()* system call returns a range of identifying information about the host system on which an application is running, in the structure pointed to by *utsbuf*.

```
#include <sys/utsname.h>

int uname(struct utsname *utsbuf);
```
                                             Returns 0 on success, or −1 on error

The *utsbuf* argument is a pointer to a *utsname* structure, which is defined as follows:

```
#define _UTSNAME_LENGTH 65

struct utsname {
    char sysname[_UTSNAME_LENGTH];      /* Implementation name */
    char nodename[_UTSNAME_LENGTH];     /* Node name on network */
    char release[_UTSNAME_LENGTH];      /* Implementation release level */
    char version[_UTSNAME_LENGTH];      /* Release version level */
    char machine[_UTSNAME_LENGTH];      /* Hardware on which system
                                           is running */
#ifdef _GNU_SOURCE                      /* Following is Linux-specific */
    char domainname[_UTSNAME_LENGTH];   /* NIS domain name of host */
#endif
};
```

SUSv3 specifies *uname()*, but leaves the lengths of the various fields of the *utsname* structure undefined, requiring only that the strings be terminated by a null byte. On Linux, these fields are each 65 bytes long, including space for the terminating null byte. On some UNIX implementations, these fields are shorter; on others (e.g., Solaris), they range up to 257 bytes.

The *sysname*, *release*, *version*, and *machine* fields of the *utsname* structure are automatically set by the kernel.

> On Linux, three files in the directory /proc/sys/kernel provide access to the same information as is returned in the *sysname*, *release*, and *version* fields of the *utsname* structure. These read-only files are, respectively, ostype, osrelease, and version. Another file, /proc/version, includes the same information as in these files, and also includes information about the kernel compilation step (i.e., the name of the user that performed the compilation, the name of host on which the compilation was performed, and the *gcc* version used).

The *nodename* field returns the value that was set using the *sethostname()* system call (see the manual page for details of this system call). Often, this name is something like the hostname prefix from the system's DNS domain name.

The *domainname* field returns the value that was set using the *setdomainname()* system call (see the manual page for details of this system call). This is the Network Information Services (NIS) domain name of the host (which is not the same thing as the host's DNS domain name).

The *gethostname()* system call, which is the converse of *sethostname()*, retrieves the system hostname. The system hostname is also viewable and settable using the *hostname(1)* command and the Linux-specific /proc/sys/kernel/hostname file.

The *getdomainname()* system call, which is the converse of *setdomainname()*, retrieves the NIS domain name. The NIS domain name is also viewable and settable using the *domainname(1)* command and the Linux-specific /proc/sys/kernel/domainname file.

The *sethostname()* and *setdomainname()* system calls are rarely used in application programs. Normally, the hostname and NIS domain name are established at boot time by startup scripts.

The program in Listing 12-2 displays the information returned by *uname()*. Here's an example of the output we might see when running this program:

```
$ ./t_uname
Node name:   tekapo
System name: Linux
Release:     2.6.30-default
Version:     #3 SMP Fri Jul 17 10:25:00 CEST 2009
Machine:     i686
Domain name:
```

Listing 12-2: Using *uname()*

─── sysinfo/t_uname.c

```c
#ifdef __linux__
#define _GNU_SOURCE
#endif
#include <sys/utsname.h>
#include "tlpi_hdr.h"

int
main(int argc, char *argv[])
{
    struct utsname uts;

    if (uname(&uts) == -1)
        errExit("uname");

    printf("Node name:   %s\n", uts.nodename);
    printf("System name: %s\n", uts.sysname);
    printf("Release:     %s\n", uts.release);
    printf("Version:     %s\n", uts.version);
    printf("Machine:     %s\n", uts.machine);
#ifdef _GNU_SOURCE
    printf("Domain name: %s\n", uts.domainname);
#endif
    exit(EXIT_SUCCESS);
}
```

─── sysinfo/t_uname.c

12.3 Summary

The /proc file system exposes a range of kernel information to application programs. Each /proc/*PID* subdirectory contains files and subdirectories that provide information about the process whose ID matches *PID*. Various other files and directories under /proc expose system-wide information that programs can read and, in some cases, modify.

The *uname()* system call allows us to discover the UNIX implementation and the type of machine on which an application is running.

Further information

Further information about the /proc file system can be found in the *proc(5)* manual page, in the kernel source file Documentation/filesystems/proc.txt, and in various files in the Documentation/sysctl directory.

12.4 Exercises

12-1. Write a program that lists the process ID and command name for all processes being run by the user named in the program's command-line argument. (You may find the *userIdFromName()* function from Listing 8-1, on page 159, useful.) This can be done by inspecting the *Name:* and *Uid:* lines of all of the /proc/*PID*/status files on the system. Walking through all of the /proc/*PID* directories on the system requires the use of *readdir(3)*, which is described in Section 18.8. Make sure your program correctly handles the possibility that a /proc/*PID* directory disappears between the time that the program determines that the directory exists and the time that it tries to open the corresponding /proc/*PID*/status file.

12-2. Write a program that draws a tree showing the hierarchical parent-child relationships of all processes on the system, going all the way back to *init*. For each process, the program should display the process ID and the command being executed. The output of the program should be similar to that produced by *pstree(1)*, although it does need not to be as sophisticated. The parent of each process on the system can be found by inspecting the *PPid:* line of all of the /proc/*PID*/status files on the system. Be careful to handle the possibility that a process's parent (and thus its /proc/*PID* directory) disappears during the scan of all /proc/*PID* directories.

12-3. Write a program that lists all processes that have a particular file pathname open. This can be achieved by inspecting the contents of all of the /proc/*PID*/fd/* symbolic links. This will require nested loops employing *readdir(3)* to scan all /proc/*PID* directories, and then the contents of all /proc/*PID*/fd entries within each /proc/*PID* directory. To read the contents of a /proc/*PID*/fd/*n* symbolic link requires the use of *readlink()*, described in Section 18.5.

13

FILE I/O BUFFERING

In the interests of speed and efficiency, I/O system calls (i.e., the kernel) and the I/O functions of the standard C library (i.e., the *stdio* functions) buffer data when operating on disk files. In this chapter, we describe both types of buffering and consider how they affect application performance. We also look at various techniques for influencing and disabling both types of buffering, and look at a technique called direct I/O, which is useful for bypassing kernel buffering in certain circumstances.

13.1 Kernel Buffering of File I/O: The Buffer Cache

When working with disk files, the *read()* and *write()* system calls don't directly initiate disk access. Instead, they simply copy data between a user-space buffer and a buffer in the kernel *buffer cache*. For example, the following call transfers 3 bytes of data from a buffer in user-space memory to a buffer in kernel space:

```
write(fd, "abc", 3);
```

At this point, *write()* returns. At some later point, the kernel writes (flushes) its buffer to the disk. (Hence, we say that the system call is not *synchronized* with the disk operation.) If, in the interim, another process attempts to read these bytes of the file, then the kernel automatically supplies the data from the buffer cache, rather than from (the outdated contents of) the file.

Correspondingly, for input, the kernel reads data from the disk and stores it in a kernel buffer. Calls to *read()* fetch data from this buffer until it is exhausted, at which point the kernel reads the next segment of the file into the buffer cache. (This is a simplification; for sequential file access, the kernel typically performs read-ahead to try to ensure that the next blocks of a file are read into the buffer cache before the reading process requires them. We say a bit more about read-ahead in Section 13.5.)

The aim of this design is to allow *read()* and *write()* to be fast, since they don't need to wait on a (slow) disk operation. This design is also efficient, since it reduces the number of disk transfers that the kernel must perform.

The Linux kernel imposes no fixed upper limit on the size of the buffer cache. The kernel will allocate as many buffer cache pages as are required, limited only by the amount of available physical memory and the demands for physical memory for other purposes (e.g., holding the text and data pages required by running processes). If available memory is scarce, then the kernel flushes some modified buffer cache pages to disk, in order to free those pages for reuse.

> Speaking more precisely, from kernel 2.4 onward, Linux no longer maintains a separate buffer cache. Instead, file I/O buffers are included in the page cache, which, for example, also contains pages from memory-mapped files. Nevertheless, in the discussion in the main text, we use the term *buffer cache*, since that term is historically common on UNIX implementations.

Effect of buffer size on I/O system call performance

The kernel performs the same number of disk accesses, regardless of whether we perform 1000 writes of a single byte or a single write of a 1000 bytes. However, the latter is preferable, since it requires a single system call, while the former requires 1000. Although much faster than disk operations, system calls nevertheless take an appreciable amount of time, since the kernel must trap the call, check the validity of the system call arguments, and transfer data between user space and kernel space (refer to Section 3.1 for further details).

The impact of performing file I/O using different buffer sizes can be seen by running the program in Listing 4-1 (on page 71) with different BUF_SIZE values. (The BUF_SIZE constant specifies how many bytes are transferred by each call to *read()* and *write()*.) Table 13-1 shows the time that this program requires to copy a file of 100 million bytes on a Linux *ext2* file system using different BUF_SIZE values. Note the following points concerning the information in this table:

- The *Elapsed* and *Total CPU* time columns have the obvious meanings. The *User CPU* and *System CPU* columns show a breakdown of the *Total CPU* time into, respectively, the time spent executing code in user mode and the time spent executing kernel code (i.e., system calls).

- The tests shown in the table were performed using a vanilla 2.6.30 kernel on an *ext2* file system with a block size of 4096 bytes.

> When we talk about a *vanilla kernel*, we mean an unpatched mainline kernel. This is in contrast to kernels that are supplied by most distributors, which often include various patches to fix bugs or add features.

- Each row shows the average of 20 runs for the given buffer size. In these tests, as in other tests shown later in this chapter, the file system was unmounted and remounted between each execution of the program to ensure that the buffer cache for the file system was empty. Timing was done using the shell *time* command.

Table 13-1: Time required to duplicate a file of 100 million bytes

BUF_SIZE	Time (seconds)			
	Elapsed	Total CPU	User CPU	System CPU
1	107.43	107.32	8.20	99.12
2	54.16	53.89	4.13	49.76
4	31.72	30.96	2.30	28.66
8	15.59	14.34	1.08	13.26
16	7.50	7.14	0.51	6.63
32	3.76	3.68	0.26	3.41
64	2.19	2.04	0.13	1.91
128	2.16	1.59	0.11	1.48
256	2.06	1.75	0.10	1.65
512	2.06	1.03	0.05	0.98
1024	2.05	0.65	0.02	0.63
4096	2.05	0.38	0.01	0.38
16384	2.05	0.34	0.00	0.33
65536	2.06	0.32	0.00	0.32

Since the total amount of data transferred (and hence the number of disk operations) is the same for the various buffer sizes, what Table 13-1 illustrates is the overhead of making *read()* and *write()* calls. With a buffer size of 1 byte, 100 million calls are made to *read()* and *write()*. With a buffer size of 4096 bytes, the number of invocations of each system call falls to around 24,000, and near optimal performance is reached. Beyond this point, there is no significant performance improvement, because the cost of making *read()* and *write()* system calls becomes negligible compared to the time required to copy data between user space and kernel space, and to perform actual disk I/O.

> The final rows of Table 13-1 allow us to make rough estimates of the times required for data transfer between user space and kernel space, and for file I/O. Since the number of system calls in these cases is relatively small, their contribution to the elapsed and CPU times is negligible. Thus, we can say that the *System CPU* time is essentially measuring the time for data transfers between user space and kernel space. The *Elapsed* time value gives us an estimate of the time required for data transfer to and from the disk. (As we'll see in a moment, this is mainly the time required for disk reads.)

In summary, if we are transferring a large amount of data to or from a file, then by buffering data in large blocks, and thus performing fewer system calls, we can greatly improve I/O performance.

The data in Table 13-1 measures a range of factors: the time to perform *read()* and *write()* system calls, the time to transfer data between buffers in kernel space and user space, and the time to transfer data between kernel buffers and the disk. Let's consider the last factor further. Obviously, transferring the contents of the input file into the buffer cache is unavoidable. However, we already saw that *write()* returns immediately after transferring data from user space to the kernel buffer cache. Since the RAM size on the test system (4 GB) far exceeds the size of the file being copied (100 MB), we can assume that by the time the program completes, the output file has not actually been written to disk. Therefore, as a further experiment, we ran a program that simply wrote arbitrary data to a file using different *write()* buffer sizes. The results are shown in Table 13-2.

Again, the data shown in Table 13-2 was obtained from kernel 2.6.30, on an *ext2* file system with a 4096-byte block size, and each row shows the average of 20 runs. We don't show the test program (`filebuff/write_bytes.c`), but it is available in the source code distribution for this book.

Table 13-2: Time required to write a file of 100 million bytes

BUF_SIZE	Time (seconds)			
	Elapsed	Total CPU	User CPU	System CPU
1	72.13	72.11	5.00	67.11
2	36.19	36.17	2.47	33.70
4	20.01	19.99	1.26	18.73
8	9.35	9.32	0.62	8.70
16	4.70	4.68	0.31	4.37
32	2.39	2.39	0.16	2.23
64	1.24	1.24	0.07	1.16
128	0.67	0.67	0.04	0.63
256	0.38	0.38	0.02	0.36
512	0.24	0.24	0.01	0.23
1024	0.17	0.17	0.01	0.16
4096	0.11	0.11	0.00	0.11
16384	0.10	0.10	0.00	0.10
65536	0.09	0.09	0.00	0.09

Table 13-2 shows the costs just for making *write()* system calls and transferring data from user space to the kernel buffer cache using different *write()* buffer sizes. For larger buffer sizes, we see significant differences from the data shown in Table 13-1. For example, for a 65,536-byte buffer size, the elapsed time in Table 13-1 is 2.06 seconds, while for Table 13-2 it is 0.09 seconds. This is because no actual disk I/O is being performed in the latter case. In other words, the majority of the time required for the large buffer cases in Table 13-1 is due to the disk reads.

As we'll see in Section 13.3, when we force output operations to block until data is transferred to the disk, the times for *write()* calls rise significantly.

Finally, it is worth noting that the information in Table 13-2 (and later, in Table 13-3) represents just one form of (naive) benchmark for a file system. Furthermore, the results will probably show some variation across file systems. File systems can be measured by various other criteria, such as performance under heavy multiuser load, speed of file creation and deletion, time required to search for a file in a large directory, space required to store small files, or maintenance of file integrity in the event of a system crash. Where the performance of I/O or other file-system operations is critical, there is no substitute for application-specific benchmarks on the target platform.

13.2 Buffering in the *stdio* Library

Buffering of data into large blocks to reduce system calls is exactly what is done by the C library I/O functions (e.g., *fprintf()*, *fscanf()*, *fgets()*, *fputs()*, *fputc()*, *fgetc()*) when operating on disk files. Thus, using the *stdio* library relieves us of the task of buffering data for output with *write()* or input via *read()*.

Setting the buffering mode of a *stdio* stream

The *setvbuf()* function controls the form of buffering employed by the *stdio* library.

```
#include <stdio.h>

int setvbuf(FILE *stream, char *buf, int mode, size_t size);
```
                              Returns 0 on success, or nonzero on error

The *stream* argument identifies the file stream whose buffering is to be modified. After the stream has been opened, the *setvbuf()* call must be made before calling any other *stdio* function on the stream. The *setvbuf()* call affects the behavior of all subsequent *stdio* operations on the specified stream.

> The streams used by the *stdio* library should not be confused with the STREAMS facility of System V. The System V STREAMS facility is not implemented in the mainline Linux kernel.

The *buf* and *size* arguments specify the buffer to be used for *stream*. These arguments may be specified in two ways:

- If *buf* is non-NULL, then it points to a block of memory of *size* bytes that is to be used as the buffer for *stream*. Since the buffer pointed to by *buf* is then used by the *stdio* library, it should be either statically allocated or dynamically allocated on the heap (using *malloc()* or similar). It should not be allocated as a local function variable on the stack, since chaos will result when that function returns and its stack frame is deallocated.

- If *buf* is NULL, then the *stdio* library automatically allocates a buffer for use with *stream* (unless we select unbuffered I/O, as described below). SUSv3 permits, but does not require, an implementation to use *size* to determine the size for this buffer. In the *glibc* implementation, *size* is ignored in this case.

The *mode* argument specifies the type of buffering and has one of the following values:

_IONBF
> Don't buffer I/O. Each *stdio* library call results in an immediate *write()* or *read()* system call. The *buf* and *size* arguments are ignored, and can be specified as NULL and 0, respectively. This is the default for *stderr*, so that error output is guaranteed to appear immediately.

_IOLBF

> Employ line-buffered I/O. This flag is the default for streams referring to terminal devices. For output streams, data is buffered until a newline character is output (unless the buffer fills first). For input streams, data is read a line at a time.

_IOFBF

> Employ fully buffered I/O. Data is read or written (via calls to *read()* or *write()*) in units equal to the size of the buffer. This mode is the default for streams referring to disk files.

The following code demonstrates the use of *setvbuf()*:

```
#define BUF_SIZE 1024
static char buf[BUF_SIZE];

if (setvbuf(stdout, buf, _IOFBF, BUF_SIZE) != 0)
    errExit("setvbuf");
```

Note that *setvbuf()* returns a nonzero value (not necessarily −1) on error.

The *setbuf()* function is layered on top of *setvbuf()*, and performs a similar task.

```
#include <stdio.h>

void setbuf(FILE *stream, char *buf);
```

Other than the fact that it doesn't return a function result, the call *setbuf(fp, buf)* is equivalent to:

```
setvbuf(fp, buf, (buf != NULL) ? _IOFBF: _IONBF, BUFSIZ);
```

The *buf* argument is specified either as NULL, for no buffering, or as a pointer to a caller-allocated buffer of BUFSIZ bytes. (BUFSIZ is defined in <stdio.h>. In the *glibc* implementation, this constant has the value 8192, which is typical.)

The *setbuffer()* function is similar to *setbuf()*, but allows the caller to specify the size of *buf*.

```
#define _BSD_SOURCE
#include <stdio.h>

void setbuffer(FILE *stream, char *buf, size_t size);
```

The call *setbuffer(fp, buf, size)* is equivalent to the following:

```
setvbuf(fp, buf, (buf != NULL) ? _IOFBF : _IONBF, size);
```

The *setbuffer()* function is not specified in SUSv3, but is available on most UNIX implementations.

Flushing a *stdio* buffer

Regardless of the current buffering mode, at any time, we can force the data in a *stdio* output stream to be written (i.e., flushed to a kernel buffer via *write()*) using the *fflush()* library function. This function flushes the output buffer for the specified *stream*.

```
#include <stdio.h>

int fflush(FILE *stream);
```
                                                    Returns 0 on success, EOF on error

If *stream* is NULL, *fflush()* flushes all *stdio* buffers that are associated with output streams.

The *fflush()* function can also be applied to an input stream. This causes any buffered input to be discarded. (The buffer will be refilled when the program next tries to read from the stream.)

A *stdio* buffer is automatically flushed when the corresponding stream is closed.

In many C library implementations, including *glibc*, if *stdin* and *stdout* refer to a terminal, then an implicit *fflush(stdout)* is performed whenever input is read from *stdin*. This has the effect of flushing any prompts written to *stdout* that don't include a terminating newline character (e.g., *printf("Date: ")*). However, this behavior is not specified in SUSv3 or C99 and is not implemented in all C libraries. Portable programs should use explicit *fflush(stdout)* calls to ensure that such prompts are displayed.

> The C99 standard makes two requirements if a stream is opened for both input and output. First, an output operation can't be directly followed by an input operation without an intervening call to *fflush()* or one of the file-positioning functions (*fseek()*, *fsetpos()*, or *rewind()*). Second, an input operation can't be directly followed by an output operation without an intervening call to one of the file-positioning functions, unless the input operation encountered end-of-file.

13.3 Controlling Kernel Buffering of File I/O

It is possible to force flushing of kernel buffers for output files. Sometimes, this is necessary if an application (e.g., a database journaling process) must ensure that output really has been written to the disk (or at least to the disk's hardware cache) before continuing.

Before we describe the system calls used to control kernel buffering, it is useful to consider a few relevant definitions from SUSv3.

Synchronized I/O data integrity and synchronized I/O file integrity

SUSv3 defines the term *synchronized I/O completion* to mean "an I/O operation that has either been successfully transferred [to the disk] or diagnosed as unsuccessful."

SUSv3 defines two different types of synchronized I/O completion. The difference between the types involves the *metadata* ("data about data") describing the file, which the kernel stores along with the data for a file. We consider file metadata in detail when we look at file i-nodes in Section 14.4, but for now, it is sufficient to note that the file metadata includes information such as the file owner and group; file permissions; file size; number of (hard) links to the file; timestamps indicating the time of the last file access, last file modification, and last metadata change; and file data block pointers.

The first type of synchronized I/O completion defined by SUSv3 is *synchronized I/O data integrity completion*. This is concerned with ensuring that a file data update transfers sufficient information to allow a later retrieval of that data to proceed.

- For a read operation, this means that the requested file data has been transferred (from the disk) to the process. If there were any pending write operations affecting the requested data, these are transferred to the disk before performing the read.

- For a write operation, this means that the data specified in the write request has been transferred (to the disk) and all file metadata required to retrieve that data has also been transferred. The key point to note here is that not all modified file metadata attributes need to be transferred to allow the file data to be retrieved. An example of a modified file metadata attribute that would need to be transferred is the file size (if the write operation extended the file). By contrast, modified file timestamps would not need to be transferred to disk before a subsequent data retrieval could proceed.

The other type of synchronized I/O completion defined by SUSv3 is *synchronized I/O file integrity completion*, which is a superset of synchronized I/O data integrity completion. The difference with this mode of I/O completion is that during a file update, *all* updated file metadata is transferred to disk, even if it is not necessary for the operation of a subsequent read of the file data.

System calls for controlling kernel buffering of file I/O

The *fsync()* system call causes the buffered data and all metadata associated with the open file descriptor *fd* to be flushed to disk. Calling *fsync()* forces the file to the synchronized I/O file integrity completion state.

```
#include <unistd.h>

int fsync(int fd);
```

Returns 0 on success, or −1 on error

An *fsync()* call returns only after the transfer to the disk device (or at least its cache) has completed.

The *fdatasync()* system call operates similarly to *fsync()*, but only forces the file to the synchronized I/O data integrity completion state.

```
#include <unistd.h>

int fdatasync(int fd);
```

Returns 0 on success, or −1 on error

Using *fdatasync()* potentially reduces the number of disk operations from the two required by *fsync()* to one. For example, if the file data has changed, but the file size has not, then calling *fdatasync()* only forces the data to be updated. (We noted above that changes to file metadata attributes such as the last modification timestamp don't need to be transferred for synchronized I/O data integrity completion.) By contrast, calling *fsync()* would also force the metadata to be transferred to disk.

Reducing the number of disk I/O operations in this manner is useful for certain applications in which performance is crucial and the accurate maintenance of certain metadata (such as timestamps) is not essential. This can make a considerable performance difference for applications that are making multiple file updates: because the file data and metadata normally reside on different parts of the disk, updating them both would require repeated seek operations backward and forward across the disk.

In Linux 2.2 and earlier, *fdatasync()* is implemented as a call to *fsync()*, and thus carries no performance gain.

> Starting with kernel 2.6.17, Linux provides the nonstandard *sync_file_range()* system call, which allows more precise control than *fdatasync()* when flushing file data. The caller can specify the file region to be flushed, and specify flags controlling whether the system call blocks on disk writes. See the *sync_file_range(2)* manual page for further details.

The *sync()* system call causes all kernel buffers containing updated file information (i.e., data blocks, pointer blocks, metadata, and so on) to be flushed to disk.

```
#include <unistd.h>

void sync(void);
```

In the Linux implementation, *sync()* returns only after all data has been transferred to the disk device (or at least to its cache). However, SUSv3 permits an implementation of *sync()* to simply schedule the I/O transfer and return before it has completed.

> A permanently running kernel thread ensures that modified kernel buffers are flushed to disk if they are not explicitly synchronized within 30 seconds. This is done to ensure that buffers don't remain unsynchronized with the corresponding disk file (and thus vulnerable to loss in the event of a system crash) for long periods. In Linux 2.6, this task is performed by the *pdflush* kernel thread. (In Linux 2.4, it is performed by the *kupdated* kernel thread.)
>
> The file /proc/sys/vm/dirty_expire_centisecs specifies the age (in hundredths of a second) that a dirty buffer must reach before it is flushed by *pdflush*. Additional files in the same directory control other aspects of the operation of *pdflush*.

Making all writes synchronous: O_SYNC

Specifying the O_SYNC flag when calling *open()* makes all subsequent output *synchronous*:

```
fd = open(pathname, O_WRONLY | O_SYNC);
```

After this *open()* call, every *write()* to the file automatically flushes the file data and metadata to the disk (i.e., writes are performed according to synchronized I/O file integrity completion).

> Older BSD systems used the O_FSYNC flag to provide O_SYNC functionality. In *glibc*, O_FSYNC is defined as a synonym for O_SYNC.

Performance impact of O_SYNC

Using the O_SYNC flag (or making frequent calls to *fsync()*, *fdatasync()*, or *sync()*) can strongly affect performance. Table 13-3 shows the time required to write 1 million bytes to a newly created file (on an *ext2* file system) for a range of buffer sizes with and without O_SYNC. The results were obtained (using the filebuff/write_bytes.c program provided in the source code distribution for this book) using a vanilla 2.6.30 kernel and an *ext2* file system with a block size of 4096 bytes. Each row shows the average of 20 runs for the given buffer size.

As can be seen from the table, O_SYNC increases elapsed times enormously—in the 1-byte buffer case, by a factor of more than 1000. Note also the large differences between the elapsed and CPU times for writes with O_SYNC. This is a consequence of the program being blocked while each buffer is actually transferred to disk.

The results shown in Table 13-3 omit a further factor that affects performance when using O_SYNC. Modern disk drives have large internal caches, and by default, O_SYNC merely causes data to be transferred to the cache. If we disable caching on the disk (using the command *hdparm −W0*), then the performance impact of O_SYNC becomes even more extreme. In the 1-byte case, the elapsed time rises from 1030 seconds to around 16,000 seconds. In the 4096-byte case, the elapsed time rises from 0.34 seconds to 4 seconds.

In summary, if we need to force flushing of kernel buffers, we should consider whether we can design our application to use large *write()* buffer sizes or make judicious use of occasional calls to *fsync()* or *fdatasync()*, instead of using the O_SYNC flag when opening the file.

Table 13-3: Impact of the O_SYNC flag on the speed of writing 1 million bytes

BUF_SIZE	Time required (seconds)			
	Without O_SYNC		With O_SYNC	
	Elapsed	Total CPU	Elapsed	Total CPU
1	0.73	0.73	1030	98.8
16	0.05	0.05	65.0	0.40
256	0.02	0.02	4.07	0.03
4096	0.01	0.01	0.34	0.03

The O_DSYNC and O_RSYNC flags

SUSv3 specifies two further open file status flags related to synchronized I/O: O_DSYNC and O_RSYNC.

The O_DSYNC flag causes writes to be performed according to the requirements of synchronized I/O data integrity completion (like *fdatasync()*). This contrasts with O_SYNC, which causes writes to be performed according to the requirements of synchronized I/O file integrity completion (like *fsync()*).

The O_RSYNC flag is specified in conjunction with either O_SYNC or O_DSYNC, and extends the write behaviors of these flags to read operations. Specifying both O_RSYNC and O_DSYNC when opening a file means that all subsequent reads are completed according to the requirements of synchronized I/O data integrity completion (i.e., prior to performing the read, all pending file writes are completed as though carried out with O_DSYNC). Specifying both O_RSYNC and O_SYNC when opening a file means that all subsequent reads are completed according to the requirements of synchronized I/O file integrity completion (i.e., prior to performing the read, all pending file writes are completed as though carried out with O_SYNC).

Before kernel 2.6.33, the O_DSYNC and O_RSYNC flags were not implemented on Linux, and the *glibc* headers defined these constants to be the same as O_SYNC. (This isn't actually correct in the case of O_RSYNC, since O_SYNC doesn't provide any functionality for read operations.)

Starting with kernel 2.6.33, Linux implements O_DSYNC, and an implementation of O_RSYNC is likely to be added in a future kernel release.

> Before kernel 2.6.33, Linux didn't fully implement O_SYNC semantics. Instead, O_SYNC was implemented as O_DSYNC. To maintain consistent behavior for applications that were built for older kernels, applications that were linked against older versions of the GNU C library continue to provide O_DSYNC semantics for O_SYNC, even on Linux 2.6.33 and later.

13.4 Summary of I/O Buffering

Figure 13-1 provides an overview of the buffering employed (for output files) by the *stdio* library and the kernel, along with the mechanisms for controlling each type of buffering. Traveling downward through the middle of this diagram, we see the transfer of user data by the *stdio* library functions to the *stdio* buffer, which is maintained in user memory space. When this buffer is filled, the *stdio* library invokes the *write()* system call, which transfers the data into the kernel buffer cache (maintained in kernel memory). Eventually, the kernel initiates a disk operation to transfer the data to the disk.

The left side of Figure 13-1 shows the calls that can be used at any time to explicitly force a flush of either of the buffers. The right side shows the calls that can be used to make flushing automatic, either by disabling buffering in the *stdio* library or by making file output system calls synchronous, so that each *write()* is immediately flushed to the disk.

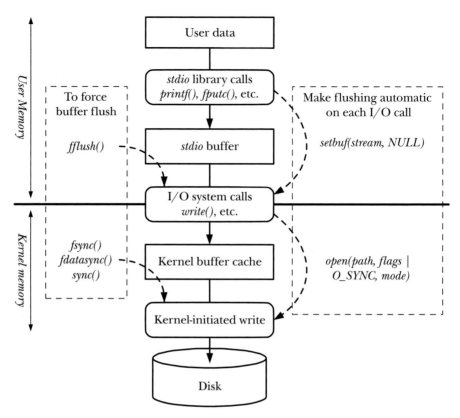

Figure 13-1: Summary of I/O buffering

13.5 Advising the Kernel About I/O Patterns

The *posix_fadvise()* system call allows a process to inform the kernel about its likely pattern for accessing file data.

```
#include <fcntl.h>

int posix_fadvise(int fd, off_t offset, off_t len, int advice);
```
                    Returns 0 on success, or a positive error number on error

The kernel may (but is not obliged to) use the information provided by *posix_fadvise()* to optimize its use of the buffer cache, thereby improving I/O performance for the process and for the system as a whole. Calling *posix_fadvise()* has no effect on the semantics of a program.

The *fd* argument is a file descriptor identifying the file about whose access patterns we wish to inform the kernel. The *offset* and *len* arguments identify the region of the file about which advice is being given: *offset* specifies the starting offset of the region, and *len* specifies the size of the region in bytes. A *len* value of 0 means all bytes from *offset* through to the end of the file. (In kernels before 2.6.6, a *len* of 0 was interpreted literally as zero bytes.)

The *advice* argument indicates the process's expected pattern of access for the file. It is specified as one of the following:

POSIX_FADV_NORMAL

> The process has no special advice to give about access patterns. This is the default behavior if no advice is given for the file. On Linux, this operation sets the file read-ahead window to the default size (128 kB).

POSIX_FADV_SEQUENTIAL

> The process expects to read data sequentially from lower offsets to higher offsets. On Linux, this operation sets the file read-ahead window to twice the default size.

POSIX_FADV_RANDOM

> The process expects to access the data in random order. On Linux, this option disables file read-ahead.

POSIX_FADV_WILLNEED

> The process expects to access the specified file region in the near future. The kernel performs read-ahead to populate the buffer cache with file data in the range specified by *offset* and *len*. Subsequent *read()* calls on the file don't block on disk I/O; instead, they simply fetch data from the buffer cache. The kernel provides no guarantees about how long the data fetched from the file will remain resident in the buffer cache. If other processes or kernel activities place a sufficiently strong demand on memory, then the pages will eventually be reused. In other words, if memory pressure is high, then we should ensure that the elapsed time between the *posix_fadvise()* call and the subsequent *read()* call(s) is short. (The Linux-specific *readahead()* system call provides functionality equivalent to the POSIX_FADV_WILLNEED operation.)

POSIX_FADV_DONTNEED

> The process expects not to access the specified file region in the near future. This advises the kernel that it can free the corresponding cache pages (if there are any). On Linux, this operation is performed in two steps. First, if the underlying device is not currently congested with a series of queued write operations, the kernel flushes any modified pages in the specified region. Second, the kernel attempts to free any cache pages for the region. For modified pages in the region, this second step will succeed only if the pages have been written to the underlying device in the first step—that is, if the device's write queue was not congested. Since congestion on the device can't be controlled by the application, an alternate way of ensuring that the cache pages can be freed is to precede the POSIX_FADV_DONTNEED operation with a *sync()* or *fdatasync()* call that specifies *fd*.

POSIX_FADV_NOREUSE

> The process expects to access data in the specified file region once, and then not to reuse it. This hint tells the kernel that it can free the pages after they have been accessed once. On Linux, this operation currently has no effect.

The specification of *posix_fadvise()* is new in SUSv3, and not all UNIX implementations support this interface. Linux provides *posix_fadvise()* since kernel 2.6.

13.6 Bypassing the Buffer Cache: Direct I/O

Starting with kernel 2.4, Linux allows an application to bypass the buffer cache when performing disk I/O, thus transferring data directly from user space to a file or disk device. This is sometimes termed *direct I/O* or *raw I/O*.

> The details described here are Linux-specific and are not standardized by SUSv3. Nevertheless, most UNIX implementations provide some form of direct I/O access to devices and files.

Direct I/O is sometimes misunderstood as being a means of obtaining fast I/O performance. However, for most applications, using direct I/O can considerably degrade performance. This is because the kernel applies a number of optimizations to improve the performance of I/O done via the buffer cache, including performing sequential read-ahead, performing I/O in clusters of disk blocks, and allowing processes accessing the same file to share buffers in the cache. All of these optimizations are lost when we use direct I/O. Direct I/O is intended only for applications with specialized I/O requirements. For example, database systems that perform their own caching and I/O optimizations don't need the kernel to consume CPU time and memory performing the same tasks.

We can perform direct I/O either on an individual file or on a block device (e.g., a disk). To do this, we specify the O_DIRECT flag when opening the file or device with *open()*.

The O_DIRECT flag is effective since kernel 2.4.10. Not all Linux file systems and kernel versions support the use of this flag. Most native file systems support O_DIRECT, but many non-UNIX file systems (e.g., VFAT) do not. It may be necessary to test the file system concerned (if a file system doesn't support O_DIRECT, then *open()* fails with the error EINVAL) or read the kernel source code to check for this support.

> If a file is opened with O_DIRECT by one process, and opened normally (i.e., so that the buffer cache is used) by another process, then there is no coherency between the contents of the buffer cache and the data read or written via direct I/O. Such scenarios should be avoided.
>
> The *raw(8)* manual page describes an older (now deprecated) technique for obtaining raw access to a disk device.

Alignment restrictions for direct I/O

Because direct I/O (on both disk devices and files) involves direct access to the disk, we must observe a number of restrictions when performing I/O:

- The data buffer being transferred must be aligned on a memory boundary that is a multiple of the block size.
- The file or device offset at which data transfer commences must be a multiple of the block size.
- The length of the data to be transferred must be a multiple of the block size.

Failure to observe any of these restrictions results in the error EINVAL. In the above list, *block size* means the physical block size of the device (typically 512 bytes).

> When performing direct I/O, Linux 2.4 is more restrictive than Linux 2.6: the alignment, length, and offset must be multiples of the *logical* block size of the underlying file system. (Typical file system logical block sizes are 1024, 2048, or 4096 bytes.)

Example program

Listing 13-1 provides a simple example of the use of O_DIRECT while opening a file for reading. This program takes up to four command-line arguments specifying, in order, the file to be read, the number of bytes to be read from the file, the offset to which the program should seek before reading from the file, and the alignment of the data buffer passed to *read()*. The last two arguments are optional, and default to offset 0 and 4096 bytes, respectively. Here are some examples of what we see when we run this program:

```
$ ./direct_read /test/x 512                    Read 512 bytes at offset 0
Read 512 bytes                                 Succeeds
$ ./direct_read /test/x 256
ERROR [EINVAL Invalid argument] read           Length is not a multiple of 512
$ ./direct_read /test/x 512 1
ERROR [EINVAL Invalid argument] read           Offset is not a multiple of 512
$ ./direct_read /test/x 4096 8192 512
Read 4096 bytes                                Succeeds
$ ./direct_read /test/x 4096 512 256
ERROR [EINVAL Invalid argument] read           Alignment is not a multiple of 512
```

> The program in Listing 13-1 uses the *memalign()* function to allocate a block of memory aligned on a multiple of its first argument. We describe *memalign()* in Section 7.1.4.

Listing 13-1: Using O_DIRECT to bypass the buffer cache

―――――――――――――――――――――――――――――― **filebuff/direct_read.c**
```c
#define _GNU_SOURCE     /* Obtain O_DIRECT definition from <fcntl.h> */
#include <fcntl.h>
#include <malloc.h>
#include "tlpi_hdr.h"

int
main(int argc, char *argv[])
{
    int fd;
    ssize_t numRead;
    size_t length, alignment;
    off_t offset;
    char *buf;

    if (argc < 3 || strcmp(argv[1], "--help") == 0)
        usageErr("%s file length [offset [alignment]]\n", argv[0]);
```

```
length = getLong(argv[2], GN_ANY_BASE, "length");
offset = (argc > 3) ? getLong(argv[3], GN_ANY_BASE, "offset") : 0;
alignment = (argc > 4) ? getLong(argv[4], GN_ANY_BASE, "alignment") : 4096;

fd = open(argv[1], O_RDONLY | O_DIRECT);
if (fd == -1)
    errExit("open");

/* memalign() allocates a block of memory aligned on an address that
   is a multiple of its first argument. By specifying this argument as
   2 * 'alignment' and then adding 'alignment' to the returned pointer,
   we ensure that 'buf' is aligned on a non-power-of-two multiple of
   'alignment'. We do this to ensure that if, for example, we ask
   for a 256-byte aligned buffer, we don't accidentally get a
   buffer that is also aligned on a 512-byte boundary. */

buf = memalign(alignment * 2, length + alignment);
if (buf == NULL)
    errExit("memalign");

buf += alignment;

if (lseek(fd, offset, SEEK_SET) == -1)
    errExit("lseek");

numRead = read(fd, buf, length);
if (numRead == -1)
    errExit("read");
printf("Read %ld bytes\n", (long) numRead);

exit(EXIT_SUCCESS);
}
```

—————————————————————————————— filebuff/direct_read.c

13.7 Mixing Library Functions and System Calls for File I/O

It is possible to mix the use of system calls and the standard C library functions to perform I/O on the same file. The *fileno()* and *fdopen()* functions assist us with this task.

```
#include <stdio.h>

int fileno(FILE *stream);
```
                        Returns file descriptor on success, or −1 on error
```
FILE *fdopen(int fd, const char *mode);
```
                        Returns (new) file pointer on success, or NULL on error

Given a stream, *fileno()* returns the corresponding file descriptor (i.e., the one that the *stdio* library has opened for this stream). This file descriptor can then be used in the usual way with I/O system calls such as *read()*, *write()*, *dup()*, and *fcntl()*.

The *fdopen()* function is the converse of *fileno()*. Given a file descriptor, it creates a corresponding stream that uses this descriptor for its I/O. The *mode* argument is the same as for *fopen()*; for example, *r* for read, *w* for write, or *a* for append. If this argument is not consistent with the access mode of the file descriptor *fd*, then *fdopen()* fails.

The *fdopen()* function is especially useful for descriptors referring to files other than regular files. As we'll see in later chapters, the system calls for creating sockets and pipes always return file descriptors. To use the *stdio* library with these file types, we must use *fdopen()* to create a corresponding file stream.

When using the *stdio* library functions in conjunction with I/O system calls to perform I/O on disk files, we must keep buffering issues in mind. I/O system calls transfer data directly to the kernel buffer cache, while the *stdio* library waits until the stream's user-space buffer is full before calling *write()* to transfer that buffer to the kernel buffer cache. Consider the following code used to write to standard output:

```
printf("To man the world is twofold, ");
write(STDOUT_FILENO, "in accordance with his twofold attitude.\n", 41);
```

In the usual case, the output of the *printf()* will typically appear *after* the output of the *write()*, so that this code yields the following output:

```
in accordance with his twofold attitude.
To man the world is twofold,
```

When intermingling I/O system calls and *stdio* functions, judicious use of *fflush()* may be required to avoid this problem. We could also use *setvbuf()* or *setbuf()* to disable buffering, but doing so might impact I/O performance for the application, since each output operation would then result in the execution of a *write()* system call.

> SUSv3 goes to some length specifying the requirements for an application to be able to mix the use of I/O system calls and *stdio* functions. See the section headed *Interaction of File Descriptors and Standard I/O Streams* under the chapter *General Information* in the *System Interfaces* (XSH) volume for details.

13.8 Summary

Buffering of input and output data is performed by the kernel, and also by the *stdio* library. In some cases, we may wish to prevent buffering, but we need to be aware of the impact this has on application performance. Various system calls and library functions can be used to control kernel and *stdio* buffering and to perform one-off buffer flushes.

A process can use *posix_fadvise()* to advise the kernel of its likely pattern for accessing data from a specified file. The kernel may use this information to optimize the use of the buffer cache, thus improving I/O performance.

The Linux-specific *open()* O_DIRECT flag allows specialized applications to bypass the buffer cache.

The *fileno()* and *fdopen()* functions assist us with the task of mixing system calls and standard C library functions to perform I/O on the same file. Given a stream, *fileno()* returns the corresponding file descriptor; *fdopen()* performs the converse operation, creating a new stream that employs a specified open file descriptor.

Further information

[Bach, 1986] describes the implementation and advantages of the buffer cache on System V. [Goodheart & Cox, 1994] and [Vahalia, 1996] also describe the rationale and implementation of the System V buffer cache. Further relevant information specific to Linux can be found in [Bovet & Cesati, 2005] and [Love, 2010].

13.9 Exercises

13-1. Using the *time* built-in command of the shell, try timing the operation of the program in Listing 4-1 (copy.c) on your system.

    a) Experiment with different file and buffer sizes. You can set the buffer size using the *-DBUF_SIZE=nbytes* option when compiling the program.

    b) Modify the *open()* system call to include the O_SYNC flag. How much difference does this make to the speed for various buffer sizes?

    c) Try performing these timing tests on a range of file systems (e.g., *ext3*, *XFS*, *Btrfs*, and *JFS*). Are the results similar? Are the trends the same when going from small to large buffer sizes?

13-2. Time the operation of the filebuff/write_bytes.c program (provided in the source code distribution for this book) for various buffer sizes and file systems.

13-3. What is the effect of the following statements?

```
fflush(fp);
fsync(fileno(fp));
```

13-4. Explain why the output of the following code differs depending on whether standard output is redirected to a terminal or to a disk file.

```
printf("If I had more time, \n");
write(STDOUT_FILENO, "I would have written you a shorter letter.\n", 43);
```

13-5. The command *tail [−n num] file* prints the last *num* lines (ten by default) of the named file. Implement this command using I/O system calls (*lseek()*, *read()*, *write()*, and so on). Keep in mind the buffering issues described in this chapter, in order to make the implementation efficient.

14

FILE SYSTEMS

In Chapters 4, 5, and 13, we looked at file I/O, with a particular focus on regular (i.e., disk) files. In this and the following chapters, we go into detail on a range of file-related topics:

- This chapter looks at file systems.

- Chapter 15 describes various attributes associated with a file, including the timestamps, ownership, and permissions.

- Chapters 16 and 17 consider two new features of Linux 2.6: extended attributes and access control lists (ACLs). Extended attributes are a method of associating arbitrary metadata with a file. ACLs are an extension of the traditional UNIX file permission model.

- Chapter 18 looks at directories and links.

The majority of this chapter is concerned with file systems, which are organized collections of files and directories. We explain a range of file-system concepts, sometimes using the traditional Linux *ext2* file system as a specific example. We also briefly describe some of the journaling file systems available on Linux.

We conclude the chapter with a discussion of the system calls used to mount and unmount a file system, and the library functions used to obtain information about mounted file systems.

14.1 Device Special Files (Devices)

This chapter frequently mentions disk devices, so we start with a brief overview of the concept of a device file.

A device special file corresponds to a device on the system. Within the kernel, each device type has a corresponding device driver, which handles all I/O requests for the device. A *device driver* is a unit of kernel code that implements a set of operations that (normally) correspond to input and output actions on an associated piece of hardware. The API provided by device drivers is fixed, and includes operations corresponding to the system calls *open()*, *close()*, *read()*, *write()*, *mmap()*, and *ioctl()*. The fact that each device driver provides a consistent interface, hiding the differences in operation of individual devices, allows for *universality of I/O* (Section 4.2).

Some devices are real, such as mice, disks, and tape drives. Others are *virtual*, meaning that there is no corresponding hardware; rather, the kernel provides (via a device driver) an abstract device with an API that is the same as a real device.

Devices can be divided into two types:

- *Character devices* handle data on a character-by-character basis. Terminals and keyboards are examples of character devices.
- *Block devices* handle data a block at a time. The size of a block depends on the type of device, but is typically some multiple of 512 bytes. Disks are a common example of block devices.

Device files appear within the file system, just like other files, usually under the /dev directory. The superuser can create a device file using the *mknod* command, and the same task can be performed in a privileged (CAP_MKNOD) program using the *mknod()* system call.

> We don't describe the *mknod()* ("make file-system i-node") system call in detail since its use is straightforward, and the only purpose for which it is required nowadays is to create device files, which is not a common application requirement. We can also use *mknod()* to create FIFOs (Section 44.7), but the *mkfifo()* function is preferred for this task. Historically, some UNIX implementations also used *mknod()* for creating directories, but this use has now been replaced by the *mkdir()* system call. Nevertheless, some UNIX implementations—but not Linux—preserve this capability in *mknod()* for backward compatibility. See the *mknod(2)* manual page for further details.

In earlier versions of Linux, /dev contained entries for all possible devices on the system, even if such devices weren't actually connected to the system. This meant that /dev could contain literally thousands of unused entries, slowing the task of programs that needed to scan the contents of that directory, and making it impossible to use the contents of the directory as a means of discovering which devices were actually present on the system. In Linux 2.6, these problems are solved by the *udev* program. The *udev* program relies on the *sysfs* file system, which exports information about devices and other kernel objects into user space via a pseudo-file system mounted under /sys.

[Kroah-Hartman, 2003] provides an overview of *udev*, and outlines the reasons it is considered superior to *devfs*, the Linux 2.4 solution to the same problems. Information about the *sysfs* file system can be found in the Linux 2.6 kernel source file `Documentation/filesystems/sysfs.txt` and in [Mochel, 2005].

Device IDs

Each device file has a *major ID number* and a *minor ID number*. The major ID identifies the general class of device, and is used by the kernel to look up the appropriate driver for this type of device. The minor ID uniquely identifies a particular device within a general class. The major and minor IDs of a device file are displayed by the *ls −l* command.

A device's major and minor IDs are recorded in the i-node for the device file. (We describe i-nodes in Section 14.4.) Each device driver registers its association with a specific major device ID, and this association provides the connection between the device special file and the device driver. The name of the device file has no relevance when the kernel looks for the device driver.

On Linux 2.4 and earlier, the total number of devices on the system is limited by the fact that device major and minor IDs are each represented using just 8 bits. The fact that major device IDs are fixed and centrally assigned (by the Linux Assigned Names and Numbers Authority; see *http://www.lanana.org/*) further exacerbates this limitation. Linux 2.6 eases this limitation by using more bits to hold the major and minor device IDs (respectively, 12 and 20 bits).

14.2 Disks and Partitions

Regular files and directories typically reside on hard disk devices. (Files and directories may also exist on other devices, such as CD-ROMs, flash memory cards, and virtual disks, but for the present discussion, we are interested primarily in hard disk devices.) In the following sections, we look at how disks are organized and divided into partitions.

Disk drives

A hard disk drive is a mechanical device consisting of one or more platters that rotate at high speed (of the order of thousands of revolutions per minute). Magnetically encoded information on the disk surface is retrieved or modified by read/write heads that move radially across the disk. Physically, information on the disk surface is located on a set of concentric circles called *tracks*. Tracks themselves are divided into a number of *sectors*, each of which consists of a series of *physical* blocks. Physical blocks are typically 512 bytes (or some multiple thereof) in size, and represent the smallest unit of information that the drive can read or write.

Although modern disks are fast, reading and writing information on the disk still takes significant time. The disk head must first move to the appropriate track (seek time), then the drive must wait until the appropriate sector rotates under the head (rotational latency), and finally the required blocks must be transferred (transfer time). The total time required to carry out such an operation is typically of the order of milliseconds. By comparison, modern CPUs are capable of executing millions of instructions in this time.

Disk partitions

Each disk is divided into one or more (nonoverlapping) *partitions*. Each partition is treated by the kernel as a separate device residing under the /dev directory.

> The system administrator determines the number, type, and size of partitions on a disk using the *fdisk* command. The command *fdisk −l* lists all partitions on a disk. The Linux-specific /proc/partitions file lists the major and minor device numbers, size, and name of each disk partition on the system.

A disk partition may hold any type of information, but usually contains one of the following:

*   a *file system* holding regular files and directories, as described in Section 14.3;
*   a *data area* accessed as a raw-mode device, as described in Section 13.6 (some database management systems use this technique); or
*   a *swap area* used by the kernel for memory management.

A swap area is created using the *mkswap(8)* command. A privileged (CAP_SYS_ADMIN) process can use the *swapon()* system call to notify the kernel that a disk partition is to be used as a swap area. The *swapoff()* system call performs the converse function, telling the kernel to cease using a disk partition as a swap area. These system calls are not standardized in SUSv3, but they exist on many UNIX implementations. See the *swapon(2)*, and *swapon(8)* manual pages for additional information.

> The Linux-specific /proc/swaps file can be used to display information about the currently enabled swap areas on the system. This information includes the size of each swap area and the amount of the area that is in use.

14.3 File Systems

A file system is an organized collection of regular files and directories. A file system is created using the *mkfs* command.

One of the strengths of Linux is that it supports a wide variety of file systems, including the following:

*   the traditional *ext2* file system;
*   various native UNIX file systems such as the Minix, System V, and BSD file systems;
*   Microsoft's FAT, FAT32, and NTFS file systems;
*   the ISO 9660 CD-ROM file system;
*   Apple Macintosh's HFS;
*   a range of network file systems, including Sun's widely used NFS (information about the Linux implementation of NFS is available at *http://nfs.sourceforge.net/*), IBM and Microsoft's SMB, Novell's NCP, and the Coda file system developed at Carnegie Mellon University; and
*   a range of journaling file systems, including *ext3*, *ext4*, *Reiserfs*, *JFS*, *XFS*, and *Btrfs*.

The file-system types currently known by the kernel can be viewed in the Linux-specific `/proc/filesystems` file.

> Linux 2.6.14 added the *Filesystem in Userspace* (FUSE) facility. This mechanism adds hooks to the kernel that allow a file system to be completely implemented via a user-space program, without needing to patch or recompile the kernel. For further details, see *http://fuse.sourceforge.net/*.

The *ext2* file system

For many years, the most widely used file system on Linux was *ext2*, the *Second Extended File System*, which is the successor to the original Linux file system, *ext*. In more recent times, the use of *ext2* has declined in favor of various journaling file systems. Sometimes, it is useful to describe generic file-system concepts in terms of a specific file-system implementation, and for this purpose, we use *ext2* as an example at various points later in this chapter.

> The *ext2* file system was written by Remy Card. The source code for *ext2* is small (around 5000 lines of C) and forms the model for several other file-system implementations. The *ext2* home page is *http://e2fsprogs.sourceforge.net/ext2.html*. This web site includes a good overview paper describing the implementation of *ext2*. *The Linux Kernel*, an online book by David Rusling available at *http://www.tldp.org/*, also describes *ext2*.

File-system structure

The basic unit for allocating space in a file system is a *logical* block, which is some multiple of contiguous physical blocks on the disk device on which the file system resides. For example, the logical block size on *ext2* is 1024, 2048, or 4096 bytes. (The logical block size is specified as an argument of the *mkfs(8)* command used to build the file system.)

> A privileged (CAP_SYS_RAWIO) program can use the FIBMAP *ioctl()* operation to determine the physical location of a specified block of a file. The third argument of the call is a value-result integer. Before the call, this argument should be set to a logical block number (the first logical block is number 0); after the call, it is set to the number of the starting physical block where that logical block is stored.

Figure 14-1 shows the relationship between disk partitions and file systems, and shows the parts of a (generic) file system.

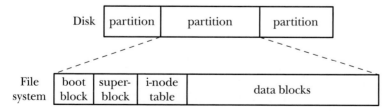

Figure 14-1: Layout of disk partitions and a file system

A file system contains the following parts:

- *Boot block*: This is always the first block in a file system. The boot block is not used by the file system; rather, it contains information used to boot the operating system. Although only one boot block is needed by the operating system, all file systems have a boot block (most of which are unused).

- *Superblock*: This is a single block, immediately following the boot block, which contains parameter information about the file system, including:
  - the size of the i-node table;
  - the size of logical blocks in this file system; and
  - the size of the file system in logical blocks.

  Different file systems residing on the same physical device can be of different types and sizes, and have different parameter settings (e.g., block size). This is one of the reasons for splitting a disk into multiple partitions.

- *I-node table*: Each file or directory in the file system has a unique entry in the i-node table. This entry records various information about the file. I-nodes are discussed in greater detail in the next section. The i-node table is sometimes also called the *i-list*.

- *Data blocks*: The great majority of space in a file system is used for the blocks of data that form the files and directories residing in the file system.

> In the specific case of the *ext2* file system, the picture is somewhat more complex than described in the main text. After the initial boot block, the file system is broken into a set of equal-sized *block groups*. Each block group contains a copy of the superblock, parameter information about the block group, and then the i-node table and data blocks for this block group. By attempting to store all of the blocks of a file within the same block group, the *ext2* file system aims to reduce seek time when sequentially accessing a file. For further information, see the Linux source code file `Documentation/filesystems/ext2.txt`, the source code of the *dumpe2fs* program that comes as part of the *e2fsprogs* package, and [Bovet & Cesati, 2005].

14.4 I-nodes

A file system's i-node table contains one i-node (short for *index node*) for each file residing in the file system. I-nodes are identified numerically by their sequential location in the i-node table. The *i-node number* (or simply *i-number*) of a file is the first field displayed by the *ls −li* command. The information maintained in an i-node includes the following:

- File type (e.g., regular file, directory, symbolic link, character device).
- Owner (also referred to as the user ID or UID) for the file.
- Group (also referred to as the group ID or GID) for the file.
- Access permissions for three categories of user: *owner* (sometimes referred to as *user*), *group*, and *other* (the rest of the world). Section 15.4 provides further details.

- Three timestamps: time of last access to the file (shown by *ls −lu*), time of last modification of the file (the default time shown by *ls −l*), and time of last status change (last change to i-node information, shown by *ls −lc*). As on other UNIX implementations, it is notable that most Linux file systems don't record the creation time of a file.

- Number of hard links to the file.

- Size of the file in bytes.

- Number of blocks actually allocated to the file, measured in units of 512-byte blocks. There may not be a simple correspondence between this number and the size of the file in bytes, since a file can contain holes (Section 4.7), and thus require fewer allocated blocks than would be expected according to its nominal size in bytes.

- Pointers to the data blocks of the file.

I-nodes and data block pointers in *ext2*

Like most UNIX file systems, the *ext2* file system doesn't store the data blocks of a file contiguously or even in sequential order (though it does attempt to store them close to one another). To locate the file data blocks, the kernel maintains a set of pointers in the i-node. The system used for doing this on the *ext2* file system is shown in Figure 14-2.

> Removing the need to store the blocks of a file contiguously allows the file system to use space in an efficient way. In particular, it reduces the incidence of *fragmentation* of free disk space—the wastage created by the existence of numerous pieces of noncontiguous free space, all of which are too small to use. Put conversely, we could say that the advantage of efficiently using the free disk space is paid for by fragmenting files in the filled disk space.

Under *ext2*, each i-node contains 15 pointers. The first 12 of these pointers (numbered 0 to 11 in Figure 14-2) point to the location in the file system of the first 12 blocks of the file. The next pointer is a *pointer to a block of pointers* that give the locations of the thirteenth and subsequent data blocks of the file. The number of pointers in this block depends on the block size of the file system. Each pointer requires 4 bytes, so there may be from 256 pointers (for a 1024-byte block size) to 1024 pointers (for a 4096-byte block size). This allows for quite large files. For even larger files, the fourteenth pointer (numbered 13 in the diagram) is a *double indirect pointer*—it points to blocks of pointers that in turn point to blocks of pointers that in turn point to data blocks of the file. And should the need for a truly enormous file arise, there is a further level of indirection: the last pointer in the i-node is a *triple-indirect pointer*.

This seemingly complex system is designed to satisfy a number of requirements. To begin with, it allows the i-node structure to be a fixed size, while at the same time allowing for files of an arbitrary size. Additionally, it allows the file system to store the blocks of a file noncontiguously, while also allowing the data to be accessed randomly via *lseek()*; the kernel just needs to calculate which pointer(s) to follow. Finally, for small files, which form the overwhelming majority of files on most systems, this scheme allows the file data blocks to be accessed rapidly via the direct pointers of the i-node.

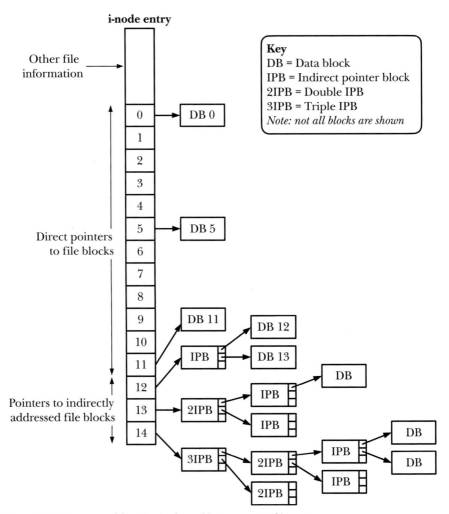

Figure 14-2: Structure of file blocks for a file in an *ext2* file system

> As an example, the author measured one system containing somewhat more than 150,000 files. Just over 30% of the files were less than 1000 bytes in size, and 80% occupied 10,000 bytes or less. Assuming a 1024-byte block size, all of the latter files could be referenced using just the 12 direct pointers, which can refer to blocks containing a total of 12,288 bytes. Using a 4096-byte block size, this limit rises to 49,152 bytes (95% of the files on the system fell under that limit).

This design also allows for enormous file sizes; for a block size of 4096 bytes, the theoretical largest file size is slightly more than 1024*1024*1024*4096, or approximately 4 terabytes (4096 GB). (We say *slightly more* because of the blocks pointed to by the direct, indirect, and double indirect pointers. These are insignificant compared to the range that can be pointed to by the triple indirect pointer.)

One other benefit conferred by this design is that files can have holes, as described in Section 4.7. Rather than allocate blocks of null bytes for the holes in a file, the file system can just mark (with the value 0) appropriate pointers in the i-node and in the indirect pointer blocks to indicate that they don't refer to actual disk blocks.

14.5 The Virtual File System (VFS)

Each of the file systems available on Linux differs in the details of its implementation. Such differences include, for example, the way in which the blocks of a file are allocated and the manner in which directories are organized. If every program that worked with files needed to understand the specific details of each file system, the task of writing programs that worked with all of the different file systems would be nearly impossible. The *virtual file system* (VFS, sometimes also referred to as the *virtual file switch*) is a kernel feature that resolves this problem by creating an abstraction layer for file-system operations (see Figure 14-3). The ideas behind the VFS are straightforward:

- The VFS defines a generic interface for file-system operations. All programs that work with files specify their operations in terms of this generic interface.

- Each file system provides an implementation for the VFS interface.

Under this scheme, programs need to understand only the VFS interface and can ignore details of individual file-system implementations.

The VFS interface includes operations corresponding to all of the usual system calls for working with file systems and directories, such as *open()*, *read()*, *write()*, *lseek()*, *close()*, *truncate()*, *stat()*, *mount()*, *umount()*, *mmap()*, *mkdir()*, *link()*, *unlink()*, *symlink()*, and *rename()*.

The VFS abstraction layer is closely modeled on the traditional UNIX file-system model. Naturally, some file systems—especially non-UNIX file systems—don't support all of the VFS operations (e.g., Microsoft's VFAT doesn't support the notion of symbolic links, created using *symlink()*). In such cases, the underlying file system passes an error code back to the VFS layer indicating the lack of support, and the VFS in turn passes this error code back to the application.

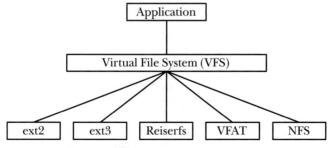

Figure 14-3: The virtual file system

14.6 Journaling File Systems

The *ext2* file system is a good example of a traditional UNIX file system, and suffers from a classic limitation of such file systems: after a system crash, a file-system consistency check (*fsck*) must be performed on reboot in order to ensure the integrity of the file system. This is necessary because, at the time of the system crash, a file update may have been only partially completed, and the file-system metadata (directory entries, i-node information, and file data block pointers) may be in an inconsistent state, so that the file system might be further damaged if these inconsistencies are not repaired. A file-system consistency check ensures the consistency of the file-system metadata. Where possible, repairs are performed; otherwise, information that is not retrievable (possibly including file data) is discarded.

The problem is that a consistency check requires examining the entire file system. On a small file system, this may take anything from several seconds to a few minutes. On a large file system, this may require several hours, which is a serious problem for systems that must maintain high availability (e.g., network servers).

Journaling file systems eliminate the need for lengthy file-system consistency checks after a system crash. A journaling file system logs (journals) all metadata updates to a special on-disk journal file before they are actually carried out. The updates are logged in groups of related metadata updates (*transactions*). In the event of a system crash in the middle of a transaction, on system reboot, the log can be used to rapidly redo any incomplete updates and bring the file system back to a consistent state. (To borrow database parlance, we can say that a journaling file system ensures that file metadata transactions are always *committed* as a complete unit.) Even very large journaling file systems can typically be available within seconds after a system crash, making them very attractive for systems with high-availability requirements.

The most notable disadvantage of journaling is that it adds time to file updates, though good design can make this overhead low.

> Some journaling file systems ensure only the consistency of file metadata. Because they don't log file data, data may still be lost in the event of a crash. The *ext3*, *ext4*, and *Reiserfs* file systems provide options for logging data updates, but, depending on the workload, this may result in lower file I/O performance.

The journaling file systems available for Linux include the following:

- *Reiserfs* was the first of the journaling file systems to be integrated into the kernel (in version 2.4.1). *Reiserfs* provides a feature called *tail packing* (or *tail merging*): small files (and the final fragment of larger files) are packed into the same disk blocks as the file metadata. Because many systems have (and some applications create) large numbers of small files, this can save a significant amount of disk space.

- The *ext3* file system was a result of a project to add journaling to *ext2* with minimal impact. The migration path from *ext2* to *ext3* is very easy (no backup and restore are required), and it is possible to migrate in the reverse direction as well. The *ext3* file system was integrated into the kernel in version 2.4.15.

- *JFS* was developed at IBM. It was integrated into the 2.4.20 kernel.

- *XFS* (*http://oss.sgi.com/projects/xfs/*) was originally developed by Silicon Graphics (SGI) in the early 1990s for Irix, its proprietary UNIX implementation. In 2001, *XFS* was ported to Linux and made available as a free software project. *XFS* was integrated into the 2.4.24 kernel.

Support for the various file systems is enabled using kernel options that are set under the *File systems* menu when configuring the kernel.

At the time of writing, work is in progress on two other file systems that provide journaling and a range of other advanced features:

- The *ext4* file system (*http://ext4.wiki.kernel.org/*) is the successor to *ext3*. The first pieces of the implementation were added in kernel 2.6.19, and various features were added in later kernel versions. Among the planned (or already implemented) features for *ext4* are extents (reservation of contiguous blocks of storage) and other allocation features that aim to reduce file fragmentation, online file-system defragmentation, faster file-system checking, and support for nanosecond timestamps.

- *Btrfs* (B-tree FS, usually pronounced "butter FS"; *http://btrfs.wiki.kernel.org/*) is a new file system designed from the ground up to provide a range of modern features, including extents, writable snapshots (which provide functionality equivalent to metadata and data journaling), checksums on data and metadata, online file-system checking, online file-system defragmentation, space-efficient packing of small files, and space-efficient indexed directories. It was integrated into the kernel in version 2.6.29.

14.7   Single Directory Hierarchy and Mount Points

On Linux, as on other UNIX systems, all files from all file systems reside under a single directory tree. At the base of this tree is the root directory, / (slash). Other file systems are *mounted* under the root directory and appear as subtrees within the overall hierarchy. The superuser uses a command of the following form to mount a file system:

```
$ mount device directory
```

This command attaches the file system on the named *device* into the directory hierarchy at the specified *directory*—the file system's *mount point*. It is possible to change the location at which a file system is mounted—the file system is unmounted using the *umount* command, and then mounted once more at a different point.

> With Linux 2.4.19 and later, things became more complicated. The kernel now supports per-process *mount namespaces*. This means that each process potentially has its own set of file-system mount points, and thus may see a different single directory hierarchy from other processes. We explain this point further when we describe the CLONE_NEWNS flag in Section 28.2.1.

To list the currently mounted file systems, we can use the command *mount*, with no arguments, as in the following example (whose output has been somewhat abridged):

```
$ mount
/dev/sda6 on / type ext4 (rw)
proc on /proc type proc (rw)
sysfs on /sys type sysfs (rw)
devpts on /dev/pts type devpts (rw,mode=0620,gid=5)
/dev/sda8 on /home type ext3 (rw,acl,user_xattr)
/dev/sda1 on /windows/C type vfat (rw,noexec,nosuid,nodev)
/dev/sda9 on /home/mtk/test type reiserfs (rw)
```

Figure 14-4 shows a partial directory and file structure for the system on which the above *mount* command was performed. This diagram shows how the mount points map onto the directory hierarchy.

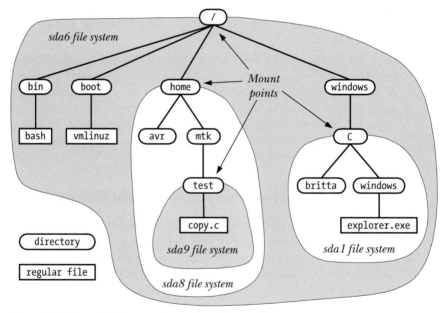

Figure 14-4: Example directory hierarchy showing file-system mount points

14.8 Mounting and Unmounting File Systems

The *mount()* and *umount()* system calls allow a privileged (CAP_SYS_ADMIN) process to mount and unmount file systems. Most UNIX implementations provide versions of these system calls. However, they are not standardized by SUSv3, and their operation varies both across UNIX implementations and across file systems.

Before looking at these system calls, it is useful to know about three files that contain information about the file systems that are currently mounted or can be mounted:

- A list of the currently mounted file systems can be read from the Linux-specific /proc/mounts virtual file. /proc/mounts is an interface to kernel data structures, so it always contains accurate information about mounted file systems.

  > With the arrival of the per-process mount namespace feature mentioned earlier, each process now has a /proc/*PID*/mounts file that lists the mount points constituting its mount namespace, and /proc/mounts is just a symbolic link to /proc/self/mounts.

- The *mount(8)* and *umount(8)* commands automatically maintain the file /etc/mtab, which contains information that is similar to that in /proc/mounts, but slightly more detailed. In particular, /etc/mtab includes file system–specific options given to *mount(8)*, which are not shown in /proc/mounts. However, because the *mount()* and *umount()* system calls don't update /etc/mtab, this file may be inaccurate if some application that mounts or unmounts devices fails to update it.

- The /etc/fstab file, maintained manually by the system administrator, contains descriptions of all of the available file systems on a system, and is used by the *mount(8)*, *umount(8)*, and *fsck(8)* commands.

The /proc/mounts, /etc/mtab, and /etc/fstab files share a common format, described in the *fstab(5)* manual page. Here is an example of a line from the /proc/mounts file:

```
/dev/sda9 /boot ext3 rw 0 0
```

This line contains six fields:

1. The name of the mounted device.
2. The mount point for the device.
3. The file-system type.
4. Mount flags. In the above example, *rw* indicates that the file system was mounted read-write.
5. A number used to control the operation of file-system backups by *dump(8)*. This field and the next are used only in the /etc/fstab file; for /proc/mounts and /etc/mtab, these fields are always 0.
6. A number used to control the order in which *fsck(8)* checks file systems at system boot time.

The *getfsent(3)* and *getmntent(3)* manual pages document functions that can be used to read records from these files.

14.8.1 Mounting a File System: *mount()*

The *mount()* system call mounts the file system contained on the device specified by *source* under the directory (the *mount point*) specified by *target*.

```
#include <sys/mount.h>

int mount(const char *source, const char *target, const char *fstype,
          unsigned long mountflags, const void *data);
```
                                    Returns 0 on success, or −1 on error

The names *source* and *target* are used for the first two arguments because *mount()* can perform other tasks than mounting a disk file system under a directory.

The *fstype* argument is a string identifying the type of file system contained on the device, such as *ext4* or *btrfs*.

The *mountflags* argument is a bit mask constructed by ORing (|) zero or more of the flags shown in Table 14-1, which are described in more detail below.

The final *mount()* argument, *data*, is a pointer to a buffer of information whose interpretation depends on the file system. For most file-system types, this argument is a string consisting of comma-separated option settings. A full list of these options can be found in the *mount(8)* manual page (or the documentation for the file system concerned, if it is not described in *mount(8)*).

Table 14-1: *mountflags* values for *mount()*

Flag	Purpose
MS_BIND	Create a bind mount (since Linux 2.4)
MS_DIRSYNC	Make directory updates synchronous (since Linux 2.6)
MS_MANDLOCK	Permit mandatory locking of files
MS_MOVE	Atomically move mount point to new location
MS_NOATIME	Don't update last access time for files
MS_NODEV	Don't allow access to devices
MS_NODIRATIME	Don't update last access time for directories
MS_NOEXEC	Don't allow programs to be executed
MS_NOSUID	Disable set-user-ID and set-group-ID programs
MS_RDONLY	Read-only mount; files can't be created or modified
MS_REC	Recursive mount (since Linux 2.4.11)
MS_RELATIME	Update last access time only if older than last modification time or last status change time (since Linux 2.6.20)
MS_REMOUNT	Remount with new *mountflags* and *data*
MS_STRICTATIME	Always update last access time (since Linux 2.6.30)
MS_SYNCHRONOUS	Make all file and directory updates synchronous

The *mountflags* argument is a bit mask of flags that modify the operation of *mount()*. Zero or more of the following flags can be specified in *mountflags*:

MS_BIND (since Linux 2.4)

> Create a bind mount. We describe this feature in Section 14.9.4. If this flag is specified, then the *fstype* and *data* arguments are ignored, as are flags in *mountflags* other than MS_REC (described below).

MS_DIRSYNC (since Linux 2.6)

> Make directory updates synchronous. This is similar to the effect of the *open()* O_SYNC flag (Section 13.3), but applies only to directory updates. The MS_SYNCHRONOUS flag described below provides a superset of the functionality of MS_DIRSYNC, ensuring that both file and directory updates are performed synchronously. The MS_DIRSYNC flag allows an application to ensure that directory updates (e.g., *open(pathname, O_CREAT)*, *rename()*, *link()*, *unlink()*, *symlink()*, and *mkdir()*) are synchronized without incurring the expense of synchronizing all file updates. The FS_DIRSYNC_FL flag (Section 15.5) serves a similar purpose to MS_DIRSYNC, with the difference that FS_DIRSYNC_FL can be applied to individual directories. In addition, on Linux, calling *fsync()* on a file descriptor that refers to a directory provides a means of synchronizing directory updates on a per-directory basis. (This Linux-specific *fsync()* behavior is not specified in SUSv3.)

MS_MANDLOCK

> Permit mandatory record locking on files in this file system. We describe record locking in Chapter 55.

MS_MOVE

> Atomically move the existing mount point specified by *source* to the new location specified by *target*. This corresponds to the *--move* option to *mount(8)*. This is equivalent to unmounting the subtree and then remounting at a different location, except that there is no point in time when the subtree is unmounted. The *source* argument should be a string specified as a *target* in a previous *mount()* call. When this flag is specified, the *fstype* and *data* arguments are ignored, as are the remaining flags in *mountflags*.

MS_NOATIME

> Don't update the last access time for files in this file system. The purpose of this flag, as well as the MS_NODIRATIME flag described below, is to eliminate the extra disk access required to update the file i-node each time a file is accessed. In some applications, maintaining this timestamp is not critical, and avoiding doing so can significantly improve performance. The MS_NOATIME flag serves a similar purpose to the FS_NOATIME_FL flag (Section 15.5), with the difference that FS_NOATIME_FL can be applied to single files. Linux also provides similar functionality via the O_NOATIME *open()* flag, which selects this behavior for individual open files (Section 4.3.1).

MS_NODEV

> Don't allow access to block and character devices on this file system. This is a security feature designed to prevent users from doing things such as inserting a removable disk containing device special files that would allow arbitrary access to the system.

MS_NODIRATIME

> Don't update the last access time for directories on this file system. (This flag provides a subset of the functionality of MS_NOATIME, which prevents updates to the last access time for all file types.)

MS_NOEXEC

> Don't allow programs (or scripts) to be executed from this file system. This is useful if the file system contains non-Linux executables.

MS_NOSUID

> Disable set-user-ID and set-group-ID programs on this file system. This is a security feature to prevent users from running set-user-ID and set-group-ID programs from removable devices.

MS_RDONLY

> Mount the file system read-only, so that no new files can be created and no existing files can be modified.

MS_REC (since Linux 2.4.11)

> This flag is used in conjunction with other flags (e.g., MS_BIND) to recursively apply the mount action to all of the mounts in a subtree.

MS_RELATIME (since Linux 2.6.20)

> Update the last access timestamp for files on this file system only if the current setting of this timestamp is less than or equal to either the last modification or the last status change timestamp. This provides some of the performance benefits of MS_NOATIME, but is useful for programs that need to know if a file has been read since it was last updated. Since Linux 2.6.30, the behavior provided by MS_RELATIME is the default (unless the MS_NOATIME flag is specified), and the MS_STRICTATIME flag is required to obtain classical behavior. In addition, since Linux 2.6.30, the last access timestamp is always updated if its current value is more than 24 hours in the past, even if the current value is more recent than the last modification and last status change timestamps. (This is useful for certain system programs that monitor directories to see whether files have recently been accessed.)

MS_REMOUNT

> Alter the *mountflags* and *data* for a file system that is already mounted (e.g., to make a read-only file system writable). When using this flag, the *target* argument should be the same as for the original *mount()* call, and the *source* and *fstype* arguments are ignored. This flag avoids the need to unmount and remount the disk, which may not be possible in some cases. For example, we can't unmount a file system if any process has files open on, or its current

working directory located within, the file system (this will always be true of the root file system). Another example of where we need to use MS_REMOUNT is with *tmpfs* (memory-based) file systems (Section 14.10), which can't be unmounted without losing their contents. Not all *mountflags* are modifiable; see the *mount(2)* manual page for details.

MS_STRICTATIME (since Linux 2.6.30)

Always update the last access timestamp when files on this file system are accessed. This was the default behavior before Linux 2.6.30. If MS_STRICTATIME is specified, then MS_NOATIME and MS_RELATIME are ignored if they are also specified in *mountflags*.

MS_SYNCHRONOUS

Make all file and directory updates on this file system synchronous. (In the case of files, this is as though files were always opened with the *open()* O_SYNC flag.)

> Starting with kernel 2.6.15, Linux provides four new mount flags to support the notion of *shared subtrees*. The new flags are MS_PRIVATE, MS_SHARED, MS_SLAVE, and MS_UNBINDABLE. (These flags can be used in conjunction with MS_REC to propagate their effects to all of the submounts under a mount subtree.) Shared subtrees are designed for use with certain advanced file-system features, such as per-process mount namespaces (see the description of CLONE_NEWNS in Section 28.2.1), and the *Filesystem in Userspace* (FUSE) facility. The shared subtree facility permits file-system mounts to be propagated between mount namespaces in a controlled fashion. Details on shared subtrees can be found in the kernel source code file Documentation/filesystems/sharedsubtree.txt and [Viro & Pai, 2006].

Example program

The program in Listing 14-1 provides a command-level interface to the *mount(2)* system call. In effect, it is a crude version of the *mount(8)* command. The following shell session log demonstrates the use of this program. We begin by creating a directory to be used as a mount point and mounting a file system:

```
$ su                                    Need privilege to mount a file system
Password:
# mkdir /testfs
# ./t_mount -t ext2 -o bsdgroups /dev/sda12 /testfs
# cat /proc/mounts | grep sda12          Verify the setup
/dev/sda12 /testfs ext3 rw 0 0           Doesn't show bsdgroups
# grep sda12 /etc/mtab
```

We find that the preceding *grep* command produces no output because our program doesn't update /etc/mtab. We continue, remounting the file system read-only:

```
# ./t_mount -f Rr /dev/sda12 /testfs
# cat /proc/mounts | grep sda12          Verify change
/dev/sda12 /testfs ext3 ro 0 0
```

The string *ro* in the line displayed from /proc/mounts indicates that this is a read-only mount.

Finally, we move the mount point to a new location within the directory hierarchy:

```
# mkdir /demo
# ./t_mount -f m /testfs /demo
# cat /proc/mounts | grep sda12          Verify change
/dev/sda12 /demo ext3 ro 0
```

Listing 14-1: Using *mount()*

── **filesys/t_mount.c**

```
#include <sys/mount.h>
#include "tlpi_hdr.h"

static void
usageError(const char *progName, const char *msg)
{
    if (msg != NULL)
        fprintf(stderr, "%s", msg);

    fprintf(stderr, "Usage: %s [options] source target\n\n", progName);
    fprintf(stderr, "Available options:\n");
#define fpe(str) fprintf(stderr, "    " str)    /* Shorter! */
    fpe("-t fstype      [e.g., 'ext2' or 'reiserfs']\n");
    fpe("-o data        [file system-dependent options,\n");
    fpe("               e.g., 'bsdgroups' for ext2]\n");
    fpe("-f mountflags  can include any of:\n");
#define fpe2(str) fprintf(stderr, "           " str)
    fpe2("b - MS_BIND        create a bind mount\n");
    fpe2("d - MS_DIRSYNC     synchronous directory updates\n");
    fpe2("l - MS_MANDLOCK    permit mandatory locking\n");
    fpe2("m - MS_MOVE        atomically move subtree\n");
    fpe2("A - MS_NOATIME     don't update atime (last access time)\n");
    fpe2("V - MS_NODEV       don't permit device access\n");
    fpe2("D - MS_NODIRATIME  don't update atime on directories\n");
    fpe2("E - MS_NOEXEC      don't allow executables\n");
    fpe2("S - MS_NOSUID      disable set-user/group-ID programs\n");
    fpe2("r - MS_RDONLY      read-only mount\n");
    fpe2("c - MS_REC         recursive mount\n");
    fpe2("R - MS_REMOUNT     remount\n");
    fpe2("s - MS_SYNCHRONOUS make writes synchronous\n");
    exit(EXIT_FAILURE);
}

int
main(int argc, char *argv[])
{
    unsigned long flags;
    char *data, *fstype;
    int j, opt;

    flags = 0;
    data = NULL;
    fstype = NULL;

    while ((opt = getopt(argc, argv, "o:t:f:")) != -1) {
        switch (opt) {
```

```
          case 'o':
              data = optarg;
              break;

          case 't':
              fstype = optarg;
              break;

          case 'f':
              for (j = 0; j < strlen(optarg); j++) {
                  switch (optarg[j]) {
                  case 'b': flags |= MS_BIND;          break;
                  case 'd': flags |= MS_DIRSYNC;       break;
                  case 'l': flags |= MS_MANDLOCK;      break;
                  case 'm': flags |= MS_MOVE;          break;
                  case 'A': flags |= MS_NOATIME;       break;
                  case 'V': flags |= MS_NODEV;         break;
                  case 'D': flags |= MS_NODIRATIME;    break;
                  case 'E': flags |= MS_NOEXEC;        break;
                  case 'S': flags |= MS_NOSUID;        break;
                  case 'r': flags |= MS_RDONLY;        break;
                  case 'c': flags |= MS_REC;           break;
                  case 'R': flags |= MS_REMOUNT;       break;
                  case 's': flags |= MS_SYNCHRONOUS;   break;
                  default:  usageError(argv[0], NULL);
                  }
              }
              break;

          default:
              usageError(argv[0], NULL);
          }
      }

      if (argc != optind + 2)
          usageError(argv[0], "Wrong number of arguments\n");

      if (mount(argv[optind], argv[optind + 1], fstype, flags, data) == -1)
          errExit("mount");

      exit(EXIT_SUCCESS);
  }
```
—— **filesys/t_mount.c**

14.8.2   Unmounting a File System: *umount()* and *umount2()*

The *umount()* system call unmounts a mounted file system.

```
#include <sys/mount.h>

int umount(const char *target);
```
                                            Returns 0 on success, or −1 on error

The *target* argument specifies the mount point of the file system to be unmounted.

On Linux 2.2 and earlier, the file system can be identified in two ways: by the mount point or by the name of the device containing the file system. Since kernel 2.4, Linux doesn't allow the latter possibility, because a single file system can now be mounted at multiple locations, so that specifying a file system for *target* would be ambiguous. We explain this point in further detail in Section 14.9.1.

It is not possible to unmount a file system that is *busy*; that is, if there are open files on the file system, or a process's current working directory is somewhere in the file system. Calling *umount()* on a busy file system yields the error EBUSY.

The *umount2()* system call is an extended version of *umount()*. It allows finer control over the unmount operation via the *flags* argument.

```
#include <sys/mount.h>

int umount2(const char *target, int flags);
```
                                        Returns 0 on success, or −1 on error

This *flags* bit-mask argument consists of zero or more of the following values ORed together:

MNT_DETACH (since Linux 2.4.11)
>   Perform a *lazy* unmount. The mount point is marked so that no process can make new accesses to it, but processes that are already using it can continue to do so. The file system is actually unmounted when all processes cease using the mount.

MNT_EXPIRE (since Linux 2.6.8)
>   Mark the mount point as *expired*. If an initial *umount2()* call is made specifying this flag, and the mount point is not busy, then the call fails with the error EAGAIN, but the mount point is marked to expire. (If the mount point is busy, then the call fails with the error EBUSY, and the mount point is not marked to expire.) A mount point remains expired as long as no process subsequently makes use of it. A second *umount2()* call specifying MNT_EXPIRE will unmount an expired mount point. This provides a mechanism to unmount a file system that hasn't been used for some period of time. This flag can't be specified with MNT_DETACH or MNT_FORCE.

MNT_FORCE
>   Force an unmount even if the device is busy (NFS mounts only). Employing this option can cause data loss.

UMOUNT_NOFOLLOW (since Linux 2.6.34)
>   Don't dereference *target* if it is a symbolic link. This flag is designed for use in certain set-user-ID-*root* programs that allow unprivileged users to perform unmounts, in order to avoid the security problems that could occur if *target* is a symbolic link that is changed to point to a different location.

14.9 Advanced Mount Features

We now look at a number of more advanced features that can be employed when mounting file systems. We demonstrate the use of most of these features using the *mount(8)* command. The same effects can also be accomplished from a program via calls to *mount(2)*.

14.9.1 Mounting a File System at Multiple Mount Points

In kernel versions before 2.4, a file system could be mounted only on a single mount point. From kernel 2.4 onward, a file system can be mounted at multiple locations within the single directory hierarchy. Because each of the mount points shows the same subtree, changes made via one mount point are visible through the other(s), as demonstrated by the following shell session:

```
$ su                               Privilege is required to use mount(8)
Password:
# mkdir /testfs                    Create two directories for mount points
# mkdir /demo
# mount /dev/sda12 /testfs         Mount file system at one mount point
# mount /dev/sda12 /demo           Mount file system at second mount point
# mount | grep sda12               Verify the setup
/dev/sda12 on /testfs type ext3 (rw)
/dev/sda12 on /demo type ext3 (rw)
# touch /testfs/myfile             Make a change via first mount point
# ls /demo                         View files at second mount point
lost+found  myfile
```

The output of the *ls* command shows that the change made via the first mount point (/testfs) was visible via the second mount point (/demo).

We present one example of why it is useful to mount a file system at multiple points when we describe bind mounts in Section 14.9.4.

> It is because a device can be mounted at multiple points that the *umount()* system call can't take a device as its argument in Linux 2.4 and later.

14.9.2 Stacking Multiple Mounts on the Same Mount Point

In kernel versions before 2.4, a mount point could be used only once. Since kernel 2.4, Linux allows multiple mounts to be stacked on a single mount point. Each new mount hides the directory subtree previously visible at that mount point. When the mount at the top of the stack is unmounted, the previously hidden mount becomes visible once more, as demonstrated by the following shell session:

```
$ su                               Privilege is required to use mount(8)
Password:
# mount /dev/sda12 /testfs         Create first mount on /testfs
# touch /testfs/myfile             Make a file in this subtree
# mount /dev/sda13 /testfs         Stack a second mount on /testfs
# mount | grep testfs              Verify the setup
/dev/sda12 on /testfs type ext3 (rw)
/dev/sda13 on /testfs type reiserfs (rw)
```

```
# touch /testfs/newfile          Create a file in this subtree
# ls /testfs                     View files in this subtree
newfile
# umount /testfs                 Pop a mount from the stack
# mount | grep testfs
/dev/sda12 on /testfs type ext3 (rw)   Now only one mount on /testfs
# ls /testfs                     Previous mount is now visible
lost+found  myfile
```

One use of mount stacking is to stack a new mount on an existing mount point that is busy. Processes that hold file descriptors open, that are *chroot()*-jailed, or that have current working directories within the old mount point continue to operate under that mount, but processes making new accesses to the mount point use the new mount. Combined with a MNT_DETACH unmount, this can provide a smooth migration off a file system without needing to take the system into single-user mode. We'll see another example of how stacking mounts is useful when we discuss the *tmpfs* file system in Section 14.10.

14.9.3 Mount Flags That Are Per-Mount Options

In kernel versions before 2.4, there was a one-to-one correspondence between file systems and mount points. Because this no longer holds in Linux 2.4 and later, some of the *mountflags* values described in Section 14.8.1 can be set on a per-mount basis. These flags are MS_NOATIME (since Linux 2.6.16), MS_NODEV, MS_NODIRATIME (since Linux 2.6.16), MS_NOEXEC, MS_NOSUID, MS_RDONLY (since Linux 2.6.26), and MS_RELATIME. The following shell session demonstrates this effect for the MS_NOEXEC flag:

```
$ su
Password:
# mount /dev/sda12 /testfs
# mount -o noexec /dev/sda12 /demo
# cat /proc/mounts | grep sda12
/dev/sda12 /testfs ext3 rw 0 0
/dev/sda12 /demo ext3 rw,noexec 0 0
# cp /bin/echo /testfs
# /testfs/echo "Art is something which is well done"
Art is something which is well done
# /demo/echo "Art is something which is well done"
bash: /demo/echo: Permission denied
```

14.9.4 Bind Mounts

Starting with kernel 2.4, Linux permits the creation of bind mounts. A *bind mount* (created using the *mount()* MS_BIND flag) allows a directory or a file to be mounted at some other location in the file-system hierarchy. This results in the directory or file being visible in both locations. A bind mount is somewhat like a hard link, but differs in two respects:

- A bind mount can cross file-system mount points (and even *chroot* jails).
- It is possible to make a bind mount for a directory.

We can create a bind mount from the shell using the *--bind* option to *mount(8)*, as shown in the following examples.

In the first example, we bind mount a directory at another location and show that files created in one directory are visible at the other location:

```
$ su                          Privilege is required to use mount(8)
Password:
# pwd
/testfs
# mkdir d1                    Create directory to be bound at another location
# touch d1/x                  Create file in the directory
# mkdir d2                    Create mount point to which d1 will be bound
# mount --bind d1 d2          Create bind mount: d1 visible via d2
# ls d2                       Verify that we can see contents of d1 via d2
x
# touch d2/y                  Create second file in directory d2
# ls d1                       Verify that this change is visible via d1
x  y
```

In the second example, we bind mount a file at another location and demonstrate that changes to the file via one mount are visible via the other mount:

```
# cat > f1                    Create file to be bound to another location
Chance is always powerful. Let your hook be always cast.
Type Control-D
# touch f2                    This is the new mount point
# mount --bind f1 f2          Bind f1 as f2
# mount | egrep '(d1|f1)'     See how mount points look
/testfs/d1 on /testfs/d2 type none (rw,bind)
/testfs/f1 on /testfs/f2 type none (rw,bind)
# cat >> f2                   Change f2
In the pool where you least expect it, will be a fish.
# cat f1                      The change is visible via original file f1
Chance is always powerful. Let your hook be always cast.
In the pool where you least expect it, will be a fish.
# rm f2                       Can't do this because it is a mount point
rm: cannot unlink `f2': Device or resource busy
# umount f2                   So unmount
# rm f2                       Now we can remove f2
```

One example of when we might use a bind mount is in the creation of a *chroot* jail (Section 18.12). Rather than replicating various standard directories (such as /lib) in the jail, we can simply create bind mounts for these directories within the jail.

14.9.5 Recursive Bind Mounts

By default, if we create a bind mount for a directory using MS_BIND, then only that directory is mounted at the new location; if there are any submounts under the source directory, they are not replicated under the mount *target*. Linux 2.4.11 added the MS_REC flag, which can be ORed with MS_BIND as part of the *flags* argument to *mount()* so that submounts *are* replicated under the mount target. This is referred to as a *recursive bind mount*. The *mount(8)* command provides the *--rbind* option to achieve the same effect from the shell, as shown in the following shell session.

We begin by creating a directory tree (src1) mounted under top. This tree includes a submount (src2) at top/sub.

```
$ su
Password:
# mkdir top                    This is our top-level mount point
# mkdir src1                   We'll mount this under top
# touch src1/aaa
# mount --bind src1 top        Create a normal bind mount
# mkdir top/sub                Create directory for a submount under top
# mkdir src2                   We'll mount this under top/sub
# touch src2/bbb
# mount --bind src2 top/sub    Create a normal bind mount
# find top                     Verify contents under top mount tree
top
top/aaa
top/sub                        This is the submount
top/sub/bbb
```

Now we create another bind mount (dir1) using top as the source. Since this new mount is nonrecursive, the submount is not replicated.

```
# mkdir dir1
# mount --bind top dir1        Here we use a normal bind mount
# find dir1
dir1
dir1/aaa
dir1/sub
```

The absence of dir1/sub/bbb in the output of *find* shows that the submount top/sub was not replicated.

Now we create a recursive bind mount (dir2) using top as the source.

```
# mkdir dir2
# mount --rbind top dir2
# find dir2
dir2
dir2/aaa
dir2/sub
dir2/sub/bbb
```

The presence of dir2/sub/bbb in the output of *find* shows that the submount top/sub was replicated.

14.10 A Virtual Memory File System: *tmpfs*

All of the file systems we have described so far in this chapter reside on disks. However, Linux also supports the notion of *virtual file systems* that reside in memory. To applications, these look just like any other file system—the same operations (*open()*, *read()*, *write()*, *link()*, *mkdir()*, and so on) can be applied to files and directories in such file systems. There is, however, one important difference: file operations are much faster, since no disk access is involved.

Various memory-based file systems have been developed for Linux. The most sophisticated of these to date is the *tmpfs* file system, which first appeared in Linux 2.4. The *tmpfs* file system differs from other memory-based file systems in that it is a *virtual* memory file system. This means that *tmpfs* uses not only RAM, but also the swap space, if RAM is exhausted. (Although the *tmpfs* file system described here is Linux-specific, most UNIX implementations provide some form of memory-based file system.)

> The *tmpfs* file system is an optional Linux kernel component that is configured via the CONFIG_TMPFS option.

To create a *tmpfs* file system, we use a command of the following form:

```
# mount -t tmpfs source target
```

The *source* can be any name; its only significance is that it appears in /proc/mounts and is displayed by the *mount* and *df* commands. As usual, *target* is the mount point for the file system. Note that it is not necessary to use *mkfs* to create a file system first, because the kernel automatically builds a file system as part of the *mount()* system call.

As an example of the use of *tmpfs*, we could employ mount stacking (so that we don't need to care if /tmp is already in use) and create a *tmpfs* file system mounted on /tmp as follows:

```
# mount -t tmpfs newtmp /tmp
# cat /proc/mounts | grep tmp
newtmp /tmp tmpfs rw 0 0
```

A command such as the above (or an equivalent entry in /etc/fstab) is sometimes used to improve the performance of applications (e.g., compilers) that make heavy use of the /tmp directory for creating temporary files.

By default, a *tmpfs* file system is permitted to grow to half the size of RAM, but the *size=nbytes mount* option can be used to set a different ceiling for the file-system size, either when the file system is created or during a later remount. (A *tmpfs* file system consumes only as much memory and swap space as is currently required for the files it holds.)

If we unmount a *tmpfs* file system, or the system crashes, then all data in the file system is lost; hence the name *tmpfs*.

Aside from use by user applications, *tmpfs* file systems also serve two special purposes:

- An invisible *tmpfs* file system, mounted internally by the kernel, is used for implementing System V shared memory (Chapter 48) and shared anonymous memory mappings (Chapter 49).
- A *tmpfs* file system mounted at /dev/shm (/run/shm on some systems) is used for the *glibc* implementation of POSIX shared memory and POSIX semaphores.

14.11 Obtaining Information About a File System: *statvfs()*

The *statvfs()* and *fstatvfs()* library functions obtain information about a mounted file system.

```
#include <sys/statvfs.h>

int statvfs(const char *pathname, struct statvfs *statvfsbuf);
int fstatvfs(int fd, struct statvfs *statvfsbuf);
```

Both return 0 on success, or −1 on error

The only difference between these two functions is in how the file system is identified. For *statvfs()*, we use *pathname* to specify the name of any file in the file system. For *fstatvfs()*, we specify an open file descriptor, *fd*, referring to any file in the file system. Both functions return a *statvfs* structure containing information about the file system in the buffer pointed to by *statvfsbuf*. This structure has the following form:

```
struct statvfs {
    unsigned long f_bsize;      /* File-system block size (in bytes) */
    unsigned long f_frsize;     /* Fundamental file-system block size
                                   (in bytes) */
    fsblkcnt_t    f_blocks;     /* Total number of blocks in file
                                   system (in units of 'f_frsize') */
    fsblkcnt_t    f_bfree;      /* Total number of free blocks */
    fsblkcnt_t    f_bavail;     /* Number of free blocks available to
                                   unprivileged process */
    fsfilcnt_t    f_files;      /* Total number of i-nodes */
    fsfilcnt_t    f_ffree;      /* Total number of free i-nodes */
    fsfilcnt_t    f_favail;     /* Number of i-nodes available to unprivileged
                                   process (set to 'f_ffree' on Linux) */
    unsigned long f_fsid;       /* File-system ID */
    unsigned long f_flag;       /* Mount flags */
    unsigned long f_namemax;    /* Maximum length of filenames on
                                   this file system */
};
```

The purpose of most of the fields in the *statvfs* structure is made clear in the comments above. We note a few further points regarding some fields:

- The *fsblkcnt_t* and *fsfilcnt_t* data types are integer types specified by SUSv3.
- For most Linux file systems, the values of *f_bsize* and *f_frsize* are the same. However, some file systems support the notion of block fragments, which can be used to allocate a smaller unit of storage at the end of the file if a full block is not required. This avoids the waste of space that would otherwise occur if a full block was allocated. On such file systems, *f_frsize* is the size of a fragment, and *f_bsize* is the size of a whole block. (The notion of fragments in UNIX file systems first appeared in the early 1980s with the 4.2BSD Fast File System, described in [McKusick et al., 1984].)

- Many native UNIX and Linux file systems support the notion of reserving a certain portion of the blocks of a file system for the superuser, so that if the file system fills up, the superuser can still log in to the system and do some work to resolve the problem. If there are reserved blocks in the file system, then the difference in values of the *f_bfree* and *f_bavail* fields in the *statvfs* structure tells us how many blocks are reserved.

- The *f_flag* field is a bit mask of the flags used to mount the file system; that is, it contains information similar to the *mountflags* argument given to *mount(2)*. However, the constants used for the bits in this field have names starting with ST_ instead of the MS_ used for *mountflags*. SUSv3 requires only the ST_RDONLY and ST_NOSUID constants, but the *glibc* implementation supports a full range of constants with names corresponding to the MS_* constants described for the *mount() mountflags* argument.

- The *f_fsid* field is used to return a unique identifier for the file system—for example, a value based on the identifier of the device on which the file system resides. On older Linux kernels, many types of file systems return 0 in this field.

SUSv3 specifies both *statvfs()* and *fstatvfs()*. On Linux (as on several other UNIX implementations), these functions are layered on top of the quite similar *statfs()* and *fstatfs()* system calls. (Some UNIX implementations provide a *statfs()* system call, but don't provide *statvfs()*.) The principal differences (aside from some differently named fields) are as follows

- The *statvfs()* and *fstatvfs()* functions return the *f_flag* field, giving information about the file-system mount flags. (The *glibc* implementation obtains this information by scanning /proc/mounts or /etc/mtab.)

- The *statfs()* and *fstatfs()* system calls return the field *f_type*, giving the type of the file system (e.g., the value 0xef53 indicates that this is an *ext2* file system).

> The filesys subdirectory in the source code distribution for this book contains two files, t_statvfs.c and t_statfs.c, demonstrating the use of *statvfs()* and *statfs()*.

14.12 Summary

Devices are represented by entries in the /dev directory. Each device has a corresponding device driver, which implements a standard set of operations, including those corresponding to the *open()*, *read()*, *write()*, and *close()* system calls. A device may be real, meaning that there is a corresponding hardware device, or virtual, meaning that no hardware device exists, but the kernel nevertheless provides a device driver that implements an API that is the same as a real device.

A hard disk is divided into one or more partitions, each of which may contain a file system. A file system is an organized collection of regular files and directories. Linux implements a wide variety of file systems, including the traditional *ext2* file system. The *ext2* file system is conceptually similar to early UNIX file systems, consisting of a boot block, a superblock, an i-node table, and a data area containing file data blocks. Each file has an entry in the file system's i-node table. This entry contains various information about the file, including its type, size, link count, ownership, permissions, timestamps, and pointers to the file's data blocks.

Linux provides a range of journaling file systems, including *Reiserfs*, *ext3*, *ext4*, *XFS*, *JFS*, and *Btrfs*. A journaling file system records metadata updates (and optionally on some file systems, data updates) to a log file before the actual file updates are performed. This means that in the event of a system crash, the log file can be replayed to quickly restore the file system to a consistent state. The key benefit of journaling file systems is that they avoid the lengthy file-system consistency checks required by conventional UNIX file systems after a system crash.

All file systems on a Linux system are mounted under a single directory tree, with the directory / at its root. The location at which a file system is mounted in the directory tree is called its mount point.

A privileged process can mount and unmount a file system using the *mount()* and *umount()* system calls. Information about a mounted file system can be retrieved using *statvfs()*.

Further information

For detailed information about devices and device drivers, see [Bovet & Cesati, 2005] and especially [Corbet et al., 2005]. Some useful information about devices can be found in the kernel source file Documentation/devices.txt.

Several books provide further information about file systems. [Tanenbaum, 2007] is a general introduction to file-system structures and implementation. [Bach, 1986] provides an introduction to the implementation of UNIX file systems, oriented primarily toward System V. [Vahalia, 1996] and [Goodheart & Cox, 1994] also describe the System V file-system implementation. [Love, 2010] and [Bovet & Cesati, 2005] describe the Linux VFS implementation.

Documentation on various file systems can be found in the kernel source subdirectory Documentation/filesystems. Individual web sites can be found describing most of the file-system implementations available on Linux.

14.13 Exercise

14-1. Write a program that measures the time required to create and then remove a large number of 1-byte files from a single directory. The program should create files with names of the form xNNNNNN, where NNNNNN is replaced by a random six-digit number. The files should be created in the random order in which their names are generated, and then deleted in increasing numerical order (i.e., an order that is different from that in which they were created). The number of files (*NF*) and the directory in which they are to be created should be specifiable on the command line. Measure the times required for different values of *NF* (e.g., in the range from 1000 to 20,000) and for different file systems (e.g., *ext2*, *ext3*, and *XFS*). What patterns do you observe on each file system as *NF* increases? How do the various file systems compare? Do the results change if the files are created in increasing numerical order (x000000, x000001, x0000002, and so on) and then deleted in the same order? If so, what do you think the reason(s) might be? Again, do the results vary across file-system types?

15

FILE ATTRIBUTES

In this chapter, we investigate various attributes of files (file metadata). We begin with a description of the *stat()* system call, which returns a structure containing many of these attributes, including file timestamps, file ownership, and file permissions. We then go on to look at various system calls used to change these attributes. (The discussion of file permissions continues in Chapter 17, where we look at access control lists.) We conclude the chapter with a discussion of i-node flags (also known as *ext2* extended file attributes), which control various aspects of the treatment of files by the kernel.

15.1 Retrieving File Information: *stat()*

The *stat()*, *lstat()*, and *fstat()* system calls retrieve information about a file, mostly drawn from the file i-node.

```
#include <sys/stat.h>

int stat(const char *pathname, struct stat *statbuf);
int lstat(const char *pathname, struct stat *statbuf);
int fstat(int fd, struct stat *statbuf);
```
                                        All return 0 on success, or −1 on error

These three system calls differ only in the way that the file is specified:

- *stat()* returns information about a named file;
- *lstat()* is similar to *stat()*, except that if the named file is a symbolic link, information about the link itself is returned, rather than the file to which the link points; and
- *fstat()* returns information about a file referred to by an open file descriptor.

The *stat()* and *lstat()* system calls don't require permissions on the file itself. However, execute (search) permission is required on all of the parent directories specified in *pathname*. The *fstat()* system call always succeeds, if provided with a valid file descriptor.

All of these system calls return a *stat* structure in the buffer pointed to by *statbuf*. This structure has the following form:

```
struct stat {
    dev_t     st_dev;       /* IDs of device on which file resides */
    ino_t     st_ino;       /* I-node number of file */
    mode_t    st_mode;      /* File type and permissions */
    nlink_t   st_nlink;     /* Number of (hard) links to file */
    uid_t     st_uid;       /* User ID of file owner */
    gid_t     st_gid;       /* Group ID of file owner */
    dev_t     st_rdev;      /* IDs for device special files */
    off_t     st_size;      /* Total file size (bytes) */
    blksize_t st_blksize;   /* Optimal block size for I/O (bytes) */
    blkcnt_t  st_blocks;    /* Number of (512B) blocks allocated */
    time_t    st_atime;     /* Time of last file access */
    time_t    st_mtime;     /* Time of last file modification */
    time_t    st_ctime;     /* Time of last status change */
};
```

The various data types used to type the fields in the *stat* structure are all specified in SUSv3. See Section 3.6.2 for further information about these types.

> According to SUSv3, when *lstat()* is applied to a symbolic link, it needs to return valid information only in the *st_size* field and in the file type component (described shortly) of the *st_mode* field. None of the other fields (e.g., the time fields) need contain valid information. This gives an implementation the freedom to not maintain these fields, which may be done for efficiency reasons. In particular, the intent of earlier UNIX standards was to allow a symbolic link to be implemented either as an i-node or as an entry in a directory. Under the latter implementation, it is not possible to implement all of the fields required by the *stat* structure. (On all major contemporary UNIX implementations, symbolic links are implemented as i-nodes. See Section 18.2 for further details.) On Linux, *lstat()* returns information in all of the *stat* fields when applied to a symbolic link. SUSv4 tightens the requirements on an implementation, requiring *lstat()* to return valid information in all fields of the *stat* structure except the permission bits of *st_mode*.

In the following pages, we look at some of the *stat* structure fields in more detail, and finish with an example program that displays the entire *stat* structure.

Device IDs and i-node number

The *st_dev* field identifies the device on which the file resides. The *st_ino* field contains the i-node number of the file. The combination of *st_dev* and *st_ino* uniquely identifies a file across all file systems. The *dev_t* type records the major and minor IDs of a device (Section 14.1).

If this is the i-node for a device, then the *st_rdev* field contains the major and minor IDs of the device.

The major and minor IDs of a *dev_t* value can be extracted using two macros: major() and minor(). The header file required to obtain the declarations of these two macros varies across UNIX implementations. On Linux, they are exposed by <sys/sysmacros.h>.

The size of the integer values returned by major() and minor() varies across UNIX implementations. For portability, we always cast the returned values to *long* when printing them (see Section 3.6.2).

File ownership

The *st_uid* and *st_gid* fields identify, respectively, the owner (user ID) and group (group ID) to which the file belongs.

Link count

The *st_nlink* field is the number of (hard) links to the file. We describe links in detail in Chapter 18.

File type and permissions

The *st_mode* field is a bit mask serving the dual purpose of identifying the file type and specifying the file permissions. The bits of this field are laid out as shown in Figure 15-1.

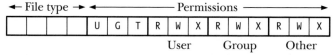

Figure 15-1: Layout of *st_mode* bit mask

The file type can be extracted from this field by ANDing (&) with the constant S_IFMT. (On Linux, 4 bits are used for the file-type component of the *st_mode* field. However, because SUSv3 makes no specification about how the file type is represented, this detail may vary across implementations.) The resulting value can then be compared with a range of constants to determine the file type, like so:

```
if ((statbuf.st_mode & S_IFMT) == S_IFREG)
    printf("regular file\n");
```

Because this is a common operation, standard macros are provided to simplify the above to the following:

```
if (S_ISREG(statbuf.st_mode))
    printf("regular file\n");
```

The full set of file-type macros (defined in <sys/stat.h>) is shown in Table 15-1. All of the file-type macros in Table 15-1 are specified in SUSv3 and appear on Linux. Some other UNIX implementations define additional file types (e.g., S_IFDOOR, for door files on Solaris). The type S_IFLNK is returned only by calls to *lstat()*, since calls to *stat()* always follow symbolic links.

The original POSIX.1 standard did not specify the constants shown in the first column of Table 15-1, although most of them appeared on most UNIX implementations. SUSv3 requires these constants.

> In order to obtain the definitions of S_IFSOCK and S_ISSOCK() from <sys/stat.h>, we must either define the _BSD_SOURCE feature test macro or define _XOPEN_SOURCE with a value greater than or equal to 500. (The rules have varied somewhat across *glibc* versions: in some cases, _XOPEN_SOURCE must be defined with a value of 600 or greater.)

Table 15-1: Macros for checking file types in the *st_mode* field of the *stat* structure

Constant	Test macro	File type
S_IFREG	S_ISREG()	Regular file
S_IFDIR	S_ISDIR()	Directory
S_IFCHR	S_ISCHR()	Character device
S_IFBLK	S_ISBLK()	Block device
S_IFIFO	S_ISFIFO()	FIFO or pipe
S_IFSOCK	S_ISSOCK()	Socket
S_IFLNK	S_ISLNK()	Symbolic link

The bottom 12 bits of the *st_mode* field define the permissions for the file. We describe the file permission bits in Section 15.4. For now, we simply note that the 9 least significant of the permission bits are the read, write, and execute permissions for each of the categories owner, group, and other.

File size, blocks allocated, and optimal I/O block size

For regular files, the *st_size* field is the total size of the file in bytes. For a symbolic link, this field contains the length (in bytes) of the pathname pointed to by the link. For a shared memory object (Chapter 54), this field contains the size of the object.

The *st_blocks* field indicates the total number of blocks allocated to the file, in 512-byte block units. This total includes space allocated for pointer blocks (see Figure 14-2, on page 258). The choice of the 512-byte unit of measurement is historical—this is the smallest block size on any of the file systems that have been implemented under UNIX. More modern file systems use larger logical block sizes. For example, under *ext2*, the value in *st_blocks* is always a multiple of 2, 4, or 8, depending on whether the *ext2* logical block size is 1024, 2048, or 4096 bytes.

> SUSv3 doesn't define the units in which *st_blocks* is measured, allowing the possibility that an implementation uses a unit other than 512 bytes. Most UNIX implementations do use 512-byte units, but HP-UX 11 uses file system–specific units (e.g., 1024 bytes in some cases).

The *st_blocks* field records the number of disk blocks actually allocated. If the file contains holes (Section 4.7), this will be smaller than might be expected from the corresponding number of bytes (*st_size*) in the file. (The disk usage command, *du −k file*, displays the actual space allocated for a file, in kilobytes; that is, a figure calculated from the *st_blocks* value for the file, rather than the *st_size* value.)

The *st_blksize* field is somewhat misleadingly named. It is not the block size of the underlying file system, but rather the optimal block size (in bytes) for I/O on files on this file system. I/O in blocks smaller than this size is less efficient (refer to Section 13.1). A typical value returned in *st_blksize* is 4096.

File timestamps

The *st_atime*, *st_mtime*, and *st_ctime* fields contain, respectively, the times of last file access, last file modification, and last status change. These fields are of type *time_t*, the standard UNIX time format of seconds since the Epoch. We say more about these fields in Section 15.2.

Example program

The program in Listing 15-1 uses *stat()* to retrieve information about the file named on its command line. If the *−l* command-line option is specified, then the program instead uses *lstat()* so that we can retrieve information about a symbolic link instead of the file to which it refers. The program prints all fields of the returned *stat* structure. (For an explanation of why we cast the *st_size* and *st_blocks* fields to *long long*, see Section 5.10.) The *filePermStr()* function used by this program is shown in Listing 15-4, on page 296.

Here is an example of the use of the program:

```
$ echo 'All operating systems provide services for programs they run' > apue
$ chmod g+s apue          Turn on set-group-ID bit; affects last status change time
$ cat apue                Affects last file access time
All operating systems provide services for programs they run
$ ./t_stat apue
File type:                regular file
Device containing i-node: major=3   minor=11
I-node number:            234363
Mode:                     102644 (rw-r--r--)
    special bits set:     set-GID
Number of (hard) links:   1
Ownership:                UID=1000   GID=100
File size:                61 bytes
Optimal I/O block size:   4096 bytes
512B blocks allocated:    8
Last file access:         Mon Jun  8 09:40:07 2011
Last file modification:   Mon Jun  8 09:39:25 2011
Last status change:       Mon Jun  8 09:39:51 2011
```

Listing 15-1: Retrieving and interpreting file *stat* information

─── **files/t_stat.c**

```c
#include <sys/sysmacros.h>
#include <sys/stat.h>
#include <time.h>
#include "file_perms.h"
#include "tlpi_hdr.h"

static void
displayStatInfo(const struct stat *sb)
{
    printf("File type:                ");

    switch (sb->st_mode & S_IFMT) {
    case S_IFREG:  printf("regular file\n");          break;
    case S_IFDIR:  printf("directory\n");             break;
    case S_IFCHR:  printf("character device\n");      break;
    case S_IFBLK:  printf("block device\n");          break;
    case S_IFLNK:  printf("symbolic (soft) link\n");  break;
    case S_IFIFO:  printf("FIFO or pipe\n");          break;
    case S_IFSOCK: printf("socket\n");                break;
    default:       printf("unknown file type?\n");    break;
    }

    printf("Device containing i-node: major=%ld   minor=%ld\n",
            (long) major(sb->st_dev), (long) minor(sb->st_dev));

    printf("I-node number:            %ld\n", (long) sb->st_ino);

    printf("Mode:                     %lo (%s)\n",
           (unsigned long) sb->st_mode, filePermStr(sb->st_mode, 0));

    if (sb->st_mode & (S_ISUID | S_ISGID | S_ISVTX))
        printf("    special bits set:     %s%s%s\n",
                (sb->st_mode & S_ISUID) ? "set-UID " : "",
                (sb->st_mode & S_ISGID) ? "set-GID " : "",
                (sb->st_mode & S_ISVTX) ? "sticky " : "");

    printf("Number of (hard) links:   %ld\n", (long) sb->st_nlink);

    printf("Ownership:                UID=%ld   GID=%ld\n",
           (long) sb->st_uid, (long) sb->st_gid);

    if (S_ISCHR(sb->st_mode) || S_ISBLK(sb->st_mode))
        printf("Device number (st_rdev):  major=%ld; minor=%ld\n",
                (long) major(sb->st_rdev), (long) minor(sb->st_rdev));

    printf("File size:                %lld bytes\n", (long long) sb->st_size);
    printf("Optimal I/O block size:   %ld bytes\n", (long) sb->st_blksize);
    printf("512B blocks allocated:    %lld\n", (long long) sb->st_blocks);

    printf("Last file access:         %s", ctime(&sb->st_atime));
    printf("Last file modification:   %s", ctime(&sb->st_mtime));
    printf("Last status change:       %s", ctime(&sb->st_ctime));
```

```
}

int
main(int argc, char *argv[])
{
    struct stat sb;
    Boolean statLink;              /* True if "-l" specified (i.e., use lstat) */
    int fname;                     /* Location of filename argument in argv[] */

    statLink = (argc > 1) && strcmp(argv[1], "-l") == 0;
                                   /* Simple parsing for "-l" */
    fname = statLink ? 2 : 1;

    if (fname >= argc || (argc > 1 && strcmp(argv[1], "--help") == 0))
        usageErr("%s [-l] file\n"
        "                -l = use lstat() instead of stat()\n", argv[0]);

    if (statLink) {
        if (lstat(argv[fname], &sb) == -1)
            errExit("lstat");
    } else {
        if (stat(argv[fname], &sb) == -1)
            errExit("stat");
    }

    displayStatInfo(&sb);

    exit(EXIT_SUCCESS);
}
```
—— **files/t_stat.c**

15.2 File Timestamps

The *st_atime*, *st_mtime*, and *st_ctime* fields of the *stat* structure contain file timestamps. These fields record, respectively, the times of last file access, last file modification, and last file status change (i.e., last change to the file's i-node information). Timestamps are recorded in seconds since the Epoch (1 January 1970; see Section 10.1).

Most native Linux and UNIX file systems support all of the timestamp fields, but some non-UNIX file systems may not.

Table 15-2 summarizes which of the timestamp fields (and in some cases, the analogous fields in the parent directory) are changed by various system calls and library functions described in this book. In the headings of this table, *a*, *m*, and *c* represent the *st_atime*, *st_mtime*, and *st_ctime* fields, respectively. In most cases, the relevant timestamp is set to the current time by the system call. The exceptions are *utime()* and similar calls (discussed in Sections 15.2.1 and 15.2.2), which can be used to explicitly set the last file access and modification times to arbitrary values.

Table 15-2: Effect of various functions on file timestamps

Function	File or directory a	m	c	Parent directory a	m	c	Notes
chmod()			•				Same for *fchmod()*
chown()			•				Same for *lchown()* and *fchown()*
exec()	•						
link()			•		•	•	Affects parent directory of second argument
mkdir()	•	•	•		•	•	
mkfifo()	•	•	•		•	•	
mknod()	•	•	•		•	•	
mmap()	•	•	•				*st_mtime* and *st_ctime* are changed only on updates to MAP_SHARED mapping
msync()		•	•				Changed only if file is modified
open(), *creat()*	•	•	•		•	•	When creating new file
open(), *creat()*		•	•				When truncating existing file
pipe()	•	•	•				
read()	•						Same for *readv()*, *pread()*, and *preadv()*
readdir()	•						*readdir()* may buffer directory entries; timestamps updated only if directory is read
removexattr()			•				Same for *fremovexattr()* and *lremovexattr()*
rename()			•		•	•	Affects timestamps in both parent directories; SUSv3 doesn't specify file *st_ctime* change, but notes that some implementations do this
rmdir()					•	•	Same for *remove(directory)*
sendfile()	•						Timestamp changed for input file
setxattr()			•				Same for *fsetxattr()* and *lsetxattr()*
symlink()	•	•	•		•	•	Sets timestamps of link (not target file)
truncate()		•	•				Same for *ftruncate()*
unlink()			•		•	•	Same for *remove(file)*; file *st_ctime* changes if previous link count was > 1
utime()	•	•	•				Same for *utimes()*, *futimes()*, *futimens()*, *lutimes()*, and *utimensat()*
write()		•	•				Same for *writev()*, *pwrite()*, and *pwritev()*

In Sections 14.8.1 and 15.5, we describe *mount(2)* options and per-file flags that prevent updates to the last access time of a file. The *open()* O_NOATIME flag described in Section 4.3.1 also serves a similar purpose. In some applications, this can be useful for performance reasons, since it reduces the number of disk operations that are required when a file is accessed.

> Although most UNIX systems don't record the creation time of a file, on recent BSD systems, this time is recorded in a *stat* field named *st_birthtime*.

Nanosecond timestamps

With version 2.6, Linux supports nanosecond resolution for the three timestamp fields of the *stat* structure. Nanosecond resolution improves the accuracy of programs that need to make decisions based on the relative order of file timestamps (e.g., *make(1)*).

SUSv3 doesn't specify nanosecond timestamps for the *stat* structure, but SUSv4 adds this specification.

Not all file systems support nanosecond timestamps. *JFS*, *XFS*, *ext4*, and *Btrfs* do, but *ext2*, *ext3*, and *Reiserfs* do not.

Under the *glibc* API (since version 2.3), the timestamp fields are each defined as a *timespec* structure (we describe this structure when we discuss *utimensat()* later in this section), which represents a time in seconds and nanoseconds components. Suitable macro definitions make the seconds component of these structures visible using the traditional field names (*st_atime*, *st_mtime*, and *st_ctime*). The nanosecond components can be accessed using field names such as *st_atim.tv_nsec*, for the nanosecond component of the last file access time.

15.2.1   Changing File Timestamps with *utime()* and *utimes()*

The last file access and modification timestamps stored in a file i-node can be explicitly changed using *utime()* or one of a related set of system calls. Programs such as *tar(1)* and *unzip(1)* use these system calls to reset file timestamps when unpacking an archive.

```
#include <utime.h>

int utime(const char *pathname, const struct utimbuf *buf);
```
Returns 0 on success, or −1 on error

The *pathname* argument identifies the file whose times we wish to modify. If *pathname* is a symbolic link, it is dereferenced. The *buf* argument can be either NULL or a pointer to a *utimbuf* structure:

```
struct utimbuf {
    time_t actime;      /* Access time */
    time_t modtime;     /* Modification time */
};
```

The fields in this structure measure time in seconds since the Epoch (Section 10.1). Two different cases determine how *utime()* works:

- If *buf* is specified as NULL, then both the last access and the last modification times are set to the current time. In this case, either the effective user ID of the process must match the file's user ID (owner), the process must have write permission on the file (logical, since a process with write permission on a file could employ other system calls that would have the side effect of changing these file timestamps), or the process must be privileged (CAP_FOWNER or CAP_DAC_OVERRIDE).

(To be accurate, on Linux, it is the process's file-system user ID, rather than its effective user ID, that is checked against the file's user ID, as described in Section 9.5.)

- If *buf* is specified as pointer to a *utimbuf* structure, then the last file access and modification times are updated using the corresponding fields of this structure. In this case, the effective user ID of the process must match the file's user ID (having write permission on the file is not sufficient) or the caller must be privileged (CAP_FOWNER).

To change just one of the file timestamps, we first use *stat()* to retrieve both times, use one of these times to initialize the *utimbuf* structure, and then set the other as desired. This is demonstrated in the following code, which makes the last modification time of a file the same as the last access time:

```
struct stat sb;
struct utimbuf utb;

if (stat(pathname, &sb) == -1)
    errExit("stat");
utb.actime = sb.st_atime;        /* Leave access time unchanged */
utb.modtime = sb.st_atime;
if (utime(pathname, &utb) == -1)
    errExit("utime");
```

A successful call to *utime()* always sets the last status change time to the current time.

Linux also provides the BSD-derived *utimes()* system call, which performs a similar task to *utime()*.

```
#include <sys/time.h>

int utimes(const char *pathname, const struct timeval tv[2]);
```
                                        Returns 0 on success, or −1 on error

The most notable difference between *utime()* and *utimes()* is that *utimes()* allows time values to be specified with microsecond accuracy (the *timeval* structure is described in Section 10.1). This provides (partial) access to the nanosecond accuracy with which file timestamps are provided in Linux 2.6. The new file access time is specified in *tv[0]*, and the new modification time is specified in *tv[1]*.

> An example of the use of *utimes()* is provided in the file files/t_utimes.c in the source code distribution for this book.

The *futimes()* and *lutimes()* library functions perform a similar task to *utimes()*. They differ from *utimes()* in the argument used to specify the file whose timestamps are to be changed.

```
#include <sys/time.h>

int futimes(int fd, const struct timeval tv[2]);
int lutimes(const char *pathname, const struct timeval tv[2]);
```
$$\text{Both return 0 on success, or } -1 \text{ on error}$$

With *futimes()*, the file is specified via an open file descriptor, *fd*.

With *lutimes()*, the file is specified via a pathname, with the difference from *utimes()* that if the pathname refers to a symbolic link, then the link is not dereferenced; instead, the timestamps of the link itself are changed.

The *futimes()* function is supported since *glibc* 2.3. The *lutimes()* function is supported since *glibc* 2.6.

15.2.2 Changing File Timestamps with *utimensat()* and *futimens()*

The *utimensat()* system call (supported since kernel 2.6.22) and the *futimens()* library function (supported since *glibc* 2.6) provide extended functionality for setting a file's last access and last modification timestamps. Among the advantages of these interfaces are the following:

- We can set timestamps with nanosecond precision. This improves on the microsecond precision provided by *utimes()*.

- It is possible to set the timestamps independently (i.e., one at a time). As shown earlier, to change just one of the timestamps using the older interfaces, we must first call *stat()* to retrieve the value of the other timestamp, and then specify the retrieved value along with the timestamp whose value we want to change. (This could lead to a race condition if another process performed an operation that updated the timestamp between these two steps.)

- We can independently set either of the timestamps to the current time. To change just one timestamp to the current time with the older interfaces, we need to employ a call to *stat()* to retrieve the setting of the timestamp whose value we wish to leave unchanged, and a call to *gettimeofday()* to obtain the current time.

These interfaces are not specified in SUSv3, but are included in SUSv4.

The *utimensat()* system call updates the timestamps of the file specified by *pathname* to the values specified in the array *times*.

```
#define _XOPEN_SOURCE 700      /* Or define _POSIX_C_SOURCE >= 200809 */
#include <sys/stat.h>

int utimensat(int dirfd, const char *pathname,
              const struct timespec times[2], int flags);
```
$$\text{Returns 0 on success, or } -1 \text{ on error}$$

If *times* is specified as NULL, then both file timestamps are updated to the current time. If *times* is not NULL, then the new last access timestamp is specified in *times[0]* and the new last modification timestamp is specified in *times[1]*. Each of the elements of the array *times* is a structure of the following form:

```
struct timespec {
    time_t tv_sec;      /* Seconds ('time_t' is an integer type) */
    long   tv_nsec;     /* Nanoseconds */
};
```

The fields in this structure specify a time in seconds and nanoseconds since the Epoch (Section 10.1).

To set one of the timestamps to the current time, we specify the special value UTIME_NOW in the corresponding *tv_nsec* field. To leave one of the timestamps unchanged, we specify the special value UTIME_OMIT in the corresponding *tv_nsec* field. In both cases, the value in the corresponding *tv_sec* field is ignored.

The *dirfd* argument can either specify AT_FDCWD, in which case the *pathname* argument is interpreted as for *utimes()*, or it can specify a file descriptor referring to a directory. The purpose of the latter choice is described in Section 18.11.

The *flags* argument can be either 0, or AT_SYMLINK_NOFOLLOW, meaning that *pathname* should not be dereferenced if it is a symbolic link (i.e., the timestamps of the symbolic link itself should be changed). By contrast, *utimes()* always dereferences symbolic links.

The following code segment sets the last access time to the current time and leaves the last modification time unchanged:

```
struct timespec times[2];

times[0].tv_sec = 0;
times[0].tv_nsec = UTIME_NOW;
times[1].tv_sec = 0;
times[1].tv_nsec = UTIME_OMIT;
if (utimensat(AT_FDCWD, "myfile", times, 0) == -1)
    errExit("utimensat");
```

The permission rules for changing timestamps with *utimensat()* (and *futimens()*) are similar to those for the older APIs, and are detailed in the *utimensat(2)* manual page.

The *futimens()* library function updates the timestamps of the file referred to by the open file descriptor *fd*.

```
#define _GNU_SOURCE
#include <sys/stat.h>

int futimens(int fd, const struct timespec times[2]);
```
                                          Returns 0 on success, or −1 on error

The *times* argument of *futimens()* is used in the same way as for *utimensat()*.

15.3 File Ownership

Each file has an associated user ID (UID) and group ID (GID). These IDs determine which user and group the file belongs to. We now look at the rules that determine the ownership of new files and describe the system calls used to change a file's ownership.

15.3.1 Ownership of New Files

When a new file is created, its user ID is taken from the effective user ID of the process. The group ID of the new file may be taken from either the effective group ID of the process (equivalent to the System V default behavior) or the group ID of the parent directory (the BSD behavior). The latter possibility is useful for creating project directories in which all files belong to a particular group and are accessible to the members of that group. Which of the two values is used as the new file's group ID is determined by various factors, including the type of file system on which the new file is created. We begin by describing the rules followed by *ext2* and a few other file systems.

> To be accurate, on Linux, all uses of the terms *effective user* or *group ID* in this section should really be *file-system user* or *group ID* (Section 9.5).

When an *ext2* file system is mounted, either the *−o grpid* (or the synonymous *−o bsdgroups*) option or the *−o nogrpid* (or the synonymous *−o sysvgroups*) option may be specified to the *mount* command. (If neither option is specified, the default is *−o nogrpid*.) If *−o grpid* is specified, then a new file always inherits its group ID from the parent directory. If *−o nogrpid* is specified, then, by default, a new file takes its group ID from the process's effective group ID. However, if the set-group-ID bit is enabled for the directory (via *chmod g+s*), then the group ID of the file is inherited from the parent directory. These rules are summarized in Table 15-3.

> In Section 18.6, we'll see that when the set-group-ID bit is set on a directory, then it is also set on new subdirectories created within that directory. In this manner, the set-group-ID behavior described in the main text is propagated down through an entire directory tree.

Table 15-3: Rules determining the group ownership of a newly created file

File system mount option	Set-group-ID bit enabled on parent directory?	Group ownership of new file taken from
−o grpid, −o bsdgroups	(ignored)	parent directory group ID
−o nogrpid, −o sysvgroups (*default*)	no	process effective group ID
	yes	parent directory group ID

At the time of writing, the only file systems that support the *grpid* and *nogrpid* mount options are *ext2, ext3, ext4,* and (since Linux 2.6.14) *XFS*. Other file systems follow the *nogrpid* rules.

15.3.2 Changing File Ownership: *chown(), fchown(),* and *lchown()*

The *chown(), lchown(),* and *fchown()* system calls change the owner (user ID) and group (group ID) of a file.

```
#include <unistd.h>

int chown(const char *pathname, uid_t owner, gid_t group);
int lchown(const char *pathname, uid_t owner, gid_t group);
int fchown(int fd, uid_t owner, gid_t group);
```

                                          All return 0 on success, or –1 on error

The distinction between these three system calls is similar to the *stat()* family of system calls:

- *chown()* changes the ownership of the file named in the *pathname* argument;
- *lchown()* does the same, except that if *pathname* is a symbolic link, ownership of the link file is changed, rather than the file to which it refers; and
- *fchown()* changes the ownership of a file referred to by the open file descriptor, *fd*.

The *owner* argument specifies the new user ID for the file, and the *group* argument specifies the new group ID for the file. To change just one of the IDs, we can specify –1 for the other argument to leave that ID unchanged.

> Prior to Linux 2.2, *chown()* did not dereference symbolic links. The semantics of *chown()* were changed with Linux 2.2, and the new *lchown()* system call was added to provide the behavior of the old *chown()* system call.

Only a privileged (CAP_CHOWN) process may use *chown()* to change the user ID of a file. An unprivileged process can use *chown()* to change the group ID of a file that it owns (i.e., the process's effective user ID matches the user ID of the file) to any of the groups of which they are a member. A privileged process can change the group ID of a file to any value.

If the owner or group of a file is changed, then the set-user-ID and set-group-ID permission bits are both turned off. This is a security precaution to ensure that a normal user could not enable the set-user-ID (or set-group-ID) bit on an executable file and then somehow make it owned by some privileged user (or group), thereby gaining that privileged identity when executing the file.

> SUSv3 leaves it unspecified whether the set-user-ID and set-group-ID bits should be turned off when the superuser changes the owner or group of an executable file. Linux 2.0 did turn these bits off in this case, while some of the early 2.2 kernels (up to 2.2.12) did not. Later 2.2 kernels returned to the 2.0 behavior, where changes by the superuser are treated the same as everyone else, and this behavior is maintained in subsequent kernel versions.

When changing the owner or group of a file, the set-group-ID permission bit is not turned off if the group-execute permission bit is already off or if we are changing the ownership of a directory. In both of these cases, the set-group-ID bit is being used for a purpose other than the creation of a set-group-ID program, and therefore it is undesirable to turn the bit off. These other uses of the set-group-ID bit are as follows:

- If the group-execute permission bit is off, then the set-group-ID permission bit is being used to enable mandatory file locking (discussed in Section 55.4).

- In the case of a directory, the set-group-ID bit is being used to control the ownership of new files created in the directory (Section 15.3.1).

The use of *chown()* is demonstrated in Listing 15-2, a program that allows the user to change the owner and group of an arbitrary number of files, specified as command-line arguments. (This program uses the *userIdFromName()* and *groupIdFromName()* functions from Listing 8-1, on page 159, to convert user and group names into corresponding numeric IDs.)

Listing 15-2: Changing the owner and group of a file

── **files/t_chown.c**

```
#include <pwd.h>
#include <grp.h>
#include "ugid_functions.h"            /* Declarations of userIdFromName()
                                          and groupIdFromName() */

#include "tlpi_hdr.h"

int
main(int argc, char *argv[])
{
    uid_t uid;
    gid_t gid;
    int j;
    Boolean errFnd;

    if (argc < 3 || strcmp(argv[1], "--help") == 0)
        usageErr("%s owner group [file...]\n"
                 "        owner or group can be '-', "
                 "meaning leave unchanged\n", argv[0]);

    if (strcmp(argv[1], "-") == 0) {            /* "-" ==> don't change owner */
        uid = -1;
    } else {                                    /* Turn user name into UID */
        uid = userIdFromName(argv[1]);
        if (uid == -1)
            fatal("No such user (%s)", argv[1]);
    }

    if (strcmp(argv[2], "-") == 0) {            /* "-" ==> don't change group */
        gid = -1;
```

```
    } else {                                          /* Turn group name into GID */
        gid = groupIdFromName(argv[2]);
        if (gid == -1)
            fatal("No group user (%s)", argv[2]);
    }

    /* Change ownership of all files named in remaining arguments */

    errFnd = FALSE;
    for (j = 3; j < argc; j++) {
        if (chown(argv[j], uid, gid) == -1) {
            errMsg("chown: %s", argv[j]);
            errFnd = TRUE;
        }
    }

    exit(errFnd ? EXIT_FAILURE : EXIT_SUCCESS);
}
```

——— **files/t_chown.c**

15.4   File Permissions

In this section, we describe the permission scheme applied to files and directories. Although we talk about permissions here mainly as they apply to regular files and directories, the rules that we describe apply to all types of files, including devices, FIFOs, and UNIX domain sockets. Furthermore, the System V and POSIX inter-process communication objects (shared memory, semaphores, and message queues) also have permission masks, and the rules that apply for these objects are similar to those for files.

15.4.1   Permissions on Regular Files

As noted in Section 15.1, the bottom 12 bits of the *st_mode* field of the *stat* structure define the permissions for a file. The first 3 of these bits are special bits known as the set-user-ID, set-group-ID, and sticky bits (labeled U, G, and T, respectively, in Figure 15-1). We say more about these bits in Section 15.4.5. The remaining 9 bits form the mask defining the permissions that are granted to various categories of users accessing the file. The file permissions mask divides the world into three categories:

- *Owner* (also known as *user*): The permissions granted to the owner of the file.

> The term *user* is used by commands such as *chmod(1)*, which uses the abbreviation *u* to refer to this permission category.

- *Group*: The permissions granted to users who are members of the file's group.
- *Other*: The permissions granted to everyone else.

Three permissions may be granted to each user category:

- *Read*: The contents of the file may be read.
- *Write*: The contents of the file may be changed.

- *Execute*: The file may be executed (i.e., it is a program or a script). In order to execute a script file (e.g., a *bash* script), both read and execute permissions are required.

The permissions and ownership of a file can be viewed using the command *ls −l*, as in the following example:

```
$ ls -l myscript.sh
-rwxr-x---    1 mtk       users        1667 Jan 15 09:22 myscript.sh
```

In the above example, the file permissions are displayed as rwxr-x--- (the initial hyphen preceding this string indicates the type of this file: a regular file). To interpret this string, we break these 9 characters into sets of 3 characters, which respectively indicate whether read, write, and execute permission are enabled. The first set indicates the permissions for owner, which has read, write, and execute permissions enabled. The next set indicates the permissions for group, which has read and execute enabled, but not write. The final set are the permissions for other, which doesn't have any permissions enabled.

The <sys/stat.h> header file defines constants that can be ANDed (&) with *st_mode* of the *stat* structure, in order to check whether particular permission bits are set. (These constants are also defined via the inclusion of <fcntl.h>, which prototypes the *open()* system call.) These constants are shown in Table 15-4.

Table 15-4: Constants for file permission bits

Constant	Octal value	Permission bit
S_ISUID	04000	Set-user-ID
S_ISGID	02000	Set-group-ID
S_ISVTX	01000	Sticky
S_IRUSR	0400	User-read
S_IWUSR	0200	User-write
S_IXUSR	0100	User-execute
S_IRGRP	040	Group-read
S_IWGRP	020	Group-write
S_IXGRP	010	Group-execute
S_IROTH	04	Other-read
S_IWOTH	02	Other-write
S_IXOTH	01	Other-execute

In addition to the constants shown in Table 15-4, three constants are defined to equate to masks for all three permissions for each of the categories owner, group, and other: S_IRWXU (0700), S_IRWXG (070), and S_IRWXO (07).

The header file in Listing 15-3 declares a function, *filePermStr()*, which, given a file permissions mask, returns a statically allocated string representation of that mask in the same style as is used by *ls(1)*.

Listing 15-3: Header file for `file_perms.c`

———files/file_perms.h
```
#ifndef FILE_PERMS_H
#define FILE_PERMS_H

#include <sys/types.h>

#define FP_SPECIAL 1            /* Include set-user-ID, set-group-ID, and sticky
                                   bit information in returned string */

char *filePermStr(mode_t perm, int flags);

#endif
```
———files/file_perms.h

If the `FP_SPECIAL` flag is set in the *filePermStr() flags* argument, then the returned string includes the settings of the set-user-ID, set-group-ID, and sticky bits, again in the style of *ls(1)*.

The implementation of the *filePermStr()* function is shown in Listing 15-4. We employ this function in the program in Listing 15-1.

Listing 15-4: Convert file permissions mask to string

———files/file_perms.c
```
#include <sys/stat.h>
#include <stdio.h>
#include "file_perms.h"                 /* Interface for this implementation */

#define STR_SIZE sizeof("rwxrwxrwx")

char *              /* Return ls(1)-style string for file permissions mask */
filePermStr(mode_t perm, int flags)
{
    static char str[STR_SIZE];

    snprintf(str, STR_SIZE, "%c%c%c%c%c%c%c%c%c",
        (perm & S_IRUSR) ? 'r' : '-', (perm & S_IWUSR) ? 'w' : '-',
        (perm & S_IXUSR) ?
            (((perm & S_ISUID) && (flags & FP_SPECIAL)) ? 's' : 'x') :
            (((perm & S_ISUID) && (flags & FP_SPECIAL)) ? 'S' : '-'),
        (perm & S_IRGRP) ? 'r' : '-', (perm & S_IWGRP) ? 'w' : '-',
        (perm & S_IXGRP) ?
            (((perm & S_ISGID) && (flags & FP_SPECIAL)) ? 's' : 'x') :
            (((perm & S_ISGID) && (flags & FP_SPECIAL)) ? 'S' : '-'),
        (perm & S_IROTH) ? 'r' : '-', (perm & S_IWOTH) ? 'w' : '-',
        (perm & S_IXOTH) ?
            (((perm & S_ISVTX) && (flags & FP_SPECIAL)) ? 't' : 'x') :
            (((perm & S_ISVTX) && (flags & FP_SPECIAL)) ? 'T' : '-'));

    return str;
}
```
———files/file_perms.c

15.4.2 Permissions on Directories

Directories have the same permission scheme as files. However, the three permissions are interpreted differently:

- *Read*: The contents (i.e., the list of filenames) of the directory may be listed (e.g., by *ls*).

  > If experimenting to verify the operation of the directory read permission bit, be aware that some Linux distributions alias the *ls* command to include flags (e.g., *–F*) that require access to i-node information for files in the directory, and this requires execute permission on the directory. To ensure that we are using an unadulterated *ls*, we can specify the full pathname of the command (/bin/ls) or precede the *ls* command with a backslash to prevent alias substitution.

- *Write*: Files may be created in and removed from the directory. Note that it is not necessary to have any permission on a file itself in order to be able to delete it.

- *Execute*: Files within the directory may be accessed. Execute permission on a directory is sometimes called *search* permission.

When accessing a file, execute permission is required on all of the directories listed in the pathname. For example, reading the file /home/mtk/x would require execute permission on /, /home, and /home/mtk (as well as read permission on the file x itself). If the current working directory is /home/mtk/sub1 and we access the relative pathname ../sub2/x, then we need execute permission on /home/mtk and /home/mtk/sub2 (but not on / or /home).

Read permission on a directory only lets us view the list of filenames in the directory. We must have execute permission on the directory in order to access the contents or the i-node information of files in the directory.

Conversely, if we have execute permission on a directory, but not read permission, then we can access a file in the directory if we know its name, but we can't list the contents of (i.e., the other filenames in) the directory. This is a simple and frequently used technique to control access to the contents of a public directory.

To add or remove files in a directory, we need both execute and write permissions on the directory.

15.4.3 Permission-Checking Algorithm

The kernel checks file permissions whenever we specify a pathname in a system call that accesses a file or directory. When the pathname given to the system call includes a directory prefix, then, in addition to checking for the required permissions on the file itself, the kernel also checks for execute permission on each of the directories in this prefix. Permission checks are made using the process's effective user ID, effective group ID, and supplementary group IDs. (To be strictly accurate, for file permission checks on Linux, the file-system user and group IDs are used instead of the corresponding effective IDs, as described in Section 9.5.)

> Once a file has been opened with *open()*, no permission checking is performed by subsequent system calls that work with the returned file descriptor (such as *read()*, *write()*, *fstat()*, *fcntl()*, and *mmap()*).

The rules applied by the kernel when checking permissions are as follows:

1. If the process is privileged, all access is granted.

2. If the effective user ID of the process is the same as the user ID (owner) of the file, then access is granted according to the *owner* permissions on the file. For example, read access is granted if the owner-read permission bit is turned on in the file permissions mask; otherwise, read access is denied.

3. If the effective group ID of the process or any of the process supplementary group IDs matches the group ID (group owner) of the file, then access is granted according to the *group* permissions on the file.

4. Otherwise, access is granted according to the *other* permissions on the file.

> In the kernel code, the above tests are actually constructed so that the test to see whether a process is privileged is performed only if the process is not granted the permissions it needs via one of the other tests. This is done to avoid unnecessarily setting the ASU process accounting flag, which indicates that the process made use of superuser privileges (Section 28.1).

The checks against owner, group, and other permissions are done in order, and checking stops as soon as the applicable rule is found. This can have an unexpected consequence: if, for example, the permissions for group exceed those of owner, then the owner will actually have fewer permissions on the file than members of the file's group, as illustrated by the following example:

```
$ echo 'Hello world' > a.txt
$ ls -l a.txt
-rw-r--r--  1 mtk    users    12 Jun 18 12:26 a.txt
$ chmod u-rw a.txt              Remove read and write permission from owner
$ ls -l a.txt
----r--r--  1 mtk    users    12 Jun 18 12:26 a.txt
$ cat a.txt
cat: a.txt: Permission denied   Owner can no longer read file
$ su avr                        Become someone else...
Password:
$ groups                        who is in the group owning the file...
users staff teach cs
$ cat a.txt                     and thus can read the file
Hello world
```

Similar remarks apply if other grants more permissions than owner or group.

Since file permissions and ownership information are maintained within a file i-node, all filenames (links) that refer to the same i-node share this information.

Linux 2.6 provides access control lists (ACLs), which make it possible to define file permissions on a per-user and per-group basis. If a file has an ACL, then a modified version of the above algorithm is used. We describe ACLs in Chapter 17.

Permission checking for privileged processes

Above, we said that if a process is privileged, all access is granted when checking permissions. We need to add one proviso to this statement. For a file that is not a directory, Linux grants execute permission to a privileged process only if that permission is granted to at least one of the permission categories for the file. On some other UNIX implementations, a privileged process can execute a file even when no permission category grants execute permission. When accessing a directory, a privileged process is always granted execute (search) permission.

> We can rephrase our description of a privileged process in terms of two Linux process capabilities: CAP_DAC_READ_SEARCH and CAP_DAC_OVERRIDE (Section 39.2). A process with the CAP_DAC_READ_SEARCH capability always has read permission for any type of file, and always has read and execute permissions for a directory (i.e., can always access files in a directory and read the list of files in a directory). A process with the CAP_DAC_OVERRIDE capability always has read and write permissions for any type of file, and also has execute permission if the file is a directory or if execute permission is granted to at least one of the permission categories for the file.

15.4.4 Checking File Accessibility: *access()*

As noted in Section 15.4.3, the *effective* user and group IDs, as well as supplementary group IDs, are used to determine the permissions a process has when accessing a file. It is also possible for a program (e.g., a set-user-ID or set-group-ID program) to check file accessibility based on the *real* user and group IDs of the process.

The *access()* system call checks the accessibility of the file specified in *pathname* based on a process's real user and group IDs (and supplementary group IDs).

```
#include <unistd.h>

int access(const char *pathname, int mode);
                    Returns 0 if all permissions are granted, otherwise –1
```

If *pathname* is a symbolic link, *access()* dereferences it.

The *mode* argument is a bit mask consisting of one or more of the constants shown in Table 15-5, ORed (|) together. If all of the permissions specified in *mode* are granted on *pathname*, then *access()* returns 0; if at least one of the requested permissions is not available (or an error occurred), then *access()* returns –1.

Table 15-5: *mode* constants for *access()*

Constant	Description
F_OK	Does the file exist?
R_OK	Can the file be read?
W_OK	Can the file be written?
X_OK	Can the file be executed?

The time gap between a call to *access()* and a subsequent operation on a file means that there is no guarantee that the information returned by *access()* will still be true at the time of the later operation (no matter how brief the interval). This situation could lead to security holes in some application designs.

Suppose, for example, that we have a set-user-ID-*root* program that uses *access()* to check that a file is accessible to the real user ID of the program, and, if so, performs an operation on the file (e.g., *open()* or *exec()*).

The problem is that if the pathname given to *access()* is a symbolic link, and a malicious user manages to change the link so that it refers to a different file before the second step, then the set-user-ID-*root* may end up operating on a file for which the real user ID does not have permission. (This is an example of the type of time-of-check, time-of-use race condition described in Section 38.6.) For this reason, recommended practice is to avoid the use of *access()* altogether (see, for example, [Borisov, 2005]). In the example just given, we can achieve this by temporarily changing the effective (or file system) user ID of the set-user-ID process, attempting the desired operation (e.g., *open()* or *exec()*), and then checking the return value and *errno* to determine whether the operation failed because of a permissions problem.

> The GNU C library provides an analogous, nonstandard function, *euidaccess()* (or synonymously, *eaccess()*), that checks file access permissions using the effective user ID of the process.

15.4.5 Set-User-ID, Set-Group-ID, and Sticky Bits

As well as the 9 bits used for owner, group, and other permissions, the file permissions mask contains 3 additional bits, known as the *set-user-ID* (bit 04000), *set-group-ID* (bit 02000), and *sticky* (bit 01000) bits. We have already discussed the use of the set-user-ID and set-group-ID permission bits for creating privileged programs in Section 9.3. The set-group-ID bit also serves two other purposes that we describe elsewhere: controlling the group ownership of new files created in a directory mounted with the *nogrpid* option (Section 15.3.1), and enabling mandatory locking on a file (Section 55.4). In the remainder of this section, we limit our discussion to the use of the sticky bit.

On older UNIX implementations, the sticky bit was provided as a way of making commonly used programs run faster. If the sticky bit was set on a program file, then the first time the program was executed, a copy of the program text was saved in the swap area—thus it *sticks* in swap, and loads faster on subsequent executions. Modern UNIX implementations have more sophisticated memory-management systems, which have rendered this use of the sticky permission bit obsolete.

> The name of the constant for the sticky permission bit shown in Table 15-4, S_ISVTX, derives from an alternative name for the sticky bit: the *saved-text* bit.

In modern UNIX implementations (including Linux), the sticky permission bit serves another, quite different purpose. For directories, the sticky bit acts as the *restricted deletion* flag. Setting this bit on a directory means that an unprivileged process can unlink (*unlink()*, *rmdir()*) and rename (*rename()*) files in the directory only if it has write permission on the directory *and* owns either the file or the directory. (A process with the CAP_FOWNER capability can bypass the latter ownership check.) This makes it possible to create a directory that is shared by many users, who can each create and delete their own files in the directory but can't delete files owned by other users. The sticky permission bit is commonly set on the /tmp directory for this reason.

A file's sticky permission bit is set via the *chmod* command (*chmod +t file*) or via the *chmod()* system call. If the sticky bit for a file is set, *ls −l* shows a lowercase or uppercase letter *T* in the other-execute permission field, depending on whether the other-execute permission bit is on or off, as in the following:

```
$ touch tfile
$ ls -l tfile
-rw-r--r--   1 mtk     users     0 Jun 23 14:44 tfile
$ chmod +t tfile
$ ls -l tfile
-rw-r--r-T   1 mtk     users     0 Jun 23 14:44 tfile
$ chmod o+x tfile
$ ls -l tfile
-rw-r--r-t   1 mtk     users     0 Jun 23 14:44 tfile
```

15.4.6 The Process File Mode Creation Mask: *umask()*

We now consider in more detail the permissions that are placed on a newly created file or directory. For new files, the kernel uses the permissions specified in the *mode* argument to *open()* or *creat()*. For new directories, permissions are set according to the *mode* argument to *mkdir()*. However, these settings are modified by the file mode creation mask, also known simply as the *umask*. The umask is a process attribute that specifies which permission bits should always be turned *off* when new files or directories are created by the process.

Often, a process just uses the umask it inherits from its parent shell, with the (usually desirable) consequence that the user can control the umask of programs executed from the shell using the shell built-in command *umask*, which changes the umask of the shell process.

The initialization files for most shells set the default umask to the octal value 022 (----w--w-). This value specifies that write permission should always be turned off for group and other. Thus, assuming the *mode* argument in a call to *open()* is 0666 (i.e., read and write permitted for all users, which is typical), then new files are created with read and write permissions for owner, and only read permission for everyone else (displayed by *ls −l* as rw-r--r--). Correspondingly, assuming that the *mode* argument to *mkdir()* is specified as 0777 (i.e., all permissions granted to all users), new directories are created with all permissions granted for owner, and just read and execute permissions for group and other (i.e., rwxr-xr-x).

The *umask()* system call changes a process's umask to the value specified in *mask*.

```
#include <sys/stat.h>

mode_t umask(mode_t mask);
```
                          Always successfully returns the previous process umask

The *mask* argument can be specified either as an octal number or by ORing (|) together the constants listed in Table 15-4.

A call to *umask()* is always successful, and returns the previous umask.

Listing 15-5 illustrates the use of *umask()* in conjunction with *open()* and *mkdir()*. When we run this program, we see the following:

```
$ ./t_umask
Requested file perms: rw-rw----      This is what we asked for
Process umask:        ----wx-wx      This is what we are denied
Actual file perms:    rw-r-----      So this is what we end up with

Requested dir. perms: rwxrwxrwx
Process umask:        ----wx-wx
Actual dir. perms:    rwxr--r--
```

In Listing 15-5, we employ the *mkdir()* and *rmdir()* system calls to create and remove a directory, and the *unlink()* system call to remove a file. We describe these system calls in Chapter 18.

Listing 15-5: Using *umask()*

—— **files/t_umask.c**

```c
#include <sys/stat.h>
#include <fcntl.h>
#include "file_perms.h"
#include "tlpi_hdr.h"

#define MYFILE "myfile"
#define MYDIR  "mydir"
#define FILE_PERMS    (S_IRUSR | S_IWUSR | S_IRGRP | S_IWGRP)
#define DIR_PERMS     (S_IRWXU | S_IRWXG | S_IRWXO)
#define UMASK_SETTING (S_IWGRP | S_IXGRP | S_IWOTH | S_IXOTH)

int
main(int argc, char *argv[])
{
    int fd;
    struct stat sb;
    mode_t u;

    umask(UMASK_SETTING);

    fd = open(MYFILE, O_RDWR | O_CREAT | O_EXCL, FILE_PERMS);
    if (fd == -1)
        errExit("open-%s", MYFILE);
    if (mkdir(MYDIR, DIR_PERMS) == -1)
        errExit("mkdir-%s", MYDIR);

    u = umask(0);               /* Retrieves (and clears) umask value */

    if (stat(MYFILE, &sb) == -1)
        errExit("stat-%s", MYFILE);
    printf("Requested file perms: %s\n", filePermStr(FILE_PERMS, 0));
    printf("Process umask:        %s\n", filePermStr(u, 0));
    printf("Actual file perms:    %s\n\n", filePermStr(sb.st_mode, 0));
```

```
    if (stat(MYDIR, &sb) == -1)
        errExit("stat-%s", MYDIR);
    printf("Requested dir. perms: %s\n", filePermStr(DIR_PERMS, 0));
    printf("Process umask:        %s\n", filePermStr(u, 0));
    printf("Actual dir. perms:    %s\n", filePermStr(sb.st_mode, 0));

    if (unlink(MYFILE) == -1)
        errMsg("unlink-%s", MYFILE);
    if (rmdir(MYDIR) == -1)
        errMsg("rmdir-%s", MYDIR);
    exit(EXIT_SUCCESS);
}
```

―― files/t_umask.c

15.4.7 Changing File Permissions: *chmod()* and *fchmod()*

The *chmod()* and *fchmod()* system calls change the permissions of a file.

```
#include <sys/stat.h>

int chmod(const char *pathname, mode_t mode);
int fchmod(int fd, mode_t mode);
```

                                    Both return 0 on success, or −1 on error

The *chmod()* system call changes the permissions of the file named in *pathname*. If this argument is a symbolic link, *chmod()* changes the permissions of the file to which it refers, rather than the permissions of the link itself. (A symbolic link is always created with read, write, and execute permissions enabled for all users, and these permission can't be changed. These permissions are ignored when dereferencing the link.)

The *fchmod()* system call changes the permissions on the file referred to by the open file descriptor *fd*.

The *mode* argument specifies the new permissions of the file, either numerically (octal) or as a mask formed by ORing (|) the permission bits listed in Table 15-4. In order to change the permissions on a file, either the process must be privileged (CAP_FOWNER) or its effective user ID must match the owner (user ID) of the file. (To be strictly accurate, on Linux, for an unprivileged process, it is the process's filesystem user ID, rather than its effective user ID, that must match the user ID of the file, as described in Section 9.5.)

To set the permissions on a file so that only read permission is granted to all users, we could use the following call:

```
    if (chmod("myfile", S_IRUSR | S_IRGRP | S_IROTH) == -1)
        errExit("chmod");
    /* Or equivalently: chmod("myfile", 0444); */
```

In order to modify selected bits of the file permissions, we first retrieve the existing permissions using *stat()*, tweak the bits we want to change, and then use *chmod()* to update the permissions:

```
struct stat sb;
mode_t mode;

if (stat("myfile", &sb) == -1)
    errExit("stat");
mode = (sb.st_mode | S_IWUSR) & ~S_IROTH;
            /* owner-write on, other-read off, remaining bits unchanged */
if (chmod("myfile", mode) == -1)
    errExit("chmod");
```

The above is equivalent to the following shell command:

```
$ chmod u+w,o-r myfile
```

In Section 15.3.1, we noted that if a directory resides on an *ext2* system mounted with the *–o bsdgroups* option, or on one mounted with the *–o sysvgroups* option *and* the set-group-ID permission bit is turned on for the directory, then a newly created file in the directory takes its ownership from the parent directory, not the effective group ID of the creating process. It may be the case that the group ID of such a file doesn't match any of the group IDs of the creating process. For this reason, when an unprivileged process (one that doesn't have the CAP_FSETID capability) calls *chmod()* (or *fchmod()*) on a file whose group ID is not equal to the effective group ID or any of the supplementary group IDs of the process, the kernel always clears the set-group-ID permission bit. This is a security measure designed to prevent a user from creating a set-group-ID program for a group of which they are not a member. The following shell commands show the attempted exploit that this measure prevents:

```
$ mount | grep test              Hmmm, /test is mounted with –o bsdgroups
/dev/sda9 on /test type ext3 (rw,bsdgroups)
$ ls -ld /test                   Directory has GID root, writable by anyone
drwxrwxrwx   3 root    root    4096 Jun 30 20:11 /test
$ id                             I'm an ordinary user, not part of root group
uid=1000(mtk) gid=100(users) groups=100(users),101(staff),104(teach)
$ cd /test
$ cp ~/myprog .                  Copy some mischievous program here
$ ls -l myprog                   Hey! It's in the root group!
-rwxr-xr-x   1 mtk     root    19684 Jun 30 20:43 myprog
$ chmod g+s myprog               Can I make it set-group-ID to root?
$ ls -l myprog                   Hmm, no...
-rwxr-xr-x   1 mtk     root    19684 Jun 30 20:43 myprog
```

15.5 I-node Flags (*ext2* Extended File Attributes)

Some Linux file systems allow various *i-node flags* to be set on files and directories. This feature is a nonstandard Linux extension.

> The modern BSDs provide a similar feature to i-node flags in the form of file flags set using *chflags(1)* and *chflags(2)*.

The first Linux file system to support i-node flags was *ext2*, and these flags are sometimes referred to as *ext2 extended file attributes*. Subsequently, support for i-node flags has been added on other file systems, including *Btrfs*, *ext3*, *ext4*, *Reiserfs* (since Linux 2.4.19), *XFS* (since Linux 2.4.25 and 2.6), and *JFS* (since Linux 2.6.17).

> The range of i-node flags supported varies somewhat across file systems. In order to use i-node flags on a *Reiserfs* file system, we must use the *mount -o attrs* option when mounting the file system.

From the shell, i-node flags can be set and viewed using the *chattr* and *lsattr* commands, as shown in the following example:

```
$ lsattr myfile
-------- myfile
$ sudo chattr +ai myfile          Turn on Append Only and Immutable flags
$ lsattr myfile
----ia-- myfile
```

Within a program, i-node flags can be retrieved and modified using the *ioctl()* system call, as detailed shortly.

I-node flags can be set on both regular files and directories. Most i-node flags are intended for use with regular files, although some of them also (or only) have meaning for directories. Table 15-6 summarizes the range of available i-node flags, showing the corresponding flag name (defined in <linux/fs.h>) that is used from programs in *ioctl()* calls, and the option letter that is used with the *chattr* command.

> Before Linux 2.6.19, the FS_* constants shown in Table 15-6 were not defined in <linux/fs.h>. Instead, there was a set of file system–specific header files that defined file system–specific constant names, all with the same value. Thus, *ext2* had EXT2_APPEND_FL, defined in <linux/ext2_fs.h>; *Reiserfs* had REISERFS_APPEND_FL, defined with the same value in <linux/reiser_fs.h>; and so on. Since each of the header files defines the corresponding constants with the same value, on older systems that don't provide the definitions in <linux/fs.h>, it is possible to include any of the header files and use the file system–specific names.

Table 15-6: I-node flags

Constant	*chattr* option	Purpose
FS_APPEND_FL	a	Append only (privilege required)
FS_COMPR_FL	c	Enable file compression (not implemented)
FS_DIRSYNC_FL	D	Synchronous directory updates (since Linux 2.6)
FS_IMMUTABLE_FL	i	Immutable (privilege required)
FS_JOURNAL_DATA_FL	j	Enable data journaling (privilege required)
FS_NOATIME_FL	A	Don't update file last access time
FS_NODUMP_FL	d	No dump
FS_NOTAIL_FL	t	No tail packing
FS_SECRM_FL	s	Secure deletion (not implemented)
FS_SYNC_FL	S	Synchronous file (and directory) updates
FS_TOPDIR_FL	T	Treat as top-level directory for Orlov (since Linux 2.6)
FS_UNRM_FL	u	File can be undeleted (not implemented)

The various FS_* flags and their meanings are as follows:

FS_APPEND_FL

> The file can be opened for writing only if the O_APPEND flag is specified (thus forcing all file updates to append to the end of the file). This flag could be used for a log file, for example. Only privileged (CAP_LINUX_IMMUTABLE) processes can set this flag.

FS_COMPR_FL

> Store the file on disk in a compressed format. This feature is not implemented as a standard part of any of the major native Linux file systems. (There are packages that implement this feature for *ext2* and *ext3*.) Given the low cost of disk storage, the CPU overhead involved in compression and decompression, and the fact that compressing a file means that it is no longer a simple matter to randomly access the file's contents (via *lseek()*), file compression is undesirable for many applications.

FS_DIRSYNC_FL (since Linux 2.6)

> Make directory updates (e.g., *open(pathname, O_CREAT)*, *link()*, *unlink()*, and *mkdir()*) synchronous. This is analogous to the synchronous file update mechanism described in Section 13.3. As with synchronous file updates, there is a performance impact associated with synchronous directory updates. This setting can be applied only to directories. (The MS_DIRSYNC mount flag described in Section 14.8.1 provides similar functionality, but on a per-mount basis.)

FS_IMMUTABLE_FL

> Make the file immutable. File data can't be updated (*write()* and *truncate()*) and metadata changes are prevented (e.g., *chmod()*, *chown()*, *unlink()*, *link()*, *rename()*, *rmdir()*, *utime()*, *setxattr()*, and *removexattr()*). Only privileged (CAP_LINUX_IMMUTABLE) processes can set this flag for a file. When this flag is set, even a privileged process can't change the file contents or metadata.

FS_JOURNAL_DATA_FL

> Enable journaling of data. This flag is supported only on the *ext3* and *ext4* file systems. These file systems provide three levels of journaling: *journal*, *ordered*, and *writeback*. All modes journal updates to file metadata, but the *journal* mode additionally journals updates to file data. On a file system that is journaling in *ordered* or *writeback* mode, a privileged (CAP_SYS_RESOURCE) process can enable journaling of data updates on a per-file basis by setting this flag. (The *mount(8)* manual page describes the difference between the *ordered* and *writeback* modes.)

FS_NOATIME_FL

> Don't update the file last access time when the file is accessed. This eliminates the need to update the file's i-node each time the file is accessed, thus improving I/O performance (see the description of the MS_NOATIME flag in Section 14.8.1).

FS_NODUMP_FL

> Don't include this file in backups made using *dump(8)*. The effect of this flag is dependent on the *–h* option described in the *dump(8)* manual page.

FS_NOTAIL_FL

> Disable tail packing. This flag is supported only on the *Reiserfs* file system. It disables the *Reiserfs* tail-packing feature, which tries to pack small files (and the final fragment of larger files) into the same disk block as the file metadata. Tail packing can also be disabled for an entire *Reiserfs* file system by mounting it with the *mount –o notail* option.

FS_SECRM_FL

> Delete the file securely. The intended purpose of this unimplemented feature is that, when removed, a file is securely deleted, meaning that it is first overwritten to prevent a disk-scanning program from reading or re-creating it. (The issue of truly secure deletion is rather complex: it can actually require multiple writes on magnetic media to securely erase previously recorded data; see [Gutmann, 1996].)

FS_SYNC_FL

> Make file updates synchronous. When applied to files, this flag causes writes to the file to be synchronous (as though the O_SYNC flag was specified on all opens of this file). When applied to a directory, this flag has the same effect as the synchronous directory updates flag described above.

FS_TOPDIR_FL (since Linux 2.6)

> This marks a directory for special treatment under the *Orlov* block-allocation strategy. The Orlov strategy is a BSD-inspired modification of the *ext2* block-allocation strategy that tries to improve the chances that related files (e.g., the files within a single directory) are placed close to each other on disk, which can improve disk seek times. For details, see [Corbet, 2002] and [Kumar, et al. 2008]. FS_TOPDIR_FL has an effect only for *ext2* and its descendants, *ext3* and *ext4*.

FS_UNRM_FL

> Allow this file to be recovered (undeleted) if it is deleted. This feature is not implemented, since it is possible to implement file-recovery mechanisms outside the kernel.

Generally, when i-node flags are set on a directory, they are automatically inherited by new files and subdirectories created in that directory. There are exceptions to this rule:

- The FS_DIRSYNC_FL (*chattr +D*) flag, which can be applied only to a directory, is inherited only by subdirectories created in that directory.

- When the FS_IMMUTABLE_FL (*chattr +i*) flag is applied to a directory, it is not inherited by files and subdirectories created within that directory, since this flag prevents new entries being added to the directory.

Within a program, i-node flags can be retrieved and modified using the *ioctl()* FS_IOC_GETFLAGS and FS_IOC_SETFLAGS operations. (These constants are defined in <linux/fs.h>.) The following code shows how to enable the FS_NOATIME_FL flag on the file referred to by the open file descriptor *fd*:

```
int attr;

if (ioctl(fd, FS_IOC_GETFLAGS, &attr) == -1)    /* Fetch current flags */
    errExit("ioctl");
attr |= FS_NOATIME_FL;
if (ioctl(fd, FS_IOC_SETFLAGS, &attr) == -1)    /* Update flags */
    errExit("ioctl");
```

In order to change the i-node flags of a file, either the effective user ID of the process must match the user ID (owner) of the file, or the process must be privileged (CAP_FOWNER). (To be strictly accurate, on Linux, for an unprivileged process it is the process's file-system user ID, rather than its effective user ID, that must match the user ID of the file, as described in Section 9.5.)

15.6 Summary

The *stat()* system call retrieves information about a file (metadata), most of which is drawn from the file i-node. This information includes file ownership, file permissions, and file timestamps.

A program can update a file's last access time and last modification time using *utime()*, *utimes()*, and various similar interfaces.

Each file has an associated user ID (owner) and group ID, as well as a set of permission bits. For permissions purposes, file users are divided into three categories: *owner* (also known as *user*), *group*, and *other*. Three permissions may be granted to each category of user: *read*, *write*, and *execute*. The same scheme is used with directories, although the permission bits have slightly different meanings. The *chown()* and *chmod()* system calls change the ownership and permissions of a file. The *umask()* system call sets a mask of permission bits that are always turned off when the calling process creates a file.

Three additional permission bits are used for files and directories. The set-user-ID and set-group-ID permission bits can be applied to program files to create programs that cause the executing process to gain privilege by assuming a different effective user or group identity (that of the program file). For directories residing on file systems mounted using the *nogrpid* (*sysvgroups*) option, the set-group-ID permission bit can be used to control whether new files created in the directory inherit their group ID from the process's effective group ID or from the parent directory's group ID. When applied to directories, the sticky permission bit acts as the restricted deletion flag.

I-node flags control the various behaviors of files and directories. Although originally defined for *ext2*, these flags are now supported on several other file systems.

15.7   Exercises

15-1. Section 15.4 contained several statements about the permissions required for various file-system operations. Use shell commands or write programs to verify or answer the following:

  a) Removing all owner permissions from a file denies the file owner access, even though group and other do have access.

  b) On a directory with read permission but not execute permission, the names of files in the directory can be listed, but the files themselves can't be accessed, regardless of the permissions on them.

  c) What permissions are required on the parent directory and the file itself in order to create a new file, open a file for reading, open a file for writing, and delete a file? What permissions are required on the source and target directory to rename a file? If the target file of a rename operation already exists, what permissions are required on that file? How does setting the sticky permission bit (*chmod +t*) of a directory affect renaming and deletion operations?

15-2. Do you expect any of a file's three timestamps to be changed by the *stat()* system call? If not, explain why.

15-3. On a system running Linux 2.6, modify the program in Listing 15-1 (t_stat.c) so that the file timestamps are displayed with nanosecond accuracy.

15-4. The *access()* system call checks permissions using the process's real user and group IDs. Write a corresponding function that performs the checks according to the process's effective user and group IDs.

15-5. As noted in Section 15.4.6, *umask()* always sets the process umask and, at the same time, returns a copy of the old umask. How can we obtain a copy of the current process umask while leaving it unchanged?

15-6. The *chmod a+rX file* command enables read permission for all categories of user, and likewise enables execute permission for all categories of user if *file* is a directory or execute permission is enabled for any of the user categories for *file*, as demonstrated in the following example:

```
$ ls -ld dir file prog
dr--------  2 mtk users    48 May  4 12:28 dir
-r--------  1 mtk users 19794 May  4 12:22 file
-r-x------  1 mtk users 19336 May  4 12:21 prog
$ chmod a+rX dir file prog
$ ls -ld dir file prog
dr-xr-xr-x  2 mtk users    48 May  4 12:28 dir
-r--r--r--  1 mtk users 19794 May  4 12:22 file
-r-xr-xr-x  1 mtk users 19336 May  4 12:21 prog
```

Write a program that uses *stat()* and *chmod()* to perform the equivalent of *chmod a+rX*.

15-7. Write a simple version of the *chattr(1)* command, which modifies file i-node flags. See the *chattr(1)* man page for details of the *chattr* command-line interface. (You don't need to implement the *-R*, *-V*, and *-v* options.)

16

EXTENDED ATTRIBUTES

This chapter describes extended attributes (EAs), which allow arbitrary metadata, in the form of name-value pairs, to be associated with file i-nodes. EAs were added to Linux in version 2.6.

16.1 Overview

EAs are used to implement access control lists (Chapter 17) and file capabilities (Chapter 39). However, the design of EAs is general enough to allow them to be used for other purposes as well. For example, EAs could be used to record a file version number, information about the MIME type or character set for the file, or (a pointer to) a graphical icon.

EAs are not specified in SUSv3. However, a similar feature is provided on a few other UNIX implementations, notably the modern BSDs (see *extattr(2)*) and Solaris 9 and later (see *fsattr(5)*).

EAs require support from the underlying file system. This support is provided in *Btrfs*, *ext2*, *ext3*, *ext4*, *JFS*, *Reiserfs*, and *XFS*.

> Support for EAs is optional for each file system, and is controlled by kernel configuration options under the *File systems* menu. EAs are supported on *Reiserfs* since Linux 2.6.7.

EA namespaces

EAs have names of the form *namespace.name*. The *namespace* component serves to separate EAs into functionally distinct classes. The *name* component uniquely identifies an EA within the given *namespace*.

Four values are supported for *namespace*: *user*, *trusted*, *system*, and *security*. These four types of EAs are used as follows:

- *User* EAs may be manipulated by unprivileged processes, subject to file permission checks: to retrieve the value of a *user* EA requires read permission on the file; to change the value of a *user* EA requires write permission. (Lack of the required permission results in an EACCES error.) In order to associate *user* EAs with a file on *ext2*, *ext3*, *ext4*, or *Reiserfs* file systems, the underlying file system must be mounted with the *user_xattr* option:

  ```
  $ mount -o user_xattr device directory
  ```

- *Trusted* EAs are like *user* EAs in that they can be manipulated by user processes. The difference is that a process must be privileged (CAP_SYS_ADMIN) in order to manipulate *trusted* EAs.

- *System* EAs are used by the kernel to associate system objects with a file. Currently, the only supported object type is an access control list (Chapter 17).

- *Security* EAs are used to store file security labels for operating system security modules, and to associate capabilities with executable files (Section 39.3.2). *Security* EAs were initially devised to support Security-Enhanced Linux (SELinux, *http://www.nsa.gov/research/selinux/*).

An i-node may have multiple associated EAs, in the same namespace or in different namespaces. The EA names within each namespace are distinct sets. In the *user* and *trusted* namespaces, EA names can be arbitrary strings. In the *system* namespace, only names explicitly permitted by the kernel (e.g., those used for access control lists) are allowed.

> *JFS* supports another namespace, *os2*, that is not implemented in other file systems. The *os2* namespace is provided to support legacy OS/2 file-system EAs. A process doesn't need to be privileged in order to create *os2* EAs.

Creating and viewing EAs from the shell

From the shell, we can use the *setfattr(1)* and *getfattr(1)* commands to set and view the EAs on a file:

```
$ touch tfile
$ setfattr -n user.x -v "The past is not dead." tfile
$ setfattr -n user.y -v "In fact, it's not even past." tfile
$ getfattr -n user.x tfile          Retrieve value of a single EA
# file: tfile                       Informational message from getfattr
user.x="The past is not dead."      The getfattr command prints a blank
                                    line after each file's attributes
$ getfattr -d tfile                 Dump values of all user EAs
# file: tfile
```

```
user.x="The past is not dead."
user.y="In fact, it's not even past."

$ setfattr -n user.x tfile          Change value of EA to be an empty string
$ getfattr -d tfile
# file: tfile
user.x
user.y="In fact, it's not even past."

$ setfattr -x user.y tfile          Remove an EA
$ getfattr -d tfile
# file: tfile
user.x
```

One of the points that the preceding shell session demonstrates is that the value of an EA may be an empty string, which is not the same as an EA that is undefined. (At the end of the shell session, the value of *user.x* is an empty string and *user.y* is undefined.)

By default, *getfattr* lists only the values of *user* EAs. The *−m* option can be used to specify a regular expression pattern that selects the EA names that are to be displayed:

```
$ getfattr -m 'pattern' file
```

The default value for *pattern* is ^user\.. We can list all EAs on a file using the following command:

```
$ getfattr -m - file
```

16.2 Extended Attribute Implementation Details

In this section, we extend the overview of the preceding section to fill in a few details of the implementation of EAs.

Restrictions on *user* extended attributes

It is only possible to place *user* EAs on regular files and directories. Other file types are excluded for the following reasons:

- For a symbolic link, all permissions are enabled for all users, and these permissions can't be changed. (Symbolic link permissions have no meaning on Linux, as detailed in Section 18.2.) This means that permissions can't be used to prevent arbitrary users from placing *user* EAs on a symbolic link. The resolution of this problem is to prevent all users from creating *user* EAs on the symbolic link.

- For device files, sockets, and FIFOs, the permissions control the access that users are granted for the purpose of performing I/O on the underlying object. Manipulating these permissions to control the creation of *user* EAs would conflict with this purpose.

Furthermore, it is not possible for an unprivileged process to place a *user* EA on a directory owned by another user if the sticky bit (Section 15.4.5) is set on the directory.

This prevents arbitrary users from attaching EAs to directories such as /tmp, which are publicly writable (and so would allow arbitrary users to manipulate EAs on the directory), but which have the sticky bit set to prevent users from deleting files owned by other users in the directory.

Implementation limits

The Linux VFS imposes the following limits on EAs on all file systems:

- The length of an EA name is limited to 255 characters.
- An EA value is limited to 64 kB.

In addition, some file systems impose more restrictive limits on the size and number of EAs that can be associated with a file:

- On *ext2, ext3*, and *ext4*, the total bytes used by the names and values of all EAs on a file is limited to the size of a single logical disk block (Section 14.3): 1024, 2048, or 4096 bytes.
- On *JFS*, there is an upper limit of 128 kB on the total bytes used by the names and values of all EAs on a file.

16.3 System Calls for Manipulating Extended Attributes

In this section, we look at the system calls used to update, retrieve, and remove EAs.

Creating and modifying EAs

The *setxattr()*, *lsetxattr()*, and *fsetxattr()* system calls set the value of one of a file's EAs.

```
#include <sys/xattr.h>

int setxattr(const char *pathname, const char *name, const void *value,
            size_t size, int flags);
int lsetxattr(const char *pathname, const char *name, const void *value,
            size_t size, int flags);
int fsetxattr(int fd, const char *name, const void *value,
            size_t size, int flags);
```
All return 0 on success, or −1 on error

The differences between these three calls are analogous to those between *stat()*, *lstat()*, and *fstat()* (Section 15.1):

- *setxattr()* identifies a file by *pathname*, and dereferences the filename if it is a symbolic link;
- *lsetxattr()* identifies a file by *pathname*, but doesn't dereference symbolic links; and
- *fsetxattr()* identifies a file by the open file descriptor *fd*.

The same distinction applies to the other groups of system calls described in the remainder of this section.

The *name* argument is a null-terminated string that defines the name of the EA. The *value* argument is a pointer to a buffer that defines the new value for the EA. The *size* argument specifies the length of this buffer.

By default, these system calls create a new EA if one with the given *name* doesn't already exist, or replace the value of an EA if it does already exist. The *flags* argument provides finer control over this behavior. It may be specified as 0 to obtain the default behavior, or as one of the following constants:

XATTR_CREATE
> Fail (EEXIST) if an EA with the given *name* already exists.

XATTR_REPLACE
> Fail (ENODATA) if an EA with the given *name* doesn't already exist.

Here is an example of the use of *setxattr()* to create a *user* EA:

```
char *value;

value = "The past is not dead.";

if (setxattr(pathname, "user.x", value, strlen(value), 0) == -1)
    errExit("setxattr");
```

Retrieving the value of an EA

The *getxattr()*, *lgetxattr()*, and *fgetxattr()* system calls retrieve the value of an EA.

```
#include <sys/xattr.h>

ssize_t getxattr(const char *pathname, const char *name, void *value,
                 size_t size);
ssize_t lgetxattr(const char *pathname, const char *name, void *value,
                  size_t size);
ssize_t fgetxattr(int fd, const char *name, void *value,
                  size_t size);
```
                    All return (nonnegative) size of EA value on success, or −1 on error

The *name* argument is a null-terminated string that identifies the EA whose value we want to retrieve. The EA value is returned in the buffer pointed to by *value*. This buffer must be allocated by the caller, and its length must be specified in *size*. On success, these system calls return the number of bytes copied into *value*.

If the file doesn't have an attribute with the given *name*, these system calls fail with the error ENODATA. If *size* is too small, these system calls fail with the error ERANGE.

It is possible to specify *size* as 0, in which case *value* is ignored but the system call still returns the size of the EA value. This provides a mechanism to determine the size of the *value* buffer required for a subsequent call to actually retrieve the EA value. Note, however, that we still have no guarantee that the returned size will be big enough when subsequently trying to retrieve the value. Another process may have assigned a bigger value to the attribute in the meantime, or removed the attribute altogether.

Removing an EA

The *removexattr()*, *lremovexattr()*, and *fremovexattr()* system calls remove an EA from a file.

```
#include <sys/xattr.h>

int removexattr(const char *pathname, const char *name);
int lremovexattr(const char *pathname, const char *name);
int fremovexattr(int fd, const char *name);
```
All return 0 on success, or –1 on error

The null-terminated string given in *name* identifies the EA that is to be removed. An attempt to remove an EA that doesn't exist fails with the error ENODATA.

Retrieving the names of all EAs associated with a file

The *listxattr()*, *llistxattr()*, and *flistxattr()* system calls return a list containing the names of all of the EAs associated with a file.

```
#include <sys/xattr.h>

ssize_t listxattr(const char *pathname, char *list, size_t size);
ssize_t llistxattr(const char *pathname, char *list, size_t size);
ssize_t flistxattr(int fd, char *list, size_t size);
```
All return number of bytes copied into list on success, or –1 on error

The list of EA names is returned as a series of null-terminated strings in the buffer pointed to by *list*. The size of this buffer must be specified in *size*. On success, these system calls return the number of bytes copied into *list*.

As with *getxattr()*, it is possible to specify *size* as 0, in which case *list* is ignored, but the system call returns the size of the buffer that would be required for a subsequent call to actually retrieve the EA name list (assuming it remains unchanged).

To retrieve a list of the EA names associated with a file requires only that the file be accessible (i.e., that we have execute access to all of the directories included in *pathname*). No permissions are required on the file itself.

For security reasons, the EA names returned in *list* may exclude attributes to which the calling process doesn't have access. For example, most file systems omit *trusted* attributes from the list returned by a call to *listxattr()* in an unprivileged process. But note the "may" in the earlier sentence, indicating that a file-system implementation is not obliged to do this. Therefore, we need to allow for the possibility that a subsequent call to *getxattr()* using an EA name returned in *list* may fail because the process doesn't have the privilege required to obtain the value of that EA. (A similar failure could also happen if another process deleted an attribute between the calls to *listxattr()* and *getxattr()*.)

Example program

The program in Listing 16-1 retrieves and displays the names and values of all EAs of the files listed on its command line. For each file, the program uses *listxattr()* to retrieve the names of all EAs associated with the file, and then executes a loop calling *getxattr()* once for each name, to retrieve the corresponding value. By default, attribute values are displayed as plain text. If the *-x* option is supplied, then the attribute values are displayed as hexadecimal strings. The following shell session log demonstrates the use of this program:

```
$ setfattr -n user.x -v "The past is not dead." tfile
$ setfattr -n user.y -v "In fact, it's not even past." tfile
$ ./xattr_view tfile
tfile:
        name=user.x; value=The past is not dead.
        name=user.y; value=In fact, it's not even past.
```

Listing 16-1: Display file extended attributes

―――――――――――――――――――――――――――――――――――――――xattr/xattr_view.c
```c
#include <sys/xattr.h>
#include "tlpi_hdr.h"

#define XATTR_SIZE 10000

static void
usageError(char *progName)
{
    fprintf(stderr, "Usage: %s [-x] file...\n", progName);
    exit(EXIT_FAILURE);
}

int
main(int argc, char *argv[])
{
    char list[XATTR_SIZE], value[XATTR_SIZE];
    ssize_t listLen, valueLen;
    int ns, j, k, opt;
    Boolean hexDisplay;

    hexDisplay = 0;
    while ((opt = getopt(argc, argv, "x")) != -1) {
        switch (opt) {
        case 'x': hexDisplay = 1;        break;
        case '?': usageError(argv[0]);
        }
    }

    if (optind >= argc)
        usageError(argv[0]);
```

```
        for (j = optind; j < argc; j++) {
            listLen = listxattr(argv[j], list, XATTR_SIZE);
            if (listLen == -1)
                errExit("listxattr");

            printf("%s:\n", argv[j]);

            /* Loop through all EA names, displaying name + value */

            for (ns = 0; ns < listLen; ns += strlen(&list[ns]) + 1) {
                printf("        name=%s; ", &list[ns]);

                valueLen = getxattr(argv[j], &list[ns], value, XATTR_SIZE);
                if (valueLen == -1) {
                    printf("couldn't get value");
                } else if (!hexDisplay) {
                    printf("value=%.*s", (int) valueLen, value);
                } else {
                    printf("value=");
                    for (k = 0; k < valueLen; k++)
                        printf("%02x ", (unsigned char) value[k]);
                }

                printf("\n");
            }

            printf("\n");
        }

        exit(EXIT_SUCCESS);
    }
```
——— **xattr/xattr_view.c**

16.4 Summary

From version 2.6 onward, Linux supports extended attributes, which allow arbitrary metadata to be associated with a file, in the form of name-value pairs.

16.5 Exercise

16-1. Write a program that can be used to create or modify a *user* EA for a file (i.e., a simple version of *setfattr(1)*). The filename and the EA name and value should be supplied as command-line arguments to the program.

17

ACCESS CONTROL LISTS

Section 15.4 described the traditional UNIX (and Linux) file permissions scheme. For many applications, this scheme is sufficient. However, some applications need finer control over the permissions granted to specific users and groups. To meet this requirement, many UNIX systems implement an extension to the traditional UNIX file permissions model known as *access control lists* (ACLs). ACLs allow file permissions to be specified per user or per group, for an arbitrary number of users and groups. Linux provides ACLs from kernel 2.6 onward.

> Support for ACLs is optional for each file system, and is controlled by kernel configuration options under the *File systems* menu. *Reiserfs* support for ACLs has been available since kernel 2.6.7.
>
> In order to be able to create ACLs on an *ext2*, *ext3*, *ext4*, or *Reiserfs* file system, the file system must be mounted with the *mount −o acl* option.

ACLs have never been formally standardized for UNIX systems. An attempt was made to do this in the form of the POSIX.1e and POSIX.2c draft standards, which aimed to specify, respectively, the application program interface (API) and the shell commands for ACLs (as well as other features, such as capabilities). Ultimately, this standardization attempt foundered, and these draft standards were withdrawn. Nevertheless, many UNIX implementations (including Linux) base their ACL implementations on these draft standards (usually on the final version, *Draft 17*). However, because there are many variations across ACL implementations (in part springing from the incompleteness of the draft standards), writing portable programs that use ACLs presents some difficulties.

This chapter provides a description of ACLs and a brief tutorial on their use. It also describes some of the library functions used for manipulating and retrieving ACLs. We won't go into detail on all of these functions because there are so many of them. (For the details, see the manual pages.)

17.1 Overview

An ACL is a series of ACL entries, each of which defines the file permissions for an individual user or group of users (see Figure 17-1).

Tag type	Tag qualifier	Permissions
ACL_USER_OBJ	-	rwx
ACL_USER	1007	r--
ACL_USER	1010	rwx
ACL_GROUP_OBJ	-	rwx
ACL_GROUP	102	r--
ACL_GROUP	103	-w-
ACL_GROUP	109	--x
ACL_MASK	-	rw-
ACL_OTHER	-	r--

Group class entries bracket ACL_USER_OBJ through ACL_GROUP (109).

Corresponds to traditional *owner* (*user*) permissions

Corresponds to traditional *group* permissions

Corresponds to traditional *other* permissions

Figure 17-1: An access control list

ACL entries

Each ACL entry consists of the following parts:

- a *tag type*, which indicates whether this entry applies to a user, to a group, or to some other category of user;
- an optional *tag qualifier*, which identifies a specific user or group (i.e., a user ID or a group ID); and
- a *permission set*, which specifies the permissions (read, write, and execute) that are granted by the entry.

The tag type has one of the following values:

ACL_USER_OBJ
> This entry specifies the permissions granted to the file owner. Each ACL contains exactly one ACL_USER_OBJ entry. This entry corresponds to the traditional file *owner* (*user*) permissions.

ACL_USER
> This entry specifies the permissions granted to the user identified by the tag qualifier. An ACL may contain zero or more ACL_USER entries, but at most one ACL_USER entry may be defined for a particular user.

ACL_GROUP_OBJ

This entry specifies permissions granted to the file group. Each ACL contains exactly one ACL_GROUP_OBJ entry. This entry corresponds to the traditional file *group* permissions, unless the ACL also contains an ACL_MASK entry.

ACL_GROUP

This entry specifies the permissions granted to the group identified by the tag qualifier. An ACL may contain zero or more ACL_GROUP entries, but at most one ACL_GROUP entry may be defined for a particular group.

ACL_MASK

This entry specifies the maximum permissions that may be granted by ACL_USER, ACL_GROUP_OBJ, and ACL_GROUP entries. An ACL contains at most one ACL_MASK entry. If the ACL contains ACL_USER or ACL_GROUP entries, then an ACL_MASK entry is mandatory. We say more about this tag type shortly.

ACL_OTHER

This entry specifies the permissions that are granted to users that don't match any other ACL entry. Each ACL contains exactly one ACL_OTHER entry. This entry corresponds to the traditional file *other* permissions.

The tag qualifier is employed only for ACL_USER and ACL_GROUP entries. It specifies either a user ID or a group ID.

Minimal and extended ACLs

A *minimal* ACL is one that is semantically equivalent to the traditional file permission set. It contains exactly three entries: one of each of the types ACL_USER_OBJ, ACL_GROUP_OBJ, and ACL_OTHER. An *extended* ACL is one that additionally contains ACL_USER, ACL_GROUP, and ACL_MASK entries.

One reason for drawing a distinction between minimal ACLs and extended ACLs is that the latter provide a semantic extension to the traditional permissions model. Another reason concerns the Linux implementation of ACLs. ACLs are implemented as *system* extended attributes (Chapter 16). The extended attribute used for maintaining a file access ACL is named *system.posix_acl_access*. This extended attribute is required only if the file has an extended ACL. The permissions information for a minimal ACL can be (and is) stored in the traditional file permission bits.

17.2   ACL Permission-Checking Algorithm

Permission checking on a file that has an ACL is performed in the same circumstances as for the traditional file permissions model (Section 15.4.3). Checks are performed in the following order, until one of the criteria is matched:

1. If the process is privileged, all access is granted. There is one exception to this statement, analogous to the traditional permissions model described in Section 15.4.3. When executing a file, a privileged process is granted execute permission only if that permission is granted via at least one of the ACL entries on the file.

2. If the effective user ID of the process matches the owner (user ID) of the file, then the process is granted the permissions specified in the ACL_USER_OBJ entry. (To be strictly accurate, on Linux, it is the process's file-system IDs, rather than its effective IDs, that are used for the checks described in this section, as described in Section 9.5.)

3. If the effective user ID of the process matches the tag qualifier in one of the ACL_USER entries, then the process is granted the permissions specified in that entry, masked (ANDed) against the value of the ACL_MASK entry.

4. If one of the process's group IDs (i.e., the effective group ID or any of the supplementary group IDs) matches the file group (this corresponds to the ACL_GROUP_OBJ entry) or the tag qualifier of any of the ACL_GROUP entries, then access is determined by checking each of the following, until a match is found:

   a) If one of the process's group IDs matches the file group, and the ACL_GROUP_OBJ entry grants the requested permissions, then this entry determines the access granted to the file. The granted access is restricted by masking (ANDing) against the value in the ACL_MASK entry, if present.

   b) If one of the process's group IDs matches the tag qualifier in an ACL_GROUP entry for the file, and that entry grants the requested permissions, then this entry determines the permissions granted. The granted access is restricted by masking (ANDing) against the value in the ACL_MASK entry.

   c) Otherwise, access is denied.

5. Otherwise, the process is granted the permissions specified in the ACL_OTHER entry.

We can clarify the rules relating to group IDs with some examples. Suppose we have a file whose group ID is 100, and that file is protected by the ACL shown in Figure 17-1. If a process whose group ID is 100 makes the call *access(file, R_OK)*, then that call would succeed (i.e., return 0). (We describe *access()* in Section 15.4.4.) On the other hand, even though the ACL_GROUP_OBJ entry grants all permissions, the call *access(file, R_OK | W_OK | X_OK)* would fail (i.e., return −1, with *errno* set to EACCES) because the ACL_GROUP_OBJ permissions are masked (ANDed) against the ACL_MASK entry, and this entry denies execute permission.

As another example using Figure 17-1, suppose we have a process that has a group ID of 102 and that also contains the group ID 103 in its supplementary group IDs. For this process, the calls *access(file, R_OK)* and *access(file, W_OK)* would both succeed, since they would match the ACL_GROUP entries for the group IDs 102 and 103, respectively. On the other hand, the call *access(file, R_OK | W_OK)* would fail because there is no matching ACL_GROUP entry that grants both read and write permissions.

17.3 Long and Short Text Forms for ACLs

When manipulating ACLs using the *setfacl* and *getfacl* commands (described in a moment) or certain ACL library functions, we specify textual representations of the ACL entries. Two formats are permitted for these textual representations:

- *Long text form* ACLs contain one ACL entry per line, and may include comments, which are started by a # character and continue to the end-of-line. The *getfacl* command displays ACLs in long text form. The *setfacl −M acl-file* option, which takes an ACL specification from a file, expects the specification to be in long text form.
- *Short text form* ACLs consist of a sequence of ACL entries separated by commas.

In both forms, each ACL entry consists of three parts separated by colons:

---

tag-type: [*tag-qualifier*] : *permissions*

The *tag-type* is one of the values shown in the first column of Table 17-1. The *tag-type* may optionally be followed by a *tag-qualifier*, which identifies a user or group, either by name or numeric identifier. The *tag-qualifier* is present only for ACL_USER and ACL_GROUP entries.

The following are all short text form ACLs corresponding to a traditional permissions mask of 0650:

```
u::rw-,g::r-x,o::---
u::rw,g::rx,o::-
user::rw,group::rx,other::-
```

The following short text form ACL includes two named users, a named group, and a mask entry:

```
u::rw,u:paulh:rw,u:annabel:rw,g::r,g:teach:rw,m::rwx,o::-
```

Table 17-1: Interpretation of ACL entry text forms

Tag text forms	Tag qualifier present?	Corresponding tag type	Entry for
u, user	N	ACL_USER_OBJ	File owner (user)
u, user	Y	ACL_USER	Specified user
g, group	N	ACL_GROUP_OBJ	File group
g, group	Y	ACL_GROUP	Specified group
m, mask	N	ACL_MASK	Mask for group class
o, other	N	ACL_OTHER	Other users

17.4 The `ACL_MASK` Entry and the ACL Group Class

If an ACL contains `ACL_USER` or `ACL_GROUP` entries, then it must contain an `ACL_MASK` entry. If the ACL doesn't contain any `ACL_USER` or `ACL_GROUP` entries, then the `ACL_MASK` entry is optional.

The `ACL_MASK` entry acts as an upper limit on the permissions granted by ACL entries in the so-called *group class*. The group class is the set of all `ACL_USER`, `ACL_GROUP`, and `ACL_GROUP_OBJ` entries in the ACL.

The purpose of the `ACL_MASK` entry is to provide consistent behavior when running ACL-unaware applications. As an example of why the mask entry is needed, suppose that the ACL on a file includes the following entries:

```
user::rwx                      # ACL_USER_OBJ
user:paulh:r-x                 # ACL_USER
group::r-x                     # ACL_GROUP_OBJ
group:teach:--x                # ACL_GROUP
other::--x                     # ACL_OTHER
```

Now suppose that a program executes the following *chmod()* call on this file:

```
chmod(pathname, 0700);        /* Set permissions to rwx------ */
```

In an ACL-unaware application, this means "Deny access to everyone except the file owner." These semantics should hold even in the presence of ACLs. In the absence of an `ACL_MASK` entry, this behavior could be implemented in various ways, but there are problems with each approach:

- Simply modifying the `ACL_GROUP_OBJ` and `ACL_OTHER` entries to have the mask `---` would be insufficient, since the user *paulh* and the group *teach* would still have some permissions on the file.

- Another possibility would be to apply the new group and other permission settings (i.e., all permissions disabled) to all of the `ACL_USER`, `ACL_GROUP`, `ACL_GROUP_OBJ`, and `ACL_OTHER` entries in the ACL:

```
user::rwx                      # ACL_USER_OBJ
user:paulh:---                 # ACL_USER
group::---                     # ACL_GROUP_OBJ
group:teach:---                # ACL_GROUP
other::---                     # ACL_OTHER
```

The problem with this approach is that the ACL-unaware application would thereby inadvertently destroy the file permission semantics established by ACL-aware applications, since the following call (for example) would not restore the `ACL_USER` and `ACL_GROUP` entries of the ACL to their former states:

```
chmod(pathname, 0751);
```

- To avoid these problems, we might consider making the ACL_GROUP_OBJ entry the limiting set for all ACL_USER and ACL_GROUP entries. However, this would mean that the ACL_GROUP_OBJ permissions would always need to be set to the union of all permissions allowed in all ACL_USER and ACL_GROUP entries. This would conflict with the use of the ACL_GROUP_OBJ entry for determining the permissions accorded to the file group.

The ACL_MASK entry was devised to solve these problems. It provides a mechanism that allows the traditional meanings of *chmod()* operations to be implemented, without destroying the file permission semantics established by ACL-aware applications. When an ACL has an ACL_MASK entry:

- all changes to traditional group permissions via *chmod()* change the setting of the ACL_MASK entry (rather than the ACL_GROUP_OBJ entry); and
- a call to *stat()* returns the ACL_MASK permissions (instead of the ACL_GROUP_OBJ permissions) in the group permission bits of the *st_mode* field (Figure 15-1, on page 281).

While the ACL_MASK entry provides a way of preserving ACL information in the face of ACL-unaware applications, the reverse is not guaranteed. The presence of ACLs overrides the effect of traditional operations on file group permissions. For example, suppose that we have placed the following ACL on a file:

```
user::rw-,group::---,mask::---,other::r--
```

If we then execute the command *chmod g+rw* on this file, the ACL becomes:

```
user::rw-,group::---,mask::rw-,other::r--
```

In this case, group still has no access to the file. One workaround for this is to modify the ACL entry for group to grant all permissions. Consequently, group will then always obtain whatever permissions are granted to the ACL_MASK entry.

17.5 The *getfacl* and *setfacl* Commands

From the shell, we can use the *getfacl* command to view the ACL on a file.

```
$ umask 022            Set shell umask to known state
$ touch tfile          Create a new file
$ getfacl tfile
# file: tfile
# owner: mtk
# group: users
user::rw-
group::r--
other::r--
```

From the output of the *getfacl* command, we see that the new file is created with a minimal ACL. When displaying the text form of this ACL, *getfacl* precedes the ACL entries with three lines showing the name and ownership of the file. We can prevent these lines from being displayed by specifying the *--omit-header* option.

Next, we demonstrate that changes to a file's permissions using the traditional *chmod* command are carried through to the ACL.

```
$ chmod u=rwx,g=rx,o=x tfile
$ getfacl --omit-header tfile
user::rwx
group::r-x
other::--x
```

The *setfacl* command modifies a file ACL. Here, we use the *setfacl* *-m* command to add an ACL_USER and an ACL_GROUP entry to the ACL:

```
$ setfacl -m u:paulh:rx,g:teach:x tfile
$ getfacl --omit-header tfile
user::rwx
user:paulh:r-x                          ACL_USER entry
group::r-x
group:teach:--x                         ACL_GROUP entry
mask::r-x                               ACL_MASK entry
other::--x
```

The *setfacl* *-m* option modifies existing ACL entries, or adds new entries if corresponding entries with the given tag type and qualifier do not already exist. We can additionally use the *-R* option to recursively apply the specified ACL to all of the files in a directory tree.

From the output of the *getfacl* command, we can see that *setfacl* automatically created an ACL_MASK entry for this ACL.

The addition of the ACL_USER and ACL_GROUP entries converts this ACL into an extended ACL, and *ls* *-l* indicates this fact by appending a plus sign (+) after the traditional file permissions mask:

```
$ ls -l tfile
-rwxr-x--x+  1 mtk      users        0 Dec 3 15:42 tfile
```

We continue by using *setfacl* to disable all permissions except execute on the ACL_MASK entry, and then view the ACL once more with *getfacl*:

```
$ setfacl -m m::x tfile
$ getfacl --omit-header tfile
user::rwx
user:paulh:r-x                  #effective:--x
group::r-x                      #effective:--x
group:teach:--x
mask::--x
other::--x
```

The #effective: comments that *getfacl* prints after the entries for the user *paulh* and the file group (group::) inform us that after masking (ANDing) against the ACL_MASK entry, the permissions granted by each of these entries will actually be less than those specified in the entry.

We then use *ls* −*l* to once more view the traditional permission bits of the file. We see that the displayed group class permission bits reflect the permissions in the ACL_MASK entry (--x), rather than those in the ACL_GROUP entry (r-x):

```
$ ls -l tfile
-rwx--x--x+   1 mtk        users              0 Dec 3 15:42 tfile
```

The *setfacl* −*x* command can be used to remove entries from an ACL. Here, we remove the entries for the user *paulh* and the group *teach* (no permissions are specified when removing entries):

```
$ setfacl -x u:paulh,g:teach tfile
$ getfacl --omit-header tfile
user::rwx
group::r-x
mask::r-x
other::--x
```

Note that during the above operation, *setfacl* automatically adjusted the mask entry to be the union of all of the group class entries. (There was just one such entry: ACL_GROUP_OBJ.) If we want to prevent such adjustment, then we must specify the −*n* option to *setfacl*.

Finally, we note that the *setfacl* −*b* option can be used to remove all extended entries from an ACL, leaving just the minimal (i.e., user, group, and other) entries.

17.6 Default ACLs and File Creation

In the discussion of ACLs so far, we have been describing *access* ACLs. As its name implies, an access ACL is used in determining the permissions that a process has when accessing the file associated with the ACL. We can create a second type of ACL on directories: a *default* ACL.

A default ACL plays no part in determining the permissions granted when accessing the directory. Instead, its presence or absence determines the ACL(s) and permissions that are placed on files and subdirectories that are created in the directory. (A default ACL is stored as an extended attribute named *system.posix_acl_default.*)

To view and set the default ACL of a directory, we use the −*d* option of the *getfacl* and *setfacl* commands.

```
$ mkdir sub
$ setfacl -d -m u::rwx,u:paulh:rx,g::rx,g:teach:rwx,o::- sub
$ getfacl -d --omit-header sub
user::rwx
user:paulh:r-x
group::r-x
group:teach:rwx
mask::rwx                    setfacl generated ACL_MASK entry automatically
other::---
```

We can remove a default ACL from a directory using the *setfacl* −*k* option.

If a directory has a default ACL, then:

- A new subdirectory created in this directory inherits the directory's default ACL as its default ACL. In other words, default ACLs propagate down through a directory tree as new subdirectories are created.

- A new file or subdirectory created in this directory inherits the directory's default ACL as its access ACL. The ACL entries that correspond to the traditional file permission bits are masked (ANDed) against the corresponding bits of the *mode* argument in the system call (*open()*, *mkdir()*, and so on) used to create the file or subdirectory. By "corresponding ACL entries," we mean:
  - ACL_USER_OBJ;
  - ACL_MASK or, if ACL_MASK is absent, then ACL_GROUP_OBJ; and
  - ACL_OTHER.

When a directory has a default ACL, the process umask (Section 15.4.6) doesn't play a part in determining the permissions in the entries of the access ACL of a new file created in that directory.

As an example of how a new file inherits its access ACL from the parent directory's default ACL, suppose we used the following *open()* call to create a new file in the directory created above:

```
open("sub/tfile", O_RDWR | O_CREAT,
        S_IRWXU | S_IXGRP | S_IXOTH);   /* rwx--x--x */
```

The new file would have the following access ACL:

```
$ getfacl --omit-header sub/tfile
user::rwx
user:paulh:r-x                  #effective:--x
group::r-x                      #effective:--x
group:teach:rwx                 #effective:--x
mask::--x
other::---
```

If a directory doesn't have a default ACL, then:

- New subdirectories created in this directory also do not have a default ACL.
- The permissions of the new file or directory are set following the traditional rules (Section 15.4.6): the file permissions are set to the value in the *mode* argument (given to *open()*, *mkdir()*, and so on), less the bits that are turned off by the process umask. This results in a minimal ACL on the new file.

17.7 ACL Implementation Limits

The various file-system implementations impose limits on the number of entries in an ACL:

- On *ext2*, *ext3*, and *ext4*, the total number of ACLs on a file is governed by the requirement that the bytes in all of the names and values of a file's extended attributes must be contained in a single logical disk block (Section 16.2). Each

ACL entry requires 8 bytes, so that the maximum number of ACL entries for a file is somewhat less (because of some overhead for the name of the extended attribute for the ACL) than one-eighth of the block size. Thus, a 4096-byte block size allows for a maximum of around 500 ACL entries. (Kernels before 2.6.11 imposed an arbitrary limitation of 32 entries for ACLs on *ext2* and *ext3*.)

- On *XFS*, an ACL is limited to 25 entries.

- On *Reiserfs* and *JFS*, ACLs can contain up to 8191 entries. This limit is a consequence of the size limitation (64 kB) imposed by the VFS on the value of an extended attribute (Section 16.2).

> At the time of writing, *Btrfs* limits ACLs to around 500 entries. However, since *Btrfs* was still under heavy development, this limit may change.

Although most of the above file systems allow large numbers of entries to be created in an ACL, this should be avoided for the following reasons:

- The maintenance of lengthy ACLs becomes a complex and potentially error-prone system administration task.

- The amount of time required to scan the ACL for the matching entry (or matching entries in the case of group ID checks) increases linearly with the number of ACL entries.

Generally, we can keep the number of ACL entries on a file down to a reasonable number by defining suitable groups in the system group file (Section 8.3) and using those groups within the ACL.

17.8 The ACL API

The POSIX.1e draft standard defined a large suite of functions and data structures for manipulating ACLs. Since they are so numerous, we won't attempt to describe the details of all of these functions. Instead, we provide an overview of their usage and conclude with an example program.

Programs that use the ACL API should include `<sys/acl.h>`. It may also be necessary to include `<acl/libacl.h>` if the program makes use of various Linux extensions to the POSIX.1e draft standard. (A list of the Linux extensions is provided in the *acl(5)* manual page.) Programs using this API must be compiled with the *–lacl* option, in order to link against the *libacl* library.

> As already noted, on Linux, ACLs are implemented using extended attributes, and the ACL API is implemented as a set of library functions that manipulate user-space data structures, and, where necessary, make calls to *getxattr()* and *setxattr()* to retrieve and modify the on-disk *system* extended attribute that holds the ACL representation. It is also possible (though not recommended) for an application to use *getxattr()* and *setxattr()* to manipulate ACLs directly.

Overview

The functions that constitute the ACL API are listed in the *acl(5)* manual page. At first sight, this plethora of functions and data structures can seem bewildering. Figure 17-2 provides an overview of the relationship between the various data structures and indicates the use of many of the ACL functions.

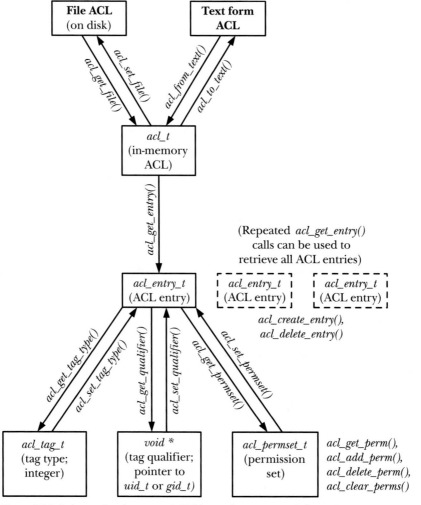

Figure 17-2: Relationship between ACL library functions and data structures

From Figure 17-2, we can see that the ACL API considers an ACL as a hierarchical object:

- An ACL consists of one or more ACL entries.
- Each ACL entry consists of a tag type, an optional tag qualifier, and a permission set.

We now look briefly at the various ACL functions. In most cases, we don't describe the error returns from each function. Functions that return an integer (*status*) typically return 0 on success and −1 on error. Functions that return a handle (pointer) return NULL on error. Errors can be diagnosed using *errno* in the usual manner.

> A *handle* is an abstract term for some technique used to refer to an object or data structure. The representation of a handle is private to the API implementation. It may be, for example, a pointer, an array index, or a hash key.

Fetching a file's ACL into memory

The *acl_get_file()* function retrieves a copy of the ACL of the file identified by *pathname*.

```
acl_t acl;

acl = acl_get_file(pathname, type);
```

This function retrieves either the access ACL or the default ACL, depending on whether *type* is specified as ACL_TYPE_ACCESS or ACL_TYPE_DEFAULT. As its function result, *acl_get_file()* returns a handle (of type *acl_t*) for use with other ACL functions.

Retrieving entries from an in-memory ACL

The *acl_get_entry()* function returns a handle (of type *acl_entry_t*) referring to one of the ACL entries within the in-memory ACL referred to by its *acl* argument. This handle is returned in the location pointed to by the final function argument.

```
acl_entry_t entry;

status = acl_get_entry(acl, entry_id, &entry);
```

The *entry_id* argument determines which entry's handle is returned. If *entry_id* is specified as ACL_FIRST_ENTRY, then a handle for the first entry in the ACL is returned. If *entry_id* is specified as ACL_NEXT_ENTRY, then a handle is returned for the entry following the last ACL entry that was retrieved. Thus, we can loop through all of the entries in an ACL by specifying *entry_id* as ACL_FIRST_ENTRY in the first call to *acl_get_entry()* and specifying *entry_id* as ACL_NEXT_ENTRY in subsequent calls.

The *acl_get_entry()* function returns 1 if it successfully fetches an ACL entry, 0 if there are no more entries, or −1 on error.

Retrieving and modifying attributes in an ACL entry

The *acl_get_tag_type()* and *acl_set_tag_type()* functions retrieve and modify the tag type in the ACL entry referred to by their *entry* argument.

```
acl_tag_t tag_type;

status = acl_get_tag_type(entry, &tag_type);
status = acl_set_tag_type(entry, tag_type);
```

The *tag_type* argument has the type *acl_tag_t* (an integer type), and has one of the values ACL_USER_OBJ, ACL_USER, ACL_GROUP_OBJ, ACL_GROUP, ACL_OTHER, or ACL_MASK.

The *acl_get_qualifier()* and *acl_set_qualifier()* functions retrieve and modify the tag qualifier in the ACL entry referred to by their *entry* argument. Here is an example, in which we assume that we have already determined that this is an ACL_USER entry by inspecting the tag type:

```
uid_t *qualp;                 /* Pointer to UID */

qualp = acl_get_qualifier(entry);
status = acl_set_qualifier(entry, qualp);
```

The tag qualifier is valid only if the tag type of this entry is ACL_USER or ACL_GROUP. In the former case, *qualp* is a pointer to a user ID (*uid_t **); in the latter case, it is a pointer to a group ID (*gid_t **).

The *acl_get_permset()* and *acl_set_permset()* functions retrieve and modify the permission set in the ACL entry referred to by their *entry* argument.

```
acl_permset_t permset;

status = acl_get_permset(entry, &permset);
status = acl_set_permset(entry, permset);
```

The *acl_permset_t* data type is a handle referring to a permission set.

The following functions are used to manipulate the contents of a permission set:

```
int is_set;

is_set = acl_get_perm(permset, perm);

status = acl_add_perm(permset, perm);
status = acl_delete_perm(permset, perm);
status = acl_clear_perms(permset);
```

In each of these calls, *perm* is specified as ACL_READ, ACL_WRITE, or ACL_EXECUTE, with the obvious meanings. These functions are used as follows:

- The *acl_get_perm()* function returns 1 (true) if the permission specified in *perm* is enabled in the permission set referred to by *permset*, or 0 if it is not. This function is a Linux extension to the POSIX.1e draft standard.

- The *acl_add_perm()* function adds the permission specified in *perm* to the permission set referred to by *permset*.

- The *acl_delete_perm()* function removes the permission specified in *perm* from the permission set referred to by *permset*. (It is not an error to remove a permission if it is not present in the set.)

- The *acl_clear_perms()* function removes all permissions from the permission set referred to by *permset*.

Creating and deleting ACL entries

The *acl_create_entry()* function creates a new entry in an existing ACL. A handle referring to the new entry is returned in the location pointed to by the second function argument.

```
acl_entry_t entry;

status = acl_create_entry(&acl, &entry);
```

The new entry can then be populated using the functions described previously.
   The *acl_delete_entry()* function removes an entry from an ACL.

```
status = acl_delete_entry(acl, entry);
```

Updating a file's ACL

The *acl_set_file()* function is the converse of *acl_get_file()*. It updates the on-disk ACL with the contents of the in-memory ACL referred to by its *acl* argument.

```
int status;

status = acl_set_file(pathname, type, acl);
```

The *type* argument is either ACL_TYPE_ACCESS, to update the access ACL, or ACL_TYPE_DEFAULT, to update a directory's default ACL.

Converting an ACL between in-memory and text form

The *acl_from_text()* function translates a string containing a long or short text form ACL into an in-memory ACL, and returns a handle that can be used to refer to the ACL in subsequent function calls.

```
acl = acl_from_text(acl_string);
```

The *acl_to_text()* function performs the reverse conversion, returning a long text form string corresponding to the ACL referred to by its *acl* argument.

```
char *str;
ssize_t len;

str = acl_to_text(acl, &len);
```

If the *len* argument is not specified as NULL, then the buffer it points to is used to return the length of the string returned as the function result.

Other functions in the ACL API

The following paragraphs describe several other commonly used ACL functions that are not shown in Figure 17-2.
   The *acl_calc_mask(&acl)* function calculates and sets the permissions in the ACL_MASK entry of the in-memory ACL whose handle is pointed to by its argument. Typically, we use this function whenever we create or modify an ACL. The ACL_MASK permissions are calculated as the union of the permissions in all ACL_USER, ACL_GROUP, and ACL_GROUP_OBJ entries. A useful property of this function is that it creates the ACL_MASK entry if it doesn't already exist. This means that if we add ACL_USER and ACL_GROUP entries to a previously minimal ACL, then we can use this function to ensure the creation of the ACL_MASK entry.

The *acl_valid(acl)* function returns 0 if the ACL referred to by its argument is valid, or –1 otherwise. An ACL is valid if all of the following are true:

- the `ACL_USER_OBJ`, `ACL_GROUP_OBJ`, and `ACL_OTHER` entries appear exactly once;
- there is an `ACL_MASK` entry if any `ACL_USER` or `ACL_GROUP` entries are present;
- there is at most one `ACL_MASK` entry;
- each `ACL_USER` entry has a unique user ID; and
- each `ACL_GROUP` entry has a unique group ID.

> The *acl_check()* and *acl_error()* functions (both are Linux extensions) are alternatives to *acl_valid()* that are less portable, but provide a more precise description of the error in a malformed ACL. See the manual pages for details.

The *acl_delete_def_file(pathname)* function removes the default ACL on the directory referred to by *pathname*.

The *acl_init(count)* function creates a new, empty ACL structure that initially contains space for at least *count* ACL entries. (The *count* argument is a hint to the system about intended usage, not a hard limit.) A handle for the new ACL is returned as the function result.

The *acl_dup(acl)* function creates a duplicate of the ACL referred to by *acl* and returns a handle for the duplicate ACL as its function result.

The *acl_free(handle)* function frees memory allocated by other ACL functions. For example, we must use *acl_free()* to free memory allocated by calls to *acl_from_text()*, *acl_to_text()*, *acl_get_file()*, *acl_init()*, and *acl_dup()*.

Example program

Listing 17-1 demonstrates the use of some of the ACL library functions. This program retrieves and displays the ACL on a file (i.e., it provides a subset of the functionality of the *getfacl* command). If the *–d* command-line option is specified, then the program displays the default ACL (of a directory) instead of the access ACL.

Here is an example of the use of this program:

```
$ touch tfile
$ setfacl -m 'u:annie:r,u:paulh:rw,g:teach:r' tfile
$ ./acl_view tfile
user_obj            rw-
user        annie   r--
user        paulh   rw-
group_obj           r--
group       teach   r--
mask                rw-
other               r--
```

> The source code distribution of this book also includes a program, acl/acl_update.c, that performs updates on an ACL (i.e., it provides a subset of the functionality of the *setfacl* command).

Listing 17-1: Display the access or default ACL on a file

```
#include <acl/libacl.h>
#include <sys/acl.h>
#include "ugid_functions.h"
#include "tlpi_hdr.h"

static void
usageError(char *progName)
{
    fprintf(stderr, "Usage: %s [-d] filename\n", progName);
    exit(EXIT_FAILURE);
}

int
main(int argc, char *argv[])
{
    acl_t acl;
    acl_type_t type;
    acl_entry_t entry;
    acl_tag_t tag;
    uid_t *uidp;
    gid_t *gidp;
    acl_permset_t permset;
    char *name;
    int entryId, permVal, opt;

    type = ACL_TYPE_ACCESS;
    while ((opt = getopt(argc, argv, "d")) != -1) {
        switch (opt) {
        case 'd': type = ACL_TYPE_DEFAULT;      break;
        case '?': usageError(argv[0]);
        }
    }

    if (optind + 1 != argc)
        usageError(argv[0]);

    acl = acl_get_file(argv[optind], type);
    if (acl == NULL)
        errExit("acl_get_file");

    /* Walk through each entry in this ACL */

    for (entryId = ACL_FIRST_ENTRY; ; entryId = ACL_NEXT_ENTRY) {

        if (acl_get_entry(acl, entryId, &entry) != 1)
            break;                      /* Exit on error or no more entries */
```

```
/* Retrieve and display tag type */

if (acl_get_tag_type(entry, &tag) == -1)
    errExit("acl_get_tag_type");

printf("%-12s", (tag == ACL_USER_OBJ) ?  "user_obj" :
                (tag == ACL_USER) ?      "user" :
                (tag == ACL_GROUP_OBJ) ? "group_obj" :
                (tag == ACL_GROUP) ?     "group" :
                (tag == ACL_MASK) ?      "mask" :
                (tag == ACL_OTHER) ?     "other" : "???");

/* Retrieve and display optional tag qualifier */

if (tag == ACL_USER) {
    uidp = acl_get_qualifier(entry);
    if (uidp == NULL)
        errExit("acl_get_qualifier");

    name = userNameFromID(*uidp);
    if (name == NULL)
        printf("%-8d ", *uidp);
    else
        printf("%-8s ", name);

    if (acl_free(uidp) == -1)
        errExit("acl_free");

} else if (tag == ACL_GROUP) {
    gidp = acl_get_qualifier(entry);
    if (gidp == NULL)
        errExit("acl_get_qualifier");

    name = groupNameFromId(*gidp);
    if (name == NULL)
        printf("%-8d ", *gidp);
    else
        printf("%-8s ", name);

    if (acl_free(gidp) == -1)
        errExit("acl_free");

} else {
    printf("         ");
}

/* Retrieve and display permissions */

if (acl_get_permset(entry, &permset) == -1)
    errExit("acl_get_permset");

permVal = acl_get_perm(permset, ACL_READ);
if (permVal == -1)
    errExit("acl_get_perm - ACL_READ");
```

```
            printf("%c", (permVal == 1) ? 'r' : '-');
            permVal = acl_get_perm(permset, ACL_WRITE);
            if (permVal == -1)
                errExit("acl_get_perm - ACL_WRITE");
            printf("%c", (permVal == 1) ? 'w' : '-');
            permVal = acl_get_perm(permset, ACL_EXECUTE);
            if (permVal == -1)
                errExit("acl_get_perm - ACL_EXECUTE");
            printf("%c", (permVal == 1) ? 'x' : '-');

            printf("\n");
        }

    if (acl_free(acl) == -1)
        errExit("acl_free");

    exit(EXIT_SUCCESS);
}
```
── acl/acl_view.c

17.9 Summary

From version 2.6 onward, Linux supports ACLs. ACLs extend the traditional
UNIX file permissions model, allowing file permissions to be controlled on a per-
user and per-group basis.

Further information

The final versions (*Draft 17*) of the draft POSIX.1e and POSIX.2c standards are
available online at *http://wt.tuxomania.net/publications/posix.1e/*.

The *acl(5)* manual page gives an overview of ACLs and some guidance on the
portability of the various ACL library functions implemented on Linux.

Details of the Linux implementation of ACLs and extended attributes can be
found in [Grünbacher, 2003]. Andreas Grünbacher maintains a web site containing information about ACLs at *http://acl.bestbits.at/*.

17.10 Exercise

17-1.   Write a program that displays the permissions from the ACL entry that
corresponds to a particular user or group. The program should take two
command-line arguments. The first argument is either of the letters *u* or *g*,
indicating whether the second argument identifies a user or group. (The functions
defined in Listing 8-1, on page 159, can be used to allow the second command-line
argument to be specified numerically or as a name.) If the ACL entry that
corresponds to the given user or group falls into the group class, then the program
should additionally display the permissions that would apply after the ACL entry
has been modified by the ACL mask entry.

18

DIRECTORIES AND LINKS

In this chapter, we conclude our discussion of file-related topics by looking at directories and links. After an overview of their implementation, we describe the system calls used to create and remove directories and links. We then look at library functions that allow a program to scan the contents of a single directory and to walk through (i.e., examine each file in) a directory tree.

Each process has two directory-related attributes: a root directory, which determines the point from which absolute pathnames are interpreted, and a current working directory, which determines the point from which relative pathnames are interpreted. We look at the system calls that allow a process to change both of these attributes.

We finish the chapter with a discussion of library functions that are used to resolve pathnames and to parse them into directory and filename components.

18.1 Directories and (Hard) Links

A *directory* is stored in the file system in a similar way to a regular file. Two things distinguish a directory from a regular file:

- A directory is marked with a different file type in its i-node entry (Section 14.4).
- A directory is a file with a special organization. Essentially, it is a table consisting of filenames and i-node numbers.

On most native Linux file systems, filenames can be up to 255 characters long. The relationship between directories and i-nodes is illustrated in Figure 18-1, which shows the partial contents of the file system i-node table and relevant directory files that are maintained for an example file (/etc/passwd).

Although a process can open a directory, it can't use *read()* to read the contents of a directory. To retrieve the contents of a directory, a process must instead use the system calls and library functions discussed later in this chapter. (On some UNIX implementations, it is possible to perform a *read()* on a directory, but this is not portable.) Nor can a process directly change a directory's contents with *write()*; it can only indirectly (i.e., request the kernel to) change the contents using system calls such as *open()* (to create a new file), *link()*, *mkdir()*, *symlink()*, *unlink()*, and *rmdir()*. (All of these system calls are described later in this chapter, except *open()*, which was described in Section 4.3.)

The i-node table is numbered starting at 1, rather than 0, because 0 in the i-node field of a directory entry indicates that the entry is unused. I-node 1 is used to record bad blocks in the file system. The root directory (/) of a file system is always stored in i-node entry 2 (as shown in Figure 18-1), so that the kernel knows where to start when resolving a pathname.

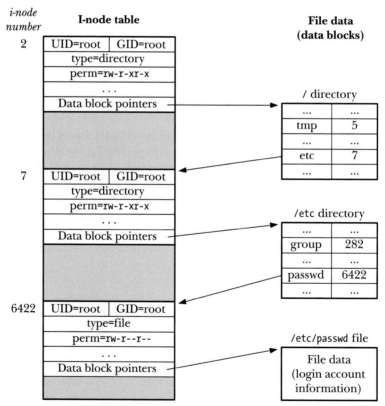

Figure 18-1: Relationship between i-node and directory structures for the file /etc/passwd

If we review the list of information stored in a file i-node (Section 14.4), we see that the i-node doesn't contain a filename; it is only the mapping within a directory list that defines the name of a file. This has a useful consequence: we can create multiple names—in the same or in different directories—each of which refers to the same i-node. These multiple names are known as *links*, or sometimes as *hard links* to distinguish them from symbolic links, which we discuss shortly.

> All native Linux and UNIX file systems support hard links. However, many non-UNIX file systems (e.g., Microsoft's VFAT) do not. (Microsoft's NTFS file system does support hard links.)

From the shell, we can create new hard links to an existing file using the *ln* command, as shown in the following shell session log:

```
$ echo -n 'It is good to collect things,' > abc
$ ls -li abc
122232 -rw-r--r--    1 mtk      users          29 Jun 15 17:07 abc
$ ln abc xyz
$ echo ' but it is better to go on walks.' >> xyz
$ cat abc
It is good to collect things, but it is better to go on walks.
$ ls -li abc xyz
122232 -rw-r--r--    2 mtk      users          63 Jun 15 17:07 abc
122232 -rw-r--r--    2 mtk      users          63 Jun 15 17:07 xyz
```

The i-node numbers displayed (as the first column) by *ls −li* confirm what was already clear from the output of the *cat* command: the names abc and xyz refer to the same i-node entry, and hence to the same file. In the third field displayed by *ls −li*, we can see the link count for the i-node. After the *ln abc xyz* command, the link count of the i-node referred to by abc has risen to 2, since there are now two names referring to the file. (The same link count is displayed for the file xyz, since it refers to the same i-node.)

If one of these filenames is removed, the other name, and the file itself, continue to exist:

```
$ rm abc
$ ls -li xyz
122232 -rw-r--r--    1 mtk      users          63 Jun 15 17:07 xyz
```

The i-node entry and data blocks for the file are removed (deallocated) only when the i-node's link count falls to 0—that is, when all of the names for the file have been removed. To summarize: the *rm* command removes a filename from a directory list, decrements the link count of the corresponding i-node by 1, and, if the link count thereby falls to 0, deallocates the i-node and the data blocks to which it refers.

All of the names (links) for a file are equivalent—none of the names (e.g., the first) has priority over any of the others. As we saw in the above example, after the first name associated with the file was removed, the physical file continued to exist, but it was then accessible only by the other name.

A question often asked in online forums is "How can I find the filename associated with the file descriptor X in my program?" The short answer is that we can't—

at least not portably and unambiguously—since a file descriptor refers to an i-node, and multiple filenames (or even, as described in Section 18.3, none at all) may refer to this i-node.

> On Linux, we can see which files a process currently has open by using *readdir()* (Section 18.8) to scan the contents of the Linux-specific /proc/*PID*/fd directory, which contains symbolic links for each of the file descriptors currently opened by the process. The *lsof(1)* and *fuser(1)* tools, which have been ported to many UNIX systems, can also be useful in this regard.

Hard links have two limitations, both of which can be circumvented by the use of symbolic links:

- Because directory entries (hard links) refer to files using just an i-node number, and i-node numbers are unique only within a file system, a hard link must reside on the same file system as the file to which it refers.

- A hard link can't be made to a directory. This prevents the creation of circular links, which would confuse many system programs.

> Early UNIX implementations permitted the superuser to create hard links to directories. This was necessary because these implementations did not provide a *mkdir()* system call. Instead, a directory was created using *mknod()*, and then links for the . and .. entries were created ([Vahalia, 1996]). Although this feature is no longer needed, some modern UNIX implementations retain it for backward compatibility.
>
> An effect similar to hard links on directories can be achieved using bind mounts (Section 14.9.4).

18.2 Symbolic (Soft) Links

A *symbolic link*, also sometimes called a *soft link*, is a special file type whose data is the name of another file. Figure 18-2 illustrates the situation where two hard links, /home/erena/this and /home/allyn/that, refer to the same file, and a symbolic link, /home/kiran/other, refers to the name /home/erena/this.

From the shell, symbolic links are created using the *ln –s* command. The *ls –F* command displays a trailing @ character at the end of symbolic links.

The pathname to which a symbolic link refers may be either absolute or relative. A relative symbolic link is interpreted relative to the location of the link itself.

Symbolic links don't have the same status as hard links. In particular, a symbolic link is not included in the link count of the file to which it refers. (Thus, the link count of i-node 61 in Figure 18-2 is 2, not 3.) Therefore, if the filename to which the symbolic link refers is removed, the symbolic link itself continues to exist, even though it can no longer be dereferenced (followed). We say that it has become a *dangling link*. It is even possible to create a symbolic link to a filename that doesn't exist at the time the link is created.

> Symbolic links were introduced by 4.2BSD. Although they were not included in POSIX.1-1990, they were subsequently incorporated into SUSv1, and thus are in SUSv3.

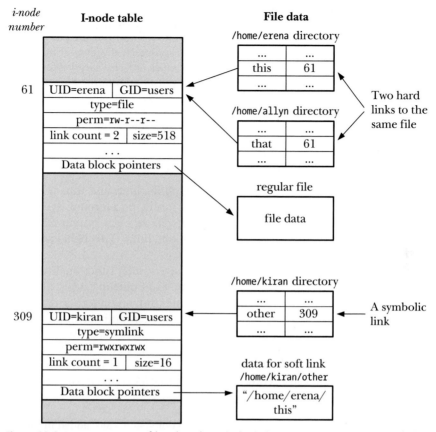

Figure 18-2: Representation of hard and symbolic links

Since a symbolic link refers to a filename, rather than an i-node number, it can be used to link to a file in a different file system. Symbolic links also do not suffer the other limitation of hard links: we can create symbolic links to directories. Tools such as *find* and *tar* can tell the difference between hard and symbolic links, and either don't follow symbolic links by default, or avoid getting trapped in circular references created using symbolic links.

It is possible to chain symbolic links (e.g., a is a symbolic link to b, which is a symbolic link to c). When a symbolic link is specified in various file-related system calls, the kernel dereferences the series of links to arrive at the final file.

SUSv3 requires that an implementation allow at least _POSIX_SYMLOOP_MAX dereferences of each symbolic link component of a pathname. The specified value for _POSIX_SYMLOOP_MAX is 8. However, before kernel 2.6.18, Linux imposed a limit of 5 dereferences when following a chain of symbolic links. Starting with kernel 2.6.18, Linux implements the SUSv3-specified minimum of 8 dereferences. Linux also imposes a total of 40 dereferences for an entire pathname. These limits are required to prevent extremely long symbolic link chains, as well as symbolic link loops, from causing stack overflows in the kernel code that resolves symbolic links.

Some UNIX file systems perform an optimization not mentioned in the main text nor shown in Figure 18-2. When the total length of the string forming the symbolic link's contents is small enough to fit in the part of the i-node that would normally be used for data pointers, the link string is instead stored there. This saves allocating a disk block and also speeds access to the symbolic link information, since it is retrieved along with the file i-node. For example, *ext2*, *ext3*, and *ext4* employ this technique to fit short symbolic strings into the 60 bytes normally used for data block pointers. In practice, this can be a very effective optimization. Of the 20,700 symbolic links on one system checked by the author, 97% were 60 bytes or smaller.

Interpretation of symbolic links by system calls

Many system calls dereference (follow) symbolic links and thus work on the file to which the link refers. Some system calls don't dereference symbolic links, but instead operate directly on the link file itself. As each system call is covered, we describe its behavior with respect to symbolic links. This behavior is also summarized in Table 18-1.

In a few cases where it is necessary to have similar functionality for both the file to which a symbolic link refers and for the symbolic link itself, alternative system calls are provided: one that dereferences the link and another that does not, with the latter prefixed by the letter *l*; for example, *stat()* and *lstat()*.

One point generally applies: symbolic links in the directory part of a pathname (i.e., all of the components preceding the final slash) are always dereferenced. Thus, in the pathname /somedir/somesubdir/file, somedir and somesubdir will always be dereferenced if they are symbolic links, and file may be dereferenced, depending on the system call to which the pathname is passed.

In Section 18.11, we describe a set of system calls, added in Linux 2.6.16, that extend the functionality of some of the interfaces shown in Table 18-1. For some of these system calls, the behavior with respect to following symbolic links can be controlled by the *flags* argument to the call.

File permissions and ownership for symbolic links

The ownership and permissions of a symbolic link are ignored for most operations (symbolic links are always created with all permissions enabled). Instead, the ownership and permissions of the file to which the link refers are used in determining whether an operation is permitted. The ownership of a symbolic link is relevant only when the link itself is being removed or renamed in a directory with the sticky permission bit set (Section 15.4.5).

18.3 Creating and Removing (Hard) Links: *link()* and *unlink()*

The *link()* and *unlink()* system calls create and remove hard links.

```
#include <unistd.h>

int link(const char *oldpath, const char *newpath);
```
                                        Returns 0 on success, or −1 on error

Table 18-1: Interpretation of symbolic links by various functions

Function	Follows links?	Notes
access()	•	
acct()	•	
bind()	•	UNIX domain sockets have pathnames
chdir()	•	
chmod()	•	
chown()	•	
chroot()	•	
creat()	•	
exec()	•	
getxattr()	•	
lchown()		
lgetxattr()		
link()		See Section 18.3
listxattr()	•	
llistxattr()		
lremovexattr()		
lsetxattr()		
lstat()		
lutimes()		
open()	•	Unless O_NOFOLLOW or O_EXCL | O_CREAT specified
opendir()	•	
pathconf()	•	
pivot_root()	•	
quotactl()	•	
readlink()		
removexattr()	•	
rename()		Links are not followed in either argument
rmdir()		Fails with ENOTDIR if argument is a symbolic link
setxattr()	•	
stat()	•	
statfs(), *statvfs()*	•	
swapon(), *swapoff()*	•	
truncate()	•	
unlink()		
uselib()	•	
utime(), *utimes()*	•	

Given the pathname of an existing file in *oldpath*, the *link()* system call creates a new link, using the pathname specified in *newpath*. If *newpath* already exists, it is not overwritten; instead, an error (EEXIST) results.

On Linux, the *link()* system call doesn't dereference symbolic links. If *oldpath* is a symbolic link, then *newpath* is created as a new hard link to the same symbolic link file. (In other words, *newpath* is also a symbolic link to the same file to which *oldpath* refers.) This behavior doesn't conform to SUSv3, which says that all functions that perform pathname resolution should dereference symbolic links unless otherwise specified (and there is no exception specified for *link()*). Most other UNIX implementations behave in the manner specified by SUSv3. One notable exception is Solaris, which provides the same behavior as Linux by default, but provides SUSv3-conformant behavior if appropriate compiler options are used. The upshot of this inconsistency across implementations is that portable applications should avoid specifying a symbolic link for the *oldpath* argument.

> SUSv4 recognizes the inconsistency across existing implementations and specifies that the choice of whether or not *link()* dereferences symbolic links is implementation-defined. SUSv4 also adds the specification of *linkat()*, which performs the same task as *link()*, but has a *flags* argument that can be used to control whether the call dereferences symbolic links. See Section 18.11 for further details.

```
#include <unistd.h>

int unlink(const char *pathname);
```
                                              Returns 0 on success, or −1 on error

The *unlink()* system call removes a link (deletes a filename) and, if that is the last link to the file, also removes the file itself. If the link specified in *pathname* doesn't exist, then *unlink()* fails with the error ENOENT.

We can't use *unlink()* to remove a directory; that task requires *rmdir()* or *remove()*, which we look at in Section 18.6.

> SUSv3 says that if *pathname* specifies a directory, then *unlink()* should fail with the error EPERM. However, on Linux, *unlink()* fails with the error EISDIR in this case. (LSB explicitly permits this deviation from SUSv3.) A portable application should be prepared to handle either value if checking for this case.

The *unlink()* system call doesn't dereference symbolic links. If *pathname* is a symbolic link, the link itself is removed, rather than the name to which it points.

An open file is deleted only when all file descriptors are closed

In addition to maintaining a link count for each i-node, the kernel also counts open file descriptions for the file (see Figure 5-2, on page 95). If the last link to a file is removed and any processes hold open descriptors referring to the file, the file won't actually be deleted until all of the descriptors are closed. This is a useful feature, because it permits us to unlink a file without needing to worry about whether some other process has it open. (However, we can't reattach a name to an open file whose link count has fallen to 0.) In addition, we can perform tricks such as creating and opening a temporary file, unlinking it immediately, and then continuing to use it within our program, relying on the fact that the file is destroyed only when we close the file descriptor—either explicitly, or implicitly when the program exits. (This is what the *tmpfile()* function described in Section 5.12 does.)

The program in Listing 18-1 demonstrates that even when the last link to a file is removed, the file is deleted only when all open file descriptors that refer to it are closed.

Listing 18-1: Removing a link with *unlink()*

─── **dirs_links/t_unlink.c**

```
#include <sys/stat.h>
#include <fcntl.h>
#include "tlpi_hdr.h"

#define CMD_SIZE 200
#define BUF_SIZE 1024

int
main(int argc, char *argv[])
{
    int fd, j, numBlocks;
    char shellCmd[CMD_SIZE];         /* Command to be passed to system() */
    char buf[BUF_SIZE];              /* Random bytes to write to file */

    if (argc < 2 || strcmp(argv[1], "--help") == 0)
        usageErr("%s temp-file [num-1kB-blocks] \n", argv[0]);

    numBlocks = (argc > 2) ? getInt(argv[2], GN_GT_0, "num-1kB-blocks")
                           : 100000;

    fd = open(argv[1], O_WRONLY | O_CREAT | O_EXCL, S_IRUSR | S_IWUSR);
    if (fd == -1)
        errExit("open");

    if (unlink(argv[1]) == -1)       /* Remove filename */
        errExit("unlink");

    for (j = 0; j < numBlocks; j++)    /* Write lots of junk to file */
        if (write(fd, buf, BUF_SIZE) != BUF_SIZE)
            fatal("partial/failed write");

    snprintf(shellCmd, CMD_SIZE, "df -k `dirname %s`", argv[1]);
    system(shellCmd);                /* View space used in file system */

    if (close(fd) == -1)             /* File is now destroyed */
        errExit("close");
    printf("********** Closed file descriptor\n");

    system(shellCmd);                /* Review space used in file system */
    exit(EXIT_SUCCESS);
}
```

─── **dirs_links/t_unlink.c**

The program in Listing 18-1 accepts two command-line arguments. The first argument identifies the name of a file that the program should create. The program opens this file and then immediately unlinks the filename. Although the filename disappears, the file itself continues to exist. The program then writes random blocks of data to the file. The number of these blocks is specified in the optional second command-line argument of the program. At this point, the program employs the *df(1)* command to display the amount of space used on the file system.

The program then closes the file descriptor, at which the point the file is removed, and uses *df(1)* once more to show that the amount of disk space in use has decreased. The following shell session demonstrates the use of the program in Listing 18-1:

```
$ ./t_unlink /tmp/tfile 1000000
Filesystem              1K-blocks       Used Available Use% Mounted on
/dev/sda10               5245020    3204044    2040976  62% /
********** Closed file descriptor
Filesystem              1K-blocks       Used Available Use% Mounted on
/dev/sda10               5245020    2201128    3043892  42% /
```

> In Listing 18-1, we use the *system()* function to execute a shell command. We describe *system()* in detail in Section 27.6.

18.4 Changing the Name of a File: *rename()*

The *rename()* system call can be used both to rename a file and to move it into another directory on the same file system.

```
#include <stdio.h>

int rename(const char *oldpath, const char *newpath);
```
                                         Returns 0 on success, or –1 on error

The *oldpath* argument is an existing pathname, which is renamed to the pathname given in *newpath*.

The *rename()* call just manipulates directory entries; it doesn't move file data. Renaming a file doesn't affect other hard links to the file, nor does it affect any processes that hold open descriptors for the file, since these descriptors refer to open file descriptions, which (after the *open()* call) have no connection with filenames.

The following rules apply to the use of *rename()*:

- If *newpath* already exists, it is overwritten.
- If *newpath* and *oldpath* refer to the same file, then no changes are made (and the call succeeds). This is rather counterintuitive. Following from the previous point, we normally expect that if two filenames x and y exist, then the call *rename("x", "y")* would remove the name x. This is not the case if x and y are links to the same file.

  > The rationale for this rule, which comes from the original BSD implementation, was probably to simplify the checks that the kernel must perform in order to guarantee that calls such as *rename("x", "x")*, *rename("x", "./x")*, and *rename("x", "somedir/../x")* don't remove the file.

- The *rename()* system call doesn't dereference symbolic links in either of its arguments. If *oldpath* is a symbolic link, then the symbolic link is renamed. If *newpath* is a symbolic link, then it is treated as a normal pathname to which *oldpath* is to be renamed (i.e., the existing *newpath* symbolic link is removed).

- If *oldpath* refers to a file other than a directory, then *newpath* can't specify the pathname of a directory (the error is EISDIR). To rename a file to a location inside a directory (i.e., move the file to another directory), *newpath* must include the new filename. The following call both moves a file into a different directory and changes its name:

```
rename("sub1/x", "sub2/y");
```

- Specifying the name of a directory in *oldpath* allows us to rename that directory. In this case, *newpath* either must not exist or must be the name of an empty directory. If *newpath* is an existing file or an existing, nonempty directory, then an error results (respectively, ENOTDIR and ENOTEMPTY).

- If *oldpath* is a directory, then *newpath* can't contain a directory prefix that is the same as *oldpath*. For example, we could not rename /home/mtk to /home/mtk/bin (the error is EINVAL).

- The files referred to by *oldpath* and *newpath* must be on the same file system. This is required because a directory is a list of hard links that refer to i-nodes in the same file system as the directory. As stated earlier, *rename()* is merely manipulating the contents of directory lists. Attempting to rename a file into a different file system fails with the error EXDEV. (To achieve the desired result, we must instead copy the contents of the file from one file system to another and then delete the old file. This is what the *mv* command does in this case.)

18.5 Working with Symbolic Links: *symlink()* and *readlink()*

We now look at the system calls used to create symbolic links and examine their contents.

The *symlink()* system call creates a new symbolic link, *linkpath*, to the pathname specified in *filepath*. (To remove a symbolic link, we use *unlink()*.)

```
#include <unistd.h>

int symlink(const char *filepath, const char *linkpath);
```
                                    Returns 0 on success, or –1 on error

If the pathname given in *linkpath* already exists, then the call fails (with *errno* set to EEXIST). The pathname specified in *filepath* may be absolute or relative.

The file or directory named in *filepath* doesn't need to exist at the time of the call. Even if it exists at that time, there is nothing to prevent it from being removed later. In this case, *linkpath* becomes a *dangling link*, and attempts to dereference it in other system calls yield an error (usually ENOENT).

If we specify a symbolic link as the *pathname* argument to *open()*, it opens the file to which the link refers. Sometimes, we would rather retrieve the content of the link itself—that is, the pathname to which it refers. The *readlink()* system call performs this task, placing a copy of the symbolic link string in the character array pointed to by *buffer*.

```
#include <unistd.h>

ssize_t readlink(const char *pathname, char *buffer, size_t bufsiz);
                    Returns number of bytes placed in buffer on success, or −1 on error
```

The *bufsiz* argument is an integer used to tell *readlink()* the number of bytes available in *buffer*.

If no errors occur, then *readlink()* returns the number of bytes actually placed in *buffer*. If the length of the link exceeds *bufsiz*, then a truncated string is placed in *buffer* (and *readlink()* returns the size of that string—that is, *bufsiz*).

Because a terminating null byte is not placed at the end of *buffer*, there is no way to distinguish the case where *readlink()* returns a truncated string from that where it returns a string that exactly fills *buffer*. One way of checking if the latter has occurred is to reallocate a larger *buffer* array and call *readlink()* again. Alternatively, we can size *buffer* using the PATH_MAX constant (described in Section 11.1), which defines the length of the longest pathname that a program should have to accommodate.

We demonstrate the use of *readlink()* in Listing 18-4.

> SUSv3 defined a new limit, SYMLINK_MAX, that an implementation should define to indicate the maximum number of bytes that can be stored in a symbolic link. This limit is required to be at least 255 bytes. At the time of writing, Linux doesn't define this limit. In the main text, we suggest the use of PATH_MAX because that limit should be at least as large as SYMLINK_MAX.
>
> In SUSv2, the return type of *readlink()* was specified as *int*, and many current implementations (as well as older *glibc* versions on Linux) follow that specification. SUSv3 changed the return type to *ssize_t*.

18.6 Creating and Removing Directories: *mkdir()* and *rmdir()*

The *mkdir()* system call creates a new directory.

```
#include <sys/stat.h>

int mkdir(const char *pathname, mode_t mode);
                                        Returns 0 on success, or −1 on error
```

The *pathname* argument specifies the pathname of the new directory. This pathname may be relative or absolute. If a file with this pathname already exists, then the call fails with the error EEXIST.

The ownership of the new directory is set according to the rules described in Section 15.3.1.

The *mode* argument specifies the permissions for the new directory. (We describe the meanings of the permission bits for directories in Sections 15.3.1, 15.3.2, and 15.4.5.) This bit-mask value may be specified by ORing (|) together constants from Table 15-4, on page 295, but, as with *open()*, it may also be specified as an octal number. The value given in *mode* is ANDed against the process umask (Section 15.4.6). In addition, the set-user-ID bit (S_ISUID) is always turned off, since it has no meaning for directories.

If the sticky bit (S_ISVTX) is set in *mode*, then it will be set on the new directory.

The setting of the set-group-ID bit (S_ISGID) in *mode* is ignored. Instead, if the set-group-ID bit is set on the parent directory, then it will also be set on the newly created directory. In Section 15.3.1, we noted that setting the set-group-ID permission bit on a directory causes new files created in the directory to take their group ID from the directory's group ID, rather than the process's effective group ID. The *mkdir()* system call propagates the set-group-ID permission bit in the manner described here so that all subdirectories under a directory will share the same behavior.

SUSv3 explicitly notes that the manner in which *mkdir()* treats the set-user-ID, set-group-ID, and sticky bits is implementation-defined. On some UNIX implementations, these 3 bits are always turned off on a new directory.

The newly created directory contains two entries: . (dot), which is a link to the directory itself, and .. (dot-dot), which is a link to the parent directory.

> SUSv3 doesn't require directories to contain . and .. entries. It requires only that an implementation correctly interpret . and .. when they appear in pathnames. A portable application should not rely on the existence of these entries in a directory.

The *mkdir()* system call creates only the last component of *pathname*. In other words, the call *mkdir("aaa/bbb/ccc", mode)* will succeed only if the directories aaa and aaa/bbb already exist. (This corresponds to the default operation of the *mkdir(1)* command, but *mkdir(1)* also provides the *-p* option to create all of the intervening directory names if they don't exist.)

> The GNU C library provides the *mkdtemp(template)* function, which is the directory analog of the *mkstemp()* function. It creates a uniquely named directory with read, write, and execute permissions enabled for the owner, and no permissions allowed for any other users. Instead of returning a file descriptor as its result, *mkdtemp()* returns a pointer to a modified string containing the actual directory name in *template*. SUSv3 doesn't specify this function, and it is not available on all UNIX implementations; it is specified in SUSv4.

The *rmdir()* system call removes the directory specified in *pathname*, which may be an absolute or a relative pathname.

```
#include <unistd.h>

int rmdir(const char *pathname);
```
> Returns 0 on success, or –1 on error

In order for *rmdir()* to succeed, the directory must be empty. If the final component of *pathname* is a symbolic link, it is not dereferenced; instead, the error ENOTDIR results.

18.7 Removing a File or Directory: *remove()*

The *remove()* library function removes a file or an empty directory.

```
#include <stdio.h>

int remove(const char *pathname);
                                        Returns 0 on success, or -1 on error
```

If *pathname* is a file, *remove()* calls *unlink()*; if *pathname* is a directory, *remove()* calls *rmdir()*.

Like *unlink()* and *rmdir()*, *remove()* doesn't dereference symbolic links. If *pathname* is a symbolic link, *remove()* removes the link itself, rather than the file to which it refers.

If we want to remove a file in preparation for creating a new file with the same name, then using *remove()* is simpler than code that checks whether a pathname refers to a file or directory and calls *unlink()* or *rmdir()*.

> The *remove()* function was invented for the standard C library, which is implemented on both UNIX and non-UNIX systems. Most non-UNIX systems don't support hard links, so removing files with a function named *unlink()* would not make sense.

18.8 Reading Directories: *opendir()* and *readdir()*

The library functions described in this section can be used to open a directory and retrieve the names of the files it contains one by one.

> The library functions for reading directories are layered on top of the *getdents()* system call (which is not part of SUSv3), but provide an interface that is easier to use. Linux also provides a *readdir(2)* system call (as opposed to the *readdir(3)* library function described here), which performs a similar task to, but is made obsolete by, *getdents()*.

The *opendir()* function opens a directory and returns a handle that can be used to refer to the directory in later calls.

```
#include <dirent.h>

DIR *opendir(const char *dirpath);
                            Returns directory stream handle, or NULL on error
```

The *opendir()* function opens the directory specified by *dirpath* and returns a pointer to a structure of type *DIR*. This structure is a so-called *directory stream*, which is a handle that the caller passes to the other functions described below. Upon return from *opendir()*, the directory stream is positioned at the first entry in the directory list.

The *fdopendir()* function is like *opendir()*, except that the directory for which a stream is to be created is specified via the open file descriptor *fd*.

```
#include <dirent.h>

DIR *fdopendir(int fd);
```
                        Returns directory stream handle, or NULL on error

The *fdopendir()* function is provided so that applications can avoid the kinds of race conditions described in Section 18.11.

After a successful call to *fdopendir()*, this file descriptor is under the control of the system, and the program should not access it in any way other than by using the functions described in the remainder of this section.

The *fdopendir()* function is specified in SUSv4 (but not in SUSv3).

The *readdir()* function reads successive entries from a directory stream.

```
#include <dirent.h>

struct dirent *readdir(DIR *dirp);
```
                Returns pointer to a statically allocated structure describing
                    next directory entry, or NULL on end-of-directory or error

Each call to *readdir()* reads the next directory entry from the directory stream referred to by *dirp* and returns a pointer to a statically allocated structure of type *dirent*, containing the following information about the entry:

```
struct dirent {
    ino_t d_ino;        /* File i-node number */
    char  d_name[];     /* Null-terminated name of file */
};
```

This structure is overwritten on each call to *readdir()*.

> We have omitted various nonstandard fields in the Linux *dirent* structure from the above definition, since their use renders an application nonportable. The most interesting of these nonstandard fields is d_type, which is also present on BSD derivatives, but not on other UNIX implementations. This field holds a value indicating the type of the file named in d_name, such as DT_REG (regular file), DT_DIR (directory), DT_LNK (symbolic link), or DT_FIFO (FIFO). (These names are analogous to the macros in Table 15-1, on page 282.) Using the information in this field saves the cost of calling *lstat()* in order to discover the file type. Note, however, that, at the time of writing, this field is fully supported only on *Btrfs*, *ext2*, *ext3*, and *ext4*.

Further information about the file referred to by *d_name* can be obtained by calling *lstat()* (or *stat()*, if a symbolic link should be dereferenced) on the pathname constructed using the *dirpath* argument that was specified to *opendir()* concatenated with (a slash and) the value returned in the *d_name* field.

The filenames returned by *readdir()* are not in sorted order, but rather in the order in which they happen to occur in the directory (this depends on the order in which the file system adds files to the directory and how it fills gaps in the directory list after files are removed). (The command *ls -f* lists files in the same unsorted order that they would be retrieved by *readdir()*.)

> We can use the function *scandir(3)* to retrieve a sorted list of files matching programmer-defined criteria; see the manual page for details. Although not specified in SUSv3, *scandir()* is provided on most UNIX implementations. SUSv4 added a specification for *scandir()*.

On end-of-directory or error, *readdir()* returns NULL, in the latter case setting *errno* to indicate the error. To distinguish these two cases, we can write the following:

```
errno = 0;
direntp = readdir(dirp);
if (direntp == NULL) {
    if (errno != 0) {
        /* Handle error */
    } else {
        /* We reached end-of-directory */
    }
}
```

If the contents of a directory change while a program is scanning it with *readdir()*, the program might not see the changes. SUSv3 explicitly notes that it is unspecified whether *readdir()* will return a filename that has been added to or removed from the directory since the last call to *opendir()* or *rewinddir()*. All filenames that have been neither added nor removed since the last such call are guaranteed to be returned.

The *rewinddir()* function moves the directory stream back to the beginning so that the next call to *readdir()* will begin again with the first file in the directory.

```
#include <dirent.h>

void rewinddir(DIR *dirp);
```

The *closedir()* function closes the open directory stream referred to by *dirp*, freeing the resources used by the stream.

```
#include <dirent.h>

int closedir(DIR *dirp);
```
                                    Returns 0 on success, or −1 on error

Two further functions, *telldir()* and *seekdir()*, which are also specified in SUSv3, allow random access within a directory stream. Refer to the manual pages for further information about these functions.

Directory streams and file descriptors

A directory stream has an associated file descriptor. The *dirfd()* function returns the file descriptor associated with the directory stream referred to by *dirp*.

```
#define _BSD_SOURCE         /* Or: #define _SVID_SOURCE */
#include <dirent.h>

int dirfd(DIR *dirp);
```
                                Returns file descriptor on success, or −1 on error

We might, for example, pass the file descriptor returned by *dirfd()* to *fchdir()* (Section 18.10) in order to change the current working directory of the process to the corresponding directory. Alternatively, we might pass the file descriptor as the *dirfd* argument of one of the functions described in Section 18.11.

The *dirfd()* function also appears on the BSDs, but is present on few other implementations. It is not specified in SUSv3, but is specified in SUSv4.

At this point, it is worth mentioning that *opendir()* automatically sets the close-on-exec flag (FD_CLOEXEC) for the file descriptor associated with the directory stream. This ensures that the file descriptor is automatically closed when an *exec()* is performed. (SUSv3 requires this behavior.) We describe the close-on-exec flag in Section 27.4.

Example program

Listing 18-2 uses *opendir()*, *readdir()*, and *closedir()* to list the contents of each of the directories specified in its command line (or in the current working directory if no arguments are supplied). Here is an example of the use of this program:

```
$ mkdir sub                   Create a test directory
$ touch sub/a sub/b           Make some files in the test directory
$ ./list_files sub            List contents of directory
sub/a
sub/b
```

Listing 18-2: Scanning a directory

―――――――――――――――――――――――――――――――――――― **dirs_links/list_files.c**

```c
#include <dirent.h>
#include "tlpi_hdr.h"

static void                  /* List all files in directory 'dirPath' */
listFiles(const char *dirpath)
{
    DIR *dirp;
    struct dirent *dp;
    Boolean isCurrent;          /* True if 'dirpath' is "." */

    isCurrent = strcmp(dirpath, ".") == 0;

    dirp = opendir(dirpath);
    if (dirp  == NULL) {
        errMsg("opendir failed on '%s'", dirpath);
        return;
    }

    /* For each entry in this directory, print directory + filename */

    for (;;) {
        errno = 0;              /* To distinguish error from end-of-directory */
        dp = readdir(dirp);
        if (dp == NULL)
            break;

        if (strcmp(dp->d_name, ".") == 0 || strcmp(dp->d_name, "..") == 0)
            continue;           /* Skip . and .. */

        if (!isCurrent)
            printf("%s/", dirpath);
        printf("%s\n", dp->d_name);
    }

    if (errno != 0)
        errExit("readdir");

    if (closedir(dirp) == -1)
        errMsg("closedir");
}

int
main(int argc, char *argv[])
{
    if (argc > 1 && strcmp(argv[1], "--help") == 0)
        usageErr("%s [dir...]\n", argv[0]);

    if (argc == 1)              /* No arguments - use current directory */
        listFiles(".");
```

```
    else
        for (argv++; *argv; argv++)
            listFiles(*argv);

    exit(EXIT_SUCCESS);
}
```

——— `dirs_links/list_files.c`

The *readdir_r()* function

The *readdir_r()* function is a variation on *readdir()*. The key semantic difference between *readdir_r()* and *readdir()* is that the former is reentrant, while the latter is not. This is because *readdir_r()* returns the file entry via the caller-allocated *entry* argument, while *readdir()* returns information via a pointer to a statically allocated structure. We discuss reentrancy in Sections 21.1.2 and 31.1.

```
#include <dirent.h>

int readdir_r(DIR *dirp, struct dirent *entry, struct dirent **result);
```
                        Returns 0 on success, or a positive error number on error

Given *dirp*, which is a directory stream previously opened via *opendir()*, *readdir_r()* places information about the next directory entry into the *dirent* structure referred to by *entry*. In addition, a pointer to this structure is placed in *result*. If the end of the directory stream is reached, then NULL is placed in *result* instead (and *readdir_r()* returns 0). On error, *readdir_r()* doesn't return –1, but instead returns a positive integer corresponding to one of the *errno* values.

On Linux, the *d_name* field of the *dirent* structure is sized as an array of 256 bytes, which is long enough to hold the largest possible filename. Although several other UNIX implementations define the same size for *d_name*, SUSv3 leaves this point unspecified, and some UNIX implementations instead define the field as a 1-byte array, leaving the calling program with the task of allocating a structure of the correct size. When doing this, we should size the *d_name* field as one greater (for the terminating null byte) than the value of the constant NAME_MAX. Portable applications should thus allocate the *dirent* structure as follows:

```
    struct dirent *entryp;
    size_t len;

    len = offsetof(struct dirent, d_name) + NAME_MAX + 1;
    entryp = malloc(len);
    if (entryp == NULL)
        errExit("malloc");
```

Using the offsetof() macro (defined in <stddef.h>) avoids any implementation-specific dependencies on the number and size of fields in the *dirent* structure preceding the *d_name* field (which is always the last field in the structure).

The offsetof() macro takes two arguments—a structure type and the name of a field within that structure—and returns a value of type *size_t* that is the offset in bytes of the field from the beginning of the structure. This macro is necessary because a compiler may insert padding bytes in a structure to satisfy alignment requirements for types such as *int*, with the result that a field's offset within a structure may be greater than the sum of the sizes of the fields that precede it.

18.9 File Tree Walking: *nftw()*

The *nftw()* function allows a program to recursively walk through an entire directory subtree performing some operation (i.e., calling some programmer-defined function) for each file in the subtree.

> The *nftw()* function is an enhancement of the older *ftw()* function, which performs a similar task. New applications should use *nftw()* (*new ftw*) because it provides more functionality, and predictable handling of symbolic links (SUSv3 permits *ftw()* either to follow or not follow symbolic links). SUSv3 specifies both *nftw()* and *ftw()*, but the latter function is marked obsolete in SUSv4.
>
> The GNU C library also provides the BSD-derived *fts* API (*fts_open()*, *fts_read()*, *fts_children()*, *fts_set()*, and *fts_close()*). These functions perform a similar task to *ftw()* and *nftw()*, but offer greater flexibility to an application walking the tree. However, this API is not standardized and is provided on few UNIX implementations other than BSD descendants, so we omit discussion of it here.

The *nftw()* function walks through the directory tree specified by *dirpath* and calls the programmer-defined function *func* once for each file in the directory tree.

```
#define _XOPEN_SOURCE 500
#include <ftw.h>

int nftw(const char *dirpath,
        int (*func) (const char *pathname, const struct stat *statbuf,
                    int typeflag, struct FTW *ftwbuf),
        int nopenfd, int flags);
```
>   Returns 0 after successful walk of entire tree, or −1 on error,
>   or the first nonzero value returned by a call to *func*

By default, *nftw()* performs an unsorted, preorder traversal of the given tree, processing each directory before processing the files and subdirectories within that directory.

While traversing the directory tree, *nftw()* opens at most one file descriptor for each level of the tree. The *nopenfd* argument specifies the maximum number of file descriptors that *nftw()* may use. If the depth of the directory tree exceeds this maximum, *nftw()* does some bookkeeping, and closes and reopens descriptors in order to avoid holding open more than *nopenfd* descriptors simultaneously (and consequently runs more slowly). The need for this argument was greater under older UNIX implementations, some of which had a limit of 20 open file descriptors per process. Modern UNIX implementations allow a process to open a large number of file descriptors, and thus we can specify a generous number here (say 20 or more).

The *flags* argument to *nftw()* is created by ORing (|) zero or more of the following constants, which modify the operation of the function:

FTW_CHDIR

Do a *chdir()* into each directory before processing its contents. This is useful if *func* is designed to do some work in the directory in which the file specified by its *pathname* argument resides.

FTW_DEPTH

Do a postorder traversal of the directory tree. This means that *nftw()* calls *func* on all of the files (and subdirectories) within a directory before executing *func* on the directory itself. (The name of this flag is somewhat misleading—*nftw()* always does a depth-first, rather than a breadth-first, traversal of the directory tree. All that this flag does is convert the traversal from preorder to postorder.)

FTW_MOUNT

Don't cross over into another file system. Thus, if one of the subdirectories of the tree is a mount point, it is not traversed.

FTW_PHYS

By default, *nftw()* dereferences symbolic links. This flag tells it not to do so. Instead, a symbolic link is passed to *func* with a *typeflag* value of FTW_SL, as described below.

For each file, *nftw()* passes four arguments when calling *func*. The first of these arguments, *pathname*, is the pathname of the file. This pathname may be absolute, if *dirpath* was specified as an absolute pathname, or relative to the current working directory of the calling process at the time of the call to *ntfw()*, if *dirpath* was expressed as a relative pathname. The second argument, *statbuf*, is a pointer to a *stat* structure (Section 15.1) containing information about this file. The third argument, *typeflag*, provides further information about the file, and has one of the following symbolic values:

FTW_D

This is a directory.

FTW_DNR

This is a directory that can't be read (and so *nftw()* doesn't traverse any of its descendants).

FTW_DP

We are doing a postorder traversal (FTW_DEPTH) of a directory, and the current item is a directory whose files and subdirectories have already been processed.

FTW_F

This is a file of any type other than a directory or symbolic link.

FTW_NS

Calling *stat()* on this file failed, probably because of permission restrictions. The value in *statbuf* is undefined.

FTW_SL

> This is a symbolic link. This value is returned only if *nftw()* is called with the
> FTW_PHYS flag.

FTW_SLN

> This item is a dangling symbolic link. This value occurs only if FTW_PHYS was
> not specified in the *flags* argument.

The fourth argument to *func*, *ftwbuf*, is a pointer to a structure defined as follows:

```
struct FTW {
    int base;       /* Offset to basename part of pathname */
    int level;      /* Depth of file within tree traversal */
};
```

The *base* field of this structure is the integer offset of the filename part (the component after the last /) of the *pathname* argument of *func*. The *level* field is the depth of this item relative to the starting point of the traversal (which is level 0).

Each time it is called, *func* must return an integer value, and this value is interpreted by *nftw()*. Returning 0 tells *nftw()* to continue the tree walk, and if all calls to *func* return 0, *nftw()* itself returns 0 to its caller. Returning a nonzero value tells *nftw()* to immediately stop the tree walk, in which case *nftw()* returns the same nonzero value as its return value.

Because *nftw()* uses dynamically allocated data structures, the only way that a program should ever prematurely terminate a directory tree walk is by returning a nonzero value from *func*. Using *longjmp()* (Section 6.8) to exit from *func* may lead to unpredictable results—at the very least, memory leaks in a program.

Example program

Listing 18-3 demonstrates the use of *nftw()*.

Listing 18-3: Using *nftw()* to walk a directory tree

──────────────────────────────────── dirs_links/nftw_dir_tree.c
```
#define _XOPEN_SOURCE 600      /* Get nftw() and S_IFSOCK declarations */
#include <ftw.h>
#include "tlpi_hdr.h"

static void
usageError(const char *progName, const char *msg)
{
    if (msg != NULL)
        fprintf(stderr, "%s\n", msg);
    fprintf(stderr, "Usage: %s [-d] [-m] [-p] [directory-path]\n", progName);
    fprintf(stderr, "\t-d Use FTW_DEPTH flag\n");
    fprintf(stderr, "\t-m Use FTW_MOUNT flag\n");
    fprintf(stderr, "\t-p Use FTW_PHYS flag\n");
    exit(EXIT_FAILURE);
}

static int                      /* Function called by nftw() */
dirTree(const char *pathname, const struct stat *sbuf, int type,
        struct FTW *ftwb)
```

```c
{
    if (type == FTW_NS) {                      /* Could not stat() file */
        printf("?");
    } else {
        switch (sbuf->st_mode & S_IFMT) {   /* Print file type */
        case S_IFREG:  printf("-"); break;
        case S_IFDIR:  printf("d"); break;
        case S_IFCHR:  printf("c"); break;
        case S_IFBLK:  printf("b"); break;
        case S_IFLNK:  printf("l"); break;
        case S_IFIFO:  printf("p"); break;
        case S_IFSOCK: printf("s"); break;
        default:       printf("?"); break; /* Should never happen (on Linux) */
        }
    }
    printf(" %s  ",
            (type == FTW_D)  ? "D  " : (type == FTW_DNR) ? "DNR" :
            (type == FTW_DP) ? "DP " : (type == FTW_F)   ? "F  " :
            (type == FTW_SL) ? "SL " : (type == FTW_SLN) ? "SLN" :
            (type == FTW_NS) ? "NS " : "   ");
    if (type != FTW_NS)
        printf("%7ld ", (long) sbuf->st_ino);
    else
        printf("        ");
    printf(" %*s", 4 * ftwb->level, "");        /* Indent suitably */
    printf("%s\n", &pathname[ftwb->base]);      /* Print basename */
    return 0;                                   /* Tell nftw() to continue */
}

int
main(int argc, char *argv[])
{
    int flags, opt;

    flags = 0;
    while ((opt = getopt(argc, argv, "dmp")) != -1) {
        switch (opt) {
        case 'd': flags |= FTW_DEPTH;   break;
        case 'm': flags |= FTW_MOUNT;   break;
        case 'p': flags |= FTW_PHYS;    break;
        default:  usageError(argv[0], NULL);
        }
    }

    if (argc > optind + 1)
        usageError(argv[0], NULL);

    if (nftw((argc > optind) ? argv[optind] : ".", dirTree, 10, flags) == -1) {
        perror("nftw");
        exit(EXIT_FAILURE);
    }
    exit(EXIT_SUCCESS);
}
```

── **dirs_links/nftw_dir_tree.c**

The program in Listing 18-3 displays an indented hierarchy of the filenames in a directory tree, one file per line, as well as the file type and i-node number. Command-line options can be used to specify settings for the *flags* argument used to call *nftw()*. The following shell session shows examples of what we see when we run this program. We first create a new empty subdirectory, which we populate with various types of files:

```
$ mkdir dir
$ touch dir/a dir/b            Create some plain files
$ ln -s a dir/sl              and a symbolic link
$ ln -s x dir/dsl             and a dangling symbolic link
$ mkdir dir/sub               and a subdirectory
$ touch dir/sub/x             with a file of its own
$ mkdir dir/sub2              and another subdirectory
$ chmod 0 dir/sub2            that is not readable
```

We then use our program to invoke *nftw()* with a *flags* argument of 0:

```
$ ./nftw_dir_tree dir
d D    2327983  dir
- F    2327984     a
- F    2327985     b
- F    2327984     sl         The symbolic link sl was resolved to a
l SLN  2327987     dsl
d D    2327988     sub
- F    2327989        x
d DNR  2327994     sub2
```

In the above output, we can see that the symbolic link sl was resolved.

We then use our program to invoke *nftw()* with a *flags* argument containing FTW_PHYS and FTW_DEPTH:

```
$ ./nftw_dir_tree -p -d dir
- F    2327984     a
- F    2327985     b
l SL   2327986     sl         The symbolic link sl was not resolved
l SL   2327987     dsl
- F    2327989        x
d DP   2327988     sub
d DNR  2327994     sub2
d DP   2327983  dir
```

From the above output, we can see that the symbolic link sl was not resolved.

The *nftw()* FTW_ACTIONRETVAL flag

Starting with version 2.3.3, *glibc* permits an additional, nonstandard flag to be specified in *flags*. This flag, FTW_ACTIONRETVAL, changes the way that *nftw()* interprets the return value from calls to *func()*. When this flag is specified, *func()* should return one of the following values:

FTW_CONTINUE

> Continue processing entries in the directory tree, as with the traditional 0 return from *func()*.

FTW_SKIP_SIBLINGS

Don't process any further entries in the current directory; resume processing in the parent directory.

FTW_SKIP_SUBTREE

If *pathname* is a directory (i.e., *typeflag* is FTW_D), then don't call *func()* for entries under that directory. Processing resumes with the next sibling of this directory.

FTW_STOP

Don't process any further entries in the directory tree, as with the traditional nonzero return from *func()*. The value FTW_STOP is returned to the caller of *nftw()*.

The _GNU_SOURCE feature test macro must be defined in order to obtain the definition of FTW_ACTIONRETVAL from <ftw.h>.

18.10 The Current Working Directory of a Process

A process's *current working directory* defines the starting point for the resolution of relative pathnames referred to by the process. A new process inherits its current working directory from its parent.

Retrieving the current working directory

A process can retrieve its current working directory using *getcwd()*.

```
#include <unistd.h>

char *getcwd(char *cwdbuf, size_t size);
```
Returns *cwdbuf* on success, or NULL on error

The *getcwd()* function places a null-terminated string containing the absolute pathname of the current working directory into the allocated buffer pointed to by *cwdbuf*. The caller must allocate the *cwdbuf* buffer to be at least *size* bytes in length. (Normally, we would size *cwdbuf* using the PATH_MAX constant.)

On success, *getcwd()* returns a pointer to *cwdbuf* as its function result. If the pathname for the current working directory exceeds *size* bytes, then *getcwd()* returns NULL, with *errno* set to ERANGE.

On Linux/x86-32, *getcwd()* returns a maximum of 4096 (PATH_MAX) bytes. If the current working directory (and *cwdbuf* and *size*) exceeds this limit, then the pathname is silently truncated, removing complete directory prefixes from the *beginning* of the string (which is still null-terminated). In other words, we can't use *getcwd()* reliably when the length of the absolute pathname for the current working directory exceeds this limit.

> In fact, the Linux *getcwd()* system call internally allocates a virtual memory page for the returned pathname. On the x86-32 architecture, the page size is 4096 bytes, but on architectures with larger page sizes (e.g., Alpha with a page size of 8192 bytes), *getcwd()* can return larger pathnames.

If the *cwdbuf* argument is NULL and *size* is 0, then the *glibc* wrapper function for *getcwd()* allocates a buffer as large as required and returns a pointer to that buffer as its function result. To avoid memory leaks, the caller must later deallocate this buffer with *free()*. Reliance on this feature should be avoided in portable applications. Most other implementations provide a simpler extension of the SUSv3 specification: if *cwdbuf* is NULL, then *getcwd()* allocates *size* bytes and uses this buffer to return the result to the caller. The *glibc getcwd()* implementation also provides this feature.

> The GNU C library also provides two other functions for obtaining the current working directory. The BSD-derived *getwd(path)* function is vulnerable to buffer overruns, since it provides no method of specifying an upper limit for the size of the returned pathname. The *get_current_dir_name()* function returns a string containing the current working directory name as its function result. This function is easy to use, but it is not portable. For security and portability, *getcwd()* is preferred over these two functions (as long as we avoid using the GNU extensions).

With suitable permissions (roughly, we own the process or have the CAP_SYS_PTRACE capability), we can determine the current working directory of any process by reading (*readlink()*) the contents of the Linux-specific /proc/*PID*/cwd symbolic link.

Changing the current working directory

The *chdir()* system call changes the calling process's current working directory to the relative or absolute pathname specified in *pathname* (which is dereferenced if it is a symbolic link).

```
#include <unistd.h>

int chdir(const char *pathname);
```
                                          Returns 0 on success, or –1 on error

The *fchdir()* system call does the same as *chdir()*, except that the directory is specified via a file descriptor previously obtained by opening the directory with *open()*.

```
#include <unistd.h>

int fchdir(int fd);
```
                                          Returns 0 on success, or –1 on error

We can use *fchdir()* to change the process's current working directory to another location, and then later return to the original location, as follows:

```
int fd;

fd = open(".", O_RDONLY);      /* Remember where we are */
chdir(somepath);               /* Go somewhere else */
fchdir(fd);                    /* Return to original directory */
close(fd);
```

The equivalent using *chdir()* is as follows:

```
char buf[PATH_MAX];

getcwd(buf, PATH_MAX);          /* Remember where we are */
chdir(somepath);                /* Go somewhere else */
chdir(buf);                     /* Return to original directory */
```

18.11 Operating Relative to a Directory File Descriptor

Starting with kernel 2.6.16, Linux provides a range of new system calls that perform similar tasks to various traditional system calls, but provide additional functionality that is useful to some applications. These system calls are summarized in Table 18-2. We describe these system calls in this chapter because they provide variations on the traditional semantics of the process's current working directory.

Table 18-2: System calls that use a directory file descriptor to interpret relative pathnames

New interface	Traditional analog	Notes
faccessat()	*access()*	Supports AT_EACCESS and AT_SYMLINK_NOFOLLOW flags
fchmodat()	*chmod()*	
fchownat()	*chown()*	Supports AT_SYMLINK_NOFOLLOW flag
fstatat()	*stat()*	Supports AT_SYMLINK_NOFOLLOW flag
linkat()	*link()*	Supports (since Linux 2.6.18) AT_SYMLINK_FOLLOW flag
mkdirat()	*mkdir()*	
mkfifoat()	*mkfifo()*	Library function layered on top of *mknodat()*
mknodat()	*mknod()*	
openat()	*open()*	
readlinkat()	*readlink()*	
renameat()	*rename()*	
symlinkat()	*symlink()*	
unlinkat()	*unlink()*	Supports AT_REMOVEDIR flag
utimensat()	*utimes()*	Supports AT_SYMLINK_NOFOLLOW flag

In order to describe these system calls, we'll use a specific example: *openat()*.

```
#define _XOPEN_SOURCE 700      /* Or define _POSIX_C_SOURCE >= 200809 */
#include <fcntl.h>

int openat(int dirfd, const char *pathname, int flags, ... /* mode_t mode */);
```
                            Returns file descriptor on success, or −1 on error

The *openat()* system call is similar to the traditional *open()* system call, but adds an argument, *dirfd*, that is used as follows:

- If *pathname* specifies a relative pathname, then it is interpreted relative to the directory referred to by the open file descriptor *dirfd*, rather than relative to the process's current working directory.
- If *pathname* specifies a relative pathname, and *dirfd* contains the special value AT_FDCWD, then *pathname* is interpreted relative to the process's current working directory (i.e., the same behavior as *open(2)*).
- If *pathname* specifies an absolute pathname, then *dirfd* is ignored.

The *flags* argument of *openat()* serves the same purpose as for *open()*. However, some of the system calls listed in Table 18-2 support a *flags* argument that is not provided by the corresponding traditional system call, and the purpose of this argument is to modify the semantics of the call. The most frequently provided flag is AT_SYMLINK_NOFOLLOW, which specifies that if *pathname* is a symbolic link, then the system call should operate on the link, rather than the file to which it refers. (The *linkat()* system call provides the AT_SYMLINK_FOLLOW flag, which performs the converse action, changing the default behavior of *linkat()* so that it dereferences *oldpath* if it is a symbolic link.) For details of the other flags, refer to the corresponding manual pages.

The system calls listed in Table 18-2 are supported for two reasons (again, we explain using the example of *openat()*):

- Using *openat()* allows an application to avoid certain race conditions that can occur when *open()* is used to open files in locations other than the current working directory. These races can occur because some component of the directory prefix of *pathname* could be changed in parallel with the *open()* call. By opening a file descriptor for the target directory, and passing that descriptor to *openat()*, such races can be avoided.
- In Chapter 29, we'll see that the working directory is a process attribute that is shared by all threads of the process. For some applications, it is useful for different threads to have different "virtual" working directories. An application can emulate this functionality using *openat()* in conjunction with directory file descriptors maintained by the application.

These system calls are not standardized in SUSv3, but are included in SUSv4. In order to expose the declaration of each of these system calls, the _XOPEN_SOURCE feature test macro must be defined with a value greater than or equal to 700 before including the appropriate header file (e.g., <fcntl.h> for *open()*). Alternatively, the _POSIX_C_SOURCE macro can be defined with a value greater than or equal to 200809. (Before *glibc* 2.10, the _ATFILE_SOURCE macro needed to be defined to expose the declarations of these system calls.)

> Solaris 9 and later provide versions of some of the interfaces listed in Table 18-2, with slightly different semantics.

18.12 Changing the Root Directory of a Process: *chroot()*

Every process has a *root directory*, which is the point from which absolute pathnames (i.e., those beginning with /) are interpreted. By default, this is the real root directory of the file system. (A new process inherits its parent's root directory.) On occasion, it is useful for a process to change its root directory, and a privileged (CAP_SYS_CHROOT) process can do this using the *chroot()* system call.

```
#define _BSD_SOURCE
#include <unistd.h>

int chroot(const char *pathname);
```
                                          Returns 0 on success, or −1 on error

The *chroot()* system call changes the process's root directory to the directory specified by *pathname* (which is dereferenced if it is a symbolic link). Thereafter, all absolute pathnames are interpreted as starting from that location in the file system. This is sometimes referred to as setting up a *chroot* jail, since the program is then confined to a particular area of the file system.

SUSv2 contained a specification for *chroot()* (marked LEGACY), but this was removed in SUSv3. Nevertheless, *chroot()* appears on most UNIX implementations.

> The *chroot()* system call is employed by the *chroot* command, which enables us to execute shell commands in a *chroot* jail.
> The root directory of any process can be found by reading (*readlink()*) the contents of the Linux-specific /proc/*PID*/root symbolic link.

The classic example of the use of *chroot()* is in the *ftpd* program (the FTP server daemon). As a security measure, when a user logs in anonymously under FTP, the *ftpd* program uses *chroot()* to set the root directory for the new process to the directory specifically reserved for anonymous logins. After the *chroot()* call, the user is limited to the file-system subtree under their new root directory, so they can't roam around the entire file system. (This relies on the fact that the root directory is its own parent; that is, /.. is a link to /, so that changing directory to / and then attempting a *cd* .. leaves the user in the same directory.)

> Some UNIX implementations (but not Linux) allow multiple hard links to a directory, so that it is possible to create a hard link within a subdirectory to its parent (or a further removed ancestor). On implementations permitting this, the presence of a hard link that reaches outside the jail directory tree compromises the jail. Symbolic links to directories outside the jail don't pose a problem—because they are interpreted within the framework of the process's new root directory, they can't reach outside the *chroot* jail.

Normally, we can't execute arbitrary programs within a *chroot* jail. This is because most programs are dynamically linked against shared libraries. Therefore, we must either limit ourselves to executing statically linked programs, or replicate a standard set of system directories containing shared libraries (including, for example, /lib and /usr/lib) within the jail (in this regard, the bind mount feature described in Section 14.9.4 can be useful).

The *chroot()* system call was not conceived as a completely secure jail mechanism. To begin with, there are various ways in which a privileged program can subsequently use a further *chroot()* call to break out of the jail. For example, a privileged (CAP_MKNOD) program can use *mknod()* to create a memory device file (similar to /dev/mem) giving access to the contents of RAM, and, from that point, anything is possible. In general, it is advisable not to include set-user-ID-*root* programs within a *chroot* jail file system.

Even with unprivileged programs, we must take care to prevent the following possible routes for breaking out of a *chroot* jail:

- Calling *chroot()* doesn't change the process's current working directory. Thus, a call to *chroot()* is typically preceded or followed by a call to *chdir()* (e.g., *chdir("/")* after the *chroot()* call). If this is not done, then a process can use relative pathnames to access files and directories outside the jail. (Some BSD derivatives prevent this possibility—if the current working directory lies outside the new root directory tree, then it is changed by the *chroot()* call to be the same as the root directory.)

- If a process holds an open file descriptor for a directory outside the jail, then the combination of *fchdir()* plus *chroot()* can be used to break out of the jail, as shown in the following code sample:

```
int fd;

fd = open("/", O_RDONLY);
chroot("/home/mtk");            /* Jailed */
fchdir(fd);
chroot(".");                    /* Out of jail */
```

  To prevent this possibility, we must close all open file descriptors referring to directories outside the jail. (Some other UNIX implementations provide the *fchroot()* system call, which can be used to achieve a similar result to the above code snippet.)

- Even preventing the preceding possibilities is insufficient to stop an arbitrary unprivileged program (i.e., one whose operation we don't have control over) from breaking out of the jail. The jailed process can still use a UNIX domain socket to receive a file descriptor (from another process) referring to a directory outside the jail. (We briefly explain the concept of passing file descriptors between processes via a socket in Section 61.13.3.) By specifying this file descriptor in a call to *fchdir()*, the program can set its current working directory outside the jail and then access arbitrary files and directories using relative pathnames.

> Some BSD derivatives provide a *jail()* system call, which addresses the points described above, as well as several others, to create a jail that is secure even for a privileged process.

18.13 Resolving a Pathname: *realpath()*

The *realpath()* library function dereferences all symbolic links in *pathname* (a null-terminated string) and resolves all references to /. and /.. to produce a null-terminated string containing the corresponding absolute pathname.

```
#include <stdlib.h>

char *realpath(const char *pathname, char *resolved_path);
```
                    Returns pointer to resolved pathname on success, or NULL on error

The resulting string is placed in the buffer pointed to by *resolved_path*, which should be a character array of at least PATH_MAX bytes. On success, *realpath()* also returns a pointer to this resolved string.

The *glibc* implementation of *realpath()* allows the caller to specify *resolved_path* as NULL. In this case, *realpath()* allocates a buffer of up to PATH_MAX bytes for the resolved pathname and returns a pointer to that buffer as the function result. (The caller must deallocate this buffer using *free()*.) SUSv3 doesn't specify this extension, but it is specified in SUSv4.

The program in Listing 18-4 uses *readlink()* and *realpath()* to read the contents of a symbolic link and to resolve the link to an absolute pathname. Here is an example of the use of this program:

```
$ pwd                           Where are we?
/home/mtk
$ touch x                        Make a file
$ ln -s x y                      and a symbolic link to it
$ ./view_symlink y
readlink: y --> x
realpath: y --> /home/mtk/x
```

Listing 18-4: Read and resolve a symbolic link

───**dirs_links/view_symlink.c**
```c
#include <sys/stat.h>
#include <limits.h>                /* For definition of PATH_MAX */
#include "tlpi_hdr.h"

#define BUF_SIZE PATH_MAX

int
main(int argc, char *argv[])
{
    struct stat statbuf;
    char buf[BUF_SIZE];
    ssize_t numBytes;

    if (argc != 2 || strcmp(argv[1], "--help") == 0)
        usageErr("%s pathname\n", argv[0]);
```

```
    if (lstat(argv[1], &statbuf) == -1)
        errExit("lstat");

    if (!S_ISLNK(statbuf.st_mode))
        fatal("%s is not a symbolic link", argv[1]);

    numBytes = readlink(argv[1], buf, BUF_SIZE - 1);
    if (numBytes == -1)
        errExit("readlink");
    buf[numBytes] = '\0';                           /* Add terminating null byte */
    printf("readlink: %s --> %s\n", argv[1], buf);

    if (realpath(argv[1], buf) == NULL)
        errExit("realpath");
    printf("realpath: %s --> %s\n", argv[1], buf);

    exit(EXIT_SUCCESS);
}
```
─── dirs_links/view_symlink.c

18.14 Parsing Pathname Strings: *dirname()* **and** *basename()*

The *dirname()* and *basename()* functions break a pathname string into directory and
filename parts. (These functions perform a similar task to the *dirname(1)* and
basename(1) commands.)

```
#include <libgen.h>

char *dirname(char *pathname);
char *basename(char *pathname);
```
Both return a pointer to a null-terminated (and possibly
statically allocated) string

For example, given the pathname /home/britta/prog.c, *dirname()* returns /home/britta
and *basename()* returns prog.c. Concatenating the string returned by *dirname()*, a
slash (/), and the string returned by *basename()* yields a complete pathname.

Note the following points regarding the operation of *dirname()* and *basename()*:

- Trailing slash characters in *pathname* are ignored.

- If *pathname* doesn't contain a slash, then *dirname()* returns the string . (dot)
  and *basename()* returns *pathname*.

- If *pathname* consists of just a slash, then both *dirname()* and *basename()* return
  the string /. Applying the concatenation rule above to create a pathname from
  these returned strings would yield the string ///. This *is* a valid pathname.
  Because multiple consecutive slashes are equivalent to a single slash, the pathname /// is equivalent to the pathname /.

- If *pathname* is a NULL pointer or an empty string, then both *dirname()* and *basename()* return the string . (dot). (Concatenating these strings yields the pathname ./., which is equivalent to ., the current directory.)

Table 18-3 shows the strings returned by *dirname()* and *basename()* for various example pathnames.

Table 18-3: Examples of strings returned by *dirname()* and *basename()*

Pathname string	*dirname()*	*basename()*
/	/	/
/usr/bin/zip	/usr/bin	zip
/etc/passwd////	/etc	passwd
/etc////passwd	/etc	passwd
etc/passwd	etc	passwd
passwd	.	passwd
passwd/	.	passwd
..	.	..
NULL	.	.

Listing 18-5: Using *dirname()* and *basename()*

─── dirs_links/t_dirbasename.c
```
#include <libgen.h>
#include "tlpi_hdr.h"

int
main(int argc, char *argv[])
{
    char *t1, *t2;
    int j;

    for (j = 1; j < argc; j++)  {
        t1 = strdup(argv[j]);
        if (t1 == NULL)
            errExit("strdup");
        t2 = strdup(argv[j]);
        if (t2 == NULL)
            errExit("strdup");

        printf("%s ==> %s + %s\n", argv[j], dirname(t1), basename(t2));

        free(t1);
        free(t2);
    }

    exit(EXIT_SUCCESS);
}
```
─── dirs_links/t_dirbasename.c

Both *dirname()* and *basename()* may modify the string pointed to by *pathname*. Therefore, if we wish to preserve a pathname string, we must pass copies of it to *dirname()* and *basename()*, as shown in Listing 18-5 (page 371). This program uses *strdup()* (which calls *malloc()*) to make copies of the strings to be passed to *dirname()* and *basename()*, and then uses *free()* to deallocate the duplicate strings.

Finally, note that both *dirname()* and *basename()* can return pointers to statically allocated strings that may be modified by future calls to the same functions.

18.15 Summary

An i-node doesn't contain a file's name. Instead, files are assigned names via entries in directories, which are tables listing filename and i-node number correspondences. These directory entries are called (hard) links. A file may have multiple links, all of which enjoy equal status. Links are created and removed using *link()* and *unlink()*. A file can be renamed using the *rename()* system call.

A symbolic (or soft) link is created using *symlink()*. Symbolic links are similar to hard links in some respects, with the differences that symbolic links can cross file-system boundaries and can refer to directories. A symbolic link is just a file containing the name of another file; this name may be retrieved using *readlink()*. A symbolic link is not included in the (target) i-node's link count, and it may be left dangling if the filename to which it refers is removed. Some system calls automatically dereference (follow) symbolic links; others do not. In some cases, two versions of a system call are provided: one that dereferences symbolic links and another that does not. Examples are *stat()* and *lstat()*.

Directories are created with *mkdir()* and removed using *rmdir()*. To scan the contents of a directory, we can use *opendir()*, *readdir()*, and related functions. The *nftw()* function allows a program to walk an entire directory tree, calling a programmer-defined function to operate on each file in the tree.

The *remove()* function can be used to remove a file (i.e., a link) or an empty directory.

Each process has a root directory, which determines the point from which absolute pathnames are interpreted, and a current working directory, which determines the point from which relative pathnames are interpreted. The *chroot()* and *chdir()* system calls are used to change these attributes. The *getcwd()* function returns a process's current working directory.

Linux provides a set of system calls (e.g., *openat()*) that behave like their traditional counterparts (e.g., *open()*), except that relative pathnames can be interpreted with respect to the directory specified by a file descriptor supplied to the call (instead of using the process's current working directory). This is useful for avoiding certain types of race conditions and for implementing per-thread virtual working directories.

The *realpath()* function resolves a pathname—dereferencing all symbolic links and resolving all references to . and .. to corresponding directories—to yield a corresponding absolute pathname. The *dirname()* and *basename()* functions can be used to parse a pathname into directory and filename components.

18.16 Exercises

18-1. In Section 4.3.2, we noted that it is not possible to open a file for writing if it is currently being executed (*open()* returns −1, with *errno* set to ETXTBSY). Nevertheless, it is possible to do the following from the shell:

```
$ cc -o longrunner longrunner.c
$ ./longrunner &                    Leave running in background
$ vi longrunner.c                   Make some changes to the source code
$ cc -o longrunner longrunner.c
```

The last command overwrites the existing executable of the same name. How is this possible? (For a clue, use *ls −li* to look at the i-node number of the executable file after each compilation.)

18-2. Why does the call to *chmod()* in the following code fail?

```
mkdir("test", S_IRUSR | S_IWUSR | S_IXUSR);
chdir("test");
fd = open("myfile", O_RDWR | O_CREAT, S_IRUSR | S_IWUSR);
symlink("myfile", "../mylink");
chmod("../mylink", S_IRUSR);
```

18-3. Implement *realpath()*.

18-4. Modify the program in Listing 18-2 (list_files.c) to use *readdir_r()* instead of *readdir()*.

18-5. Implement a function that performs the equivalent of *getcwd()*. A useful tip for solving this problem is that you can find the name of the current working directory by using *opendir()* and *readdir()* to walk through each of the entries in the parent directory (..) to find an entry with the same i-node and device number as the current working directory (i.e., respectively, the *st_ino* and *st_dev* fields in the *stat* structure returned by *stat()* and *lstat()*). Thus, it is possible to construct the directory path by walking up the directory tree (*chdir("..")*) one step at a time and performing such scans. The walk can be finished when the parent directory is the same as the current working directory (recall that /.. is the same as /). The caller should be left in the same directory in which it started, regardless of whether your *getcwd()* function succeeds or fails (*open()* plus *fchdir()* are handy for this purpose).

18-6. Modify the program in Listing 18-3 (nftw_dir_tree.c) to use the FTW_DEPTH flag. Note the difference in the order in which the directory tree is traversed.

18-7. Write a program that uses *nftw()* to traverse a directory tree and finishes by printing out counts and percentages of the various types (regular, directory, symbolic link, and so on) of files in the tree.

18-8. Implement *nftw()*. (This will require the use of the *opendir()*, *readdir()*, *closedir()*, and *stat()* system calls, among others.)

18-9. In Section 18.10, we showed two different techniques (using *fchdir()* and *chdir()*, respectively) to return to the previous current working directory after changing the current working directory to another location. Suppose we are performing such an operation repeatedly. Which method do you expect to be more efficient? Why? Write a program to confirm your answer.

19

MONITORING FILE EVENTS

Some applications need to be able to monitor files or directories in order to determine whether events have occurred for the monitored objects. For example, a graphical file manager needs to be able to determine when files are added or removed from the directory that is currently being displayed, or a daemon may want to monitor its configuration file in order to know if the file has been changed.

Starting with kernel 2.6.13, Linux provides the *inotify* mechanism, which allows an application to monitor file events. This chapter describes the use of *inotify*.

The *inotify* mechanism replaces an older mechanism, *dnotify*, which provided a subset of the functionality of *inotify*. We describe *dnotify* briefly at the end of this chapter, focusing on why *inotify* is better.

The *inotify* and *dnotify* mechanisms are Linux-specific. (A few other systems provide similar mechanisms. For example, the BSDs provide the *kqueue* API.)

> A few libraries provide an API that is more abstract and portable than *inotify* and *dnotify*. The use of these libraries may be preferable for some applications. Some of these libraries employ *inotify* or *dnotify*, on systems where they are available. Two such libraries are FAM (File Alteration Monitor, *http://oss.sgi.com/projects/fam/*) and Gamin (*http://www.gnome.org/~veillard/gamin/*).

19.1 Overview

The key steps in the use of the *inotify* API are as follows:

1. The application uses *inotify_init()* to create an *inotify instance*. This system call returns a file descriptor that is used to refer to the *inotify* instance in later operations.

2. The application informs the kernel about which files are of interest by using *inotify_add_watch()* to add items to the watch list of the *inotify* instance created in the previous step. Each watch item consists of a pathname and an associated bit mask. The bit mask specifies the set of events to be monitored for the pathname. As its function result, *inotify_add_watch()* returns a *watch descriptor*, which is used to refer to the watch in later operations. (The *inotify_rm_watch()* system call performs the converse task, removing a watch that was previously added to an *inotify* instance.)

3. In order to obtain event notifications, the application performs *read()* operations on the *inotify* file descriptor. Each successful *read()* returns one or more *inotify_event* structures, each containing information about an event that occurred on one of the pathnames being watched via this *inotify* instance.

4. When the application has finished monitoring, it closes the *inotify* file descriptor. This automatically removes all watch items associated with the *inotify* instance.

The *inotify* mechanism can be used to monitor files or directories. When monitoring a directory, the application will be informed about events for the directory itself and for files inside the directory.

The *inotify* monitoring mechanism is not recursive. If an application wants to monitor events within an entire directory subtree, it must issue *inotify_add_watch()* calls for each directory in the tree.

An *inotify* file descriptor can be monitored using *select()*, *poll()*, *epoll*, and, since Linux 2.6.25, signal-driven I/O. If events are available to be read, then these interfaces indicate the *inotify* file descriptor as being readable. See Chapter 63 for further details of these interfaces.

> The *inotify* mechanism is an optional Linux kernel component that is configured via the options CONFIG_INOTIFY and CONFIG_INOTIFY_USER.

19.2 The *inotify* API

The *inotify_init()* system call creates a new *inotify* instance.

```
#include <sys/inotify.h>

int inotify_init(void);
```
                                        Returns file descriptor on success, or –1 on error

As its function result, *inotify_init()* returns a file descriptor. This file descriptor is the handle that is used to refer to the *inotify* instance in subsequent operations.

Starting with kernel 2.6.27, Linux supports a new, nonstandard system call, *inotify_init1()*. This system call performs the same task as *inotify_init()*, but provides an additional argument, *flags*, that can be used to modify the behavior of the system call. Two flags are supported. The IN_CLOEXEC flag causes the kernel to enable the close-on-exec flag (FD_CLOEXEC) for the new file descriptor. This flag is useful for the same reasons as the *open()* O_CLOEXEC flag described in Section 4.3.1. The IN_NONBLOCK flag causes the kernel to enable the O_NONBLOCK flag on the underlying open file description, so that future reads will be nonblocking. This saves additional calls to *fcntl()* to achieve the same result.

The *inotify_add_watch()* system call either adds a new watch item to or modifies an existing watch item in the watch list for the *inotify* instance referred to by the file descriptor *fd*. (Refer to Figure 19-1.)

```
#include <sys/inotify.h>

int inotify_add_watch(int fd, const char *pathname, uint32_t mask);
```
                              Returns watch descriptor on success, or −1 on error

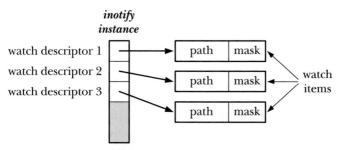

Figure 19-1: An *inotify* instance and associated kernel data structures

The *pathname* argument identifies the file for which a watch item is to be created or modified. The caller must have read permission for this file. (The file permission check is performed once, at the time of the *inotify_add_watch()* call. As long as the watch item continues to exist, the caller will continue to receive file notifications even if the file permissions are later changed so that the caller no longer has read permission on the file.)

The *mask* argument is a bit mask that specifies the events to be monitored for *pathname*. We say more about the bit values that can be specified in *mask* shortly.

If *pathname* has not previously been added to the watch list for *fd*, then *inotify_add_watch()* creates a new watch item in the list and returns a new, nonnegative watch descriptor, which is used to refer to the watch item in later operations. This watch descriptor is unique for this *inotify* instance.

If *pathname* has previously been added to the watch list for *fd*, then *inotify_add_watch()* modifies the mask of the existing watch item for *pathname* and returns the watch descriptor for that item. (This watch descriptor will be the same as that returned by the *inotify_add_watch()* call that initially added *pathname* to this watch list.) We say more about how the mask may be modified when we describe the IN_MASK_ADD flag in the next section.

The *inotify_rm_watch()* system call removes the watch item specified by *wd* from the *inotify* instance referred to by the file descriptor *fd*.

```
#include <sys/inotify.h>

int inotify_rm_watch(int fd, int wd);
```
                                              Returns 0 on success, or −1 on error

The *wd* argument is a watch descriptor returned by a previous call to *inotify_add_watch()*.

Removing a watch causes an IN_IGNORED event to be generated for this watch descriptor. We say more about this event shortly.

19.3   *inotify* **Events**

When we create or modify a watch using *inotify_add_watch()*, the *mask* bit-mask argument identifies the events to be monitored for the given *pathname*. The event bits that may be specified in *mask* are indicated by the *In* column of Table 19-1.

Table 19-1: *inotify* events

Bit value	In	Out	Description
IN_ACCESS	•	•	File was accessed (*read()*)
IN_ATTRIB	•	•	File metadata changed
IN_CLOSE_WRITE	•	•	File opened for writing was closed
IN_CLOSE_NOWRITE	•	•	File opened read-only was closed
IN_CREATE	•	•	File/directory created inside watched directory
IN_DELETE	•	•	File/directory deleted from within watched directory
IN_DELETE_SELF	•	•	Watched file/directory was itself deleted
IN_MODIFY	•	•	File was modified
IN_MOVE_SELF	•	•	Watched file/directory was itself moved
IN_MOVED_FROM	•	•	File moved out of watched directory
IN_MOVED_TO	•	•	File moved into watched directory
IN_OPEN	•	•	File was opened
IN_ALL_EVENTS	•		Shorthand for all of the above input events
IN_MOVE	•		Shorthand for IN_MOVED_FROM | IN_MOVED_TO
IN_CLOSE	•		Shorthand for IN_CLOSE_WRITE | IN_CLOSE_NOWRITE
IN_DONT_FOLLOW	•		Don't dereference symbolic link (since Linux 2.6.15)
IN_MASK_ADD	•		Add events to current watch mask for *pathname*
IN_ONESHOT	•		Monitor *pathname* for just one event
IN_ONLYDIR	•		Fail if *pathname* is not a directory (since Linux 2.6.15)
IN_IGNORED		•	Watch was removed by application or by kernel
IN_ISDIR		•	Filename returned in *name* is a directory
IN_Q_OVERFLOW		•	Overflow on event queue
IN_UNMOUNT		•	File system containing object was unmounted

The meanings of most of the bits in Table 19-1 are evident from their names. The following list clarifies a few details:

- The IN_ATTRIB event occurs when file metadata such as permissions, ownership, link count, extended attributes, user ID, or group ID, is changed.

- The IN_DELETE_SELF event occurs when an object (i.e., a file or a directory) that is being monitored is deleted. The IN_DELETE event occurs when the monitored object is a directory and one of the files that it contains is deleted.

- The IN_MOVE_SELF event occurs when an object that is being monitored is renamed. The IN_MOVED_FROM and IN_MOVED_TO events occur when an object is renamed within monitored directories. The former event occurs for the directory containing the old name, and the latter event occurs for the directory containing the new name.

- The IN_DONT_FOLLOW, IN_MASK_ADD, IN_ONESHOT, and IN_ONLYDIR bits don't specify events to be monitored. Instead, they control the operation of the *inotify_add_watch()* call.

- IN_DONT_FOLLOW specifies that *pathname* should not be dereferenced if it is a symbolic link. This permits an application to monitor a symbolic link, rather than the file to which it refers.

- If we perform an *inotify_add_watch()* call that specifies a pathname that is already being watched via this *inotify* file descriptor, then, by default, the given *mask* is used to replace the current mask for this watch item. If IN_MASK_ADD is specified, then the current mask is instead modified by ORing it with the value given in *mask*.

- IN_ONESHOT permits an application to monitor *pathname* for a single event. After that event, the watch item is automatically removed from the watch list.

- IN_ONLYDIR permits an application to monitor a pathname only if it is a directory. If *pathname* is not a directory, then *inotify_add_watch()* fails with the error ENOTDIR. Using this flag prevents race conditions that could otherwise occur if we wanted to ensure that we are monitoring a directory.

19.4 Reading *inotify* Events

Having registered items in the watch list, an application can determine which events have occurred by using *read()* to read events from the *inotify* file descriptor. If no events have occurred so far, then *read()* blocks until an event occurs (unless the O_NONBLOCK status flag has been set for the file descriptor, in which case the *read()* fails immediately with the error EAGAIN if no events are available).

After events have occurred, each *read()* returns a buffer (see Figure 19-2) containing one or more structures of the following type:

```
struct inotify_event {
    int      wd;        /* Watch descriptor on which event occurred */
    uint32_t mask;      /* Bits describing event that occurred */
    uint32_t cookie;    /* Cookie for related events (for rename()) */
    uint32_t len;       /* Size of 'name' field */
    char     name[];    /* Optional null-terminated filename */
};
```

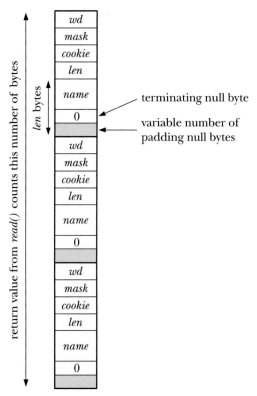

Figure 19-2: An input buffer containing three *inotify_event* structures

The *wd* field tells us the watch descriptor for which this event occurred. This field contains one of the values returned by a previous call to *inotify_add_watch()*. The *wd* field is useful when an application is monitoring multiple files or directories via the same *inotify* file descriptor. It provides the link that allows the application to determine the particular file or directory for which the event occurred. (To do this, the application must maintain a bookkeeping data structure that relates watch descriptors to pathnames.)

The *mask* field returns a bit mask that describes the event. The range of bits that can appear in *mask* is indicated via the *Out* column of Table 19-1. Note the following additional details about specific bits:

- An IN_IGNORED event is generated when a watch is removed. This can occur for two reasons: the application used an *inotify_rm_watch()* call to explicitly remove the watch, or the watch was implicitly removed by the kernel because the monitored object was deleted or the file system where it resides was unmounted. An IN_IGNORED event is not generated when a watch that was established with IN_ONESHOT is automatically removed because an event was triggered.

- If the subject of the event is a directory, then, in addition to some other bit, the IN_ISDIR bit will be set in *mask*.

- The `IN_UNMOUNT` event informs the application that the file system containing the monitored object has been unmounted. After this event, a further event containing the `IN_IGNORED` bit will be delivered.

- We describe the `IN_Q_OVERFLOW` in Section 19.5, which discusses limits on queued *inotify* events.

The *cookie* field is used to tie related events together. Currently, this field is used only when a file is renamed. When this happens, an `IN_MOVED_FROM` event is generated for the directory from which the file is renamed, and then an `IN_MOVED_TO` event is generated for the directory to which the file is renamed. (If a file is given a new name within the same directory, then both events occur for the same directory.) These two events will have the same unique value in their *cookie* field, thus allowing the application to associate them. For all other types of event, the *cookie* field is set to 0.

When an event occurs for a file within a monitored directory, the *name* field is used to return a null-terminated string that identifies the file. If the event occurs for the monitored object itself, then the *name* field is unused, and the *len* field will contain 0.

The *len* field indicates how many bytes are actually allocated for the *name* field. This field is necessary because there may be additional padding bytes between the end of the string stored in *name* and the start of the next *inotify_event* structure contained in the buffer returned by *read()* (see Figure 19-2). The length of an individual *inotify* event is thus *sizeof(struct inotify_event) + len*.

If the buffer passed to *read()* is too small to hold the next *inotify_event* structure, then *read()* fails with the error `EINVAL` to warn the application of this fact. (In kernels before 2.6.21, *read()* returned 0 for this case. The change to the use of an `EINVAL` error provides a clearer indication that a programming error has been made.) The application could respond by performing another *read()* with a larger buffer. However, the problem can be avoided altogether by ensuring that the buffer is always large enough to hold at least one event: the buffer given to *read()* should be at least *(sizeof(struct inotify_event) + NAME_MAX + 1)* bytes, where `NAME_MAX` is the maximum length of a filename, plus one for the terminating null byte.

Using a larger buffer size than the minimum allows an application to efficiently retrieve multiple events with a single *read()*. A *read()* from an *inotify* file descriptor reads the minimum of the number of events that are available and the number of events that will fit in the supplied buffer.

> The call *ioctl(fd, FIONREAD, &numbytes)* returns the number of bytes that are currently available to read from the *inotify* instance referred to by the file descriptor *fd*.

The events read from an *inotify* file descriptor form an ordered queue. Thus, for example, it is guaranteed that when a file is renamed, the `IN_MOVED_FROM` event will be read before the `IN_MOVED_TO` event.

When appending a new event to the end of the event queue, the kernel will coalesce that event with the event at the tail of the queue (so that the new event is not in fact queued), if the two events have the same values for *wd*, *mask*, *cookie*, and *name*. This is done because many applications don't need to know about repeated instances of the same event, and dropping the excess events reduces the amount of (kernel) memory required for the event queue. However, this means we can't use *inotify* to reliably determine how many times or how often a recurrent event occurs.

Example program

Although there is a lot of detail in the preceding description, the *inotify* API is actually quite simple to use. Listing 19-1 demonstrates the use of *inotify*.

Listing 19-1: Using the *inotify* API

——————————————————————————————————— *inotify/demo_inotify.c*
```
#include <sys/inotify.h>
#include <limits.h>
#include "tlpi_hdr.h"

static void                /* Display information from inotify_event structure */
displayInotifyEvent(struct inotify_event *i)
{
    printf("    wd =%2d; ", i->wd);
    if (i->cookie > 0)
        printf("cookie =%4d; ", i->cookie);

    printf("mask = ");
    if (i->mask & IN_ACCESS)        printf("IN_ACCESS ");
    if (i->mask & IN_ATTRIB)        printf("IN_ATTRIB ");
    if (i->mask & IN_CLOSE_NOWRITE) printf("IN_CLOSE_NOWRITE ");
    if (i->mask & IN_CLOSE_WRITE)   printf("IN_CLOSE_WRITE ");
    if (i->mask & IN_CREATE)        printf("IN_CREATE ");
    if (i->mask & IN_DELETE)        printf("IN_DELETE ");
    if (i->mask & IN_DELETE_SELF)   printf("IN_DELETE_SELF ");
    if (i->mask & IN_IGNORED)       printf("IN_IGNORED ");
    if (i->mask & IN_ISDIR)         printf("IN_ISDIR ");
    if (i->mask & IN_MODIFY)        printf("IN_MODIFY ");
    if (i->mask & IN_MOVE_SELF)     printf("IN_MOVE_SELF ");
    if (i->mask & IN_MOVED_FROM)    printf("IN_MOVED_FROM ");
    if (i->mask & IN_MOVED_TO)      printf("IN_MOVED_TO ");
    if (i->mask & IN_OPEN)          printf("IN_OPEN ");
    if (i->mask & IN_Q_OVERFLOW)    printf("IN_Q_OVERFLOW ");
    if (i->mask & IN_UNMOUNT)       printf("IN_UNMOUNT ");
    printf("\n");

    if (i->len > 0)
        printf("        name = %s\n", i->name);
}
```

```c
#define BUF_LEN (10 * (sizeof(struct inotify_event) + NAME_MAX + 1))

int
main(int argc, char *argv[])
{
    int inotifyFd, wd, j;
    char buf[BUF_LEN] __attribute__((aligned(8)));
    ssize_t numRead;
    char *p;
    struct inotify_event *event;

    if (argc < 2 || strcmp(argv[1], "--help") == 0)
        usageErr("%s pathname... \n", argv[0]);

①  inotifyFd = inotify_init();                /* Create inotify instance */
    if (inotifyFd == -1)
        errExit("inotify_init");

    for (j = 1; j < argc; j++) {
②      wd = inotify_add_watch(inotifyFd, argv[j], IN_ALL_EVENTS);
        if (wd == -1)
            errExit("inotify_add_watch");

        printf("Watching %s using wd %d\n", argv[j], wd);
    }

    for (;;) {                                 /* Read events forever */
③      numRead = read(inotifyFd, buf, BUF_LEN);
        if (numRead == 0)
            fatal("read() from inotify fd returned 0!");

        if (numRead == -1)
            errExit("read");

        printf("Read %ld bytes from inotify fd\n", (long) numRead);

        /* Process all of the events in buffer returned by read() */

        for (p = buf; p < buf + numRead; ) {
            event = (struct inotify_event *) p;
④          displayInotifyEvent(event);

            p += sizeof(struct inotify_event) + event->len;
        }
    }

    exit(EXIT_SUCCESS);
}
```

—— **inotify/demo_inotify.c**

The program in Listing 19-1 performs the following steps:

- Use *inotify_init()* to create an *inotify* file descriptor ①.
- Use *inotify_add_watch()* to add a watch item for each of the files named in the command-line argument of the program ②. Each watch item watches for all possible events.
- Execute an infinite loop that:
  - Reads a buffer of events from the *inotify* file descriptor ③.
  - Calls the *displayInotifyEvent()* function to display the contents of each of the *inotify_event* structures within that buffer ④.

The following shell session demonstrates the use of the program in Listing 19-1. We start an instance of the program that runs in the background monitoring two directories:

```
$ ./demo_inotify dir1 dir2 &
[1] 5386
Watching dir1 using wd 1
Watching dir2 using wd 2
```

Then we execute commands that generate events in the two directories. We begin by creating a file using *cat(1)*:

```
$ cat > dir1/aaa
Read 64 bytes from inotify fd
    wd = 1; mask = IN_CREATE
        name = aaa
    wd = 1; mask = IN_OPEN
        name = aaa
```

The above output produced by the background program shows that *read()* fetched a buffer containing two events. We continue by typing some input for the file and then the terminal *end-of-file* character:

```
Hello world
Read 32 bytes from inotify fd
    wd = 1; mask = IN_MODIFY
        name = aaa
Type Control-D
Read 32 bytes from inotify fd
    wd = 1; mask = IN_CLOSE_WRITE
        name = aaa
```

We then rename the file into the other monitored directory. This results in two events, one for the directory from which the file moves (watch descriptor 1), and the other for the destination directory (watch descriptor 2):

```
$ mv dir1/aaa dir2/bbb
Read 64 bytes from inotify fd
    wd = 1; cookie = 548; mask = IN_MOVED_FROM
        name = aaa
    wd = 2; cookie = 548; mask = IN_MOVED_TO
        name = bbb
```

These two events share the same *cookie* value, allowing the application to link them.

When we create a subdirectory under one of the monitored directories, the mask in the resulting event includes the IN_ISDIR bit, indicating that the subject of the event is a directory:

```
$ mkdir dir2/ddd
Read 32 bytes from inotify fd
    wd = 2; mask = IN_CREATE IN_ISDIR
        name = ddd
```

At this point, it is worth repeating that *inotify* monitoring is not recursive. If the application wanted to monitor events in the newly created subdirectory, then it would need to issue a further *inotify_add_watch()* call specifying the pathname of the subdirectory.

Finally, we remove one of the monitored directories:

```
$ rmdir dir1
Read 32 bytes from inotify fd
    wd = 1; mask = IN_DELETE_SELF
    wd = 1; mask = IN_IGNORED
```

The last event, IN_IGNORED, was generated to inform the application that the kernel has removed this watch item from the watch list.

19.5   Queue Limits and /proc Files

Queuing *inotify* events requires kernel memory. For this reason, the kernel places various limits on the operation of the *inotify* mechanism. The superuser can configure these limits via three files in the directory /proc/sys/fs/inotify:

max_queued_events

> When *inotify_init()* is called, this value is used to set an upper limit on the number of events that can be queued on the new *inotify* instance. If this limit is reached, then an IN_Q_OVERFLOW event is generated and excess events are discarded. The *wd* field for the overflow event will have the value −1.

max_user_instances

> This is a limit on the number of *inotify* instances that can be created per real user ID.

max_user_watches

> This is a limit on the number of watch items that can be created per real user ID.

Typical default values for these three files are 16,384, 128, and 8192, respectively.

19.6 An Older System for Monitoring File Events: *dnotify*

Linux provides another mechanism for monitoring file events. This mechanism, known as *dnotify*, has been available since kernel 2.4, but has been made obsolete by *inotify*. The *dnotify* mechanism suffers a number of limitations compared with *inotify*:

- The *dnotify* mechanism provides notification of events by sending signals to the application. Using signals as a notification mechanism complicates application design (Section 22.12). It also makes the use of *dnotify* within a library difficult, since the calling program might change the disposition of the notification signal(s). The *inotify* mechanism doesn't use signals.

- The monitoring unit of *dnotify* is a directory. The application is informed when an operation is performed on any file in that directory. By contrast, *inotify* can be used to monitor directories or individual files.

- In order to monitor a directory, *dnotify* requires the application to open a file descriptor for that directory. The use of file descriptors causes two problems. First, because it is busy, the file system containing the directory can't be unmounted. Second, because one file descriptor is required for each directory, an application can end up consuming a large number of file descriptors. Because *inotify* doesn't use file descriptors, it avoids these problems.

- The information provided by *dnotify* about file events is less precise than that provided by *inotify*. When a file is changed inside a monitored directory, *dnotify* tells us that an event has occurred, but doesn't tell us which file was involved in the event. The application must determine this by caching information about the directory contents. Furthermore, *inotify* provides more detailed information than *dnotify* about the type of event that has occurred.

- In some circumstances, *dnotify* doesn't provide reliable notification of file events.

Further information about *dnotify* can be found under the description of the F_NOTIFY operation in the *fcntl(2)* manual page, and in the kernel source file Documentation/dnotify.txt.

19.7 Summary

The Linux-specific *inotify* mechanism allows an application to obtain notifications when events (files are opened, closed, created, deleted, modified, renamed, and so on) occur for a set of monitored files and directories. The *inotify* mechanism supersedes the older *dnotify* mechanism.

19.8 Exercise

19-1. Write a program that logs all file creations, deletions, and renames under the directory named in its command-line argument. The program should monitor events in all of the subdirectories under the specified directory. To obtain a list of all of these subdirectories, you will need to make use of *nftw()* (Section 18.9). When a new subdirectory is added under the tree or a directory is deleted, the set of monitored subdirectories should be updated accordingly.

20

SIGNALS: FUNDAMENTAL CONCEPTS

This chapter and the next two chapters discuss signals. Although the fundamental concepts are simple, our discussion is quite lengthy, since there are many details to cover.

This chapter covers the following topics:

- the various different signals and their purposes;

- the circumstances in which the kernel may generate a signal for a process, and the system calls that one process may use to send a signal to another process;

- how a process responds to a signal by default, and the means by which a process can change its response to a signal, in particular, through the use of a signal handler, a programmer-defined function that is automatically invoked on receipt of a signal;

- the use of the process signal mask to block signals, and the associated notion of pending signals; and

- how a process can suspend execution and wait for the delivery of a signal.

20.1 Concepts and Overview

A *signal* is a notification to a process that an event has occurred. Signals are sometimes described as *software interrupts*. Signals are analogous to hardware interrupts in that they interrupt the normal flow of execution of a program; in most cases, it is not possible to predict exactly when a signal will arrive.

One process can (if it has suitable permissions) send a signal to another process. In this use, signals can be employed as a synchronization technique, or even as a primitive form of interprocess communication (IPC). It is also possible for a process to send a signal to itself. However, the usual source of many signals sent to a process is the kernel. Among the types of events that cause the kernel to generate a signal for a process are the following:

- A hardware exception occurred, meaning that the hardware detected a fault condition that was notified to the kernel, which in turn sent a corresponding signal to the process concerned. Examples of hardware exceptions include executing a malformed machine-language instruction, dividing by 0, or referencing a part of memory that is inaccessible.

- The user typed one of the terminal special characters that generate signals. These characters include the *interrupt* character (usually *Control-C*) and the *suspend* character (usually *Control-Z*).

- A software event occurred. For example, input became available on a file descriptor, the terminal window was resized, a timer went off, the process's CPU time limit was exceeded, or a child of this process terminated.

Each signal is defined as a unique (small) integer, starting sequentially from 1. These integers are defined in <signal.h> with symbolic names of the form SIGxxxx. Since the actual numbers used for each signal vary across implementations, it is these symbolic names that are always used in programs. For example, when the user types the *interrupt* character, SIGINT (signal number 2) is delivered to a process.

Signals fall into two broad categories. The first set constitutes the *traditional* or *standard* signals, which are used by the kernel to notify processes of events. On Linux, the standard signals are numbered from 1 to 31. We describe the standard signals in this chapter. The other set of signals consists of the *realtime* signals, whose differences from standard signals are described in Section 22.8.

A signal is said to be *generated* by some event. Once generated, a signal is later *delivered* to a process, which then takes some action in response to the signal. Between the time it is generated and the time it is delivered, a signal is said to be *pending*.

Normally, a pending signal is delivered to a process as soon as it is next scheduled to run, or immediately if the process is already running (e.g., if the process sent a signal to itself). Sometimes, however, we need to ensure that a segment of code is not interrupted by the delivery of a signal. To do this, we can add a signal to the process's *signal mask*—a set of signals whose delivery is currently *blocked*. If a signal is generated while it is blocked, it remains pending until it is later unblocked (removed from the signal mask). Various system calls allow a process to add and remove signals from its signal mask.

Upon delivery of a signal, a process carries out one of the following default actions, depending on the signal:

- The signal is *ignored*; that is, it is discarded by the kernel and has no effect on the process. (The process never even knows that it occurred.)

- The process is *terminated* (killed). This is sometimes referred to as *abnormal process termination*, as opposed to the normal process termination that occurs when a process terminates using *exit()*.

- A *core dump file* is generated, and the process is terminated. A core dump file contains an image of the virtual memory of the process, which can be loaded into a debugger in order to inspect the state of the process at the time that it terminated.

- The process is *stopped*—execution of the process is suspended.

- Execution of the process is *resumed* after previously being stopped.

Instead of accepting the default for a particular signal, a program can change the action that occurs when the signal is delivered. This is known as setting the *disposition* of the signal. A program can set one of the following dispositions for a signal:

- The *default action* should occur. This is useful to undo an earlier change of the disposition of the signal to something other than its default.

- The signal is *ignored*. This is useful for a signal whose default action would be to terminate the process.

- A *signal handler* is executed.

A signal handler is a function, written by the programmer, that performs appropriate tasks in response to the delivery of a signal. For example, the shell has a handler for the SIGINT signal (generated by the *interrupt* character, *Control-C*) that causes it to stop what it is currently doing and return control to the main input loop, so that the user is once more presented with the shell prompt. Notifying the kernel that a handler function should be invoked is usually referred to as *installing* or *establishing* a signal handler. When a signal handler is invoked in response to the delivery of a signal, we say that the signal has been *handled* or, synonymously, *caught*.

Note that it isn't possible to set the disposition of a signal to *terminate* or *dump core* (unless one of these is the default disposition of the signal). The nearest we can get to this is to install a handler for the signal that then calls either *exit()* or *abort()*. The *abort()* function (Section 21.2.2) generates a SIGABRT signal for the process, which causes it to dump core and terminate.

> The Linux-specific /proc/*PID*/status file contains various bit-mask fields that can be inspected to determine a process's treatment of signals. The bit masks are displayed as hexadecimal numbers, with the least significant bit representing signal 1, the next bit to the left representing signal 2, and so on. These fields are *SigPnd* (per-thread pending signals), *ShdPnd* (process-wide pending signals; since Linux 2.6), *SigBlk* (blocked signals), *SigIgn* (ignored signals), and *SigCgt* (caught signals). (The difference between the *SigPnd* and *ShdPnd* fields will become clear when we describe the handling of signals in multithreaded processes in Section 33.2.) The same information can also be obtained using various options to the *ps(1)* command.

Signals appeared in very early UNIX implementations, but have gone through some significant changes since their inception. In early implementations, signals could be lost (i.e., not delivered to the target process) in certain circumstances. Furthermore, although facilities were provided to block delivery of signals while critical code was executed, in some circumstances, blocking was not reliable. These problems were remedied in 4.2BSD, which provided so-called *reliable signals*. (One further BSD innovation was the addition of extra signals to support shell job control, which we describe in Section 34.7.)

System V also added reliable semantics to signals, but employed a model incompatible with BSD. These incompatibilities were resolved only with the arrival of the POSIX.1-1990 standard, which adopted a specification for reliable signals largely based on the BSD model.

We consider the details of reliable and unreliable signals in Section 22.7, and briefly describe the older BSD and System V signal APIs in Section 22.13.

20.2 Signal Types and Default Actions

Earlier, we mentioned that the standard signals are numbered from 1 to 31 on Linux. However, the Linux *signal(7)* manual page lists more than 31 signal names. The excess names can be accounted for in a variety of ways. Some of the names are simply synonyms for other names, and are defined for source compatibility with other UNIX implementations. Other names are defined but unused. The following list describes the various signals:

SIGABRT

> A process is sent this signal when it calls the *abort()* function (Section 21.2.2). By default, this signal terminates the process with a core dump. This achieves the intended purpose of the *abort()* call: to produce a core dump for debugging.

SIGALRM

> The kernel generates this signal upon the expiration of a real-time timer set by a call to *alarm()* or *setitimer()*. A real-time timer is one that counts according to wall clock time (i.e., the human notion of elapsed time). For further details, see Section 23.1.

SIGBUS

> This signal ("bus error") is generated to indicate certain kinds of memory-access errors. One such error can occur when using memory mappings created with *mmap()*, if we attempt to access an address that lies beyond the end of the underlying memory-mapped file, as described in Section 49.4.3.

SIGCHLD

> This signal is sent (by the kernel) to a parent process when one of its children terminates (either by calling *exit()* or as a result of being killed by a signal). It may also be sent to a process when one of its children is stopped or resumed by a signal. We consider SIGCHLD in detail in Section 26.3.

SIGCLD

    This is a synonym for SIGCHLD.

SIGCONT

    When sent to a stopped process, this signal causes the process to resume (i.e., to be rescheduled to run at some later time). When received by a process that is not currently stopped, this signal is ignored by default. A process may catch this signal, so that it carries out some action when it resumes. This signal is covered in more detail in Sections 22.2 and 34.7.

SIGEMT

    In UNIX systems generally, this signal is used to indicate an implementation-dependent hardware error. On Linux, this signal is used only in the Sun SPARC implementation. The suffix EMT derives from *emulator trap*, an assembler mnemonic on the Digital PDP-11.

SIGFPE

    This signal is generated for certain types of arithmetic errors, such as divide-by-zero. The suffix FPE is an abbreviation for *floating-point exception*, although this signal can also be generated for integer arithmetic errors. The precise details of when this signal is generated depend on the hardware architecture and the settings of CPU control registers. For example, on x86-32, integer divide-by-zero always yields a SIGFPE, but the handling of floating-point divide-by-zero depends on whether the FE_DIVBYZERO exception has been enabled. If this exception is enabled (using *feenableexcept()*), then a floating-point divide-by-zero generates SIGFPE; otherwise, it yields the IEEE-standard result for the operands (a floating-point representation of infinity). See the *fenv(3)* manual page and <fenv.h> for further information.

SIGHUP

    When a terminal disconnect (hangup) occurs, this signal is sent to the controlling process of the terminal. We describe the concept of a controlling process and the various circumstances in which SIGHUP is sent in Section 34.6. A second use of SIGHUP is with daemons (e.g., *init*, *httpd*, and *inetd*). Many daemons are designed to respond to the receipt of SIGHUP by reinitializing themselves and rereading their configuration files. The system administrator triggers these actions by manually sending SIGHUP to the daemon, either by using an explicit *kill* command or by executing a program or script that does the same.

SIGILL

    This signal is sent to a process if it tries to execute an illegal (i.e., incorrectly formed) machine-language instruction.

SIGINFO

    On Linux, this signal name is a synonym for SIGPWR. On BSD systems, the SIGINFO signal, generated by typing *Control-T*, is used to obtain status information about the foreground process group.

SIGINT

> When the user types the terminal *interrupt* character (usually *Control-C*), the terminal driver sends this signal to the foreground process group. The default action for this signal is to terminate the process.

SIGIO

> Using the *fcntl()* system call, it is possible to arrange for this signal to be generated when an I/O event (e.g., input becoming available) occurs on certain types of open file descriptors, such as those for terminals and sockets. This feature is described further in Section 63.3.

SIGIOT

> On Linux, this is a synonym for SIGABRT. On some other UNIX implementations, this signal indicates an implementation-defined hardware fault.

SIGKILL

> This is the *sure kill* signal. It can't be blocked, ignored, or caught by a handler, and thus always terminates a process.

SIGLOST

> This signal name exists on Linux, but is unused. On some other UNIX implementations, the NFS client sends this signal to local processes holding locks if the NFS client fails to regain locks held by those processes following the recovery of a remote NFS server that crashed. (This feature is not standardized in NFS specifications.)

SIGPIPE

> This signal is generated when a process tries to write to a pipe, a FIFO, or a socket for which there is no corresponding reader process. This normally occurs because the reading process has closed its file descriptor for the IPC channel. See Section 44.2 for further details.

SIGPOLL

> This signal, which is derived from System V, is a synonym for SIGIO on Linux.

SIGPROF

> The kernel generates this signal upon the expiration of a profiling timer set by a call to *setitimer()* (Section 23.1). A profiling timer is one that counts the CPU time used by a process. Unlike a virtual timer (see SIGVTALRM below), a profiling timer counts CPU time used in both user mode and kernel mode.

SIGPWR

> This is the *power failure* signal. On systems that have an uninterruptible power supply (UPS), it is possible to set up a daemon process that monitors the backup battery level in the event of a power failure. If the battery power is about to run out (after an extended power outage), then the monitoring process sends SIGPWR to the *init* process, which interprets this signal as a request to shut down the system in a quick and orderly fashion.

SIGQUIT

When the user types the *quit* character (usually *Control-*) on the keyboard, this signal is sent to the foreground process group. By default, this signal terminates a process and causes it to produce a core dump, which can then be used for debugging. Using SIGQUIT in this manner is useful with a program that is stuck in an infinite loop or is otherwise not responding. By typing *Control-* and then loading the resulting core dump with the *gdb* debugger and using the *backtrace* command to obtain a stack trace, we can find out which part of the program code was executing. ([Matloff, 2008] describes the use of *gdb*.)

SIGSEGV

This very popular signal is generated when a program makes an invalid memory reference. A memory reference may be invalid because the referenced page doesn't exist (e.g., it lies in an unmapped area somewhere between the heap and the stack), the process tried to update a location in read-only memory (e.g., the program text segment or a region of mapped memory marked read-only), or the process tried to access a part of kernel memory while running in user mode (Section 2.1). In C, these events often result from dereferencing a pointer containing a bad address (e.g., an uninitialized pointer) or passing an invalid argument in a function call. The name of this signal derives from the term *segmentation violation*.

SIGSTKFLT

Documented in *signal(7)* as "stack fault on coprocessor," this signal is defined, but is unused on Linux.

SIGSTOP

This is the *sure stop* signal. It can't be blocked, ignored, or caught by a handler; thus, it always stops a process.

SIGSYS

This signal is generated if a process makes a "bad" system call. This means that the process executed an instruction that was interpreted as a system call trap, but the associated system call number was not valid (refer to Section 3.1).

SIGTERM

This is the standard signal used for terminating a process and is the default signal sent by the *kill* and *killall* commands. Users sometimes explicitly send the SIGKILL signal to a process using *kill -KILL* or *kill -9*. However, this is generally a mistake. A well-designed application will have a handler for SIGTERM that causes the application to exit gracefully, cleaning up temporary files and releasing other resources beforehand. Killing a process with SIGKILL bypasses the SIGTERM handler. Thus, we should always first attempt to terminate a process using SIGTERM, and reserve SIGKILL as a last resort for killing runaway processes that don't respond to SIGTERM.

SIGTRAP

> This signal is used to implement debugger breakpoints and system call tracing, as performed by *strace(1)* (Appendix A). See the *ptrace(2)* manual page for further information.

SIGTSTP

> This is the job-control *stop* signal, sent to stop the foreground process group when the user types the *suspend* character (usually *Control-Z*) on the keyboard. Chapter 34 describes process groups (jobs) and job control in detail, as well as details of when and how a program may need to handle this signal. The name of this signal derives from "terminal stop."

SIGTTIN

> When running under a job-control shell, the terminal driver sends this signal to a background process group when it attempts to *read()* from the terminal. This signal stops a process by default.

SIGTTOU

> This signal serves an analogous purpose to SIGTTIN, but for terminal output by background jobs. When running under a job-control shell, if the TOSTOP (*terminal output stop*) option has been enabled for the terminal (perhaps via the command *stty tostop*), the terminal driver sends SIGTTOU to a background process group when it attempts to *write()* to the terminal (see Section 34.7.1). This signal stops a process by default.

SIGUNUSED

> As the name implies, this signal is unused. On Linux 2.4 and later, this signal name is synonymous with SIGSYS on many architectures. In other words, this signal number is no longer unused on those architectures, although the signal name remains for backward compatibility.

SIGURG

> This signal is sent to a process to indicate the presence of *out-of-band* (also known as *urgent*) data on a socket (Section 61.13.1).

SIGUSR1

> This signal and SIGUSR2 are available for programmer-defined purposes. The kernel never generates these signals for a process. Processes may use these signals to notify one another of events or to synchronize with each other. In early UNIX implementations, these were the only two signals that could be freely used in applications. (In fact, processes can send one another any signal, but this has the potential for confusion if the kernel also generates one of the signals for a process.) Modern UNIX implementations provide a large set of realtime signals that are also available for programmer-defined purposes (Section 22.8).

SIGUSR2

> See the description of SIGUSR1.

SIGVTALRM

> The kernel generates this signal upon expiration of a virtual timer set by a call to *setitimer()* (Section 23.1). A virtual timer is one that counts the user-mode CPU time used by a process.

SIGWINCH

> In a windowing environment, this signal is sent to the foreground process group when the terminal window size changes (as a consequence either of the user manually resizing it, or of a program resizing it via a call to *ioctl()*, as described in Section 62.9). By installing a handler for this signal, programs such as *vi* and *less* can know to redraw their output after a change in window size.

SIGXCPU

> This signal is sent to a process when it exceeds its CPU time resource limit (RLIMIT_CPU, described in Section 36.3).

SIGXFSZ

> This signal is sent to a process if it attempts (using *write()* or *truncate()*) to increase the size of a file beyond the process's file size resource limit (RLIMIT_FSIZE, described in Section 36.3).

Table 20-1 summarizes a range of information about signals on Linux. Note the following points about this table:

- The *signal number* column shows the number assigned to this signal on various hardware architectures. Except where otherwise indicated, signals have the same number on all architectures. Architectural differences in signal numbers are indicated in parentheses, and occur on the Sun SPARC and SPARC64 (S), HP/Compaq/Digital Alpha (A), MIPS (M), and HP PA-RISC (P) architectures. In this column, *undef* indicates that a symbol is undefined on the indicated architectures.

- The *SUSv3* column indicates whether the signal is standardized in SUSv3.

- The *Default* column indicates the default action of the signal: *term* means that the signal terminates the process, *core* means that the process produces a core dump file and terminates, *ignore* means that the signal is ignored, *stop* means that the signal stops the process, and *cont* means that the signal resumes a stopped process.

> Certain of the signals listed previously are not shown in Table 20-1: SIGCLD (synonym for SIGCHLD), SIGINFO (unused), SIGIOT (synonym for SIGABRT), SIGLOST (unused), and SIGUNUSED (synonym for SIGSYS on many architectures).

Table 20-1: Linux signals

Name	Signal number	Description	SUSv3	Default
SIGABRT	6	Abort process	•	core
SIGALRM	14	Real-time timer expired	•	term
SIGBUS	7 (SAMP=10)	Memory access error	•	core
SIGCHLD	17 (SA=20, MP=18)	Child terminated or stopped	•	ignore
SIGCONT	18 (SA=19, M=25, P=26)	Continue if stopped	•	cont
SIGEMT	undef (SAMP=7)	Hardware fault		term
SIGFPE	8	Arithmetic exception	•	core
SIGHUP	1	Hangup	•	term
SIGILL	4	Illegal instruction	•	core
SIGINT	2	Terminal interrupt	•	term
SIGIO / SIGPOLL	29 (SA=23, MP=22)	I/O possible	•	term
SIGKILL	9	Sure kill	•	term
SIGPIPE	13	Broken pipe	•	term
SIGPROF	27 (M=29, P=21)	Profiling timer expired	•	term
SIGPWR	30 (SA=29, MP=19)	Power about to fail		term
SIGQUIT	3	Terminal quit	•	core
SIGSEGV	11	Invalid memory reference	•	core
SIGSTKFLT	16 (SAM=undef, P=36)	Stack fault on coprocessor		term
SIGSTOP	19 (SA=17, M=23, P=24)	Sure stop	•	stop
SIGSYS	31 (SAMP=12)	Invalid system call	•	core
SIGTERM	15	Terminate process	•	term
SIGTRAP	5	Trace/breakpoint trap	•	core
SIGTSTP	20 (SA=18, M=24, P=25)	Terminal stop	•	stop
SIGTTIN	21 (M=26, P=27)	Terminal read from BG	•	stop
SIGTTOU	22 (M=27, P=28)	Terminal write from BG	•	stop
SIGURG	23 (SA=16, M=21, P=29)	Urgent data on socket	•	ignore
SIGUSR1	10 (SA=30, MP=16)	User-defined signal 1	•	term
SIGUSR2	12 (SA=31, MP=17)	User-defined signal 2	•	term
SIGVTALRM	26 (M=28, P=20)	Virtual timer expired	•	term
SIGWINCH	28 (M=20, P=23)	Terminal window size change		ignore
SIGXCPU	24 (M=30, P=33)	CPU time limit exceeded	•	core
SIGXFSZ	25 (M=31, P=34)	File size limit exceeded	•	core

Note the following points regarding the default behavior shown for certain signals in Table 20-1:

- On Linux 2.2, the default action for the signals SIGXCPU, SIGXFSZ, SIGSYS, and SIGBUS is to terminate the process without producing a core dump. From kernel 2.4 onward, Linux conforms to the requirements of SUSv3, with these signals causing termination with a core dump. On several other UNIX implementations, SIGXCPU and SIGXFSZ are treated in the same way as on Linux 2.2.

- SIGPWR is typically ignored by default on those other UNIX implementations where it appears.

- SIGIO is ignored by default on several UNIX implementations (particularly BSD derivatives).

- Although not specified by any standards, SIGEMT appears on most UNIX implementations. However, this signal typically results in termination with a core dump on other implementations.

- In SUSv1, the default action for SIGURG was specified as process termination, and this is the default in some older UNIX implementations. SUSv2 adopted the current specification (ignore).

20.3 Changing Signal Dispositions: *signal()*

UNIX systems provide two ways of changing the disposition of a signal: *signal()* and *sigaction()*. The *signal()* system call, which is described in this section, was the original API for setting the disposition of a signal, and it provides a simpler interface than *sigaction()*. On the other hand, *sigaction()* provides functionality that is not available with *signal()*. Furthermore, there are variations in the behavior of *signal()* across UNIX implementations (Section 22.7), which mean that it should never be used for establishing signal handlers in portable programs. Because of these portability issues, *sigaction()* is the (strongly) preferred API for establishing a signal handler. After we explain the use of *sigaction()* in Section 20.13, we'll always employ that call when establishing signal handlers in our example programs.

> Although documented in section 2 of the Linux manual pages, *signal()* is actually implemented in *glibc* as a library function layered on top of the *sigaction()* system call.

```
#include <signal.h>

void ( *signal(int sig, void (*handler)(int)) ) (int);
```
                    Returns previous signal disposition on success, or SIG_ERR on error

The function prototype for *signal()* requires some decoding. The first argument, *sig*, identifies the signal whose disposition we wish to change. The second argument, *handler*, is the address of the function that should be called when this signal is delivered. This function returns nothing (*void*) and takes one integer argument. Thus, a signal handler has the following general form:

```
void
handler(int sig)
{
    /* Code for the handler */
}
```

We describe the purpose of the *sig* argument to the handler function in Section 20.4.

The return value of *signal()* is the previous disposition of the signal. Like the *handler* argument, this is a pointer to a function returning nothing and taking one integer argument. In other words, we could write code such as the following to temporarily establish a handler for a signal, and then reset the disposition of the signal to whatever it was previously:

```
void (*oldHandler)(int);

oldHandler = signal(SIGINT, newHandler);
if (oldHandler == SIG_ERR)
    errExit("signal");

/* Do something else here. During this time, if SIGINT is
   delivered, newHandler will be used to handle the signal. */

if (signal(SIGINT, oldHandler) == SIG_ERR)
    errExit("signal");
```

> It is not possible to use *signal()* to retrieve the current disposition of a signal without at the same time changing that disposition. To do that, we must use *sigaction()*.

We can make the prototype for *signal()* much more comprehensible by using the following type definition for a pointer to a signal handler function:

```
typedef void (*sighandler_t)(int);
```

This enables us to rewrite the prototype for *signal()* as follows:

```
sighandler_t signal(int sig, sighandler_t handler);
```

> If the _GNU_SOURCE feature test macro is defined, then *glibc* exposes the non-standard *sighandler_t* data type in the <signal.h> header file.

Instead of specifying the address of a function as the *handler* argument of *signal()*, we can specify one of the following values:

SIG_DFL
> Reset the disposition of the signal to its default (Table 20-1). This is useful for undoing the effect of an earlier call to *signal()* that changed the disposition for the signal.

SIG_IGN
> Ignore the signal. If the signal is generated for this process, the kernel silently discards it. The process never even knows that the signal occurred.

A successful call to *signal()* returns the previous disposition of the signal, which may be the address of a previously installed handler function, or one of the constants SIG_DFL or SIG_IGN. On error, *signal()* returns the value SIG_ERR.

20.4 Introduction to Signal Handlers

A *signal handler* (also called a *signal catcher*) is a function that is called when a specified signal is delivered to a process. We describe the fundamentals of signal handlers in this section, and then go into the details in Chapter 21.

Invocation of a signal handler may interrupt the main program flow at any time; the kernel calls the handler on the process's behalf, and when the handler returns, execution of the program resumes at the point where the handler interrupted it. This sequence is illustrated in Figure 20-1.

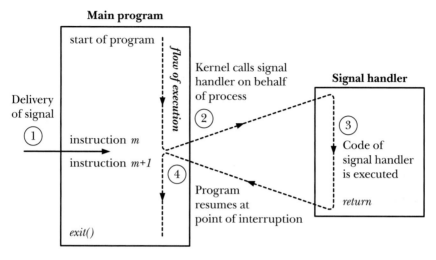

Figure 20-1: Signal delivery and handler execution

Although signal handlers can do virtually anything, they should, in general, be designed to be as simple as possible. We expand on this point in Section 21.1.

Listing 20-1: Installing a handler for SIGINT

——————————————————————————————————————— signals/ouch.c

```
#include <signal.h>
#include "tlpi_hdr.h"

static void
sigHandler(int sig)
{
    printf("Ouch!\n");                  /* UNSAFE (see Section 21.1.2) */
}

int
main(int argc, char *argv[])
{
    int j;

    if (signal(SIGINT, sigHandler) == SIG_ERR)
        errExit("signal");

    for (j = 0; ; j++) {
        printf("%d\n", j);
        sleep(3);                       /* Loop slowly... */
    }
}
```

——————————————————————————————————————— signals/ouch.c

Listing 20-1 (on page 399) shows a simple example of a signal handler function and a main program that establishes it as the handler for the SIGINT signal. (The terminal driver generates this signal when we type the terminal *interrupt* character, usually *Control-C.*) The handler simply prints a message and returns.

The main program continuously loops. On each iteration, the program increments a counter whose value it prints, and then the program sleeps for a few seconds. (To sleep in this manner, we use the *sleep()* function, which suspends the execution of its caller for a specified number of seconds. We describe this function in Section 23.4.1.)

When we run the program in Listing 20-1, we see the following:

```
$ ./ouch
0                           Main program loops, displaying successive integers
Type Control-C
Ouch!                       Signal handler is executed, and returns
1                           Control has returned to main program
2
Type Control-C again
Ouch!
3
Type Control-\ (the terminal quit character)
Quit (core dumped)
```

When the kernel invokes a signal handler, it passes the number of the signal that caused the invocation as an integer argument to the handler. (This is the *sig* argument in the handler of Listing 20-1). If a signal handler catches only one type of signal, then this argument is of little use. We can, however, establish the same handler to catch different types of signals and use this argument to determine which signal caused the handler to be invoked.

This is illustrated in Listing 20-2, a program that establishes the same handler for SIGINT and SIGQUIT. (SIGQUIT is generated by the terminal driver when we type the terminal *quit* character, usually *Control-\.*) The code of the handler distinguishes the two signals by examining the *sig* argument, and takes different actions for each signal. In the *main()* function, we use *pause()* (described in Section 20.14) to block the process until a signal is caught.

The following shell session log demonstrates the use of this program:

```
$ ./intquit
Type Control-C
Caught SIGINT (1)
Type Control-C again
Caught SIGINT (2)
and again
Caught SIGINT (3)
Type Control-\
Caught SIGQUIT - that's all folks!
```

In Listing 20-1 and Listing 20-2, we use *printf()* to display the message from the signal handler. For reasons that we discuss in Section 21.1.2, real-world applications should generally never call *stdio* functions from within a signal handler. However, in various example programs, we'll nevertheless call *printf()* from a signal handler as a simple means of seeing when the handler is called.

Listing 20-2: Establishing the same handler for two different signals

―――――――――――――――――――――――――――――― `signals/intquit.c`
```c
#include <signal.h>
#include "tlpi_hdr.h"

static void
sigHandler(int sig)
{
    static int count = 0;

    /* UNSAFE: This handler uses non-async-signal-safe functions
       (printf(), exit(); see Section 21.1.2) */

    if (sig == SIGINT) {
        count++;
        printf("Caught SIGINT (%d)\n", count);
        return;                   /* Resume execution at point of interruption */
    }

    /* Must be SIGQUIT - print a message and terminate the process */

    printf("Caught SIGQUIT - that's all folks!\n");
    exit(EXIT_SUCCESS);
}

int
main(int argc, char *argv[])
{
    /* Establish same handler for SIGINT and SIGQUIT */

    if (signal(SIGINT, sigHandler) == SIG_ERR)
        errExit("signal");
    if (signal(SIGQUIT, sigHandler) == SIG_ERR)
        errExit("signal");

    for (;;)                    /* Loop forever, waiting for signals */
        pause();                /* Block until a signal is caught */
}
```
―――――――――――――――――――――――――――――― `signals/intquit.c`

20.5 Sending Signals: *kill()*

One process can send a signal to another process using the *kill()* system call, which is the analog of the *kill* shell command. (The term *kill* was chosen because the default action of most of the signals that were available on early UNIX implementations was to terminate the process.)

```
#include <signal.h>

int kill(pid_t pid, int sig);
```
                                    Returns 0 on success, or −1 on error

The *pid* argument identifies one or more processes to which the signal specified by *sig* is to be sent. Four different cases determine how *pid* is interpreted:

- If *pid* is greater than 0, the signal is sent to the process with the process ID specified by *pid*.

- If *pid* equals 0, the signal is sent to every process in the same process group as the calling process, including the calling process itself. (SUSv3 states that the signal should be sent to all processes in the same process group, excluding an "unspecified set of system processes" and adds the same qualification to each of the remaining cases.)

- If *pid* is less than −1, the signal is sent to all of the processes in the process group whose ID equals the absolute value of *pid*. Sending a signal to all of the processes in a process group finds particular use in shell job control (Section 34.7).

- If *pid* equals −1, the signal is sent to every process for which the calling process has permission to send a signal, except *init* (process ID 1) and the calling process. If a privileged process makes this call, then all processes on the system will be signaled, except for these last two. For obvious reasons, signals sent in this way are sometimes called *broadcast signals*. (SUSv3 doesn't require that the calling process be excluded from receiving the signal; Linux follows the BSD semantics in this regard.)

If no process matches the specified *pid*, *kill()* fails and sets *errno* to ESRCH ("No such process").

A process needs appropriate permissions to be able send a signal to another process. The permission rules are as follows:

- A privileged (CAP_KILL) process may send a signal to any process.

- The *init* process (process ID 1), which runs with user and group of *root*, is a special case. It can be sent only signals for which it has a handler installed. This prevents the system administrator from accidentally killing *init*, which is fundamental to the operation of the system.

- An unprivileged process can send a signal to another process if the real or effective user ID of the sending process matches the real user ID or saved set-user-ID of the receiving process, as shown in Figure 20-2. This rule allows users to send signals to set-user-ID programs that they have started, regardless of the current setting of the target process's effective user ID. Furthermore, on Linux and other systems that provide the *setresuid()* system call, a set-user-ID program can take advantage of this rule to prevent itself being sent signals by the user that owns the executable, by using *setresuid()* to make its saved set-user-ID the same as the real user ID. (SUSv3 mandates the rules shown in Figure 20-2, but Linux followed slightly different rules in kernel versions before 2.0, as described in the *kill(2)* manual page.)

- The SIGCONT signal is treated specially. An unprivileged process may send this signal to any other process in the same session, regardless of user ID checks. This rule allows job-control shells to restart stopped jobs (process groups), even if the processes of the job have changed their user IDs (i.e., they are privileged processes that have used the system calls described in Section 9.7 to change their credentials).

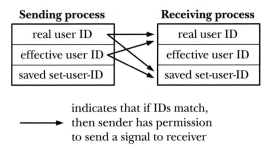

Figure 20-2: Permissions required for an unprivileged process to send a signal

If a process doesn't have permissions to send a signal to the requested *pid*, then *kill()* fails, setting *errno* to EPERM. Where *pid* specifies a set of processes (i.e., *pid* is negative), *kill()* succeeds if at least one of them could be signaled.

We demonstrate the use of *kill()* in Listing 20-3.

20.6 Checking for the Existence of a Process

The *kill()* system call can serve another purpose. If the *sig* argument is specified as 0 (the so-called *null signal*), then no signal is sent. Instead, *kill()* merely performs error checking to see if the process can be signaled. Read another way, this means we can use the null signal to test if a process with a specific process ID exists. If sending a null signal fails with the error ESRCH, then we know the process doesn't exist. If the call fails with the error EPERM (meaning the process exists, but we don't have permission to send a signal to it) or succeeds (meaning we do have permission to send a signal to the process), then we know that the process exists.

Verifying the existence of a particular process ID doesn't guarantee that a particular program is still running. Because the kernel recycles process IDs as processes are born and die, the same process ID may, over time, refer to a different process. Furthermore, a particular process ID may exist, but be a zombie (i.e., a process that has died, but whose parent has not yet performed a *wait()* to obtain its termination status, as described in Section 26.2).

Various other techniques can also be used to check whether a particular process is running, including the following:

- *The wait() system calls*: These calls are described in Chapter 26. They can be employed only if the monitored process is a child of the caller.
- *Semaphores and exclusive file locks*: If the process that is being monitored continuously holds a semaphore or a file lock, then, if we can acquire the semaphore or lock, we know the process has terminated. We describe semaphores in Chapters 47 and 53 and file locks in Chapter 55.

- *IPC channels such as pipes and FIFOs*: We set up the monitored process so that it holds a file descriptor open for writing on the channel as long as it is alive. Meanwhile, the monitoring process holds open a read descriptor for the channel, and it knows that the monitored process has terminated when the write end of the channel is closed (because it sees end-of-file). The monitoring process can determine this either by reading from its file descriptor or by monitoring the descriptor using one of the techniques described in Chapter 63.

- *The /proc/PID interface*: For example, if a process with the process ID 12345 exists, then the directory /proc/12345 will exist, and we can check this using a call such as *stat()*.

All of these techniques, except the last, are unaffected by recycling of process IDs.

Listing 20-3 demonstrates the use of *kill()*. This program takes two command-line arguments, a process ID and a signal number, and uses *kill()* to send the signal to the specified process. If signal 0 (the null signal) is specified, then the program reports on the existence of the target process.

20.7 Other Ways of Sending Signals: *raise()* and *killpg()*

Sometimes, it is useful for a process to send a signal to itself. (We see an example of this in Section 34.7.3.) The *raise()* function performs this task.

```
#include <signal.h>

int raise(int sig);
```

                                        Returns 0 on success, or nonzero on error

In a single-threaded program, a call to *raise()* is equivalent to the following call to *kill()*:

```
kill(getpid(), sig);
```

On a system that supports threads, *raise(sig)* is implemented as:

```
pthread_kill(pthread_self(), sig)
```

We describe the *pthread_kill()* function in Section 33.2.3, but for now it is sufficient to say that this implementation means that the signal will be delivered to the specific thread that called *raise()*. By contrast, the call *kill(getpid(), sig)* sends a signal to the calling *process*, and that signal may be delivered to any thread in the process.

> The *raise()* function originates from C89. The C standards don't cover operating system details such as process IDs, but *raise()* can be specified within the C standard because it doesn't require reference to process IDs.

When a process sends itself a signal using *raise()* (or *kill()*), the signal is delivered immediately (i.e., before *raise()* returns to the caller).

Note that *raise()* returns a nonzero value (not necessarily −1) on error. The only error that can occur with *raise()* is EINVAL, because *sig* was invalid. Therefore, where we specify one of the SIGxxxx constants, we don't check the return status of this function.

Listing 20-3: Using the *kill()* system call

——————————————————————————————— signals/t_kill.c

```c
#include <signal.h>
#include "tlpi_hdr.h"

int
main(int argc, char *argv[])
{
    int s, sig;

    if (argc != 3 || strcmp(argv[1], "--help") == 0)
        usageErr("%s pid sig-num\n", argv[0]);

    sig = getInt(argv[2], 0, "sig-num");

    s = kill(getLong(argv[1], 0, "pid"), sig);

    if (sig != 0) {
        if (s == -1)
            errExit("kill");

    } else {                        /* Null signal: process existence check */
        if (s == 0) {
            printf("Process exists and we can send it a signal\n");
        } else {
            if (errno == EPERM)
                printf("Process exists, but we don't have "
                        "permission to send it a signal\n");
            else if (errno == ESRCH)
                printf("Process does not exist\n");
            else
                errExit("kill");
        }
    }

    exit(EXIT_SUCCESS);
}
```

——————————————————————————————— signals/t_kill.c

The *killpg()* function sends a signal to all of the members of a process group.

```
#include <signal.h>

int killpg(pid_t pgrp, int sig);
```
                                    Returns 0 on success, or −1 on error

A call to *killpg()* is equivalent to the following call to *kill()*:

```
kill(-pgrp, sig);
```

If *pgrp* is specified as 0, then the signal is sent to all processes in the same process group as the caller. SUSv3 leaves this point unspecified, but most UNIX implementations interpret this case in the same way as Linux.

Signals: Fundamental Concepts   **405**

20.8 Displaying Signal Descriptions

Each signal has an associated printable description. These descriptions are listed in the array *sys_siglist*. For example, we can refer to *sys_siglist[SIGPIPE]* to get the description for SIGPIPE (broken pipe). However, rather than using the *sys_siglist* array directly, the *strsignal()* function is preferable.

```
#define _BSD_SOURCE
#include <signal.h>

extern const char *const sys_siglist[];

#define _GNU_SOURCE
#include <string.h>

char *strsignal(int sig);
```
                              Returns pointer to signal description string

The *strsignal()* function performs bounds checking on the *sig* argument, and then returns a pointer to a printable description of the signal, or a pointer to an error string if the signal number was invalid. (On some other UNIX implementations, *strsignal()* returns NULL if *sig* is invalid.)

Aside from bounds checking, another advantage of *strsignal()* over the direct use of *sys_siglist* is that *strsignal()* is locale-sensitive (Section 10.4), so that signal descriptions will be displayed in the local language.

An example of the use of *strsignal()* is shown in Listing 20-4.

The *psignal()* function displays (on standard error) the string given in its argument *msg*, followed by a colon, and then the signal description corresponding to *sig*. Like *strsignal()*, *psignal()* is locale-sensitive.

```
#include <signal.h>

void psignal(int sig, const char *msg);
```

Although *psignal()*, *strsignal()*, and *sys_siglist* are not standardized as part of SUSv3, they are nevertheless available on many UNIX implementations. (SUSv4 adds specifications for *psignal()* and *strsignal()*.)

20.9 Signal Sets

Many signal-related system calls need to be able to represent a group of different signals. For example, *sigaction()* and *sigprocmask()* allow a program to specify a group of signals that are to be blocked by a process, while *sigpending()* returns a group of signals that are currently pending for a process. (We describe these system calls shortly.)

Multiple signals are represented using a data structure called a *signal set*, provided by the system data type *sigset_t*. SUSv3 specifies a range of functions for manipulating signal sets, and we now describe these functions.

> On Linux, as on most UNIX implementations, the *sigset_t* data type is a bit mask. However, SUSv3 doesn't require this. A signal set could conceivably be represented using some other kind of structure. SUSv3 requires only that the type of *sigset_t* be assignable. Thus, it must be implemented using either some scalar type (e.g., an integer) or a C structure (perhaps containing an array of integers).

The *sigemptyset()* function initializes a signal set to contain no members. The *sigfillset()* function initializes a set to contain all signals (including all realtime signals).

```
#include <signal.h>

int sigemptyset(sigset_t *set);
int sigfillset(sigset_t *set);
```
                                      Both return 0 on success, or –1 on error

One of *sigemptyset()* or *sigfillset()* *must* be used to initialize a signal set. This is because C doesn't initialize automatic variables, and the initialization of static variables to 0 can't portably be relied upon as indicating an empty signal set, since signal sets may be implemented using structures other than bit masks. (For the same reason, it is incorrect to use *memset(3)* to zero the contents of a signal set in order to mark it as empty.)

After initialization, individual signals can be added to a set using *sigaddset()* and removed using *sigdelset()*.

```
#include <signal.h>

int sigaddset(const sigset_t *set, int sig);
int sigdelset(const sigset_t *set, int sig);
```
                                      Both return 0 on success, or –1 on error

For both *sigaddset()* and *sigdelset()*, the *sig* argument is a signal number.

The *sigismember()* function is used to test for membership of a set.

```
#include <signal.h>

int sigismember(const sigset_t *set, int sig);
```
              Returns 1 if *sig* is a member of *set*, 0 if it is not, or –1 on error

The *sigismember()* function returns 1 (true) if *sig* is a member of *set*, 0 (false) if it is not a member, or –1 on error (e.g., *sig* is not a valid signal number).

The GNU C library implements three nonstandard functions that perform tasks that are complementary to the standard signal set functions just described.

```
#define _GNU_SOURCE
#include <signal.h>

int sigandset(sigset_t *dest, sigset_t *left, sigset_t *right);
int sigorset(sigset_t *dest, sigset_t *left, sigset_t *right);
```
                                    Both return 0 on success, or −1 on error
```
int sigisemptyset(const sigset_t *set);
```
                                    Returns 1 if *set* is empty, otherwise 0

These functions perform the following tasks:

- *sigandset()* places the intersection of the sets *left* and *right* in the set *dest*;
- *sigorset()* places the union of the sets *left* and *right* in the set *dest*; and
- *sigisemptyset()* returns true if *set* contains no signals.

Example program

Using the functions described in this section, we can write the functions shown in Listing 20-4, which we employ in various later programs. The first of these, *printSigset()*, displays the signals that are members of the specified signal set. This function uses the NSIG constant, which is defined in <signal.h> to be one greater than the highest signal number. We use NSIG as the upper bound in a loop that tests all signal numbers for membership of a set.

> Although NSIG is not specified in SUSv3, it is defined on most UNIX implementations. However, it may be necessary to use implementation-specific compiler options to make it visible. For example, on Linux, we must define one of the feature test macros _BSD_SOURCE, _SVID_SOURCE, or _GNU_SOURCE.

The *printSigMask()* and *printPendingSigs()* functions employ *printSigset()* to display, respectively, the process signal mask and the set of currently pending signals. The *printSigMask()* and *printPendingSigs()* functions use the *sigprocmask()* and *sigpending()* system calls, respectively. We describe the *sigprocmask()* and *sigpending()* system calls in Sections 20.10 and 20.11.

Listing 20-4: Functions for displaying signal sets

————————————————————————————————— **signals/signal_functions.c**

```
#define _GNU_SOURCE
#include <string.h>
#include <signal.h>
#include "signal_functions.h"        /* Declares functions defined here */
#include "tlpi_hdr.h"

/* NOTE: All of the following functions employ fprintf(), which
   is not async-signal-safe (see Section 21.1.2). As such, these
```

```
        functions are also not async-signal-safe (i.e., beware of
        indiscriminately calling them from signal handlers). */

void                    /* Print list of signals within a signal set */
printSigset(FILE *of, const char *prefix, const sigset_t *sigset)
{
    int sig, cnt;

    cnt = 0;
    for (sig = 1; sig < NSIG; sig++) {
        if (sigismember(sigset, sig)) {
            cnt++;
            fprintf(of, "%s%d (%s)\n", prefix, sig, strsignal(sig));
        }
    }

    if (cnt == 0)
        fprintf(of, "%s<empty signal set>\n", prefix);
}

int                     /* Print mask of blocked signals for this process */
printSigMask(FILE *of, const char *msg)
{
    sigset_t currMask;

    if (msg != NULL)
        fprintf(of, "%s", msg);

    if (sigprocmask(SIG_BLOCK, NULL, &currMask) == -1)
        return -1;

    printSigset(of, "\t\t", &currMask);

    return 0;
}

int                     /* Print signals currently pending for this process */
printPendingSigs(FILE *of, const char *msg)
{
    sigset_t pendingSigs;

    if (msg != NULL)
        fprintf(of, "%s", msg);

    if (sigpending(&pendingSigs) == -1)
        return -1;

    printSigset(of, "\t\t", &pendingSigs);

    return 0;
}
```
————————————————————————————————————— signals/signal_functions.c

20.10 The Signal Mask (Blocking Signal Delivery)

For each process, the kernel maintains a *signal mask*—a set of signals whose delivery to the process is currently blocked. If a signal that is blocked is sent to a process, delivery of that signal is delayed until it is unblocked by being removed from the process signal mask. (In Section 33.2.1, we'll see that the signal mask is actually a per-thread attribute, and that each thread in a multithreaded process can independently examine and modify its signal mask using the *pthread_sigmask()* function.)

A signal may be added to the signal mask in the following ways:

* When a signal handler is invoked, the signal that caused its invocation can be automatically added to the signal mask. Whether or not this occurs depends on the flags used when the handler is established using *sigaction()*.

* When a signal handler is established with *sigaction()*, it is possible to specify an additional set of signals that are to be blocked when the handler is invoked.

* The *sigprocmask()* system call can be used at any time to explicitly add signals to, and remove signals from, the signal mask.

We delay discussion of the first two cases until we examine *sigaction()* in Section 20.13, and discuss *sigprocmask()* now.

```
#include <signal.h>

int sigprocmask(int how, const sigset_t *set, sigset_t *oldset);
```
                                                    Returns 0 on success, or –1 on error

---

We can use *sigprocmask()* to change the process signal mask, to retrieve the existing mask, or both. The *how* argument determines the changes that *sigprocmask()* makes to the signal mask:

SIG_BLOCK
> The signals specified in the signal set pointed to by *set* are added to the signal mask. In other words, the signal mask is set to the union of its current value and *set*.

SIG_UNBLOCK
> The signals in the signal set pointed to by *set* are removed from the signal mask. Unblocking a signal that is not currently blocked doesn't cause an error to be returned.

SIG_SETMASK
> The signal set pointed to by *set* is assigned to the signal mask.

In each case, if the *oldset* argument is not NULL, it points to a *sigset_t* buffer that is used to return the previous signal mask.

If we want to retrieve the signal mask without changing it, then we can specify NULL for the *set* argument, in which case the *how* argument is ignored.

To temporarily prevent delivery of a signal, we can use the series of calls shown in Listing 20-5 to block the signal, and then unblock it by resetting the signal mask to its previous state.

Listing 20-5: Temporarily blocking delivery of a signal

```
sigset_t blockSet, prevMask;

/* Initialize a signal set to contain SIGINT */

sigemptyset(&blockSet);
sigaddset(&blockSet, SIGINT);

/* Block SIGINT, save previous signal mask */

if (sigprocmask(SIG_BLOCK, &blockSet, &prevMask) == -1)
    errExit("sigprocmask1");

/* ... Code that should not be interrupted by SIGINT ... */

/* Restore previous signal mask, unblocking SIGINT */

if (sigprocmask(SIG_SETMASK, &prevMask, NULL) == -1)
    errExit("sigprocmask2");
```

SUSv3 specifies that if any pending signals are unblocked by a call to *sigprocmask()*, then at least one of those signals will be delivered before the call returns. In other words, if we unblock a pending signal, it is delivered to the process immediately.

Attempts to block SIGKILL and SIGSTOP are silently ignored. If we attempt to block these signals, *sigprocmask()* neither honors the request nor generates an error. This means that we can use the following code to block all signals except SIGKILL and SIGSTOP:

```
sigfillset(&blockSet);
if (sigprocmask(SIG_BLOCK, &blockSet, NULL) == -1)
    errExit("sigprocmask");
```

20.11 Pending Signals

If a process receives a signal that it is currently blocking, that signal is added to the process's set of pending signals. When (and if) the signal is later unblocked, it is then delivered to the process. To determine which signals are pending for a process, we can call *sigpending()*.

```
#include <signal.h>

int sigpending(sigset_t *set);
```

                                        Returns 0 on success, or −1 on error

The *sigpending()* system call returns the set of signals that are pending for the calling process in the *sigset_t* structure pointed to by *set*. We can then examine *set* using the *sigismember()* function described in Section 20.9.

If we change the disposition of a pending signal, then, when the signal is later unblocked, it is handled according to its new disposition. Although not often used, one application of this technique is to prevent the delivery of a pending signal by setting its disposition to SIG_IGN, or to SIG_DFL if the default action for the signal is *ignore*. As a result, the signal is removed from the process's set of pending signals and thus not delivered.

20.12 Signals Are Not Queued

The set of pending signals is only a mask; it indicates whether or not a signal has occurred, but not how many times it has occurred. In other words, if the same signal is generated multiple times while it is blocked, then it is recorded in the set of pending signals, and later delivered, just once. (One of the differences between standard and realtime signals is that realtime signals are queued, as discussed in Section 22.8.)

Listing 20-6 and Listing 20-7 show two programs that can be used to observe that signals are not queued. The program in Listing 20-6 takes up to four command-line arguments, as follows:

```
$ ./sig_sender PID num-sigs sig-num [sig-num-2]
```

The first argument is the process ID of a process to which the program should send signals. The second argument specifies the number of signals to be sent to the target process. The third argument specifies the signal number that is to be sent to the target process. If a signal number is supplied as the fourth argument, then the program sends one instance of that signal after sending the signals specified by the previous arguments. In the example shell session below, we use this final argument to send a SIGINT signal to the target process; the purpose of sending this signal will become clear in a moment.

Listing 20-6: Sending multiple signals

── signals/sig_sender.c
```c
#include <signal.h>
#include "tlpi_hdr.h"

int
main(int argc, char *argv[])
{
    int numSigs, sig, j;
    pid_t pid;

    if (argc < 4 || strcmp(argv[1], "--help") == 0)
        usageErr("%s pid num-sigs sig-num [sig-num-2]\n", argv[0]);
```

```
    pid = getLong(argv[1], 0, "PID");
    numSigs = getInt(argv[2], GN_GT_0, "num-sigs");
    sig = getInt(argv[3], 0, "sig-num");

    /* Send signals to receiver */

    printf("%s: sending signal %d to process %ld %d times\n",
            argv[0], sig, (long) pid, numSigs);

    for (j = 0; j < numSigs; j++)
        if (kill(pid, sig) == -1)
            errExit("kill");

    /* If a fourth command-line argument was specified, send that signal */

    if (argc > 4)
        if (kill(pid, getInt(argv[4], 0, "sig-num-2")) == -1)
            errExit("kill");

    printf("%s: exiting\n", argv[0]);
    exit(EXIT_SUCCESS);
}
```

── **signals/sig_sender.c**

The program shown in Listing 20-7 is designed to catch and report statistics on signals sent by the program in Listing 20-6. This program performs the following steps:

- The program sets up a single handler to catch all signals ②. (It isn't possible to catch SIGKILL and SIGSTOP, but we ignore the error that occurs when trying to establish a handler for these signals.) For most types of signals, the handler ① simply counts the signal using an array. If SIGINT is received, the handler sets a flag (*gotSigint*) that causes the program to exit its main loop (the while loop described below). (We explain the use of the volatile qualifier and the *sig_atomic_t* data type used to declare the *gotSigint* variable in Section 21.1.3.)

- If a command-line argument was supplied to the program, then the program blocks all signals for the number of seconds specified by that argument, and then, prior to unblocking the signals, displays the set of pending signals ③. This allows us to send signals to the process before it commences the following step.

- The program executes a while loop that consumes CPU time until *gotSigint* is set ④. (Sections 20.14 and 22.9 describe the use of *pause()* and *sigsuspend()*, which are more CPU-efficient ways of waiting for the arrival of a signal.)

- After exiting the while loop, the program displays counts of all signals received ⑤.

We first use these two programs to illustrate that a blocked signal is delivered only once, no matter how many times it is generated. We do this by specifying a sleep interval for the receiver and sending all signals before the sleep interval completes.

```
$ ./sig_receiver 15 &                        Receiver blocks signals for 15 secs
[1] 5368
./sig_receiver: PID is 5368
./sig_receiver: sleeping for 15 seconds
```

```
$ ./sig_sender 5368 1000000 10 2          Send SIGUSR1 signals, plus a SIGINT
./sig_sender: sending signal 10 to process 5368 1000000 times
./sig_sender: exiting
./sig_receiver: pending signals are:
            2 (Interrupt)
            10 (User defined signal 1)
./sig_receiver: signal 10 caught 1 time
[1]+  Done                    ./sig_receiver 15
```

The command-line arguments to the sending program specified the SIGUSR1 and SIGINT signals, which are signals 10 and 2, respectively, on Linux/x86.

From the output above, we can see that even though one million signals were sent, only one was delivered to the receiver.

Even if a process doesn't block signals, it may receive fewer signals than are sent to it. This can happen if the signals are sent so fast that they arrive before the receiving process has a chance to be scheduled for execution by the kernel, with the result that the multiple signals are recorded just once in the process's pending signal set. If we execute the program in Listing 20-7 with no command-line arguments (so that it doesn't block signals and sleep), we see the following:

```
$ ./sig_receiver &
[1] 5393
./sig_receiver: PID is 5393
$ ./sig_sender 5393 1000000 10 2
./sig_sender: sending signal 10 to process 5393 1000000 times
./sig_sender: exiting
./sig_receiver: signal 10 caught 52 times
[1]+  Done                    ./sig_receiver
```

Of the million signals sent, just 52 were caught by the receiving process. (The precise number of signals caught will vary depending on the vagaries of decisions made by the kernel scheduling algorithm.) The reason for this is that each time the sending program is scheduled to run, it sends multiple signals to the receiver. However, only one of these signals is marked as pending and then delivered when the receiver has a chance to run.

Listing 20-7: Catching and counting signals

—————————————————————————————————————— **signals/sig_receiver.c**

```
#define _GNU_SOURCE
#include <signal.h>
#include "signal_functions.h"         /* Declaration of printSigset() */
#include "tlpi_hdr.h"

static int sigCnt[NSIG];              /* Counts deliveries of each signal */
static volatile sig_atomic_t gotSigint = 0;
                                      /* Set nonzero if SIGINT is delivered */

static void
① handler(int sig)
{
```

```
        if (sig == SIGINT)
            gotSigint = 1;
        else
            sigCnt[sig]++;
    }

    int
    main(int argc, char *argv[])
    {
        int n, numSecs;
        sigset_t pendingMask, blockingMask, emptyMask;

        printf("%s: PID is %ld\n", argv[0], (long) getpid());

②      for (n = 1; n < NSIG; n++)          /* Same handler for all signals */
            (void) signal(n, handler);      /* Ignore errors */

        /* If a sleep time was specified, temporarily block all signals,
           sleep (while another process sends us signals), and then
           display the mask of pending signals and unblock all signals */

③      if (argc > 1) {
            numSecs = getInt(argv[1], GN_GT_0, NULL);

            sigfillset(&blockingMask);
            if (sigprocmask(SIG_SETMASK, &blockingMask, NULL) == -1)
                errExit("sigprocmask");

            printf("%s: sleeping for %d seconds\n", argv[0], numSecs);
            sleep(numSecs);

            if (sigpending(&pendingMask) == -1)
                errExit("sigpending");

            printf("%s: pending signals are: \n", argv[0]);
            printSigset(stdout, "\t\t", &pendingMask);

            sigemptyset(&emptyMask);         /* Unblock all signals */
            if (sigprocmask(SIG_SETMASK, &emptyMask, NULL) == -1)
                errExit("sigprocmask");
        }

④      while (!gotSigint)                   /* Loop until SIGINT caught */
            continue;

⑤      for (n = 1; n < NSIG; n++)           /* Display number of signals received */
            if (sigCnt[n] != 0)
                printf("%s: signal %d caught %d time%s\n", argv[0], n,
                        sigCnt[n], (sigCnt[n] == 1) ? "" : "s");

        exit(EXIT_SUCCESS);
    }
```

—————————————————————————————————— **signals/sig_receiver.c**

20.13 Changing Signal Dispositions: *sigaction()*

The *sigaction()* system call is an alternative to *signal()* for setting the disposition of a signal. Although *sigaction()* is somewhat more complex to use than *signal()*, in return it provides greater flexibility. In particular, *sigaction()* allows us to retrieve the disposition of a signal without changing it, and to set various attributes controlling precisely what happens when a signal handler is invoked. Additionally, as we'll elaborate in Section 22.7, *sigaction()* is more portable than *signal()* when establishing a signal handler.

```
#include <signal.h>

int sigaction(int sig, const struct sigaction *act, struct sigaction *oldact);
```
                                                    Returns 0 on success, or −1 on error

The *sig* argument identifies the signal whose disposition we want to retrieve or change. This argument can be any signal except SIGKILL or SIGSTOP.

The *act* argument is a pointer to a structure specifying a new disposition for the signal. If we are interested only in finding the existing disposition of the signal, then we can specify NULL for this argument. The *oldact* argument is a pointer to a structure of the same type, and is used to return information about the signal's previous disposition. If we are not interested in this information, then we can specify NULL for this argument. The structures pointed to by *act* and *oldact* are of the following type:

```
struct sigaction {
    void    (*sa_handler)(int);     /* Address of handler */
    sigset_t sa_mask;               /* Signals blocked during handler
                                       invocation */
    int      sa_flags;              /* Flags controlling handler invocation */
    void    (*sa_restorer)(void);   /* Not for application use */
};
```

> The *sigaction* structure is actually somewhat more complex than shown here. We consider further details in Section 21.4.

The *sa_handler* field corresponds to the *handler* argument given to *signal()*. It specifies the address of a signal handler, or one of the constants SIG_IGN or SIG_DFL. The *sa_mask* and *sa_flags* fields, which we discuss in a moment, are interpreted only if *sa_handler* is the address of a signal handler—that is, a value other than SIG_IGN or SIG_DFL. The remaining field, *sa_restorer*, is not intended for use in applications (and is not specified by SUSv3).

> The *sa_restorer* field is used internally to ensure that on completion of a signal handler, a call is made to the special-purpose *sigreturn()* system call, which restores the process's execution context so that it can continue execution at the point where it was interrupted by the signal handler. An example of this usage can be found in the *glibc* source file sysdeps/unix/sysv/linux/i386/sigaction.c.

The *sa_mask* field defines a set of signals that are to be blocked during invocation of the handler defined by *sa_handler*. When the signal handler is invoked, any signals in this set that are not currently part of the process signal mask are automatically added to the mask before the handler is called. These signals remain in the process signal mask until the signal handler returns, at which time they are automatically removed. The *sa_mask* field allows us to specify a set of signals that aren't permitted to interrupt execution of this handler. In addition, the signal that caused the handler to be invoked is automatically added to the process signal mask. This means that a signal handler won't recursively interrupt itself if a second instance of the same signal arrives while the handler is executing. Because blocked signals are not queued, if any of these signals are repeatedly generated during the execution of the handler, they are (later) delivered only once.

The *sa_flags* field is a bit mask specifying various options controlling how the signal is handled. The following bits may be ORed (|) together in this field:

SA_NOCLDSTOP

> If *sig* is SIGCHLD, don't generate this signal when a child process is stopped or resumed as a consequence of receiving a signal. Refer to Section 26.3.2.

SA_NOCLDWAIT

> (since Linux 2.6) If *sig* is SIGCHLD, don't transform children into zombies when they terminate. For further details, see Section 26.3.3.

SA_NODEFER

> When this signal is caught, don't automatically add it to the process signal mask while the handler is executing. The name SA_NOMASK is provided as a historical synonym for SA_NODEFER, but the latter name is preferable because it is standardized in SUSv3.

SA_ONSTACK

> Invoke the handler for this signal using an alternate stack installed by *sigaltstack()*. Refer to Section 21.3.

SA_RESETHAND

> When this signal is caught, reset its disposition to the default (i.e., SIG_DFL) before invoking the handler. (By default, a signal handler remains established until it is explicitly disestablished by a further call to *sigaction()*.) The name SA_ONESHOT is provided as a historical synonym for SA_RESETHAND, but the latter name is preferable because it is standardized in SUSv3.

SA_RESTART

> Automatically restart system calls interrupted by this signal handler. See Section 21.5.

SA_SIGINFO

> Invoke the signal handler with additional arguments providing further information about the signal. We describe this flag in Section 21.4.

All of the above options are specified in SUSv3.

An example of the use of *sigaction()* is shown in Listing 21-1.

20.14 Waiting for a Signal: *pause()*

Calling *pause()* suspends execution of the process until the call is interrupted by a signal handler (or until an unhandled signal terminates the process).

```
#include <unistd.h>

int pause(void);
```
                                          Always returns −1 with *errno* set to EINTR

When a signal is handled, *pause()* is interrupted and always returns −1 with *errno* set to EINTR. (We say more about the EINTR error in Section 21.5.)

An example of the use of *pause()* is provided in Listing 20-2.

In Sections 22.9, 22.10, and 22.11, we look at various other ways that a program can suspend execution while waiting for a signal.

20.15 Summary

A signal is a notification that some kind of event has occurred, and may be sent to a process by the kernel, by another process, or by itself. There is a range of standard signal types, each of which has a unique number and purpose.

Signal delivery is typically asynchronous, meaning that the point at which the signal interrupts execution of the process is unpredictable. In some cases (e.g., hardware-generated signals), signals are delivered synchronously, meaning that delivery occurs predictably and reproducibly at a certain point in the execution of a program.

By default, a signal either is ignored, terminates a process (with or without a core dump), stops a running process, or restarts a stopped process. The particular default action depends on the signal type. Alternatively, a program can use *signal()* or *sigaction()* to explicitly ignore a signal or to establish a programmer-defined signal handler function that is invoked when the signal is delivered. For portability reasons, establishing a signal handler is best performed using *sigaction()*.

A process (with suitable permissions) can send a signal to another process using *kill()*. Sending the null signal (0) is a way of determining if a particular process ID is in use.

Each process has a signal mask, which is the set of signals whose delivery is currently blocked. Signals can be added to and removed from the signal mask using *sigprocmask()*.

If a signal is received while it is blocked, then it remains pending until it is unblocked. Standard signals can't be queued; that is, a signal can be marked as pending (and thus later delivered) only once. A process can use the *sigpending()* system call to retrieve a signal set (a data structure used to represent multiple different signals) identifying the signals that it has pending.

The *sigaction()* system call provides more control and flexibility than *signal()* when setting the disposition of a signal. First, we can specify a set of additional signals to be blocked when a handler is invoked. In addition, various flags can be used to control the actions that occur when a signal handler is invoked. For example, there are flags that select the older unreliable signal semantics (not blocking the signal causing invocation of a handler, and having the disposition of the signal reset to its default before the handler is called).

Using *pause()*, a process can suspend execution until a signal arrives.

Further information

[Bovet & Cesati, 2005] and [Maxwell, 1999] provide background on the implementation of signals in Linux. [Goodheart & Cox, 1994] details the implementation of signals on System V Release 4. The GNU C library manual (available online at *http://www.gnu.org/*) contains an extensive description of signals.

20.16 Exercises

20-1. As noted in Section 20.3, *sigaction()* is more portable than *signal()* for establishing a signal handler. Replace the use of *signal()* by *sigaction()* in the program in Listing 20-7 (sig_receiver.c).

20-2. Write a program that shows that when the disposition of a pending signal is changed to be SIG_IGN, the program never sees (catches) the signal.

20-3. Write programs that verify the effect of the SA_RESETHAND and SA_NODEFER flags when establishing a signal handler with *sigaction()*.

20-4. Implement the *siginterrupt()* function described in Section 21.5 using *sigaction()*.

21

SIGNALS: SIGNAL HANDLERS

This chapter continues the description of signals begun in the previous chapter. It focuses on signal handlers, and extends the discussion started in Section 20.4. Among the topics we consider are the following:

- how to design a signal handler, which necessitates a discussion of reentrancy and async-signal-safe functions;

- alternatives to performing a normal return from a signal handler, in particular, the use of a nonlocal goto for this purpose;

- handling of signals on an alternate stack;

- the use of the *sigaction()* SA_SIGINFO flag to allow a signal handler to obtain more detailed information about the signal that caused its invocation; and

- how a blocking system call may be interrupted by a signal handler, and how the call can be restarted if desired.

21.1 Designing Signal Handlers

In general, it is preferable to write simple signal handlers. One important reason for this is to reduce the risk of creating race conditions. Two common designs for signal handlers are the following:

- The signal handler sets a global flag and exits. The main program periodically checks this flag and, if it is set, takes appropriate action. (If the main program cannot perform such periodic checks because it needs to monitor one or more file descriptors to see if I/O is possible, then the signal handler can also write a single byte to a dedicated pipe whose read end is included among the file descriptors monitored by the main program. We show an example of this technique in Section 63.5.2.)

- The signal handler performs some type of cleanup and then either terminates the process or uses a nonlocal goto (Section 21.2.1) to unwind the stack and return control to a predetermined location in the main program.

In the following sections, we explore these ideas, as well as other concepts that are important in the design of signal handlers.

21.1.1 Signals Are Not Queued (Revisited)

In Section 20.10, we noted that delivery of a signal is blocked during the execution of its handler (unless we specify the SA_NODEFER flag to *sigaction()*). If the signal is (again) generated while the handler is executing, then it is marked as pending and later delivered when the handler returns. We also already noted that signals are not queued. If the signal is generated more than once while the handler is executing, then it is still marked as pending, and it will later be delivered only once.

That signals can "disappear" in this way has implications for how we design signal handlers. To begin with, we can't reliably count the number of times a signal is generated. Furthermore, we may need to code our signal handlers to deal with the possibility that multiple events of the type corresponding to the signal have occurred. We'll see an example of this when we consider the use of the SIGCHLD signal in Section 26.3.1.

21.1.2 Reentrant and Async-Signal-Safe Functions

Not all system calls and library functions can be safely called from a signal handler. To understand why requires an explanation of two concepts: reentrant functions and async-signal-safe functions.

Reentrant and nonreentrant functions

To explain what a reentrant function is, we need to first distinguish between single-threaded and multithreaded programs. Classical UNIX programs have a single *thread of execution*: the CPU processes instructions for a single logical flow of execution through the program. In a multithreaded program, there are multiple, independent, concurrent logical flows of execution within the same process.

In Chapter 29, we'll see how to explicitly create programs that contain multiple threads of execution. However, the concept of multiple threads of execution is also relevant for programs that employ signal handlers. Because a signal handler may asynchronously interrupt the execution of a program at any point in time, the main program and the signal handler in effect form two independent (although not concurrent) threads of execution within the same process.

A function is said to be *reentrant* if it can safely be simultaneously executed by multiple threads of execution in the same process. In this context, "safe" means that the function achieves its expected result, regardless of the state of execution of any other thread of execution.

> The SUSv3 definition of a reentrant function is one "whose effect, when called by two or more threads, is guaranteed to be as if the threads each executed the function one after the other in an undefined order, even if the actual execution is interleaved."

A function may be *nonreentrant* if it updates global or static data structures. (A function that employs only local variables is guaranteed to be reentrant.) If two invocations of (i.e., two threads executing) the function simultaneously attempt to update the same global variable or data structure, then these updates are likely to interfere with each other and produce incorrect results. For example, suppose that one thread of execution is in the middle of updating a linked list data structure to add a new list item when another thread also attempts to update the same linked list. Since adding a new item to the list requires updating multiple pointers, if another thread interrupts these steps and updates the same pointers, chaos will result.

Such possibilities are in fact rife within the standard C library. For example, we already noted in Section 7.1.3 that *malloc()* and *free()* maintain a linked list of freed memory blocks available for reallocation from the heap. If a call to *malloc()* in the main program is interrupted by a signal handler that also calls *malloc()*, then this linked list can be corrupted. For this reason, the *malloc()* family of functions, and other library functions that use them, are nonreentrant.

Other library functions are nonreentrant because they return information using statically allocated memory. Examples of such functions (described elsewhere in this book) include *crypt()*, *getpwnam()*, *gethostbyname()*, and *getservbyname()*. If a signal handler also uses one of these functions, then it will overwrite information returned by any earlier call to the same function from within the main program (or vice versa).

Functions can also be nonreentrant if they use static data structures for their internal bookkeeping. The most obvious examples of such functions are the members of the *stdio* library (*printf()*, *scanf()*, and so on), which update internal data structures for buffered I/O. Thus, when using *printf()* from within a signal handler, we may sometimes see strange output—or even a program crash or data corruption—if the handler interrupts the main program in the middle of executing a call to *printf()* or another *stdio* function.

Even if we are not using nonreentrant library functions, reentrancy issues can still be relevant. If a signal handler updates programmer-defined global data structures that are also updated within the main program, then we can say that the signal handler is nonreentrant with respect to the main program.

If a function is nonreentrant, then its manual page will normally provide an explicit or implicit indication of this fact. In particular, watch out for statements that the function uses or returns information in statically allocated variables.

Example program

Listing 21-1 demonstrates the nonreentrant nature of the *crypt()* function (Section 8.5). As command-line arguments, this program accepts two strings. The program performs the following steps:

1. Call *crypt()* to encrypt the string in the first command-line argument, and copy this string to a separate buffer using *strdup()*.

2. Establish a handler for SIGINT (generated by typing *Control-C*). The handler calls *crypt()* to encrypt the string supplied in the second command-line argument.

3. Enter an infinite for loop that uses *crypt()* to encrypt the string in the first command-line argument and check that the returned string is the same as that saved in step 1.

In the absence of a signal, the strings will always match in step 3. However, if a SIGINT signal arrives and the execution of the signal handler interrupts the main program just after the execution of the *crypt()* call in the for loop, but before the check to see if the strings match, then the main program will report a mismatch. When we run the program, this is what we see:

```
$ ./non_reentrant abc def
Repeatedly type Control-C to generate SIGINT
Mismatch on call 109871 (mismatch=1 handled=1)
Mismatch on call 128061 (mismatch=2 handled=2)
Many lines of output removed
Mismatch on call 727935 (mismatch=149 handled=156)
Mismatch on call 729547 (mismatch=150 handled=157)
Type Control-\ to generate SIGQUIT
Quit (core dumped)
```

Comparing the *mismatch* and *handled* values in the above output, we see that in the majority of cases where the signal handler is invoked, it overwrites the statically allocated buffer between the call to *crypt()* and the string comparison in *main()*.

Listing 21-1: Calling a nonreentrant function from both *main()* and a signal handler

—— **signals/nonreentrant.c**

```c
#define _XOPEN_SOURCE 600
#include <unistd.h>
#include <signal.h>
#include <string.h>
#include "tlpi_hdr.h"

static char *str2;              /* Set from argv[2] */
static int handled = 0;         /* Counts number of calls to handler */

static void
handler(int sig)
{
    crypt(str2, "xx");
    handled++;
}
```

```c
int
main(int argc, char *argv[])
{
    char *cr1;
    int callNum, mismatch;
    struct sigaction sa;

    if (argc != 3)
        usageErr("%s str1 str2\n", argv[0]);

    str2 = argv[2];                         /* Make argv[2] available to handler */
    cr1 = strdup(crypt(argv[1], "xx"));  /* Copy statically allocated string
                                                to another buffer */
    if (cr1 == NULL)
        errExit("strdup");

    sigemptyset(&sa.sa_mask);
    sa.sa_flags = 0;
    sa.sa_handler = handler;
    if (sigaction(SIGINT, &sa, NULL) == -1)
        errExit("sigaction");

    /* Repeatedly call crypt() using argv[1]. If interrupted by a
       signal handler, then the static storage returned by crypt()
       will be overwritten by the results of encrypting argv[2], and
       strcmp() will detect a mismatch with the value in 'cr1'. */

    for (callNum = 1, mismatch = 0; ; callNum++) {
        if (strcmp(crypt(argv[1], "xx"), cr1) != 0) {
            mismatch++;
            printf("Mismatch on call %d (mismatch=%d handled=%d)\n",
                    callNum, mismatch, handled);
        }
    }
}
```

——————————————————————————————————————— signals/nonreentrant.c

Standard async-signal-safe functions

An *async-signal-safe* function is one that the implementation guarantees to be safe when called from a signal handler. A function is async-signal-safe either because it is reentrant or because it is not interruptible by a signal handler.

Table 21-1 lists the functions that various standards require to be async-signal-safe. In this table, the functions whose names are not followed by a *v2* or *v3* were specified as async-signal-safe in POSIX.1-1990. SUSv2 added the functions marked *v2* to the list, and those marked *v3* were added by SUSv3. Individual UNIX implementations may make other functions async-signal-safe, but all standards-conformant UNIX implementations must ensure that at least these functions are async-signal-safe (if they are provided by the implementation; not all of these functions are provided on Linux).

SUSv4 makes the following changes to Table 21-1:

- The following functions are removed: *fpathconf()*, *pathconf()*, and *sysconf()*.

- The following functions are added: *execl()*, *execv()*, *faccessat()*, *fchmodat()*, *fchownat()*, *fexecve()*, *fstatat()*, *futimens()*, *linkat()*, *mkdirat()*, *mkfifoat()*, *mknod()*, *mknodat()*, *openat()*, *readlinkat()*, *renameat()*, *symlinkat()*, *unlinkat()*, *utimensat()*, and *utimes()*.

Table 21-1: Functions required to be async-signal-safe by POSIX.1-1990, SUSv2, and SUSv3

_Exit() (v3)	*getpid()*	*sigdelset()*
_exit()	*getppid()*	*sigemptyset()*
abort() (v3)	*getsockname() (v3)*	*sigfillset()*
accept() (v3)	*getsockopt() (v3)*	*sigismember()*
access()	*getuid()*	*signal() (v2)*
aio_error() (v2)	*kill()*	*sigpause() (v2)*
aio_return() (v2)	*link()*	*sigpending()*
aio_suspend() (v2)	*listen() (v3)*	*sigprocmask()*
alarm()	*lseek()*	*sigqueue() (v2)*
bind() (v3)	*lstat() (v3)*	*sigset() (v2)*
cfgetispeed()	*mkdir()*	*sigsuspend()*
cfgetospeed()	*mkfifo()*	*sleep()*
cfsetispeed()	*open()*	*socket() (v3)*
cfsetospeed()	*pathconf()*	*sockatmark() (v3)*
chdir()	*pause()*	*socketpair() (v3)*
chmod()	*pipe()*	*stat()*
chown()	*poll() (v3)*	*symlink() (v3)*
clock_gettime() (v2)	*posix_trace_event() (v3)*	*sysconf()*
close()	*pselect() (v3)*	*tcdrain()*
connect() (v3)	*raise() (v2)*	*tcflow()*
creat()	*read()*	*tcflush()*
dup()	*readlink() (v3)*	*tcgetattr()*
dup2()	*recv() (v3)*	*tcgetpgrp()*
execle()	*recvfrom() (v3)*	*tcsendbreak()*
execve()	*recvmsg() (v3)*	*tcsetattr()*
fchmod() (v3)	*rename()*	*tcsetpgrp()*
fchown() (v3)	*rmdir()*	*time()*
fcntl()	*select() (v3)*	*timer_getoverrun() (v2)*
fdatasync() (v2)	*sem_post() (v2)*	*timer_gettime() (v2)*
fork()	*send() (v3)*	*timer_settime() (v2)*
fpathconf() (v2)	*sendmsg() (v3)*	*times()*
fstat()	*sendto() (v3)*	*umask()*
fsync() (v2)	*setgid()*	*uname()*
ftruncate() (v3)	*setpgid()*	*unlink()*
getegid()	*setsid()*	*utime()*
geteuid()	*setsockopt() (v3)*	*wait()*
getgid()	*setuid()*	*waitpid()*
getgroups()	*shutdown() (v3)*	*write()*
getpeername() (v3)	*sigaction()*	
getpgrp()	*sigaddset()*	

SUSv3 notes that all functions not listed in Table 21-1 are considered to be unsafe with respect to signals, but points out that a function is unsafe only when invocation of a signal handler interrupts the execution of an unsafe function, and the handler itself also calls an unsafe function. In other words, when writing signal handlers, we have two choices:

- Ensure that the code of the signal handler itself is reentrant and that it calls only async-signal-safe functions.
- Block delivery of signals while executing code in the main program that calls unsafe functions or works with global data structures also updated by the signal handler.

The problem with the second approach is that, in a complex program, it can be difficult to ensure that a signal handler will never interrupt the main program while it is calling an unsafe function. For this reason, the above rules are often simplified to the statement that we must not call unsafe functions from within a signal handler.

> If we set up the same handler function to deal with several different signals or use the SA_NODEFER flag to *sigaction()*, then a handler may interrupt itself. As a consequence, the handler may be nonreentrant if it updates global (or static) variables, even if they are not used by the main program.

Use of *errno* inside signal handlers

Because they may update *errno*, use of the functions listed in Table 21-1 can nevertheless render a signal handler nonreentrant, since they may overwrite the *errno* value that was set by a function called from the main program. The workaround is to save the value of *errno* on entry to a signal handler that uses any of the functions in Table 21-1 and restore the *errno* value on exit from the handler, as in the following example:

```
void
handler(int sig)
{
    int savedErrno;

    savedErrno = errno;

    /* Now we can execute a function that might modify errno */

    errno = savedErrno;
}
```

Use of unsafe functions in example programs in this book

Although *printf()* is not async-signal-safe, we use it in signal handlers in various example programs in this book. We do so because *printf()* provides an easy and concise way to demonstrate that a signal handler has been called, and to display the contents of relevant variables within the handler. For similar reasons, we occasionally use a few other unsafe functions in signal handlers, including other *stdio* functions and *strsignal()*.

Real-world applications should avoid calling non-async-signal-safe functions from signal handlers. To make this clear, each signal handler in the example programs that uses one of these functions is marked with a comment indicating that the usage is unsafe:

```
printf("Some message\n");            /* UNSAFE */
```

21.1.3 Global Variables and the *sig_atomic_t* Data Type

Notwithstanding reentrancy issues, it can be useful to share global variables between the main program and a signal handler. This can be safe as long as the main program correctly handles the possibility that the signal handler may change the global variable at any time. For example, one common design is to make a signal handler's sole action the setting of a global flag. This flag is periodically checked by the main program, which then takes appropriate action in response to the delivery of the signal (and clears the flag). When global variables are accessed in this way from a signal handler, we should always declare them using the volatile keyword (see Section 6.8) in order to prevent the compiler from performing optimizations that result in the variable being stored in a register.

Reading and writing global variables may involve more than one machine-language instruction, and a signal handler may interrupt the main program in the middle of such an instruction sequence. (We say that access to the variable is *nonatomic*.) For this reason, the C language standards and SUSv3 specify an integer data type, *sig_atomic_t*, for which reads and writes are guaranteed to be atomic. Thus, a global flag variable that is shared between the main program and a signal handler should be declared as follows:

```
volatile sig_atomic_t flag;
```

We show an example of the use of the *sig_atomic_t* data type in Listing 22-5, on page 466.

Note that the C increment (++) and decrement (--) operators don't fall within the guarantee provided for *sig_atomic_t*. On some hardware architectures, these operations may not be atomic (refer to Section 30.1 for more details). All that we are guaranteed to be safely allowed to do with a *sig_atomic_t* variable is set it within the signal handler, and check it in the main program (or vice versa).

C99 and SUSv3 specify that an implementation should define two constants (in <stdint.h>), SIG_ATOMIC_MIN and SIG_ATOMIC_MAX, that define the range of values that may be assigned to variables of type *sig_atomic_t*. The standards require that this range be at least −127 to 127 if *sig_atomic_t* is represented as a signed value, or 0 to 255 if it is represented as an unsigned value. On Linux, these two constants equate to the negative and positive limits for signed 32-bit integers.

21.2 Other Methods of Terminating a Signal Handler

All of the signal handlers that we have looked at so far complete by returning to the main program. However, simply returning from a signal handler sometimes isn't desirable, or in some cases, isn't even useful. (We'll see an example of where returning from a signal handler isn't useful when we discuss hardware-generated signals in Section 22.4.)

There are various other ways of terminating a signal handler:

- Use *_exit()* to terminate the process. Beforehand, the handler may carry out some cleanup actions. Note that we can't use *exit()* to terminate a signal handler, because it is not one of safe functions listed in Table 21-1. It is unsafe because it flushes *stdio* buffers prior to calling *_exit()*, as described in Section 25.1.

- Use *kill()* or *raise()* to send a signal that kills the process (i.e., a signal whose default action is process termination).

- Perform a nonlocal goto from the signal handler.

- Use the *abort()* function to terminate the process with a core dump.

The last two of these options are described in further detail in the following sections.

21.2.1 Performing a Nonlocal Goto from a Signal Handler

Section 6.8 described the use of *setjmp()* and *longjmp()* to perform a nonlocal goto from a function to one of its callers. We can also use this technique from a signal handler. This provides a way to recover after delivery of a signal caused by a hardware exception (e.g., a memory access error), and also allows us to catch a signal and return control to a particular point in a program. For example, upon receipt of a SIGINT signal (normally generated by typing *Control-C*), the shell performs a nonlocal goto to return control to its main input loop (and thus read a new command).

However, there is a problem with using the standard *longjmp()* function to exit from a signal handler. We noted earlier that, upon entry to the signal handler, the kernel automatically adds the invoking signal, as well as any signals specified in the *act.sa_mask* field, to the process signal mask, and then removes these signals from the mask when the handler does a normal return.

What happens to the signal mask if we exit the signal handler using *longjmp()*? The answer depends on the genealogy of the particular UNIX implementation. Under System V, *longjmp()* doesn't restore the signal mask, so that blocked signals are not unblocked upon leaving the handler. Linux follows the System V behavior. (This is usually not what we want, since it leaves the signal that caused invocation of the handler blocked.) Under BSD-derived implementations, *setjmp()* saves the signal mask in its *env* argument, and the saved signal mask is restored by *longjmp()*. (BSD-derived implementations also provide two other functions, *_setjmp()* and *_longjmp()*, which have the System V semantics.) In other words, we can't portably use *longjmp()* to exit a signal handler.

> If we define the _BSD_SOURCE feature test macro when compiling a program, then (the *glibc*) *setjmp()* follows the BSD semantics.

Because of this difference in the two main UNIX variants, POSIX.1-1990 chose not to specify the handling of the signal mask by *setjmp()* and *longjmp()*. Instead, it defined a pair of new functions, *sigsetjmp()* and *siglongjmp()*, that provide explicit control of the signal mask when performing a nonlocal goto.

```
#include <setjmp.h>

int sigsetjmp(sigjmp_buf env, int savesigs);
```

                    Returns 0 on initial call, nonzero on return via *siglongjmp()*

```
void siglongjmp(sigjmp_buf env, int val);
```

The *sigsetjmp()* and *siglongjmp()* functions operate similarly to *setjmp()* and *longjmp()*. The only differences are in the type of the *env* argument (*sigjmp_buf* instead of *jmp_buf*) and the extra *savesigs* argument to *sigsetjmp()*. If *savesigs* is nonzero, then the process signal mask that is current at the time of the *sigsetjmp()* call is saved in *env* and restored by a later *siglongjmp()* call specifying the same *env* argument. If *savesigs* is 0, then the process signal mask is not saved and restored.

The *longjmp()* and *siglongjmp()* functions are not listed among the async-signal-safe functions in Table 21-1. This is because calling any non-async-signal-safe function after performing a nonlocal goto carries the same risks as calling that function from within the signal handler. Furthermore, if a signal handler interrupts the main program while it is part-way through updating a data structure, and the handler exits by performing a nonlocal goto, then the incomplete update may leave that data structure in an inconsistent state. One technique that can help to avoid problems is to use *sigprocmask()* to temporarily block the signal while sensitive updates are being performed.

Example program

Listing 21-2 demonstrates the difference in signal mask handling for the two types of nonlocal gotos. This program establishes a handler for SIGINT. The program is designed to allow either *setjmp()* plus *longjmp()* or *sigsetjmp()* plus *siglongjmp()* to be used to exit the signal handler, depending on whether the program is compiled with the USE_SIGSETJMP macro defined. The program displays the current settings of the signal mask both on entry to the signal handler and after the nonlocal goto has transferred control from the handler back to the main program.

When we build the program so that *longjmp()* is used to exit the signal handler, this is what we see when we run the program:

```
$ make -s sigmask_longjmp          Default compilation causes setjmp() to be used
$ ./sigmask_longjmp
Signal mask at startup:
                <empty signal set>
Calling setjmp()
Type Control-C to generate SIGINT
Received signal 2 (Interrupt), signal mask is:
                2 (Interrupt)
After jump from handler, signal mask is:
                2 (Interrupt)
(At this point, typing Control-C again has no effect, since SIGINT is blocked)
Type Control-\ to kill the program
Quit
```

From the program output, we can see that, after a *longjmp()* from the signal handler, the signal mask remains set to the value to which it was set on entry to the signal handler.

> In the above shell session, we built the program using the makefile supplied with the source code distribution for this book. The *-s* option tells *make* not to echo the commands that it is executing. We use this option to avoid cluttering the session log. ([Mecklenburg, 2005] provides a description of the GNU *make* program.)

When we compile the same source file to build an executable that uses *siglongjmp()* to exit the handler, we see the following:

```
$ make -s sigmask_siglongjmp          Compiles using cc -DUSE_SIGSETJMP
$ ./sigmask_siglongjmp
Signal mask at startup:
                <empty signal set>
Calling sigsetjmp()
Type Control-C
Received signal 2 (Interrupt), signal mask is:
                2 (Interrupt)
After jump from handler, signal mask is:
                <empty signal set>
```

At this point, SIGINT is not blocked, because *siglongjmp()* restored the signal mask to its original state. Next, we type *Control-C* again, so that the handler is once more invoked:

```
Type Control-C
Received signal 2 (Interrupt), signal mask is:
                2 (Interrupt)
After jump from handler, signal mask is:
                <empty signal set>
Type Control-\ to kill the program
Quit
```

From the above output, we can see that *siglongjmp()* restores the signal mask to the value it had at the time of the *sigsetjmp()* call (i.e., an empty signal set).

Listing 21-2 also demonstrates a useful technique for use with a signal handler that performs a nonlocal goto. Because a signal can be generated at any time, it may actually occur before the target of the goto has been set up by *sigsetjmp()* (or *setjmp()*). To prevent this possibility (which would cause the handler to perform a nonlocal goto using an uninitialized *env* buffer), we employ a guard variable, *canJump*, to indicate whether the *env* buffer has been initialized. If *canJump* is false, then instead of doing a nonlocal goto, the handler simply returns. An alternative approach is to arrange the program code so that the call to *sigsetjmp()* (or *setjmp()*) occurs before the signal handler is established. However, in complex programs, it may be difficult to ensure that these two steps are performed in that order, and the use of a guard variable may be simpler.

Note that using #ifdef was the simplest way of writing the program in Listing 21-2 in a standards-conformant fashion. In particular, we could not have replaced the #ifdef with the following run-time check:

```
if (useSiglongjmp)
    s = sigsetjmp(senv, 1);
else
    s = setjmp(env);
if (s == 0)
    ...
```

This is not permitted because SUSv3 doesn't allow *setjmp()* and *sigsetjmp()* to be used within an assignment statement (see Section 6.8).

Listing 21-2: Performing a nonlocal goto from a signal handler

───signals/sigmask_longjmp.c
```c
#define _GNU_SOURCE        /* Get strsignal() declaration from <string.h> */
#include <string.h>
#include <setjmp.h>
#include <signal.h>
#include "signal_functions.h"           /* Declaration of printSigMask() */
#include "tlpi_hdr.h"

static volatile sig_atomic_t canJump = 0;
                        /* Set to 1 once "env" buffer has been
                           initialized by [sig]setjmp() */
#ifdef USE_SIGSETJMP
static sigjmp_buf senv;
#else
static jmp_buf env;
#endif

static void
handler(int sig)
{
    /* UNSAFE: This handler uses non-async-signal-safe functions
       (printf(), strsignal(), printSigMask(); see Section 21.1.2) */

    printf("Received signal %d (%s), signal mask is:\n", sig,
            strsignal(sig));
    printSigMask(stdout, NULL);

    if (!canJump) {
        printf("'env' buffer not yet set, doing a simple return\n");
        return;
    }

#ifdef USE_SIGSETJMP
    siglongjmp(senv, 1);
#else
    longjmp(env, 1);
#endif
}
```

```
int
main(int argc, char *argv[])
{
    struct sigaction sa;

    printSigMask(stdout, "Signal mask at startup:\n");

    sigemptyset(&sa.sa_mask);
    sa.sa_flags = 0;
    sa.sa_handler = handler;
    if (sigaction(SIGINT, &sa, NULL) == -1)
        errExit("sigaction");

#ifdef USE_SIGSETJMP
    printf("Calling sigsetjmp()\n");
    if (sigsetjmp(senv, 1) == 0)
#else
    printf("Calling setjmp()\n");
    if (setjmp(env) == 0)
#endif
        canJump = 1;                    /* Executed after [sig]setjmp() */

    else                                /* Executed after [sig]longjmp() */
        printSigMask(stdout, "After jump from handler, signal mask is:\n" );

    for (;;)                            /* Wait for signals until killed */
        pause();
}
```

─── signals/sigmask_longjmp.c

21.2.2 Terminating a Process Abnormally: *abort()*

The *abort()* function terminates the calling process and causes it to produce a core dump.

```
#include <stdlib.h>

void abort(void);
```

The *abort()* function terminates the calling process by raising a SIGABRT signal. The default action for SIGABRT is to produce a core dump file and terminate the process. The core dump file can then be used within a debugger to examine the state of the program at the time of the *abort()* call.

SUSv3 requires that *abort()* override the effect of blocking or ignoring SIGABRT. Furthermore, SUSv3 specifies that *abort()* must terminate the process unless the process catches the signal with a handler that doesn't return. This last statement requires a moment's thought. Of the methods of terminating a signal handler described in Section 21.2, the one that is relevant here is the use of a nonlocal goto to exit the handler. If this is done, then the effect of *abort()* will be nullified; otherwise, *abort()* always terminates the process. In most implementations, termination is guaranteed as follows: if the process still hasn't terminated after raising SIGABRT once (i.e., a handler catches the signal and returns, so that execution of *abort()* is resumed), *abort()* resets the handling of SIGABRT to SIG_DFL and raises a second SIGABRT, which is guaranteed to kill the process.

If *abort()* does successfully terminate the process, then it also flushes and closes *stdio* streams.

An example of the use of *abort()* is provided in the error-handling functions of Listing 3-3, on page 54.

21.3 Handling a Signal on an Alternate Stack: *sigaltstack()*

Normally, when a signal handler is invoked, the kernel creates a frame for it on the process stack. However, this may not be possible if a process attempts to extend the stack beyond the maximum possible size. For example, this may occur because the stack grows so large that it encounters a region of mapped memory (Section 48.5) or the upwardly growing heap, or it reaches the RLIMIT_STACK resource limit (Section 36.3).

When a process attempts to grow its stack beyond the maximum possible size, the kernel generates a SIGSEGV signal for the process. However, since the stack space is exhausted, the kernel can't create a frame for any SIGSEGV handler that the program may have established. Consequently, the handler is not invoked, and the process is terminated (the default action for SIGSEGV).

If we instead need to ensure that the SIGSEGV signal is handled in these circumstances, we can do the following:

1. Allocate an area of memory, called an *alternate signal stack*, to be used for the stack frame of a signal handler.
2. Use the *sigaltstack()* system call to inform the kernel of the existence of the alternate signal stack.
3. When establishing the signal handler, specify the SA_ONSTACK flag, to tell the kernel that the frame for this handler should be created on the alternate stack.

The *sigaltstack()* system call both establishes an alternate signal stack and returns information about any alternate signal stack that is already established.

```
#include <signal.h>

int sigaltstack(const stack_t *sigstack, stack_t *old_sigstack);
```
                                        Returns 0 on success, or −1 on error

The *sigstack* argument points to a structure specifying the location and attributes of the new alternate signal stack. The *old_sigstack* argument points to a structure used to return information about the previously established alternate signal stack (if there was one). Either one of these arguments can be specified as NULL. For example, we can find out about the existing alternate signal stack, without changing it, by specifying `NULL` for the *sigstack* argument. Otherwise, each of these arguments points to a structure of the following type:

```
typedef struct {
    void  *ss_sp;       /* Starting address of alternate stack */
    int    ss_flags;    /* Flags: SS_ONSTACK, SS_DISABLE */
    size_t ss_size;     /* Size of alternate stack */
} stack_t;
```

The *ss_sp* and *ss_size* fields specify the size and location of the alternate signal stack. When actually using the alternate signal stack, the kernel automatically takes care of aligning the value given in *ss_sp* to an address boundary that is suitable for the hardware architecture.

Typically, the alternate signal stack is either statically allocated or dynamically allocated on the heap. SUSv3 specifies the constant `SIGSTKSZ` to be used as a typical value when sizing the alternate stack, and `MINSIGSTKSZ` as the minimum size required to invoke a signal handler. On Linux/x86-32, these constants are defined with the values 8192 and 2048, respectively.

The kernel doesn't resize an alternate signal stack. If the stack overflows the space we have allocated for it, then chaos results (e.g., overwriting of variables beyond the limits of the stack). This is not usually a problem—because we normally use an alternate signal stack to handle the special case of the standard stack over-flowing, typically only one or a few frames are allocated on the stack. The job of the `SIGSEGV` handler is either to perform some cleanup and terminate the process or to unwind the standard stack using a nonlocal goto.

The *ss_flags* field contains one of the following values:

`SS_ONSTACK`
> If this flag is set when retrieving information about the currently estab-lished alternate signal stack (*old_sigstack*), it indicates that the process is currently executing on the alternate signal stack. Attempts to establish a new alternate signal stack while the process is already running on an alter-nate signal stack result in an error (`EPERM`) from *sigaltstack()*.

`SS_DISABLE`
> Returned in *old_sigstack*, this flag indicates that there is no currently estab-lished alternate signal stack. When specified in *sigstack*, this disables a currently established alternate signal stack.

Listing 21-3 demonstrates the establishment and use of an alternate signal stack. After establishing an alternate signal stack and a handler for `SIGSEGV`, this program calls a function that infinitely recurses, so that the stack overflows and the process is sent a `SIGSEGV` signal. When we run the program, this is what we see:

```
$ ulimit -s unlimited
$ ./t_sigaltstack
Top of standard stack is near 0xbffff6b8
Alternate stack is at          0x804a948-0x804cfff
Call     1 - top of stack near 0xbff0b3ac
Call     2 - top of stack near 0xbfe1714c
```
Many intervening lines of output removed
```
Call 2144 - top of stack near 0x4034120c
```

```
    Call 2145 - top of stack near 0x4024cfac
    Caught signal 11 (Segmentation fault)
    Top of handler stack near      0x804c860
```

In this shell session, the *ulimit* command is used to remove any RLIMIT_STACK resource limit that may have been set in the shell. We explain this resource limit in Section 36.3.

Listing 21-3: Using *sigaltstack()*

––– **signals/t_sigaltstack.c**
```
#define _GNU_SOURCE             /* Get strsignal() declaration from <string.h> */
#include <string.h>
#include <signal.h>
#include "tlpi_hdr.h"

static void
sigsegvHandler(int sig)
{
    int x;

    /* UNSAFE: This handler uses non-async-signal-safe functions
       (printf(), strsignal(), fflush(); see Section 21.1.2) */

    printf("Caught signal %d (%s)\n", sig, strsignal(sig));
    printf("Top of handler stack near      %10p\n", (void *) &x);
    fflush(NULL);

    _exit(EXIT_FAILURE);                /* Can't return after SIGSEGV */
}

static void              /* A recursive function that overflows the stack */
overflowStack(int callNum)
{
    char a[100000];                     /* Make this stack frame large */

    printf("Call %4d - top of stack near %10p\n", callNum, &a[0]);
    overflowStack(callNum+1);
}

int
main(int argc, char *argv[])
{
    stack_t sigstack;
    struct sigaction sa;
    int j;

    printf("Top of standard stack is near %10p\n", (void *) &j);

    /* Allocate alternate stack and inform kernel of its existence */

    sigstack.ss_sp = malloc(SIGSTKSZ);
    if (sigstack.ss_sp == NULL)
        errExit("malloc");
```

```
        sigstack.ss_size = SIGSTKSZ;
        sigstack.ss_flags = 0;
        if (sigaltstack(&sigstack, NULL) == -1)
            errExit("sigaltstack");
        printf("Alternate stack is at          %10p-%p\n",
                sigstack.ss_sp, (char *) sbrk(0) - 1);

        sa.sa_handler = sigsegvHandler;     /* Establish handler for SIGSEGV */
        sigemptyset(&sa.sa_mask);
        sa.sa_flags = SA_ONSTACK;           /* Handler uses alternate stack */
        if (sigaction(SIGSEGV, &sa, NULL) == -1)
            errExit("sigaction");

        overflowStack(1);
    }
```

———— signals/t_sigaltstack.c

21.4 The SA_SIGINFO Flag

Setting the SA_SIGINFO flag when establishing a handler with *sigaction()* allows the handler to obtain additional information about a signal when it is delivered. In order to obtain this information, we must declare the handler as follows:

```
void handler(int sig, siginfo_t *siginfo, void *ucontext);
```

The first argument, *sig*, is the signal number, as for a standard signal handler. The second argument, *siginfo*, is a structure used to provide the additional information about the signal. We describe this structure below. The last argument, *ucontext*, is also described below.

Since the above signal handler has a different prototype from a standard signal handler, C typing rules mean that we can't use the *sa_handler* field of the *sigaction* structure to specify the address of the handler. Instead, we must use an alternative field: *sa_sigaction*. In other words, the definition of the *sigaction* structure is somewhat more complex than was shown in Section 20.13. In full, the structure is defined as follows:

```
struct sigaction {
    union {
        void (*sa_handler)(int);
        void (*sa_sigaction)(int, siginfo_t *, void *);
    } __sigaction_handler;
    sigset_t    sa_mask;
    int         sa_flags;
    void        (*sa_restorer)(void);
};

/* Following defines make the union fields look like simple fields
   in the parent structure */

#define sa_handler   __sigaction_handler.sa_handler
#define sa_sigaction __sigaction_handler.sa_sigaction
```

The *sigaction* structure uses a union to combine the *sa_sigaction* and *sa_handler* fields. (Most other UNIX implementations similarly use a union for this purpose.) Using a union is possible because only one of these fields is required during a particular call to *sigaction()*. (However, this can lead to strange bugs if we naively expect to be able to set the *sa_handler* and *sa_sigaction* fields independently of one another, perhaps because we reuse a single *sigaction* structure in multiple *sigaction()* calls to establish handlers for different signals.)

Here is an example of the use of SA_SIGINFO to establish a signal handler:

```
struct sigaction act;

sigemptyset(&act.sa_mask);
act.sa_sigaction = handler;
act.sa_flags = SA_SIGINFO;

if (sigaction(SIGINT, &act, NULL) == -1)
    errExit("sigaction");
```

For complete examples of the use of the SA_SIGINFO flag, see Listing 22-3 (page 462) and Listing 23-5 (page 500).

The *siginfo_t* structure

The *siginfo_t* structure passed as the second argument to a signal handler that is established with SA_SIGINFO has the following form:

```
typedef struct {
    int      si_signo;      /* Signal number */
    int      si_code;       /* Signal code */
    int      si_trapno;     /* Trap number for hardware-generated signal
                               (unused on most architectures) */
    union sigval si_value;  /* Accompanying data from sigqueue() */
    pid_t    si_pid;        /* Process ID of sending process */
    uid_t    si_uid;        /* Real user ID of sender */
    int      si_errno;      /* Error number (generally unused) */
    void     *si_addr;      /* Address that generated signal
                               (hardware-generated signals only) */
    int      si_overrun;    /* Overrun count (Linux 2.6, POSIX timers) */
    int      si_timerid;    /* (Kernel-internal) Timer ID
                               (Linux 2.6, POSIX timers) */
    long     si_band;       /* Band event (SIGPOLL/SIGIO) */
    int      si_fd;         /* File descriptor (SIGPOLL/SIGIO) */
    int      si_status;     /* Exit status or signal (SIGCHLD) */
    clock_t si_utime;       /* User CPU time (SIGCHLD) */
    clock_t si_stime;       /* System CPU time (SIGCHLD) */
} siginfo_t;
```

The _POSIX_C_SOURCE feature test macro must be defined with a value greater than or equal to 199309 in order to make the declaration of the *siginfo_t* structure visible from <signal.h>.

On Linux, as on most UNIX implementations, many of the fields in the *siginfo_t* structure are combined into a union, since not all of the fields are needed for each signal. (See <bits/siginfo.h> for details.)

Upon entry to a signal handler, the fields of the *siginfo_t* structure are set as follows:

si_signo

This field is set for all signals. It contains the number of the signal causing invocation of the handler—that is, the same value as the *sig* argument to the handler.

si_code

This field is set for all signals. It contains a code providing further information about the origin of the signal, as shown in Table 21-2.

si_value

This field contains the accompanying data for a signal sent via *sigqueue()*. We describe *sigqueue()* in Section 22.8.1.

si_pid

For signals sent via *kill()* or *sigqueue()*, this field is set to the process ID of the sending process.

si_uid

For signals sent via *kill()* or *sigqueue()*, this field is set to the real user ID of the sending process. The system provides the real user ID of the sending process because that is more informative than providing the effective user ID. Consider the permission rules for sending signals described in Section 20.5: if the effective user ID grants the sender permission to send the signal, then that user ID must either be 0 (i.e., a privileged process), or be the same as the real user ID or saved set-user-ID of the receiving process. In this case, it could be useful for the receiver to know the sender's real user ID, which may be different from the effective user ID (e.g., if the sender is a set-user-ID program).

si_errno

If this field is set to a nonzero value, then it contains an error number (like *errno*) that identifies the cause of the signal. This field is generally unused on Linux.

si_addr

This field is set only for hardware-generated SIGBUS, SIGSEGV, SIGILL, and SIGFPE signals. For the SIGBUS and SIGSEGV signals, this field contains the address that caused the invalid memory reference. For the SIGILL and SIGFPE signals, this field contains the address of the program instruction that caused the signal.

The following fields, which are nonstandard Linux extensions, are set only on the delivery of a signal generated on expiration of a POSIX timer (see Section 23.6):

si_timerid

This field contains an ID that the kernel uses internally to identify the timer.

si_overrun

This field is set to the overrun count for the timer.

The following two fields are set only for the delivery of a SIGIO signal (Section 63.3):

si_band

> This field contains the "band event" value associated with the I/O event. (In versions of *glibc* up until 2.3.2, *si_band* was typed as *int*.)

si_fd

> This field contains the number of the file descriptor associated with the I/O event. This field is not specified in SUSv3, but it is present on many other implementations.

The following fields are set only for the delivery of a SIGCHLD signal (Section 26.3):

si_status

> This field contains either the exit status of the child (if *si_code* is CLD_EXITED) or the number of the signal sent to the child (i.e., the number of the signal that terminated or stopped the child, as described in Section 26.1.3).

si_utime

> This field contains the user CPU time used by the child process. In kernels before 2.6, and since 2.6.27, this is measured in system clock ticks (divide by *sysconf(_SC_CLK_TCK)*). In 2.6 kernels before 2.6.27, a bug meant that this field reported times measured in (user-configurable) jiffies (see Section 10.6). This field is not specified in SUSv3, but it is present on many other implementations.

si_stime

> This field contains the system CPU time used by the child process. See the description of the *si_utime* field. This field is not specified in SUSv3, but it is present on many other implementations.

The *si_code* field provides further information about the origin of the signal, using the values shown in Table 21-2. Not all of the signal-specific values shown in the second column of this table occur on all UNIX implementations and hardware architectures (especially in the case of the four hardware-generated signals SIGBUS, SIGSEGV, SIGILL, and SIGFPE), although all of these constants are defined on Linux and most appear in SUSv3.

Note the following additional points about the values shown in Table 21-2:

- The values SI_KERNEL and SI_SIGIO are Linux-specific. They are not specified in SUSv3 and do not appear on other UNIX implementations.
- SI_SIGIO is employed only in Linux 2.2. From kernel 2.4 onward, Linux instead employs the POLL_* constants shown in the table.

> SUSv4 specifies the *psiginfo()* function, whose purpose is similar to *psignal()* (Section 20.8). The *psiginfo()* function takes two arguments: a pointer to a *siginfo_t* structure and a message string. It prints the message string on standard error, followed by information about the signal described in the *siginfo_t* structure. The *psiginfo()* function is provided by *glibc* since version 2.10. The *glibc* implementation prints the signal description, the origin of the signal (as indicated by the *si_code* field), and, for some signals, other fields from the *siginfo_t* structure. The *psiginfo()* function is new in SUSv4, and it is not available on all systems.

Table 21-2: Values returned in the *si_code* field of the *siginfo_t* structure

Signal	*si_code* value	Origin of signal
Any	SI_ASYNCIO	Completion of an asynchronous I/O (AIO) operation
	SI_KERNEL	Sent by the kernel (e.g., a signal from terminal driver)
	SI_MESGQ	Message arrival on POSIX message queue (since Linux 2.6.6)
	SI_QUEUE	A realtime signal from a user process via *sigqueue()*
	SI_SIGIO	SIGIO signal (Linux 2.2 only)
	SI_TIMER	Expiration of a POSIX (realtime) timer
	SI_TKILL	A user process via *tkill()* or *tgkill()* (since Linux 2.4.19)
	SI_USER	A user process via *kill()*
SIGBUS	BUS_ADRALN	Invalid address alignment
	BUS_ADRERR	Nonexistent physical address
	BUS_MCEERR_AO	Hardware memory error; action optional (since Linux 2.6.32)
	BUS_MCEERR_AR	Hardware memory error; action required (since Linux 2.6.32)
	BUS_OBJERR	Object-specific hardware error
SIGCHLD	CLD_CONTINUED	Child continued by SIGCONT (since Linux 2.6.9)
	CLD_DUMPED	Child terminated abnormally, with core dump
	CLD_EXITED	Child exited
	CLD_KILLED	Child terminated abnormally, without core dump
	CLD_STOPPED	Child stopped
	CLD_TRAPPED	Traced child has stopped
SIGFPE	FPE_FLTDIV	Floating-point divide-by-zero
	FPE_FLTINV	Invalid floating-point operation
	FPE_FLTOVF	Floating-point overflow
	FPE_FLTRES	Floating-point inexact result
	FPE_FLTUND	Floating-point underflow
	FPE_INTDIV	Integer divide-by-zero
	FPE_INTOVF	Integer overflow
	FPE_SUB	Subscript out of range
SIGILL	ILL_BADSTK	Internal stack error
	ILL_COPROC	Coprocessor error
	ILL_ILLADR	Illegal addressing mode
	ILL_ILLOPC	Illegal opcode
	ILL_ILLOPN	Illegal operand
	ILL_ILLTRP	Illegal trap
	ILL_PRVOPC	Privileged opcode
	ILL_PRVREG	Privileged register
SIGPOLL/ SIGIO	POLL_ERR	I/O error
	POLL_HUP	Device disconnected
	POLL_IN	Input data available
	POLL_MSG	Input message available
	POLL_OUT	Output buffers available
	POLL_PRI	High-priority input available
SIGSEGV	SEGV_ACCERR	Invalid permissions for mapped object
	SEGV_MAPERR	Address not mapped to object

(continued)

Table 21-2: Values returned in the *si_code* field of the *siginfo_t* structure (continued)

Signal	*si_code* value	Origin of signal
SIGTRAP	TRAP_BRANCH	Process branch trap
	TRAP_BRKPT	Process breakpoint
	TRAP_HWBKPT	Hardware breakpoint/watchpoint
	TRAP_TRACE	Process trace trap

The *ucontext* argument

The final argument passed to a handler established with the SA_SIGINFO flag, *ucontext*, is a pointer to a structure of type *ucontext_t* (defined in <ucontext.h>). (SUSv3 uses a *void* pointer for this argument because it doesn't specify any of the details of the argument.) This structure provides so-called user-context information describing the process state prior to invocation of the signal handler, including the previous process signal mask and saved register values (e.g., program counter and stack pointer). This information is rarely used in signal handlers, so we don't go into further details.

> Another use of *ucontext_t* structures is with the functions *getcontext()*, *makecontext()*, *setcontext()*, and *swapcontext()*, which allow a process to retrieve, create, change, and swap execution contexts, respectively. (These operations are somewhat like *setjmp()* and *longjmp()*, but more general.) These functions can be used to implement coroutines, where the thread of execution of a process alternates between two (or more) functions. SUSv3 specifies these functions, but marks them obsolete. SUSv4 removes the specifications, and suggests that applications should be rewritten to use POSIX threads instead. The *glibc* manual provides further information about these functions.

21.5 Interruption and Restarting of System Calls

Consider the following scenario:

1. We establish a handler for some signal.
2. We make a blocking system call, for example, a *read()* from a terminal device, which blocks until input is supplied.
3. While the system call is blocked, the signal for which we established a handler is delivered, and its signal handler is invoked.

What happens after the signal handler returns? By default, the system call fails with the error EINTR ("Interrupted function"). This can be a useful feature. In Section 23.3, we'll see how to use a timer (which results in the delivery of a SIGALRM signal) to set a timeout on a blocking system call such as *read()*.

Often, however, we would prefer to continue the execution of an interrupted system call. To do this, we could use code such as the following to manually restart a system call in the event that it is interrupted by a signal handler:

```
while ((cnt = read(fd, buf, BUF_SIZE)) == -1 && errno == EINTR)
    continue;                       /* Do nothing loop body */

if (cnt == -1)                      /* read() failed with other than EINTR */
    errExit("read");
```

If we frequently write code such as the above, it can be useful to define a macro such as the following:

```
#define NO_EINTR(stmt) while ((stmt) == -1 && errno == EINTR);
```

Using this macro, we can rewrite the earlier *read()* call as follows:

```
NO_EINTR(cnt = read(fd, buf, BUF_SIZE));

if (cnt == -1)                  /* read() failed with other than EINTR */
    errExit("read");
```

> The GNU C library provides a (nonstandard) macro with the same purpose as our NO_EINTR() macro in <unistd.h>. The macro is called TEMP_FAILURE_RETRY() and is made available if the _GNU_SOURCE feature test macro is defined.

Even if we employ a macro like NO_EINTR(), having signal handlers interrupt system calls can be inconvenient, since we must add code to each blocking system call (assuming that we want to restart the call in each case). Instead, we can specify the SA_RESTART flag when establishing the signal handler with *sigaction()*, so that system calls are automatically restarted by the kernel on the process's behalf. This means that we don't need to handle a possible EINTR error return for these system calls.

The SA_RESTART flag is a per-signal setting. In other words, we can allow handlers for some signals to interrupt blocking system calls, while others permit automatic restarting of system calls.

System calls (and library functions) for which SA_RESTART is effective

Unfortunately, not all blocking system calls automatically restart as a result of specifying SA_RESTART. The reasons for this are partly historical:

- Restarting of system calls was introduced in 4.2BSD, and covered interrupted calls to *wait()* and *waitpid()*, as well as the following I/O system calls: *read()*, *readv()*, *write()*, *writev()*, and blocking *ioctl()* operations. The I/O system calls are interruptible, and hence automatically restarted by SA_RESTART, only when operating on a "slow" device. Slow devices include terminals, pipes, FIFOs, and sockets. On these file types, various I/O operations may block. (By contrast, disk files don't fall into the category of slow devices, because disk I/O operations generally can be immediately satisfied via the buffer cache. If a disk I/O is required, the kernel puts the process to sleep until the I/O completes.)
- A number of other blocking system calls are derived from System V, which did not initially provide for restarting of system calls.

On Linux, the following blocking system calls (and library functions layered on top of system calls) are automatically restarted if interrupted by a signal handler established using the SA_RESTART flag:

- The system calls used to wait for a child process (Section 26.1): *wait()*, *waitpid()*, *wait3()*, *wait4()*, and *waitid()*.
- The I/O system calls *read()*, *readv()*, *write()*, *writev()*, and *ioctl()* when applied to "slow" devices. In cases where data has already been partially transferred at the

time of signal delivery, the input and output system calls will be interrupted, but return a success status: an integer indicating how many bytes were successfully transferred.

- The *open()* system call, in cases where it can block (e.g., when opening FIFOs, as described in Section 44.7).

- Various system calls used with sockets: *accept()*, *accept4()*, *connect()*, *send()*, *sendmsg()*, *sendto()*, *recv()*, *recvfrom()*, and *recvmsg()*. (On Linux, these system calls are not automatically restarted if a timeout has been set on the socket using *setsockopt()*. See the *signal(7)* manual page for details.)

- The system calls used for I/O on POSIX message queues: *mq_receive()*, *mq_timedreceive()*, *mq_send()*, and *mq_timedsend()*.

- The system calls and library functions used to place file locks: *flock()*, *fcntl()*, and *lockf()*.

- The FUTEX_WAIT operation of the Linux-specific *futex()* system call.

- The *sem_wait()* and *sem_timedwait()* functions used to decrement a POSIX semaphore. (On some UNIX implementations, *sem_wait()* *is* restarted if the SA_RESTART flag is specified.)

- The functions used to synchronize POSIX threads: *pthread_mutex_lock()*, *pthread_mutex_trylock()*, *pthread_mutex_timedlock()*, *pthread_cond_wait()*, and *pthread_cond_timedwait()*.

In kernels before 2.6.22, *futex()*, *sem_wait()*, and *sem_timedwait()* always failed with the error EINTR when interrupted, regardless of the setting of the SA_RESTART flag.

The following blocking system calls (and library functions layered on top of system calls) are never automatically restarted (even if SA_RESTART is specified):

- The *poll()*, *ppoll()*, *select()*, and *pselect()* I/O multiplexing calls. (SUSv3 explicitly states that the behavior of *select()* and *pselect()* when interrupted by a signal handler is unspecified, regardless of the setting of SA_RESTART.)

- The Linux-specific *epoll_wait()* and *epoll_pwait()* system calls.

- The Linux-specific *io_getevents()* system call.

- The blocking system calls used with System V message queues and semaphores: *semop()*, *semtimedop()*, *msgrcv()*, and *msgsnd()*. (Although System V did not originally provide automatic restarting of system calls, on some UNIX implementations, these system calls *are* restarted if the SA_RESTART flag is specified.)

- A *read()* from an *inotify* file descriptor.

- The system calls and library functions designed to suspend execution of a program for a specified period: *sleep()*, *nanosleep()*, and *clock_nanosleep()*.

- The system calls designed specifically to wait until a signal is delivered: *pause()*, *sigsuspend()*, *sigtimedwait()*, and *sigwaitinfo()*.

Modifying the SA_RESTART flag for a signal

The *siginterrupt()* function changes the SA_RESTART setting associated with a signal.

```
#include <signal.h>

int siginterrupt(int sig, int flag);
```

                                        Returns 0 on success, or -1 on error

If *flag* is true (1), then a handler for the signal *sig* will interrupt blocking system
calls. If *flag* is false (0), then blocking system calls will be restarted after execution
of a handler for *sig*.

The *siginterrupt()* function works by using *sigaction()* to fetch a copy of the signal's
current disposition, tweaking the SA_RESTART flag in the returned *oldact* structure,
and then calling *sigaction()* once more to update the signal's disposition.

SUSv4 marks *siginterrupt()* obsolete, recommending the use of *sigaction()*
instead for this purpose.

Unhandled stop signals can generate EINTR for some Linux system calls

On Linux, certain blocking system calls can return EINTR even in the absence of a
signal handler. This can occur if the system call is blocked and the process is
stopped by a signal (SIGSTOP, SIGTSTP, SIGTTIN, or SIGTTOU), and then resumed by delivery
of a SIGCONT signal.

The following system calls and functions exhibit this behavior: *epoll_pwait()*,
epoll_wait(), *read()* from an *inotify* file descriptor, *semop()*, *semtimedop()*, *sigtimedwait()*,
and *sigwaitinfo()*.

In kernels before 2.6.24, *poll()* also exhibited this behavior, as did *sem_wait()*,
sem_timedwait(), *futex(FUTEX_WAIT)*, in kernels before 2.6.22, *msgrcv()* and *msgsnd()*
in kernels before 2.6.9, and *nanosleep()* in Linux 2.4 and earlier.

In Linux 2.4 and earlier, *sleep()* can also be interrupted in this manner, but,
instead of returning an error, it returns the number of remaining unslept seconds.

The upshot of this behavior is that if there is a chance that our program may be
stopped and restarted by signals, then we may need to include code to restart these
system calls, even in a program that doesn't install handlers for the stop signals.

21.6 Summary

In this chapter, we considered a range of factors that affect the operation and
design of signal handlers.

Because signals are not queued, a signal handler must sometimes be coded to
deal with the possibility that multiple events of a particular type have occurred,
even though only one signal was delivered. The issue of reentrancy affects how we
can update global variables and limits the set of functions that we can safely call
from a signal handler.

Instead of returning, a signal handler can terminate in a variety of other ways,
including calling _exit(), terminating the process by sending a signal (*kill()*, *raise()*,
or *abort()*), or performing a nonlocal goto. Using *sigsetjmp()* and *siglongjmp()* provides a program with explicit control of the treatment of the process signal mask
when a nonlocal goto is performed.

We can use *sigaltstack()* to define an alternate signal stack for a process. This is an area of memory that is used instead of the standard process stack when invoking a signal handler. An alternate signal stack is useful in cases where the standard stack has been exhausted by growing too large (at which point the kernel sends a SIGSEGV signal to the process).

The *sigaction()* SA_SIGINFO flag allows us to establish a signal handler that receives additional information about a signal. This information is supplied via a *siginfo_t* structure whose address is passed as an argument to the signal handler.

When a signal handler interrupts a blocked system call, the system call fails with the error EINTR. We can take advantage of this behavior to, for example, set a timer on a blocking system call. Interrupted system calls can be manually restarted if desired. Alternatively, establishing the signal handler with the *sigaction()* SA_RESTART flag causes many (but not all) system calls to be automatically restarted.

Further information

See the sources listed in Section 20.15.

21.7 Exercise

21-1. Implement *abort()*.

22

SIGNALS: ADVANCED FEATURES

This chapter completes the discussion of signals that we began in Chapter 20, covering a number of more advanced topics, including the following:

- core dump files;
- special cases regarding signal delivery, disposition, and handling;
- synchronous and asynchronous generation of signals;
- when and in what order signals are delivered;
- realtime signals;
- the use of *sigsuspend()* to set the process signal mask and wait for a signal to arrive;
- the use of *sigwaitinfo()* (and *sigtimedwait()*) to synchronously wait for a signal to arrive;
- the use of *signalfd()* to receive a signal via a file descriptor; and
- the older BSD and System V signal APIs.

22.1 Core Dump Files

Certain signals cause a process to create a core dump and terminate (Table 20-1, page 396). A core dump is a file containing a memory image of the process at the time it terminated. (The term *core* derives from an old memory technology.) This memory image can be loaded into a debugger in order to examine the state of a program's code and data at the moment when the signal arrived.

One way of causing a program to produce a core dump is to type the *quit* character (usually *Control-*), which causes the SIGQUIT signal to be generated:

```
$ ulimit -c unlimited                      Explained in main text
$ sleep 30
Type Control-\
Quit (core dumped)
$ ls -l core                               Shows core dump file for sleep(1)
-rw-------   1 mtk    users     57344 Nov 30 13:39 core
```

In this example, the message *Quit (core dumped)* is printed by the shell, which detects that its child (the process running *sleep*) was killed by SIGQUIT and did a core dump.

The core dump file was created in the working directory of the process, with the name core. This is the default location and name for a core dump file; shortly, we explain how these defaults can be changed.

> Many implementations provide a tool (e.g., *gcore* on FreeBSD and Solaris) to obtain a core dump of a running process. Similar functionality is available on Linux by attaching to a running process using *gdb* and then using the *gcore* command.

Circumstances in which core dump files are not produced

A core dump is not produced in the following circumstances:

- The process doesn't have permission to write the core dump file. This could happen because the process doesn't have write permission for the directory in which the core dump file is to be created, or because a file with the same name already exists and either is not writable or is not a regular file (e.g., it is a directory or a symbolic link).

- A regular file with the same name already exists, and is writable, but there is more than one (hard) link to the file.

- The directory in which the core dump file is to be created doesn't exist.

- The process resource limit on the size of a core dump file is set to 0. This limit, RLIMIT_CORE, is discussed in more detail in Section 36.3. In the example above, we used the *ulimit* command (*limit* in the C shell) to ensure that there is no limit on the size of core files.

- The process resource limit on the size of a file that may be produced by the process is set to 0. We describe this limit, RLIMIT_FSIZE, in Section 36.3.

- The binary executable file that the process is executing doesn't have read permission enabled. This prevents users from using a core dump to obtain a copy of the code of a program that they would otherwise be unable to read.

- The file system on which the current working directory resides is mounted read-only, is full, or has run out of i-nodes. Alternatively, the user has reached their quota limit on the file system.

- Set-user-ID (set-group-ID) programs executed by a user other than the file owner (group owner) don't generate core dumps. This prevents malicious users from dumping the memory of a secure program and examining it for sensitive information such as passwords.

> Using the PR_SET_DUMPABLE operation of the Linux-specific *prctl()* system call, we can set the *dumpable* flag for a process, so that when a set-user-ID (set-group-ID) program is run by a user other than the owner (group owner), a core dump can be produced. The PR_SET_DUMPABLE operation is available from Linux 2.4 onward. See the *prctl(2)* manual page for further details. In addition, since kernel 2.6.13, the /proc/sys/fs/suid_dumpable file provides system-wide control over whether or not set-user-ID and set-group-ID processes produce core dumps. For details, see the *proc(5)* manual page.

Since kernel 2.6.23, the Linux-specific /proc/*PID*/coredump_filter can be used on a per-process basis to determine which types of memory mappings are written to a core dump file. (We explain memory mappings in Chapter 49.) The value in this file is a mask of four bits corresponding to the four types of memory mappings: private anonymous mappings, private file mappings, shared anonymous mappings, and shared file mappings. The default value of the file provides traditional Linux behavior: only private anonymous and shared anonymous mappings are dumped. See the *core(5)* manual page for further details.

Naming the core dump file: /proc/sys/kernel/core_pattern

Starting with Linux 2.6, the format string contained in the Linux-specific /proc/sys/kernel/core_pattern file controls the naming of all core dump files produced on the system. By default, this file contains the string *core*. A privileged user can define this file to include any of the format specifiers shown in Table 22-1. These format specifiers are replaced by the value indicated in the right column of the table. Additionally, the string may include slashes (/). In other words, we can control not just the name of the core file, but also the (absolute or relative) directory in which it is created. After all format specifiers have been replaced, the resulting pathname string is truncated to a maximum of 128 characters (64 characters before Linux 2.6.19).

Since kernel 2.6.19, Linux supports an additional syntax in the core_pattern file. If this file contains a string starting with the pipe symbol (|), then the remaining characters in the file are interpreted as a program—with optional arguments that may include the % specifiers shown in Table 22-1—that is to be executed when a process dumps core. The core dump is written to the standard input of that program instead of to a file. See the *core(5)* manual page for further details.

> Some other UNIX implementations provide facilities similar to core_pattern. For example, in BSD derivatives, the program name is appended to the filename, thus core.*progname*. Solaris provides a tool (*coreadm*) that allows the user to choose the filename and directory where core dump files are placed.

Table 22-1: Format specifiers for `/proc/sys/kernel/core_pattern`

Specifier	Replaced by
%c	Core file size soft resource limit (bytes; since Linux 2.6.24)
%e	Executable filename (without path prefix)
%g	Real group ID of dumped process
%h	Name of host system
%p	Process ID of dumped process
%s	Number of signal that terminated process
%t	Time of dump, in seconds since the Epoch
%u	Real user ID of dumped process
%%	A single % character

22.2 Special Cases for Delivery, Disposition, and Handling

For certain signals, special rules apply regarding delivery, disposition, and handling, as described in this section.

SIGKILL and SIGSTOP

It is not possible to change the default action for SIGKILL, which always terminates a process, and SIGSTOP, which always stops a process. Both *signal()* and *sigaction()* return an error on attempts to change the disposition of these signals. These two signals also can't be blocked. This is a deliberate design decision. Disallowing changes to the default actions of these signals means that they can always be used to kill or stop a runaway process.

SIGCONT and stop signals

As noted earlier, the SIGCONT signal is used to continue a process previously stopped by one of the stop signals (SIGSTOP, SIGTSTP, SIGTTIN, and SIGTTOU). Because of their unique purpose, in certain situations the kernel deals with these signals differently from other signals.

If a process is currently stopped, the arrival of a SIGCONT signal always causes the process to resume, even if the process is currently blocking or ignoring SIGCONT. This feature is necessary because it would otherwise be impossible to resume such stopped processes. (If the stopped process was blocking SIGCONT, and had established a handler for SIGCONT, then, after the process is resumed, the handler is invoked only when SIGCONT is later unblocked.)

> If any other signal is sent to a stopped process, the signal is not actually delivered to the process until it is resumed via receipt of a SIGCONT signal. The one exception is SIGKILL, which always kills a process—even one that is currently stopped.

Whenever SIGCONT is delivered to a process, any pending stop signals for the process are discarded (i.e., the process never sees them). Conversely, if any of the stop signals is delivered to a process, then any pending SIGCONT signal is automatically discarded. These steps are taken in order to prevent the action of a SIGCONT signal from being subsequently undone by a stop signal that was actually sent beforehand, and vice versa.

Don't change the disposition of ignored terminal-generated signals

If, at the time it was execed, a program finds that the disposition of a terminal-generated signal has been set to SIG_IGN (ignore), then generally the program should not attempt to change the disposition of the signal. This is not a rule enforced by the system, but rather a convention that should be followed when writing applications. We explain the reasons for this in Section 34.7.3. The signals for which this convention is relevant are SIGHUP, SIGINT, SIGQUIT, SIGTTIN, SIGTTOU, and SIGTSTP.

22.3 Interruptible and Uninterruptible Process Sleep States

We need to add a proviso to our earlier statement that SIGKILL and SIGSTOP always act immediately on a process. At various times, the kernel may put a process to sleep, and two sleep states are distinguished:

- TASK_INTERRUPTIBLE: The process is waiting for some event. For example, it is waiting for terminal input, for data to be written to a currently empty pipe, or for the value of a System V semaphore to be increased. A process may spend an arbitrary length of time in this state. If a signal is generated for a process in this state, then the operation is interrupted and the process is woken up by the delivery of a signal. When listed by *ps(1)*, processes in the TASK_INTERRUPTIBLE state are marked by the letter *S* in the STAT (process state) field.

- TASK_UNINTERRUPTIBLE: The process is waiting on certain special classes of event, such as the completion of a disk I/O. If a signal is generated for a process in this state, then the signal is not delivered until the process emerges from this state. Processes in the TASK_UNINTERRUPTIBLE state are listed by *ps(1)* with a *D* in the STAT field.

Because a process normally spends only very brief periods in the TASK_UNINTERRUPTIBLE state, the fact that a signal is delivered only when the process leaves this state is invisible. However, in rare circumstances, a process may remain hung in this state, perhaps as the result of a hardware failure, an NFS problem, or a kernel bug. In such cases, SIGKILL won't terminate the hung process. If the underlying problem can't otherwise be resolved, then we must restart the system in order to eliminate the process.

The TASK_INTERRUPTIBLE and TASK_UNINTERRUPTIBLE states are present on most UNIX implementations. Starting with kernel 2.6.25, Linux adds a third state to address the hanging process problem just described:

- TASK_KILLABLE: This state is like TASK_UNINTERRUPTIBLE, but wakes the process if a fatal signal (i.e., one that would kill the process) is received. By converting relevant parts of the kernel code to use this state, various scenarios where a hung process requires a system restart can be avoided. Instead, the process can be killed by sending it a fatal signal. The first piece of kernel code to be converted to use TASK_KILLABLE was NFS.

22.4 Hardware-Generated Signals

SIGBUS, SIGFPE, SIGILL, and SIGSEGV can be generated as a consequence of a hardware exception or, less usually, by being sent by *kill()*. In the case of a hardware exception, SUSv3 specifies that the behavior of a process is undefined if it returns from a handler for the signal, or if it ignores or blocks the signal. The reasons for this are as follows:

- *Returning from the signal handler*: Suppose that a machine-language instruction generates one of these signals, and a signal handler is consequently invoked. On normal return from the handler, the program attempts to resume execution at the point where it was interrupted. But this is the very instruction that generated the signal in the first place, so the signal is generated once more. The consequence is usually that the program goes into an infinite loop, repeatedly calling the signal handler.

- *Ignoring the signal*: It makes little sense to ignore a hardware-generated signal, as it is unclear how a program should continue execution after, say, an arithmetic exception. When one of these signals is generated as a consequence of a hardware exception, Linux forces its delivery, even if the program has requested that the signal be ignored.

- *Blocking the signal*: As with the previous case, it makes little sense to block a hardware-generated signal, as it is unclear how a program should then continue execution. On Linux 2.4 and earlier, the kernel simply ignores attempts to block a hardware-generated signal; the signal is delivered to the process anyway, and then either terminates the process or is caught by a signal handler, if one has been established. Starting with Linux 2.6, if the signal is blocked, then the process is always immediately killed by that signal, even if the process has installed a handler for the signal. (The rationale for the Linux 2.6 change in the treatment of blocked hardware-generated signals was that the Linux 2.4 behavior hid bugs and could cause deadlocks in threaded programs.)

> The signals/demo_SIGFPE.c program in the source code distribution for this book can be used to demonstrate the results of ignoring or blocking SIGFPE or catching the signal with a handler that performs a normal return.

The correct way to deal with hardware-generated signals is either to accept their default action (process termination) or to write handlers that don't perform a normal return. Other than returning normally, a handler can complete execution by calling *_exit()* to terminate the process or by calling *siglongjmp()* (Section 21.2.1) to ensure that control passes to some point in the program other than the instruction that generated the signal.

22.5 Synchronous and Asynchronous Signal Generation

We have already seen that a process generally can't predict when it will receive a signal. We now need to qualify this observation by distinguishing between *synchronous* and *asynchronous* signal generation.

The model we have implicitly considered so far is *asynchronous* signal generation, in which the signal is sent either by another process or generated by the kernel for an event that occurs independently of the execution of the process (e.g., the user types the *interrupt* character or a child of this process terminates). For asynchronously generated signals, the earlier statement that a process can't predict when the signal will be delivered holds true.

However, in some cases, a signal is generated while the process itself is executing. We have already seen two examples of this:

• The hardware-generated signals (SIGBUS, SIGFPE, SIGILL, SIGSEGV, and SIGEMT) described in Section 22.4 are generated as a consequence of executing a specific machine-language instruction that results in a hardware exception.

• A process can use *raise()*, *kill()*, or *killpg()* to send a signal to itself.

In these cases, the generation of the signal is *synchronous*—the signal is delivered immediately (unless it is blocked, but see Section 22.4 for a discussion of what happens when blocking hardware-generated signals). In other words, the earlier statement about the unpredictability of the delivery of a signal doesn't apply. For synchronously generated signals, delivery is predictable and reproducible.

Note that synchronicity is an attribute of how a signal is generated, rather than of the signal itself. All signals may be generated synchronously (e.g., when a process sends itself a signal using *kill()*) or asynchronously (e.g., when the signal is sent by another process using *kill()*).

22.6 Timing and Order of Signal Delivery

As the first topic of this section, we consider exactly when a pending signal is delivered. We then consider what happens if multiple pending blocked signals are simultaneously unblocked.

When is a signal delivered?

As noted in Section 22.5, synchronously generated signals are delivered immediately. For example, a hardware exception triggers an immediate signal, and when a process sends itself a signal using *raise()*, the signal is delivered before the *raise()* call returns.

When a signal is generated asynchronously, there may be a (small) delay while the signal is pending between the time when it was generated and the time it is actually delivered, even if we have not blocked the signal. The reason for this is that the kernel delivers a pending signal to a process only at the next switch from kernel mode to user mode while executing that process. In practice, this means the signal is delivered at one of the following times:

• when the process is rescheduled after it earlier timed out (i.e., at the start of a time slice); or

• at completion of a system call (delivery of the signal may cause a blocking system call to complete prematurely).

Order of delivery of multiple unblocked signals

If a process has multiple pending signals that are unblocked using *sigprocmask()*, then all of these signals are immediately delivered to the process.

As currently implemented, the Linux kernel delivers the signals in ascending order. For example, if pending SIGINT (signal 2) and SIGQUIT (signal 3) signals were both simultaneously unblocked, then the SIGINT signal would be delivered before SIGQUIT, regardless of the order in which the two signals were generated.

We can't, however, rely on (standard) signals being delivered in any particular order, since SUSv3 says that the delivery order of multiple signals is implementation-defined. (This statement applies only to standard signals. As we'll see in Section 22.8, the standards governing realtime signals do provide guarantees about the order in which multiple unblocked realtime signals are delivered.)

When multiple unblocked signals are awaiting delivery, if a switch between kernel mode and user mode occurs during the execution of a signal handler, then the execution of that handler will be interrupted by the invocation of a second signal handler (and so on), as shown in Figure 22-1.

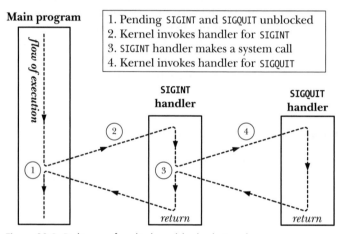

Figure 22-1: Delivery of multiple unblocked signals

22.7 Implementation and Portability of *signal()*

In this section, we show how to implement *signal()* using *sigaction()*. The implementation is straightforward, but needs to account for the fact that, historically and across different UNIX implementations, *signal()* has had different semantics. In particular, early implementations of signals were unreliable, meaning that:

- On entry to a signal handler, the disposition of the signal was reset to its default. (This corresponds to the SA_RESETHAND flag described in Section 20.13.) In order to have the signal handler invoked again for a subsequent delivery of the same signal, the programmer needed to make a call to *signal()* from within the handler to explicitly reestablish the handler. The problem in this scenario is that there is a small window of time between entering the signal handler and reestablishment of the handler, during which, if the signal arrives a second time, it would be processed according to its default disposition.

- Delivery of further occurrences of a signal was not blocked during execution of a signal handler. (This corresponds to the SA_NODEFER flag described in Section 20.13.) This meant that if the signal was delivered again while the handler was still executing, then the handler would be recursively invoked. Given a sufficiently rapid stream of signals, the resulting recursive invocations of the handler could overflow the stack.

As well as being unreliable, early UNIX implementations did not provide automatic restarting of system calls (i.e., the behavior described for the SA_RESTART flag in Section 21.5).

The 4.2BSD reliable signals implementation rectified these limitations, and several other UNIX implementations followed suit. However, the older semantics live on today in the System V implementation of *signal()*, and even contemporary standards such as SUSv3 and C99 leave these aspects of *signal()* deliberately unspecified.

Tying the above information together, we implement *signal()* as shown in Listing 22-1. By default, this implementation provides the modern signal semantics. If compiled with *–DOLD_SIGNAL*, then it provides the earlier unreliable signal semantics and doesn't enable automatic restarting of system calls.

Listing 22-1: An implementation of *signal()*

———————————————————————————————— signals/signal.c

```
#include <signal.h>

typedef void (*sighandler_t)(int);

sighandler_t
signal(int sig, sighandler_t handler)
{
    struct sigaction newDisp, prevDisp;

    newDisp.sa_handler = handler;
    sigemptyset(&newDisp.sa_mask);
#ifdef OLD_SIGNAL
    newDisp.sa_flags = SA_RESETHAND | SA_NODEFER;
#else
    newDisp.sa_flags = SA_RESTART;
#endif

    if (sigaction(sig, &newDisp, &prevDisp) == -1)
        return SIG_ERR;
    else
        return prevDisp.sa_handler;
}
```

———————————————————————————————— signals/signal.c

Some *glibc* details

The *glibc* implementation of the *signal()* library function has changed over time. In newer versions of the library (*glibc 2* and later), the modern semantics are provided by default. In older versions of the library, the earlier unreliable (System V-compatible) semantics are provided.

> The Linux kernel contains an implementation of *signal()* as a system call. This implementation provides the older, unreliable semantics. However, *glibc* bypasses this system call by providing a *signal()* library function that calls *sigaction()*.

If we want to obtain unreliable signal semantics with modern versions of *glibc*, we can explicitly replace our calls to *signal()* with calls to the (nonstandard) *sysv_signal()* function.

```
#define _GNU_SOURCE
#include <signal.h>

void ( *sysv_signal(int sig, void (*handler)(int)) ) (int);
```
                    Returns previous signal disposition on success, or SIG_ERR on error

The *sysv_signal()* function takes the same arguments as *signal()*.

If the _BSD_SOURCE feature test macro is not defined when compiling a program, *glibc* implicitly redefines all calls to *signal()* to be calls to *sysv_signal()*, meaning that *signal()* has unreliable semantics. By default, _BSD_SOURCE *is* defined, but it is disabled (unless also explicitly defined) if other feature test macros such as _SVID_SOURCE or _XOPEN_SOURCE are defined when compiling a program.

sigaction() is the preferred API for establishing a signal handler

Because of the System V versus BSD (and old versus recent *glibc*) portability issues described above, it is good practice always to use *sigaction()*, rather than *signal()*, to establish signal handlers. We follow this practice throughout the remainder of this book. (An alternative is to write our own version of *signal()*, probably similar to Listing 22-1, specifying exactly the flags that we require, and employ that version with our applications.) Note, however, that it is portable (and shorter) to use *signal()* to set the disposition of a signal to SIG_IGN or SIG_DFL, and we'll often use *signal()* for that purpose.

22.8 Realtime Signals

Realtime signals were defined in POSIX.1b to remedy a number of limitations of standard signals. They have the following advantages over standard signals:

- Realtime signals provide an increased range of signals that can be used for application-defined purposes. Only two standard signals are freely available for application-defined purposes: SIGUSR1 and SIGUSR2.

- Realtime signals are queued. If multiple instances of a realtime signal are sent to a process, then the signal is delivered multiple times. By contrast, if we send further instances of a standard signal that is already pending for a process, that signal is delivered only once.

- When sending a realtime signal, it is possible to specify data (an integer or pointer value) that accompanies the signal. The signal handler in the receiving process can retrieve this data.

- The order of delivery of different realtime signals is guaranteed. If multiple different realtime signals are pending, then the lowest-numbered signal is delivered first. In other words, signals are prioritized, with lower-numbered signals having higher priority. When multiple signals of the same type are queued, they are delivered—along with their accompanying data—in the order in which they were sent.

SUSv3 requires that an implementation provide a minimum of _POSIX_RTSIG_MAX (defined as 8) different realtime signals. The Linux kernel defines 33 different realtime signals, numbered from 32 to 64. The <limits.h> header file defines the constant RTSIG_MAX to indicate the number of available realtime signals, and the constants SIGRTMIN and SIGRTMAX to indicate the lowest and highest available realtime signal numbers.

> On systems employing the LinuxThreads threading implementation, SIGRTMIN is defined as 35 (rather than 32) to allow for the fact that LinuxThreads makes internal use of the first three realtime signals. On systems employing the NPTL threading implementation, SIGRTMIN is defined as 34 to allow for the fact that NPTL makes internal use of the first two realtime signals.

Realtime signals are not individually identified by different constants in the manner of standard signals. However, an application should not hard-code integer values for them, since the range used for realtime signals varies across UNIX implementations. Instead, a realtime signal number can be referred to by adding a value to SIGRTMIN; for example, the expression *(SIGRTMIN + 1)* refers to the second realtime signal.

Be aware that SUSv3 doesn't require SIGRTMAX and SIGRTMIN to be simple integer values. They may be defined as functions (as they are on Linux). This means that we can't write code for the preprocessor such as the following:

```
#if SIGRTMIN+100 > SIGRTMAX            /* WRONG! */
#error "Not enough realtime signals"
#endif
```

Instead, we must perform equivalent checks at run time.

Limits on the number of queued realtime signals

Queuing realtime signals (with associated data) requires that the kernel maintain data structures listing the signals queued to each process. Since these data structures consume kernel memory, the kernel places limits on the number of realtime signals that may be queued.

SUSv3 allows an implementation to place an upper limit on the number of realtime signals (of all types) that may be queued by a process, and requires that this limit be at least _POSIX_SIGQUEUE_MAX (defined as 32). An implementation can define the constant SIGQUEUE_MAX to indicate the number of realtime signals it allows to be queued. It can also make this information available through the following call:

```
lim = sysconf(_SC_SIGQUEUE_MAX);
```

In systems with *glibc* versions before 2.4, this call returns –1. Since *glibc* 2.4, the return value depends on the kernel version. Before Linux 2.6.8, the call returns the value in the Linux-specific /proc/sys/kernel/rtsig-max file. This file defines a system-wide limit on the number of realtime signals that may be queued to all processes. The default value is 1024, but a privileged process can change it. The Linux-specific /proc/sys/kernel/rtsig-nr file shows the number of currently queued realtime signals.

Starting with Linux 2.6.8, these /proc files disappear. In their place, the RLIMIT_SIGPENDING resource limit (Section 36.3) limits the number of signals that can be queued to all processes owned by a particular real user ID. Since *glibc* 2.10, the *sysconf()* call returns the RLIMIT_SIGPENDING limit. (The SigQ field of the Linux-specific /proc/*PID*/status file displays the number of realtime signals pending for a process.)

Using realtime signals

In order for a pair of processes to send and receive realtime signals, SUSv3 requires the following:

- The sending process sends the signal plus its accompanying data using the *sigqueue()* system call.

  > A realtime signal can also be sent using *kill()*, *killpg()*, and *raise()*. However, SUSv3 leaves it as implementation-dependent whether realtime signals sent using these interfaces are queued. On Linux, these interfaces do queue real-time signals, but on many other UNIX implementations, they do not.

- The receiving process establishes a handler for the signal using a call to *sigaction()* that specifies the SA_SIGINFO flag. This causes the signal handler to be invoked with additional arguments, one of which includes the data accompanying the realtime signal.

  > On Linux, it is possible to queue realtime signals even if the receiving process doesn't specify the SA_SIGINFO flag when establishing the signal handler (although it is not then possible to obtain the data associated with the signal in this case). However, SUSv3 doesn't require implementations to guarantee this behavior, so we can't portably rely on it.

22.8.1 Sending Realtime Signals

The *sigqueue()* system call sends the realtime signal specified by *sig* to the process specified by *pid*.

```
#define _POSIX_C_SOURCE 199309
#include <signal.h>

int sigqueue(pid_t pid, int sig, const union sigval value);
```
                                        Returns 0 on success, or –1 on error

The same permissions are required to send a signal using *sigqueue()* as are required with *kill()* (see Section 20.5). A null signal (i.e., signal 0) can be sent, with the same meaning as for *kill()*. (Unlike *kill()*, we can't use *sigqueue()* to send a signal to an entire process group by specifying a negative value in *pid*.)

Listing 22-2: Using *sigqueue()* to send realtime signals

── signals/t_sigqueue.c

```
#define _POSIX_C_SOURCE 199309
#include <signal.h>
#include "tlpi_hdr.h"

int
main(int argc, char *argv[])
{
    int sig, numSigs, j, sigData;
    union sigval sv;

    if (argc < 4 || strcmp(argv[1], "--help") == 0)
        usageErr("%s pid sig-num data [num-sigs]\n", argv[0]);

    /* Display our PID and UID, so that they can be compared with the
       corresponding fields of the siginfo_t argument supplied to the
       handler in the receiving process */

    printf("%s: PID is %ld, UID is %ld\n", argv[0],
            (long) getpid(), (long) getuid());

    sig = getInt(argv[2], 0, "sig-num");
    sigData = getInt(argv[3], GN_ANY_BASE, "data");
    numSigs = (argc > 4) ? getInt(argv[4], GN_GT_0, "num-sigs") : 1;

    for (j = 0; j < numSigs; j++) {
        sv.sival_int = sigData + j;
        if (sigqueue(getLong(argv[1], 0, "pid"), sig, sv) == -1)
            errExit("sigqueue %d", j);
    }

    exit(EXIT_SUCCESS);
}
```

── signals/t_sigqueue.c

The *value* argument specifies the data to accompany the signal. This argument has the following form:

```
union sigval {
    int    sival_int;      /* Integer value for accompanying data */
    void *sival_ptr;       /* Pointer value for accompanying data */
};
```

The interpretation of this argument is application-dependent, as is the choice of whether to set the *sival_int* or the *sival_ptr* field of the union. The *sival_ptr* field is seldom useful with *sigqueue()*, since a pointer value that is useful in one process is rarely meaningful in another process. However, this field is useful in other functions that employ *sigval* unions, as we'll see when we consider POSIX timers in Section 23.6 and POSIX message queue notification in Section 52.6.

> Several UNIX implementations, including Linux, define a *sigval_t* data type as a synonym for *union sigval*. However, this type is not specified in SUSv3 and is not available on some implementations. Portable applications should avoid using it.

A call to *sigqueue()* may fail if the limit on the number of queued signals has been reached. In this case, *errno* is set to EAGAIN, indicating that we need to send the signal again (at some later time when some of the currently queued signals have been delivered).

An example of the use of *sigqueue()* is provided in Listing 22-2 (page 459). This program takes up to four arguments, of which the first three are mandatory: a target process ID, a signal number, and an integer value to accompany the realtime signal. If more than one instance of the specified signal is to be sent, the optional fourth argument specifies the number of instances; in this case, the accompanying integer data value is incremented by one for each successive signal. We demonstrate the use of this program in Section 22.8.2.

22.8.2 Handling Realtime Signals

We can handle realtime signals just like standard signals, using a normal (single-argument) signal handler. Alternatively, we can handle a realtime signal using a three-argument signal handler established using the SA_SIGINFO flag (Section 21.4). Here is an example of using SA_SIGINFO to establish a handler for the sixth realtime signal:

```
struct sigaction act;

sigemptyset(&act.sa_mask);
act.sa_sigaction = handler;
act.sa_flags = SA_RESTART | SA_SIGINFO;

if (sigaction(SIGRTMIN + 5, &act, NULL) == -1)
    errExit("sigaction");
```

When we employ the SA_SIGINFO flag, the second argument passed to the signal handler is a *siginfo_t* structure that contains additional information about the realtime signal. We described this structure in detail in Section 21.4. For a realtime signal, the following fields are set in the *siginfo_t* structure:

- The *si_signo* field is the same value as is passed in the first argument of the signal handler.
- The *si_code* field indicates the source of the signal, and contains one of the values shown in Table 21-2 (page 441). For a realtime signal sent via *sigqueue()*, this field always has the value SI_QUEUE.
- The *si_value* field contains the data specified in the *value* argument (the *sigval* union) by the process that sent the signal using *sigqueue()*. As noted already, the interpretation of this data is application-defined. (The *si_value* field doesn't contain valid information if the signal was sent using *kill()*.)
- The *si_pid* and *si_uid* fields contain, respectively, the process ID and real user ID of the process sending the signal.

Listing 22-3 provides an example of handling realtime signals. This program catches signals and displays various fields from the *siginfo_t* structure passed to the signal handler. The program takes two optional integer command-line arguments.

If the first argument is supplied, the main program blocks all signals, and then sleeps for the number of seconds specified by this argument. During this time, we can queue multiple realtime signals to the process and observe what happens when the signals are unblocked. The second argument specifies the number of seconds that the signal handler should sleep before returning. Specifying a nonzero value (the default is 1 second) is useful for slowing down the program so that we can more easily see what is happening when multiple signals are handled.

We can use the program in Listing 22-3, along with the program in Listing 22-2 (t_sigqueue.c) to explore the behavior of realtime signals, as shown in the following shell session log:

```
$ ./catch_rtsigs 60 &
[1] 12842
$ ./catch_rtsigs: PID is 12842          Shell prompt mixed with program output
./catch_rtsigs: signals blocked - sleeping 60 seconds
Press Enter to see next shell prompt
$ ./t_sigqueue 12842 54 100 3          Send signal three times
./t_sigqueue: PID is 12843, UID is 1000
$ ./t_sigqueue 12842 43 200
./t_sigqueue: PID is 12844, UID is 1000
$ ./t_sigqueue 12842 40 300
./t_sigqueue: PID is 12845, UID is 1000
```

Eventually, the *catch_rtsigs* program completes sleeping, and displays messages as the signal handler catches various signals. (We see a shell prompt mixed with the next line of the program's output because the *catch_rtsigs* program is writing output from the background.) We first observe that realtime signals are delivered lowest-numbered signal first, and that the *siginfo_t* structure passed to the handler includes the process ID and user ID of the process that sent the signal:

```
$ ./catch_rtsigs: sleep complete
caught signal 40
    si_signo=40, si_code=-1 (SI_QUEUE), si_value=300
    si_pid=12845, si_uid=1000
caught signal 43
    si_signo=43, si_code=-1 (SI_QUEUE), si_value=200
    si_pid=12844, si_uid=1000
```

The remaining output is produced by the three instances of the same realtime signal. Looking at the *si_value* values, we can see that these signals were delivered in the order they were sent:

```
caught signal 54
    si_signo=54, si_code=-1 (SI_QUEUE), si_value=100
    si_pid=12843, si_uid=1000
caught signal 54
    si_signo=54, si_code=-1 (SI_QUEUE), si_value=101
    si_pid=12843, si_uid=1000
caught signal 54
    si_signo=54, si_code=-1 (SI_QUEUE), si_value=102
    si_pid=12843, si_uid=1000
```

We continue by using the shell *kill* command to send a signal to the *catch_rtsigs* program. As before, we see that the *siginfo_t* structure received by the handler includes the process ID and user ID of the sending process, but in this case, the *si_code* value is SI_USER:

```
Press Enter to see next shell prompt
$ echo $$                          Display PID of shell
12780
$ kill -40 12842                   Uses kill(2) to send a signal
$ caught signal 40
    si_signo=40, si_code=0 (SI_USER), si_value=0
    si_pid=12780, si_uid=1000      PID is that of the shell
Press Enter to see next shell prompt
$ kill 12842                       Kill catch_rtsigs by sending SIGTERM
Caught 6 signals
Press Enter to see notification from shell about terminated background job
[1]+  Done                        ./catch_rtsigs 60
```

Listing 22-3: Handling realtime signals

———————————————————————————————————— signals/catch_rtsigs.c

```c
#define _GNU_SOURCE
#include <string.h>
#include <signal.h>
#include "tlpi_hdr.h"

static volatile int handlerSleepTime;
static volatile int sigCnt = 0;            /* Number of signals received */
static volatile sig_atomic_t allDone = 0;

static void              /* Handler for signals established using SA_SIGINFO */
siginfoHandler(int sig, siginfo_t *si, void *ucontext)
{
    /* UNSAFE: This handler uses non-async-signal-safe functions
       (printf()); see Section 21.1.2) */

    /* SIGINT or SIGTERM can be used to terminate program */

    if (sig == SIGINT || sig == SIGTERM) {
        allDone = 1;
        return;
    }

    sigCnt++;
    printf("caught signal %d\n", sig);

    printf("    si_signo=%d, si_code=%d (%s), ", si->si_signo, si->si_code,
            (si->si_code == SI_USER) ? "SI_USER" :
            (si->si_code == SI_QUEUE) ? "SI_QUEUE" : "other");
    printf("si_value=%d\n", si->si_value.sival_int);
    printf("    si_pid=%ld, si_uid=%ld\n", (long) si->si_pid, (long) si->si_uid);

    sleep(handlerSleepTime);
}
```

```c
int
main(int argc, char *argv[])
{
    struct sigaction sa;
    int sig;
    sigset_t prevMask, blockMask;

    if (argc > 1 && strcmp(argv[1], "--help") == 0)
        usageErr("%s [block-time [handler-sleep-time]]\n", argv[0]);

    printf("%s: PID is %ld\n", argv[0], (long) getpid());

    handlerSleepTime = (argc > 2) ?
                getInt(argv[2], GN_NONNEG, "handler-sleep-time") : 1;

    /* Establish handler for most signals. During execution of the handler,
       mask all other signals to prevent handlers recursively interrupting
       each other (which would make the output hard to read). */

    sa.sa_sigaction = siginfoHandler;
    sa.sa_flags = SA_SIGINFO;
    sigfillset(&sa.sa_mask);

    for (sig = 1; sig < NSIG; sig++)
        if (sig != SIGTSTP && sig != SIGQUIT)
            sigaction(sig, &sa, NULL);

    /* Optionally block signals and sleep, allowing signals to be
       sent to us before they are unblocked and handled */

    if (argc > 1) {
        sigfillset(&blockMask);
        sigdelset(&blockMask, SIGINT);
        sigdelset(&blockMask, SIGTERM);

        if (sigprocmask(SIG_SETMASK, &blockMask, &prevMask) == -1)
            errExit("sigprocmask");

        printf("%s: signals blocked - sleeping %s seconds\n", argv[0], argv[1]);
        sleep(getInt(argv[1], GN_GT_0, "block-time"));
        printf("%s: sleep complete\n", argv[0]);

        if (sigprocmask(SIG_SETMASK, &prevMask, NULL) == -1)
            errExit("sigprocmask");
    }

    while (!allDone)                    /* Wait for incoming signals */
        pause();

    printf("Caught %d signals\n", sigCnt);
    exit(EXIT_SUCCESS);
}
```

———————————————————————————————————— **signals/catch_rtsigs.c**

22.9 Waiting for a Signal Using a Mask: *sigsuspend()*

Before we explain what *sigsuspend()* does, we first describe a situation where we need to use it. Consider the following scenario that is sometimes encountered when programming with signals:

1. We temporarily block a signal so that the handler for the signal doesn't interrupt the execution of some critical section of code.
2. We unblock the signal, and then suspend execution until the signal is delivered.

In order to do this, we might try using code such as that shown in Listing 22-4.

Listing 22-4: Incorrectly unblocking and waiting for a signal

```
sigset_t prevMask, intMask;
struct sigaction sa;

sigemptyset(&intMask);
sigaddset(&intMask, SIGINT);

sigemptyset(&sa.sa_mask);
sa.sa_flags = 0;
sa.sa_handler = handler;

if (sigaction(SIGINT, &sa, NULL) == -1)
    errExit("sigaction");

/* Block SIGINT prior to executing critical section. (At this
   point we assume that SIGINT is not already blocked.) */

if (sigprocmask(SIG_BLOCK, &intMask, &prevMask) == -1)
    errExit("sigprocmask - SIG_BLOCK");

/* Critical section: do some work here that must not be
   interrupted by the SIGINT handler */

/* End of critical section - restore old mask to unblock SIGINT */

if (sigprocmask(SIG_SETMASK, &prevMask, NULL) == -1)
    errExit("sigprocmask - SIG_SETMASK");

/* BUG: what if SIGINT arrives now... */

pause();                                /* Wait for SIGINT */
```

There is a problem with the code in Listing 22-4. Suppose that the SIGINT signal is delivered after execution of the second *sigprocmask()*, but before the *pause()* call. (The signal might actually have been generated at any time during the execution of the critical section, and then be delivered only when it is unblocked.) Delivery of the SIGINT signal will cause the handler to be invoked, and after the handler returns and the main program resumes, the *pause()* call will block until a *second* instance of SIGINT is delivered. This defeats the purpose of the code, which was to unblock SIGINT and then wait for its *first* occurrence.

Even if the likelihood of SIGINT being generated between the start of the critical section (i.e., the first *sigprocmask()* call) and the *pause()* call is small, this nevertheless constitutes a bug in the above code. This time-dependent bug is an example of a race condition (Section 5.1). Normally, race conditions occur where two processes or threads share common resources. However, in this case, the main program is racing against its own signal handler.

To avoid this problem, we require a means of *atomically* unblocking a signal and suspending the process. That is the purpose of the *sigsuspend()* system call.

```
#include <signal.h>

int sigsuspend(const sigset_t *mask);
```
                                              (Normally) returns −1 with *errno* set to EINTR

The *sigsuspend()* system call replaces the process signal mask by the signal set pointed to by *mask*, and then suspends execution of the process until a signal is caught and its handler returns. Once the handler returns, *sigsuspend()* restores the process signal mask to the value it had prior to the call.

Calling *sigsuspend()* is equivalent to atomically performing these operations:

```
sigprocmask(SIG_SETMASK, &mask, &prevMask);    /* Assign new mask */
pause();
sigprocmask(SIG_SETMASK, &prevMask, NULL);     /* Restore old mask */
```

Although restoring the old signal mask (i.e., the last step in the above sequence) may at first appear inconvenient, it is essential to avoid race conditions in situations where we need to repeatedly wait for signals. In such situations, the signals must remain blocked except during the *sigsuspend()* calls. If we later need to unblock the signals that were blocked prior to the *sigsuspend()* call, we can employ a further call to *sigprocmask()*.

When *sigsuspend()* is interrupted by delivery of a signal, it returns −1, with *errno* set to EINTR. If *mask* doesn't point to a valid address, *sigsuspend()* fails with the error EFAULT.

Example program

Listing 22-5 demonstrates the use of *sigsuspend()*. This program performs the following steps:

- Display the initial value of the process signal mask using the *printSigMask()* function (Listing 20-4, on page 408) ①.
- Block SIGINT and SIGQUIT, and save the original process signal mask ②.
- Establish the same handler for both SIGINT and SIGQUIT ③. This handler displays a message, and, if it was invoked via delivery of SIGQUIT, sets the global variable *gotSigquit*.

- Loop until *gotSigquit* is set ④. Each loop iteration performs the following steps:
  - Display the current value of the signal mask using our *printSigMask()* function.
  - Simulate a critical section by executing a CPU busy loop for a few seconds.
  - Display the mask of pending signals using our *printPendingSigs()* function (Listing 20-4).
  - Uses *sigsuspend()* to unblock SIGINT and SIGQUIT and wait for a signal (if one is not already pending).
- Use *sigprocmask()* to restore the process signal mask to its original state ⑤, and then display the signal mask using *printSigMask()* ⑥.

Listing 22-5: Using *sigsuspend()*

─── signals/t_sigsuspend.c

```
#define _GNU_SOURCE       /* Get strsignal() declaration from <string.h> */
#include <string.h>
#include <signal.h>
#include <time.h>
#include "signal_functions.h"          /* Declarations of printSigMask()
                                          and printPendingSigs() */
#include "tlpi_hdr.h"

static volatile sig_atomic_t gotSigquit = 0;

static void
handler(int sig)
{
    printf("Caught signal %d (%s)\n", sig, strsignal(sig));
                                        /* UNSAFE (see Section 21.1.2) */
    if (sig == SIGQUIT)
        gotSigquit = 1;
}

int
main(int argc, char *argv[])
{
    int loopNum;
    time_t startTime;
    sigset_t origMask, blockMask;
    struct sigaction sa;

①    printSigMask(stdout, "Initial signal mask is:\n");

    sigemptyset(&blockMask);
    sigaddset(&blockMask, SIGINT);
    sigaddset(&blockMask, SIGQUIT);
②    if (sigprocmask(SIG_BLOCK, &blockMask, &origMask) == -1)
        errExit("sigprocmask - SIG_BLOCK");

    sigemptyset(&sa.sa_mask);
    sa.sa_flags = 0;
    sa.sa_handler = handler;
```

```
③    if (sigaction(SIGINT, &sa, NULL) == -1)
         errExit("sigaction");
     if (sigaction(SIGQUIT, &sa, NULL) == -1)
         errExit("sigaction");

④    for (loopNum = 1; !gotSigquit; loopNum++) {
         printf("=== LOOP %d\n", loopNum);

         /* Simulate a critical section by delaying a few seconds */

         printSigMask(stdout, "Starting critical section, signal mask is:\n");
         for (startTime = time(NULL); time(NULL) < startTime + 4; )
             continue;                    /* Run for a few seconds elapsed time */

         printPendingSigs(stdout,
                 "Before sigsuspend() - pending signals:\n");
         if (sigsuspend(&origMask) == -1 && errno != EINTR)
             errExit("sigsuspend");
     }

⑤    if (sigprocmask(SIG_SETMASK, &origMask, NULL) == -1)
         errExit("sigprocmask - SIG_SETMASK");

⑥    printSigMask(stdout, "=== Exited loop\nRestored signal mask to:\n");

     /* Do other processing... */

     exit(EXIT_SUCCESS);
}
```
—— signals/t_sigsuspend.c

The following shell session log shows an example of what we see when running the program in Listing 22-5:

```
$ ./t_sigsuspend
Initial signal mask is:
                <empty signal set>
=== LOOP 1
Starting critical section, signal mask is:
                2 (Interrupt)
                3 (Quit)
```
Type Control-C; SIGINT is generated, but remains pending because it is blocked
```
Before sigsuspend() - pending signals:
                2 (Interrupt)
Caught signal 2 (Interrupt)        sigsuspend() is called, signals are unblocked
```

The last line of output appeared when the program called *sigsuspend()*, which caused SIGINT to be unblocked. At that point, the signal handler was called and displayed that line of output.

The main program continues its loop:

```
=== LOOP 2
Starting critical section, signal mask is:
                2 (Interrupt)
                3 (Quit)
Type Control-\ to generate SIGQUIT
Before sigsuspend() - pending signals:
                3 (Quit)
Caught signal 3 (Quit)            sigsuspend() is called, signals are unblocked
=== Exited loop                   Signal handler set gotSigquit
Restored signal mask to:
                <empty signal set>
```

This time, we typed *Control-*, which caused the signal handler to set the *gotSigquit* flag, which in turn caused the main program to terminate its loop.

22.10 Synchronously Waiting for a Signal

In Section 22.9, we saw how to use a signal handler plus *sigsuspend()* to suspend execution of a process until a signal is delivered. However, the need to write a signal handler and to handle the complexities of asynchronous delivery makes this approach cumbersome for some applications. Instead, we can use the *sigwaitinfo()* system call to synchronously *accept* a signal.

```
#define _POSIX_C_SOURCE 199309
#include <signal.h>

int sigwaitinfo(const sigset_t *set, siginfo_t *info);
```
                              Returns signal number on success, or −1 on error

The *sigwaitinfo()* system call suspends execution of the process until one of the signals in the signal set pointed to by *set* becomes pending. If one of the signals in *set* is already pending at the time of the call, *sigwaitinfo()* returns immediately. One of the signals is removed from the process's list of pending signals, and the signal number is returned as the function result. If the *info* argument is not NULL, then it points to a *siginfo_t* structure that is initialized to contain the same information provided to a signal handler taking a *siginfo_t* argument (Section 21.4).

The delivery order and queuing characteristics of signals accepted by *sigwaitinfo()* are the same as for signals caught by a signal handler; that is, standard signals are not queued, and realtime signals are queued and delivered lowest signal number first.

As well as saving us the extra baggage of writing a signal handler, waiting for signals using *sigwaitinfo()* is somewhat faster than the combination of a signal handler plus *sigsuspend()* (see Exercise 22-3).

It usually makes sense to use *sigwaitinfo()* only in conjunction with blocking the set of signals for which we were interested in waiting. (We can fetch a pending signal with *sigwaitinfo()* even while that signal is blocked.) If we fail to do this and a signal arrives before the first, or between successive calls to *sigwaitinfo()*, then the signal will be handled according to its current disposition.

According to SUSv3, calling *sigwaitinfo()* without blocking the signals in *set* results in undefined behavior.

An example of the use of *sigwaitinfo()* is shown in Listing 22-6. This program first blocks all signals, then delays for the number of seconds specified in its optional command-line argument. This allows signals to be sent to the program before *sigwaitinfo()*. The program then loops continuously using *sigwaitinfo()* to accept incoming signals, until SIGINT or SIGTERM is received.

The following shell session log demonstrates the use of the program in Listing 22-6. We run the program in the background, specifying that it should delay 60 seconds before calling *sigwaitinfo()*, and then send it two signals:

```
$ ./t_sigwaitinfo 60 &
./t_sigwaitinfo: PID is 3837
./t_sigwaitinfo: signals blocked
./t_sigwaitinfo: about to delay 60 seconds
[1] 3837
$ ./t_sigqueue 3837 43 100             Send signal 43
./t_sigqueue: PID is 3839, UID is 1000
$ ./t_sigqueue 3837 42 200             Send signal 42
./t_sigqueue: PID is 3840, UID is 1000
```

Eventually, the program completes its sleep interval, and the *sigwaitinfo()* loop accepts the queued signals. (We see a shell prompt mixed with the next line of the program's output because the *t_sigwaitinfo* program is writing output from the background.) As with realtime signals caught with a handler, we see that signals are delivered lowest number first, and that the *siginfo_t* structure passed to the signal handler allows us to obtain the process ID and user ID of the sending process:

```
$ ./t_sigwaitinfo: finished delay
got signal: 42
    si_signo=42, si_code=-1 (SI_QUEUE), si_value=200
    si_pid=3840, si_uid=1000
got signal: 43
    si_signo=43, si_code=-1 (SI_QUEUE), si_value=100
    si_pid=3839, si_uid=1000
```

We continue, using the shell *kill* command to send a signal to the process. This time, we see that the *si_code* field is set to SI_USER (instead of SI_QUEUE):

```
Press Enter to see next shell prompt
$ echo $$                                Display PID of shell
3744
$ kill -USR1 3837                        Shell sends SIGUSR1 using kill()
$ got signal: 10                         Delivery of SIGUSR1
    si_signo=10, si_code=0 (SI_USER), si_value=100
    si_pid=3744, si_uid=1000             3744 is PID of shell
Press Enter to see next shell prompt
$ kill %1                                Terminate program with SIGTERM
$
Press Enter to see notification of background job termination
[1]+  Done                  ./t_sigwaitinfo 60
```

In the output for the accepted SIGUSR1 signal, we see that the *si_value* field has the value 100. This is the value to which the field was initialized by the preceding signal that was sent using *sigqueue()*. We noted earlier that the *si_value* field contains valid information only for signals sent using *sigqueue()*.

Listing 22-6: Synchronously waiting for a signal with *sigwaitinfo()*

―――――――――――――――――――――――――――――――――――― **signals/t_sigwaitinfo.c**
```
#define _GNU_SOURCE
#include <string.h>
#include <signal.h>
#include <time.h>
#include "tlpi_hdr.h"

int
main(int argc, char *argv[])
{
    int sig;
    siginfo_t si;
    sigset_t allSigs;

    if (argc > 1 && strcmp(argv[1], "--help") == 0)
        usageErr("%s [delay-secs]\n", argv[0]);

    printf("%s: PID is %ld\n", argv[0], (long) getpid());

    /* Block all signals (except SIGKILL and SIGSTOP) */

    sigfillset(&allSigs);
    if (sigprocmask(SIG_SETMASK, &allSigs, NULL) == -1)
        errExit("sigprocmask");
    printf("%s: signals blocked\n", argv[0]);

    if (argc > 1) {             /* Delay so that signals can be sent to us */
        printf("%s: about to delay %s seconds\n", argv[0], argv[1]);
        sleep(getInt(argv[1], GN_GT_0, "delay-secs"));
        printf("%s: finished delay\n", argv[0]);
    }

    for (;;) {                  /* Fetch signals until SIGINT (^C) or SIGTERM */
        sig = sigwaitinfo(&allSigs, &si);
        if (sig == -1)
            errExit("sigwaitinfo");

        if (sig == SIGINT || sig == SIGTERM)
            exit(EXIT_SUCCESS);

        printf("got signal: %d (%s)\n", sig, strsignal(sig));
        printf("    si_signo=%d, si_code=%d (%s), si_value=%d\n",
                si.si_signo, si.si_code,
                (si.si_code == SI_USER) ? "SI_USER" :
                    (si.si_code == SI_QUEUE) ? "SI_QUEUE" : "other",
                si.si_value.sival_int);
```

```
        printf("    si_pid=%ld, si_uid=%ld\n",
                (long) si.si_pid, (long) si.si_uid);
    }
}
```

── **signals/t_sigwaitinfo.c**

The *sigtimedwait()* system call is a variation on *sigwaitinfo()*. The only difference is that *sigtimedwait()* allows us to specify a time limit for waiting.

```
#define _POSIX_C_SOURCE 199309
#include <signal.h>

int sigtimedwait(const sigset_t *set, siginfo_t *info,
                const struct timespec *timeout);
```
                Returns signal number on success, or –1 on error or timeout (EAGAIN)

The *timeout* argument specifies the maximum time that *sigtimedwait()* should wait for a signal. It is a pointer to a structure of the following type:

```
struct timespec {
    time_t tv_sec;     /* Seconds ('time_t' is an integer type) */
    long   tv_nsec;    /* Nanoseconds */
};
```

The fields of the *timespec* structure are filled in to specify the maximum number of seconds and nanoseconds that *sigtimedwait()* should wait. Specifying both fields of the structure as 0 causes an immediate timeout—that is, a poll to check if any of the specified set of signals is pending. If the call times out without a signal being delivered, *sigtimedwait()* fails with the error EAGAIN.

If the *timeout* argument is specified as NULL, then *sigtimedwait()* is exactly equivalent to *sigwaitinfo()*. SUSv3 leaves the meaning of a NULL *timeout* unspecified, and some UNIX implementations instead interpret this as a poll request that returns immediately.

22.11 Fetching Signals via a File Descriptor

Starting with kernel 2.6.22, Linux provides the (nonstandard) *signalfd()* system call, which creates a special file descriptor from which signals directed to the caller can be read. The *signalfd* mechanism provides an alternative to the use of *sigwaitinfo()* for synchronously accepting signals.

```
#include <sys/signalfd.h>

int signalfd(int fd, const sigset_t *mask, int flags);
```
                        Returns file descriptor on success, or –1 on error

The *mask* argument is a signal set that specifies the signals that we want to be able to read via the *signalfd* file descriptor. As with *sigwaitinfo()*, we should normally also block all of the signals in *mask* using *sigprocmask()*, so that the signals don't get handled according to their default dispositions before we have a chance to read them.

If *fd* is specified as −1, then *signalfd()* creates a new file descriptor that can be used to read the signals in *mask*; otherwise, it modifies the mask associated with *fd*, which must be a file descriptor created by a previous call to *signalfd()*.

In the initial implementation, the *flags* argument was reserved for future use and had to be specified as 0. However, since Linux 2.6.27, two flags are supported:

SFD_CLOEXEC
> Set the close-on-exec flag (FD_CLOEXEC) for the new file descriptor. This flag is useful for the same reasons as the *open()* O_CLOEXEC flag described in Section 4.3.1.

SFD_NONBLOCK
> Set the O_NONBLOCK flag on the underlying open file description, so that future reads will be nonblocking. This saves additional calls to *fcntl()* to achieve the same result.

Having created the file descriptor, we can then read signals from it using *read()*. The buffer given to *read()* must be large enough to hold at least one *signalfd_siginfo* structure, defined as follows in <sys/signalfd.h>:

```
struct signalfd_siginfo {
    uint32_t  ssi_signo;    /* Signal number */
    int32_t   ssi_errno;    /* Error number (generally unused) */
    int32_t   ssi_code;     /* Signal code */
    uint32_t  ssi_pid;      /* Process ID of sending process */
    uint32_t  ssi_uid;      /* Real user ID of sender */
    int32_t   ssi_fd;       /* File descriptor (SIGPOLL/SIGIO) */
    uint32_t  ssi_tid;      /* (Kernel-internal) timer ID (POSIX timers) */
    uint32_t  ssi_band;     /* Band event (SIGPOLL/SIGIO) */
    uint32_t  ssi_overrun;  /* Overrun count (POSIX timers) */
    uint32_t  ssi_trapno;   /* Trap number */
    int32_t   ssi_status;   /* Exit status or signal (SIGCHLD) */
    int32_t   ssi_int;      /* Integer sent by sigqueue() */
    uint64_t  ssi_ptr;      /* Pointer sent by sigqueue() */
    uint64_t  ssi_utime;    /* User CPU time (SIGCHLD) */
    uint64_t  ssi_stime;    /* System CPU time (SIGCHLD) */
    uint64_t  ssi_addr;     /* Address that generated signal
                               (hardware-generated signals only) */
};
```

The fields in this structure return the same information as the similarly named fields in the traditional *siginfo_t* structure (Section 21.4).

Each call to *read()* returns as many *signalfd_siginfo* structures as there are signals pending and will fit in the supplied buffer. If no signals are pending at the time of the call, then *read()* blocks until a signal arrives. We can also use the *fcntl()* F_SETFL operation (Section 5.3) to set the O_NONBLOCK flag for the file descriptor, so that reads are nonblocking and will fail with the error EAGAIN if no signals are pending.

When a signal is read from a *signalfd* file descriptor, it is consumed and ceases to be pending for the process.

Listing 22-7: Using *signalfd()* to read signals

```
─────────────────────────────────────────signals/signalfd_sigval.c
#include <sys/signalfd.h>
#include <signal.h>
#include "tlpi_hdr.h"

int
main(int argc, char *argv[])
{
    sigset_t mask;
    int sfd, j;
    struct signalfd_siginfo fdsi;
    ssize_t s;

    if (argc < 2 || strcmp(argv[1], "--help") == 0)
        usageErr("%s sig-num...\n", argv[0]);

    printf("%s: PID = %ld\n", argv[0], (long) getpid());

    sigemptyset(&mask);
    for (j = 1; j < argc; j++)
        sigaddset(&mask, atoi(argv[j]));

    if (sigprocmask(SIG_BLOCK, &mask, NULL) == -1)
        errExit("sigprocmask");

    sfd = signalfd(-1, &mask, 0);
    if (sfd == -1)
        errExit("signalfd");

    for (;;) {
        s = read(sfd, &fdsi, sizeof(struct signalfd_siginfo));
        if (s != sizeof(struct signalfd_siginfo))
            errExit("read");

        printf("%s: got signal %d", argv[0], fdsi.ssi_signo);
        if (fdsi.ssi_code == SI_QUEUE) {
            printf("; ssi_pid = %d; ", fdsi.ssi_pid);
            printf("ssi_int = %d", fdsi.ssi_int);
        }
        printf("\n");
    }
}
─────────────────────────────────────────signals/signalfd_sigval.c
```

A *signalfd* file descriptor can be monitored along with other descriptors using *select()*, *poll()*, and *epoll* (described in Chapter 63). Among other uses, this feature provides an alternative to the self-pipe trick described in Section 63.5.2. If signals are pending, then these techniques indicate the file descriptor as being readable.

When we no longer require a *signalfd* file descriptor, we should close it, in order to release the associated kernel resources.

Listing 22-7 (on page 473) demonstrates the use of *signalfd()*. This program creates a mask of the signal numbers specified in its command-line arguments, blocks those signals, and then creates a *signalfd* file descriptor to read those signals. It then loops, reading signals from the file descriptor and displaying some of the information from the returned *signalfd_siginfo* structure. In the following shell session, we run the program in Listing 22-7 in the background and send it a realtime signal with accompanying data using the program in Listing 22-2 (t_sigqueue.c):

```
$ ./signalfd_sigval 44 &
./signalfd_sigval: PID = 6267
[1] 6267
$ ./t_sigqueue 6267 44 123          Send signal 44 with data 123 to PID 6267
./t_sigqueue: PID is 6269, UID is 1000
./signalfd_sigval: got signal 44; ssi_pid=6269; ssi_int=123
$ kill %1                           Kill program running in background
```

22.12 Interprocess Communication with Signals

From one viewpoint, we can consider signals as a form of interprocess communication (IPC). However, signals suffer a number of limitations as an IPC mechanism. First, by comparison with other methods of IPC that we examine in later chapters, programming with signals is cumbersome and difficult. The reasons for this are as follows:

- The asynchronous nature of signals means that we face various problems, including reentrancy requirements, race conditions, and the correct handling of global variables from signal handlers. (Most of these problems do not occur if we are using *sigwaitinfo()* or *signalfd()* to synchronously fetch signals.)

- Standard signals are not queued. Even for realtime signals, there are upper limits on the number of signals that may be queued. This means that in order to avoid loss of information, the process receiving the signals must have a method of informing the sender that it is ready to receive another signal. The most obvious method of doing this is for the receiver to send a signal to the sender.

A further problem is that signals carry only a limited amount of information: the signal number, and in the case of realtime signals, a word (an integer or a pointer) of additional data. This low bandwidth makes signals slow by comparison with other methods of IPC such as pipes.

As a consequence of the above limitations, signals are rarely used for IPC.

22.13 Earlier Signal APIs (System V and BSD)

Our discussion of signals has focused on the POSIX signal API. We now briefly look at the historical APIs provided by System V and BSD. Although all new applications should use the POSIX API, we may encounter these obsolete APIs when porting (usually older) applications from other UNIX implementations. Because Linux (like many other UNIX implementations) provides System V and BSD compatibility APIs, often all that is required to port programs using these older APIs is to recompile them on Linux.

The System V signal API

As noted earlier, one important difference in the System V signal API is that when a handler is established with *signal()*, we get the older, unreliable signal semantics. This means that the signal is not added to the process signal mask, the disposition of the signal is reset to the default when the handler is called, and system calls are not automatically restarted.

Below, we briefly describe the functions in the System V signal API. The manual pages provide full details. SUSv3 specifies all of these functions, but notes that the modern POSIX equivalents are preferred. SUSv4 marks these functions obsolete.

```
#define _XOPEN_SOURCE 500
#include <signal.h>

void (*sigset(int sig, void (*handler)(int)))(int);
```
> On success: returns the previous disposition of *sig*, or SIG_HOLD
> if *sig* was previously blocked; on error −1 is returned

To establish a signal handler with reliable semantics, System V provided the *sigset()* call (with a prototype similar to that of *signal()*). As with *signal()*, the *handler* argument for *sigset()* can be specified as SIG_IGN, SIG_DFL, or the address of a signal handler. Alternatively, it can be specified as SIG_HOLD, to add the signal to the process signal mask while leaving the disposition of the signal unchanged.

If *handler* is specified as anything other than SIG_HOLD, *sig* is removed from the process signal mask (i.e., if *sig* was blocked, it is unblocked).

```
#define _XOPEN_SOURCE 500
#include <signal.h>

int sighold(int sig);
int sigrelse(int sig);
int sigignore(int sig);
```
> All return 0 on success, or −1 on error

```
int sigpause(int sig);
```
> Always returns −1 with *errno* set to EINTR

The *sighold()* function adds a signal to the process signal mask. The *sigrelse()* function removes a signal from the signal mask. The *sigignore()* function sets a signal's disposition to *ignore*. The *sigpause()* function is similar to *sigsuspend()*, but removes just one signal from the process signal mask before suspending the process until the arrival of a signal.

The BSD signal API

The POSIX signal API drew heavily on the 4.2BSD API, so the BSD functions are mainly direct analogs of those in POSIX.

As with the functions in the System V signal API described above, we present the prototypes of the functions in the BSD signal API, and briefly explain the operation of each function. Once again, the manual pages provide full details.

```
#define _BSD_SOURCE
#include <signal.h>

int sigvec(int sig, const struct sigvec *vec, struct sigvec *ovec);
```
                                          Returns 0 on success, or −1 on error

The *sigvec()* function is analogous to *sigaction()*. The *vec* and *ovec* arguments are pointers to structures of the following type:

```
struct sigvec {
    void (*sv_handler)(int);
    int  sv_mask;
    int  sv_flags;
};
```

The fields of the *sigvec* structure correspond closely with those of the *sigaction* structure. The first notable difference is that the *sv_mask* field (the analog of *sa_mask*) was an integer rather than a *sigset_t*, which meant that, on 32-bit architectures, there was a maximum of 31 different signals. The other difference is the use of the SV_INTERRUPT flag in the *sv_flags* field (the analog of *sa_flags*). Since system call restarting was the default on 4.2BSD, this flag was used to specify that slow system calls should be interrupted by signal handlers. (This contrasts with the POSIX API, where we must explicitly specify SA_RESTART in order to enable restarting of system calls when establishing a signal handler with *sigaction()*.)

```
#define _BSD_SOURCE
#include <signal.h>

int sigblock(int mask);
int sigsetmask(int mask);
```
                                          Both return previous signal mask
```
int sigpause(int sigmask);
```
                                          Always returns −1 with *errno* set to EINTR
```
int sigmask(int sig);
```
                                          Returns signal mask value with bit *sig* set

The *sigblock()* function adds a set of signals to the process signal mask. It is analogous to the *sigprocmask()* `SIG_BLOCK` operation. The *sigsetmask()* call specifies an absolute value for the signal mask. It is analogous to the *sigprocmask()* `SIG_SETMASK` operation.

The *sigpause()* function is analogous to *sigsuspend()*. Note that this function is defined with different calling signatures in the System V and BSD APIs. The GNU C library provides the System V version by default, unless we specify the `_BSD_SOURCE` feature test macro when compiling a program.

The *sigmask()* macro turns a signal number into the corresponding 32-bit mask value. Such bit masks can then be ORed together to create a set of signals, as in the following:

```
sigblock(sigmask(SIGINT) | sigmask(SIGQUIT));
```

22.14 Summary

Certain signals cause a process to create a core dump and terminate. Core dumps contain information that can be used by a debugger to inspect the state of a process at the time that it terminated. By default, a core dump file is named core, but Linux provides the /proc/sys/kernel/core_pattern file to control the naming of core dump files.

A signal may be generated asynchronously or synchronously. Asynchronous generation occurs when a signal is sent to a process by the kernel or by another process. A process can't predict precisely when an asynchronously generated signal will be delivered. (We noted that asynchronous signals are normally delivered the next time the receiving process switches from kernel mode to user mode.) Synchronous generation occurs when the process itself executes code that directly generates the signal—for example, by executing an instruction that causes a hardware exception or by calling *raise()*. The delivery of a synchronously generated signal is precisely predictable (it occurs immediately).

Realtime signals are a POSIX addition to the original signal model, and differ from standard signals in that they are queued, have a specified delivery order, and can be sent with an accompanying piece of data. Realtime signals are designed to be used for application-defined purposes. A realtime signal is sent using the *sigqueue()* system call, and an additional argument (the *siginfo_t* structure) is supplied to the signal handler so that it can obtain the data accompanying the signal, as well as the process ID and real user ID of the sending process.

The *sigsuspend()* system call allows a program to atomically modify the process signal mask and suspend execution until a signal arrives. The atomicity of *sigsuspend()* is essential to avoid race conditions when unblocking a signal and then suspending execution until that signal arrives.

We can use *sigwaitinfo()* and *sigtimedwait()* to synchronously wait for a signal. This saves us the work of designing and writing a signal handler, which may be unnecessary if our only aim is to wait for the delivery of a signal.

Like *sigwaitinfo()* and *sigtimedwait()*, the Linux-specific *signalfd()* system call can be used to synchronously wait for a signal. The distinctive feature of this interface is that signals can be read via a file descriptor. This file descriptor can also be monitored using *select()*, *poll()*, and *epoll*.

Although signals can be viewed as a method of IPC, many factors make them generally unsuitable for this purpose, including their asynchronous nature, the fact that they are not queued, and their low bandwidth. More usually, signals are used as a method of process synchronization and for a variety of other purposes (e.g., event notification, job control, and timer expiration).

Although the fundamental signal concepts are straightforward, our discussion has stretched over three chapters, since there were many details to cover. Signals play an important role in various parts of the system call API, and we'll revisit their use in several later chapters. In addition, various signal-related functions are specific to threads (e.g., *pthread_kill()* and *pthread_sigmask()*), and we defer discussion of these functions until Section 33.2.

Further information

See the sources listed in Section 20.15.

22.15 Exercises

22-1. Section 22.2 noted that if a stopped process that has established a handler for and blocked SIGCONT is later resumed as a consequence of receiving a SIGCONT, then the handler is invoked only when SIGCONT is unblocked. Write a program to verify this. Recall that a process can be stopped by typing the terminal *suspend* character (usually *Control-Z*) and can be sent a SIGCONT signal using the command *kill -CONT* (or implicitly, using the shell *fg* command).

22-2. If both a realtime and a standard signal are pending for a process, SUSv3 leaves it unspecified which is delivered first. Write a program that shows what Linux does in this case. (Have the program set up a handler for all signals, block signals for a period of time so that you can send various signals to it, and then unblock all signals.)

22-3. Section 22.10 stated that accepting signals using *sigwaitinfo()* is faster than the use of a signal handler plus *sigsuspend()*. The program signals/sig_speed_sigsuspend.c, supplied in the source code distribution for this book, uses *sigsuspend()* to alternately send signals back and forward between a parent and a child process. Time the operation of this program to exchange one million signals between the two processes. (The number of signals to exchange is provided as a command-line argument to the program.) Create a modified version of the program that instead uses *sigwaitinfo()*, and time that version. What is the speed difference between the two programs?

22-4. Implement the System V functions *sigset()*, *sighold()*, *sigrelse()*, *sigignore()*, and *sigpause()* using the POSIX signal API.

23

TIMERS AND SLEEPING

A timer allows a process to schedule a notification for itself to occur at some time in the future. Sleeping allows a process (or thread) to suspend execution for a period of time. This chapter describes the interfaces used for setting timers and for sleeping. It covers the following topics:

- the classical UNIX APIs for setting interval timers (*setitimer()* and *alarm()*) to notify a process when a certain amount of time has passed;
- the APIs that allow a process to sleep for a specified interval;
- the POSIX.1b clocks and timers APIs; and
- the Linux-specific *timerfd* facility, which allows the creation of timers whose expirations can be read from a file descriptor.

23.1 Interval Timers

The *setitimer()* system call establishes an *interval timer*, which is a timer that expires at a future point in time and (optionally) at regular intervals after that.

```
#include <sys/time.h>

int setitimer(int which, const struct itimerval *new_value,
              struct itimerval *old_value);
```

                                        Returns 0 on success, or −1 on error

Using *setitimer()*, a process can establish three different types of timers, by specifying *which* as one of the following:

ITIMER_REAL

> Create a timer that counts down in real (i.e., wall clock) time. When the timer expires, a SIGALRM signal is generated for the process.

ITIMER_VIRTUAL

> Create a timer that counts down in process virtual time (i.e., user-mode CPU time). When the timer expires, a SIGVTALRM signal is generated for the process.

ITIMER_PROF

> Create a *profiling* timer. A profiling timer counts in process time (i.e., the sum of both user-mode and kernel-mode CPU time). When the timer expires, a SIGPROF signal is generated for the process.

The default disposition of all of the timer signals is to terminate the process. Unless this is the desired result, we must establish a handler for the signal delivered by the timer.

The *new_value* and *old_value* arguments are pointers to *itimerval* structures, defined as follows:

```
struct itimerval {
    struct timeval it_interval;    /* Interval for periodic timer */
    struct timeval it_value;       /* Current value (time until
                                      next expiration) */
};
```

Each of the fields in the *itimerval* structure is in turn a structure of type *timeval*, containing seconds and microseconds fields:

```
struct timeval {
    time_t     tv_sec;             /* Seconds */
    suseconds_t tv_usec;           /* Microseconds (long int) */
};
```

The *it_value* substructure of the *new_value* argument specifies the delay until the timer is to expire. The *it_interval* substructure specifies whether this is to be a periodic timer. If both fields of *it_interval* are set to 0, then the timer expires just once, at the time given by *it_value*. If one or both of the *it_interval* fields are nonzero, then, after each expiration of the timer, the timer will be reset to expire again at the specified interval.

A process has only one of each of the three types of timers. If we call *setitimer()* a second time, it will change the characteristics of any existing timer corresponding to *which*. If we call *setitimer()* with both fields of *new_value.it_value* set to 0, then any existing timer is disabled.

If *old_value* is not NULL, then it points to an *itimerval* structure that is used to return the previous value of the timer. If both fields of *old_value.it_value* are 0, then the timer was previously disabled. If both fields of *old_value.it_interval* are 0, then the previous timer was set to expire just once, at the time given by *old_value.it_value*. Retrieving the previous settings of the timer can be useful if we want to restore the settings after the new timer has expired. If we are not interested in the previous value of the timer, we can specify *old_value* as NULL.

As a timer progresses, it counts down from the initial value (*it_value*) toward 0. When the timer reaches 0, the corresponding signal is sent to the process, and then, if the interval (*it_interval*) is nonzero, the timer value (*it_value*) is reloaded with the interval value, and counting down toward 0 recommences.

At any time, we can use *getitimer()* to retrieve the current state of the timer in order to see how much time is left before it next expires.

```
#include <sys/time.h>

int getitimer(int which, struct itimerval *curr_value);
```

                                        Returns 0 on success, or -1 on error

The *getitimer()* system call returns the current state of the timer specified by *which*, in the buffer pointed to by *curr_value*. This is exactly the same information as is returned via the *old_value* argument of *setitimer()*, with the difference that we don't need to change the timer settings in order to retrieve the information. The *curr_value.it_value* substructure returns the amount of time remaining until the timer next expires. This value changes as the timer counts down, and is reset on timer expiration if a nonzero *it_interval* value was specified when the timer was set. The *curr_value.it_interval* substructure returns the interval for this timer; this value remains unchanged until a subsequent call to *setitimer()*.

Timers established using *setitimer()* (and *alarm()*, which we discuss shortly) are preserved across *exec()*, but are not inherited by a child created by *fork()*.

> SUSv4 marks *getitimer()* and *setitimer()* obsolete, noting that the POSIX timers API (Section 23.6) is preferred.

Example program

Listing 23-1 demonstrates the use of *setitimer()* and *getitimer()*. This program performs the following steps:

- Establish a handler for the SIGALRM signal ③.
- Set the value and interval fields for a real (ITIMER_REAL) timer using the values supplied in its command-line arguments ④. If these arguments are absent, the program sets a timer that expires just once, after 2 seconds.
- Execute a continuous loop ⑤, consuming CPU time and periodically calling the function *displayTimes()* ①, which displays the elapsed real time since the program began, as well as the current state of the ITIMER_REAL timer.

Each time the timer expires, the SIGALRM handler is invoked, and it sets a global flag, *gotAlarm* ②. Whenever this flag is set, the loop in the main program calls *displayTimes()* in order to show when the handler was called and the state of the timer ⑥. (We designed the signal handler in this manner to avoid calling non-async-signal-safe functions from within the handler, for the reasons described in Section 21.1.2.) If the timer has a zero interval, then the program exits on delivery of the first signal; otherwise, it catches up to three signals before terminating ⑦.

When we run the program in Listing 23-1, we see the following:

```
$ ./real_timer 1 800000 1 0          Initial value 1.8 seconds, interval 1 second
          Elapsed   Value  Interval
START:      0.00
Main:       0.50    1.30    1.00     Timer counts down until expiration
Main:       1.00    0.80    1.00
Main:       1.50    0.30    1.00
ALARM:      1.80    1.00    1.00     On expiration, timer is reloaded from interval
Main:       2.00    0.80    1.00
Main:       2.50    0.30    1.00
ALARM:      2.80    1.00    1.00
Main:       3.00    0.80    1.00
Main:       3.50    0.30    1.00
ALARM:      3.80    1.00    1.00
That's all folks
```

Listing 23-1: Using a real-time timer

—— timers/real_timer.c
```c
#include <signal.h>
#include <sys/time.h>
#include <time.h>
#include "tlpi_hdr.h"

static volatile sig_atomic_t gotAlarm = 0;
                        /* Set nonzero on receipt of SIGALRM */

/* Retrieve and display the real time, and (if 'includeTimer' is
   TRUE) the current value and interval for the ITIMER_REAL timer */

static void
displayTimes(const char *msg, Boolean includeTimer)
{
    struct itimerval itv;
    static struct timeval start;
    struct timeval curr;
    static int callNum = 0;             /* Number of calls to this function */

    if (callNum == 0)                   /* Initialize elapsed time meter */
        if (gettimeofday(&start, NULL) == -1)
            errExit("gettimeofday");

    if (callNum % 20 == 0)              /* Print header every 20 lines */
        printf("       Elapsed  Value Interval\n");
```

```c
        if (gettimeofday(&curr, NULL) == -1)
            errExit("gettimeofday");
        printf("%-7s %6.2f", msg, curr.tv_sec - start.tv_sec +
                            (curr.tv_usec - start.tv_usec) / 1000000.0);

        if (includeTimer) {
            if (getitimer(ITIMER_REAL, &itv) == -1)
                errExit("getitimer");
            printf("   %6.2f  %6.2f",
                    itv.it_value.tv_sec + itv.it_value.tv_usec / 1000000.0,
                    itv.it_interval.tv_sec + itv.it_interval.tv_usec / 1000000.0);
        }

        printf("\n");
        callNum++;
    }

    static void
    sigalrmHandler(int sig)
    {
②       gotAlarm = 1;
    }

    int
    main(int argc, char *argv[])
    {
        struct itimerval itv;
        clock_t prevClock;
        int maxSigs;               /* Number of signals to catch before exiting */
        int sigCnt;                /* Number of signals so far caught */
        struct sigaction sa;

        if (argc > 1 && strcmp(argv[1], "--help") == 0)
            usageErr("%s [secs [usecs [int-secs [int-usecs]]]]\n", argv[0]);

        sigemptyset(&sa.sa_mask);
        sa.sa_flags = 0;
        sa.sa_handler = sigalrmHandler;
③       if (sigaction(SIGALRM, &sa, NULL) == -1)
            errExit("sigaction");

         /* Set timer from the command-line arguments */

        itv.it_value.tv_sec = (argc > 1) ? getLong(argv[1], 0, "secs") : 2;
        itv.it_value.tv_usec = (argc > 2) ? getLong(argv[2], 0, "usecs") : 0;
        itv.it_interval.tv_sec = (argc > 3) ? getLong(argv[3], 0, "int-secs") : 0;
        itv.it_interval.tv_usec = (argc > 4) ? getLong(argv[4], 0, "int-usecs") : 0;

      /* Exit after 3 signals, or on first signal if interval is 0 */

      maxSigs = (itv.it_interval.tv_sec == 0 &&
                  itv.it_interval.tv_usec == 0) ? 1 : 3;
```

```
          displayTimes("START:", FALSE);
④     if (setitimer(ITIMER_REAL, &itv, NULL) == -1)
              errExit("setitimer");

      prevClock = clock();
      sigCnt = 0;

⑤     for (;;) {

          /* Inner loop consumes at least 0.5 seconds CPU time */

          while (((clock() - prevClock) * 10 / CLOCKS_PER_SEC) < 5) {
⑥            if (gotAlarm) {                    /* Did we get a signal? */
                  gotAlarm = 0;
                  displayTimes("ALARM:", TRUE);

                  sigCnt++;
⑦                if (sigCnt >= maxSigs) {
                      printf("That's all folks\n");
                      exit(EXIT_SUCCESS);
                  }
              }
          }

          prevClock = clock();
          displayTimes("Main: ", TRUE);
      }
  }
```

——— *timers/real_timer.c*

A simpler timer interface: *alarm()*

The *alarm()* system call provides a simple interface for establishing a real-time timer
that expires once, with no repeating interval. (Historically, *alarm()* was the original
UNIX API for setting a timer.)

```
#include <unistd.h>

unsigned int alarm(unsigned int seconds);
```
> Always succeeds, returning number of seconds remaining on
> any previously set timer, or 0 if no timer previously was set

The *seconds* argument specifies the number of seconds in the future when the timer
is to expire. At that time, a SIGALRM signal is delivered to the calling process.

Setting a timer with *alarm()* overrides any previously set timer. We can disable
an existing timer using the call *alarm(0)*.

As its return value, *alarm()* gives us the number of seconds remaining until the
expiration of any previously set timer, or 0 if no timer was set.

An example of the use of *alarm()* is shown in Section 23.3.

> In some later example programs in this book, we use *alarm()* to start a timer without establishing a corresponding SIGALRM handler, as a technique for ensuring that a process is killed if it is not otherwise terminated.

Interactions between *setitimer()* and *alarm()*

On Linux, *alarm()* and *setitimer()* share the same per-process real-time timer, which means that setting a timer with one of these functions changes any timer previously set by either of the functions. This may not be the case on other UNIX implementations (i.e., these functions could control independent timers). SUSv3 explicitly leaves unspecified the interactions between *setitimer()* and *alarm()*, as well as the interactions of these functions with the *sleep()* function described in Section 23.4.1. For maximum portability, we should ensure that our applications use only one of *setitimer()* and *alarm()* for setting real-time timers.

23.2 Scheduling and Accuracy of Timers

Depending on system load and the scheduling of processes, a process may not be scheduled to run until some short time (i.e., usually some small fraction of a second) after actual expiration of the timer. Notwithstanding this, the expiration of a periodic timer established by *setitimer()*, or the other interfaces described later in this chapter, will remain regular. For example, if a real-time timer is set to expire every 2 seconds, then the delivery of individual timer events may be subject to the delays just described, but the scheduling of subsequent expirations will nevertheless be at exactly the next 2-second interval. In other words, interval timers are not subject to creeping errors.

Although the *timeval* structure used by *setitimer()* allows for microsecond precision, the accuracy of a timer has traditionally been limited by the frequency of the software clock (Section 10.6). If a timer value does not exactly match a multiple of the granularity of the software clock, then the timer value is rounded up. This means that if, for example, we specified an interval timer to go off each 19,100 microseconds (i.e., just over 19 milliseconds), then, assuming a jiffy value of 4 milliseconds, we would actually get a timer that expired every 20 milliseconds.

High-resolution timers

On modern Linux kernels, the preceding statement that timer resolution is limited by the frequency of the software clock no longer holds true. Since kernel 2.6.21, Linux optionally supports high-resolution timers. If this support is enabled (via the CONFIG_HIGH_RES_TIMERS kernel configuration option), then the accuracy of the various timer and sleep interfaces that we describe in this chapter is no longer constrained by the size of the kernel jiffy. Instead, these calls can be as accurate as the underlying hardware allows. On modern hardware, accuracy down to a microsecond is typical.

> The availability of high-resolution timers can be determined by examining the clock resolution returned by *clock_getres()*, described in Section 23.5.1.

23.3 Setting Timeouts on Blocking Operations

One use of real-time timers is to place an upper limit on the time for which a blocking system call can remain blocked. For example, we may wish to cancel a *read()* from a terminal if the user has not entered a line of input within a certain time. We can do this as follows:

1. Call *sigaction()* to establish a handler for SIGALRM, omitting the SA_RESTART flag, so that system calls are not restarted (refer to Section 21.5).

2. Call *alarm()* or *setitimer()* to establish a timer specifying the upper limit of time for which we wish the system call to block.

3. Make the blocking system call.

4. After the system call returns, call *alarm()* or *setitimer()* once more to disable the timer (in case the system call completed before the timer expired).

5. Check to see whether the blocking system call failed with *errno* set to EINTR (interrupted system call).

Listing 23-2 demonstrates this technique for *read()*, using *alarm()* to establish the timer.

Listing 23-2: Performing a *read()* with timeout

———————————————————————————————— timers/timed_read.c
```
#include <signal.h>
#include "tlpi_hdr.h"

#define BUF_SIZE 200

static void      /* SIGALRM handler: interrupts blocked system call */
handler(int sig)
{
    printf("Caught signal\n");           /* UNSAFE (see Section 21.1.2) */
}

int
main(int argc, char *argv[])
{
    struct sigaction sa;
    char buf[BUF_SIZE];
    ssize_t numRead;
    int savedErrno;

    if (argc > 1 && strcmp(argv[1], "--help") == 0)
        usageErr("%s [num-secs [restart-flag]]\n", argv[0]);

    /* Set up handler for SIGALRM. Allow system calls to be interrupted,
       unless second command-line argument was supplied. */

    sa.sa_flags = (argc > 2) ? SA_RESTART : 0;
    sigemptyset(&sa.sa_mask);
```

```
    sa.sa_handler = handler;
    if (sigaction(SIGALRM, &sa, NULL) == -1)
        errExit("sigaction");

    alarm((argc > 1) ? getInt(argv[1], GN_NONNEG, "num-secs") : 10);

    numRead = read(STDIN_FILENO, buf, BUF_SIZE);

    savedErrno = errno;              /* In case alarm() changes it */
    alarm(0);                        /* Ensure timer is turned off */
    errno = savedErrno;

    /* Determine result of read() */

    if (numRead == -1) {
        if (errno == EINTR)
            printf("Read timed out\n");
        else
            errMsg("read");
    } else {
        printf("Successful read (%ld bytes): %.*s",
                (long) numRead, (int) numRead, buf);
    }

    exit(EXIT_SUCCESS);
}
```

—— **timers/timed_read.c**

Note that there is a theoretical race condition in the program in Listing 23-2. If the timer expires after the call to *alarm()*, but before the *read()* call is started, then the *read()* call won't be interrupted by the signal handler. Since the timeout value used in scenarios like this is normally relatively large (at least several seconds) this is highly unlikely to occur, so that, in practice, this is a viable technique. [Stevens & Rago, 2005] proposes an alternative technique using *longjmp()*. A further alternative when dealing with I/O system calls is to use the timeout feature of the *select()* or *poll()* system calls (Chapter 63), which also have the advantage of allowing us to simultaneously wait for I/O on multiple descriptors.

23.4 Suspending Execution for a Fixed Interval (Sleeping)

Sometimes, we want to suspend execution of a process for a fixed amount of time. While it is possible to do this using a combination of *sigsuspend()* and the timer functions already described, it is easier to use one of the sleep functions instead.

23.4.1 Low-Resolution Sleeping: *sleep()*

The *sleep()* function suspends execution of the calling thread for the number of seconds specified in the *seconds* argument or until a signal is caught (thus interrupting the call).

```
#include <unistd.h>

unsigned int sleep(unsigned int seconds);
```

> Returns 0 on normal completion, or number of
> unslept seconds if prematurely terminated

If the sleep completes, *sleep()* returns 0. If the sleep is interrupted by a signal, *sleep()* returns the number of remaining (unslept) seconds. As with timers set by *alarm()* and *setitimer()*, system load may mean that the process is rescheduled only at some (normally short) time after the completion of the *sleep()* call.

SUSv3 leaves possible interactions of *sleep()* with *alarm()* and *setitimer()* unspecified. On Linux, *sleep()* is implemented as a call to *nanosleep()* (Section 23.4.2), with the consequence that there is no interaction between *sleep()* and the timer functions. However, on many implementations, especially older ones, *sleep()* is implemented using *alarm()* and a handler for the SIGALRM signal. For portability, we should avoid mixing the use of *sleep()* with *alarm()* and *setitimer()*.

23.4.2 High-Resolution Sleeping: *nanosleep()*

The *nanosleep()* function performs a similar task to *sleep()*, but provides a number of advantages, including finer resolution when specifying the sleep interval.

```
#define _POSIX_C_SOURCE 199309
#include <time.h>

int nanosleep(const struct timespec *request, struct timespec *remain);
```

> Returns 0 on successfully completed sleep,
> or −1 on error or interrupted sleep

The *request* argument specifies the duration of the sleep interval and is a pointer to a structure of the following form:

```
struct timespec {
    time_t tv_sec;          /* Seconds */
    long   tv_nsec;         /* Nanoseconds */
};
```

The *tv_nsec* field specifies a nanoseconds value. It must be a number in the range 0 to 999,999,999.

A further advantage of *nanosleep()* is that SUSv3 explicitly specifies that it should not be implemented using signals. This means that, unlike the situation with *sleep()*, we can portably mix calls to *nanosleep()* with calls to *alarm()* or *setitimer()*.

Although it is not implemented using signals, *nanosleep()* may still be interrupted by a signal handler. In this case, *nanosleep()* returns −1, with *errno* set to the usual EINTR and, if the argument *remain* is not NULL, the buffer it points to returns the remaining unslept time. If desired, we can use the returned value to restart the system call and complete the sleep. This is demonstrated in Listing 23-3. As command-line arguments, this program expects seconds and nanosecond values for *nanosleep()*. The program loops repeatedly, executing *nanosleep()* until the total sleep interval is passed. If *nanosleep()* is interrupted by the handler for SIGINT (generated by typing *Control-C*), then the call is restarted using the value returned in *remain*. When we run this program, we see the following:

```
$ ./t_nanosleep 10 0                    Sleep for 10 seconds
Type Control-C
Slept for:  1.853428 secs
Remaining:  8.146617000
Type Control-C
Slept for:  4.370860 secs
Remaining:  5.629800000
Type Control-C
Slept for:  6.193325 secs
Remaining:  3.807758000
Slept for: 10.008150 secs
Sleep complete
```

Although *nanosleep()* allows nanosecond precision when specifying the sleep interval, the accuracy of the sleep interval is limited to the granularity of the software clock (Section 10.6). If we specify an interval that is not a multiple of the software clock, then the interval is rounded up.

> As noted earlier, on systems that support high-resolution timers, the accuracy of the sleep interval can be much finer than the granularity of the software clock.

This rounding behavior means that if signals are received at a high rate, then there is a problem with the approach employed in the program in Listing 23-3. The problem is that each restart of *nanosleep()* will be subject to rounding errors, since the returned *remain* time is unlikely to be an exact multiple of the granularity of the software clock. Consequently, each restarted *nanosleep()* will sleep longer than the value returned in *remain* by the previous call. In the case of an extremely high rate of signal delivery (i.e., as or more frequent than the software clock granularity), the process may never be able to complete its sleep. On Linux 2.6, this problem can be avoided by making use of *clock_nanosleep()* with the TIMER_ABSTIME option. We describe *clock_nanosleep()* in Section 23.5.4.

> In Linux 2.4 and earlier, there is an eccentricity in the implementation of *nanosleep()*. Suppose that a process performing a *nanosleep()* call is stopped by a signal. When the process is later resumed via delivery of SIGCONT, then the *nanosleep()* call fails with the error EINTR, as expected. However, if the program subsequently restarts the *nanosleep()* call, then the time that the process has spent in the stopped state is *not* counted against the sleep interval, so that the process will sleep longer than expected. This eccentricity is eliminated in Linux 2.6, where the *nanosleep()* call automatically resumes on delivery of the SIGCONT signal, and the time spent in the stopped state is counted against the sleep interval.

Listing 23-3: Using *nanosleep()*

```
#define _POSIX_C_SOURCE 199309
#include <sys/time.h>
#include <time.h>
#include <signal.h>
#include "tlpi_hdr.h"

static void
sigintHandler(int sig)
{
    return;                    /* Just interrupt nanosleep() */
}

int
main(int argc, char *argv[])
{
    struct timeval start, finish;
    struct timespec request, remain;
    struct sigaction sa;
    int s;

    if (argc != 3 || strcmp(argv[1], "--help") == 0)
        usageErr("%s secs nanosecs\n", argv[0]);

    request.tv_sec = getLong(argv[1], 0, "secs");
    request.tv_nsec = getLong(argv[2], 0, "nanosecs");

    /* Allow SIGINT handler to interrupt nanosleep() */

    sigemptyset(&sa.sa_mask);
    sa.sa_flags = 0;
    sa.sa_handler = sigintHandler;
    if (sigaction(SIGINT, &sa, NULL) == -1)
        errExit("sigaction");

    if (gettimeofday(&start, NULL) == -1)
        errExit("gettimeofday");

    for (;;) {
        s = nanosleep(&request, &remain);
        if (s == -1 && errno != EINTR)
            errExit("nanosleep");

        if (gettimeofday(&finish, NULL) == -1)
            errExit("gettimeofday");
        printf("Slept for: %9.6f secs\n", finish.tv_sec - start.tv_sec +
                    (finish.tv_usec - start.tv_usec) / 1000000.0);

        if (s == 0)
            break;                        /* nanosleep() completed */

        printf("Remaining: %2ld.%09ld\n", (long) remain.tv_sec,
                remain.tv_nsec);
```

```
        request = remain;              /* Next sleep is with remaining time */
    }

    printf("Sleep complete\n");
    exit(EXIT_SUCCESS);
}
```
—— timers/t_nanosleep.c

23.5 POSIX Clocks

POSIX clocks (originally defined in POSIX.1b) provide an API for accessing clocks
that measure time with nanosecond precision. Nanosecond time values are represented using the same *timespec* structure as is used by *nanosleep()* (Section 23.4.2).

On Linux, programs using this API must be compiled with the *−lrt* option, in
order to link against the *librt* (realtime) library.

The main system calls in the POSIX clocks API are *clock_gettime()*, which
retrieves the current value of a clock; *clock_getres()*, which returns the resolution of
a clock; and *clock_settime()*, which updates a clock.

23.5.1 Retrieving the Value of a Clock: *clock_gettime()*

The *clock_gettime()* system call returns the time according to the clock specified in
clockid.

```
#define _POSIX_C_SOURCE 199309
#include <time.h>

int clock_gettime(clockid_t clockid, struct timespec *tp);
int clock_getres(clockid_t clockid, struct timespec *res);
                              Both return 0 on success, or −1 on error
```

The time value is returned in the *timespec* structure pointed to by *tp*. Although the
timespec structure affords nanosecond precision, the granularity of the time value
returned by *clock_gettime()* may be coarser than this. The *clock_getres()* system call
returns, via the argument *res*, a pointer to a *timespec* structure containing the resolution of the clock specified in *clockid*.

The *clockid_t* data type is a type specified by SUSv3 for representing a clock
identifier. The first column of Table 23-1 lists the values that can be specified for
clockid.

Table 23-1: POSIX.1b clock types

Clock ID	Description
CLOCK_REALTIME	Settable system-wide real-time clock
CLOCK_MONOTONIC	Nonsettable monotonic clock
CLOCK_PROCESS_CPUTIME_ID	Per-process CPU-time clock (since Linux 2.6.12)
CLOCK_THREAD_CPUTIME_ID	Per-thread CPU-time clock (since Linux 2.6.12)

The CLOCK_REALTIME clock is a system-wide clock that measures wall-clock time. By contrast with the CLOCK_MONOTONIC clock, the setting of this clock can be changed.

SUSv3 specifies that the CLOCK_MONOTONIC clock measures time since some "unspecified point in the past" that doesn't change after system startup. This clock is useful for applications that must not be affected by discontinuous changes to the system clock (e.g., a manual change to the system time). On Linux, this clock measures the time since system startup.

The CLOCK_PROCESS_CPUTIME_ID clock measures the user and system CPU time consumed by the calling process. The CLOCK_THREAD_CPUTIME_ID clock performs the analogous task for an individual thread within a process.

All of the clocks in Table 23-1 are specified in SUSv3, but only CLOCK_REALTIME is mandatory and widely supported on UNIX implementations.

> Linux 2.6.28 adds a new clock type, CLOCK_MONOTONIC_RAW, to those listed in Table 23-1. This is a nonsettable clock that is similar to CLOCK_MONOTONIC, but it gives access to a pure hardware-based time that is unaffected by NTP adjustments. This nonstandard clock is intended for use in specialized clock-synchronization applications.
>
> Linux 2.6.32 adds two more new clocks to those listed in Table 23-1: CLOCK_REALTIME_COARSE and CLOCK_MONOTONIC_COARSE. These clocks are similar to CLOCK_REALTIME and CLOCK_MONOTONIC, but intended for applications that want to obtain lower-resolution timestamps at minimal cost. These nonstandard clocks don't cause any access to the hardware clock (which can be expensive for some hardware clock sources), and the resolution of the returned value is the jiffy (Section 10.6).

23.5.2 Setting the Value of a Clock: *clock_settime()*

The *clock_settime()* system call sets the clock specified by *clockid* to the time supplied in the buffer pointed to by *tp*.

```
#define _POSIX_C_SOURCE 199309
#include <time.h>

int clock_settime(clockid_t clockid, const struct timespec *tp);
```
                                        Returns 0 on success, or −1 on error

If the time specified by *tp* is not a multiple of the clock resolution as returned by *clock_getres()*, the time is rounded downward.

A privileged (CAP_SYS_TIME) process may set the CLOCK_REALTIME clock. The initial value of this clock is typically the time since the Epoch. None of the other clocks in Table 23-1 are modifiable.

> According to SUSv3, an implementation may allow the CLOCK_PROCESS_CPUTIME_ID and CLOCK_THREAD_CPUTIME_ID clocks to be settable. At the time of writing, these clocks are read-only on Linux.

23.5.3 Obtaining the Clock ID of a Specific Process or Thread

The functions described in this section allow us to obtain the ID of a clock that measures the CPU time consumed by a particular process or thread. We can use the returned clock ID in a call to *clock_gettime()* in order to find out the CPU time consumed by the process or thread.

The *clock_getcpuclockid()* function returns the identifier of the CPU-time clock of the process whose ID is *pid*, in the buffer pointed to by *clockid*.

```
#include <time.h>

int clock_getcpuclockid(pid_t pid, clockid_t *clockid);
```
                        Returns 0 on success, or a positive error number on error

If *pid* is 0, *clock_getcpuclockid()* returns the ID of the CPU-time clock of the calling process.

The *pthread_getcpuclockid()* function is the POSIX threads analog of the *clock_getcpuclockid()* function. It returns the identifier of the clock measuring the CPU time consumed by a specific thread of the calling process.

```
#include <pthread.h>
#include <time.h>

int pthread_getcpuclockid(pthread_t thread, clockid_t *clockid);
```
                        Returns 0 on success, or a positive error number on error

The *thread* argument is a POSIX thread ID that identifies the thread whose CPU-time clock ID we want to obtain. The clock ID is returned in the buffer pointed to by *clockid*.

23.5.4 Improved High-Resolution Sleeping: *clock_nanosleep()*

Like *nanosleep()*, the Linux-specific *clock_nanosleep()* system call suspends the calling process until either a specified interval of time has passed or a signal arrives. In this section, we describe the features that distinguish *clock_nanosleep()* from *nanosleep()*.

```
#include <time.h>

int clock_nanosleep(clockid_t clockid, int flags,
        const struct timespec *request, struct timespec *remain);
```
                        Returns 0 on successfully completed sleep,
                or a positive error number on error or interrupted sleep

The *request* and *remain* arguments serve similar purposes to the analogous arguments for *nanosleep()*.

By default (i.e., if *flags* is 0), the sleep interval specified in *request* is relative (like *nanosleep()*). However, if we specify TIMER_ABSTIME in *flags* (see the example in Listing 23-4), then *request* specifies an absolute time as measured by the clock identified by *clockid*. This feature is essential in applications that need to sleep accurately until a specific time. If we instead try retrieving the current time, calculating the difference until the desired target time, and doing a relative sleep, then there is a possibility that the process may be preempted in the middle of these steps, and consequently sleep for longer than desired.

As described in Section 23.4.2, this "oversleeping" problem is particularly marked for a process that uses a loop to restart a sleep that is interrupted by a signal handler. If signals are delivered at a high rate, then a relative sleep (of the type performed by *nanosleep()*) can lead to large inaccuracies in the time a process spends sleeping. We can avoid the oversleeping problem by making an initial call to *clock_gettime()* to retrieve the time, adding the desired amount to that time, and then calling *clock_nanosleep()* with the TIMER_ABSTIME flag (and restarting the system call if it is interrupted by a signal handler).

When the TIMER_ABSTIME flag is specified, the *remain* argument is unused (it is unnecessary). If the *clock_nanosleep()* call is interrupted by a signal handler, then the sleep can be restarted by repeating the call with the same *request* argument.

Another feature that distinguishes *clock_nanosleep()* from *nanosleep()* is that we can choose the clock that is used to measure the sleep interval. We specify the desired clock in *clockid*: CLOCK_REALTIME, CLOCK_MONOTONIC, or CLOCK_PROCESS_CPUTIME_ID. See Table 23-1 for a description of these clocks.

Listing 23-4 demonstrates the use of *clock_nanosleep()* to sleep for 20 seconds against the CLOCK_REALTIME clock using an absolute time value.

Listing 23-4: Using *clock_nanosleep()*

```
struct timespec request;

/* Retrieve current value of CLOCK_REALTIME clock */

if (clock_gettime(CLOCK_REALTIME, &request) == -1)
    errExit("clock_gettime");

request.tv_sec += 20;                  /* Sleep for 20 seconds from now */

s = clock_nanosleep(CLOCK_REALTIME, TIMER_ABSTIME, &request, NULL);
if (s != 0) {
    if (s == EINTR)
        printf("Interrupted by signal handler\n");
    else
        errExitEN(s, "clock_nanosleep");
}
```

23.6 POSIX Interval Timers

The classical UNIX interval timers set by *setitimer()* suffer a number of limitations:

- We can set only one timer of each of the three types, ITIMER_REAL, ITIMER_VIRTUAL, and ITIMER_PROF.

- The only way of being notified of timer expiration is via delivery of a signal. Furthermore, we can't change the signal that is generated when the timer expires.

- If an interval timer expires multiple times while the corresponding signal is blocked, then the signal handler is called only once. In other words, we have no way of knowing whether there was a *timer overrun*.

- Timers are limited to microsecond resolution. However, some systems have hardware clocks that provide finer resolution than this, and, on such systems, it is desirable to have software access to this greater resolution.

POSIX.1b defined an API to address these limitations, and this API is implemented in Linux 2.6.

> On older Linux systems, an incomplete version of this API was provided via a threads-based implementation in *glibc*. However, this user-space implementation doesn't provide all of the features described here.

The POSIX timer API divides the life of a timer into the following steps:

- The *timer_create()* system call creates a new timer and defines the method by which it will notify the process when it expires.

- The *timer_settime()* system call arms (starts) or disarms (stops) a timer.

- The *timer_delete()* system call deletes a timer that is no longer required.

POSIX timers are not inherited by a child created by *fork()*. They are disarmed and deleted during an *exec()* or on process termination.

On Linux, programs using the POSIX timer API must be compiled with the *-lrt* option, in order to link against the *librt* (realtime) library.

23.6.1 Creating a Timer: *timer_create()*

The *timer_create()* function creates a new timer that measures time using the clock specified by *clockid*.

```
#define _POSIX_C_SOURCE 199309
#include <signal.h>
#include <time.h>

int timer_create(clockid_t clockid, struct sigevent *evp, timer_t *timerid);
```
                                               Returns 0 on success, or −1 on error

The *clockid* can specify any of the values shown in Table 23-1, or the *clockid* value returned by *clock_getcpuclockid()* or *pthread_getcpuclockid()*. The *timerid* argument points to a buffer that returns a handle used to refer to the timer in later system calls. This buffer is typed as *timer_t*, which is a data type specified by SUSv3 for representing a timer identifier.

The *evp* argument determines how the program is to be notified when the timer expires. It points to a structure of type *sigevent*, defined as follows:

```
union sigval {
    int    sival_int;          /* Integer value for accompanying data */
    void *sival_ptr;           /* Pointer value for accompanying data */
};

struct sigevent {
    int           sigev_notify;   /* Notification method */
    int           sigev_signo;    /* Timer expiration signal */
    union sigval sigev_value;     /* Value accompanying signal or
                                     passed to thread function */
    union {
        pid_t      _tid;          /* ID of thread to be signaled */
        struct {
            void (*_function) (union sigval);
                                  /* Thread notification function */
            void  *_attribute;    /* Really 'pthread_attr_t *' */
        } _sigev_thread;
    } _sigev_un;
};

#define sigev_notify_function     _sigev_un._sigev_thread._function
#define sigev_notify_attributes   _sigev_un._sigev_thread._attribute
#define sigev_notify_thread_id    _sigev_un._tid
```

The *sigev_notify* field of this structure is set to one of the values shown in Table 23-2.

Table 23-2: Values for the *sigev_notify* field of the *sigevent* structure

sigev_notify value	Notification method	SUSv3
SIGEV_NONE	No notification; monitor timer using *timer_gettime()*	•
SIGEV_SIGNAL	Send signal *sigev_signo* to process	•
SIGEV_THREAD	Call *sigev_notify_function* as start function of new thread	•
SIGEV_THREAD_ID	Send signal *sigev_signo* to thread *sigev_notify_thread_id*	

Further details on the *sigev_notify* field constants, and the fields in the *sigval* structure that are associated with each constant value, are as follows:

SIGEV_NONE

Don't provide notification of timer expiration. The process can still monitor the progress of the timer using *timer_gettime()*.

SIGEV_SIGNAL

When the timer expires, generate the signal specified in the *sigev_signo* field for the process. The *sigev_value* field specifies data (an integer or a pointer) to accompany the signal (Section 22.8.1). This data can be retrieved via the *si_value* field of the *siginfo_t* structure that is passed to the handler for this signal or returned by a call to *sigwaitinfo()* or *sigtimedwait()*.

SIGEV_THREAD

When the timer expires, call the function specified in the *sigev_notify_function* field. This function is invoked *as if* it were the start function in a new thread. The "as if" wording is from SUSv3, and allows an implementation to generate the notifications for a periodic timer either by having each notification delivered to a new unique thread or by having the notifications delivered in series to a single new thread. The *sigev_notify_attributes* field can be specified as NULL or as a pointer to a *pthread_attr_t* structure that defines attributes for the thread (Section 29.8). The union *sigval* value specified in *sigev_value* is passed as the sole argument of the function.

SIGEV_THREAD_ID

This is similar to SIGEV_SIGNAL, but the signal is sent to the thread whose thread ID matches *sigev_notify_thread_id*. This thread must be in the same process as the calling thread. (With SIGEV_SIGNAL notification, a signal is queued to the process as a whole, and, if there are multiple threads in the process, the signal will be delivered to an arbitrarily selected thread in the process. See Section 33.2 for a discussion of the interaction of threads and signals.) The *sigev_notify_thread_id* field can be set to the value returned by *clone()* or the value returned by *gettid()*. The SIGEV_THREAD_ID flag is intended for use by threading libraries. (It requires a threading implementation that employs the CLONE_THREAD option, described in Section 28.2.1. The modern NPTL threading implementation employs CLONE_THREAD, but the older LinuxThreads threading implementation does not.)

All of the above constants are specified in SUSv3, except for SIGEV_THREAD_ID, which is Linux-specific.

The *evp* argument may be specified as NULL, which is equivalent to specifying *sigev_notify* as SIGEV_SIGNAL, *sigev_signo* as SIGALRM (this may be different on other systems, since SUSv3 merely says "a default signal number"), and *sigev_value.sival_int* as the timer ID.

As currently implemented, the kernel preallocates one queued realtime signal structure for each POSIX timer that is created using *timer_create()*. The intent of this preallocation is to ensure that at least one such structure is available for queuing a signal when the timer expires. This means that the number of POSIX timers that may be created is subject to the limitations on the number of realtime signals that can be queued (refer to Section 22.8).

23.6.2 Arming and Disarming a Timer: *timer_settime()*

Once we have created a timer, we can arm (start) or disarm (stop) it using *timer_settime()*.

```
#define _POSIX_C_SOURCE 199309
#include <time.h>

int timer_settime(timer_t timerid, int flags, const struct itimerspec *value,
                  struct itimerspec *old_value);
```

> > > Returns 0 on success, or −1 on error

The *timerid* argument of *timer_settime()* is a timer handle returned by a previous call to *timer_create()*.

The *value* and *old_value* arguments are analogous to the *setitimer()* arguments of the same name: *value* specifies the new settings for the timer, and *old_value* is used to return the previous timer settings (see the description of *timer_gettime()* below). If we are not interested in the previous settings, we can specify *old_value* as NULL. The *value* and *old_value* arguments are pointers to *itimerspec* structures, defined as follows:

```
struct itimerspec {
    struct timespec it_interval;    /* Interval for periodic timer */
    struct timespec it_value;       /* First expiration */
};
```

Each of the fields of the *itimerspec* structure is in turn a structure of type *timespec*, which specifies time values as a number of seconds and nanoseconds:

```
struct timespec {
    time_t tv_sec;                  /* Seconds */
    long   tv_nsec;                 /* Nanoseconds */
};
```

The *it_value* field specifies when the timer will first expire. If either subfield of *it_interval* is nonzero, then this is a periodic timer that, after the initial expiry specified by *it_value*, will expire with the frequency specified in these subfields. If both subfields of *it_interval* are 0, this timer expires just once.

If *flags* is specified as 0, then *value.it_value* is interpreted relative to the clock value at the time of the call to *timer_settime()* (i.e., like *setitimer()*). If *flags* is specified as TIMER_ABSTIME, then *value.it_value* is interpreted as an absolute time (i.e., measured from the clock's zero point). If that time has already passed on the clock, the timer expires immediately.

To arm a timer, we make a call to *timer_settime()* in which either or both of the subfields of *value.it_value* are nonzero. If the timer was previously armed, *timer_settime()* replaces the previous settings.

If the timer value and interval are not multiples of the resolution of the corresponding clock (as returned by *clock_getres()*), these values are rounded up to the next multiple of the resolution.

On each expiration of the timer, the process is notified using the method defined in the *timer_create()* call that created this timer. If the *it_interval* structure contains nonzero values, these values are used to reload the *it_value* structure.

To disarm a timer, we make a call to *timer_settime()* specifying both fields of *value.it_value* as 0.

23.6.3 Retrieving the Current Value of a Timer: *timer_gettime()*

The *timer_gettime()* system call returns the interval and remaining time for the POSIX timer identified by *timerid*.

```
#define _POSIX_C_SOURCE 199309
#include <time.h>

int timer_gettime(timer_t timerid, struct itimerspec *curr_value);
```
                                          Returns 0 on success, or −1 on error

The interval and the time until the next expiration of the timer are returned in the *itimerspec* structure pointed to by *curr_value*. The *curr_value.it_value* field returns the time until next timer expiration, even if this timer was established as an absolute timer using TIMER_ABSTIME.

If both fields of the returned *curr_value.it_value* structure are 0, then the timer is currently disarmed. If both fields of the returned *curr_value.it_interval* structure are 0, then the timer expires just once, at the time given in *curr_value.it_value*.

23.6.4 Deleting a Timer: *timer_delete()*

Each POSIX timer consumes a small amount of system resources. Therefore, when we have finished using a timer, we should free these resources by using *timer_delete()* to remove the timer.

```
#define _POSIX_C_SOURCE 199309
#include <time.h>

int timer_delete(timer_t timerid);
```
                                          Returns 0 on success, or −1 on error

The *timerid* argument is a handle returned by a previous call to *timer_create()*. If the timer was armed, then it is automatically disarmed before removal. If there is already a pending signal from an expiration of this timer, that signal remains pending. (SUSv3 leaves this point unspecified, so other UNIX implementations may behave differently.) Timers are deleted automatically when a process terminates.

23.6.5 Notification via a Signal

If we elect to receive timer notifications via a signal, then we can accept the signal via a signal handler, or by calling *sigwaitinfo()* or *sigtimedwait()*. Both mechanisms allow the receiving process to obtain a *siginfo_t* structure (Section 21.4) that provides further information about the signal. (To take advantage of this feature in a signal handler, we specify the SA_SIGINFO flag when establishing the handler.) The following fields are set in the *siginfo_t* structure:

- *si_signo*: This field contains the signal generated by this timer.
- *si_code*: This field is set to SI_TIMER, indicating that this signal was generated because of the expiration of a POSIX timer.
- *si_value*: This field is set to the value that was supplied in *evp.sigev_value* when the timer was created using *timer_create()*. Specifying different *evp.sigev_value* values provides a means of distinguishing expirations of multiple timers that deliver the same signal.

When calling *timer_create()*, *evp.sigev_value.sival_ptr* is typically assigned the address of the *timerid* argument given in the same call (see Listing 23-5). This allows the signal handler (or the *sigwaitinfo()* call) to obtain the ID of the timer that generated the signal. (Alternatively, *evp.sigev_value.sival_ptr* may be assigned the address of a structure that contains the *timerid* given to *timer_create()*.)

Linux also supplies the following nonstandard field in the *siginfo_t* structure:

- *si_overrun*: This field contains the overrun count for this timer (described in Section 23.6.6).

> Linux also supplies another nonstandard field: *si_timerid*. This field contains an identifier that is used internally by the system to identify the timer (it is not the same as the ID returned by *timer_create()*). It is not useful to applications.

Listing 23-5 demonstrates the use of signals as the notification mechanism for a POSIX timer.

Listing 23-5: POSIX timer notification using a signal

```
────────────────────────────────────────────────── timers/ptmr_sigev_signal.c
#define _POSIX_C_SOURCE 199309
#include <signal.h>
#include <time.h>
#include "curr_time.h"                  /* Declares currTime() */
#include "itimerspec_from_str.h"        /* Declares itimerspecFromStr() */
#include "tlpi_hdr.h"

#define TIMER_SIG SIGRTMAX              /* Our timer notification signal */

   static void
① handler(int sig, siginfo_t *si, void *uc)
   {
       timer_t *tidptr;

       tidptr = si->si_value.sival_ptr;

       /* UNSAFE: This handler uses non-async-signal-safe functions
          (printf(); see Section 21.1.2) */
```

```
        printf("[%s] Got signal %d\n", currTime("%T"), sig);
        printf("    *sival_ptr        = %ld\n", (long) *tidptr);
        printf("    timer_getoverrun() = %d\n", timer_getoverrun(*tidptr));
    }

    int
    main(int argc, char *argv[])
    {
        struct itimerspec ts;
        struct sigaction  sa;
        struct sigevent   sev;
        timer_t *tidlist;
        int j;

        if (argc < 2)
            usageErr("%s secs[/nsecs][:int-secs[/int-nsecs]]...\n", argv[0]);

        tidlist = calloc(argc - 1, sizeof(timer_t));
        if (tidlist == NULL)
            errExit("malloc");

        /* Establish handler for notification signal */

        sa.sa_flags = SA_SIGINFO;
        sa.sa_sigaction = handler;
        sigemptyset(&sa.sa_mask);
②      if (sigaction(TIMER_SIG, &sa, NULL) == -1)
            errExit("sigaction");

        /* Create and start one timer for each command-line argument */

        sev.sigev_notify = SIGEV_SIGNAL;    /* Notify via signal */
        sev.sigev_signo = TIMER_SIG;        /* Notify using this signal */

        for (j = 0; j < argc - 1; j++) {
③          itimerspecFromStr(argv[j + 1], &ts);

            sev.sigev_value.sival_ptr = &tidlist[j];
                /* Allows handler to get ID of this timer */

④          if (timer_create(CLOCK_REALTIME, &sev, &tidlist[j]) == -1)
                errExit("timer_create");
            printf("Timer ID: %ld (%s)\n", (long) tidlist[j], argv[j + 1]);

⑤          if (timer_settime(tidlist[j], 0, &ts, NULL) == -1)
                errExit("timer_settime");
        }

⑥      for (;;)                            /* Wait for incoming timer signals */
            pause();
    }
```
── **timers/ptmr_sigev_signal.c**

Each of the command-line arguments of the program in Listing 23-5 specifies the initial value and interval for a timer. The syntax of these arguments is described in the program's "usage" message and demonstrated in the shell session below. This program performs the following steps:

- Establish a handler for the signal that is used for timer notifications ②.
- For each command-line argument, create ④ and arm ⑤ a POSIX timer that uses the SIGEV_SIGNAL notification mechanism. The *itimerspecFromStr()* function that we use to convert ③ the command-line arguments to *itimerspec* structures is shown in Listing 23-6.
- On each timer expiration, the signal specified in *sev.sigev_signo* will be delivered to the process. The handler for this signal displays the value that was supplied in *sev.sigev_value.sival_ptr* (i.e., the timer ID, *tidlist[j]*) and the overrun value for the timer ①.
- Having created and armed the timers, wait for timer expirations by executing a loop that repeatedly calls *pause()* ⑥.

Listing 23-6 shows the function that converts each of the command-line arguments for the program in Listing 23-5 into a corresponding *itimerspec* structure. The format of the string arguments interpreted by this function is shown in a comment at the top of the listing (and demonstrated in the shell session below).

Listing 23-6: Converting time-plus-interval string to an *itimerspec* value

—— timers/itimerspec_from_str.c

```
#include <string.h>
#include <stdlib.h>
#include "itimerspec_from_str.h"        /* Declares function defined here */

/* Convert a string of the following form to an itimerspec structure:
   "value.sec[/value.nanosec][:interval.sec[/interval.nanosec]]".
   Optional components that are omitted cause 0 to be assigned to the
   corresponding structure fields. */

void
itimerspecFromStr(char *str, struct itimerspec *tsp)
{
    char *dupstr, *cptr, *sptr;

    dupstr = strdup(str);

    cptr = strchr(dupstr, ':');
    if (cptr != NULL)
        *cptr = '\0';

    sptr = strchr(dupstr, '/');
    if (sptr != NULL)
        *sptr = '\0';

    tsp->it_value.tv_sec = atoi(dupstr);
    tsp->it_value.tv_nsec = (sptr != NULL) ? atoi(sptr + 1) : 0;
```

```
        if (cptr == NULL) {
            tsp->it_interval.tv_sec = 0;
            tsp->it_interval.tv_nsec = 0;
        } else {
            sptr = strchr(cptr + 1, '/');
            if (sptr != NULL)
                *sptr = '\0';
            tsp->it_interval.tv_sec = atoi(cptr + 1);
            tsp->it_interval.tv_nsec = (sptr != NULL) ? atoi(sptr + 1) : 0;
        }
        free(dupstr);
    }
```
—— timers/itimerspec_from_str.c

We demonstrate the use of the program in Listing 23-5 in the following shell session, creating a single timer with an initial timer expiry of 2 seconds and an interval of 5 seconds.

```
$ ./ptmr_sigev_signal 2:5
Timer ID: 134524952 (2:5)
[15:54:56] Got signal 64                    SIGRTMAX is signal 64 on this system
    *sival_ptr        = 134524952          sival_ptr points to the variable tid
    timer_getoverrun() = 0
[15:55:01] Got signal 64
    *sival_ptr        = 134524952
    timer_getoverrun() = 0
Type Control-Z to suspend the process
[1]+  Stopped         ./ptmr_sigev_signal 2:5
```

After suspending the program, we pause for a few seconds, allowing several timer expirations to occur before we resume the program:

```
$ fg
./ptmr_sigev_signal 2:5
[15:55:34] Got signal 64
    *sival_ptr        = 134524952
    timer_getoverrun() = 5
Type Control-C to kill the program
```

The last line of program output shows that five timer overruns occurred, meaning that six timer expirations occurred since the previous signal delivery.

23.6.6 Timer Overruns

Suppose that we have chosen to receive notification of timer expiration via delivery of a signal (i.e., *sigev_notify* is SIGEV_SIGNAL). Suppose further that the timer expires multiple times before the associated signal is caught or accepted. This could occur as the result of a delay before the process is next scheduled. Alternatively, it could occur because delivery of the associated signal was blocked, either explicitly via *sigprocmask()*, or implicitly during the execution of the handler for the signal. How do we know that such *timer overruns* have happened?

We might suppose that using a realtime signal would help solve this problem, since multiple instances of a realtime signal are queued. However, this approach turns out to be unworkable, because there are limits on the number of realtime signals that can be queued. Therefore, the POSIX.1b committee decided on a different approach: if we choose to receive timer notification via a signal, then multiple instances of the signal are never queued, even if we use a realtime signal. Instead, after receiving the signal (either via a signal handler or by using *sigwaitinfo()*), we can fetch the *timer overrun count*, which is the number of extra timer expirations that occurred between the time the signal was generated and the time it was received. For example, if the timer has expired three times since the last signal was received, then the overrun count is 2.

After receiving a timer signal, we can obtain the timer overrun count in two ways:

- Call *timer_getoverrun()*, which we describe below. This is the SUSv3-specified way of obtaining the overrun count.
- Use the value in the *si_overrun* field of the *siginfo_t* structure returned with the signal. This approach saves the overhead of the *timer_getoverrun()* system call, but is a nonportable Linux extension.

The timer overrun count is reset each time we receive the timer signal. If the timer expired just once since the timer signal was handled or accepted, then the overrun count will be 0 (i.e., there were no overruns).

```
#define _POSIX_C_SOURCE 199309
#include <time.h>

int timer_getoverrun(timer_t timerid);
```
                              Returns timer overrun count on success, or −1 on error

The *timer_getoverrun()* function returns the overrun count for the timer specified by its *timerid* argument.

The *timer_getoverrun()* function is one of those specified as being async-signal-safe in SUSv3 (Table 21-1, on page 426), so it is safe to call it from within a signal handler.

23.6.7 Notification via a Thread

The SIGEV_THREAD flag allows a program to obtain notification of timer expiration via the invocation of a function in a separate thread. Understanding this flag requires knowledge of POSIX threads that we present later, in Chapters 29 and 30. Readers unfamiliar with POSIX threads may want to read those chapters before examining the example program that we present in this section.

Listing 23-7 demonstrates the use of SIGEV_THREAD. This program takes the same command-line arguments as the program in Listing 23-5. The program performs the following steps:

- For each command-line argument, the program creates ⑥ and arms ⑦ a POSIX timer that uses the SIGEV_THREAD notification mechanism ③.
- Each time this timer expires, the function specified by *sev.sigev_notify_function* ④ will be invoked in a separate thread. When this function is invoked, it receives

the value specified in *sev.sigev_value.sival_ptr* as an argument. We assign the address of the timer ID (*tidlist[j]*) to this field ⑤ so that the notification function can obtain the ID of the timer that caused its invocation.

- Having created and armed all of the timers, the main program enters a loop that waits for timer expirations ⑧. Each time through the loop, the program uses *pthread_cond_wait()* to wait for a condition variable (*cond*) to be signaled by the thread that is handling a timer notification.

- The *threadFunc()* function is invoked on each timer expiration ①. After printing a message, it increments the value of the global variable *expireCnt*. To allow for the possibility of timer overruns, the value returned by *timer_getoverrun()* is also added to *expireCnt*. (We explained timer overruns in Section 23.6.6 in relation to the SIGEV_SIGNAL notification mechanism. Timer overruns can also come into play with the SIGEV_THREAD mechanism, because a timer might expire multiple times before the notification function is invoked.) The notification function also signals the condition variable *cond* so that the main program knows to check that a timer has expired ②.

The following shell session log demonstrates the use of the program in Listing 23-7. In this example, the program creates two timers: one with an initial expiry of 5 seconds and an interval of 5 seconds, and the other with an initial expiration of 10 seconds and an interval of 10 seconds.

```
$ ./ptmr_sigev_thread 5:5 10:10
Timer ID: 134525024 (5:5)
Timer ID: 134525080 (10:10)
[13:06:22] Thread notify
    timer ID=134525024
    timer_getoverrun()=0
main(): expireCnt = 1
[13:06:27] Thread notify
    timer ID=134525080
    timer_getoverrun()=0
main(): expireCnt = 2
[13:06:27] Thread notify
    timer ID=134525024
    timer_getoverrun()=0
main(): expireCnt = 3
```
Type Control-Z to suspend the program
```
[1]+  Stopped         ./ptmr_sigev_thread 5:5 10:10
$ fg                                    Resume execution
./ptmr_sigev_thread 5:5 10:10
[13:06:45] Thread notify
    timer ID=134525024
    timer_getoverrun()=2                There were timer overruns
main(): expireCnt = 6
[13:06:45] Thread notify
    timer ID=134525080
    timer_getoverrun()=0
main(): expireCnt = 7
```
Type Control-C to kill the program

Listing 23-7: POSIX timer notification using a thread function

─── timers/ptmr_sigev_thread.c

```
#include <signal.h>
#include <time.h>
#include <pthread.h>
#include "curr_time.h"            /* Declaration of currTime() */
#include "tlpi_hdr.h"
#include "itimerspec_from_str.h"  /* Declares itimerspecFromStr() */

static pthread_mutex_t mtx = PTHREAD_MUTEX_INITIALIZER;
static pthread_cond_t cond = PTHREAD_COND_INITIALIZER;

static int expireCnt = 0;         /* Number of expirations of all timers */

static void                       /* Thread notification function */
① threadFunc(union sigval sv)
{
    timer_t *tidptr;
    int s;

    tidptr = sv.sival_ptr;

    printf("[%s] Thread notify\n", currTime("%T"));
    printf("    timer ID=%ld\n", (long) *tidptr);
    printf("    timer_getoverrun()=%d\n", timer_getoverrun(*tidptr));

    /* Increment counter variable shared with main thread and signal
       condition variable to notify main thread of the change. */

    s = pthread_mutex_lock(&mtx);
    if (s != 0)
        errExitEN(s, "pthread_mutex_lock");

    expireCnt += 1 + timer_getoverrun(*tidptr);

    s = pthread_mutex_unlock(&mtx);
    if (s != 0)
        errExitEN(s, "pthread_mutex_unlock");

②   s = pthread_cond_signal(&cond);
    if (s != 0)
        errExitEN(s, "pthread_cond_signal");
}

int
main(int argc, char *argv[])
{
    struct sigevent sev;
    struct itimerspec ts;
    timer_t *tidlist;
    int s, j;
```

```
            if (argc < 2)
                usageErr("%s secs[/nsecs][:int-secs[/int-nsecs]]...\n", argv[0]);

            tidlist = calloc(argc - 1, sizeof(timer_t));
            if (tidlist == NULL)
                errExit("malloc");

③          sev.sigev_notify = SIGEV_THREAD;            /* Notify via thread */
④          sev.sigev_notify_function = threadFunc;     /* Thread start function */
            sev.sigev_notify_attributes = NULL;
                    /* Could be pointer to pthread_attr_t structure */

            /* Create and start one timer for each command-line argument */

            for (j = 0; j < argc - 1; j++) {
                itimerspecFromStr(argv[j + 1], &ts);

⑤              sev.sigev_value.sival_ptr = &tidlist[j];
                        /* Passed as argument to threadFunc() */

⑥              if (timer_create(CLOCK_REALTIME, &sev, &tidlist[j]) == -1)
                    errExit("timer_create");
                printf("Timer ID: %ld (%s)\n", (long) tidlist[j], argv[j + 1]);

⑦              if (timer_settime(tidlist[j], 0, &ts, NULL) == -1)
                    errExit("timer_settime");
            }

            /* The main thread waits on a condition variable that is signaled
               on each invocation of the thread notification function. We
               print a message so that the user can see that this occurred. */

            s = pthread_mutex_lock(&mtx);
            if (s != 0)
                errExitEN(s, "pthread_mutex_lock");

⑧          for (;;) {
                s = pthread_cond_wait(&cond, &mtx);
                if (s != 0)
                    errExitEN(s, "pthread_cond_wait");
                printf("main(): expireCnt = %d\n", expireCnt);
            }
        }
```

—— timers/ptmr_sigev_thread.c

23.7 Timers That Notify via File Descriptors: The *timerfd* API

Starting with kernel 2.6.25, Linux provides another API for creating timers. The
Linux-specific *timerfd* API creates a timer whose expiration notifications can be
read from a file descriptor. This is useful because the file descriptor can be monitored along with other descriptors using *select()*, *poll()*, and *epoll* (described in Chapter 63). (With the other timer APIs discussed in this chapter, it requires some effort

to be able to simultaneously monitor one or more timers along with a set of file descriptors.)

The operation of the three new system calls in this API is analogous to the operation of the *timer_create()*, *timer_settime()*, and *timer_gettime()* system calls described in Section 23.6.

The first of the new system calls is *timerfd_create()*, which creates a new timer object and returns a file descriptor referring to that object.

```
#include <sys/timerfd.h>

int timerfd_create(int clockid, int flags);
```
                                    Returns file descriptor on success, or –1 on error

The value of *clockid* can be either CLOCK_REALTIME or CLOCK_MONOTONIC (see Table 23-1).

In the initial implementation of *timerfd_create()*, the *flags* argument was reserved for future use and had to be specified as 0. However, since Linux 2.6.27, two flags are supported:

TFD_CLOEXEC
> Set the close-on-exec flag (FD_CLOEXEC) for the new file descriptor. This flag is useful for the same reasons as the *open()* O_CLOEXEC flag described in Section 4.3.1.

TFD_NONBLOCK
> Set the O_NONBLOCK flag on the underlying open file description, so that future reads will be nonblocking. This saves additional calls to *fcntl()* to achieve the same result.

When we have finished using a timer created by *timerfd_create()*, we should *close()* the associated file descriptor, so that the kernel can free the resources associated with the timer.

The *timerfd_settime()* system call arms (starts) or disarms (stops) the timer referred to by the file descriptor *fd*.

```
#include <sys/timerfd.h>

int timerfd_settime(int fd, int flags, const struct itimerspec *new_value,
                    struct itimerspec *old_value);
```
                                    Returns 0 on success, or –1 on error

The *new_value* argument specifies the new settings for the timer. The *old_value* argument can be used to return the previous settings of the timer (see the description of *timerfd_gettime()* below for details). If we are not interested in the previous settings, we can specify *old_value* as NULL. Both of these arguments are *itimerspec* structures that are used in the same way as for *timer_settime()* (see Section 23.6.2).

The *flags* argument is similar to the corresponding argument for *timer_settime()*. It may either be 0, meaning that *new_value.it_value* is interpreted relative to the time of the call to *timerfd_settime()*, or it can be TFD_TIMER_ABSTIME, meaning that *new_value.it_value* is interpreted as an absolute time (i.e., measured from the clock's zero point).

The *timerfd_gettime()* system call returns the interval and remaining time for the timer identified by the file descriptor *fd*.

```
#include <sys/timerfd.h>

int timerfd_gettime(int fd, struct itimerspec *curr_value);
```
                                                    Returns 0 on success, or –1 on error

As with *timer_gettime()*, the interval and the time until the next expiration of the timer are returned in the *itimerspec* structure pointed to by *curr_value*. The *curr_value.it_value* field returns the time until the next timer expiration, even if this timer was established as an absolute timer using TFD_TIMER_ABSTIME. If both fields of the returned *curr_value.it_value* structure are 0, then the timer is currently disarmed. If both fields of the returned *curr_value.it_interval* structure are 0, then the timer expires just once, at the time given in *curr_value.it_value*.

Interactions of *timerfd* with *fork()* and *exec()*

During a *fork()*, a child process inherits copies of file descriptors created by *timerfd_create()*. These file descriptors refer to the same timer objects as the corresponding descriptors in the parent, and timer expirations can be read in either process.

File descriptors created by *timerfd_create()* are preserved across an *exec()* (unless the descriptors are marked close-on-exec, as described in Section 27.4), and armed timers will continue to generate timer expirations after the *exec()*.

Reading from the *timerfd* file descriptor

Once we have armed a timer with *timerfd_settime()*, we can use *read()* to read information about timer expirations from the associated file descriptor. For this purpose, the buffer given to *read()* must be large enough to hold an unsigned 8-byte integer (*uint64_t*).

If one or more expirations have occurred since the timer settings were last modified using *timerfd_settime()* or the last *read()* was performed, then *read()* returns immediately, and the returned buffer contains the number of expirations that have occurred. If no timer expirations have occurred, then *read()* blocks until the next expiration occurs. It is also possible to use the *fcntl()* F_SETFL operation (Section 5.3) to set the O_NONBLOCK flag for the file descriptor, so that reads are nonblocking, and will fail with the error EAGAIN if no timer expirations have occurred.

As stated earlier, a *timerfd* file descriptor can be monitored using *select()*, *poll()*, and *epoll*. If the timer has expired, then the file descriptor indicates as being readable.

Example program

Listing 23-8 demonstrates the use of the *timerfd* API. This program takes two command-line arguments. The first argument is mandatory, and specifies the initial time and interval for a timer. (This argument is interpreted using the *itimerspecFromStr()* function shown in Listing 23-6.) The second argument, which is optional, specifies the maximum number of expirations of the timer that the program should wait for before terminating; the default for this argument is 1.

The program creates a timer using *timerfd_create()*, and arms it using *timerfd_settime()*. It then loops, reading expiration notifications from the file descriptor until the specified number of expirations has been reached. After each *read()*, the program displays the time elapsed since the timer was started, the number of expirations read, and the total number of expirations so far.

In the following shell session log, the command-line arguments specify a timer with a 1-second initial value and 1-second interval, and a maximum of 100 expirations.

```
$ ./demo_timerfd 1:1 100
1.000: expirations read: 1; total=1
2.000: expirations read: 1; total=2
3.000: expirations read: 1; total=3
Type Control-Z to suspend program in background for a few seconds
[1]+  Stopped                 ./demo_timerfd 1:1 100
$ fg                                         Resume program in foreground
./demo_timerfd 1:1 100
14.205: expirations read: 11; total=14    Multiple expirations since last read()
15.000: expirations read: 1; total=15
16.000: expirations read: 1; total=16
Type Control-C to terminate the program
```

From the above output, we can see that multiple timer expirations occurred while the program was suspended in the background, and all of these expirations were returned on the first *read()* after the program resumed execution.

Listing 23-8: Using the *timerfd* API

```
────────────────────────────────────────────────── timers/demo_timerfd.c
#include <sys/timerfd.h>
#include <time.h>
#include <stdint.h>                    /* Definition of uint64_t */
#include "itimerspec_from_str.h"       /* Declares itimerspecFromStr() */
#include "tlpi_hdr.h"

int
main(int argc, char *argv[])
{
    struct itimerspec ts;
    struct timespec start, now;
    int maxExp, fd, secs, nanosecs;
    uint64_t numExp, totalExp;
    ssize_t s;

    if (argc < 2 || strcmp(argv[1], "--help") == 0)
        usageErr("%s secs[/nsecs][:int-secs[/int-nsecs]] [max-exp]\n", argv[0]);

    itimerspecFromStr(argv[1], &ts);
    maxExp = (argc > 2) ? getInt(argv[2], GN_GT_0, "max-exp") : 1;
```

```
    fd = timerfd_create(CLOCK_REALTIME, 0);
    if (fd == -1)
        errExit("timerfd_create");

    if (timerfd_settime(fd, 0, &ts, NULL) == -1)
        errExit("timerfd_settime");

    if (clock_gettime(CLOCK_MONOTONIC, &start) == -1)
        errExit("clock_gettime");

    for (totalExp = 0; totalExp < maxExp;) {

        /* Read number of expirations on the timer, and then display
           time elapsed since timer was started, followed by number
           of expirations read and total expirations so far. */

        s = read(fd, &numExp, sizeof(uint64_t));
        if (s != sizeof(uint64_t))
            errExit("read");

        totalExp += numExp;

        if (clock_gettime(CLOCK_MONOTONIC, &now) == -1)
            errExit("clock_gettime");

        secs = now.tv_sec - start.tv_sec;
        nanosecs = now.tv_nsec - start.tv_nsec;
        if (nanosecs < 0) {
            secs--;
            nanosecs += 1000000000;
        }

        printf("%d.%03d: expirations read: %llu; total=%llu\n",
                secs, (nanosecs + 500000) / 1000000,
                (unsigned long long) numExp, (unsigned long long) totalExp);
    }

    exit(EXIT_SUCCESS);
}
```
—— timers/demo_timerfd.c

23.8 Summary

A process can use *setitimer()* or *alarm()* to set a timer, so that it receives a signal after
the passage of a specified amount of real or process time. One use of timers is to
set an upper limit on the time for which a system call can block.

Applications that need to suspend execution for a specified interval of real
time can use a variety of sleep functions for this purpose.

Linux 2.6 implements the POSIX.1b extensions that define an API for high-
precision clocks and timers. POSIX.1b timers provide a number of advantages over
traditional (*setitimer()*) UNIX timers. We can: create multiple timers; choose the signal
that is delivered on timer expiration; retrieve the timer overrun count in order to

determine if a timer has expired multiple times since the last expiration notification; and choose to receive timer notifications via execution of a thread function instead of delivery of a signal.

The Linux-specific *timerfd* API provides a set of interfaces for creating timers that is similar to the POSIX timers API, but allows timer notifications to be read via a file descriptor. This file descriptor can be monitored using *select()*, *poll()*, and *epoll*.

Further information

Under the rationale for individual functions, SUSv3 provides useful notes on the (standard) timer and sleep interface described in this chapter. [Gallmeister, 1995] discusses POSIX.1b clocks and timers.

23.9 Exercises

23-1. Although *alarm()* is implemented as a system call within the Linux kernel, this is redundant. Implement *alarm()* using *setitimer()*.

23-2. Try running the program in Listing 23-3 (t_nanosleep.c) in the background with a 60-second sleep interval, while using the following command to send as many SIGINT signals as possible to the background process:

```
$ while true; do kill -INT pid; done
```

You should observe that the program sleeps rather longer than expected. Replace the use of *nanosleep()* with the use of *clock_gettime()* (use a CLOCK_REALTIME clock) and *clock_nanosleep()* with the TIMER_ABSTIME flag. (This exercise requires Linux 2.6.) Repeat the test with the modified program and explain the difference.

23-3. Write a program to show that if the *evp* argument to *timer_create()* is specified as NULL, then this is equivalent to specifying *evp* as a pointer to a *sigevent* structure with *sigev_notify* set to SIGEV_SIGNAL, *sigev_signo* set to SIGALRM, and *si_value.sival_int* set to the timer ID.

23-4. Modify the program in Listing 23-5 (ptmr_sigev_signal.c) to use *sigwaitinfo()* instead of a signal handler.

24

PROCESS CREATION

In this and the next four chapters, we look at how a process is created and terminates, and how a process can execute a new program. This chapter covers process creation. However, before diving into that subject, we present a short overview of the main system calls covered in these chapters.

24.1 Overview of *fork()*, *exit()*, *wait()*, **and** *execve()*

The principal topics of this and the next few chapters are the system calls *fork()*, *exit()*, *wait()*, and *execve()*. Each of these system calls has variants, which we'll also look at. For now, we provide an overview of these four system calls and how they are typically used together.

- The *fork()* system call allows one process, the parent, to create a new process, the child. This is done by making the new child process an (almost) exact duplicate of the parent: the child obtains copies of the parent's stack, data, heap, and text segments (Section 6.3). The term *fork* derives from the fact that we can envisage the parent process as dividing to yield two copies of itself.

- The *exit(status)* library function terminates a process, making all resources (memory, open file descriptors, and so on) used by the process available for subsequent reallocation by the kernel. The *status* argument is an integer that determines the termination status for the process. Using the *wait()* system call, the parent can retrieve this status.

The *exit()* library function is layered on top of the *_exit()* system call. In Chapter 25, we explain the difference between the two interfaces. In the meantime, we'll just note that, after a *fork()*, generally only one of the parent and child terminate by calling *exit()*; the other process should terminate using *_exit()*.

- The *wait(&status)* system call has two purposes. First, if a child of this process has not yet terminated by calling *exit()*, then *wait()* suspends execution of the process until one of its children has terminated. Second, the termination status of the child is returned in the status argument of *wait()*.

- The *execve(pathname, argv, envp)* system call loads a new program (*pathname*, with argument list *argv*, and environment list *envp*) into a process's memory. The existing program text is discarded, and the stack, data, and heap segments are freshly created for the new program. This operation is often referred to as *execing* a new program. Later, we'll see that several library functions are layered on top of *execve()*, each of which provides a useful variation in the programming interface. Where we don't care about these interface variations, we follow the common convention of referring to these calls generically as *exec()*, but be aware that there is no system call or library function with this name.

Some other operating systems combine the functionality of *fork()* and *exec()* into a single operation—a so-called *spawn*—that creates a new process that then executes a specified program. By comparison, the UNIX approach is usually simpler and more elegant. Separating these two steps makes the APIs simpler (the *fork()* system call takes *no* arguments) and allows a program a great degree of flexibility in the actions it performs between the two steps. Moreover, it is often useful to perform a *fork()* without a following *exec()*.

> SUSv3 specifies the optional *posix_spawn()* function, which combines the effect of *fork()* and *exec()*. This function, and several related APIs specified by SUSv3, are implemented on Linux in *glibc*. SUSv3 specifies *posix_spawn()* to permit portable applications to be written for hardware architectures that don't provide swap facilities or memory-management units (this is typical of many embedded systems). On such architectures, a traditional *fork()* is difficult or impossible to implement.

Figure 24-1 provides an overview of how *fork()*, *exit()*, *wait()*, and *execve()* are commonly used together. (This diagram outlines the steps taken by the shell in executing a command: the shell continuously executes a loop that reads a command, performs various processing on it, and then forks a child process to exec the command.)

The use of *execve()* shown in this diagram is optional. Sometimes, it is instead useful to have the child carry on executing the same program as the parent. In either case, the execution of the child is ultimately terminated by a call to *exit()* (or by delivery of a signal), yielding a termination status that the parent can obtain via *wait()*.

The call to *wait()* is likewise optional. The parent can simply ignore its child and continue executing. However, we'll see later that the use of *wait()* is usually desirable, and is often employed within a handler for the SIGCHLD signal, which the kernel generates for a parent process when one of its children terminates. (By default, SIGCHLD is ignored, which is why we label it as being optionally delivered in the diagram.)

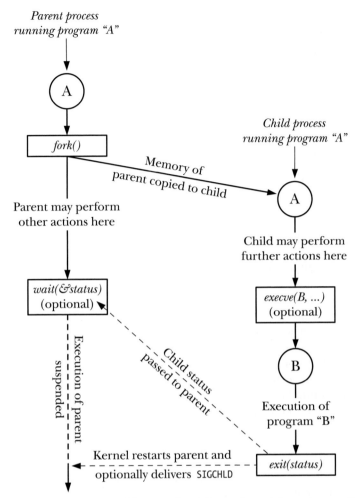

Figure 24-1: Overview of the use of *fork()*, *exit()*, *wait()*, and *execve()*

24.2 Creating a New Process: *fork()*

In many applications, creating multiple processes can be a useful way of dividing up a task. For example, a network server process may listen for incoming client requests and create a new child process to handle each request; meanwhile, the server process continues to listen for further client connections. Dividing tasks up in this way often makes application design simpler. It also permits greater concurrency (i.e., more tasks or requests can be handled simultaneously).

The *fork()* system call creates a new process, the *child*, which is an almost exact duplicate of the calling process, the *parent*.

```
#include <unistd.h>

pid_t fork(void);
```

> In parent: returns process ID of child on success, or −1 on error;
> in successfully created child: always returns 0

The key point to understanding *fork()* is to realize that after it has completed its work, two processes exist, and, in each process, execution continues from the point where *fork()* returns.

The two processes are executing the same program text, but they have separate copies of the stack, data, and heap segments. The child's stack, data, and heap segments are initially exact duplicates of the corresponding parts of the parent's memory. After the *fork()*, each process can modify the variables in its stack, data, and heap segments without affecting the other process.

Within the code of a program, we can distinguish the two processes via the value returned from *fork()*. For the parent, *fork()* returns the process ID of the newly created child. This is useful because the parent may create, and thus need to track, several children (via *wait()* or one of its relatives). For the child, *fork()* returns 0. If necessary, the child can obtain its own process ID using *getpid()*, and the process ID of its parent using *getppid()*.

If a new process can't be created, *fork()* returns −1. Possible reasons for failure are that the resource limit (RLIMIT_NPROC, described in Section 36.3) on the number of processes permitted to this (real) user ID has been exceeded or that the system-wide limit on the number of processes that can be created has been reached.

The following idiom is sometimes employed when calling *fork()*:

```
pid_t childPid;            /* Used in parent after successful fork()
                              to record PID of child */
switch (childPid = fork()) {
case -1:                   /* fork() failed */
    /* Handle error */

case 0:                    /* Child of successful fork() comes here */
    /* Perform actions specific to child */

default:                   /* Parent comes here after successful fork() */
    /* Perform actions specific to parent */
}
```

It is important to realize that after a *fork()*, it is indeterminate which of the two processes is next scheduled to use the CPU. In poorly written programs, this indeterminacy can lead to errors known as race conditions, which we describe further in Section 24.4.

Listing 24-1 demonstrates the use of *fork()*. This program creates a child that modifies the copies of global and automatic variables that it inherits during the *fork()*.

The use of *sleep()* (in the code executed by the parent) in this program permits the child to be scheduled for the CPU before the parent, so that the child can complete its work and terminate before the parent continues execution. Using *sleep()* in this manner is not a foolproof method of guaranteeing this result; we look at a better method in Section 24.5.

When we run the program in Listing 24-1, we see the following output:

```
$ ./t_fork
PID=28557 (child)  idata=333 istack=666
PID=28556 (parent) idata=111 istack=222
```

The above output demonstrates that the child process gets its own copy of the stack and data segments at the time of the *fork()*, and it is able to modify variables in these segments without affecting the parent.

Listing 24-1: Using *fork()*

─── procexec/t_fork.c
```c
#include "tlpi_hdr.h"

static int idata = 111;             /* Allocated in data segment */

int
main(int argc, char *argv[])
{
    int istack = 222;               /* Allocated in stack segment */
    pid_t childPid;

    switch (childPid = fork()) {
    case -1:
        errExit("fork");

    case 0:
        idata *= 3;
        istack *= 3;
        break;

    default:
        sleep(3);                   /* Give child a chance to execute */
        break;
    }

    /* Both parent and child come here */

    printf("PID=%ld %s idata=%d istack=%d\n", (long) getpid(),
            (childPid == 0) ? "(child) " : "(parent)", idata, istack);

    exit(EXIT_SUCCESS);
}
```
─── procexec/t_fork.c

24.2.1 File Sharing Between Parent and Child

When a *fork()* is performed, the child receives duplicates of all of the parent's file descriptors. The duplicated file descriptors in the child refer to the same open file descriptions as the corresponding descriptors in the parent. As we saw in Section 5.4, the open file description contains the current file offset (as modified by *read()*, *write()*, and *lseek()*) and the open file status flags (set by *open()* and changed by the *fcntl()* F_SETFL operation). Consequently, these attributes of an open file are shared between the parent and child. For example, if the child updates the file offset, this change is visible through the corresponding descriptor in the parent.

The fact that these attributes are shared by the parent and child after a *fork()* is demonstrated by the program in Listing 24-2. This program opens a temporary file using *mkstemp()*, and then calls *fork()* to create a child process. The child changes the file offset and open file status flags of the temporary file, and exits. The parent then retrieves the file offset and flags to verify that it can see the changes made by the child. When we run the program, we see the following:

```
$ ./fork_file_sharing
File offset before fork(): 0
O_APPEND flag before fork() is: off
Child has exited
File offset in parent: 1000
O_APPEND flag in parent is: on
```

> For an explanation of why we cast the return value from *lseek()* to *long long* in Listing 24-2, see Section 5.10.

Listing 24-2: Sharing of file offset and open file status flags between parent and child

────────────────────────────── procexec/fork_file_sharing.c

```c
#include <sys/stat.h>
#include <fcntl.h>
#include <sys/wait.h>
#include "tlpi_hdr.h"

int
main(int argc, char *argv[])
{
    int fd, flags;
    char template[] = "/tmp/testXXXXXX";

    setbuf(stdout, NULL);                    /* Disable buffering of stdout */

    fd = mkstemp(template);
    if (fd == -1)
        errExit("mkstemp");

    printf("File offset before fork(): %lld\n",
            (long long) lseek(fd, 0, SEEK_CUR));

    flags = fcntl(fd, F_GETFL);
    if (flags == -1)
        errExit("fcntl - F_GETFL");
    printf("O_APPEND flag before fork() is: %s\n",
            (flags & O_APPEND) ? "on" : "off");
```

```
        switch (fork()) {
        case -1:
            errExit("fork");

        case 0:     /* Child: change file offset and status flags */
            if (lseek(fd, 1000, SEEK_SET) == -1)
                errExit("lseek");

            flags = fcntl(fd, F_GETFL);         /* Fetch current flags */
            if (flags == -1)
                errExit("fcntl - F_GETFL");
            flags |= O_APPEND;                  /* Turn O_APPEND on */
            if (fcntl(fd, F_SETFL, flags) == -1)
                errExit("fcntl - F_SETFL");
            _exit(EXIT_SUCCESS);

        default:    /* Parent: can see file changes made by child */
            if (wait(NULL) == -1)
                errExit("wait");                /* Wait for child exit */
            printf("Child has exited\n");

            printf("File offset in parent: %lld\n",
                    (long long) lseek(fd, 0, SEEK_CUR));

            flags = fcntl(fd, F_GETFL);
            if (flags == -1)
                errExit("fcntl - F_GETFL");
            printf("O_APPEND flag in parent is: %s\n",
                    (flags & O_APPEND) ? "on" : "off");
            exit(EXIT_SUCCESS);
        }
    }
```

—— procexec/fork_file_sharing.c

Sharing of open file attributes between the parent and child processes is frequently useful. For example, if the parent and child are both writing to a file, sharing the file offset ensures that the two processes don't overwrite each other's output. It does not, however, prevent the output of the two processes from being randomly intermingled. If this is not desired, then some form of process synchronization is required. For example, the parent can use the *wait()* system call to pause until the child has exited. This is what the shell does, so that it prints its prompt only after the child process executing a command has terminated (unless the user explicitly runs the command in the background by placing an ampersand character at the end of the command).

If sharing of open file attributes in this manner is not required, then an application should be designed so that, after a *fork()*, the parent and child use different file descriptors, with each process closing unused descriptors (i.e., those used by the other process) immediately after forking. (If one of the processes performs an *exec()*, the close-on-exec flag described in Section 27.4 can also be useful.) These steps are shown in Figure 24-2.

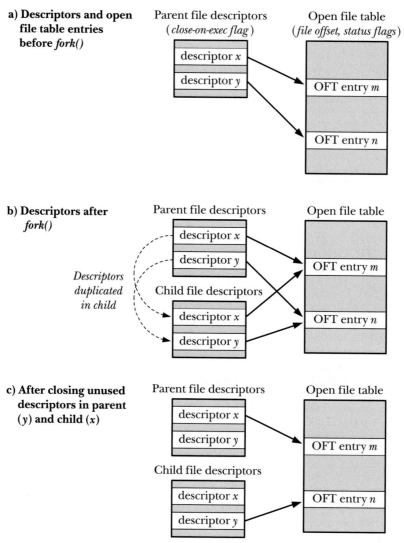

a) **Descriptors and open file table entries before** *fork()*

Parent file descriptors
(*close-on-exec flag*)

descriptor *x*
descriptor *y*

Open file table
(*file offset, status flags*)

OFT entry *m*

OFT entry *n*

b) **Descriptors after** *fork()*

Parent file descriptors

descriptor *x*
descriptor *y*

Descriptors duplicated in child

Child file descriptors

descriptor *x*
descriptor *y*

Open file table

OFT entry *m*

OFT entry *n*

c) **After closing unused descriptors in parent (***y***) and child (***x***)**

Parent file descriptors

descriptor *x*
descriptor *y*

Child file descriptors

descriptor *x*
descriptor *y*

Open file table

OFT entry *m*

OFT entry *n*

Figure 24-2: Duplication of file descriptors during *fork()*, and closing of unused descriptors

24.2.2 Memory Semantics of *fork()*

Conceptually, we can consider *fork()* as creating copies of the parent's text, data, heap, and stack segments. (Indeed, in some early UNIX implementations, such duplication was literally performed: a new process image was created by copying the parent's memory to swap space, and making that swapped-out image the child process while the parent kept its own memory.) However, actually performing a simple copy of the parent's virtual memory pages into the new child process would be wasteful for a number of reasons—one being that a *fork()* is often followed by an immediate *exec()*, which replaces the process's text with a new program and reinitializes the process's data, heap, and stack segments. Most modern UNIX implementations, including Linux, use two techniques to avoid such wasteful copying:

- The kernel marks the text segment of each process as read-only, so that a process can't modify its own code. This means that the parent and child can share the same text segment. The *fork()* system call creates a text segment for the child by building a set of per-process page-table entries that refer to the same physical memory page frames already used by the parent.

- For the pages in the data, heap, and stack segments of the parent process, the kernel employs a technique known as *copy-on-write*. (The implementation of copy-on-write is described in [Bach, 1986] and [Bovet & Cesati, 2005].) Initially, the kernel sets things up so that the page-table entries for these segments refer to the same physical memory pages as the corresponding page-table entries in the parent, and the pages themselves are marked read-only. After the *fork()*, the kernel traps any attempts by either the parent or the child to modify one of these pages, and makes a duplicate copy of the about-to-be-modified page. This new page copy is assigned to the faulting process, and the corresponding page-table entry for the other process is adjusted appropriately. From this point on, the parent and child can each modify their private copies of the page, without the changes being visible to the other process. Figure 24-3 illustrates the copy-on-write technique.

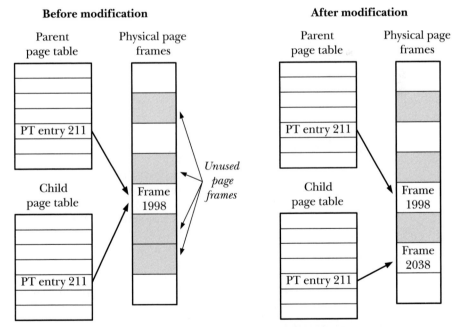

Figure 24-3: Page tables before and after modification of a shared copy-on-write page

Controlling a process's memory footprint

We can combine the use of *fork()* and *wait()* to control the memory footprint of a process. The process's memory footprint is the range of virtual memory pages used by the process, as affected by factors such as the adjustment of the stack as functions are called and return, calls to *exec()*, and, of particular interest to this discussion, modification of the heap as a consequence of calls to *malloc()* and *free()*.

Suppose that we bracket a call to some function, *func()*, using *fork()* and *wait()* in the manner shown in Listing 24-3. After executing this code, we know that the memory footprint of the parent is unchanged from the point before *func()* was called, since all possible changes will have occurred in the child process. This can be useful for the following reasons:

- If we know that *func()* causes memory leaks or excessive fragmentation of the heap, this technique eliminates the problem. (We might not otherwise be able to deal with these problems if we don't have access to the source code of *func()*.)

- Suppose that we have some algorithm that performs memory allocation while doing a tree analysis (for example, a game program that analyzes a range of possible moves and their responses). We could code such a program to make calls to *free()* to deallocate all of the allocated memory. However, in some cases, it is simpler to employ the technique we describe here in order to allow us to backtrack, leaving the caller (the parent) with its original memory footprint unchanged.

In the implementation shown in Listing 24-3, the result of *func()* must be expressed in the 8 bits that *exit()* passes from the terminating child to the parent calling *wait()*. However, we could employ a file, a pipe, or some other interprocess communication technique to allow *func()* to return larger results.

Listing 24-3: Calling a function without changing the process's memory footprint

——— *from* **procexec/footprint.c**

```
pid_t childPid;
int status;

childPid = fork();
if (childPid == -1)
    errExit("fork");

if (childPid == 0)              /* Child calls func() and */
    exit(func(arg));           /* uses return value as exit status */

/* Parent waits for child to terminate. It can determine the
   result of func() by inspecting 'status'. */

if (wait(&status) == -1)
    errExit("wait");
```

——— *from* **procexec/footprint.c**

24.3 The *vfork()* System Call

Early BSD implementations were among those in which *fork()* performed a literal duplication of the parent's data, heap, and stack. As noted earlier, this is wasteful, especially if the *fork()* is followed by an immediate *exec()*. For this reason, later versions of BSD introduced the *vfork()* system call, which was far more efficient than BSD's *fork()*, although it operated with slightly different (in fact, somewhat strange) semantics.

Modern UNIX implementations employing copy-on-write for implementing *fork()* are much more efficient than older *fork()* implementations, thus largely eliminating the need for *vfork()*. Nevertheless, Linux (like many other UNIX implementations) provides a *vfork()* system call with BSD semantics for programs that require the fastest possible fork. However, because the unusual semantics of *vfork()* can lead to some subtle program bugs, its use should normally be avoided, except in the rare cases where it provides worthwhile performance gains.

Like *fork()*, *vfork()* is used by the calling process to create a new child process. However, *vfork()* is expressly designed to be used in programs where the child performs an immediate *exec()* call.

```
#include <unistd.h>

pid_t vfork(void);
```
                    In parent: returns process ID of child on success, or –1 on error;
                                in successfully created child: always returns 0

Two features distinguish the *vfork()* system call from *fork()* and make it more efficient:

- No duplication of virtual memory pages or page tables is done for the child process. Instead, the child shares the parent's memory until it either performs a successful *exec()* or calls *_exit()* to terminate.

- Execution of the parent process is suspended until the child has performed an *exec()* or *_exit()*.

These points have some important implications. Since the child is using the parent's memory, any changes made by the child to the data, heap, or stack segments will be visible to the parent once it resumes. Furthermore, if the child performs a function return between the *vfork()* and a later *exec()* or *_exit()*, this will also affect the parent. This is similar to the example described in Section 6.8 of trying to *longjmp()* into a function from which a return has already been performed. Similar chaos—typically a segmentation fault (SIGSEGV)—is likely to result.

There are a few things that the child process can do between *vfork()* and *exec()* without affecting the parent. Among these are operations on open file descriptors (but not *stdio* file streams). Since the file descriptor table for each process is maintained in kernel space (Section 5.4) and is duplicated during *vfork()*, the child process can perform file descriptor operations without affecting the parent.

> SUSv3 says that the behavior of a program is undefined if it: a) modifies any data other than a variable of type *pid_t* used to store the return value of *vfork()*; b) returns from the function in which *vfork()* was called; or c) calls any other function before successfully calling *_exit()* or performing an *exec()*.
>
> When we look at the *clone()* system call in Section 28.2, we'll see that a child created using *fork()* or *vfork()* also obtains its own copies of a few other process attributes.

The semantics of *vfork()* mean that after the call, the child is guaranteed to be scheduled for the CPU before the parent. In Section 24.2, we noted that this is not a guarantee made by *fork()*, after which either the parent or the child may be scheduled first.

Listing 24-4 shows the use of *vfork()*, demonstrating both of the semantic features that distinguish it from *fork()*: the child shares the parent's memory, and the parent is suspended until the child terminates or calls *exec()*. When we run this program, we see the following output:

```
$ ./t_vfork
Child executing              Even though child slept, parent was not scheduled
Parent executing
istack=666
```

From the last line of output, we can see that the change made by the child to the variable *istack* was performed on the parent's variable.

Listing 24-4: Using *vfork()*

```
────────────────────────────────────────────────────────────procexec/t_vfork.c
#include "tlpi_hdr.h"

int
main(int argc, char *argv[])
{
    int istack = 222;

    switch (vfork()) {
    case -1:
        errExit("vfork");

    case 0:              /* Child executes first, in parent's memory space */
        sleep(3);                    /* Even if we sleep for a while,
                                        parent still is not scheduled */
        write(STDOUT_FILENO, "Child executing\n", 16);
        istack *= 3;                 /* This change will be seen by parent */
        _exit(EXIT_SUCCESS);

    default:             /* Parent is blocked until child exits */
        write(STDOUT_FILENO, "Parent executing\n", 17);
        printf("istack=%d\n", istack);
        exit(EXIT_SUCCESS);
    }
}
────────────────────────────────────────────────────────────procexec/t_vfork.c
```

Except where speed is absolutely critical, new programs should avoid the use of *vfork()* in favor of *fork()*. This is because, when *fork()* is implemented using copy-on-write semantics (as is done on most modern UNIX implementations), it approaches the speed of *vfork()*, and we avoid the eccentric behaviors associated with *vfork()* described above. (We show some speed comparisons between *fork()* and *vfork()* in Section 28.3.)

SUSv3 marks *vfork()* as obsolete, and SUSv4 goes further, removing the specification of *vfork()*. SUSv3 leaves many details of the operation of *vfork()* unspecified, allowing the possibility that it is implemented as a call to *fork()*. When implemented in this manner, the BSD semantics for *vfork()* are not preserved. Some UNIX systems do indeed implement *vfork()* as a call to *fork()*, and Linux also did this in kernel 2.0 and earlier.

Where it is used, *vfork()* should generally be immediately followed by a call to *exec()*. If the *exec()* call fails, the child process should terminate using *_exit()*. (The child of a *vfork()* should not terminate by calling *exit()*, since that would cause the parent's *stdio* buffers to be flushed and closed. We go into more detail on this point in Section 25.4.)

Other uses of *vfork()*—in particular, those relying on its unusual semantics for memory sharing and process scheduling—are likely to render a program nonportable, especially to implementations where *vfork()* is implemented simply as a call to *fork()*.

24.4 Race Conditions After *fork()*

After a *fork()*, it is indeterminate which process—the parent or the child—next has access to the CPU. (On a multiprocessor system, they may both simultaneously get access to a CPU.) Applications that implicitly or explicitly rely on a particular sequence of execution in order to achieve correct results are open to failure due to *race conditions*, which we described in Section 5.1. Such bugs can be hard to find, as their occurrence depends on scheduling decisions that the kernel makes according to system load.

We can use the program in Listing 24-5 to demonstrate this indeterminacy. This program loops, using *fork()* to create multiple children. After each *fork()*, both parent and child print a message containing the loop counter value and a string indicating whether the process is the parent or child. For example, if we asked the program to produce just one child, we might see the following:

```
$ ./fork_whos_on_first 1
0 parent
0 child
```

We can use this program to create a large number of children, and then analyze the output to see whether the parent or the child is the first to print its message each time. Analyzing the results when using this program to create 1 million children on a Linux/x86-32 2.2.19 system showed that the parent printed its message first in all but 332 cases (i.e., in 99.97% of the cases).

> The results from running the program in Listing 24-5 were analyzed using the script procexec/fork_whos_on_first.count.awk, which is provided in the source code distribution for this book.

From these results, we may surmise that, on Linux 2.2.19, execution always continues with the parent process after a *fork()*. The reason that the child occasionally printed its message first was that, in 0.03% of cases, the parent's CPU time slice ran out before it had time to print its message. In other words, if this example represented a case where we were relying on the parent to always be scheduled first after *fork()*, then things would usually go right, but one time out of every 3000, things would go wrong. Of course, if the application expected that the parent should be able to carry out a larger piece of work before the child was scheduled, the possibility of things going wrong would be greater. Trying to debug such errors in a complex program can be difficult.

Listing 24-5: Parent and child race to write a message after *fork()*

─────────────────────────────────────── procexec/fork_whos_on_first.c

```c
#include <sys/wait.h>
#include "tlpi_hdr.h"

int
main(int argc, char *argv[])
{
    int numChildren, j;
    pid_t childPid;

    if (argc > 1 && strcmp(argv[1], "--help") == 0)
        usageErr("%s [num-children]\n", argv[0]);

    numChildren = (argc > 1) ? getInt(argv[1], GN_GT_0, "num-children") : 1;

    setbuf(stdout, NULL);                 /* Make stdout unbuffered */

    for (j = 0; j < numChildren; j++) {
        switch (childPid = fork()) {
        case -1:
            errExit("fork");

        case 0:
            printf("%d child\n", j);
            _exit(EXIT_SUCCESS);

        default:
            printf("%d parent\n", j);
            wait(NULL);                   /* Wait for child to terminate */
            break;
        }
    }

    exit(EXIT_SUCCESS);
}
```

─────────────────────────────────────── procexec/fork_whos_on_first.c

Although Linux 2.2.19 always continues execution with the parent after a *fork()*, we can't rely on this being the case on other UNIX implementations, or even across different versions of the Linux kernel. During the 2.4 stable kernel series, experiments were briefly made with a "child first after *fork()*" patch, which completely reverses the results obtained from 2.2.19. Although this change was later dropped from the 2.4 kernel series, it was subsequently adopted in Linux 2.6. Thus, programs that assume the 2.2.19 behavior would be broken by the 2.6 kernel.

Some more recent experiments reversed the kernel developers' assessment of whether it was better to run the child or the parent first after *fork()*, and, since Linux 2.6.32, it is once more the parent that is, by default, run first after a *fork()*. This default can be changed by assigning a nonzero value to the Linux-specific /proc/sys/kernel/sched_child_runs_first file.

To see the argument for the "children first after *fork()*" behavior, consider what happens with copy-on-write semantics when the child of a *fork()* performs an immediate *exec()*. In this case, as the parent carries on after the *fork()* to modify data and stack pages, the kernel duplicates the to-be-modified pages for the child. Since the child performs an *exec()* as soon as it is scheduled to run, this duplication is wasted. According to this argument, it is better to schedule the child first, so that by the time the parent is next scheduled, no page copying is required. Using the program in Listing 24-5 to create 1 million child processes on one busy Linux/x86-32 system running kernel 2.6.30 showed that, in 99.98% of cases, the child process displayed its message first. (The precise percentage depends on factors such as system load.) Testing this program on other UNIX implementations showed wide variation in the rules that govern which process runs first after *fork()*.

The argument for switching back to "parent first after *fork()*" in Linux 2.6.32 was based on the observation that, after a *fork()*, the parent's state is already active in the CPU and its memory-management information is already cached in the hardware memory management unit's translation look-aside buffer (TLB). Therefore, running the parent first should result in better performance. This was informally verified by measuring the time required for kernel builds under the two behaviors.

In conclusion, it is worth noting that the performance differences between the two behaviors are rather small, and won't affect most applications.

From the preceding discussion, it is clear that we can't assume a particular order of execution for the parent and child after a *fork()*. If we need to guarantee a particular order, we must use some kind of synchronization technique. We describe several synchronization techniques in later chapters, including semaphores, file locks, and sending messages between processes using pipes. One other method, which we describe next, is to use signals.

24.5 Avoiding Race Conditions by Synchronizing with Signals

After a *fork()*, if either process needs to wait for the other to complete an action, then the active process can send a signal after completing the action; the other process waits for the signal.

Listing 24-6 demonstrates this technique. In this program, we assume that it is the parent that must wait on the child to carry out some action. The signal-related calls in the parent and child can be swapped if the child must wait on the parent. It is even possible for both parent and child to signal each other multiple times in order to coordinate their actions, although, in practice, such coordination is more likely to be done using semaphores, file locks, or message passing.

> [Stevens & Rago, 2005] suggests encapsulating such synchronization steps (block signal, send signal, catch signal) into a standard set of functions for process synchronization. The advantage of such encapsulation is that we can then later replace the use of signals by another IPC mechanism, if desired.

Note that we block the synchronization signal (SIGUSR1) before the *fork()* call in Listing 24-6. If the parent tried blocking the signal after the *fork()*, it would remain vulnerable to the very race condition we are trying to avoid. (In this program, we assume that the state of the signal mask in the child is irrelevant; if necessary, we can unblock SIGUSR1 in the child after the *fork()*.)

The following shell session log shows what happens when we run the program in Listing 24-6:

```
$ ./fork_sig_sync
[17:59:02 5173] Child started - doing some work
[17:59:02 5172] Parent about to wait for signal
[17:59:04 5173] Child about to signal parent
[17:59:04 5172] Parent got signal
```

Listing 24-6: Using signals to synchronize process actions

─── procexec/fork_sig_sync.c
```c
#include <signal.h>
#include "curr_time.h"                    /* Declaration of currTime() */
#include "tlpi_hdr.h"

#define SYNC_SIG SIGUSR1                   /* Synchronization signal */

static void                /* Signal handler - does nothing but return */
handler(int sig)
{
}

int
main(int argc, char *argv[])
{
    pid_t childPid;
    sigset_t blockMask, origMask, emptyMask;
    struct sigaction sa;

    setbuf(stdout, NULL);                  /* Disable buffering of stdout */

    sigemptyset(&blockMask);
    sigaddset(&blockMask, SYNC_SIG);       /* Block signal */
    if (sigprocmask(SIG_BLOCK, &blockMask, &origMask) == -1)
        errExit("sigprocmask");

    sigemptyset(&sa.sa_mask);
    sa.sa_flags = SA_RESTART;
    sa.sa_handler = handler;
    if (sigaction(SYNC_SIG, &sa, NULL) == -1)
        errExit("sigaction");

    switch (childPid = fork()) {
    case -1:
        errExit("fork");

    case 0: /* Child */

        /* Child does some required action here... */
```

```
        printf("[%s %ld] Child started - doing some work\n",
                currTime("%T"), (long) getpid());
        sleep(2);                   /* Simulate time spent doing some work */

        /* And then signals parent that it's done */

        printf("[%s %ld] Child about to signal parent\n",
                currTime("%T"), (long) getpid());
        if (kill(getppid(), SYNC_SIG) == -1)
            errExit("kill");

        /* Now child can do other things... */

        _exit(EXIT_SUCCESS);

    default: /* Parent */

        /* Parent may do some work here, and then waits for child to
           complete the required action */

        printf("[%s %ld] Parent about to wait for signal\n",
                currTime("%T"), (long) getpid());
        sigemptyset(&emptyMask);
        if (sigsuspend(&emptyMask) == -1 && errno != EINTR)
            errExit("sigsuspend");
        printf("[%s %ld] Parent got signal\n", currTime("%T"), (long) getpid());

        /* If required, return signal mask to its original state */

        if (sigprocmask(SIG_SETMASK, &origMask, NULL) == -1)
            errExit("sigprocmask");

        /* Parent carries on to do other things... */

        exit(EXIT_SUCCESS);
    }
}
```
── procexec/fork_sig_sync.c

24.6 Summary

The *fork()* system call creates a new process (the child) by making an almost exact
duplicate of the calling process (the parent). The *vfork()* system call is a more efficient
version of *fork()*, but is usually best avoided because of its unusual semantics,
whereby the child uses the parent's memory until it either performs an *exec()* or
terminates; in the meantime, execution of the parent process is suspended.

After a *fork()* call, we can't rely on the order in which the parent and the child
are next scheduled to use the CPU(s). Programs that make assumptions about the
order of execution are susceptible to errors known as race conditions. Because the
occurrence of such errors depends on external factors such as system load, they
can be difficult to find and debug.

Further information

[Bach, 1986] and [Goodheart & Cox, 1994] provide details of the implementation of *fork()*, *execve()*, *wait()*, and *exit()* on UNIX systems. [Bovet & Cesati, 2005] and [Love, 2010] provide Linux-specific implementation details of process creation and termination.

24.7 Exercises

24-1. After a program executes the following series of *fork()* calls, how many new processes will result (assuming that none of the calls fails)?

```
fork();
fork();
fork();
```

24-2. Write a program to demonstrate that after a *vfork()*, the child process can close a file descriptor (e.g., descriptor 0) without affecting the corresponding file descriptor in the parent.

24-3. Assuming that we can modify the program source code, how could we get a core dump of a process at a given point in the program, while letting the process continue execution?

24-4. Experiment with the program in Listing 24-5 (fork_whos_on_first.c) on other UNIX implementations to determine how these implementations schedule the parent and child processes after a *fork()*.

24-5. Suppose that in the program in Listing 24-6, the child process also needed to wait on the parent to complete some actions. What changes to the program would be required in order to enforce this?

25

PROCESS TERMINATION

This chapter describes what happens when a process terminates. We begin by describing the use of *exit()* and *_exit()* to terminate a process. We then discuss the use of exit handlers to automatically perform cleanups when a process calls *exit()*. We conclude by considering some interactions between *fork()*, *stdio* buffers, and *exit()*.

25.1 Terminating a Process: *_exit()* and *exit()*

A process may terminate in two general ways. One of these is *abnormal* termination, caused by the delivery of a signal whose default action is to terminate the process (with or without a core dump), as described in Section 20.1. Alternatively, a process can terminate *normally*, using the *_exit()* system call.

```
#include <unistd.h>

void _exit(int status);
```

The *status* argument given to *_exit()* defines the *termination status* of the process, which is available to the parent of this process when it calls *wait()*. Although defined as an *int*, only the bottom 8 bits of *status* are actually made available to the parent. By convention, a termination status of 0 indicates that a process completed successfully, and a nonzero status value indicates that the process terminated unsuccessfully. There are no fixed rules about how nonzero status values are to be interpreted; different applications follow their own conventions, which should be described in their documentation. SUSv3 specifies two constants, EXIT_SUCCESS (0) and EXIT_FAILURE (1), that are used in most programs in this book.

A process is always successfully terminated by _exit() (i.e., _exit() never returns).

> Although any value in the range 0 to 255 can be passed to the parent via the *status* argument to _exit(), specifying values greater than 128 can cause confusion in shell scripts. The reason is that, when a command is terminated by a signal, the shell indicates this fact by setting the value of the variable *$?* to 128 plus the signal number, and this value is indistinguishable from that yielded when a process calls _exit() with the same *status* value.

Programs generally don't call _exit() directly, but instead call the *exit()* library function, which performs various actions before calling _exit().

```
#include <stdlib.h>

void exit(int status);
```

The following actions are performed by *exit()*:

- Exit handlers (functions registered with *atexit()* and *on_exit()*) are called, in reverse order of their registration (Section 25.3).
- The *stdio* stream buffers are flushed.
- The _exit() system call is invoked, using the value supplied in *status*.

> Unlike _exit(), which is UNIX-specific, *exit()* is defined as part of the standard C library; that is, it is available with every C implementation.

One other way in which a process may terminate is to return from *main()*, either explicitly, or implicitly, by falling off the end of the *main()* function. Performing an explicit *return n* is generally equivalent to calling *exit(n)*, since the run-time function that invokes *main()* uses the return value from *main()* in a call to *exit()*.

> There is one circumstance in which calling *exit()* and returning from *main()* are not equivalent. If any steps performed during exit processing access variables local to *main()*, then doing a return from *main()* results in undefined behavior. For example, this could occur if a variable that is local to *main()* is specified in a call to *setvbuf()* or *setbuf()* (Section 13.2).

Performing a return without specifying a value, or falling off the end of the *main()* function, also results in the caller of *main()* invoking *exit()*, but with results that vary depending on the version of the C standard supported and the compilation options employed:

- In C89, the behavior in these circumstances is undefined; the program can terminate with an arbitrary *status* value. This is the behavior that occurs by default with *gcc* on Linux, where the exit status of the program is taken from some random value lying on the stack or in a particular CPU register. Terminating a program in this way should be avoided.

- The C99 standard requires that falling off the end of the main program should be equivalent to calling *exit(0)*. This is the behavior we obtain on Linux if we compile a program using *gcc −std=c99*.

25.2 Details of Process Termination

During both normal and abnormal termination of a process, the following actions occur:

- Open file descriptors, directory streams (Section 18.8), message catalog descriptors (see the *catopen(3)* and *catgets(3)* manual pages), and conversion descriptors (see the *iconv_open(3)* manual page) are closed.

- As a consequence of closing file descriptors, any file locks (Chapter 55) held by this process are released.

- Any attached System V shared memory segments are detached, and the *shm_nattch* counter corresponding to each segment is decremented by one. (Refer to Section 48.8.)

- For each System V semaphore for which a *semadj* value has been set by the process, that *semadj* value is added to the semaphore value. (Refer to Section 47.8.)

- If this is the controlling process for a controlling terminal, then the SIGHUP signal is sent to each process in the controlling terminal's foreground process group, and the terminal is disassociated from the session. We consider this point further in Section 34.6.

- Any POSIX named semaphores that are open in the calling process are closed as though *sem_close()* were called.

- Any POSIX message queues that are open in the calling process are closed as though *mq_close()* were called.

- If, as a consequence of this process exiting, a process group becomes orphaned and there are any stopped processes in that group, then all processes in the group are sent a SIGHUP signal followed by a SIGCONT signal. We consider this point further in Section 34.7.4.

- Any memory locks established by this process using *mlock()* or *mlockall()* (Section 50.2) are removed.

- Any memory mappings established by this process using *mmap()* are unmapped.

25.3 Exit Handlers

Sometimes, an application needs to automatically perform some operations on process termination. Consider the example of an application library that, if used during the life of the process, needs to have some cleanup actions performed automatically when the process exits. Since the library doesn't have control of when and how the process exits, and can't mandate that the main program call a library-specific cleanup function before exiting, cleanup is not guaranteed to occur. One approach in such situations is to use an *exit handler* (older System V manuals used the term *program termination routine*).

An exit handler is a programmer-supplied function that is registered at some point during the life of the process and is then automatically called during *normal* process termination via *exit()*. Exit handlers are not called if a program calls *_exit()* directly or if the process is terminated abnormally by a signal.

> To some extent, the fact that exit handlers are not called when a process is terminated by a signal limits their utility. The best we can do is to establish handlers for the signals that might be sent to the process, and have these handlers set a flag that causes the main program to call *exit()*. (Because *exit()* is not one of the async-signal-safe functions listed in Table 21-1, on page 426, we generally can't call it from a signal handler.) Even then, this doesn't handle the case of SIGKILL, whose default action can't be changed. This is one more reason we should avoid using SIGKILL to terminate a process (as noted in Section 20.2), and instead use SIGTERM, which is the default signal sent by the *kill* command.

Registering exit handlers

The GNU C library provides two ways of registering exit handlers. The first method, specified in SUSv3, is to use the *atexit()* function.

```
#include <stdlib.h>

int atexit(void (*func)(void));
```
                                            Returns 0 on success, or nonzero on error

The *atexit()* function adds *func* to a list of functions that are called when the process terminates. The function *func* should be defined to take no arguments and return no value, thus having the following general form:

```
void
func(void)
{
    /* Perform some actions */
}
```

Note that *atexit()* returns a nonzero value (not necessarily −1) on error.

It is possible to register multiple exit handlers (and even the same exit handler multiple times). When the program invokes *exit()*, these functions are called *in reverse order* of registration. This ordering is logical because, typically, functions that are registered earlier are those that carry out more fundamental types of cleanups that may need to be performed after later-registered functions.

Essentially, any desired action can be performed inside an exit handler, including registering additional exit handlers, which are placed at the head of the list of exit handlers that remain to be called. However, if one of the exit handlers fails to return—either because it called *_exit()* or because the process was terminated by a signal (e.g., the exit handler called *raise()*)—then the remaining exit handlers are not called. In addition, the remaining actions that would normally be performed by *exit()* (i.e., flushing *stdio* buffers) are not performed.

> SUSv3 states that if an exit handler itself calls *exit()*, the results are undefined. On Linux, the remaining exit handlers are invoked as normal. However, on some systems, this causes all of the exit handlers to once more be invoked, which can result in an infinite recursion (until a stack overflow kills the process). Portable applications should avoid calling *exit()* inside an exit handler.

SUSv3 requires that an implementation allow a process to be able to register at least 32 exit handlers. Using the call *sysconf(_SC_ATEXIT_MAX)*, a program can determine the implementation-defined upper limit on the number of exit handlers that can be registered. (However, there is no way to find out how many exit handlers have already been registered.) By chaining the registered exit handlers in a dynamically allocated linked list, *glibc* allows a virtually unlimited number of exit handlers to be registered. On Linux, *sysconf(_SC_ATEXIT_MAX)* returns 2,147,483,647 (i.e., the maximum signed 32-bit integer). In other words, something else will break (e.g., lack of memory) before we reach the limit on the number of functions that can be registered.

A child process created via *fork()* inherits a copy of its parent's exit handler registrations. When a process performs an *exec()*, all exit handler registrations are removed. (This is necessarily so, since an *exec()* replaces the code of the exit handlers along with the rest of the existing program code.)

> We can't deregister an exit handler that has been registered with *atexit()* (or *on_exit()*, described below). However, we can have the exit handler check whether a global flag is set before it performs its actions, and disable the exit handler by clearing the flag.

Exit handlers registered with *atexit()* suffer a couple of limitations. The first is that when called, an exit handler doesn't know what status was passed to *exit()*. Occasionally, knowing the status could be useful; for example, we may like to perform different actions depending on whether the process is exiting successfully or unsuccessfully. The second limitation is that we can't specify an argument to the exit handler when it is called. Such a facility could be useful to define an exit handler that performs different actions depending on its argument, or to register a function multiple times, each time with a different argument.

To address these limitations, *glibc* provides a (nonstandard) alternative method of registering exit handlers: *on_exit()*.

```
#define _BSD_SOURCE          /* Or: #define _SVID_SOURCE */
#include <stdlib.h>

int on_exit(void (*func)(int, void *), void *arg);
```
                                    Returns 0 on success, or nonzero on error

The *func* argument of *on_exit()* is a pointer to a function of the following type:

    void

```
func(int status, void *arg)
{
    /* Perform cleanup actions */
}
```

When called, *func()* is passed two arguments: the *status* argument supplied to *exit()*, and a copy of the *arg* argument supplied to *on_exit()* at the time the function was registered. Although defined as a pointer type, *arg* is open to programmer-defined interpretation. It could be used as a pointer to some structure; equally, through judicious use of casting, it could be treated as an integer or other scalar type.

Like *atexit()*, *on_exit()* returns a nonzero value (not necessarily –1) on error.

As with *atexit()*, multiple exit handlers can be registered with *on_exit()*. Functions registered using *atexit()* and *on_exit()* are placed on the same list. If both methods are used in the same program, then the exit handlers are called in reverse order of their registration using the two methods.

Although more flexible than *atexit()*, *on_exit()* should be avoided in programs intended to be portable, since it is not covered by any standards and is available on few other UNIX implementations.

Example program

Listing 25-1 demonstrates the use of *atexit()* and *on_exit()* to register exit handlers. When we run this program, we see the following output:

```
$ ./exit_handlers
on_exit function called: status=2, arg=20
atexit function 2 called
atexit function 1 called
on_exit function called: status=2, arg=10
```

Listing 25-1: Using exit handlers

––– procexec/exit_handlers.c
```
#define _BSD_SOURCE     /* Get on_exit() declaration from <stdlib.h> */
#include <stdlib.h>
#include "tlpi_hdr.h"

static void
atexitFunc1(void)
{
    printf("atexit function 1 called\n");
}

static void
atexitFunc2(void)
{
    printf("atexit function 2 called\n");
}

static void
onexitFunc(int exitStatus, void *arg)
{
    printf("on_exit function called: status=%d, arg=%ld\n",
            exitStatus, (long) arg);
```

```
}

int
main(int argc, char *argv[])
{
    if (on_exit(onexitFunc, (void *) 10) != 0)
        fatal("on_exit 1");
    if (atexit(atexitFunc1) != 0)
        fatal("atexit 1");
    if (atexit(atexitFunc2) != 0)
        fatal("atexit 2");
    if (on_exit(onexitFunc, (void *) 20) != 0)
        fatal("on_exit 2");

    exit(2);
}
```

─── procexec/exit_handlers.c

25.4 Interactions Between *fork()*, *stdio* Buffers, and *_exit()*

The output yielded by the program in Listing 25-2 demonstrates a phenomenon
that is at first puzzling. When we run this program with standard output directed to
the terminal, we see the expected result:

```
$ ./fork_stdio_buf
Hello world
Ciao
```

However, when we redirect standard output to a file, we see the following:

```
$ ./fork_stdio_buf > a
$ cat a
Ciao
Hello world
Hello world
```

In the above output, we see two strange things: the line written by *printf()* appears
twice, and the output of *write()* precedes that of *printf()*.

Listing 25-2: Interaction of *fork()* and *stdio* buffering

─── procexec/fork_stdio_buf.c
```
#include "tlpi_hdr.h"

int
main(int argc, char *argv[])
{
    printf("Hello world\n");
    write(STDOUT_FILENO, "Ciao\n", 5);

    if (fork() == -1)
        errExit("fork");

    /* Both child and parent continue execution here */
```

```
        exit(EXIT_SUCCESS);
}
```

――――――――――――――――――――――――――――― **procexec/fork_stdio_buf.c**

To understand why the message written with *printf()* appears twice, recall that the *stdio* buffers are maintained in a process's user-space memory (refer to Section 13.2). Therefore, these buffers are duplicated in the child by *fork()*. When standard output is directed to a terminal, it is line-buffered by default, with the result that the newline-terminated string written by *printf()* appears immediately. However, when standard output is directed to a file, it is block-buffered by default. Thus, in our example, the string written by *printf()* is still in the parent's *stdio* buffer at the time of the *fork()*, and this string is duplicated in the child. When the parent and the child later call *exit()*, they both flush their copies of the *stdio* buffers, resulting in duplicate output.

We can prevent this duplicated output from occurring in one of the following ways:

- As a specific solution to the *stdio* buffering issue, we can use *fflush()* to flush the *stdio* buffer prior to a *fork()* call. Alternatively, we could use *setvbuf()* or *setbuf()* to disable buffering on the *stdio* stream.

- Instead of calling *exit()*, the child can call *_exit()*, so that it doesn't flush *stdio* buffers. This technique exemplifies a more general principle: in an application that creates child processes that don't exec new programs, typically only one of the processes (most often the parent) should terminate via *exit()*, while the other processes should terminate via *_exit()*. This ensures that only one process calls exit handlers and flushes *stdio* buffers, which is usually desirable.

> Other approaches that allow both the parent and child to call *exit()* are possible (and sometimes necessary). For example, it may be possible to design exit handlers so that they operate correctly even if called from multiple processes, or to have the application install exit handlers only after the call to *fork()*. Furthermore, sometimes we may actually want all processes to flush their *stdio* buffers after a *fork()*. In this case, we may choose to terminate the processes using *exit()*, or use explicit calls to *fflush()* in each process, as appropriate.

The output of the *write()* in the program in Listing 25-2 doesn't appear twice, because *write()* transfers data directly to a kernel buffer, and this buffer is not duplicated during a *fork()*.

By now, the reason for the second strange aspect of the program's output when redirected to a file should be clear. The output of *write()* appears before that from *printf()* because the output of *write()* is immediately transferred to the kernel buffer cache, while the output from *printf()* is transferred only when the *stdio* buffers are flushed by the call to *exit()*. (In general, care is required when mixing *stdio* functions and system calls to perform I/O on the same file, as described in Section 13.7.)

25.5 Summary

A process can terminate either abnormally or normally. Abnormal termination occurs on delivery of certain signals, some of which also cause the process to produce a core dump file.

Normal termination is accomplished by calling _exit() or, more usually, exit(), which is layered on top of _exit(). Both _exit() and exit() take an integer argument whose least significant 8 bits define the termination status of the process. By convention, a status of 0 is used to indicate successful termination, and a nonzero status indicates unsuccessful termination.

As part of both normal and abnormal process termination, the kernel performs various cleanup steps. Terminating a process normally by calling exit() additionally causes exit handlers registered using atexit() and on_exit() to be called (in reverse order of registration), and causes stdio buffers to be flushed.

Further information

Refer to the sources of further information listed in Section 24.6.

25.6 Exercise

25-1. If a child process makes the call exit(-1), what exit status will be seen by the parent?

26

MONITORING CHILD PROCESSES

In many application designs, a parent process needs to know when one of its child processes changes state—when the child terminates or is stopped by a signal. This chapter describes two techniques used to monitor child processes: the *wait()* system call (and its variants) and the use of the SIGCHLD signal.

26.1 Waiting on a Child Process

In many applications where a parent creates child processes, it is useful for the parent to be able to monitor the children to find out when and how they terminate. This facility is provided by *wait()* and a number of related system calls.

26.1.1 The *wait()* System Call

The *wait()* system call waits for one of the children of the calling process to terminate and returns the termination status of that child in the buffer pointed to by *status*.

```
#include <sys/wait.h>

pid_t wait(int *status);
```
                              Returns process ID of terminated child, or –1 on error

The *wait()* system call does the following:

1. If no (previously unwaited-for) child of the calling process has yet terminated, the call blocks until one of the children terminates. If a child has already terminated by the time of the call, *wait()* returns immediately.

2. If *status* is not NULL, information about how the child terminated is returned in the integer to which *status* points. We describe the information returned in *status* in Section 26.1.3.

3. The kernel adds the process CPU times (Section 10.7) and resource usage statistics (Section 36.1) to running totals for all children of this parent process.

4. As its function result, *wait()* returns the process ID of the child that has terminated.

On error, *wait()* returns –1. One possible error is that the calling process has no (previously unwaited-for) children, which is indicated by the *errno* value ECHILD. This means that we can use the following loop to wait for all children of the calling process to terminate:

```
while ((childPid = wait(NULL)) != -1)
    continue;
if (errno != ECHILD)                    /* An unexpected error... */
    errExit("wait");
```

Listing 26-1 demonstrates the use of *wait()*. This program creates multiple child processes, one per (integer) command-line argument. Each child sleeps for the number of seconds specified in the corresponding command-line argument and then exits. In the meantime, after all children have been created, the parent process repeatedly calls *wait()* to monitor the termination of its children. This loop continues until *wait()* returns –1. (This is not the only approach: we could alternatively exit the loop when the number of terminated children, *numDead*, matches the number of children created.) The following shell session log shows what happens when we use the program to create three children:

```
$ ./multi_wait 7 1 4
[13:41:00] child 1 started with PID 21835, sleeping 7 seconds
[13:41:00] child 2 started with PID 21836, sleeping 1 seconds
[13:41:00] child 3 started with PID 21837, sleeping 4 seconds
[13:41:01] wait() returned child PID 21836 (numDead=1)
[13:41:04] wait() returned child PID 21837 (numDead=2)
[13:41:07] wait() returned child PID 21835 (numDead=3)
No more children - bye!
```

> If there are multiple terminated children at a particular moment, SUSv3 leaves unspecified the order in which these children will be reaped by a sequence of *wait()* calls; that is, the order depends on the implementation. Even across versions of the Linux kernel, the behavior varies.

Listing 26-1: Creating and waiting for multiple children

── **procexec/multi_wait.c**

```c
#include <sys/wait.h>
#include <time.h>
#include "curr_time.h"              /* Declaration of currTime() */
#include "tlpi_hdr.h"

int
main(int argc, char *argv[])
{
    int numDead;        /* Number of children so far waited for */
    pid_t childPid;     /* PID of waited for child */
    int j;

    if (argc < 2 || strcmp(argv[1], "--help") == 0)
        usageErr("%s sleep-time...\n", argv[0]);

    setbuf(stdout, NULL);           /* Disable buffering of stdout */

    for (j = 1; j < argc; j++) {    /* Create one child for each argument */
        switch (fork()) {
        case -1:
            errExit("fork");

        case 0:                     /* Child sleeps for a while then exits */
            printf("[%s] child %d started with PID %ld, sleeping %s "
                    "seconds\n", currTime("%T"), j, (long) getpid(), argv[j]);
            sleep(getInt(argv[j], GN_NONNEG, "sleep-time"));
            _exit(EXIT_SUCCESS);

        default:                    /* Parent just continues around loop */
            break;
        }
    }

    numDead = 0;
    for (;;) {                      /* Parent waits for each child to exit */
        childPid = wait(NULL);
        if (childPid == -1) {
            if (errno == ECHILD) {
                printf("No more children - bye!\n");
                exit(EXIT_SUCCESS);
            } else {                /* Some other (unexpected) error */
                errExit("wait");
            }
        }

        numDead++;
        printf("[%s] wait() returned child PID %ld (numDead=%d)\n",
                currTime("%T"), (long) childPid, numDead);
    }
}
```

── **procexec/multi_wait.c**

26.1.2 The *waitpid()* System Call

The *wait()* system call has a number of limitations, which *waitpid()* was designed to address:

- If a parent process has created multiple children, it is not possible to *wait()* for the completion of a specific child; we can only wait for the next child that terminates.
- If no child has yet terminated, *wait()* always blocks. Sometimes, it would be preferable to perform a nonblocking wait so that if no child has yet terminated, we obtain an immediate indication of this fact.
- Using *wait()*, we can find out only about children that have terminated. It is not possible to be notified when a child is stopped by a signal (such as SIGSTOP or SIGTTIN) or when a stopped child is resumed by delivery of a SIGCONT signal.

```
#include <sys/wait.h>

pid_t waitpid(pid_t pid, int *status, int options);
```
                          Returns process ID of child, 0 (see text), or −1 on error

The return value and *status* arguments of *waitpid()* are the same as for *wait()*. (See Section 26.1.3 for an explanation of the value returned in *status*.) The *pid* argument enables the selection of the child to be waited for, as follows:

- If *pid* is greater than 0, wait for the child whose *process ID* equals *pid*.
- If *pid* equals 0, wait for any child in the *same process group as the caller* (parent). We describe process groups in Section 34.2.
- If *pid* is less than −1, wait for any child whose *process group* identifier equals the absolute value of *pid*.
- If *pid* equals −1, wait for *any* child. The call *wait(&status)* is equivalent to the call *waitpid(−1, &status, 0)*.

The *options* argument is a bit mask that can include (OR) zero or more of the following flags (all of which are specified in SUSv3):

WUNTRACED
> In addition to returning information about terminated children, also return information when a child is *stopped* by a signal.

WCONTINUED (since Linux 2.6.10)
> Also return status information about stopped children that have been resumed by delivery of a SIGCONT signal.

WNOHANG
> If no child specified by *pid* has yet changed state, then return immediately, instead of blocking (i.e., perform a "poll"). In this case, the return value of *waitpid()* is 0. If the calling process has no children that match the specification in *pid*, *waitpid()* fails with the error ECHILD.

We demonstrate the use of *waitpid()* in Listing 26-3.

In its rationale for *waitpid()*, SUSv3 notes that the name WUNTRACED is a historical artifact of this flag's origin in BSD, where a process could be stopped in one of two ways: as a consequence of being traced by the *ptrace()* system call, or by being stopped by a signal (i.e., not being traced). When a child is being traced by *ptrace()*, then delivery of *any* signal (other than SIGKILL) causes the child to be stopped, and a SIGCHLD signal is consequently sent to the parent. This behavior occurs even if the child is ignoring the signal. However, if the child is blocking the signal, then it is not stopped (unless the signal is SIGSTOP, which can't be blocked).

26.1.3 The Wait Status Value

The *status* value returned by *wait()* and *waitpid()* allows us to distinguish the following events for the child:

- The child terminated by calling _exit() (or exit()), specifying an integer *exit status*.
- The child was terminated by the delivery of an unhandled signal.
- The child was stopped by a signal, and *waitpid()* was called with the WUNTRACED flag.
- The child was resumed by a SIGCONT signal, and *waitpid()* was called with the WCONTINUED flag.

We use the term *wait status* to encompass all of the above cases. The designation *termination status* is used to refer to the first two cases. (In the shell, we can obtain the termination status of the last command executed by examining the contents of the variable *$?*.)

Although defined as an *int*, only the bottom 2 bytes of the value pointed to by *status* are actually used. The way in which these 2 bytes are filled depends on which of the above events occurred for the child, as depicted in Figure 26-1.

> Figure 26-1 shows the layout of the wait status value for Linux/x86-32. The details vary across implementations. SUSv3 doesn't specify any particular layout for this information, or even require that it is contained in the bottom 2 bytes of the value pointed to by *status*. Portable applications should always use the macros described in this section to inspect this value, rather than directly inspecting its bit-mask components.

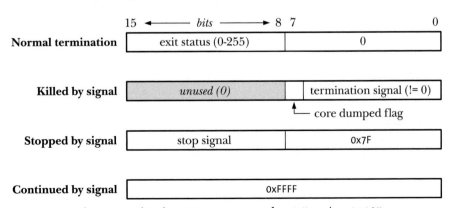

Figure 26-1: Value returned in the *status* argument of *wait()* and *waitpid()*

The <sys/wait.h> header file defines a standard set of macros that can be used to dissect a wait status value. When applied to a *status* value returned by *wait()* or *waitpid()*, only one of the macros in the list below will return true. Additional macros are provided to further dissect the *status* value, as noted in the list.

WIFEXITED(status)

> This macro returns true if the child process exited normally. In this case, the macro WEXITSTATUS(status) returns the exit status of the child process. (As noted in Section 25.1, only the least significant byte of the child's exit status is available to the parent.)

WIFSIGNALED(status)

> This macro returns true if the child process was killed by a signal. In this case, the macro WTERMSIG(status) returns the number of the signal that caused the process to terminate, and the macro WCOREDUMP(status) returns true if the child process produced a core dump file. The WCOREDUMP() macro is not specified by SUSv3, but is available on most UNIX implementations.

WIFSTOPPED(status)

> This macro returns true if the child process was stopped by a signal. In this case, the macro WSTOPSIG(status) returns the number of the signal that stopped the process.

WIFCONTINUED(status)

> This macro returns true if the child was resumed by delivery of SIGCONT. This macro is available since Linux 2.6.10.

Note that although the name *status* is also used for the argument of the above macros, they expect a plain integer, rather than a pointer to an integer as required by *wait()* and *waitpid()*.

Example program

The *printWaitStatus()* function of Listing 26-2 uses all of the macros described above. This function dissects and prints the contents of a wait status value.

Listing 26-2: Displaying the status value returned by *wait()* and related calls

———————————————————————————————— procexec/print_wait_status.c
```
#define _GNU_SOURCE     /* Get strsignal() declaration from <string.h> */
#include <string.h>
#include <sys/wait.h>
#include "print_wait_status.h"   /* Declaration of printWaitStatus() */
#include "tlpi_hdr.h"

/* NOTE: The following function employs printf(), which is not
   async-signal-safe (see Section 21.1.2). As such, this function is
   also not async-signal-safe (i.e., beware of calling it from a
   SIGCHLD handler). */

void                    /* Examine a wait() status using the W* macros */
printWaitStatus(const char *msg, int status)
{
```

```
    if (msg != NULL)
        printf("%s", msg);

    if (WIFEXITED(status)) {
        printf("child exited, status=%d\n", WEXITSTATUS(status));

    } else if (WIFSIGNALED(status)) {
        printf("child killed by signal %d (%s)",
                WTERMSIG(status), strsignal(WTERMSIG(status)));
#ifdef WCOREDUMP            /* Not in SUSv3, may be absent on some systems */
        if (WCOREDUMP(status))
            printf(" (core dumped)");
#endif
        printf("\n");

    } else if (WIFSTOPPED(status)) {
        printf("child stopped by signal %d (%s)\n",
                WSTOPSIG(status), strsignal(WSTOPSIG(status)));

#ifdef WIFCONTINUED         /* SUSv3 has this, but older Linux versions and
                               some other UNIX implementations don't */
    } else if (WIFCONTINUED(status)) {
        printf("child continued\n");
#endif

    } else {                /* Should never happen */
        printf("what happened to this child? (status=%x)\n",
                (unsigned int) status);
    }
}
```

—— procexec/print_wait_status.c

The *printWaitStatus()* function is used in Listing 26-3. This program creates a child process that either loops continuously calling *pause()* (during which time signals can be sent to the child) or, if an integer command-line argument was supplied, exits immediately using this integer as the exit status. In the meantime, the parent monitors the child via *waitpid()*, printing the returned status value and passing this value to *printWaitStatus()*. The parent exits when it detects that the child has either exited normally or been terminated by a signal.

The following shell session shows a few example runs of the program in Listing 26-3. We begin by creating a child that immediately exits with a status of 23:

```
$ ./child_status 23
Child started with PID = 15807
waitpid() returned: PID=15807; status=0x1700 (23,0)
child exited, status=23
```

In the next run, we start the program in the background, and then send SIGSTOP and SIGCONT signals to the child:

```
$ ./child_status &
[1] 15870
$ Child started with PID = 15871
```

```
kill -STOP 15871
$ waitpid() returned: PID=15871; status=0x137f (19,127)
child stopped by signal 19 (Stopped (signal))
kill -CONT 15871
$ waitpid() returned: PID=15871; status=0xffff (255,255)
child continued
```

The last two lines of output will appear only on Linux 2.6.10 and later, since earlier kernels don't support the *waitpid()* WCONTINUED option. (This shell session is made slightly hard to read by the fact that output from the program executing in the background is in some cases intermingled with the prompt produced by the shell.)

We continue the shell session by sending a SIGABRT signal to terminate the child:

```
kill -ABRT 15871
$ waitpid() returned: PID=15871; status=0x0006 (0,6)
child killed by signal 6 (Aborted)
```
Press Enter, in order to see shell notification that background job has terminated
```
[1]+  Done                    ./child_status
$ ls -l core
ls: core: No such file or directory
$ ulimit -c                                          Display RLIMIT_CORE limit
0
```

Although the default action of SIGABRT is to produce a core dump file and terminate the process, no core file was produced. This is because core dumps were disabled—the RLIMIT_CORE soft resource limit (Section 36.3), which specifies the maximum size of a core file, was set to 0, as shown by the *ulimit* command above.

We repeat the same experiment, but this time enabling core dumps before sending SIGABRT to the child:

```
$ ulimit -c unlimited                                Allow core dumps
$ ./child_status &
[1] 15902
$ Child started with PID = 15903
kill -ABRT 15903                                     Send SIGABRT to child
$ waitpid() returned: PID=15903; status=0x0086 (0,134)
child killed by signal 6 (Aborted) (core dumped)
```
Press Enter, in order to see shell notification that background job has terminated
```
[1]+  Done                    ./child_status
$ ls -l core                                         This time we get a core dump
-rw-------  1 mtk     users      65536 May  6 21:01 core
```

Listing 26-3: Using *waitpid()* to retrieve the status of a child process

─── procexec/child_status.c

```
#include <sys/wait.h>
#include "print_wait_status.h"        /* Declares printWaitStatus() */
#include "tlpi_hdr.h"

int
main(int argc, char *argv[])
{
    int status;
    pid_t childPid;
```

```
        if (argc > 1 && strcmp(argv[1], "--help") == 0)
            usageErr("%s [exit-status]\n", argv[0]);

        switch (fork()) {
        case -1: errExit("fork");

        case 0:                 /* Child: either exits immediately with given
                                   status or loops waiting for signals */
            printf("Child started with PID = %ld\n", (long) getpid());
            if (argc > 1)                     /* Status supplied on command line? */
                exit(getInt(argv[1], 0, "exit-status"));
            else                              /* Otherwise, wait for signals */
                for (;;)
                    pause();
            exit(EXIT_FAILURE);               /* Not reached, but good practice */

        default:                /* Parent: repeatedly wait on child until it
                                   either exits or is terminated by a signal */
            for (;;) {
                childPid = waitpid(-1, &status, WUNTRACED
#ifdef WCONTINUED       /* Not present on older versions of Linux */
                                    | WCONTINUED
#endif
                        );
                if (childPid == -1)
                    errExit("waitpid");

                /* Print status in hex, and as separate decimal bytes */

                printf("waitpid() returned: PID=%ld; status=0x%04x (%d,%d)\n",
                        (long) childPid,
                        (unsigned int) status, status >> 8, status & 0xff);
                printWaitStatus(NULL, status);

                if (WIFEXITED(status) || WIFSIGNALED(status))
                    exit(EXIT_SUCCESS);
            }
        }
    }
```

── procexec/child_status.c

26.1.4 Process Termination from a Signal Handler

As shown in Table 20-1 (on page 396), some signals terminate a process by default.
In some circumstances, we may wish to have certain cleanup steps performed
before a process terminates. For this purpose, we can arrange to have a handler
catch such signals, perform the cleanup steps, and then terminate the process. If
we do this, we should bear in mind that the termination status of a process is available to its parent via *wait()* or *waitpid()*. For example, calling *_exit(EXIT_SUCCESS)*
from the signal handler will make it appear to the parent process that the child terminated successfully.

   If the child needs to inform the parent that it terminated because of a signal,
then the child's signal handler should first disestablish itself, and then raise the

same signal once more, which this time will terminate the process. The signal handler would contain code such as the following:

```
void
handler(int sig)
{
    /* Perform cleanup steps */

    signal(sig, SIG_DFL);          /* Disestablish handler */
    raise(sig);                    /* Raise signal again */
}
```

26.1.5 The *waitid()* System Call

Like *waitpid()*, *waitid()* returns the status of child processes. However, *waitid()* provides extra functionality that is unavailable with *waitpid()*. This system call derives from System V, but is now specified in SUSv3. It was added to Linux in kernel 2.6.9.

> Before Linux 2.6.9, a version of *waitid()* was provided via an implementation in *glibc*. However, because a full implementation of this interface requires kernel support, the *glibc* implementation provided no more functionality than was available using *waitpid()*.

```
#include <sys/wait.h>

int waitid(idtype_t idtype, id_t id, siginfo_t *infop, int options);
```
> Returns 0 on success or if WNOHANG was specified and there were no children to wait for, or −1 on error

The *idtype* and *id* arguments specify which child(ren) to wait for, as follows:

- If *idtype* is P_ALL, wait for any child; *id* is ignored.
- If *idtype* is P_PID, wait for the child whose process ID equals *id*.
- If *idtype* is P_PGID, wait for any child whose process group ID equals *id*.

> Note that unlike *waitpid()*, it is not possible to specify 0 in *id* to mean any process in the same process group as the caller. Instead, we must explicitly specify the caller's process group ID using the value returned by *getpgrp()*.

The most significant difference between *waitpid()* and *waitid()* is that *waitid()* provides more precise control of the child events that should be waited for. We control this by ORing one or more of the following flags in *options*:

WEXITED
> Wait for children that have terminated, either normally or abnormally.

WSTOPPED
> Wait for children that have been stopped by a signal.

WCONTINUED
> Wait for children that have been resumed by a SIGCONT signal.

The following additional flags may be ORed in *options*:

WNOHANG

> This flag has the same meaning as for *waitpid()*. If none of the children matching the specification in *id* has status information to return, then return immediately (a poll). In this case, the return value of *waitid()* is 0. If the calling process has no children that match the specification in *id*, *waitid()* instead fails with the error ECHILD.

WNOWAIT

> Normally, once a child has been waited for using *waitid()*, then that "status event" is consumed. However, if WNOWAIT is specified, then the child status is returned, but the child remains in a waitable state, and we can later wait for it again to retrieve the same information.

On success, *waitid()* returns 0, and the *siginfo_t* structure (Section 21.4) pointed to by *infop* is updated to contain information about the child. The following fields are filled in the *siginfo_t* structure:

si_code

> This field contains one of the following values: CLD_EXITED, indicating that the child terminated by calling *_exit()*; CLD_KILLED, indicating that the child was killed by a signal; CLD_STOPPED, indicating that the child was stopped by a signal; or CLD_CONTINUED, indicating that the (previously stopped) child resumed execution as a consequence of receiving a (SIGCONT) signal.

si_pid

> This field contains the process ID of the child whose state has changed.

si_signo

> This field is always set to SIGCHLD.

si_status

> This field contains either the exit status of the child, as passed to *_exit()*, or the signal that caused the child to stop, continue, or terminate. We can determine which type of information is in this field by examining the *si_code* field.

si_uid

> This field contains the real user ID of the child. Most other UNIX implementations don't set this field.

> > On Solaris, two additional fields are filled in: *si_stime* and *si_utime*. These contain the system and user CPU time used by the child, respectively. SUSv3 doesn't require these fields to be set by *waitid()*.

One detail of the operation of *waitid()* needs further clarification. If WNOHANG is specified in *options*, then a 0 return value from *waitid()* can mean one of two things: a child had already changed state at the time of the call (and information about the child is returned in the *siginfo_t* structure pointed to by *infop*), or there was no child whose state has changed. For the case where no child has changed state, some UNIX implementations (including Linux), zero out the returned *siginfo_t* structure. This provides a method of distinguishing the two possibilities: we can check whether the value in *si_pid* is 0 or nonzero. Unfortunately, this behavior is not required by SUSv3, and some UNIX implementations leave the *siginfo_t* structure unchanged in this case. (A future corrigendum to SUSv4 is likely to add a requirement that *si_pid* and *si_signo* are zeroed in this case.) The only portable way to distinguish these two cases is to zero out the *siginfo_t* structure before calling *waitid()*, as in the following code:

```
siginfo_t info;
...
memset(&info, 0, sizeof(siginfo_t));
if (waitid(idtype, id, &info, options | WNOHANG) == -1)
    errExit("waitid");
if (info.si_pid == 0) {
    /* No children changed state */
} else {
    /* A child changed state; details are provided in 'info' */
}
```

26.1.6 The *wait3()* and *wait4()* System Calls

The *wait3()* and *wait4()* system calls perform a similar task to *waitpid()*. The principal semantic difference is that *wait3()* and *wait4()* return *resource usage* information about the terminated child in the structure pointed to by the *rusage* argument. This information includes the amount of CPU time used by the process and memory-management statistics. We defer detailed discussion of the *rusage* structure until Section 36.1, where we describe the *getrusage()* system call.

```
#define _BSD_SOURCE          /* Or #define _XOPEN_SOURCE 500 for wait3() */
#include <sys/resource.h>
#include <sys/wait.h>

pid_t wait3(int *status, int options, struct rusage *rusage);
pid_t wait4(pid_t pid, int *status, int options, struct rusage *rusage);
                              Both return process ID of child, or -1 on error
```

Excluding the use of the *rusage* argument, a call to *wait3()* is equivalent to the following *waitpid()* call:

```
waitpid(-1, &status, options);
```

Similarly, *wait4()* is equivalent to the following:

```
waitpid(pid, &status, options);
```

In other words, *wait3()* waits for any child, while *wait4()* can be used to select a specific child or children upon which to wait.

On some UNIX implementations, *wait3()* and *wait4()* return resource usage information only for terminated children. On Linux, resource usage information can also be retrieved for stopped children if the WUNTRACED flag is specified in *options*.

The names for these two system calls refer to the number of arguments they each take. Both system calls originated in BSD, but are now available on most

UNIX implementations. Neither is standardized in SUSv3. (SUSv2 did specify *wait3()*, but marked it LEGACY.)

We usually avoid the use of *wait3()* and *wait4()* in this book. Typically, we don't need the extra information returned by these calls. Also, lack of standardization limits their portability.

26.2 Orphans and Zombies

The lifetimes of parent and child processes are usually not the same—either the parent outlives the child or vice versa. This raises two questions:

- Who becomes the parent of an *orphaned* child? The orphaned child is adopted by *init*, the ancestor of all processes, whose process ID is 1. In other words, after a child's parent terminates, a call to *getppid()* will return the value 1. This can be used as a way of determining if a child's true parent is still alive (this assumes a child that was created by a process other than *init*).

    > Using the PR_SET_PDEATHSIG operation of the Linux-specific *prctl()* system call, it is possible to arrange that a process receives a specified signal when it becomes an orphan.

- What happens to a child that terminates before its parent has had a chance to perform a *wait()*? The point here is that, although the child has finished its work, the parent should still be permitted to perform a *wait()* at some later time to determine how the child terminated. The kernel deals with this situation by turning the child into a *zombie*. This means that most of the resources held by the child are released back to the system to be reused by other processes. The only part of the process that remains is an entry in the kernel's process table recording (among other things) the child's process ID, termination status, and resource usage statistics (Section 36.1).

Regarding zombies, UNIX systems imitate the movies—a zombie process can't be killed by a signal, not even the (silver bullet) SIGKILL. This ensures that the parent can always eventually perform a *wait()*.

When the parent does perform a *wait()*, the kernel removes the zombie, since the last remaining information about the child is no longer required. On the other hand, if the parent terminates without doing a *wait()*, then the *init* process adopts the child and automatically performs a *wait()*, thus removing the zombie process from the system.

If a parent creates a child, but fails to perform a *wait()*, then an entry for the zombie child will be maintained indefinitely in the kernel's process table. If a large number of such zombie children are created, they will eventually fill the kernel process table, preventing the creation of new processes. Since the zombies can't be killed by a signal, the only way to remove them from the system is to kill their parent (or wait for it to exit), at which time the zombies are adopted and waited on by *init*, and consequently removed from the system.

These semantics have important implications for the design of long-lived parent processes, such as network servers and shells, that create numerous children. To put things another way, in such applications, a parent process should perform *wait()* calls in order to ensure that dead children are always removed from the system, rather than becoming long-lived zombies. The parent may perform such *wait()* calls either synchronously, or asynchronously, in response to delivery of the SIGCHLD signal, as described in Section 26.3.1.

Listing 26-4 demonstrates the creation of a zombie and that a zombie can't be killed by SIGKILL. When we run this program, we see the following output:

```
$ ./make_zombie
Parent PID=1013
Child (PID=1014) exiting
 1013 pts/4    00:00:00 make_zombie                    Output from ps(1)
 1014 pts/4    00:00:00 make_zombie <defunct>
After sending SIGKILL to make_zombie (PID=1014):
 1013 pts/4    00:00:00 make_zombie                    Output from ps(1)
 1014 pts/4    00:00:00 make_zombie <defunct>
```

In the above output, we see that *ps(1)* displays the string <defunct> to indicate a process in the zombie state.

> The program in Listing 26-4 uses the *system()* function to execute the shell command given in its character-string argument. We describe *system()* in detail in Section 27.6.

Listing 26-4: Creating a zombie child process

─── procexec/make_zombie.c

```c
#include <signal.h>
#include <libgen.h>              /* For basename() declaration */
#include "tlpi_hdr.h"

#define CMD_SIZE 200

int
main(int argc, char *argv[])
{
    char cmd[CMD_SIZE];
    pid_t childPid;

    setbuf(stdout, NULL);        /* Disable buffering of stdout */

    printf("Parent PID=%ld\n", (long) getpid());

    switch (childPid = fork()) {
    case -1:
        errExit("fork");

    case 0:     /* Child: immediately exits to become zombie */
        printf("Child (PID=%ld) exiting\n", (long) getpid());
        _exit(EXIT_SUCCESS);
```

```
        default:     /* Parent */
            sleep(3);                    /* Give child a chance to start and exit */
            snprintf(cmd, CMD_SIZE, "ps | grep %s", basename(argv[0]));
            system(cmd);                 /* View zombie child */

            /* Now send the "sure kill" signal to the zombie */

            if (kill(childPid, SIGKILL) == -1)
                errMsg("kill");
            sleep(3);                    /* Give child a chance to react to signal */
            printf("After sending SIGKILL to zombie (PID=%ld):\n", (long) childPid);
            system(cmd);                 /* View zombie child again */

            exit(EXIT_SUCCESS);
        }
    }
```

—— procexec/make_zombie.c

26.3 The SIGCHLD Signal

The termination of a child process is an event that occurs asynchronously. A parent
can't predict when one of its children will terminate. (Even if the parent sends a
SIGKILL signal to a child, the exact time of termination is still dependent on when
the child is next scheduled for use of a CPU.) We have already seen that the parent
should use *wait()* (or similar) in order to prevent the accumulation of zombie children, and have looked at two ways in which this can be done:

- The parent can call *wait()*, or *waitpid()* without specifying the WNOHANG flag, in
  which case the call will block if a child has not already terminated.
- The parent can periodically perform a nonblocking check (a poll) for dead children via a call to *waitpid()* specifying the WNOHANG flag.

Both of these approaches can be inconvenient. On the one hand, we may not want
the parent to be blocked waiting for a child to terminate. On the other hand, making
repeated nonblocking *waitpid()* calls wastes CPU time and adds complexity to an
application design. To get around these problems, we can employ a handler for the
SIGCHLD signal.

26.3.1 Establishing a Handler for SIGCHLD

The SIGCHLD signal is sent to a parent process whenever one of its children termi-
nates. By default, this signal is ignored, but we can catch it by installing a signal handler.
Within the signal handler, we can use *wait()* (or similar) to reap the zombie child.
However, there is a subtlety to consider in this approach.

In Sections 20.10 and 20.12, we observed that when a signal handler is called,
the signal that caused its invocation is temporarily blocked (unless the *sigaction()*
SA_NODEFER flag was specified), and also that standard signals, of which SIGCHLD is one,
are not queued. Consequently, if a second and third child terminate in quick

succession while a SIGCHLD handler is executing for an already terminated child, then, although SIGCHLD is generated twice, it is queued only once to the parent. As a result, if the parent's SIGCHLD handler called *wait()* only once each time it was invoked, the handler might fail to reap some zombie children.

The solution is to loop inside the SIGCHLD handler, repeatedly calling *waitpid()* with the WNOHANG flag until there are no more dead children to be reaped. Often, the body of a SIGCHLD handler simply consists of the following code, which reaps any dead children without checking their status:

```
while (waitpid(-1, NULL, WNOHANG) > 0)
    continue;
```

The above loop continues until *waitpid()* returns either 0, indicating no more zombie children, or -1, indicating an error (probably ECHILD, meaning that there are no more children).

Design issues for SIGCHLD handlers

Suppose that, at the time we establish a handler for SIGCHLD, there is already a terminated child for this process. Does the kernel then immediately generate a SIGCHLD signal for the parent? SUSv3 leaves this point unspecified. Some System V–derived implementations do generate a SIGCHLD in these circumstances; other implementations, including Linux, do not. A portable application can make this difference invisible by establishing the SIGCHLD handler before creating any children. (This is usually the natural way of doing things, of course.)

A further point to consider is the issue of reentrancy. In Section 21.1.2, we noted that using a system call (e.g., *waitpid()*) from within a signal handler may change the value of the global variable *errno*. Such a change could interfere with attempts by the main program to explicitly set *errno* (see, for example, the discussion of *getpriority()* in Section 35.1) or check its value after a failed system call. For this reason, it is sometimes necessary to code a SIGCHLD handler to save *errno* in a local variable on entry to the handler, and then restore the *errno* value just prior to returning. An example of this is shown in Listing 26-5.

Example program

Listing 26-5 provides an example of a more complex SIGCHLD handler. This handler displays the process ID and wait status of each reaped child ①. In order to see that multiple SIGCHLD signals are not queued while the handler is already invoked, execution of the handler is artificially lengthened by a call to *sleep()* ②. The main program creates one child process for each (integer) command-line argument ④. Each of these children sleeps for the number of seconds specified in the corresponding command-line argument and then exits ⑤. In the following example of the execution of this program, we see that even though three children terminate, SIGCHLD is only queued twice to the parent:

```
$ ./multi_SIGCHLD 1 2 4
16:45:18 Child 1 (PID=17767) exiting
16:45:18 handler: Caught SIGCHLD          First invocation of handler
16:45:18 handler: Reaped child 17767 - child exited, status=0
```

```
16:45:19 Child 2 (PID=17768) exiting        These children terminate during...
16:45:21 Child 3 (PID=17769) exiting        first invocation of handler
16:45:23 handler: returning                 End of first invocation of handler
16:45:23 handler: Caught SIGCHLD            Second invocation of handler
16:45:23 handler: Reaped child 17768 - child exited, status=0
16:45:23 handler: Reaped child 17769 - child exited, status=0
16:45:28 handler: returning
16:45:28 All 3 children have terminated; SIGCHLD was caught 2 times
```

Note the use of *sigprocmask()* to block the SIGCHLD signal before any children are created in Listing 26-5 ③. This is done to ensure correct operation of the *sigsuspend()* loop in the parent. If we failed to block SIGCHLD in this way, and a child terminated between the test of the value of *numLiveChildren* and the execution of the *sigsuspend()* call (or alternatively a *pause()* call), then the *sigsuspend()* call would block forever waiting for a signal that has already been caught ⑥. The requirement for dealing with this type of race condition was detailed in Section 22.9.

Listing 26-5: Reaping dead children via a handler for SIGCHLD

── procexec/multi_SIGCHLD.c

```
#include <signal.h>
#include <sys/wait.h>
#include "print_wait_status.h"
#include "curr_time.h"
#include "tlpi_hdr.h"

static volatile int numLiveChildren = 0;
                /* Number of children started but not yet waited on */

static void
sigchldHandler(int sig)
{
    int status, savedErrno;
    pid_t childPid;

    /* UNSAFE: This handler uses non-async-signal-safe functions
       (printf(), printWaitStatus(), currTime(); see Section 21.1.2) */

    savedErrno = errno;        /* In case we modify 'errno' */

    printf("%s handler: Caught SIGCHLD\n", currTime("%T"));

    while ((childPid = waitpid(-1, &status, WNOHANG)) > 0) {
        printf("%s handler: Reaped child %ld - ", currTime("%T"),
                (long) childPid);
        printWaitStatus(NULL, status);
        numLiveChildren--;
    }

    if (childPid == -1 && errno != ECHILD)
        errMsg("waitpid");
```

① (marginal annotation beside the `while` loop)

```
②      sleep(5);                     /* Artificially lengthen execution of handler */
        printf("%s handler: returning\n", currTime("%T"));

        errno = savedErrno;
    }

    int
    main(int argc, char *argv[])
    {
        int j, sigCnt;
        sigset_t blockMask, emptyMask;
        struct sigaction sa;

        if (argc < 2 || strcmp(argv[1], "--help") == 0)
            usageErr("%s child-sleep-time...\n", argv[0]);

        setbuf(stdout, NULL);          /* Disable buffering of stdout */

        sigCnt = 0;
        numLiveChildren = argc - 1;

        sigemptyset(&sa.sa_mask);
        sa.sa_flags = 0;
        sa.sa_handler = sigchldHandler;
        if (sigaction(SIGCHLD, &sa, NULL) == -1)
            errExit("sigaction");

        /* Block SIGCHLD to prevent its delivery if a child terminates
           before the parent commences the sigsuspend() loop below */

        sigemptyset(&blockMask);
        sigaddset(&blockMask, SIGCHLD);
③      if (sigprocmask(SIG_SETMASK, &blockMask, NULL) == -1)
            errExit("sigprocmask");

④      for (j = 1; j < argc; j++) {
            switch (fork()) {
            case -1:
                errExit("fork");

            case 0:          /* Child - sleeps and then exits */
⑤              sleep(getInt(argv[j], GN_NONNEG, "child-sleep-time"));
                printf("%s Child %d (PID=%ld) exiting\n", currTime("%T"),
                        j, (long) getpid());
                _exit(EXIT_SUCCESS);

            default:         /* Parent - loops to create next child */
                break;
            }
        }
```

```
    /* Parent comes here: wait for SIGCHLD until all children are dead */

    sigemptyset(&emptyMask);
    while (numLiveChildren > 0) {
⑥       if (sigsuspend(&emptyMask) == -1 && errno != EINTR)
            errExit("sigsuspend");
        sigCnt++;
    }

    printf("%s All %d children have terminated; SIGCHLD was caught "
            "%d times\n", currTime("%T"), argc - 1, sigCnt);

    exit(EXIT_SUCCESS);
}
```

─── procexec/multi_SIGCHLD.c

26.3.2 Delivery of SIGCHLD for Stopped Children

Just as *waitpid()* can be used to monitor stopped children, so is it possible for a parent
process to receive the SIGCHLD signal when one of its children is stopped by a signal. This
behavior is controlled by the SA_NOCLDSTOP flag when using *sigaction()* to establish a
handler for the SIGCHLD signal. If this flag is omitted, a SIGCHLD signal is delivered to
the parent when one of its children stops; if the flag is present, SIGCHLD is not delivered for stopped children. (The implementation of *signal()* given in Section 22.7
doesn't specify SA_NOCLDSTOP.)

> Since SIGCHLD is ignored by default, the SA_NOCLDSTOP flag has a meaning only if
> we are establishing a handler for SIGCHLD. Furthermore, SIGCHLD is the only signal
> for which the SA_NOCLDSTOP flag has an effect.

SUSv3 also allows for a parent to be sent a SIGCHLD signal if one of its stopped children is resumed by being sent a SIGCONT signal. (This corresponds to the WCONTINUED
flag for *waitpid()*.) This feature is implemented in Linux since kernel 2.6.9.

26.3.3 Ignoring Dead Child Processes

There is a further possibility for dealing with dead child processes. Explicitly setting
the disposition of SIGCHLD to SIG_IGN causes any child process that subsequently terminates to be immediately removed from the system instead of being converted
into a zombie. In this case, since the status of the child process is simply discarded,
a subsequent call to *wait()* (or similar) can't return any information for the terminated child.

> Note that even though the default disposition for SIGCHLD is to be ignored,
> explicitly setting the disposition to SIG_IGN causes the different behavior
> described here. In this respect, SIGCHLD is treated uniquely among signals.

On Linux, as on many UNIX implementations, setting the disposition of SIGCHLD to
SIG_IGN doesn't affect the status of any existing zombie children, which must still be
waited upon in the usual way. On some other UNIX implementations (e.g., Solaris 8),
setting the disposition of SIGCHLD to SIG_IGN *does* remove existing zombie children.

The SIG_IGN semantics for SIGCHLD have a long history, deriving from System V. SUSv3 specifies the behavior described here, but these semantics were left unspecified in the original POSIX.1 standard. Thus, on some older UNIX implementations, ignoring SIGCHLD has no effect on the creation of zombies. The only completely portable way of preventing the creation of zombies is to call *wait()* or *waitpid()*, possibly from within a handler established for SIGCHLD.

Deviations from SUSv3 in older Linux kernels

SUSv3 specifies that if the disposition of SIGCHLD is set to SIG_IGN, the resource usage information for the child should be discarded and not included in the totals returned when the parent makes a call to *getrusage()* specifying the RUSAGE_CHILDREN flag (Section 36.1). However, on Linux versions before kernel 2.6.9, the CPU times and resources used by the child *are* recorded and are visible in calls to *getrusage()*. This nonconformance is fixed in Linux 2.6.9 and later.

> Setting the disposition of SIGCHLD to SIG_IGN should also prevent the child CPU times from being included in the structure returned by *times()* (Section 10.7). However, on Linux kernels before 2.6.9, a similar nonconformance applies for the information returned by *times()*.

SUSv3 specifies that if the disposition of SIGCHLD is set to SIG_IGN, and the parent has no terminated children that have been transformed into zombies and have not yet been waited for, then a call to *wait()* (or *waitpid()*) should block until *all* of the parent's children have terminated, at which point the call should terminate with the error ECHILD. Linux 2.6 conforms to this requirement. However, in Linux 2.4 and earlier, *wait()* blocks only until the *next* child terminates, and then returns the process ID and status of that child (i.e., the behavior is the same as if the disposition of SIGCHLD had not been set to SIG_IGN).

The *sigaction()* SA_NOCLDWAIT flag

SUSv3 specifies the SA_NOCLDWAIT flag, which can be used when setting the disposition of the SIGCHLD signal using *sigaction()*. This flag produces behavior similar to that when the disposition of SIGCHLD is set to SIG_IGN. This flag was not implemented in Linux 2.4 and earlier, but is implemented in Linux 2.6.

The principal difference between setting the disposition of SIGCHLD to SIG_IGN and employing SA_NOCLDWAIT is that, when establishing a handler with SA_NOCLDWAIT, SUSv3 leaves it unspecified whether or not a SIGCHLD signal is sent to the parent when a child terminates. In other words, an implementation is permitted to deliver SIGCHLD when SA_NOCLDWAIT is specified, and an application could catch this signal (although the SIGCHLD handler would not be able to reap the child status using *wait()*, since the kernel has already discarded the zombie). On some UNIX implementations, including Linux, the kernel does generate a SIGCHLD signal for the parent process. On other UNIX implementations, SIGCHLD is not generated.

> When setting the SA_NOCLDWAIT flag for the SIGCHLD signal, older Linux kernels demonstrate the same details of nonconformance to SUSv3 as were described above for setting the disposition of SIGCHLD to SIG_IGN.

The System V SIGCLD signal

On Linux, the name SIGCLD is provided as a synonym for the SIGCHLD signal. The reason for the existence of both names is historical. The SIGCHLD signal originated on BSD, and this name was adopted by POSIX, which largely standardized on the BSD signal model. System V provided the corresponding SIGCLD signal, with slightly different semantics.

The key difference between BSD SIGCHLD and System V SIGCLD lies in what happens when the disposition of the signal was set to SIG_IGN:

- On historical (and some contemporary) BSD implementations, the system continues to generate zombies for unwaited-for children, even when SIGCHLD is ignored.

- On System V, using *signal()* (but not *sigaction()*) to ignore SIGCLD has the result that zombies are not generated when children died.

As already noted, the original POSIX.1 standard left the result of ignoring SIGCHLD unspecified, thus permitting the System V behavior. Nowadays, this System V behavior is specified as part of SUSv3 (which nevertheless holds to the name SIGCHLD). Modern System V derivatives use the standard name SIGCHLD for this signal, but continue to provide the synonym SIGCLD. Further details on SIGCLD can be found in [Stevens & Rago, 2005].

26.4 Summary

Using *wait()* and *waitpid()* (and other related functions), a parent process can obtain the status of its terminated and stopped children. This status indicates whether a child process terminated normally (with an exit status indicating either success or failure), terminated abnormally, was stopped by a signal, or was resumed by a SIGCONT signal.

If a child's parent terminates, the child becomes an orphan and is adopted by the *init* process, whose process ID is 1.

When a child process terminates, it becomes a zombie, and is removed from the system only when its parent calls *wait()* (or similar) to retrieve the child's status. Long-running programs such as shells and daemons should be designed so that they always reap the status of the child processes they create, since a process in the zombie state can't be killed, and unreaped zombies will eventually clog the kernel process table.

A common way of reaping dead child processes is to establish a handler for the SIGCHLD signal. This signal is delivered to a parent process whenever one of its children terminates, and optionally when a child is stopped by a signal. Alternatively, but somewhat less portably, a process may elect to set the disposition of SIGCHLD to SIG_IGN, in which case the status of terminated children is immediately discarded (and thus can't later be retrieved by the parent), and the children don't become zombies.

Further information

Refer to the sources of further information listed in Section 24.6.

26.5 Exercises

26-1. Write a program to verify that when a child's parent terminates, a call to *getppid()* returns 1 (the process ID of *init*).

26-2. Suppose that we have three processes related as grandparent, parent, and child, and that the grandparent doesn't immediately perform a *wait()* after the parent exits, so that the parent becomes a zombie. When do you expect the grandchild to be adopted by *init* (so that *getppid()* in the grandchild returns 1): after the parent terminates or after the grandparent does a *wait()*? Write a program to verify your answer.

26-3. Replace the use of *waitpid()* with *waitid()* in Listing 26-3 (`child_status.c`). The call to *printWaitStatus()* will need to be replaced by code that prints relevant fields from the *siginfo_t* structure returned by *waitid()*.

26-4. Listing 26-4 (`make_zombie.c`) uses a call to *sleep()* to allow the child process a chance to execute and terminate before the parent executes *system()*. This approach produces a theoretical race condition. Modify the program to eliminate the race condition by using signals to synchronize the parent and child.

27

PROGRAM EXECUTION

This chapter follows from our discussion of process creation and termination in the previous chapters. We now look at how a process can use the *execve()* system call to replace the program that it is running by a completely new program. We then show how to implement the *system()* function, which allows its caller to execute an arbitrary shell command.

27.1 Executing a New Program: *execve()*

The *execve()* system call loads a new program into a process's memory. During this operation, the old program is discarded, and the process's stack, data, and heap are replaced by those of the new program. After executing various C library run-time startup code and program initialization code (e.g., C++ static constructors or C functions declared with the *gcc* constructor attribute described in Section 42.4), the new program commences execution at its *main()* function.

The most frequent use of *execve()* is in the child produced by a *fork()*, although it is also occasionally used in applications without a preceding *fork()*.

Various library functions, all with names beginning with *exec*, are layered on top of the *execve()* system call. Each of these functions provides a different interface to the same functionality. The loading of a new program by any of these calls is commonly referred to as an *exec* operation, or simply by the notation *exec()*. We begin with a description of *execve()* and then describe the library functions.

```
#include <unistd.h>

int execve(const char *pathname, char *const argv[], char *const envp[]);
```
                              Never returns on success; returns −1 on error

The *pathname* argument contains the pathname of the new program to be loaded into the process's memory. This pathname can be absolute (indicated by an initial /) or relative to the current working directory of the calling process.

The *argv* argument specifies the command-line arguments to be passed to the new program. This array corresponds to, and has the same form as, the second (*argv*) argument to a C *main()* function; it is a NULL-terminated list of pointers to character strings. The value supplied for *argv[0]* corresponds to the command name. Typically, this value is the same as the basename (i.e., the final component) of *pathname*.

The final argument, *envp*, specifies the environment list for the new program. The *envp* argument corresponds to the *environ* array of the new program; it is a NULL-terminated list of pointers to character strings of the form *name=value* (Section 6.7).

> The Linux-specific /proc/*PID*/exe file is a symbolic link containing the absolute pathname of the executable file being run by the corresponding process.

After an *execve()*, the process ID of the process remains the same, because the same process continues to exist. A few other process attributes also remain unchanged, as described in Section 28.4.

If the set-user-ID (set-group-ID) permission bit of the program file specified by *pathname* is set, then, when the file is execed, the effective user (group) ID of the process is changed to be the same as the owner (group) of the program file. This is a mechanism for temporarily granting privileges to users while running a specific program (see Section 9.3).

After optionally changing the effective IDs, and regardless of whether they were changed, an *execve()* copies the value of the process's effective user ID into its saved set-user-ID, and copies the value of the process's effective group ID into its saved set-group-ID.

Since it replaces the program that called it, a successful *execve()* never returns. We never need to check the return value from *execve()*; it will always be −1. The very fact that it returned informs us that an error occurred, and, as usual, we can use *errno* to determine the cause. Among the errors that may be returned in *errno* are the following:

EACCES

> The *pathname* argument doesn't refer to a regular file, the file doesn't have execute permission enabled, or one of the directory components of *pathname* is not searchable (i.e., execute permission is denied on the directory). Alternatively, the file resides on a file system that was mounted with the MS_NOEXEC flag (Section 14.8.1).

ENOENT

> The file referred to by *pathname* doesn't exist.

ENOEXEC

> The file referred to by *pathname* is marked as being executable, but it is not in a recognizable executable format. Possibly, it is a script that doesn't begin with a line (starting with the characters #!) specifying a script interpreter.

ETXTBSY

> The file referred to by *pathname* is open for writing by one or more processes (Section 4.3.2).

E2BIG

> The total space required by the argument list and environment list exceeds the allowed maximum.

The errors listed above may also be generated if any of these conditions apply to the interpreter file defined to execute a script (refer to Section 27.3) or to the ELF interpreter being used to execute the program.

> The Executable and Linking Format (ELF) is a widely implemented specification describing the layout of executable files. Normally, during an exec, a process image is constructed using the segments of the executable file (Section 6.3). However, the ELF specification also allows for an executable file to define an interpreter (the PT_INTERP ELF program header element) to be used to execute the program. If an interpreter is defined, the kernel constructs the process image from the segments of the specified interpreter executable file. It is then the responsibility of the interpreter to load and execute the program. We say a little more about the ELF interpreter in Chapter 41 and provide some pointers to further information in that chapter.

Example program

Listing 27-1 demonstrates the use of *execve()*. This program creates an argument list and an environment for a new program, and then calls *execve()*, using its command-line argument (*argv[1]*) as the pathname to be executed.

Listing 27-2 shows a program that is designed to be executed by the program in Listing 27-1. This program simply displays its command-line arguments and environment list (the latter is accessed using the global *environ* variable, as described in Section 6.7).

The following shell session demonstrates the use of the programs in Listing 27-1 and Listing 27-2 (in this example, a relative pathname is used to specify the program to be execed):

```
$ ./t_execve ./envargs
argv[0] = envargs                    All of the output is printed by envargs
argv[1] = hello world
argv[2] = goodbye
environ: GREET=salut
environ: BYE=adieu
```

Listing 27-1: Using *execve()* to execute a new program

```c
#include "tlpi_hdr.h"

int
main(int argc, char *argv[])
{
    char *argVec[10];           /* Larger than required */
    char *envVec[] = { "GREET=salut", "BYE=adieu", NULL };

    if (argc != 2 || strcmp(argv[1], "--help") == 0)
        usageErr("%s pathname\n", argv[0]);

    argVec[0] = strrchr(argv[1], '/');       /* Get basename from argv[1] */
    if (argVec[0] != NULL)
        argVec[0]++;
    else
        argVec[0] = argv[1];
    argVec[1] = "hello world";
    argVec[2] = "goodbye";
    argVec[3] = NULL;            /* List must be NULL-terminated */

    execve(argv[1], argVec, envVec);
    errExit("execve");          /* If we get here, something went wrong */
}
```

Listing 27-2: Display argument list and environment

```c
#include "tlpi_hdr.h"

extern char **environ;

int
main(int argc, char *argv[])
{
    int j;
    char **ep;

    for (j = 0; j < argc; j++)
        printf("argv[%d] = %s\n", j, argv[j]);

    for (ep = environ; *ep != NULL; ep++)
        printf("environ: %s\n", *ep);

    exit(EXIT_SUCCESS);
}
```

27.2 The *exec()* Library Functions

The library functions described in this section provide alternative APIs for performing an *exec()*. All of these functions are layered on top of *execve()*, and they differ from one another and from *execve()* only in the way in which the program name, argument list, and environment of the new program are specified.

```
#include <unistd.h>

int execle(const char *pathname, const char *arg, ...
            /* , (char *) NULL, char *const envp[] */ );
int execlp(const char *filename, const char *arg, ...
            /* , (char *) NULL */);
int execvp(const char *filename, char *const argv[]);
int execv(const char *pathname, char *const argv[]);
int execl(const char *pathname, const char *arg, ...
            /* , (char *) NULL */);
```

                    None of the above returns on success; all return −1 on error

The final letters in the names of these functions provide a clue to the differences between them. These differences are summarized in Table 27-1 and detailed in the following list:

- Most of the *exec()* functions expect a pathname as the specification of the new program to be loaded. However, *execlp()* and *execvp()* allow the program to be specified using just a filename. The filename is sought in the list of directories specified in the PATH environment variable (explained in more detail below). This is the kind of searching that the shell performs when given a command name. To indicate this difference in operation, the names of these functions contain the letter *p* (for PATH). The PATH variable is not used if the filename contains a slash (/), in which case it is treated as a relative or absolute pathname.

- Instead of using an array to specify the *argv* list for the new program, *execle()*, *execlp()*, and *execl()* require the programmer to specify the arguments as a list of strings within the call. The first of these arguments corresponds to *argv[0]* in the *main* function of the new program, and is thus typically the same as the *filename* argument or the basename component of the *pathname* argument. A NULL pointer must terminate the argument list, so that these calls can locate the end of the list. (This requirement is indicated by the commented *(char *) NULL* in the above prototypes; for a discussion of why the cast is required before the NULL, see Appendix C.) The names of these functions contain the letter *l* (for *list*) to distinguish them from those functions requiring the argument list as a NULL-terminated array. The names of the functions that require the argument list as an array (*execve()*, *execvp()*, and *execv()*) contain the letter *v* (for *vector*).

- The *execve()* and *execle()* functions allow the programmer to explicitly specify the environment for the new program using *envp*, a NULL-terminated array of pointers to character strings. The names of these functions end with the letter *e* (for *environment*) to indicate this fact. All of the other *exec()* functions use the caller's existing environment (i.e., the contents of *environ*) as the environment for the new program.

> Version 2.11 of *glibc* added a nonstandard function, *execvpe(file, argv, envp)*. This function is like *execvp()*, but instead of taking the environment for the new program from *environ*, the caller specifies the new environment via the *envp* argument (like *execve()* and *execle()*).

In the next few pages, we demonstrate the use of some of these *exec()* variants.

Table 27-1: Summary of differences between the *exec()* functions

Function	Specification of program file (-, p)	Specification of arguments (v, l)	Source of environment (e, -)
execve()	pathname	array	*envp* argument
execle()	pathname	list	*envp* argument
execlp()	filename + PATH	list	caller's *environ*
execvp()	filename + PATH	array	caller's *environ*
execv()	pathname	array	caller's *environ*
execl()	pathname	list	caller's *environ*

27.2.1 The PATH Environment Variable

The *execvp()* and *execlp()* functions allow us to specify just the name of the file to be executed. These functions make use of the PATH environment variable to search for the file. The value of PATH is a string consisting of colon-separated directory names called *path prefixes*. As an example, the following PATH value specifies five directories:

```
$ echo $PATH
/home/mtk/bin:/usr/local/bin:/usr/bin:/bin:.
```

The PATH value for a login shell is set by system-wide and user-specific shell startup scripts. Since a child process inherits a copy of its parent's environment variables, each process that the shell creates to execute a command inherits a copy of the shell's PATH.

The directory pathnames specified in PATH can be either absolute (commencing with an initial /) or relative. A relative pathname is interpreted with respect to the current working directory of the calling process. The current working directory can be specified using . (dot), as in the above example.

> It is also possible to specify the current working directory by including a zero-length prefix in PATH, by employing consecutive colons, an initial colon, or a trailing colon (e.g., /usr/bin:/bin:). SUSv3 declares this technique obsolete; the current working directory should be explicitly specified using . (dot).

If the PATH variable is not defined, then *execvp()* and *execlp()* assume a default path list of .:/usr/bin:/bin.

As a security measure, the superuser account (*root*) is normally set up so that the current working directory is excluded from PATH. This prevents *root* from accidentally executing a file from the current working directory (which may have been deliberately placed there by a malicious user) with the same name as a standard command or with a name that is a misspelling of a common command (e.g., *sl* instead of *ls*). In some Linux distributions, the default value for PATH also excludes the current working directory for unprivileged users. We assume such a PATH definition in all of the shell session logs shown in this book, which is why we always prefix ./ to the names of programs executed from the current working directory. (This also has the useful side effect of visually distinguishing our programs from standard commands in the shell session logs shown in this book.)

The *execvp()* and *execlp()* functions search for the filename in each of the directories named in PATH, starting from the beginning of the list and continuing until a file with the given name is successfully execed. Using the PATH environment variable in this way is useful if we don't know the run-time location of an executable file or don't want to create a hard-coded dependency on that location.

The use of *execvp()* and *execlp()* in set-user-ID or set-group-ID programs should be avoided, or at least approached with great caution. In particular, the PATH environment variable should be carefully controlled to prevent the execing of a malicious program. In practice, this means that the application should override any previously defined PATH value with a known-secure directory list.

Listing 27-3 provides an example of the use of *execlp()*. The following shell session log demonstrates the use of this program to invoke the *echo* command (/bin/echo):

```
$ which echo
/bin/echo
$ ls -l /bin/echo
-rwxr-xr-x    1 root        15428 Mar 19 21:28 /bin/echo
$ echo $PATH                          Show contents of PATH environment variable
/home/mtk/bin:/usr/local/bin:/usr/bin:/bin          /bin is in PATH
$ ./t_execlp echo                     execlp() uses PATH to successfully find echo
hello world
```

The string *hello world* that appears above was supplied as the third argument of the call to *execlp()* in the program in Listing 27-3.

We continue by redefining PATH to omit /bin, which is the directory containing the *echo* program:

```
$ PATH=/home/mtk/bin:/usr/local/bin:/usr/bin
$ ./t_execlp echo
ERROR [ENOENT No such file or directory] execlp
$ ./t_execlp /bin/echo
hello world
```

As can be seen, when we supply a filename (i.e., a string containing no slashes) to *execlp()*, the call fails, since a file named echo was not found in any of the directories listed in PATH. On the other hand, when we provide a pathname containing one or more slashes, *execlp()* ignores the contents of PATH.

Listing 27-3: Using *execlp()* to search for a filename in PATH

—————————————————————————————— `procexec/t_execlp.c`
```
#include "tlpi_hdr.h"

int
main(int argc, char *argv[])
{
    if (argc != 2 || strcmp(argv[1], "--help") == 0)
        usageErr("%s pathname\n", argv[0]);

    execlp(argv[1], argv[1], "hello world", (char *) NULL);
    errExit("execlp");          /* If we get here, something went wrong */
}
```
—————————————————————————————— `procexec/t_execlp.c`

27.2.2 Specifying Program Arguments as a List

When we know the number of arguments for an *exec()* at the time we write a program, we can use *execle()*, *execlp()*, or *execl()* to specify the arguments as a list within the function call. This can be convenient, since it requires less code than assembling the arguments in an *argv* vector. The program in Listing 27-4 achieves the same result as the program in Listing 27-1 but using *execle()* instead of *execve()*.

Listing 27-4: Using *execle()* to specify program arguments as a list

—————————————————————————————— `procexec/t_execle.c`
```
#include "tlpi_hdr.h"

int
main(int argc, char *argv[])
{
    char *envVec[] = { "GREET=salut", "BYE=adieu", NULL };
    char *filename;

    if (argc != 2 || strcmp(argv[1], "--help") == 0)
        usageErr("%s pathname\n", argv[0]);

    filename = strrchr(argv[1], '/');       /* Get basename from argv[1] */
    if (filename != NULL)
        filename++;
    else
        filename = argv[1];

    execle(argv[1], filename, "hello world", "goodbye", (char *) NULL, envVec);
    errExit("execle");          /* If we get here, something went wrong */
}
```
—————————————————————————————— `procexec/t_execle.c`

27.2.3 Passing the Caller's Environment to the New Program

The *execlp()*, *execvp()*, *execl()*, and *execv()* functions don't permit the programmer to explicitly specify an environment list; instead, the new program inherits its environment from the calling process (Section 6.7). This may, or may not, be desirable. For security reasons, it is sometimes preferable to ensure that a program is execed with a known environment list. We consider this point further in Section 38.8.

Listing 27-5 demonstrates that the new program inherits its environment from the caller during an *execl()* call. This program first uses *putenv()* to make a change to the environment that it inherits from the shell as a result of *fork()*. Then the *printenv* program is execed to display the values of the USER and SHELL environment variables. When we run this program, we see the following:

```
$ echo $USER $SHELL          Display some of the shell's environment variables
blv /bin/bash
$ ./t_execl
Initial value of USER: blv   Copy of environment was inherited from the shell
britta                       These two lines are displayed by execed printenv
/bin/bash
```

Listing 27-5: Passing the caller's environment to the new program using *execl()*

—— procexec/t_execl.c

```c
#include <stdlib.h>
#include "tlpi_hdr.h"

int
main(int argc, char *argv[])
{
    printf("Initial value of USER: %s\n", getenv("USER"));
    if (putenv("USER=britta") != 0)
        errExit("putenv");

    execl("/usr/bin/printenv", "printenv", "USER", "SHELL", (char *) NULL);
    errExit("execl");          /* If we get here, something went wrong */
}
```

—— procexec/t_execl.c

27.2.4 Executing a File Referred to by a Descriptor: *fexecve()*

Since version 2.3.2, *glibc* provides *fexecve()*, which behaves just like *execve()*, but specifies the file to be execed via the open file descriptor *fd*, rather than as a pathname. Using *fexecve()* is useful for applications that want to open a file, verify its contents by performing a checksum, and then execute the file.

```
#define _GNU_SOURCE
#include <unistd.h>

int fexecve(int fd, char *const argv[], char *const envp[]);
```

                              Doesn't return on success; returns −1 on error

Without *fexecve()*, we could *open()* and read the file to verify its contents, and then exec it. However, this would allow the possibility that, between opening the file and execing it, the file was replaced (holding an open file descriptor doesn't prevent a new file with the same name from being created), so that the content that was execed was different from the content that was checked.

27.3 Interpreter Scripts

An *interpreter* is a program that reads commands in text form and executes them. (This contrasts with a *compiler*, which translates input source code into a machine language that can then be executed on a real or virtual machine.) Examples of interpreters include the various UNIX shells and programs such as *awk*, *sed*, *perl*, *python*, and *ruby*. In addition to being able to read and execute commands interactively, interpreters usually provide a facility to read and execute commands from a text file, referred to as a *script*.

UNIX kernels allow interpreter scripts to be run in the same way as a binary program file, as long as two requirements are met. First, execute permission must be enabled for the script file. Second, the file must contain an initial line that specifies the pathname of the interpreter to be used to run the script. This line has the following form:

#! *interpreter-path* [*optional-arg*]

The #! characters must be placed at the start of the line; optionally, a space may separate these characters from the interpreter pathname. The PATH environment variable is *not* used in interpreting this pathname, so that an absolute pathname usually should be specified. A relative pathname is also possible, though unusual; it is interpreted relative to the current working directory of the process starting the interpreter. White space separates the interpreter pathname from an optional argument, whose purpose we explain shortly. The optional argument should not contain white-space characters.

As an example, UNIX shell scripts usually begin with the following line, which specifies that the shell is to be used to execute the script:

```
#!/bin/sh
```

> The optional argument in the first line of the interpreter script file should not contain white space because the behavior in this case is highly implementation-dependent. On Linux, white space in *optional-arg* is not interpreted specially—all of the text from the start of the argument to the end of the line is interpreted as a single word (which is given as an argument to the interpreter, as we describe below). Note that this treatment of spaces contrasts with the shell, where white space delimits the words of a command line.
>
> While some UNIX implementations treat white space in *optional-arg* in the same way as Linux, other implementations do not. On FreeBSD before version 6.0, multiple space-delimited optional arguments may follow *interpreter-path* (and these are passed as separate words to the interpreter); since version 6.0, FreeBSD behaves like Linux. On Solaris 8, white-space characters terminate *optional-arg*, and any remaining text in the #! line is ignored.

The Linux kernel places a 127-character limit on the length of the #! line of a script (excluding the newline character at the end of the line). Additional characters are silently ignored.

The #! technique for interpreter scripts is not specified in SUSv3, but is available on most UNIX implementations.

The limit placed on the length of the #! line varies across UNIX implementations. For example, the limit is 64 characters in OpenBSD 3.1 and 1024 characters on Tru64 5.1. On some historical implementations (e.g., SunOS 4), this limit was as low as 32 characters.

Execution of interpreter scripts

Since a script doesn't contain binary machine code, when *execve()* is used to run the script, obviously something different from usual must be occurring when the script is executed. If *execve()* detects that the file it has been given commences with the 2-byte sequence #!, then it extracts the remainder of the line (the pathname and argument), and execs the interpreter file with the following list of arguments:

---

interpreter-path [*optional-arg*] *script-path arg...*

Here, *interpreter-path* and *optional-arg* are taken from the #! line of the script, *script-path* is the pathname given to *execve()*, and *arg...* is the list of any further arguments specified via the *argv* argument to *execve()* (but excluding *argv[0]*). The origin of each of the script arguments is summarized in Figure 27-1.

Script file (located at *script-path*)

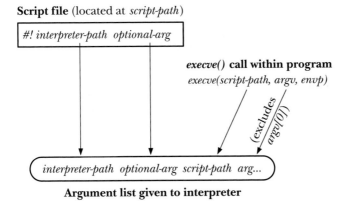

Argument list given to interpreter

Figure 27-1: The argument list supplied to an execed script

We can demonstrate the origin of the interpreter arguments by writing a script that uses the program in Listing 6-2 (necho.c, on page 123) as an interpreter. This program simply echoes all of its command-line arguments. We then use the program in Listing 27-1 to exec the script:

```
$ cat > necho.script              Create script
#!/home/mtk/bin/necho some argument
Some junk
Type Control-D
$ chmod +x necho.script           Make script executable
$ ./t_execve necho.script         And exec the script
argv[0] = /home/mtk/bin/necho     First 3 arguments are generated by kernel
argv[1] = some argument           Script argument is treated as a single word
argv[2] = necho.script            This is the script path
argv[3] = hello world             This was argVec[1] given to execve()
argv[4] = goodbye                 And this was argVec[2]
```

In this example, our "interpreter" (necho) ignores the contents of its script file (necho.script), and the second line of the script (*Some junk*) has no effect on its execution.

> The Linux 2.2 kernel passes only the basename part of the *interpreter-path* as the first argument when invoking a script. Consequently, on Linux 2.2, the line displaying *argv[0]* would show just the value *necho*.

Most UNIX shells and interpreters treat the # character as the start of a comment. Thus, these interpreters ignore the initial #! line when interpreting the script.

Using the script *optional-arg*

One use of the *optional-arg* in a script's initial #! line is to specify command-line options for the interpreter. This feature is useful with certain interpreters, such as *awk*.

> The *awk* interpreter has been part of the UNIX system since the late 1970s. The *awk* language is described in a number of books, including one by its creators [Aho et al., 1988], whose initials gave the language its name. Its forte is rapid prototyping of text-processing applications. In its design—a weakly typed language, with a rich set of text-handling primitives, and a syntax based on C—*awk* is the ancestor of many widely used contemporary scripting languages, such as JavaScript and PHP.

A script can be supplied to *awk* in two different ways. The default is to provide the script as the first command-line argument to *awk*:

```
$ awk 'script' input-file...
```

Alternatively, an *awk* script can reside inside a file, as in the following *awk* script, which prints out the length of the longest line of its input:

```
$ cat longest_line.awk
#!/usr/bin/awk
length > max { max = length; }
END          { print max; }
```

Suppose that we try execing this script using the following C code:

```
execl("longest_line.awk", "longest_line.awk", "input.txt", (char *) NULL);
```

This *execl()* call in turn employs *execve()* with the following argument list to invoke *awk*:

```
/usr/bin/awk longest_line.awk input.txt
```

This *execve()* call fails, because *awk* interprets the string *longest_line.awk* as a script containing an invalid *awk* command. We need a way of informing *awk* that this argument is actually the name of a file containing the script. We can do this by adding the *–f* option as the optional argument in the script's #! line. This tells *awk* that the following argument is a script file:

```
#!/usr/bin/awk -f
length > max { max = length; }
END          { print max; }
```

Now, our *execl()* call results in the following argument list being used:

```
/usr/bin/awk -f longest_line.awk input.txt
```

This successfully invokes *awk* using the script longest_line.awk to process the file input.txt.

Executing scripts with *execlp()* and *execvp()*

Normally, the absence of a #! line at the start of a script causes the *exec()* functions to fail. However, *execlp()* and *execvp()* do things somewhat differently. Recall that these are the functions that use the PATH environment variable to obtain a list of directories in which to search for a file to be executed. If either of these functions finds a file that has execute permission turned on, but is not a binary executable and does not start with a #! line, then they exec the shell to interpret the file. On Linux, this means that such files are treated as though they started with a line containing the string #!/bin/sh.

27.4 File Descriptors and *exec()*

By default, all file descriptors opened by a program that calls *exec()* remain open across the *exec()* and are available for use by the new program. This is frequently useful, because the calling program may open files on particular descriptors, and these files are automatically available to the new program, without it needing to know the names of, or open, the files.

The shell takes advantage of this feature to handle I/O redirection for the programs that it executes. For example, suppose we enter the following shell command:

```
$ ls /tmp > dir.txt
```

The shell performs the following steps to execute this command:

1. A *fork()* is performed to create a child process that is also running a copy of the shell (and thus has a copy of the command).

2. The child shell opens dir.txt for output using file descriptor 1 (standard output). This can be done in either of the following ways:

   a) The child shell closes descriptor 1 (STDOUT_FILENO) and then opens the file dir.txt. Since *open()* always uses the lowest available file descriptor, and standard input (descriptor 0) remains open, the file will be opened on descriptor 1.

   b) The shell opens dir.txt, obtaining a new file descriptor. Then, if that file descriptor is not standard output, the shell uses *dup2()* to force standard output to be a duplicate of the new descriptor and closes the new descriptor, since it is no longer required. (This method is safer than the preceding method, since it doesn't rely on lower-numbered descriptors being open.) The code sequence is something like the following:

```
fd = open("dir.txt", O_WRONLY | O_CREAT,
            S_IRUSR | S_IWUSR | S_IRGRP | S_IWGRP | S_IROTH | S_IWOTH);
            /* rw-rw-rw- */
if (fd != STDOUT_FILENO) {
    dup2(fd, STDOUT_FILENO);
    close(fd);
}
```

3. The child shell execs the *ls* program. The *ls* program writes its output to standard output, which is the file `dir.txt`.

> The explanation given here of how the shell performs I/O redirections simplifies some points. In particular, certain commands—so-called shell *built-in* commands—are executed directly by the shell, without performing a *fork()* or an *exec()*. Such commands must be treated somewhat differently for the purposes of I/O redirection.
>
> A shell command is implemented as a built-in for either of two reasons: efficiency and to obtain side effects within the shell. Some frequently used commands—such as *pwd*, *echo*, and *test*—are sufficiently simple that it is a worthwhile efficiency to implement them inside the shell. Other commands are implemented within the shell so that they have side effects on the shell itself—that is, they change information stored by the shell, or modify attributes of or affect the execution of the shell process. For example, the *cd* command must change the working directory of the shell itself, and so can't be executed within a separate process. Other examples of commands that are built in for their side effects include *exec*, *exit*, *read*, *set*, *source*, *ulimit*, *umask*, *wait*, and the shell job-control commands (*jobs*, *fg*, and *bg*). The full set of built-in commands understood by a shell is documented in the shell's manual page.

The close-on-exec flag (FD_CLOEXEC)

Sometimes, it may be desirable to ensure that certain file descriptors are closed before an *exec()*. In particular, if we *exec()* an unknown program (i.e., one that we did not write) from a privileged process, or a program that doesn't need descriptors for files we have already opened, then it is secure programming practice to ensure that all unnecessary file descriptors are closed before the new program is loaded. We could do this by calling *close()* on all such descriptors, but this suffers the following limitations:

- The file descriptor may have been opened by a library function. This function has no mechanism to force the main program to close the file descriptor before the *exec()* is performed. (As a general principle, library functions should always set the close-on-exec flag, using the technique described below, for any files that they open.)

- If the *exec()* call fails for some reason, we may want to keep the file descriptors open. If they are already closed, it may be difficult, or impossible, to reopen them so that they refer to the same files.

For these reasons, the kernel provides a close-on-exec flag for each file descriptor. If this flag is set, then the file descriptor is automatically closed during a successful *exec()*, but left open if the *exec()* fails. The close-on-exec flag for a file descriptor can be accessed using the *fcntl()* system call (Section 5.2). The *fcntl()* F_GETFD operation retrieves a copy of the file descriptor flags:

```
int flags;

flags = fcntl(fd, F_GETFD);
if (flags == -1)
    errExit("fcntl");
```

After retrieving these flags, we can modify the FD_CLOEXEC bit and use a second *fcntl()* call specifying F_SETFD to update the flags:

```
flags |= FD_CLOEXEC;
if (fcntl(fd, F_SETFD, flags) == -1)
    errExit("fcntl");
```

> FD_CLOEXEC is actually the only bit used in the file descriptor flags. This bit corresponds to the value 1. In older programs, we may sometimes see the close-on-exec flag set using just the call *fcntl(fd, F_SETFD, 1)*, relying on the fact that there are no other bits that can be affected by this operation. Theoretically, this may not always be so (in the future, some UNIX system might implement additional flag bits), so we should use the technique shown in the main text.
>
> Many UNIX implementations, including Linux, also allow the close-on-exec flag to be modified using two unstandardized *ioctl()* calls: *ioctl(fd, FIOCLEX)* to set the close-on-exec flag for *fd*, and *ioctl(fd, FIONCLEX)* to clear the flag.

When *dup()*, *dup2()*, or *fcntl()* is used to create a duplicate of a file descriptor, the close-on-exec flag is always cleared for the duplicate descriptor. (This behavior is historical and an SUSv3 requirement.)

Listing 27-6 demonstrates the manipulation of the close-on-exec flag. Depending on the presence of a command-line argument (any string), this program first sets the close-on-exec flag for standard output and then execs the *ls* program. Here is what we see when we run the program:

```
$ ./closeonexec                    Exec ls without closing standard output
-rwxr-xr-x   1 mtk    users   28098 Jun 15 13:59 closeonexec
$ ./closeonexec n                  Sets close-on-exec flag for standard output
ls: write error: Bad file descriptor
```

In the second run shown above, *ls* detects that its standard output is closed and prints an error message on standard error.

Listing 27-6: Setting the close-on-exec flag for a file descriptor

─── **procexec/closeonexec.c**
```
#include <fcntl.h>
#include "tlpi_hdr.h"

int
main(int argc, char *argv[])
{
    int flags;

    if (argc > 1) {
        flags = fcntl(STDOUT_FILENO, F_GETFD);              /* Fetch flags */
        if (flags == -1)
            errExit("fcntl - F_GETFD");

        flags |= FD_CLOEXEC;                       /* Turn on FD_CLOEXEC */

        if (fcntl(STDOUT_FILENO, F_SETFD, flags) == -1)     /* Update flags */
            errExit("fcntl - F_SETFD");
    }

    execlp("ls", "ls", "-l", argv[0], (char *) NULL);
    errExit("execlp");
}
```
─── **procexec/closeonexec.c**

27.5 Signals and *exec()*

During an *exec()*, the text of the existing process is discarded. This text may include signal handlers established by the calling program. Because the handlers disappear, the kernel resets the dispositions of all handled signals to SIG_DFL. The dispositions of all other signals (i.e., those with dispositions of SIG_IGN or SIG_DFL) are left unchanged by an *exec()*. This behavior is required by SUSv3.

SUSv3 makes a special case for an ignored SIGCHLD signal. (We noted in Section 26.3.3 that ignoring SIGCHLD prevents the creation of zombies.) SUSv3 leaves it unspecified whether an ignored SIGCHLD remains ignored across an *exec()* or its disposition is reset to SIG_DFL. Linux does the former, but some other UNIX implementations (e.g., Solaris) do the latter. This implies that, in programs that ignore SIGCHLD, for maximum portability, we should perform a *signal(SIGCHLD, SIG_DFL)* call prior to an *exec()*, and ensure that we don't write programs that rely on the initial disposition of SIGCHLD being anything other than SIG_DFL.

The destruction of the old program's data, heap, and stack also means that any alternate signal stack established by a call to *sigaltstack()* (Section 21.3) is lost. Since an alternate signal stack is not preserved across an *exec()*, the SA_ONSTACK bit is also cleared for all signals.

During an *exec()*, the process signal mask and set of pending signals are both preserved. This feature allows us to block and queue signals for the newly execed program. However, SUSv3 notes that many existing applications wrongly assume that they are started with the disposition of certain signals set to SIG_DFL or that these signals are unblocked. (In particular, the C standards provide a much weaker specification of signals, which doesn't specify signal blocking; therefore, C programs written on non-UNIX systems won't know to unblock signals.) For this reason, SUSv3 recommends that signals should not be blocked or ignored across an *exec()* of an arbitrary program. Here, "arbitrary" means a program that we did not write. It is acceptable to block or ignore signals when execing a program we have written or one with known behavior with respect to signals.

27.6 Executing a Shell Command: *system()*

The *system()* function allows the calling program to execute an arbitrary shell command. In this section, we describe the operation of *system()*, and in the next section we show how *system()* can be implemented using *fork()*, *exec()*, *wait()*, and *exit()*.

> In Section 44.5, we look at the *popen()* and *pclose()* functions, which can also be used to execute a shell command, but allow the calling program to either read the output of the command or to send input to the command.

```
#include <stdlib.h>

int system(const char *command);
```
                              See main text for a description of return value

The *system()* function creates a child process that invokes a shell to execute *command*. Here is an example of a call to *system()*:

```
system("ls | wc");
```

The principal advantages of *system()* are simplicity and convenience:

- We don't need to handle the details of calling *fork()*, *exec()*, *wait()*, and *exit()*.
- Error and signal handling are performed by *system()* on our behalf.
- Because *system()* uses the shell to execute *command*, all of the usual shell processing, substitutions, and redirections are performed on *command* before it is executed. This makes it easy to add an "execute a shell command" feature to an application. (Many interactive applications provide such a feature in the form of a ! command.)

The main cost of *system()* is inefficiency. Executing a command using *system()* requires the creation of at least two processes—one for the shell and one or more for the command(s) it executes—each of which performs an *exec()*. If efficiency or speed is a requirement, it is preferable to use explicit *fork()* and *exec()* calls to execute the desired program.

The return value of *system()* is as follows:

- If *command* is a NULL pointer, then *system()* returns a nonzero value if a shell is available, and 0 if no shell is available. This case arises out of the C programming language standards, which are not tied to any operating system, so a shell might not be available if *system()* is running on a non-UNIX system. Furthermore, even though all UNIX implementations have a shell, this shell might not be available if the program called *chroot()* before calling *system()*. If *command* is non-NULL, then the return value for *system()* is determined according to the remaining rules in this list.

- If a child process could not be created or its termination status could not be retrieved, then *system()* returns –1.

- If a shell could not be execed in the child process, then *system()* returns a value as though the child shell had terminated with the call *_exit(127)*.

- If all system calls succeed, then *system()* returns the termination status of the child shell used to execute *command*. The termination status of a shell is the exit status of the last command it executes; if that command is killed by a signal, most shells exit with the value *128+n*, where *n* is the signal number. (If the child shell is itself killed by a signal, the termination status is as described in Section 26.1.3.)

> It is impossible (using the value returned by *system()*) to distinguish the case where *system()* fails to exec a shell from the case where the shell exits with the status 127 (the latter possibility can occur if the shell could not find a program with the given name to exec).

In the last two cases, the value returned by *system()* is a *wait status* of the same form returned by *waitpid()*. This means we should use the functions described in Section 26.1.3 to dissect this value, and we can display the value using our *printWaitStatus()* function (Listing 26-2, on page 546).

Example program

Listing 27-7 demonstrates the use of *system()*. This program executes a loop that reads a command string, executes it using *system()*, and then analyzes and displays the value returned by *system()*. Here is a sample run:

```
$ ./t_system
Command: whoami
mtk
system() returned: status=0x0000 (0,0)
child exited, status=0
Command: ls | grep XYZ                    Shell terminates with the status of...
system() returned: status=0x0100 (1,0)    its last command (grep), which...
child exited, status=1                     found no match, and so did an exit(1)
Command: exit 127
system() returned: status=0x7f00 (127,0)
(Probably) could not invoke shell         Actually, not true in this case
Command: sleep 100
Type Control-Z to suspend foreground process group
[1]+  Stopped              ./t_system
$ ps | grep sleep                         Find PID of sleep
29361 pts/6    00:00:00 sleep
$ kill 29361                              And send a signal to terminate it
$ fg                                      Bring t_system back into foreground
./t_system
system() returned: status=0x000f (0,15)
child killed by signal 15 (Terminated)
Command: ^D$                              Type Control-D to terminate program
```

Listing 27-7: Executing shell commands with *system()*

—————————————————————————————— procexec/t_system.c
```
#include <sys/wait.h>
#include "print_wait_status.h"
#include "tlpi_hdr.h"

#define MAX_CMD_LEN 200

int
main(int argc, char *argv[])
{
    char str[MAX_CMD_LEN];      /* Command to be executed by system() */
    int status;                 /* Status return from system() */

    for (;;) {                  /* Read and execute a shell command */
        printf("Command: ");
        fflush(stdout);
        if (fgets(str, MAX_CMD_LEN, stdin) == NULL)
            break;              /* end-of-file */

        status = system(str);
        printf("system() returned: status=0x%04x (%d,%d)\n",
                (unsigned int) status, status >> 8, status & 0xff);

        if (status == -1) {
            errExit("system");
        } else {
            if (WIFEXITED(status) && WEXITSTATUS(status) == 127)
                printf("(Probably) could not invoke shell\n");
            else                /* Shell successfully executed command */
                printWaitStatus(NULL, status);
        }
    }

    exit(EXIT_SUCCESS);
}
```
—————————————————————————————— procexec/t_system.c

Avoid using *system()* in set-user-ID and set-group-ID programs

Set-user-ID and set-group-ID programs should never use *system()* while operating under the program's privileged identifier. Even when such programs don't allow the user to specify the text of the command to be executed, the shell's reliance on various environment variables to control its operation means that the use of *system()* inevitably opens the door for a system security breach.

For example, in older Bourne shells, the IFS environment variable, which defined the internal field separator used to break a command line into separate words, was the source of a number of successful system break-ins. If we defined IFS to have the value *a*, then the shell would treat the command string *shar* as the word *sh* followed by the argument *r*, and invoke another shell to execute the script file named r in the current working directory, instead of the intended purpose (executing a command named *shar*). This particular security hole was fixed by applying IFS only to the words produced by shell expansions. In addition, modern shells reset IFS (to a string consisting of the three characters space, tab, and newline) on shell startup to ensure that scripts behave consistently if they inherit a strange IFS value. As a further security measure, *bash* reverts to the real user (group) ID when invoked from a set-user-ID (set-group-ID) program.

Secure programs that need to spawn another program should use *fork()* and one of the *exec()* functions—other than *execlp()* or *execvp()*—directly.

27.7 Implementing *system()*

In this section, we explain how to implement *system()*. We begin with a simple implementation, explain what pieces are missing from that implementation, and then present a complete implementation.

A simple implementation of *system()*

The *−c* option of the *sh* command provides an easy way to execute a string containing arbitrary shell commands:

```
$ sh -c "ls | wc"
      38      38     444
```

Thus, to implement *system()*, we need to use *fork()* to create a child that then does an *execl()* with arguments corresponding to the above *sh* command:

```
execl("/bin/sh", "sh", "-c", command, (char *) NULL);
```

To collect the status of the child created by *system()*, we use a *waitpid()* call that specifies the child's process ID. (Using *wait()* would not suffice, because *wait()* waits for any child, which could accidentally collect the status of some other child created by the calling process.) A simple, and incomplete, implementation of *system()* is shown in Listing 27-8.

Listing 27-8: An implementation of *system()* that excludes signal handling

——————————————————————————————— **procexec/simple_system.c**

```
#include <unistd.h>
#include <sys/wait.h>
#include <sys/types.h>

int
system(char *command)
{
    int status;
    pid_t childPid;

    switch (childPid = fork()) {
    case -1: /* Error */
        return -1;
```

```
    case 0: /* Child */
        execl("/bin/sh", "sh", "-c", command, (char *) NULL);
        _exit(127);                     /* Failed exec */

    default: /* Parent */
        if (waitpid(childPid, &status, 0) == -1)
            return -1;
        else
            return status;
    }
}
```

── **procexec/simple_system.c**

Treating signals correctly inside *system()*

What adds complexity to the implementation of *system()* is the correct treatment with signals.

The first signal to consider is SIGCHLD. Suppose that the program calling *system()* is also directly creating children, and has established a handler for SIGCHLD that performs its own *wait()*. In this situation, when a SIGCHLD signal is generated by the termination of the child created by *system()*, it is possible that the signal handler of the main program will be invoked—and collect the child's status—before *system()* has a chance to call *waitpid()*. (This is an example of a race condition.) This has two undesirable consequences:

- The calling program would be deceived into thinking that one of the children that it created has terminated.

- The *system()* function would be unable to obtain the termination status of the child that it created.

Therefore, *system()* must block delivery of SIGCHLD while it is executing.

The other signals to consider are those generated by the terminal *interrupt* (usually *Control-C*) and *quit* (usually *Control-*) characters, SIGINT and SIGQUIT, respectively. Consider what is happening when we execute the following call:

```
system("sleep 20");
```

At this point, three processes are running: the process executing the calling program, a shell, and *sleep*, as shown in Figure 27-2.

> As an efficiency measure, when the string given to the *-c* option is a simple command (as opposed to a pipeline or a sequence), some shells (including *bash*) directly exec the command, rather than forking a child shell. For shells that perform such an optimization, Figure 27-2 is not strictly accurate, since there will be only two processes (the calling process and *sleep*). Nevertheless, the arguments in this section about how *system()* should handle signals still apply.

All of the processes shown in Figure 27-2 form part of the foreground process group for the terminal. (We consider process groups in detail in Section 34.2.) Therefore, when we type the *interrupt* or *quit* characters, all three processes are sent the corresponding signal. The shell ignores SIGINT and SIGQUIT while waiting for its child. However, both the calling program and the *sleep* process would, by default, be killed by these signals.

How should the calling process and the executed command respond to these signals? SUSv3 specifies the following:

- SIGINT and SIGQUIT should be ignored in the calling process while the command is being executed.

- In the child, SIGINT and SIGQUIT should be treated as they would be if the calling process did a *fork()* and *exec()*; that is, the disposition of handled signals is reset to the default, and the disposition of other signals remains unchanged.

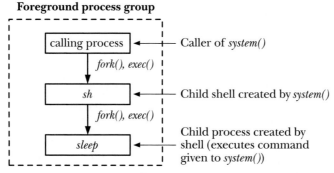

Figure 27-2: Arrangement of processes during execution of *system("sleep 20")*

Dealing with signals in the manner specified by SUSv3 is the most reasonable approach, for the following reasons:

- It would not make sense to have both processes responding to these signals, since this could lead to confusing behaviors for the user of the application.

- Similarly, it would not make sense to ignore these signals in the process executing the command while treating them according to their default dispositions in the calling process. This would allow the user to do things such as killing the calling process while the executed command was left running. It is also inconsistent with the fact that the calling process has actually given up control (i.e., is blocked in a *waitpid()* call) while the command passed to *system()* is being executed.

- The command executed by *system()* may be an interactive application, and it makes sense to have this application respond to terminal-generated signals.

SUSv3 requires the treatment of SIGINT and SIGQUIT described above, but notes that this could have an undesirable effect in a program that invisibly uses *system()* to perform some task. While the command is being executed, typing *Control-C* or *Control-* will kill only the child of *system()*, while the application (unexpectedly, to the user) continues to run. A program that uses *system()* in this way should check the termination status returned by *system()*, and take appropriate action if it detects that the command was killed by a signal.

An improved *system()* implementation

Listing 27-9 shows an implementation of *system()* conforming to the rules described above. Note the following points about this implementation:

- As noted earlier, if *command* is a NULL pointer, then *system()* should return non-zero if a shell is available or 0 if no shell is available. The only way to reliably determine this information is to try to execute a shell. We do this by recursively calling *system()* to execute the : shell command and checking for a return status of 0 from the recursive call ①. The : command is a shell built-in command that does nothing, but always returns a success status. We could have executed the shell command *exit 0* to achieve the same result. (Note that it isn't sufficient to use *access()* to check whether the file /bin/sh exists and has execute permission enabled. In a *chroot()* environment, even if the shell executable is present, it may not be able to be executed if it is dynamically linked and the required shared libraries are not available.)

- It is only in the parent process (the caller of *system()*) that SIGCHLD needs to be blocked ②, and SIGINT and SIGQUIT need to be ignored ③. However, we must perform these actions prior to the *fork()* call, because, if they were done in the parent after the *fork()*, we would create a race condition. (Suppose, for example, that the child exited before the parent had a chance to block SIGCHLD.) Consequently, the child must undo these changes to the signal attributes, as described shortly.

- In the parent, we ignore errors from the *sigaction()* and *sigprocmask()* calls used to manipulate signal dispositions and the signal mask ② ③ ⑨. We do this for two reasons. First, these calls are very unlikely to fail. In practice, the only thing that can realistically go wrong with these calls is an error in specifying their arguments, and such an error should be eliminated during initial debugging. Second, we assume that the caller is more interested in knowing if *fork()* or *waitpid()* failed than in knowing if these signal-manipulation calls failed. For similar reasons, we bracket the signal-manipulation calls used at the end of *system()* with code to save ⑧ and restore *errno* ⑩, so that if *fork()* or *waitpid()* fails, then the caller can determine why. If we returned −1 because these signal-manipulation calls failed, then the caller might wrongly assume that *system()* failed to execute *command*.

    > SUSv3 merely says that *system()* should return −1 if a child process could not be created or its status could not be obtained. No mention is made of a −1 return because of failures in signal-manipulation operations by *system()*.

- Error checking is not performed for signal-related system calls in the child ④ ⑤. On the one hand, there is no way of reporting such an error (the use of *_exit(127)* is reserved for reporting an error when execing the shell); on the other hand, such failures don't affect the caller of *system()*, which is a separate process.

- On return from *fork()* in the child, the disposition of SIGINT and SIGQUIT is SIG_IGN (i.e., the disposition inherited from the parent). However, as noted earlier, in the child, these signals should be treated as if the caller of *system()* did a *fork()* and an *exec()*. A *fork()* leaves the treatment of signals unchanged in the child. An *exec()* resets the dispositions of handled signals to their defaults and leaves the dispositions of other signals unchanged (Section 27.5). Therefore, if the dispositions of SIGINT and SIGQUIT in the caller were other than SIG_IGN, then the child resets the dispositions to SIG_DFL ④.

  > Some implementations of *system()* instead reset the SIGINT and SIGQUIT dispositions to those that were in effect in the caller, relying on the fact that the subsequent *execl()* will automatically reset the disposition of handled signals to their defaults. However, this could result in potentially undesirable behavior if the caller is handling either of these signals. In this case, if a signal was delivered to the child in the small time interval before the call to *execl()*, then the handler would be invoked in the child. (By contrast, in the implementation shown in Listing 27-9, there is a small window of time before the *execl()* call where these signals will be ignored rather than being handled according to the dispositions that were in effect in the caller.)

- If the *execl()* call in the child fails, then we use *_exit()* to terminate the process ⑥, rather than *exit()*, in order to prevent flushing of any unwritten data in the child's copy of the *stdio* buffers.

- In the parent, we must use *waitpid()* to wait specifically for the child that we created ⑦. If we used *wait()*, then we might inadvertently fetch the status of some other child created by the calling program.

- Although the implementation of *system()* doesn't require the use of a signal handler, the calling program may have established signal handlers, and one of these could interrupt a blocked call to *waitpid()*. SUSv3 explicitly requires that the wait be restarted in this case. Therefore, we use a loop to restart *waitpid()* if it fails with the error EINTR ⑦; any other error from *waitpid()* causes this loop to terminate.

Listing 27-9: Implementation of *system()*

—— procexec/system.c

```
#include <unistd.h>
#include <signal.h>
#include <sys/wait.h>
#include <sys/types.h>
#include <errno.h>

int
system(const char *command)
{
    sigset_t blockMask, origMask;
    struct sigaction saIgnore, saOrigQuit, saOrigInt, saDefault;
    pid_t childPid;
    int status, savedErrno;

①  if (command == NULL)                /* Is a shell available? */
        return system(":") == 0;
```

```
        sigemptyset(&blockMask);              /* Block SIGCHLD */
        sigaddset(&blockMask, SIGCHLD);
②       sigprocmask(SIG_BLOCK, &blockMask, &origMask);

        saIgnore.sa_handler = SIG_IGN;        /* Ignore SIGINT and SIGQUIT */
        saIgnore.sa_flags = 0;
        sigemptyset(&saIgnore.sa_mask);
③       sigaction(SIGINT, &saIgnore, &saOrigInt);
        sigaction(SIGQUIT, &saIgnore, &saOrigQuit);

        switch (childPid = fork()) {
        case -1: /* fork() failed */
            status = -1;
            break;                            /* Carry on to reset signal attributes */

        case 0: /* Child: exec command */
            saDefault.sa_handler = SIG_DFL;
            saDefault.sa_flags = 0;
            sigemptyset(&saDefault.sa_mask);

④          if (saOrigInt.sa_handler != SIG_IGN)
                sigaction(SIGINT, &saDefault, NULL);
            if (saOrigQuit.sa_handler != SIG_IGN)
                sigaction(SIGQUIT, &saDefault, NULL);

⑤          sigprocmask(SIG_SETMASK, &origMask, NULL);

            execl("/bin/sh", "sh", "-c", command, (char *) NULL);
⑥          _exit(127);                        /* We could not exec the shell */

        default: /* Parent: wait for our child to terminate */
⑦          while (waitpid(childPid, &status, 0) == -1) {
                if (errno != EINTR) {         /* Error other than EINTR */
                    status = -1;
                    break;                    /* So exit loop */
                }
            }
            break;
        }

        /* Unblock SIGCHLD, restore dispositions of SIGINT and SIGQUIT */

⑧       savedErrno = errno;                   /* The following may change 'errno' */

⑨       sigprocmask(SIG_SETMASK, &origMask, NULL);
        sigaction(SIGINT, &saOrigInt, NULL);
        sigaction(SIGQUIT, &saOrigQuit, NULL);

⑩       errno = savedErrno;

        return status;
    }
```

Further details on *system()*

Portable applications should ensure that *system()* is not called with the disposition of SIGCHLD set to SIG_IGN, because it is impossible for the *waitpid()* call to obtain the status of the child in this case. (Ignoring SIGCHLD causes the status of a child process to be immediately discarded, as described in Section 26.3.3.)

On some UNIX implementations, *system()* handles the case that it is called with the disposition of SIGCHLD set to SIG_IGN by temporarily setting the disposition of SIGCHLD to SIG_DFL. This is workable, as long as the UNIX implementation is one of those that (unlike Linux) reaps existing zombie children when the disposition of SIGCHLD is reset to SIG_IGN. (If the implementation doesn't do this, then implementing *system()* in this way would have the negative consequence that if another child that was created by the caller terminated during the execution of *system()*, it would become a zombie that might never be reaped.)

On some UNIX implementations (notably Solaris), /bin/sh is not a standard POSIX shell. If we want to ensure that we exec a standard shell, then we must use the *confstr()* library function to obtain the value of the _CS_PATH configuration variable. This value is a PATH-style list of directories containing the standard system utilities. We can assign this list to PATH, and then use *execlp()* to exec the standard shell as follows:

```
char path[PATH_MAX];

if (confstr(_CS_PATH, path, PATH_MAX) == 0)
    _exit(127);
if (setenv("PATH", path, 1) == -1)
    _exit(127);
execlp("sh", "sh", "-c", command, (char *) NULL);
_exit(127);
```

27.8 Summary

Using *execve()*, a process can replace the program that it is currently running by a new program. Arguments to the *execve()* call allow the specification of the argument list (*argv*) and environment list for the new program. Various similarly named library functions are layered on top of *execve()* and provide different interfaces to the same functionality.

All of the *exec()* functions can be used to load a binary executable file or to execute an interpreter script. When a process execs a script, the script's interpreter program replaces the program currently being executed by the process. The script's interpreter is normally identified by an initial line (starting with the characters #!) in the script that specifies the pathname of the interpreter. If no such line is present, then the script is executable only via *execlp()* or *execvp()*, and these functions exec the shell as the script interpreter.

We showed how *fork()*, *exec()*, *exit()*, and *wait()* can be combined to implement the *system()* function, which can be used to execute an arbitrary shell command.

Further information

Refer to the sources of further information listed in Section 24.6.

27.9 Exercises

27-1. The final command in the following shell session uses the program in Listing 27-3 to exec the program *xyz*. What happens?

```
$ echo $PATH
/usr/local/bin:/usr/bin:/bin:./dir1:./dir2
$ ls -l dir1
total 8
-rw-r--r--   1 mtk       users        7860 Jun 13 11:55 xyz
$ ls -l dir2
total 28
-rwxr-xr-x   1 mtk       users       27452 Jun 13 11:55 xyz
$ ./t_execlp xyz
```

27-2. Use *execve()* to implement *execlp()*. You will need to use the *stdarg(3)* API to handle the variable-length argument list supplied to *execlp()*. You will also need to use functions in the *malloc* package to allocate space for the argument and environment vectors. Finally, note that an easy way of checking whether a file exists in a particular directory and is executable is simply to try execing the file.

27-3. What output would we see if we make the following script executable and *exec()* it?

```
#!/bin/cat -n
Hello world
```

27-4. What is the effect of the following code? In what circumstances might it be useful?

```
childPid = fork();
if (childPid == -1)
    errExit("fork1");
if (childPid == 0) {      /* Child */
    switch (fork()) {
    case -1: errExit("fork2");

    case 0:               /* Grandchild */
        /* ----- Do real work here ----- */
        exit(EXIT_SUCCESS);            /* After doing real work */

    default:
        exit(EXIT_SUCCESS);            /* Make grandchild an orphan */
    }
}

/* Parent falls through to here */

if (waitpid(childPid, &status, 0) == -1)
    errExit("waitpid");

/* Parent carries on to do other things */
```

27-5. When we run the following program, we find it produces no output. Why is this?

```
#include "tlpi_hdr.h"

int
main(int argc, char *argv[])
{
    printf("Hello world");
    execlp("sleep", "sleep", "0", (char *) NULL);
}
```

27-6. Suppose that a parent process has established a handler for SIGCHLD and also blocked this signal. Subsequently, one of its children exits, and the parent then does a *wait()* to collect the child's status. What happens when the parent unblocks SIGCHLD? Write a program to verify your answer. What is the relevance of the result for a program calling the *system()* function?

28

PROCESS CREATION AND PROGRAM EXECUTION IN MORE DETAIL

This chapter extends the material presented in Chapters 24 to 27 by covering a variety of topics related to process creation and program execution. We describe process accounting, a kernel feature that writes an accounting record for each process on the system as it terminates. We then look at the Linux-specific *clone()* system call, which is the low-level API that is used to create threads on Linux. We follow this with some comparisons of the performance of *fork()*, *vfork()*, and *clone()*. We conclude with a summary of the effects of *fork()* and *exec()* on the attributes of a process.

28.1 Process Accounting

When process accounting is enabled, the kernel writes an accounting record to the system-wide process accounting file as each process terminates. This accounting record contains various information maintained by the kernel about the process, including its termination status and how much CPU time it consumed. The accounting file can be analyzed by standard tools (*sa(8)* summarizes information from the accounting file, and *lastcomm(1)* lists information about previously executed commands) or by tailored applications.

In kernels before 2.6.10, a separate process accounting record was written for each thread created using the NPTL threading implementation. Since kernel 2.6.10, a single accounting record is written for the entire process when the last thread terminates. Under the older LinuxThreads threading implementation, a single process accounting record is always written for each thread.

Historically, the primary use of process accounting was to charge users for consumption of system resources on multiuser UNIX systems. However, process accounting can also be useful for obtaining information about a process that was not otherwise monitored and reported on by its parent.

Although available on most UNIX implementations, process accounting is not specified in SUSv3. The format of the accounting records, as well as the location of the accounting file, vary somewhat across implementations. We describe the details for Linux in this section, noting some variations from other UNIX implementations along the way.

On Linux, process accounting is an optional kernel component that is configured via the option CONFIG_BSD_PROCESS_ACCT.

Enabling and disabling process accounting

The *acct()* system call is used by a privileged (CAP_SYS_PACCT) process to enable and disable process accounting. This system call is rarely used in application programs. Normally, process accounting is enabled at each system restart by placing appropriate commands in the system boot scripts.

```
#define _BSD_SOURCE
#include <unistd.h>

int acct(const char *acctfile);
```

                                                Returns 0 on success, or −1 on error

To enable process accounting, we supply the pathname of an *existing* regular file in *acctfile*. A typical pathname for the accounting file is /var/log/pacct or /usr/account/pacct. To disable process accounting, we specify *acctfile* as NULL.

The program in Listing 28-1 uses *acct()* to switch process accounting on and off. The functionality of this program is similar to the shell *accton(8)* command.

Listing 28-1: Turning process accounting on and off

—— procexec/acct_on.c
```
#define _BSD_SOURCE
#include <unistd.h>
#include "tlpi_hdr.h"

int
main(int argc, char *argv[])
{
    if (argc > 2 || (argc > 1 && strcmp(argv[1], "--help") == 0))
        usageErr("%s [file]\n", argv[0]);
```

```
    if (acct(argv[1]) == -1)
        errExit("acct");

    printf("Process accounting %s\n",
            (argv[1] == NULL) ? "disabled" : "enabled");
    exit(EXIT_SUCCESS);
}
```

── procexec/acct_on.c

Process accounting records

Once process accounting is enabled, an *acct* record is written to the accounting file
as each process terminates. The *acct* structure is defined in <sys/acct.h> as follows:

```
typedef u_int16_t comp_t;   /* See text */

struct acct {
    char      ac_flag;      /* Accounting flags (see text) */
    u_int16_t ac_uid;       /* User ID of process */
    u_int16_t ac_gid;       /* Group ID of process */
    u_int16_t ac_tty;       /* Controlling terminal for process (may be
                               0 if none, e.g., for a daemon) */
    u_int32_t ac_btime;     /* Start time (time_t; seconds since the Epoch) */
    comp_t    ac_utime;     /* User CPU time (clock ticks) */
    comp_t    ac_stime;     /* System CPU time (clock ticks) */
    comp_t    ac_etime;     /* Elapsed (real) time (clock ticks) */
    comp_t    ac_mem;       /* Average memory usage (kilobytes) */
    comp_t    ac_io;        /* Bytes transferred by read(2) and write(2)
                               (unused) */
    comp_t    ac_rw;        /* Blocks read/written (unused) */
    comp_t    ac_minflt;    /* Minor page faults (Linux-specific) */
    comp_t    ac_majflt;    /* Major page faults (Linux-specific) */
    comp_t    ac_swaps;     /* Number of swaps (unused; Linux-specific) */
    u_int32_t ac_exitcode;  /* Process termination status */
#define ACCT_COMM 16
    char      ac_comm[ACCT_COMM+1];
                            /* (Null-terminated) command name
                               (basename of last execed file) */
    char      ac_pad[10];   /* Padding (reserved for future use) */
};
```

Note the following points regarding the *acct* structure:

- The *u_int16_t* and *u_int32_t* data types are 16-bit and 32-bit unsigned integers.
- The *ac_flag* field is a bit mask recording various events for the process. The bits
  that can appear in this field are shown in Table 28-1. As indicated in the table,
  some of these bits are not present on all UNIX implementations. A few other
  implementations provide additional bits in this field.
- The *ac_comm* field records the name of the last command (program file) executed by this process. The kernel records this value on each *execve()*. On some
  other UNIX implementations, this field is limited to 8 characters.

- The *comp_t* type is a kind of floating-point number. Values of this type are sometimes called *compressed clock ticks*. The floating-point value consists of a 3-bit, base-8 exponent, followed by a 13-bit mantissa; the exponent can represent a factor in the range $8^0 = 1$ to 8^7 (2,097,152). For example, a mantissa of 125 and an exponent of 1 represent the value 1000. Listing 28-2 defines a function (*comptToLL()*) to convert this type to *long long*. We need to use the type *long long* because the 32 bits used to represent an *unsigned long* on x86-32 are insufficient to hold the largest value that can be represented in *comp_t*, which is $(2^{13} - 1) * 8^7$.

- The three time fields defined with the type *comp_t* represent time in system clock ticks. Therefore, we must divide these times by the value returned by *sysconf(_SC_CLK_TCK)* in order to convert them to seconds.

- The *ac_exitcode* field holds the termination status of the process (described in Section 26.1.3). Most other UNIX implementations instead provide a single-byte field named *ac_stat*, which records only the signal that killed the process (if it was killed by a signal) and a bit indicating whether that signal caused the process to dump core. BSD-derived implementations don't provide either field.

Table 28-1: Bit values for the *ac_flag* field of process accounting records

Bit	Description
AFORK	Process was created by *fork()*, but did not *exec()* before terminating
ASU	Process made use of superuser privileges
AXSIG	Process was terminated by a signal (not present on some implementations)
ACORE	Process produced a core dump (not present on some implementations)

Because accounting records are written only as processes terminate, they are ordered by termination time (a value not recorded in the record), rather than by process start time (*ac_btime*).

> If the system crashes, no accounting record is written for any processes that are still executing.

Since writing records to the accounting file can rapidly consume disk space, Linux provides the /proc/sys/kernel/acct virtual file for controlling the operation of process accounting. This file contains three numbers, defining (in order) the parameters *high-water*, *low-water*, and *frequency*. Typical defaults for these three parameters are 4, 2, and 30. If process accounting is enabled and the amount of free disk space falls below *low-water* percent, accounting is suspended. If the amount of free disk space later rises above *high-water* percent, then accounting is resumed. The *frequency* value specifies how often, in seconds, checks should be made on the percentage of free disk space.

Example program

The program in Listing 28-2 displays selected fields from the records in a process accounting file. The following shell session demonstrates the use of this program. We begin by creating a new, empty process accounting file and enabling process accounting:

```
$ su                            Need privilege to enable process accounting
Password:
# touch pacct
# ./acct_on pacct               This process will be first entry in accounting file
Process accounting enabled
# exit                          Cease being superuser
```

At this point, three processes have already terminated since we enabled process accounting. These processes executed the *acct_on*, *su*, and *bash* programs. The *bash* process was started by *su* to run the privileged shell session.

Now we run a series of commands to add further records to the accounting file:

```
$ sleep 15 &
[1] 18063
$ ulimit -c unlimited           Allow core dumps (shell built-in)
$ cat                           Create a process
Type Control-\ (generates SIGQUIT, signal 3) to kill cat process
Quit (core dumped)
$
Press Enter to see shell notification of completion of sleep before next shell prompt
[1]+  Done              sleep 15
$ grep xxx badfile              grep fails with status of 2
grep: badfile: No such file or directory
$ echo $?                       The shell obtained status of grep (shell built-in)
2
```

The next two commands run programs that we presented in previous chapters (Listing 27-1, on page 566, and Listing 24-1, on page 517). The first command runs a program that execs the file /bin/echo; this results in an accounting record with the command name *echo*. The second command creates a child process that doesn't perform an *exec()*.

```
$ ./t_execve /bin/echo
hello world goodbye
$ ./t_fork
PID=18350 (child) idata=333 istack=666
PID=18349 (parent) idata=111 istack=222
```

Finally, we use the program in Listing 28-2 to view the contents of the accounting file:

```
$ ./acct_view pacct
command  flags  term.  user  start time            CPU   elapsed
                status                              time  time
acct_on  -S--      0   root  2010-07-23 17:19:05   0.00   0.00
bash     ----      0   root  2010-07-23 17:18:55   0.02  21.10
su       -S--      0   root  2010-07-23 17:18:51   0.01  24.94
cat      --XC   0x83   mtk   2010-07-23 17:19:55   0.00   1.72
sleep    ----      0   mtk   2010-07-23 17:19:42   0.00  15.01
grep     ----  0x200   mtk   2010-07-23 17:20:12   0.00   0.00
echo     ----      0   mtk   2010-07-23 17:21:15   0.01   0.01
t_fork   F---      0   mtk   2010-07-23 17:21:36   0.00   0.00
t_fork   ----      0   mtk   2010-07-23 17:21:36   0.00   3.01
```

In the output, we see one line for each process that was created in the shell session. The *ulimit* and *echo* commands are shell built-in commands, so they don't result in the creation of new processes. Note that the entry for *sleep* appeared in the accounting file after the *cat* entry because the *sleep* command terminated after the *cat* command.

Most of the output is self-explanatory. The *flags* column shows single letters indicating which of the *ac_flag* bits is set in each record (see Table 28-1). Section 26.1.3 describes how to interpret the termination status values shown in the *term. status* column.

Listing 28-2: Displaying data from a process accounting file

—————————————————————————————————————— procexec/acct_view.c

```c
#include <fcntl.h>
#include <time.h>
#include <sys/stat.h>
#include <sys/acct.h>
#include <limits.h>
#include "ugid_functions.h"              /* Declaration of userNameFromId() */
#include "tlpi_hdr.h"

#define TIME_BUF_SIZE 100

static long long                  /* Convert comp_t value into long long */
comptToLL(comp_t ct)
{
    const int EXP_SIZE = 3;              /* 3-bit, base-8 exponent */
    const int MANTISSA_SIZE = 13;       /* Followed by 13-bit mantissa */
    const int MANTISSA_MASK = (1 << MANTISSA_SIZE) - 1;
    long long mantissa, exp;

    mantissa = ct & MANTISSA_MASK;
    exp = (ct >> MANTISSA_SIZE) & ((1 << EXP_SIZE) - 1);
    return mantissa << (exp * 3);        /* Power of 8 = left shift 3 bits */
}

int
main(int argc, char *argv[])
{
    int acctFile;
    struct acct ac;
    ssize_t numRead;
    char *s;
    char timeBuf[TIME_BUF_SIZE];
    struct tm *loc;
    time_t t;

    if (argc != 2 || strcmp(argv[1], "--help") == 0)
        usageErr("%s file\n", argv[0]);

    acctFile = open(argv[1], O_RDONLY);
    if (acctFile == -1)
        errExit("open");
```

```
#define _GNU_SOURCE
#include <sched.h>

int clone(int (*func) (void *), void *child_stack, int flags, void *func_arg, ...
        /* pid_t *ptid, struct user_desc *tls, pid_t *ctid */ );
```
                        Returns process ID of child on success, or −1 on error

Like *fork()*, a new process created with *clone()* is an almost exact duplicate of the parent.

Unlike *fork()*, the cloned child doesn't continue from the point of the call, but instead commences by calling the function specified in the *func* argument; we'll refer to this as the *child function*. When called, the child function is passed the value specified in *func_arg*. Using appropriate casting, the child function can freely interpret this argument; for example, as an *int* or as a pointer to a structure. (Interpreting it as a pointer is possible because the cloned child either obtains a copy of or shares the calling process's memory.)

> Within the kernel, *fork()*, *vfork()*, and *clone()* are ultimately implemented by the same function (*do_fork()* in kernel/fork.c). At this level, cloning is much closer to forking: *sys_clone()* doesn't have the *func* and *func_arg* arguments, and after the call, *sys_clone()* returns in the child in the same manner as *fork()*. The main text describes the *clone()* wrapper function that *glibc* provides for *sys_clone()*. (This function is defined in architecture-specific *glibc* assembler sources, such as in sysdeps/unix/sysv/linux/i386/clone.S.) This wrapper function invokes *func* after *sys_clone()* returns in the child.

The cloned child process terminates either when *func* returns (in which case its return value is the exit status of the process) or when the process makes a call to *exit()* (or *_exit()*). The parent process can wait for the cloned child in the usual manner using *wait()* or similar.

Since a cloned child may (like *vfork()*) share the parent's memory, it can't use the parent's stack. Instead, the caller must allocate a suitably sized block of memory for use as the child's stack and pass a pointer to that block in the argument *child_stack*. On most hardware architectures, the stack grows downward, so the *child_stack* argument should point to the high end of the allocated block.

> The architecture-dependence on the direction of stack growth is a defect in the design of *clone()*. On the Intel IA-64 architecture, an improved clone API is provided, in the form of *clone2()*. This system call defines the range of the stack of the child in a way that doesn't depend on the direction of stack growth, by supplying both the start address and size of the stack. See the manual page for details.

The *clone()* *flags* argument serves two purposes. First, its lower byte specifies the child's *termination signal*, which is the signal to be sent to the parent when the child terminates. (If a cloned child is *stopped* by a signal, the parent still receives SIGCHLD.) This byte may be 0, in which case no signal is generated. (Using the Linux-specific /proc/*PID*/stat file, we can determine the termination signal of any process; see the *proc(5)* manual page for further details.)

With *fork()* and *vfork()*, we have no way to select the termination signal; it is always SIGCHLD.

The remaining bytes of the *flags* argument hold a bit mask that controls the operation of *clone()*. We summarize these bit-mask values in Table 28-2, and describe them in more detail in Section 28.2.1.

Table 28-2: The *clone()* *flags* bit-mask values

Flag	Effect if present
CLONE_CHILD_CLEARTID	Clear *ctid* when child calls *exec()* or *_exit()* (2.6 onward)
CLONE_CHILD_SETTID	Write thread ID of child into *ctid* (2.6 onward)
CLONE_FILES	Parent and child share table of open file descriptors
CLONE_FS	Parent and child share attributes related to file system
CLONE_IO	Child shares parent's I/O context (2.6.25 onward)
CLONE_NEWIPC	Child gets new System V IPC namespace (2.6.19 onward)
CLONE_NEWNET	Child gets new network namespace (2.6.24 onward)
CLONE_NEWNS	Child gets copy of parent's mount namespace (2.4.19 onward)
CLONE_NEWPID	Child gets new process-ID namespace (2.6.19 onward)
CLONE_NEWUSER	Child gets new user-ID namespace (2.6.23 onward)
CLONE_NEWUTS	Child gets new UTS (*uname()*) namespace (2.6.19 onward)
CLONE_PARENT	Make child's parent same as caller's parent (2.4 onward)
CLONE_PARENT_SETTID	Write thread ID of child into *ptid* (2.6 onward)
CLONE_PID	Obsolete flag used only by system boot process (up to 2.4)
CLONE_PTRACE	If parent is being traced, then trace child also
CLONE_SETTLS	*tls* describes thread-local storage for child (2.6 onward)
CLONE_SIGHAND	Parent and child share signal dispositions
CLONE_SYSVSEM	Parent and child share semaphore undo values (2.6 onward)
CLONE_THREAD	Place child in same thread group as parent (2.4 onward)
CLONE_UNTRACED	Can't force CLONE_PTRACE on child (2.6 onward)
CLONE_VFORK	Parent is suspended until child calls *exec()* or *_exit()*
CLONE_VM	Parent and child share virtual memory

The remaining arguments to *clone()* are *ptid*, *tls*, and *ctid*. These arguments relate to the implementation of threads, in particular the use of thread IDs and thread-local storage. We cover the use of these arguments when describing the *flags* bit-mask values in Section 28.2.1. (In Linux 2.4 and earlier, these three arguments are not provided by *clone()*. They were specifically added in Linux 2.6 to support the NPTL POSIX threads implementation.)

Example program

Listing 28-3 shows a simple example of the use of *clone()* to create a child process. The main program does the following:

- Open a file descriptor (for /dev/null) that will be closed by the child ②.
- Set the value for the *clone()* *flags* argument to CLONE_FILES ③ if a command-line argument was supplied, so that the parent and child will share a single file descriptor table. If no command-line argument was supplied, *flags* is set to 0.

- Allocate a stack for use by the child ④.

- If CHILD_SIG is nonzero and is not equal to SIGCHLD, ignore it, in case it is a signal that would terminate the process ⑤. We don't ignore SIGCHLD, because doing so would prevent waiting on the child to collect its status.

- Call *clone()* to create the child ⑥. The third (bit-mask) argument includes the termination signal. The fourth argument (*func_arg*) specifies the file descriptor opened earlier (at ②).

- Wait for the child to terminate ⑦.

- Check whether the file descriptor (opened at ②) is still open by trying to *write()* to it ⑧. The program reports whether the *write()* succeeds or fails.

Execution of the cloned child begins in *childFunc()*, which receives (in the argument *arg*) the file descriptor opened by the main program (at ②). The child closes this file descriptor and then terminates by performing a return ①.

Listing 28-3: Using *clone()* to create a child process

—— *procexec/t_clone.c*

```
#define _GNU_SOURCE
#include <signal.h>
#include <sys/wait.h>
#include <fcntl.h>
#include <sched.h>
#include "tlpi_hdr.h"

#ifndef CHILD_SIG
#define CHILD_SIG SIGUSR1       /* Signal to be generated on termination
                                   of cloned child */
#endif

static int                      /* Startup function for cloned child */
childFunc(void *arg)
{
①   if (close(*((int *) arg)) == -1)
        errExit("close");

    return 0;                   /* Child terminates now */
}

int
main(int argc, char *argv[])
{
    const int STACK_SIZE = 65536;    /* Stack size for cloned child */
    char *stack;                     /* Start of stack buffer */
    char *stackTop;                  /* End of stack buffer */
    int s, fd, flags;

②   fd = open("/dev/null", O_RDWR);  /* Child will close this fd */
    if (fd == -1)
        errExit("open");
```

```
                 /* If argc > 1, child shares file descriptor table with parent */

    ③          flags = (argc > 1) ? CLONE_FILES : 0;

                 /* Allocate stack for child */

    ④          stack = malloc(STACK_SIZE);
                 if (stack == NULL)
                     errExit("malloc");
                 stackTop = stack + STACK_SIZE;         /* Assume stack grows downward */

                 /* Ignore CHILD_SIG, in case it is a signal whose default is to
                    terminate the process; but don't ignore SIGCHLD (which is ignored
                    by default), since that would prevent the creation of a zombie. */

    ⑤          if (CHILD_SIG != 0 && CHILD_SIG != SIGCHLD)
                     if (signal(CHILD_SIG, SIG_IGN) == SIG_ERR)
                         errExit("signal");

                 /* Create child; child commences execution in childFunc() */

    ⑥          if (clone(childFunc, stackTop, flags | CHILD_SIG, (void *) &fd) == -1)
                     errExit("clone");

                 /* Parent falls through to here. Wait for child; __WCLONE is
                    needed for child notifying with signal other than SIGCHLD. */

    ⑦          if (waitpid(-1, NULL, (CHILD_SIG != SIGCHLD) ? __WCLONE : 0) == -1)
                     errExit("waitpid");
                 printf("child has terminated\n");

                 /* Did close() of file descriptor in child affect parent? */

    ⑧          s = write(fd, "x", 1);
                 if (s == -1 && errno == EBADF)
                     printf("file descriptor %d has been closed\n", fd);
                 else if (s == -1)
                     printf("write() on file descriptor %d failed "
                             "unexpectedly (%s)\n", fd, strerror(errno));
                 else
                     printf("write() on file descriptor %d succeeded\n", fd);

                 exit(EXIT_SUCCESS);
             }
```

—— procexec/t_clone.c

When we run the program in Listing 28-3 without a command-line argument, we
see the following:

```
$ ./t_clone                              Doesn't use CLONE_FILES
child has terminated
write() on file descriptor 3 succeeded   Child's close() did not affect parent
```

When we run the program with a command-line argument, we can see that the two processes share the file descriptor table:

```
$ ./t_clone x                          Uses CLONE_FILES
child has terminated
file descriptor 3 has been closed      Child's close() affected parent
```

We show a more complex example of the use of *clone()* in the file procexec/demo_clone.c in the source code distribution for this book.

28.2.1 The *clone() flags* Argument

The *clone() flags* argument is a combination (ORing) of the bit-mask values described in the following pages. Rather than presenting these flags in alphabetical order, we present them in an order that eases explanation, and begin with those flags that are used in the implementation of POSIX threads. From the point of view of implementing threads, many uses of the word *process* below can be replaced by *thread*.

At this point, it is worth remarking that, to some extent, we are playing with words when trying to draw a distinction between the terms *thread* and *process*. It helps a little to introduce the term *kernel scheduling entity* (KSE), which is used in some texts to refer to the objects that are dealt with by the kernel scheduler. Really, threads and processes are simply KSEs that provide for greater and lesser degrees of sharing of attributes (virtual memory, open file descriptors, signal dispositions, process ID, and so on) with other KSEs. The POSIX threads specification provides just one out of various possible definitions of which attributes should be shared between threads.

In the course of the following descriptions, we'll sometimes mention the two main implementations of POSIX threads available on Linux: the older LinuxThreads implementation and the more recent NPTL implementation. Further information about these two implementations can be found in Section 33.5.

> Starting in kernel 2.6.16, Linux provides a new system call, *unshare()*, which allows a child created using *clone()* (or *fork()* or *vfork()*) to undo some of the attribute sharing (i.e., reverse the effects of some of the *clone() flags* bits) that was established when the child was created. For details, see the *unshare(2)* manual page.

Sharing file descriptor tables: CLONE_FILES

If the CLONE_FILES flag is specified, the parent and the child share the same table of open file descriptors. This means that file descriptor allocation or deallocation (*open()*, *close()*, *dup()*, *pipe()*, *socket()*, and so on) in either process will be visible in the other process. If the CLONE_FILES flag is not set, then the file descriptor table is not shared, and the child gets a copy of the parent's table at the time of the *clone()* call. These copied descriptors refer to the same open file descriptions as the corresponding descriptors in the parent (as with *fork()* and *vfork()*).

The specification of POSIX threads requires that all of the threads in a process share the same open file descriptors.

Sharing file system–related information: CLONE_FS

If the CLONE_FS flag is specified, then the parent and the child share file system–related information—umask, root directory, and current working directory. This means that calls to *umask()*, *chdir()*, or *chroot()* in either process will affect the other process. If the CLONE_FS flag is not set, then the parent and child have separate copies of this information (as with *fork()* and *vfork()*).

The attribute sharing provided by CLONE_FS is required by POSIX threads.

Sharing signal dispositions: CLONE_SIGHAND

If the CLONE_SIGHAND flag is set, then the parent and child share the same table of signal dispositions. Using *sigaction()* or *signal()* to change a signal's disposition in either process will affect that signal's disposition in the other process. If the CLONE_SIGHAND flag is not set, then signal dispositions are not shared; instead, the child gets a copy of the parent's signal disposition table (as with *fork()* and *vfork()*). The CLONE_SIGHAND flag doesn't affect the process signal mask and the set of pending signals, which are always distinct for the two processes. From Linux 2.6 onward, CLONE_VM must also be included in *flags* if CLONE_SIGHAND is specified.

Sharing of signal dispositions is required by POSIX threads.

Sharing the parent's virtual memory: CLONE_VM

If the CLONE_VM flag is set, then the parent and child share the same virtual memory pages (as with *vfork()*). Updates to memory or calls to *mmap()* or *munmap()* by either process will be visible to the other process. If the CLONE_VM flag is not set, then the child receives a copy of the parent's virtual memory (as with *fork()*).

Sharing the same virtual memory is one of the defining attributes of threads, and is required by POSIX threads.

Thread groups: CLONE_THREAD

If the CLONE_THREAD flag is set, then the child is placed in the same thread group as the parent. If this flag is not set, the child is placed in its own new thread group.

Thread groups were introduced in Linux 2.4 to allow threading libraries to support the POSIX threads requirement that all of the threads in a process share a single process ID (i.e., *getpid()* in each of the threads should return the same value). A thread group is a group of KSEs that share the same *thread group identifier* (TGID), as shown in Figure 28-1. For the remainder of the discussion of CLONE_THREAD, we'll refer to these KSEs as *threads*.

Since Linux 2.4, *getpid()* returns the calling thread's TGID. In other words, a TGID is the same thing as a process ID.

> The *clone()* implementation in Linux 2.2 and earlier did not provide CLONE_THREAD. Instead, LinuxThreads implemented POSIX threads as processes that shared various attributes (e.g., virtual memory) but had distinct process IDs. For compatibility reasons, even on modern Linux kernels, the LinuxThreads implementation doesn't use the CLONE_THREAD flag, so that threads in that implementation continue to have distinct process IDs.

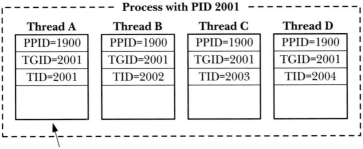

Figure 28-1: A thread group containing four threads

Thread group leader (TID matches TGID)

Each thread within a thread group is distinguished by a unique *thread identifier* (TID). Linux 2.4 introduced a new system call, *gettid()*, to allow a thread to obtain its own thread ID (this is the same value as is returned to the thread that calls *clone()*). A thread ID is represented using the same data type that is used for a process ID, *pid_t*. Thread IDs are unique system-wide, and the kernel guarantees that no thread ID will be the same as any process ID on the system, except when a thread is the thread group leader for a process.

The first thread in a new thread group has a thread ID that is the same as its thread group ID. This thread is referred to as the *thread group leader*.

> The thread IDs that we are discussing here are not the same as the thread IDs (the *pthread_t* data type) used by POSIX threads. The latter identifiers are generated and maintained internally (in user space) by a POSIX threads implementation.

All of the threads in a thread group have the same parent process ID—that of the thread group leader. Only after all of the threads in a thread group have terminated is a SIGCHLD signal (or other termination signal) sent to that parent process. These semantics correspond to the requirements of POSIX threads.

When a CLONE_THREAD thread terminates, no signal is sent to the thread that created it using *clone()*. Correspondingly, it is not possible to use *wait()* (or similar) to wait for a thread created using CLONE_THREAD. This accords with POSIX requirements. A POSIX thread is not the same thing as a process, and can't be waited for using *wait()*; instead, it must be joined using *pthread_join()*. To detect the termination of a thread created using CLONE_THREAD, a special synchronization primitive, called a *futex*, is used (see the discussion of the CLONE_PARENT_SETTID flag below).

If any of the threads in a thread group performs an *exec()*, then all threads other than the thread group leader are terminated (this behavior corresponds to the semantics required for POSIX threads), and the new program is execed in the thread group leader. In other words, in the new program, *gettid()* will return the thread ID of the thread group leader. During an *exec()*, the termination signal that this process should send to its parent is reset to SIGCHLD.

If one of the threads in a thread group creates a child using *fork()* or *vfork()*, then any thread in the group can monitor that child using *wait()* or similar.

From Linux 2.6 onward, CLONE_SIGHAND must also be included in *flags* if CLONE_THREAD is specified. This corresponds to further POSIX threads requirements;

for details, see the description of how POSIX threads and signals interact in Section 33.2. (The kernel handling of signals for CLONE_THREAD thread groups mirrors the POSIX requirements for how the threads in a process should react to signals.)

Threading library support: CLONE_PARENT_SETTID, CLONE_CHILD_SETTID, and CLONE_CHILD_CLEARTID

The CLONE_PARENT_SETTID, CLONE_CHILD_SETTID, and CLONE_CHILD_CLEARTID flags were added in Linux 2.6 to support the implementation of POSIX threads. These flags affect how *clone()* treats its *ptid* and *ctid* arguments. CLONE_PARENT_SETTID and CLONE_CHILD_CLEARTID are used in the NPTL threading implementation.

If the CLONE_PARENT_SETTID flag is set, then the kernel writes the thread ID of the child thread into the location pointed to by *ptid*. The thread ID is copied into *ptid* before the memory of the parent is duplicated. This means that, even if the CLONE_VM flag is not specified, both the parent and the child can see the child's thread ID in this location. (As noted above, the CLONE_VM flag is specified when creating POSIX threads.)

The CLONE_PARENT_SETTID flag exists in order to provide a reliable means for a threading implementation to obtain the ID of the new thread. Note that it isn't sufficient to obtain the thread ID of the new thread via the return value of *clone()*, like so:

```
tid = clone(...);
```

The problem is that this code can lead to various race conditions, because the assignment occurs only after *clone()* returns. For example, suppose that the new thread terminates, and the handler for its termination signal is invoked before the assignment to *tid* completes. In this case, the handler can't usefully access *tid*. (Within a threading library, *tid* might be an item in a global bookkeeping structure used to track the status of all threads.) Programs that invoke *clone()* directly often can be designed to work around this race condition. However, a threading library can't control the actions of the program that calls it. Using CLONE_PARENT_SETTID to ensure that the new thread ID is placed in the location pointed to by *ptid* before *clone()* returns allows a threading library to avoid such race conditions.

If the CLONE_CHILD_SETTID flag is set, then *clone()* writes the thread ID of the child thread into the location pointed to by *ctid*. The setting of *ctid* is done only in the child's memory, but this will affect the parent if CLONE_VM is also specified. Although NPTL doesn't need CLONE_CHILD_SETTID, this flag is provided to allow flexibility for other possible threading library implementations.

If the CLONE_CHILD_CLEARTID flag is set, then *clone()* zeros the memory location pointed to by *ctid* when the child terminates.

The *ctid* argument is the mechanism (described in a moment) by which the NPTL threading implementation obtains notification of the termination of a thread. Such notification is required by the *pthread_join()* function, which is the POSIX threads mechanism by which one thread can wait for the termination of another thread.

When a thread is created using *pthread_create()*, NPTL makes a *clone()* call in which *ptid* and *ctid* point to the same location. (This is why CLONE_CHILD_SETTID is not required by NPTL.) The CLONE_PARENT_SETTID flag causes that location to be initialized with the new thread's ID. When the child terminates and *ctid* is cleared, that change is visible to all threads in the process (since the CLONE_VM flag is also specified).

The kernel treats the location pointed to by *ctid* as a *futex*, an efficient synchronization mechanism. (See the *futex(2)* manual page for further details of futexes.) Notification of thread termination can be obtained by performing a *futex()* system call that blocks waiting for a change in the value at the location pointed to by *ctid*. (Behind the scenes, this is what *pthread_join()* does.) At the same time that the kernel clears *ctid*, it also wakes up any kernel scheduling entity (i.e., thread) that is blocked performing a futex wait on that address. (At the POSIX threads level, this causes the *pthread_join()* call to unblock.)

Thread-local storage: CLONE_SETTLS

If the CLONE_SETTLS flag is set, then the *tls* argument points to a *user_desc* structure describing the thread-local storage buffer to be used for this thread. This flag was added in Linux 2.6 to support the NPTL implementation of thread-local storage (Section 31.4). For details of the *user_desc* structure, see the definition and use of this structure in the 2.6 kernel sources and the *set_thread_area(2)* manual page.

Sharing System V semaphore undo values: CLONE_SYSVSEM

If the CLONE_SYSVSEM flag is set, then the parent and child share a single list of System V semaphore undo values (Section 47.8). If this flag is not set, then the parent and child have separate undo lists, and the child's undo list is initially empty.

The CLONE_SYSVSEM flag is available from kernel 2.6 onward, and provides the sharing semantics required by POSIX threads.

Per-process mount namespaces: CLONE_NEWNS

From kernel 2.4.19 onward, Linux supports the notion of per-process *mount namespaces*. A mount namespace is the set of mount points maintained by calls to *mount()* and *umount()*. The mount namespace affects how pathnames are resolved to actual files, as well as the operation of system calls such as *chdir()* and *chroot()*.

By default, the parent and the child share a mount namespace, which means that changes to the namespace by one process using *mount()* and *umount()* are visible in the other process (as with *fork()* and *vfork()*). A privileged (CAP_SYS_ADMIN) process may specify the CLONE_NEWNS flag so that the child obtains a copy of the parent's mount namespace. Thereafter, changes to the namespace by one process are not visible in the other process. (In earlier 2.4.*x* kernels, as well as in older kernels, we can consider all processes on the system as sharing a single system-wide mount namespace.)

Per-process mount namespaces can be used to create environments that are similar to *chroot()* jails, but which are more secure and flexible; for example, a jailed process can be provided with a mount point that is not visible to other processes on the system. Mount namespaces are also useful in setting up virtual server environments.

Specifying both CLONE_NEWNS and CLONE_FS in the same call to *clone()* is nonsensical and is not permitted.

Making the child's parent the same as the caller's: CLONE_PARENT

By default, when we create a new process with *clone()*, the parent of that process (as returned by *getppid()*) is the process that calls *clone()* (as with *fork()* and *vfork()*). If the CLONE_PARENT flag is set, then the parent of the child will be the caller's parent. In other words, CLONE_PARENT is the equivalent of setting *child.PPID = caller.PPID*. (In the default case, without CLONE_PARENT, it would be *child.PPID = caller.PID*.) The parent process (*child.PPID*) is the process that is signaled when the child terminates.

The CLONE_PARENT flag is available in Linux 2.4 and later. Originally, it was designed to be useful for POSIX threads implementations, but the 2.6 kernel pursued an approach to supporting threads (the use of CLONE_THREAD, described above) that removed the need for this flag.

Making the child's PID the same as the parent's PID: CLONE_PID (obsolete)

If the CLONE_PID flag is set, then the child has the same process ID as the parent. If this flag is not set, then the parent and child have different process IDs (as with *fork()* and *vfork()*). Only the system boot process (process ID 0) may specify this flag; it is used when initializing a multiprocessor system.

The CLONE_PID flag is not intended for use in user applications. In Linux 2.6, it has been removed, and is superseded by CLONE_IDLETASK, which causes the process ID of the new process to be set to 0. CLONE_IDLETASK is available only for internal use within the kernel (if specified in the *flags* argument of *clone()*, it is ignored). It is used to create the invisible per-CPU *idle process*, of which multiple instances may exist on multiprocessor systems.

Process tracing: CLONE_PTRACE and CLONE_UNTRACED

If the CLONE_PTRACE flag is set and the calling process is being traced, then the child is also traced. For details on process tracing (used by debuggers and the *strace* command), refer to the *ptrace(2)* manual page.

From kernel 2.6 onward, the CLONE_UNTRACED flag can be set, meaning that a tracing process can't force CLONE_PTRACE on this child. The CLONE_UNTRACED flag is used internally by the kernel in the creation of kernel threads.

Suspending the parent until the child exits or execs: CLONE_VFORK

If the CLONE_VFORK flag is set, then the execution of the parent is suspended until the child releases its virtual memory resources via a call to *exec()* or *_exit()* (as with *vfork()*).

New *clone()* flags to support containers

A number of new *clone() flags* values were added in Linux 2.6.19 and later: CLONE_IO, CLONE_NEWIPC, CLONE_NEWNET, CLONE_NEWPID, CLONE_NEWUSER, and CLONE_NEWUTS. (See the *clone(2)* manual page for the details of these flags.)

Most of these flags are provided to support the implementation of *containers* ([Bhattiprolu et al., 2008]). A container is a form of lightweight virtualization, whereby groups of processes running on the same kernel can be isolated from one another in environments that appear to be separate machines. Containers can also be nested, one inside the other. The containers approach contrasts with full virtualization, where each virtualized environment is running a distinct kernel.

To implement containers, the kernel developers had to provide a layer of indirection within the kernel around each of the global system resources—such as process IDs, the networking stack, the identifiers returned by *uname()*, System V IPC objects, and user and group ID namespaces—so that each container can provide its own instance of these resources.

There are various possible uses for containers, including the following:

- controlling allocation of resources on the system, such as network bandwidth or CPU time (e.g., one container might be granted 75% of the CPU time, while the other gets 25%);

- providing multiple lightweight virtual servers on a single host machine;

- freezing a container, so that execution of all processes in the container is suspended, later to be restarted, possibly after migrating to a different machine; and

- allowing an application's state to be dumped (checkpointed) and then later restored (perhaps after an application crash, or a planned or unplanned system shutdown) to continue computation from the time of the checkpoint.

Use of *clone()* flags

Roughly, we can say that a *fork()* corresponds to a *clone()* call with *flags* specified as just SIGCHLD, while a *vfork()* corresponds to a *clone()* call specifying *flags* as follows:

```
CLONE_VM | CLONE_VFORK | SIGCHLD
```

> Since version 2.3.3, the *glibc* wrapper *fork()* provided as part of the NPTL threading implementation bypasses the kernel's *fork()* system call and invokes *clone()*. This wrapper function invokes any fork handlers that have been established by the caller using *pthread_atfork()* (see Section 33.3).

The LinuxThreads threading implementation uses *clone()* (with just the first four arguments) to create threads by specifying *flags* as follows:

```
CLONE_VM | CLONE_FILES | CLONE_FS | CLONE_SIGHAND
```

The NPTL threading implementation uses *clone()* (with all seven arguments) to create threads by specifying *flags* as follows:

```
CLONE_VM | CLONE_FILES | CLONE_FS | CLONE_SIGHAND | CLONE_THREAD |
CLONE_SETTLS | CLONE_PARENT_SETTID | CLONE_CHILD_CLEARTID | CLONE_SYSVSEM
```

28.2.2 Extensions to *waitpid()* for Cloned Children

To wait for children produced by *clone()*, the following additional (Linux-specific) values can be included in the *options* bit-mask argument for *waitpid()*, *wait3()*, and *wait4()*:

__WCLONE

> If set, then wait for *clone* children only. If not set, then wait for *nonclone* children only. In this context, a *clone* child is one that delivers a signal other than SIGCHLD to its parent on termination. This bit is ignored if __WALL is also specified.

__WALL (since Linux 2.4)
>   Wait for all children, regardless of type (*clone* or *nonclone*).

__WNOTHREAD (since Linux 2.4)
>   By default, the wait calls wait not only for children of the calling process, but also for children of any other processes in the same thread group as the caller. Specifying the __WNOTHREAD flag limits the wait to children of the calling process.

These flags can't be used with *waitid()*.

28.3 Speed of Process Creation

Table 28-3 shows some speed comparisons for different methods of process creation. The results were obtained using a test program that executed a loop that repeatedly created a child process and then waited for it to terminate. The table compares the various methods using three different process memory sizes, as indicated by the *Total virtual memory* value. The differences in memory size were simulated by having the program *malloc()* additional memory on the heap prior to performing the timings.

> Values for process size (*Total virtual memory*) in Table 28-3 are taken from the *VSZ* value displayed by the command *ps -o "pid vsz cmd"*.

Table 28-3: Time required to create 100,000 processes using *fork()*, *vfork()*, and *clone()*

Method of process creation	Total Virtual Memory					
	1.70 MB		2.70 MB		11.70 MB	
	Time (secs)	Rate	Time (secs)	Rate	Time (secs)	Rate
fork()	22.27 (7.99)	4544	26.38 (8.98)	4135	126.93 (52.55)	1276
vfork()	3.52 (2.49)	28955	3.55 (2.50)	28621	3.53 (2.51)	28810
clone()	2.97 (2.14)	34333	2.98 (2.13)	34217	2.93 (2.10)	34688
fork() + *exec()*	135.72 (12.39)	764	146.15 (16.69)	719	260.34 (61.86)	435
vfork() + *exec()*	107.36 (6.27)	969	107.81 (6.35)	964	107.97 (6.38)	960

For each process size, two types of statistics are provided in Table 28-3:

- The first statistic consists of two time measurements. The main (larger) measurement is the total elapsed (real) time to perform 100,000 process creation operations. The second time, shown in parentheses, is the CPU time consumed by the parent process. Since these tests were run on an otherwise unloaded machine, the difference between the two time values represents the total time consumed by child processes created during the test.

- The second statistic for each test shows the rate at which processes were created per (real) second.

Statistics shown are the average of 20 runs for each case, and were obtained using kernel 2.6.27 running on an x86-32 system.

The first three data rows show times for simple process creation (without execing a new program in the child). In each case, the child processes exit immediately after they are created, and the parent waits for each child to terminate before creating the next.

The first row contains values for the *fork()* system call. From the data, we can see that as a process gets larger, *fork()* takes longer. These time differences show the additional time required to duplicate increasingly large page tables for the child and mark all data, heap, and stack segment page entries as read-only. (No *pages* are copied, since the child doesn't modify its data or stack segments.)

The second data row provides the same statistics for *vfork()*. We see that as the process size increases, the times remain the same—because no page tables or pages are copied during a *vfork()*, the virtual memory size of the calling process has no effect. The difference between the *fork()* and *vfork()* statistics represents the total time required for copying process page tables in each case.

> Small variations in the *vfork()* and *clone()* values in Table 28-3 are due to sampling errors and scheduling variations. Even when creating processes up to 300 MB in size, times for these two system calls remained constant.

The third data row shows statistics for process creation using *clone()* with the following flags:

```
CLONE_VM | CLONE_VFORK | CLONE_FS | CLONE_SIGHAND | CLONE_FILES
```

The first two of these flags emulate the behavior of *vfork()*. The remaining flags specify that the parent and child should share their file-system attributes (umask, root directory, and current working directory), table of signal dispositions, and table of open file descriptors. The difference between the *clone()* and *vfork()* data represents the small amount of additional work performed in *vfork()* to copy this information into the child process. The cost of copying file-system attributes and the table of signal dispositions is constant. However, the cost of copying the table of open file descriptors varies according to the number of descriptors. For example, opening 100 file descriptors in the parent process raised the *vfork()* real time (in the first column of the table) from 3.52 to 5.04 seconds, but left times for *clone()* unaffected.

> The timings for *clone()* are for the *glibc clone()* wrapper function, rather than direct calls to *sys_clone()*. Other tests (not summarized here) revealed negligible timing differences between using *sys_clone()* and calling *clone()* with a child function that immediately exited.

The differences between *fork()* and *vfork()* are quite marked. However, the following points should be kept in mind:

- The final data column, where *vfork()* is more than 30 times faster than *fork()*, corresponds to a large process. Typical processes would lie somewhere closer to the first two columns of the table.

- Because the times required for process creation are typically much smaller than those required for an *exec()*, the differences are much less marked if a *fork()* or *vfork()* is followed by an *exec()*. This is illustrated by the final pair of data rows in Table 28-3, where each child performs an *exec()*, rather than immediately exiting. The program execed was the *true* command (/bin/true, chosen because it produces no output). In this case, we see that the relative differences between *fork()* and *vfork()* are much lower.

> In fact, the data shown in Table 28-3 doesn't reveal the full cost of an *exec()*, because the child execs the same program in each loop of the test. As a result, the cost of disk I/O to read the program into memory is essentially eliminated, because the program will be read into the kernel buffer cache on the first *exec()*, and then remain there. If each loop of the test execed a different program (e.g., a differently named copy of the same program), then we would observe a greater cost for an *exec()*.

28.4 Effect of *exec()* and *fork()* on Process Attributes

A process has numerous attributes, some of which we have already described in earlier chapters, and others that we explore in later chapters. Regarding these attributes, two questions arise:

- What happens to these attributes when a process performs an *exec()*?
- Which attributes are inherited by a child when a *fork()* is performed?

Table 28-4 summarizes the answers to these questions. The *exec()* column indicates which attributes are preserved during an *exec()*. The *fork()* column indicates which attributes are inherited (or in some cases, shared) by a child after *fork()*. Other than the attributes indicated as being Linux-specific, all listed attributes appear in standard UNIX implementations, and their handling during *exec()* and *fork()* conforms to the requirements of SUSv3.

Table 28-4: Effect of *exec()* and *fork()* on process attributes

Process attribute	*exec()*	*fork()*	Interfaces affecting attribute; additional notes
Process address space			
Text segment	No	Shared	Child process shares text segment with parent.
Stack segment	No	Yes	Function entry/exit; *alloca()*, *longjmp()*, *siglongjmp()*.
Data and heap segments	No	Yes	*brk()*, *sbrk()*.
Environment variables	See notes	Yes	*putenv()*, *setenv()*; direct modification of *environ*. Overwritten by *execle()* and *execve()* and preserved by remaining *exec()* calls.
Memory mappings	No	Yes; see notes	*mmap()*, *munmap()*. A mapping's MAP_NORESERVE flag is inherited across *fork()*. Mappings that have been marked with *madvise(MADV_DONTFORK)* are not inherited across *fork()*.
Memory locks	No	No	*mlock()*, *munlock()*.

Table 28-4: Effect of *exec()* and *fork()* on process attributes (continued)

Process attribute	exec()	fork()	Interfaces affecting attribute; additional notes
Process identifiers and credentials			
Process ID	Yes	No	
Parent process ID	Yes	No	
Process group ID	Yes	Yes	*setpgid()*.
Session ID	Yes	Yes	*setsid()*.
Real IDs	Yes	Yes	*setuid()*, *setgid()*, and related calls.
Effective and saved set IDs	See notes	Yes	*setuid()*, *setgid()*, and related calls. Chapter 9 explains how *exec()* affects these IDs.
Supplementary group IDs	Yes	Yes	*setgroups()*, *initgroups()*.
Files, file I/O, and directories			
Open file descriptors	See notes	Yes	*open()*, *close()*, *dup()*, *pipe()*, *socket()*, and so on. File descriptors are preserved across *exec()* unless marked close-on-exec. Descriptors in child and parent refer to same open file descriptions; see Section 5.4.
Close-on-exec flag	Yes (if off)	Yes	*fcntl(F_SETFD)*.
File offsets	Yes	Shared	*lseek()*, *read()*, *write()*, *readv()*, *writev()*. Child shares file offsets with parent.
Open file status flags	Yes	Shared	*open()*, *fcntl(F_SETFL)*. Child shares open file status flags with parent.
Asynchronous I/O operations	See notes	No	*aio_read()*, *aio_write()*, and related calls. Outstanding operations are canceled during an *exec()*.
Directory streams	No	Yes; see notes	*opendir()*, *readdir()*. SUSv3 states that child gets a copy of parent's directory streams, but these copies may or may not share the directory stream position. On Linux, the directory stream position is not shared.
File system			
Current working directory	Yes	Yes	*chdir()*.
Root directory	Yes	Yes	*chroot()*.
File mode creation mask	Yes	Yes	*umask()*.
Signals			
Signal dispositions	See notes	Yes	*signal()*, *sigaction()*. During an *exec()*, signals with dispositions set to default or ignore are unchanged; caught signals revert to their default dispositions. See Section 27.5.
Signal mask	Yes	Yes	Signal delivery, *sigprocmask()*, *sigaction()*.
Pending signal set	Yes	No	Signal delivery; *raise()*, *kill()*, *sigqueue()*.
Alternate signal stack	No	Yes	*sigaltstack()*.

(continued)

Table 28-4: Effect of *exec( )* and *fork( )* on process attributes (continued)

Process attribute	*exec( )*	*fork( )*	Interfaces affecting attribute; additional notes
Timers			
Interval timers	Yes	No	*setitimer( ).*
Timers set by *alarm( )*	Yes	No	*alarm( ).*
POSIX timers	No	No	*timer_create( )* and related calls.
POSIX threads			
Threads	No	See notes	During *fork( )*, only calling thread is replicated in child.
Thread cancelability state and type	No	Yes	After an *exec( )*, the cancelability type and state are reset to PTHREAD_CANCEL_ENABLE and PTHREAD_CANCEL_DEFERRED, respectively
Mutexes and condition variables	No	Yes	See Section 33.3 for details of the treatment of mutexes and other thread resources during *fork( ).*
Priority and scheduling			
Nice value	Yes	Yes	*nice( )*, *setpriority( ).*
Scheduling policy and priority	Yes	Yes	*sched_setscheduler( )*, *sched_setparam( ).*
Resources and CPU time			
Resource limits	Yes	Yes	*setrlimit( ).*
Process and child CPU times	Yes	No	As returned by *times( ).*
Resource usages	Yes	No	As returned by *getrusage( ).*
Interprocess communication			
System V shared memory segments	No	Yes	*shmat( )*, *shmdt( ).*
POSIX shared memory	No	Yes	*shm_open( )* and related calls.
POSIX message queues	No	Yes	*mq_open( )* and related calls. Descriptors in child and parent refer to same open message queue descriptions. A child doesn't inherit its parent's message notification registrations.
POSIX named semaphores	No	Shared	*sem_open( )* and related calls. Child shares references to same semaphores as parent.
POSIX unnamed semaphores	No	See notes	*sem_init( )* and related calls. If semaphores are in a shared memory region, then child shares semaphores with parent; otherwise, child has its own copy of the semaphores.
System V semaphore adjustments	Yes	No	*semop( ).* See Section 47.8.
File locks	Yes	See notes	*flock( ).* Child inherits a reference to the same lock as parent.
Record locks	See notes	No	*fcntl(F_SETLK).* Locks are preserved across *exec( )* unless a file descriptor referring to the file is marked close-on-exec; see Section 55.3.5.

Table 28-4: Effect of *exec( )* and *fork( )* on process attributes (continued)

Process attribute	exec()	fork()	Interfaces affecting attribute; additional notes
Miscellaneous			
Locale settings	No	Yes	*setlocale( )*. As part of C run-time initialization, the equivalent of *setlocale(LC_ALL, "C")* is executed after a new program is execed.
Floating-point environment	No	Yes	When a new program is execed, the state of the floating-point environment is reset to the default; see *fenv(3)*.
Controlling terminal	Yes	Yes	
Exit handlers	No	Yes	*atexit( ), on_exit( )*.
Linux-specific			
File-system IDs	See notes	Yes	*setfsuid( ), setfsgid( )*. These IDs are also changed any time the corresponding effective IDs are changed.
timerfd timers	Yes	See notes	*timerfd_create( )*; child inherits file descriptors referring to same timers as parent.
Capabilities	See notes	Yes	*capset( )*. The handling of capabilities during an *exec( )* is described in Section 39.5.
Capability bounding set	Yes	Yes	
Capabilities *securebits* flags	See notes	Yes	All *securebits* flags are preserved during an *exec( )* except SECBIT_KEEP_CAPS, which is always cleared.
CPU affinity	Yes	Yes	*sched_setaffinity( )*.
SCHED_RESET_ON_FORK	Yes	No	See Section 35.3.2.
Allowed CPUs	Yes	Yes	See *cpuset(7)*.
Allowed memory nodes	Yes	Yes	See *cpuset(7)*.
Memory policy	Yes	Yes	See *set_mempolicy(2)*.
File leases	Yes	See notes	*fcntl(F_SETLEASE)*. Child inherits a reference to the same lease as parent.
Directory change notifications	Yes	No	The *dnotify* API, available via *fcntl(F_NOTIFY)*.
prctl(PR_SET_DUMPABLE)	See notes	Yes	During an *exec( )*, the PR_SET_DUMPABLE flag is set, unless execing a set-user-ID or set-group-ID program, in which case it is cleared.
prctl(PR_SET_PDEATHSIG)	Yes	No	
prctl(PR_SET_NAME)	No	Yes	
oom_adj	Yes	Yes	See Section 49.9.
coredump_filter	Yes	Yes	See Section 22.1.

28.5 Summary

When process accounting is enabled, the kernel writes an accounting record to a file for each process that terminates on the system. This record contains statistics on the resources used by the process.

Like *fork()*, the Linux-specific *clone()* system call creates a new process, but allows finer control over which attributes are shared between the parent and child. This system call is used primarily for implementing threading libraries.

We compared the speed of process creation using *fork()*, *vfork()*, and *clone()*. Although *vfork()* is faster than *fork()*, the time difference between these system calls is small by comparison with the time required for a child process to do a subsequent *exec()*.

When a child process is created via *fork()*, it inherits copies of (or in some cases shares) certain process attributes from its parent, while other process attributes are not inherited. For example, a child inherits copies of its parent's file descriptor table and signal dispositions, but doesn't inherit its parent's interval timers, record locks, or set of pending signals. Correspondingly, when a process performs an *exec()*, certain process attributes remain unchanged, while others are reset to defaults. For example, the process ID remains the same, file descriptors remain open (unless marked close-on-exec), interval timers are preserved, and pending signals remain pending, but handled signals are reset to their default disposition and shared memory segments are detached.

Further information

Refer to the sources of further information listed in Section 24.6. Chapter 17 of [Frisch, 2002] describes the administration of process accounting, as well as some of the variations across UNIX implementations. [Bovet & Cesati, 2005] describes the implementation of the *clone()* system call.

28.6 Exercise

28-1. Write a program to see how fast the *fork()* and *vfork()* system calls are on your system. Each child process should immediately exit, and the parent should *wait()* on each child before creating the next. Compare the relative differences for these two system calls with those of Table 28-3. The shell built-in command *time* can be used to measure the execution time of a program.

29

THREADS: INTRODUCTION

In this and the next few chapters, we describe POSIX threads, often known as *Pthreads*. We won't attempt to cover the entire Pthreads API, since it is rather large. Various sources of further information about threads are listed at the end of this chapter.

These chapters mainly describe the standard behavior specified for the Pthreads API. In Section 33.5, we discuss those points where the two main Linux threading implementations—LinuxThreads and Native POSIX Threads Library (NPTL)—deviate from the standard.

In this chapter, we provide an overview of the operation of threads, and then look at how threads are created and how they terminate. We conclude with a discussion of some factors that may influence the choice of a multithreaded approach versus a multiprocess approach when designing an application.

29.1 Overview

Like processes, threads are a mechanism that permits an application to perform multiple tasks concurrently. A single process can contain multiple threads, as illustrated in Figure 29-1. All of these threads are independently executing the same program, and they all share the same global memory, including the initialized data, uninitialized data, and heap segments. (A traditional UNIX process is simply a special case of a multithreaded process; it is a process that contains just one thread.)

We have simplified things somewhat in Figure 29-1. In particular, the location of the per-thread stacks may be intermingled with shared libraries and shared memory regions, depending on the order in which threads are created, shared libraries loaded, and shared memory regions attached. Furthermore, the location of the per-thread stacks can vary depending on the Linux distribution.

The threads in a process can execute concurrently. On a multiprocessor system, multiple threads can execute in parallel. If one thread is blocked on I/O, other threads are still eligible to execute. (Although it is sometimes useful to create a separate thread purely for the purpose of performing I/O, it is often preferable to employ one of the alternative I/O models that we describe in Chapter 63.)

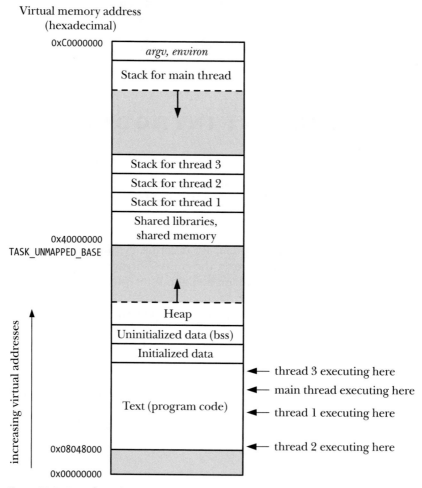

Figure 29-1: Four threads executing in a process (Linux/x86-32)

Threads offer advantages over processes in certain applications. Consider the traditional UNIX approach to achieving concurrency by creating multiple processes. An example of this is a network server design in which a parent process accepts incoming connections from clients, and then uses *fork()* to create a separate child process to handle communication with each client (refer to Section 60.3). Such a design makes it possible to serve multiple clients simultaneously. While this approach works well for many scenarios, it does have the following limitations in some applications:

- It is difficult to share information between processes. Since the parent and child don't share memory (other than the read-only text segment), we must use some form of interprocess communication in order to exchange information between processes.

- Process creation with *fork()* is relatively expensive. Even with the copy-on-write technique described in Section 24.2.2, the need to duplicate various process attributes such as page tables and file descriptor tables means that a *fork()* call is still time-consuming.

Threads address both of these problems:

- Sharing information between threads is easy and fast. It is just a matter of copying data into shared (global or heap) variables. However, in order to avoid the problems that can occur when multiple threads try to update the same information, we must employ the synchronization techniques described in Chapter 30.

- Thread creation is faster than process creation—typically, ten times faster or better. (On Linux, threads are implemented using the *clone()* system call, and Table 28-3, on page 610, shows the differences in speed between *fork()* and *clone()*.) Thread creation is faster because many of the attributes that must be duplicated in a child created by *fork()* are instead shared between threads. In particular, copy-on-write duplication of pages of memory is not required, nor is duplication of page tables.

Besides global memory, threads also share a number of other attributes (i.e., these attributes are global to a process, rather than specific to a thread). These attributes include the following:

- process ID and parent process ID;
- process group ID and session ID;
- controlling terminal;
- process credentials (user and group IDs);
- open file descriptors;
- record locks created using *fcntl()*;
- signal dispositions;
- file system–related information: umask, current working directory, and root directory;
- interval timers (*setitimer()*) and POSIX timers (*timer_create()*);
- System V semaphore undo (*semadj*) values (Section 47.8);
- resource limits;
- CPU time consumed (as returned by *times()*);
- resources consumed (as returned by *getrusage()*); and
- nice value (set by *setpriority()* and *nice()*).

Among the attributes that are distinct for each thread are the following:

- thread ID (Section 29.5);
- signal mask;
- thread-specific data (Section 31.3);
- alternate signal stack (*sigaltstack()*);
- the *errno* variable;
- floating-point environment (see *fenv(3)*);
- realtime scheduling policy and priority (Sections 35.2 and 35.3);
- CPU affinity (Linux-specific, described in Section 35.4);
- capabilities (Linux-specific, described in Chapter 39); and
- stack (local variables and function call linkage information).

> As can be seen from Figure 29-1, all of the per-thread stacks reside within the same virtual address space. This means that, given a suitable pointer, it is possible for threads to share data on each other's stacks. This is occasionally useful, but it requires careful programming to handle the dependency that results from the fact that a local variable remains valid only for the lifetime of the stack frame in which it resides. (If a function returns, the memory region used by its stack frame may be reused by a later function call. If the thread terminates, a new thread may reuse the memory region used for the terminated thread's stack.) Failing to correctly handle this dependency can create bugs that are hard to track down.

29.2   Background Details of the Pthreads API

In the late 1980s and early 1990s, several different threading APIs existed. In 1995, POSIX.1c standardized the POSIX threads API, and this standard was later incorporated into SUSv3.

Several concepts apply to the Pthreads API as a whole, and we briefly introduce these before looking in detail at the API.

Pthreads data types

The Pthreads API defines a number of data types, some of which are listed in Table 29-1. We describe most of these data types in the following pages.

Table 29-1: Pthreads data types

Data type	Description
pthread_t	Thread identifier
pthread_mutex_t	Mutex
pthread_mutexattr_t	Mutex attributes object
pthread_cond_t	Condition variable
pthread_condattr_t	Condition variable attributes object
pthread_key_t	Key for thread-specific data
pthread_once_t	One-time initialization control context
pthread_attr_t	Thread attributes object

SUSv3 doesn't specify how these data types should be represented, and portable programs should treat them as opaque data. By this, we mean that a program should avoid any reliance on knowledge of the structure or contents of a variable of one of these types. In particular, we can't compare variables of these types using the C == operator.

Threads and *errno*

In the traditional UNIX API, *errno* is a global integer variable. However, this doesn't suffice for threaded programs. If a thread made a function call that returned an error in a global *errno* variable, then this would confuse other threads that might also be making function calls and checking *errno*. In other words, race conditions would result. Therefore, in threaded programs, each thread has its own *errno* value. On Linux, a thread-specific *errno* is achieved in a similar manner to most other UNIX implementations: *errno* is defined as a macro that expands into a function call returning a modifiable lvalue that is distinct for each thread. (Since the lvalue is modifiable, it is still possible to write assignment statements of the form *errno = value* in threaded programs.)

To summarize, the *errno* mechanism has been adapted for threads in a manner that leaves error reporting unchanged from the traditional UNIX API.

> The original POSIX.1 standard followed K&R C usage in allowing a program to declare *errno* as *extern int errno*. SUSv3 doesn't permit this usage (the change actually occurred in 1995 in POSIX.1c). Nowadays, a program is required to declare *errno* by including <errno.h>, which enables the implementation of a per-thread *errno*.

Return value from Pthreads functions

The traditional method of returning status from system calls and some library functions is to return 0 on success and −1 on error, with *errno* being set to indicate the error. The functions in the Pthreads API do things differently. All Pthreads functions return 0 on success or a positive value on failure. The failure value is one of the same values that can be placed in *errno* by traditional UNIX system calls.

Because each reference to *errno* in a threaded program carries the overhead of a function call, our example programs don't directly assign the return value of a Pthreads function to *errno*. Instead, we use an intermediate variable and employ our *errExitEN()* diagnostic function (Section 3.5.2), like so:

```
pthread_t thread;
int s;

s = pthread_create(&thread, NULL, func, &arg);
if (s != 0)
    errExitEN(s, "pthread_create");
```

Compiling Pthreads programs

On Linux, programs that use the Pthreads API must be compiled with the *cc −pthread* option. The effects of this option include the following:

- The _REENTRANT preprocessor macro is defined. This causes the declarations of a few reentrant functions to be exposed.
- The program is linked with the *libpthread* library (the equivalent of *−lpthread*).

> The precise options for compiling a multithreaded program vary across implementations (and compilers). Some other implementations (e.g., Tru64) also use *cc −pthread*; Solaris and HP-UX use *cc −mt*.

29.3 Thread Creation

When a program is started, the resulting process consists of a single thread, called the *initial* or *main* thread. In this section, we look at how to create additional threads.

The *pthread_create()* function creates a new thread.

```
#include <pthread.h>

int pthread_create(pthread_t *thread, const pthread_attr_t *attr,
                   void *(*start)(void *), void *arg);
```
>   Returns 0 on success, or a positive error number on error

The new thread commences execution by calling the function identified by *start* with the argument *arg* (i.e., *start(arg)*). The thread that calls *pthread_create()* continues execution with the next statement that follows the call. (This behavior is the same as the *glibc* wrapper function for the *clone()* system call described in Section 28.2.)

The *arg* argument is declared as *void **, meaning that we can pass a pointer to any type of object to the *start* function. Typically, *arg* points to a global or heap variable, but it can also be specified as NULL. If we need to pass multiple arguments to *start*, then *arg* can be specified as a pointer to a structure containing the arguments as separate fields. With judicious casting, we can even specify *arg* as an *int*.

> Strictly speaking, the C standards don't define the results of casting *int* to *void ** and vice versa. However, most C compilers permit these operations, and they produce the desired result; that is, *int j == (int) ((void *) j)*.

The return value of *start* is likewise of type *void **, and it can be employed in the same way as the *arg* argument. We'll see how this value is used when we describe the *pthread_join()* function below.

> Caution is required when using a cast integer as the return value of a thread's start function. The reason for this is that PTHREAD_CANCELED, the value returned when a thread is canceled (see Chapter 32), is usually some implementation-defined integer value cast to *void **. If a thread's start function returns the same integer value, then, to another thread that is doing a *pthread_join()*, it will

wrongly appear that the thread was canceled. In an application that employs thread cancellation and chooses to return cast integer values from a thread's start functions, we must ensure that a normally terminating thread does not return an integer whose value matches PTHREAD_CANCELED on that Pthreads implementation. A portable application would need to ensure that normally terminating threads don't return integer values that match PTHREAD_CANCELED on any of the implementations on which the application is to run.

The *thread* argument points to a buffer of type *pthread_t* into which the unique identifier for this thread is copied before *pthread_create()* returns. This identifier can be used in later Pthreads calls to refer to the thread.

> SUSv3 explicitly notes that the implementation need not initialize the buffer pointed to by *thread* before the new thread starts executing; that is, the new thread may start running before *pthread_create()* returns to its caller. If the new thread needs to obtain its own ID, then it must do so using *pthread_self()* (described in Section 29.5).

The *attr* argument is a pointer to a *pthread_attr_t* object that specifies various attributes for the new thread. We say some more about these attributes in Section 29.8. If *attr* is specified as NULL, then the thread is created with various default attributes, and this is what we'll do in most of the example programs in this book.

After a call to *pthread_create()*, a program has no guarantees about which thread will next be scheduled to use the CPU (on a multiprocessor system, both threads may simultaneously execute on different CPUs). Programs that implicitly rely on a particular order of scheduling are open to the same sorts of race conditions that we described in Section 24.4. If we need to enforce a particular order of execution, we must use one of the synchronization techniques described in Chapter 30.

29.4 Thread Termination

The execution of a thread terminates in one of the following ways:

- The thread's start function performs a return specifying a return value for the thread.
- The thread calls *pthread_exit()* (described below).
- The thread is canceled using *pthread_cancel()* (described in Section 32.1).
- Any of the threads calls *exit()*, or the main thread performs a return (in the *main()* function), which causes all threads in the process to terminate immediately.

The *pthread_exit()* function terminates the calling thread, and specifies a return value that can be obtained in another thread by calling *pthread_join()*.

```
#include <pthread.h>

void pthread_exit(void *retval);
```

Calling *pthread_exit()* is equivalent to performing a return in the thread's start function, with the difference that *pthread_exit()* can be called from any function that has been called by the thread's start function.

The *retval* argument specifies the return value for the thread. The value pointed to by *retval* should not be located on the thread's stack, since the contents of that stack become undefined on thread termination. (For example, that region of the process's virtual memory might be immediately reused by the stack for a new thread.) The same statement applies to the value given to a return statement in the thread's start function.

If the main thread calls *pthread_exit()* instead of calling *exit()* or performing a return, then the other threads continue to execute.

29.5 Thread IDs

Each thread within a process is uniquely identified by a thread ID. This ID is returned to the caller of *pthread_create()*, and a thread can obtain its own ID using *pthread_self()*.

```
#include <pthread.h>

pthread_t pthread_self(void);
```
                              Returns the thread ID of the calling thread

Thread IDs are useful within applications for the following reasons:

- Various Pthreads functions use thread IDs to identify the thread on which they are to act. Examples of such functions include *pthread_join()*, *pthread_detach()*, *pthread_cancel()*, and *pthread_kill()*, all of which we describe in this and the following chapters.

- In some applications, it can be useful to tag dynamic data structures with the ID of a particular thread. This can serve to identify the thread that created or "owns" a data structure, or can be used by one thread to identify a specific thread that should subsequently do something with that data structure.

The *pthread_equal()* function allows us to check whether two thread IDs are the same.

```
#include <pthread.h>

int pthread_equal(pthread_t t1, pthread_t t2);
```
                    Returns nonzero value if *t1* and *t2* are equal, otherwise 0

For example, to check if the ID of the calling thread matches a thread ID saved in the variable *tid*, we could write the following:

```
if (pthread_equal(tid, pthread_self())
    printf("tid matches self\n");
```

The *pthread_equal()* function is needed because the *pthread_t* data type must be treated as opaque data. On Linux, *pthread_t* happens to be defined as an *unsigned long*, but on other implementations, it could be a pointer or a structure.

> In NPTL, *pthread_t* is actually a pointer that has been cast to *unsigned long*.

SUSv3 doesn't require *pthread_t* to be implemented as a scalar type; it could be a structure. Therefore, we can't portably use code such as the following to display a thread ID (though it does work on many implementations, including Linux, and is sometimes useful for debugging purposes):

```
pthread_t thr;

printf("Thread ID = %ld\n", (long) thr);        /* WRONG! */
```

In the Linux threading implementations, thread IDs are unique across processes. However, this is not necessarily the case on other implementations, and SUSv3 explicitly notes that an application can't portably use a thread ID to identify a thread in another process. SUSv3 also notes that an implementation is permitted to reuse a thread ID after a terminated thread has been joined with *pthread_join()* or after a detached thread has terminated. (We explain *pthread_join()* in the next section, and detached threads in Section 29.7.)

> POSIX thread IDs are not the same as the thread IDs returned by the Linux-specific *gettid()* system call. POSIX thread IDs are assigned and maintained by the threading implementation. The thread ID returned by *gettid()* is a number (similar to a process ID) that is assigned by the kernel. Although each POSIX thread has a unique kernel thread ID in the Linux NPTL threading implementation, an application generally doesn't need to know about the kernel IDs (and won't be portable if it depends on knowing them).

29.6 Joining with a Terminated Thread

The *pthread_join()* function waits for the thread identified by *thread* to terminate. (If that thread has already terminated, *pthread_join()* returns immediately.) This operation is termed *joining*.

```
#include <pthread.h>

int pthread_join(pthread_t thread, void **retval);
```
                        Returns 0 on success, or a positive error number on error

If *retval* is a non-NULL pointer, then it receives a copy of the terminated thread's return value—that is, the value that was specified when the thread performed a return or called *pthread_exit()*.

Calling *pthread_join()* for a thread ID that has been previously joined can lead to unpredictable behavior; for example, it might instead join with a thread created later that happened to reuse the same thread ID.

If a thread is not detached (see Section 29.7), then we must join with it using *pthread_join()*. If we fail to do this, then, when the thread terminates, it produces the thread equivalent of a zombie process (Section 26.2). Aside from wasting system resources, if enough thread zombies accumulate, we won't be able to create additional threads.

The task that *pthread_join()* performs for threads is similar to that performed by *waitpid()* for processes. However, there are some notable differences:

- Threads are peers. Any thread in a process can use *pthread_join()* to join with any other thread in the process. For example, if thread A creates thread B, which creates thread C, then it is possible for thread A to join with thread C, or vice versa. This differs from the hierarchical relationship between processes. When a parent process creates a child using *fork()*, it is the only process that can *wait()* on that child. There is no such relationship between the thread that calls *pthread_create()* and the resulting new thread.

- There is no way of saying "join with any thread" (for processes, we can do this using the call *waitpid(−1, &status, options)*); nor is there a way to do a nonblocking join (analogous to the *waitpid()* WNOHANG flag). There are ways to achieve similar functionality using condition variables; we show an example in Section 30.2.4.

> The limitation that *pthread_join()* can join only with a specific thread ID is intentional. The idea is that a program should join only with the threads that it "knows" about. The problem with a "join with any thread" operation stems from the fact that there is no hierarchy of threads, so such an operation could indeed join with *any* thread, including one that was privately created by a library function. (The condition-variable technique that we show in Section 30.2.4 allows a thread to join only with any other thread that it knows about.) As a consequence, the library would no longer be able to join with that thread in order to obtain its status, and it would erroneously try to join with a thread ID that had already been joined. In other words, a "join with any thread" operation is incompatible with modular program design.

Example program

The program in Listing 29-1 creates another thread and then joins with it.

Listing 29-1: A simple program using Pthreads

—— *threads/simple_thread.c*

```
#include <pthread.h>
#include "tlpi_hdr.h"

static void *
threadFunc(void *arg)
{
    char *s = (char *) arg;

    printf("%s", s);

    return (void *) strlen(s);
}
```

```
int
main(int argc, char *argv[])
{
    pthread_t t1;
    void *res;
    int s;

    s = pthread_create(&t1, NULL, threadFunc, "Hello world\n");
    if (s != 0)
        errExitEN(s, "pthread_create");

    printf("Message from main()\n");
    s = pthread_join(t1, &res);
    if (s != 0)
        errExitEN(s, "pthread_join");

    printf("Thread returned %ld\n", (long) res);

    exit(EXIT_SUCCESS);
}
```
———————————————————————————————— **threads/simple_thread.c**

When we run the program in Listing 29-1, we see the following:

```
$ ./simple_thread
Message from main()
Hello world
Thread returned 12
```

Depending on how the two threads were scheduled, the order of the first two lines of output might be reversed.

29.7 Detaching a Thread

By default, a thread is *joinable*, meaning that when it terminates, another thread can obtain its return status using *pthread_join()*. Sometimes, we don't care about the thread's return status; we simply want the system to automatically clean up and remove the thread when it terminates. In this case, we can mark the thread as *detached*, by making a call to *pthread_detach()* specifying the thread's identifier in *thread*.

```
#include <pthread.h>

int pthread_detach(pthread_t thread);
```
                        Returns 0 on success, or a positive error number on error

As an example of the use of *pthread_detach()*, a thread can detach itself using the following call:

```
pthread_detach(pthread_self());
```

Once a thread has been detached, it is no longer possible to use *pthread_join()* to obtain its return status, and the thread can't be made joinable again.

Detaching a thread doesn't make it immune to a call to *exit()* in another thread or a return in the main thread. In such an event, all threads in the process are immediately terminated, regardless of whether they are joinable or detached. To put things another way, *pthread_detach()* simply controls what happens after a thread terminates, not how or when it terminates.

29.8 Thread Attributes

We mentioned earlier that the *pthread_create()* *attr* argument, whose type is *pthread_attr_t*, can be used to specify the attributes used in the creation of a new thread. We won't go into the details of these attributes (for those details, see the references listed at the end of this chapter) or show the prototypes of the various Pthreads functions that can be used to manipulate a *pthread_attr_t* object. We'll just mention that these attributes include information such as the location and size of the thread's stack, the thread's scheduling policy and priority (akin to the process realtime scheduling policies and priorities described in Sections 35.2 and 35.3), and whether the thread is joinable or detached.

As an example of the use of thread attributes, the code shown in Listing 29-2 creates a new thread that is made detached at the time of thread creation (rather than subsequently, using *pthread_detach()*). This code first initializes a thread attributes structure with default values, sets the attribute required to create a detached thread, and then creates a new thread using the thread attributes structure. Once the thread has been created, the attributes object is no longer needed, and so is destroyed.

Listing 29-2: Creating a thread with the detached attribute

── *from* **threads/detached_attrib.c**

```
pthread_t thr;
pthread_attr_t attr;
int s;

s = pthread_attr_init(&attr);                  /* Assigns default values */
if (s != 0)
    errExitEN(s, "pthread_attr_init");

s = pthread_attr_setdetachstate(&attr, PTHREAD_CREATE_DETACHED);
if (s != 0)
    errExitEN(s, "pthread_attr_setdetachstate");

s = pthread_create(&thr, &attr, threadFunc, (void *) 1);
if (s != 0)
    errExitEN(s, "pthread_create");

s = pthread_attr_destroy(&attr);               /* No longer needed */
if (s != 0)
    errExitEN(s, "pthread_attr_destroy");
```

── *from* **threads/detached_attrib.c**

29.9 Threads Versus Processes

In this section, we briefly consider some of the factors that might influence our choice of whether to implement an application as a group of threads or as a group of processes. We begin by considering the advantages of a multithreaded approach:

- Sharing data between threads is easy. By contrast, sharing data between processes requires more work (e.g., creating a shared memory segment or using a pipe).
- Thread creation is faster than process creation; context-switch time may be lower for threads than for processes.

Using threads can have some disadvantages compared to using processes:

- When programming with threads, we need to ensure that the functions we call are thread-safe or are called in a thread-safe manner. (We describe the concept of thread safety in Section 31.1.) Multiprocess applications don't need to be concerned with this.
- A bug in one thread (e.g., modifying memory via an incorrect pointer) can damage all of the threads in the process, since they share the same address space and other attributes. By contrast, processes are more isolated from one another.
- Each thread is competing for use of the finite virtual address space of the host process. In particular, each thread's stack and thread-specific data (or thread-local storage) consumes a part of the process virtual address space, which is consequently unavailable for other threads. Although the available virtual address space is large (e.g., typically 3 GB on x86-32), this factor may be a significant limitation for processes employing large numbers of threads or threads that require large amounts of memory. By contrast, separate processes can each employ the full range of available virtual memory (subject to the limitations of RAM and swap space).

The following are some other points that may influence our choice of threads versus processes:

- Dealing with signals in a multithreaded application requires careful design. (As a general principle, it is usually desirable to avoid the use of signals in multithreaded programs.) We say more about threads and signals in Section 33.2.
- In a multithreaded application, all threads must be running the same program (although perhaps in different functions). In a multiprocess application, different processes can run different programs.
- Aside from data, threads also share certain other information (e.g., file descriptors, signal dispositions, current working directory, and user and group IDs). This may be an advantage or a disadvantage, depending on the application.

29.10 Summary

In a multithreaded process, multiple threads are concurrently executing the same program. All of the threads share the same global and heap variables, but each thread has a private stack for local variables. The threads in a process also share a number of other attributes, including process ID, open file descriptors, signal dispositions, current working directory, and resource limits.

The key difference between threads and processes is the easier sharing of information that threads provide, and this is the main reason that some application designs map better onto a multithread design than onto a multiprocess design. Threads can also provide better performance for some operations (e.g., thread creation is faster than process creation), but this factor is usually secondary in influencing the choice of threads versus processes.

Threads are created using *pthread_create()*. Each thread can then independently terminate using *pthread_exit()*. (If any thread calls *exit()*, then all threads immediately terminate.) Unless a thread has been marked as detached (e.g., via a call to *pthread_detach()*), it must be joined by another thread using *pthread_join()*, which returns the termination status of the joined thread.

Further information

[Butenhof, 1996] provides an exposition of Pthreads that is both readable and thorough. [Robbins & Robbins, 2003] also provides good coverage of Pthreads. [Tanenbaum, 2007] provides a more theoretical introduction to thread concepts, covering topics such as mutexes, critical regions, conditional variables, and deadlock detection and avoidance. [Vahalia, 1996] provides background on the implementation of threads.

29.11 Exercises

29-1. What possible outcomes might there be if a thread executes the following code:

```
pthread_join(pthread_self(), NULL);
```

Write a program to see what actually happens on Linux. If we have a variable, *tid*, containing a thread ID, how can a thread prevent itself from making a call, *pthread_join(tid, NULL)*, that is equivalent to the above statement?

29-2. Aside from the absence of error checking and various variable and structure declarations, what is the problem with the following program?

```
static void *
threadFunc(void *arg)
{
    struct someStruct *pbuf = (struct someStruct *) arg;

    /* Do some work with structure pointed to by 'pbuf' */
}

int
main(int argc, char *argv[])
{
    struct someStruct buf;

    pthread_create(&thr, NULL, threadFunc, (void *) &buf);
    pthread_exit(NULL);
}
```

30

THREADS: THREAD
SYNCHRONIZATION

In this chapter, we describe two tools that threads can use to synchronize their actions: mutexes and condition variables. Mutexes allow threads to synchronize their use of a shared resource, so that, for example, one thread doesn't try to access a shared variable at the same time as another thread is modifying it. Condition variables perform a complementary task: they allow threads to inform each other that a shared variable (or other shared resource) has changed state.

30.1 Protecting Accesses to Shared Variables: Mutexes

One of the principal advantages of threads is that they can share information via global variables. However, this easy sharing comes at a cost: we must take care that multiple threads do not attempt to modify the same variable at the same time, or that one thread doesn't try to read the value of a variable while another thread is modifying it. The term *critical section* is used to refer to a section of code that accesses a shared resource and whose execution should be *atomic*; that is, its execution should not be interrupted by another thread that simultaneously accesses the same shared resource.

Listing 30-1 provides a simple example of the kind of problems that can occur when shared resources are not accessed atomically. This program creates two threads, each of which executes the same function. The function executes a loop that repeatedly increments a global variable, *glob*, by copying *glob* into the local variable *loc*, incrementing *loc*, and copying *loc* back to *glob*. (Since *loc* is an automatic variable allocated on the per-thread stack, each thread has its own copy of this variable.) The number of iterations of the loop is determined by the command-line argument supplied to the program, or by a default value, if no argument is supplied.

Listing 30-1: Incorrectly incrementing a global variable from two threads

———————————————————————— **threads/thread_incr.c**
```
#include <pthread.h>
#include "tlpi_hdr.h"

static volatile int glob = 0;    /* "volatile" prevents compiler optimizations
                                    of arithmetic operations on 'glob' */

static void *                    /* Loop 'arg' times incrementing 'glob' */
threadFunc(void *arg)
{
    int loops = *((int *) arg);
    int loc, j;

    for (j = 0; j < loops; j++) {
        loc = glob;
        loc++;
        glob = loc;
    }

    return NULL;
}

int
main(int argc, char *argv[])
{
    pthread_t t1, t2;
    int loops, s;

    loops = (argc > 1) ? getInt(argv[1], GN_GT_0, "num-loops") : 10000000;

    s = pthread_create(&t1, NULL, threadFunc, &loops);
    if (s != 0)
        errExitEN(s, "pthread_create");
    s = pthread_create(&t2, NULL, threadFunc, &loops);
    if (s != 0)
        errExitEN(s, "pthread_create");

    s = pthread_join(t1, NULL);
    if (s != 0)
        errExitEN(s, "pthread_join");
    s = pthread_join(t2, NULL);
    if (s != 0)
        errExitEN(s, "pthread_join");

    printf("glob = %d\n", glob);
    exit(EXIT_SUCCESS);
}
```
———————————————————————— **threads/thread_incr.c**

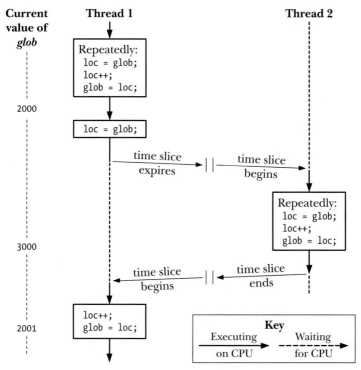

Figure 30-1: Two threads incrementing a global variable without synchronization

When we run the program in Listing 30-1 specifying that each thread should increment the variable 1000 times, all seems well:

```
$ ./thread_incr 1000
glob = 2000
```

However, what has probably happened here is that the first thread completed all of its work and terminated before the second thread even started. When we ask both threads to do a lot more work, we see a rather different result:

```
$ ./thread_incr 10000000
glob = 16517656
```

At the end of this sequence, the value of *glob* should have been 20 million. The problem here results from execution sequences such as the following (see also Figure 30-1, above):

1. Thread 1 fetches the current value of *glob* into its local variable *loc*. Let's assume that the current value of *glob* is 2000.

2. The scheduler time slice for thread 1 expires, and thread 2 commences execution.

3. Thread 2 performs multiple loops in which it fetches the current value of *glob* into its local variable *loc*, increments *loc*, and assigns the result to *glob*. In the first of these loops, the value fetched from *glob* will be 2000. Let's suppose that by the time the time slice for thread 2 has expired, *glob* has been increased to 3000.

4. Thread 1 receives another time slice and resumes execution where it left off. Having previously (step 1) copied the value of *glob* (2000) into its *loc*, it now increments *loc* and assigns the result (2001) to *glob*. At this point, the effect of the increment operations performed by thread 2 is lost.

If we run the program in Listing 30-1 multiple times with the same command-line argument, we see that the printed value of *glob* fluctuates wildly:

```
$ ./thread_incr 10000000
glob = 10880429
$ ./thread_incr 10000000
glob = 13493953
```

This nondeterministic behavior is a consequence of the vagaries of the kernel's CPU scheduling decisions. In complex programs, this nondeterministic behavior means that such errors may occur only rarely, be hard to reproduce, and therefore be difficult to find.

It might seem that we could eliminate the problem by replacing the three statements inside the for loop in the *threadFunc()* function in Listing 30-1 with a single statement:

```
glob++;                /* or: ++glob; */
```

However, on many hardware architectures (e.g., RISC architectures), the compiler would still need to convert this single statement into machine code whose steps are equivalent to the three statements inside the loop in *threadFunc()*. In other words, despite its simple appearance, even a C increment operator may not be atomic, and it might demonstrate the behavior that we described above.

To avoid the problems that can occur when threads try to update a shared variable, we must use a *mutex* (short for *mutual exclusion*) to ensure that only one thread at a time can access the variable. More generally, mutexes can be used to ensure atomic access to any shared resource, but protecting shared variables is the most common use.

A mutex has two states: *locked* and *unlocked*. At any moment, at most one thread may hold the lock on a mutex. Attempting to lock a mutex that is already locked either blocks or fails with an error, depending on the method used to place the lock.

When a thread locks a mutex, it becomes the owner of that mutex. Only the mutex owner can unlock the mutex. This property improves the structure of code that uses mutexes and also allows for some optimizations in the implementation of mutexes. Because of this ownership property, the terms *acquire* and *release* are sometimes used synonymously for lock and unlock.

In general, we employ a different mutex for each shared resource (which may consist of multiple related variables), and each thread employs the following protocol for accessing a resource:

- lock the mutex for the shared resource;
- access the shared resource; and
- unlock the mutex.

If multiple threads try to execute this block of code (a *critical section*), the fact that only one thread can hold the mutex (the others remain blocked) means that only one thread at a time can enter the block, as illustrated in Figure 30-2.

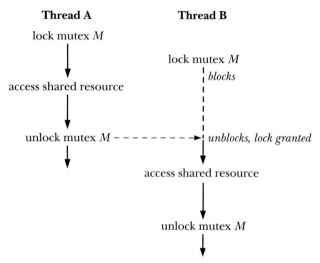

Figure 30-2: Using a mutex to protect a critical section

Finally, note that mutex locking is advisory, rather than mandatory. By this, we mean that a thread is free to ignore the use of a mutex and simply access the corresponding shared variable(s). In order to safely handle shared variables, all threads must cooperate in their use of a mutex, abiding by its locking rules.

30.1.1 Statically Allocated Mutexes

A mutex can either be allocated as a static variable or be created dynamically at run time (for example, in a block of memory allocated via *malloc()*). Dynamic mutex creation is somewhat more complex, and we delay discussion of it until Section 30.1.5.

A mutex is a variable of the type *pthread_mutex_t*. Before it can be used, a mutex must always be initialized. For a statically allocated mutex, we can do this by assigning it the value PTHREAD_MUTEX_INITIALIZER, as in the following example:

```
pthread_mutex_t mtx = PTHREAD_MUTEX_INITIALIZER;
```

> According to SUSv3, applying the operations that we describe in the remainder of this section to a *copy* of a mutex yields results that are undefined. Mutex operations should always be performed only on the original mutex that has been statically initialized using PTHREAD_MUTEX_INITIALIZER or dynamically initialized using *pthread_mutex_init()* (described in Section 30.1.5).

30.1.2 Locking and Unlocking a Mutex

After initialization, a mutex is unlocked. To lock and unlock a mutex, we use the *pthread_mutex_lock()* and *pthread_mutex_unlock()* functions.

```
#include <pthread.h>

int pthread_mutex_lock(pthread_mutex_t *mutex);
int pthread_mutex_unlock(pthread_mutex_t *mutex);
```
                     Both return 0 on success, or a positive error number on error

To lock a mutex, we specify the mutex in a call to *pthread_mutex_lock()*. If the mutex is currently unlocked, this call locks the mutex and returns immediately. If the mutex is currently locked by another thread, then *pthread_mutex_lock()* blocks until the mutex is unlocked, at which point it locks the mutex and returns.

If the calling thread itself has already locked the mutex given to *pthread_mutex_lock()*, then, for the default type of mutex, one of two implementation-defined possibilities may result: the thread deadlocks, blocked trying to lock a mutex that it already owns, or the call fails, returning the error EDEADLK. On Linux, the thread deadlocks by default. (We describe some other possible behaviors when we look at mutex types in Section 30.1.7.)

The *pthread_mutex_unlock()* function unlocks a mutex previously locked by the calling thread. It is an error to unlock a mutex that is not currently locked, or to unlock a mutex that is locked by another thread.

If more than one other thread is waiting to acquire the mutex unlocked by a call to *pthread_mutex_unlock()*, it is indeterminate which thread will succeed in acquiring it.

Example program

Listing 30-2 is a modified version of the program in Listing 30-1. It uses a mutex to protect access to the global variable *glob*. When we run this program with a similar command line to that used earlier, we see that *glob* is always reliably incremented:

```
$ ./thread_incr_mutex 10000000
glob = 20000000
```

Listing 30-2: Using a mutex to protect access to a global variable

─── **threads/thread_incr_mutex.c**
```
#include <pthread.h>
#include "tlpi_hdr.h"

static volatile int glob = 0;
static pthread_mutex_t mtx = PTHREAD_MUTEX_INITIALIZER;

static void *                    /* Loop 'arg' times incrementing 'glob' */
threadFunc(void *arg)
{
    int loops = *((int *) arg);
    int loc, j, s;

    for (j = 0; j < loops; j++) {
        s = pthread_mutex_lock(&mtx);
        if (s != 0)
            errExitEN(s, "pthread_mutex_lock");
```

```
        loc = glob;
        loc++;
        glob = loc;

        s = pthread_mutex_unlock(&mtx);
        if (s != 0)
            errExitEN(s, "pthread_mutex_unlock");
    }

    return NULL;
}

int
main(int argc, char *argv[])
{
    pthread_t t1, t2;
    int loops, s;

    loops = (argc > 1) ? getInt(argv[1], GN_GT_0, "num-loops") : 10000000;

    s = pthread_create(&t1, NULL, threadFunc, &loops);
    if (s != 0)
        errExitEN(s, "pthread_create");
    s = pthread_create(&t2, NULL, threadFunc, &loops);
    if (s != 0)
        errExitEN(s, "pthread_create");

    s = pthread_join(t1, NULL);
    if (s != 0)
        errExitEN(s, "pthread_join");
    s = pthread_join(t2, NULL);
    if (s != 0)
        errExitEN(s, "pthread_join");

    printf("glob = %d\n", glob);
    exit(EXIT_SUCCESS);
}
```

——————————————————————————————————————— **threads/thread_incr_mutex.c**

pthread_mutex_trylock() **and** *pthread_mutex_timedlock()*

The Pthreads API provides two variants of the *pthread_mutex_lock()* function: *pthread_mutex_trylock()* and *pthread_mutex_timedlock()*. (See the manual pages for prototypes of these functions.)

The *pthread_mutex_trylock()* function is the same as *pthread_mutex_lock()*, except that if the mutex is currently locked, *pthread_mutex_trylock()* fails, returning the error EBUSY.

The *pthread_mutex_timedlock()* function is the same as *pthread_mutex_lock()*, except that the caller can specify an additional argument, *abstime*, that places a limit on the time that the thread will sleep while waiting to acquire the mutex. If the time interval specified by its *abstime* argument expires without the caller becoming the owner of the mutex, *pthread_mutex_timedlock()* returns the error ETIMEDOUT.

The *pthread_mutex_trylock()* and *pthread_mutex_timedlock()* functions are much less frequently used than *pthread_mutex_lock()*. In most well-designed applications, a thread should hold a mutex for only a short time, so that other threads are not prevented from executing in parallel. This guarantees that other threads that are blocked on the mutex will soon be granted a lock on the mutex. A thread that uses *pthread_mutex_trylock()* to periodically poll the mutex to see if it can be locked risks being starved of access to the mutex while other queued threads are successively granted access to the mutex via *pthread_mutex_lock()*.

30.1.3 Performance of Mutexes

What is the cost of using a mutex? We have shown two different versions of a program that increments a shared variable: one without mutexes (Listing 30-1) and one with mutexes (Listing 30-2). When we run these two programs on an x86-32 system running Linux 2.6.31 (with NPTL), we find that the version without mutexes requires a total of 0.35 seconds to execute 10 million loops in each thread (and produces the wrong result), while the version with mutexes requires 3.1 seconds.

At first, this seems expensive. But, consider the main loop executed by the version that does not employ a mutex (Listing 30-1). In that version, the *threadFunc()* function executes a for loop that increments a loop control variable, compares that variable against another variable, performs two assignments and another increment operation, and then branches back to the top of the loop. The version that uses a mutex (Listing 30-2) performs the same steps, and locks and unlocks the mutex each time around the loop. In other words, the cost of locking and unlocking a mutex is somewhat less than ten times the cost of the operations that we listed for the first program. This is relatively cheap. Furthermore, in the typical case, a thread would spend much more time doing other work, and perform relatively fewer mutex lock and unlock operations, so that the performance impact of using a mutex is not significant in most applications.

To put this further in perspective, running some simple test programs on the same system showed that 20 million loops locking and unlocking a file region using *fcntl()* (Section 55.3) require 44 seconds, and 20 million loops incrementing and decrementing a System V semaphore (Chapter 47) require 28 seconds. The problem with file locks and semaphores is that they always require a system call for the lock and unlock operations, and each system call has a small, but appreciable, cost (Section 3.1). By contrast, mutexes are implemented using atomic machine-language operations (performed on memory locations visible to all threads) and require system calls only in case of lock contention.

> On Linux, mutexes are implemented using *futexes* (an acronym derived from *fast user space mutexes*), and lock contentions are dealt with using the *futex()* system call. We don't describe futexes in this book (they are not intended for direct use in user-space applications), but details can be found in [Drepper, 2004 (a)], which also describes how mutexes are implemented using futexes. [Franke et al., 2002] is a (now outdated) paper written by the developers of futexes, which describes the early futex implementation and looks at the performance gains derived from futexes.

30.1.4 Mutex Deadlocks

Sometimes, a thread needs to simultaneously access two or more different shared resources, each of which is governed by a separate mutex. When more than one thread is locking the same set of mutexes, deadlock situations can arise. Figure 30-3 shows an example of a deadlock in which each thread successfully locks one mutex, and then tries to lock the mutex that the other thread has already locked. Both threads will remain blocked indefinitely.

Thread A	Thread B
1. *pthread_mutex_lock(mutex1);*	1. *pthread_mutex_lock(mutex2);*
2. *pthread_mutex_lock(mutex2);*	2. *pthread_mutex_lock(mutex1);*
blocks	blocks

Figure 30-3: A deadlock when two threads lock two mutexes

The simplest way to avoid such deadlocks is to define a mutex hierarchy. When threads can lock the same set of mutexes, they should always lock them in the same order. For example, in the scenario in Figure 30-3, the deadlock could be avoided if the two threads always lock the mutexes in the order *mutex1* followed by *mutex2*. Sometimes, there is a logically obvious hierarchy of mutexes. However, even if there isn't, it may be possible to devise an arbitrary hierarchical order that all threads should follow.

An alternative strategy that is less frequently used is "try, and then back off." In this strategy, a thread locks the first mutex using *pthread_mutex_lock()*, and then locks the remaining mutexes using *pthread_mutex_trylock()*. If any of the *pthread_mutex_trylock()* calls fails (with EBUSY), then the thread releases all mutexes, and then tries again, perhaps after a delay interval. This approach is less efficient than a lock hierarchy, since multiple iterations may be required. On the other hand, it can be more flexible, since it doesn't require a rigid mutex hierarchy. An example of this strategy is shown in [Butenhof, 1996].

30.1.5 Dynamically Initializing a Mutex

The static initializer value PTHREAD_MUTEX_INITIALIZER can be used only for initializing a statically allocated mutex with default attributes. In all other cases, we must dynamically initialize the mutex using *pthread_mutex_init()*.

```
#include <pthread.h>

int pthread_mutex_init(pthread_mutex_t *mutex, const pthread_mutexattr_t *attr);
```
Returns 0 on success, or a positive error number on error

The *mutex* argument identifies the mutex to be initialized. The *attr* argument is a pointer to a *pthread_mutexattr_t* object that has previously been initialized to define the attributes for the mutex. (We say some more about mutex attributes in the next section.) If *attr* is specified as NULL, then the mutex is assigned various default attributes.

SUSv3 specifies that initializing an already initialized mutex results in undefined behavior; we should not do this.

Among the cases where we must use *pthread_mutex_init()* rather than a static initializer are the following:

- The mutex was dynamically allocated on the heap. For example, suppose that we create a dynamically allocated linked list of structures, and each structure in the list includes a *pthread_mutex_t* field that holds a mutex that is used to protect access to that structure.

- The mutex is an automatic variable allocated on the stack.

- We want to initialize a statically allocated mutex with attributes other than the defaults.

When an automatically or dynamically allocated mutex is no longer required, it should be destroyed using *pthread_mutex_destroy()*. (It is not necessary to call *pthread_mutex_destroy()* on a mutex that was statically initialized using PTHREAD_MUTEX_INITIALIZER.)

```
#include <pthread.h>

int pthread_mutex_destroy(pthread_mutex_t *mutex);
```
                            Returns 0 on success, or a positive error number on error

It is safe to destroy a mutex only when it is unlocked, and no thread will subsequently try to lock it. If the mutex resides in a region of dynamically allocated memory, then it should be destroyed before freeing that memory region. An automatically allocated mutex should be destroyed before its host function returns.

A mutex that has been destroyed with *pthread_mutex_destroy()* can subsequently be reinitialized by *pthread_mutex_init()*.

30.1.6 Mutex Attributes

As noted earlier, the *pthread_mutex_init()* *attr* argument can be used to specify a *pthread_mutexattr_t* object that defines the attributes of a mutex. Various Pthreads functions can be used to initialize and retrieve the attributes in a *pthread_mutexattr_t* object. We won't go into all of the details of mutex attributes or show the prototypes of the various functions that can be used to initialize the attributes in a *pthread_mutexattr_t* object. However, we'll describe one of the attributes that can be set for a mutex: its type.

30.1.7 Mutex Types

In the preceding pages, we made a number of statements about the behavior of mutexes:

- A single thread may not lock the same mutex twice.

- A thread may not unlock a mutex that it doesn't currently own (i.e., that it did not lock).

- A thread may not unlock a mutex that is not currently locked.

Precisely what happens in each of these cases depends on the *type* of the mutex. SUSv3 defines the following mutex types:

PTHREAD_MUTEX_NORMAL

> (Self-)deadlock detection is not provided for this type of mutex. If a thread tries to lock a mutex that it has already locked, then deadlock results. Unlocking a mutex that is not locked or that is locked by another thread produces undefined results. (On Linux, both of these operations succeed for this mutex type.)

PTHREAD_MUTEX_ERRORCHECK

> Error checking is performed on all operations. All three of the above scenarios cause the relevant Pthreads function to return an error. This type of mutex is typically slower than a normal mutex, but can be useful as a debugging tool to discover where an application is violating the rules about how a mutex should be used.

PTHREAD_MUTEX_RECURSIVE

> A recursive mutex maintains the concept of a lock count. When a thread first acquires the mutex, the lock count is set to 1. Each subsequent lock operation by the same thread increments the lock count, and each unlock operation decrements the count. The mutex is released (i.e., made available for other threads to acquire) only when the lock count falls to 0. Unlocking an unlocked mutex fails, as does unlocking a mutex that is currently locked by another thread.

The Linux threading implementation provides nonstandard static initializers for each of the above mutex types (e.g., PTHREAD_RECURSIVE_MUTEX_INITIALIZER_NP), so that the use of *pthread_mutex_init()* is not required to initialize these mutex types for statically allocated mutexes. However, portable applications should avoid the use of these initializers.

In addition to the above mutex types, SUSv3 defines the PTHREAD_MUTEX_DEFAULT type, which is the default type of mutex if we use PTHREAD_MUTEX_INITIALIZER or specify *attr* as NULL in a call to *pthread_mutex_init()*. The behavior of this mutex type is deliberately undefined in all three of the scenarios described at the start of this section, which allows maximum flexibility for efficient implementation of mutexes. On Linux, a PTHREAD_MUTEX_DEFAULT mutex behaves like a PTHREAD_MUTEX_NORMAL mutex.

The code shown in Listing 30-3 demonstrates how to set the type of a mutex, in this case to create an *error-checking* mutex.

Listing 30-3: Setting the mutex type

```
pthread_mutex_t mtx;
pthread_mutexattr_t mtxAttr;
int s, type;

s = pthread_mutexattr_init(&mtxAttr);
if (s != 0)
    errExitEN(s, "pthread_mutexattr_init");
```

```
    s = pthread_mutexattr_settype(&mtxAttr, PTHREAD_MUTEX_ERRORCHECK);
    if (s != 0)
        errExitEN(s, "pthread_mutexattr_settype");

    s = pthread_mutex_init(&mtx, &mtxAttr);
    if (s != 0)
        errExitEN(s, "pthread_mutex_init");

    s = pthread_mutexattr_destroy(&mtxAttr);          /* No longer needed */
    if (s != 0)
        errExitEN(s, "pthread_mutexattr_destroy");
```

30.2 Signaling Changes of State: Condition Variables

A mutex prevents multiple threads from accessing a shared variable at the same time. A condition variable allows one thread to inform other threads about changes in the state of a shared variable (or other shared resource) and allows the other threads to wait (block) for such notification.

A simple example that doesn't use condition variables serves to demonstrate why they are useful. Suppose that we have a number of threads that produce some "result units" that are consumed by the main thread, and that we use a mutex-protected variable, *avail*, to represent the number of produced units awaiting consumption:

```
static pthread_mutex_t mtx = PTHREAD_MUTEX_INITIALIZER;

static int avail = 0;
```

> The code segments shown in this section can be found in the file threads/ prod_no_condvar.c in the source code distribution for this book.

In the producer threads, we would have code such as the following:

```
/* Code to produce a unit omitted */

s = pthread_mutex_lock(&mtx);
if (s != 0)
    errExitEN(s, "pthread_mutex_lock");

avail++;    /* Let consumer know another unit is available */

s = pthread_mutex_unlock(&mtx);
if (s != 0)
    errExitEN(s, "pthread_mutex_unlock");
```

And in the main (consumer) thread, we could employ the following code:

```
for (;;) {
    s = pthread_mutex_lock(&mtx);
    if (s != 0)
        errExitEN(s, "pthread_mutex_lock");
```

```
        while (avail > 0) {          /* Consume all available units */
            /* Do something with produced unit */
            avail--;
        }

        s = pthread_mutex_unlock(&mtx);
        if (s != 0)
            errExitEN(s, "pthread_mutex_unlock");
    }
```

The above code works, but it wastes CPU time, because the main thread continu-ally loops, checking the state of the variable *avail*. A *condition variable* remedies this problem. It allows a thread to sleep (wait) until another thread notifies (signals) it that it must do something (i.e., that some "condition" has arisen that the sleeper must now respond to).

A condition variable is always used in conjunction with a mutex. The mutex provides mutual exclusion for accessing the shared variable, while the condition variable is used to signal changes in the variable's state. (The use of the term *signal* here has nothing to do with the signals described in Chapters 20 to 22; rather, it is used in the sense of *indicate*.)

30.2.1 Statically Allocated Condition Variables

As with mutexes, condition variables can be allocated statically or dynamically. We defer discussion of dynamically allocated condition variables until Section 30.2.5, and consider statically allocated condition variables here.

A condition variable has the type *pthread_cond_t*. As with a mutex, a condition variable must be initialized before use. For a statically allocated condition variable, this is done by assigning it the value PTHREAD_COND_INITIALIZER, as in the following example:

```
pthread_cond_t cond = PTHREAD_COND_INITIALIZER;
```

> According to SUSv3, applying the operations that we describe in the remain-der of this section to a *copy* of a condition variable yields results that are unde-fined. Operations should always be performed only on the original condition variable that has been statically initialized using PTHREAD_COND_INITIALIZER or dynamically initialized using *pthread_cond_init()* (described in Section 30.2.5).

30.2.2 Signaling and Waiting on Condition Variables

The principal condition variable operations are *signal* and *wait*. The signal opera-tion is a notification to one or more waiting threads that a shared variable's state has changed. The wait operation is the means of blocking until such a notification is received.

The *pthread_cond_signal()* and *pthread_cond_broadcast()* functions both signal the condition variable specified by *cond*. The *pthread_cond_wait()* function blocks a thread until the condition variable *cond* is signaled.

```
#include <pthread.h>

int pthread_cond_signal(pthread_cond_t *cond);
int pthread_cond_broadcast(pthread_cond_t *cond);
int pthread_cond_wait(pthread_cond_t *cond, pthread_mutex_t *mutex);
```
                    All return 0 on success, or a positive error number on error

The difference between *pthread_cond_signal()* and *pthread_cond_broadcast()* lies in what happens if multiple threads are blocked in *pthread_cond_wait()*. With *pthread_cond_signal()*, we are simply guaranteed that at least one of the blocked threads is woken up; with *pthread_cond_broadcast()*, all blocked threads are woken up.

Using *pthread_cond_broadcast()* always yields correct results (since all threads should be programmed to handle redundant and spurious wake-ups), but *pthread_cond_signal()* can be more efficient. However, *pthread_cond_signal()* should be used only if just one of the waiting threads needs to be woken up to handle the change in state of the shared variable, and it doesn't matter which one of the waiting threads is woken up. This scenario typically applies when all of the waiting threads are designed to perform exactly the same task. Given these assumptions, *pthread_cond_signal()* can be more efficient than *pthread_cond_broadcast()*, because it avoids the following possibility:

1. All waiting threads are awoken.
2. One thread is scheduled first. This thread checks the state of the shared variable(s) (under protection of the associated mutex) and sees that there is work to be done. The thread performs the required work, changes the state of the shared variable(s) to indicate that the work has been done, and unlocks the associated mutex.
3. Each of the remaining threads in turn locks the mutex and tests the state of the shared variable. However, because of the change made by the first thread, these threads see that there is no work to be done, and so unlock the mutex and go back to sleep (i.e., call *pthread_cond_wait()* once more).

By contrast, *pthread_cond_broadcast()* handles the case where the waiting threads are designed to perform different tasks (in which case they probably have different predicates associated with the condition variable).

A condition variable holds no state information. It is simply a mechanism for communicating information about the application's state. If no thread is waiting on the condition variable at the time that it is signaled, then the signal is lost. A thread that later waits on the condition variable will unblock only when the variable is signaled once more.

The *pthread_cond_timedwait()* function is the same as *pthread_cond_wait()*, except that the *abstime* argument specifies an upper limit on the time that the thread will sleep while waiting for the condition variable to be signaled.

```
#include <pthread.h>

int pthread_cond_timedwait(pthread_cond_t *cond, pthread_mutex_t *mutex,
                           const struct timespec *abstime);
```
Returns 0 on success, or a positive error number on error

The *abstime* argument is a *timespec* structure (Section 23.4.2) specifying an absolute time expressed as seconds and nanoseconds since the Epoch (Section 10.1). If the time interval specified by *abstime* expires without the condition variable being signaled, then *pthread_cond_timedwait()* returns the error ETIMEDOUT.

Using a condition variable in the producer-consumer example

Let's revise our previous example to use a condition variable. The declarations of our global variable and associated mutex and condition variable are as follows:

```
static pthread_mutex_t mtx = PTHREAD_MUTEX_INITIALIZER;
static pthread_cond_t cond = PTHREAD_COND_INITIALIZER;

static int avail = 0;
```

> The code segments shown in this section can be found in the file threads/prod_condvar.c in the source code distribution for this book.

The code in the producer threads is the same as before, except that we add a call to *pthread_cond_signal()*:

```
s = pthread_mutex_lock(&mtx);
if (s != 0)
    errExitEN(s, "pthread_mutex_lock");

avail++;                    /* Let consumer know another unit is available */

s = pthread_mutex_unlock(&mtx);
if (s != 0)
    errExitEN(s, "pthread_mutex_unlock");

s = pthread_cond_signal(&cond);        /* Wake sleeping consumer */
if (s != 0)
    errExitEN(s, "pthread_cond_signal");
```

Before considering the code of the consumer, we need to explain *pthread_cond_wait()* in greater detail. We noted earlier that a condition variable always has an associated mutex. Both of these objects are passed as arguments to *pthread_cond_wait()*, which performs the following steps:

- unlock the mutex specified by *mutex*;
- block the calling thread until another thread signals the condition variable *cond*; and
- relock *mutex*.

The *pthread_cond_wait()* function is designed to perform these steps because, normally, we access a shared variable in the following manner:

```
s = pthread_mutex_lock(&mtx);
if (s != 0)
    errExitEN(s, "pthread_mutex_lock");

while (/* Check that shared variable is not in state we want */)
    pthread_cond_wait(&cond, &mtx);

/* Now shared variable is in desired state; do some work */

s = pthread_mutex_unlock(&mtx);
if (s != 0)
    errExitEN(s, "pthread_mutex_unlock");
```

(We explain why the *pthread_cond_wait()* call is placed within a while loop rather than an if statement in the next section.)

In the above code, both accesses to the shared variable must be mutex-protected for the reasons that we explained earlier. In other words, there is a natural association of a mutex with a condition variable:

1. The thread locks the mutex in preparation for checking the state of the shared variable.

2. The state of the shared variable is checked.

3. If the shared variable is not in the desired state, then the thread must unlock the mutex (so that other threads can access the shared variable) before it goes to sleep on the condition variable.

4. When the thread is reawakened because the condition variable has been signaled, the mutex must once more be locked, since, typically, the thread then immediately accesses the shared variable.

The *pthread_cond_wait()* function automatically performs the mutex unlocking and locking required in the last two of these steps. In the third step, releasing the mutex and blocking on the condition variable are performed atomically. In other words, it is not possible for some other thread to acquire the mutex and signal the condition variable before the thread calling *pthread_cond_wait()* has blocked on the condition variable.

> There is a corollary to the observation that there is a natural relationship between a condition variable and a mutex: all threads that concurrently wait on a particular condition variable must specify the same mutex in their *pthread_cond_wait()* (or *pthread_cond_timedwait()*) calls. In effect, a *pthread_cond_wait()* call dynamically binds a condition variable to a unique mutex for the duration of the call. SUSv3 notes that the result of using more than one mutex for concurrent *pthread_cond_wait()* calls on the same condition variable is undefined.
>
> Chapter 32, which describes thread cancellation, notes that *pthread_cond_wait()* is a cancellation point. If a thread is canceled while blocked in a call to *pthread_cond_wait()*, then the mutex is relocked before the first cancellation cleanup handler is called. This means a cleanup handler can safely unlock the mutex (as is done, for example, in Listing 32-2).

Putting the above details together, we can now modify the main (consumer) thread to use *pthread_cond_wait()*, as follows:

```
for (;;) {
    s = pthread_mutex_lock(&mtx);
    if (s != 0)
        errExitEN(s, "pthread_mutex_lock");

    while (avail == 0) {            /* Wait for something to consume */
        s = pthread_cond_wait(&cond, &mtx);
        if (s != 0)
            errExitEN(s, "pthread_cond_wait");
    }

    while (avail > 0) {             /* Consume all available units */
        /* Do something with produced unit */
        avail--;
    }

    s = pthread_mutex_unlock(&mtx);
    if (s != 0)
        errExitEN(s, "pthread_mutex_unlock");

    /* Perhaps do other work here that doesn't require mutex lock */
}
```

We conclude with one final observation about the use of *pthread_cond_signal()* (and *pthread_cond_broadcast()*). In the producer code shown earlier, we called *pthread_mutex_unlock()*, and then called *pthread_cond_signal()*; that is, we first unlocked the mutex associated with the shared variable, and then signaled the corresponding condition variable. We could have reversed these two steps; SUSv3 permits them to be done in either order.

> [Butenhof, 1996] points out that, on some implementations, unlocking the mutex and then signaling the condition variable may yield better performance than performing these steps in the reverse sequence. If the mutex is unlocked only after the condition variable is signaled, the thread performing *pthread_cond_wait()* may wake up while the mutex is still locked, and then immediately go back to sleep again when it finds that the mutex is locked. This results in two superfluous context switches. Some implementations eliminate this problem by employing a technique called *wait morphing*, which moves the signaled thread from the condition variable wait queue to the mutex wait queue without performing a context switch if the mutex is locked.

30.2.3 Testing a Condition Variable's Predicate

Each condition variable has an associated predicate involving one or more shared variables. For example, in the code segment in the preceding section, the predicate associated with *cond* is *(avail == 0)*. This code segment demonstrates a general design principle: a *pthread_cond_wait()* call must be governed by a while loop rather than an if statement. This is so because, on return from *pthread_cond_wait()*, there are no guarantees about the state of the predicate; therefore, we should immediately recheck the predicate and resume sleeping if it is not in the desired state.

We can't make any assumptions about the state of the predicate upon return from *pthread_cond_wait()*, for the following reasons:

- *Other threads may be woken up first.* Perhaps several threads were waiting to acquire the mutex associated with the condition variable. Even if the thread that signaled the mutex set the predicate to the desired state, it is still possible that another thread might acquire the mutex first and change the state of the associated shared variable(s), and thus the state of the predicate.

- *Designing for "loose" predicates may be simpler.* Sometimes, it is easier to design applications based on condition variables that indicate *possibility* rather than *certainty*. In other words, signaling a condition variable would mean "there *may be* something" for the signaled thread to do, rather than "there *is* something" to do. Using this approach, the condition variable can be signaled based on approximations of the predicate's state, and the signaled thread can ascertain if there really is something to do by rechecking the predicate.

- *Spurious wake-ups can occur.* On some implementations, a thread waiting on a condition variable may be woken up even though no other thread actually signaled the condition variable. Such spurious wake-ups are a (rare) consequence of the techniques required for efficient implementation on some multiprocessor systems, and are explicitly permitted by SUSv3.

30.2.4 Example Program: Joining Any Terminated Thread

We noted earlier that *pthread_join()* can be used to join with only a specific thread. It provides no mechanism for joining with *any* terminated thread. We now show how a condition variable can be used to circumvent this restriction.

The program in Listing 30-4 creates one thread for each of its command-line arguments. Each thread sleeps for the number of seconds specified in the corresponding command-line argument and then terminates. The sleep interval is our means of simulating the idea of a thread that does work for a period of time.

The program maintains a set of global variables recording information about all of the threads that have been created. For each thread, an element in the global *thread* array records the ID of the thread (the *tid* field) and its current state (the *state* field). The *state* field has one of the following values: TS_ALIVE, meaning the thread is alive; TS_TERMINATED, meaning the thread has terminated but not yet been joined; or TS_JOINED, meaning the thread has terminated and been joined.

As each thread terminates, it assigns the value TS_TERMINATED to the *state* field for its element in the *thread* array, increments a global counter of terminated but as yet unjoined threads (*numUnjoined*), and signals the condition variable *threadDied*.

The main thread employs a loop that continuously waits on the condition variable *threadDied*. Whenever *threadDied* is signaled and there are terminated threads that have not been joined, the main thread scans the *thread* array, looking for elements with *state* set to TS_TERMINATED. For each thread in this state, *pthread_join()* is called using the corresponding *tid* field from the *thread* array, and then the *state* is set to TS_JOINED. The main loop terminates when all of the threads created by the main thread have died—that is, when the global variable *numLive* is 0.

The following shell session log demonstrates the use of the program in Listing 30-4:

```
$ ./thread_multijoin 1 1 2 3 3          Create 5 threads
Thread 0 terminating
Thread 1 terminating
Reaped thread 0 (numLive=4)
Reaped thread 1 (numLive=3)
Thread 2 terminating
Reaped thread 2 (numLive=2)
Thread 3 terminating
Thread 4 terminating
Reaped thread 3 (numLive=1)
Reaped thread 4 (numLive=0)
```

Finally, note that although the threads in the example program are created as join-able and are immediately reaped on termination using *pthread_join()*, we don't need to use this approach in order to find out about thread termination. We could have made the threads detached, removed the use of *pthread_join()*, and simply used the *thread* array (and associated global variables) as the means of recording the termination of each thread.

Listing 30-4: A main thread that can join with any terminated thread

── **threads/thread_multijoin.c**

```c
#include <pthread.h>
#include "tlpi_hdr.h"

static pthread_cond_t threadDied = PTHREAD_COND_INITIALIZER;
static pthread_mutex_t threadMutex = PTHREAD_MUTEX_INITIALIZER;
                /* Protects all of the following global variables */

static int totThreads = 0;      /* Total number of threads created */
static int numLive = 0;         /* Total number of threads still alive or
                                   terminated but not yet joined */
static int numUnjoined = 0;     /* Number of terminated threads that
                                   have not yet been joined */
enum tstate {                   /* Thread states */
    TS_ALIVE,                   /* Thread is alive */
    TS_TERMINATED,              /* Thread terminated, not yet joined */
    TS_JOINED                   /* Thread terminated, and joined */
};

static struct {                 /* Info about each thread */
    pthread_t tid;              /* ID of this thread */
    enum tstate state;          /* Thread state (TS_* constants above) */
    int sleepTime;              /* Number seconds to live before terminating */
} *thread;

static void *                   /* Start function for thread */
threadFunc(void *arg)
{
    int idx = (int) arg;
    int s;
```

```
        sleep(thread[idx].sleepTime);       /* Simulate doing some work */
        printf("Thread %d terminating\n", idx);

        s = pthread_mutex_lock(&threadMutex);
        if (s != 0)
            errExitEN(s, "pthread_mutex_lock");

        numUnjoined++;
        thread[idx].state = TS_TERMINATED;

        s = pthread_mutex_unlock(&threadMutex);
        if (s != 0)
            errExitEN(s, "pthread_mutex_unlock");
        s = pthread_cond_signal(&threadDied);
        if (s != 0)
            errExitEN(s, "pthread_cond_signal");

        return NULL;
    }

    int
    main(int argc, char *argv[])
    {
        int s, idx;

        if (argc < 2 || strcmp(argv[1], "--help") == 0)
            usageErr("%s nsecs...\n", argv[0]);

        thread = calloc(argc - 1, sizeof(*thread));
        if (thread == NULL)
            errExit("calloc");

        /* Create all threads */

        for (idx = 0; idx < argc - 1; idx++) {
            thread[idx].sleepTime = getInt(argv[idx + 1], GN_NONNEG, NULL);
            thread[idx].state = TS_ALIVE;
            s = pthread_create(&thread[idx].tid, NULL, threadFunc, (void *) idx);
            if (s != 0)
                errExitEN(s, "pthread_create");
        }

        totThreads = argc - 1;
        numLive = totThreads;

        /* Join with terminated threads */

        while (numLive > 0) {
            s = pthread_mutex_lock(&threadMutex);
            if (s != 0)
                errExitEN(s, "pthread_mutex_lock");
```

```
            while (numUnjoined == 0) {
                s = pthread_cond_wait(&threadDied, &threadMutex);
                if (s != 0)
                    errExitEN(s, "pthread_cond_wait");
            }

            for (idx = 0; idx < totThreads; idx++) {
                if (thread[idx].state == TS_TERMINATED) {
                    s = pthread_join(thread[idx].tid, NULL);
                    if (s != 0)
                        errExitEN(s, "pthread_join");

                    thread[idx].state = TS_JOINED;
                    numLive--;
                    numUnjoined--;

                    printf("Reaped thread %d (numLive=%d)\n", idx, numLive);
                }
            }

            s = pthread_mutex_unlock(&threadMutex);
            if (s != 0)
                errExitEN(s, "pthread_mutex_unlock");
        }

        exit(EXIT_SUCCESS);
    }
```
—— **threads/thread_multijoin.c**

30.2.5 Dynamically Allocated Condition Variables

The *pthread_cond_init()* function is used to dynamically initialize a condition variable. The circumstances in which we need to use *pthread_cond_init()* are analogous to those where *pthread_mutex_init()* is needed to dynamically initialize a mutex (Section 30.1.5); that is, we must use *pthread_cond_init()* to initialize automatically and dynamically allocated condition variables, and to initialize a statically allocated condition variable with attributes other than the defaults.

```
#include <pthread.h>

int pthread_cond_init(pthread_cond_t *cond, const pthread_condattr_t *attr);
```
                    Returns 0 on success, or a positive error number on error

---

The *cond* argument identifies the condition variable to be initialized. As with mutexes, we can specify an *attr* argument that has been previously initialized to determine attributes for the condition variable. Various Pthreads functions can be used to initialize the attributes in the *pthread_condattr_t* object pointed to by *attr*. If *attr* is NULL, a default set of attributes is assigned to the condition variable.

SUSv3 specifies that initializing an already initialized condition variable results in undefined behavior; we should not do this.

When an automatically or dynamically allocated condition variable is no longer required, then it should be destroyed using *pthread_cond_destroy()*. It is not necessary to call *pthread_cond_destroy()* on a condition variable that was statically initialized using PTHREAD_COND_INITIALIZER.

```
#include <pthread.h>

int pthread_cond_destroy(pthread_cond_t *cond);
```
                          Returns 0 on success, or a positive error number on error

It is safe to destroy a condition variable only when no threads are waiting on it. If the condition variable resides in a region of dynamically allocated memory, then it should be destroyed before freeing that memory region. An automatically allocated condition variable should be destroyed before its host function returns.

A condition variable that has been destroyed with *pthread_cond_destroy()* can subsequently be reinitialized by *pthread_cond_init()*.

30.3 Summary

The greater sharing provided by threads comes at a cost. Threaded applications must employ synchronization primitives such as mutexes and condition variables in order to coordinate access to shared variables. A mutex provides exclusive access to a shared variable. A condition variable allows one or more threads to wait for notification that some other thread has changed the state of a shared variable.

Further information

Refer to the sources of further information listed in Section 29.10.

30.4 Exercises

30-1. Modify the program in Listing 30-1 (thread_incr.c) so that each loop in the thread's start function outputs the current value of *glob* and some identifier that uniquely identifies the thread. The unique identifier for the thread could be specified as an argument to the *pthread_create()* call used to create the thread. For this program, that would require changing the argument of the thread's start function to be a pointer to a structure containing the unique identifier and a loop limit value. Run the program, redirecting output to a file, and then inspect the file to see what happens to *glob* as the kernel scheduler alternates execution between the two threads.

30-2. Implement a set of thread-safe functions that update and search an unbalanced binary tree. This library should include functions (with the obvious purposes) of the following form:

```
initialize(tree);
add(tree, char *key, void *value);
delete(tree, char *key)
Boolean lookup(char *key, void **value)
```

In the above prototypes, *tree* is a structure that points to the root of the tree (you will need to define a suitable structure for this purpose). Each element of the tree holds a key-value pair. You will also need to define the structure for each element to include a mutex that protects that element so that only one thread at a time can access it. The *initialize()*, *add()*, and *lookup()* functions are relatively simple to implement. The *delete()* operation requires a little more effort.

> Removing the need to maintain a balanced tree greatly simplifies the locking requirements of the implementation, but carries the risk that certain patterns of input would result in a tree that performs poorly. Maintaining a balanced tree necessitates moving nodes between subtrees during the *add()* and *delete()* operations, which requires much more complex locking strategies.

31

THREADS: THREAD SAFETY AND PER-THREAD STORAGE

This chapter extends the discussion of the POSIX threads API, providing a description of thread-safe functions and one-time initialization. We also discuss how to use thread-specific data or thread-local storage to make an existing function thread-safe without changing the function's interface.

31.1 Thread Safety (and Reentrancy Revisited)

A function is said to be *thread-safe* if it can safely be invoked by multiple threads at the same time; put conversely, if a function is not thread-safe, then we can't call it from one thread while it is being executed in another thread. For example, the following function (similar to code that we looked at in Section 30.1) is not thread-safe:

```
static int glob = 0;

static void
incr(int loops)
{
    int loc, j;
```

```
    for (j = 0; j < loops; j++) {
        loc = glob;
        loc++;
        glob = loc;
    }
}
```

If multiple threads invoke this function concurrently, the final value in *glob* is unpredictable. This function illustrates the typical reason that a function is not thread-safe: it employs global or static variables that are shared by all threads.

There are various methods of rendering a function thread-safe. One way is to associate a mutex with the function (or perhaps with all of the functions in a library, if they all share the same global variables), lock that mutex when the function is called, and unlock it when the function returns. This approach has the virtue of simplicity. On the other hand, it means that only one thread at a time can execute the function—we say that access to the function is *serialized*. If the threads spend a significant amount of time executing this function, then this serialization results in a loss of concurrency, because the threads of a program can no longer execute in parallel.

A more sophisticated solution is to associate the mutex with a shared variable. We then determine which parts of the function are critical sections that access the shared variable, and acquire and release the mutex only during the execution of these critical sections. This allows multiple threads to execute the function at the same time and to operate in parallel, except when more than one thread needs to execute a critical section.

Non-thread-safe functions

To facilitate the development of threaded applications, all of the functions specified in SUSv3 are required to be implemented in a thread-safe manner, except those listed in Table 31-1. (Many of these functions are not discussed in this book.)

In addition to the functions listed in Table 31-1, SUSv3 specifies the following:

- The *ctermid()* and *tmpnam()* functions need not be thread-safe if passed a NULL argument.

- The *wcrtomb()* and *wcsrtombs()* functions need not be thread-safe if their final argument (*ps*) is NULL.

SUSv4 modifies the list of functions in Table 31-1 as follows:

- The *ecvt()*, *fcvt()*, *gcvt()*, *gethostbyname()*, and *gethostbyaddr()* functions are removed, since these functions have been removed from the standard.

- The *strsignal()* and *system()* functions are added. The *system()* function is non-reentrant because the manipulations that it must make to signal dispositions have a process-wide effect.

The standards do not prohibit an implementation from making the functions in Table 31-1 thread-safe. However, even if some of these functions are thread-safe on some implementations, a portable application can't rely on this to be the case on all implementations.

Table 31-1: Functions that SUSv3 does not require to be thread-safe

asctime()	fcvt()	getpwnam()	nl_langinfo()
basename()	ftw()	getpwuid()	ptsname()
catgets()	gcvt()	getservbyname()	putc_unlocked()
crypt()	getc_unlocked()	getservbyport()	putchar_unlocked()
ctime()	getchar_unlocked()	getservent()	putenv()
dbm_clearerr()	getdate()	getutxent()	pututxline()
dbm_close()	getenv()	getutxid()	rand()
dbm_delete()	getgrent()	getutxline()	readdir()
dbm_error()	getgrgid()	gmtime()	setenv()
dbm_fetch()	getgrnam()	hcreate()	setgrent()
dbm_firstkey()	gethostbyaddr()	hdestroy()	setkey()
dbm_nextkey()	gethostbyname()	hsearch()	setpwent()
dbm_open()	gethostent()	inet_ntoa()	setutxent()
dbm_store()	getlogin()	l64a()	strerror()
dirname()	getnetbyaddr()	lgamma()	strtok()
dlerror()	getnetbyname()	lgammaf()	ttyname()
drand48()	getnetent()	lgammal()	unsetenv()
ecvt()	getopt()	localeconv()	wcstombs()
encrypt()	getprotobyname()	localtime()	wctomb()
endgrent()	getprotobynumber()	lrand48()	
endpwent()	getprotoent()	mrand48()	
endutxent()	getpwent()	nftw()	

Reentrant and nonreentrant functions

Although the use of critical sections to implement thread safety is a significant improvement over the use of per-function mutexes, it is still somewhat inefficient because there is a cost to locking and unlocking a mutex. A *reentrant function* achieves thread safety without the use of mutexes. It does this by avoiding the use of global and static variables. Any information that must be returned to the caller, or maintained between calls to the function, is stored in buffers allocated by the caller. (We first encountered reentrancy when discussing the treatment of global variables within signal handlers in Section 21.1.2.) However, not all functions can be made reentrant. The usual reasons are the following:

- By their nature, some functions must access global data structures. The functions in the *malloc* library provide a good example. These functions maintain a global linked list of free blocks on the heap. The functions of the *malloc* library are made thread-safe through the use of mutexes.

- Some functions (defined before the invention of threads) have an interface that by definition is nonreentrant, because they return pointers to storage statically allocated by the function, or they employ static storage to maintain information between successive calls to the same (or a related) function. Most of the functions in Table 31-1 fall into this category. For example, the *asctime()* function (Section 10.2.3) returns a pointer to a statically allocated buffer containing a date-time string.

For several of the functions that have nonreentrant interfaces, SUSv3 specifies reentrant equivalents with names ending with the suffix _r. These functions require the caller to allocate a buffer whose address is then passed to the function and used to return the result. This allows the calling thread to use a local (stack) variable for the function result buffer. For this purpose, SUSv3 specifies *asctime_r()*, *ctime_r()*, *getgrgid_r()*, *getgrnam_r()*, *getlogin_r()*, *getpwnam_r()*, *getpwuid_r()*, *gmtime_r()*, *localtime_r()*, *rand_r()*, *readdir_r()*, *strerror_r()*, *strtok_r()*, and *ttyname_r()*.

> Some implementations also provide additional reentrant equivalents of other traditional nonreentrant functions. For example, *glibc* provides *crypt_r()*, *gethostbyname_r()*, *getservbyname_r()*, *getutent_r()*, *getutid_r()*, *getutline_r()*, and *ptsname_r()*. However, a portable application can't rely on these functions being present on other implementations. In some cases, SUSv3 doesn't specify these reentrant equivalents because alternatives to the traditional functions exist that are both superior and reentrant. For example, *getaddrinfo()* is the modern, reentrant alternative to *gethostbyname()* and *getservbyname()*.

31.2 One-Time Initialization

Sometimes, a threaded application needs to ensure that some initialization action occurs just once, regardless of how many threads are created. For example, a mutex may need to be initialized with special attributes using *pthread_mutex_init()*, and that initialization must occur just once. If we are creating the threads from the main program, then this is generally easy to achieve—we perform the initialization before creating any threads that depend on the initialization. However, in a library function, this is not possible, because the calling program may create the threads before the first call to the library function. Therefore, the library function needs a method of performing the initialization the first time that it is called from any thread.

A library function can perform one-time initialization using the *pthread_once()* function.

```
#include <pthread.h>

int pthread_once(pthread_once_t *once_control, void (*init)(void));
```
                                  Returns 0 on success, or a positive error number on error

The *pthread_once()* function uses the state of the argument *once_control* to ensure that the caller-defined function pointed to by *init* is called just once, no matter how many times or from how many different threads the *pthread_once()* call is made.

The *init* function is called without any arguments, and thus has the following form:

```
void
init(void)
{
    /* Function body */
}
```

The *once_control* argument is a pointer to a variable that must be statically initialized with the value PTHREAD_ONCE_INIT:

```
pthread_once_t once_var = PTHREAD_ONCE_INIT;
```

The first call to *pthread_once()* that specifies a pointer to a particular *pthread_once_t* variable modifies the value of the variable pointed to by *once_control* so that subsequent calls to *pthread_once()* don't invoke *init*.

One common use of *pthread_once()* is in conjunction with thread-specific data, which we describe next.

> The main reason for the existence of *pthread_once()* is that in early versions of Pthreads, it was not possible to statically initialize a mutex. Instead, the use of *pthread_mutex_init()* was required ([Butenhof, 1996]). Given the later addition of statically allocated mutexes, it is possible for a library function to perform one-time initialization using a statically allocated mutex and a static Boolean variable. Nevertheless, *pthread_once()* is retained as a convenience.

31.3 Thread-Specific Data

The most efficient way of making a function thread-safe is to make it reentrant. All new library functions should be implemented in this way. However, for an existing nonreentrant library function (one that was perhaps designed before the use of threads became common), this approach usually requires changing the function's interface, which means modifying all of the programs that use the function.

Thread-specific data is a technique for making an existing function thread-safe without changing its interface. A function that uses thread-specific data may be slightly less efficient than a reentrant function, but allows us to leave the programs that call the function unchanged.

Thread-specific data allows a function to maintain a separate copy of a variable for each thread that calls the function, as illustrated in Figure 31-1. Thread-specific data is persistent; each thread's variable continues to exist between the thread's invocations of the function. This allows the function to maintain per-thread information between calls to the function, and allows the function to pass distinct result buffers (if required) to each calling thread.

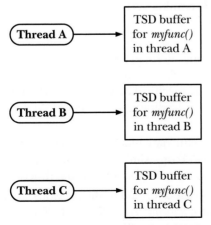

Figure 31-1: Thread-specific data (TSD) provides per-thread storage for a function

31.3.1 Thread-Specific Data from the Library Function's Perspective

In order to understand the use of the thread-specific data API, we need to consider things from the point of view of a library function that uses thread-specific data:

- The function must allocate a separate block of storage for each thread that calls the function. This block needs to be allocated once, the first time the thread calls the function.

- On each subsequent call from the same thread, the function needs to be able to obtain the address of the storage block that was allocated the first time this thread called the function. The function can't maintain a pointer to the block in an automatic variable, since automatic variables disappear when the function returns; nor can it store the pointer in a static variable, since only one instance of each static variable exists in the process. The Pthreads API provides functions to handle this task.

- Different (i.e., independent) functions may each need thread-specific data. Each function needs a method of identifying its thread-specific data (a key), as distinct from the thread-specific data used by other functions.

- The function has no direct control over what happens when the thread terminates. When the thread terminates, it is probably executing code outside the function. Nevertheless, there must be some mechanism (a destructor) to ensure that the storage block allocated for this thread is automatically deallocated when the thread terminates. If this is not done, then a memory leak could occur as threads are continuously created, call the function, and then terminate.

31.3.2 Overview of the Thread-Specific Data API

The general steps that a library function performs in order to use thread-specific data are as follows:

1. The function creates a *key*, which is the means of differentiating the thread-specific data item used by this function from the thread-specific data items used by other functions. The key is created by calling the *pthread_key_create()* function. Creating a key needs to be done only once, when the first thread calls the function. For this purpose, *pthread_once()* is employed. Creating a key doesn't allocate any blocks of thread-specific data.

2. The call to *pthread_key_create()* serves a second purpose: it allows the caller to specify the address of the programmer-defined destructor function that is used to deallocate each of the storage blocks allocated for this key (see the next step). When a thread that has thread-specific data terminates, the Pthreads API automatically invokes the destructor, passing it a pointer to the data block for this thread.

3. The function allocates a thread-specific data block for each thread from which it is called. This is done using *malloc()* (or a similar function). This allocation is done once for each thread, the first time the thread calls the function.

4. In order to save a pointer to the storage allocated in the previous step, the function employs two Pthreads functions: *pthread_setspecific()* and *pthread_getspecific()*. A call to *pthread_setspecific()* is a request to the Pthreads implementation to say

"save this pointer, recording the fact that it is associated with a particular key (the one for this function) and a particular thread (the calling thread)." Calling *pthread_getspecific()* performs the complementary task, returning the pointer previously associated with a given key for the calling thread. If no pointer was previously associated with a particular key and thread, then *pthread_getspecific()* returns NULL. This is how a function can determine that it is being called for the first time by this thread, and thus must allocate the storage block for the thread.

31.3.3 Details of the Thread-Specific Data API

In this section, we provide details of each of the functions mentioned in the previous section, and elucidate the operation of thread-specific data by describing how it is typically implemented. The next section shows how to use thread-specific data to write a thread-safe implementation of the standard C library function *strerror()*.

Calling *pthread_key_create()* creates a new thread-specific data key that is returned to the caller in the buffer pointed to by *key*.

```
#include <pthread.h>

int pthread_key_create(pthread_key_t *key, void (*destructor)(void *));
```
                        Returns 0 on success, or a positive error number on error

Because the returned key is used by all threads in the process, *key* should point to a global variable.

The *destructor* argument points to a programmer-defined function of the following form:

```
void
dest(void *value)
{
    /* Release storage pointed to by 'value' */
}
```

Upon termination of a thread that has a non-NULL value associated with *key*, the destructor function is automatically invoked by the Pthreads API and given that value as its argument. The passed value is normally a pointer to this thread's thread-specific data block for this key. If a destructor is not required, then *destructor* can be specified as NULL.

> If a thread has multiple thread-specific data blocks, then the order in which the destructors are called is unspecified. Destructor functions should be designed to operate independently of one another.

Looking at the implementation of thread-specific data helps us to understand how it is used. A typical implementation (NPTL is typical), involves the following arrays:

- a single global (i.e., process-wide) array of information about thread-specific data keys; and

- a set of per-thread arrays, each containing pointers to all of the thread-specific data blocks allocated for a particular thread (i.e., this array contains the pointers stored by calls to *pthread_setspecific()*).

In this implementation, the *pthread_key_t* value returned by *pthread_key_create()* is simply an index into the global array, which we label *pthread_keys*, whose form is shown in Figure 31-2. Each element of this array is a structure containing two fields. The first field indicates whether this array element is in use (i.e., has been allocated by a previous call to *pthread_key_create()*). The second field is used to store the pointer to the destructor function for the thread-specific data blocks for this key (i.e., it is a copy of the *destructor* argument to *pthread_key_create()*).

pthread_keys[0]	"in use" flag
	destructor pointer
pthread_keys[1]	"in use" flag
	destructor pointer
pthread_keys[2]	"in use" flag
	destructor pointer
	. . .

Figure 31-2: Implementation of thread-specific data keys

The *pthread_setspecific()* function requests the Pthreads API to save a copy of *value* in a data structure that associates it with the calling thread and with *key*, a key returned by a previous call to *pthread_key_create()*. The *pthread_getspecific()* function performs the converse operation, returning the value that was previously associated with the given *key* for this thread.

```
#include <pthread.h>

int pthread_setspecific(pthread_key_t key, const void *value);
```
                    Returns 0 on success, or a positive error number on error
```
void *pthread_getspecific(pthread_key_t key);
```
          Returns pointer, or NULL if no thread-specific data is associated with *key*

The *value* argument given to *pthread_setspecific()* is normally a pointer to a block of memory that has previously been allocated by the caller. This pointer will be passed as the argument for the destructor function for this *key* when the thread terminates.

> The *value* argument doesn't need to be a pointer to a block of memory. It could be some scalar value that can be assigned (with a cast) to *void **. In this case, the earlier call to *pthread_key_create()* would specify *destructor* as NULL.

Figure 31-3 shows a typical implementation of the data structure used to store *value*. In this diagram, we assume that *pthread_keys[1]* was allocated to a function named *myfunc()*. For each thread, the Pthreads API maintains an array of pointers to thread-specific data blocks. The elements of each of these thread-specific arrays have a one-to-one correspondence with the elements of the global *pthread_keys* array shown in Figure 31-2. The *pthread_setspecific()* function sets the element corresponding to *key* in the array for the calling thread.

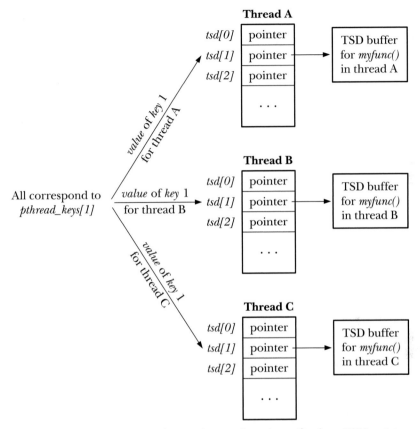

Figure 31-3: Data structure used to implement thread-specific data (TSD) pointers

When a thread is first created, all of its thread-specific data pointers are initialized to NULL. This means that when our library function is called by a thread for the first time, it must begin by using *pthread_getspecific()* to check whether the thread already has an associated value for *key*. If it does not, then the function allocates a block of memory and saves a pointer to the block using *pthread_setspecific()*. We show an example of this in the thread-safe *strerror()* implementation presented in the next section.

31.3.4 Employing the Thread-Specific Data API

When we first described the standard *strerror()* function in Section 3.4, we noted that it may return a pointer to a statically allocated string as its function result. This means that *strerror()* may not be thread-safe. In the next few pages, we look at a non-thread-safe implementation of *strerror()*, and then show how thread-specific data can be used to make this function thread-safe.

On many UNIX implementations, including Linux, the *strerror()* function provided by the standard C library *is* thread-safe. However, we use the example of *strerror()* anyway, because SUSv3 doesn't require this function to be thread-safe, and its implementation provides a simple example of the use of thread-specific data.

Listing 31-1 shows a simple non-thread-safe implementation of *strerror()*. This function makes use of a pair of global variables defined by *glibc*: *_sys_errlist* is an array of pointers to strings corresponding to the error numbers in *errno* (thus, for example, *_sys_errlist[EINVAL]* points to the string *Invalid argument*), and *_sys_nerr* specifies the number of elements in *_sys_errlist*.

Listing 31-1: An implementation of *strerror()* that is not thread-safe

```
────────────────────────────────────────────threads/strerror.c
#define _GNU_SOURCE         /* Get '_sys_nerr' and '_sys_errlist'
                               declarations from <stdio.h> */
#include <stdio.h>
#include <string.h>         /* Get declaration of strerror() */

#define MAX_ERROR_LEN 256   /* Maximum length of string
                               returned by strerror() */

static char buf[MAX_ERROR_LEN];  /* Statically allocated return buffer */

char *
strerror(int err)
{
    if (err < 0 || err >= _sys_nerr || _sys_errlist[err] == NULL) {
        snprintf(buf, MAX_ERROR_LEN, "Unknown error %d", err);
    } else {
        strncpy(buf, _sys_errlist[err], MAX_ERROR_LEN - 1);
        buf[MAX_ERROR_LEN - 1] = '\0';          /* Ensure null termination */
    }

    return buf;
}
────────────────────────────────────────────threads/strerror.c
```

We can use the program in Listing 31-2 to demonstrate the consequences of the fact that the *strerror()* implementation in Listing 31-1 is not thread-safe. This program calls *strerror()* from two different threads, but displays the returned value only after both threads have called *strerror()*. Even though each thread specifies a different value (EINVAL and EPERM) as the argument to *strerror()*, this is what we see when we compile and link this program with the version of *strerror()* shown in Listing 31-1:

```
$ ./strerror_test
Main thread has called strerror()
Other thread about to call strerror()
Other thread: str (0x804a7c0) = Operation not permitted
Main thread:  str (0x804a7c0) = Operation not permitted
```

Both threads displayed the *errno* string corresponding to EPERM, because the call to *strerror()* by the second thread (in *threadFunc*) overwrote the buffer that was written by the call to *strerror()* in the main thread. Inspection of the output shows that the local variable *str* in the two threads points to the same memory address.

Listing 31-2: Calling *strerror()* from two different threads

———————————————————————————————————— `threads/strerror_test.c`

```
#include <stdio.h>
#include <string.h>          /* Get declaration of strerror() */
#include <pthread.h>
#include "tlpi_hdr.h"

static void *
threadFunc(void *arg)
{
    char *str;

    printf("Other thread about to call strerror()\n");
    str = strerror(EPERM);
    printf("Other thread: str (%p) = %s\n", str, str);

    return NULL;
}

int
main(int argc, char *argv[])
{
    pthread_t t;
    int s;
    char *str;

    str = strerror(EINVAL);
    printf("Main thread has called strerror()\n");

    s = pthread_create(&t, NULL, threadFunc, NULL);
    if (s != 0)
        errExitEN(s, "pthread_create");

    s = pthread_join(t, NULL);
    if (s != 0)
        errExitEN(s, "pthread_join");

    printf("Main thread:  str (%p) = %s\n", str, str);

    exit(EXIT_SUCCESS);
}
```
——————————————————————————————————— `threads/strerror_test.c`

Listing 31-3 shows a reimplementation of *strerror()* that uses thread-specific data to ensure thread safety.

The first step performed by the revised *strerror()* is to call *pthread_once()* ④ to ensure that the first invocation of this function (from any thread) calls *createKey()* ②. The *createKey()* function calls *pthread_key_create()* to allocate a thread-specific data key that is stored in the global variable *strerrorKey* ③. The call to *pthread_key_create()* also records the address of the destructor ① that will be used to free the thread-specific buffers corresponding to this key.

The *strerror()* function then calls *pthread_getspecific()* ⑤ to retrieve the address of this thread's unique buffer corresponding to *strerrorKey*. If *pthread_getspecific()* returns NULL, then this thread is calling *strerror()* for the first time, and so the function allocates a new buffer using *malloc()* ⑥, and saves the address of the buffer using *pthread_setspecific()* ⑦. If the *pthread_getspecific()* call returns a non-NULL value, then that pointer refers to an existing buffer that was allocated when this thread previously called *strerror()*.

The remainder of this *strerror()* implementation is similar to the implementation that we showed earlier, with the difference that *buf* is the address of a thread-specific data buffer, rather than a static variable.

Listing 31-3: A thread-safe implementation of *strerror()* using thread-specific data

```
────────────────────────────────────────────────── threads/strerror_tsd.c
    #define _GNU_SOURCE         /* Get '_sys_nerr' and '_sys_errlist'
                                   declarations from <stdio.h> */

    #include <stdio.h>
    #include <string.h>         /* Get declaration of strerror() */
    #include <pthread.h>
    #include "tlpi_hdr.h"

    static pthread_once_t once = PTHREAD_ONCE_INIT;
    static pthread_key_t strerrorKey;

    #define MAX_ERROR_LEN 256    /* Maximum length of string in per-thread
                                    buffer returned by strerror() */

    static void                  /* Free thread-specific data buffer */
①  destructor(void *buf)
    {
        free(buf);
    }

    static void                  /* One-time key creation function */
②  createKey(void)
    {
        int s;

        /* Allocate a unique thread-specific data key and save the address
           of the destructor for thread-specific data buffers */

③      s = pthread_key_create(&strerrorKey, destructor);
        if (s != 0)
            errExitEN(s, "pthread_key_create");
    }
```

```
char *
strerror(int err)
{
    int s;
    char *buf;

    /* Make first caller allocate key for thread-specific data */

④  s = pthread_once(&once, createKey);
    if (s != 0)
        errExitEN(s, "pthread_once");

⑤  buf = pthread_getspecific(strerrorKey);
    if (buf == NULL) {              /* If first call from this thread, allocate
                                       buffer for thread, and save its location */
⑥      buf = malloc(MAX_ERROR_LEN);
        if (buf == NULL)
            errExit("malloc");

⑦      s = pthread_setspecific(strerrorKey, buf);
        if (s != 0)
            errExitEN(s, "pthread_setspecific");
    }

    if (err < 0 || err >= _sys_nerr || _sys_errlist[err] == NULL) {
        snprintf(buf, MAX_ERROR_LEN, "Unknown error %d", err);
    } else {
        strncpy(buf, _sys_errlist[err], MAX_ERROR_LEN - 1);
        buf[MAX_ERROR_LEN - 1] = '\0';              /* Ensure null termination */
    }

    return buf;
}
```
——— **threads/strerror_tsd.c**

If we compile and link our test program (Listing 31-2) with the new version of
strerror() (Listing 31-3) to create an executable file, strerror_test_tsd, then we see
the following results when running the program:

```
$ ./strerror_test_tsd
Main thread has called strerror()
Other thread about to call strerror()
Other thread: str (0x804b158) = Operation not permitted
Main thread:  str (0x804b008) = Invalid argument
```

From this output, we see that the new version of *strerror()* is thread-safe. We also see
that the address pointed to by the local variable *str* in the two threads is different.

31.3.5 Thread-Specific Data Implementation Limits

As implied by our description of how thread-specific data is typically implemented, an implementation may need to impose limits on the number of thread-specific data keys that it supports. SUSv3 requires that an implementation support at least 128 (_POSIX_THREAD_KEYS_MAX) keys. An application can determine how many keys an implementation actually supports either via the definition of PTHREAD_KEYS_MAX (defined in <limits.h>) or by calling *sysconf(_SC_THREAD_KEYS_MAX)*. Linux supports up to 1024 keys.

Even 128 keys should be more than sufficient for most applications. This is because each library function should employ only a small number of keys—often just one. If a function requires multiple thread-specific data values, these can usually be placed in a single structure that has just one associated thread-specific data key.

31.4 Thread-Local Storage

Like thread-specific data, thread-local storage provides persistent per-thread storage. This feature is nonstandard, but it is provided in the same or a similar form on many other UNIX implementations (e.g., Solaris and FreeBSD).

The main advantage of thread-local storage is that it is much simpler to use than thread-specific data. To create a thread-local variable, we simply include the __thread specifier in the declaration of a global or static variable:

```
static __thread char buf[MAX_ERROR_LEN];
```

Each thread has its own copy of the variables declared with this specifier. The variables in a thread's thread-local storage persist until the thread terminates, at which time the storage is automatically deallocated.

Note the following points about the declaration and use of thread-local variables:

- The __thread keyword must immediately follow the static or extern keyword, if either of these is specified in the variable's declaration.
- The declaration of a thread-local variable can include an initializer, in the same manner as a normal global or static variable declaration.
- The C address (&) operator can be used to obtain the address of a thread-local variable.

Thread-local storage requires support from the kernel (provided in Linux 2.6), the Pthreads implementation (provided in NPTL), and the C compiler (provided on x86-32 with *gcc* 3.3 and later).

Listing 31-4 shows a thread-safe implementation of *strerror()* using thread-local storage. If we compile and link our test program (Listing 31-2) with this version of *strerror()* to create an executable file, strerror_test_tls, then we see the following results when running the program:

```
$ ./strerror_test_tls
Main thread has called strerror()
Other thread about to call strerror()
Other thread: str (0x40376ab0) = Operation not permitted
Main thread:  str (0x40175080) = Invalid argument
```

Listing 31-4: A thread-safe implementation of *strerror()* using thread-local storage

––– **threads/strerror_tls.c**

```
#define _GNU_SOURCE             /* Get '_sys_nerr' and '_sys_errlist'
                                   declarations from <stdio.h> */

#include <stdio.h>
#include <string.h>             /* Get declaration of strerror() */
#include <pthread.h>

#define MAX_ERROR_LEN 256       /* Maximum length of string in per-thread
                                   buffer returned by strerror() */

static __thread char buf[MAX_ERROR_LEN];
                                /* Thread-local return buffer */

char *
strerror(int err)
{
    if (err < 0 || err >= _sys_nerr || _sys_errlist[err] == NULL) {
        snprintf(buf, MAX_ERROR_LEN, "Unknown error %d", err);
    } else {
        strncpy(buf, _sys_errlist[err], MAX_ERROR_LEN - 1);
        buf[MAX_ERROR_LEN - 1] = '\0';          /* Ensure null termination */
    }

    return buf;
}
```

––– **threads/strerror_tls.c**

31.5 Summary

A function is said to be thread-safe if it can safely be invoked from multiple threads at the same time. The usual reason a function is not thread-safe is that it makes use of global or static variables. One way to render a non-thread-safe function safe in a multithreaded application is to guard all calls to the function with a mutex lock. This approach suffers the problem that it reduces concurrency, because only one thread can be in the function at any time. An approach that allows greater concurrency is to add mutex locks around just those parts of the function that manipulate shared variables (the critical sections).

Mutexes can be used to render most functions thread-safe, but they carry a performance penalty because there is a cost to locking and unlocking a mutex. By avoiding the use of global and static variables, a reentrant function achieves thread-safety without the use of mutexes.

Most of the functions specified in SUSv3 are required to be thread-safe. SUSv3 also lists a small set of functions that are not required to be thread-safe. Typically, these are functions that employ static storage to return information to the caller or to maintain information between successive calls. By definition, such functions are not reentrant, and mutexes can't be used to make them thread-safe. We considered two roughly equivalent coding techniques—thread-specific data and thread-local storage—that can be used to render an unsafe function thread-safe without needing to change its interface. Both of these techniques allow a function to allocate persistent, per-thread storage.

Further information

Refer to the sources of further information listed in Section 29.10.

31.6 Exercises

31-1. Implement a function, *one_time_init(control, init)*, that performs the equivalent of *pthread_once()*. The *control* argument should be a pointer to a statically allocated structure containing a Boolean variable and a mutex. The Boolean variable indicates whether the function *init* has already been called, and the mutex controls access to that variable. To keep the implementation simple, you can ignore possibilities such as *init()* failing or being canceled when first called from a thread (i.e., it is not necessary to devise a scheme whereby, if such an event occurs, the next thread that calls *one_time_init()* reattempts the call to *init()*).

31-2. Use thread-specific data to write thread-safe versions of *dirname()* and *basename()* (Section 18.14).

32

THREADS: THREAD CANCELLATION

Typically, multiple threads execute in parallel, with each thread performing its task until it decides to terminate by calling *pthread_exit()* or returning from the thread's start function.

Sometimes, it can be useful to *cancel* a thread; that is, to send it a request asking it to terminate now. This could be useful, for example, if a group of threads is performing a calculation, and one thread detects an error condition that requires the other threads to terminate. Alternatively, a GUI-driven application may provide a cancel button to allow the user to terminate a task that is being performed by a thread in the background; in this case, the main thread (controlling the GUI) needs to tell the background thread to terminate.

In this chapter, we describe the POSIX threads cancellation mechanism.

32.1 Canceling a Thread

The *pthread_cancel()* function sends a cancellation request to the specified *thread*.

```
#include <pthread.h>

int pthread_cancel(pthread_t thread);
```
                    Returns 0 on success, or a positive error number on error

Having made the cancellation request, *pthread_cancel()* returns immediately; that is, it doesn't wait for the target thread to terminate.

Precisely what happens to the target thread, and when it happens, depends on that thread's cancellation state and type, as described in the next section.

32.2 Cancellation State and Type

The *pthread_setcancelstate()* and *pthread_setcanceltype()* functions set flags that allow a thread to control how it responds to a cancellation request.

```
#include <pthread.h>

int pthread_setcancelstate(int state, int *oldstate);
int pthread_setcanceltype(int type, int *oldtype);
```
                        Both return 0 on success, or a positive error number on error

The *pthread_setcancelstate()* function sets the calling thread's cancelability state to the value given in *state*. This argument has one of the following values:

PTHREAD_CANCEL_DISABLE

> The thread is not cancelable. If a cancellation request is received, it remains pending until cancelability is enabled.

PTHREAD_CANCEL_ENABLE

> The thread is cancelable. This is the default cancelability state in newly created threads.

The thread's previous cancelability state is returned in the location pointed to by *oldstate*.

> If we are not interested in the previous cancelability state, Linux allows *oldstate* to be specified as NULL. This is the case on many other implementations as well; however, SUSv3 doesn't specify this feature, so portable applications can't rely on it. We should always specify a non-NULL value for *oldstate*.

Temporarily disabling cancellation (PTHREAD_CANCEL_DISABLE) is useful if a thread is executing a section of code where *all* of the steps must be completed.

If a thread is cancelable (PTHREAD_CANCEL_ENABLE), then the treatment of a cancellation request is determined by the thread's cancelability type, which is specified by the *type* argument in a call to *pthread_setcanceltype()*. This argument has one of the following values:

PTHREAD_CANCEL_ASYNCHRONOUS

> The thread may be canceled at any time (perhaps, but not necessarily, immediately). Asynchronous cancelability is rarely useful, and we defer discussion of it until Section 32.6.

PTHREAD_CANCEL_DEFERRED

> The cancellation remains pending until a cancellation point (see the next section) is reached. This is the default cancelability type in newly created threads. We say more about deferred cancelability in the following sections.

The thread's previous cancelability type is returned in the location pointed to by *oldtype*.

> As with the *pthread_setcancelstate() oldstate* argument, many implementations, including Linux, allow *oldtype* to be specified as NULL if we are not interested in the previous cancelability type. Again, SUSv3 doesn't specify this feature, and portable applications can't rely on it We should always specify a non-NULL value for *oldtype*.

When a thread calls *fork()*, the child inherits the calling thread's cancelability type and state. When a thread calls *exec()*, the cancelability state and type of the main thread of the new program are reset to PTHREAD_CANCEL_ENABLE and PTHREAD_CANCEL_DEFERRED, respectively.

32.3 Cancellation Points

When cancelability is enabled and deferred, a cancellation request is acted upon only when a thread next reaches a *cancellation point*. A cancellation point is a call to one of a set of functions defined by the implementation.

SUSv3 specifies that the functions shown in Table 32-1 *must* be cancellation points if they are provided by an implementation. Most of these are functions that are capable of blocking the thread for an indefinite period of time.

Table 32-1: Functions required to be cancellation points by SUSv3

accept()	*nanosleep()*	*sem_timedwait()*
aio_suspend()	*open()*	*sem_wait()*
clock_nanosleep()	*pause()*	*send()*
close()	*poll()*	*sendmsg()*
connect()	*pread()*	*sendto()*
creat()	*pselect()*	*sigpause()*
fcntl(F_SETLKW)	*pthread_cond_timedwait()*	*sigsuspend()*
fsync()	*pthread_cond_wait()*	*sigtimedwait()*
fdatasync()	*pthread_join()*	*sigwait()*
getmsg()	*pthread_testcancel()*	*sigwaitinfo()*
getpmsg()	*putmsg()*	*sleep()*
lockf(F_LOCK)	*putpmsg()*	*system()*
mq_receive()	*pwrite()*	*tcdrain()*
mq_send()	*read()*	*usleep()*
mq_timedreceive()	*readv()*	*wait()*
mq_timedsend()	*recv()*	*waitid()*
msgrcv()	*recvfrom()*	*waitpid()*
msgsnd()	*recvmsg()*	*write()*
msync()	*select()*	*writev()*

In addition to the functions in Table 32-1, SUSv3 specifies a larger group of functions that an implementation *may* define as cancellation points. These include the *stdio* functions, the *dlopen* API, the *syslog* API, *nftw()*, *popen()*, *semop()*, *unlink()*, and various functions that retrieve information from system files such as the *utmp* file. A portable program must correctly handle the possibility that a thread may be canceled when calling these functions.

SUSv3 specifies that aside from the two lists of functions that must and may be cancellation points, none of the other functions in the standard may act as cancellation points (i.e., a portable program doesn't need to handle the possibility that calling these other functions could precipitate thread cancellation).

SUSv4 adds *openat()* to the list of functions that must be cancellation points, and removes *sigpause()* (it moves to the list of functions that *may* be cancellation points) and *usleep()* (which is dropped from the standard).

> An implementation is free to mark additional functions that are not specified in the standard as cancellation points. Any function that might block (perhaps because it might access a file) is a likely candidate to be a cancellation point. Within *glibc*, many nonstandard functions are marked as cancellation points for this reason.

Upon receiving a cancellation request, a thread whose cancelability is enabled and deferred terminates when it next reaches a cancellation point. If the thread was not detached, then some other thread in the process must join with it, in order to prevent it from becoming a zombie thread. When a canceled thread is joined, the value returned in the second argument to *pthread_join()* is a special thread return value: PTHREAD_CANCELED.

Example program

Listing 32-1 shows a simple example of the use of *pthread_cancel()*. The main program creates a thread that executes an infinite loop, sleeping for a second and printing the value of a loop counter. (This thread will terminate only if it is sent a cancellation request or if the process exits.) Meanwhile, the main program sleeps for 3 seconds, and then sends a cancellation request to the thread that it created. When we run this program, we see the following:

```
$ ./thread_cancel
New thread started
Loop 1
Loop 2
Loop 3
Thread was canceled
```

Listing 32-1: Canceling a thread with *pthread_cancel()*

———————————————————————————————— threads/thread_cancel.c

```
#include <pthread.h>
#include "tlpi_hdr.h"

static void *
threadFunc(void *arg)
{
    int j;
```

```
    printf("New thread started\n");      /* May be a cancellation point */
    for (j = 1; ; j++) {
        printf("Loop %d\n", j);          /* May be a cancellation point */
        sleep(1);                        /* A cancellation point */
    }

    /* NOTREACHED */
    return NULL;
}

int
main(int argc, char *argv[])
{
    pthread_t thr;
    int s;
    void *res;

    s = pthread_create(&thr, NULL, threadFunc, NULL);
    if (s != 0)
        errExitEN(s, "pthread_create");

    sleep(3);                            /* Allow new thread to run a while */

    s = pthread_cancel(thr);
    if (s != 0)
        errExitEN(s, "pthread_cancel");

    s = pthread_join(thr, &res);
    if (s != 0)
        errExitEN(s, "pthread_join");

    if (res == PTHREAD_CANCELED)
        printf("Thread was canceled\n");
    else
        printf("Thread was not canceled (should not happen!)\n");

    exit(EXIT_SUCCESS);
}
```
———————————————————————————————————— *threads/thread_cancel.c*

32.4 Testing for Thread Cancellation

In Listing 32-1, the thread created by *main()* accepted the cancellation request
because it executed a function that was a cancellation point (*sleep()* is a cancellation
point; *printf()* may be one). However, suppose a thread executes a loop that contains no cancellation points (e.g., a compute-bound loop). In this case, the thread
would never honor the cancellation request.

The purpose of *pthread_testcancel()* is simply to be a cancellation point. If a cancellation is pending when this function is called, then the calling thread is terminated.

```
#include <pthread.h>

void pthread_testcancel(void);
```

A thread that is executing code that does not otherwise include cancellation points can periodically call *pthread_testcancel()* to ensure that it responds in a timely fashion to a cancellation request sent by another thread.

32.5 Cleanup Handlers

If a thread with a pending cancellation were simply terminated when it reached a cancellation point, then shared variables and Pthreads objects (e.g., mutexes) might be left in an inconsistent state, perhaps causing the remaining threads in the process to produce incorrect results, deadlock, or crash. To get around this problem, a thread can establish one or more *cleanup handlers*—functions that are automatically executed if the thread is canceled. A cleanup handler can perform tasks such as modifying the values of global variables and unlocking mutexes before the thread is terminated.

Each thread can have a stack of cleanup handlers. When a thread is canceled, the cleanup handlers are executed working down from the top of the stack; that is, the most recently established handler is called first, then the next most recently established, and so on. When all of the cleanup handlers have been executed, the thread terminates.

The *pthread_cleanup_push()* and *pthread_cleanup_pop()* functions respectively add and remove handlers on the calling thread's stack of cleanup handlers.

```
#include <pthread.h>

void pthread_cleanup_push(void (*routine)(void*), void *arg);
void pthread_cleanup_pop(int execute);
```

The *pthread_cleanup_push()* function adds the function whose address is specified in *routine* to the top of the calling thread's stack of cleanup handlers. The *routine* argument is a pointer to a function that has the following form:

```
void
routine(void *arg)
{
    /* Code to perform cleanup */
}
```

The *arg* value given to *pthread_cleanup_push()* is passed as the argument of the cleanup handler when it is invoked. This argument is typed as *void **, but, using judicious casting, other data types can be passed in this argument.

Typically, a cleanup action is needed only if a thread is canceled during the execution of a particular section of code. If the thread reaches the end of that section without being canceled, then the cleanup action is no longer required. Thus, each call to *pthread_cleanup_push()* has an accompanying call to *pthread_cleanup_pop()*. This function removes the topmost function from the stack of cleanup handlers. If the *execute* argument is nonzero, the handler is also executed. This is convenient if we want to perform the cleanup action even if the thread was not canceled.

Although we have described *pthread_cleanup_push()* and *pthread_cleanup_pop()* as functions, SUSv3 permits them to be implemented as macros that expand to statement sequences that include an opening ({) and closing (}) brace, respectively. Not all UNIX implementations do things this way, but Linux and many others do. This means that each use of *pthread_cleanup_push()* must be paired with exactly one corresponding *pthread_cleanup_pop()* in the same lexical block. (On implementations that do things this way, variables declared between the *pthread_cleanup_push()* and *pthread_cleanup_pop()* will be limited to that lexical scope.) For example, it is not correct to write code such as the following:

```
pthread_cleanup_push(func, arg);
...
if (cond) {
    pthread_cleanup_pop(0);
}
```

As a coding convenience, any cleanup handlers that have not been popped are also executed automatically if a thread terminates by calling *pthread_exit()* (but not if it does a simple return).

Example program

The program in Listing 32-2 provides a simple example of the use of a cleanup handler. The main program creates a thread ⑧ whose first actions are to allocate a block of memory ③ whose location is stored in *buf*, and then lock the mutex *mtx* ④. Since the thread may be canceled, it uses *pthread_cleanup_push()* ⑤ to install a cleanup handler that is called with the address stored in *buf*. If it is invoked, the cleanup handler deallocates the freed memory ① and unlocks the mutex ②.

The thread then enters a loop waiting for the condition variable *cond* to be signaled ⑥. This loop will terminate in one of two ways, depending on whether the program is supplied with a command-line argument:

- If no command-line argument is supplied, the thread is canceled by *main()* ⑨. In this case, cancellation will occur at the call to *pthread_cond_wait()* ⑥, which is one of the cancellation points shown in Table 32-1. As part of cancellation, the cleanup handler established using *pthread_cleanup_push()* is invoked automatically. (When a *pthread_cond_wait()* call is canceled, the mutex is automatically relocked before the cleanup handler is invoked. This means the mutex can be safely unlocked in the cleanup handler.)

- If a command-line argument is supplied, the condition variable is signaled ⑩ after the associated global variable, *glob*, is first set to a nonzero value. In this case, the thread falls through to execute *pthread_cleanup_pop()* ⑦, which, given a nonzero argument, also causes the cleanup handler to be invoked.

The main program joins with the terminated thread ⑪, and reports whether the thread was canceled or terminated normally.

Listing 32-2: Using cleanup handlers

———————————————————————————————————— **threads/thread_cleanup.c**

```c
#include <pthread.h>
#include "tlpi_hdr.h"

static pthread_cond_t cond = PTHREAD_COND_INITIALIZER;
static pthread_mutex_t mtx = PTHREAD_MUTEX_INITIALIZER;
static int glob = 0;                    /* Predicate variable */

static void      /* Free memory pointed to by 'arg' and unlock mutex */
cleanupHandler(void *arg)
{
    int s;

    printf("cleanup: freeing block at %p\n", arg);
①  free(arg);

    printf("cleanup: unlocking mutex\n");
②  s = pthread_mutex_unlock(&mtx);
    if (s != 0)
        errExitEN(s, "pthread_mutex_unlock");
}

static void *
threadFunc(void *arg)
{
    int s;
    void *buf = NULL;                   /* Buffer allocated by thread */

③  buf = malloc(0x10000);              /* Not a cancellation point */
    printf("thread:  allocated memory at %p\n", buf);

④  s = pthread_mutex_lock(&mtx);       /* Not a cancellation point */
    if (s != 0)
        errExitEN(s, "pthread_mutex_lock");

⑤  pthread_cleanup_push(cleanupHandler, buf);

    while (glob == 0) {
⑥      s = pthread_cond_wait(&cond, &mtx);    /* A cancellation point */
        if (s != 0)
            errExitEN(s, "pthread_cond_wait");
    }

    printf("thread:  condition wait loop completed\n");
⑦  pthread_cleanup_pop(1);            /* Executes cleanup handler */
    return NULL;
}

int
main(int argc, char *argv[])
{
    pthread_t thr;
    void *res;
    int s;
```

```
⑧      s = pthread_create(&thr, NULL, threadFunc, NULL);
       if (s != 0)
           errExitEN(s, "pthread_create");

       sleep(2);                  /* Give thread a chance to get started */

       if (argc == 1) {           /* Cancel thread */
           printf("main:    about to cancel thread\n");
⑨          s = pthread_cancel(thr);
           if (s != 0)
               errExitEN(s, "pthread_cancel");

       } else {                   /* Signal condition variable */
           printf("main:    about to signal condition variable\n");
           glob = 1;
⑩          s = pthread_cond_signal(&cond);
           if (s != 0)
               errExitEN(s, "pthread_cond_signal");
       }

⑪      s = pthread_join(thr, &res);
       if (s != 0)
           errExitEN(s, "pthread_join");
       if (res == PTHREAD_CANCELED)
           printf("main:    thread was canceled\n");
       else
           printf("main:    thread terminated normally\n");

       exit(EXIT_SUCCESS);
   }
```
———————————————————————————————————— **threads/thread_cleanup.c**

If we invoke the program in Listing 32-2 without any command-line arguments,
then *main()* calls *pthread_cancel()*, the cleanup handler is invoked automatically, and
we see the following:

```
$ ./thread_cleanup
thread:  allocated memory at 0x804b050
main:    about to cancel thread
cleanup: freeing block at 0x804b050
cleanup: unlocking mutex
main:    thread was canceled
```

If we invoke the program with a command-line argument, then *main()* sets *glob* to 1 and
signals the condition variable, the cleanup handler is invoked by *pthread_cleanup_pop()*,
and we see the following:

```
$ ./thread_cleanup s
thread:  allocated memory at 0x804b050
main:    about to signal condition variable
thread:  condition wait loop completed
cleanup: freeing block at 0x804b050
cleanup: unlocking mutex
main:    thread terminated normally
```

32.6 Asynchronous Cancelability

When a thread is made asynchronously cancelable (cancelability type PTHREAD_CANCEL_ASYNCHRONOUS), it may be canceled at any time (i.e., at any machine-language instruction); delivery of a cancellation is not held off until the thread next reaches a cancellation point.

The problem with asynchronous cancellation is that, although cleanup handlers are still invoked, the handlers have no way of determining the state of a thread. In the program in Listing 32-2, which employs the deferred cancelability type, the thread can be canceled only when it executes the call to *pthread_cond_wait()*, which is the only cancellation point. By this time, we know that *buf* has been initialized to point to a block of allocated memory and that the mutex *mtx* has been locked. However, with asynchronous cancelability, the thread could be canceled at any point; for example, before the *malloc()* call, between the *malloc()* call and locking the mutex, or after locking the mutex. The cleanup handler has no way of knowing where cancellation has occurred, or precisely which cleanup steps are required. Furthermore, the thread might even be canceled *during* the *malloc()* call, after which chaos is likely to result (Section 7.1.3).

As a general principle, an asynchronously cancelable thread can't allocate any resources or acquire any mutexes, semaphores, or locks. This precludes the use of a wide range of library functions, including most of the Pthreads functions. (SUSv3 makes exceptions for *pthread_cancel()*, *pthread_setcancelstate()*, and *pthread_setcanceltype()*, which are explicitly required to be *async-cancel-safe*; that is, an implementation must make them safe to call from a thread that is asynchronously cancelable.) In other words, there are few circumstances where asynchronous cancellation is useful. One such circumstance is canceling a thread that is in a compute-bound loop.

32.7 Summary

The *pthread_cancel()* function allows one thread to send another thread a cancellation request, which is a request that the target thread should terminate.

How the target thread reacts to this request is determined by its cancelability state and type. If the cancelability state is currently set to disabled, the request will remain pending until the cancelability state is set to enabled. If cancelability is enabled, the cancelability type determines when the target thread reacts to the request. If the type is deferred, the cancellation occurs when the thread next calls one of a number of functions specified as cancellation points by SUSv3. If the type is asynchronous, cancellation may occur at any time (this is rarely useful).

A thread can establish a stack of cleanup handlers, which are programmer-defined functions that are invoked automatically to perform cleanups (e.g., restoring the states of shared variables, or unlocking mutexes) if the thread is canceled.

Further information

Refer to the sources of further information listed in Section 29.10.

33

THREADS: FURTHER DETAILS

This chapter provides further details on various aspects of POSIX threads. We discuss the interaction of threads with aspects of the traditional UNIX API—in particular, signals and the process control primitives (*fork()*, *exec()*, and *_exit()*). We also provide an overview of the two POSIX threads implementations available on Linux—LinuxThreads and NPTL—and note where each of these implementations deviates from the SUSv3 specification of Pthreads.

33.1 Thread Stacks

Each thread has its own stack whose size is fixed when the thread is created. On Linux/x86-32, for all threads other than the main thread, the default size of the per-thread stack is 2 MB. (On some 64-bit architectures, the default size is higher; for example, it is 32 MB on IA-64.) The main thread has a much larger space for stack growth (refer to Figure 29-1, on page 618).

Occasionally, it is useful to change the size of a thread's stack. The *pthread_attr_setstacksize()* function sets a thread attribute (Section 29.8) that determines the size of the stack in threads created using the thread attributes object. The related *pthread_attr_setstack()* function can be used to control both the size and the location of the stack, but setting the location of a stack can decrease application portability. The manual pages provide details of these functions.

One reason to change the size of per-thread stacks is to allow for larger stacks for threads that allocate large automatic variables or make nested function calls of great depth (perhaps because of recursion). Alternatively, an application may want to reduce the size of per-thread stacks to allow for a greater number of threads within a process. For example, on x86-32, where the user-accessible virtual address space is 3 GB, the default stack size of 2 MB means that we can create a maximum of around 1500 threads. (The precise maximum depends on how much virtual memory is consumed by the text and data segments, shared libraries, and so on.) The minimum stack that can be employed on a particular architecture can be determined by calling *sysconf(_SC_THREAD_STACK_MIN)*. For the NPTL implementation on Linux/x86-32, this call returns the value 16,384.

> Under the NPTL threading implementation, if the stack size resource limit (RLIMIT_STACK) is set to anything other than *unlimited*, then it is used as the default stack size when creating new threads. This limit must be set *before* the program is executed, typically by using the *ulimit −s* shell built-in command (*limit stacksize* in the C shell) before executing the program. It is not sufficient to use *setrlimit()* within the main program to set the limit, because NPTL makes its determination of the default stack size during the run-time initialization that occurs before *main()* is invoked.

33.2 Threads and Signals

The UNIX signal model was designed with the UNIX process model in mind, and predated the arrival of Pthreads by a couple of decades. As a result, there are some significant conflicts between the signal and thread models. These conflicts arose primarily from the need to maintain the traditional signal semantics for single-threaded processes (i.e., the signal semantics of traditional programs should not be changed by Pthreads), while at the same time developing a signal model that would be usable within a multithreaded process.

The differences between the signal and thread models mean that combining signals and threads is complex, and should be avoided whenever possible. Nevertheless, sometimes we must deal with signals in a threaded program. In this section, we discuss the interactions between threads and signals, and describe various functions that are useful in threaded programs that deal with signals.

33.2.1 How the UNIX Signal Model Maps to Threads

To understand how UNIX signals map to the Pthreads model, we need to know which aspects of the signal model are process-wide (i.e., are shared by all of the threads in the process) as opposed to those aspects that are specific to individual threads within the process. The following list summarizes the key points:

- Signal actions are process-wide. If any unhandled signal whose default action is *stop* or *terminate* is delivered to any thread in a process, then all of the threads in the process are stopped or terminated.

- Signal dispositions are process-wide; all threads in a process share the same disposition for each signal. If one thread uses *sigaction()* to establish a handler for, say, SIGINT, then that handler may be invoked from any thread to which the SIGINT is delivered. Similarly, if one thread sets the disposition of a signal to *ignore*, then that signal is ignored by all threads.

- A signal may be directed to either the process as a whole or to a specific thread. A signal is thread-directed if:

  - it is generated as the direct result of the execution of a specific hardware instruction within the context of the thread (i.e., the hardware exceptions described in Section 22.4: SIGBUS, SIGFPE, SIGILL, and SIGSEGV);

  - it is a SIGPIPE signal generated when the thread tried to write to a broken pipe; or

  - it is sent using *pthread_kill()* or *pthread_sigqueue()*, which are functions (described in Section 33.2.3) that allow one thread to send a signal to another thread within the same process.

  All signals generated by other mechanisms are process-directed. Examples are signals sent from another process using *kill()* or *sigqueue()*; signals such as SIGINT and SIGTSTP, generated when the user types one of the terminal special characters that generate a signal; and signals generated for software events such as the resizing of a terminal window (SIGWINCH) or the expiration of a timer (e.g., SIGALRM).

- When a signal is delivered to a multithreaded process that has established a signal handler, the kernel arbitrarily selects one thread in the process to which to deliver the signal and invokes the handler in that thread. This behavior is consistent with maintaining the traditional signal semantics. It would not make sense for a process to perform the signal handling actions multiple times in response to a single signal.

- The signal mask is per-thread. (There is no notion of a process-wide signal mask that governs all threads in a multithreaded process.) Threads can independently block or unblock different signals using *pthread_sigmask()*, a new function defined by the Pthreads API. By manipulating the per-thread signal masks, an application can control which thread(s) may handle a signal that is directed to the whole process.

- The kernel maintains a record of the signals that are pending for the process as a whole, as well as a record of the signals that are pending for each thread. A call to *sigpending()* returns the union of the set of signals that are pending for the process and those that are pending for the calling thread. In a newly created thread, the per-thread set of pending signals is initially empty. A thread-directed signal can be delivered only to the target thread. If the thread is blocking the signal, it will remain pending until the thread unblocks the signal (or terminates).

- If a signal handler interrupts a call to *pthread_mutex_lock()*, then the call is always automatically restarted. If a signal handler interrupts a call to *pthread_cond_wait()*, then the call either is restarted automatically (this is what Linux does) or returns 0, indicating a spurious wake-up (in which case a well-designed application will recheck the corresponding predicate and restart the call, as described in Section 30.2.3). SUSv3 requires these two functions to behave as described here.

- The alternate signal stack is per-thread (refer to the description of *sigaltstack()* in Section 21.3). A newly created thread doesn't inherit the alternate signal stack from its creator.

More precisely, SUSv3 specifies that there is a separate alternate signal stack for each kernel scheduling entity (KSE). On a system with a 1:1 threading implementation, as on Linux, there is one KSE per thread (see Section 33.4).

33.2.2 Manipulating the Thread Signal Mask

When a new thread is created, it inherits a copy of the signal mask of the thread that created it. A thread can use *pthread_sigmask()* to change its signal mask, to retrieve the existing mask, or both.

```
#include <signal.h>

int pthread_sigmask(int how, const sigset_t *set, sigset_t *oldset);
```
Returns 0 on success, or a positive error number on error

Other than the fact that it operates on the thread signal mask, the use of *pthread_sigmask()* is the same as the use of *sigprocmask()* (Section 20.10).

> SUSv3 notes that the use of *sigprocmask()* within a multithreaded program is unspecified. We can't portably employ *sigprocmask()* in a multithreaded program. In practice, *sigprocmask()* and *pthread_sigmask()* are identical on many implementations, including Linux.

33.2.3 Sending a Signal to a Thread

The *pthread_kill()* function sends the signal *sig* to a thread in the same process as the caller. The target thread is identified by the argument *thread*.

```
#include <signal.h>

int pthread_kill(pthread_t thread, int sig);
```
Returns 0 on success, or a positive error number on error

Because a thread ID is guaranteed to be unique only within a process (see Section 29.5), we can't use *pthread_kill()* to send a signal to a thread in another process.

> The *pthread_kill()* function is implemented using the Linux-specific *tgkill(tgid, tid, sig)* system call, which sends the signal *sig* to the thread identified by *tid* (a kernel thread ID of the type returned by *gettid()*) within the thread group identified by *tgid*. See the *tgkill(2)* manual page for further details.

The Linux-specific *pthread_sigqueue()* function combines the functionality of *pthread_kill()* and *sigqueue()* (Section 22.8.1): it sends a signal with accompanying data to a thread in the same process as the caller.

```
#define _GNU_SOURCE
#include <signal.h>

int pthread_sigqueue(pthread_t thread, int sig, const union sigval value);
```
                        Returns 0 on success, or a positive error number on error

As with *pthread_kill()*, *sig* specifies the signal to be sent, and *thread* identifies the target thread. The *value* argument specifies the data to accompany the signal, and is used in the same way as the equivalent argument of *sigqueue()*.

> The *pthread_sigqueue()* function was added to *glibc* in version 2.11 and requires support from the kernel. This support is provided by the *rt_tgsigqueueinfo()* system call, which was added in Linux 2.6.31.

33.2.4 Dealing with Asynchronous Signals Sanely

In Chapters 20 to 22, we discussed various factors—such as reentrancy issues, the need to restart interrupted system calls, and avoiding race conditions—that can make it complex to deal with asynchronously generated signals via signal handlers. Furthermore, none of the functions in the Pthreads API is among the set of async-signal-safe functions that we can safely call from within a signal handler (Section 21.1.2). For these reasons, multithreaded programs that must deal with asynchronously generated signals generally should not use a signal handler as the mechanism to receive notification of signal delivery. Instead, the preferred approach is the following:

- All threads block all of the asynchronous signals that the process might receive. The simplest way to do this is to block the signals in the main thread before any other threads are created. Each subsequently created thread will inherit a copy of the main thread's signal mask.

- Create a single dedicated thread that accepts incoming signals using *sigwaitinfo()*, *sigtimedwait()*, or *sigwait()*. We described *sigwaitinfo()* and *sigtimedwait()* in Section 22.10. We describe *sigwait()* below.

The advantage of this approach is that asynchronously generated signals are received synchronously. As it accepts incoming signals, the dedicated thread can safely modify shared variables (under mutex control) and call non-async-signal-safe functions. It can also signal condition variables, and employ other thread and process communication and synchronization mechanisms.

The *sigwait()* function waits for the delivery of one of the signals in the signal set pointed to by *set*, accepts that signal, and returns it in *sig*.

```
#include <signal.h>

int sigwait(const sigset_t *set, int *sig);
```
                        Returns 0 on success, or a positive error number on error

The operation of *sigwait()* is the same as *sigwaitinfo()*, except that:

- instead of returning a *siginfo_t* structure describing the signal, *sigwait()* returns just the signal number; and
- the return value is consistent with other thread-related functions (rather than the 0 or −1 returned by traditional UNIX system calls).

If multiple threads are waiting for the same signal with *sigwait()*, only one of the threads will actually accept the signal when it arrives. Which of the threads this will be is indeterminate.

33.3 Threads and Process Control

Like the signals mechanism, *exec()*, *fork()*, and *exit()* predate the Pthreads API. In the following paragraphs, we note some details concerning the use of these system calls in threaded programs.

Threads and *exec()*

When any thread calls one of the *exec()* functions, the calling program is completely replaced. All threads, except the one that called *exec()*, vanish immediately. None of the threads executes destructors for thread-specific data or calls cleanup handlers. All of the (process-private) mutexes and condition variables belonging to the process also disappear. After an *exec()*, the thread ID of the remaining thread is unspecified.

Threads and *fork()*

When a multithreaded process calls *fork()*, only the calling thread is replicated in the child process. (The ID of the thread in the child is the same as the ID of the thread that called *fork()* in the parent.) All of the other threads vanish in the child; no thread-specific data destructors or cleanup handlers are executed for those threads. This can lead to various problems:

- Although only the calling thread is replicated in the child, the states of global variables, as well as all Pthreads objects such as mutexes and condition variables, are preserved in the child. (This is so because these Pthreads objects are allocated within the parent's memory, and the child gets a duplicate of that memory.) This can lead to tricky scenarios. For example, suppose that another thread had locked a mutex at the time of the *fork()* and is part-way through updating a global data structure. In this case, the thread in the child would not be able to unlock the mutex (since it is not the mutex owner) and would block if it tried to acquire the mutex. Furthermore, the child's copy of the global data structure is probably in an inconsistent state, because the thread that was updating it vanished part-way through the update.
- Since destructors for thread-specific data and cleanup handlers are not called, a *fork()* in a multithreaded program can cause memory leaks in the child. Furthermore, the thread-specific data items created by other threads are likely to be inaccessible to the thread in the new child, since it doesn't have pointers referring to these items.

Because of these problems, the usual recommendation is that the only use of *fork()* in a multithreaded process should be one that is followed by an immediate *exec()*. The *exec()* causes all of the Pthreads objects in the child process to disappear as the new program overwrites the memory of the process.

For programs that must use a *fork()* that is not followed by an *exec()*, the Pthreads API provides a mechanism for defining *fork handlers*. Fork handlers are established using a *pthread_atfork()* call of the following form:

```
pthread_atfork(prepare_func, parent_func, child_func);
```

Each *pthread_atfork()* call adds *prepare_func* to a list of functions that will be automatically executed (in reverse order of registration) before the new child process is created when *fork()* is called. Similarly, *parent_func* and *child_func* are added to a list of functions that will be called automatically (in order of registration), in, respectively, the parent and child process, just before *fork()* returns.

Fork handlers are sometimes useful for library code that makes use of threads. In the absence of fork handlers, there would be no way for the library to deal with applications that naively make use of the library and call *fork()*, unaware that the library has created some threads.

The child produced by *fork()* inherits fork handlers from the thread that called *fork()*. During an *exec()*, fork handlers are not preserved (they can't be, since the code of the handlers is overwritten during the *exec()*).

Further details on fork handlers, and examples of their use, can be found in [Butenhof, 1996].

> On Linux, fork handlers are not called if a program using the NPTL threading library calls *vfork()*. However, in a program using LinuxThreads, fork handlers are called in this case.

Threads and *exit()*

If any thread calls *exit()* or, equivalently, the main thread does a return, all threads vanish after higher-level cleanups have been performed (e.g., calling C++ destructors); no thread-specific data destructors or cleanup handlers are executed.

33.4 Thread Implementation Models

In this section, we go into some theory, briefly considering three different models for implementing a threading API. This provides useful background for Section 33.5, where we consider the Linux threading implementations. The differences between these implementation models hinge on how threads are mapped onto *kernel scheduling entities* (KSEs), which are the units to which the kernel allocates the CPU and other system resources. (In traditional UNIX implementations that predate threads, the term *kernel scheduling entity* is synonymous with the term *process*.)

Many-to-one (M:1) implementations (user-level threads)

In M:1 threading implementations, all of the details of thread creation, scheduling, and synchronization (mutex locking, waiting on condition variables, and so on) are handled entirely within the process by a user-space threading library. The kernel knows nothing about the existence of multiple threads within the process.

M:1 implementations have a few advantages. The greatest advantage is that many threading operations—for example, creating and terminating a thread, context switching between threads, and mutex and condition variable operations—are fast, since a switch to kernel mode is not required. Furthermore, since kernel support for the threading library is not required, an M:1 implementation can be relatively easily ported from one system to another.

However, M:1 implementations suffer from some serious disadvantages:

- When a thread makes a system call such as *read()*, control passes from the user-space threading library to the kernel. This means that if the *read()* call blocks, then all threads in the process are blocked.

- The kernel can't schedule the threads of a process. Since the kernel is unaware of the existence of multiple threads within the process, it can't schedule the separate threads to different processors on multiprocessor hardware. Nor is it possible to meaningfully assign a thread in one process a higher priority than a thread in another process, since the scheduling of the threads is handled entirely within the process.

One-to-one (1:1) implementations (kernel-level threads)

In a 1:1 threading implementation, each thread maps onto a separate KSE. The kernel handles each thread's scheduling separately. Thread synchronization operations are implemented using system calls into the kernel.

1:1 implementations eliminate the disadvantages suffered by M:1 implementations. A blocking system call does not cause all of the threads in a process to block, and the kernel can schedule the threads of a process onto different CPUs on multiprocessor hardware.

However, operations such as thread creation, context switching, and synchronization are slower on a 1:1 implementation, since a switch into kernel mode is required. Furthermore, the overhead required to maintain a separate KSE for each of the threads in an application that contains a large number of threads may place a significant load on the kernel scheduler, degrading overall system performance.

Despite these disadvantages, a 1:1 implementation is usually preferred over an M:1 implementation. Both of the Linux threading implementations—LinuxThreads and NPTL—employ the 1:1 model.

> During the development of NPTL, significant effort went into rewriting the kernel scheduler and devising a threading implementation that would allow the efficient execution of multithreaded processes containing many thousands of threads. Subsequent testing showed that this goal was achieved.

Many-to-many (M:N) implementations (two-level model)

M:N implementations aim to combine the advantages of the 1:1 and M:1 models, while eliminating their disadvantages.

In the M:N model, each process can have multiple associated KSEs, and several threads may map to each KSE. This design permits the kernel to distribute the threads of an application across multiple CPUs, while eliminating the possible scaling problems associated with applications that employ large numbers of threads.

The most significant disadvantage of the M:N model is complexity. The task of thread scheduling is shared between the kernel and the user-space threading library, which must cooperate and communicate information with one another. Managing signals according to the requirements of SUSv3 is also complex under an M:N implementation.

> An M:N implementation was initially considered for the NPTL threading implementation, but rejected as requiring changes to the kernel that were too wide ranging and perhaps unnecessary, given the ability of the Linux scheduler to scale well, even when dealing with large numbers of KSEs.

33.5 Linux Implementations of POSIX Threads

Linux has two main implementations of the Pthreads API:

- *LinuxThreads*: This is the original Linux threading implementation, developed by Xavier Leroy.
- *NPTL (Native POSIX Threads Library)*: This is the modern Linux threading implementation, developed by Ulrich Drepper and Ingo Molnar as a successor to LinuxThreads. NPTL provides performance that is superior to LinuxThreads, and it adheres more closely to the SUSv3 specification for Pthreads. Support for NPTL required changes to the kernel, and these changes appeared in Linux 2.6.

> For a while, it appeared that the successor to LinuxThreads would be another implementation, called Next Generation POSIX Threads (NGPT), a threading implementation developed at IBM. NGPT employed an M:N design and performed significantly better than LinuxThreads. However, the NPTL developers decided to pursue a new implementation. This approach was justified—the 1:1-design NPTL was shown to perform better than NGPT. Following the release of NPTL, development of NGPT was discontinued.

In the following sections, we consider further details of these two implementations, and note the points where they deviate from the SUSv3 requirements for Pthreads.

At this point, it is worth emphasizing that the LinuxThreads implementation is now obsolete; it is not supported in *glibc* 2.4 and later. All new thread library development occurs only in NPTL.

33.5.1 LinuxThreads

For many years, LinuxThreads was the main threading implementation on Linux, and it was sufficient for implementing a variety of threaded applications. The essentials of the LinuxThreads implementation are as follows:

- Threads are created using a *clone()* call that specifies the following flags:

    ```
    CLONE_VM | CLONE_FILES | CLONE_FS | CLONE_SIGHAND
    ```

    This means that LinuxThreads threads share virtual memory, file descriptors, file system–related information (umask, root directory, and current working directory), and signal dispositions. However, threads don't share process IDs and parent process IDs.

- In addition to the threads created by the application, LinuxThreads creates an additional "manager" thread that handles thread creation and termination.

- The implementation uses signals for its internal operation. With kernels that support realtime signals (Linux 2.2 and later), the first three realtime signals are used. With older kernels, SIGUSR1 and SIGUSR2 are used. Applications can't use these signals. (The use of signals results in high latency for various thread synchronization operations.)

LinuxThreads deviations from specified behavior

LinuxThreads doesn't conform to the SUSv3 specification for Pthreads on a number of points. (The LinuxThreads implementation was constrained by the kernel features available at the time that it was developed; it was as conformant as practicable within those constraints.) The following list summarizes the nonconformances:

- Calls to *getpid()* return a different value in each of the threads of a process. Calls to *getppid()* in threads other than the main thread return the process ID of the manager thread, which reflects the fact that every thread other than the main thread is created by the manager thread. Calls to *getppid()* in the other threads should return the same value as a call to *getppid()* in the main thread.

- If one thread creates a child using *fork()*, then any other thread should be able to obtain the termination status of that child using *wait()* (or similar). However, this is not so; only the thread that created the child process can *wait()* for it.

- If a thread calls *exec()*, then, as required by SUSv3, all other threads are terminated. However, if the *exec()* is done from any thread other than the main thread, then the resulting process will have the same process ID as the calling thread—that is, a process ID that is different from the main thread's process ID. According to SUSv3, the process ID should be the same as that of the main thread.

- Threads don't share credentials (user and group IDs). When a multithreaded process is executing a set-user-ID program, this can lead to scenarios in which one thread can't send a signal to another thread using *pthread_kill()*, because the credentials of the two threads have been changed in such a way that the sending thread no longer has permission to signal the target thread (refer to Figure 20-2, on page 403). Furthermore, since the LinuxThreads implementation uses signals internally, various Pthreads operations can fail or hang if a thread changes its credentials.

- Various aspects of the SUSv3 specification for the interaction between threads and signals are not honored:
  - A signal that is sent to a process using *kill()* or *sigqueue()* should be delivered to, and handled by, an arbitrary thread in the target process that is not blocking the signal. However, since LinuxThreads threads have different process IDs, a signal can be targeted only at a specific thread. If that thread is blocking the signal, it remains pending, even if there are other threads that are not blocking the signal.

- LinuxThreads doesn't support the notion of signals that are pending for a process as whole; only per-thread pending signals are supported.

- If a signal is directed at a process group that contains a multithreaded application, then the signal will be handled by all threads in the application (i.e., all threads that have established a signal handler), rather than by a single (arbitrary) thread. Such a signal may, for example, be generated by typing one of the terminal characters that generates a job-control signal for the foreground process group.

- The alternate signal stack settings (established by *sigaltstack()*) are per-thread. However, because a new thread wrongly inherits its alternate signal stack settings from the caller of *pthread_create()*, the two threads share an alternate signal stack. SUSv3 requires that a new thread should start with no alternate signal stack defined. The consequence of this LinuxThreads nonconformance is that if two threads happen to simultaneously handle different signals on their shared alternate signal stacks at the same time, chaos is likely to result (e.g., a program crash). This problem may be very hard to reproduce and debug, since its occurrence depends on the probably rare event that the two signals are handled at the same time.

> In a program using LinuxThreads, a new thread could make a call to *sigaltstack()* to ensure that it uses a different alternate signal stack from the thread that created it (or no stack at all). However, portable programs (and library functions that create threads) won't know to do this, since it is not a requirement on other implementations. Furthermore, even if we employ this technique, there is still a possible race condition: the new thread could receive and handle a signal on the alternate stack before it has a chance to call *sigaltstack()*.

- Threads don't share a common session ID and process group ID. The *setsid()* and *setpgid()* system calls can't be used to change the session or process group membership of a multithreaded process.

- Record locks established using *fcntl()* are not shared. Overlapping lock requests of the same type are not merged.

- Threads don't share resource limits. SUSv3 specifies that resource limits are process-wide attributes.

- The CPU time returned by *times()* and the resource usage information returned by *getrusage()* are per-thread. These system calls should return process-wide totals.

- Some versions of *ps(1)* show all of the threads in a process (including the manager thread) as separate items with distinct process IDs.

- Threads don't share the nice value set by *setpriority()*.

- Interval timers created using *setitimer()* are not shared between threads.

- Threads don't share System V semaphore undo (*semadj*) values.

Other problems with LinuxThreads

In addition to the above deviations from SUSv3, the LinuxThreads implementation has the following problems:

- If the manager thread is killed, then the remaining threads must be manually cleaned up.

- A core dump of a multithreaded program may not include all of the threads of the process (or even the one that triggered the core dump).

- The nonstandard *ioctl()* TIOCNOTTY operation can remove the process's association with a controlling terminal only when called from the main thread.

33.5.2 NPTL

NPTL was designed to address most of the shortcomings of LinuxThreads. In particular:

- NPTL provides much closer conformance to the SUSv3 specification for Pthreads.

- Applications that employ large numbers of threads scale much better under NPTL than under LinuxThreads.

> NPTL allows an application to create large numbers of threads. The NPTL implementers were able to run test programs that created 100,000 threads. With LinuxThreads, the practical limit on the number of threads is a few thousand. (Admittedly, very few applications need such large numbers of threads.)

Work on implementing NPTL began in 2002 and progressed over the next year or so. In parallel, various changes were made within the Linux kernel to accommodate the requirements of NPTL. The changes that appeared in the Linux 2.6 kernel to support NPTL included the following:

- refinements to the implementation of thread groups (Section 28.2.1);
- the addition of futexes as a synchronization mechanism (futexes are a generic mechanism that was designed not just for NPTL);
- the addition of new system calls (*get_thread_area()* and *set_thread_area()*) to support thread-local storage;
- support for threaded core dumps and debugging of multithreaded processes;
- modifications to support management of signals in a manner consistent with the Pthreads model;
- the addition of a new *exit_group()* system call to terminate all of the threads in a process (starting with *glibc* 2.3, *_exit()*—and thus also the *exit()* library function—is aliased as a wrapper that invokes *exit_group()*, while a call to *pthread_exit()* invokes the true *_exit()* system call in the kernel, which terminates just the calling thread);
- a rewrite of the kernel scheduler to allow efficient scheduling of very large numbers (i.e., thousands) of KSEs;

- improved performance for the kernel's process termination code; and
- extensions to the *clone()* system call (Section 28.2).

The essentials of the NPTL implementation are as follows:

- Threads are created using a *clone()* call that specifies the following flags:

```
CLONE_VM | CLONE_FILES | CLONE_FS | CLONE_SIGHAND |
CLONE_THREAD | CLONE_SETTLS | CLONE_PARENT_SETTID |
CLONE_CHILD_CLEARTID | CLONE_SYSVSEM
```

   NPTL threads share all of the information that LinuxThreads threads share, and more. The CLONE_THREAD flag means that a thread is placed in the same thread group as its creator and shares the same process ID and parent process ID. The CLONE_SYSVSEM flag means that a thread shares System V semaphore undo values with its creator.

   > When we use *ps(1)* to list a multithreaded process running under NPTL, we see just a single line of output. To see information about the threads within a process, we can use the *ps −L* option.

- The implementation makes internal use of the first two realtime signals. Applications can't use these signals.

   > One of these signals is used to implement thread cancellation. The other signal is used as part of a technique that ensures that all of the threads in a process have the same user and group IDs. This technique is required because, at the kernel level, threads have distinct user and group credentials. Therefore, the NPTL implementation does some work in the wrapper function for each system call that changes user and group IDs (*setuid()*, *setresuid()*, and so on, and their group analogs) that causes the IDs to be changed in all of the threads of the process.

- Unlike LinuxThreads, NPTL doesn't use manager threads.

NPTL standards conformance

These changes mean that NPTL achieves much closer SUSv3 conformance than LinuxThreads. At the time of writing, the following nonconformance remains:

- Threads don't share a nice value.

There are some additional NPTL nonconformances in earlier 2.6.*x* kernels:

- In kernels before 2.6.16, the alternate signal stack was per-thread, but a new thread wrongly inherited alternate signal stack settings (established by *sigaltstack()*) from the caller of *pthread_create()*, with the consequence that the two threads shared an alternate signal stack.
- In kernels before 2.6.16, only a thread group leader (i.e., the main thread) could start a new session by calling *setsid()*.
- In kernels before 2.6.16, only a thread group leader could use *setpgid()* to make the host process a process group leader.

- In kernels prior to 2.6.12, interval timers created using *setitimer()* were not shared between the threads of a process.

- In kernels prior to 2.6.10, resource limit settings were not shared between the threads of a process.

- In kernels prior to 2.6.9, the CPU time returned by *times()* and the resource usage information returned by *getrusage()* were per-thread.

NPTL was designed to be ABI-compatible with LinuxThreads. This means that programs that were linked against a GNU C library providing LinuxThreads don't need to be relinked in order to use NPTL. However, some behaviors may change when the program is run with NPTL, primarily because NPTL adheres more closely to the SUSv3 specification for Pthreads.

33.5.3 Which Threading Implementation?

Some Linux distributions ship with a GNU C library that provides both LinuxThreads and NPTL, with the default being determined by the dynamic linker according to the underlying kernel on which the system is running. (These distributions are by now historical because, since version 2.4, *glibc* no longer provides LinuxThreads.) Therefore, we may sometimes need to answer the following questions:

- Which threading implementation is available in a particular Linux distribution?

- On a Linux distribution that provides both LinuxThreads and NPTL, which implementation is used by default, and how can we explicitly select the implementation that is used by a program?

Discovering the threading implementation

We can use a few techniques to discover the threading implementation that is available on a particular system, or to discover the default implementation that will be employed when a program is run on a system that provides both threading implementations.

On a system providing *glibc* version 2.3.2 or later, we can use the following command to discover which threading implementation the system provides, or, if it provides both implementation, then which one is used by default:

```
$ getconf GNU_LIBPTHREAD_VERSION
```

On a system where NPTL is the only or the default implementation, this will display a string such as the following:

```
NPTL 2.3.4
```

> Since *glibc* 2.3.2, a program can obtain similar information by using *confstr(3)* to retrieve the value of the *glibc*-specific _CS_GNU_LIBPTHREAD_VERSION configuration variable.

On systems with older GNU C libraries, we must do a little more work. First, the following command can be used to show the pathname of the GNU C library that is used when we run a program (here, we use the example of the standard *ls* program, which resides at /bin/ls):

```
$ ldd /bin/ls | grep libc.so
        libc.so.6 => /lib/tls/libc.so.6 (0x40050000)
```

> We say a little more about the *ldd* (list dynamic dependencies) program in Section 41.5.

The pathname of the GNU C library is shown after the =>. If we execute this pathname as a command, then *glibc* displays a range of information about itself. We can *grep* through this information to select the line that displays the threading implementation:

```
$ /lib/tls/libc.so.6 | egrep -i 'threads|nptl'
        Native POSIX Threads Library by Ulrich Drepper et al
```

We include *nptl* in the *egrep* regular expression because some *glibc* releases containing NPTL instead display a string like this:

```
        NPTL 0.61 by Ulrich Drepper
```

Since the *glibc* pathname may vary from one Linux distribution to another, we can employ shell command substitution to produce a command line that will display the threading implementation in use on any Linux system, as follows:

```
$ $(ldd /bin/ls | grep libc.so | awk '{print $3}') | egrep -i 'threads|nptl'
        Native POSIX Threads Library by Ulrich Drepper et al
```

Selecting the threading implementation used by a program

On a Linux system that provides both NPTL and LinuxThreads, it is sometimes useful to be able to explicitly control which threading implementation is used. The most common example of this requirement is when we have an older program that depends on some (probably nonstandard) behavior of LinuxThreads, so that we want to force the program to run with that threading implementation, instead of the default NPTL.

For this purpose, we can employ a special environment variable understood by the dynamic linker: LD_ASSUME_KERNEL. As its name suggests, this environment variable tells the dynamic linker to operate as though it is running on top of a particular Linux kernel version. By specifying a kernel version that doesn't provide support for NPTL (e.g., 2.2.5), we can ensure that LinuxThreads is used. Thus, we could run a multithreaded program with LinuxThreads using the following command:

```
$ LD_ASSUME_KERNEL=2.2.5 ./prog
```

When we combine this environment variable setting with the command that we described earlier to show the threading implementation that is used, we see something like the following:

```
$ export LD_ASSUME_KERNEL=2.2.5
$ $(ldd /bin/ls | grep libc.so | awk '{print $3}') | egrep -i 'threads|nptl'
        linuxthreads-0.10 by Xavier Leroy
```

The range of kernel version numbers that can be specified in LD_ASSUME_KERNEL is subject to some limits. In several common distributions that supply both NPTL and LinuxThreads, specifying the version number as 2.2.5 is sufficient to ensure the use of LinuxThreads. For a fuller description of the use of this environment variable, see *http://people.redhat.com/drepper/assumekernel.html*.

33.6 Advanced Features of the Pthreads API

Some advanced features of the Pthreads API include the following:

- *Realtime scheduling*: We can set realtime scheduling policies and priorities for threads. This is similar to the process realtime scheduling system calls described in Section 35.3.

- *Process shared mutexes and condition variables*: SUSv3 specifies an option to allow mutexes and condition variables to be shared between processes (rather than just among the threads of a single process). In this case, the condition variable or mutex must be located in a region of memory shared between the processes. NPTL supports this feature.

- *Advanced thread-synchronization primitives*: These facilities include barriers, read-write locks, and spin locks.

Further details on all of these features can be found in [Butenhof, 1996].

33.7 Summary

Threads don't mix well with signals; multithreaded application designs should avoid the use of signals whenever possible. If a multithreaded application must deal with asynchronous signals, usually the cleanest way to do so is to block signals in all threads, and have a single dedicated thread that accepts incoming signals using *sigwait()* (or similar). This thread can then safely perform tasks such as modifying shared variables (under mutex control) and calling non-async-signal-safe functions.

Two threading implementations are commonly available on Linux: LinuxThreads and NPTL. LinuxThreads has been available on Linux for many years, but there are a number of points where it doesn't conform to the requirements of SUSv3 and it is now obsolete. The more recent NPTL implementation provides closer SUSv3 conformance and superior performance, and is the implementation provided in modern Linux distributions.

Further information

Refer to the sources of further information listed in Section 29.10.

The author of LinuxThreads documented the implementation in a web page that can be found at *http://pauillac.inria.fr/~xleroy/linuxthreads/*. The NPTL implementation is described by its implementers in a (now somewhat out-of-date) paper that is available online at *http://people.redhat.com/drepper/nptl-design.pdf*.

33.8 Exercises

33-1. Write a program to demonstrate that different threads in the same process can have different sets of pending signals, as returned by *sigpending()*. You can do this by using *pthread_kill()* to send different signals to two different threads that have blocked these signals, and then have each of the threads call *sigpending()* and display information about pending signals. (You may find the functions in Listing 20-4 useful.)

33-2. Suppose that a thread creates a child using *fork()*. When the child terminates, is it guaranteed that the resulting SIGCHLD signal will be delivered to the thread that called *fork()* (as opposed to some other thread in the process)?

34

PROCESS GROUPS, SESSIONS, AND JOB CONTROL

Process groups and sessions form a two-level hierarchical relationship between processes: a process group is a collection of related processes, and a session is a collection of related process groups. The meaning of the term *related* in each case will become clear in the course of this chapter.

Process groups and sessions are abstractions defined to support shell job control, which allows interactive users to run commands in the foreground or in the background. The term *job* is often used synonymously with the term *process group*.

This chapter describes process groups, sessions, and job control.

34.1 Overview

A *process group* is a set of one or more processes sharing the same *process group identifier* (PGID). A process group ID is a number of the same type (*pid_t*) as a process ID. A process group has a *process group leader*, which is the process that becomes the first member of the group and whose process ID becomes the process group ID of the group. A new process inherits its parent's process group ID.

A process group has a *lifetime*, which is the period of time beginning when the leader joins the group and ending when the last member process leaves the group. A process may leave a process group either by terminating or by joining another process group. The process group leader need not be the last member of a process group.

A *session* is a collection of process groups. A process's session membership is determined by its *session identifier* (SID), which, like the process group ID, is a number of type *pid_t*. A *session leader* is the process that creates a new session and whose process ID becomes the session ID. A new process inherits its parent's session ID.

All of the processes in a session share a single *controlling terminal*. The controlling terminal is established when the session leader first opens a terminal device. A terminal may be the controlling terminal of at most one session.

At any point in time, one of the process groups in a session is the *foreground process group* for the terminal, and the others are *background process groups*. Only processes in the foreground process group can read input from the controlling terminal. When the user types one of the signal-generating terminal characters on the controlling terminal, a signal is sent to all members of the foreground process group. These characters are the *interrupt* character (usually *Control-C*), which generates SIGINT; the *quit* character (usually *Control-*), which generates SIGQUIT; and the *suspend* character (usually *Control-Z*), which generates SIGTSTP.

As a consequence of establishing the connection to (i.e., opening) the controlling terminal, the session leader becomes the *controlling process* for the terminal. The principal significance of being the controlling process is that the kernel sends this process a SIGHUP signal if a terminal disconnect occurs.

> By inspecting the Linux-specific /proc/*PID*/stat files, we can determine the process group ID and session ID of any process. We can also determine the device ID of the process's controlling terminal (expressed as a single decimal integer containing both major and minor IDs) and the process ID of the controlling process for that terminal. See the *proc(5)* manual page for further details.

The main use of sessions and process groups is for shell job control. Looking at a specific example from this domain helps clarify these concepts. For an interactive login, the controlling terminal is the one on which the user logs in. The login shell becomes the session leader and the controlling process for the terminal, and is also made the sole member of its own process group. Each command or pipeline of commands started from the shell results in the creation of one or more processes, and the shell places all of these processes in a new process group. (These processes are initially the only members of that process group, although any child processes that they create will also be members of the group.) A command or pipeline is created as a background process group if it is terminated with an ampersand (&). Otherwise, it becomes the foreground process group. All processes created during the login session are part of the same session.

> In a windowing environment, the controlling terminal is a pseudoterminal, and there is a separate session for each terminal window, with the window's startup shell being the session leader and controlling process for the terminal.
>
> Process groups occasionally find uses in areas other than job control, since they have two useful properties: a parent process can wait on any of its children in a particular process group (Section 26.1.2), and a signal can be sent to all of the members of a process group (Section 20.5).

Figure 34-1 shows the process group and session relationships between the various processes resulting from the execution of the following commands:

```
$ echo $$                          Display the PID of the shell
400
$ find / 2> /dev/null | wc -l &    Creates 2 processes in background group
[1] 659
$ sort < longlist | uniq -c        Creates 2 processes in foreground group
```

At this point, the shell (*bash*), *find*, *wc*, *sort*, and *uniq* are all running.

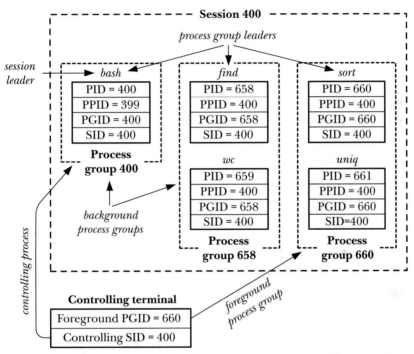

Figure 34-1: Relationships between process groups, sessions, and the controlling terminal

34.2 Process Groups

Each process has a numeric process group ID that defines the process group to which it belongs. A new process inherits its parent's process group ID. A process can obtain its process group ID using *getpgrp()*.

```
#include <unistd.h>

pid_t getpgrp(void);
                Always successfully returns process group ID of calling process
```

If the value returned by *getpgrp()* matches the caller's process ID, this process is the leader of its process group.

The *setpgid()* system call changes the process group of the process whose process ID is *pid* to the value specified in *pgid*.

```
#include <unistd.h>

int setpgid(pid_t pid, pid_t pgid);
```
                                                    Returns 0 on success, or –1 on error

If *pid* is specified as 0, the calling process's process group ID is changed. If *pgid* is specified as 0, then the process group ID of the process specified by *pid* is made the same as its process ID. Thus, the following *setpgid()* calls are equivalent:

```
setpgid(0, 0);
setpgid(getpid(), 0);
setpgid(getpid(), getpid());
```

If *setpgid()* changes the process group ID of the target process (the process specified by *pid*) to be the same as its process ID, then the target process is made the leader of a new process group whose ID is the same as the process ID. If *setpgid()* changes the process group ID of the target process to a value different from its process ID, then the target process is moved to the existing process group specified by *pgid*. If *setpgid()* leaves the process group ID of the target process unchanged, then the call has no effect on the target process.

The typical callers of *setpgid()* (and *setsid()*, described in Section 34.3) are programs such as the shell and *login(1)*. In Section 37.2, we'll see that a program also calls *setsid()* as one of the steps on the way to becoming a daemon.

Several restrictions apply when calling *setpgid()*:

- The *pid* argument may specify only the calling process or one of its children. Violation of this rule results in the error ESRCH.

- When moving a process between groups, the calling process and the process specified by *pid* (which may be one and the same), as well as the target process group, must all be part of the same session. Violation of this rule results in the error EPERM.

- The *pid* argument may not specify a process that is a session leader. Violation of this rule results in the error EPERM.

- A process may not change the process group ID of one of its children after that child has performed an *exec()*. Violation of this rule results in the error EACCES. The rationale for this constraint is that it could confuse a program if its process group ID were changed after it had commenced.

Using *setpgid()* in a job-control shell

The restriction that a process may not change the process group ID of one of its children after that child has performed an *exec()* affects the programming of job-control shells, which have the following requirements:

- All of the processes in a job (i.e., a command or a pipeline) must be placed in a single process group. (We can see the desired result by looking at the two process groups created by *bash* in Figure 34-1.) This step permits the shell to use *killpg()* (or, equivalently, *kill()* with a negative *pid* argument) to simultaneously send job-control signals to all of the members of the process group. Naturally, this step must be carried out before any job-control signals are sent.

- Each of the child processes must be transferred to the process group before it execs a program, since the program itself is ignorant of manipulations of the process group ID.

For each process in the job, either the parent or the child could use *setpgid()* to change the process group ID of the child. However, because the scheduling of the parent and child is indeterminate after a *fork()* (Section 24.4), we can't rely on the parent changing the child's process group ID before the child does an *exec()*; nor can we rely on the child changing its process group ID before the parent tries to send any job-control signals to it. (Dependence on either one of these behaviors would result in a race condition.) Therefore, job-control shells are programmed so that the parent and the child process both call *setpgid()* to change the child's process group ID to the same value immediately after a *fork()*, and the parent ignores any occurrence of the EACCES error on the *setpgid()* call. In other words, in a job-control shell, we'll find code something like that shown in Listing 34-1.

Listing 34-1: How a job-control shell sets the process group ID of a child process

```
pid_t childPid;
pid_t pipelinePgid;        /* PGID to which processes in a pipeline
                              are to be assigned */

/* Other code */

childPid = fork();
switch (childPid) {
case -1: /* fork() failed */
    /* Handle error */

case 0: /* Child */
    if (setpgid(0, pipelinePgid) == -1)
        /* Handle error */
    /* Child carries on to exec the required program */

default: /* Parent (shell) */
    if (setpgid(childPid, pipelinePgid) == -1 && errno != EACCES)
        /* Handle error */
    /* Parent carries on to do other things */
}
```

Things are slightly more complex than shown in Listing 34-1, since, when creating the processes for a pipeline, the parent shell records the process ID of the first process in the pipeline and uses this as the process group ID (*pipelinePgid*) for all of the processes in the group.

Other (obsolete) interfaces for retrieving and modifying process group IDs

The different suffixes in the names of the *getpgrp()* and *setpgid()* system calls deserve explanation.

In the beginning, 4.2BSD provided a *getpgrp(pid)* system call that returned the process group ID of the process specified by *pid*. In practice, *pid* was always used to specify the calling process. Consequently, the POSIX committee deemed the call to be more complex than necessary, and instead adopted the System V *getpgrp()* call, which took no arguments and returned the process group ID of the calling process.

In order to change the process group ID, 4.2BSD provided the call *setpgrp(pid, pgid)*, which operated in a similar manner to *setpgid()*. The principal difference was that the BSD *setpgrp()* could be used to set the process group ID to any value. (We noted earlier that *setpgid()* can't transfer a process into a process group in a different session.) This resulted in some security issues and was also more flexible than required for implementing job control. Consequently, the POSIX committee settled on a more restrictive function and gave it the name *setpgid()*.

To further complicate matters, SUSv3 specifies *getpgid(pid)*, with the same semantics as the old BSD *getpgrp()*, and also weakly specifies an alternative, System V–derived version of *setpgrp()*, taking no arguments, as being approximately equivalent to *setpgid(0, 0)*.

Although the *setpgid()* and *getpgrp()* system calls that we described earlier are sufficient for implementing shell job control, Linux, like most other UNIX implementations, also provides *getpgid(pid)* and *setpgrp(void)*. For backward compatibility, many BSD-derived implementations continue to provide *setprgp(pid, pgid)* as a synonym for *setpgid(pid, pgid)*.

If we explicitly define the _BSD_SOURCE feature test macro when compiling a program, then *glibc* provides the BSD-derived versions of *setpgrp()* and *getpgrp()*, instead of the default versions.

34.3 Sessions

A *session* is a collection of process groups. The session membership of a process is defined by its numeric session ID. A new process inherits its parent's session ID. The *getsid()* system call returns the session ID of the process specified by *pid*.

```
#define _XOPEN_SOURCE 500
#include <unistd.h>

pid_t getsid(pid_t pid);
```
                        Returns session ID of specified process, or –1 on error

If *pid* is specified as 0, *getsid()* returns the session ID of the calling process.

On a few UNIX implementations (e.g., HP-UX 11), *getsid()* can be used to retrieve the session ID of a process only if it is in the same session as the calling process. (SUSv3 permits this possibility.) In other words, the call merely serves, by its success or failure (EPERM), to inform us if the specified process is in the same session as the caller. This restriction doesn't apply on Linux or on most other implementations.

If the calling process is not a process group leader, *setsid()* creates a new session.

```
#include <unistd.h>

pid_t setsid(void);
```
                              Returns session ID of new session, or −1 on error

The *setsid()* system call creates a new session as follows:

- The calling process becomes the leader of a new session, and is made the leader of a new process group within that session. The calling process's process group ID and session ID are set to the same value as its process ID.
- The calling process has no controlling terminal. Any previously existing connection to a controlling terminal is broken.

If the calling process is a process group leader, *setsid()* fails with the error EPERM. The simplest way of ensuring that this doesn't happen is to perform a *fork()* and have the parent exit while the child carries on to call *setsid()*. Since the child inherits its parent's process group ID and receives its own unique process ID, it can't be a process group leader.

The restriction against a process group leader being able to call *setsid()* is necessary because, without it, the process group leader would be able to place itself in another (new) session, while other members of the process group remained in the original session. (A new process group would not be created, since, by definition, the process group leader's process group ID is already the same as its process ID.) This would violate the strict two-level hierarchy of sessions and process groups, whereby all members of a process group must be part of the same session.

> When a new process is created via *fork()*, the kernel ensures not only that it has a unique process ID, but also that the process ID doesn't match the process group ID or session ID of any existing process. Thus, even if the leader of a process group or a session has exited, a new process can't reuse the leader's process ID and thereby accidentally become the leader of an existing session or process group.

Listing 34-2 demonstrates the use of *setsid()* to create a new session. To check that it no longer has a controlling terminal, this program attempts to open the special file /dev/tty (described in the next section). When we run this program, we see the following:

```
$ ps -p $$ -o 'pid pgid sid command'          $$ is PID of shell
  PID  PGID   SID COMMAND
12243 12243 12243 bash                         PID, PGID, and SID of shell
$ ./t_setsid
$ PID=12352, PGID=12352, SID=12352
ERROR [ENXIO Device not configured] open /dev/tty
```

As can be seen from the output, the process successfully places itself in a new process group within a new session. Since this session has no controlling terminal, the *open()* call fails. (In the penultimate line of program output above, we see a shell prompt mixed with the program output, because the shell notices that the parent process has exited after the *fork()* call, and so prints its next prompt before the child has completed.)

Listing 34-2: Creating a new session

────────────────────────────────────── pgsjc/t_setsid.c
```
#define _XOPEN_SOURCE 500
#include <unistd.h>
#include <fcntl.h>
#include "tlpi_hdr.h"

int
main(int argc, char *argv[])
{
    if (fork() != 0)                /* Exit if parent, or on error */
        _exit(EXIT_SUCCESS);

    if (setsid() == -1)
        errExit("setsid");

    printf("PID=%ld, PGID=%ld, SID=%ld\n", (long) getpid(),
            (long) getpgrp(), (long) getsid(0));

    if (open("/dev/tty", O_RDWR) == -1)
        errExit("open /dev/tty");
    exit(EXIT_SUCCESS);
}
```
────────────────────────────────────── pgsjc/t_setsid.c

34.4 Controlling Terminals and Controlling Processes

All of the processes in a session may have a (single) controlling terminal. Upon creation, a session has no controlling terminal; the controlling terminal is established when the session leader first opens a terminal that is not already the controlling terminal for a session, unless the O_NOCTTY flag is specified when calling *open()*. A terminal may be the controlling terminal for at most one session.

> SUSv3 specifies the function *tcgetsid(int fd)* (prototyped in <termios.h>), which returns the ID of the session associated with the controlling terminal specified by *fd*. This function is provided in *glibc* (where it is implemented using the *ioctl()* TIOCGSID operation).

The controlling terminal is inherited by the child of a *fork()* and preserved across an *exec()*.

When a session leader opens a controlling terminal, it simultaneously becomes the controlling process for the terminal. If a terminal disconnect subsequently occurs, the kernel sends the controlling process a SIGHUP signal to inform it of this event. We go into further detail on this point in Section 34.6.2.

If a process has a controlling terminal, opening the special file /dev/tty obtains a file descriptor for that terminal. This is useful if standard input and output are redirected, and a program wants to ensure that it is communicating with the controlling terminal. For example, the *getpass()* function described in Section 8.5 opens /dev/tty for this purpose. If the process doesn't have a controlling terminal, opening /dev/tty fails with the error ENXIO.

Removing a process's association with the controlling terminal

The *ioctl(fd, TIOCNOTTY)* operation can be used to remove a process's association with its controlling terminal, specified via the file descriptor *fd*. After this call, attempts to open /dev/tty will fail. (Although not specified in SUSv3, the TIOCNOTTY operation is supported on most UNIX implementations.)

If the calling process is the controlling process for the terminal, then as for the termination of the controlling process (Section 34.6.2), the following steps occur:

1. All processes in the session lose their association with the controlling terminal.
2. The controlling terminal loses its association with the session, and can therefore be acquired as the controlling terminal by another session leader.
3. The kernel sends a SIGHUP signal (and a SIGCONT signal) to all members of the foreground process group, to inform them of the loss of the controlling terminal.

Establishing a controlling terminal on BSD

SUSv3 leaves the manner in which a session acquires a controlling terminal unspecified, merely stating that specifying the O_NOCTTY flag when opening a terminal guarantees that the terminal won't become a controlling terminal for the session. The Linux semantics that we have described above derive from System V.

On BSD systems, opening a terminal in the session leader never causes the terminal to become a controlling terminal, regardless of whether the O_NOCTTY flag is specified. Instead, the session leader uses the *ioctl()* TIOCSCTTY operation to explicitly establish the terminal referred to by the file descriptor *fd* as the controlling terminal:

```
if (ioctl(fd, TIOCSCTTY, 0) == -1)
    errExit("ioctl");
```

This operation can be performed only if the session doesn't already have a controlling terminal.

The TIOCSCTTY operation is also available on Linux, but it is not widespread on other (non-BSD) implementations.

Obtaining a pathname that refers to the controlling terminal: *ctermid()*

The *ctermid()* function returns a pathname referring to the controlling terminal.

```
#include <stdio.h>              /* Defines L_ctermid constant */

char *ctermid(char *ttyname);
```
Returns pointer to string containing pathname of controlling terminal, or NULL if pathname could not be determined

---

The *ctermid()* function returns the controlling terminal's pathname in two different ways: via the function result and via the buffer pointed to by *ttyname*.

If *ttyname* is not NULL, then it should be a buffer of at least L_ctermid bytes, and the pathname is copied into this array. In this case, the function return value is also a pointer to this buffer. If *ttyname* is NULL, *ctermid()* returns a pointer to a statically allocated buffer containing the pathname. When *ttyname* is NULL, *ctermid()* is not reentrant.

On Linux and other UNIX implementations, *ctermid()* typically yields the string /dev/tty. The purpose of this function is to ease portability to non-UNIX systems.

34.5 Foreground and Background Process Groups

The controlling terminal maintains the notion of a foreground process group. Within a session, only one process group can be in the foreground at a particular moment; all of the other process groups in the session are background process groups. The foreground process group is the only process group that can freely read and write on the controlling terminal. When one of the signal-generating terminal characters is typed on the controlling terminal, the terminal driver delivers the corresponding signal to the members of the foreground process group. We describe further details in Section 34.7.

> In theory, situations can arise where a session has no foreground process group. This could happen, for example, if all processes in the foreground process group terminate, and no other process notices this fact and moves itself into the foreground. In practice, such situations are rare. Normally, the shell is the process monitoring the status of the foreground process group, and it moves itself back into the foreground when it notices (via *wait()*) that the foreground process group has terminated.

The *tcgetpgrp()* and *tcsetpgrp()* functions respectively retrieve and change the process group of a terminal. These functions are used primarily by job-control shells.

```
#include <unistd.h>

pid_t tcgetpgrp(int fd);
```
                     Returns process group ID of terminal's foreground process group,
                                                                 or −1 on error
```
int tcsetpgrp(int fd, pid_t pgid);
```
                                             Returns 0 on success, or −1 on error

The *tcgetpgrp()* function returns the process group ID of the foreground process group of the terminal referred to by the file descriptor *fd*, which must be the controlling terminal of the calling process.

> If there is no foreground process group for this terminal, *tcgetpgrp()* returns a value greater than 1 that doesn't match the ID of any existing process group. (This is the behavior specified by SUSv3.)

The *tcsetpgrp()* function changes the foreground process group for a terminal. If the calling process has a controlling terminal, and the file descriptor *fd* refers to that terminal, then *tcsetpgrp()* sets the foreground process group of the terminal to the value specified in *pgid*, which must match the process group ID of one of the processes in the calling process's session.

Both *tcgetpgrp()* and *tcsetpgrp()* are standardized in SUSv3. On Linux, as on many other UNIX implementations, these functions are implemented using two unstandardized *ioctl()* operations: TIOCGPGRP and TIOCSPGRP.

34.6 The SIGHUP Signal

When a controlling process loses its terminal connection, the kernel sends it a SIGHUP signal to inform it of this fact. (A SIGCONT signal is also sent, to ensure that the process is restarted in case it had been previously stopped by a signal.) Typically, this may occur in two circumstances:

- When a "disconnect" is detected by the terminal driver, indicating a loss of signal on a modem or terminal line.
- When a terminal window is closed on a workstation. This occurs because the last open file descriptor for the master side of the pseudoterminal associated with the terminal window is closed.

The default action of SIGHUP is to terminate a process. If the controlling process instead handles or ignores this signal, then further attempts to read from the terminal return end-of-file.

> SUSv3 states that if both a terminal disconnect occurs and one of the conditions giving rise to an EIO error from *read()* exists, then it is unspecified whether *read()* returns end-of-file or fails with the error EIO. Portable programs must allow for both possibilities. We look at the circumstances in which *read()* may fail with the EIO error in Sections 34.7.2 and 34.7.4.

The delivery of SIGHUP to the controlling process can set off a kind of chain reaction, resulting in the delivery of SIGHUP to many other processes. This may occur in two ways:

- The controlling process is typically a shell. The shell establishes a handler for SIGHUP, so that, before terminating, it can send a SIGHUP to each of the jobs that it has created. This signal terminates those jobs by default, but if instead they catch the signal, then they are thus informed of the shell's demise.
- Upon termination of the controlling process for a terminal, the kernel disassociates all processes in the session from the controlling terminal, disassociates the controlling terminal from the session (so that it may be acquired as the controlling terminal by another session leader), and informs the members of the foreground process group of the terminal of the loss of their controlling terminal by sending them a SIGHUP signal.

We go into the details of each of these two cases in the next sections.

The SIGHUP signal also finds other uses. In Section 34.7.4, we'll see that SIGHUP is generated when a process group becomes orphaned. In addition, manually sending SIGHUP is conventionally used as a way of triggering a daemon process to reinitialize itself or reread its configuration file. (By definition, a daemon process doesn't have a controlling terminal, and so can't otherwise receive SIGHUP from the kernel.) We describe the use of SIGHUP with daemon processes in Section 37.4.

34.6.1 Handling of SIGHUP by the Shell

In a login session, the shell is normally the controlling process for the terminal. Most shells are programmed so that, when run interactively, they establish a handler for SIGHUP. This handler terminates the shell, but beforehand sends a SIGHUP signal to each of the process groups (both foreground and background) created by the shell. (The SIGHUP signal may be followed by a SIGCONT signal, depending on the shell and whether or not the job is currently stopped.) How the processes in these groups respond to SIGHUP is application-dependent; if no special action is taken, they are terminated by default.

> Some job-control shells also send SIGHUP to stopped background jobs if the shell exits normally (e.g., when we explicitly log out or type *Control-D* in a shell window). This is done by both *bash* and the Korn shell (after printing a message on the first logout attempt).
>
> The *nohup(1)* command can be used to make a command immune to the SIGHUP signal—that is, start it with the disposition of SIGHUP set to SIG_IGN. The *bash* built-in command *disown* serves a similar purpose, removing a job from the shell's list of jobs, so that the job is not sent SIGHUP when the shell terminates.

We can use the program in Listing 34-3 to demonstrate that when the shell receives SIGHUP, it in turn sends SIGHUP to the jobs it has created. The main task of this program is to create a child process, and then have both the parent and the child pause to catch SIGHUP and display a message if it is received. If the program is given an optional command-line argument (which may be any string), the child places itself in a different process group (within the same session). This is useful to show that the shell doesn't send SIGHUP to a process group that it did not create, even if it is in the same session as the shell. (Since the final for loop of the program loops forever, this program uses *alarm()* to establish a timer to deliver SIGALRM. The arrival of an unhandled SIGALRM signal guarantees process termination, if the process is not otherwise terminated.)

Listing 34-3: Catching SIGHUP

---
　　　　　　　　　　　　　　　　　　　　　　　　　　　　　　　　　　 pgsjc/catch_SIGHUP.c
```
#define _XOPEN_SOURCE 500
#include <unistd.h>
#include <signal.h>
#include "tlpi_hdr.h"

static void
handler(int sig)
{
}
```

```
int
main(int argc, char *argv[])
{
    pid_t childPid;
    struct sigaction sa;

    setbuf(stdout, NULL);          /* Make stdout unbuffered */

    sigemptyset(&sa.sa_mask);
    sa.sa_flags = 0;
    sa.sa_handler = handler;
    if (sigaction(SIGHUP, &sa, NULL) == -1)
        errExit("sigaction");

    childPid = fork();
    if (childPid == -1)
        errExit("fork");

    if (childPid == 0 && argc > 1)
        if (setpgid(0, 0) == -1)            /* Move to new process group */
            errExit("setpgid");

    printf("PID=%ld; PPID=%ld; PGID=%ld; SID=%ld\n", (long) getpid(),
            (long) getppid(), (long) getpgrp(), (long) getsid(0));

    alarm(60);                     /* An unhandled SIGALRM ensures this process
                                      will die if nothing else terminates it */
    for(;;) {                      /* Wait for signals */
        pause();
        printf("%ld: caught SIGHUP\n", (long) getpid());
    }
}
```

—————————————————————————————————————— **pgsjc/catch_SIGHUP.c**

Suppose that we enter the following commands in a terminal window in order to run two instances of the program in Listing 34-3, and then we close the terminal window:

```
$ echo $$                                    PID of shell is ID of session
5533
$ ./catch_SIGHUP > samegroup.log 2>&1 &
$ ./catch_SIGHUP x > diffgroup.log 2>&1
```

The first command results in the creation of two processes that remain in the process group created by the shell. The second command creates a child that places itself in a separate process group.

When we look at samegroup.log, we see that it contains the following output, indicating that both members of this process group were signaled by the shell:

```
$ cat samegroup.log
PID=5612; PPID=5611; PGID=5611; SID=5533      Child
PID=5611; PPID=5533; PGID=5611; SID=5533      Parent
5611: caught SIGHUP
5612: caught SIGHUP
```

When we examine `diffgroup.log`, we find the following output, indicating that when the shell received SIGHUP, it did not send a signal to the process group that it did not create:

```
$ cat diffgroup.log
PID=5614; PPID=5613; PGID=5614; SID=5533      Child
PID=5613; PPID=5533; PGID=5613; SID=5533      Parent
5613: caught SIGHUP                           Parent was signaled, but not child
```

34.6.2 SIGHUP and Termination of the Controlling Process

If the SIGHUP signal that is sent to the controlling process as the result of a terminal disconnect causes the controlling process to terminate, then SIGHUP is sent to all of the members of the terminal's foreground process group (refer to Section 25.2). This behavior is a consequence of the termination of the controlling process, rather than a behavior associated specifically with the SIGHUP signal. If the controlling process terminates for any reason, then the foreground process group is signaled with SIGHUP.

> On Linux, the SIGHUP signal is followed by a SIGCONT signal to ensure that the process group is resumed if it had earlier been stopped by a signal. However, SUSv3 doesn't specify this behavior, and most other UNIX implementations don't send a SIGCONT in this circumstance.

We can use the program in Listing 34-4 to demonstrate that termination of the controlling process causes a SIGHUP signal to be sent to all members of the terminal's foreground process group. This program creates one child process for each of its command-line arguments ②. If the corresponding command-line argument is the letter *d*, then the child process places itself in its own (different) process group ③; otherwise, the child remains in the same process group as its parent. (We use the letter *s* to specify the latter action, although any letter other than *d* can be used.) Each child then establishes a handler for SIGHUP ④. To ensure that they terminate if no event occurs that would otherwise terminate them, the parent and the children both call *alarm()* to set a timer that delivers a SIGALRM signal after 60 seconds ⑤. Finally, all processes (including the parent) print out their process ID and process group ID ⑥ and then loop waiting for signals to arrive ⑦. When a signal is delivered, the handler prints the process ID of the process and signal number ①.

Listing 34-4: Catching SIGHUP when a terminal disconnect occurs

── pgsjc/disc_SIGHUP.c
```c
#define _GNU_SOURCE        /* Get strsignal() declaration from <string.h> */
#include <string.h>
#include <signal.h>
#include "tlpi_hdr.h"

static void                /* Handler for SIGHUP */
handler(int sig)
{
①     printf("PID %ld: caught signal %2d (%s)\n", (long) getpid(),
            sig, strsignal(sig));
                           /* UNSAFE (see Section 21.1.2) */
}
```

```
int
main(int argc, char *argv[])
{
    pid_t parentPid, childPid;
    int j;
    struct sigaction sa;

    if (argc < 2 || strcmp(argv[1], "--help") == 0)
        usageErr("%s {d|s}... [ > sig.log 2>&1 ]\n", argv[0]);

    setbuf(stdout, NULL);              /* Make stdout unbuffered */

    parentPid = getpid();
    printf("PID of parent process is:      %ld\n", (long) parentPid);
    printf("Foreground process group ID is: %ld\n",
            (long) tcgetpgrp(STDIN_FILENO));

②  for (j = 1; j < argc; j++) {       /* Create child processes */
        childPid = fork();
        if (childPid == -1)
            errExit("fork");

        if (childPid == 0) {           /* If child... */
③          if (argv[j][0] == 'd')     /* 'd' --> to different pgrp */
                if (setpgid(0, 0) == -1)
                    errExit("setpgid");

            sigemptyset(&sa.sa_mask);
            sa.sa_flags = 0;
            sa.sa_handler = handler;
④          if (sigaction(SIGHUP, &sa, NULL) == -1)
                errExit("sigaction");
            break;                     /* Child exits loop */
        }
    }

    /* All processes fall through to here */

⑤  alarm(60);          /* Ensure each process eventually terminates */

⑥  printf("PID=%ld PGID=%ld\n", (long) getpid(), (long) getpgrp());
    for (;;)
⑦      pause();        /* Wait for signals */
}
```

—— **pgsjc/disc_SIGHUP.c**

Suppose that we run the program in Listing 34-4 in a terminal window with the following command:

$ exec ./disc_SIGHUP d s s > sig.log 2>&1

The *exec* command is a shell built-in command that causes the shell to do an *exec()*, replacing itself with the named program. Since the shell was the controlling process for the terminal, our program is now the controlling process and will receive

SIGHUP when the terminal window is closed. After closing the terminal window, we find the following lines in the file sig.log:

```
PID of parent process is:        12733
Foreground process group ID is: 12733
PID=12755 PGID=12755              First child is in a different process group
PID=12756 PGID=12733              Remaining children are in same PG as parent
PID=12757 PGID=12733
PID=12733 PGID=12733              This is the parent process
PID 12756: caught signal  1 (Hangup)
PID 12757: caught signal  1 (Hangup)
```

Closing the terminal window caused SIGHUP to be sent to the controlling process (the parent), which terminated as a result. We see that the two children that were in the same process group as the parent (i.e., the foreground process group for the terminal) also both received SIGHUP. However, the child that was in a separate (background) process group did not receive this signal.

34.7 Job Control

Job control is a feature that first appeared around 1980 in the C shell on BSD. Job control permits a shell user to simultaneously execute multiple commands (jobs), one in the foreground and the others in the background. Jobs can be stopped and resumed, and moved between the foreground and background, as described in the following paragraphs.

> In the initial POSIX.1 standard, support for job control was optional. Later UNIX standards made support mandatory.

In the days of character-based dumb terminals (physical terminal devices that were limited to displaying ASCII characters), many shell users knew how to use shell job-control commands. With the advent of bit-mapped monitors running the X Window System, knowledge of shell job control is less common. However, job control remains a useful feature. Using job control to manage multiple simultaneous commands can be faster and simpler than switching back and forth between multiple windows. For those readers unfamiliar with job control, we begin with a short tutorial on its use. We then go on to look at a few details of the implementation of job control and consider the implications of job control for application design.

34.7.1 Using Job Control Within the Shell

When we enter a command terminated by an ampersand (&), it is run as a background job, as illustrated by the following examples:

```
$ grep -r SIGHUP /usr/src/linux >x &
[1] 18932                        Job 1: process running grep has PID 18932
$ sleep 60 &
[2] 18934                        Job 2: process running sleep has PID 18934
```

Each job that is placed in the background is assigned a unique job number by the shell. This job number is shown in square brackets after the job is started in the background, and also when the job is manipulated or monitored by various job-control commands. The number following the job number is the process ID of the process created to execute the command, or, in the case of a pipeline, the process ID of the last process in the pipeline. In the commands described in the following paragraphs, jobs can be referred to using the notation %*num*, where *num* is the number assigned to this job by the shell.

In many cases, the %*num* argument can be omitted, in which case the *current* job is used by default. The current job is the last job that was stopped in the foreground (using the *suspend* character described below), or, if there is no such job, then the last job that was started in the background. (There are some variations in the details of how different shells determine which background job is considered the current job.) In addition, the notation %% or %+ refers to the current job, and the notation %- refers to the *previous current* job. The current and previous current jobs are marked by a plus (+) and a minus (-) sign, respectively, in the output produced by the *jobs* command, which we describe next.

The *jobs* shell built-in command lists all background jobs:

```
$ jobs
[1]- Running         grep -r SIGHUP /usr/src/linux >x &
[2]+ Running         sleep 60 &
```

At this point, the shell is the foreground process for the terminal. Since only a foreground process can read input from the controlling terminal and receive terminal-generated signals, sometimes it is necessary to move a background job into the foreground. This is done using the *fg* shell built-in command:

```
$ fg %1
grep -r SIGHUP /usr/src/linux >x
```

As demonstrated in this example, the shell redisplays a job's command line whenever the job is moved between the foreground and the background. Below, we'll see that the shell also does this whenever the job's state changes in the background.

When a job is running in the foreground, we can suspend it using the terminal *suspend* character (normally *Control-Z*), which sends the SIGTSTP signal to the terminal's foreground process group:

```
Type Control-Z
[1]+ Stopped         grep -r SIGHUP /usr/src/linux >x
```

After we typed *Control-Z*, the shell displays the command that has been stopped in the background. If desired, we can use the *fg* command to resume the job in the foreground, or use the *bg* command to resume it in the background. In both cases, the shell resumes the stopped job by sending it a SIGCONT signal.

```
$ bg %1
[1]+ grep -r SIGHUP /usr/src/linux >x &
```

We can stop a background job by sending it a SIGSTOP signal:

```
$ kill -STOP %1
[1]+ Stopped         grep -r SIGHUP /usr/src/linux >x
$ jobs
[1]+ Stopped         grep -r SIGHUP /usr/src/linux >x
[2]- Running         sleep 60 &
$ bg %1                              Restart job in background
[1]+ grep -r SIGHUP /usr/src/linux >x &
```

> The Korn and C shells provide the command *stop* as a shorthand for *kill –stop*.

When a background job eventually completes, the shell prints a message prior to displaying the next shell prompt:

```
Press Enter to see a further shell prompt
[1]- Done            grep -r SIGHUP /usr/src/linux >x
[2]+ Done            sleep 60
$
```

Only processes in the foreground job may read from the controlling terminal. This restriction prevents multiple jobs from competing for terminal input. If a background job tries to read from the terminal, it is sent a SIGTTIN signal. The default action of SIGTTIN is to stop the job:

```
$ cat > x.txt &
[1] 18947
$
Press Enter once more in order to see job state changes displayed prior to next shell prompt
[1]+ Stopped         cat >x.txt
$
```

> It may not always be necessary to press the *Enter* key to see the job state changes in the previous example and some of the following examples. Depending on kernel scheduling decisions, the shell may receive notification about changes in the state of the background job before the next shell prompt is displayed.

At this point, we must bring the job into the foreground (*fg*), and provide the required input. If desired, we can then continue execution of the job in the background by first suspending it and then resuming it in the background (*bg*). (Of course, in this particular example, *cat* would immediately be stopped again, since it would once more try to read from the terminal.)

By default, background jobs are allowed to perform output to the controlling terminal. However, if the TOSTOP flag (*terminal output stop*, Section 62.5) is set for the terminal, then attempts by background jobs to perform terminal output result in the generation of a SIGTTOU signal. (We can set the TOSTOP flag using the *stty* command, which is described in Section 62.3.) Like SIGTTIN, a SIGTTOU signal stops the job.

```
$ stty tostop                        Enable TOSTOP flag for this terminal
$ date &
[1] 19023
$
Press Enter once more to see job state changes displayed prior to next shell prompt
[1]+ Stopped         date
```

We can then see the output of the job by bringing it into the foreground:

```
$ fg
date
Tue Dec 28 16:20:51 CEST 2010
```

The various states of a job under job control, as well as the shell commands and terminal characters (and the accompanying signals) used to move a job between these states, are summarized in Figure 34-2. This figure also includes a notional *terminated* state for a job. This state can be reached by sending various signals to the job, including SIGINT and SIGQUIT, which can be generated from the keyboard.

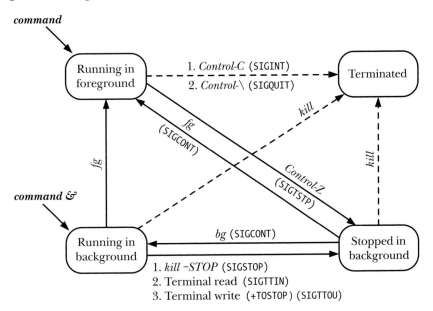

Figure 34-2: Job-control states

34.7.2 Implementing Job Control

In this section, we examine various aspects of the implementation of job control, and conclude with an example program that makes the operation of job control more transparent.

Although optional in the original POSIX.1 standard, later standards, including SUSv3, require that an implementation support job control. This support requires the following:

- The implementation must provide certain job-control signals: SIGTSTP, SIGSTOP, SIGCONT, SIGTTOU, and SIGTTIN. In addition, the SIGCHLD signal (Section 26.3) is also necessary, since it allows the shell (the parent of all jobs) to find out when one of its children terminates or is stopped.

- The terminal driver must support generation of the job-control signals, so that when certain characters are typed, or terminal I/O and certain other terminal operations (described below) are performed from a background job, an appropriate signal (as shown in Figure 34-2) is sent to the relevant process group. In order to be able to carry out these actions, the terminal driver must also record the session ID (controlling process) and foreground process group ID associated with a terminal (Figure 34-1).

- The shell must support job control (most modern shells do so). This support is provided in the form of the commands described earlier to move a job between the foreground and background and monitor the state of jobs. Certain of these commands send signals to a job (as shown in Figure 34-2). In addition, when performing operations that move a job between the *running in foreground* and any of the other states, the shell uses calls to *tcsetpgrp()* to adjust the terminal driver's record of the foreground process group.

> In Section 20.5, we saw that signals can generally be sent to a process only if the real or effective user ID of the sending process matches the real user ID or saved set-user-ID of the receiving process. However, SIGCONT is an exception to this rule. The kernel allows a process (e.g., the shell) to send SIGCONT to any process in the same session, regardless of process credentials. This relaxation of the rules for SIGCONT is required so that if a user starts a set-user-ID program that changes its credentials (in particular, its real user ID), it is still possible to resume it with SIGCONT if it is stopped.

The SIGTTIN and SIGTTOU signals

SUSv3 specifies (and Linux implements) some special cases that apply with respect to the generation of the SIGTTIN and SIGTTOU signals for background jobs:

- SIGTTIN is not sent if the process is currently blocking or ignoring this signal. Instead, a *read()* from the controlling terminal fails, setting *errno* to EIO. The rationale for this behavior is that the process would otherwise have no way of knowing that the *read()* was not permitted.

- Even if the terminal TOSTOP flag is set, SIGTTOU is not sent if the process is currently blocking or ignoring this signal. Instead, a *write()* to the controlling terminal is permitted (i.e., the TOSTOP flag is ignored).

- Regardless of the setting of the TOSTOP flag, certain functions that change terminal driver data structures result in the generation of SIGTTOU for a background process if it tries to apply them to its controlling terminal. These functions include *tcsetpgrp()*, *tcsetattr()*, *tcflush()*, *tcflow()*, *tcsendbreak()*, and *tcdrain()*. (These functions are described in Chapter 62.) If SIGTTOU is being blocked or ignored, these calls succeed.

Example program: demonstrating the operation of job control

The program in Listing 34-5 allows us to see how the shell organizes the commands in a pipeline into a job (process group). This program also allows us to monitor certain of the signals sent and the changes made to the terminal's foreground process group setting under job control. The program is designed so that multiple instances can be run in a pipeline, as in the following example:

```
$ ./job_mon | ./job_mon | ./job_mon
```

The program in Listing 34-5 performs the following steps:

- On startup, the program installs a single handler for SIGINT, SIGTSTP, and SIGCONT ④. The handler carries out the following steps:
  - Display the foreground process group for the terminal ①. To avoid multiple identical lines of output, this is done only by the process group leader.
  - Display the ID of the process, the process's position in the pipeline, and the signal received ②.
  - The handler must do some extra work if it catches SIGTSTP, since, when caught, this signal doesn't stop a process. So, to actually stop the process, the handler raises the SIGSTOP signal ③, which always stops a process. (We refine this treatment of SIGTSTP in Section 34.7.3.)

- If the program is the initial process in the pipeline, it prints headings for the output produced by all of the processes ⑥. In order to test whether it is the initial (or final) process in the pipeline, the program uses the *isatty()* function (described in Section 62.10) to check whether its standard input (or output) is a terminal ⑤. If the specified file descriptor refers to a pipe, *isatty()* returns false (0).

- The program builds a message to be passed to its successor in the pipeline. This message is an integer indicating the position of this process in the pipeline. Thus, for the initial process, the message contains the number 1. If the program is the initial process in the pipeline, the message is initialized to 0. If it is not the initial process in the pipeline, the program first reads this message from its predecessor ⑦. The program increments the message value before proceeding to the next steps ⑧.

- Regardless of its position in the pipeline, the program displays a line containing its pipeline position, process ID, parent process ID, process group ID, and session ID ⑨.

- Unless it is the last command in the pipeline, the program writes an integer message for its successor in the pipeline ⑩.

- Finally, the program loops forever, using *pause()* to wait for signals ⑪.

Listing 34-5: Observing the treatment of a process under job control

––– **pgsjc/job_mon.c**
```
#define _GNU_SOURCE      /* Get declaration of strsignal() from <string.h> */
#include <string.h>
#include <signal.h>
#include <fcntl.h>
#include "tlpi_hdr.h"

static int cmdNum;              /* Our position in pipeline */

static void                     /* Handler for various signals */
handler(int sig)
{
    /* UNSAFE: This handler uses non-async-signal-safe functions
       (fprintf(), strsignal(); see Section 21.1.2) */
```

```
①        if (getpid() == getpgrp())              /* If process group leader */
             fprintf(stderr, "Terminal FG process group: %ld\n",
                     (long) tcgetpgrp(STDERR_FILENO));
②        fprintf(stderr, "Process %ld (%d) received signal %d (%s)\n",
                 (long) getpid(), cmdNum, sig, strsignal(sig));

         /* If we catch SIGTSTP, it won't actually stop us. Therefore we
            raise SIGSTOP so we actually get stopped. */

③        if (sig == SIGTSTP)
             raise(SIGSTOP);
     }

     int
     main(int argc, char *argv[])
     {
         struct sigaction sa;

         sigemptyset(&sa.sa_mask);
         sa.sa_flags = SA_RESTART;
         sa.sa_handler = handler;
④        if (sigaction(SIGINT, &sa, NULL) == -1)
             errExit("sigaction");
         if (sigaction(SIGTSTP, &sa, NULL) == -1)
             errExit("sigaction");
         if (sigaction(SIGCONT, &sa, NULL) == -1)
             errExit("sigaction");

         /* If stdin is a terminal, this is the first process in pipeline:
            print a heading and initialize message to be sent down pipe */

⑤        if (isatty(STDIN_FILENO)) {
             fprintf(stderr, "Terminal FG process group: %ld\n",
                     (long) tcgetpgrp(STDIN_FILENO));
⑥           fprintf(stderr, "Command  PID PPID PGRP   SID\n");
             cmdNum = 0;

         } else {               /* Not first in pipeline, so read message from pipe */
⑦           if (read(STDIN_FILENO, &cmdNum, sizeof(cmdNum)) <= 0)
                 fatal("read got EOF or error");
         }

⑧        cmdNum++;
⑨        fprintf(stderr, "%4d    %5ld %5ld %5ld %5ld\n", cmdNum,
                 (long) getpid(), (long) getppid(),
                 (long) getpgrp(), (long) getsid(0));

         /* If not the last process, pass a message to the next process */

         if (!isatty(STDOUT_FILENO))    /* If not tty, then should be pipe */
⑩           if (write(STDOUT_FILENO, &cmdNum, sizeof(cmdNum)) == -1)
                 errMsg("write");

⑪        for (;;)               /* Wait for signals */
             pause();
     }
```

—— pgsjc/job_mon.c

The following shell session demonstrates the use of the program in Listing 34-5. We begin by displaying the process ID of the shell (which is the session leader, and the leader of a process group of which it is the sole member), and then create a background job containing two processes:

```
$ echo $$                                      Show PID of the shell
1204
$ ./job_mon | ./job_mon &                      Start a job containing 2 processes
[1] 1227
Terminal FG process group: 1204
Command   PID  PPID  PGRP   SID
    1     1226  1204  1226  1204
    2     1227  1204  1226  1204
```

From the above output, we can see that the shell remains the foreground process for the terminal. We can also see that the new job is in the same session as the shell and that all of the processes are in the same process group. Looking at the process IDs, we can see that the processes in the job were created in the same order as the commands were given on the command line. (Most shells do things this way, but some shell implementations create the processes in a different order.)

We continue, creating a second background job consisting of three processes:

```
$ ./job_mon | ./job_mon | ./job_mon &
[2] 1230
Terminal FG process group: 1204
Command   PID  PPID  PGRP   SID
    1     1228  1204  1228  1204
    2     1229  1204  1228  1204
    3     1230  1204  1228  1204
```

We see that the shell is still the foreground process group for the terminal. We also see that the processes for the new job are in the same session as the shell, but are in a different process group from the first job. Now we bring the second job into the foreground and send it a SIGINT signal:

```
$ fg
./job_mon | ./job_mon | ./job_mon
Type Control-C to generate SIGINT (signal 2)
Process 1230 (3) received signal 2 (Interrupt)
Process 1229 (2) received signal 2 (Interrupt)
Terminal FG process group: 1228
Process 1228 (1) received signal 2 (Interrupt)
```

From the above output, we see that the SIGINT signal was delivered to all of the processes in the foreground process group. We also see that this job is now the foreground process group for the terminal. Next, we send a SIGTSTP signal to the job:

```
Type Control-Z to generate SIGTSTP (signal 20 on Linux/x86-32).
Process 1230 (3) received signal 20 (Stopped)
Process 1229 (2) received signal 20 (Stopped)
Terminal FG process group: 1228
Process 1228 (1) received signal 20 (Stopped)

[2]+  Stopped        ./job_mon | ./job_mon | ./job_mon
```

Now all members of the process group are stopped. The output indicates that process group 1228 was the foreground job. However, after this job was stopped, the shell became the foreground process group, although we can't tell this from the output.

We then proceed by restarting the job using the *bg* command, which delivers a SIGCONT signal to the processes in the job:

```
$ bg                                        Resume job in background
[2]+ ./job_mon | ./job_mon | ./job_mon &
Process 1230 (3) received signal 18 (Continued)
Process 1229 (2) received signal 18 (Continued)
Terminal FG process group: 1204            The shell is in the foreground
Process 1228 (1) received signal 18 (Continued)
$ kill %1 %2                                We've finished: clean up
[1]-  Terminated     ./job_mon | ./job_mon
[2]+  Terminated     ./job_mon | ./job_mon | ./job_mon
```

34.7.3 Handling Job-Control Signals

Because the operation of job control is transparent to most applications, they don't need to take special action for dealing with job-control signals. One exception is programs that perform screen handling, such as *vi* and *less*. Such programs control the precise layout of text on a terminal and change various terminal settings, including settings that allow terminal input to be read a character (rather than a line) at a time. (We describe the various terminal settings in Chapter 62.)

Screen-handling programs need to handle the terminal stop signal (SIGTSTP). The signal handler should reset the terminal into canonical (line-at-a-time) input mode and place the cursor at the bottom-left corner of the terminal. When resumed, the program sets the terminal back into the mode required by the program, checks the terminal window size (which may have been changed by the user in the meantime), and redraws the screen with the desired contents.

> When we suspend or exit a terminal-handling program, such as *vi* on an *xterm* or other terminal emulator, we typically see that the terminal is redrawn with the text that was visible before the program was started. The terminal emulator achieves this effect by catching two character sequences that programs employing the *terminfo* or *termcap* packages are required to output when assuming and releasing control of terminal layout. The first of these sequences, called *smcup* (normally *Escape* followed by [?1049h), causes the terminal emulator to switch to its "alternate" screen. The second sequence, called *rmcup* (normally *Escape* followed by [?1049l), causes the terminal emulator to revert to its default screen, thus resulting in the reappearance of the original text that was on display before the screen-handling program took control of the terminal.

When handling SIGTSTP, we should be aware of some subtleties. We have already noted the first of these in Section 34.7.2: if SIGTSTP is caught, then it doesn't perform its default action of stopping a process. We dealt with this issue in Listing 34-5 by having the handler for SIGTSTP raise the SIGSTOP signal. Since SIGSTOP can't be caught, blocked, or ignored, it is guaranteed to immediately stop the process. However, this approach is not quite correct. In Section 26.1.3, we saw that a parent process can use the wait status value returned by *wait()* or *waitpid()* to determine which signal caused one of its child to stop. If we raise the SIGSTOP signal in the handler for SIGTSTP, it will (misleadingly) appear to the parent that the child was stopped by SIGSTOP.

The proper approach in this situation is to have the SIGTSTP handler raise a further SIGTSTP signal to stop the process, as follows:

1. The handler resets the disposition of SIGTSTP to its default (SIG_DFL).

2. The handler raises SIGTSTP.

3. Since SIGTSTP was blocked on entry to the handler (unless the SA_NODEFER flag was specified), the handler unblocks this signal. At this point, the pending SIGTSTP raised in the previous step performs its default action: the process is immediately suspended.

4. At some later time, the process will be resumed upon receipt of SIGCONT. At this point, execution of the handler continues.

5. Before returning, the handler reblocks the SIGTSTP signal and reestablishes itself to handle the next occurrence of the SIGTSTP signal.

The step of reblocking the SIGTSTP signal is needed to prevent the handler from being recursively called if another SIGTSTP signal was delivered after the handler reestablished itself, but before the handler returned. As noted in Section 22.7, recursive invocations of a signal handler could cause stack overflow if a rapid stream of signals is delivered. Blocking the signal also avoids problems if the signal handler needs to perform some other actions (e.g., saving or restoring values from global variables) after reestablishing the handler but before returning.

Example program

The handler in Listing 34-6 implements the steps described above to correctly handle SIGTSTP. (We show another example of the handling of the SIGTSTP signal in Listing 62-4, on page 1313.) After establishing the SIGTSTP handler, the *main()* function of this program sits in a loop waiting for signals. Here is an example of what we see when running this program:

```
$ ./handling_SIGTSTP
Type Control-Z, sending SIGTSTP
Caught SIGTSTP                      This message is printed by SIGTSTP handler

[1]+  Stopped         ./handling_SIGTSTP
$ fg                               Sends SIGCONT
./handling_SIGTSTP
Exiting SIGTSTP handler            Execution of handler continues; handler returns
Main                               pause() call in main() was interrupted by handler
Type Control-C to terminate the program
```

In a screen-handling program such as *vi*, the *printf()* calls inside the signal handler in Listing 34-6 would be replaced by code that caused the program to modify the terminal mode and redraw the terminal display, as outlined above. (Because of the need to avoid calling non-async-signal-safe functions, described in Section 21.1.2, the handler should do this by setting a flag to inform the main program to redraw the screen.)

Note that the SIGTSTP handler may interrupt certain blocking system calls (as described in Section 21.5). This point is illustrated in the above program output by the fact that, after the *pause()* call is interrupted, the main program prints the message *Main*.

Listing 34-6: Handling SIGTSTP

———————————————————————————————— pgsjc/handling_SIGTSTP.c
```
#include <signal.h>
#include "tlpi_hdr.h"

static void                         /* Handler for SIGTSTP */
tstpHandler(int sig)
{
    sigset_t tstpMask, prevMask;
    int savedErrno;
    struct sigaction sa;

    savedErrno = errno;             /* In case we change 'errno' here */

    printf("Caught SIGTSTP\n");      /* UNSAFE (see Section 21.1.2) */

    if (signal(SIGTSTP, SIG_DFL) == SIG_ERR)
        errExit("signal");          /* Set handling to default */

    raise(SIGTSTP);                 /* Generate a further SIGTSTP */

    /* Unblock SIGTSTP; the pending SIGTSTP immediately suspends the program */

    sigemptyset(&tstpMask);
    sigaddset(&tstpMask, SIGTSTP);
    if (sigprocmask(SIG_UNBLOCK, &tstpMask, &prevMask) == -1)
        errExit("sigprocmask");

    /* Execution resumes here after SIGCONT */

    if (sigprocmask(SIG_SETMASK, &prevMask, NULL) == -1)
        errExit("sigprocmask");      /* Reblock SIGTSTP */

    sigemptyset(&sa.sa_mask);        /* Reestablish handler */
    sa.sa_flags = SA_RESTART;
    sa.sa_handler = tstpHandler;
    if (sigaction(SIGTSTP, &sa, NULL) == -1)
        errExit("sigaction");

    printf("Exiting SIGTSTP handler\n");
    errno = savedErrno;
}

int
main(int argc, char *argv[])
{
    struct sigaction sa;
```

```
                /* Only establish handler for SIGTSTP if it is not being ignored */

                if (sigaction(SIGTSTP, NULL, &sa) == -1)
                    errExit("sigaction");

                if (sa.sa_handler != SIG_IGN) {
                    sigemptyset(&sa.sa_mask);
                    sa.sa_flags = SA_RESTART;
                    sa.sa_handler = tstpHandler;
                    if (sigaction(SIGTSTP, &sa, NULL) == -1)
                        errExit("sigaction");
                }

                for (;;) {                           /* Wait for signals */
                    pause();
                    printf("Main\n");
                }
            }
```

—————————————————————————————————— *pgsjc/handling_SIGTSTP.c*

Dealing with ignored job-control and terminal-generated signals

The program in Listing 34-6 establishes a signal handler for SIGTSTP only if that signal is not being ignored. This is an instance of the more general rule that applications should handle job-control and terminal-generated signals only if these signals were not previously being ignored. In the case of job-control signals (SIGTSTP, SIGTTIN, and SIGTTOU), this prevents an application from attempting to handle these signals if it is started from a non-job-control shell (such as the traditional Bourne shell). In a non-job-control shell, the dispositions of these signals are set to SIG_IGN; only job-control shells set the dispositions of these signals to SIG_DFL.

A similar statement also applies to the other signals that can be generated from the terminal: SIGINT, SIGQUIT, and SIGHUP. In the case of SIGINT and SIGQUIT, the reason is that when a command is executed in the background under non-job-control shells, the resulting process is not placed in a separate process group. Instead, the process stays in the same group as the shell, and the shell sets the disposition of SIGINT and SIGQUIT to be ignored before execing the command. This ensures that the process is not killed if the user types the terminal *interrupt* or *quit* characters (which should affect only the job that is notionally in the foreground). If the process subsequently undoes the shell's manipulations of the dispositions of these signals, then it once more becomes vulnerable to receiving them.

The SIGHUP signal is ignored if a command is executed via *nohup(1)*. This prevents the command from being killed as a consequence of a terminal hangup. Thus, an application should not attempt to change the disposition if it is being ignored.

34.7.4 Orphaned Process Groups (and SIGHUP Revisited)

In Section 26.2, we saw that an orphaned process is one that has been adopted by *init* (process ID 1) after its parent terminated. Within a program, we can create an orphaned child using the following code:

```
                if (fork() != 0)                 /* Exit if parent (or on error) */
                    exit(EXIT_SUCCESS);
```

Suppose that we include this code in a program executed from the shell. Figure 34-3 shows the state of processes before and after the parent exits.

After the parent terminates, the child process in Figure 34-3 is not only an orphaned process, it is also part of an *orphaned process group*. SUSv3 defines a process group as orphaned if "the parent of every member is either itself a member of the group or is not a member of the group's session." Put another way, a process group is not orphaned if at least one of its members has a parent in the same session but in a different process group. In Figure 34-3, the process group containing the child is orphaned because the child is in a process group on its own and its parent (*init*) is in a different session.

> By definition, a session leader is in an orphaned process group. This follows because *setsid()* creates a new process group in the new session, and the parent of the session leader is in a different session.

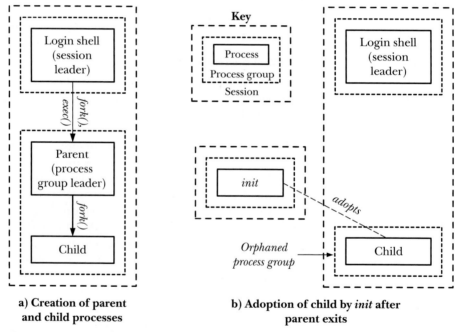

a) Creation of parent and child processes

b) Adoption of child by *init* after parent exits

Figure 34-3: Steps in the creation of an orphaned process group

To see why orphaned process groups are important, we need to view things from the perspective of shell job control. Consider the following scenario based on Figure 34-3:

1. Before the parent process exits, the child was stopped (perhaps because the parent sent it a stop signal).

2. When the parent process exits, the shell removes the parent's process group from its list of jobs. The child is adopted by *init* and becomes a background process for the terminal. The process group containing the child is orphaned.

3. At this point, there is no process that monitors the state of the stopped child via *wait()*.

Since the shell did not create the child process, it is not aware of the child's existence or that the child is part of the same process group as the deceased parent. Furthermore, the *init* process checks only for a terminated child, and then reaps the resulting zombie process. Consequently, the stopped child might languish forever, since no other process knows to send it a SIGCONT signal in order to cause it to resume execution.

Even if a stopped process in an orphaned process group has a still-living parent in a different session, that parent is not guaranteed to be able to send SIGCONT to the stopped child. A process may send SIGCONT to any other process in the same session, but if the child is in a different session, the normal rules for sending signals apply (Section 20.5), so the parent may not be able to send a signal to the child if the child is a privileged process that has changed its credentials.

To prevent scenarios such as the one described above, SUSv3 specifies that if a process group becomes orphaned and has any stopped members, then all members of the group are sent a SIGHUP signal, to inform them that they have become disconnected from their session, followed by a SIGCONT signal, to ensure that they resume execution. If the orphaned process group doesn't have any stopped members, no signals are sent.

A process group may become orphaned either because the last parent in a different process group in the same session terminated or because of the termination of the last process within the group that had a parent in another group. (The latter case is the one illustrated in Figure 34-3.) In either case, the treatment of a newly orphaned process group containing stopped children is the same.

> Sending SIGHUP and SIGCONT to a newly orphaned process group that contains stopped members is done in order to eliminate a specific loophole in the job-control framework. There is nothing to prevent the members of an already-orphaned process group from later being stopped if another process (with suitable privileges) sends them a stop signal. In this case, the processes will remain stopped until some process (again with suitable privileges) sends them a SIGCONT signal.
>
> When called by a member of an orphaned process group, the *tcsetpgrp()* function (Section 34.5) fails with the error ENOTTY, and calls to the *tcsetattr()*, *tcflush()*, *tcflow()*, *tcsendbreak()*, and *tcdrain()* functions (all described in Chapter 62) fail with the error EIO.

Example program

The program in Listing 34-7 demonstrates the treatment of orphaned processes that we have just described. After establishing handlers for SIGHUP and SIGCONT ②, this program creates one child process for each command-line argument ③. Each child then stops itself (by raising SIGSTOP) ④, or waits for signals (using *pause()*) ⑤. The choice of action by the child is determined by whether or not the corresponding command-line argument starts with the letter *s* (for *stop*). (We use a command-line argument starting with the letter *p* to specify the converse action of calling *pause()*, although any character other than the letter *s* can be used.)

After creating all of the children, the parent sleeps for a few seconds to allow the children time to get set up ⑥. (As noted in Section 24.2, using *sleep()* in this way is an imperfect, but sometimes viable method of accomplishing this result.) The parent then exits ⑦, at which point the process group containing the children becomes orphaned. If any of the children receives a signal as a consequence of the process group becoming orphaned, the signal handler is invoked, and it displays the child's process ID and the signal number ①.

Listing 34-7: SIGHUP and orphaned process groups

─────────────────────────────────────── pgsjc/orphaned_pgrp_SIGHUP.c

```
#define _GNU_SOURCE        /* Get declaration of strsignal() from <string.h> */
#include <string.h>
#include <signal.h>
#include "tlpi_hdr.h"

static void                /* Signal handler */
handler(int sig)
{
①     printf("PID=%ld: caught signal %d (%s)\n", (long) getpid(),
            sig, strsignal(sig));    /* UNSAFE (see Section 21.1.2) */
}

int
main(int argc, char *argv[])
{
    int j;
    struct sigaction sa;

    if (argc < 2 || strcmp(argv[1], "--help") == 0)
        usageErr("%s {s|p} ...\n", argv[0]);

    setbuf(stdout, NULL);              /* Make stdout unbuffered */

    sigemptyset(&sa.sa_mask);
    sa.sa_flags = 0;
    sa.sa_handler = handler;
②   if (sigaction(SIGHUP, &sa, NULL) == -1)
        errExit("sigaction");
    if (sigaction(SIGCONT, &sa, NULL) == -1)
        errExit("sigaction");

    printf("parent: PID=%ld, PPID=%ld, PGID=%ld, SID=%ld\n",
            (long) getpid(), (long) getppid(),
            (long) getpgrp(), (long) getsid(0));

    /* Create one child for each command-line argument */

③   for (j = 1; j < argc; j++) {
        switch (fork()) {
        case -1:
            errExit("fork");

        case 0:         /* Child */
            printf("child:  PID=%ld, PPID=%ld, PGID=%ld, SID=%ld\n",
                    (long) getpid(), (long) getppid(),
                    (long) getpgrp(), (long) getsid(0));

            if (argv[j][0] == 's') {    /* Stop via signal */
                printf("PID=%ld stopping\n", (long) getpid());
```

```
④                  raise(SIGSTOP);
             } else {                    /* Wait for signal */
                 alarm(60);              /* So we die if not SIGHUPed */
                 printf("PID=%ld pausing\n", (long) getpid());
⑤                pause();
             }
             _exit(EXIT_SUCCESS);

        default:        /* Parent carries on round loop */
            break;
        }
    }

    /* Parent falls through to here after creating all children */

⑥   sleep(3);                        /* Give children a chance to start */
    printf("parent exiting\n");
⑦   exit(EXIT_SUCCESS);              /* And orphan them and their group */
}
```
—————————————————————————————— pgsjc/orphaned_pgrp_SIGHUP.c

The following shell session log shows the results of two different runs of the program in Listing 34-7:

```
$ echo $$                    Display PID of shell, which is also the session ID
4785
$ ./orphaned_pgrp_SIGHUP s p
parent: PID=4827, PPID=4785, PGID=4827, SID=4785
child:  PID=4828, PPID=4827, PGID=4827, SID=4785
PID=4828 stopping
child:  PID=4829, PPID=4827, PGID=4827, SID=4785
PID=4829 pausing
parent exiting
$ PID=4828: caught signal 18 (Continued)
PID=4828: caught signal 1 (Hangup)
PID=4829: caught signal 18 (Continued)
PID=4829: caught signal 1 (Hangup)
Press Enter to get another shell prompt
$ ./orphaned_pgrp_SIGHUP p p
parent: PID=4830, PPID=4785, PGID=4830, SID=4785
child:  PID=4831, PPID=4830, PGID=4830, SID=4785
PID=4831 pausing
child:  PID=4832, PPID=4830, PGID=4830, SID=4785
PID=4832 pausing
parent exiting
```

The first run creates two children in the to-be-orphaned process group: one stops itself and the other pauses. (In this run, the shell prompt appears in the middle of the children's output because the shell notices that the parent has already exited.) As can be seen, both children receive SIGCONT and SIGHUP after the parent exits. (The SIGCONT output appears first because the SIGCONT handler interrupted the SIGHUP handler before the latter handler had a chance to print its output.) In the second run, two children are created, neither stops itself, and consequently no signals are sent when the parent exits.

Orphaned process groups and the SIGTSTP, SIGTTIN, and SIGTTOU signals

Orphaned process groups also affect the semantics for delivery of the SIGTSTP, SIGTTIN, and SIGTTOU signals.

In Section 34.7.1, we saw that SIGTTIN is sent to a background process if it tries to *read()* from the controlling terminal, and SIGTTOU is sent to a background process that tries to *write()* to the controlling terminal if the terminal's TOSTOP flag is set. However, it makes no sense to send these signals to an orphaned process group since, once stopped, it will never be resumed again. For this reason, instead of sending SIGTTIN or SIGTTOU, the kernel causes *read()* or *write()* to fail with the error EIO.

For similar reasons, if delivery of SIGTSTP, SIGTTIN, or SIGTTOU would stop a member of an orphaned process group, then the signal is silently discarded. (If the signal is being handled, then it is delivered to the process.) This behavior occurs no matter how the signal is sent—for example, whether the signal is generated by the terminal driver or sent by an explicit call to *kill()*.

34.8 Summary

Sessions and process groups (also known as jobs) form a two-level hierarchy of processes: a session is a collection of process groups, and a process group is a collection of processes. A session leader is the process that created the session using *setsid()*. A process group leader is the first member of a process group. All of the members of a process group share the same process group ID (which is the same as the process ID of the process group leader), and all processes in the process groups that constitute a session have the same session ID (which is the same as the process ID of the session leader). Each session may have a controlling terminal (/dev/tty), which is established when the session leader opens a terminal device. Opening the controlling terminal also causes the session leader to become the controlling process for the terminal.

Sessions and process groups were defined to support shell job control (although occasionally they find other uses in applications). Under job control, the shell is the session leader and controlling process for the terminal on which it is running. Each job (a simple command or a pipeline) executed by the shell is created as a separate process group, and the shell provides commands to move a job between three states: running in the foreground, running in the background, and stopped in the background.

To support job control, the terminal driver maintains a record of the foreground process group (job) for the controlling terminal. The terminal driver delivers job-control signals to the foreground job when certain characters are typed. These signals either terminate or stop the foreground job.

The notion of the terminal's foreground job is also used to arbitrate terminal I/O requests. Only processes in the foreground job may read from the controlling terminal. Background jobs are prevented from reading by delivery of the SIGTTIN signal, whose default action is to stop the job. If the terminal TOSTOP is set, then background jobs are also prevented from writing to the controlling terminal by delivery of a SIGTTOU signal, whose default action is to stop the job.

When a terminal disconnect occurs, the kernel delivers a SIGHUP signal to the controlling process to inform it of the fact. Such an event may result in a chain reaction whereby a SIGHUP signal is delivered to many other processes. First, if the controlling process is a shell (as is typically the case), then, before terminating, the shell sends SIGHUP to each of the process groups it has created. Second, if delivery of SIGHUP results in termination of a controlling process, then the kernel also sends SIGHUP to all of the members of the foreground process group of the controlling terminal.

In general, applications don't need to be cognizant of job-control signals. One exception is when a program performs screen-handling operations. Such programs need to correctly handle the SIGTSTP signal, resetting terminal attributes to sane values before the process is suspended, and restoring the correct (application-specific) terminal attributes when the application is once more resumed following delivery of a SIGCONT signal.

A process group is considered to be orphaned if none of its member processes has a parent in a different process group in the same session. Orphaned process groups are significant because there is no process outside the group that can both monitor the state of any stopped processes within the group and is always allowed to send a SIGCONT signal to these stopped processes in order to restart them. This could result in such stopped processes languishing forever on the system. To avoid this possibility, when a process group with stopped member processes becomes orphaned, all members of the process group are sent a SIGHUP signal, followed by a SIGCONT signal, to notify them that they have become orphaned and ensure that they are restarted.

Further information

Chapter 9 of [Stevens & Rago, 2005] covers similar material to this chapter, and includes a description of the steps that occur during login to establish the session for a login shell. The *glibc* manual contains a lengthy description of the functions relating to job control and the implementation of job control within the shell. The SUSv3 rationale contains an extensive discussion of sessions, process groups, and job control.

34.9 Exercises

34-1. Suppose a parent process performs the following steps:

```
/* Call fork() to create a number of child processes, each of which
   remains in same process group as the parent */

/* Sometime later... */
signal(SIGUSR1, SIG_IGN);     /* Parent makes itself immune to SIGUSR1 */

killpg(getpgrp(), SIGUSR1);   /* Send signal to children created earlier */
```

What problem might be encountered with this application design? (Consider shell pipelines.) How could this problem be avoided?

34-2. Write a program to verify that a parent process can change the process group ID of one of its children before the child performs an *exec()*, but not afterward.

34-3. Write a program to verify that a call to *setsid()* from a process group leader fails.

34-4. Modify the program in Listing 34-4 (`disc_SIGHUP.c`) to verify that, if the controlling process doesn't terminate as a consequence of receiving SIGHUP (i.e., it instead ignores or catches the signal and continues execution), then the kernel doesn't send SIGHUP to the members of the foreground process group.

34-5. Suppose that, in the signal handler of Listing 34-6, the code that unblocks the SIGTSTP signal was moved to the start of the handler. What potential race condition does this create?

34-6. Write a program to verify that when a process in an orphaned process group attempts to *read()* from the controlling terminal, the *read()* fails with the error EIO.

34-7. Write a program to verify that if one of the signals SIGTTIN, SIGTTOU, or SIGTSTP is sent to a member of an orphaned process group, then the signal is discarded (i.e., has no effect) if it would stop the process (i.e., the disposition is SIG_DFL), but is delivered if a handler is installed for the signal.

35

PROCESS PRIORITIES
AND SCHEDULING

This chapter discusses various system calls and process attributes that determine when and which processes obtain access to the CPU(s). We begin by describing the *nice* value, a process characteristic that influences the amount of CPU time that a process is allocated by the kernel scheduler. We follow this with a description of the POSIX realtime scheduling API. This API allows us to define the policy and priority used for scheduling processes, giving us much tighter control over how processes are allocated to the CPU. We conclude with a discussion of the system calls for setting a process's CPU affinity mask, which determines the set of CPUs on which a process running on a multiprocessor system will run.

35.1 Process Priorities (Nice Values)

On Linux, as with most other UNIX implementations, the default model for scheduling processes for use of the CPU is *round-robin time-sharing*. Under this model, each process in turn is permitted to use the CPU for a brief period of time, known as a *time slice* or *quantum*. Round-robin time-sharing satisfies two important requirements of an interactive multitasking system:

- *Fairness*: Each process gets a share of the CPU.
- *Responsiveness*: A process doesn't need to wait for long periods before it receives use of the CPU.

Under the round-robin time-sharing algorithm, processes can't exercise direct control over when and for how long they will be able to use the CPU. By default, each process in turn receives use of the CPU until its time slice runs out or it voluntarily gives up the CPU (for example, by putting itself to sleep or performing a disk read). If all processes attempt to use the CPU as much as possible (i.e., no process ever sleeps or blocks on an I/O operation), then they will receive a roughly equal share of the CPU.

However, one process attribute, the *nice value*, allows a process to indirectly influence the kernel's scheduling algorithm. Each process has a nice value in the range −20 (high priority) to +19 (low priority); the default is 0 (refer to Figure 35-1). In traditional UNIX implementations, only privileged processes can assign themselves (or other processes) a negative (high) priority. (We'll explain some Linux differences in Section 35.3.2.) Unprivileged processes can only lower their priority, by assuming a nice value greater than the default of 0. By doing this, they are being "nice" to other processes, and this fact gives the attribute its name.

The nice value is inherited by a child created via *fork()* and preserved across an *exec()*.

> Rather than returning the actual nice value, the *getpriority()* system call service routine returns a number in the range 1 (low priority) to 40 (high priority), calculated according to the formula *unice = 20 − knice*. This is done to avoid having a negative return value from a system call service routine, which is used to indicate an error. (See the description of system call service routines in Section 3.1.) Applications are unaware of the manipulated value returned by the system call service routine, since the C library *getpriority()* wrapper function reverses the calculation, returning the value *20 − unice* to the calling program.

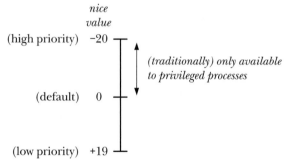

Figure 35-1: Range and interpretation of the process nice value

Effect of the nice value

Processes are not scheduled in a strict hierarchy by nice value; rather, the nice value acts as weighting factor that causes the kernel scheduler to favor processes with higher priorities. Giving a process a low priority (i.e., high nice value) won't cause it to be completely starved of the CPU, but causes it to receive relatively less CPU time. The extent to which the nice value influences the scheduling of a process has varied across Linux kernel versions, as well as across UNIX systems.

> Starting in kernel 2.6.23, a new kernel scheduling algorithm means that relative differences in nice values have a much stronger effect than in previous kernels. As a result, processes with low priorities receive less CPU than before, and processes with high priorities obtain a greater proportion of the CPU.

Retrieving and modifying priorities

The *getpriority()* and *setpriority()* system calls allow a process to retrieve and change its own nice value or that of another process.

```
#include <sys/resource.h>

int getpriority(int which, id_t who);
```
                    Returns (possibly negative) nice value of specified process on success,
                                                                   or –1 on error
```
int setpriority(int which, id_t who, int prio);
```
                                          Returns 0 on success, or –1 on error

Both system calls take the arguments *which* and *who*, identifying the process(es) whose priority is to be retrieved or modified. The *which* argument determines how *who* is interpreted. This argument takes one of the following values:

PRIO_PROCESS
: Operate on the process whose process ID equals *who*. If *who* is 0, use the caller's process ID.

PRIO_PGRP
: Operate on all of the members of the process group whose process group ID equals *who*. If *who* is 0, use the caller's process group.

PRIO_USER
: Operate on all processes whose real user ID equals *who*. If *who* is 0, use the caller's real user ID.

The *id_t* data type, used for the *who* argument, is an integer type of sufficient size to accommodate a process ID or a user ID.

The *getpriority()* system call returns the nice value of the process specified by *which* and *who*. If multiple processes match the criteria specified (which may occur if *which* is PRIO_PGRP or PRIO_USER), then the nice value of the process with the highest priority (i.e., lowest numerical value) is returned. Since *getpriority()* may legitimately return a value of –1 on a successful call, we must test for an error by setting *errno* to 0 prior to the call, and then checking for a –1 return status and a nonzero *errno* value after the call.

The *setpriority()* system call sets the nice value of the process(es) specified by *which* and *who* to the value specified in *prio*. Attempts to set a nice value to a number outside the permitted range (–20 to +19) are silently bounded to this range.

> Historically, the nice value was changed using the call *nice(incr)*, which added *incr* to the calling process's nice value. This function is still available, but it is superseded by the more general *setpriority()* system call.
>
> The command-line analogs of *setpriority()* are *nice(1)*, which can be used by unprivileged users to run a command with a lower priority or by privileged users to run a command with a raised priority, and *renice(8)*, which can be used by the superuser to change the nice value of an existing process.

A privileged (CAP_SYS_NICE) process can change the priority of any process. An unprivileged process may change its own priority (by specifying *which* as PRIO_PROCESS, and *who* as 0) or the priority of another (target) process, if its effective user ID matches the real or effective user ID of the target process. The Linux permission rules for *setpriority()* differ from SUSv3, which specifies that an unprivileged process can change the priority of another process if its real or effective user ID matches the effective user ID of the target process. UNIX implementations show some variation on this point. Some follow the SUSv3 rules, but others—notably the BSDs—behave in the same way as Linux.

> In Linux kernels before 2.6.12, the permission rules for calls to *setpriority()* by unprivileged processes are different from later kernels (and also deviate from SUSv3). An unprivileged process can change the priority of another process if its real or effective user ID matches the real user ID of the target process. From Linux 2.6.12 onward, the permissions checks were changed to be consistent with other similar APIs available on Linux, such as *sched_setscheduler()* and *sched_setaffinity()*.

In Linux kernels before 2.6.12, an unprivileged process may use *setpriority()* only to (irreversibly) lower its own or another process's priority. A privileged (CAP_SYS_NICE) process can use *setpriority()* to raise priorities.

Since kernel 2.6.12, Linux provides the RLIMIT_NICE resource limit, which permits unprivileged processes to raise priorities. An unprivileged process can set its own nice value to the maximum specified by the formula $20 - rlim\_cur$, where *rlim_cur* is the current RLIMIT_NICE soft resource limit. As an example, if a process's RLIMIT_NICE soft limit is 25, then its nice value can be set to −5. From this formula, and the knowledge that the nice value has the range +19 (low) to −20 (high), we can deduce that the effectively useful range of the RLIMIT_NICE limit is 1 (low) to 40 (high). (RLIMIT_NICE doesn't use the number range +19 to −20 because some negative resource-limit values have special meanings—for example, RLIM_INFINITY has the same representation as −1.)

An unprivileged process can make a *setpriority()* call to change the nice value of another (target) process, if the effective user ID of the process calling *setpriority()* matches the real or effective user ID of the target process, and the change to the nice value is consistent with the target process's RLIMIT_NICE limit.

The program in Listing 35-1 uses *setpriority()* to change the nice value of the process(es) specified by its command-line arguments (which correspond to the arguments of *setpriority()*), and then calls *getpriority()* to verify the change.

Listing 35-1: Modifying and retrieving a process's nice value

—————————————————————————————— `procpri/t_setpriority.c`

```
#include <sys/time.h>
#include <sys/resource.h>
#include "tlpi_hdr.h"

int
main(int argc, char *argv[])
{
    int which, prio;
    id_t who;
```

```
    if (argc != 4 || strchr("pgu", argv[1][0]) == NULL)
        usageErr("%s {p|g|u} who priority\n"
                "       set priority of: p=process; g=process group; "
                "u=processes for user\n", argv[0]);

    /* Set nice value according to command-line arguments */

    which = (argv[1][0] == 'p') ? PRIO_PROCESS :
                (argv[1][0] == 'g') ? PRIO_PGRP : PRIO_USER;
    who = getLong(argv[2], 0, "who");
    prio = getInt(argv[3], 0, "prio");

    if (setpriority(which, who, prio) == -1)
        errExit("setpriority");

    /* Retrieve nice value to check the change */

    errno = 0;                      /* Because successful call may return -1 */
    prio = getpriority(which, who);
    if (prio == -1 && errno != 0)
        errExit("getpriority");

    printf("Nice value = %d\n", prio);

    exit(EXIT_SUCCESS);
}
```

── **procpri/t_setpriority.c**

35.2 Overview of Realtime Process Scheduling

The standard kernel scheduling algorithm usually provides adequate performance
and responsiveness for the mixture of interactive and background processes typically
run on a system. However, realtime applications have more stringent requirements
of a scheduler, including the following:

- A realtime application must provide a guaranteed maximum response time for
  external inputs. In many cases, these guaranteed maximum response times
  must be quite small (e.g., of the order of a fraction of a second). For example, a
  slow response by a vehicle navigation system could be catastrophic. To satisfy
  this requirement, the kernel must provide the facility for a high-priority process
  to obtain control of the CPU in a timely fashion, preempting any process that
  may currently be running.

  > A time-critical application may need to take other steps to avoid unacceptable
  > delays. For example, to avoid being delayed by a page fault, an application can
  > lock all of its virtual memory into RAM using *mlock()* or *mlockall()* (described in
  > Section 50.2).

- A high-priority process should be able to maintain exclusive access to the CPU
  until it completes or voluntarily relinquishes the CPU.

- A realtime application should be able to control the precise order in which its component processes are scheduled.

SUSv3 specifies a realtime process scheduling API (originally defined in POSIX.1b) that partly addresses these requirements. This API provides two realtime scheduling policies: SCHED_RR and SCHED_FIFO. Processes operating under either of these policies always have priority over processes scheduled using the standard round-robin time-sharing policy described in Section 35.1, which the realtime scheduling API identifies using the constant SCHED_OTHER.

Each of the realtime policies allows for a range of priority levels. SUSv3 requires that an implementation provide at least 32 discrete priorities for the realtime policies. In each scheduling policy, runnable processes with higher priority always have precedence over lower-priority processes when seeking access to the CPU.

> The statement that runnable processes with higher priority always have precedence over lower-priority processes needs to be qualified for multiprocessor Linux systems (including hyperthreaded systems). On a multiprocessor system, each CPU has a separate run queue (this provides better performance than a single system-wide run queue), and processes are prioritized only per CPU run queue. For example, on a dual-processor system with three processes, process A with realtime priority 20 could be queued waiting for CPU 0, which is currently running process B with priority 30, even though CPU 1 is running process C with a priority of 10.
>
> Realtime applications that employ multiple processes (or threads) can use the CPU affinity API described in Section 35.4 to avoid any problems that might result from this scheduling behavior. For example, on a four-processor system, all noncritical processes could be isolated onto a single CPU, leaving the other three CPUs available for use by the application.

Linux provides 99 realtime priority levels, numbered 1 (lowest) to 99 (highest), and this range applies in both realtime scheduling policies. The priorities in each policy are equivalent. This means that, given two processes with the same priority, one operating under the SCHED_RR policy and the other under SCHED_FIFO, either may be the next one eligible for execution, depending on the order in which they were scheduled. In effect, each priority level maintains a queue of runnable processes, and the next process to run is selected from the front of the highest-priority nonempty queue.

POSIX realtime versus hard realtime

Applications with all of the requirements listed at the start of this section are sometimes referred to as *hard* realtime applications. However, the POSIX realtime process scheduling API doesn't satisfy all of these requirements. In particular, it provides no way for an application to guarantee response times for handling input. To make such guarantees requires operating system features that are not part of the mainline Linux kernel (nor most other standard operating systems). The POSIX API merely provides us with so-called *soft* realtime, allowing us to control which processes are scheduled for use of the CPU.

Adding support for hard realtime applications is difficult to achieve without imposing an overhead on the system that conflicts with the performance requirements of the time-sharing applications that form the majority of applications on typical desktop and server systems. This is why most UNIX kernels—including, historically, Linux—have not natively supported realtime applications. Nevertheless, starting from around version 2.6.18, various features have been added to the Linux kernel with the eventual aim of allowing Linux to natively provide full support for hard realtime applications, without imposing the aforementioned overhead for time-sharing operation.

35.2.1 The SCHED_RR Policy

Under the SCHED_RR (round-robin) policy, processes of equal priority are executed in a round-robin time-sharing fashion. A process receives a fixed-length time slice each time it uses the CPU. Once scheduled, a process employing the SCHED_RR policy maintains control of the CPU until either:

- it reaches the end of its time slice;
- it voluntarily relinquishes the CPU, either by performing a blocking system call or by calling the *sched_yield()* system call (described in Section 35.3.3);
- it terminates; or
- it is preempted by a higher-priority process.

For the first two events above, when a process running under the SCHED_RR policy loses access to the CPU, it is placed at the back of the queue for its priority level. In the final case, when the higher-priority process has ceased execution, the preempted process continues execution, consuming the remainder of its time slice (i.e., the preempted process remains at the head of the queue for its priority level).

In both the SCHED_RR and the SCHED_FIFO policies, the currently running process may be preempted for one of the following reasons:

- a higher-priority process that was blocked became unblocked (e.g., an I/O operation on which it was waiting completed);
- the priority of another process was raised to a higher level than the currently running process; or
- the priority of the currently running process was decreased to a lower value than that of some other runnable process.

The SCHED_RR policy is similar to the standard round-robin time-sharing scheduling algorithm (SCHED_OTHER), in that it allows a group of processes with the same priority to share access to the CPU. The most notable difference is that the SCHED_RR policy has strictly distinct priority levels, with higher-priority processes always taking precedence over lower-priority processes. By contrast, a low nice value (i.e., high priority) doesn't give a process exclusive access to the CPU; it merely gives the process a favorable weighting in scheduling decisions. As noted in Section 35.1, a process with a low priority (i.e., high nice value) always receives at least some CPU time. The other important difference is that the SCHED_RR policy allows us to precisely control the order in which processes are scheduled.

35.2.2 The SCHED_FIFO Policy

The SCHED_FIFO (first-in, first-out) policy is similar to the SCHED_RR policy. The major difference is that there is no time slice. Once a SCHED_FIFO process gains access to the CPU, it executes until either:

- it voluntarily relinquishes the CPU (in the same manner as described for the SCHED_RR policy above);
- it terminates; or
- it is preempted by a higher-priority process (in the same circumstances as described for the SCHED_RR policy above).

In the first case, the process is placed at the back of the queue for its priority level. In the last case, when the higher-priority process has ceased execution (by blocking or terminating), the preempted process continues execution (i.e., the preempted process remains at the head of the queue for its priority level).

35.2.3 The SCHED_BATCH and SCHED_IDLE Policies

The Linux 2.6 kernel series added two nonstandard scheduling policies: SCHED_BATCH and SCHED_IDLE. Although these policies are set via the POSIX realtime scheduling API, they are not actually realtime policies.

The SCHED_BATCH policy, added in kernel 2.6.16, is similar to the default SCHED_OTHER policy. This policy is intended for batch-style execution of processes. The scheduler takes account of the nice value, but assumes that this is a CPU-intensive job that does not require low latency scheduling in response to wake-up events, and thus mildly disfavors it in scheduling decisions.

The SCHED_IDLE policy, added in kernel 2.6.23, is also similar to SCHED_OTHER, but schedules the process with a very low priority (lower even than a nice value of +19). The process nice value has no meaning for this policy. It is intended for running low-priority jobs that will receive a significant proportion of the CPU only if no other job on the system requires the CPU.

35.3 Realtime Process Scheduling API

We now look at the various system calls constituting the realtime process scheduling API. These system calls allow us to control process scheduling policies and priorities.

> Although realtime scheduling has been a part of Linux since version 2.0 of the kernel, several problems persisted for a long time in the implementation. A number of features of the implementation remained broken in the 2.2 kernel, and even in early 2.4 kernels. Most of these problems were rectified by about kernel 2.4.20.

35.3.1 Realtime Priority Ranges

The *sched_get_priority_min()* and *sched_get_priority_max()* system calls return the available priority range for a scheduling policy.

```
#include <sched.h>

int sched_get_priority_min(int policy);
int sched_get_priority_max(int policy);
```
                    Both return nonnegative integer priority on success, or −1 on error

For both system calls, *policy* specifies the scheduling policy about which we wish to obtain information. For this argument, we specify either SCHED_RR or SCHED_FIFO. The *sched_get_priority_min()* system call returns the minimum priority for the specified policy, and *sched_get_priority_max()* returns the maximum priority. On Linux, these system calls return the numbers 1 and 99, respectively, for both the SCHED_RR and SCHED_FIFO policies. In other words, the priority ranges of the two realtime policies completely coincide, and SCHED_RR and SCHED_FIFO processes with the same priority are equally eligible for scheduling. (Which one is scheduled first depends on their order in the queue for that priority level.)

The range of realtime priorities differs from one UNIX implementation to another. Therefore, instead of hard-coding priority values into an application, we should specify priorities relative to the return value from one of these functions. Thus, the lowest SCHED_RR priority would be specified as *sched_get_priority_min(SCHED_RR)*, the next higher priority as *sched_get_priority_min(SCHED_RR) + 1*, and so on.

> SUSv3 doesn't require that the SCHED_RR and SCHED_FIFO policies use the same priority ranges, but they do so on most UNIX implementations. For example, on Solaris 8, the priority range for both policies is 0 to 59, and on FreeBSD 6.1, it is 0 to 31.

35.3.2 Modifying and Retrieving Policies and Priorities

In this section, we look at the system calls that modify and retrieve scheduling policies and priorities.

Modifying scheduling policies and priorities

The *sched_setscheduler()* system call changes both the scheduling policy and the priority of the process whose process ID is specified in *pid*. If *pid* is specified as 0, the attributes of the calling process are changed.

```
#include <sched.h>

int sched_setscheduler(pid_t pid, int policy, const struct sched_param *param);
```
                                        Returns 0 on success, or −1 on error

The *param* argument is a pointer to a structure of the following form:

```
struct sched_param {
    int sched_priority;        /* Scheduling priority */
};
```

SUSv3 defines the *param* argument as a structure to allow an implementation to include additional implementation-specific fields, which may be useful if an implementation provides additional scheduling policies. However, like most UNIX implementations, Linux provides just the *sched_priority* field, which specifies the scheduling priority. For the SCHED_RR and SCHED_FIFO policies, this must be a value in the range indicated by *sched_get_priority_min()* and *sched_get_priority_max()*; for other policies, the priority must be 0.

The *policy* argument determines the scheduling policy for the process. It is specified as one of the policies shown in Table 35-1.

Table 35-1: Linux realtime and nonrealtime scheduling policies

Policy	Description	SUSv3
SCHED_FIFO	Realtime first-in first-out	•
SCHED_RR	Realtime round-robin	•
SCHED_OTHER	Standard round-robin time-sharing	•
SCHED_BATCH	Similar to SCHED_OTHER, but intended for batch execution (since Linux 2.6.16)	
SCHED_IDLE	Similar to SCHED_OTHER, but with priority even lower than nice value +19 (since Linux 2.6.23)	

A successful *sched_setscheduler()* call moves the process specified by *pid* to the back of the queue for its priority level.

SUSv3 specifies that the return value of a successful *sched_setscheduler()* call should be the previous scheduling policy. However, Linux deviates from the standard in that a successful call returns 0. A portable application should test for success by checking that the return status is not −1.

The scheduling policy and priority are inherited by a child created via *fork()*, and they are preserved across an *exec()*.

The *sched_setparam()* system call provides a subset of the functionality of *sched_setscheduler()*. It modifies the scheduling priority of a process while leaving the policy unchanged.

```
#include <sched.h>

int sched_setparam(pid_t pid, const struct sched_param *param);
```
                                        Returns 0 on success, or −1 on error

The *pid* and *param* arguments are the same as for *sched_setscheduler()*.

A successful *sched_setparam()* call moves the process specified by *pid* to the back of the queue for its priority level.

The program in Listing 35-2 uses *sched_setscheduler()* to set the policy and priority of the processes specified by its command-line arguments. The first argument is a letter specifying a scheduling policy, the second is an integer priority, and the remaining arguments are the process IDs of the processes whose scheduling attributes are to be changed.

Listing 35-2: Modifying process scheduling policies and priorities

─── *procpri/sched_set.c*

```c
#include <sched.h>
#include "tlpi_hdr.h"

int
main(int argc, char *argv[])
{
    int j, pol;
    struct sched_param sp;

    if (argc < 3 || strchr("rfobi", argv[1][0]) == NULL)
        usageErr("%s policy priority [pid...]\n"
                "   policy is 'r' (RR), 'f' (FIFO), "
#ifdef SCHED_BATCH              /* Linux-specific */
                "'b' (BATCH), "
#endif
#ifdef SCHED_IDLE              /* Linux-specific */
                "'i' (IDLE), "
#endif
                "or 'o' (OTHER)\n",
                argv[0]);

    pol = (argv[1][0] == 'r') ? SCHED_RR :
                (argv[1][0] == 'f') ? SCHED_FIFO :
#ifdef SCHED_BATCH
                (argv[1][0] == 'b') ? SCHED_BATCH :
#endif
#ifdef SCHED_IDLE
                (argv[1][0] == 'i') ? SCHED_IDLE :
#endif
                SCHED_OTHER;
    sp.sched_priority = getInt(argv[2], 0, "priority");

    for (j = 3; j < argc; j++)
        if (sched_setscheduler(getLong(argv[j], 0, "pid"), pol, &sp) == -1)
            errExit("sched_setscheduler");

    exit(EXIT_SUCCESS);
}
```

─── *procpri/sched_set.c*

Privileges and resource limits affecting changes to scheduling parameters

In kernels before 2.6.12, a process generally must be privileged (CAP_SYS_NICE) to make changes to scheduling policies and priorities. The one exception to this requirement is that an unprivileged process can change the scheduling policy of a process to SCHED_OTHER if the effective user ID of the caller matches either the real or effective user ID of the target process.

Since kernel 2.6.12, the rules about setting realtime scheduling policies and priorities have changed with the introduction of a new, nonstandard resource limit, RLIMIT_RTPRIO. As with older kernels, privileged (CAP_SYS_NICE) processes can make arbitrary changes to the scheduling policy and priority of any process. However, an unprivileged process can also change scheduling policies and priorities, according to the following rules:

- If the process has a nonzero RLIMIT_RTPRIO soft limit, then it can make arbitrary changes to its scheduling policy and priority, subject to the constraint that the upper limit on the realtime priority that it may set is the maximum of its current realtime priority (if the process is currently operating under a realtime policy) and the value of its RLIMIT_RTPRIO soft limit.

- If the value of a process's RLIMIT_RTPRIO soft limit is 0, then the only change that it can make is to lower its realtime scheduling priority or to switch from a realtime policy to a nonrealtime policy.

- The SCHED_IDLE policy is special. A process that is operating under this policy can't make any changes to its policy, regardless of the value of the RLIMIT_RTPRIO resource limit.

- Policy and priority changes can also be performed from another unprivileged process, as long as the effective user ID of that process matches either the real or effective user ID of the target process.

- A process's soft RLIMIT_RTPRIO limit determines only what changes can be made to its own scheduling policy and priority, either by the process itself or by another unprivileged process. A nonzero limit doesn't give an unprivileged process the ability to change the scheduling policy and priority of other processes.

> Starting with kernel 2.6.25, Linux adds the concept of realtime scheduling groups, configurable via the CONFIG_RT_GROUP_SCHED kernel option, which also affect the changes that can be made when setting realtime scheduling policies. See the kernel source file Documentation/scheduler/sched-rt-group.txt for details.

Retrieving scheduling policies and priorities

The *sched_getscheduler()* and *sched_getparam()* system calls retrieve the scheduling policy and priority of a process.

```
#include <sched.h>

int sched_getscheduler(pid_t pid);
```
                              Returns scheduling policy, or −1 on error
```
int sched_getparam(pid_t pid, struct sched_param *param);
```
                              Returns 0 on success, or −1 on error

For both of these system calls, *pid* specifies the ID of the process about which information is to be retrieved. If *pid* is 0, information is retrieved about the calling process. Both system calls can be used by an unprivileged process to retrieve information about any process, regardless of credentials.

The *sched_getparam()* system call returns the realtime priority of the specified process in the *sched_priority* field of the *sched_param* structure pointed to by *param*.

Upon successful execution, *sched_getscheduler()* returns one of the policies shown earlier in Table 35-1.

The program in Listing 35-3 uses *sched_getscheduler()* and *sched_getparam()* to retrieve the policy and priority of all of the processes whose process IDs are given as command-line arguments. The following shell session demonstrates the use of this program, as well as the program in Listing 35-2:

```
$ su                                    Assume privilege so we can set realtime policies
Password:
# sleep 100 &                           Create a process
[1] 2006
# ./sched_view 2006                     View initial policy and priority of sleep process
2006: OTHER  0
# ./sched_set f 25 2006                 Switch process to SCHED_FIFO policy, priority 25
# ./sched_view 2006                     Verify change
2006: FIFO  25
```

Listing 35-3: Retrieving process scheduling policies and priorities

—————————————————————————————————————— procpri/sched_view.c
```c
#include <sched.h>
#include "tlpi_hdr.h"

int
main(int argc, char *argv[])
{
    int j, pol;
    struct sched_param sp;

    for (j = 1; j < argc; j++) {
        pol = sched_getscheduler(getLong(argv[j], 0, "pid"));
        if (pol == -1)
            errExit("sched_getscheduler");

        if (sched_getparam(getLong(argv[j], 0, "pid"), &sp) == -1)
            errExit("sched_getparam");

        printf("%s: %-5s %2d\n", argv[j],
                (pol == SCHED_OTHER) ? "OTHER" :
                (pol == SCHED_RR) ? "RR" :
                (pol == SCHED_FIFO) ? "FIFO" :
#ifdef SCHED_BATCH              /* Linux-specific */
                (pol == SCHED_BATCH) ? "BATCH" :
#endif
#ifdef SCHED_IDLE                 /* Linux-specific */
                (pol == SCHED_IDLE) ? "IDLE" :
#endif
                "???", sp.sched_priority);
    }

    exit(EXIT_SUCCESS);
}
```
—————————————————————————————————————— procpri/sched_view.c

Preventing realtime processes from locking up the system

Since SCHED_RR and SCHED_FIFO processes preempt any lower-priority processes (e.g., the shell under which the program is run), when developing applications that use these policies, we need to be aware of the possibility that a runaway realtime process could lock up the system by hogging the CPU. Programmatically, there are a few of ways to avoid this possibility:

- Establish a suitably low soft CPU time resource limit (RLIMIT_CPU, described in Section 36.3) using *setrlimit()*. If the process consumes too much CPU time, it will be sent a SIGXCPU signal, which kills the process by default.

- Set an alarm timer using *alarm()*. If the process continues running for a wall clock time that exceeds the number of seconds specified in the *alarm()* call, then it will be killed by a SIGALRM signal.

- Create a watchdog process that runs with a high realtime priority. This process can loop repeatedly, sleeping for a specified interval, and then waking and monitoring the status of other processes. Such monitoring could include measuring the value of the CPU time clock for each process (see the discussion of the *clock_getcpuclockid()* function in Section 23.5.3) and checking its scheduling policy and priority using *sched_getscheduler()* and *sched_getparam()*. If a process is deemed to be misbehaving, the watchdog thread could lower the process's priority, or stop or terminate it by sending an appropriate signal.

- Since kernel 2.6.25, Linux provides a nonstandard resource limit, RLIMIT_RTTIME, for controlling the amount of CPU time that can be consumed in a single burst by a process running under a realtime scheduling policy. Specified in microseconds, RLIMIT_RTTIME limits the amount of CPU time that the process may consume without performing a system call that blocks. When the process does perform such a call, the count of consumed CPU time is reset to 0. The count of consumed CPU time is not reset if the process is preempted by a higher-priority process, is scheduled off the CPU because its time slice expired (for a SCHED_RR process), or calls *sched_yield()* (Section 35.3.3). If the process reaches its limit of CPU time, then, as with RLIMIT_CPU, it will be sent a SIGXCPU signal, which kills the process by default.

> The changes in kernel 2.6.25 can also help prevent runaway realtime processes from locking up the system. For details, see the kernel source file Documentation/scheduler/sched-rt-group.txt.

Preventing child processes from inheriting privileged scheduling policies

Linux 2.6.32 added SCHED_RESET_ON_FORK as a value that can be specified in *policy* when calling *sched_setscheduler()*. This is a flag value that is ORed with one of the policies in Table 35-1. If this flag is set, then children that are created by this process using *fork()* do not inherit privileged scheduling policies and priorities. The rules are as follows:

- If the calling process has a realtime scheduling policy (SCHED_RR or SCHED_FIFO), then the policy in child processes is reset to the standard round-robin time-sharing policy, SCHED_OTHER.

- If the process has a negative (i.e., high) nice value, then the nice value in child processes is reset to 0.

The SCHED_RESET_ON_FORK flag was designed to be used in media-playback applications. It permits the creation of single processes that have realtime scheduling policies that can't be passed to child processes. Using the SCHED_RESET_ON_FORK flag prevents the creation of fork bombs that try to evade the ceiling set by the RLIMIT_RTTIME resource limit by creating multiple children running under realtime scheduling policies.

Once the SCHED_RESET_ON_FORK flag has been enabled for a process, only a privileged process (CAP_SYS_NICE) can disable it. When a child process is created, its reset-on-fork flag is disabled.

35.3.3 Relinquishing the CPU

A realtime process may voluntarily relinquish the CPU in two ways: by invoking a system call that blocks the process (e.g., a *read()* from a terminal) or by calling *sched_yield()*.

```
#include <sched.h>

int sched_yield(void);
```
                                               Returns 0 on success, or –1 on error

The operation of *sched_yield()* is simple. If there are any other queued runnable processes at the same priority level as the calling process, then the calling process is placed at the back of the queue, and the process at the head of the queue is scheduled to use the CPU. If no other runnable processes are queued at this priority, then *sched_yield()* does nothing; the calling process simply continues using the CPU.

Although SUSv3 permits a possible error return from *sched_yield()*, this system call always succeeds on Linux, as well as on many other UNIX implementations. Portable applications should nevertheless always check for an error return.

The use of *sched_yield()* for nonrealtime processes is undefined.

35.3.4 The SCHED_RR Time Slice

The *sched_rr_get_interval()* system call enables us to find out the length of the time slice allocated to a SCHED_RR process each time it is granted use of the CPU.

```
#include <sched.h>

int sched_rr_get_interval(pid_t pid, struct timespec *tp);
```
                                               Returns 0 on success, or –1 on error

As with the other process scheduling system calls, *pid* identifies the process about which we want to obtain information, and specifying *pid* as 0 means the calling process. The time slice is returned in the *timespec* structure pointed to by *tp*:

```
struct timespec {
    time_t tv_sec;        /* Seconds */
    long   tv_nsec;       /* Nanoseconds */
};
```

On recent 2.6 kernels, the realtime round-robin time slice is 0.1 seconds.

35.4 CPU Affinity

When a process is rescheduled to run on a multiprocessor system, it doesn't necessarily run on the same CPU on which it last executed. The usual reason it may run on another CPU is that the original CPU is already busy.

When a process changes CPUs, there is a performance impact: in order for a line of the process's data to be loaded into the cache of the new CPU, it must first be invalidated (i.e., either discarded if it is unmodified, or flushed to main memory if it was modified), if present in the cache of the old CPU. (To prevent cache inconsistencies, multiprocessor architectures allow data to be kept in only one CPU cache at a time.) This invalidation costs execution time. Because of this performance impact, the Linux (2.6) kernel tries to ensure *soft* CPU affinity for a process—wherever possible, the process is rescheduled to run on the same CPU.

> A *cache line* is the cache analog of a page in a virtual memory management system. It is the size of the unit used for transfers between the CPU cache and main memory. Typical line sizes range from 32 to 128 bytes. For further information, see [Schimmel, 1994] and [Drepper, 2007].
>
> One of the fields in the Linux-specific /proc/*PID*/stat file displays the number of the CPU on which a process is currently executing or last executed. See the *proc(5)* manual page for details.

Sometimes, it is desirable to set *hard* CPU affinity for a process, so that it is explicitly restricted to always running on one, or a subset, of the available CPUs. Among the reasons we may want to do this are the following:

- We can avoid the performance impacts caused by invalidation of cached data.
- If multiple threads (or processes) are accessing the same data, then we may obtain performance benefits by confining them all to the same CPU, so that they don't contend for the data and thus cause cache misses.
- For a time-critical application, it may be desirable to confine most processes on the system to other CPUs, while reserving one or more CPUs for the time-critical application.

> The *isolcpus* kernel boot option can be used to isolate one or more CPUs from the normal kernel scheduling algorithms. The only way to move a process on or off a CPU that has been isolated is via the CPU affinity system calls described in this section. The *isolcpus* boot option is the preferred method of implementing the last of the scenarios listed above. For details, see the kernel source file Documentation/kernel-parameters.txt.
>
> Linux also provides a *cpuset* kernel option, which can be used on systems containing large numbers of CPUs to achieve more sophisticated control over how the CPUs and memory are allocated to processes. For details, see the kernel source file Documentation/cpusets.txt.

Linux 2.6 provides a pair of nonstandard system calls to modify and retrieve the hard CPU affinity of a process: *sched_setaffinity()* and *sched_getaffinity()*.

> Many other UNIX implementations provide interfaces for controlling CPU affinity. For example, HP-UX and Solaris provide a *pset_bind()* system call.

The *sched_setaffinity()* system call sets the CPU affinity of the process specified by *pid*. If *pid* is 0, the CPU affinity of the calling process is changed.

```
#define _GNU_SOURCE
#include <sched.h>

int sched_setaffinity(pid_t pid, size_t len, cpu_set_t *set);
```
                                            Returns 0 on success, or −1 on error

The CPU affinity to be assigned to the process is specified in the *cpu_set_t* structure pointed to by *set*.

> CPU affinity is actually a per-thread attribute that can be adjusted independently for each of the threads in a thread group. If we want to change the CPU affinity of a specific thread in a multithreaded process, we can specify *pid* as the value returned by a call to *gettid()* in that thread. Specifying *pid* as 0 means the calling thread.

Although the *cpu_set_t* data type is implemented as a bit mask, we should treat it as an opaque structure. All manipulations of the structure should be done using the macros CPU_ZERO(), CPU_SET(), CPU_CLR(), and CPU_ISSET().

```
#define _GNU_SOURCE
#include <sched.h>

void CPU_ZERO(cpu_set_t *set);
void CPU_SET(int cpu, cpu_set_t *set);
void CPU_CLR(int cpu, cpu_set_t *set);

int CPU_ISSET(int cpu, cpu_set_t *set);
```
                            Returns true (1) if *cpu* is in *set*, or false (0) otherwise

These macros operate on the CPU set pointed to by *set* as follows:

- CPU_ZERO() initializes *set* to be empty.
- CPU_SET() adds the CPU *cpu* to *set*.
- CPU_CLR() removes the CPU *cpu* from *set*.
- CPU_ISSET() returns true if the CPU *cpu* is a member of *set*.

> The GNU C library also provides a number of other macros for working with CPU sets. See the *CPU_SET(3)* manual page for details.

The CPUs in a CPU set are numbered starting at 0. The <sched.h> header file defines the constant CPU_SETSIZE to be one greater than the maximum CPU number that can be represented in a *cpu_set_t* variable. CPU_SETSIZE has the value 1024.

The *len* argument given to *sched_setaffinity()* should specify the number of bytes in the *set* argument (i.e., *sizeof(cpu_set_t)*).

The following code confines the process identified by *pid* to running on any CPU other than the first CPU of a four-processor system:

```
cpu_set_t set;

CPU_ZERO(&set);
CPU_SET(1, &set);
CPU_SET(2, &set);
CPU_SET(3, &set);

sched_setaffinity(pid, sizeof(cpu_set_t), &set);
```

If the CPUs specified in *set* don't correspond to any CPUs on the system, then *sched_setaffinity()* fails with the error EINVAL.

If *set* doesn't include the CPU on which the calling process is currently running, then the process is migrated to one of the CPUs in *set*.

An unprivileged process may set the CPU affinity of another process only if its effective user ID matches the real or effective user ID of the target process. A privileged (CAP_SYS_NICE) process may set the CPU affinity of any process.

The *sched_getaffinity()* system call retrieves the CPU affinity mask of the process specified by *pid*. If *pid* is 0, the CPU affinity mask of the calling process is returned.

```
#define _GNU_SOURCE
#include <sched.h>

int sched_getaffinity(pid_t pid, size_t len, cpu_set_t *set);
```
                                              Returns 0 on success, or −1 on error

The CPU affinity mask is returned in the *cpu_set_t* structure pointed to by *set*. The *len* argument should be set to indicate the number of bytes in this structure (i.e., *sizeof(cpu_set_t)*). We can use the CPU_ISSET() macro to determine which CPUs are in the returned *set*.

If the CPU affinity mask of the target process has not otherwise been modified, *sched_getaffinity()* returns a set containing all of the CPUs on the system.

No permission checking is performed by *sched_getaffinity()*; an unprivileged process can retrieve the CPU affinity mask of any process on the system.

A child process created by *fork()* inherits its parent's CPU affinity mask, and this mask is preserved across an *exec()*.

The *sched_setaffinity()* and *sched_getaffinity()* system calls are Linux-specific.

> The t_sched_setaffinity.c and t_sched_getaffinity.c programs in the procpri subdirectory in the source code distribution for this book demonstrate the use of *sched_setaffinity()* and *sched_getaffinity()*.

35.5 Summary

The default kernel scheduling algorithm employs a round-robin time-sharing policy. By default, all processes have equal access to the CPU under this policy, but we can set a process's nice value to a number in the range −20 (high priority) to +19 (low priority) to cause the scheduler to favor or disfavor that process. However, even if we give a process the lowest priority, it is not completely starved of the CPU.

Linux also implements the POSIX realtime scheduling extensions. These allow an application to precisely control the allocation of the CPU to processes. Processes operating under the two realtime scheduling policies, SCHED_RR (round-robin) and SCHED_FIFO (first-in, first-out), always have priority over processes operating under nonrealtime policies. Realtime processes have priorities in the range 1 (low) to 99 (high). As long as it is runnable, a higher-priority process completely excludes lower-priority processes from the CPU. A process operating under the SCHED_FIFO policy maintains exclusive access to the CPU until either it terminates, it voluntarily relinquishes the CPU, or it is preempted because a higher-priority process became runnable. Similar rules apply to the SCHED_RR policy, with the addition that if multiple processes are running at the same priority, then the CPU is shared among these processes in a round-robin fashion.

A process's CPU affinity mask can be used to restrict the process to running on a subset of the CPUs available on a multiprocessor system. This can improve the performance of certain types of applications.

Further information

[Love, 2010] provides background detail on process priorities and scheduling on Linux. [Gallmeister, 1995] provides further information about the POSIX realtime scheduling API. Although targeted at POSIX threads, much of the discussion of the realtime scheduling API in [Butenhof, 1996] is useful background to the realtime scheduling discussion in this chapter.

For further information about CPU affinity and controlling the allocation of threads to CPUs and memory nodes on multiprocessor systems, see the kernel source file Documentation/cpusets.txt, and the *mbind(2)*, *set_mempolicy(2)*, and *cpuset(7)* manual pages.

35.6 Exercises

35-1. Implement the *nice(1)* command.

35-2. Write a set-user-ID-*root* program that is the realtime scheduling analog of *nice(1)*. The command-line interface of this program should be as follows:

```
# ./rtsched policy priority command arg...
```

In the above command, *policy* is *r* for SCHED_RR or *f* for SCHED_FIFO. This program should drop its privileged ID before execing the command, for the reasons described in Sections 9.7.1 and 38.3.

35-3. Write a program that places itself under the SCHED_FIFO scheduling policy and then creates a child process. Both processes should execute a function that causes the process to consume a maximum of 3 seconds of CPU time. (This can be done by using a loop in which the *times()* system call is repeatedly called to determine the amount of CPU time so far consumed.) After each quarter of a second of consumed CPU time, the function should print a message that displays the process ID and the amount of CPU time so far consumed. After each second of consumed CPU time, the function should call *sched_yield()* to yield the CPU to the other process. (Alternatively, the processes could raise each other's scheduling priority using *sched_setparam()*.) The program's output should demonstrate that the two processes alternately execute for 1 second of CPU time. (Note carefully the advice given in Section 35.3.2 about preventing a runaway realtime process from hogging the CPU.)

> If your system has multiple CPUs, then, in order to demonstrate the behavior described in this exercise, you will need to confine all processes to a single CPU. This can be done by calling *sched_setaffinity()* before creating the child process or from the command line by using the *taskset* command.

35-4. If two processes use a pipe to exchange a large amount of data on a multiprocessor system, the communication should be faster if the processes run on the same CPU than if they run on different CPUs. The reason is that when the two processes run on the same CPU, the pipe data will be more quickly accessed because it can remain in that CPU's cache. By contrast, when the processes run on separate CPUs, the benefits of the CPU cache are lost. If you have access to a multiprocessor system, write a program that uses *sched_setaffinity()* to demonstrate this effect, by forcing the processes either onto the same CPUs or onto different CPUs. (Chapter 44 describes the use of pipes.)

> The advantage in favor of processes running on the same CPU won't hold true on hyperthreaded systems and on some modern multiprocessor architectures where the CPUs do share the cache. In these cases, the advantage will be in favor of processes running on different CPUs. Information about the CPU topology of a multiprocessor system can be obtained by inspecting the contents of the Linux-specific /proc/cpuinfo file.

36

PROCESS RESOURCES

Each process consumes system resources such as memory and CPU time. This chapter looks at resource-related system calls. We begin with the *getrusage()* system call, which allows a process to monitor the resources that it has used or that its children have used. We then look at the *setrlimit()* and *getrlimit()* system calls, which can be used to change and retrieve limits on the calling process's consumption of various resources.

36.1 Process Resource Usage

The *getrusage()* system call retrieves statistics about various system resources used by the calling process or by all of its children.

```
#include <sys/resource.h>

int getrusage(int who, struct rusage *res_usage);
```
Returns 0 on success, or –1 on error

The *who* argument specifies the process(es) for which resource usage information is to be retrieved. It has one of the following values:

RUSAGE_SELF

> Return information about the calling process.

RUSAGE_CHILDREN

> Return information about all children of the calling process that have terminated and been waited for.

RUSAGE_THREAD (since Linux 2.6.26)

> Return information about the calling thread. This value is Linux-specific.

The *res_usage* argument is a pointer to a structure of type *rusage*, defined as shown in Listing 36-1.

Listing 36-1: Definition of the *rusage* structure

```
struct rusage {
    struct timeval ru_utime;      /* User CPU time used */
    struct timeval ru_stime;      /* System CPU time used */
    long           ru_maxrss;     /* Maximum size of resident set (kilobytes)
                                     [used since Linux 2.6.32] */
    long           ru_ixrss;      /* Integral (shared) text memory size
                                     (kilobyte-seconds) [unused] */
    long           ru_idrss;      /* Integral (unshared) data memory used
                                     (kilobyte-seconds) [unused] */
    long           ru_isrss;      /* Integral (unshared) stack memory used
                                     (kilobyte-seconds) [unused] */
    long           ru_minflt;     /* Soft page faults (I/O not required) */
    long           ru_majflt;     /* Hard page faults (I/O required) */
    long           ru_nswap;      /* Swaps out of physical memory [unused] */
    long           ru_inblock;    /* Block input operations via file
                                     system [used since Linux 2.6.22] */
    long           ru_oublock;    /* Block output operations via file
                                     system [used since Linux 2.6.22] */
    long           ru_msgsnd;     /* IPC messages sent [unused] */
    long           ru_msgrcv;     /* IPC messages received [unused] */
    long           ru_nsignals;   /* Signals received [unused] */
    long           ru_nvcsw;      /* Voluntary context switches (process
                                     relinquished CPU before its time slice
                                     expired) [used since Linux 2.6] */
    long           ru_nivcsw;     /* Involuntary context switches (higher
                                     priority process became runnable or time
                                     slice ran out) [used since Linux 2.6] */
};
```

As indicated in the comments in Listing 36-1, on Linux, many of the fields in the *rusage* structure are not filled in by *getrusage()* (or *wait3()* and *wait4()*), or they are filled in only by more recent kernel versions. Some of the fields that are unused on Linux are used on other UNIX implementations. These fields are provided on Linux so that, if they are implemented at a future date, the *rusage* structure does not need to undergo a change that would break existing application binaries.

Although *getrusage()* appears on most UNIX implementations, it is only weakly specified in SUSv3 (which specifies only the fields *ru_utime* and *ru_stime*). In part, this is because the meaning of much of the information in the *rusage* structure is implementation-dependent.

The *ru_utime* and *ru_stime* fields are structures of type *timeval* (Section 10.1), which return the number of seconds and microseconds of CPU time consumed by a process in user mode and kernel mode, respectively. (Similar information is retrieved by the *times()* system call described in Section 10.7.)

> The Linux-specific /proc/*PID*/stat files expose some resource usage information (CPU time and page faults) about all processes on the system. See the *proc(5)* manual page for further details.

The *rusage* structure returned by the *getrusage()* RUSAGE_CHILDREN operation includes the resource usage statistics of all of the descendants of the calling process. For example, if we have three processes related as parent, child, and grandchild, then, when the child does a *wait()* on the grandchild, the resource usage values of the grandchild are added to the child's RUSAGE_CHILDREN values; when the parent performs a *wait()* for the child, the resource usage values of both the child and the grandchild are added to the parent's RUSAGE_CHILDREN values. Conversely, if the child does not *wait()* on the grandchild, then the grandchild's resource usages are not recorded in the RUSAGE_CHILDREN values of the parent.

For the RUSAGE_CHILDREN operation, the *ru_maxrss* field returns the maximum resident set size among all of the descendants of the calling process (rather than a sum for all descendants).

> SUSv3 specifies that if SIGCHLD is being ignored (so that children are not turned into zombies that can be waited on), then the child statistics should not be added to the values returned by RUSAGE_CHILDREN. However, as noted in Section 26.3.3, in kernels before 2.6.9, Linux deviates from this requirement—if SIGCHLD is ignored, then the resource usage values for dead children *are* included in the values returned for RUSAGE_CHILDREN.

36.2 Process Resource Limits

Each process has a set of resource limits that can be used to restrict the amounts of various system resources that the process may consume. For example, we may want to set resource limits on a process before execing an arbitrary program, if we are concerned that it may consume excessive resources. We can set the resource limits of the shell using the *ulimit* built-in command (*limit* in the C shell). These limits are inherited by the processes that the shell creates to execute user commands.

> Since kernel 2.6.24, the Linux-specific /proc/*PID*/limits file can be used to view all of the resource limits of any process. This file is owned by the real user ID of the corresponding process and its permissions allow reading only by that user ID (or by a privileged process).

The *getrlimit()* and *setrlimit()* system calls allow a process to fetch and modify its resource limits.

```
#include <sys/resource.h>

int getrlimit(int resource, struct rlimit *rlim);
int setrlimit(int resource, const struct rlimit *rlim);
```
                                    Both return 0 on success, or –1 on error

The *resource* argument identifies the resource limit to be retrieved or changed. The *rlim* argument is used to return resource limit values (*getrlimit()*) or to specify new resource limit values (*setrlimit()*), and is a pointer to a structure containing two fields:

```
struct rlimit {
    rlim_t rlim_cur;        /* Soft limit (actual process limit) */
    rlim_t rlim_max;        /* Hard limit (ceiling for rlim_cur) */
};
```

These fields correspond to the two associated limits for a resource: the *soft* (*rlim_cur*) and *hard* (*rlim_max*) limits. (The *rlim_t* data type is an integer type.) The soft limit governs the amount of the resource that may be consumed by the process. A process can adjust the soft limit to any value from 0 up to the hard limit. For most resources, the sole purpose of the hard limit is to provide this ceiling for the soft limit. A privileged (CAP_SYS_RESOURCE) process can adjust the hard limit in either direction (as long as its value remains greater than the soft limit), but an unprivileged process can adjust the hard limit only to a lower value (irreversibly). The value RLIM_INFINITY in *rlim_cur* or *rlim_max* means infinity (no limit on the resource), both when retrieved via *getrlimit()* and when set via *setrlimit()*.

In most cases, resource limits are enforced for both privileged and unprivileged processes. They are inherited by child processes created via *fork()* and are preserved across an *exec()*.

The values that can be specified for the *resource* argument of *getrlimit()* and *setrlimit()* are summarized in Table 36-1 and detailed in Section 36.3.

Although a resource limit is a per-process attribute, in some cases, the limit is measured against not just that process's consumption of the corresponding resource, but also against the sum of resources consumed by all processes with the same real user ID. The RLIMIT_NPROC limit, which places a limit on the number of processes that can be created, is a good example of the rationale for this approach. Applying this limit against only the number of children that the process itself created would be ineffective, since each child that the process created would also be able to create further children, which could create more children, and so on. Instead, the limit is measured against the count of all processes that have the same real user ID. Note, however, that the resource limit is checked only in the processes where it has been set (i.e., the process itself and its descendants, which inherit the limit). If another process owned by the same real user ID has not set the limit (i.e., the limit is infinite) or has set a different limit, then that process's capacity to create children will be checked according to the limit that it has set.

As we describe each resource limit below, we note those limits that are measured against the resources consumed by all processes with the same real user ID. If not otherwise specified, then a resource limit is measured only against the process's own consumption of the resource.

Be aware that, in many cases, the shell commands for getting and setting resource limits (*ulimit* in *bash* and the Korn shell, and *limit* in the C shell) use different units from those used in *getrlimit()* and *setrlimit()*. For example, the shell commands typically express the limits on the size of various memory segments in kilobytes.

Table 36-1: Resource values for *getrlimit()* and *setrlimit()*

resource	Limit on	SUSv3
RLIMIT_AS	Process virtual memory size (bytes)	•
RLIMIT_CORE	Core file size (bytes)	•
RLIMIT_CPU	CPU time (seconds)	•
RLIMIT_DATA	Process data segment (bytes)	•
RLIMIT_FSIZE	File size (bytes)	•
RLIMIT_MEMLOCK	Locked memory (bytes)	
RLIMIT_MSGQUEUE	Bytes allocated for POSIX message queues for real user ID (since Linux 2.6.8)	
RLIMIT_NICE	Nice value (since Linux 2.6.12)	
RLIMIT_NOFILE	Maximum file descriptor number plus one	•
RLIMIT_NPROC	Number of processes for real user ID	
RLIMIT_RSS	Resident set size (bytes; not implemented)	
RLIMIT_RTPRIO	Realtime scheduling priority (since Linux 2.6.12)	
RLIMIT_RTTIME	Realtime CPU time (microseconds; since Linux 2.6.25)	
RLIMIT_SIGPENDING	Number of queued signals for real user ID (since Linux 2.6.8)	
RLIMIT_STACK	Size of stack segment (bytes)	•

Example program

Before going into the specifics of each resource limit, we look at a simple example of the use of resource limits. Listing 36-2 defines the function *printRlimit()*, which displays a message, along with the soft and hard limits for a specified resource.

> The *rlim_t* data type is typically represented in the same way as *off_t*, to handle the representation of RLIMIT_FSIZE, the file size resource limit. For this reason, when printing *rlim_t* values (as in Listing 36-2), we cast them to *long long* and use the %lld *printf()* specifier, as explained in Section 5.10.

The program in Listing 36-3 calls *setrlimit()* to set the soft and hard limits on the number of processes that a user may create (RLIMIT_NPROC), uses the *printRlimit()* function of Listing 36-2 to display the limits before and after the change, and then creates as many processes as possible. When we run this program, setting the soft limit to 30 and the hard limit to 100, we see the following:

```
$ ./rlimit_nproc 30 100
Initial maximum process limits:  soft=1024; hard=1024
New maximum process limits:      soft=30; hard=100
Child 1 (PID=15674) started
Child 2 (PID=15675) started
Child 3 (PID=15676) started
Child 4 (PID=15677) started
ERROR [EAGAIN Resource temporarily unavailable] fork
```

In this example, the program managed to create only 4 new processes, because 26 processes were already running for this user.

Listing 36-2: Displaying process resource limits

—— **procres/print_rlimit.c**
```
#include <sys/resource.h>
#include "print_rlimit.h"              /* Declares function defined here */
#include "tlpi_hdr.h"

int                     /* Print 'msg' followed by limits for 'resource' */
printRlimit(const char *msg, int resource)
{
    struct rlimit rlim;

    if (getrlimit(resource, &rlim) == -1)
        return -1;

    printf("%s soft=", msg);
    if (rlim.rlim_cur == RLIM_INFINITY)
        printf("infinite");
#ifdef RLIM_SAVED_CUR              /* Not defined on some implementations */
    else if (rlim.rlim_cur == RLIM_SAVED_CUR)
        printf("unrepresentable");
#endif
    else
        printf("%lld", (long long) rlim.rlim_cur);

    printf("; hard=");
    if (rlim.rlim_max == RLIM_INFINITY)
        printf("infinite\n");
#ifdef RLIM_SAVED_MAX              /* Not defined on some implementations */
    else if (rlim.rlim_max == RLIM_SAVED_MAX)
        printf("unrepresentable");
#endif
    else
        printf("%lld\n", (long long) rlim.rlim_max);

    return 0;
}
```
—— **procres/print_rlimit.c**

Listing 36-3: Setting the RLIMIT_NPROC resource limit

—— **procres/rlimit_nproc.c**
```
#include <sys/resource.h>
#include "print_rlimit.h"                  /* Declaration of printRlimit() */
#include "tlpi_hdr.h"

int
main(int argc, char *argv[])
{
    struct rlimit rl;
    int j;
    pid_t childPid;
```

```
    if (argc < 2 || argc > 3 || strcmp(argv[1], "--help") == 0)
        usageErr("%s soft-limit [hard-limit]\n", argv[0]);

    printRlimit("Initial maximum process limits: ", RLIMIT_NPROC);

    /* Set new process limits (hard == soft if not specified) */

    rl.rlim_cur = (argv[1][0] == 'i') ? RLIM_INFINITY :
                                getInt(argv[1], 0, "soft-limit");
    rl.rlim_max = (argc == 2) ? rl.rlim_cur :
                (argv[2][0] == 'i') ? RLIM_INFINITY :
                                getInt(argv[2], 0, "hard-limit");
    if (setrlimit(RLIMIT_NPROC, &rl) == -1)
        errExit("setrlimit");

    printRlimit("New maximum process limits:     ", RLIMIT_NPROC);

    /* Create as many children as possible */

    for (j = 1; ; j++) {
        switch (childPid = fork()) {
        case -1: errExit("fork");

        case 0: _exit(EXIT_SUCCESS);            /* Child */

        default:        /* Parent: display message about each new child
                            and let the resulting zombies accumulate */
            printf("Child %d (PID=%ld) started\n", j, (long) childPid);
            break;
        }
    }
}
```

─── procres/rlimit_nproc.c

Unrepresentable limit values

In some programming environments, the *rlim_t* data type may not be able to represent
the full range of values that could be maintained for a particular resource limit.
This may be the case on a system that offers multiple programming environments
in which the size of the *rlim_t* data type differs. Such systems can arise if a large-file
compilation environment with a 64-bit *off_t* is added to a system on which *off_t* was
traditionally 32 bits. (In each environment, *rlim_t* would be the same size as *off_t*.)
This leads to the situation where a program with a small *rlim_t* can, after being
execed by a program with a 64-bit *off_t*, inherit a resource limit (e.g., the file size
limit) that is greater than the maximum *rlim_t* value.

   To assist portable applications in handling the possibility that a resource limit
may be unrepresentable, SUSv3 specifies two constants to indicate unrepresentable limit values: RLIM_SAVED_CUR and RLIM_SAVED_MAX. If a soft resource limit can't be
represented in *rlim_t*, then *getrlimit()* will return RLIM_SAVED_CUR in the *rlim_cur* field.
RLIM_SAVED_MAX performs an analogous function for an unrepresentable hard limit
returned in the *rlim_max* field.

If all possible resource limit values can be represented in *rlim_t*, then SUSv3 permits an implementation to define `RLIM_SAVED_CUR` and `RLIM_SAVED_MAX` to be the same as `RLIM_INFINITY`. This is how these constants are defined on Linux, implying that all possible resource limit values can be represented in *rlim_t*. However, this is not the case on 32-bit architectures such as x86-32. On those architectures, in a large-file compilation environment (i.e., setting the `_FILE_OFFSET_BITS` feature test macro to 64 as described in Section 5.10), the *glibc* definition of *rlim_t* is 64 bits wide, but the kernel data type for representing a resource limit is *unsigned long*, which is only 32 bits wide. Current versions of *glibc* deal with this situation as follows: if a program compiled with `_FILE_OFFSET_BITS=64` tries to set a resource limit to a value larger than can be represented in a 32-bit *unsigned long*, then the *glibc* wrapper for *setrlimit()* silently converts the value to `RLIM_INFINITY`. In other words, the requested setting of the resource limit is not honored.

> Because utilities that handle files are normally compiled with `_FILE_OFFSET_BITS=64` in many x86-32 distributions, the failure to honor resource limits larger than the value that can be represented in 32 bits is a problem that can affect not only application programmers, but also end users.
>
> One could argue that it might be better for the *glibc* *setrlimit()* wrapper to give an error if the requested resource limit exceeds the capacity of a 32-bit *unsigned long*. However, the fundamental problem is a kernel limitation, and the behavior described in the main text is the approach that the *glibc* developers have taken to dealing with it.

36.3 Details of Specific Resource Limits

In this section, we provide details on each of the resource limits available on Linux, noting those that are Linux-specific.

RLIMIT_AS

The `RLIMIT_AS` limit specifies the maximum size for the process's virtual memory (address space), in bytes. Attempts (*brk()*, *sbrk()*, *mmap()*, *mremap()*, and *shmat()*) to exceed this limit fail with the error `ENOMEM`. In practice, the most common place where a program may hit this limit is in calls to functions in the *malloc* package, which make use of *sbrk()* and *mmap()*. Upon encountering this limit, stack growth can also fail with the consequences listed below for `RLIMIT_STACK`.

RLIMIT_CORE

The `RLIMIT_CORE` limit specifies the maximum size, in bytes, for core dump files produced when a process is terminated by certain signals (Section 22.1). Production of a core dump file will stop at this limit. Specifying a limit of 0 prevents creation of core dump files, which is sometimes useful because core dump files can be very large, and end users usually don't know what to do with them. Another reason for disabling core dumps is security—to prevent the contents of a program's memory from being dumped to disk. If the `RLIMIT_FSIZE` limit is lower than this limit, core dump files are limited to `RLIMIT_FSIZE` bytes.

RLIMIT_CPU

The RLIMIT_CPU limit specifies the maximum number of seconds of CPU time (in both system and user mode) that can be used by the process. SUSv3 requires that the SIGXCPU signal be sent to the process when the soft limit is reached, but leaves other details unspecified. (The default action for SIGXCPU is to terminate a process with a core dump.) It is possible to establish a handler for SIGXCPU that does whatever processing is desired and then returns control to the main program. Thereafter, (on Linux) SIGXCPU is sent once per second of consumed CPU time. If the process continues executing until the hard CPU limit is reached, then the kernel sends it a SIGKILL signal, which always terminates the process.

UNIX implementations vary in the details of how they deal with processes that continue consuming CPU time after handling a SIGXCPU signal. Most continue to deliver SIGXCPU at regular intervals. If aiming for portable use of this signal, we should code an application so that, on first receipt of this signal, it does whatever cleanup is required and terminates. (Alternatively, the program could change the resource limit after receiving the signal.)

RLIMIT_DATA

The RLIMIT_DATA limit specifies the maximum size, in bytes, of the process's data segment (the sum of the initialized data, uninitialized data, and heap segments described in Section 6.3). Attempts (*sbrk()* and *brk()*) to extend the data segment (program break) beyond this limit fail with the error ENOMEM. As with RLIMIT_AS, the most common place where a program may hit this limit is in calls to functions in the *malloc* package.

RLIMIT_FSIZE

The RLIMIT_FSIZE limit specifies the maximum size of files that the process may create, in bytes. If a process attempts to extend a file beyond the soft limit, it is sent a SIGXFSZ signal, and the system call (e.g., *write()* or *truncate()*) fails with the error EFBIG. The default action for SIGXFSZ is to terminate a process and produce a core dump. It is possible to instead catch this signal and return control to the main program. However, any further attempt to extend the file will yield the same signal and error.

RLIMIT_MEMLOCK

The RLIMIT_MEMLOCK limit (BSD-derived; absent from SUSv3 and available only on Linux and the BSDs) specifies the maximum number of bytes of virtual memory that a process may lock into physical memory, to prevent the memory from being swapped out. This limit affects the *mlock()* and *mlockall()* system calls, and the locking options for the *mmap()* and *shmctl()* system calls. We describe the details in Section 50.2.

If the MCL_FUTURE flag is specified when calling *mlockall()*, then the RLIMIT_MEMLOCK limit may also cause later calls to *brk()*, *sbrk()*, *mmap()*, or *mremap()* to fail.

RLIMIT_MSGQUEUE

The RLIMIT_MSGQUEUE limit (Linux-specific; since Linux 2.6.8) specifies the maximum number of bytes that can be allocated for POSIX message queues for the real user

ID of the calling process. When a POSIX message queue is created using *mq_open()*, bytes are deducted against this limit according to the following formula:

```
bytes = attr.mq_maxmsg * sizeof(struct msg_msg *) +
        attr.mq_maxmsg * attr.mq_msgsize;
```

In this formula, *attr* is the *mq_attr* structure that is passed as the fourth argument to *mq_open()*. The addend that includes *sizeof(struct msg_msg *)* ensures that the user can't queue an unlimited number of zero-length messages. (The *msg_msg* structure is a data type used internally by the kernel.) This is necessary because, although zero-length messages contain no data, they do consume some system memory for bookkeeping overhead.

The `RLIMIT_MSGQUEUE` limit affects only the calling process. Other processes belonging to this user are not affected unless they also set this limit or inherit it.

RLIMIT_NICE

The `RLIMIT_NICE` limit (Linux-specific; since Linux 2.6.12) specifies a ceiling on the nice value that may be set for this process using *sched_setscheduler()* and *nice()*. The ceiling is calculated as $20 - rlim\_cur$, where *rlim_cur* is the current `RLIMIT_NICE` soft resource limit. Refer to Section 35.1 for further details.

RLIMIT_NOFILE

The `RLIMIT_NOFILE` limit specifies a number one greater than the maximum file descriptor number that a process may allocate. Attempts (e.g., *open()*, *pipe()*, *socket()*, *accept()*, *shm_open()*, *dup()*, *dup2()*, *fcntl(F_DUPFD)*, and *epoll_create()*) to allocate descriptors beyond this limit fail. In most cases, the error is `EMFILE`, but for *dup2(fd, newfd)* it is `EBADF`, and for *fcntl(fd, F_DUPFD, newfd)* with *newfd* is greater than or equal to the limit, it is `EINVAL`.

Changes to the `RLIMIT_NOFILE` limit are reflected in the value returned by *sysconf(_SC_OPEN_MAX)*. SUSv3 permits, but doesn't require, an implementation to return different values for a call to *sysconf(_SC_OPEN_MAX)* before and after changing the `RLIMIT_NOFILE` limit; other implementations may not behave the same as Linux on this point.

> SUSv3 states that if an application sets the soft or hard `RLIMIT_NOFILE` limit to a value less than or equal to the number of the highest file descriptor that the process currently has open, unexpected behavior may occur.
>
> On Linux, we can check which file descriptors a process currently has open by using *readdir()* to scan the contents of the /proc/*PID*/fd directory, which contains symbolic links for each of the file descriptors currently opened by the process.

The kernel imposes a ceiling on the value to which the `RLIMIT_NOFILE` limit may be raised. In kernels before 2.6.25, this ceiling is a hard-coded value defined by the kernel constant `NR_OPEN`, whose value is 1,048,576. (A kernel rebuild is required to raise this ceiling.) Since kernel 2.6.25, the limit is defined by the value in the Linux-specific /proc/sys/fs/nr_open file. The default value in this file is 1,048,576; this can be modified by the superuser. Attempts to set the soft or hard `RLIMIT_NOFILE` limit higher than the ceiling value yield the error `EPERM`.

There is also a system-wide limit on the total number of files that may be opened by all processes. This limit can be retrieved and modified via the Linux-specific /proc/sys/fs/file-max file. (Referring to Section 5.4, we can define file-max more precisely as a system-wide limit on the number of open file descriptions.) Only privileged (CAP_SYS_ADMIN) processes can exceed the file-max limit. In an unprivileged process, a system call that encounters the file-max limit fails with the error ENFILE.

RLIMIT_NPROC

The RLIMIT_NPROC limit (BSD-derived; absent from SUSv3 and available only on Linux and the BSDs) specifies the maximum number of processes that may be created for the real user ID of the calling process. Attempts (*fork()*, *vfork()*, and *clone()*) to exceed this limit fail with the error EAGAIN.

The RLIMIT_NPROC limit affects only the calling process. Other processes belonging to this user are not affected unless they also set or inherit this limit. This limit is not enforced for privileged (CAP_SYS_ADMIN or CAP_SYS_RESOURCE) processes.

> Linux also imposes a system-wide limit on the number of processes that can be created by all users. On Linux 2.4 and later, the Linux-specific /proc/sys/kernel/threads-max file can be used to retrieve and modify this limit.
>
> To be precise, the RLIMIT_NPROC resource limit and the threads-max file are actually limits on the numbers of threads that can be created, rather than the number of processes.

The manner in which the default value for the RLIMIT_NPROC resource limit is set has varied across kernel versions. In Linux 2.2, it was calculated according to a fixed formula. In Linux 2.4 and later, it is calculated using a formula based on the amount of available physical memory.

> SUSv3 doesn't specify the RLIMIT_NPROC resource limit. The SUSv3-mandated method for retrieving (but not changing) the maximum number of processes permitted to a user ID is via the call *sysconf(_SC_CHILD_MAX)*. This *sysconf()* call is supported on Linux, but in kernel versions before 2.6.23, the call does not return accurate information—it always returns the value 999. Since Linux 2.6.23 (and with *glibc* 2.4 and later), this call correctly reports the limit (by checking the value of the RLIMIT_NPROC resource limit).
>
> There is no portable way of discovering how many processes have already been created for a specific user ID. On Linux, we can try scanning all of the /proc/*PID*/status files on the system and examining the information under the Uid entry (which lists the four process user IDs in the order: real, effective, saved set, and file system) in order to estimate the number of processes currently owned by a user. Be aware, however, that by the time we have completed such a scan, this information may already have changed.

RLIMIT_RSS

The RLIMIT_RSS limit (BSD-derived; absent from SUSv3, but widely available) specifies the maximum number of pages in the process's resident set; that is, the total number of virtual memory pages currently in physical memory. This limit is provided on Linux, but it currently has no effect.

In older Linux 2.4 kernels (up to and including 2.4.29), RLIMIT_RSS did have an effect on the behavior of the *madvise()* MADV_WILLNEED operation (Section 50.4). If this operation could not be performed as a result of encountering the RLIMIT_RSS limit, the error EIO was returned in *errno*.

RLIMIT_RTPRIO

The RLIMIT_RTPRIO limit (Linux-specific; since Linux 2.6.12) specifies a ceiling on the realtime priority that may be set for this process using *sched_setscheduler()* and *sched_setparam()*. Refer to Section 35.3.2 for further details.

RLIMIT_RTTIME

The RLIMIT_RTTIME limit (Linux-specific; since Linux 2.6.25) specifies the maximum amount of CPU time in microseconds that a process running under a realtime scheduling policy may consume without sleeping (i.e., performing a blocking system call). The behavior if this limit is reached is the same as for RLIMIT_CPU: if the process reaches the soft limit, then a SIGXCPU signal is sent to the process, and further SIGXCPU signals are sent for each additional second of CPU time consumed. On reaching the hard limit, a SIGKILL signal is sent. Refer to Section 35.3.2 for further details.

RLIMIT_SIGPENDING

The RLIMIT_SIGPENDING limit (Linux-specific; since Linux 2.6.8) specifies the maximum number of signals that may be queued for the real user ID of the calling process. Attempts (*sigqueue()*) to exceed this limit fail with the error EAGAIN.

The RLIMIT_SIGPENDING limit affects only the calling process. Other processes belonging to this user are not affected unless they also set or inherit this limit.

As initially implemented, the default value for the RLIMIT_SIGPENDING limit was 1024. Since kernel 2.6.12, the default value has been changed to be the same as the default value for RLIMIT_NPROC.

For the purposes of checking the RLIMIT_SIGPENDING limit, the count of queued signals includes both realtime and standard signals. (Standard signals can be queued only once to a process.) However, this limit is enforced only for *sigqueue()*. Even if the number of signals specified by this limit has already been queued to processes belonging to this real user ID, it is still possible to use *kill()* to queue one instance of each of the signals (including realtime signals) that are not already queued to a process.

From kernel 2.6.12 onward, the SigQ field of the Linux-specific /proc/*PID*/status file displays the current and maximum number of queued signals for the real user ID of the process.

RLIMIT_STACK

The RLIMIT_STACK limit specifies the maximum size of the process stack, in bytes. Attempts to grow the stack beyond this limit result in the generation of a SIGSEGV signal for the process. Since the stack is exhausted, the only way to catch this signal is by establishing an alternate signal stack, as described in Section 21.3.

Since Linux 2.6.23, the RLIMIT_STACK limit also determines the amount of space available for holding the process's command-line arguments and environment variables. See the *execve(2)* manual page for details.

36.4 Summary

Processes consume various system resources. The *getrusage()* system call allows a process to monitor certain of the resources consumed by itself and by its children.

The *setrlimit()* and *getrlimit()* system calls allow a process to set and retrieve limits on its consumption of various resources. Each resource limit has two components: a soft limit, which is what the kernel enforces when checking a process's resource consumption, and a hard limit, which acts as a ceiling on the value of the soft limit. An unprivileged process can set the soft limit for a resource to any value in the range from 0 up to the hard limit, but can only lower the hard limit. A privileged process can make any changes to either limit value, as long as the soft limit is less than or equal to the hard limit. If a process encounters a soft limit, it is typically informed of the fact either by receiving a signal or via failure of the system call that attempts to exceed the limit.

36.5 Exercises

36-1. Write a program that shows that the *getrusage()* RUSAGE_CHILDREN flag retrieves information about only the children for which a *wait()* call has been performed. (Have the program create a child process that consumes some CPU time, and then have the parent call *getrusage()* before and after calling *wait()*.)

36-2. Write a program that executes a command and then displays its resource usage. This is analogous to what the *time(1)* command does. Thus, we would use this program as follows:

```
$ ./rusage command arg...
```

36-3. Write programs to determine what happens if a process's consumption of various resources already exceeds the soft limit specified in a call to *setrlimit()*.

37

DAEMONS

This chapter examines the characteristics of daemon processes and looks at the steps required to turn a process into a daemon. We also look at how to log messages from a daemon using the *syslog* facility.

37.1 Overview

A *daemon* is a process with the following characteristics:

- It is long-lived. Often, a daemon is created at system startup and runs until the system is shut down.
- It runs in the background and has no controlling terminal. The lack of a controlling terminal ensures that the kernel never automatically generates any job-control or terminal-related signals (such as SIGINT, SIGTSTP, and SIGHUP) for a daemon.

Daemons are written to carry out specific tasks, as illustrated by the following examples:

- *cron*: a daemon that executes commands at a scheduled time.
- *sshd*: the secure shell daemon, which permits logins from remote hosts using a secure communications protocol.

- *httpd*: the HTTP server daemon (Apache), which serves web pages.
- *inetd*: the Internet superserver daemon (described in Section 60.5), which listens for incoming network connections on specified TCP/IP ports and launches appropriate server programs to handle these connections.

Many standard daemons run as privileged processes (i.e., effective user ID of 0), and thus should be coded following the guidelines provided in Chapter 38.

It is a convention (not universally observed) that daemons have names ending with the letter *d*.

> On Linux, certain daemons are run as *kernel threads*. The code of such daemons is part of the kernel, and they are typically created during system startup. When listed using *ps(1)*, the names of these daemons are surrounded by square brackets ([ ]). One example of a kernel thread is *pdflush*, which periodically flushes dirty pages (e.g., pages from the buffer cache) to disk.

37.2 Creating a Daemon

To become a daemon, a program performs the following steps:

1. Perform a *fork()*, after which the parent exits and the child continues. (As a consequence, the daemon becomes a child of the *init* process.) This step is done for two reasons:
   - Assuming the daemon was started from the command line, the parent's termination is noticed by the shell, which then displays another shell prompt and leaves the child to continue in the background.
   - The child process is guaranteed not to be a process group leader, since it inherited its process group ID from its parent and obtained its own unique process ID, which differs from the inherited process group ID. This is required in order to be able to successfully perform the next step.

2. The child process calls *setsid()* (Section 34.3) to start a new session and free itself of any association with a controlling terminal.

3. If the daemon never opens any terminal devices thereafter, then we don't need to worry about the daemon reacquiring a controlling terminal. If the daemon might later open a terminal device, then we must take steps to ensure that the device does not become the controlling terminal. We can do this in two ways:
   - Specify the O_NOCTTY flag on any *open()* that may apply to a terminal device.
   - Alternatively, and more simply, perform a second *fork()* after the *setsid()* call, and again have the parent exit and the (grand)child continue. This ensures that the child is not the session leader, and thus, according to the System V conventions for the acquisition of a controlling terminal (which Linux follows), the process can never reacquire a controlling terminal (Section 34.4).

     > On implementations following the BSD conventions, a process can obtain a controlling terminal only through an explicit *ioctl()* TIOCSCTTY operation, and so this second *fork()* has no effect with regard to the acquisition of a controlling terminal, but the superfluous *fork()* does no harm.

4. Clear the process umask (Section 15.4.6), to ensure that, when the daemon creates files and directories, they have the requested permissions.

5. Change the process's current working directory, typically to the root directory (/). This is necessary because a daemon usually runs until system shutdown; if the daemon's current working directory is on a file system other than the one containing /, then that file system can't be unmounted (Section 14.8.2). Alternatively, the daemon can change its working directory to a location where it does its job or a location defined in its configuration file, as long as we know that the file system containing this directory never needs to be unmounted. For example, *cron* places itself in /var/spool/cron.

6. Close all open file descriptors that the daemon has inherited from its parent. (A daemon may need to keep certain inherited file descriptors open, so this step is optional, or open to variation.) This is done for a variety of reasons. Since the daemon has lost its controlling terminal and is running in the background, it makes no sense for the daemon to keep file descriptors 0, 1, and 2 open if these refer to the terminal. Furthermore, we can't unmount any file systems on which the long-lived daemon holds files open. And, as usual, we should close unused open file descriptors because file descriptors are a finite resource.

> Some UNIX implementations (e.g., Solaris 9 and some of the recent BSD releases) provide a function named *closefrom(n)* (or similar), which closes all file descriptors greater than or equal to *n*. This function isn't available on Linux.

7. After having closed file descriptors 0, 1, and 2, a daemon normally opens /dev/null and uses *dup2()* (or similar) to make all those descriptors refer to this device. This is done for two reasons:

    – It ensures that if the daemon calls library functions that perform I/O on these descriptors, those functions won't unexpectedly fail.

    – It prevents the possibility that the daemon later opens a file using descriptor 1 or 2, which is then written to—and thus corrupted—by a library function that expects to treat these descriptors as standard output and standard error.

    > /dev/null is a virtual device that always discards the data written to it. When we want to eliminate the standard output or error of a shell command, we can redirect it to this file. Reads from this device always return end-of-file.

We now show the implementation of a function, *becomeDaemon()*, that performs the steps described above in order to turn the caller into a daemon.

```
#include <syslog.h>

int becomeDaemon(int flags);
```
                                           Returns 0 on success, or −1 on error

The *becomeDaemon()* function takes a bit-mask argument, *flags*, that allows the caller to selectively inhibit some of the steps, as described in the comments in the header file in Listing 37-1.

Listing 37-1: Header file for `become_daemon.c`

———————————————————————————————————— **daemons/become_daemon.h**

```
#ifndef BECOME_DAEMON_H                  /* Prevent double inclusion */
#define BECOME_DAEMON_H

/* Bit-mask values for 'flags' argument of becomeDaemon() */

#define BD_NO_CHDIR           01    /* Don't chdir("/") */
#define BD_NO_CLOSE_FILES     02    /* Don't close all open files */
#define BD_NO_REOPEN_STD_FDS  04    /* Don't reopen stdin, stdout, and
                                        stderr to /dev/null */
#define BD_NO_UMASK0          010   /* Don't do a umask(0) */

#define BD_MAX_CLOSE  8192          /* Maximum file descriptors to close if
                                        sysconf(_SC_OPEN_MAX) is indeterminate */

int becomeDaemon(int flags);

#endif
```

———————————————————————————————————— **daemons/become_daemon.h**

The implementation of the *becomeDaemon()* function is shown in Listing 37-2.

> The GNU C library provides a nonstandard function, *daemon()*, that turns the caller into a daemon. The *glibc daemon()* function doesn't have an equivalent of the *flags* argument of our *becomeDaemon()* function.

Listing 37-2: Creating a daemon process

———————————————————————————————————— **daemons/become_daemon.c**

```
#include <sys/stat.h>
#include <fcntl.h>
#include "become_daemon.h"
#include "tlpi_hdr.h"

int                                 /* Returns 0 on success, -1 on error */
becomeDaemon(int flags)
{
    int maxfd, fd;

    switch (fork()) {               /* Become background process */
    case -1: return -1;
    case 0:  break;                 /* Child falls through... */
    default: _exit(EXIT_SUCCESS);   /* while parent terminates */
    }

    if (setsid() == -1)             /* Become leader of new session */
        return -1;

    switch (fork()) {               /* Ensure we are not session leader */
    case -1: return -1;
    case 0:  break;
    default: _exit(EXIT_SUCCESS);
    }
```

```
    if (!(flags & BD_NO_UMASK0))
        umask(0);                       /* Clear file mode creation mask */

    if (!(flags & BD_NO_CHDIR))
        chdir("/");                     /* Change to root directory */

    if (!(flags & BD_NO_CLOSE_FILES)) { /* Close all open files */
        maxfd = sysconf(_SC_OPEN_MAX);
        if (maxfd == -1)                /* Limit is indeterminate... */
            maxfd = BD_MAX_CLOSE;       /* so take a guess */

        for (fd = 0; fd < maxfd; fd++)
            close(fd);
    }

    if (!(flags & BD_NO_REOPEN_STD_FDS)) {
        close(STDIN_FILENO);            /* Reopen standard fd's to /dev/null */

        fd = open("/dev/null", O_RDWR);

        if (fd != STDIN_FILENO)         /* 'fd' should be 0 */
            return -1;
        if (dup2(STDIN_FILENO, STDOUT_FILENO) != STDOUT_FILENO)
            return -1;
        if (dup2(STDIN_FILENO, STDERR_FILENO) != STDERR_FILENO)
            return -1;
    }

    return 0;
}
```

——————————————————————————————————— daemons/become_daemon.c

If we write a program that makes the call *becomeDaemon(0)* and then sleeps for a while, we can use *ps(1)* to look at some of the attributes of the resulting process:

```
$ ./test_become_daemon
$ ps -C test_become_daemon -o "pid ppid pgid sid tty command"
  PID  PPID  PGID    SID TT      COMMAND
24731     1 24730 24730 ?       ./test_become_daemon
```

> We don't show the source code for daemons/test_become_daemon.c, since it is trivial, but the program is provided in the source code distribution for this book.

In the output of *ps*, the ? under the *TT* heading indicates that the process has no controlling terminal. From the fact that the process ID is not the same as the session ID (SID), we can also see that the process is not the leader of its session, and so won't reacquire a controlling terminal if it opens a terminal device. This is as things should be for a daemon.

37.3 Guidelines for Writing Daemons

As previously noted, a daemon typically terminates only when the system shuts down. Many standard daemons are stopped by application-specific scripts executed during system shutdown. Those daemons that are not terminated in this fashion will receive a SIGTERM signal, which the *init* process sends to all of its children during system shutdown. By default, SIGTERM terminates a process. If the daemon needs to perform any cleanup before terminating, it should do so by establishing a handler for this signal. This handler must be designed to perform such cleanup quickly, since *init* follows up the SIGTERM signal with a SIGKILL signal after 5 seconds. (This doesn't mean that the daemon can perform 5 seconds' worth of CPU work; *init* signals all of the processes on the system at the same time, and they may all be attempting to clean up within that 5 seconds.)

Since daemons are long-lived, we must be particularly wary of possible memory leaks (Section 7.1.3) and file descriptor leaks (where an application fails to close all of the file descriptors it opens). If such bugs affect a daemon, the only remedy is to kill it and restart it after (fixing the bug).

Many daemons need to ensure that just one instance of the daemon is active at one time. For example, it makes no sense to have two copies of the *cron* daemon both trying to execute scheduled jobs. In Section 55.6, we look at a technique for achieving this.

37.4 Using SIGHUP to Reinitialize a Daemon

The fact that many daemons should run continuously presents a couple of programming hurdles:

- Typically, a daemon reads operational parameters from an associated configuration file on startup. Sometimes, it is desirable to be able to change these parameters "on the fly," without needing to stop and restart the daemon.

- Some daemons produce log files. If the daemon never closes the log file, then it may grow endlessly, eventually clogging the file system. (In Section 18.3, we noted that even if we remove the last name of a file, the file continues to exist as long as any process has it open.) What we need is a way of telling the daemon to close its log file and open a new file, so that we can rotate log files as required.

The solution to both of these problems is to have the daemon establish a handler for SIGHUP, and perform the required steps upon receipt of this signal. In Section 34.4, we noted that SIGHUP is generated for the controlling process on disconnection of a controlling terminal. Since a daemon has no controlling terminal, the kernel never generates this signal for a daemon. Therefore, daemons can use SIGHUP for the purpose described here.

> The *logrotate* program can be used to automate rotation of daemon log files. See the *logrotate(8)* manual page for details.

Listing 37-3 provides an example of how a daemon can employ SIGHUP. This program establishes a handler for SIGHUP ②, becomes a daemon ③, opens the log file ④, and reads its configuration file ⑤. The SIGHUP handler ① just sets a global flag variable, *hupReceived*, which is checked by the main program. The main program sits in a loop, printing a message to the log file every 15 seconds ⑧. The calls to *sleep()* ⑥ in this loop are intended to simulate some sort of processing performed by a real application. After each return from *sleep()* in this loop, the program checks to see whether *hupReceived* has been set ⑦; if so, it reopens the log file, rereads the configuration file, and clears the *hupReceived* flag.

For brevity, the functions *logOpen()*, *logClose()*, *logMessage()*, and *readConfigFile()* are omitted from Listing 37-3, but are provided with the source code distribution of this book. The first three functions do what we would expect from their names. The *readConfigFile()* function simply reads a line from the configuration file and echoes it to the log file.

> Some daemons use an alternative method to reinitialize themselves on receipt of SIGHUP: they close all files and then restart themselves with an *exec()*.

The following is an example of what we might see when running the program in Listing 37-3. We begin by creating a dummy configuration file and then launching the daemon:

```
$ echo START > /tmp/ds.conf
$ ./daemon_SIGHUP
$ cat /tmp/ds.log                              View log file
2011-01-17 11:18:34: Opened log file
2011-01-17 11:18:34: Read config file: START
```

Now we modify the configuration file and rename the log file before sending SIGHUP to the daemon:

```
$ echo CHANGED > /tmp/ds.conf
$ date +'%F %X'; mv /tmp/ds.log /tmp/old_ds.log
2011-01-17 11:19:03 AM
$ date +'%F %X'; killall -HUP daemon_SIGHUP
2011-01-17 11:19:23 AM
$ ls /tmp/*ds.log                              Log file was reopened
/tmp/ds.log  /tmp/old_ds.log
$ cat /tmp/old_ds.log                          View old log file
2011-01-17 11:18:34: Opened log file
2011-01-17 11:18:34: Read config file: START
2011-01-17 11:18:49: Main: 1
2011-01-17 11:19:04: Main: 2
2011-01-17 11:19:19: Main: 3
2011-01-17 11:19:23: Closing log file
```

The output of *ls* shows that we have both an old and a new log file. When we use *cat* to view the contents of the old log file, we see that even after the *mv* command was used to rename the file, the daemon continued to log messages there. At this point, we could delete the old log file if we no longer need it. When we look at the new log file, we see that the configuration file has been reread:

```
$ cat /tmp/ds.log
2011-01-17 11:19:23: Opened log file
2011-01-17 11:19:23: Read config file: CHANGED
2011-01-17 11:19:34: Main: 4
$ killall daemon_SIGHUP                         Kill our daemon
```

Note that a daemon's log and configuration files are typically placed in standard directories, not in the /tmp directory, as is done in the program in Listing 37-3. By convention, configuration files are placed in /etc or one of its subdirectories, while log files are often placed in /var/log. Daemon programs commonly provide command-line options to specify alternative locations instead of the defaults.

Listing 37-3: Using SIGHUP to reinitialize a daemon

——— **daemons/daemon_SIGHUP.c**

```
#include <sys/stat.h>
#include <signal.h>
#include "become_daemon.h"
#include "tlpi_hdr.h"

static const char *LOG_FILE = "/tmp/ds.log";
static const char *CONFIG_FILE = "/tmp/ds.conf";

/* Definitions of logMessage(), logOpen(), logClose(), and
   readConfigFile() are omitted from this listing */

static volatile sig_atomic_t hupReceived = 0;
                                    /* Set nonzero on receipt of SIGHUP */

static void
sighupHandler(int sig)
{
①     hupReceived = 1;
}

int
main(int argc, char *argv[])
{
    const int SLEEP_TIME = 15;    /* Time to sleep between messages */
    int count = 0;                /* Number of completed SLEEP_TIME intervals */
    int unslept;                  /* Time remaining in sleep interval */
    struct sigaction sa;

    sigemptyset(&sa.sa_mask);
    sa.sa_flags = SA_RESTART;
    sa.sa_handler = sighupHandler;
②     if (sigaction(SIGHUP, &sa, NULL) == -1)
        errExit("sigaction");

③     if (becomeDaemon(0) == -1)
        errExit("becomeDaemon");

④     logOpen(LOG_FILE);
⑤     readConfigFile(CONFIG_FILE);

    unslept = SLEEP_TIME;

    for (;;) {
⑥         unslept = sleep(unslept);       /* Returns > 0 if interrupted */

⑦         if (hupReceived) {              /* If we got SIGHUP... */
            hupReceived = 0;              /* Get ready for next SIGHUP */
```

```
        logClose();
        logOpen(LOG_FILE);
        readConfigFile(CONFIG_FILE);
    }

    if (unslept == 0) {                 /* On completed interval */
        count++;
⑧       logMessage("Main: %d", count);
        unslept = SLEEP_TIME;          /* Reset interval */
    }
  }
}
```

── **daemons/daemon_SIGHUP.c**

37.5 Logging Messages and Errors Using *syslog*

When writing a daemon, one problem we encounter is how to display error messages. Since a daemon runs in the background, we can't display messages on an associated terminal, as we would typically do with other programs. One possible alternative is to write messages to an application-specific log file, as is done in the program in Listing 37-3. The main problem with this approach is that it is difficult for a system administrator to manage multiple application log files and monitor them all for error messages. The *syslog* facility was devised to address this problem.

37.5.1 Overview

The *syslog* facility provides a single, centralized logging facility that can be used to log messages by all applications on the system. An overview of this facility is provided in Figure 37-1.

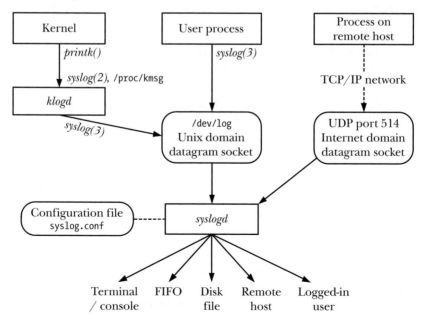

Figure 37-1: Overview of system logging

The *syslog* facility has two principal components: the *syslogd* daemon and the *syslog(3)* library function.

The *System Log* daemon, *syslogd*, accepts log messages from two different sources: a UNIX domain socket, /dev/log, which holds locally produced messages, and (if enabled) an Internet domain socket (UDP port 514), which holds messages sent across a TCP/IP network. (On some other UNIX implementations, the *syslog* socket is located at /var/run/log.)

Each message processed by *syslogd* has a number of attributes, including a *facility*, which specifies the type of program generating the message, and a *level*, which specifies the severity (priority) of the message. The *syslogd* daemon examines the *facility* and *level* of each message, and then passes it along to any of several possible destinations according to the dictates of an associated configuration file, /etc/syslog.conf. Possible destinations include a terminal or virtual console, a disk file, a FIFO, one or more (or all) logged-in users, or a process (typically another *syslogd* daemon) on another system connected via a TCP/IP network. (Sending the message to a process on another system is useful for reducing administrative overhead by consolidating messages from multiple systems to a single location.) A single message may be sent to multiple destinations (or none at all), and messages with different combinations of *facility* and *level* can be targeted to different destinations or to different instances of destinations (i.e., different consoles, different disk files, and so on).

> Sending *syslog* messages to another system via a TCP/IP network can also help in detecting system break-ins. Break-ins often leave traces in the system log, but attackers usually try to cover up their activities by erasing log records. With remote logging, an attacker would need to break into another system in order to do that.

The *syslog(3)* library function can be used by any process to log a message. This function, which we describe in detail in a moment, uses its supplied arguments to construct a message in a standard format that is then placed on the /dev/log socket for reading by *syslogd*.

An alternative source of the messages placed on /dev/log is the *Kernel Log* daemon, *klogd*, which collects kernel log messages (produced by the kernel using its *printk()* function). These messages are collected using either of two equivalent Linux-specific interfaces—the /proc/kmsg file and the *syslog(2)* system call—and then placed on /dev/log using the *syslog(3)* library function.

> Although *syslog(2)* and *syslog(3)* share the same name, they perform quite different tasks. An interface to *syslog(2)* is provided in *glibc* under the name *klogctl()*. Unless explicitly indicated otherwise, when we refer to *syslog()* in this section, we mean *syslog(3)*.
>
> Some modern implementations of *syslogd*, such as *rsyslog* and *syslog-ng*, dispense with the need for a separate *klogd* daemon by instead themselves reading directly from /proc/kmsg.

The *syslog* facility originally appeared in 4.2BSD, but is now provided on most UNIX implementations. SUSv3 has standardized *syslog(3)* and related functions, but leaves the implementation and operation of *syslogd*, as well as the format of the syslog.conf file, unspecified. The Linux implementation of *syslogd* differs from the original BSD facility in permitting some extensions to the message-processing rules that can be specified in `syslog.conf`.

37.5.2 The *syslog* API

The *syslog* API consists of three main functions:

- The *openlog()* function establishes default settings that apply to subsequent calls to *syslog()*. The use of *openlog()* is optional. If it is omitted, a connection to the logging facility is established with default settings on the first call to *syslog()*.
- The *syslog()* function logs a message.
- The *closelog()* function is called after we have finished logging messages, to disestablish the connection with the log.

None of these functions returns a status value. In part, this is because system logging should always be available (the system administrator is soon likely to notice if it is not). Furthermore, if an error occurs with system logging, there is typically little that the application can usefully do to report it.

> The GNU C library also provides the function *void vsyslog(int priority, const char *format, va_list args)*. This function performs the same task as *syslog()*, but takes an argument list previously processed by the *stdarg(3)* API. (Thus, *vsyslog()* is to *syslog()* what *vprintf()* is to *printf()*.) SUSv3 doesn't specify *vsyslog()*, and it is not available on all UNIX implementations.

Establishing a connection to the system log

The *openlog()* function optionally establishes a connection to the system log facility and sets defaults that apply to subsequent *syslog()* calls.

```
#include <syslog.h>

void openlog(const char *ident, int log_options, int facility);
```

The *ident* argument is a pointer to a string that is included in each message written by *syslog()*; typically, the program name is specified for this argument. Note that *openlog()* merely copies the value of this pointer. As long as it continues to call *syslog()*, the application should ensure that the referenced string is not later changed.

> If *ident* is specified as NULL, then, like some other implementations, the *glibc* *syslog* implementation automatically uses the program name as the *ident* value. However, this feature is not required by SUSv3, and is not provided on some implementations. Portable applications should avoid reliance on it.

The *log_options* argument to *openlog()* is a bit mask created by ORing together any of the following constants:

LOG_CONS
> If there is an error sending to the system logger, then write the message to the system console (/dev/console).

LOG_NDELAY

Open the connection to the logging system (i.e., the underlying UNIX domain socket, /dev/log) immediately. By default (LOG_ODELAY), the connection is opened only when (and if) the first message is logged with *syslog()*. The LOG_NDELAY flag is useful in programs that need to precisely control when the file descriptor for /dev/log is allocated. One example of such a requirement is in a program that calls *chroot()*. After a *chroot()* call, the /dev/log pathname will no longer be visible, and so an *openlog()* call specifying LOG_NDELAY must be performed before the *chroot()*. The *tftpd* (Trivial File Transfer) daemon is an example of a program that uses LOG_NDELAY for this purpose.

LOG_NOWAIT

Don't *wait()* for any child process that may have been created in order to log the message. On implementations that create a child process for logging messages, LOG_NOWAIT is needed if the caller is also creating and waiting for children, so that *syslog()* doesn't attempt to wait for a child that has already been reaped by the caller. On Linux, LOG_NOWAIT has no effect, since no child processes are created when logging a message.

LOG_ODELAY

This flag is the converse of LOG_NDELAY—connecting to the logging system is delayed until the first message is logged. This is the default, and need not be specified.

LOG_PERROR

Write messages to standard error as well as to the system log. Typically, daemon processes close standard error or redirect it to /dev/null, in which case, LOG_PERROR is not useful.

LOG_PID

Log the caller's process ID with each message. Employing LOG_PID in a server that forks multiple children allows us to distinguish which process logged a particular message.

All of the above constants are specified in SUSv3, except LOG_PERROR, which appears on many (but not all) other UNIX implementations.

The *facility* argument to *openlog()* specifies the default *facility* value to be used in subsequent calls to *syslog()*. Possible values for this argument are listed in Table 37-1.

The majority of the *facility* values in Table 37-1 appear in SUSv3, as indicated by the *SUSv3* column of the table. Exceptions are LOG_AUTHPRIV and LOG_FTP, which appear on only a few other UNIX implementations, and LOG_SYSLOG, which appears on most implementations. The LOG_AUTHPRIV value is useful for logging messages containing passwords or other sensitive information to a different location than LOG_AUTH.

The LOG_KERN *facility* value is used for kernel messages. Log messages for this facility can't be generated from user-space programs. The LOG_KERN constant has the value 0. If it is used in a *syslog()* call, the 0 translates to "use the default level."

Table 37-1: *facility* values for *openlog()* and the *priority* argument of *syslog()*

Value	Description	SUSv3
LOG_AUTH	Security and authorization messages (e.g., *su*)	•
LOG_AUTHPRIV	Private security and authorization messages	
LOG_CRON	Messages from the *cron* and *at* daemons	•
LOG_DAEMON	Messages from other system daemons	•
LOG_FTP	Messages from the *ftp* daemon (*ftpd*)	
LOG_KERN	Kernel messages (can't be generated from a user process)	•
LOG_LOCAL0	Reserved for local use (also LOG_LOCAL1 to LOG_LOCAL7)	•
LOG_LPR	Messages from the line printer system (*lpr, lpd, lpc*)	•
LOG_MAIL	Messages from the mail system	•
LOG_NEWS	Messages related to Usenet network news	•
LOG_SYSLOG	Internal messages from the *syslogd* daemon	
LOG_USER	Messages generated by user processes (default)	•
LOG_UUCP	Messages from the UUCP system	•

Logging a message

To write a log message, we call *syslog()*.

```
#include <syslog.h>

void syslog(int priority, const char *format, ...);
```

The *priority* argument is created by ORing together a *facility* value and a *level* value. The *facility* indicates the general category of the application logging the message, and is specified as one of the values listed in Table 37-1. If omitted, the *facility* defaults to the value specified in a previous *openlog()* call, or to LOG_USER if that call was omitted. The *level* value indicates the severity of the message, and is specified as one of the values in Table 37-2. All of the *level* values listed in this table appear in SUSv3.

Table 37-2: *level* values for the *priority* argument of *syslog()* (from highest to lowest severity)

Value	Description
LOG_EMERG	Emergency or panic condition (system is unusable)
LOG_ALERT	Condition requiring immediate action (e.g., corrupt system database)
LOG_CRIT	Critical condition (e.g., error on disk device)
LOG_ERR	General error condition
LOG_WARNING	Warning message
LOG_NOTICE	Normal condition that may require special handling
LOG_INFO	Informational message
LOG_DEBUG	Debugging message

The remaining arguments to *syslog()* are a format string and corresponding arguments in the manner of *printf()*. One difference from *printf()* is that the format string doesn't need to include a terminating newline character. Also, the format string may include the 2-character sequence %m, which is replaced by the error string corresponding to the current value of *errno* (i.e., the equivalent of *strerror(errno)*).

The following code demonstrates the use of *openlog()* and *syslog()*:

```
openlog(argv[0], LOG_PID | LOG_CONS | LOG_NOWAIT, LOG_LOCAL0);
syslog(LOG_ERR, "Bad argument: %s", argv[1]);
syslog(LOG_USER | LOG_INFO, "Exiting");
```

Since no *facility* is specified in the first *syslog()* call, the default specified by *openlog()* (LOG_LOCAL0) is used. In the second *syslog()* call, explicitly specifying LOG_USER overrides the default established by *openlog()*.

> From the shell, we can use the *logger(1)* command to add entries to the system log. This command allows specification of the *level* (*priority*) and *ident* (*tag*) to be associated with the logged messages. For further details, see the *logger(1)* manual page. The *logger* command is (weakly) specified in SUSv3, and a version of this command is provided on most UNIX implementations.

It is an error to use *syslog()* to write some user-supplied string in the following manner:

```
syslog(priority, user_supplied_string);
```

The problem with this code is that it leaves the application open to so-called *format-string attacks*. If the user-supplied string contains format specifiers (e.g., %s), then the results are unpredictable and, from a security point of view, potentially dangerous. (The same observation applies to the use of the conventional *printf()* function.) We should instead rewrite the above call as follows:

```
syslog(priority, "%s", user_supplied_string);
```

Closing the log

When we have finished logging, we can call *closelog()* to deallocate the file descriptor used for the /dev/log socket.

```
#include <syslog.h>

void closelog(void);
```

Since a daemon typically keeps a connection open to the system log continuously, it is common to omit calling *closelog()*.

Filtering log messages

The *setlogmask()* function sets a mask that filters the messages written by *syslog()*.

```
#include <syslog.h>

int setlogmask(int mask_priority);
```
                                        Returns previous log priority mask

Any message whose *level* is not included in the current mask setting is discarded.
The default mask value allows all severity levels to be logged.

The macro LOG_MASK() (defined in <syslog.h>) converts the *level* values of Table 37-2
to bit values suitable for passing to *setlogmask()*. For example, to discard all messages
except those with priorities of LOG_ERR and above, we would make the following call:

```
setlogmask(LOG_MASK(LOG_EMERG) | LOG_MASK(LOG_ALERT) |
           LOG_MASK(LOG_CRIT) | LOG_MASK(LOG_ERR));
```

The LOG_MASK() macro is specified by SUSv3. Most UNIX implementations (including Linux) also provide the unspecified macro LOG_UPTO(), which creates a bit mask
filtering all messages of a certain *level* and above. Using this macro, we can simplify
the previous *setlogmask()* call to the following:

```
setlogmask(LOG_UPTO(LOG_ERR));
```

37.5.3 The /etc/syslog.conf File

The /etc/syslog.conf configuration file controls the operation of the *syslogd* daemon.
This file consists of rules and comments (starting with a # character). Rules have the
following general form:

---

facility.*level*   *action*

Together, the *facility* and *level* are referred to as the *selector*, since they select the
messages to which the rule applies. These fields are strings corresponding to the values
listed in Table 37-1 and Table 37-2. The *action* specifies where to send the messages
matching this *selector*. White space separates the *selector* and the *action* parts of a
rule. The following are examples of rules:

```
*.err                          /dev/tty10
auth.notice                    root
*.debug;mail.none;news.none    -/var/log/messages
```

The first rule says that messages from all facilities (*) with a *level* of err (LOG_ERR) or
higher should be sent to the /dev/tty10 console device. The second rule says that
authorization facility (LOG_AUTH) messages with a *level* of notice (LOG_NOTICE) or higher
should be sent to any consoles or terminals where *root* is logged in. This particular
rule would allow a logged-in *root* user to immediately see messages about failed *su*
attempts, for example.

The last rule demonstrates several of the more advanced features of rule syntax. A rule can contain multiple selectors separated by semicolons. The first selector specifies *all* messages, using the * wildcard for *facility* and debug for *level*,
meaning all messages of level debug (the lowest level) and higher. (On Linux, as on

some other UNIX implementations, it is possible to specify *level* as *, with the same meaning as debug. However, this feature is not available to all *syslog* implementations.) Normally, a rule that contains multiple selectors matches messages corresponding to any of the selectors, but specifying a *level* of none has the effect of *excluding* all messages belonging to the corresponding *facility*. Thus, this rule sends all messages except those for the mail and news facilities to the file /var/log/messages. The hyphen (-) preceding the name of this file specifies that a sync to the disk does not occur on each write to the file (refer to Section 13.3). This means that writes are faster, but some data may be lost if the system crashes soon after the write.

Whenever we change the syslog.conf file, we must ask the daemon to reinitialize itself from this file in the usual fashion:

```
$ killall -HUP syslogd          Send SIGHUP to syslogd
```

> Further features of the syslog.conf rule syntax allow for much more powerful rules than we have shown. Full details are provided in the *syslog.conf(5)* manual page.

37.6   Summary

A daemon is a long-lived process that has no controlling terminal (i.e., it runs in the background). Daemons perform specific tasks, such as providing a network login facility or serving web pages. To become a daemon, a program performs a standard sequence of steps, including calls to *fork()* and *setsid()*.

Where appropriate, daemons should correctly handle the arrival of the SIGTERM and SIGHUP signals. The SIGTERM signal should result in an orderly shutdown of the daemon, while the SIGHUP signal provides a way to trigger the daemon to reinitialize itself by rereading its configuration file and reopening any log files it may be using.

The *syslog* facility provides a convenient way for daemons (and other applications) to log error and other messages to a central location. These messages are processed by the *syslogd* daemon, which redistributes the messages according to the dictates of the syslog.conf configuration file. Messages may be redistributed to a number of targets, including terminals, disk files, logged-in users, and, via a TCP/IP network, to other processes on remote hosts (typically other *syslogd* daemons).

Further information

Perhaps the best source of further information about writing daemons is the source code of various existing daemons.

37.7   Exercise

37-1.   Write a program (similar to *logger(1)*) that uses *syslog(3)* to write arbitrary messages to the system log file. As well as accepting a single command-line argument containing the message to be logged, the program should permit an option to specify the *level* of the message.

38

WRITING SECURE
PRIVILEGED PROGRAMS

Privileged programs have access to features and resources (files, devices, and so on) that are not available to ordinary users. A program can run with privileges by two general means:

- The program was started under a privileged user ID. Many daemons and network servers, which are typically run as *root*, fall into this category.

- The program has its set-user-ID or set-group-ID permission bit set. When a set-user-ID (set-group-ID) program is execed, it changes the effective user (group) ID of the process to be the same as the owner (group) of the program file. (We first described set-user-ID and set-group-ID programs in Section 9.3.) In this chapter, we'll sometimes use the term set-user-ID-*root* to distinguish a set-user-ID program that gives superuser privileges to a process from one that gives a process another effective identity.

If a privileged program contains bugs, or can be subverted by a malicious user, then the security of the system or an application can be compromised. From a security viewpoint, we should write programs so as to minimize both the chance of a compromise and the damage that can be done if a compromise does occur. These topics form the subject of this chapter, which provides a set of recommended practices for secure programming, and describes various pitfalls that should be avoided when writing privileged programs.

38.1 Is a Set-User-ID or Set-Group-ID Program Required?

One of the best pieces of advice concerning set-user-ID and set-group-ID programs is to avoid writing them whenever possible. If there is an alternative way of performing a task that doesn't involve giving a program privilege, we should generally employ that alternative, since it eliminates the possibility of a security compromise.

Sometimes, we can isolate the functionality that needs privilege into a separate program that performs a single task, and exec that program in a child process as required. This technique can be especially useful for libraries. One example of such a use is provided by the *pt_chown* program described in Section 64.2.2.

Even in cases where a set-user-ID or set-group-ID is needed, it isn't always necessary for a set-user-ID program to give a process *root* credentials. If giving a process some other credentials suffices, then this option should be preferred, since running with *root* privileges opens the gates to possible security compromises.

Consider a set-user-ID program that needs to allow users to update a file on which they do not have write permission. A safer way to do this is to create a dedicated group account (group ID) for this program, change the group ownership of the file to that group (and make the file writable by that group), and write a set-group-ID program that sets the process's effective group ID to the dedicated group ID. Since the dedicated group ID is not otherwise privileged, this greatly limits the damage that can be done if the program contains bugs or can otherwise be subverted.

38.2 Operate with Least Privilege

A set-user-ID (or set-group-ID) program typically requires privileges only to perform certain operations. While the program (especially one assuming superuser privileges) is performing other work, it should disable these privileges. When privileges will never again be required, they should be dropped permanently. In other words, the program should always operate with the *least privilege* required to accomplish the tasks that it is currently performing. The saved set-user-ID facility was designed for this purpose (Section 9.4).

Hold privileges only while they are required

In a set-user-ID program, we can use the following sequence of *seteuid()* calls to temporarily drop and then reacquire privileges:

```
uid_t orig_euid;

orig_euid = geteuid();
if (seteuid(getuid()) == -1)                /* Drop privileges */
    errExit("seteuid");

/* Do unprivileged work */

if (seteuid(orig_euid) == -1)               /* Reacquire privileges */
    errExit("seteuid");

/* Do privileged work */
```

The first call makes the effective user ID of the calling process the same as its real ID. The second call restores the effective user ID to the value held in the saved set-user-ID.

For set-group-ID programs, the saved set-group-ID saves the program's initial effective group ID, and *setegid()* is used to drop and reacquire privilege. We describe *seteuid()*, *setegid()*, and other similar system calls mentioned in the following recommendations in Chapter 9 and summarize them in Table 9-1 (on page 181).

The safest practice is to drop privileges immediately on program startup, and then temporarily reacquire them as needed at later points in the program. If, at a certain point, privileges will never be required again, then the program should drop them irreversibly, by ensuring that the saved set-user-ID is also changed. This eliminates the possibility of the program being tricked into reacquiring privilege, perhaps via the stack-crashing technique described in Section 38.9.

Drop privileges permanently when they will never again be required

If a set-user-ID or set-group-ID program finishes all tasks that require privileges, then it should drop its privileges permanently in order to eliminate any security risk that could occur because the program is compromised by a bug or other unexpected behavior. Dropping privileges permanently is accomplished by resetting all process user (group) IDs to the same value as the real user (group) ID.

From a set-user-ID-*root* program whose effective user ID is currently 0, we can reset all user IDs using the following code:

```
if (setuid(getuid()) == -1)
    errExit("setuid");
```

However, the above code does *not* reset the saved set-user-ID if the effective user ID of the calling process is currently nonzero: when called from a program whose effective user ID is nonzero, *setuid()* changes only the effective user ID (Section 9.7.1). In other words, in a set-user-ID-*root* program, the following sequence doesn't permanently drop the user ID 0:

```
/* Initial UIDs:    real=1000 effective=0 saved=0 */

/* 1. Usual call to temporarily drop privilege */

orig_euid = geteuid();
if (seteuid(getuid()) == -1)
    errExit("seteuid");

/* UIDs changed to: real=1000 effective=1000 saved=0 */

/* 2. Looks like the right way to permanently drop privilege (WRONG!) */

if (setuid(getuid()) == -1)
    errExit("setuid");

/* UIDs unchanged:  real=1000 effective=1000 saved=0 */
```

Instead, we must regain privilege prior to dropping it permanently, by inserting the following call between steps 1 and 2 above:

```
if (seteuid(orig_euid) == -1)
    errExit("seteuid");
```

On the other hand, if we have a set-user-ID program owned by a user other than *root*, then, because *setuid()* is insufficient to change the saved set-user-ID, we must use either *setreuid()* or *setresuid()* to permanently drop the privileged identifier. For example, we could achieve the desired result using *setreuid()*, as follows:

```
if (setreuid(getuid(), getuid()) == -1)
    errExit("setreuid");
```

This code relies on a feature of the Linux implementation of *setreuid()*: if the first (*ruid*) argument is not −1, then the saved set-user-ID is also set to the same value as the (new) effective user ID. SUSv3 doesn't specify this feature, but many other implementations behave the same way as Linux. SUSv4 does specify this feature.

The *setregid()* or *setresgid()* system call must likewise be used to permanently drop a privileged group ID in a set-group-ID program, since, when the effective user ID of a program is nonzero, *setgid()* changes only the effective group ID of the calling process.

General points on changing process credentials

In the preceding pages, we described techniques for temporarily and permanently dropping privileges. We now add a few general points regarding the use of these techniques:

- The semantics of some of the system calls that change process credentials vary across systems. Furthermore, the semantics of some of these system calls vary depending on whether or not the caller is privileged (effective user ID of 0). For details, see Chapter 9, and especially Section 9.7.4. Because of these variations, [Tsafrir et al., 2008] recommends that applications should use system-specific *nonstandard* system calls for changing process credentials, since, in many cases, these nonstandard system calls provide simpler and more consistent semantics than their standard counterparts. On Linux, this would translate to using *setresuid()* and *setresgid()* to change user and group credentials. Although these system calls are not present on all systems, their use is likely to be less prone to error. ([Tsafrir et al., 2008] proposes a library of functions that make credential changes using what they consider to be the best interfaces available on each platform.)

- On Linux, even if the caller has an effective user ID of 0, system calls for changing credentials may not behave as expected if the program has explicitly manipulated its capabilities. For example, if the CAP_SETUID capability has been disabled, then attempts to change process user IDs will fail or, even worse, silently change only some of the requested user IDs.

- Because of the possibilities listed in the two preceding points, it is highly recommended practice (see, for example, [Tsafrir et al., 2008]) to not only check that a credential-changing system call has succeeded, but also to verify that the change occurred as expected. For example, if we are temporarily dropping or reacquiring a privileged user ID using *seteuid()*, then we should follow that call with a *geteuid()* call that verifies that the effective user ID is what we expect. Similarly, if we are dropping a privileged user ID permanently, then we should verify that the real user ID, effective user ID, and saved set-user-ID have all been successfully changed to the unprivileged user ID. Unfortunately, while there are standard system calls for retrieving the real and effective IDs, there are no standard system calls for retrieving the saved set IDs. Linux and a few other systems provide *getresuid()* and *getresgid()* for this purpose; on some other systems, we may need to employ techniques such as parsing information in /proc files.

- Some credential changes can be made only by processes with an effective user ID of 0. Therefore, when changing multiple IDs—supplementary group IDs, group IDs, and user IDs—we should drop the privileged effective user ID last when dropping privileged IDs. Conversely, we should raise the privileged effective user ID first when raising privileged IDs.

38.3 Be Careful When Executing a Program

Caution is required when a privileged program executes another program, either directly, via an *exec()*, or indirectly, via *system()*, *popen()*, or a similar library function.

Drop privileges permanently before execing another program

If a set-user-ID (or set-group-ID) program executes another program, then it should ensure that all process user (group) IDs are reset to the same value as the real user (group) ID, so that the new program doesn't start with privileges and also can't reacquire them. One way to do this is to reset all of the IDs before performing the *exec()*, using the techniques described in Section 38.2.

The same result can be achieved by preceding the *exec()* with the call *setuid(getuid())*. Even though this *setuid()* call changes only the effective user ID in a process whose effective user ID is nonzero, privileges are nevertheless dropped because (as described in Section 9.4) a successful *exec()* goes on to copy the effective user ID to the saved set-user-ID. (If the *exec()* fails, then the saved set-user-ID is left unchanged. This may be useful if the program then needs to perform other privileged work because the *exec()* failed.)

A similar approach (i.e., *setgid(getgid())*) can be used with set-group-ID programs, since a successful *exec()* also copies the effective group ID to the saved set-group-ID.

As an example, suppose that we have a set-user-ID program owned by user ID 200. When this program is executed by a user whose ID is 1000, the user IDs of the resulting process will be as follows:

```
real=1000 effective=200 saved=200
```

If this program subsequently executes the call *setuid(getuid())*, then the process user IDs are changed to the following:

```
real=1000 effective=1000 saved=200
```

When the process executes an unprivileged program, the effective user ID of the process is copied to the saved set-user-ID, resulting in the following set of process user IDs:

```
real=1000 effective=1000 saved=1000
```

Avoid executing a shell (or other interpreter) with privileges

Privileged programs running under user control should never exec a shell, either directly or indirectly (via *system()*, *popen()*, *execlp()*, *execvp()*, or other similar library functions). The complexity and power of shells (and other unconstrained interpreters such as *awk*) mean that it is virtually impossible to eliminate all security loopholes, even if the execed shell doesn't allow interactive access. The consequent risk is that the user may be able to execute arbitrary shell commands under the effective user ID of the process. If a shell must be execed, ensure that privileges are permanently dropped beforehand.

> An example of the kind of security loophole that can occur when execing a shell is noted in the discussion of *system()* in Section 27.6.

A few UNIX implementations honor the set-user-ID and set-group-ID permission bits when they are applied to interpreter scripts (Section 27.3), so that, when the script is run, the process executing the script assumes the identity of some other (privileged) user. Because of the security risks just described, Linux, like some other UNIX implementations, silently ignores the set-user-ID and set-group-ID permission bits when execing a script. Even on implementations where set-user-ID and set-group-ID scripts are permitted, their use should be avoided.

Close all unnecessary file descriptors before an *exec()*

In Section 27.4, we noted that, by default, file descriptors remain open across an *exec()*. A privileged program may open a file that normal processes can't access. The resulting open file descriptor represents a privileged resource. The file descriptor should be closed before an *exec()*, so that the execed program can't access the associated file. We can do this either by explicitly closing the file descriptor or by setting its close-on-exec flag (Section 27.4).

38.4   Avoid Exposing Sensitive Information

When a program reads passwords or other sensitive information, it should perform whatever processing is required, and then immediately erase the information from memory. (We show an example of this in Section 8.5.) Leaving such information in memory is a security risk, for the following reasons:

- The virtual memory page containing the data may be swapped out (unless it is locked in memory using *mlock()* or similar), and could then be read from the swap area by a privileged program.

- If the process receives a signal that causes it to produce a core dump file, then that file may be read to obtain the information.

Following on from the last point, as a general principle, a secure program should prevent core dumps, so that a core dump file can't be inspected for sensitive information. A program can ensure that a core dump file is not created by using *setrlimit()* to set the RLIMIT_CORE resource limit to 0 (see Section 36.3).

> By default, Linux doesn't permit a set-user-ID program to perform a core dump in response to a signal (Section 22.1), even if the program has dropped all privileges. However, other UNIX implementations may not provide this security feature.

38.5 Confine the Process

In this section, we consider ways in which we can confine a program to limit the damage that is done if the program is compromised.

Consider using capabilities

The Linux capabilities scheme divides the traditional all-or-nothing UNIX privilege scheme into distinct units called *capabilities*. A process can independently enable or disable individual capabilities. By enabling just those capabilities that it requires, a program operates with less privilege than it would have if run with full *root* privileges. This reduces the potential for damage if the program is compromised.

Furthermore, using capabilities and the *securebits* flags, we can create a process that has a limited set of capabilities but is not owned by *root* (i.e., all of its user IDs are nonzero). Such a process can no longer use *exec()* to regain a full set of capabilities. We describe capabilities and the *securebits* flags in Chapter 39.

Consider using a *chroot* jail

A useful security technique in certain cases is to establish a *chroot* jail to limit the set of directories and files that a program may access. (Make sure to also call *chdir()* to change the process's current working directory to a location within the jail.) Note, however, that a *chroot* jail is insufficient to confine a set-user-ID-*root* program (see Section 18.12).

> An alternative to using a *chroot* jail is a *virtual server*, which is a server implemented on top of a virtual kernel. Because each virtual kernel is isolated from other virtual kernels that may be running on the same hardware, a virtual server is more secure and flexible than a *chroot* jail. (Several other modern operating systems also provide their own implementations of virtual servers.) The oldest virtualization implementation on Linux is User-Mode Linux (UML), which is a standard part of the Linux 2.6 kernel. Further information about UML can be found at *http://user-mode-linux.sourceforge.net/*. More recent virtual kernel projects include Xen (*http://www.cl.cam.ac.uk/Research/SRG/netos/xen/*) and KVM (*http://kvm.qumranet.com/*).

38.6 Beware of Signals and Race Conditions

A user may send arbitrary signals to a set-user-ID program that they have started. Such signals may arrive at any time and with any frequency. We need to consider the race conditions that can occur if a signal is delivered at *any* point in the execution of the program. Where appropriate, signals should be caught, blocked, or ignored to prevent possible security problems. Furthermore, the design of signal handlers should be as simple as possible, in order to reduce the risk of inadvertently creating a race condition.

This issue is particularly relevant with the signals that stop a process (e.g., SIGTSTP and SIGSTOP). The problematic scenario is the following:

1. A set-user-ID program determines some information about its run-time environment.

2. The user manages to stop the process running the program and change details of the run-time environment. Such changes may include modifying the permissions on a file, changing the target of a symbolic link, or removing a file that the program depends on.

3. The user resumes the process with a SIGCONT signal. At this point, the program will continue execution based on now false assumptions about its run-time environment, and these assumptions may lead to a security breach.

The situation described here is really just a special case of a *time-of-check, time-of-use* race condition. A privileged process should avoid performing operations based on previous verifications that may no longer hold (refer to the discussion of the *access()* system call in Section 15.4.4 for a specific example). This guideline applies even when the user can't send signals to the process. The ability to stop a process simply allows a user to widen the interval between the time of the check and the time of use.

> Although it may be difficult on a single attempt to stop a process between the time of check and time of use, a malicious user could execute a set-user-ID program repeatedly, and use another program or a shell script to repeatedly send stop signals to the set-user-ID program and change the run-time environment. This greatly improves the chances of subverting the set-user-ID program.

38.7 Pitfalls When Performing File Operations and File I/O

If a privileged process needs to create a file, then we must take care of that file's ownership and permissions to ensure that there is never a point, no matter how brief, when the file is vulnerable to malicious manipulation. The following guidelines apply:

- The process umask (Section 15.4.6) should be set to a value that ensures that the process never creates publicly writable files, since these could be modified by a malicious user.

- Since the ownership of a file is taken from the effective user ID of the creating process, judicious use of *seteuid()* or *setreuid()* to temporarily change process credentials may be required in order ensure that a newly created file doesn't belong to the wrong user. Since the group ownership of the file *may* be taken from process's effective group ID (see Section 15.3.1), a similar statement applies with respect to set-group-ID programs, and the corresponding group ID calls can be used to avoid such problems. (To be strictly accurate, on Linux, the owner of a new file is determined by the process's file-system user ID, which normally has the same value as the process's effective user ID; refer to Section 9.5.)

- If a set-user-ID-*root* program must create a file that initially it must own, but which will eventually be owned by another user, the file should be created so that it is initially not writable by other users, either by using a suitable *mode* argument to *open()* or by setting the process umask before calling *open()*. Afterward, the program can change its ownership with *fchown()*, and then change its permissions, if necessary, with *fchmod()*. The key point is that a set-user-ID program should ensure that it never creates a file that is owned by the program owner and that is even momentarily writable by other users.

- Checks on file attributes should be performed on open file descriptors (e.g., *open()* followed by *fstat()*), rather than by checking the attributes associated with a pathname and then opening the file (e.g., *stat()* followed by *open()*). The latter method creates a time-of-use, time-of-check problem.

- If a program must ensure that it is the creator of a file, then the O_EXCL flag should be used when calling *open()*.

- A privileged program should avoid creating or relying on files in publicly writable directories such as /tmp, since this leaves the program vulnerable to malicious attempts to create unauthorized files with names expected by the privileged program. A program that absolutely must create a file in a publicly writable directory should at least ensure that the file has an unpredictable name, by using a function such as *mkstemp()* (Section 5.12).

38.8 Don't Trust Inputs or the Environment

Privileged programs should avoid making assumptions about the input they are given, or the environment in which they are running.

Don't trust the environment list

Set-user-ID and set-group-ID programs should not assume that the values of environment variables are reliable. Two variables that are particularly relevant are PATH and IFS.

PATH determines where the shell (and thus *system()* and *popen()*), as well as *execlp()* and *execvp()*, search for programs. A malicious user can set PATH to a value that may trick a set-user-ID program employing one of these functions into executing an arbitrary program with privilege. If these functions are to be used, PATH should be set to a trustworthy list of directories (but better still, absolute pathnames should be specified when execing programs). However, as already noted, it is best to drop privileges before execing a shell or employing one of the aforementioned functions.

IFS specifies the delimiting characters that the shell interprets as separating the words of a command line. This variable should be set to an empty string, which means that only white-space characters are interpreted by the shell as word separators. Some shells always set IFS in this way on startup. (Section 27.6 describes one vulnerability relating to IFS that appeared in older Bourne shells.)

In some cases, it may be safest to erase the entire environment list (Section 6.7), and then restore selected environment variables with known-safe values, especially when executing other programs or calling libraries that may be affected by environment variable settings.

Handle untrusted user inputs defensively

A privileged program should carefully validate all inputs from untrusted sources before taking action based on those inputs. Such validation may include verifying that numbers fall within acceptable limits, and that strings are of an acceptable length and consist of acceptable characters. Among inputs that may need to be validated in this way are those coming from user-created files, command-line arguments, interactive inputs, CGI inputs, email messages, environment variables, interprocess communication channels (FIFOs, shared memory, and so on) accessible by untrusted users, and network packets.

Avoid unreliable assumptions about the process's run-time environment

A set-user-ID program should avoid making unreliable assumptions about its initial run-time environment. For example, standard input, output, or error may have been closed. (These descriptors might have been closed in the program that execs the set-user-ID program.) In this case, opening a file could inadvertently reuse descriptor 1 (for example), so that, while the program thinks it is writing to standard output, it is actually writing to the file it opened.

There are many other possibilities to consider. For example, a process may exhaust various resource limits, such as the limit on the number of processes that may be created, the CPU time resource limit, or the file size resource limit, with the result that various system calls may fail or various signals may be generated. Malicious users may attempt to deliberately engineer resource exhaustion in an attempt to subvert a program.

38.9 Beware of Buffer Overruns

Beware of buffer overruns (overflows), where an input value or copied string exceeds the allocated buffer space. Never use *gets()*, and employ functions such as *scanf()*, *sprintf()*, *strcpy()*, and *strcat()* with caution (e.g., guarding their use with if statements that prevent buffer overruns).

Buffer overruns allow techniques such as *stack crashing* (also known as *stack smashing*), whereby a malicious user employs a buffer overrun to place carefully coded bytes into a stack frame in order to force the privileged program to execute arbitrary code. (Several online sources explain the details of stack crashing; see also [Erickson, 2008] and [Anley, 2007].) Buffer overruns are probably the single most common source of security breaches on computer systems, as evidenced by the frequency of advisories posted by CERT (*http://www.cert.org/*) and to Bugtraq (*http://www.securityfocus.com/*). Buffer overruns are particularly dangerous in network servers, since they leave a system open to remote attack from anywhere on a network.

In order to make stack crashing more difficult—in particular, to make such attacks much more time-consuming when conducted remotely against network servers—from kernel 2.6.12 onward, Linux implements *address-space randomization*. This technique randomly varies the location of the stack over an 8 MB range at the top of virtual memory. In addition, the locations of memory mappings may also be randomized, if the soft RLIMIT_STACK limit is not infinite and the Linux-specific /proc/sys/vm/legacy_va_layout file contains the value 0.

More recent x86-32 architectures provide hardware support for marking page tables as *NX* ("no execute"). This feature is used to prevent execution of program code on the stack, thus making stack crashing more difficult.

There are safe alternatives to many of the functions mentioned above—for example, *snprintf()*, *strncpy()*, and *strncat()*—that allow the caller to specify the maximum number of characters that should be copied. These functions take the specified maximum into account in order to avoid overrunning the target buffer. In general, these alternatives are preferable, but must still be handled with care. In particular, note the following points:

- With most of these functions, if the specified maximum is reached, then a truncated version of the source string is placed in the target buffer. Since such a truncated string may be meaningless in terms of the semantics of the program, the caller must check if truncation occurred (e.g., using the return value from *snprintf()*), and take appropriate action if it has.

- Using *strncpy()* can carry a performance impact. If, in the call *strncpy(s1, s2, n)*, the string pointed to by *s2* is less than *n* bytes in length, then padding null bytes are written to *s1* to ensure that *n* bytes in total are written.

- If the maximum size value given to *strncpy()* is not long enough to permit the inclusion of the terminating null character, then the target string is *not* null-terminated.

> Some UNIX implementations provide the *strlcpy()* function, which, given a length argument *n*, copies at most *n − 1* bytes to the destination buffer and always appends a null character at the end of the buffer. However, this function is not specified in SUSv3 and is not implemented in *glibc*. Furthermore, in cases where the caller is not carefully checking string lengths, this function only substitutes one problem (buffer overflows) for another (silently discarding data).

38.10 Beware of Denial-of-Service Attacks

With the increase in Internet-based services has come a corresponding increase in the opportunities for remote denial-of-service attacks. These attacks attempt to make a service unavailable to legitimate clients, either by sending the server malformed data that causes it to crash or by overloading it with bogus requests.

> Local denial-of-service attacks are also possible. The most well-known example is when a user runs a simple fork bomb (a program that repeatedly forks, thus consuming all of the process slots on the system). However, the origin of local denial-of-service attacks is much easier to determine, and they can generally be prevented by suitable physical and password security measures.

Dealing with malformed requests is straightforward—a server should be programmed to rigorously check its inputs and avoid buffer overruns, as described above.

Overload attacks are more difficult to deal with. Since the server can't control the behavior of remote clients or the rate at which they submit requests, such attacks are impossible to prevent. (The server may not even be able to determine the true origin of the attack, since the source IP address of a network packet can be spoofed. Alternatively, distributed attacks may enlist unwitting intermediary hosts to direct an attack at a target system.) Nevertheless, various measures can be taken to minimize the risk and consequences of an overload attack:

- The server should perform load throttling, dropping requests when the load exceeds some predetermined limit. This will have the consequence of dropping legitimate requests, but prevents the server and host machine from becoming overloaded. The use of resource limits and disk quotas may also be helpful in limiting excessive loads. (Refer to *http://sourceforge.net/projects/linuxquota/* for more information on disk quotas.)

- A server should employ timeouts for communication with a client, so that if the client (perhaps deliberately) doesn't respond, the server is not tied up indefinitely waiting on the client.

- In the event of an overload, the server should log suitable messages so that the system administrator is notified of the problem. (However, logging should be throttled, so that logging itself does not overload the system.)

- The server should be programmed so that it doesn't crash in the face of an unexpected load. For example, bounds checking should be rigorously performed to ensure that excessive requests don't overflow a data structure.

- Data structures should be designed to avoid *algorithmic-complexity attacks*. For example, a binary tree may be balanced and deliver acceptable performance under typical loads. However, an attacker could construct a sequence of inputs that result in an unbalanced tree (the equivalent of a linked list in the worst case), which could cripple performance. [Crosby & Wallach, 2003] details the nature of such attacks and discusses data-structuring techniques that can be used to avoid them.

38.11 Check Return Statuses and Fail Safely

A privileged program should always check to see whether system calls and library functions succeed, and whether they return expected values. (This is true for all programs, of course, but is especially important for privileged programs.) Various system calls can fail, even for a program running as *root*. For example, *fork()* may fail if the system-wide limit on the number of processes is encountered, an *open()* for writing may fail on a read-only file system, or *chdir()* may fail if the target directory doesn't exist.

Even where a system call succeeds, it may be necessary to check its result. For example, where it matters, a privileged program should check that a successful *open()* has not returned one of the three standard file descriptors: 0, 1, or 2.

Finally, if a privileged program encounters an unexpected situation, then the appropriate behavior is usually either to terminate or, in the case of a server, to drop the client request. Attempting to fix unexpected problems typically requires making assumptions that may not be justified in all circumstances and may lead to the creation of security loopholes. In such situations, it is safer to have the program terminate, or to have the server log a message and discard the client's request.

38.12 Summary

Privileged programs have access to system resources that are not available to ordinary users. If such programs can be subverted, then the security of the system can be compromised. In this chapter, we presented a set of guidelines for writing privileged programs. The aim of these guidelines is twofold: to minimize the chances of a privileged program being subverted, and to minimize the damage that can be done in the event that a privileged program is subverted.

Further information

[Viega & McGraw, 2002] covers a broad range of topics relating to the design and implementation of secure software. General information about security on UNIX systems, as well as a chapter on secure-programming techniques can be found in [Garfinkel et al., 2003]. Computer security is covered at some length in [Bishop, 2005], and at even greater length by the same author in [Bishop, 2003]. [Peikari & Chuvakin, 2004] describes computer security with a focus on the various means by which system may be attacked. [Erickson, 2008] and [Anley, 2007] both provide a thorough discussion of various security exploits, providing enough detail for wise programmers to avoid these exploits. [Chen et al., 2002] is a paper describing and analyzing the UNIX set-user-ID model. [Tsafrir et al., 2008] revises and enhances the discussion of various points in [Chen et al., 2002]. [Drepper, 2009] provides a wealth of tips on secure and defensive programming on Linux.

Several sources of information about writing secure programs are available online, including the following:

- Matt Bishop has written a range of security-related papers, which are available online at *http://nob.cs.ucdavis.edu/~bishop/secprog*. The most interesting of these is "How to Write a Setuid Program," (originally published in *;login: 12(1) Jan/Feb 1986*). Although somewhat dated, this paper contains a wealth of useful tips.

- The *Secure Programming for Linux and Unix HOWTO*, written by David Wheeler, is available at *http://www.dwheeler.com/secure-programs/*.

- A useful checklist for writing set-user-ID programs is available online at *http://www.homeport.org/~adam/setuid.7.html*.

38.13 Exercises

38-1. Log in as a normal, unprivileged user, create an executable file (or copy an existing file such as /bin/sleep), and enable the set-user-ID permission bit on that file (*chmod u+s*). Try modifying the file (e.g., *cat >> file*). What happens to the file permissions as a result (*ls −l*)? Why does this happen?

38-2. Write a set-user-ID-*root* program similar to the *sudo(8)* program. This program should take command-line options and arguments as follows:

```
$ ./douser [-u user ] program-file arg1 arg2 ...
```

The *douser* program executes *program-file*, with the given arguments, as though it was run by *user*. (If the −u option is omitted, then *user* should default to *root*.) Before executing *program-file*, *douser* should request the password for *user*, authenticate it against the standard password file (see Listing 8-2, on page 164), and then set all of the process user and group IDs to the correct values for that user.

39

CAPABILITIES

This chapter describes the Linux capabilities scheme, which divides the traditional all-or-nothing UNIX privilege scheme into individual capabilities that can be independently enabled or disabled. Using capabilities allows a program to perform some privileged operations, while preventing it from performing others.

39.1 Rationale for Capabilities

The traditional UNIX privilege scheme divides processes into two categories: those whose effective user ID is 0 (superuser), which bypass all privilege checks, and all other processes, which are subject to privilege checking according to their user and group IDs.

The coarse granularity of this scheme is a problem. If we want to allow a process to perform some operation that is permitted only to the superuser—for example, changing the system time—then we must run that process with an effective user ID of 0. (If an unprivileged user needs to perform such operations, this is typically implemented using a set-user-ID-*root* program.) However, this grants the process privileges to perform a host of other actions as well—for example, bypassing all permission checks when accessing files—thus opening the door for a range of security breaches if the program behaves in unexpected ways (which may be the consequence of unforeseen circumstances, or because of deliberate manipulation by a malicious user). The traditional way of dealing with this problem was outlined in Chapter 38: we drop effective privileges (i.e., change from an effective user ID of 0, while maintaining 0 in the saved set-user-ID) and temporarily reacquire them only when needed.

The Linux capability scheme refines the handling of this problem. Rather than using a single privilege (i.e., effective user ID of 0) when performing security checks in the kernel, the superuser privilege is divided into distinct units, called *capabilities*. Each privileged operation is associated with a particular capability, and a process can perform that operation only if it has the corresponding capability (regardless of its effective user ID). Put another way, everywhere in this book that we talk about a privileged process on Linux, what we really mean is a process that has the relevant capability for performing a particular operation.

Most of the time, the Linux capability scheme is invisible to us. The reason for this is that when an application that is unaware of capabilities assumes an effective user ID of 0, the kernel grants that process the complete range of capabilities.

The Linux capabilities implementation is based on the POSIX 1003.1e draft standard (*http://wt.tuxomania.net/publications/posix.1e/*). This standardization effort foundered in the late 1990s before it was completed, but various capabilities implementations are nevertheless based on the draft standard. (Some of the capabilities listed in Table 39-1 are defined in the POSIX.1e draft, but many are Linux extensions.)

> Capability schemes are provided in a few other UNIX implementations, such as in Sun's Solaris 10 and earlier Trusted Solaris releases, SGI's Trusted Irix, and as part of the TrustedBSD project for FreeBSD ([Watson, 2000]). Similar schemes exist in some other operating systems; for example, the privilege mechanism in Digital's VMS system.

39.2 The Linux Capabilities

Table 39-1 lists the Linux capabilities and provides an abbreviated (and incomplete) guide to the operations to which they apply.

39.3 Process and File Capabilities

Each process has three associated capability sets—termed *permitted*, *effective*, and *inheritable*—that can contain zero or more of the capabilities listed in Table 39-1. Each file can likewise have three associated capability sets, with the same names. (For reasons that will become evident, the file effective capability set is really just a single bit that is either enabled or disabled.) We go into the details of each of these capability sets in the following sections.

39.3.1 Process Capabilities

For each process, the kernel maintains three capability sets (implemented as bit masks) in which zero or more of the capabilities specified in Table 39-1 are enabled. The three sets are as follows:

- *Permitted*: These are the capabilities that a process *may* employ. The permitted set is a limiting superset for the capabilities that can be added to the effective and inheritable sets. If a process drops a capability from its permitted set, it can never reacquire that capability (unless it execs a program that once more confers the capability).

- *Effective*: These are the capabilities used by the kernel to perform privilege checking for the process. As long as it maintains a capability in its permitted set, a process can temporarily disable the capability by dropping it from the effective set, and then later restoring it to that set.

- *Inheritable*: These are capabilities that may be carried over to the permitted set when a program is execed by this process.

We can view hexadecimal representations of the three capability sets for any process in the three fields CapInh, CapPrm, and CapEff in the Linux-specific /proc/*PID*/status file.

> The *getpcaps* program (part of the *libcap* package described in Section 39.7) can be used to display the capabilities of a process in an easier-to-read format.

A child process produced via *fork()* inherits copies of its parent's capability sets. We describe the treatment of capability sets during an *exec()* in Section 39.5.

> In reality, capabilities are a per-thread attribute that can be adjusted independently for each of the threads in a process. The capabilities of a specific thread within a multithreaded process are shown in the /proc/*PID*/task/*TID*/status file. The /proc/*PID*/status file shows the capabilities of the main thread.
>
> Before kernel 2.6.25, Linux represented capability sets using 32 bits. The addition of further capabilities in kernel 2.6.25 required a move to 64-bit sets.

39.3.2 File Capabilities

If a file has associated capability sets, then these sets are used to determine the capabilities that are given to a process if it execs that file. There are three file capability sets:

- *Permitted*: This is a set of capabilities that may be added to the process's permitted set during an *exec()*, regardless of the process's existing capabilities.

- *Effective*: This is just a single bit. If it is enabled, then, during an *exec()*, the capabilities that are enabled in the process's new permitted set are also enabled in the process's new effective set. If the file effective bit is disabled, then, after an *exec()*, the process's new effective set is initially empty.

- *Inheritable*: This set is masked against the process's inheritable set to determine a set of capabilities that are to be enabled in the process's permitted set after an *exec()*.

Section 39.5 provides details of how file capabilities are used during an *exec()*.

> The permitted and inheritable file capabilities were formerly known as *forced* and *allowed*. Those terms are now obsolete, but they are still informative. The permitted file capabilities are the ones that are *forced* into the process's permitted set during an *exec()*, regardless of the process's existing capabilities. The inheritable file capabilities are the ones that the file *allows* into the process's permitted set during an *exec()*, if those capabilities are also enabled in the process's inheritable capability set.
>
> The capabilities associated with a file are stored in a *security* extended attribute (Section 16.1) named *security.capability*. The CAP_SETFCAP capability is required to update this extended attribute.

Table 39-1: Operations permitted by each Linux capability

Capability	Permits process to
CAP_AUDIT_CONTROL	(Since Linux 2.6.11) Enable and disable kernel audit logging; change filtering rules for auditing; retrieve auditing status and filtering rules
CAP_AUDIT_WRITE	(Since Linux 2.6.11) Write records to the kernel auditing log
CAP_CHOWN	Change file's user ID (owner) or change file's group ID to a group of which process is not a member (*chown()*)
CAP_DAC_OVERRIDE	Bypass file read, write, and execute permission checks (DAC is an abbreviation for discretionary access control); read contents of cwd, exe, and root symbolic links in /proc/*PID*
CAP_DAC_READ_SEARCH	Bypass file read permission checks and directory read and execute (search) permission checks
CAP_FOWNER	Generally ignore permission checks on operations that normally require the process's file-system user ID to match the file's user ID (*chmod()*, *utime()*); set i-node flags on arbitrary files; set and modify ACLs on arbitrary files; ignore effect of directory sticky bit when deleting files (*unlink()*, *rmdir()*, *rename()*); specify O_NOATIME flag for arbitrary files in *open()* and *fcntl(F_SETFL)*
CAP_FSETID	Modify a file without having the kernel turn off set-user-ID and set-group-ID bits (*write()*, *truncate()*); enable set-group-ID bit for a file whose group ID doesn't match the process's file-system group ID or supplementary group IDs (*chmod()*)
CAP_IPC_LOCK	Override memory-locking restrictions (*mlock()*, *mlockall()*, *shmctl(SHM_LOCK)*, *shmctl(SHM_UNLOCK)*); employ *shmget()* SHM_HUGETLB flag and *mmap()* MAP_HUGETLB flag.
CAP_IPC_OWNER	Bypass permission checks for operations on System V IPC objects
CAP_KILL	Bypass permission checks for sending signals (*kill()*, *sigqueue()*)
CAP_LEASE	(Since Linux 2.4) Establish leases on arbitrary files (*fcntl(F_SETLEASE)*)
CAP_LINUX_IMMUTABLE	Set append and immutable i-node flags
CAP_MAC_ADMIN	(Since Linux 2.6.25) Configure or make state changes for mandatory access control (MAC) (implemented by some Linux security modules)
CAP_MAC_OVERRIDE	(Since Linux 2.6.25) Override MAC (implemented by some Linux security modules)
CAP_MKNOD	(Since Linux 2.4) Use *mknod()* to create devices
CAP_NET_ADMIN	Perform various network-related operations (e.g., setting privileged socket options, enabling multicasting, configuring network interfaces, and modifying routing tables)
CAP_NET_BIND_SERVICE	Bind to privileged socket ports
CAP_NET_BROADCAST	(Unused) Perform socket broadcasts and listen to multicasts
CAP_NET_RAW	Use raw and packet sockets
CAP_SETGID	Make arbitrary changes to process group IDs (*setgid()*, *setegid()*, *setregid()*, *setresgid()*, *setfsgid()*, *setgroups()*, *initgroups()*); forge group ID when passing credentials via UNIX domain socket (SCM_CREDENTIALS)
CAP_SETFCAP	(Since Linux 2.6.24) Set file capabilities

Table 39-1: Operations permitted by each Linux capability (continued)

Capability	Permits process to
CAP_SETPCAP	If file capabilities are not supported, grant and remove capabilities in the process's permitted set to or from any other process (including self); if file capabilities are supported, add any capability in the process's capability bounding set to its inheritable set, drop capabilities from the bounding set, and change *securebits* flags
CAP_SETUID	Make arbitrary changes to process user IDs (*setuid()*, *seteuid()*, *setreuid()*, *setresuid()*, *setfsuid()*); forge user ID when passing credentials via UNIX domain socket (SCM_CREDENTIALS)
CAP_SYS_ADMIN	Exceed /proc/sys/fs/file-max limit in system calls that open files (e.g., *open()*, *shm_open()*, *pipe()*, *socket()*, *accept()*, *exec()*, *acct()*, *epoll_create()*); perform various system administration operations, including *quotactl()* (control disk quotas), *mount()* and *umount()*, *swapon()* and *swapoff()*, *pivot_root()*, *sethostname()* and *setdomainname()*; perform various *syslog(2)* operations; override RLIMIT_NPROC resource limit (*fork()*); call *lookup_dcookie()*; set *trusted* and *security* extended attributes; perform IPC_SET and IPC_RMID operations on arbitrary System V IPC objects; forge process ID when passing credentials via UNIX domain socket (SCM_CREDENTIALS); use *ioprio_set()* to assign IOPRIO_CLASS_RT scheduling class; employ TIOCCONS *ioctl()*; employ namespace-creation flags with *clone()* and *unshare()*; perform KEYCTL_CHOWN and KEYCTL_SETPERM *keyctl()* operations; administer *random(4)* device; various device-specific operations
CAP_SYS_BOOT	Use *reboot()* to reboot the system; call *kexec_load()*
CAP_SYS_CHROOT	Use *chroot()* to set process root directory
CAP_SYS_MODULE	Load and unload kernel modules (*init_module()*, *delete_module()*, *create_module()*)
CAP_SYS_NICE	Raise nice value (*nice()*, *setpriority()*); change nice value for arbitrary processes (*setpriority()*); set SCHED_RR and SCHED_FIFO realtime scheduling policies for calling process; reset SCHED_RESET_ON_FORK flag; set scheduling policies and priorities for arbitrary processes (*sched_setscheduler()*, *sched_setparam()*); set I/O scheduling class and priority for arbitrary processes (*ioprio_set()*); set CPU affinity for arbitrary processes (*sched_setaffinity()*); use *migrate_pages()* to migrate arbitrary processes and allow processes to be migrated to arbitrary nodes; apply *move_pages()* to arbitrary processes; use MPOL_MF_MOVE_ALL flag with *mbind()* and *move_pages()*
CAP_SYS_PACCT	Use *acct()* to enable or disable process accounting
CAP_SYS_PTRACE	Trace arbitrary processes using *ptrace()*; access /proc/*PID*/environ for arbitrary processes; apply *get_robust_list()* to arbitrary processes
CAP_SYS_RAWIO	Perform operations on I/O ports using *iopl()* and *ioperm()*; access /proc/kcore; open /dev/mem and /dev/kmem
CAP_SYS_RESOURCE	Use reserved space on file systems; make *ioctl()* calls controlling *ext3* journaling; override disk quota limits; increase hard resource limits (*setrlimit()*); override RLIMIT_NPROC resource limit (*fork()*); raise *msg_qbytes* limit for a System V message queue above limit in /proc/sys/kernel/msgmnb; bypass various POSIX message queue limits defined by files under /proc/sys/fs/mqueue
CAP_SYS_TIME	Modify system clock (*settimeofday()*, *stime()*, *adjtime()*, *adjtimex()*); set hardware clock
CAP_SYS_TTY_CONFIG	Perform virtual hangup of terminal or pseudoterminal using *vhangup()*

39.3.3 Purpose of the Process Permitted and Effective Capability Sets

The *process permitted* capability set defines the capabilities that a process *may* employ. The *process effective* capability set defines the capabilities that are currently in effect for the process—that is, the set of capabilities that the kernel uses when checking whether the process has the necessary privilege to perform a particular operation.

The permitted capability set imposes an upper bound on the effective set. A process can *raise* a capability in its effective set only if that capability is in the permitted set. (The terms *add* to and *set* are sometimes used synonymously with *raise*. The converse operation is *drop*, or synonymously, *remove* or *clear*.)

> The relationship between the effective and permitted capability sets is analogous to that between the effective user ID and the saved set-user-ID for a set-user-ID-*root* program. Dropping a capability from the effective set is analogous to temporarily dropping an effective user ID of 0, while maintaining 0 in the saved set-user-ID. Dropping a capability from both the effective and permitted capability sets is analogous to permanently dropping superuser privileges by setting both the effective user ID and the saved set-user-ID to nonzero values.

39.3.4 Purpose of the File Permitted and Effective Capability Sets

The *file permitted* capability set provides a mechanism by which an executable file can give capabilities to a process. It specifies a group of capabilities that are to be assigned to the process's permitted capability set during an *exec()*.

The *file effective* capability set is a single flag (bit) that is either enabled or disabled. To understand why this set consists of just a single bit, we need to consider the two cases that occur when a program is execed:

- The program may be *capability-dumb*, meaning that it doesn't know about capabilities (i.e., it is designed as a traditional set-user-ID-*root* program). Such a program won't know that it needs to raise capabilities in its effective set in order to be able to perform privileged operations. For such programs, an *exec()* should have the effect that all of the process's new permitted capabilities are automatically also assigned to its effective set. This result is achieved by enabling the file effective bit.

- The program may be *capability-aware*, meaning that it has been designed with the capabilities framework in mind, and it will make the appropriate system calls (discussed later) to raise and drop capabilities in its effective set. For such programs, least-privilege considerations mean that, after an *exec()*, all capabilities should initially be disabled in the process's effective capability set. This result is achieved by disabling the file effective capability bit.

39.3.5 Purpose of the Process and File Inheritable Sets

At first glance, the use of permitted and effective sets for processes and files might seem a sufficient framework for a capabilities system. However, there are some situations where they do not suffice. For example, what if a process performing an *exec()* wants to preserve some of its current capabilities across the *exec()*? It might appear that the capabilities implementation could provide this feature simply by preserving the process's permitted capabilities across an *exec()*. However, this approach would not handle the following cases:

- Performing the *exec()* might require certain privileges (e.g., CAP_DAC_OVERRIDE) that we don't want to preserve across the *exec()*.

- Suppose that we explicitly dropped some permitted capabilities that we didn't want to preserve across the *exec()*, but then the *exec()* failed. In this case, the program might need some of the permitted capabilities that it has already (irrevocably) dropped.

For these reasons, a process's permitted capabilities are not preserved across an *exec()*. Instead, another capability set is introduced: the *inheritable set*. The inheritable set provides a mechanism by which a process can preserve some of its capabilities across an *exec()*.

The *process inheritable* capability set specifies a group of capabilities that may be assigned to the process's permitted capability set during an *exec()*. The corresponding *file inheritable* set is masked (ANDed) against the process inherited capability set to determine the capabilities that are actually added to the process's permitted capability set during an *exec()*.

> There is a further, philosophical reason for not simply preserving the process permitted capability set across an *exec()*. The idea of the capabilities system is that all privileges given to a process are granted or controlled by the file that the process execs. Although the process inheritable set specifies capabilities that are passed across an *exec()*, these capabilities are masked by the file inheritable set.

39.3.6 Assigning and Viewing File Capabilities from the Shell

The *setcap(8)* and *getcap(8)* commands, contained in the *libcap* package described in Section 39.7, can be used to manipulate file capabilities sets. We demonstrate the use of these commands with a short example using the standard *date(1)* program. (This program is an example of a capability-dumb application according to the definition in Section 39.3.4.) When run with privilege, *date(1)* can be used to change the system time. The *date* program is not set-user-ID-*root*, so normally the only way to run it with privilege is to become the superuser.

We begin by displaying the current system time, and then try to change the time as an unprivileged user:

```
$ date
Tue Dec 28 15:54:08 CET 2010
$ date -s '2018-02-01 21:39'
date: cannot set date: Operation not permitted
Thu Feb  1 21:39:00 CET 2018
```

Above, we see that the *date* command failed to change the system time, but nevertheless displayed its argument in the standard format.

Next, we become the superuser, which allows us to successfully change the system time:

```
$ sudo date -s '2018-02-01 21:39'
root's password:
Thu Feb  1 21:39:00 CET 2018
$ date
Thu Feb  1 21:39:02 CET 2018
```

We now make a copy of the *date* program and assign it the capability that it needs:

```
$ whereis -b date                          Find location of date binary
date: /bin/date
$ cp /bin/date .
$ sudo setcap "cap_sys_time=pe" date
root's password:
$ getcap date
date = cap_sys_time+ep
```

The *setcap* command shown above assigns the CAP_SYS_TIME capability to the permitted (*p*) and effective (*e*) capability sets of the executable file. We then used the *getcap* command to verify the capabilities assigned to the file. (The syntax used by *setcap* and *getcap* for representing capability sets is described in the *cap_from_text(3)* manual page provided in the *libcap* package.)

The file capabilities of our copy of the *date* program allow the program to be used by unprivileged users to set the system time:

```
$ ./date -s '2010-12-28 15:55'
Tue Dec 28 15:55:00 CET 2010
$ date
Tue Dec 28 15:55:02 CET 2010
```

39.4 The Modern Capabilities Implementation

A complete implementation of capabilities requires the following:

- For each privileged operation, the kernel should check whether the process has the relevant capability, rather than checking for an effective (or file system) user ID of 0.

- The kernel must provide system calls allowing a process's capabilities to be retrieved and modified.

- The kernel must support the notion of attaching capabilities to an executable file, so that the process gains the associated capabilities when that file is execed. This is analogous to the set-user-ID bit, but allows the independent specification of all capabilities on the executable file. In addition, the system must provide a set of programming interfaces and commands for setting and viewing the capabilities attached to an executable file.

Up to and including kernel 2.6.23, Linux met only the first two of these requirements. Since kernel 2.6.24, it is possible to attach capabilities to a file. Various other features were added in kernels 2.6.25 and 2.6.26 in order to complete the capabilities implementation.

For most of our discussion of capabilities, we'll focus on the modern implementation. In Section 39.10, we consider how the implementation differed before file capabilities were introduced. Furthermore, file capabilities are an optional kernel component in modern kernels, but for the main part of our discussion, we'll assume that this component is enabled. Later, we'll describe the differences that occur if file capabilities are not enabled. (In several respects, the behavior is similar to that of Linux in kernels before 2.6.24, where file capabilities were not implemented.)

In the following sections, we go into more detail on the Linux capabilities implementation.

39.5 Transformation of Process Capabilities During *exec()*

During an *exec()*, the kernel sets new capabilities for the process based on the process's current capabilities and the capability sets of the file being executed. The kernel calculates the new capabilities of the process using the following rules:

```
P'(permitted) = (P(inheritable) & F(inheritable)) | (F(permitted) & cap_bset)

P'(effective) = F(effective) ? P'(permitted) : 0

P'(inheritable) = P(inheritable)
```

In the above rules, *P* denotes the value of a capability set prior to the *exec()*, *P'* denotes the value of a capability set after the *exec()*, and *F* denotes a file capability set. The identifier *cap_bset* denotes the value of the capability bounding set. Note that *exec()* leaves the process inheritable capability set unchanged.

39.5.1 Capability Bounding Set

The capability bounding set is a security mechanism that is used to limit the capabilities that a process can gain during an *exec()*. This set is used as follows:

- During an *exec()*, the capability bounding set is ANDed with the file permitted capabilities to determine the permitted capabilities that are to be granted to the new program. In other words, an executable file's permitted capability set can't grant a permitted capability to a process if the capability is not in the bounding set.

- The capability bounding set is a limiting superset for the capabilities that can be added to the process's inheritable set. This means that, unless the capability is in the bounding set, a process can't add one of its permitted capabilities to its inheritable set and then—via the first of the capability transformation rules described above—have that capability preserved in its permitted set when it execs a file that has the capability in its inheritable set.

The capability bounding set is a per-process attribute that is inherited by a child created via *fork()*, and preserved across an *exec()*. On a kernel that supports file capabilities, *init* (the ancestor of all processes) starts with a capability bounding set that contains all capabilities.

If a process has the CAP_SETPCAP capability, then it can (irreversibly) remove capabilities from its bounding set using the *prctl()* PR_CAPBSET_DROP operation. (Dropping a capability from the bounding set doesn't affect the process permitted, effective, and inheritable capability sets.) A process can determine if a capability is in its bounding set using the *prctl()* PR_CAPBSET_READ operation.

> More precisely, the capability bounding set is a per-thread attribute. Starting with Linux 2.6.26, this attribute is displayed as the CapBnd field in the Linux-specific /proc/*PID*/task/*TID*/status file. The /proc/*PID*/status file shows the bounding set of a process's main thread.

39.5.2 Preserving *root* Semantics

In order to preserve the traditional semantics for the *root* user (i.e., *root* has all privileges) when executing a file, any capability sets associated with the file are ignored. Instead, for the purposes of the algorithm shown in Section 39.5, the file capability sets are notionally defined as follows during an *exec()*:

- If a set-user-ID-*root* program is being execed, or the real or effective user ID of the process calling *exec()* is 0, then the file inheritable and permitted sets are defined to be all ones.

- If a set-user-ID-*root* program is being execed, or the effective user ID of the process calling *exec()* is 0, then the file effective bit is defined to be set.

Assuming that we are execing a set-user-ID-*root* program, these notional definitions of the file capability sets mean that the calculation of the process's new permitted and effective capability sets in Section 39.5 simplifies to the following:

```
P'(permitted) = P(inheritable) | cap_bset
P'(effective) = P'(permitted)
```

39.6 Effect on Process Capabilities of Changing User IDs

To preserve compatibility with the traditional meanings for transitions between 0 and nonzero user IDs, the kernel does the following when changing process user IDs (using *setuid()*, and so on):

1. If the real user ID, effective user ID, or saved set-user-ID previously had the value 0 and, as a result of the changes to the user IDs, all three of these IDs have a nonzero value, then the permitted and effective capability sets are cleared (i.e., all capabilities are permanently dropped).

2. If the effective user ID is changed from 0 to a nonzero value, then the effective capability set is cleared (i.e., the effective capabilities are dropped, but those in the permitted set can be raised again).

3. If the effective user ID is changed from a nonzero value to 0, then the permitted capability set is copied into the effective capability set (i.e., all permitted capabilities become effective).

4. If the file-system user ID is changed from 0 to a nonzero value, then the following file-related capabilities are cleared from the effective capability set: CAP_CHOWN, CAP_DAC_OVERRIDE, CAP_DAC_READ_SEARCH, CAP_FOWNER, CAP_FSETID, CAP_LINUX_IMMUTABLE (since Linux 2.6.30), CAP_MAC_OVERRIDE, and CAP_MKNOD (since Linux 2.6.30). Conversely, if the file-system user ID is changed from a nonzero value to 0, then any of these capabilities that are enabled in the permitted set are enabled in the effective set. These manipulations are done to maintain the traditional semantics for manipulations of the Linux-specific file-system user ID.

39.7 Changing Process Capabilities Programmatically

A process can raise or drop capabilities from its capability sets using either the *capset()* system call or, preferably, the *libcap* API, which we describe below. Changes to process capabilities are subject to the following rules:

1. If the process doesn't have the CAP_SETPCAP capability in its effective set, then the new *inheritable* set must be a subset of the combination (union) of the existing inheritable and permitted sets.

2. The new *inheritable* set must be a subset of the combination (union) of the existing inheritable set and the capability bounding set.

3. The new *permitted* set must be a subset of the existing permitted set. In other words, a process can't grant itself permitted capabilities that it doesn't have. Put another way, a capability dropped from the permitted set can't be reacquired.

4. The new *effective* set is allowed to contain only capabilities that are also in the new permitted set.

The *libcap* API

Up to this point, we have deliberately not shown the prototype of the *capset()* system call, or its counterpart *capget()*, which retrieves a process's capabilities. This is because the use of these system calls should be avoided. Instead, the functions in the *libcap* library should be employed. These functions provide an interface that conforms with the withdrawn draft POSIX 1003.1e standard, along with some Linux extensions.

For reasons of space, we don't describe the *libcap* API in detail. As an overview, we note that programs employing these functions typically carry out the following steps:

1. Use the *cap_get_proc()* function to retrieve a copy of the process's current capability sets from the kernel and place it in a structure that the function allocates in user space. (Alternatively, we may use the *cap_init()* function to create a new, empty capability set structure.) In the *libcap* API, the *cap_t* data type is a pointer used to refer to such structures.

2. Use the *cap_set_flag()* function to update the user-space structure to raise (CAP_SET) and drop (CAP_CLEAR) capabilities from the permitted, effective, and inheritable sets stored in the user-space structure retrieved in the previous step.

3. Use the *cap_set_proc()* function to pass the user-space structure back to the kernel in order to change the process's capabilities.

4. Use the *cap_free()* function to free the structure that was allocated by the *libcap* API in the first step.

> At the time of writing, work is in progress on *libcap-ng*, a new, improved capabilities library API. Details can be found at *https://people.redhat.com/sgrubb/libcap-ng/*.

Example program

In Listing 8-2, on page 164, we presented a program that authenticates a username plus password against the standard password database. We noted that the program requires privilege in order to read the shadow password file, which is protected to prevent reading by users other than *root* or members of the *shadow* group. The traditional way of providing this program with the privileges that it requires would be to run it under a *root* login or to make it a set-user-ID-*root* program. We now present a modified version of this program that employs capabilities and the *libcap* API.

In order to read the shadow password file as a normal user, we need to bypass the standard file permission checks. Scanning the capabilities listed in Table 39-1, we see that the appropriate capability is CAP_DAC_READ_SEARCH. Our modified version of the password authentication program is shown in Listing 39-1. This program uses the *libcap* API to raise CAP_DAC_READ_SEARCH in its effective capability set just before accessing the shadow password file, and then drops the capability again immediately after this access. In order for an unprivileged user to employ the program, we must set this capability in the file permitted capability set, as shown in the following shell session:

```
$ sudo setcap "cap_dac_read_search=p" check_password_caps
root's password:
$ getcap check_password_caps
check_password_caps = cap_dac_read_search+p
$ ./check_password_caps
Username: mtk
Password:
Successfully authenticated: UID=1000
```

Listing 39-1: A capability-aware program that authenticates a user

——— cap/check_password_caps.c
```c
#define _BSD_SOURCE        /* Get getpass() declaration from <unistd.h> */
#define _XOPEN_SOURCE      /* Get crypt() declaration from <unistd.h> */
#include <sys/capability.h>
#include <unistd.h>
#include <limits.h>
#include <pwd.h>
#include <shadow.h>
#include "tlpi_hdr.h"

/* Change setting of capability in caller's effective capabilities */

static int
modifyCap(int capability, int setting)
```

```
{
    cap_t caps;
    cap_value_t capList[1];

    /* Retrieve caller's current capabilities */

    caps = cap_get_proc();
    if (caps == NULL)
        return -1;

    /* Change setting of 'capability' in the effective set of 'caps'. The
        third argument, 1, is the number of items in the array 'capList'. */

    capList[0] = capability;
    if (cap_set_flag(caps, CAP_EFFECTIVE, 1, capList, setting) == -1) {
        cap_free(caps);
        return -1;
    }

    /* Push modified capability sets back to kernel, to change
        caller's capabilities */

    if (cap_set_proc(caps) == -1) {
        cap_free(caps);
        return -1;
    }

    /* Free the structure that was allocated by libcap */

    if (cap_free(caps) == -1)
        return -1;

    return 0;
}

static int                  /* Raise capability in caller's effective set */
raiseCap(int capability)
{
    return modifyCap(capability, CAP_SET);
}

/* An analogous dropCap() (unneeded in this program), could be
    defined as: modifyCap(capability, CAP_CLEAR); */

static int                  /* Drop all capabilities from all sets */
dropAllCaps(void)
{
    cap_t empty;
    int s;

    empty = cap_init();
    if (empty == NULL)
        return -1;

    s = cap_set_proc(empty);
```

```
        if (cap_free(empty) == -1)
            return -1;

        return s;
    }

    int
    main(int argc, char *argv[])
    {
        char *username, *password, *encrypted, *p;
        struct passwd *pwd;
        struct spwd *spwd;
        Boolean authOk;
        size_t len;
        long lnmax;

        lnmax = sysconf(_SC_LOGIN_NAME_MAX);
        if (lnmax == -1)                        /* If limit is indeterminate */
            lnmax = 256;                        /* make a guess */

        username = malloc(lnmax);
        if (username == NULL)
            errExit("malloc");

        printf("Username: ");
        fflush(stdout);
        if (fgets(username, lnmax, stdin) == NULL)
            exit(EXIT_FAILURE);                 /* Exit on EOF */

        len = strlen(username);
        if (username[len - 1] == '\n')
            username[len - 1] = '\0';           /* Remove trailing '\n' */

        pwd = getpwnam(username);
        if (pwd == NULL)
            fatal("couldn't get password record");

        /* Only raise CAP_DAC_READ_SEARCH for as long as we need it */

        if (raiseCap(CAP_DAC_READ_SEARCH) == -1)
            fatal("raiseCap() failed");

        spwd = getspnam(username);
        if (spwd == NULL && errno == EACCES)
            fatal("no permission to read shadow password file");

        /* At this point, we won't need any more capabilities,
           so drop all capabilities from all sets */

        if (dropAllCaps() == -1)
            fatal("dropAllCaps() failed");

        if (spwd != NULL)                       /* If there is a shadow password record */
            pwd->pw_passwd = spwd->sp_pwdp;     /* Use the shadow password */
```

```
    password = getpass("Password: ");

    /* Encrypt password and erase cleartext version immediately */

    encrypted = crypt(password, pwd->pw_passwd);
    for (p = password; *p != '\0'; )
        *p++ = '\0';

    if (encrypted == NULL)
        errExit("crypt");

    authOk = strcmp(encrypted, pwd->pw_passwd) == 0;
    if (!authOk) {
        printf("Incorrect password\n");
        exit(EXIT_FAILURE);
    }

    printf("Successfully authenticated: UID=%ld\n", (long) pwd->pw_uid);

    /* Now do authenticated work... */

    exit(EXIT_SUCCESS);
}
```

                                                      ———————————— cap/check_password_caps.c

39.8 Creating Capabilities-Only Environments

In the preceding pages, we have described various ways in which a process with the
user ID 0 (*root*) is treated specially with respect to capabilities:

- When a process with one or more user IDs that equal 0 sets all of its user IDs to
  nonzero values, its permitted and effective capability sets are cleared. (See
  Section 39.6.)

- When a process with an effective user ID of 0 changes that user ID to a nonzero value, it loses its effective capabilities. When the reverse change is made,
  the permitted capability set is copied to the effective set. A similar procedure is
  followed for a subset of capabilities when the process's file-system user ID is
  switched between 0 and nonzero values. (See Section 39.6.)

- If a process with real or effective user ID of *root* execs a program, or any process execs a set-user-ID-*root* program, then the file inheritable and permitted
  sets are notionally defined to be all ones. If the process's effective user ID is 0,
  or it is execing a set-user-ID-*root* program, then the file effective bit is notionally
  defined to be 1. (See Section 39.5.2.) In the usual cases (i.e., both the real and
  effective user ID are *root*, or a set-user-ID-*root* program is being execed), this
  means the process gets all capabilities in its permitted and effective sets.

In a fully capability-based system, the kernel would not need to perform any of
these special treatments of *root*. There would be no set-user-ID-*root* programs, and
file capabilities would be used to grant just the minimum capabilities that a program requires.

Since existing applications aren't engineered to make use of the file-capabilities infrastructure, the kernel must maintain the traditional handling of processes with the user ID 0. Nevertheless, we may want an application to run in a purely capability-based environment in which *root* gets none of the special treatments described above. Starting with kernel 2.6.26, and if file capabilities are enabled in the kernel, Linux provides the *securebits* mechanism, which controls a set of per-process flags that enable or disable each of the three special treatments for *root*. (To be precise, the *securebits* flags are actually a per-thread attribute.)

The *securebits* mechanism controls the flags shown in Table 39-2. The flags exist as related pairs of a *base* flag and a corresponding *locked* flag. Each of the base flags controls one of the special treatments of *root* described above. Setting the corresponding locked flag is a one-time operation that prevents further changes to the associated base flag—once set, the locked flag can't be unset.

Table 39-2: The *securebits* flags

Flag	Meaning if set
SECBIT_KEEP_CAPS	Don't drop permitted capabilities when a process with one or more 0 user IDs sets all of its user IDs to nonzero values. This flag has an effect only if SECBIT_NO_SETUID_FIXUP is not also set. This flag is cleared on an *exec()*.
SECBIT_NO_SETUID_FIXUP	Don't change capabilities when user IDs are switched between 0 and nonzero values (i.e., during the transitions described in Section 39.6).
SECBIT_NOROOT	If a process with a real or effective user ID of 0 does an *exec()*, or it execs a set-user-ID-*root* program, don't grant it capabilities (unless the executable has file capabilities).
SECBIT_KEEP_CAPS_LOCKED	Lock SECBIT_KEEP_CAPS.
SECBIT_NO_SETUID_FIXUP_LOCKED	Lock SECBIT_NO_SETUID_FIXUP.
SECBIT_NOROOT_LOCKED	Lock SECBIT_NOROOT.

The *securebits* flag settings are inherited in a child created by *fork()*. All of the flag settings are preserved during *exec()*, except SECBIT_KEEP_CAPS, which is cleared for historical compatibility with the PR_SET_KEEPCAPS setting, described below.

A process can retrieve the *securebits* flags using the *prctl()* PR_GET_SECUREBITS operation. If a process has the CAP_SETPCAP capability, it can modify the *securebits* flags using the *prctl()* PR_SET_SECUREBITS operations. A purely capability-based application can irreversibly disable special treatment of *root* for the calling process and all of its descendants using the following call:

```
if (prctl(PR_SET_SECUREBITS,
        /* SECBIT_KEEP_CAPS off */
        SECBIT_NO_SETUID_FIXUP | SECBIT_NO_SETUID_FIXUP_LOCKED |
        SECBIT_NOROOT | SECBIT_NOROOT_LOCKED)
    == -1)
    errExit("prctl");
```

After this call, the only way in which this process and its descendants can obtain capabilities is by executing programs that have file capabilities.

The SECBIT_KEEP_CAPS flag prevents capabilities from being dropped when a process with one or more user IDs with the value 0 sets all of its user IDs to nonzero values. Roughly speaking, SECBIT_KEEP_CAPS provides half of the functionality provided by SECBIT_NO_SETUID_FIXUP. (As noted in Table 39-2, SECBIT_KEEP_CAPS has an effect only if SECBIT_NO_SETUID_FIXUP is not set.) This flag exists to provide a *securebits* flag that mirrors the older *prctl()* PR_SET_KEEPCAPS operation, which controls the same attribute. (The one difference between the two mechanisms is that a process doesn't need the CAP_SETPCAP capability to employ the *prctl()* PR_SET_KEEPCAPS operation.)

> Earlier, we noted that all of the *securebits* flags are preserved during an *exec()*, except SECBIT_KEEP_CAPS. The setting of the SECBIT_KEEP_CAPS bit was made the converse of the other *securebits* settings in order to maintain consistency with the treatment of the attribute set by the *prctl()* PR_SET_KEEPCAPS operation.

The *prctl()* PR_SET_KEEPCAPS operation is designed for use by set-user-ID-*root* programs running on older kernels that don't support file capabilities. Such programs can still improve their security by programmatically dropping and raising capabilities as required (refer to Section 39.10).

However, even if such a set-user-ID-*root* program drops all capabilities except those that it requires, it still maintains two important privileges: the ability to access files owned by *root* and the ability to regain capabilities by execing a program (Section 39.5.2). The only way of permanently dropping these privileges is to set all of the process's user IDs to nonzero values. But doing that normally results in the clearing of the permitted and effective capability sets (see the four points in Section 39.6 concerning the effect of user ID changes on capabilities). This defeats the purpose, which is to permanently drop user ID 0, while maintaining some capabilities. To allow this possibility, the *prctl()* PR_SET_KEEPCAPS operation can be used to set the process attribute that prevents the permitted capability set from being cleared when all user IDs are changed to a nonzero value. (The process's effective capability set is always cleared in this case, regardless of the setting of the "keep capabilities" attribute.)

39.9 Discovering the Capabilities Required by a Program

Suppose we have a program that is unaware of capabilities and that is provided only in binary form, or we have a program whose source code is too large for us to easily read to determine which capabilities might be required to run it. If the program requires privileges, but shouldn't be a set-user-ID-*root* program, then how can we determine the permitted capabilities to assign to the executable file with *setcap(8)*? There are two ways to answer this question:

- Use *strace(1)* (Appendix A) to see which system call fails with the error EPERM, the error used to indicate the lack of a required capability. By consulting the system call's manual page or the kernel source code, we can then deduce what capability is required. This approach isn't perfect, because an EPERM error can occasionally be generated for other reasons, some of which may have nothing to do with the capability requirements for the program. Furthermore, programs may legitimately make a system call that requires privilege, and then change their behavior after determining that they don't have privilege for a particular operation. It can sometimes be difficult to distinguish such "false positives" when trying to determine the capabilities that an executable really does need.

- Use a kernel probe to produce monitoring output when the kernel is asked to perform capability checks. An example of how to do this is provided in [Hallyn, 2007], an article written by one of the developers of file capabilities. For each request to check a capability, the probe shown in the article logs the kernel function that was called, the capability that was requested, and the name of the requesting program. Although this approach requires more work than the use of *strace(1)*, it can also help us more accurately determine the capabilities that a program requires.

39.10 Older Kernels and Systems Without File Capabilities

In this section, we describe various differences in the implementation of capabilities in older kernels. We also describe the differences that occur on kernels where file capabilities are not supported. There are two scenarios where Linux doesn't support file capabilities:

- Before Linux 2.6.24, file capabilities were not implemented.
- In Linux kernel versions 2.6.24 through to 2.6.32, file capabilities can be disabled if the kernel is built without the CONFIG_SECURITY_FILE_CAPABILITIES option. (This also disables the *securebits* mechanism described in Section 39.8.)

> Although Linux introduced capabilities and allowed them to be attached to processes starting with kernel 2.2, the implementation of file capabilities appeared only several years later. The reasons that file capabilities remained unimplemented for so long were matters of policy, rather than technical difficulties. (Extended attributes, described in Chapter 16, which are used to implement file capabilities, had been available since kernel 2.6.) The weight of opinion among kernel developers was that requiring system administrators to set and monitor different sets of capabilities—some of whose consequences are subtle but far-reaching—for each privileged program would create an unmanageably complex administration task. By contrast, system administrators are familiar with the existing UNIX privilege model, know to treat set-user-ID programs with due caution, and can locate the set-user-ID and set-group-ID programs on a system using simple *find* commands. Nevertheless, the developers of file capabilities made the case that file capabilities could be made administratively workable, and eventually provided a convincing enough argument that file capabilities were integrated into the kernel.

The CAP_SETPCAP capability

On kernels that don't support file capabilities (i.e., any kernel before 2.6.24, and kernels since 2.6.24 with file capabilities disabled), the semantics of the CAP_SETPCAP capability are different. Subject to rules that are analogous to those described in Section 39.7, a process that has the CAP_SETPCAP capability in its effective set can theoretically change the capabilities of processes other than itself. Changes can be made to the capabilities of another process, all of the members of a specified process group, or all processes on the system except *init* and the caller itself. The final case excludes *init* because it is fundamental to the operation of the system. It also excludes the caller because the caller may be attempting to remove capabilities from every other process on the system, and we don't want to remove the capabilities from the calling process itself.

However, changing the capabilities of other processes is only a theoretical possibility. On older kernels, and on modern kernels where support for file capabilities is disabled, the capability bounding set (discussed next) always masks out the `CAP_SETPCAP` capability.

The capability bounding set

Since Linux 2.6.25, the capability bounding set is a per-process attribute. However, on older kernels, the capability bounding set is a system-wide attribute that affects all processes on the system. The system-wide capability bounding set is initialized so that it always masks out `CAP_SETPCAP` (described above).

> On kernels after 2.6.25, removing capabilities from the per-process bounding set is supported only if file capabilities are enabled in the kernel. In that case, *init*, the ancestor of all processes, starts with a bounding set containing all capabilities, and a copy of that bounding set is inherited by other processes created on the system. If file capabilities are disabled, then, because of the differences in the semantics of `CAP_SETPCAP` described above, *init* starts with a bounding set that contains all capabilities except `CAP_SETPCAP`.

There is one further change in the semantics of the capability bounding set in Linux 2.6.25. As noted earlier (Section 39.5.1), on Linux 2.6.25 and later, the per-process capability bounding set acts as a limiting superset for the capabilities that can be added to the process's inheritable set. In Linux 2.6.24 and earlier, the system-wide capability bounding set doesn't have this masking effect. (It is not needed, because these kernels don't support file capabilities.)

The system-wide capability bounding set is accessible via the Linux-specific /proc/ sys/kernel/cap-bound file. A process must have the `CAP_SYS_MODULE` capability to be able to change the contents of cap-bound. However, only the *init* process can turn bits on in this mask; other privileged processes can only turn bits off. The upshot of these limitations is that on a system where file capabilities are not supported, we can never give the `CAP_SETPCAP` capability to a process. This is reasonable, since that capability can be used to subvert the entire kernel privilege-checking system. (In the unlikely case that we want to change this limitation, we must either load a kernel module that changes the value in the set, modify the source code of the *init* program, or change the initialization of the capability bounding set in the kernel source code and perform a kernel rebuild.)

> Confusingly, although it is a bit mask, the value in the system-wide cap-bound file is displayed as a signed decimal number. For example, the initial value of this file is −257. This is the two's complement interpretation of the bit mask with all bits except *(1 << 8)* turned on (i.e., in binary, 11111111 11111111 11111110 11111111); `CAP_SETPCAP` has the value 8.

Using capabilities within a program on a system without file capabilities

Even on a system that doesn't support file capabilities, we can nevertheless employ capabilities to improve the security of a program. We do this as follows:

1. Run the program in a process with an effective user ID of 0 (typically a set-user-ID-*root* program). Such a process is granted all capabilities (except CAP_SETPCAP, as noted earlier) in its permitted and effective sets.

2. On program startup, use the *libcap* API to drop all capabilities from the effective set, and drop all capabilities except those that we may later need from the permitted set.

3. Employ the call *prctl(PR_SET_KEEPCAPS, 1)* so that the next step does not drop capabilities (see Section 39.8).

4. Set all user IDs to nonzero values, to prevent the process from accessing files owned by *root* or gaining capabilities by doing an *exec()*.

    > We could replace the two preceding steps by a single step that sets the SECBIT_NOROOT flag, if we want to prevent the process from regaining privileges on an *exec()*, but must allow it to access files owned by *root*. (Of course, allowing access to files owned by *root* leaves open the risk of some security vulnerability.)

5. During the rest of the program's lifetime, use the *libcap* API to raise and drop the remaining permitted capabilities from the effective set as needed in order to perform privileged tasks.

Some applications built for Linux kernels before version 2.6.24 employed this approach.

> Among the kernel developers who argued against the implementation of capabilities for executable files, one of the perceived virtues of the approach described in the main text was that the developer of an application knows which capabilities an executable requires. By contrast, a system administrator may not be able to easily determine this information.

39.11 Summary

The Linux capabilities scheme divides privileged operations into distinct categories, and allows a process to be granted some capabilities, while being denied others. This scheme represents an improvement over the traditional all-or-nothing privilege mechanism, whereby a process has either privileges to perform all operations (user ID 0) or no privileges (nonzero user ID). Since kernel 2.6.24, Linux supports attaching capabilities to files, so that a process can gain selected capabilities by execing a program.

39.12 Exercise

39-1. Modify the program in Listing 35-2 (sched_set.c, on page 743) to use file capabilities, so that it can be used by an unprivileged user.

40

LOGIN ACCOUNTING

Login accounting is concerned with recording which users are currently logged in to the system, and recording past logins and logouts. This chapter looks at the login accounting files and the library functions used to retrieve and update the information they contain. We also describe the steps that an application providing a login service should perform in order to update these files when a user logs in and out.

40.1 Overview of the utmp and wtmp Files

UNIX systems maintain two data files containing information about users logging in and out of the system:

- The utmp file maintains a record of users currently logged in to the system (as well as certain other information that we describe later). As each user logs in, a record is written to the utmp file. One of the fields in this record, *ut_user*, records the login name of the user. This record is later erased on logout. Programs such as *who(1)* use the information in the utmp file to display a list of currently logged-in users.

- The wtmp file is an audit trail of all user logins and logouts (as well as certain other information that we describe later). On each login, a record containing the same information as is written to the utmp file is appended to the wtmp file. On logout, a further record is appended to the file. This record contains the same information, except that the *ut_user* field is zeroed out. The *last(1)* command can be used to display and filter the contents of the wtmp file.

On Linux, the `utmp` file resides at `/var/run/utmp`, and the `wtmp` file resides at `/var/log/wtmp`. In general, applications don't need to know about these pathnames, since they are compiled into *glibc*. Programs that do need to refer to the locations of these files should use the `_PATH_UTMP` and `_PATH_WTMP` pathname constants, defined in `<paths.h>` (and `<utmpx.h>`), rather than explicitly coding pathnames into the program.

> SUSv3 doesn't standardize any symbolic names for the pathnames of the `utmp` and `wtmp` files. The names `_PATH_UTMP` and `_PATH_WTMP` are used on Linux and the BSDs. Many other UNIX implementations instead define the constants `UTMP_FILE` and `WTMP_FILE` for these pathnames. Linux also defines these names in `<utmp.h>`, but doesn't define them in `<utmpx.h>` or `<paths.h>`.

40.2 The *utmpx* API

The `utmp` and `wtmp` files have been present in the UNIX system since early times, but underwent steady evolution and divergence across various UNIX implementations, especially BSD versus System V. System V Release 4 greatly extended the API, in the process creating a new (parallel) *utmpx* structure and associated utmpx and wtmpx files. The letter *x* was likewise included in the names of header files and additional functions for processing these new files. Many other UNIX implementations also added their own extensions to the API.

In this chapter, we describe the Linux *utmpx* API, which is a hybrid of the BSD and System V implementations. Linux doesn't follow System V in creating parallel utmpx and wtmpx files; instead, the `utmp` and `wtmp` files contain all of the required information. However, for compatibility with other UNIX implementations, Linux provides both the traditional *utmp* and the System V–derived *utmpx* APIs for accessing the contents of these files. On Linux, these two APIs return exactly the same information. (One of the few differences between the two APIs is that the *utmp* API contains reentrant versions of a few functions, while the *utmpx* API does not.) However, we confine our discussion to the *utmpx* interface, since that is the API specified in SUSv3 and is thus preferred for portability to other UNIX implementations.

The SUSv3 specification doesn't cover all aspects of the *utmpx* API (e.g., the locations of the `utmp` and `wtmp` files are not specified). The precise contents of the login accounting files differ somewhat across implementations, and various implementations provide additional login accounting functions that are not specified in SUSv3.

> Chapter 17 of [Frisch, 2002] summarizes some of the variations in the location and use of the `wtmp` and `utmp` files across different UNIX implementations. It also describes the use of the *ac(1)* command, which can be used to summarize login information from the `wtmp` file.

40.3 The *utmpx* Structure

The `utmp` and `wtmp` files consist of *utmpx* records. The *utmpx* structure is defined in `<utmpx.h>`, as shown in Listing 40-1.

The SUSv3 specification of the *utmpx* structure doesn't include the *ut_host*, *ut_exit*, *ut_session*, or *ut_addr_v6* fields. The *ut_host* and *ut_exit* fields are present on most other implementations; *ut_session* is present on a few other implementations; and *ut_addr_v6* is Linux-specific. SUSv3 specifies the *ut_line* and *ut_user* fields, but leaves their lengths unspecified.

The *int32_t* data type used to define the *ut_addr_v6* field of the *utmpx* structure is a 32-bit integer.

Listing 40-1: Definition of the *utmpx* structure

```
#define _GNU_SOURCE          /* Without _GNU_SOURCE the two field
struct exit_status {            names below are prepended by "__" */
    short e_termination;   /* Process termination status (signal) */
    short e_exit;          /* Process exit status */
};

#define __UT_LINESIZE    32
#define __UT_NAMESIZE    32
#define __UT_HOSTSIZE    256

struct utmpx {
    short ut_type;                  /* Type of record */
    pid_t ut_pid;                   /* PID of login process */
    char  ut_line[__UT_LINESIZE];   /* Terminal device name */
    char  ut_id[4];                 /* Suffix from terminal name, or
                                       ID field from inittab(5) */

    char  ut_user[__UT_NAMESIZE];   /* Username */
    char  ut_host[__UT_HOSTSIZE];   /* Hostname for remote login, or kernel
                                       version for run-level messages */

    struct exit_status ut_exit;     /* Exit status of process marked
                                       as DEAD_PROCESS (not filled
                                       in by init(8) on Linux) */

    long  ut_session;               /* Session ID */
    struct timeval ut_tv;           /* Time when entry was made */
    int32_t ut_addr_v6[4];          /* IP address of remote host (IPv4
                                       address uses just ut_addr_v6[0],
                                       with other elements set to 0) */

    char  __unused[20];             /* Reserved for future use */
};
```

Each of the string fields in the *utmpx* structure is null-terminated unless it completely fills the corresponding array.

For login processes, the information stored in the *ut_line* and *ut_id* fields is derived from the name of the terminal device. The *ut_line* field contains the complete filename of the terminal device. The *ut_id* field contains the suffix part of the filename—that is, the string following *tty*, *pts*, or *pty* (the last two are for System V–style and BSD-style pseudoterminals, respectively). Thus, for the terminal /dev/tty2, *ut_line* would be *tty2* and *ut_id* would be *2*.

In a windowing environment, some terminal emulators use the *ut_session* field to record the session ID for the terminal window. (Refer to Section 34.3 for an explanation of session IDs.)

The *ut_type* field is an integer defining the type of record being written to the file. The following set of constants (with their corresponding numeric values shown in parentheses) can be used as values for this field:

EMPTY (0)
> This record doesn't contain valid accounting information.

RUN_LVL (1)
> This record indicates a change in the system's run-level during system startup or shutdown. (Information about run-levels can be found in the *init(8)* manual page.) The _GNU_SOURCE feature test macro must be defined in order to obtain the definition of this constant from <utmpx.h>.

BOOT_TIME (2)
> This record contains the time of system boot in the *ut_tv* field. The usual author of RUN_LVL and BOOT_TIME records is *init*. These records are written to both the utmp file and the wtmp file.

NEW_TIME (3)
> This record contains the new time after a system clock change, recorded in the *ut_tv* field.

OLD_TIME (4)
> This record contains the old time before a system clock change, recorded in the *ut_tv* field. Records of type OLD_TIME and NEW_TIME are written to the utmp and wtmp files by the NTP (or a similar) daemon when it makes changes to the system clock.

INIT_PROCESS (5)
> This is a record for a process spawned by *init*, such as a *getty* process. Refer to the *inittab(5)* manual page for details.

LOGIN_PROCESS (6)
> This is a record for a session leader process for a user login, such as a *login(1)* process.

USER_PROCESS (7)
> This is a record for a user process, usually a login session, with the username appearing in the *ut_user* field. The login session may have been started by *login(1)* or by some application offering a remote login facility, such as *ftp* or *ssh*.

DEAD_PROCESS (8)
> This record identifies a process that has exited.

We show the numeric values of these constants because various applications depend on the constants having the above numerical order. For example, in the source code of the *agetty* program, we find checks such as the following:

```
utp->ut_type >= INIT_PROCESS && utp->ut_type <= DEAD_PROCESS
```

Records of the type INIT_PROCESS usually correspond to invocations of *getty(8)* (or a similar program, such as *agetty(8)* or *mingetty(8)*). On system boot, the *init* process creates a child for each terminal line and virtual console, and each child execs the *getty* program. The *getty* program opens the terminal, prompts the user for a login name, and then execs *login(1)*. After successfully validating the user and performing various other steps, *login* forks a child that execs the user's login shell. The complete life of such a login session is represented by four records written to the wtmp file in the following order:

- an INIT_PROCESS record, written by *init*;
- a LOGIN_PROCESS record, written by *getty*;
- a USER_PROCESS record, written by *login*; and
- a DEAD_PROCESS record, written by *init* when it detects the death of the child *login* process (which occurs on user logout).

Further details on the operation of *getty* and *login* during user login can be found in Chapter 9 of [Stevens & Rago, 2005].

> Some versions of *init* spawn the *getty* process before updating the wtmp file. Consequently, *init* and *getty* race with each other to update the wtmp file, with the result that the INIT_PROCESS and LOGIN_PROCESS records may be written in the opposite order from that described in the main text.

40.4 Retrieving Information from the utmp and wtmp Files

The functions described in this section retrieve records from files containing *utmpx*-format records. By default, these functions use the standard utmp file, but this can be changed using the *utmpxname()* function (described below).

These functions employ the notion of a *current location* within the file from which they are retrieving records. This location is updated by each function.

The *setutxent()* function rewinds the utmp file to the beginning.

```
#include <utmpx.h>

void setutxent(void);
```

Normally, we should call *setutxent()* before employing any of the *getutx*()* functions (described below). This prevents possible confusion that might result if some third-party function that we have called has previously made use of these functions. Depending on the task being performed, it may also be necessary to call *setutxent()* again at appropriate points later in a program.

The *setutxent()* function and the *getutx*()* functions open the utmp file if it is not already open. When we have finished using the file, we can close it with the *endutxent()* function.

```
#include <utmpx.h>

void endutxent(void);
```

The *getutxent()*, *getutxid()*, and *getutxline()* functions read a record from the utmp file and return a pointer to a (statically allocated) *utmpx* structure.

```
#include <utmpx.h>

struct utmpx *getutxent(void);
struct utmpx *getutxid(const struct utmpx *ut);
struct utmpx *getutxline(const struct utmpx *ut);
```

All return a pointer to a statically allocated *utmpx* structure,
or NULL if no matching record or EOF was encountered

The *getutxent()* function retrieves the next sequential record from the utmp file. The *getutxid()* and *getutxline()* functions perform searches, starting from the current file location, for a record matching the criteria specified in the *utmpx* structure pointed to by the *ut* argument.

The *getutxid()* function searches the utmp file for a record based on the values specified in the *ut_type* and *ut_id* fields of the *ut* argument:

- If the *ut_type* field is RUN_LVL, BOOT_TIME, NEW_TIME, or OLD_TIME, then *getutxid()* finds the next record whose *ut_type* field matches the specified value. (Records of these types don't correspond to user logins.) This permits searches for records of changes to the system time and run-level.

- If the *ut_type* field is one of the remaining valid values (INIT_PROCESS, LOGIN_PROCESS, USER_PROCESS, or DEAD_PROCESS), then *getutxid()* finds the next record whose *ut_type* field matches *any* of these values and whose *ut_id* field matches that specified in its *ut* argument. This permits scanning the file for records corresponding to a particular terminal.

The *getutxline()* function searches forward for a record whose *ut_type* field is either LOGIN_PROCESS or USER_PROCESS, and whose *ut_line* field matches that specified in the *ut* argument. This is useful for finding records corresponding to user logins.

Both *getutxid()* and *getutxline()* return NULL if the search fails (i.e., end-of-file is encountered without finding a matching record).

On some UNIX implementations, *getutxline()* and *getutxid()* treat the static area used for returning the *utmpx* structure as a kind of cache. If they determine that the record placed in this cache by a previous *getutx*()* call matches the criteria specified in *ut*, then no file read is performed; the call simply returns the same record once more (SUSv3 permits this behavior). Therefore, to prevent the same record from being repeatedly returned when calling *getutxline()* and *getutxid()* within a loop, we must zero out this static data structure, using code such as the following:

```
struct utmpx *res = NULL;

/* Other code omitted */

if (res != NULL)              /* If 'res' was set via a previous call */
    memset(res, 0, sizeof(struct utmpx));
res = getutxline(&ut);
```

The *glibc* implementation doesn't perform this type of caching, but we should nevertheless employ this technique for the sake of portability.

> Because the *getutx*()* functions return a pointer to a statically allocated structure, they are not reentrant. The GNU C library provides reentrant versions of the traditional *utmp* functions (*getutent_r()*, *getutid_r()*, and *getutline_r()*), but doesn't provide reentrant versions of their *utmpx* counterparts. (SUSv3 doesn't specify the reentrant versions.)

By default, all of the *getutx*()* functions work on the standard utmp file. If we want to use another file, such as the wtmp file, then we must first call *utmpxname()*, specifying the desired pathname.

```
#define _GNU_SOURCE
#include <utmpx.h>

int utmpxname(const char *file);
```
                                              Returns 0 on success, or −1 on error

The *utmpxname()* function merely records a copy of the pathname given to it. It doesn't open the file, but does close any file previously opened by one of the other calls. This means that *utmpxname()* doesn't return an error if an invalid pathname is specified. Instead, when one of the *getutx*()* functions is later called, it will return an error (i.e., NULL, with *errno* set to ENOENT) when it fails to open the file.

> Although not specified in SUSv3, most UNIX implementations provide *utmpxname()* or the analogous *utmpname()* function.

Example program

The program in Listing 40-2 uses some of the functions described in this section to dump the contents of a *utmpx*-format file. The following shell session log demonstrates the results when we use this program to dump the contents of /var/run/utmp (the default used by these functions if *utmpxname()* is not called):

```
$ ./dump_utmpx
user      type       PID line   id  host      date/time
LOGIN     LOGIN_PR   1761 tty1   1             Sat Oct 23 09:29:37 2010
LOGIN     LOGIN_PR   1762 tty2   2             Sat Oct 23 09:29:37 2010
lynley    USER_PR   10482 tty3   3             Sat Oct 23 10:19:43 2010
david     USER_PR    9664 tty4   4             Sat Oct 23 10:07:50 2010
liz       USER_PR    1985 tty5   5             Sat Oct 23 10:50:12 2010
mtk       USER_PR   10111 pts/0  /0            Sat Oct 23 09:30:57 2010
```

For brevity, we edited out much of the output produced by the program. The lines matching tty1 to tty5 are for logins on virtual consoles (/dev/tty[1-6]). The last line of output is for an *xterm* session on a pseudoterminal.

The following output produced by dumping /var/log/wtmp shows that when a user logs in and out, two records are written to the wtmp file. (We edited out all of the other output produced by the program.) By searching sequentially through the wtmp file (using *getutxline()*), these records can be matched via the *ut_line* field.

```
$ ./dump_utmpx /var/log/wtmp
user     type        PID line   id  host        date/time
lynley   USER_PR   10482 tty3    3              Sat Oct 23 10:19:43 2010
         DEAD_PR   10482 tty3    3   2.4.20-4G Sat Oct 23 10:32:54 2010
```

Listing 40-2: Displaying the contents of a *utmpx*-format file

―――――――――――――――――――――――――――――― loginacct/dump_utmpx.c

```c
#define _GNU_SOURCE
#include <time.h>
#include <utmpx.h>
#include <paths.h>
#include "tlpi_hdr.h"

int
main(int argc, char *argv[])
{
    struct utmpx *ut;

    if (argc > 1 && strcmp(argv[1], "--help") == 0)
        usageErr("%s [utmp-pathname]\n", argv[0]);

    if (argc > 1)               /* Use alternate file if supplied */
        if (utmpxname(argv[1]) == -1)
            errExit("utmpxname");

    setutxent();

    printf("user     type        PID line   id  host        date/time\n");

    while ((ut = getutxent()) != NULL) {          /* Sequential scan to EOF */
        printf("%-8s ", ut->ut_user);
        printf("%-9.9s ",
                (ut->ut_type == EMPTY)        ?   "EMPTY" :
                (ut->ut_type == RUN_LVL)      ?   "RUN_LVL" :
                (ut->ut_type == BOOT_TIME)    ?   "BOOT_TIME" :
                (ut->ut_type == NEW_TIME)     ?   "NEW_TIME" :
                (ut->ut_type == OLD_TIME)     ?   "OLD_TIME" :
                (ut->ut_type == INIT_PROCESS) ?   "INIT_PR" :
                (ut->ut_type == LOGIN_PROCESS) ?  "LOGIN_PR" :
                (ut->ut_type == USER_PROCESS) ?   "USER_PR" :
                (ut->ut_type == DEAD_PROCESS) ?   "DEAD_PR" : "???");
        printf("%5ld %-6.6s %-3.5s %-9.9s ", (long) ut->ut_pid,
                ut->ut_line, ut->ut_id, ut->ut_host);
        time_t tv_sec = ut->ut_tv.tv_sec;
        printf("%s", ctime((time_t *) &tv_sec));
    }
    endutxent();
    exit(EXIT_SUCCESS);
}
```

―――――――――――――――――――――――――――――― loginacct/dump_utmpx.c

40.5 Retrieving the Login Name: *getlogin()*

The *getlogin()* function returns the name of the user logged in on the controlling terminal of the calling process. This function uses the information maintained in the utmp file.

```
#include <unistd.h>

char *getlogin(void);
```
                    Returns pointer to username string, or NULL on error

The *getlogin()* function calls *ttyname()* (Section 62.10) to find the name of the terminal associated with the calling process's standard input. It then searches the utmp file for a record whose *ut_line* value matches this terminal name. If a matching record is found, then *getlogin()* returns the *ut_user* string from that record.

If a match is not found or an error occurs, then *getlogin()* returns NULL and sets *errno* to indicate the error. One reason *getlogin()* may fail is that the process doesn't have a terminal associated with its standard input (ENOTTY), perhaps because it is daemon. Another possibility is that this terminal session is not recorded in utmp; for example, some software terminal emulators don't create entries in the utmp file.

Even in the (unusual) case where a user ID has multiple login names in /etc/passwd, *getlogin()* is able to return the actual username that was used to log in on this terminal because it relies on the utmp file. By contrast, using *getpwuid(getuid())* always retrieves the first matching record from /etc/passwd, regardless of the name that was used to log in.

> A reentrant version of *getlogin()* is specified by SUSv3, in the form of *getlogin_r()*, and this function is provided by *glibc*.
>
> The LOGNAME environment variable can also be used to find a user's login name. However, the value of this variable can be changed by the user, which means that it can't be used to securely identify a user.

40.6 Updating the utmp and wtmp Files for a Login Session

When writing an application that creates a login session (in the manner of, say, *login* or *sshd*), we should update the utmp and wtmp files as follows:

- On login, a record should be written to the utmp file to indicate that this user logged in. The application must check whether a record for this terminal already exists in the utmp file. If a previous record exists, it is overwritten; otherwise, a new record is appended to the file. Often, calling *pututxline()* (described shortly) is enough to ensure that these steps are correctly performed (see Listing 40-3 for an example). The output *utmpx* record should have at least the *ut_type*, *ut_user*, *ut_tv*, *ut_pid*, *ut_id*, and *ut_line* fields filled in. The *ut_type* field should be set to USER_PROCESS. The *ut_id* field should contain the suffix of the name of the device (i.e., the terminal or pseudoterminal) on which the user is logging in, and the *ut_line* field should contain the name of the login device, with the leading /dev/ string removed. (Examples of the contents of these two fields are shown in the sample runs of the program in Listing 40-2.) A record containing exactly the same information is appended to the wtmp file.

> The terminal name acts (via the *ut_line* and *ut_id* fields) as a unique key for records in the utmp file.

- On logout, the record previously written to the utmp file should be erased. This is done by creating a record with *ut_type* set to DEAD_PROCESS, and with the same *ut_id* and *ut_line* values as the record written during login, but with the *ut_user* field zeroed out. This record is written over the earlier record. A copy of the same record is appended to the wtmp file.

> If we fail to clean up the *utmp* record on logout, perhaps because of a program crash, then, on the next reboot, *init* automatically cleans up the record, setting its *ut_type* to DEAD_PROCESS and zeroing out various other fields of the record.

The utmp and wtmp files are normally protected so that only privileged users can perform updates on these files. The accuracy of *getlogin()* depends on the integrity of the utmp file. For this, as well as other reasons, the permissions on the utmp and wtmp files should never be set to allow writing by unprivileged users.

What qualifies as a login session? As we might expect, logins via *login*, *telnet*, and *ssh* are recorded in the login accounting files. Most *ftp* implementations also create login accounting records. However, are login accounting records created for each terminal window started on the system or for invocations of *su*, for example? The answer to that question varies across UNIX implementations.

> Under some terminal emulator programs (e.g., *xterm*), command-line options or other mechanisms can be used to determine whether the program updates the login accounting files.

The *pututxline()* function writes the *utmpx* structure pointed to by *ut* into the /var/run/utmp file (or an alternative file if *utmpxname()* was previously called).

```
#include <utmpx.h>

struct utmpx *pututxline(const struct utmpx *ut);
```
                Returns pointer to copy of successfully updated record on success,
                                                         or NULL on error

Before writing the record, *pututxline()* first uses *getutxid()* to search forward for a record that may be overwritten. If such a record is found, it is overwritten; otherwise, a new record is appended to the end of the file. In many cases, an application precedes a call to *pututxline()* by a call to one of the *getutx*()* functions, which sets the current file location to the correct record—that is, one matching the *getutxid()*-style criteria in the *utmpx* structure pointed to by *ut*. If *pututxline()* determines that this has occurred, it doesn't call *getutxid()*.

> If *pututxline()* makes an internal call to *getutxid()*, this call doesn't change the static area used by the *getutx*()* functions to return the *utmpx* structure. SUSv3 requires this behavior from an implementation.

When updating the wtmp file, we simply open the file and append a record to it. Because this is a standard operation, *glibc* encapsulates it in the *updwtmpx()* function.

```
#define _GNU_SOURCE
#include <utmpx.h>

void updwtmpx(const char *wtmpx_file, const struct utmpx *ut);
```

The *updwtmpx()* function appends the *utmpx* record pointed to by *ut* to the file specified in *wtmpx_file*.

SUSv3 doesn't specify *updwtmpx()*, and it appears on only a few other UNIX implementations. Other implementations provide related functions—*login(3)*, *logout(3)*, and *logwtmp(3)*—which are also in *glibc* and described in the manual pages. If such functions are not present, we need to write our own equivalents. (The implementation of these functions is not complex.)

Example program

Listing 40-3 uses the functions described in this section to update the utmp and wtmp files. This program performs the required updates to utmp and wtmp in order to log in the user named on the command line, and then, after sleeping a few seconds, log them out again. Normally, such actions would be associated with the creation and termination of a login session for a user. This program uses *ttyname()* to retrieve the name of the terminal device associated with a file descriptor. We describe *ttyname()* in Section 62.10.

The following shell session log demonstrates the operation of the program in Listing 40-3. We assume privilege in order to be able to update the login accounting files, and then use the program to create a record for the user *mtk*:

```
$ su
Password:
# ./utmpx_login mtk
Creating login entries in utmp and wtmp
        using pid 1471, line pts/7, id /7
Type Control-Z to suspend program
[1]+  Stopped                 ./utmpx_login mtk
```

While the *utmpx_login* program was sleeping, we typed *Control-Z* to suspend the program and push it into the background. Next, we use the program in Listing 40-2 to examine the contents of the utmp file:

```
# ./dump_utmpx /var/run/utmp
user     type        PID line   id  host     date/time
cecilia  USER_PR     249 tty1   1            Fri Feb  1 21:39:07 2008
mtk      USER_PR    1471 pts/7  /7           Fri Feb  1 22:08:06 2008
# who
cecilia  tty1     Feb  1 21:39
mtk      pts/7    Feb  1 22:08
```

Above, we used the *who(1)* command to show that the output of *who* derives from utmp.

Next we use our program to examine the contents of the wtmp file:

```
# ./dump_utmpx /var/log/wtmp
user     type        PID line   id  host       date/time
cecilia  USER_PR     249 tty1   1              Fri Feb  1 21:39:07 2008
mtk      USER_PR    1471 pts/7  /7             Fri Feb  1 22:08:06 2008
# last mtk
mtk      pts/7                      Fri Feb  1 22:08    still logged in
```

Above, we used the *last(1)* command to show that the output of *last* derives from wtmp. (For brevity, we have edited the output of the *dump_utmpx* and *last* commands in this shell session log to remove lines of output that are irrelevant to our discussion.)

Next, we use the *fg* command to resume the *utmpx_login* program in the foreground. It subsequently writes logout records to the utmp and wtmp files.

```
# fg
./utmpx_login mtk
Creating logout entries in utmp and wtmp
```

We then once more examine the contents of the utmp file. We see that the utmp record was overwritten:

```
# ./dump_utmpx /var/run/utmp
user     type        PID line   id  host       date/time
cecilia  USER_PR     249 tty1   1              Fri Feb  1 21:39:07 2008
         DEAD_PR    1471 pts/7  /7             Fri Feb  1 22:09:09 2008
# who
cecilia  tty1     Feb  1 21:39
```

The final line of output shows that *who* ignored the DEAD_PROCESS record.

When we examine the wtmp file, we see that the wtmp record was superseded:

```
# ./dump_utmpx /var/log/wtmp
user     type        PID line   id  host       date/time
cecilia  USER_PR     249 tty1   1              Fri Feb  1 21:39:07 2008
mtk      USER_PR    1471 pts/7  /7             Fri Feb  1 22:08:06 2008
         DEAD_PR    1471 pts/7  /7             Fri Feb  1 22:09:09 2008
# last mtk
mtk      pts/7                      Fri Feb  1 22:08 - 22:09  (00:01)
```

The final line of output above demonstrates that *last* matches the login and logout records in wtmp to show the starting and ending times of the completed login session.

Listing 40-3: Updating the utmp and wtmp files

─── loginacct/utmpx_login.c
```
#define _GNU_SOURCE
#include <time.h>
#include <utmpx.h>
#include <paths.h>              /* Definitions of _PATH_UTMP and _PATH_WTMP */
#include "tlpi_hdr.h"
```

```
int
main(int argc, char *argv[])
{
    struct utmpx ut;
    char *devName;

    if (argc < 2 || strcmp(argv[1], "--help") == 0)
        usageErr("%s username [sleep-time]\n", argv[0]);

    /* Initialize login record for utmp and wtmp files */

    memset(&ut, 0, sizeof(struct utmpx));
    ut.ut_type = USER_PROCESS;         /* This is a user login */
    strncpy(ut.ut_user, argv[1], sizeof(ut.ut_user));
    if (time((time_t *) &ut.ut_tv.tv_sec) == -1)
        errExit("time");                /* Stamp with current time */
    ut.ut_pid = getpid();

    /* Set ut_line and ut_id based on the terminal associated with
       'stdin'. This code assumes terminals named "/dev/[pt]t[sy]*".
       The "/dev/" dirname is 5 characters; the "[pt]t[sy]" filename
       prefix is 3 characters (making 8 characters in all). */

    devName = ttyname(STDIN_FILENO);
    if (devName == NULL)
        errExit("ttyname");
    if (strlen(devName) <= 8)            /* Should never happen */
        fatal("Terminal name is too short: %s", devName);

    strncpy(ut.ut_line, devName + 5, sizeof(ut.ut_line));
    strncpy(ut.ut_id, devName + 8, sizeof(ut.ut_id));

    printf("Creating login entries in utmp and wtmp\n");
    printf("        using pid %ld, line %.*s, id %.*s\n",
            (long) ut.ut_pid, (int) sizeof(ut.ut_line), ut.ut_line,
            (int) sizeof(ut.ut_id), ut.ut_id);

    setutxent();                        /* Rewind to start of utmp file */
    if (pututxline(&ut) == NULL)        /* Write login record to utmp */
        errExit("pututxline");
    updwtmpx(_PATH_WTMP, &ut);          /* Append login record to wtmp */

    /* Sleep a while, so we can examine utmp and wtmp files */

    sleep((argc > 2) ? getInt(argv[2], GN_NONNEG, "sleep-time") : 15);

    /* Now do a "logout"; use values from previously initialized 'ut',
       except for changes below */

    ut.ut_type = DEAD_PROCESS;          /* Required for logout record */
    time((time_t *) &ut.ut_tv.tv_sec);  /* Stamp with logout time */
    memset(&ut.ut_user, 0, sizeof(ut.ut_user));
                                        /* Logout record has null username */
```

```
        printf("Creating logout entries in utmp and wtmp\n");
        setutxent();                      /* Rewind to start of utmp file */
        if (pututxline(&ut) == NULL)      /* Overwrite previous utmp record */
            errExit("pututxline");
        updwtmpx(_PATH_WTMP, &ut);        /* Append logout record to wtmp */

        endutxent();
        exit(EXIT_SUCCESS);
    }
```

── loginacct/utmpx_login.c

40.7   The lastlog File

The lastlog file records the time each user last logged in to the system. (This is different from the wtmp file, which records all logins and logouts by all users.) Among other things, the lastlog file allows the *login* program to inform users (at the start of a new login session) when they last logged in. In addition to updating utmp and wtmp, applications providing login services should also update lastlog.

As with the utmp and wtmp files, there is variation in the location and format of the lastlog file. (A few UNIX implementations don't provide this file.) On Linux, this file resides at /var/log/lastlog, and a constant, _PATH_LASTLOG, is defined in <paths.h> to point to this location. Like the utmp and wtmp files, the lastlog file is normally protected so that it can be read by all users but can be updated only by privileged processes.

The records in the lastlog file have the following format (defined in <lastlog.h>):

```
#define UT_NAMESIZE           32
#define UT_HOSTSIZE          256

struct lastlog {
    time_t ll_time;                   /* Time of last login */
    char   ll_line[UT_NAMESIZE];      /* Terminal for remote login */
    char   ll_host[UT_HOSTSIZE];      /* Hostname for remote login */
};
```

Note that these records don't include a username or user ID. Instead, the lastlog file consists of a series of records that are indexed by user ID. Thus, to find the lastlog record for user ID 1000, we would seek to byte *(1000 * sizeof(struct lastlog))* of the file. This is demonstrated in Listing 40-4, a program that allows us to view the lastlog records for the user(s) listed on its command line. This is similar to the functionality offered by the *lastlog(1)* command. Here is an example of the output produced by running this program:

```
$ ./view_lastlog annie paulh
annie    tty2              Mon Jan 17 11:00:12 2011
paulh    pts/11            Sat Aug 14 09:22:14 2010
```

Performing updates on lastlog is similarly a matter of opening the file, seeking to the correct location, and performing a write.

Since the lastlog file is indexed by user ID, it is not possible to distinguish logins under different usernames that have the same user ID. (In Section 8.1, we noted that it is possible, though unusual, to have multiple login names with the same user ID.)

Listing 40-4: Displaying information from the lastlog file

———————————————————————————— loginacct/view_lastlog.c

```c
#include <time.h>
#include <lastlog.h>
#include <paths.h>                      /* Definition of _PATH_LASTLOG */
#include <fcntl.h>
#include "ugid_functions.h"             /* Declaration of userIdFromName() */
#include "tlpi_hdr.h"

int
main(int argc, char *argv[])
{
    struct lastlog llog;
    int fd, j;
    uid_t uid;

    if (argc > 1 && strcmp(argv[1], "--help") == 0)
        usageErr("%s [username...]\n", argv[0]);

    fd = open(_PATH_LASTLOG, O_RDONLY);
    if (fd == -1)
        errExit("open");

    for (j = 1; j < argc; j++) {
        uid = userIdFromName(argv[j]);
        if (uid == -1) {
            printf("No such user: %s\n", argv[j]);
            continue;
        }

        if (lseek(fd, uid * sizeof(struct lastlog), SEEK_SET) == -1)
            errExit("lseek");

        if (read(fd, &llog, sizeof(struct lastlog)) <= 0) {
            printf("read failed for %s\n", argv[j]);    /* EOF or error */
            continue;
        }

        time_t ll_time = llog.ll_time;
        printf("%-8.8s %-6.6s %-20.20s %s", argv[j], llog.ll_line,
                llog.ll_host, ctime(&ll_time));
    }

    close(fd);
    exit(EXIT_SUCCESS);
}
```

———————————————————————————— loginacct/view_lastlog.c

40.8 Summary

Login accounting records the users currently logged in, as well as all past logins. This information is maintained in three files: the utmp file, which maintains a record of all currently logged-in users; the wtmp file, which is an audit trail of all logins and logouts; and the lastlog file, which records the time of last login for each user. Various commands, such as *who* and *last*, use the information in these files.

The C library provides functions to retrieve and update the information in the login accounting files. Applications providing login services should use these functions to update the login accounting files, so that commands depending on this information operate correctly.

Further information

Aside from the *utmp(5)* manual page, the most useful place to find further information about the login accounting functions is in the source code of the various applications that use these functions. See, for example, the sources of *mingetty* (or *agetty*), *login*, *init*, *telnet*, *ssh*, and *ftp*.

40.9 Exercises

40-1. Implement *getlogin()*. As noted in Section 40.5, *getlogin()* may not work correctly for processes running under some software terminal emulators; in that case, test from a virtual console instead.

40-2. Modify the program in Listing 40-3 (utmpx_login.c) so that it updates the lastlog file in addition to the utmp and wtmp files.

40-3. Read the manual pages for *login(3)*, *logout(3)*, and *logwtmp(3)*. Implement these functions.

40-4. Implement a simple version of *who(1)*.

41

FUNDAMENTALS OF SHARED LIBRARIES

Shared libraries are a technique for placing library functions into a single unit that can be shared by multiple processes at run time. This technique can save both disk space and RAM. This chapter covers the fundamentals of shared libraries. The next chapter covers a number of advanced features of shared libraries.

41.1 Object Libraries

One way of building a program is simply to compile each of its source files to produce corresponding object files, and then link all of these object files together to produce the executable program, like so:

```
$ cc -g -c prog.c mod1.c mod2.c mod3.c
$ cc -g -o prog_nolib prog.o mod1.o mod2.o mod3.o
```

> Linking is actually performed by the separate linker program, *ld*. When we link a program using the *cc* (or *gcc*) command, the compiler invokes *ld* behind the scenes. On Linux, the linker should always be invoked indirectly via *gcc*, since *gcc* ensures that *ld* is invoked with the correct options and links the program against the correct library files.

In many cases, however, we may have source files that are used by several programs. As a first step toward saving ourselves some work, we could compile these source files just once, and then link them into different executables as required. Although this technique saves us compilation time, it still suffers from the disadvantage that we must name all of the object files during the link phase. Furthermore, our directories may be inconveniently cluttered with a large number of object files.

To get around these problems, we can group a set of object files into a single unit, known as an *object library*. Object libraries are of two types: *static* and *shared*. Shared libraries are the more modern type of object library, and provide several advantages over static libraries, as we describe in Section 41.3.

An aside: including debugger information when compiling a program

In the *cc* command shown above, we used the *-g* option to include debugging information in the compiled program. In general, it is a good idea to always create programs and libraries that allow debugging. (In earlier times, debugging information was sometimes omitted so that the resulting executable used less disk and RAM, but nowadays disk and RAM are cheap.)

In addition, on some architectures, such as x86-32, the *-fomit-frame-pointer* option should not be specified because this makes debugging impossible. (On some architectures, such as x86-64, this option is enabled by default since it doesn't prevent debugging.) For the same reason, executables and libraries should not be stripped of debugging information using *strip(1)*.

41.2   Static Libraries

Before starting our discussion of shared libraries, we begin with a brief description of static libraries in order to make clear the differences and advantages of shared libraries.

Static libraries, also known as *archives*, were the first type of library to be provided on UNIX systems. They provide the following benefits:

- We can place a set of commonly used object files into a single library file that can then be used to build multiple executables, without needing to recompile the original source files when building each application.

- Link commands become simpler. Instead of listing a long series of object files on the link command line, we specify just the name of the static library. The linker knows how to search the static library and extract the objects required by the executable.

Creating and maintaining a static library

In effect, a static library is simply a file holding copies of all of the object files added to it. The archive also records various attributes of each of the component object files, including file permissions, numeric user and group IDs, and last modification time. By convention, static libraries have names of the form lib*name*.a.

A static library is created and maintained using the *ar(1)* command, which has the following general form:

```
$ ar options archive object-file...
```

The *options* argument consists of a series of letters, one of which is the *operation code*, while the others are *modifiers* that influence the way the operation is carried out. Some commonly used operation codes are the following:

- *r* (replace): Insert an object file into the archive, replacing any previous object file of the same name. This is the standard method for creating and updating an archive. Thus, we might build an archive with the following commands:

  ```
  $ cc -g -c mod1.c mod2.c mod3.c
  $ ar r libdemo.a mod1.o mod2.o mod3.o
  $ rm mod1.o mod2.o mod3.o
  ```

  As shown above, after building the library, we can delete the original object files if desired, since they are no longer required.

- *t* (table of contents): Display a table of contents of the archive. By default, this lists just the names of the object files in the archive. By adding the *v* (verbose) modifier, we additionally see all of the other attributes recorded in the archive for each object file, as in the following example:

  ```
  $ ar tv libdemo.a
  rw-r--r-- 1000/100 1001016 Nov 15 12:26 2009 mod1.o
  rw-r--r-- 1000/100 406668 Nov 15 12:21 2009 mod2.o
  rw-r--r-- 1000/100  46672 Nov 15 12:21 2009 mod3.o
  ```

  The additional attributes that we see for each object are, from left to right, its permissions when it was added to the archive, its user ID and group ID, its size, and the date and time when it was last modified.

- *d* (delete): Delete a named module from the archive, as in this example:

  ```
  $ ar d libdemo.a mod3.o
  ```

Using a static library

We can link a program against a static library in two ways. The first is to name the static library as part of the link command, as in the following:

```
$ cc -g -c prog.c
$ cc -g -o prog prog.o libdemo.a
```

Alternatively, we can place the library in one of the standard directories searched by the linker (e.g., /usr/lib), and then specify the library name (i.e., the filename of the library without the lib prefix and .a suffix) using the *-l* option:

```
$ cc -g -o prog prog.o -ldemo
```

If the library resides in a directory not normally searched by the linker, we can specify that the linker should search this additional directory using the *-L* option:

```
$ cc -g -o prog prog.o -Lmylibdir -ldemo
```

Although a static library may contain many object modules, the linker includes only those modules that the program requires.

Having linked the program, we can run it in the usual way:

```
$ ./prog
Called mod1-x1
Called mod2-x2
```

41.3 Overview of Shared Libraries

When a program is built by linking against a static library (or, for that matter, without using a library at all), the resulting executable file includes copies of all of the object files that were linked into the program. Thus, when several different executables use the same object modules, each executable has its own copy of the object modules. This redundancy of code has several disadvantages:

- Disk space is wasted storing multiple copies of the same object modules. Such wastage can be considerable.

- If several different programs using the same modules are running at the same time, then each holds separate copies of the object modules in virtual memory, thus increasing the overall virtual memory demands on the system.

- If a change is required (perhaps a security or bug fix) to an object module in a static library, then all executables using that module must be relinked in order to incorporate the change. This disadvantage is further compounded by the fact that the system administrator needs to be aware of which applications were linked against the library.

Shared libraries were designed to address these shortcomings. The key idea of a shared library is that a single copy of the object modules is shared by all programs requiring the modules. The object modules are not copied into the linked executable; instead, a single copy of the library is loaded into memory at run time, when the first program requiring modules from the shared library is started. When other programs using the same shared library are later executed, they use the copy of the library that is already loaded into memory. The use of shared libraries means that executable programs require less space on disk and (when running) in virtual memory.

> Although the code of a shared library is shared among multiple processes, its variables are not. Each process that uses the library has its own copies of the global and static variables that are defined within the library.

Shared libraries provide the following further advantages:

- Because overall program size is smaller, in some cases, programs can be loaded into memory and started more quickly. This point holds true only for large shared libraries that are already in use by another program. The first program to load a shared library will actually take longer to start, since the shared library must be found and loaded into memory.

- Since object modules are not copied into the executable files, but instead maintained centrally in the shared library, it is possible (subject to limitations described in Section 41.8) to make changes to the object modules without requiring programs to be relinked in order to see the changes. Such changes can be carried out even while running programs are using an existing version of the shared library.

The principal costs of this added functionality are the following:

- Shared libraries are more complex than static libraries, both at the conceptual level, and at the practical level of creating shared libraries and building the programs that use them.

- Shared libraries must be compiled to use position-independent code (described in Section 41.4.2), which has a performance overhead on most architectures because it requires the use of an extra register ([Hubička, 2003]).

- *Symbol relocation* must be performed at run time. During symbol relocation, references to each symbol (a variable or function) in a shared library need to be modified to correspond to the actual run-time location at which the symbol is placed in virtual memory. Because of this relocation process, a program using a shared library may take a little more time to execute than its statically linked equivalent.

> One further use of shared libraries is as a building block in the *Java Native Interface* (JNI), which allows Java code to directly access features of the underlying operating system by calling C functions within a shared library. For further information, see [Liang, 1999] and [Rochkind, 2004].

41.4 Creating and Using Shared Libraries—A First Pass

To begin understanding how shared libraries operate, we look at the minimum sequence of steps required to build and use a shared library. For the moment, we'll ignore the convention that is normally used to name shared library files. This convention, described in Section 41.6, allows programs to automatically load the most up-to-date version of the libraries they require, and also allows multiple incompatible versions (so-called *major versions*) of a library to coexist peacefully.

In this chapter, we concern ourselves only with Executable and Linking Format (ELF) shared libraries, since ELF is the format employed for executables and shared libraries in modern versions of Linux, as well as in many other UNIX implementations.

> ELF supersedes the older *a.out* and *COFF* formats.

41.4.1 Creating a Shared Library

In order to build a shared version of the static library we created earlier, we perform the following steps:

```
$ gcc -g -c -fPIC -Wall mod1.c mod2.c mod3.c
$ gcc -g -shared -o libfoo.so mod1.o mod2.o mod3.o
```

The first of these commands creates the three object modules that are to be put into the library. (We explain the *cc −fPIC* option in the next section.) The *cc −shared* command creates a shared library containing the three object modules.

By convention, shared libraries have the prefix lib and the suffix .so (for *shared object*).

In our examples, we use the *gcc* command, rather than the equivalent *cc* command, to emphasize that the command-line options we are using to create shared libraries are compiler-dependent. Using a different C compiler on another UNIX implementation will probably require different options.

Note that it is possible to compile the source files and create the shared library in a single command:

```
$ gcc -g -fPIC -Wall mod1.c mod2.c mod3.c -shared -o libfoo.so
```

However, to clearly distinguish the compilation and library building steps, we'll write the two as separate commands in the examples shown in this chapter.

Unlike static libraries, it is not possible to add or remove individual object modules from a previously built shared library. As with normal executables, the object files within a shared library no longer maintain distinct identities.

41.4.2 Position-Independent Code

The *cc –fPIC* option specifies that the compiler should generate *position-independent code*. This changes the way that the compiler generates code for operations such as accessing global, static, and external variables; accessing string constants; and taking the addresses of functions. These changes allow the code to be located at any virtual address at run time. This is necessary for shared libraries, since there is no way of knowing at link time where the shared library code will be located in memory. (The run-time memory location of a shared library depends on various factors, such as the amount of memory already taken up by the program that is loading the library and which other shared libraries the program has already loaded.)

On Linux/x86-32, it is possible to create a shared library using modules compiled without the *–fPIC* option. However, doing so loses some of the benefits of shared libraries, since pages of program text containing position-dependent memory references are not shared across processes. On some architectures, it is impossible to build shared libraries without the *–fPIC* option.

In order to determine whether an existing object file has been compiled with the *–fPIC* option, we can check for the presence of the name _GLOBAL_OFFSET_TABLE_ in the object file's symbol table, using either of the following commands:

```
$ nm mod1.o | grep _GLOBAL_OFFSET_TABLE_
$ readelf -s mod1.o | grep _GLOBAL_OFFSET_TABLE_
```

Conversely, if either of the following equivalent commands yields any output, then the specified shared library includes at least one object module that was not compiled with *–fPIC*:

```
$ objdump --all-headers libfoo.so | grep TEXTREL
$ readelf -d libfoo.so | grep TEXTREL
```

The string TEXTREL indicates the presence of an object module whose text segment contains a reference that requires run-time relocation.

We say more about the *nm*, *readelf*, and *objdump* commands in Section 41.5.

41.4.3 Using a Shared Library

In order to use a shared library, two steps must occur that are not required for programs that use static libraries:

- Since the executable file no longer contains copies of the object files that it requires, it must have some mechanism for identifying the shared library that it needs at run time. This is done by embedding the name of the shared library inside the executable during the link phase. (In ELF parlance, the library dependency is recorded in a DT_NEEDED tag in the executable.) The list of all of a program's shared library dependencies is referred to as its *dynamic dependency list*.

- At run time, there must be some mechanism for resolving the embedded library name—that is, for finding the shared library file corresponding to the name specified in the executable file—and then loading the library into memory, if it is not already present.

Embedding the name of the library inside the executable happens automatically when we link our program with a shared library:

```
$ gcc -g -Wall -o prog prog.c libfoo.so
```

If we now attempt to run our program, we receive the following error message:

```
$ ./prog
./prog: error in loading shared libraries: libfoo.so: cannot
open shared object file: No such file or directory
```

This brings us to the second required step: *dynamic linking*, which is the task of resolving the embedded library name at run time. This task is performed by the *dynamic linker* (also called the *dynamic linking loader* or the *run-time linker*). The dynamic linker is itself a shared library, named /lib/ld-linux.so.2, which is employed by every ELF executable that uses shared libraries.

> The pathname /lib/ld-linux.so.2 is normally a symbolic link pointing to the dynamic linker executable file. This file has the name ld-*version*.so, where *version* is the *glibc* version installed on the system—for example, ld-2.11.so. The pathname of the dynamic linker differs on some architectures. For example, on IA-64, the dynamic linker symbolic link is named /lib/ld-linux-ia64.so.2.

The dynamic linker examines the list of shared libraries required by a program and uses a set of predefined rules in order to find the library files in the file system. Some of these rules specify a set of standard directories in which shared libraries normally reside. For example, many shared libraries reside in /lib and /usr/lib. The error message above occurs because our library resides in the current working directory, which is not part of the standard list searched by the dynamic linker.

> Some architectures (e.g., zSeries, PowerPC64, and x86-64) support execution of both 32-bit and 64-bit programs. On such systems, the 32-bit libraries reside in */lib subdirectories, and the 64-bit libraries reside in */lib64 subdirectories.

The LD_LIBRARY_PATH environment variable

One way of informing the dynamic linker that a shared library resides in a non-standard directory is to specify that directory as part of a colon-separated list of directories in the LD_LIBRARY_PATH environment variable. (Semicolons can also be used to separate the directories, in which case the list must be quoted to prevent the shell from interpreting the semicolons.) If LD_LIBRARY_PATH is defined, then the dynamic linker searches for the shared library in the directories it lists before looking in the standard library directories. (Later, we'll see that a production application should never rely on LD_LIBRARY_PATH, but for now, this variable provides us with a simple way of getting started with shared libraries.) Thus, we can run our program with the following command:

```
$ LD_LIBRARY_PATH=. ./prog
Called mod1-x1
Called mod2-x2
```

The (*bash*, Korn, and Bourne) shell syntax used in the above command creates an environment variable definition within the process executing *prog*. This definition tells the dynamic linker to search for shared libraries in ., the current working directory.

> An empty directory specification in the LD_LIBRARY_PATH list (e.g., the middle specification in *dirx::diry*) is equivalent to ., the current working directory (but note that setting LD_LIBRARY_PATH to an empty string does not achieve the same result). We avoid this usage (SUSv3 discourages the corresponding usage in the PATH environment variable).

Static linking and dynamic linking contrasted

Commonly, the term *linking* is used to describe the use of the linker, *ld*, to combine one or more compiled object files into a single executable file. Sometimes, the term *static* linking is used to distinguish this step from *dynamic* linking, the run-time loading of the shared libraries used by an executable. (Static linking is sometimes also referred to as *link editing*, and a static linker such as *ld* is sometimes referred to as a link editor.) Every program—including those that use shared libraries—goes through a static-linking phase. At run time, a program that employs shared libraries additionally undergoes dynamic linking.

41.4.4 The Shared Library Soname

In the example presented so far, the name that was embedded in the executable and sought by the dynamic linker at run time was the actual name of the shared library file. This is referred to as the library's *real name*. However, it is possible—in fact, usual—to create a shared library with a kind of alias, called a *soname* (the DT_SONAME tag in ELF parlance).

If a shared library has a soname, then, during static linking, the soname is embedded in the executable file instead of the real name, and subsequently used by the dynamic linker when searching for the library at run time. The purpose of the soname is to provide a level of indirection that permits an executable to use, at run time, a version of the shared library that is different from (but compatible with) the library against which it was linked.

In Section 41.6, we'll look at the conventions used for the shared library real name and soname. For now, we show a simplified example to demonstrate the principles.

The first step in using a soname is to specify it when the shared library is created:

```
$ gcc -g -c -fPIC -Wall mod1.c mod2.c mod3.c
$ gcc -g -shared -Wl,-soname,libbar.so -o libfoo.so mod1.o mod2.o mod3.o
```

The *–Wl,–soname,libbar.so* option is an instruction to the linker to mark the shared library libfoo.so with the soname libbar.so.

If we want to determine the soname of an existing shared library, we can use either of the following commands:

```
$ objdump -p libfoo.so | grep SONAME
  SONAME        libbar.so
$ readelf -d libfoo.so | grep SONAME
 0x0000000e (SONAME)       Library soname: [libbar.so]
```

Having created a shared library with a soname, we then create the executable as usual:

```
$ gcc -g -Wall -o prog prog.c libfoo.so
```

However, this time, the linker detects that the library libfoo.so contains the soname libbar.so and embeds the latter name inside the executable.

Now when we attempt to run the program, this is what we see:

```
$ LD_LIBRARY_PATH=. ./prog
prog: error in loading shared libraries: libbar.so: cannot open
shared object file: No such file or directory
```

The problem here is that the dynamic linker can't find anything named libbar.so. When using a soname, one further step is required: we must create a symbolic link from the soname to the real name of the library. This symbolic link must be created in one of the directories searched by the dynamic linker. Thus, we could run our program as follows:

```
$ ln -s libfoo.so libbar.so        Create soname symbolic link in current directory
$ LD_LIBRARY_PATH=. ./prog
Called mod1-x1
Called mod2-x2
```

Figure 41-1 shows the compilation and linking steps involved in producing a shared library with an embedded soname, linking a program against that shared library, and creating the soname symbolic link needed to run the program.

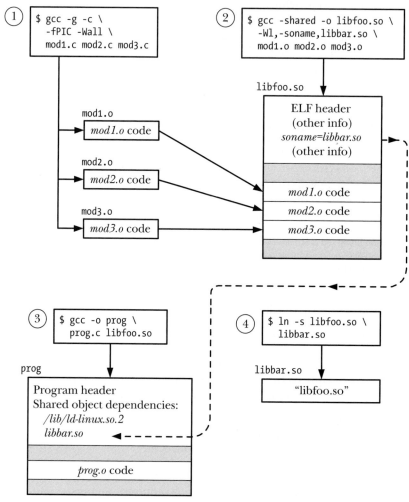

Figure 41-1: Creating a shared library and linking a program against it

Figure 41-2 shows the steps that occur when the program created in Figure 41-1 is loaded into memory in preparation for execution.

> To find out which shared libraries a process is currently using, we can list the contents of the corresponding Linux-specific /proc/*PID*/maps file (Section 48.5).

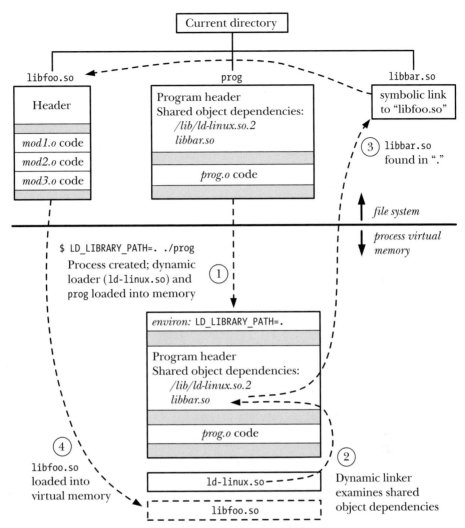

Figure 41-2: Execution of a program that loads a shared library

41.5 Useful Tools for Working with Shared Libraries

In this section, we briefly describe a few tools that are useful for analyzing shared libraries, executable files, and compiled object (.o) files.

The *ldd* command

The *ldd(1)* (list dynamic dependencies) command displays the shared libraries that a program (or a shared library) requires to run. Here's an example:

```
$ ldd prog
        libdemo.so.1 => /usr/lib/libdemo.so.1 (0x40019000)
        libc.so.6 => /lib/tls/libc.so.6 (0x4017b000)
        /lib/ld-linux.so.2 => /lib/ld-linux.so.2 (0x40000000)
```

The *ldd* command resolves each library reference (employing the same search conventions as the dynamic linker) and displays the results in the following form:

library-name => *resolves-to-path*

For most ELF executables, *ldd* will list entries for at least ld-linux.so.2, the dynamic linker, and libc.so.6, the standard C library.

> The name of the C library is different on some architectures. For example, this library is named libc.so.6.1 on IA-64 and Alpha.

The *objdump* and *readelf* commands

The *objdump* command can be used to obtain various information—including disassembled binary machine code—from an executable file, compiled object, or shared library. It can also be used to display information from the headers of the various ELF sections of these files; in this usage, it resembles *readelf*, which displays similar information, but in a different format. Sources of further information about *objdump* and *readelf* are listed at the end of this chapter.

The *nm* command

The *nm* command lists the set of symbols defined within an object library or executable program. One use of this command is to find out which of several libraries defines a symbol. For example, to find out which library defines the *crypt()* function, we could do the following:

```
$ nm -A /usr/lib/lib*.so 2> /dev/null | grep ' crypt$'
/usr/lib/libcrypt.so:00007080 W crypt
```

The *–A* option to *nm* specifies that the library name should be listed at the start of each line displaying a symbol. This is necessary because, by default, *nm* lists the library name once, and then, on subsequent lines, all of the symbols it contains, which isn't useful for the kind of filtering shown in the above example. In addition, we discard standard error output in order to hide error messages about files in formats unrecognized by *nm*. From the above output, we can see that *crypt()* is defined in the *libcrypt* library.

41.6 Shared Library Versions and Naming Conventions

Let's consider what is entailed by shared library versioning. Typically, successive versions of a shared library are compatible with one another, meaning that the functions in each module present the same calling interface and are semantically equivalent (i.e., they achieve identical results). Such differing but compatible versions are referred to as *minor versions* of a shared library. Occasionally, however, it is necessary to create a new *major version* of a library—one that is incompatible with a previous version. (In Section 41.8, we'll see more precisely what may cause such incompatibilities.) At the same time, it must still be possible to continue running programs that require the older version of the library.

To deal with these versioning requirements, a standard naming convention is employed for shared library real names and sonames.

Real names, sonames, and linker names

Each incompatible version of a shared library is distinguished by a unique *major version identifier*, which forms part of its real name. By convention, the major version identifier takes the form of a number that is sequentially incremented with each incompatible release of the library. In addition to the major version identifier, the real name also includes a *minor version identifier*, which distinguishes compatible minor versions within the library major version. The real name employs the format convention lib*name*.so.*major-id*.*minor-id*.

Like the major version identifier, the minor version identifier can be any string, but, by convention, it is either a number, or two numbers separated by a dot, with the first number identifying the minor version, and the second number indicating a patch level or revision number within the minor version. Some examples of real names of shared libraries are the following:

```
libdemo.so.1.0.1
libdemo.so.1.0.2        Minor version, compatible with version 1.0.1
libdemo.so.2.0.0        New major version, incompatible with version 1.*
libreadline.so.5.0
```

The soname of the shared library includes the same major version identifier as its corresponding real library name, but excludes the minor version identifier. Thus, the soname has the form lib*name*.so.*major-id*.

Usually, the soname is created as a relative symbolic link in the directory that contains the real name. The following are some examples of sonames, along with the real names to which they might be symbolically linked:

```
libdemo.so.1        -> libdemo.so.1.0.2
libdemo.so.2        -> libdemo.so.2.0.0
libreadline.so.5    -> libreadline.so.5.0
```

For a particular major version of a shared library, there may be several library files distinguished by different minor version identifiers. Normally, the soname corresponding to each major library version points to the most recent minor version within the major version (as shown in the above examples for libdemo.so). This setup allows for the correct versioning semantics during the run-time operation of shared libraries. Because the static-linking phase embeds a copy of the (minor version–independent) soname in the executable, and the soname symbolic link may subsequently be modified to point to a newer (minor) version of the shared library, it is possible to ensure that an executable loads the most up-to-date minor version of the library at run time. Furthermore, since different major versions of a library have different sonames, they can happily coexist and be accessed by the programs that require them.

In addition to the real name and soname, a third name is usually defined for each shared library: the *linker name*, which is used when linking an executable against the shared library. The linker name is a symbolic link containing just the library name without the major or minor version identifiers, and thus has the form lib*name*.so. The linker name allows us to construct version-independent link commands that automatically operate with the correct (i.e., most up-to-date) version of the shared library.

Typically, the linker name is created in the same directory as the file to which it refers. It can be linked either to the real name or to the soname of the most recent major version of the library. Usually, a link to the soname is preferable, so that changes to the soname are automatically reflected in the linker name. (In Section 41.7, we'll see that the *ldconfig* program automates the task of keeping sonames up to date, and thus implicitly maintains linker names if we use the convention just described.)

If we want to link a program against an older major version of a shared library, we can't use the linker name. Instead, as part of the link command, we would need to indicate the required (major) version by specifying a particular real name or soname.

The following are some examples of linker names:

```
libdemo.so        -> libdemo.so.2
libreadline.so    -> libreadline.so.5
```

Table 41-1 summarizes information about the shared library real name, soname, and linker name, and Figure 41-3 portrays the relationship between these names.

Table 41-1: Summary of shared library names

Name	Format	Description
real name	lib*name*.so.*maj*.*min*	File holding library code; one instance per major-plus-minor version of the library.
soname	lib*name*.so.*maj*	One instance per major version of library; embedded in executable at link time; used at run time to find library via a symbolic link with same name that points to corresponding (most up-to-date) real name.
linker name	lib*name*.so	Symbolic link to latest real name or (more usually) latest soname; single instance; allows construction of version-independent link commands.

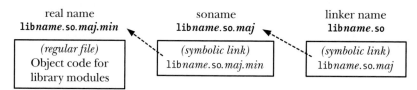

Figure 41-3: Conventional arrangement of shared library names

Creating a shared library using standard conventions

Putting all of the above information together, we now show how to build our demonstration library following the standard conventions. First, we create the object files:

```
$ gcc -g -c -fPIC -Wall mod1.c mod2.c mod3.c
```

Then we create the shared library with the real name libdemo.so.1.0.1 and the soname libdemo.so.1.

```
$ gcc -g -shared -Wl,-soname,libdemo.so.1 -o libdemo.so.1.0.1 \
        mod1.o mod2.o mod3.o
```

Next, we create appropriate symbolic links for the soname and linker name:

```
$ ln -s libdemo.so.1.0.1 libdemo.so.1
$ ln -s libdemo.so.1 libdemo.so
```

We can employ *ls* to verify the setup (with *awk* used to select the fields of interest):

```
$ ls -l libdemo.so* | awk '{print $1, $9, $10, $11}'
lrwxrwxrwx libdemo.so -> libdemo.so.1
lrwxrwxrwx libdemo.so.1 -> libdemo.so.1.0.1
-rwxr-xr-x libdemo.so.1.0.1
```

Then we can build our executable using the linker name (note that the link command makes no mention of version numbers), and run the program as usual:

```
$ gcc -g -Wall -o prog prog.c -L. -ldemo
$ LD_LIBRARY_PATH=. ./prog
Called mod1-x1
Called mod2-x2
```

41.7 Installing Shared Libraries

In the examples up to now, we created a shared library in a user-private directory, and then used the LD_LIBRARY_PATH environment variable to ensure that the dynamic linker searched that directory. Both privileged and unprivileged users may use this technique. However, this technique should not be employed in production applications. More usually, a shared library and its associated symbolic links are installed in one of a number of standard library directories, in particular, one of the following:

- /usr/lib, the directory in which most standard libraries are installed;
- /lib, the directory into which libraries required during system startup should be installed (since, during system startup, /usr/lib may not be mounted yet);
- /usr/local/lib, the directory into which nonstandard or experimental libraries should be installed (placing libraries in this directory is also useful if /usr/lib is a network mount shared among multiple systems and we want to install a library just for use on this system); or
- one of the directories listed in /etc/ld.so.conf (described shortly).

In most cases, copying a file into one of these directories requires superuser privilege.

After installation, the symbolic links for the soname and linker name must be created, usually as relative symbolic links in the same directory as the library file. Thus, to install our demonstration library in /usr/lib (whose permissions only allow updates by *root*), we would do the following:

```
$ su
Password:
# mv libdemo.so.1.0.1 /usr/lib
```

```
# cd /usr/lib
# ln -s libdemo.so.1.0.1 libdemo.so.1
# ln -s libdemo.so.1 libdemo.so
```

The last two lines in this shell session create the soname and linker name symbolic links.

ldconfig

The *ldconfig(8)* program addresses two potential problems with shared libraries:

- Shared libraries can reside in a variety of directories. If the dynamic linker needed to search all of these directories in order to find a library, then loading libraries could be very slow.

- As new versions of libraries are installed or old versions are removed, the soname symbolic links may become out of date.

The *ldconfig* program solves these problems by performing two tasks:

1. It searches a standard set of directories and creates or updates a cache file, /etc/ld.so.cache, to contain a list of the (latest minor versions of each of the) major library versions in all of these directories. The dynamic linker in turn uses this cache file when resolving library names at run time. To build the cache, *ldconfig* searches the directories specified in the file /etc/ld.so.conf and then /lib and /usr/lib. The /etc/ld.so.conf file consists of a list of directory pathnames (these should be specified as absolute pathnames), separated by newlines, spaces, tabs, commas, or colons. In some distributions, the directory /usr/local/lib is included in this list. (If not, we may need to add it manually.)

   The command *ldconfig –p* displays the current contents of /etc/ld.so.cache.

2. It examines the latest minor version (i.e., the version with the highest minor number) of each major version of each library to find the embedded soname and then creates (or updates) relative symbolic links for each soname in the same directory.

In order to correctly perform these actions, *ldconfig* expects libraries to be named according to the conventions described earlier (i.e., library real names include major and minor identifiers that increase appropriately from one library version to the next).

By default, *ldconfig* performs both of the above actions. Command-line options can be used to selectively inhibit either action: the *–N* option prevents rebuilding of the cache, and the *–X* option inhibits the creation of the soname symbolic links. In addition, the *–v* (*verbose*) option causes *ldconfig* to display output describing its actions.

We should run *ldconfig* whenever a new library is installed, an existing library is updated or removed, or the list of directories in /etc/ld.so.conf is changed.

As an example of the operation of *ldconfig*, suppose we wanted to install two different major versions of a library. We would do this as follows:

```
$ su
Password:
# mv libdemo.so.1.0.1 libdemo.so.2.0.0 /usr/lib
```

```
# ldconfig -v | grep libdemo
        libdemo.so.1 -> libdemo.so.1.0.1 (changed)
        libdemo.so.2 -> libdemo.so.2.0.0 (changed)
```

Above, we filter the output of *ldconfig*, so that we see just the information relating to libraries named libdemo.

Next, we list the files named libdemo in /usr/lib to verify the setup of the soname symbolic links:

```
# cd /usr/lib
# ls -l libdemo* | awk '{print $1, $9, $10, $11}'
lrwxrwxrwx libdemo.so.1 -> libdemo.so.1.0.1
-rwxr-xr-x libdemo.so.1.0.1
lrwxrwxrwx libdemo.so.2 -> libdemo.so.2.0.0
-rwxr-xr-x libdemo.so.2.0.0
```

We must still create the symbolic link for the linker name, as shown in the next command:

```
# ln -s libdemo.so.2 libdemo.so
```

However, if we install a new 2.*x* minor version of our library, then, since the linker name points to the latest soname, *ldconfig* has the effect of also keeping the linker name up to date, as the following example shows:

```
# mv libdemo.so.2.0.1 /usr/lib
# ldconfig -v | grep libdemo
        libdemo.so.1 -> libdemo.so.1.0.1
        libdemo.so.2 -> libdemo.so.2.0.1 (changed)
```

If we are building and using a private library (i.e., one that is not installed in one of the standard directories), we can have *ldconfig* create the soname symbolic link for us by using the −*n* option. This specifies that *ldconfig* should process only libraries in the directories on the command line and should not update the cache file. In the following example, we use *ldconfig* to process libraries in the current working directory:

```
$ gcc -g -c -fPIC -Wall mod1.c mod2.c mod3.c
$ gcc -g -shared -Wl,-soname,libdemo.so.1 -o libdemo.so.1.0.1 \
        mod1.o mod2.o mod3.o
$ /sbin/ldconfig -nv .
.:
        libdemo.so.1 -> libdemo.so.1.0.1
$ ls -l libdemo.so* | awk '{print $1, $9, $10, $11}'
lrwxrwxrwx libdemo.so.1 -> libdemo.so.1.0.1
-rwxr-xr-x libdemo.so.1.0.1
```

In the above example, we specified the full pathname when running *ldconfig*, because we were using an unprivileged account whose PATH environment variable did not include the /sbin directory.

41.8 Compatible Versus Incompatible Libraries

Over time, we may need to make changes to the code of a shared library. Such changes result in a new version of the library that is either *compatible* with previous version(s), meaning that we need to change only the minor version identifier of the library's real name, or *incompatible*, meaning that we must define a new major version of the library.

A change to a library is compatible with an existing library version if *all* of the following conditions hold true:

- The semantics of each public function and variable in the library remain unchanged. In other words, each function keeps the same argument list, and continues to produce its specified effect on global variables and returned arguments, and returns the same result value. Thus, changes that result in an improvement in performance or fix a bug (resulting in closer conformance to specified behavior) can be regarded as compatible changes.
- No function or variable in the library's public API is removed. It is, however, compatible to add new functions and variables to the public API.
- Structures allocated within and returned by each function remain unchanged. Similarly, public structures exported by the library remain unchanged. One exception to this rule is that, under certain circumstances, new items may be added to the end of an existing structure, though even this may be subject to pitfalls if, for example, the calling program tries to allocate arrays of this structure type. Library designers sometimes circumvent this limitation by defining exported structures to be larger than is required in the initial release of the library, with some extra padding fields being "reserved for future use."

If none of these conditions is violated, then the new library name can be updated by adjusting the minor version of the existing name. Otherwise, a new major version of the library should be created.

41.9 Upgrading Shared Libraries

One of the advantages of shared libraries is that a new major or minor version of a library can be installed even while running programs are using an existing version. All that we need to do is create the new library version, install it in the appropriate directory, and update the soname and linker name symbolic links as required (or, more usually, have *ldconfig* do the job for us). To produce a new minor version (i.e., a compatible upgrade) of the shared library /usr/lib/libdemo.1.0.1, we would do the following:

```
$ su
Password:
# gcc -g -c -fPIC -Wall mod1.c mod2.c mod3.c
# gcc -g -shared -Wl,-soname,libdemo.so.1 -o libdemo.so.1.0.2 \
        mod1.o mod2.o mod3.o
# mv libdemo.so.1.0.2 /usr/lib
# ldconfig -v | grep libdemo
        libdemo.so.1 -> libdemo.so.1.0.2 (changed)
```

Assuming the linker name was already correctly set up (i.e., to point to the library soname), we would not need to modify it.

Already running programs will continue to use the previous minor version of the shared library. Only when they are terminated and restarted will they too use the new minor version of the shared library.

If we subsequently wanted to create a new major version (2.0.0) of the shared library, we would do the following:

```
# gcc -g -c -fPIC -Wall mod1.c mod2.c mod3.c
# gcc -g -shared -Wl,-soname,libdemo.so.2 -o libdemo.so.2.0.0 \
        mod1.o mod2.o mod3.o
# mv libdemo.so.2.0.0 /usr/lib
# ldconfig -v | grep libdemo
        libdemo.so.1 -> libdemo.so.1.0.2
        libdemo.so.2 -> libdemo.so.2.0.0 (changed)
# cd /usr/lib
# ln -sf libdemo.so.2 libdemo.so
```

As can be seen in the above output, *ldconfig* automatically creates a soname symbolic link for the new major version. However, as the last command shows, we must manually update the linker name symbolic link.

41.10 Specifying Library Search Directories in an Object File

We have already seen two ways of informing the dynamic linker of the location of shared libraries: using the LD_LIBRARY_PATH environment variable and installing a shared library into one of the standard library directories (/lib, /usr/lib, or one of the directories listed in /etc/ld.so.conf).

There is a third way: during the static editing phase, we can insert into the executable a list of directories that should be searched at run time for shared libraries. This is useful if we have libraries that reside in fixed locations that are not among the standard locations searched by the dynamic linker. To do this, we employ the *–rpath* linker option when creating an executable:

```
$ gcc -g -Wall -Wl,-rpath,/home/mtk/pdir -o prog prog.c libdemo.so
```

The above command copies the string */home/mtk/pdir* into the run-time library path (*rpath*) list of the executable *prog*, so, that when the program is run, the dynamic linker will also search this directory when resolving shared library references.

If necessary, the *–rpath* option can be specified multiple times; all of the directories are concatenated into a single ordered *rpath* list placed in the executable file. Alternatively, multiple directories can be specified as a colon-separated list within a single *–rpath* option. At run time, the dynamic linker searches the directories in the order they were specified in the *–rpath* option(s).

> An alternative to the *–rpath* option is the LD_RUN_PATH environment variable. This variable can be assigned a string containing a series of colon-separated directories that are to be used as the *rpath* list when building the executable file. LD_RUN_PATH is employed only if the *–rpath* option is not specified when building the executable.

Using the *–rpath* linker option when building a shared library

The *–rpath* linker option can also be useful when building a shared library. Suppose we have one shared library, libx1.so, that depends on another, libx2.so, as shown in Figure 41-4. Suppose also that these libraries reside in the nonstandard directories d1 and d2, respectively. We now go through the steps required to build these libraries and the program that uses them.

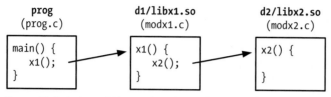

prog (prog.c)	d1/libx1.so (modx1.c)	d2/libx2.so (modx2.c)

Figure 41-4: A shared library that depends on another shared library

First, we build libx2.so, in the directory pdir/d2. (To keep the example simple, we dispense with library version numbering and explicit sonames.)

```
$ cd /home/mtk/pdir/d2
$ gcc -g -c -fPIC -Wall modx2.c
$ gcc -g -shared -o libx2.so modx2.o
```

Next, we build libx1.so, in the directory pdir/d1. Since libx1.so depends on libx2.so, which is not in a standard directory, we specify the latter's run-time location with the *–rpath* linker option. This could be different from the link-time location of the library (specified by the *–L* option), although in this case the two locations are the same.

```
$ cd /home/mtk/pdir/d1
$ gcc -g -c -Wall -fPIC modx1.c
$ gcc -g -shared -o libx1.so modx1.o -Wl,-rpath,/home/mtk/pdir/d2 \
        -L/home/mtk/pdir/d2 -lx2
```

Finally, we build the main program, in the pdir directory. Since the main program makes use of libx1.so, and this library resides in a nonstandard directory, we again employ the *–rpath* linker option:

```
$ cd /home/mtk/pdir
$ gcc -g -Wall -o prog prog.c -Wl,-rpath,/home/mtk/pdir/d1 \
        -L/home/mtk/pdir/d1 -lx1
```

Note that we did not need to mention libx2.so when linking the main program. Since the linker is capable of analyzing the *rpath* list in libx1.so, it can find libx2.so, and thus is able to satisfy the requirement that all symbols can be resolved at static link time.

We can use the following commands to examine prog and libx1.so in order to see the contents of their *rpath* lists:

```
$ objdump -p prog | grep PATH
  RPATH        /home/mtk/pdir/d1          libx1.so will be sought here at run time
$ objdump -p d1/libx1.so | grep PATH
  RPATH        /home/mtk/pdir/d2          libx2.so will be sought here at run time
```

We can also view the *rpath* lists by grepping the output of the *readelf --dynamic* (or, equivalently, *readelf -d*) command.

We can use the *ldd* command to show the complete set of dynamic dependencies of prog:

```
$ ldd prog
        libx1.so => /home/mtk/pdir/d1/libx1.so (0x40017000)
        libc.so.6 => /lib/tls/libc.so.6 (0x40024000)
        libx2.so => /home/mtk/pdir/d2/libx2.so (0x4014c000)
        /lib/ld-linux.so.2 => /lib/ld-linux.so.2 (0x40000000)
```

The ELF DT_RPATH and DT_RUNPATH entries

In the original ELF specification, only one type of *rpath* list could be embedded in an executable or shared library. This corresponded to the DT_RPATH tag in an ELF file. Later ELF specifications deprecated DT_RPATH, and introduced a new tag, DT_RUNPATH, for representing *rpath* lists. The difference between these two types of *rpath* lists is their relative precedence with respect to the LD_LIBRARY_PATH environment variable when the dynamic linker searches for shared libraries at run time: DT_RPATH has higher precedence, while DT_RUNPATH has lower precedence (refer to Section 41.11).

By default, the linker creates the *rpath* list as a DT_RPATH tag. To have the linker instead create the *rpath* list as a DT_RUNPATH entry, we must additionally employ the *--enable-new-dtags* (*enable new dynamic tags*) linker option. If we rebuild our program using this option, and inspect the resulting executable file with *objdump*, we see the following:

```
$ gcc -g -Wall -o prog prog.c -Wl,--enable-new-dtags \
        -Wl,-rpath,/home/mtk/pdir/d1 -L/home/mtk/pdir/d1 -lx1
$ objdump -p prog | grep PATH
  RPATH         /home/mtk/pdir/d1
  RUNPATH       /home/mtk/pdir/d1
```

As can be seen, the executable contains both DT_RPATH and DT_RUNPATH tags. The linker duplicates the *rpath* list in this way for the benefit of older dynamic linkers that may not understand the DT_RUNPATH tag. (Support for DT_RUNPATH was added in version 2.2 of *glibc*.) Dynamic linkers that understand the DT_RUNPATH tag ignore the DT_RPATH tag (see Section 41.11).

Using $ORIGIN in *rpath*

Suppose that we want to distribute an application that uses some of its own shared libraries, but we don't want to require the user to install the libraries in one of the standard directories. Instead, we would like to allow the user to unpack the application under an arbitrary directory of their choice and then immediately be able to run the application. The problem is that the application has no way of determining where its shared libraries are located, unless it requests the user to set LD_LIBRARY_PATH or we require the user to run some sort of installation script that identifies the required directories. Neither of these approaches is desirable.

To get around this problem, the dynamic linker is built to understand a special string, $ORIGIN (or, equivalently, ${ORIGIN}), in an *rpath* specification. The dynamic linker interprets this string to mean "the directory containing the application." This means that we can, for example, build an application with the following command:

```
$ gcc -Wl,-rpath,'$ORIGIN'/lib ...
```

This presumes that at run time the application's shared libraries will reside in the subdirectory lib under the directory that contains the application executable. We can then provide the user with a simple installation package that contains the application and associated libraries, and the user can install the package in any location and then run the application (i.e., a so-called "turn-key application").

41.11 Finding Shared Libraries at Run Time

When resolving library dependencies, the dynamic linker first inspects each dependency string to see if it contains a slash (/), which can occur if we specified an explicit library pathname when linking the executable. If a slash is found, then the dependency string is interpreted as a pathname (either absolute or relative), and the library is loaded using that pathname. Otherwise, the dynamic linker searches for the shared library using the following rules:

1. If the executable has any directories listed in its DT_RPATH run-time library path list (*rpath*) and the executable does *not* contain a DT_RUNPATH list, then these directories are searched (in the order that they were supplied when linking the program).

2. If the LD_LIBRARY_PATH environment variable is defined, then each of the colon-separated directories listed in its value is searched in turn. If the executable is a set-user-ID or set-group-ID program, then LD_LIBRARY_PATH is ignored. This is a security measure to prevent users from tricking the dynamic linker into loading a private version of a library with the same name as a library required by the executable.

3. If the executable has any directories listed in its DT_RUNPATH run-time library path list, then these directories are searched (in the order that they were supplied when linking the program).

4. The file /etc/ld.so.cache is checked to see if it contains an entry for the library.

5. The directories /lib and /usr/lib are searched (in that order).

41.12 Run-Time Symbol Resolution

Suppose that a global symbol (i.e., a function or variable) is defined in multiple locations, such as in an executable and in a shared library, or in multiple shared libraries. How is a reference to that symbol resolved?

For example, suppose that we have a main program and a shared library, both of which define a global function, *xyz()*, and another function within the shared library calls *xyz()*, as shown in Figure 41-5.

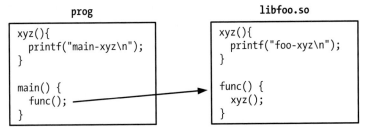

```
     prog                          libfoo.so

xyz(){                        xyz(){
  printf("main-xyz\n");         printf("foo-xyz\n");
}                             }

main() {                      func() {
  func();                       xyz();
}                             }
```

Figure 41-5: Resolving a global symbol reference

When we build the shared library and the executable program, and then run the program, this is what we see:

```
$ gcc -g -c -fPIC -Wall -c foo.c
$ gcc -g -shared -o libfoo.so foo.o
$ gcc -g -o prog prog.c libfoo.so
$ LD_LIBRARY_PATH=. ./prog
main-xyz
```

From the last line of output, we can see that the definition of *xyz()* in the main program overrides (interposes) the one in the shared library.

Although this may at first appear surprising, there is a good historical reason why things are done this way. The first shared library implementations were designed so that the default semantics for symbol resolution exactly mirrored those of applications linked against static equivalents of the same libraries. This means that the following semantics apply:

- A definition of a global symbol in the main program overrides a definition in a library.
- If a global symbol is defined in multiple libraries, then a reference to that symbol is bound to the first definition found by scanning libraries in the left-to-right order in which they were listed on the static link command line.

Although these semantics make the transition from static to shared libraries relatively straightforward, they can cause some problems. The most significant problem is that these semantics conflict with the model of a shared library as implementing a self-contained subsystem. By default, a shared library can't guarantee that a reference to one of its own global symbols will actually be bound to the library's definition of that symbol. Consequently, the properties of a shared library can change when it is aggregated into a larger unit. This can lead to applications breaking in unexpected ways, and also makes it difficult to perform divide-and-conquer debugging (i.e., trying to reproduce a problem using fewer or different shared libraries).

In the above scenario, if we wanted to ensure that the invocation of *xyz()* in the shared library actually called the version of the function defined within the library, then we could use the *–Bsymbolic* linker option when building the shared library:

```
$ gcc -g -c -fPIC -Wall foo.c
$ gcc -g -shared -Wl,-Bsymbolic -o libfoo.so foo.o
$ gcc -g -o prog prog.c libfoo.so
$ LD_LIBRARY_PATH=. ./prog
foo-xyz
```

The *–Bsymbolic* linker option specifies that references to global symbols within a shared library should be preferentially bound to definitions (if they exist) within that library. (Note that, regardless of this option, calling *xyz()* from the main program would always invoke the version of *xyz()* defined in the main program.)

41.13 Using a Static Library Instead of a Shared Library

Although it is almost always preferable to use shared libraries, there are occasional situations where static libraries may be appropriate. In particular, the fact that a statically linked application contains all of the code that it requires at run time can be advantageous. For example, static linking is useful if the user can't, or doesn't wish to, install a shared library on the system where the program is to be used, or if the program is to be run in an environment (perhaps a *chroot* jail, for example) where shared libraries are unavailable. In addition, even a compatible shared library upgrade may unintentionally introduce a bug that breaks an application. By linking an application statically, we can ensure that it is immune to changes in the shared libraries on a system and that it has all of the code it requires to run (at the expense of a larger program size, and consequent increased disk and memory requirements).

By default, where the linker has a choice of a shared and a static library of the same name (e.g., we link using *–Lsomedir –ldemo*, and both libdemo.so and libdemo.a exist), the shared version of the library is used. To force usage of the static version of the library, we may do one of the following:

- Specify the pathname of the static library (including the .a extension) on the *gcc* command line.
- Specify the *–static* option to *gcc*.
- Use the *gcc* options *–Wl,–Bstatic* and *–Wl,–Bdynamic* to explicitly toggle the linker's choice between static and shared libraries. These options can be intermingled with *–l* options on the *gcc* command line. The linker processes the options in the order in which they are specified.

41.14 Summary

An object library is an aggregation of compiled object modules that can be employed by programs that are linked against the library. Like other UNIX implementations, Linux provides two types of object libraries: static libraries, which were the only type of library available under early UNIX systems, and the more modern shared libraries.

Because they provide several advantages over static libraries, shared libraries are the predominant type of library in use on contemporary UNIX systems. The advantages of shared libraries spring primarily from the fact that when a program is linked against the library, copies of the object modules required by the program are not included in the resulting executable. Instead, the (static) linker merely includes information in the executable file about the shared libraries that are required at run time. When the file is executed, the dynamic linker uses this information to load the required shared libraries. At run time, all programs using the same shared library share a single copy of that library in memory. Since shared libraries are not copied into executable files, and a single memory-resident copy of the shared library is employed by all programs at run time, shared libraries reduce the amount of disk space and memory required by the system.

The shared library soname provides a level of indirection in resolving shared library references at run time. If a shared library has a soname, then this name, rather than the library's real name, is recorded in the resulting executable produced by the static linker. A versioning scheme, whereby a shared library is given a real name of the form lib*name*.so.*major-id.minor-id*, while the soname has the form lib*name*.so.*major-id*, allows for the creation of programs that automatically employ the latest minor version of the shared library (without requiring the programs to be relinked), while also allowing for the creation of new, incompatible major versions of the library.

In order to find a shared library at run time, the dynamic linker follows a standard set of search rules, which include searching a set of directories (e.g., /lib and /usr/lib) in which most shared libraries are installed.

Further information

Various information related to static and shared libraries can be found in the *ar(1)*, *gcc(1)*, *ld(1)*, *ldconfig(8)*, *ld.so(8)*, *dlopen(3)*, *readelf(1)*, and *objdump(1)* manual pages and in the *info* documentation for *ld*. [Drepper, 2004 (b)] covers many of the finer details of writing shared libraries on Linux. Further useful information can also be found in David Wheeler's *Program Library HOWTO*, which is online at the LDP web site, *http://www.tldp.org/*. The GNU shared library scheme has many similarities to that implemented in Solaris, and therefore it is worth reading Sun's *Linker and Libraries Guide* (available at *http://docs.sun.com/*) for further information and examples. [Levine, 2000] provides an introduction to the operation of static and dynamic linkers.

Information about GNU *Libtool*, a tool that shields the programmer from the implementation-specific details of building shared libraries, can be found online at *http://www.gnu.org/software/libtool* and in [Vaughan et al., 2000].

The document *Executable and Linking Format*, from the *Tools Interface Standards* committee, provides details on ELF. This document can be found online at *http://refspecs.freestandards.org/elf/elf.pdf*. [Lu, 1995] also provides a lot of useful detail on ELF.

41.15 Exercise

41-1. Try compiling a program with and without the *–static* option, to see the difference in size between an executable dynamically linked with the C library and one that is linked against the static version of the C library.

42

ADVANCED FEATURES
OF SHARED LIBRARIES

The previous chapter covered the fundamentals of shared libraries. This chapter describes a number of advanced features of shared libraries, including the following:

- dynamically loading shared libraries;
- controlling the visibility of symbols defined by a shared library;
- using linker scripts to create versioned symbols;
- using initialization and finalization functions to automatically execute code when a library is loaded and unloaded;
- shared library preloading; and
- using LD_DEBUG to monitor the operation of the dynamic linker.

42.1 Dynamically Loaded Libraries

When an executable starts, the dynamic linker loads all of the shared libraries in the program's dynamic dependency list. Sometimes, however, it can be useful to load libraries at a later time. For example, a plug-in is loaded only when it is needed. This functionality is provided by an API to the dynamic linker. This API, usually referred to as the *dlopen* API, originated on Solaris, and much of it is now specified in SUSv3.

The *dlopen* API enables a program to open a shared library at run time, search for a function by name in that library, and then call the function. A shared library loaded at run time in this way is commonly referred to as a *dynamically loaded library*, and is created in the same way as any other shared library.

The core *dlopen* API consists of the following functions (all of which are specified in SUSv3):

- The *dlopen()* function opens a shared library, returning a handle used by subsequent calls.

- The *dlsym()* function searches a library for a symbol (a string containing the name of a function or variable) and returns its address.

- The *dlclose()* function closes a library previously opened by *dlopen()*.

- The *dlerror()* function returns an error-message string, and is used after a failure return from one of the preceding functions.

The *glibc* implementation also includes a number of related functions, some of which we describe below.

To build programs that use the *dlopen* API on Linux, we must specify the *–ldl* option, in order to link against the *libdl* library.

42.1.1   Opening a Shared Library: *dlopen()*

The *dlopen()* function loads the shared library named in *libfilename* into the calling process's virtual address space and increments the count of open references to the library.

```
#include <dlfcn.h>

void *dlopen(const char *libfilename, int flags);
```
                          Returns library handle on success, or NULL on error

If *libfilename* contains a slash (/), *dlopen()* interprets it as an absolute or relative pathname. Otherwise, the dynamic linker searches for the shared library using the rules described in Section 41.11.

On success, *dlopen()* returns a handle that can be used to refer to the library in subsequent calls to functions in the *dlopen* API. If an error occurred (e.g., the library couldn't be found), *dlopen()* returns NULL.

If the shared library specified by *libfilename* contains dependencies on other shared libraries, *dlopen()* also automatically loads those libraries. This procedure occurs recursively if necessary. We refer to the set of such loaded libraries as this library's *dependency tree*.

It is possible to call *dlopen()* multiple times on the same library file. The library is loaded into memory only once (by the initial call), and all calls return the same *handle* value. However, the *dlopen* API maintains a reference count for each library handle. This count is incremented by each call to *dlopen()* and decremented by each call to *dlclose()*; only when the count reaches 0 does *dlclose()* unload the library from memory.

The *flags* argument is a bit mask that must include exactly one of the constants RTLD_LAZY or RTLD_NOW, with the following meanings:

RTLD_LAZY

Undefined function symbols in the library should be resolved only as the code is executed. If a piece of code requiring a particular symbol is not executed, that symbol is never resolved. Lazy resolution is performed only for function references; references to variables are always resolved immediately. Specifying the RTLD_LAZY flag provides behavior that corresponds to the normal operation of the dynamic linker when loading the shared libraries identified in an executable's dynamic dependency list.

RTLD_NOW

All undefined symbols in the library should be immediately resolved before *dlopen()* completes, regardless of whether they will ever be required. As a consequence, opening the library is slower, but any potential undefined function symbol errors are detected immediately instead of at some later time. This can be useful when debugging an application, or simply to ensure that an application fails immediately on an unresolved symbol, rather than doing so only after executing for a long time.

> By setting the environment variable LD_BIND_NOW to a nonempty string, we can force the dynamic linker to immediately resolve all symbols (i.e., like RTLD_NOW) when loading the shared libraries identified in an executable's dynamic dependency list. This environment variable is effective in *glibc* 2.1.1 and later. Setting LD_BIND_NOW overrides the effect of the *dlopen()* RTLD_LAZY flag.

It is also possible to include further values in *flags*. The following flags are specified in SUSv3:

RTLD_GLOBAL

Symbols in this library and its dependency tree are made available for resolving references in other libraries loaded by this process and also for lookups via *dlsym()*.

RTLD_LOCAL

This is the converse of RTLD_GLOBAL and the default if neither constant is specified. It specifies that symbols in this library and its dependency tree are not available to resolve references in subsequently loaded libraries.

SUSv3 doesn't specify a default if neither RTLD_GLOBAL nor RTLD_LOCAL is specified. Most UNIX implementations assume the same default (RTLD_LOCAL) as Linux, but a few assume a default of RTLD_GLOBAL.

Linux also supports a number of flags that are not specified in SUSv3:

RTLD_NODELETE (since *glibc* 2.2)

Don't unload the library during a *dlclose()*, even if the reference count falls to 0. This means that the library's static variables are not reinitialized if the library is later reloaded by *dlopen()*. (We can achieve a similar effect for libraries loaded automatically by the dynamic linker by specifying the *gcc −Wl,−znodelete* option when creating the library.)

`RTLD_NOLOAD` (since *glibc* 2.2)

> Don't load the library. This serves two purposes. First, we can use this flag to check if a particular library is currently loaded as part of the process's address space. If it is, *dlopen()* returns the library's handle; if it is not, *dlopen()* returns `NULL`. Second, we can use this flag to "promote" the *flags* of an already loaded library. For example, we can specify `RTLD_NOLOAD | RTLD_GLOBAL` in *flags* when using *dlopen()* on a library previously opened with `RTLD_LOCAL`.

`RTLD_DEEPBIND` (since *glibc* 2.3.4)

> When resolving symbol references made by this library, search for definitions in the library before searching for definitions in libraries that have already been loaded. This allows a library to be self-contained, using its own symbol definitions in preference to global symbols with the same name defined in other shared libraries that have already been loaded. (This is similar to the effect of the *−Bsymbolic* linker option described in Section 41.12.)

The `RTLD_NODELETE` and `RTLD_NOLOAD` flags are also implemented in the Solaris *dlopen* API, but are available on few other UNIX implementations. The `RTLD_DEEPBIND` flag is Linux-specific.

As a special case, we can specify *libfilename* as `NULL`. This causes *dlopen()* to return a handle for the main program. (SUSv3 refers to this as a handle for the "global symbol object.") Specifying this handle in a subsequent call to *dlsym()* causes the requested symbol to be sought in the main program, followed by all shared libraries loaded at program startup, and then all libraries dynamically loaded with the `RTLD_GLOBAL` flag.

42.1.2 Diagnosing Errors: *dlerror()*

If we receive an error return from *dlopen()* or one of the other functions in the *dlopen* API, we can use *dlerror()* to obtain a pointer to a string that indicates the cause of the error.

```
#include <dlfcn.h>

const char *dlerror(void);
```
> > Returns pointer to error-diagnostic string, or `NULL` if
> > no error has occurred since previous call to *dlerror()*

The *dlerror()* function returns `NULL` if no error has occurred since the last call to *dlerror()*. We'll see how this is useful in the next section.

42.1.3 Obtaining the Address of a Symbol: *dlsym()*

The *dlsym()* function searches for the named *symbol* (a function or variable) in the library referred to by *handle* and in the libraries in that library's dependency tree.

```
#include <dlfcn.h>

void *dlsym(void *handle, char *symbol);
```
                              Returns address of *symbol*, or NULL if *symbol* is not found

If *symbol* is found, *dlsym()* returns its address; otherwise, *dlsym()* returns NULL. The
handle argument is normally a library handle returned by a previous call to *dlopen()*.
Alternatively, it may be one of the so-called pseudohandles described below.

> A related function, *dlvsym(handle, symbol, version)*, is similar to *dlsym()*, but can
> be used to search a symbol-versioned library for a symbol definition whose ver-
> sion matches the string specified in *version*. (We describe symbol versioning in
> Section 42.3.2.) The _GNU_SOURCE feature test macro must be defined in order to
> obtain the declaration of this function from <dlfcn.h>.

The value of a symbol returned by *dlsym()* may be NULL, which is indistinguishable
from the "symbol not found" return. In order to differentiate the two possibilities,
we must call *dlerror()* beforehand (to make sure that any previously held error
string is cleared) and then if, after the call to *dlsym()*, *dlerror()* returns a non-NULL
value, we know that an error occurred.

If *symbol* is the name of a variable, then we can assign the return value of *dlsym()*
to an appropriate pointer type, and obtain the value of the variable by dereferencing the pointer:

```
int *ip;

ip = (int *) dlsym(handle, symbol);
if (ip != NULL)
    printf("Value is %d\n", *ip);
```

If *symbol* is the name of a function, then the pointer returned by *dlsym()* can be used
to call the function. We can store the value returned by *dlsym()* in a pointer of the
appropriate type, such as the following:

```
int (*funcp)(int);          /* Pointer to a function taking an integer
                               argument and returning an integer */
```

However, we can't simply assign the result of *dlsym()* to such a pointer, as in the following example:

```
funcp = dlsym(handle, symbol);
```

The reason is that the ISO C standard leaves the results of casting between function
pointers and *void* * undefined. The solution is to use the following (somewhat
clumsy) cast:

```
*(void **) (&funcp) = dlsym(handle, symbol);
```

Having used *dlsym()* to obtain a pointer to the function, we can then call the function using the usual C syntax for dereferencing function pointers:

```
res = (*funcp)(somearg);
```

Instead of the *(void **)* syntax shown above, one might consider using the following seemingly equivalent code when assigning the return value of *dlsym()*:

```
(void *) funcp = dlsym(handle, symbol);
```

However, for this code, *gcc –pedantic* warns that "ANSI C forbids the use of cast expressions as lvalues." The *(void **)* syntax doesn't incur this warning because we are assigning to an address *pointed to* by the assignment's lvalue.

On many UNIX implementations, we can use casts such as the following to eliminate warnings from the C compiler:

```
funcp = (int (*) (int)) dlsym(handle, symbol);
```

However, the specification of *dlsym()* in SUSv3 *Technical Corrigendum Number 1* notes that the ISO C standard nevertheless requires compilers to generate a warning for such a conversion, and proposes the *(void **)* syntax shown above.

> SUSv3 TC1 noted that because of the need for the *(void **)* syntax, a future version of the standard may define separate *dlsym()*-like APIs for handling data and function pointers. However, SUSv4 contains no changes with respect to this point.

Using library pseudohandles with *dlsym()*

Instead of specifying a library handle returned by a call to *dlopen()*, either of the following *pseudohandles* may be specified as the *handle* argument for *dlsym()*:

RTLD_DEFAULT
> Search for *symbol* starting with the main program, and then proceeding in order through the list of all shared libraries loaded, including those libraries dynamically loaded by *dlopen()* with the RTLD_GLOBAL flag. This corresponds to the default search model employed by the dynamic linker.

RTLD_NEXT
> Search for *symbol* in shared libraries loaded after the one invoking *dlsym()*. This is useful when creating a wrapper function with the same name as a function defined elsewhere. For example, in our main program, we may define our own version of *malloc()* (which perhaps does some bookkeeping of memory allocation), and this function can invoke the real *malloc()* by first obtaining its address via the call *func = dlsym(RTLD_NEXT, "malloc")*.

The pseudohandle values listed above are not required by SUSv3 (which nevertheless reserves them for future use), and are not available on all UNIX implementations. In order to get the definitions of these constants from <dlfcn.h>, we must define the _GNU_SOURCE feature test macro.

Example program

Listing 42-1 demonstrates the use of the *dlopen* API. This program takes two command-line arguments: the name of a shared library to load and the name of a function to execute within that library. The following examples demonstrate the use of this program:

```
$ ./dynload ./libdemo.so.1 x1
```

```
Called mod1-x1
$ LD_LIBRARY_PATH=. ./dynload libdemo.so.1 x1
Called mod1-x1
```

In the first of the above commands, *dlopen()* notes that the library path includes a slash and thus interprets it as a relative pathname (in this case, to a library in the current working directory). In the second command, we specify a library search path in LD_LIBRARY_PATH. This search path is interpreted according to the usual rules of the dynamic linker (in this case, likewise to find the library in the current working directory).

Listing 42-1: Using the *dlopen* API

———————————————————————————————— shlibs/dynload.c
```c
#include <dlfcn.h>
#include "tlpi_hdr.h"

int
main(int argc, char *argv[])
{
    void *libHandle;            /* Handle for shared library */
    void (*funcp)(void);        /* Pointer to function with no arguments */
    const char *err;

    if (argc != 3 || strcmp(argv[1], "--help") == 0)
        usageErr("%s lib-path func-name\n", argv[0]);

    /* Load the shared library and get a handle for later use */

    libHandle = dlopen(argv[1], RTLD_LAZY);
    if (libHandle == NULL)
        fatal("dlopen: %s", dlerror());

    /* Search library for symbol named in argv[2] */

    (void) dlerror();                           /* Clear dlerror() */
    *(void **) (&funcp) = dlsym(libHandle, argv[2]);
    err = dlerror();
    if (err != NULL)
        fatal("dlsym: %s", err);

    /* Try calling the address returned by dlsym() as a function
       that takes no arguments. */

    (*funcp)();

    dlclose(libHandle);                         /* Close the library */

    exit(EXIT_SUCCESS);
}
```
———————————————————————————————— shlibs/dynload.c

Advanced Features of Shared Libraries **865**

42.1.4 Closing a Shared Library: *dlclose()*

The *dlclose()* function closes a library.

```
#include <dlfcn.h>

int dlclose(void *handle);
```
                                          Returns 0 on success, or –1 on error

The *dlclose()* function decrements the system's counter of open references to the library referred to by *handle*. If this reference count falls to 0, and no symbols in the library are required by other libraries, then the library is unloaded. This procedure is also (recursively) performed for the libraries in this library's dependency tree. An implicit *dlclose()* of all libraries is performed on process termination.

> From *glibc* 2.2.3 onward, a function within a shared library can use *atexit()* (or *on_exit()*) to establish a function that is called automatically when the library is unloaded.

42.1.5 Obtaining Information About Loaded Symbols: *dladdr()*

Given an address in *addr* (typically, one obtained by an earlier call to *dlsym()*), *dladdr()* returns a structure containing information about that address.

```
#define _GNU_SOURCE
#include <dlfcn.h>

int dladdr(const void *addr, Dl_info *info);
```
          Returns nonzero value if *addr* was found in a shared library, otherwise 0

The *info* argument is a pointer to a caller-allocated structure that has the following form:

```
typedef struct {
    const char *dli_fname;      /* Pathname of shared library
                                   containing 'addr' */
    void       *dli_fbase;      /* Base address at which shared
                                   library is loaded */
    const char *dli_sname;      /* Name of symbol whose definition
                                   overlaps 'addr' */
    void       *dli_saddr;      /* Actual value of the symbol
                                   returned in 'dli_sname' */
} Dl_info;
```

The first two fields of the *Dl_info* structure specify the pathname and run-time base address of the shared library containing the address specified in *addr*. The last two fields return information about that address. Assuming that *addr* points to the exact address of a symbol in the shared library, then *dli_saddr* returns the same value as was passed in *addr*.

SUSv3 doesn't specify *dladdr()*, and this function is not available on all UNIX implementations.

42.1.6 Accessing Symbols in the Main Program

Suppose that we use *dlopen()* to dynamically load a shared library, use *dlsym()* to obtain the address of a function *x()* from that library, and then call *x()*. If *x()* in turn calls a function *y()*, then *y()* would normally be sought in one of the shared libraries loaded by the program.

Sometimes, it is desirable instead to have *x()* invoke an implementation of *y()* in the main program. (This is similar to a callback mechanism.) In order to do this, we must make the (global-scope) symbols in the main program available to the dynamic linker, by linking the program using the *--export-dynamic* linker option:

```
$ gcc -Wl,--export-dynamic main.c
```
(plus further options and arguments)

Equivalently, we can write the following:

```
$ gcc -export-dynamic main.c
```

Using either of these options allows a dynamically loaded library to access global symbols in the main program.

> The *gcc −rdynamic* option and the *gcc −Wl,−E* option are further synonyms for *−Wl,--export−dynamic*.

42.2 Controlling Symbol Visibility

A well-designed shared library should make visible only those symbols (functions and variables) that form part of its specified application binary interface (ABI). The reasons for this are as follows:

- If the shared library designer accidentally exports unspecified interfaces, then authors of applications that use the library may choose to employ these interfaces. This creates a compatibility problem for future upgrades of the shared library. The library developer expects to be able to change or remove any interfaces other than those in the documented ABI, while the library user expects to continue using the same interfaces (with the same semantics) that they currently employ.

- During run-time symbol resolution, any symbols that are exported by a shared library might interpose definitions that are provided in other shared libraries (Section 41.12).

- Exporting unnecessary symbols increases the size of the dynamic symbol table that must be loaded at run time.

All of these problems can be minimized or avoided altogether if the library designer ensures that only the symbols required by the library's specified ABI are exported. The following techniques can be used to control the export of symbols:

- In a C program, we can use the static keyword to make a symbol private to a source-code module, thus rendering it unavailable for binding by other object files.

As well as making a symbol private to a source-code module, the static keyword also has a converse effect. If a symbol is marked as static, then all references to the symbol in the same source file will be bound to that definition of the symbol. Consequently, these references won't be subject to run-time interposition by definitions from other shared libraries (in the manner described in Section 41.12). This effect of the static keyword is similar to the *–Bsymbolic* linker option described in Section 41.12, with the difference that the static keyword affects a single symbol within a single source file.

- The GNU C complier, *gcc*, provides a compiler-specific attribute declaration that performs a similar task to the static keyword:

```
void
__attribute__ ((visibility("hidden")))
func(void) {
    /* Code */
}
```

Whereas the static keyword limits the visibility of a symbol to a single source code file, the hidden attribute makes the symbol available across all source code files that compose the shared library, but prevents it from being visible outside the library.

> As with the static keyword, the hidden attribute also has the converse effect of preventing symbol interposition at run time.

- Version scripts (Section 42.3) can be used to precisely control symbol visibility and to select the version of a symbol to which a reference is bound.
- When dynamically loading a shared library (Section 42.1.1), the *dlopen()* RTLD_GLOBAL flag can be used to specify that the symbols defined by the library should be made available for binding by subsequently loaded libraries, and the *––export-dynamic* linker option (Section 42.1.6) can be used to make the global symbols of the main program available to dynamically loaded libraries.

For further details on the topic of symbol visibility, see [Drepper, 2004 (b)].

42.3 Linker Version Scripts

A *version script* is a text file containing instructions for the linker, *ld*. In order to use a version script, we must specify the *––version-script* linker option:

```
$ gcc -Wl,--version-script,myscriptfile.map ...
```

Version scripts are commonly (but not universally) identified using the extension .map. The following sections describe some uses of version scripts.

42.3.1 Controlling Symbol Visibility with Version Scripts

One use of version scripts is to control the visibility of symbols that might otherwise accidentally be made global (i.e., visible to applications linking against the library). As a simple example, suppose that we are building a shared library from the three source files vis_comm.c, vis_f1.c, and vis_f2.c, which respectively define the functions *vis_comm()*, *vis_f1()*, and *vis_f2()*. The *vis_comm()* function is called by *vis_f1()* and *vis_f2()*, but is not intended for direct use by applications linked against the library. Suppose we build the shared library in the usual way:

```
$ gcc -g -c -fPIC -Wall vis_comm.c vis_f1.c vis_f2.c
$ gcc -g -shared -o vis.so vis_comm.o vis_f1.o vis_f2.o
```

If we use the following *readelf* command to list the dynamic symbols exported by the library, we see the following:

```
$ readelf --syms --use-dynamic vis.so | grep vis_
    30  12: 00000790    59  FUNC GLOBAL DEFAULT  10 vis_f1
    25  13: 000007d0    73  FUNC GLOBAL DEFAULT  10 vis_f2
    27  16: 00000770    20  FUNC GLOBAL DEFAULT  10 vis_comm
```

This shared library exported three symbols: *vis_comm()*, *vis_f1()*, and *vis_f2()*. However, we would like to ensure that only the symbols *vis_f1()* and *vis_f2()* are exported by the library. We can achieve this result using the following version script:

```
$ cat vis.map
VER_1 {
    global:
        vis_f1;
        vis_f2;
    local:
        *;
};
```

The identifier *VER_1* is an example of a *version tag*. As we'll see in the discussion of symbol versioning in Section 42.3.2, a version script may contain multiple *version nodes*, each grouped within braces ({}) and prefixed with a unique version tag. If we are using a version script only for the purpose of controlling symbol visibility, then the version tag is redundant; nevertheless, older versions of *ld* required it. Modern versions of *ld* allow the version tag to be omitted; in this case, the version node is said to have an anonymous version tag, and no other version nodes may be present in the script.

Within the version node, the global keyword begins a semicolon-separated list of symbols that are made visible outside the library. The local keyword begins a list of symbols that are to be hidden from the outside world. The asterisk (*) here illustrates the fact that we can use wildcard patterns in these symbol specifications. The wildcard characters are the same as those used for shell filename matching—for example, * and ?. (See the *glob(7)* manual page for further details.) In this example, using an asterisk for the local specification says that everything that wasn't explicitly declared global is hidden. If we did not say this, then *vis_comm()* would still be visible, since the default is to make C global symbols visible outside the shared library.

We can then build our shared library using the version script as follows:

```
$ gcc -g -c -fPIC -Wall vis_comm.c vis_f1.c vis_f2.c
$ gcc -g -shared -o vis.so vis_comm.o vis_f1.o vis_f2.o \
        -Wl,--version-script,vis.map
```

Using *readelf* once more shows that *vis_comm()* is no longer externally visible:

```
$ readelf --syms --use-dynamic vis.so | grep vis_
    25   0: 00000730    73   FUNC GLOBAL DEFAULT  11 vis_f2
    29  16: 000006f0    59   FUNC GLOBAL DEFAULT  11 vis_f1
```

42.3.2 Symbol Versioning

Symbol versioning allows a single shared library to provide multiple versions of the same function. Each program uses the version of the function that was current when the program was (statically) linked against the shared library. As a result, we can make an incompatible change to a shared library without needing to increase the library's major version number. Carried to an extreme, symbol versioning can replace the traditional shared library major and minor versioning scheme. Symbol versioning is used in this manner in *glibc* 2.1 and later, so that all versions of *glibc* from 2.0 onward are supported within a single major library version (libc.so.6).

We demonstrate the use of symbol versioning with a simple example. We begin by creating the first version of a shared library using a version script:

```
$ cat sv_lib_v1.c
#include <stdio.h>

void xyz(void) { printf("v1 xyz\n"); }
$ cat sv_v1.map
VER_1 {
        global: xyz;
        local:  *;      # Hide all other symbols
};
$ gcc -g -c -fPIC -Wall sv_lib_v1.c
$ gcc -g -shared -o libsv.so sv_lib_v1.o -Wl,--version-script,sv_v1.map
```

> Within a version script, the hash character (#) starts a comment.

(To keep the example simple, we avoid the use of explicit library sonames and library major version numbers.)

At this stage, our version script, sv_v1.map, serves only to control the visibility of the shared library's symbols; *xyz()* is exported, but all other symbols (of which there are none in this small example) are hidden. Next, we create a program, *p1*, which makes use of this library:

```
$ cat sv_prog.c
#include <stdlib.h>

int
main(int argc, char *argv[])
{
    void xyz(void);

    xyz();

    exit(EXIT_SUCCESS);
}
$ gcc -g -o p1 sv_prog.c libsv.so
```

When we run this program, we see the expected result:

```
$ LD_LIBRARY_PATH=. ./p1
v1 xyz
```

Now, suppose that we want to modify the definition of *xyz()* within our library, while still ensuring that program *p1* continues to use the old version of this function. To do this, we must define two versions of *xyz()* within our library:

```
$ cat sv_lib_v2.c
#include <stdio.h>

__asm__(".symver xyz_old,xyz@VER_1");
__asm__(".symver xyz_new,xyz@@VER_2");

void xyz_old(void) { printf("v1 xyz\n"); }

void xyz_new(void) { printf("v2 xyz\n"); }

void pqr(void) { printf("v2 pqr\n"); }
```

Our two versions of *xyz()* are provided by the functions *xyz_old()* and *xyz_new()*. The *xyz_old()* function corresponds to our original definition of *xyz()*, which is the one that should continue to be used by program *p1*. The *xyz_new()* function provides the definition of *xyz()* to be used by programs linking against the new version of the library.

The two .symver assembler directives are the glue that ties these two functions to different version tags in the modified version script (shown in a moment) that we use to create the new version of the shared library. The first of these directives says that *xyz_old()* is the implementation of *xyz()* to be used for applications linked against version tag *VER_1* (i.e., program *p1* in our example), and that *xyz_new()* is the implementation of *xyz()* to be used by applications linked against version tag *VER_2*.

The use of @@ rather than @ in the second .symver directive indicates that this is the default definition of *xyz()* to which applications should bind when statically linked against this shared library. Exactly one of the .symver directives for a symbol should be marked using @@.

The corresponding version script for our modified library is as follows:

```
$ cat sv_v2.map
VER_1 {
        global: xyz;
        local: *;       # Hide all other symbols
};

VER_2 {
        global: pqr;
} VER_1;
```

This version script provides a new version tag, *VER_2*, which depends on the tag *VER_1*. This dependency is indicated by the following line:

```
} VER_1;
```

Version tag dependencies indicate the relationships between successive library versions. Semantically, the only effect of version tag dependencies on Linux is that a version node inherits global and local specifications from the version node upon which it depends.

Dependencies can be chained, so that we could have another version node tagged *VER_3*, which depended on *VER_2*, and so on.

The version tag names have no meanings in themselves. Their relationship with one another is determined only by the specified version dependencies, and we chose the names *VER_1* and *VER_2* merely to be suggestive of these relationships. To assist maintenance, recommended practice is to use version tags that include the package name and a version number. For example, *glibc* uses version tags with names such as *GLIBC_2.0*, *GLIBC_2.1*, and so on.

The *VER_2* version tag also specifies that the new function *pqr()* is to be exported by the library and bound to the *VER_2* version tag. If we didn't declare *pqr()* in this manner, then the local specification that *VER_2* version tag inherited from the *VER_1* version tag would make *pqr()* invisible outside the library. Note also that if we omitted the local specification altogether, then the symbols *xyz_old()* and *xyz_new()* would also be exported by the library (which is typically not what we want).

We now build the new version of our library in the usual way:

```
$ gcc -g -c -fPIC -Wall sv_lib_v2.c
$ gcc -g -shared -o libsv.so sv_lib_v2.o -Wl,--version-script,sv_v2.map
```

Now we can create a new program, *p2*, which uses the new definition of *xyz()*, while program *p1* uses the old version of *xyz()*.

```
$ gcc -g -o p2 sv_prog.c libsv.so
$ LD_LIBRARY_PATH=. ./p2
v2 xyz                                          Uses xyz@VER_2
$ LD_LIBRARY_PATH=. ./p1
v1 xyz                                          Uses xyz@VER_1
```

The version tag dependencies of an executable are recorded at static link time. We can use *objdump –t* to display the symbol tables of each executable, thus showing the different version tag dependencies of each program:

```
$ objdump -t p1 | grep xyz
08048380        F *UND*  0000002e              xyz@@VER_1
$ objdump -t p2 | grep xyz
080483a0        F *UND*  0000002e              xyz@@VER_2
```

We can also use *readelf –s* to obtain similar information.

> Further information about symbol versioning can be found using the command *info ld scripts version* and at *http://people.redhat.com/drepper/symbol-versioning*.

42.4 Initialization and Finalization Functions

It is possible to define one or more functions that are executed automatically when a shared library is loaded and unloaded. This allows us to perform initialization and finalization actions when working with shared libraries. Initialization and finalization functions are executed regardless of whether the library is loaded automatically or loaded explicitly using the *dlopen* interface (Section 42.1).

Initialization and finalization functions are defined using the *gcc* constructor and destructor attributes. Each function that is to be executed when the library is loaded should be defined as follows:

```
void __attribute__ ((constructor)) some_name_load(void)
{
    /* Initialization code */
}
```

Unload functions are similarly defined:

```
void __attribute__ ((destructor)) some_name_unload(void)
{
    /* Finalization code */
}
```

The function names *some_name_load()* and *some_name_unload()* can be replaced by any desired names.

> It is also possible to use the *gcc* constructor and destructor attributes to create initialization and finalization functions in a main program.

The _init() and _fini() functions

An older technique for shared library initialization and finalization is to create two functions, *_init()* and *_fini()*, as part of the library. The *void _init(void)* function contains code that is to be executed when the library is first loaded by a process. The *void _fini(void)* function contains code that is to be executed when the library is unloaded.

If we create *_init()* and *_fini()* functions, then we must specify the *gcc* –*nostartfiles* option when building the shared library, in order to prevent the linker from including default versions of these functions. (Using the *–Wl,–init* and *–Wl,–fini* linker options, we can choose alternative names for these two functions if desired.)

Use of *_init()* and *_fini()* is now considered obsolete in favor of the *gcc* constructor and destructor attributes, which, among other advantages, allow us to define multiple initialization and finalization functions.

42.5   Preloading Shared Libraries

For testing purposes, it can sometimes be useful to selectively override functions (and other symbols) that would normally be found by the dynamic linker using the rules described in Section 41.11. To do this, we can define the environment variable LD_PRELOAD as a string consisting of space-separated or colon-separated names of shared libraries that should be loaded before any other shared libraries. Since these libraries are loaded first, any functions they define will automatically be used if required by the executable, thus overriding any other functions of the same name that the dynamic linker would otherwise have searched for. For example, suppose that we have a program that calls functions *x1()* and *x2()*, defined in our *libdemo* library. When we run this program, we see the following output:

```
$ ./prog
Called mod1-x1 DEMO
Called mod2-x2 DEMO
```

(In this example, we assume that the shared library is in one of the standard directories, and thus we don't need to use the LD_LIBRARY_PATH environment variable.)

We could selectively override the function *x1()* by creating another shared library, libalt.so, which contains a different definition of *x1()*. Preloading this library when running the program would result in the following:

```
$ LD_PRELOAD=libalt.so ./prog
Called mod1-x1 ALT
Called mod2-x2 DEMO
```

Here, we see that the version of *x1()* defined in libalt.so is invoked, but that the call to *x2()*, for which no definition is provided in libalt.so, results in the invocation of the *x2()* function defined in libdemo.so.

The LD_PRELOAD environment variable controls preloading on a per-process basis. Alternatively, the file /etc/ld.so.preload, which lists libraries separated by white space, can be used to perform the same task on a system-wide basis. (Libraries specified by LD_PRELOAD are loaded before those specified in /etc/ld.so.preload.)

For security reasons, set-user-ID and set-group-ID programs ignore LD_PRELOAD.

42.6 Monitoring the Dynamic Linker: LD_DEBUG

Sometimes, it is useful to monitor the operation of the dynamic linker in order to know, for example, where it is searching for libraries. We can use the LD_DEBUG environment variable to do this. By setting this variable to one (or more) of a set of standard keywords, we can obtain various kinds of tracing information from the dynamic linker.

If we assign the value *help* to LD_DEBUG, the dynamic linker displays help information about LD_DEBUG, and the specified command is *not* executed:

```
$ LD_DEBUG=help date
Valid options for the LD_DEBUG environment variable are:

    libs       display library search paths
    reloc      display relocation processing
    files      display progress for input file
    symbols    display symbol table processing
    bindings   display information about symbol binding
    versions   display version dependencies
    all        all previous options combined
    statistics display relocation statistics
    unused     determine unused DSOs
    help       display this help message and exit

To direct the debugging output into a file instead of standard output
a filename can be specified using the LD_DEBUG_OUTPUT environment variable.
```

The following example shows an abridged version of the output provided when we request tracing of information about library searches:

```
$ LD_DEBUG=libs date
    10687:      find library=librt.so.1 [0]; searching
    10687:       search cache=/etc/ld.so.cache
    10687:        trying file=/lib/librt.so.1
    10687:      find library=libc.so.6 [0]; searching
    10687:       search cache=/etc/ld.so.cache
    10687:        trying file=/lib/libc.so.6
    10687:      find library=libpthread.so.0 [0]; searching
    10687:       search cache=/etc/ld.so.cache
    10687:        trying file=/lib/libpthread.so.0
    10687:      calling init: /lib/libpthread.so.0
    10687:      calling init: /lib/libc.so.6
    10687:      calling init: /lib/librt.so.1
    10687:      initialize program: date
    10687:      transferring control: date
Tue Dec 28 17:26:56 CEST 2010
    10687:      calling fini: date [0]
    10687:      calling fini: /lib/librt.so.1 [0]
    10687:      calling fini: /lib/libpthread.so.0 [0]
    10687:      calling fini: /lib/libc.so.6 [0]
```

The value 10687 displayed at the start of each line is the process ID of the process being traced. This is useful if we are monitoring several processes (e.g., parent and child).

By default, LD_DEBUG output is written to standard error, but we can direct it elsewhere by assigning a pathname to the LD_DEBUG_OUTPUT environment variable.

If desired, we can assign multiple options to LD_DEBUG by separating them with commas (no spaces should appear). The output of the *symbols* option (which traces symbol resolution by the dynamic linker) is particularly voluminous.

LD_DEBUG is effective both for libraries implicitly loaded by the dynamic linker and for libraries dynamically loaded by *dlopen()*.

For security reasons, LD_DEBUG is (since *glibc* 2.2.5) ignored in set-user-ID and set-group-ID programs.

42.7 Summary

The dynamic linker provides the *dlopen* API, which allows programs to explicitly load additional shared libraries at run time. This allows programs to implement plug-in functionality.

An important aspect of shared library design is controlling symbol visibility, so that the library exports only those symbols (functions and variables) that should actually be used by programs linked against the library. We looked at a range of techniques that can be used to control symbol visibility. Among these techniques was the use of version scripts, which provide fine-grained control of symbol visibility.

We also showed how version scripts can be used to implement a scheme that allows a single shared library to export multiple definitions of a symbol for use by different applications linked against the library. (Each application uses the definition that was current when the application was statically linked against the library.) This technique provides an alternative to the traditional library versioning approach of using major and minor version numbers in the shared library real name.

Defining initialization and finalization functions within a shared library allows us to automatically execute code when the library is loaded and unloaded.

The LD_PRELOAD environment variable allows us to preload shared libraries. Using this mechanism, we can selectively override functions and other symbols that the dynamic linker would normally find in other shared libraries.

We can assign various values to the LD_DEBUG environment variable in order to monitor the operation of the dynamic linker.

Further information

Refer to the sources of further information listed in Section 41.14.

42.8 Exercises

42-1. Write a program to verify that if a library is closed with *dlclose()*, it is not unloaded if any of its symbols are used by another library.

42-2. Add a *dladdr()* call to the program in Listing 42-1 (dynload.c) in order to retrieve information about the address returned by *dlsym()*. Print out the values of the fields of the returned *Dl_info* structure, and verify that they are as expected.

43

INTERPROCESS COMMUNICATION OVERVIEW

This chapter presents a brief overview of the facilities that processes and threads can use to communicate with one another and to synchronize their actions. The following chapters provide more details about these facilities.

43.1 A Taxonomy of IPC Facilities

Figure 43-1 summarizes the rich variety of UNIX communication and synchronization facilities, dividing them into three broad functional categories:

- *Communication*: These facilities are concerned with exchanging data between processes.
- *Synchronization*: These facilities are concerned with synchronizing the actions of processes or threads.
- *Signals*: Although signals are intended primarily for other purposes, they can be used as a synchronization technique in certain circumstances. More rarely, signals can be used as a communication technique: the signal number itself is a form of information, and realtime signals can be accompanied by associated data (an integer or a pointer). Signals are described in detail in Chapters 20 to 22.

Although some of these facilities are concerned with synchronization, the general term *interprocess communication* (IPC) is often used to describe them all.

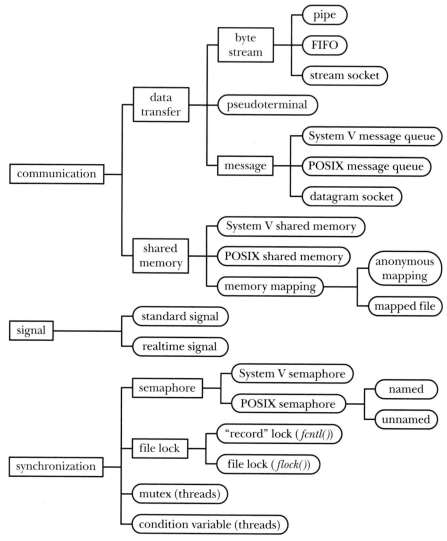

Figure 43-1: A taxonomy of UNIX IPC facilities

As Figure 43-1 illustrates, often several facilities provide similar IPC functionality. There are a couple of reasons for this:

- Similar facilities evolved on different UNIX variants, and later came to be ported to other UNIX systems. For example, FIFOs were developed on System V, while (stream) sockets were developed on BSD.

- New facilities have been developed to address design deficiencies in similar earlier facilities. For example, the POSIX IPC facilities (message queues, semaphores, and shared memory) were designed as an improvement on the older System V IPC facilities.

In some cases, facilities that are grouped together in Figure 43-1 actually provide significantly different functionality. For example, stream sockets can be used to communicate over a network, while FIFOs can be used only for communication between processes on the same machine.

43.2 Communication Facilities

The various communication facilities shown in Figure 43-1 allow processes to exchange data with one another. (These facilities can also be used to exchange data between the threads of a single process, but this is seldom necessary, since threads can exchange information via shared global variables.)

We can break the communication facilities into two categories:

- *Data-transfer facilities*: The key factor distinguishing these facilities is the notion of writing and reading. In order to communicate, one process writes data to the IPC facility, and another process reads the data. These facilities require two data transfers between user memory and kernel memory: one transfer from user memory to kernel memory during writing, and another transfer from kernel memory to user memory during reading. (Figure 43-2 shows this situation for a pipe.)

- *Shared memory*: Shared memory allows processes to exchange information by placing it in a region of memory that is shared between the processes. (The kernel accomplishes this by making page-table entries in each process point to the same pages of RAM, as shown in Figure 49-2, on page 1026.) A process can make data available to other processes by placing it in the shared memory region. Because communication doesn't require system calls or data transfer between user memory and kernel memory, shared memory can provide very fast communication.

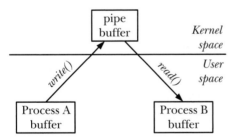

Figure 43-2: Exchanging data between two processes using a pipe

Data transfer

We can further break data-transfer facilities into the following subcategories:

- *Byte stream*: The data exchanged via pipes, FIFOs, and stream sockets is an undelimited byte stream. Each read operation may read an arbitrary number of bytes from the IPC facility, regardless of the size of blocks written by the writer. This model mirrors the traditional UNIX "file as a sequence of bytes" model.

- *Message*: The data exchanged via System V message queues, POSIX message queues, and datagram sockets takes the form of delimited messages. Each read operation reads a whole message, as written by the writer process. It is not possible to read part of a message, leaving the remainder on the IPC facility; nor is it possible to read multiple messages in a single read operation.

- *Pseudoterminals*: A pseudoterminal is a communication facility intended for use in specialized situations. We provide details in Chapter 64.

A few general features distinguish data-transfer facilities from shared memory:

- Although a data-transfer facility may have multiple readers, reads are destructive. A read operation consumes data, and that data is not available to any other process.

    The MSG_PEEK flag can be used to perform a nondestructive read from a socket (Section 61.3). UDP (Internet domain datagram) sockets allow a single message to be broadcast or multicast to multiple recipients (Section 61.12).

- Synchronization between the reader and writer processes is automatic. If a reader attempts to fetch data from a data-transfer facility that currently has no data, then (by default) the read operation will block until some process writes data to the facility.

Shared memory

Most modern UNIX systems provide three flavors of shared memory: System V shared memory, POSIX shared memory, and memory mappings. We consider the differences between them when describing the facilities in later chapters (see Section 54.5 in particular).

Note the following general points about shared memory:

- Although shared memory provides fast communication, this speed advantage is offset by the need to synchronize operations on the shared memory. For example, one process should not attempt to access a data structure in the shared memory while another process is updating it. A semaphore is the usual synchronization method used with shared memory.

- Data placed in shared memory is visible to all of the processes that share that memory. (This contrasts with the destructive read semantics described above for data-transfer facilities.)

43.3 Synchronization Facilities

The synchronization facilities shown in Figure 43-1 allow processes to coordinate their actions. Synchronization allows processes to avoid doing things such as simultaneously updating a shared memory region or the same part of a file. Without synchronization, such simultaneous updates could cause an application to produce incorrect results.

UNIX systems provide the following synchronization facilities:

- *Semaphores*: A semaphore is a kernel-maintained integer whose value is never permitted to fall below 0. A process can decrease or increase the value of a semaphore. If an attempt is made to decrease the value of the semaphore below 0, then the kernel blocks the operation until the semaphore's value increases to a level that permits the operation to be performed. (Alternatively, the process can request a nonblocking operation; then, instead of blocking, the kernel causes the operation to return immediately with an error indicating that the operation can't be performed immediately.) The meaning of a semaphore is determined by the application. A process decrements a semaphore (from, say, 1 to 0) in order to reserve exclusive access to some shared resource, and after completing work on the resource, increments the semaphore so that the shared resource is released for use by some other process. The use of a binary semaphore—a semaphore whose value is limited to 0 or 1—is common. However, an application that deals with multiple instances of a shared resource would employ a semaphore whose maximum value equals the number of shared resources. Linux provides both System V semaphores and POSIX semaphores, which have essentially similar functionality.

- *File locks*: File locks are a synchronization method explicitly designed to coordinate the actions of multiple processes operating on the same file. They can also be used to coordinate access to other shared resources. File locks come in two flavors: read (shared) locks and write (exclusive) locks. Any number of processes can hold a read lock on the same file (or region of a file). However, when one process holds a write lock on a file (or file region), other processes are prevented from holding either read or write locks on that file (or file region). Linux provides file-locking facilities via the *flock()* and *fcntl()* system calls. The *flock()* system call provides a simple locking mechanism, allowing processes to place a shared or an exclusive lock on an entire file. Because of its limited functionality, *flock()* locking facility is rarely used nowadays. The *fcntl()* system call provides record locking, allowing processes to place multiple read and write locks on different regions of the same file.

- *Mutexes and condition variables*: These synchronization facilities are normally used with POSIX threads, as described in Chapter 30.

> Some UNIX implementations, including Linux systems with a *glibc* that provides the NPTL threading implementation, also allow mutexes and condition variables to be shared between processes. SUSv3 permits, but doesn't require, an implementation to support process-shared mutexes and condition variables. They are not available on all UNIX systems, and so are not commonly employed for process synchronization.

When performing interprocess synchronization, our choice of facility is typically determined by the functional requirements. When coordinating access to a file, file record locking is usually the best choice. Semaphores are often the better choice for coordinating access to other types of shared resource.

Communication facilities can also be used for synchronization. For example, in Section 44.3, we show how a pipe can be used to synchronize the actions of a parent process with its children. More generally, any of the data-transfer facilities can be used for synchronization, with the synchronization operation taking the form of exchanging messages via the facility.

Since kernel 2.6.22, Linux provides an additional, nonstandard synchronization mechanism via the *eventfd()* system call. This system call creates an *eventfd* object that has an associated 8-byte unsigned integer maintained by the kernel. The system call returns a file descriptor that refers to the object. Writing an integer to this file descriptor adds that integer to the object's value. A *read()* from the file descriptor blocks if the object's value is 0. If the object has a non-zero value, a *read()* returns that value and resets it to 0. In addition, *poll()*, *select()*, or *epoll* can be used to test if the object has a nonzero value; if it does, the file descriptor indicates as being readable. An application that wishes to use an *eventfd* object for synchronization must first create the object using *eventfd()*, and then call *fork()* to create related processes that inherit file descriptors referring to the object. For further details, see the *eventfd(2)* manual page.

43.4 Comparing IPC Facilities

When it comes to IPC, we face a range of choices that can at first seem bewildering. In later chapters that describe each IPC facility, we include sections that compare each facility against other similar facilities. In the following pages, we consider a number of general points that may determine the choice of IPC facility.

IPC object identification and handles for open objects

In order to access an IPC object, a process must have some means of identifying the object, and once the object has been "opened," the process must use some type of handle to refer to the open object. Table 43-1 summarizes these properties for the various types of IPC facilities.

Table 43-1: Identifiers and handles for various types of IPC facilities

Facility type	Name used to identify object	Handle used to refer to object in programs
Pipe	no name	file descriptor
FIFO	pathname	file descriptor
UNIX domain socket	pathname	file descriptor
Internet domain socket	IP address + port number	file descriptor
System V message queue	System V IPC key	System V IPC identifier
System V semaphore	System V IPC key	System V IPC identifier
System V shared memory	System V IPC key	System V IPC identifier
POSIX message queue	POSIX IPC pathname	*mqd_t* (message queue descriptor)
POSIX named semaphore	POSIX IPC pathname	*sem_t* * (semaphore pointer)
POSIX unnamed semaphore	no name	*sem_t* * (semaphore pointer)
POSIX shared memory	POSIX IPC pathname	file descriptor
Anonymous mapping	no name	none
Memory-mapped file	pathname	file descriptor
flock() lock	pathname	file descriptor
fcntl() lock	pathname	file descriptor

Functionality

There are functional differences between the various IPC facilities that can be relevant in determining which facility to use. We begin by summarizing the differences between data-transfer facilities and shared memory:

- Data-transfer facilities involve read and write operations, with transferred data being consumable by just one reader process. Flow control between writer and reader, as well as synchronization (so that a reader is blocked when trying to read data from a facility that is currently empty) is automatically handled by the kernel. This model fits well with many application designs.

- Other application designs more naturally suit a shared-memory model. Shared memory allows one process to make data visible to any number of other processes sharing the same memory region. Communication "operations" are simple—a process can access data in shared memory in the same manner as it accesses any other memory in its virtual address space. On the other hand, the need to handle synchronization (and perhaps flow control) can add to the complexity of a shared-memory design. This model fits well with application designs that need to maintain shared state (e.g., a shared data structure).

With respect to the various data-transfer facilities, the following points are worth noting:

- Some data-transfer facilities transfer data as a byte stream (pipes, FIFOs, and stream sockets); others are message-oriented (message queues and datagram sockets). Which approach is preferable depends on the application. (An application can also impose a message-oriented model on a byte-stream facility, by using delimiter characters, fixed-length messages, or message headers that encode the length of the total message; see Section 44.8.)

- A distinctive feature of System V and POSIX message queues, compared with other data-transfer facilities, is the ability to assign a numeric type or priority to a message, so that messages can be delivered in a different order from that in which they were sent.

- Pipes, FIFOs, and sockets are implemented using file descriptors. These IPC facilities all support a range of alternative I/O models that we describe in Chapter 63: I/O multiplexing (the *select()* and *poll()* system calls), signal-driven I/O, and the Linux-specific *epoll* API. The primary benefit of these techniques is that they allow an application to simultaneously monitor multiple file descriptors to see whether I/O is possible on any of them. By contrast, System V message queues don't employ file descriptors and don't support these techniques.

    > On Linux, POSIX message queues are also implemented using file descriptors and support the alternative I/O techniques described above. However, this behavior is not specified in SUSv3, and is not supported on most other implementations.

- POSIX message queues provide a notification facility that can send a signal to a process, or instantiate a new thread, when a message arrives on a previously empty queue.

- UNIX domain sockets provide a feature that allows a file descriptor to be passed from one process to another. This allows one process to open a file and make it available to another process that otherwise might not be able to access the file. We briefly describe this feature in Section 61.13.3.

- UDP (Internet domain datagram) sockets allow a sender to broadcast or multicast a message to multiple recipients. We briefly describe this feature in Section 61.12.

With respect to process-synchronization facilities, the following points are worth noting:

- Record locks placed using *fcntl()* are considered to be owned by the process placing the lock. The kernel uses this ownership property to detect deadlocks (situations where two or more processes are holding locks that block each other's further lock requests). If a deadlock situation occurs, the kernel denies the lock request of one of the processes, returning an error from the *fcntl()* call to indicate that a deadlock occurred. System V and POSIX semaphores don't have an ownership property; no deadlock detection occurs for semaphores.

- Record locks placed using *fcntl()* are automatically released when the process that owns the locks terminates. System V semaphores provide a similar feature in the form of an "undo" feature, but this feature is not reliable in all circumstances (Section 47.8). POSIX semaphores don't provide an analog of this feature.

Network communication

Of all of the IPC methods shown in Figure 43-1, only sockets permit processes to communicate over a network. Sockets are generally used in one of two domains: the UNIX domain, which allows communication between processes on the same system, and the *Internet* domain, which allows communication between processes on different hosts connected via a TCP/IP network. Often, only minor changes are required to convert a program that uses UNIX domain sockets into one that uses Internet domain sockets, so an application that is built using UNIX domain sockets can be made network-capable with relatively little effort.

Portability

Modern UNIX implementations support most of the IPC facilities shown in Figure 43-1. However, the POSIX IPC facilities (message queues, semaphores, and shared memory) are not quite as widely available as their System V IPC counterparts, especially on older UNIX systems. (An implementation of POSIX message queues and full support for POSIX semaphores have appeared on Linux only in the 2.6.*x* kernel series.) Therefore, from a portability point of view, System V IPC may be preferable to POSIX IPC.

System V IPC design issues

The System V IPC facilities were designed independently of the traditional UNIX I/O model, and consequently suffer a few peculiarities that make their programming interfaces more complicated to use. The corresponding POSIX IPC facilities were designed to address these problems. The following points are of particular note:

- The System V IPC facilities are connectionless. These facilities provide no notion of a handle (like a file descriptor) referring to an open IPC object. In later chapters, we'll sometimes talk of "opening" a System V IPC object, but this is really just shorthand to describe the process of obtaining an identifer that refers to the object. The kernel does not record the process as having "opened" the object (unlike other types of IPC objects). This means that the kernel can't maintain a reference count of the number of processes that are currently using an object. Consequently, it can require additional programming effort for an application to be able to know when an object can safely be deleted.

- The programming interfaces for the System V IPC facilities are inconsistent with the traditional UNIX I/O model (they use integer key values and IPC identifiers instead of pathnames and file descriptors). The programming interfaces are also overly complex. This last point applies particularly to System V semaphores (refer to Sections 47.11 and 53.5).

By contrast, the kernel counts open references for POSIX IPC objects. This simplifies decisions about when an object can be deleted. Furthermore, the POSIX IPC facilities provide an interface that is simpler and more consistent with the traditional UNIX model.

Accessibility

The second column of Table 43-2 summarizes an important characteristic of each type of IPC object: the permissions scheme that governs which processes can access the object. The following list adds some details on the various schemes:

- For some IPC facilities (e.g., FIFOs and sockets), object names live in the file system, and accessibility is determined according to the associated file permissions mask, which specifies permissions for owner, group, and other (Section 15.4). Although System V IPC objects don't reside in the file system, each object has an associated permissions mask whose semantics are similar to those for files.

- A few IPC facilities (pipes, anonymous memory mappings) are marked as being accessible only by related processes. Here, *related* means related via *fork()*. In order for two processes to access the object, one of them must create the object and then call *fork()*. As a consequence of the *fork()*, the child process inherits a handle referring to the object, allowing both processes to share the object.

- The accessibility of a POSIX unnamed semaphore is determined by the accessibility of the shared memory region containing the semaphore.

- In order to place a lock on a file, a process must have a file descriptor referring to the file (i.e., in practice, it must have permission to open the file).

- There are no restrictions on accessing (i.e., connecting or sending a datagram to) an Internet domain socket. If necessary, access control must be implemented within the application.

Table 43-2: Accessibility and persistence for various types of IPC facilities

Facility type	Accessibility	Persistence
Pipe	only by related processes	process
FIFO	permissions mask	process
UNIX domain socket	permissions mask	process
Internet domain socket	by any process	process
System V message queue	permissions mask	kernel
System V semaphore	permissions mask	kernel
System V shared memory	permissions mask	kernel
POSIX message queue	permissions mask	kernel
POSIX named semaphore	permissions mask	kernel
POSIX unnamed semaphore	permissions of underlying memory	depends
POSIX shared memory	permissions mask	kernel
Anonymous mapping	only by related processes	process
Memory-mapped file	permissions mask	file system
flock() file lock	*open()* of file	process
fcntl() file lock	*open()* of file	process

Persistence

The term *persistence* refers to the lifetime of an IPC object. (Refer to the third column of Table 43-2.) We can distinguish three types of persistence:

- *Process persistence*: A process-persistent IPC object remains in existence only as long as it is held open by at least one process. If the object is closed by all processes, then all kernel resources associated with the object are freed, and any unread data is destroyed. Pipes, FIFOs, and sockets are examples of IPC facilities with process persistence.

> The persistence of a FIFO's data is not the same as the persistence of its name. A FIFO has a name in the file system that persists even after all file descriptors referring to the FIFO have been closed.

- *Kernel persistence*: A kernel-persistent IPC object exists until either it is explicitly deleted or the system is shut down. The lifetime of the object is independent of whether any process holds the object open. This means that, for example, one process can create an object, write data to it, and then close it (or terminate). At a later point, another process can open the object and read the data. Examples of facilities with kernel persistence are System V IPC and POSIX IPC. We exploit this property in the example programs that we present when describing these facilities in later chapters: for each facility, we implement separate programs that create an object, delete an object, and perform communication or synchronization.

- *File-system persistence*: An IPC object with file-system persistence retains its information even when the system is rebooted. The object exists until it is explicitly deleted. The only type of IPC object that demonstrates file-system persistence is shared memory based on a memory-mapped file.

Performance

In some circumstances, different IPC facilities may show notable differences in performance. However, in later chapters, we generally refrain from making performance comparisons, for the following reasons:

- The performance of an IPC facility may not be a significant factor in the overall performance of an application, and it may not be the only factor in determining the choice of an IPC facility.

- The relative performance of the various IPC facilities may vary across UNIX implementations or between different versions of the Linux kernel.

- Most importantly, the performance of an IPC facility will vary depending on the precise manner and environment in which it is used. Relevant factors include the size of the data units exchanged in each IPC operation, the amount of unread data that may be outstanding on the IPC facility, whether or not a process context switch is required for each unit of data exchanged, and other load on the system.

If IPC performance is crucial, there is no substitute for application-specific benchmarks run under an environment that matches the target system. To this end, it may be worth writing an abstract software layer that hides details of the IPC facility from the application and then testing performance when different IPC facilities are substituted underneath the abstract layer.

43.5 Summary

In this chapter, we provided an overview of various facilities that processes (and threads) can use to communicate with one another and to synchronize their actions.

Among the communication facilities provided on Linux are pipes, FIFOs, sockets, message queues, and shared memory. Synchronization facilities provided on Linux include semaphores and file locks.

In many cases, we have a choice of several possible techniques for communication and synchronization when performing a given task. In the course of this chapter, we compared the different techniques in various ways, with the aim of highlighting some differences that may influence the choice of one technique over another.

In the following chapters, we go into each of the communication and synchronization facilities in much more detail.

43.6 Exercises

43-1. Write a program that measures the bandwidth provided by pipes. As command-line arguments, the program should accept the number of data blocks to be sent and the size of each data block. After creating a pipe, the program splits into two process: a child that writes the data blocks to the pipe as fast as possible, and a parent that reads the data blocks. After all data has been read, the parent should print the elapsed time required and the bandwidth (bytes transferred per second). Measure the bandwidth for different data block sizes.

43-2. Repeat the preceding exercise for System V message queues, POSIX message queues, UNIX domain stream sockets, and UNIX domain datagram sockets. Use these programs to compare the relative performance of the various IPC facilities on Linux. If you have access to other UNIX implementations, perform the same comparisons on those systems.

44

PIPES AND FIFOS

This chapter describes pipes and FIFOs. Pipes are the oldest method of IPC on the UNIX system, having appeared in Third Edition UNIX in the early 1970s. Pipes provide an elegant solution to a frequent requirement: having created two processes to run different programs (commands), how can the shell allow the output produced by one process to be used as the input to the other process? Pipes can be used to pass data between related processes (the meaning of *related* will become clear later). FIFOs are a variation on the pipe concept. The important difference is that FIFOs can be used for communication between *any* processes.

44.1 Overview

Every user of the shell is familiar with the use of pipes in commands such as the following, which counts the number of files in a directory:

```
$ ls | wc -l
```

In order to execute the above command, the shell creates two processes, executing *ls* and *wc*, respectively. (This is done using *fork()* and *exec()*, which are described in Chapters 24 and 27.) Figure 44-1 shows how the two processes employ the pipe.

Among other things, Figure 44-1 is intended to illustrate how pipes got their name. We can think of a pipe as a piece of plumbing that allows data to flow from one process to another.

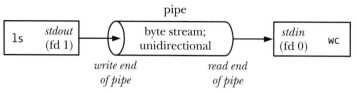

Figure 44-1: Using a pipe to connect two processes

One point to note in Figure 44-1 is that the two processes are connected to the pipe so that the writing process (*ls*) has its standard output (file descriptor 1) joined to the write end of the pipe, while the reading process (*wc*) has its standard input (file descriptor 0) joined to the read end of the pipe. In effect, these two processes are unaware of the existence of the pipe; they just read from and write to the standard file descriptors. The shell must do some work in order to set things up in this way, and we see how this is done in Section 44.4.

In the following paragraphs, we cover a number of important characteristics of pipes.

A pipe is a byte stream

When we say that a pipe is a byte stream, we mean that there is no concept of messages or message boundaries when using a pipe. The process reading from a pipe can read blocks of data of any size, regardless of the size of blocks written by the writing process. Furthermore, the data passes through the pipe sequentially—bytes are read from a pipe in exactly the order they were written. It is not possible to randomly access the data in a pipe using *lseek()*.

If we want to implement the notion of discrete messages in a pipe, we must do this within our application. While this is feasible (refer to Section 44.8), it may be preferable to use alternative IPC mechanisms, such as message queues and datagram sockets, which we discuss in later chapters.

Reading from a pipe

Attempts to read from a pipe that is currently empty block until at least one byte has been written to the pipe. If the write end of a pipe is closed, then a process reading from the pipe will see end-of-file (i.e., *read()* returns 0) once it has read all remaining data in the pipe.

Pipes are unidirectional

Data can travel only in one direction through a pipe. One end of the pipe is used for writing, and the other end is used for reading.

On some other UNIX implementations—notably those derived from System V Release 4—pipes are bidirectional (so-called *stream pipes*). Bidirectional pipes are not specified by any UNIX standards, so that, even on implementations where they are provided, it is best to avoid reliance on their semantics. As an alternative, we can use UNIX domain stream socket pairs (created using the *socketpair()* system call described in Section 57.5), which provide a standardized bidirectional communication mechanism that is semantically equivalent to stream pipes.

Writes of up to `PIPE_BUF` bytes are guaranteed to be atomic

If multiple processes are writing to a single pipe, then it is guaranteed that their data won't be intermingled if they write no more than `PIPE_BUF` bytes at a time.

SUSv3 requires that `PIPE_BUF` be at least `_POSIX_PIPE_BUF` (512). An implementation should define `PIPE_BUF` (in `<limits.h>`) and/or allow the call *fpathconf(fd, _PC_PIPE_BUF)* to return the actual upper limit for atomic writes. `PIPE_BUF` varies across UNIX implementations; for example, it is 512 bytes on FreeBSD 6.0, 4096 bytes on Tru64 5.1, and 5120 bytes on Solaris 8. On Linux, `PIPE_BUF` has the value 4096.

When writing blocks of data larger than `PIPE_BUF` bytes to a pipe, the kernel may transfer the data in multiple smaller pieces, appending further data as the reader removes bytes from the pipe. (The *write()* call blocks until all of the data has been written to the pipe.) When there is only a single process writing to a pipe (the usual case), this doesn't matter. However, if there are multiple writer processes, then writes of large blocks may be broken into segments of arbitrary size (which may be smaller than `PIPE_BUF` bytes) and interleaved with writes by other processes.

The `PIPE_BUF` limit affects exactly when data is transferred to the pipe. When writing up to `PIPE_BUF` bytes, *write()* will block if necessary until sufficient space is available in the pipe so that it can complete the operation atomically. When more than `PIPE_BUF` bytes are being written, *write()* transfers as much data as possible to fill the pipe, and then blocks until data has been removed from the pipe by some reading process. If such a blocked *write()* is interrupted by a signal handler, then the call unblocks and returns a count of the number of bytes successfully transferred, which will be less than was requested (a so-called *partial write*).

> On Linux 2.2, pipe writes of *any* size are atomic, unless interrupted by a signal handler. On Linux 2.4 and later, any write greater than `PIPE_BUF` bytes may be interleaved with writes by other processes. (The kernel code implementing pipes underwent substantial changes between kernel versions 2.2 and 2.4.)

Pipes have a limited capacity

A pipe is simply a buffer maintained in kernel memory. This buffer has a maximum capacity. Once a pipe is full, further writes to the pipe block until the reader removes some data from the pipe.

SUSv3 makes no requirement about the capacity of a pipe. In Linux kernels before 2.6.11, the pipe capacity is the same as the system page size (e.g., 4096 bytes on x86-32); since Linux 2.6.11, the pipe capacity is 65,536 bytes. Other UNIX implementations have different pipe capacities.

In general, an application never needs to know the exact capacity of a pipe. If we want to prevent the writer process(es) from blocking, the process(es) reading from the pipe should be designed to read data as soon as it is available.

> In theory, there is no reason why a pipe couldn't operate with smaller capacities, even with a single-byte buffer. The reason for employing large buffer sizes is efficiency: each time a writer fills the pipe, the kernel must perform a context switch to allow the reader to be scheduled so that it can empty some data from the pipe. Employing a larger buffer size means that fewer context switches are required.
>
> Starting with Linux 2.6.35, the capacity of a pipe can be modified. The Linux-specific call *fcntl(fd, F_SETPIPE_SZ, size)* changes the capacity of the pipe referred to by *fd* to be at least *size* bytes. An unprivileged process can

change the pipe capacity to any value in the range from the system page size up to the value in /proc/sys/fs/pipe-max-size. The default value for pipe-max-size is 1,048,576 bytes. A privileged (CAP_SYS_RESOURCE) process can override this limit. When allocating space for the pipe, the kernel may round *size* up to some value convenient for the implementation. The *fcntl(fd, F_GETPIPE_SZ)* call returns the actual size allocated for the pipe.

44.2 Creating and Using Pipes

The *pipe()* system call creates a new pipe.

```
#include <unistd.h>

int pipe(int filedes[2]);
```
                                        Returns 0 on success, or −1 on error

A successful call to *pipe()* returns two open file descriptors in the array *filedes*: one for the read end of the pipe (*filedes[0]*) and one for the write end (*filedes[1]*).

As with any file descriptor, we can use the *read()* and *write()* system calls to perform I/O on the pipe. Once written to the write end of a pipe, data is immediately available to be read from the read end. A *read()* from a pipe obtains the lesser of the number of bytes requested and the number of bytes currently available in the pipe (but blocks if the pipe is empty).

We can also use the *stdio* functions (*fprintf()*, *fscanf()*, and so on) with pipes by first using *fdopen()* to obtain a file stream corresponding to one of the descriptors in *filedes* (Section 13.7). However, when doing this, we must be aware of the *stdio* buffering issues described in Section 44.6.

> The call *ioctl(fd, FIONREAD, &cnt)* returns the number of unread bytes in the pipe or FIFO referred to by the file descriptor *fd*. This feature is also available on some other implementations, but is not specified in SUSv3.

Figure 44-2 shows the situation after a pipe has been created by *pipe()*, with the calling process having file descriptors referring to each end.

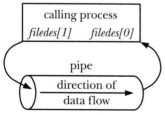

Figure 44-2: Process file descriptors after creating a pipe

A pipe has few uses within a single process (we consider one in Section 63.5.2). Normally, we use a pipe to allow communication between two processes. To connect two processes using a pipe, we follow the *pipe()* call with a call to *fork()*. During a *fork()*, the child process inherits copies of its parent's file descriptors (Section 24.2.1), bringing about the situation shown on the left side of Figure 44-3.

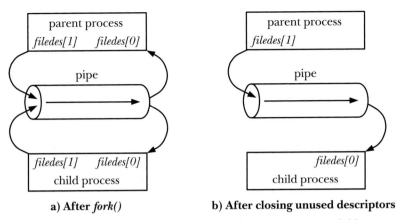

a) After *fork()*	b) After closing unused descriptors

Figure 44-3: Setting up a pipe to transfer data from a parent to a child

While it is possible for the parent and child to both read from and write to the pipe, this is not usual. Therefore, immediately after the *fork()*, one process closes its descriptor for the write end of the pipe, and the other closes its descriptor for the read end. For example, if the parent is to send data to the child, then it would close its read descriptor for the pipe, *filedes[0]*, while the child would close its write descriptor for the pipe, *filedes[1]*, bringing about the situation shown on the right side of Figure 44-3. The code to create this setup is shown in Listing 44-1.

Listing 44-1: Steps in creating a pipe to transfer data from a parent to a child

```
int filedes[2];

if (pipe(filedes) == -1)              /* Create the pipe */
    errExit("pipe");

switch (fork()) {                     /* Create a child process */
case -1:
    errExit("fork");

case 0:   /* Child */
    if (close(filedes[1]) == -1)      /* Close unused write end */
        errExit("close");

    /* Child now reads from pipe */
    break;

default: /* Parent */
    if (close(filedes[0]) == -1)      /* Close unused read end */
        errExit("close");

    /* Parent now writes to pipe */
    break;
}
```

One reason that it is not usual to have both the parent and child reading from a single pipe is that if two processes try to simultaneously read from a pipe, we can't be sure which process will be the first to succeed—the two processes race for data. Preventing such races would require the use of some synchronization mechanism. However, if we require bidirectional communication, there is a simpler way: just create two pipes, one for sending data in each direction between the two processes. (If employing this technique, then we need to be wary of deadlocks that may occur if both processes block while trying to read from empty pipes or while trying to write to pipes that are already full.)

While it is possible to have multiple processes writing to a pipe, it is typical to have only a single writer. (We show one example of where it is useful to have multiple writers to a pipe in Section 44.3.) By contrast, there are situations where it can be useful to have multiple writers on a FIFO, and we see an example of this in Section 44.8.

> Starting with kernel 2.6.27, Linux supports a new, nonstandard system call, *pipe2()*. This system call performs the same task as *pipe()*, but supports an additional argument, *flags*, that can be used to modify the behavior of the system call. Two flags are supported. The O_CLOEXEC flag causes the kernel to enable the close-on-exec flag (FD_CLOEXEC) for the two new file descriptors. This flag is useful for the same reasons as the *open()* O_CLOEXEC flag described in Section 4.3.1. The O_NONBLOCK flag causes the kernel to mark both underlying open file descriptions as nonblocking, so that future I/O operations will be nonblocking. This saves additional calls to *fcntl()* to achieve the same result.

Pipes allow communication between related processes

In the discussion so far, we have talked about using pipes for communication between a parent and a child process. However, pipes can be used for communication between any two (or more) related processes, as long as the pipe was created by a common ancestor before the series of *fork()* calls that led to the existence of the processes. (This is what we meant when we referred to *related processes* at the beginning of this chapter.) For example, a pipe could be used for communication between a process and its grandchild. The first process creates the pipe, and then forks a child that in turn forks to yield the grandchild. A common scenario is that a pipe is used for communication between two siblings—their parent creates the pipe, and then creates the two children. This is what the shell does when building a pipeline.

> There is an exception to the statement that pipes can be used to communicate only between related processes. Passing a file descriptor over a UNIX domain socket (a technique that we briefly describe in Section 61.13.3) makes it possible to pass a file descriptor for a pipe to an unrelated process.

Closing unused pipe file descriptors

Closing unused pipe file descriptors is more than a matter of ensuring that a process doesn't exhaust its limited set of file descriptors—it is essential to the correct use of pipes. We now consider why the unused file descriptors for both the read and write ends of the pipe must be closed.

The process reading from the pipe closes its write descriptor for the pipe, so that, when the other process completes its output and closes its write descriptor, the reader sees end-of-file (once it has read any outstanding data in the pipe).

If the reading process doesn't close the write end of the pipe, then, after the other process closes its write descriptor, the reader won't see end-of-file, even after it has read all data from the pipe. Instead, a *read()* would block waiting for data, because the kernel knows that there is still at least one write descriptor open for the pipe. That this descriptor is held open by the reading process itself is irrelevant; in theory, that process could still write to the pipe, even if it is blocked trying to read. For example, the *read()* might be interrupted by a signal handler that writes data to the pipe. (This is a realistic scenario, as we'll see in Section 63.5.2.)

The writing process closes its read descriptor for the pipe for a different reason. When a process tries to write to a pipe for which no process has an open read descriptor, the kernel sends the SIGPIPE signal to the writing process. By default, this signal kills a process. A process can instead arrange to catch or ignore this signal, in which case the *write()* on the pipe fails with the error EPIPE (broken pipe). Receiving the SIGPIPE signal or getting the EPIPE error is a useful indication about the status of the pipe, and this is why unused read descriptors for the pipe should be closed.

> Note that the treatment of a *write()* that is interrupted by a SIGPIPE handler is special. Normally, when a *write()* (or other "slow" system call) is interrupted by a signal handler, the call is either automatically restarted or fails with the error EINTR, depending on whether the handler was installed with the *sigaction()* SA_RESTART flag (Section 21.5). The behavior in the case of SIGPIPE is different because it makes no sense either to automatically restart the *write()* or to simply indicate that the *write()* was interrupted by a handler (thus implying that the *write()* could usefully be manually restarted). In neither case can a subsequent *write()* attempt succeed, because the pipe will still be broken.

If the writing process doesn't close the read end of the pipe, then, even after the other process closes the read end of the pipe, the writing process will still be able to write to the pipe. Eventually, the writing process will fill the pipe, and a further attempt to write will block indefinitely.

One final reason for closing unused file descriptors is that it is only after all file descriptors in all processes that refer to a pipe are closed that the pipe is destroyed and its resources released for reuse by other processes. At this point, any unread data in the pipe is lost.

Example program

The program in Listing 44-2 demonstrates the use of a pipe for communication between parent and child processes. This example demonstrates the byte-stream nature of pipes referred to earlier—the parent writes its data in a single operation, while the child reads data from the pipe in small blocks.

The main program calls *pipe()* to create a pipe ①, and then calls *fork()* to create a child ②. After the *fork()*, the parent process closes its file descriptor for the read end of the pipe ⑧, and writes the string given as the program's command-line argument to the write end of the pipe ⑨. The parent then closes the write end of the pipe ⑩, and calls *wait()* to wait for the child to terminate ⑪. After closing its file descriptor for the write end of the pipe ③, the child process enters a loop where it reads ④ blocks of data (of up to BUF_SIZE bytes) from the pipe and writes ⑥ them to standard output. When the child encounters end-of-file on the pipe ⑤, it exits the loop ⑦, writes a trailing newline character, closes its descriptor for the read end of the pipe, and terminates.

Here's an example of what we might see when running the program in Listing 44-2:

```
$ ./simple_pipe 'It was a bright cold day in April, '\
'and the clocks were striking thirteen.'
It was a bright cold day in April, and the clocks were striking thirteen.
```

Listing 44-2: Using a pipe to communicate between a parent and child process

—————————————————————————————————————— `pipes/simple_pipe.c`

```
#include <sys/wait.h>
#include "tlpi_hdr.h"

#define BUF_SIZE 10

int
main(int argc, char *argv[])
{
    int pfd[2];                          /* Pipe file descriptors */
    char buf[BUF_SIZE];
    ssize_t numRead;

    if (argc != 2 || strcmp(argv[1], "--help") == 0)
        usageErr("%s string\n", argv[0]);

①   if (pipe(pfd) == -1)                 /* Create the pipe */
        errExit("pipe");

②   switch (fork()) {
    case -1:
        errExit("fork");

    case 0:              /* Child  - reads from pipe */
③       if (close(pfd[1]) == -1)            /* Write end is unused */
            errExit("close - child");

        for (;;) {              /* Read data from pipe, echo on stdout */
④           numRead = read(pfd[0], buf, BUF_SIZE);
            if (numRead == -1)
                errExit("read");
⑤           if (numRead == 0)
                break;                      /* End-of-file */
⑥           if (write(STDOUT_FILENO, buf, numRead) != numRead)
                fatal("child - partial/failed write");
        }

⑦       write(STDOUT_FILENO, "\n", 1);
        if (close(pfd[0]) == -1)
          errExit("close");
        exit(EXIT_SUCCESS);

    default:              /* Parent - writes to pipe */
⑧       if (close(pfd[0]) == -1)            /* Read end is unused */
            errExit("close - parent");
```

```
⑨          if (write(pfd[1], argv[1], strlen(argv[1])) != strlen(argv[1]))
               fatal("parent - partial/failed write");

⑩          if (close(pfd[1]) == -1)                 /* Child will see EOF */
               errExit("close");
⑪          wait(NULL);                              /* Wait for child to finish */
           exit(EXIT_SUCCESS);
       }
   }
```

─── pipes/simple_pipe.c

44.3   Pipes as a Method of Process Synchronization

In Section 24.5, we looked at how signals could be used to synchronize the actions
of parent and child processes in order to avoid race conditions. Pipes can be used
to achieve a similar result, as shown by the skeleton program in Listing 44-3. This
program creates multiple child processes (one for each command-line argument),
each of which is intended to accomplish some action, simulated in the example
program by sleeping for some time. The parent waits until all children have completed their actions.

To perform the synchronization, the parent builds a pipe ① before creating the
child processes ②. Each child inherits a file descriptor for the write end of the pipe
and closes this descriptor once it has completed its action ③. After all of the children have closed their file descriptors for the write end of the pipe, the parent's
read() ⑤ from the pipe will complete, returning end-of-file (0). At this point, the
parent is free to carry on to do other work. (Note that closing the unused write end
of the pipe in the parent ④ is essential to the correct operation of this technique;
otherwise, the parent would block forever when trying to read from the pipe.)

The following is an example of what we see when we use the program in Listing 44-3 to create three children that sleep for 4, 2, and 6 seconds:

```
$ ./pipe_sync 4 2 6
08:22:16  Parent started
08:22:18  Child 2 (PID=2445) closing pipe
08:22:20  Child 1 (PID=2444) closing pipe
08:22:22  Child 3 (PID=2446) closing pipe
08:22:22  Parent ready to go
```

Listing 44-3: Using a pipe to synchronize multiple processes

─── pipes/pipe_sync.c

```c
#include "curr_time.h"              /* Declaration of currTime() */
#include "tlpi_hdr.h"

int
main(int argc, char *argv[])
{
    int pfd[2];                     /* Process synchronization pipe */
    int j, dummy;
```

```
        if (argc < 2 || strcmp(argv[1], "--help") == 0)
            usageErr("%s sleep-time...\n", argv[0]);

        setbuf(stdout, NULL);                    /* Make stdout unbuffered, since we
                                                    terminate child with _exit() */
        printf("%s  Parent started\n", currTime("%T"));

①      if (pipe(pfd) == -1)
            errExit("pipe");

        for (j = 1; j < argc; j++) {
②          switch (fork()) {
            case -1:
                errExit("fork %d", j);

            case 0: /* Child */
                if (close(pfd[0]) == -1)         /* Read end is unused */
                    errExit("close");

                /* Child does some work, and lets parent know it's done */

                sleep(getInt(argv[j], GN_NONNEG, "sleep-time"));
                                                 /* Simulate processing */
                printf("%s  Child %d (PID=%ld) closing pipe\n",
                        currTime("%T"), j, (long) getpid());
③              if (close(pfd[1]) == -1)
                    errExit("close");

                /* Child now carries on to do other things... */

                _exit(EXIT_SUCCESS);

            default: /* Parent loops to create next child */
                break;
            }
        }

        /* Parent comes here; close write end of pipe so we can see EOF */

④      if (close(pfd[1]) == -1)                  /* Write end is unused */
            errExit("close");

        /* Parent may do other work, then synchronizes with children */

⑤      if (read(pfd[0], &dummy, 1) != 0)
            fatal("parent didn't get EOF");
        printf("%s  Parent ready to go\n", currTime("%T"));

        /* Parent can now carry on to do other things... */

        exit(EXIT_SUCCESS);
    }
```

                                                    —— **pipes/pipe_sync.c**

Synchronization using pipes has an advantage over the earlier example of synchronization using signals: it can be used to coordinate the actions of one process with multiple other (related) processes. The fact that multiple (standard) signals can't be queued makes signals unsuitable in this case. (Conversely, signals have the advantage that they can be broadcast by one process to all of the members of a process group.)

Other synchronization topologies are possible (e.g., using multiple pipes). Furthermore, this technique could be extended so that, instead of closing the pipe, each child writes a message to the pipe containing its process ID and some status information. Alternatively, each child might write a single byte to the pipe. The parent process could then count and analyze these messages. This approach guards against the possibility of the child accidentally terminating, rather than explicitly closing the pipe.

44.4 Using Pipes to Connect Filters

When a pipe is created, the file descriptors used for the two ends of the pipe are the next lowest-numbered descriptors available. Since, in normal circumstances, descriptors 0, 1, and 2 are already in use for a process, some higher-numbered descriptors will be allocated for the pipe. So how do we bring about the situation shown in Figure 44-1, where two filters (i.e., programs that read from *stdin* and write to *stdout*) are connected using a pipe, such that the standard output of one program is directed into the pipe and the standard input of the other is taken from the pipe? And in particular, how can we do this without modifying the code of the filters themselves?

The answer is to use the techniques described in Section 5.5 for duplicating file descriptors. Traditionally, the following series of calls was used to accomplish the desired result:

```
int pfd[2];

pipe(pfd);              /* Allocates (say) file descriptors 3 and 4 for pipe */

/* Other steps here, e.g., fork() */

close(STDOUT_FILENO);        /* Free file descriptor 1 */
dup(pfd[1]);                 /* Duplication uses lowest free file
                                descriptor, i.e., fd 1 */
```

The end result of the above steps is that the process's standard output is bound to the write end of the pipe. A corresponding set of calls can be used to bind a process's standard input to the read end of the pipe.

Note that these steps depend on the assumption that file descriptors 0, 1, and 2 for a process are already open. (The shell normally ensures this for each program it executes.) If file descriptor 0 happened to be closed between the call to *pipe()* and the calls to *close()* and *dup()*, then we would erroneously bind the process's standard *input* to the write end of the pipe. To avoid this possibility, we can replace the calls to *close()* and *dup()* with the following *dup2()* call, which allows us to explicitly specify the descriptor to be bound to the pipe end:

```
dup2(pfd[1], STDOUT_FILENO);    /* Close descriptor 1, and reopen bound
                                   to write end of pipe */
```

After duplicating *pfd[1]*, we now have two file descriptors referring to the write end of the pipe: descriptor 1 and *pfd[1]*. Since unused pipe file descriptors should be closed, after the *dup2()* call, we close the superfluous descriptor:

```
close(pfd[1]);
```

The code we have shown so far relies on standard output having been previously open. Suppose that, prior to the *pipe()* call, standard input and standard output had both been closed. In this case, *pipe()* would have allocated these two descriptors to the pipe, perhaps with *pfd[0]* having the value 0 and *pfd[1]* having the value 1. Consequently, the preceding *dup2()* and *close()* calls would be equivalent to the following:

```
dup2(1, 1);          /* Does nothing */
close(1);            /* Closes sole descriptor for write end of pipe */
```

Therefore, it is good defensive programming practice to bracket these calls with an if statement of the following form:

```
if (pfd[1] != STDOUT_FILENO) {
    dup2(pfd[1], STDOUT_FILENO);
    close(pfd[1]);
}
```

Example program

The program in Listing 44-4 uses the techniques described in this section to bring about the setup shown in Figure 44-1. After building a pipe, this program creates two child processes. The first child binds its standard output to the write end of the pipe and then execs *ls*. The second child binds its standard input to the read end of the pipe and then execs *wc*.

Listing 44-4: Using a pipe to connect *ls* and *wc*

————————————————————————————————— pipes/pipe_ls_wc.c

```
#include <sys/wait.h>
#include "tlpi_hdr.h"

int
main(int argc, char *argv[])
{
    int pfd[2];                              /* Pipe file descriptors */

    if (pipe(pfd) == -1)                     /* Create pipe */
        errExit("pipe");

    switch (fork()) {
    case -1:
        errExit("fork");

    case 0:             /* First child: exec 'ls' to write to pipe */
        if (close(pfd[0]) == -1)                 /* Read end is unused */
            errExit("close 1");
```

```
                /* Duplicate stdout on write end of pipe; close duplicated descriptor */

            if (pfd[1] != STDOUT_FILENO) {              /* Defensive check */
                if (dup2(pfd[1], STDOUT_FILENO) == -1)
                    errExit("dup2 1");
                if (close(pfd[1]) == -1)
                    errExit("close 2");
            }

            execlp("ls", "ls", (char *) NULL);          /* Writes to pipe */
            errExit("execlp ls");

        default:                /* Parent falls through to create next child */
            break;
        }

        switch (fork()) {
        case -1:
            errExit("fork");

        case 0:                  /* Second child: exec 'wc' to read from pipe */
            if (close(pfd[1]) == -1)                     /* Write end is unused */
                errExit("close 3");

            /* Duplicate stdin on read end of pipe; close duplicated descriptor */

            if (pfd[0] != STDIN_FILENO) {                /* Defensive check */
                if (dup2(pfd[0], STDIN_FILENO) == -1)
                    errExit("dup2 2");
                if (close(pfd[0]) == -1)
                    errExit("close 4");
            }

            execlp("wc", "wc", "-l", (char *) NULL);     /* Reads from pipe */
            errExit("execlp wc");

        default:                    /* Parent falls through */
            break;
        }

        /* Parent closes unused file descriptors for pipe, and waits for children */

        if (close(pfd[0]) == -1)
            errExit("close 5");
        if (close(pfd[1]) == -1)
            errExit("close 6");
        if (wait(NULL) == -1)
            errExit("wait 1");
        if (wait(NULL) == -1)
            errExit("wait 2");

        exit(EXIT_SUCCESS);
    }
```
                                                              ──── **pipes/pipe_ls_wc.c**

When we run the program in Listing 44-4, we see the following:

```
$ ./pipe_ls_wc
     24
$ ls | wc -l                    Verify the results using shell commands
     24
```

44.5 Talking to a Shell Command via a Pipe: *popen()*

A common use for pipes is to execute a shell command and either read its output
or send it some input. The *popen()* and *pclose()* functions are provided to simplify
this task.

```
#include <stdio.h>

FILE *popen(const char *command, const char *mode);

                                        Returns file stream, or NULL on error
int pclose(FILE *stream);

                        Returns termination status of child process, or −1 on error
```

The *popen()* function creates a pipe, and then forks a child process that execs a
shell, which in turn creates a child process to execute the string given in *command*.
The *mode* argument is a string that determines whether the calling process will read
from the pipe (*mode* is *r*) or write to it (*mode* is *w*). (Since pipes are unidirectional,
two-way communication with the executed *command* is not possible.) The value of
mode determines whether the standard output of the executed command is connected to the write end of the pipe or its standard input is connected to the read
end of the pipe, as shown in Figure 44-4.

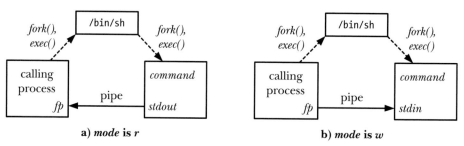

Figure 44-4: Overview of process relationships and pipe usage for *popen()*

On success, *popen()* returns a file stream pointer that can be used with the *stdio*
library functions. If an error occurs (e.g., *mode* is not *r* or *w*, pipe creation fails, or
the *fork()* to create the child fails), then *popen()* returns NULL and sets *errno* to indicate the cause of the error.

After the *popen()* call, the calling process uses the pipe to read the output of
command or to send input to it. Just as with pipes created using *pipe()*, when reading
from the pipe, the calling process encounters end-of-file once *command* has closed

the write end of the pipe; when writing to the pipe, it is sent a SIGPIPE signal, and gets the EPIPE error, if *command* has closed the read end of the pipe.

Once I/O is complete, the *pclose()* function is used to close the pipe and wait for the child shell to terminate. (The *fclose()* function should not be used, since it doesn't wait for the child.) On success, *pclose()* yields the termination status (Section 26.1.3) of the child shell (which is the termination status of the last command that the shell executed, unless the shell was killed by a signal). As with *system()* (Section 27.6), if a shell could not be execed, then *pclose()* returns a value as though the child shell had terminated with the call *_exit(127)*. If some other error occurs, *pclose()* returns –1. One possible error is that the termination status could not be obtained. We explain how this may occur shortly.

When performing a wait to obtain the status of the child shell, SUSv3 requires that *pclose()*, like *system()*, should automatically restart the internal call that it makes to *waitpid()* if that call is interrupted by a signal handler.

In general, we can make the same statements for *popen()* as were made in Section 27.6 for *system()*. Using *popen()* offers convenience. It builds the pipe, performs descriptor duplication, closes unused descriptors, and handles all of the details of *fork()* and *exec()* on our behalf. In addition, shell processing is performed on the command. This convenience comes at the cost of efficiency. At least two extra processes must be created: one for the shell and one or more for the command(s) executed by the shell. As with *system()*, *popen()* should never be used from privileged programs.

While there are several similarities between *system()* and *popen()* plus *pclose()*, there are also significant differences. These stem from the fact that, with *system()*, the execution of the shell command is encapsulated within a single function call, whereas with *popen()*, the calling process runs in parallel with the shell command and then calls *pclose()*. The differences are as follows:

- Since the calling process and the executed command are operating in parallel, SUSv3 requires that *popen()* should *not* ignore SIGINT and SIGQUIT. If generated from the keyboard, these signals are sent to both the calling process and the executed command. This occurs because both processes reside in the same process group, and terminal-generated signals are sent to all of the members of the (foreground) process group, as described in Section 34.5.

- Since the calling process may create other child processes between the execution of *popen()* and *pclose()*, SUSv3 requires that *popen()* should *not* block SIGCHLD. This means that if the calling process performs a wait operation before the *pclose()* call, it may retrieve the status of the child created by *popen()*. In this case, when *pclose()* is later called, it will return –1, with *errno* set to ECHILD, indicating that *pclose()* could not retrieve the status of the child.

Example program

Listing 44-5 demonstrates the use of *popen()* and *pclose()*. This program repeatedly reads a filename wildcard pattern ②, and then uses *popen()* to obtain the results from passing this pattern to the *ls* command ⑤. (Techniques similar to this were used on older UNIX implementations to perform filename generation, also known as *globbing*, prior to the existence of the *glob()* library function.)

Listing 44-5: Globbing filename patterns with *popen()*

——————————————————————————————— `pipes/popen_glob.c`

```
    #include <ctype.h>
    #include <limits.h>
    #include "print_wait_status.h"          /* For printWaitStatus() */
    #include "tlpi_hdr.h"

①  #define POPEN_FMT "/bin/ls -d %s 2> /dev/null"
    #define PAT_SIZE 50
    #define PCMD_BUF_SIZE (sizeof(POPEN_FMT) + PAT_SIZE)

    int
    main(int argc, char *argv[])
    {
        char pat[PAT_SIZE];                 /* Pattern for globbing */
        char popenCmd[PCMD_BUF_SIZE];
        FILE *fp;                           /* File stream returned by popen() */
        Boolean badPattern;                 /* Invalid characters in 'pat'? */
        int len, status, fileCnt, j;
        char pathname[PATH_MAX];

        for (;;) {                          /* Read pattern, display results of globbing */
            printf("pattern: ");
            fflush(stdout);
②          if (fgets(pat, PAT_SIZE, stdin) == NULL)
                break;                      /* EOF */
            len = strlen(pat);
            if (len <= 1)                   /* Empty line */
                continue;

            if (pat[len - 1] == '\n')       /* Strip trailing newline */
                pat[len - 1] = '\0';

            /* Ensure that the pattern contains only valid characters,
               i.e., letters, digits, underscore, dot, and the shell
               globbing characters. (Our definition of valid is more
               restrictive than the shell, which permits other characters
               to be included in a filename if they are quoted.) */

③          for (j = 0, badPattern = FALSE; j < len && !badPattern; j++)
                if (!isalnum((unsigned char) pat[j]) &&
                        strchr("_*?[^-].", pat[j]) == NULL)
                    badPattern = TRUE;

            if (badPattern) {
                printf("Bad pattern character: %c\n", pat[j - 1]);
                continue;
            }

            /* Build and execute command to glob 'pat' */

④          snprintf(popenCmd, PCMD_BUF_SIZE, POPEN_FMT, pat);

⑤          fp = popen(popenCmd, "r");
```

```
        if (fp == NULL) {
            printf("popen() failed\n");
            continue;
        }

        /* Read resulting list of pathnames until EOF */

        fileCnt = 0;
        while (fgets(pathname, PATH_MAX, fp) != NULL) {
            printf("%s", pathname);
            fileCnt++;
        }

        /* Close pipe, fetch and display termination status */

        status = pclose(fp);
        printf("    %d matching file%s\n", fileCnt, (fileCnt != 1) ? "s" : "");
        printf("    pclose() status = %#x\n", (unsigned int) status);
        if (status != -1)
            printWaitStatus("\t", status);
    }

    exit(EXIT_SUCCESS);
}
```

── *pipes/popen_glob.c*

The following shell session demonstrates the use of the program in Listing 44-5. In this example, we first provide a pattern that matches two filenames, and then a pattern that matches no filename:

```
$ ./popen_glob
pattern: popen_glob*                    Matches two filenames
popen_glob
popen_glob.c
    2 matching files
    pclose() status = 0
        child exited, status=0
pattern: x*                             Matches no filename
    0 matching files
    pclose() status = 0x100              ls(1) exits with status 1
        child exited, status=1
pattern: ^D$                            Type Control-D to terminate
```

The construction of the command ①④ for globbing in Listing 44-5 requires some explanation. Actual globbing of a pattern is performed by the shell. The *ls* command is merely being used to list the matching filenames, one per line. We could have tried using the *echo* command instead, but this would have had the undesirable result that if a pattern matched no filenames, then the shell would leave the pattern unchanged, and *echo* would simply display the pattern. By contrast, if *ls* is given the name of a file that doesn't exist, it prints an error message on *stderr* (which we dispose of by redirecting *stderr* to /dev/null), prints nothing on *stdout*, and exits with a status of 1.

Note also the input checking performed in Listing 44-5 ③. This is done to prevent invalid input causing *popen()* to execute an unexpected shell command. Suppose that these checks were omitted, and the user entered the following input:

```
pattern: ; rm *
```

The program would then pass the following command to *popen()*, with disastrous results:

```
/bin/ls -d ; rm * 2> /dev/null
```

Such checking of input is always required in programs that use *popen()* (or *system()*) to execute a shell command built from user input. (An alternative would be for the application to quote any characters other than those being checked for, so that those characters don't undergo special processing by the shell.)

44.6 Pipes and *stdio* Buffering

Since the file stream pointer returned by a call to *popen()* doesn't refer to a terminal, the *stdio* library applies block buffering to the file stream (Section 13.2). This means that when we call *popen()* with a *mode* of *w*, then, by default, output is sent to the child process at the other end of the pipe only when the *stdio* buffer is filled or we close the pipe with *pclose()*. In many cases, this presents no problem. If, however, we need to ensure that the child process receives data on the pipe immediately, then we can either use periodic calls to *fflush()* or disable *stdio* buffering using the call *setbuf(fp, NULL)*. This technique can also be used if we create a pipe using the *pipe()* system call and then use *fdopen()* to obtain a *stdio* stream corresponding to the write end of the pipe.

If the process calling *popen()* is reading from the pipe (i.e., *mode* is *r*), things may not be so straightforward. In this case, if the child process is using the *stdio* library, then—unless it includes explicit calls to *fflush()* or *setbuf()*—its output will be available to the calling process only when the child either fills the *stdio* buffer or calls *fclose()*. (The same statement applies if we are reading from a pipe created using *pipe()* and the process writing on the other end is using the *stdio* library.) If this is a problem, there is little we can do unless we can modify the source code of the program running in the child process to include calls to *setbuf()* or *fflush()*.

If modifying the source code is not an option, then instead of using a pipe, we could use a pseudoterminal. A pseudoterminal is an IPC channel that appears to the process on one end as though it is a terminal. Consequently, the *stdio* library line buffers output. We describe pseudoterminals in Chapter 64.

44.7 FIFOs

Semantically, a FIFO is similar to a pipe. The principal difference is that a FIFO has a name within the file system and is opened in the same way as a regular file. This allows a FIFO to be used for communication between unrelated processes (e.g., a client and server).

Once a FIFO has been opened, we use the same I/O system calls as are used with pipes and other files (i.e., *read()*, *write()*, and *close()*). Just as with pipes, a FIFO has a write end and a read end, and data is read from the pipe in the same order as it is written. This fact gives FIFOs their name: *first in, first out*. FIFOs are also sometimes known as *named pipes*.

As with pipes, when all descriptors referring to a FIFO have been closed, any outstanding data is discarded.

We can create a FIFO from the shell using the *mkfifo* command:

```
$ mkfifo [ -m mode ] pathname
```

The *pathname* is the name of the FIFO to be created, and the *−m* option is used to specify a permission *mode* in the same way as for the *chmod* command.

When applied to a FIFO (or pipe), *fstat()* and *stat()* return a file type of S_IFIFO in the *st_mode* field of the *stat* structure (Section 15.1). When listed with *ls −l*, a FIFO is shown with the type *p* in the first column, and *ls −F* appends a pipe symbol (|) to the FIFO pathname.

The *mkfifo()* function creates a new FIFO with the given *pathname*.

```
#include <sys/stat.h>

int mkfifo(const char *pathname, mode_t mode);
```
                                         Returns 0 on success, or −1 on error

The *mode* argument specifies the permissions for the new FIFO. These permissions are specified by ORing the desired combination of constants from Table 15-4, on page 295. As usual, these permissions are masked against the process umask value (Section 15.4.6).

> Historically, FIFOs were created using the system call *mknod(pathname, S_IFIFO, 0)*. POSIX.1-1990 specified *mkfifo()* as a simpler API avoiding the generality of *mknod()*, which allows creation of various types of files, including device files. (SUSv3 specifies *mknod()*, but weakly, defining only its use for creating FIFOs.) Most UNIX implementations provide *mkfifo()* as a library function layered on top of *mknod()*.

Once a FIFO has been created, any process can open it, subject to the usual file permission checks (Section 15.4.3).

Opening a FIFO has somewhat unusual semantics. Generally, the only sensible use of a FIFO is to have a reading process and a writing process on each end. Therefore, by default, opening a FIFO for reading (the *open()* O_RDONLY flag) blocks until another process opens the FIFO for writing (the *open()* O_WRONLY flag). Conversely, opening the FIFO for writing blocks until another process opens the FIFO for reading. In other words, opening a FIFO synchronizes the reading and writing processes. If the opposite end of a FIFO is already open (perhaps because a pair of processes have already opened each end of the FIFO), then *open()* succeeds immediately.

Under most UNIX implementations (including Linux), it is possible to circumvent the blocking behavior when opening FIFOs by specifying the O_RDWR flag when opening a FIFO. In this case, *open()* returns immediately with a file descriptor that can be used for reading and writing on the FIFO. Doing this rather subverts the I/O model for FIFOs, and SUSv3 explicitly notes that opening a FIFO with the O_RDWR flag is unspecified; therefore, for portability reasons, this technique should be avoided. In circumstances where we need to prevent blocking when opening a FIFO, the *open()* O_NONBLOCK flag provides a standardized method for doing so (refer to Section 44.9).

> Avoiding the use of the O_RDWR flag when opening a FIFO can be desirable for a another reason. After such an *open()*, the calling process will never see end-of-file when reading from the resulting file descriptor, because there will always be at least one descriptor open for writing to the FIFO—the same descriptor from which the process is reading.

Using FIFOs and *tee(1)* to create a dual pipeline

One of the characteristics of shell pipelines is that they are linear; each process in the pipeline reads data produced by its predecessor and sends data to its successor. Using FIFOs, it is possible to create a fork in a pipeline, so that a duplicate copy of the output of a process is sent to another process in addition to its successor in the pipeline. In order to do this, we need to use the *tee* command, which writes two copies of what it reads from its standard input: one to standard output and the other to the file named in its command-line argument.

Making the *file* argument to *tee* a FIFO allows us to have two processes simultaneously reading the duplicate output produced by *tee*. We demonstrate this in the following shell session, which creates a FIFO named myfifo, starts a background *wc* command that opens the FIFO for reading (this will block until the FIFO is opened for writing), and then executes a pipeline that sends the output of *ls* to *tee*, which both passes the output further down the pipeline to *sort* and sends it to the myfifo FIFO. (The *−k5n* option to *sort* causes the output of *ls* to be sorted in increasing numerical order on the fifth space-delimited field.)

```
$ mkfifo myfifo
$ wc -l < myfifo &
$ ls -l | tee myfifo | sort -k5n
(Resulting output not shown)
```

Diagrammatically, the above commands create the situation shown in Figure 44-5.

> The *tee* program is so named because of its shape. We can consider *tee* as functioning similarly to a pipe, but with an additional branch that sends duplicate output. Diagrammatically, this has the shape of a capital letter *T* (see Figure 44-5). In addition to the purpose described here, *tee* is also useful for debugging pipelines and for saving the results produced at some intervening point in a complex pipeline.

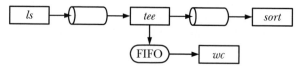

Figure 44-5: Using a FIFO and *tee(1)* to create a dual pipeline

44.8 A Client-Server Application Using FIFOs

In this section, we present a simple client-server application that employs FIFOs for IPC. The server provides the (trivial) service of assigning unique sequential numbers to each client that requests them. In the course of discussing this application, we introduce a few concepts and techniques in server design.

Application overview

In the example application, all clients send their requests to the server using a single server FIFO. The header file (Listing 44-6) defines the well-known name (/tmp/seqnum_sv) that the server uses for its FIFO. This name is fixed, so that all clients know how to contact the server. (In this example application, we create the FIFOs in the /tmp directory, since this allows us to conveniently run the programs without change on most systems. However, as noted in Section 38.7, creating files in publicly writable directories such as /tmp can lead to various security vulnerabilities and should be avoided in real-world applications.)

> In client-server applications, we'll repeatedly encounter the concept of a *well-known address* or name used by a server to make its service visible to clients. Using a well-known address is one solution to the problem of how clients can know where to contact a server. Another possible solution is to provide some kind of name server with which servers can register the names of their services. Each client then contacts the name server to obtain the location of the service it desires. This solution allows the location of servers to be flexible, at the cost of some extra programming effort. Of course, clients and servers then need to know where to contact the name server; typically, it resides at a well-known address.

It is not, however, possible to use a single FIFO to send responses to all clients, since multiple clients would race to read from the FIFO, and possibly read each other's response messages rather than their own. Therefore, each client creates a unique FIFO that the server uses for delivering the response for that client, and the server needs to know how to find each client's FIFO. One possible way to do this is for the client to generate its FIFO pathname, and then pass the pathname as part of its request message. Alternatively, the client and server can agree on a convention for constructing a client FIFO pathname, and, as part of its request, the client can pass the server the information required to construct the pathname specific to this client. This latter solution is used in our example. Each client's FIFO name is built from a template (CLIENT_FIFO_TEMPLATE) consisting of a pathname containing the client's process ID. The inclusion of the process ID provides an easy way of generating a name unique to this client.

Figure 44-6 shows how this application uses FIFOs for communication between the client and server processes of our application.

The header file (Listing 44-6) defines the formats for the request messages sent from clients to the server, and for the response messages sent from the server to clients.

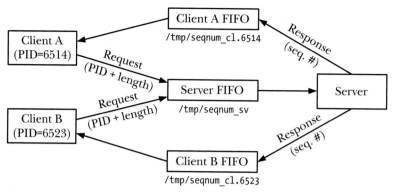

Figure 44-6: Using FIFOs in a single-server, multiple-client application

Recall that the data in pipes and FIFOs is a byte stream; boundaries between multiple messages are not preserved. This means that when multiple messages are being delivered to a single process, such as the server in our example, then the sender and receiver must agree on some convention for separating the messages. Various approaches are possible:

- Terminate each message with a *delimiter character*, such as a newline character. (For an example of this technique, see the *readLine()* function in Listing 59-1, on page 1201.) In this case, either the delimiter character must be one that never appears as part of the message, or we must adopt a convention for escaping the delimiter if it does occur within the message. For example, if we use a newline delimiter, then the characters \ plus newline could be used to represent a real newline character within the message, while \\ could represent a real \. One drawback of this approach is that the process reading messages must scan data from the FIFO a byte at a time until the delimiter character is found.

- Include a *fixed-size header with a length field* in each message specifying the number of bytes in the remaining variable-length component of the message. In this case, the reading process first reads the header from the FIFO, and then uses the header's length field to determine the number of bytes to read for the remainder of the message. This approach has the advantage of efficiently allowing messages of arbitrary size, but could lead to problems if a malformed message (e.g., bad *length* field) is written to the pipe.

- Use *fixed-length messages*, and have the server always read messages of this fixed size. This has the advantage of being simple to program. However, it places an upper limit on our message size and means that some channel capacity is wasted (since short messages must be padded to the fixed length). Furthermore, if one of the clients accidentally or deliberately sends a message that is not of the right length, then all subsequent messages will be out of step; in this situation, the server can't easily recover.

These three techniques are illustrated in Figure 44-7. Be aware that for each of these techniques, the total length of each message must be smaller than PIPE_BUF bytes in order to avoid the possibility of messages being broken up by the kernel and interleaved with messages from other writers.

In the three techniques described in the main text, a single channel (FIFO) is used for all messages from all clients. An alternative is to use a *single connection for each message*. The sender opens the communication channel, sends its message, and then closes the channel. The reading process knows that the message is complete when it encounters end-of-file. If multiple writers hold a FIFO open, then this approach is not feasible, because the reader won't see end-of-file when one of the writers closes the FIFO. This approach is, however, feasible when using stream sockets, where a server process creates a unique communication channel for each incoming client connection.

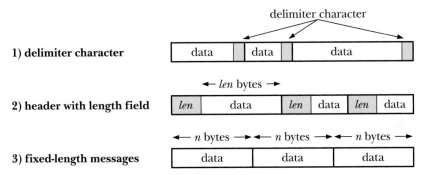

Figure 44-7: Separating messages in a byte stream

In our example application, we use the third of the techniques described above, with each client sending messages of a fixed size to the server. This message is defined by the *request* structure defined in Listing 44-6. Each request to the server includes the client's process ID, which enables the server to construct the name of the FIFO used by the client to receive a response. The request also contains a field (*seqLen*) specifying how many sequence numbers should be allocated to this client. The response message sent from server to client consists of a single field, *seqNum*, which is the starting value of the range of sequence numbers allocated to this client.

Listing 44-6: Header file for fifo_seqnum_server.c and fifo_seqnum_client.c

———————————————————————————————— pipes/fifo_seqnum.h

```
#include <sys/types.h>
#include <sys/stat.h>
#include <fcntl.h>
#include "tlpi_hdr.h"

#define SERVER_FIFO "/tmp/seqnum_sv"
                            /* Well-known name for server's FIFO */
#define CLIENT_FIFO_TEMPLATE "/tmp/seqnum_cl.%ld"
                            /* Template for building client FIFO name */
#define CLIENT_FIFO_NAME_LEN (sizeof(CLIENT_FIFO_TEMPLATE) + 20)
                            /* Space required for client FIFO pathname
                               (+20 as a generous allowance for the PID) */

struct request {                /* Request (client --> server) */
    pid_t pid;                  /* PID of client */
    int seqLen;                 /* Length of desired sequence */
};
```

```
struct response {                    /* Response (server --> client) */
    int seqNum;                      /* Start of sequence */
};
```

── pipes/fifo_seqnum.h

Server program

Listing 44-7 is the code for the server. The server performs the following steps:

- Create the server's well-known FIFO ① and open the FIFO for reading ②. The server must be run before any clients, so that the server FIFO exists by the time a client attempts to open it. The server's *open()* blocks until the first client opens the other end of the server FIFO for writing.

- Open the server's FIFO once more ③, this time for writing. This will never block, since the FIFO has already been opened for reading. This second open is a convenience to ensure that the server doesn't see end-of-file if all clients close the write end of the FIFO.

- Ignore the SIGPIPE signal ④, so that if the server attempts to write to a client FIFO that doesn't have a reader, then, rather than being sent a SIGPIPE signal (which kills a process by default), it receives an EPIPE error from the *write()* system call.

- Enter a loop that reads and responds to each incoming client request ⑤. To send the response, the server constructs the name of the client FIFO ⑥ and then opens that FIFO ⑦.

- If the server encounters an error in opening the client FIFO, it abandons that client's request ⑧.

This is an example of an *iterative server*, in which the server reads and handles each client request before going on to handle the next client. An iterative server design is suitable when each client request can be quickly processed and responded to, so that other client requests are not delayed. An alternative design is a *concurrent server*, in which the main server process employs a separate child process (or thread) to handle each client request. We discuss server design further in Chapter 60.

Listing 44-7: An iterative server using FIFOs

──────────────────────────────────── pipes/fifo_seqnum_server.c

```
#include <signal.h>
#include "fifo_seqnum.h"

int
main(int argc, char *argv[])
{
    int serverFd, dummyFd, clientFd;
    char clientFifo[CLIENT_FIFO_NAME_LEN];
    struct request req;
    struct response resp;
    int seqNum = 0;                      /* This is our "service" */
```

```
        /* Create well-known FIFO, and open it for reading */

        umask(0);                               /* So we get the permissions we want */
①      if (mkfifo(SERVER_FIFO, S_IRUSR | S_IWUSR | S_IWGRP) == -1
                && errno != EEXIST)
            errExit("mkfifo %s", SERVER_FIFO);
②      serverFd = open(SERVER_FIFO, O_RDONLY);
        if (serverFd == -1)
            errExit("open %s", SERVER_FIFO);

        /* Open an extra write descriptor, so that we never see EOF */

③      dummyFd = open(SERVER_FIFO, O_WRONLY);
        if (dummyFd == -1)
            errExit("open %s", SERVER_FIFO);

④      if (signal(SIGPIPE, SIG_IGN) == SIG_ERR)
            errExit("signal");

⑤      for (;;) {                              /* Read requests and send responses */
            if (read(serverFd, &req, sizeof(struct request))
                    != sizeof(struct request)) {
                fprintf(stderr, "Error reading request; discarding\n");
                continue;                       /* Either partial read or error */
            }

            /* Open client FIFO (previously created by client) */

⑥          snprintf(clientFifo, CLIENT_FIFO_NAME_LEN, CLIENT_FIFO_TEMPLATE,
                    (long) req.pid);
⑦          clientFd = open(clientFifo, O_WRONLY);
            if (clientFd == -1) {               /* Open failed, give up on client */
                errMsg("open %s", clientFifo);
⑧              continue;
            }

            /* Send response and close FIFO */

            resp.seqNum = seqNum;
            if (write(clientFd, &resp, sizeof(struct response))
                    != sizeof(struct response))
                fprintf(stderr, "Error writing to FIFO %s\n", clientFifo);
            if (close(clientFd) == -1)
                errMsg("close");

            seqNum += req.seqLen;               /* Update our sequence number */
        }
    }
```

─── **pipes/fifo_seqnum_server.c**

Client program

Listing 44-8 is the code for the client. The client performs the following steps:

- Create a FIFO to be used for receiving a response from the server ②. This is done before sending the request, in order to ensure that the FIFO exists by the time the server attempts to open it and send a response message.

- Construct a message for the server containing the client's process ID and a number (taken from an optional command-line argument) specifying the length of the sequence that the client wishes the server to assign to it ④. (If no command-line argument is supplied, the default sequence length is 1.)

- Open the server FIFO ⑤ and send the message to the server ⑥.

- Open the client FIFO ⑦, and read and print the server's response ⑧.

The only other detail of note is the exit handler ①, established with *atexit()* ③, which ensures that the client's FIFO is deleted when the process exits. Alternatively, we could have simply placed an *unlink()* call immediately after the *open()* of the client FIFO. This would work because, at that point, after they have both performed blocking *open()* calls, the server and the client would each hold open file descriptors for the FIFO, and removing the FIFO name from the file system doesn't affect these descriptors or the open file descriptions to which they refer.

Here is an example of what we see when we run the client and server programs:

```
$ ./fifo_seqnum_server &
[1] 5066
$ ./fifo_seqnum_client 3          Request a sequence of three numbers
0                                 Assigned sequence begins at 0
$ ./fifo_seqnum_client 2          Request a sequence of two numbers
3                                 Assigned sequence begins at 3
$ ./fifo_seqnum_client            Request a single number
5
```

Listing 44-8: Client for the sequence-number server

```
―――――――――――――――――――――――――――――――――――――― pipes/fifo_seqnum_client.c
#include "fifo_seqnum.h"

static char clientFifo[CLIENT_FIFO_NAME_LEN];

static void              /* Invoked on exit to delete client FIFO */
① removeFifo(void)
{
    unlink(clientFifo);
}

int
main(int argc, char *argv[])
{
    int serverFd, clientFd;
    struct request req;
    struct response resp;
```

```
    if (argc > 1 && strcmp(argv[1], "--help") == 0)
        usageErr("%s [seq-len]\n", argv[0]);

    /* Create our FIFO (before sending request, to avoid a race) */

    umask(0);                       /* So we get the permissions we want */
②  snprintf(clientFifo, CLIENT_FIFO_NAME_LEN, CLIENT_FIFO_TEMPLATE,
            (long) getpid());
    if (mkfifo(clientFifo, S_IRUSR | S_IWUSR | S_IWGRP) == -1
                && errno != EEXIST)
        errExit("mkfifo %s", clientFifo);

③  if (atexit(removeFifo) != 0)
        errExit("atexit");

    /* Construct request message, open server FIFO, and send request */

④  req.pid = getpid();
    req.seqLen = (argc > 1) ? getInt(argv[1], GN_GT_0, "seq-len") : 1;

⑤  serverFd = open(SERVER_FIFO, O_WRONLY);
    if (serverFd == -1)
        errExit("open %s", SERVER_FIFO);

⑥  if (write(serverFd, &req, sizeof(struct request)) !=
            sizeof(struct request))
        fatal("Can't write to server");

    /* Open our FIFO, read and display response */

⑦  clientFd = open(clientFifo, O_RDONLY);
    if (clientFd == -1)
        errExit("open %s", clientFifo);

⑧  if (read(clientFd, &resp, sizeof(struct response))
            != sizeof(struct response))
        fatal("Can't read response from server");

    printf("%d\n", resp.seqNum);
    exit(EXIT_SUCCESS);
}
```
——————————————————————————————————— pipes/fifo_seqnum_client.c

44.9 Nonblocking I/O

As noted earlier, when a process opens one end of a FIFO, it blocks if the other end
of the FIFO has not yet been opened. Sometimes, it is desirable not to block, and
for this purpose, the O_NONBLOCK flag can be specified when calling *open()*:

```
    fd = open("fifopath", O_RDONLY | O_NONBLOCK);
    if (fd == -1)
        errExit("open");
```

If the other end of the FIFO is already open, then the O_NONBLOCK flag has no effect on the *open()* call—it successfully opens the FIFO immediately, as usual. The O_NONBLOCK flag changes things only if the other end of the FIFO is not yet open, and the effect depends on whether we are opening the FIFO for reading or writing:

- If the FIFO is being opened for reading, and no process currently has the write end of the FIFO open, then the *open()* call succeeds immediately (just as though the other end of the FIFO was already open).
- If the FIFO is being opened for writing, and the other end of the FIFO is not already open for reading, then *open()* fails, setting *errno* to ENXIO.

The asymmetry of the O_NONBLOCK flag depending on whether the FIFO is being opened for reading or for writing can be explained as follows. It is okay to open a FIFO for reading when there is no writer at the other end of the FIFO, since any attempt to read from the FIFO simply returns no data. However, attempting to write to a FIFO for which there is no reader would result in the generation of the SIGPIPE signal and an EPIPE error from *write()*.

Table 44-1 summarizes the semantics of opening a FIFO, including the effects of O_NONBLOCK described above.

Table 44-1: Semantics of *open()* for a FIFO

Type of *open()*		Result of *open()*	
open for	**additional flags**	**other end of FIFO open**	**other end of FIFO closed**
reading	none (blocking)	succeeds immediately	blocks
	O_NONBLOCK	succeeds immediately	succeeds immediately
writing	none (blocking)	succeeds immediately	blocks
	O_NONBLOCK	succeeds immediately	fails (ENXIO)

Using the O_NONBLOCK flag when opening a FIFO serves two main purposes:

- It allows a single process to open both ends of a FIFO. The process first opens the FIFO for reading specifying O_NONBLOCK, and then opens the FIFO for writing.
- It prevents deadlocks between processes opening two FIFOs.

A *deadlock* is a situation where two or more process are blocked because each is waiting on the other process(es) to complete some action. The two processes shown in Figure 44-8 are deadlocked. Each process is blocked waiting to open a FIFO for reading. This blocking would not happen if each process could perform its second step (opening the other FIFO for writing). This particular deadlock problem could be solved by reversing the order of steps 1 and 2 in process Y, while leaving the order in process X unchanged, or vice versa. However, such an arrangement of steps may not be easy to achieve in some applications. Instead, we can resolve the problem by having either process, or both, specify the O_NONBLOCK flag when opening the FIFOs for reading.

Process X	Process Y
1. Open FIFO A for reading	1. Open FIFO B for reading
blocks	*blocks*
2. Open FIFO B for writing	2. Open FIFO A for writing

Figure 44-8: Deadlock between processes opening two FIFOs

Nonblocking *read()* and *write()*

The O_NONBLOCK flag affects not only the semantics of *open()* but also—because the flag then remains set for the open file description—the semantics of subsequent *read()* and *write()* calls. We describe these effects in the next section.

Sometimes, we need to change the state of the O_NONBLOCK flag for a FIFO (or another type of file) that is already open. Scenarios where this need may arise include the following:

- We opened a FIFO using O_NONBLOCK, but we want subsequent *read()* and *write()* calls to operate in blocking mode.

- We want to enable nonblocking mode for a file descriptor that was returned by *pipe()*. More generally, we might want to change the nonblocking status of any file descriptor that was obtained other than from a call to *open()*—for example, one of the three standard descriptors that are automatically opened for each new program run by the shell or a file descriptor returned by *socket()*.

- For some application-specific purpose, we need to switch the setting of the O_NONBLOCK setting of a file descriptor on and off.

For these purposes, we can use *fcntl()* to enable or disable the O_NONBLOCK open file status flag. To enable the flag, we write the following (omitting error checking):

```
int flags;

flags = fcntl(fd, F_GETFL);      /* Fetch open file status flags */
flags |= O_NONBLOCK;             /* Enable O_NONBLOCK bit */
fcntl(fd, F_SETFL, flags);       /* Update open file status flags */
```

And to disable it, we write the following:

```
flags = fcntl(fd, F_GETFL);
flags &= ~O_NONBLOCK;            /* Disable O_NONBLOCK bit */
fcntl(fd, F_SETFL, flags);
```

44.10 Semantics of *read()* and *write()* on Pipes and FIFOs

Table 44-2 summarizes the operation of *read()* for pipes and FIFOs, and includes the effect of the O_NONBLOCK flag.

The only difference between blocking and nonblocking reads occurs when no data is present and the write end is open. In this case, a normal *read()* blocks, while a nonblocking *read()* fails with the error EAGAIN.

Table 44-2: Semantics of reading *n* bytes from a pipe or FIFO containing *p* bytes

O_NONBLOCK enabled?	Data bytes available in pipe or FIFO (*p*)			
	p = 0, write end open	*p = 0*, write end closed	*p < n*	*p >= n*
No	block	return 0 (EOF)	read *p* bytes	read *n* bytes
Yes	fail (EAGAIN)	return 0 (EOF)	read *p* bytes	read *n* bytes

The impact of the O_NONBLOCK flag when writing to a pipe or FIFO is made complex by interactions with the PIPE_BUF limit. The *write()* behavior is summarized in Table 44-3.

Table 44-3: Semantics of writing *n* bytes to a pipe or FIFO

O_NONBLOCK enabled?	Read end open		Read end closed
	n <= PIPE_BUF	*n > PIPE_BUF*	
No	Atomically write *n* bytes; may block until sufficient data is read for *write()* to be performed	Write *n* bytes; may block until sufficient data is read for *write()* to complete; data may be interleaved with writes by other processes	SIGPIPE + EPIPE
Yes	If sufficient space is available to immediately write *n* bytes, then *write()* succeeds atomically; otherwise, it fails (EAGAIN)	If there is sufficient space to immediately write some bytes, then write between 1 and *n* bytes (which may be interleaved with data written by other processes); otherwise, *write()* fails (EAGAIN)	

The O_NONBLOCK flag causes a *write()* on a pipe or FIFO to fail (with the error EAGAIN) in any case where data can't be transferred immediately. This means that if we are writing up to PIPE_BUF bytes, then the *write()* will fail if there is not sufficient space in the pipe or FIFO, because the kernel can't complete the operation immediately and can't perform a partial write, since that would break the requirement that writes of up to PIPE_BUF bytes are atomic.

When writing more than PIPE_BUF bytes at a time, a write is not required to be atomic. For this reason, *write()* transfers as many bytes as possible (a partial write) to fill up the pipe or FIFO. In this case, the return value from *write()* is the number of bytes actually transferred, and the caller must retry later in order to write the remaining bytes. However, if the pipe or FIFO is full, so that not even one byte can be transferred, then *write()* fails with the error EAGAIN.

44.11 Summary

Pipes were the first method of IPC under the UNIX system, and they are used frequently by the shell, as well as in other applications. A pipe is a unidirectional, limited-capacity byte stream that can be used for communication between related processes. Although blocks of data of any size can be written to a pipe, only writes that do not exceed PIPE_BUF bytes are guaranteed to be atomic. As well as being used as a method of IPC, pipes can also be used for process synchronization.

When using pipes, we must be careful to close unused descriptors in order to ensure that reading processes detect end-of-file and writing processes receive the SIGPIPE signal or the EPIPE error. (Usually, it is easiest to have the application writing to a pipe ignore SIGPIPE and detect a "broken" pipe via the EPIPE error.)

The *popen()* and *pclose()* functions allow a program to transfer data to or from a standard shell command, without needing to handle the details of creating a pipe, execing a shell, and closing unused file descriptors.

FIFOs operate in exactly the same way as pipes, except that they are created using *mkfifo()*, have a name in the file system, and can be opened by any process with appropriate permissions. By default, opening a FIFO for reading blocks until another process opens the FIFO for writing, and vice versa.

In the course of this chapter, we looked at a number of related topics. First, we saw how to duplicate file descriptors in such a manner that the standard input or output of a filter can be bound to a pipe. While presenting a client-server example using FIFOs, we touched on a number of topics in client-server design, including the use of a well-known address for a server and iterative versus concurrent server design. In developing the example FIFO application, we noted that, although data transmitted through a pipe is a byte stream, it is sometimes useful for communicating processes to package the data into messages, and we looked at various ways in which this could be accomplished.

Finally, we noted the effect of the O_NONBLOCK (nonblocking I/O) flag when opening and performing I/O on a FIFO. The O_NONBLOCK flag is useful if we don't want to block while opening a FIFO. It is also useful if we don't want reads to block if no data is available, or writes to block if there is insufficient space within a pipe or FIFO.

Further information

The implementation of pipes is discussed in [Bach, 1986] and [Bovet & Cesati, 2005]. Useful details about pipes and FIFOs can also be found in [Vahalia, 1996].

44.12 Exercises

44-1. Write a program that uses two pipes to enable bidirectional communication between a parent and child process. The parent process should loop reading a block of text from standard input and use one of the pipes to send the text to the child, which converts it to uppercase and sends it back to the parent via the other pipe. The parent reads the data coming back from the child and echoes it on standard output before continuing around the loop once more.

44-2. Implement *popen()* and *pclose()*. Although these functions are simplified by not requiring the signal handling employed in the implementation of *system()* (Section 27.7), you will need to be careful to correctly bind the pipe ends to file streams in each process, and to ensure that all unused descriptors referring to the pipe ends are closed. Since children created by multiple calls to *popen()* may be running at one time, you will need to maintain a data structure that associates the file stream pointers allocated by *popen()* with the corresponding child process IDs. (If using an array for this purpose, the value returned by the *fileno()* function, which obtains the file descriptor corresponding to a file stream, can be used to index the array.) Obtaining the correct process ID from this structure will allow *pclose()* to select the child upon which to wait. This structure will also assist with the SUSv3 requirement that any still-open file streams created by earlier calls to *popen()* must be closed in the new child process.

44-3. The server in Listing 44-7 (fifo_seqnum_server.c) always starts assigning sequence numbers from 0 each time it is started. Modify the program to use a backup file that is updated each time a sequence number is assigned. (The *open()* O_SYNC flag, described in Section 4.3.1, may be useful.) At startup, the program should check for the existence of this file, and if it is present, use the value it contains to initialize the sequence number. If the backup file can't be found on startup, the program should create a new file and start assigning sequence numbers beginning at 0. (An alternative to this technique would be to use memory-mapped files, described in Chapter 49.)

44-4. Add code to the server in Listing 44-7 (fifo_seqnum_server.c) so that if the program receives the SIGINT or SIGTERM signals, it removes the server FIFO and terminates.

44-5. The server in Listing 44-7 (fifo_seqnum_server.c) performs a second O_WRONLY open of the FIFO so that it never sees end-of-file when reading from the reading descriptor (*serverFd*) of the FIFO. Instead of doing this, an alternative approach could be tried: whenever the server sees end-of-file on the reading descriptor, it closes the descriptor, and then once more opens the FIFO for reading. (This open would block until the next client opened the FIFO for writing.) What is wrong with this approach?

44-6. The server in Listing 44-7 (fifo_seqnum_server.c) assumes that the client process is well behaved. If a misbehaving client created a client FIFO and sent a request to the server, but did not open its FIFO, then the server's attempt to open the client FIFO would block, and other client's requests would be indefinitely delayed. (If done maliciously, this would constitute a *denial-of-service attack*.) Devise a scheme to deal with this problem. Extend the server (and possibly the client in Listing 44-8) accordingly.

44-7. Write programs to verify the operation of nonblocking opens and nonblocking I/O on FIFOs (see Section 44.9).

45

INTRODUCTION TO SYSTEM V IPC

System V IPC is the label used to refer to three different mechanisms for interprocess communication:

- *Message queues* can be used to pass messages between processes. Message queues are somewhat like pipes, but differ in two important respects. First, message boundaries are preserved, so that readers and writers communicate in units of messages, rather than via an undelimited byte stream. Second, each message includes an integer *type* field, and it is possible to select messages by type, rather than reading them in the order in which they were written.

- *Semaphores* permit multiple processes to synchronize their actions. A semaphore is a kernel-maintained integer value that is visible to all processes that have the necessary permissions. A process indicates to its peers that it is performing some action by making an appropriate modification to the value of the semaphore.

- *Shared memory* enables multiple processes to share the same region (called a *segment*) of memory (i.e., the same page frames are mapped into the virtual memory of multiple processes). Since access to user-space memory is a fast operation, shared memory is one of the quickest methods of IPC: once one process has updated the shared memory, the change is immediately visible to other processes sharing the same segment.

Although these three IPC mechanisms are quite diverse in function, there are good reasons for discussing them together. One reason is that they were developed together, first appearing in the mid-1970s in Columbus UNIX. This was a Bell-internal UNIX implementation used for database and transaction-processing systems for telephone company record keeping and administration. Around 1983, these IPC mechanisms made their way into mainstream UNIX by appearing in System V—hence the appellation System V IPC.

A more significant reason for discussing the System V IPC mechanisms together is that their programming interfaces share a number of common characteristics, so that many of the same concepts apply to all of these mechanisms.

> Because System V IPC is required by SUSv3 for XSI conformance, it is sometimes alternatively labeled *XSI IPC*.

This chapter provides an overview of the System V IPC mechanisms and details those features that are common to all three mechanisms. The three mechanisms are then discussed individually in the following chapters.

> System V IPC is a kernel option that is configured via the CONFIG_SYSVIPC option.

45.1 API Overview

Table 45-1 summarizes the header files and system calls used for working with System V IPC objects.

Some implementations require the inclusion of <sys/types.h> before including the header files shown in Table 45-1. Some older UNIX implementations may also require the inclusion of <sys/ipc.h>. (No versions of the Single UNIX Specification required these header files.)

> On most hardware architectures on which Linux is implemented, a single system call (*ipc(2)*) acts as the entry point to the kernel for all System V IPC operations, and all of the calls listed in Table 45-1 are actually implemented as library functions layered on top of this system call. (Two exceptions to this arrangement are Alpha and IA-64, where the functions listed in the table really are implemented as individual system calls.) This somewhat unusual approach is an artifact of the initial implementation of System V IPC as a loadable kernel module. Although they are actually library functions on most Linux architectures, throughout this chapter, we'll refer to the functions in Table 45-1 as system calls. Only implementers of C libraries need to use *ipc(2)*; any other use in applications is not portable.

Table 45-1: Summary of programming interfaces for System V IPC objects

Interface	Message queues	Semaphores	Shared memory
Header file	<sys/msg.h>	<sys/sem.h>	<sys/shm.h>
Associated data structure	*msqid_ds*	*semid_ds*	*shmid_ds*
Create/open object	*msgget()*	*semget()*	*shmget()* + *shmat()*
Close object	(none)	(none)	*shmdt()*
Control operations	*msgctl()*	*semctl()*	*shmctl()*
Performing IPC	*msgsnd()*—write message	*semop()*—test/adjust	access memory in
	msgrcv()—read message	semaphore	shared region

Creating and opening a System V IPC object

Each System V IPC mechanism has an associated *get* system call (*msgget()*, *semget()*, or *shmget()*), which is analogous to the *open()* system call used for files. Given an integer *key* (analogous to a filename), the *get* call either:

- creates a new IPC object with the given key and returns a unique identifier for that object; or
- returns the identifier of an existing IPC object with the given key.

We'll (loosely) term the second use *opening* an existing IPC object. In this case, all that the *get* call is doing is converting one number (the key) into another number (the identifier).

> In the context of System V IPC, the *object* doesn't carry any of the connotations associated with object-oriented programming. The term merely serves to distinguish the System V IPC mechanisms from files. Although there are several analogies between files and System V IPC objects, the use of IPC objects differs in several important respects from the standard UNIX file I/O model, and this is a source of some complications when using the System V IPC mechanisms.

An IPC *identifier* is analogous to a file descriptor in that it is used in all subsequent system calls to refer to the IPC object. There is, however, an important semantic difference. Whereas a file descriptor is a process attribute, an IPC identifier is a property of the object itself and is visible system-wide. All processes accessing the same object use the same identifier. This means that if we know an IPC object already exists, we can skip the *get* call, provided we have some other means of knowing the identifier of the object. For example, the process that created the object might write the identifier to a file that can then be read by other processes.

The following example shows how to create a System V message queue:

```
id = msgget(key, IPC_CREAT | S_IRUSR | S_IWUSR);
if (id == -1)
    errExit("msgget");
```

As with all of the *get* calls, the key is the first argument, and the identifier is returned as the function result. We specify the permissions to be placed on the new object as part of the final (*flags*) argument to the *get* call, using the same bit-mask constants as are used for files (Table 15-4, on page 295). In the above example, permission is granted to just the owner of the object to read and write messages on the queue.

The process umask (Section 15.4.6) is not applied to the permissions placed on a newly created IPC object.

> Several UNIX implementations define the following bit-mask constants for IPC permissions: MSG_R, MSG_W, SEM_R, SEM_A, SHM_R, and SHM_W. These correspond to owner (user) read and write permissions for each IPC mechanism. To get the corresponding group and other permission bit masks, these constants can be right-shifted 3 and 6 bits. These constants are not specified by SUSv3, which employs the same bit masks as are used for files, and are not defined in *glibc* headers.

Each process that wants to access the same IPC object performs a *get* call specifying the same key in order to obtain the same identifier for that object. We consider how to choose a key for an application in Section 45.2.

If no IPC object corresponding to the given key currently exists, and IPC_CREAT (analogous to the *open()* O_CREAT flag) was specified as part of the *flags* argument, then the *get* call creates a new IPC object. If no corresponding IPC object currently exists, and IPC_CREAT was not specified (and the key was not specified as IPC_PRIVATE, described in Section 45.2), then the *get* call fails with the error ENOENT.

A process can guarantee that it is the one creating an IPC object by specifying the IPC_EXCL flag (analogous to the *open()* O_EXCL flag). If IPC_EXCL is specified and the IPC object corresponding to the given key already exists, then the *get* call fails with the error EEXIST.

IPC object deletion and object persistence

The *ctl* system call (*msgctl()*, *semctl()*, *shmctl()*) for each System V IPC mechanism performs a range of *control operations* for the object. Many of these operations are specific to the IPC mechanism, but a few are generic to all IPC mechanisms. An example of a generic control operation is IPC_RMID, which is used to delete an object. For example, we can use the following call to delete a shared memory object:

```
if (shmctl(id, IPC_RMID, NULL) == -1)
    errExit("shmctl");
```

For message queues and semaphores, deletion of the IPC object is immediate, and any information contained within the object is destroyed, regardless of whether any other process is still using the object. (This is one of a number of points where the operation of System V IPC objects is not analogous to files. In Section 18.3, we saw that if we remove the last link to a file, then the file is actually removed only after all open file descriptors referring to it have been closed.)

Deletion of shared memory objects occurs differently. Following the *shmctl(id, IPC_RMID, NULL)* call, the shared memory segment is removed only after all processes using the segment detach it (using *shmdt()*). (This is much closer to the situation with file deletion.)

System V IPC objects have kernel persistence. Once created, an object continues to exist until it is explicitly deleted or the system is shut down. This property of System V IPC objects can be advantageous. It is possible for a process to create an object, modify its state, and then exit, leaving the object to be accessed by some process that is started at a later time. It can also be disadvantageous for the following reasons:

- There are system-imposed limits on the number of IPC objects of each type. If we fail to remove unused objects, we may eventually encounter application errors as a result of reaching these limits.

- When deleting a message queue or semaphore object, a multiprocess application may not be able to easily determine which will be the last process requiring access to the object, and thus when the object can be safely deleted. The problem is that these objects are *connectionless*—the kernel doesn't keep a record of which processes have the object open. (This disadvantage doesn't apply for shared memory segments, because of their different deletion semantics, described above.)

45.2 IPC Keys

System V IPC keys are integer values represented using the data type *key_t*. The IPC *get* calls translate a key into the corresponding integer IPC identifier. These calls guarantee that if we create a new IPC object, then that object will have a unique identifier, and that if we specify the key of an existing object, then we'll always obtain the (same) identifier for that object. (Internally, the kernel maintains data structures mapping keys to identifiers for each IPC mechanism, as described in Section 45.5.)

So, how do we provide a unique key—one that guarantees that we won't accidentally obtain the identifier of an existing IPC object used by some other application? There are three possibilities:

- Randomly choose some integer key value, which is typically placed in a header file included by all programs using the IPC object. The difficulty with this approach is that we may accidentally choose a value used by another application.
- Specify the IPC_PRIVATE constant as the *key* value to the *get* call when creating the IPC object, which always results in the creation of a new IPC object that is guaranteed to have a unique identifier.
- Employ the *ftok()* function to generate a (likely unique) key.

Using either IPC_PRIVATE or *ftok()* is the usual technique.

Generating a unique identifier with IPC_PRIVATE

When creating a new IPC object, the key may be specified as IPC_PRIVATE, as follows:

```
id = msgget(IPC_PRIVATE, S_IRUSR | S_IWUSR);
```

In this case, it is not necessary to specify the IPC_CREAT or IPC_EXCL flags.

This technique is especially useful in multiprocess applications where the parent process creates the IPC object prior to performing a *fork()*, with the result that the child inherits the identifier of the IPC object. We can also use this technique in client-server applications (i.e., those involving unrelated processes), but the clients must have a means of obtaining the identifiers of the IPC objects created by the server (and vice versa). For example, after creating an IPC object, the server could then write its identifier to a file that can be read by the clients.

Generating a unique key with *ftok()*

The *ftok()* (*file to key*) function returns a key value suitable for use in a subsequent call to one of the System V IPC *get* system calls.

```
#include <sys/ipc.h>

key_t ftok(char *pathname, int proj);
```
                                        Returns integer key on success, or −1 on error

Suppose a client engages in an extended dialogue with a server, with multiple IPC operations being performed by each process (e.g., multiple messages exchanged, a sequence of semaphore operations, or multiple updates to shared memory). What happens if the server process crashes or is deliberately halted and then restarted? At this point, it would make no sense to blindly reuse the existing IPC object created by the previous server process, since the new server process has no knowledge of the historical information associated with the current state of the IPC object. (For example, there may be a secondary request within a message queue that was sent by a client in response to an earlier message from the old server process.)

In such a scenario, the only option for the server may be to abandon all existing clients, delete the IPC objects created by the previous server process, and create new instances of the IPC objects. A newly started server handles the possibility that a previous instance of the server terminated prematurely by first trying to create an IPC object by specifying both the IPC_CREAT and the IPC_EXCL flags within the *get* call. If the *get* call fails because an object with the specified key already exists, then the server assumes the object was created by an old server process; it therefore uses the IPC_RMID *ctl* operation to delete the object, and once more performs a *get* call to create the object. (This may be combined with other steps to ensure that another server process is not currently running, such as those described in Section 55.6.) For a message queue, these steps might appear as shown in Listing 45-1.

Listing 45-1: Cleanup of IPC objects within a server

——————————————————————————————— svipc/svmsg_demo_server.c
```c
#include <sys/types.h>
#include <sys/ipc.h>
#include <sys/msg.h>
#include <sys/stat.h>
#include "tlpi_hdr.h"

#define KEY_FILE "/some-path/some-file"
                            /* Should be an existing file or one
                               that this program creates */
int
main(int argc, char *argv[])
{
    int msqid;
    key_t key;
    const int MQ_PERMS = S_IRUSR | S_IWUSR | S_IWGRP;    /* rw--w---- */

    /* Optional code here to check if another server process is
       already running */

    /* Generate the key for the message queue */

    key = ftok(KEY_FILE, 1);
    if (key == -1)
        errExit("ftok");
```

```
    /* While msgget() fails, try creating the queue exclusively */

    while ((msqid = msgget(key, IPC_CREAT | IPC_EXCL | MQ_PERMS)) == -1) {
        if (errno == EEXIST) {              /* MQ with the same key already
                                               exists - remove it and try again */
            msqid = msgget(key, 0);
            if (msqid == -1)
                errExit("msgget() failed to retrieve old queue ID");
            if (msgctl(msqid, IPC_RMID, NULL) == -1)
                errExit("msgget() failed to delete old queue");
            printf("Removed old message queue (id=%d)\n", msqid);

        } else {                            /* Some other error --> give up */
            errExit("msgget() failed");
        }
    }

    /* Upon loop exit, we've successfully created the message queue,
       and we can then carry on to do other work... */

    exit(EXIT_SUCCESS);
}
```
── **svipc/svmsg_demo_server.c**

Even if a restarted server re-created the IPC objects, there still would be a potential problem if supplying the same key to the *get* call always generated the same identifier whenever a new IPC object was created. Consider the solution just outlined from the point of view of the client. If the IPC objects re-created by the server use the same identifiers, then the client would have no way of becoming aware that the server has been restarted and that the IPC objects don't contain the expected historical information.

To solve this problem, the kernel employs an algorithm (described in the next section) that normally ensures that when a new IPC object is created, the object's identifier will be different, even when the same key is supplied. Consequently, any clients of the old server process that attempt to use the old identifier will receive an error from the relevant IPC system call.

> Solutions such as that shown in Listing 45-1 don't completely solve the problem of identifying a server restart when using System V shared memory, since a shared memory object is deleted only when all processes have detached it from their virtual address space. However, shared memory objects are typically used in conjunction with System V semaphores, which *are* immediately deleted in response to an IPC_RMID operation. This means that a client process will become aware of a server restart when it tries to access the deleted semaphore object.

45.5 Algorithm Employed by System V IPC *get* Calls

Figure 45-1 shows some of the structures used internally by the kernel to represent information about System V IPC objects (in this case semaphores, but the details are similar for other IPC mechanisms), including the fields used to calculate IPC keys. For each IPC mechanism (shared memory, message queue, or semaphore), the kernel maintains an associated *ipc_ids* structure that records various global information about all instances of that IPC mechanism. This information includes a dynamically sized array of pointers, *entries*, to the associated data structure for each object instance (*semid_ds* structures in the case of semaphores). The current size of the *entries* array is recorded in the *size* field, with the *max_id* field holding the index of the highest currently in-use element.

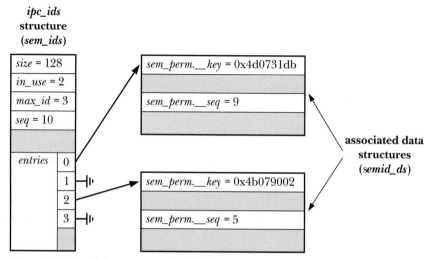

Figure 45-1: Kernel data structures used to represent System V IPC (semaphore) objects

When an IPC *get* call is made, the algorithm used on Linux (other systems use similar algorithms) is approximately as follows:

1. The list of associated data structures (pointed to by elements of the *entries* array) is searched for one whose *key* field matches that specified in the *get* call.

   a) If no match is found, and IPC_CREAT was not specified, then the error ENOENT is returned.

   b) If a match is found, but both IPC_CREAT and IPC_EXCL were specified, then the error EEXIST is returned.

   c) Otherwise, if a match is found, then the following step is skipped.

2. If no match was found, and IPC_CREAT was specified, then a new mechanism-specific associated data structure (*semid_ds* in Figure 45-1) is allocated and initialized. This also involves updating various fields of the *ipc_ids* structure, and may involve resizing the *entries* array. A pointer to the new structure is placed in the first free element of *entries*. Two substeps are included as part of this initialization:

   a) The *key* value supplied in the *get* call is copied into the *xxx_perm.__key* field of the newly allocated structure.

   b) The current value of the *seq* field of the *ipc_ids* structure is copied into the *xxx_perm.__seq* field of the associated data structure, and the *seq* field is incremented by one.

3. The identifier for the IPC object is calculated using the following formula:

```
identifier = index + xxx_perm.__seq * SEQ_MULTIPLIER
```

In the formula used to calculate the IPC identifier, *index* is the index of this object instance within the *entries* array, and SEQ_MULTIPLIER is a constant defined with the value 32,768 (IPCMNI in the kernel source file include/linux/ipc.h). For example, in Figure 45-1, the identifier generated for the semaphore with the *key* value 0x4b079002 would be (2 + 5 * 32,768) = 163,842.

Note the following points about the algorithm employed by the *get* calls:

*   Even if a new IPC object is created with the same key, it will almost certainly have a different identifier, since the identifier is calculated based on the *seq* value saved in the associated data structure, and this value is incremented by one during the creation of each object of this type.

    > The algorithm employed within the kernel wraps the *seq* value back to 0 when it reaches the value (INT_MAX / IPCMNI)—that is, 2,147,483,647 / 32,768 = 65,535. Thus, a new IPC object could have the same identifier as a previous object if 65,535 objects are created in the interim and the new object reuses the same element in the *entries* array as the previous object (i.e., this element must also have been freed in the interim). However, the chances of this occurring are small.

*   The algorithm generates a distinct set of identifier values for each index of the *entries* array.
*   Since the constant IPCMNI defines an upper limit on the number of System V objects of each type, the algorithm guarantees that each existing IPC object has a unique identifier.
*   Given an identifier value, the corresponding index into the *entries* array can be quickly calculated using this equation:

```
index = identifier % SEQ_MULTIPLIER
```

Being able to rapidly perform this calculation is necessary for the efficient operation of those IPC system calls that are supplied with the identifier of an IPC object (i.e., those calls in Table 45-1 other than the *get* calls).

In passing, it is worth noting that two different errors can result if a process makes an IPC system call (e.g., *msgctl()*, *semop()*, or *shmat()*) that specifies an identifier that doesn't correspond to an existing object. If the corresponding index of *entries* is empty, the error EINVAL results. If the index points to an associated data structure, but the sequence number stored in that structure doesn't yield the same identifier value, then it is assumed that an old object pointed to by this array index has been deleted and the index reused. This scenario is diagnosed with the error EIDRM.

45.6 The *ipcs* and *ipcrm* Commands

The *ipcs* and *ipcrm* commands are the System V IPC analogs of the *ls* and *rm* file commands. Using *ipcs*, we can obtain information about IPC objects on the system. By default, *ipcs* displays all objects, as in the following example:

```
$ ipcs

------ Shared Memory Segments --------
key          shmid      owner      perms     bytes      nattch    status
0x6d0731db 262147       mtk        600       8192       2

------ Semaphore Arrays --------
key          semid      owner      perms     nsems
0x6107c0b8 0            cecilia    660       6
0x6107c0b6 32769        britta     660       1

------ Message Queues --------
key          msqid      owner      perms     used-bytes   messages
0x71075958 229376       cecilia    620       12           2
```

On Linux, *ipcs(1)* originally used the IPC_STAT *ctl* operation (Section 45.3) so that it could display information only about IPC objects for which we have read permission, regardless of whether we own the objects. More recent versions of *ipcs* use the /proc/sysvipc interfaces (Section 45.7) and can display all objects, regardless of permissions.

By default, for each object, *ipcs* displays the key, the identifier, the owner, and the permissions (expressed as an octal number), followed by information specific to the object:

- For shared memory, *ipcs* displays the size of the shared memory region, the number of processes that currently have the shared memory region attached to their virtual address space, and status flags. The status flags indicate whether the region has been locked into RAM to prevent swapping (Section 48.7) and whether the region has been marked to be destroyed when all processes have detached it.
- For semaphores, *ipcs* displays the size of the semaphore set.
- For message queues, *ipcs* displays the total number of bytes of data and the number of messages in the queue.

The *ipcs(1)* manual page documents various options for displaying other information about IPC objects.

The *ipcrm* command deletes an IPC object. The general form of this command is one of the following:

```
$ ipcrm -X key
$ ipcrm -x id
```

In the above, we either specify *key* as an IPC object key or *id* as an IPC object identifier, and the letter *x* is replaced by an uppercase or lowercase *q* (for message queues), *s* (for semaphores), or *m* (for shared memory). Thus, we could use the following command to delete the semaphore set with the identifier 65538:

```
$ ipcrm -s 65538
```

45.7 Obtaining a List of All IPC Objects

Linux provides two nonstandard methods of obtaining a list of all IPC objects on the system:

- files within the /proc/sysvipc directory that list all IPC objects; and
- the use of Linux-specific *ctl* calls.

We describe the files in /proc/sysvipc directory here, and defer discussion of the *ctl* calls until Section 46.6, where we provide an example program that lists all System V message queues on the system.

> Some other UNIX implementations have their own nonstandard methods of obtaining a list of all IPC identifiers; for example, Solaris provides the *msgids()*, *semids()*, and *shmids()* system calls for this purpose.

Three read-only files in the /proc/sysvipc directory provide the same information as can be obtained via *ipcs*:

- /proc/sysvipc/msg lists all messages queues and their attributes.
- /proc/sysvipc/sem lists all semaphore sets and their attributes.
- /proc/sysvipc/shm lists all shared memory segments and their attributes.

Unlike the *ipcs* command, these files always show all objects of the corresponding type, regardless of whether read permission is available on the objects.

An example of the contents of /proc/sysvipc/sem is the following (with some white space removed to fit this example on the page):

```
$ cat /proc/sysvipc/sem
key      semid perms   nsems   uid   gid   cuid  cgid   otime        ctime
  0   16646144   600       4  1000   100   1000   100        0   1010166460
```

The three /proc/sysvipc files provide a (nonportable) method for programs and scripts to walk through a list of all of the existing IPC objects of a given type.

> The best that we can achieve by way of a portable approach to obtaining a list of all IPC objects of a given type is to parse the output of *ipcs(1)*.

45.8 IPC Limits

Since System V IPC objects consume system resources, the kernel places various limits on each class of IPC object in order to prevent resources from being exhausted. The methods for placing limits on System V IPC objects are not specified by SUSv3, but most UNIX implementations (including Linux) follow a similar framework for the types of limits that may be placed. As we cover each System V IPC mechanism in the following chapters, we discuss the associated limits and note differences from other UNIX implementations.

Although the types of limits that can be placed on each class of IPC object are generally similar across various UNIX implementations, the methods of viewing and changing these limits are not. The methods described in the following chapters are Linux-specific (they generally involve the use of files in the /proc/sys/kernel directory); things are done differently on other implementations.

On Linux, the *ipcs -l* command can be used to list the limits on each of the IPC mechanisms. Programs can employ the Linux-specific IPC_INFO *ctl* operation to retrieve the same information.

45.9 Summary

System V IPC is the name given to three IPC mechanisms that first appeared widely in System V, and have subsequently been ported to most UNIX implementations and incorporated into various standards. The three IPC mechanisms are message queues, which allow processes to exchange messages; semaphores, which allow processes to synchronize access to shared resources; and shared memory, which allows two or more processes to share the same pages of memory.

The three IPC mechanisms have many similarities in their APIs and semantics. For each IPC mechanism, a *get* system call creates or opens an object. Given an integer *key*, the *get* calls return an integer *identifier* used to refer to the object in subsequent system calls. Each IPC mechanism also has a corresponding *ctl* call that is used to delete an object and to retrieve and modify various attributes (e.g., ownership and permissions) in an object's associated data structure.

The algorithm used to generate identifiers for new IPC objects is designed to minimize the possibility of the same identifier being (immediately) reused if an object is deleted, even if the same key is used to create a new object. This enables client-server applications to function correctly—a restarted server process is able to detect and remove IPC objects created by its predecessor, and this action invalidates the identifiers held by any clients of the previous server process.

The *ipcs* command lists the System V IPC objects that currently exist on the system. The *ipcrm* command is used to remove System V IPC objects.

On Linux, files in the /proc/sysvipc directory can be used to obtain information about all of the System V IPC objects on the system.

Each IPC mechanism has an associated set of limits that can be used to avoid exhaustion of system resources by preventing the creation of an arbitrary number of IPC objects. Various files under the /proc/sys/kernel directory can be used to view and modify these limits.

Further information

Information about the implementation of System V IPC on Linux can be found in [Maxwell, 1999] and [Bovet & Cesati, 2005]. [Goodheart & Cox, 1994] describes the implementation of System V IPC for System V Release 4.

45.10 Exercises

45-1. Write a program to verify that the algorithm employed by *ftok()* uses the file's i-node number, minor device number, and *proj* value, as described in Section 45.2. (It is sufficient to print all of these values, as well as the return value from *ftok()*, in hexadecimal, and inspect the results for a few examples.)

45-2. Implement *ftok()*.

45-3. Verify (by experiment) the statements made in Section 45.5 about the algorithm used to generate System V IPC identifiers.

46

SYSTEM V MESSAGE QUEUES

This chapter describes System V message queues. Message queues allow processes to exchange data in the form of messages. Although message queues are similar to pipes and FIFOs in some respects, they also differ in important ways:

- The handle used to refer to a message queue is the identifier returned by a call to *msgget()*. These identifiers are not the same as the file descriptors used for most other forms of I/O on UNIX systems.

- Communication via message queues is message-oriented; that is, the reader receives whole messages, as written by the writer. It is not possible to read part of a message, leaving the remainder in the queue, or to read multiple messages at a time. This contrasts with pipes, which provide an undifferentiated stream of bytes (i.e., with pipes, the reader can read an arbitrary number of bytes at a time, irrespective of the size of data blocks written by the writer).

- In addition to containing data, each message has an integer *type*. Messages can be retrieved from a queue in first-in, first-out order or retrieved by type.

At the end of this chapter (Section 46.9), we summarize a number of limitations of System V message queues. These limitations lead us to the conclusion that, where possible, new applications should avoid the use of System V message queues in favor of other IPC mechanisms such as FIFOs, POSIX message queues, and sockets. However, when message queues were initially devised, these alternative mechanisms were unavailable or were not widespread across UNIX implementations.

Consequently, there are various existing applications that employ message queues, and this fact forms one of the primary motivations for describing them.

46.1 Creating or Opening a Message Queue

The *msgget()* system call creates a new message queue or obtains the identifier of an existing queue.

```
#include <sys/types.h>        /* For portability */
#include <sys/msg.h>

int msgget(key_t key, int msgflg);
```
                  Returns message queue identifier on success, or –1 on error

The *key* argument is a key generated using one of the methods described in Section 45.2 (i.e., usually the value IPC_PRIVATE or a key returned by *ftok()*). The *msgflg* argument is a bit mask that specifies the permissions (Table 15-4, on page 295) to be placed on a new message queue or checked against an existing queue. In addition, zero or more of the following flags can be ORed (|) in *msgflg* to control the operation of *msgget()*:

IPC_CREAT
> If no message queue with the specified *key* exists, create a new queue.

IPC_EXCL
> If IPC_CREAT was also specified, and a queue with the specified *key* already exists, fail with the error EEXIST.

These flags are described in more detail in Section 45.1.

The *msgget()* system call begins by searching the set of all existing message queues for one with the specified key. If a matching queue is found, the identifier of that queue is returned (unless both IPC_CREAT and IPC_EXCL were specified in *msgflg*, in which case an error is returned). If no matching queue was found and IPC_CREAT was specified in *msgflg*, a new queue is created and its identifier is returned.

The program in Listing 46-1 provides a command-line interface to the *msgget()* system call. The program permits the use of command-line options and arguments to specify all possibilities for the *key* and *msgflg* arguments to *msgget()*. Details of the command format accepted by this program are shown in the *usageError()* function. Upon successful queue creation, the program prints the queue identifier. We demonstrate the use of this program in Section 46.2.2.

Listing 46-1: Using *msgget()*

── svmsg/svmsg_create.c
```
#include <sys/types.h>
#include <sys/ipc.h>
#include <sys/msg.h>
#include <sys/stat.h>
#include "tlpi_hdr.h"
```

```
static void                 /* Print usage info, then exit */
usageError(const char *progName, const char *msg)
{
    if (msg != NULL)
        fprintf(stderr, "%s", msg);
    fprintf(stderr, "Usage: %s [-cx] {-f pathname | -k key | -p} "
                    "[octal-perms]\n", progName);
    fprintf(stderr, "    -c          Use IPC_CREAT flag\n");
    fprintf(stderr, "    -x          Use IPC_EXCL flag\n");
    fprintf(stderr, "    -f pathname  Generate key using ftok()\n");
    fprintf(stderr, "    -k key      Use 'key' as key\n");
    fprintf(stderr, "    -p          Use IPC_PRIVATE key\n");
    exit(EXIT_FAILURE);
}

int
main(int argc, char *argv[])
{
    int numKeyFlags;            /* Counts -f, -k, and -p options */
    int flags, msqid, opt;
    unsigned int perms;
    long lkey;
    key_t key;

    /* Parse command-line options and arguments */

    numKeyFlags = 0;
    flags = 0;

    while ((opt = getopt(argc, argv, "cf:k:px")) != -1) {
        switch (opt) {
        case 'c':
            flags |= IPC_CREAT;
            break;

        case 'f':               /* -f pathname */
            key = ftok(optarg, 1);
            if (key == -1)
                errExit("ftok");
            numKeyFlags++;
            break;

        case 'k':               /* -k key (octal, decimal or hexadecimal) */
            if (sscanf(optarg, "%li", &lkey) != 1)
                cmdLineErr("-k option requires a numeric argument\n");
            key = lkey;
            numKeyFlags++;
            break;

        case 'p':
            key = IPC_PRIVATE;
            numKeyFlags++;
            break;
```

```
        case 'x':
            flags |= IPC_EXCL;
            break;

        default:
            usageError(argv[0], "Bad option\n");
        }
    }

    if (numKeyFlags != 1)
        usageError(argv[0], "Exactly one of the options -f, -k, "
                            "or -p must be supplied\n");

    perms = (optind == argc) ? (S_IRUSR | S_IWUSR) :
                getInt(argv[optind], GN_BASE_8, "octal-perms");

    msqid = msgget(key, flags | perms);
    if (msqid == -1)
        errExit("msgget");

    printf("%d\n", msqid);
    exit(EXIT_SUCCESS);
}
```

————————————————————————————————— svmsg/svmsg_create.c

46.2 Exchanging Messages

The *msgsnd()* and *msgrcv()* system calls perform I/O on message queues. The first argument to both system calls (*msqid*) is a message queue identifier. The second argument, *msgp*, is a pointer to a programmer-defined structure used to hold the message being sent or received. This structure has the following general form:

```
struct mymsg {
    long mtype;                    /* Message type */
    char mtext[];                  /* Message body */
}
```

This definition is really just shorthand for saying that the first part of a message contains the message type, specified as a long integer, while the remainder of the message is a programmer-defined structure of arbitrary length and content; it need not be an array of characters. Thus, the *msgp* argument is typed as *void ** to allow it to be a pointer to any type of structure.

A zero-length *mtext* field is permitted, and is sometimes useful if the information to be conveyed can be encoded solely in the message type or if the existence of a message is in itself sufficient information for the receiving process.

46.2.1 Sending Messages

The *msgsnd()* system call writes a message to a message queue.

```
#include <sys/types.h>          /* For portability */
#include <sys/msg.h>

int msgsnd(int msqid, const void *msgp, size_t msgsz, int msgflg);
```

Returns 0 on success, or −1 on error

To send a message with *msgsnd()*, we must set the *mtype* field of the message structure to a value greater than 0 (we see how this value is used when we discuss *msgrcv()* in the next section) and copy the desired information into the programmer-defined *mtext* field. The *msgsz* argument specifies the number of bytes contained in the *mtext* field.

> When sending messages with *msgsnd()*, there is no concept of a partial write as with *write()*. This is why a successful *msgsnd()* needs only to return 0, rather than the number of bytes sent.

The final argument, *msgflg*, is a bit mask of flags controlling the operation of *msgsnd()*. Only one such flag is defined:

IPC_NOWAIT
> Perform a nonblocking send. Normally, if a message queue is full, *msgsnd()* blocks until enough space has become available to allow the message to be placed on the queue. However, if this flag is specified, then *msgsnd()* returns immediately with the error EAGAIN.

A *msgsnd()* call that is blocked because the queue is full may be interrupted by a signal handler. In this case, *msgsnd()* always fails with the error EINTR. (As noted in Section 21.5, *msgsnd()* is among those system calls that are never automatically restarted, regardless of the setting of the SA_RESTART flag when the signal handler is established.)

Writing a message to a message queue requires write permission on the queue.

The program in Listing 46-2 provides a command-line interface to the *msgsnd()* system call. The command-line format accepted by this program is shown in the *usageError()* function. Note that this program doesn't use the *msgget()* system call. (We noted that a process doesn't need to use a *get* call in order to access an IPC object in Section 45.1.) Instead, we specify the message queue by providing its identifier as a command-line argument. We demonstrate the use of this program in Section 46.2.2.

Listing 46-2: Using *msgsnd()* to send a message

———————————————————————————————— svmsg/svmsg_send.c

```
#include <sys/types.h>
#include <sys/msg.h>
#include "tlpi_hdr.h"

#define MAX_MTEXT 1024

struct mbuf {
    long mtype;                      /* Message type */
    char mtext[MAX_MTEXT];           /* Message body */
};
```

```
static void                   /* Print (optional) message, then usage description */
usageError(const char *progName, const char *msg)
{
    if (msg != NULL)
        fprintf(stderr, "%s", msg);
    fprintf(stderr, "Usage: %s [-n] msqid msg-type [msg-text]\n", progName);
    fprintf(stderr, "    -n        Use IPC_NOWAIT flag\n");
    exit(EXIT_FAILURE);
}

int
main(int argc, char *argv[])
{
    int msqid, flags, msgLen;
    struct mbuf msg;                  /* Message buffer for msgsnd() */
    int opt;                          /* Option character from getopt() */

    /* Parse command-line options and arguments */

    flags = 0;
    while ((opt = getopt(argc, argv, "n")) != -1) {
        if (opt == 'n')
            flags |= IPC_NOWAIT;
        else
            usageError(argv[0], NULL);
    }

    if (argc < optind + 2 || argc > optind + 3)
        usageError(argv[0], "Wrong number of arguments\n");

    msqid = getInt(argv[optind], 0, "msqid");
    msg.mtype = getInt(argv[optind + 1], 0, "msg-type");

    if (argc > optind + 2) {          /* 'msg-text' was supplied */
        msgLen = strlen(argv[optind + 2]) + 1;
        if (msgLen > MAX_MTEXT)
            cmdLineErr("msg-text too long (max: %d characters)\n", MAX_MTEXT);

        memcpy(msg.mtext, argv[optind + 2], msgLen);

    } else {                          /* No 'msg-text' ==> zero-length msg */
        msgLen = 0;
    }

    /* Send message */

    if (msgsnd(msqid, &msg, msgLen, flags) == -1)
        errExit("msgsnd");

    exit(EXIT_SUCCESS);
}
```

—————————————————————————————————— svmsg/svmsg_send.c

46.2.2 Receiving Messages

The *msgrcv()* system call reads (and removes) a message from a message queue, and copies its contents into the buffer pointed to by *msgp*.

```
#include <sys/types.h>        /* For portability */
#include <sys/msg.h>

ssize_t msgrcv(int msqid, void *msgp, size_t maxmsgsz, long msgtyp, int msgflg);
```
                    Returns number of bytes copied into *mtext* field, or –1 on error

The maximum space available in the *mtext* field of the *msgp* buffer is specified by the argument *maxmsgsz*. If the body of the message to be removed from the queue exceeds *maxmsgsz* bytes, then no message is removed from the queue, and *msgrcv()* fails with the error E2BIG. (This default behavior can be changed using the MSG_NOERROR flag described shortly.)

Messages need not be read in the order in which they were sent. Instead, we can select messages according to the value in the *mtype* field. This selection is controlled by the *msgtyp* argument, as follows:

- If *msgtyp* equals 0, the first message from the queue is removed and returned to the calling process.

- If *msgtyp* is greater than 0, the first message in the queue whose *mtype* equals *msgtyp* is removed and returned to the calling process. By specifying different values for *msgtyp*, multiple processes can read from a message queue without racing to read the same messages. One useful technique is to have each process select messages matching its process ID.

- If *msgtyp* is less than 0, treat the waiting messages as a *priority queue*. The first message of the lowest *mtype* less than or equal to the absolute value of *msgtyp* is removed and returned to the calling process.

An example helps clarify the behavior when *msgtyp* is less than 0. Suppose that we have a message queue containing the sequence of messages shown in Figure 46-1 and we performed a series of *msgrcv()* calls of the following form:

```
msgrcv(id, &msg, maxmsgsz, -300, 0);
```

These *msgrcv()* calls would retrieve messages in the order 2 (type 100), 5 (type 100), 3 (type 200), and 1 (type 300). A further call would block, since the type of the remaining message (400) exceeds 300.

The *msgflg* argument is a bit mask formed by ORing together zero or more of the following flags:

IPC_NOWAIT
:   Perform a nonblocking receive. Normally, if no message matching *msgtyp* is in the queue, *msgrcv()* blocks until such a message becomes available. Specifying the IPC_NOWAIT flag causes *msgrcv()* to instead return immediately

with the error ENOMSG. (The error EAGAIN would be more consistent, as occurs on a nonblocking *msgsnd()* or a nonblocking read from a FIFO. However, failing with ENOMSG is historical behavior, and required by SUSv3.)

MSG_EXCEPT

This flag has an effect only if *msgtyp* is greater than 0, in which case it forces the complement of the usual operation; that is, the first message from the queue whose *mtype* is *not* equal to *msgtyp* is removed from the queue and returned to the caller. This flag is Linux-specific, and is made available from <sys/msg.h> only if _GNU_SOURCE is defined. Performing a series of calls of the form *msgrcv(id, &msg, maxmsgsz, 100, MSG_EXCEPT)* on the message queue shown in Figure 46-1 would retrieve messages in the order 1, 3, 4, and then block.

MSG_NOERROR

By default, if the size of the *mtext* field of the message exceeds the space available (as defined by the *maxmsgsz* argument), *msgrcv()* fails. If the MSG_NOERROR flag is specified, then *msgrcv()* instead removes the message from the queue, truncates its *mtext* field to *maxmsgsz* bytes, and returns it to the caller. The truncated data is lost.

Upon successful completion, *msgrcv()* returns the size of the *mtext* field of the received message; on error, −1 is returned.

queue position	Message type (*mtype*)	Message body (*mtext*)
1	300	...
2	100	...
3	200	...
4	400	...
5	100	...

Figure 46-1: Example of a message queue containing messages of different types

As with *msgsnd()*, if a blocked *msgrcv()* call is interrupted by a signal handler, then the call fails with the error EINTR, regardless of the setting of the SA_RESTART flag when the signal handler was established.

Reading a message from a message queue requires read permission on the queue.

Example program

The program in Listing 46-3 provides a command-line interface to the *msgrcv()* system call. The command-line format accepted by this program is shown in the *usageError()* function. Like the program in Listing 46-2, which demonstrated the use of *msgsnd()*, this program doesn't use the *msgget()* system call, but instead expects a message queue identifier as its command-line argument.

The following shell session demonstrates the use of the programs in Listing 46-1, Listing 46-2, and Listing 46-3. We begin by creating a message queue using the IPC_PRIVATE key, and then write three messages with different types to the queue:

```
$ ./svmsg_create -p
32769                                    ID of message queue
$ ./svmsg_send 32769 20 "I hear and I forget."
$ ./svmsg_send 32769 10 "I see and I remember."
$ ./svmsg_send 32769 30 "I do and I understand."
```

We then use the program in Listing 46-3 to read messages with a type less than or equal to 20 from the queue:

```
$ ./svmsg_receive -t -20 32769
Received: type=10; length=22; body=I see and I remember.
$ ./svmsg_receive -t -20 32769
Received: type=20; length=21; body=I hear and I forget.
$ ./svmsg_receive -t -20 32769
```

The last of the above commands blocked, because there was no message in the queue whose type was less than or equal to 20. So, we continue by typing *Control-C* to terminate the command, and then execute a command that reads a message of any type from the queue:

```
Type Control-C to terminate program
$ ./svmsg_receive 32769
Received: type=30; length=23; body=I do and I understand.
```

Listing 46-3: Using *msgrcv()* to read a message

─── **svmsg/svmsg_receive.c**

```c
#define _GNU_SOURCE     /* Get definition of MSG_EXCEPT */
#include <sys/types.h>
#include <sys/msg.h>
#include "tlpi_hdr.h"

#define MAX_MTEXT 1024

struct mbuf {
    long mtype;                 /* Message type */
    char mtext[MAX_MTEXT];      /* Message body */
};

static void
usageError(const char *progName, const char *msg)
{
    if (msg != NULL)
        fprintf(stderr, "%s", msg);
    fprintf(stderr, "Usage: %s [options] msqid [max-bytes]\n", progName);
    fprintf(stderr, "Permitted options are:\n");
    fprintf(stderr, "    -e        Use MSG_NOERROR flag\n");
    fprintf(stderr, "    -t type   Select message of given type\n");
    fprintf(stderr, "    -n        Use IPC_NOWAIT flag\n");
```

```c
#ifdef MSG_EXCEPT
    fprintf(stderr, "    -x        Use MSG_EXCEPT flag\n");
#endif
    exit(EXIT_FAILURE);
}

int
main(int argc, char *argv[])
{
    int msqid, flags, type;
    ssize_t msgLen;
    size_t maxBytes;
    struct mbuf msg;            /* Message buffer for msgrcv() */
    int opt;                    /* Option character from getopt() */

    /* Parse command-line options and arguments */

    flags = 0;
    type = 0;
    while ((opt = getopt(argc, argv, "ent:x")) != -1) {
        switch (opt) {
        case 'e':       flags |= MSG_NOERROR;   break;
        case 'n':       flags |= IPC_NOWAIT;    break;
        case 't':       type = atoi(optarg);    break;
#ifdef MSG_EXCEPT
        case 'x':       flags |= MSG_EXCEPT;    break;
#endif
        default:        usageError(argv[0], NULL);
        }
    }

    if (argc < optind + 1 || argc > optind + 2)
        usageError(argv[0], "Wrong number of arguments\n");

    msqid = getInt(argv[optind], 0, "msqid");
    maxBytes = (argc > optind + 1) ?
                getInt(argv[optind + 1], 0, "max-bytes") : MAX_MTEXT;

    /* Get message and display on stdout */

    msgLen = msgrcv(msqid, &msg, maxBytes, type, flags);
    if (msgLen == -1)
        errExit("msgrcv");

    printf("Received: type=%ld; length=%ld", msg.mtype, (long) msgLen);
    if (msgLen > 0)
        printf("; body=%s", msg.mtext);
    printf("\n");

    exit(EXIT_SUCCESS);
}
```

—— **svmsg/svmsg_receive.c**

46.3 Message Queue Control Operations

The *msgctl()* system call performs control operations on the message queue identified by *msqid*.

```
#include <sys/types.h>          /* For portability */
#include <sys/msg.h>

int msgctl(int msqid, int cmd, struct msqid_ds *buf);
```
                                                    Returns 0 on success, or −1 on error

The *cmd* argument specifies the operation to be performed on the queue. It can be one of the following:

IPC_RMID

> Immediately remove the message queue object and its associated *msqid_ds* data structure. All messages remaining in the queue are lost, and any blocked reader or writer processes are immediately awakened, with *msgsnd()* or *msgrcv()* failing with the error EIDRM. The third argument to *msgctl()* is ignored for this operation.

IPC_STAT

> Place a copy of the *msqid_ds* data structure associated with this message queue in the buffer pointed to by *buf*. We describe the *msqid_ds* structure in Section 46.4.

IPC_SET

> Update selected fields of the *msqid_ds* data structure associated with this message queue using values provided in the buffer pointed to by *buf*.

Further details about these operations, including the privileges and permissions required by the calling process, are described in Section 45.3. We describe some other values for *cmd* in Section 46.6.

The program in Listing 46-4 demonstrates the use of *msgctl()* to delete a message queue.

Listing 46-4: Deleting System V message queues

── svmsg/svmsg_rm.c

```
#include <sys/types.h>
#include <sys/msg.h>
#include "tlpi_hdr.h"

int
main(int argc, char *argv[])
{
    int j;
```

```
        if (argc > 1 && strcmp(argv[1], "--help") == 0)
            usageErr("%s [msqid...]\n", argv[0]);

        for (j = 1; j < argc; j++)
            if (msgctl(getInt(argv[j], 0, "msqid"), IPC_RMID, NULL) == -1)
                errExit("msgctl %s", argv[j]);

        exit(EXIT_SUCCESS);
    }
```

—— svmsg/svmsg_rm.c

46.4 Message Queue Associated Data Structure

Each message queue has an associated *msqid_ds* data structure of the following form:

```
struct msqid_ds {
    struct ipc_perm msg_perm;          /* Ownership and permissions */
    time_t          msg_stime;         /* Time of last msgsnd() */
    time_t          msg_rtime;         /* Time of last msgrcv() */
    time_t          msg_ctime;         /* Time of last change */
    unsigned long   __msg_cbytes;      /* Number of bytes in queue */
    msgqnum_t       msg_qnum;          /* Number of messages in queue */
    msglen_t        msg_qbytes;        /* Maximum bytes in queue */
    pid_t           msg_lspid;         /* PID of last msgsnd() */
    pid_t           msg_lrpid;         /* PID of last msgrcv() */
};
```

> The purpose of the abbreviated spelling *msq* in the name *msqid_ds* is to confuse the programmer. This is the only message queue interface employing this spelling.

The *msgqnum_t* and *msglen_t* data types—used to type the *msg_qnum* and *msg_qbytes* fields—are unsigned integer types specified in SUSv3.

The fields of the *msqid_ds* structure are implicitly updated by the various message queue system calls, and certain fields can be explicitly updated using the *msgctl()* IPC_SET operation. The details are as follows:

msg_perm

When the message queue is created, the fields of this substructure are initialized as described in Section 45.3. The *uid*, *gid*, and *mode* subfields can be updated via IPC_SET.

msg_stime

When the queue is created, this field is set to 0; each later successful *msgsnd()* sets this field to the current time. This field and the other timestamp fields in the *msqid_ds* structure are typed as *time_t*; they store time in seconds since the Epoch.

msg_rtime

This field is set to 0 when the message queue is created, and then set to the current time on each successful *msgrcv()*.

msg_ctime

> This field is set to the current time when the message queue is created and whenever an `IPC_SET` operation is successfully performed.

__msg_cbytes

> This field is set to 0 when the message queue is created, and then adjusted during each successful *msgsnd()* and *msgrcv()* to reflect the total number of bytes contained in the *mtext* fields of all messages in the queue.

msg_qnum

> When the message queue is created, this field is set to 0. It is then incremented by each successful *msgsnd()* and decremented by each successful *msgrcv()* to reflect the total number of messages in the queue.

msg_qbytes

> The value in this field defines an upper limit on the number of bytes in the *mtext* fields of all messages in the message queue. This field is initialized to the value of the `MSGMNB` limit when the queue is created. A privileged (`CAP_SYS_RESOURCE`) process can use the `IPC_SET` operation to adjust *msg_qbytes* to any value in the range 0 to `INT_MAX` (2,147,483,647) bytes. An unprivileged process can adjust *msg_qbytes* to any value in the range 0 to `MSGMNB`. A privileged user can modify the value contained in the Linux-specific /proc/ sys/kernel/msgmnb file in order to change the initial *msg_qbytes* setting for all subsequently created message queues, as well as the upper limit for subsequent changes to *msg_qbytes* by unprivileged processes. We say more about message queue limits in Section 46.5.

msg_lspid

> This field is set to 0 when the queue is created, and then set to the process ID of the calling process on each successful *msgsnd()*.

msg_lrpid

> This field is set to 0 when the message queue is created, and then set to the process ID of the calling process on each successful *msgrcv()*.

All of the above fields are specified by SUSv3, with the exception of *__msg_cbytes*. Nevertheless, most UNIX implementations provide an equivalent of the *__msg_cbytes* field.

The program in Listing 46-5 demonstrates the use of the `IPC_STAT` and `IPC_SET` operations to modify the *msg_qbytes* setting of a message queue.

Listing 46-5: Changing the *msg_qbytes* setting of a System V message queue

── **svmsg/svmsg_chqbytes.c**

```
#include <sys/types.h>
#include <sys/msg.h>
#include "tlpi_hdr.h"

int
main(int argc, char *argv[])
{
    struct msqid_ds ds;
    int msqid;
```

```
    if (argc != 3 || strcmp(argv[1], "--help") == 0)
        usageErr("%s msqid max-bytes\n", argv[0]);

    /* Retrieve copy of associated data structure from kernel */

    msqid = getInt(argv[1], 0, "msqid");
    if (msgctl(msqid, IPC_STAT, &ds) == -1)
        errExit("msgctl");

    ds.msg_qbytes = getInt(argv[2], 0, "max-bytes");

    /* Update associated data structure in kernel */

    if (msgctl(msqid, IPC_SET, &ds) == -1)
        errExit("msgctl");

    exit(EXIT_SUCCESS);
}
```
—— svmsg/svmsg_chqbytes.c

46.5 Message Queue Limits

Most UNIX implementations impose various limits on the operation of System V
message queues. Here, we describe the limits under Linux and note a few differences from other UNIX implementations.

The following limits are enforced on Linux. The system call affected by the
limit and the error that results if the limit is reached are noted in parentheses.

MSGMNI

> This is a system-wide limit on the number of message queue identifiers (in
> other words, message queues) that can be created. (*msgget()*, ENOSPC)

MSGMAX

> This is a system-wide limit specifying the maximum number of (*mtext*) bytes
> that can be written in a single message. (*msgsnd()*, EINVAL)

MSGMNB

> This is the maximum number of (*mtext*) bytes that can be held in a message
> queue at one time. This limit is a system-wide parameter that is used to ini-
> tialize the *msg_qbytes* field of the *msqid_ds* data structure associated with this
> message queue. Subsequently, the *msg_qbytes* value can be modified on a
> per-queue basis, as described in Section 46.4. If a queue's *msg_qbytes* limit is
> reached, then *msgsnd()* blocks, or fails with the error EAGAIN if IPC_NOWAIT
> was set.

Some UNIX implementations also define the following further limits:

MSGTQL

> This is a system-wide limit on the number of messages that can be placed
> on all message queues on the system.

MSGPOOL

> This is a system-wide limit on the size of the buffer pool that is used to hold
> data in all message queues on the system.

Although Linux doesn't impose either of the above limits, it does limit the number of messages on an individual queue to the value specified by the queue's *msg_qbytes* setting. This limitation is relevant only if we are writing zero-length messages to a queue. It has the effect that the limit on the number of zero-length messages is the same as the limit on the number of 1-byte messages that can be written to the queue. This is necessary to prevent an infinite number of zero-length messages being written to the queue. Although they contain no data, each zero-length message consumes a small amount of memory for system bookkeeping overhead.

At system startup, the message queue limits are set to default values. These defaults have varied somewhat across kernel versions. (Some distributors' kernels set different defaults from those provided by vanilla kernels.) On Linux, the limits can be viewed or changed via files in the /proc file system. Table 46-1 shows the /proc file corresponding to each limit. As an example, here are the default limits that we see for Linux 2.6.31 on one x86-32 system:

```
$ cd /proc/sys/kernel
$ cat msgmni
748
$ cat msgmax
8192
$ cat msgmnb
16384
```

Table 46-1: System V message queue limits

Limit	Ceiling value (x86-32)	Corresponding file in /proc/sys/kernel
MSGMNI	32768 (IPCMNI)	msgmni
MSGMAX	Depends on available memory	msgmax
MSGMNB	2147483647 (INT_MAX)	msgmnb

The ceiling value column of Table 46-1 shows the maximum value to which each limit can be raised on the x86-32 architecture. Note that although the MSGMNB limit can be raised to the value INT_MAX, some other limit (e.g., lack of memory) will be reached before a message queue can be loaded with so much data.

The Linux-specific *msgctl()* IPC_INFO operation retrieves a structure of type *msginfo*, which contains the values of the various message queue limits:

```
struct msginfo buf;

msgctl(0, IPC_INFO, (struct msqid_ds *) &buf);
```

Details about IPC_INFO and the *msginfo* structure can be found in the *msgctl(2)* manual page.

46.6 Displaying All Message Queues on the System

In Section 45.7, we looked at one way to obtain a list of all of the IPC objects on the system: via a set of files in the /proc file system. We now look at a second method of obtaining the same information: via a set of Linux-specific IPC *ctl* (*msgctl()*, *semctl()*, and *shmctl()*) operations. (The *ipcs* program employs these operations.) These operations are as follows:

- MSG_INFO, SEM_INFO, and SHM_INFO: The MSG_INFO operation serves two purposes. First, it returns a structure detailing resources consumed by all message queues on the system. Second, as the function result of the *ctl* call, it returns the index of the maximum item in the *entries* array pointing to data structures for the message queue objects (see Figure 45-1, on page 932). The SEM_INFO and SHM_INFO operations perform an analogous task for semaphore sets and shared memory segments, respectively. We must define the _GNU_SOURCE feature test macro to obtain the definitions of these three constants from the corresponding System V IPC header files.

  > An example showing the use of MSG_INFO to retrieve a *msginfo* structure containing information about resources used by all message queue objects is provided in the file svmsg/svmsg_info.c in the source code distribution for this book.

- MSG_STAT, SEM_STAT, and SHM_STAT: Like the IPC_STAT operation, these operations retrieve the associated data structure for an IPC object. However, they differ in two respects. First, instead of expecting an IPC identifier as the first argument of the *ctl* call, these operations expect an index into the *entries* array. Second, if the operation is successful, then, as its function result, the *ctl* call returns the identifier of the IPC object corresponding to that index. We must define the _GNU_SOURCE feature test macro to obtain the definitions of these three constants from the corresponding System V IPC header files.

To list all message queues on the system, we can do the following:

1. Use a MSG_INFO operation to find out the maximum index (*maxind*) of the *entries* array for message queues.

2. Perform a loop for all values from 0 up to and including *maxind*, employing a MSG_STAT operation for each value. During this loop, we ignore the errors that may occur if an item of the *entries* array is empty (EINVAL) or if we don't have permissions on the object to which it refers (EACCES).

Listing 46-6 provides an implementation of the above steps for message queues. The following shell session log demonstrates the use of this program:

```
$ ./svmsg_ls
maxind: 4

index     ID      key       messages
  2     98306   0x00000000      0
  4    163844   0x000004d2      2
$ ipcs -q                              Check above against output of ipcs

------ Message Queues --------
key         msqid    owner   perms   used-bytes   messages
0x00000000 98306     mtk     600     0            0
0x000004d2 163844    mtk     600     12           2
```

Listing 46-6: Displaying all System V message queues on the system

─── svmsg/svmsg_ls.c

```c
#define _GNU_SOURCE
#include <sys/types.h>
#include <sys/msg.h>
#include "tlpi_hdr.h"

int
main(int argc, char *argv[])
{
    int maxind, ind, msqid;
    struct msqid_ds ds;
    struct msginfo msginfo;

    /* Obtain size of kernel 'entries' array */

    maxind = msgctl(0, MSG_INFO, (struct msqid_ds *) &msginfo);
    if (maxind == -1)
        errExit("msgctl-MSG_INFO");

    printf("maxind: %d\n\n", maxind);
    printf("index       id       key       messages\n");

    /* Retrieve and display information from each element of 'entries' array */

    for (ind = 0; ind <= maxind; ind++) {
        msqid = msgctl(ind, MSG_STAT, &ds);
        if (msqid == -1) {
            if (errno != EINVAL && errno != EACCES)
                errMsg("msgctl-MSG_STAT");          /* Unexpected error */
            continue;                               /* Ignore this item */
        }

        printf("%4d %8d  0x%08lx %7ld\n", ind, msqid,
                (unsigned long) ds.msg_perm.__key, (long) ds.msg_qnum);
    }

    exit(EXIT_SUCCESS);
}
```

─── svmsg/svmsg_ls.c

46.7 Client-Server Programming with Message Queues

In this section, we consider two of various possible designs for client-server applications using System V message queues:

- The use of a single message queue for exchanging messages in both directions between server and client.

- The use of separate message queues for the server and for each client. The server's queue is used to receive incoming client requests, and responses are sent to clients via the individual client queues.

Which approach we choose depends on the requirements of our application. We next consider some of the factors that may influence our choice.

Using a single message queue for server and clients

Using a single message queue may be suitable when the messages exchanged between servers and clients are small. However, note the following points:

- Since multiple processes may attempt to read messages at the same time, we must use the message type (*mtype*) field to allow each process to select only those messages intended for it. One way to accomplish this is to use the client's process ID as the message type for messages sent from the server to the client. The client can send its process ID as part of its message(s) to the server. Furthermore, messages to the server must also be distinguished by a unique message type. For this purpose, we can use the number 1, which, being the process ID of the permanently running *init* process, can never be the process ID of a client process. (An alternative would be to use the server's process ID as the message type; however, it is difficult for the clients to obtain this information.) This numbering scheme is shown in Figure 46-2.

- Message queues have a limited capacity. This has the potential to cause a couple of problems. One of these is that multiple simultaneous clients could fill the message queue, resulting in a deadlock situation, where no new client requests can be submitted and the server is blocked from writing any responses. The other problem is that a poorly behaved or intentionally malicious client may fail to read responses from the server. This can lead to the queue becoming clogged with unread messages, preventing any communication between clients and server. (Using two queues—one for messages from clients to the server, and the other for messages from the server to the clients—would solve the first of these problems, but not the second.)

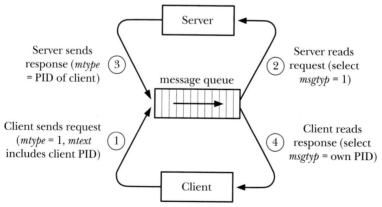

Figure 46-2: Using a single message queue for client-server IPC

Using one message queue per client

Using one message queue per client (as well as one for the server) is preferable where large messages need to be exchanged, or where there is potential for the problems listed above when using a single message queue. Note the following points regarding this approach:

- Each client must create its own message queue (typically using the IPC_PRIVATE key) and inform the server of the queue's identifier, usually by transmitting the identifier as part of the client's message(s) to the server.

- There is a system-wide limit (MSGMNI) on the number of message queues, and the default value for this limit is quite low on some systems. If we expect to have a large number of simultaneous clients, we may need to raise this limit.

- The server should allow for the possibility that the client's message queue no longer exists (perhaps because the client prematurely deleted it).

We say more about using one message queue per client in the next section.

46.8 A File-Server Application Using Message Queues

In this section, we describe a client-server application that uses one message queue per client. The application is a simple file server. The client sends a request message to the server's message queue asking for the contents of a named file. The server responds by returning the file contents as a series of messages to the client's private message queue. Figure 46-3 provides an overview of the application.

Because the server performs no authentication of the client, any user that can run the client can obtain any of the files accessible to the server. A more sophisticated server would require some type of authentication from the client before serving the requested file.

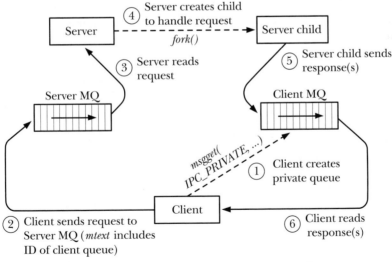

Figure 46-3: Client-server IPC using one message queue per client

Common header file

Listing 46-7 is the header file included by both the server and the client. This header defines the well-known key to be used for the server's message queue

(SERVER_KEY), and defines the formats of the messages to be passed between the client and the server.

The *requestMsg* structure defines the format of the request sent from the client to the server. In this structure, the *mtext* component consists of two fields: the identifier of the client's message queue and the pathname of the file requested by the client. The constant REQ_MSG_SIZE equates to the combined size of these two fields and is used as the *msgsz* argument in calls to *msgsnd()* using this structure.

The *responseMsg* structure defines the format of the response messages sent from the server back to the client. The *mtype* field is used in response messages to supply information about the message content, as defined by the RESP_MT_* constants.

Listing 46-7: Header file for svmsg_file_server.c and svmsg_file_client.c

———————————————————————————————— **svmsg/svmsg_file.h**
```
#include <sys/types.h>
#include <sys/msg.h>
#include <sys/stat.h>
#include <stddef.h>                      /* For definition of offsetof() */
#include <limits.h>
#include <fcntl.h>
#include <signal.h>
#include <sys/wait.h>
#include "tlpi_hdr.h"

#define SERVER_KEY 0x1aaaaaa1            /* Key for server's message queue */

struct requestMsg {                      /* Requests (client to server) */
    long mtype;                          /* Unused */
    int  clientId;                       /* ID of client's message queue */
    char pathname[PATH_MAX];             /* File to be returned */
};

/* REQ_MSG_SIZE computes size of 'mtext' part of 'requestMsg' structure.
   We use offsetof() to handle the possibility that there are padding
   bytes between the 'clientId' and 'pathname' fields. */

#define REQ_MSG_SIZE (offsetof(struct requestMsg, pathname) - \
                    offsetof(struct requestMsg, clientId) + PATH_MAX)

#define RESP_MSG_SIZE 8192

struct responseMsg {                     /* Responses (server to client) */
    long mtype;                          /* One of RESP_MT_* values below */
    char data[RESP_MSG_SIZE];            /* File content / response message */
};

/* Types for response messages sent from server to client */

#define RESP_MT_FAILURE 1                /* File couldn't be opened */
#define RESP_MT_DATA    2                /* Message contains file data */
#define RESP_MT_END     3                /* File data complete */
```
———————————————————————————————— **svmsg/svmsg_file.h**

Server program

Listing 46-8 is the server program for the application. Note the following points about the server:

- The server is designed to handle requests concurrently. A concurrent server design is preferable to the iterative design employed in Listing 44-7 (page 912), since we want to avoid the possibility that a client request for a large file would cause all other client requests to wait.

- Each client request is handled by creating a child process that serves the requested file ⑧. In the meantime, the main server process waits upon further client requests. Note the following points about the server child:
  - Since the child produced via *fork()* inherits a copy of the parent's stack, it thus obtains a copy of the request message read by the main server process.
  - The server child terminates after handling its associated client request ⑨.

- In order to avoid the creation of zombie processes (Section 26.2), the server establishes a handler for SIGCHLD ⑥ and calls *waitpid()* within this handler ①.

- The *msgrcv()* call in the parent server process may block, and consequently be interrupted by the SIGCHLD handler. To handle this possibility, a loop is used to restart the call if it fails with the EINTR error ⑦.

- The server child executes the *serveRequest()* function ②, which sends three message types back to the client. A response with an *mtype* of RESP_MT_FAILURE indicates that the server could not open the requested file ③; RESP_MT_DATA is used for a series of messages containing file data ④; and RESP_MT_END (with a zero-length *data* field) is used to indicate that transmission of file data is complete ⑤.

We consider a number of ways to improve and extend the server program in Exercise 46-4.

Listing 46-8: A file server using System V message queues

—————————————————————————————————————— svmsg/svmsg_file_server.c

```
#include "svmsg_file.h"

static void                 /* SIGCHLD handler */
grimReaper(int sig)
{
    int savedErrno;

    savedErrno = errno;                    /* waitpid() might change 'errno' */
①  while (waitpid(-1, NULL, WNOHANG) > 0)
        continue;
    errno = savedErrno;
}
```

```
    static void                   /* Executed in child process: serve a single client */
②  serveRequest(const struct requestMsg *req)
    {
        int fd;
        ssize_t numRead;
        struct responseMsg resp;

        fd = open(req->pathname, O_RDONLY);
        if (fd == -1) {                        /* Open failed: send error text */
③          resp.mtype = RESP_MT_FAILURE;
            snprintf(resp.data, sizeof(resp.data), "%s", "Couldn't open");
            msgsnd(req->clientId, &resp, strlen(resp.data) + 1, 0);
            exit(EXIT_FAILURE);                /* and terminate */
        }

        /* Transmit file contents in messages with type RESP_MT_DATA. We don't
           diagnose read() and msgsnd() errors since we can't notify client. */

④      resp.mtype = RESP_MT_DATA;
        while ((numRead = read(fd, resp.data, RESP_MSG_SIZE)) > 0)
            if (msgsnd(req->clientId, &resp, numRead, 0) == -1)
                break;

        /* Send a message of type RESP_MT_END to signify end-of-file */

⑤      resp.mtype = RESP_MT_END;
        msgsnd(req->clientId, &resp, 0, 0);          /* Zero-length mtext */
    }

    int
    main(int argc, char *argv[])
    {
        struct requestMsg req;
        pid_t pid;
        ssize_t msgLen;
        int serverId;
        struct sigaction sa;

        /* Create server message queue */

        serverId = msgget(SERVER_KEY, IPC_CREAT | IPC_EXCL |
                                    S_IRUSR | S_IWUSR | S_IWGRP);
        if (serverId == -1)
            errExit("msgget");

        /* Establish SIGCHLD handler to reap terminated children */

        sigemptyset(&sa.sa_mask);
        sa.sa_flags = SA_RESTART;
        sa.sa_handler = grimReaper;
⑥      if (sigaction(SIGCHLD, &sa, NULL) == -1)
            errExit("sigaction");
```

```
                  /* Read requests, handle each in a separate child process */

                  for (;;) {
                      msgLen = msgrcv(serverId, &req, REQ_MSG_SIZE, 0, 0);
                      if (msgLen == -1) {
⑦                        if (errno == EINTR)            /* Interrupted by SIGCHLD handler? */
                              continue;                  /* ... then restart msgrcv() */
                          errMsg("msgrcv");              /* Some other error */
                          break;                         /* ... so terminate loop */
                      }

⑧                     pid = fork();                      /* Create child process */
                      if (pid == -1) {
                          errMsg("fork");
                          break;
                      }

                      if (pid == 0) {                    /* Child handles request */
                          serveRequest(&req);
⑨                         _exit(EXIT_SUCCESS);
                      }

                      /* Parent loops to receive next client request */
                  }

                  /* If msgrcv() or fork() fails, remove server MQ and exit */

                  if (msgctl(serverId, IPC_RMID, NULL) == -1)
                      errExit("msgctl");
                  exit(EXIT_SUCCESS);
              }
```
——————————————————————————————— **svmsg/svmsg_file_server.c**

Client program

Listing 46-9 is the client program for the application. Note the following:

- The client creates a message queue with the IPC_PRIVATE key ② and uses *atexit()* ③ to establish an exit handler ① to ensure that the queue is deleted when the client exits.

- The client passes the identifier for its queue, as well as the pathname of the file to be served, in a request to the server ④.

- The client handles the possibility that the first response message sent by the server may be a failure notification (*mtype* equals RESP_MT_FAILURE) by printing the text of the error message returned by the server and exiting ⑤.

- If the file is successfully opened, then the client loops ⑥, receiving a series of messages containing the file contents (*mtype* equals RESP_MT_DATA). The loop is terminated by receipt of an end-of-file message (*mtype* equals RESP_MT_END).

This simple client doesn't handle various possibilities resulting from failures in the server. We consider some improvements in Exercise 46-5.

Listing 46-9: Client for file server using System V message queues

svmsg/svmsg_file_client.c

```
#include "svmsg_file.h"

static int clientId;

static void
removeQueue(void)
{
    if (msgctl(clientId, IPC_RMID, NULL) == -1)
①       errExit("msgctl");
}

int
main(int argc, char *argv[])
{
    struct requestMsg req;
    struct responseMsg resp;
    int serverId, numMsgs;
    ssize_t msgLen, totBytes;

    if (argc != 2 || strcmp(argv[1], "--help") == 0)
        usageErr("%s pathname\n", argv[0]);

    if (strlen(argv[1]) > sizeof(req.pathname) - 1)
        cmdLineErr("pathname too long (max: %ld bytes)\n",
                (long) sizeof(req.pathname) - 1);

    /* Get server's queue identifier; create queue for response */

    serverId = msgget(SERVER_KEY, S_IWUSR);
    if (serverId == -1)
        errExit("msgget - server message queue");

②   clientId = msgget(IPC_PRIVATE, S_IRUSR | S_IWUSR | S_IWGRP);
    if (clientId == -1)
        errExit("msgget - client message queue");

③   if (atexit(removeQueue) != 0)
        errExit("atexit");

    /* Send message asking for file named in argv[1] */

    req.mtype = 1;                      /* Any type will do */
    req.clientId = clientId;
    strncpy(req.pathname, argv[1], sizeof(req.pathname) - 1);
    req.pathname[sizeof(req.pathname) - 1] = '\0';
                                        /* Ensure string is terminated */

④   if (msgsnd(serverId, &req, REQ_MSG_SIZE, 0) == -1)
        errExit("msgsnd");
```

```
    /* Get first response, which may be failure notification */

    msgLen = msgrcv(clientId, &resp, RESP_MSG_SIZE, 0, 0);
    if (msgLen == -1)
        errExit("msgrcv");

⑤  if (resp.mtype == RESP_MT_FAILURE) {
        printf("%s\n", resp.data);        /* Display msg from server */
        exit(EXIT_FAILURE);
    }

    /* File was opened successfully by server; process messages
       (including the one already received) containing file data */

    totBytes = msgLen;                     /* Count first message */
⑥  for (numMsgs = 1; resp.mtype == RESP_MT_DATA; numMsgs++) {
        msgLen = msgrcv(clientId, &resp, RESP_MSG_SIZE, 0, 0);
        if (msgLen == -1)
            errExit("msgrcv");

        totBytes += msgLen;
    }

    printf("Received %ld bytes (%d messages)\n", (long) totBytes, numMsgs);

    exit(EXIT_SUCCESS);
}
```
—— svmsg/svmsg_file_client.c

The following shell session demonstrates the use of the programs in Listing 46-8
and Listing 46-9:

```
$ ./svmsg_file_server &                  Run server in background
[1] 9149
$ wc -c /etc/services                    Show size of file that client will request
764360 /etc/services
$ ./svmsg_file_client /etc/services
Received 764360 bytes (95 messages)      Bytes received matches size above
$ kill %1                                Terminate server
[1]+  Terminated       ./svmsg_file_server
```

46.9 Disadvantages of System V Message Queues

UNIX systems provide a number of mechanisms for transmitting data from one process to another on the same system, either in the form of an undelimited byte stream
(pipes, FIFOs, and UNIX domain stream sockets) or as delimited messages (System V
message queues, POSIX message queues, and UNIX domain datagram sockets).

A distinctive feature of System V message queues is the ability to attach a
numeric type to each message. This provides for two possibilities that may be useful

to applications: reading processes may select messages by type, or they may employ a priority-queue strategy so that higher-priority messages (i.e., those with lower message type values) are read first.

However, System V message queues have a number of disadvantages:

- Message queues are referred to by identifiers, rather than the file descriptors used by most other UNIX I/O mechanisms. This means that a variety of file descriptor–based I/O techniques described in Chapter 63 (e.g., *select()*, *poll()*, and *epoll*) can't be applied to message queues. Furthermore, writing programs that simultaneously handle inputs from both message queues and file descriptor–based I/O mechanisms requires code that is more complex than code that deals with file descriptors alone. (We look at one way of combining the two I/O models in Exercise 63-3.)

- The use of keys, rather than filenames, to identify message queues results in additional programming complexity and also requires the use of *ipcs* and *ipcrm* instead of *ls* and *rm*. The *ftok()* function usually generates a unique key, but it is not guaranteed to do so. Employing the IPC_PRIVATE key guarantees a unique queue identifier, but leaves us with the task of making that identifier visible to other processes that require it.

- Message queues are connectionless, and the kernel doesn't maintain a count of the number of processes referring to the queue as is done with pipes, FIFOs, and sockets. Consequently, it can be difficult to answer the following questions:
  - When is it safe for an application to delete a message queue? (Premature deletion of the queue results in immediate loss of data, regardless of whether any process might later be interested in reading from the queue.)
  - How can an application ensure that an unused queue is deleted?

- There are limits on the total number of message queues, the size of messages, and the capacity of individual queues. These limits are configurable, but if an application operates outside the range of the default limits, this requires extra work when installing the application.

In summary, System V message queues are often best avoided. In situations where we require the facility to select messages by type, we should consider alternatives. POSIX message queues (Chapter 52) are one such alternative. As a further alternative, solutions involving multiple file descriptor–based communication channels may provide functionality similar to selecting messages by type, while at the same time allowing the use of the alternative I/O models described in Chapter 63. For example, if we need to transmit "normal" and "priority" messages, we could use a pair of FIFOs or UNIX domain sockets for the two message types, and then employ *select()* or *poll()* to monitor file descriptors for both channels.

46.10 Summary

System V message queues allow processes to communicate by exchanging messages consisting of a numeric type plus a body containing arbitrary data. The distinguishing features of message queues are that message boundaries are preserved and that the receiver(s) can select messages by type, rather than reading messages in first-in, first-out order.

Various factors led us to conclude that other IPC mechanisms are usually preferable to System V message queues. One major difficulty is that message queues are not referred to using file descriptors. This means that we can't employ various alternative I/O models with message queues; in particular, it is complex to simultaneously monitor both message queues and file descriptors to see if I/O is possible. Furthermore, the fact that message queues are connectionless (i.e., not reference counted) makes it difficult for an application to know when a queue may be deleted safely.

46.11 Exercises

46-1. Experiment with the programs in Listing 46-1 (svmsg_create.c), Listing 46-2 (svmsg_send.c), and Listing 46-3 (svmsg_receive.c) to confirm your understanding of the *msgget()*, *msgsnd()*, and *msgrcv()* system calls.

46-2. Recode the sequence-number client-server application of Section 44.8 to use System V message queues. Use a single message queue to transmit messages from both client to server and server to client. Employ the conventions for message types described in Section 46.8.

46-3. In the client-server application of Section 46.8, why does the client pass the identifier of its message queue in the body of the message (in the *clientId* field), rather than in the message type (*mtype*)?

46-4. Make the following changes to the client-server application of Section 46.8:

a) Replace the use of a hard-coded message queue key with code in the server that uses IPC_PRIVATE to generate a unique identifier, and then writes this identifier to a well-known file. The client must read the identifier from this file. The server should remove this file if it terminates.

b) In the *serveRequest()* function of the server program, system call errors are not diagnosed. Add code that logs errors using *syslog()* (Section 37.5).

c) Add code to the server so that it becomes a daemon on startup (Section 37.2).

d) In the server, add a handler for SIGTERM and SIGINT that performs a tidy exit. The handler should remove the message queue and (if the earlier part of this exercise was implemented) the file created to hold the server's message queue identifier. Include code in the handler to terminate the server by disestablishing the handler, and then once more raising the same signal that invoked the handler (see Section 26.1.4 for the rationale and steps required for this task).

e) The server child doesn't handle the possibility that the client may terminate prematurely, in which case the server child would fill the client's message queue, and then block indefinitely. Modify the server to handle this possibility by establishing a timeout when calling *msgsnd()*, as described in Section 23.3. If the server child deems that the client has disappeared, it should attempt to delete the client's message queue, and then exit (after perhaps logging a message via *syslog( )*).

46-5. The client shown in Listing 46-9 (svmsg_file_client.c) doesn't handle various possibilities for failure in the server. In particular, if the server message queue fills up (perhaps because the server terminated and the queue was filled by other clients), then the *msgsnd( )* call will block indefinitely. Similarly, if the server fails to send a response to the client, then the *msgrcv( )* call will block indefinitely. Add code to the client that sets timeouts (Section 23.3) on these calls. If either call times out, then the program should report an error to the user and terminate.

46-6. Write a simple chat application (similar to *talk(1)*, but without the *curses* interface) using System V messages queues. Use a single message queue for each client.

47

SYSTEM V SEMAPHORES

This chapter describes System V semaphores. Unlike the IPC mechanisms described in previous chapters, System V semaphores are not used to transfer data between processes. Instead, they allow processes to synchronize their actions. One common use of a semaphore is to synchronize access to a block of shared memory, in order to prevent one process from accessing the shared memory at the same time as another process is updating it.

A semaphore is a kernel-maintained integer whose value is restricted to being greater than or equal to 0. Various operations (i.e., system calls) can be performed on a semaphore, including the following:

- setting the semaphore to an absolute value;
- adding a number to the current value of the semaphore;
- subtracting a number from the current value of the semaphore; and
- waiting for the semaphore value to be equal to 0.

The last two of these operations may cause the calling process to block. When lowering a semaphore value, the kernel blocks any attempt to decrease the value below 0. Similarly, waiting for a semaphore to equal 0 blocks the calling process if the semaphore value is not currently 0. In both cases, the calling process remains blocked until some other process alters the semaphore to a value that allows the operation to proceed, at which point the kernel wakes the blocked process. Figure 47-1 shows the use of a semaphore to synchronize the actions of two processes that alternately move the semaphore value between 0 and 1.

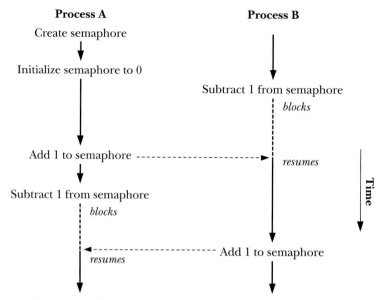

Figure 47-1: Using a semaphore to synchronize two processes

In terms of controlling the actions of a process, a semaphore has no meaning in and of itself. Its meaning is determined only by the associations given to it by the processes using the semaphore. Typically, processes agree on a convention that associates a semaphore with a shared resource, such as a region of shared memory. Other uses of semaphores are also possible, such as synchronization between parent and child processes after *fork()*. (In Section 24.5, we looked at the use of signals to accomplish the same task.)

47.1 Overview

The general steps for using a System V semaphore are the following:

- Create or open a semaphore set using *semget()*.
- Initialize the semaphores in the set using the *semctl()* SETVAL or SETALL operation. (Only one process should do this.)
- Perform operations on semaphore values using *semop()*. The processes using the semaphore typically use these operations to indicate acquisition and release of a shared resource.
- When all processes have finished using the semaphore set, remove the set using the *semctl()* IPC_RMID operation. (Only one process should do this.)

Most operating systems provide some type of semaphore primitive for use in application programs. However, System V semaphores are rendered unusually complex by the fact that they are allocated in groups called *semaphore sets*. The number of semaphores in a set is specified when the set is created using the *semget()* system call. While it is common to operate on a single semaphore at a time, the *semop()* system call allows us to atomically perform a group of operations on multiple semaphores in the same set.

Because System V semaphores are created and initialized in separate steps, race conditions can result if two processes try to perform these steps at the same time. Describing this race condition and how to avoid it requires that we describe *semctl()* before describing *semop()*, which means that there is quite a lot of material to cover before we have all of the details required to fully understand semaphores.

In the meantime, we provide Listing 47-1 as a simple example of the use of the various semaphore system calls. This program operates in two modes:

- Given a single integer command-line argument, the program creates a new semaphore set containing a single semaphore, and initializes the semaphore to the value supplied in the command-line argument. The program displays the identifier of the new semaphore set.

- Given two command-line arguments, the program interprets them as (in order) the identifier of an existing semaphore set and a value to be added to the first semaphore (numbered 0) in that set. The program carries out the specified operation on that semaphore. To enable us to monitor the semaphore operation, the program prints messages before and after the operation. Each of these messages begins with the process ID, so that we can distinguish the output of multiple instances of the program.

The following shell session log demonstrates the use of the program in Listing 47-1. We begin by creating a semaphore that is initialized to 0:

```
$ ./svsem_demo 0
Semaphore ID = 98307                        ID of new semaphore set
```

We then execute a background command that tries to decrease the semaphore value by 2:

```
$ ./svsem_demo 98307 -2 &
23338: about to semop at  10:19:42
[1] 23338
```

This command blocked, because the value of the semaphore can't be decreased below 0. Now, we execute a command that adds 3 to the semaphore value:

```
$ ./svsem_demo 98307 +3
23339: about to semop at  10:19:55
23339: semop completed at 10:19:55
23338: semop completed at 10:19:55
[1]+  Done                ./svsem_demo 98307 -2
```

The semaphore increment operation succeeded immediately, and caused the semaphore decrement operation in the background command to proceed, since that operation could now be performed without leaving the semaphore's value below 0.

Listing 47-1: Creating and operating on System V semaphores

```c
#include <sys/types.h>
#include <sys/sem.h>
#include <sys/stat.h>
#include "curr_time.h"         /* Declaration of currTime() */
#include "semun.h"             /* Definition of semun union */
#include "tlpi_hdr.h"

int
main(int argc, char *argv[])
{
    int semid;

    if (argc < 2 || argc > 3 || strcmp(argv[1], "--help") == 0)
        usageErr("%s init-value\n"
                "   or: %s semid operation\n", argv[0], argv[0]);

    if (argc == 2) {            /* Create and initialize semaphore */
        union semun arg;

        semid = semget(IPC_PRIVATE, 1, S_IRUSR | S_IWUSR);
        if (semid == -1)
            errExit("semid");

        arg.val = getInt(argv[1], 0, "init-value");
        if (semctl(semid, /* semnum= */ 0, SETVAL, arg) == -1)
            errExit("semctl");

        printf("Semaphore ID = %d\n", semid);

    } else {                    /* Perform an operation on first semaphore */

        struct sembuf sop;      /* Structure defining operation */

        semid = getInt(argv[1], 0, "semid");

        sop.sem_num = 0;        /* Specifies first semaphore in set */
        sop.sem_op = getInt(argv[2], 0, "operation");
                                /* Add, subtract, or wait for 0 */
        sop.sem_flg = 0;        /* No special options for operation */

        printf("%ld: about to semop at  %s\n", (long) getpid(), currTime("%T"));
        if (semop(semid, &sop, 1) == -1)
            errExit("semop");

        printf("%ld: semop completed at %s\n", (long) getpid(), currTime("%T"));
    }

    exit(EXIT_SUCCESS);
}
```

47.2 Creating or Opening a Semaphore Set

The *semget()* system call creates a new semaphore set or obtains the identifier of an existing set.

```
#include <sys/types.h>          /* For portability */
#include <sys/sem.h>

int semget(key_t key, int nsems, int semflg);
```
                    Returns semaphore set identifier on success, or –1 on error

The *key* argument is a key generated using one of the methods described in Section 45.2 (i.e., usually the value IPC_PRIVATE or a key returned by *ftok()*).

If we are using *semget()* to create a new semaphore set, then *nsems* specifies the number of semaphores in that set, and must be greater than 0. If we are using *semget()* to obtain the identifier of an existing set, then *nsems* must be less than or equal to the size of the set (or the error EINVAL results). It is not possible to change the number of semaphores in an existing set.

The *semflg* argument is a bit mask specifying the permissions to be placed on a new semaphore set or checked against an existing set. These permissions are specified in the same manner as for files (Table 15-4, on page 295). In addition, zero or more of the following flags can be ORed (|) in *semflg* to control the operation of *semget()*:

IPC_CREAT
> If no semaphore set with the specified *key* exists, create a new set.

IPC_EXCL
> If IPC_CREAT was also specified, and a semaphore set with the specified *key* already exists, fail with the error EEXIST.

These flags are described in more detail in Section 45.1.

On success, *semget()* returns the identifier for the new or existing semaphore set. Subsequent system calls referring to individual semaphores must specify both the semaphore set identifier and the number of the semaphore within that set. The semaphores within a set are numbered starting at 0.

47.3 Semaphore Control Operations

The *semctl()* system call performs a variety of control operations on a semaphore set or on an individual semaphore within a set.

```
#include <sys/types.h>          /* For portability */
#include <sys/sem.h>

int semctl(int semid, int semnum, int cmd, ... /* union semun arg */);
```
                    Returns nonnegative integer on success (see text); returns –1 on error

The *semid* argument is the identifier of the semaphore set on which the operation is to be performed. For those operations performed on a single semaphore, the *semnum* argument identifies a particular semaphore within the set. For other operations, this argument is ignored, and we can specify it as 0. The *cmd* argument specifies the operation to be performed.

Certain operations require a fourth argument to *semctl()*, which we refer to by the name *arg* in the remainder of this section. This argument is a union defined as shown in Listing 47-2. We must explicitly define this union in our programs. We do this in our example programs by including the header file in Listing 47-2.

Although placing the definition of the *semun* union in a standard header file would be sensible, SUSv3 requires the programmer to explicitly define it instead. Nevertheless, some UNIX implementations do provide this definition in <sys/sem.h>. Older versions of *glibc* (up to and including version 2.0) also provided this definition. In conformance with SUSv3, more recent versions of *glibc* do not, and the macro _SEM_SEMUN_UNDEFINED is defined with the value 1 in <sys/sem.h> to indicate this fact (i.e., an application compiled against *glibc* can test this macro to determine if the program must itself define the *semun* union).

Listing 47-2: Definition of the *semun* union

————————————————————————————————— svsem/semun.h

```
#ifndef SEMUN_H
#define SEMUN_H              /* Prevent accidental double inclusion */

#include <sys/types.h>       /* For portability */
#include <sys/sem.h>

union semun {                /* Used in calls to semctl() */
    int                val;
    struct semid_ds *  buf;
    unsigned short *   array;
#if defined(__linux__)
    struct seminfo *   __buf;
#endif
};

#endif
```

————————————————————————————————— svsem/semun.h

SUSv2 and SUSv3 specify that the final argument to *semctl()* is optional. However, a few (mainly older) UNIX implementations (and older versions of *glibc*) prototyped *semctl()* as follows:

```
int semctl(int semid, int semnum, int cmd, union semun arg);
```

This meant that the fourth argument was required even in the cases where it is not actually used (e.g., the IPC_RMID and GETVAL operations described below). For full portability, we specify a dummy final argument to *semctl()* in those calls where it is not required.

In the remainder of this section, we consider the various control operations that can be specified for *cmd*.

Generic control operations

The following operations are the same ones that can be applied to other types of System V IPC objects. In each case, the *semnum* argument is ignored. Further details about these operations, including the privileges and permissions required by the calling process, are provided in Section 45.3.

IPC_RMID

Immediately remove the semaphore set and its associated *semid_ds* data structure. Any processes blocked in *semop()* calls waiting on semaphores in this set are immediately awakened, with *semop()* reporting the error EIDRM. The *arg* argument is not required.

IPC_STAT

Place a copy of the *semid_ds* data structure associated with this semaphore set in the buffer pointed to by *arg.buf*. We describe the *semid_ds* structure in Section 47.4.

IPC_SET

Update selected fields of the *semid_ds* data structure associated with this semaphore set using values in the buffer pointed to by *arg.buf*.

Retrieving and initializing semaphore values

The following operations retrieve or initialize the value(s) of an individual semaphore or of all semaphores in a set. Retrieving a semaphore value requires read permission on the semaphore, while initializing the value requires alter (write) permission.

GETVAL

As its function result, *semctl()* returns the value of the *semnum*-th semaphore in the semaphore set specified by *semid*. The *arg* argument is not required.

SETVAL

The value of the *semnum*-th semaphore in the set referred to by *semid* is initialized to the value specified in *arg.val*.

GETALL

Retrieve the values of all of the semaphores in the set referred to by *semid*, placing them in the array pointed to by *arg.array*. The programmer must ensure that this array is of sufficient size. (The number of semaphores in a set can be obtained from the *sem_nsems* field of the *semid_ds* data structure retrieved by an IPC_STAT operation.) The *semnum* argument is ignored. An example of the use of the GETALL operation is provided in Listing 47-3.

SETALL

Initialize all semaphores in the set referred to by *semid*, using the values supplied in the array pointed to by *arg.array*. The *semnum* argument is ignored. Listing 47-4 demonstrates the use of the SETALL operation.

If another process is waiting to perform an operation on the semaphore(s) modified by the SETVAL or SETALL operations, and the change(s) made would permit that operation to proceed, then the kernel wakes up that process.

Changing the value of a semaphore with SETVAL or SETALL clears the undo entries for that semaphore in all processes. We describe semaphore undo entries in Section 47.8.

Note that the information returned by GETVAL and GETALL may already be out of date by the time the calling process comes to use it. Any program that depends on the information returned by these operations being unchanged may be subject to time-of-check, time-of-use race conditions (Section 38.6).

Retrieving per-semaphore information

The following operations return (via the function result value) information about the *semnum*-th semaphore of the set referred to by *semid*. For all of these operations, read permission is required on the semaphore set, and the *arg* argument is not required.

GETPID

> Return the process ID of the last process to perform a *semop()* on this semaphore; this is referred to as the *sempid* value. If no process has yet performed a *semop()* on this semaphore, 0 is returned.

GETNCNT

> Return the number of processes currently waiting for the value of this semaphore to increase; this is referred to as the *semncnt* value.

GETZCNT

> Return the number of processes currently waiting for the value of this semaphore to become 0; this is referred to as the *semzcnt* value.

As with the GETVAL and GETALL operations described above, the information returned by the GETPID, GETNCNT, and GETZCNT operations may already be out of date by the time the calling process comes to use it.

Listing 47-3 demonstrates the use of these three operations.

47.4 Semaphore Associated Data Structure

Each semaphore set has an associated *semid_ds* data structure of the following form:

```
struct semid_ds {
    struct ipc_perm sem_perm;      /* Ownership and permissions */
    time_t          sem_otime;     /* Time of last semop() */
    time_t          sem_ctime;     /* Time of last change */
    unsigned long   sem_nsems;     /* Number of semaphores in set */
};
```

> SUSv3 requires all of the fields that we show in the *semid_ds* structure. Some other UNIX implementations include additional nonstandard fields. On Linux 2.4 and later, the *sem_nsems* field is typed as *unsigned long*. SUSv3 specifies the type of this field as *unsigned short*, and it is so defined in Linux 2.2 and on most other UNIX implementations.

The fields of the *semid_ds* structure are implicitly updated by various semaphore system calls, and certain subfields of the *sem_perm* field can be explicitly updated using the *semctl()* IPC_SET operation. The details are as follows:

sem_perm
> When the semaphore set is created, the fields of this substructure are initialized as described in Section 45.3. The *uid*, *gid*, and *mode* subfields can be updated via IPC_SET.

sem_otime
> This field is set to 0 when the semaphore set is created, and then set to the current time on each successful *semop()*, or when the semaphore value is modified as a consequence of a SEM_UNDO operation (Section 47.8). This field and *sem_ctime* are typed as *time_t*, and store time in seconds since the Epoch.

sem_ctime
> This field is set to the current time when the semaphore set is created and on each successful IPC_SET, SETALL, or SETVAL operation. (On some UNIX implementations, the SETALL and SETVAL operations don't modify *sem_ctime*.)

sem_nsems
> When the set is created, this field is initialized to the number of semaphores in the set.

In the remainder of this section, we show two example programs that make use of the *semid_ds* data structure and some of the *semctl()* operations described in Section 47.3. We demonstrate the use of both of these programs in Section 47.6.

Monitoring a semaphore set

The program in Listing 47-3 makes use of various *semctl()* operations to display information about the existing semaphore set whose identifier is provided as its command-line argument. The program first displays the time fields from the *semid_ds* data structure. Then, for each semaphore in the set, the program displays the semaphore's current value, as well as its *sempid*, *semncnt*, and *semzcnt* values.

Listing 47-3: A semaphore monitoring program

—————————————————————————————————— svsem/svsem_mon.c

```
#include <sys/types.h>
#include <sys/sem.h>
#include <time.h>
#include "semun.h"                      /* Definition of semun union */
#include "tlpi_hdr.h"

int
main(int argc, char *argv[])
{
    struct semid_ds ds;
    union semun arg, dummy;             /* Fourth argument for semctl() */
    int semid, j;
```

```
    if (argc != 2 || strcmp(argv[1], "--help") == 0)
        usageErr("%s semid\n", argv[0]);

    semid = getInt(argv[1], 0, "semid");

    arg.buf = &ds;
    if (semctl(semid, 0, IPC_STAT, arg) == -1)
        errExit("semctl");

    printf("Semaphore changed: %s", ctime(&ds.sem_ctime));
    printf("Last semop():      %s", ctime(&ds.sem_otime));

    /* Display per-semaphore information */

    arg.array = calloc(ds.sem_nsems, sizeof(arg.array[0]));
    if (arg.array == NULL)
        errExit("calloc");
    if (semctl(semid, 0, GETALL, arg) == -1)
        errExit("semctl-GETALL");

    printf("Sem #  Value  SEMPID  SEMNCNT  SEMZCNT\n");

    for (j = 0; j < ds.sem_nsems; j++)
        printf("%3d   %5d   %5d %5d    %5d\n", j, arg.array[j],
                semctl(semid, j, GETPID, dummy),
                semctl(semid, j, GETNCNT, dummy),
                semctl(semid, j, GETZCNT, dummy));

    exit(EXIT_SUCCESS);
}
```

—— svsem/svsem_mon.c

Initializing all semaphores in a set

The program in Listing 47-4 provides a command-line interface for initializing all
of the semaphores in an existing set. The first command-line argument is the identifier of the semaphore set to be initialized. The remaining command-line arguments specify the values to which the semaphores are to be initialized (there must
be as many of these arguments as there are semaphores in the set).

Listing 47-4: Using the SETALL operation to initialize a System V semaphore set

—— svsem/svsem_setall.c
```
#include <sys/types.h>
#include <sys/sem.h>
#include "semun.h"                      /* Definition of semun union */
#include "tlpi_hdr.h"

int
main(int argc, char *argv[])
{
    struct semid_ds ds;
    union semun arg;                    /* Fourth argument for semctl() */
    int j, semid;
```

```
    if (argc < 3 || strcmp(argv[1], "--help") == 0)
        usageErr("%s semid val...\n", argv[0]);

    semid = getInt(argv[1], 0, "semid");

    /* Obtain size of semaphore set */

    arg.buf = &ds;
    if (semctl(semid, 0, IPC_STAT, arg) == -1)
        errExit("semctl");

    if (ds.sem_nsems != argc - 2)
        cmdLineErr("Set contains %ld semaphores, but %d values were supplied\n",
                (long) ds.sem_nsems, argc - 2);

    /* Set up array of values; perform semaphore initialization */

    arg.array = calloc(ds.sem_nsems, sizeof(arg.array[0]));
    if (arg.array == NULL)
        errExit("calloc");

    for (j = 2; j < argc; j++)
        arg.array[j - 2] = getInt(argv[j], 0, "val");

    if (semctl(semid, 0, SETALL, arg) == -1)
        errExit("semctl-SETALL");
    printf("Semaphore values changed (PID=%ld)\n", (long) getpid());

    exit(EXIT_SUCCESS);
}
```

_____ **svsem/svsem_setall.c**

47.5 Semaphore Initialization

According to SUSv3, an implementation is not required to initialize the values of
the semaphores in a set created by *semget()*. Instead, the programmer must explicitly
initialize the semaphores using the *semctl()* system call. (On Linux, the semaphores
returned by *semget()* are in fact initialized to 0, but we can't portably rely on this.) As
stated earlier, the fact that semaphore creation and initialization must be performed by separate system calls, instead of in a single atomic step, leads to possible
race conditions when initializing a semaphore. In this section, we detail the nature
of the race and look at a method of avoiding it based on an idea described in
[Stevens, 1999].

Suppose that we have an application consisting of multiple peer processes
employing a semaphore to coordinate their actions. Since no single process is guaranteed to be the first to use the semaphore (this is what is meant by the term *peer*),
each process must be prepared to create and initialize the semaphore if it doesn't
already exist. For this purpose, we might consider employing the code shown in
Listing 47-5.

Listing 47-5: Incorrectly initializing a System V semaphore

––– *from* **svsem/svsem_bad_init.c**

```
/* Create a set containing 1 semaphore */

semid = semget(key, 1, IPC_CREAT | IPC_EXCL | perms);

if (semid != -1) {                      /* Successfully created the semaphore */
    union semun arg;

    /* XXXX */

    arg.val = 0;                        /* Initialize semaphore */
    if (semctl(semid, 0, SETVAL, arg) == -1)
        errExit("semctl");

} else {                                /* We didn't create the semaphore */
    if (errno != EEXIST)                /* Unexpected error from semget() */
        errExit("semget");

    semid = semget(key, 1, perms);  /* Retrieve ID of existing set */
    if (semid == -1)
        errExit("semget");
}

/* Now perform some operation on the semaphore */

sops[0].sem_op = 1;                     /* Add 1... */
sops[0].sem_num = 0;                    /* to semaphore 0 */
sops[0].sem_flg = 0;
if (semop(semid, sops, 1) == -1)
    errExit("semop");
```

––– *from* **svsem/svsem_bad_init.c**

The problem with the code in Listing 47-5 is that if two processes execute it at the same time, then the sequence shown in Figure 47-2 could occur, if the first process's time slice happens to expire at the point marked XXXX in the code. This sequence is problematic for two reasons. First, process B performs a *semop()* on an uninitialized semaphore (i.e., one whose value is arbitrary). Second, the *semctl()* call in process A overwrites the changes made by process B.

The solution to this problem relies on a historical, and now standardized, feature of the initialization of the *sem_otime* field in the *semid_ds* data structure associated with the semaphore set. When a semaphore set is first created, the *sem_otime* field is initialized to 0, and it is changed only by a subsequent *semop()* call. We can exploit this feature to eliminate the race condition described above. We do this by inserting extra code to force the second process (i.e., the one that does not create the semaphore) to wait until the first process has both initialized the semaphore *and* executed a *semop()* call that updates the *sem_otime* field, but does not modify the semaphore's value. The modified code is shown in Listing 47-6.

> Unfortunately, the solution to the initialization problem described in the main text doesn't work on all UNIX implementations. In some versions of the modern BSD derivatives, *semop()* doesn't update the *sem_otime* field.

Listing 47-6: Initializing a System V semaphore

─────────────────────────────────────── *from* **svsem/svsem_good_init.c**

```
semid = semget(key, 1, IPC_CREAT | IPC_EXCL | perms);

if (semid != -1) {                      /* Successfully created the semaphore */
    union semun arg;
    struct sembuf sop;

    arg.val = 0;                        /* So initialize it to 0 */
    if (semctl(semid, 0, SETVAL, arg) == -1)
        errExit("semctl");

    /* Perform a "no-op" semaphore operation - changes sem_otime
       so other processes can see we've initialized the set. */

    sop.sem_num = 0;                    /* Operate on semaphore 0 */
    sop.sem_op = 0;                     /* Wait for value to equal 0 */
    sop.sem_flg = 0;
    if (semop(semid, &sop, 1) == -1)
        errExit("semop");

} else {                                /* We didn't create the semaphore set */
    const int MAX_TRIES = 10;
    int j;
    union semun arg;
    struct semid_ds ds;

    if (errno != EEXIST)               /* Unexpected error from semget() */
        errExit("semget");

    semid = semget(key, 1, perms);   /* Retrieve ID of existing set */
    if (semid == -1)
        errExit("semget");

    /* Wait until another process has called semop() */

    arg.buf = &ds;
    for (j = 0; j < MAX_TRIES; j++) {
        if (semctl(semid, 0, IPC_STAT, arg) == -1)
            errExit("semctl");
        if (ds.sem_otime != 0)          /* semop() performed? */
            break;                       /* Yes, quit loop */
        sleep(1);                       /* If not, wait and retry */
    }

    if (ds.sem_otime == 0)              /* Loop ran to completion! */
        fatal("Existing semaphore not initialized");
}

/* Now perform some operation on the semaphore */
```

─────────────────────────────────────── *from* **svsem/svsem_good_init.c**

We can use variations of the technique shown in Listing 47-6 to ensure that multiple semaphores in a set are correctly initialized, or that a semaphore is initialized to a nonzero value.

This rather complex solution to the race problem is not required in all applications. We don't need it if one process is guaranteed to be able to create and initialize the semaphore before any other processes attempt to use it. This would be the case, for example, if a parent creates and initializes the semaphore before creating child processes with which it shares the semaphore. In such cases, it is sufficient for the first process to follow its *semget()* call by a *semctl()* SETVAL or SETALL operation.

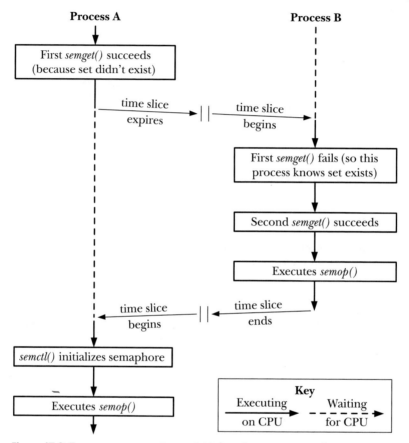

Figure 47-2: Two processes racing to initialize the same semaphore

47.6 Semaphore Operations

The *semop()* system call performs one or more operations on the semaphores in the semaphore set identified by *semid*.

```
#include <sys/types.h>          /* For portability */
#include <sys/sem.h>

int semop(int semid, struct sembuf *sops, size_t nsops);
```
                                          Returns 0 on success, or −1 on error

The *sops* argument is a pointer to an array that contains the operations to be performed, and *nsops* gives the size of this array (which must contain at least one element). The operations are performed atomically and in array order. The elements of the *sops* array are structures of the following form:

```
struct sembuf {
    unsigned short sem_num;    /* Semaphore number */
    short          sem_op;     /* Operation to be performed */
    short          sem_flg;    /* Operation flags (IPC_NOWAIT and SEM_UNDO) */
};
```

The *sem_num* field identifies the semaphore within the set upon which the operation is to be performed. The *sem_op* field specifies the operation to be performed:

- If *sem_op* is greater than 0, the value of *sem_op* is added to the semaphore value. As a result, other processes waiting to decrease the semaphore value may be awakened and perform their operations. The calling process must have alter (write) permission on the semaphore.

- If *sem_op* equals 0, the value of the semaphore is checked to see whether it currently equals 0. If it does, the operation completes immediately; otherwise, *semop()* blocks until the semaphore value becomes 0. The calling process must have read permission on the semaphore.

- If *sem_op* is less than 0, decrease the value of the semaphore by the absolute value of *sem_op*. If the current value of the semaphore is greater than or equal to the absolute value of *sem_op*, the operation completes immediately. Otherwise, *semop()* blocks until the semaphore value has been increased to a level that permits the operation to be performed without resulting in a negative value. The calling process must have alter permission on the semaphore.

Semantically, increasing the value of a semaphore corresponds to making a resource available so that others can use it, while decreasing the value of a semaphore corresponds to reserving a resource for (exclusive) use by this process. When decreasing the value of a semaphore, the operation is blocked if the semaphore value is too low—that is, if some other process has already reserved the resource.

When a *semop()* call blocks, the process remains blocked until one of the following occurs:

- Another process modifies the value of the semaphore such that the requested operation can proceed.

- A signal interrupts the *semop()* call. In this case, the error EINTR results. (As noted in Section 21.5, *semop()* is never automatically restarted after being interrupted by a signal handler.)

- Another process deletes the semaphore referred to by *semid*. In this case, *semop()* fails with the error EIDRM.

We can prevent *semop()* from blocking when performing an operation on a particular semaphore by specifying the IPC_NOWAIT flag in the corresponding *sem_flg* field. In this case, if *semop()* would have blocked, it instead fails with the error EAGAIN.

While it is usual to operate on a single semaphore at a time, it is possible to make a *semop()* call that performs operations on multiple semaphores in a set. The key point to note is that this group of operations is performed atomically; that is, *semop()* either performs all of the operations immediately, if possible, or blocks until it would be possible to perform all of the operations simultaneously.

> Few systems document the fact that *semop()* performs operations in array order, although all systems known to the author do so, and a few applications depend on this behavior. SUSv4 adds text that explicitly requires this behavior.

Listing 47-7 demonstrates the use of *semop()* to perform operations on three semaphores in a set. The operations on semaphores 0 and 2 may not be able to proceed immediately, depending on the current values of the semaphores. If the operation on semaphore 0 can't be performed immediately, then none of the requested operations is performed, and *semop()* blocks. On the other hand, if the operation on semaphore 0 could be performed immediately, but the operation on semaphore 2 could not, then—because the IPC_NOWAIT flag was specified—none of the requested operations is performed, and *semop()* returns immediately with the error EAGAIN.

The *semtimedop()* system call performs the same task as *semop()*, except that the *timeout* argument specifies an upper limit on the time for which the call will block.

```
#define _GNU_SOURCE
#include <sys/types.h>        /* For portability */
#include <sys/sem.h>

int semtimedop(int semid, struct sembuf *sops, size_t nsops,
               struct timespec *timeout);
```
                                            Returns 0 on success, or –1 on error

The *timeout* argument is a pointer to a *timespec* structure (Section 23.4.2), which allows a time interval to be expressed as a number of seconds and nanoseconds. If the specified time interval expires before it is possible to complete the semaphore operation, *semtimedop()* fails with the error EAGAIN. If *timeout* is specified as NULL, *semtimedop()* is exactly the same as *semop()*.

The *semtimedop()* system call is provided as a more efficient method of setting a timeout on a semaphore operation than using *setitimer()* plus *semop()*. The small performance benefit that this confers is significant for certain applications (notably, some database systems) that need to frequently perform such operations. However, *semtimedop()* is not specified in SUSv3 and is present on only a few other UNIX implementations.

> The *semtimedop()* system call appeared as a new feature in Linux 2.6 and was subsequently back-ported into Linux 2.4, starting with kernel 2.4.22.

Listing 47-7: Using *semop()* to perform operations on multiple System V semaphores

```
struct sembuf sops[3];

sops[0].sem_num = 0;                /* Subtract 1 from semaphore 0 */
sops[0].sem_op = -1;
sops[0].sem_flg = 0;

sops[1].sem_num = 1;                /* Add 2 to semaphore 1 */
sops[1].sem_op = 2;
sops[1].sem_flg = 0;

sops[2].sem_num = 2;                /* Wait for semaphore 2 to equal 0 */
sops[2].sem_op = 0;
sops[2].sem_flg = IPC_NOWAIT;       /* But don't block if operation
                                       can't be performed immediately */
if (semop(semid, sops, 3) == -1) {
    if (errno == EAGAIN)            /* Semaphore 2 would have blocked */
        printf("Operation would have blocked\n");
    else
        errExit("semop");          /* Some other error */
}
```

Example program

The program in Listing 47-8 provides a command-line interface to the *semop()* system call. The first argument to this program is the identifier of the semaphore set upon which operations are to be performed.

Each of the remaining command-line arguments specifies a group of semaphore operations to be performed in a single *semop()* call. The operations within a single command-line argument are delimited by commas. Each operation has one of the following forms:

- *semnum+value*: add *value* to semaphore *semnum*.
- *semnum-value*: subtract *value* from semaphore *semnum*.
- *semnum=0*: test semaphore *semnum* to see if it equals 0.

At the end of each operation, we can optionally include an *n*, a *u*, or both. The letter *n* means include IPC_NOWAIT in the *sem_flg* value for this operation. The letter *u* means include SEM_UNDO in *sem_flg*. (We describe the SEM_UNDO flag in Section 47.8.)

The following command line specifies two *semop()* calls on the semaphore set whose identifier is 0:

```
$ ./svsem_op 0 0=0 0-1,1-2n
```

The first command-line argument specifies a *semop()* call that waits until semaphore zero equals 0. The second argument specifies a *semop()* call that subtracts 1 from semaphore 0, and subtracts 2 from semaphore 1. For the operation on semaphore 0, *sem_flg* is 0; for the operation on semaphore 1, *sem_flg* is IPC_NOWAIT.

Listing 47-8: Performing System V semaphore operations with *semop()*

—— **svsem/svsem_op.c**

```c
#include <sys/types.h>
#include <sys/sem.h>
#include <ctype.h>
#include "curr_time.h"          /* Declaration of currTime() */
#include "tlpi_hdr.h"

#define MAX_SEMOPS 1000         /* Maximum operations that we permit for
                                   a single semop() */

static void
usageError(const char *progName)
{
    fprintf(stderr, "Usage: %s semid op[,op...] ...\n\n", progName);
    fprintf(stderr, "'op' is either: <sem#>{+|-}<value>[n][u]\n");
    fprintf(stderr, "           or: <sem#>=0[n]\n");
    fprintf(stderr, "    \"n\" means include IPC_NOWAIT in 'op'\n");
    fprintf(stderr, "    \"u\" means include SEM_UNDO in 'op'\n\n");
    fprintf(stderr, "The operations in each argument are "
                    "performed in a single semop() call\n\n");
    fprintf(stderr, "e.g.: %s 12345 0+1,1-2un\n", progName);
    fprintf(stderr, "      %s 12345 0=0n 1+1,2-1u 1=0\n", progName);
    exit(EXIT_FAILURE);
}

/* Parse comma-delimited operations in 'arg', returning them in the
   array 'sops'. Return number of operations as function result. */

static int
parseOps(char *arg, struct sembuf sops[])
{
    char *comma, *sign, *remaining, *flags;
    int numOps;                 /* Number of operations in 'arg' */

    for (numOps = 0, remaining = arg; ; numOps++) {
        if (numOps >= MAX_SEMOPS)
            cmdLineErr("Too many operations (maximum=%d): \"%s\"\n",
                       MAX_SEMOPS, arg);

        if (*remaining == '\0')
            fatal("Trailing comma or empty argument: \"%s\"", arg);
        if (!isdigit((unsigned char) *remaining))
            cmdLineErr("Expected initial digit: \"%s\"\n", arg);

        sops[numOps].sem_num = strtol(remaining, &sign, 10);

        if (*sign == '\0' || strchr("+-=", *sign) == NULL)
            cmdLineErr("Expected '+', '-', or '=' in \"%s\"\n", arg);
        if (!isdigit((unsigned char) *(sign + 1)))
            cmdLineErr("Expected digit after '%c' in \"%s\"\n", *sign, arg);

        sops[numOps].sem_op = strtol(sign + 1, &flags, 10);
```

```c
            if (*sign == '-')                           /* Reverse sign of operation */
                sops[numOps].sem_op = - sops[numOps].sem_op;
            else if (*sign == '=')                      /* Should be '=0' */
                if (sops[numOps].sem_op != 0)
                    cmdLineErr("Expected \"=0\" in \"%s\"\n", arg);

            sops[numOps].sem_flg = 0;
            for (;; flags++) {
                if (*flags == 'n')
                    sops[numOps].sem_flg |= IPC_NOWAIT;
                else if (*flags == 'u')
                    sops[numOps].sem_flg |= SEM_UNDO;
                else
                    break;
            }

            if (*flags != ',' && *flags != '\0')
                cmdLineErr("Bad trailing character (%c) in \"%s\"\n", *flags, arg);

            comma = strchr(remaining, ',');
            if (comma == NULL)
                break;                                  /* No comma --> no more ops */
            else
                remaining = comma + 1;
    }

    return numOps + 1;
}

int
main(int argc, char *argv[])
{
    struct sembuf sops[MAX_SEMOPS];
    int ind, nsops;

    if (argc < 2 || strcmp(argv[1], "--help") == 0)
        usageError(argv[0]);

    for (ind = 2; argv[ind] != NULL; ind++) {
        nsops = parseOps(argv[ind], sops);

        printf("%5ld, %s: about to semop()  [%s]\n", (long) getpid(),
                currTime("%T"), argv[ind]);

        if (semop(getInt(argv[1], 0, "semid"), sops, nsops) == -1)
            errExit("semop (PID=%ld)", (long) getpid());

        printf("%5ld, %s: semop() completed [%s]\n", (long) getpid(),
                currTime("%T"), argv[ind]);
    }

    exit(EXIT_SUCCESS);
}
```
——————————————————————————————————— svsem/svsem_op.c

Using the program in Listing 47-8, along with various others shown in this chapter, we can study the operation of System V semaphores, as demonstrated in the following shell session. We begin by using a program that creates a semaphore set containing two semaphores, which we initialize to 1 and 0:

```
$ ./svsem_create -p 2
32769                                           ID of semaphore set
$ ./svsem_setall 32769 1 0
Semaphore values changed (PID=3658)
```

> We don't show the code of the svsem/svsem_create.c program in this chapter, but it is provided in the source code distribution for this book. This program performs the same function for semaphores as the program in Listing 46-1 (on page 938) performs for message queues; that is, it creates a semaphore set. The only notable difference is that svsem_create.c takes an additional argument specifying the size of the semaphore set to be created.

Next, we start three background instances of the program in Listing 47-8 to perform *semop()* operations on the semaphore set. The program prints messages before and after each semaphore operation. These messages include the time, so that we can see when each operation starts and when it completes, and the process ID, so that we can track the operation of multiple instances of the program. The first command makes a request to decrease both semaphores by 1:

```
$ ./svsem_op 32769 0-1,1-1 &                    Operation 1
  3659, 16:02:05: about to semop()  [0-1,1-1]
[1] 3659
```

In the above output, we see that the program printed a message saying that the *semop()* operation is about to be performed, but did not print any further messages, because the *semop()* call blocks. The call blocks because semaphore 1 has the value 0.

Next, we execute a command that makes a request to decrease semaphore 1 by 1:

```
$ ./svsem_op 32769 1-1 &                         Operation 2
  3660, 16:02:22: about to semop()  [1-1]
[2] 3660
```

This command also blocks. Next, we execute a command that waits for the value of semaphore 0 to equal 0:

```
$ ./svsem_op 32769 0=0 &                          Operation 3
  3661, 16:02:27: about to semop()  [0=0]
[3] 3661
```

Again, this command blocks, in this case because the value of semaphore 0 is currently 1.

Now, we use the program in Listing 47-3 to inspect the semaphore set:

```
$ ./svsem_mon 32769
Semaphore changed: Sun Jul 25 16:01:53 2010
Last semop():      Thu Jan  1 01:00:00 1970
Sem # Value  SEMPID  SEMNCNT  SEMZCNT
  0     1      0        1        1
  1     0      0        2        0
```

When a semaphore set is created, the *sem_otime* field of the associated *semid_ds* data structure is initialized to 0. A calendar time value of 0 corresponds to the Epoch (Section 10.1), and *ctime()* displays this as 1 AM, 1 January 1970, since the local timezone is Central Europe, one hour ahead of UTC.

Examining the output further, we can see that, for semaphore 0, the *semncnt* value is 1 because operation 1 is waiting to decrease the semaphore value, and *semzcnt* is 1 because operation 3 is waiting for this semaphore to equal 0. For semaphore 1, the *semncnt* value of 2 reflects the fact that operation 1 and operation 2 are waiting to decrease the semaphore value.

Next, we try a nonblocking operation on the semaphore set. This operation waits for semaphore 0 to equal 0. Since this operation can't be immediately performed, *semop()* fails with the error EAGAIN:

```
$ ./svsem_op 32769 0=0n                                    Operation 4
  3673, 16:03:13: about to semop()  [0=0n]
ERROR [EAGAIN/EWOULDBLOCK Resource temporarily unavailable] semop (PID=3673)
```

Now we add 1 to semaphore 1. This causes two of the earlier blocked operations (1 and 3) to unblock:

```
$ ./svsem_op 32769 1+1                                     Operation 5
  3674, 16:03:29: about to semop()  [1+1]
  3659, 16:03:29: semop() completed [0-1,1-1]             Operation 1 completes
  3661, 16:03:29: semop() completed [0=0]                 Operation 3 completes
  3674, 16:03:29: semop() completed [1+1]                 Operation 5 completes
[1]   Done                  ./svsem_op 32769 0-1,1-1
[3]+  Done                  ./svsem_op 32769 0=0
```

When we use our monitoring program to inspect the state of the semaphore set, we see that the *sem_otime* field of the associated *semid_ds* data structure has been updated, and the *sempid* values of both semaphores have been updated. We also see that the *semncnt* value for semaphore 1 is 1, since operation 2 is still blocked, waiting to decrease the value of this semaphore:

```
$ ./svsem_mon 32769
Semaphore changed: Sun Jul 25 16:01:53 2010
Last semop():      Sun Jul 25 16:03:29 2010
Sem #  Value  SEMPID  SEMNCNT  SEMZCNT
  0      0     3661      0        0
  1      0     3659      1        0
```

From the above output, we see that the *sem_otime* value has been updated. We also see that semaphore 0 was last operated on by process ID 3661 (operation 3) and semaphore 1 was last operated on by process ID 3659 (operation 1).

Finally, we remove the semaphore set. This causes the still blocked operation 2 to fail with the error EIDRM:

```
$ ./svsem_rm 32769
ERROR [EIDRM Identifier removed] semop (PID=3660)
```

> We don't show the source code for the svsem/svsem_rm.c program in this chapter, but it is provided in the source code distribution for this book. This program removes the semaphore set identified by its command-line argument.

47.7 Handling of Multiple Blocked Semaphore Operations

If multiple processes are blocked trying to decrease the value of a semaphore by the same amount, then it is indeterminate which process will be permitted to perform the operation first when it becomes possible (i.e., which process is able to perform the operation will depend on vagaries of the kernel process scheduling algorithm).

On the other hand, if processes are blocked trying to decrease a semaphore value by different amounts, then the requests are served in the order in which they become possible. Suppose that a semaphore currently has the value 0, and process A requests to decrease the semaphore's value by 2, and then process B requests to decrease the value by 1. If a third process then adds 1 to the semaphore, process B would be the first to unblock and perform its operation, even though process A was the first to request an operation against the semaphore. In poorly designed applications, such scenarios can lead to *starvation*, whereby a process remains blocked forever because the state of the semaphore is never such that the requested operation proceeds. Continuing our example, we can envisage scenarios where multiple processes adjust the semaphore in such a way that its value is never more than 1, with the result that process A remains blocked forever.

Starvation can also occur if a process is blocked trying to perform operations on multiple semaphores. Consider the following scenario, performed on a pair of semaphores, both of which initially have the value 0:

1. Process A makes a request to subtract 1 from semaphores 0 and 1 (*blocks*).
2. Process B makes a request to subtract 1 from semaphore 0 (*blocks*).
3. Process C adds 1 to semaphore 0.

At this point, process B unblocks and completes its request, even though it placed its request later than process A. Again, it is possible to devise scenarios in which process A is starved while other processes adjust and block on the values of the individual semaphores.

47.8 Semaphore Undo Values

Suppose that, having adjusted the value of a semaphore (e.g., decreased the semaphore value so that it is now 0), a process then terminates, either deliberately or accidentally. By default, the semaphore's value is left unchanged. This may constitute a problem for other processes using the semaphore, since they may be blocked waiting on that semaphore—that is, waiting for the now-terminated process to undo the change it made.

To avoid such problems, we can employ the SEM_UNDO flag when changing the value of a semaphore via *semop()*. When this flag is specified, the kernel records the effect of the semaphore operation, and then undoes the operation if the process terminates. The undo happens regardless of whether the process terminates normally or abnormally.

The kernel doesn't need to keep a record of all operations performed using SEM_UNDO. It suffices to record the *sum* of all of the semaphore adjustments performed using SEM_UNDO in a per-semaphore, per-process integer total called the *semadj* (semaphore adjustment) value. When the process terminates, all that is necessary is to subtract this total from the semaphore's current value.

> Since Linux 2.6, processes (threads) created using *clone()* share *semadj* values if the CLONE_SYSVSEM flag is employed. Such sharing is required for a conforming implementation of POSIX threads. The NPTL threading implementation employs CLONE_SYSVSEM for the implementation of *pthread_create()*.

When a semaphore value is set using the *semctl()* SETVAL or SETALL operation, the corresponding *semadj* values are cleared (i.e., set to 0) in all processes using the semaphore. This makes sense, since absolutely setting the value of a semaphore destroys the value associated with the historical record maintained in the *semadj* total.

A child created via *fork()* doesn't inherit its parent's *semadj* values; it doesn't make sense for a child to undo its parent's semaphore operations. On the other hand, *semadj* values are preserved across an *exec()*. This permits us to adjust a semaphore value using SEM_UNDO, and then *exec()* a program that performs no operation on the semaphore, but does automatically adjust the semaphore on process termination. (This can be used as a technique that allows another process to discover when this process terminates.)

Example of the effect of SEM_UNDO

The following shell session log shows the effect of performing operations on two semaphores: one operation with the SEM_UNDO flag and one without. We begin by creating a set containing two semaphores that we initialize to 0:

```
$ ./svsem_create -p 2
131073
$ ./svsem_setall 131073 0 0
Semaphore values changed (PID=2220)
```

Next, we execute a command that adds 1 to both semaphores and then terminates. The operation on semaphore 0 specifies the SEM_UNDO flag:

```
$ ./svsem_op 131073 0+1u 1+1
 2248, 06:41:56: about to semop()
 2248, 06:41:56: semop() completed
```

Now, we use the program in Listing 47-3 to check the state of the semaphores:

```
$ ./svsem_mon 131073
Semaphore changed: Sun Jul 25 06:41:34 2010
Last semop():      Sun Jul 25 06:41:56 2010
Sem #  Value  SEMPID  SEMNCNT  SEMZCNT
  0      0    2248       0        0
  1      1    2248       0        0
```

Looking at the semaphore values in the last two lines of the above output, we can see that the operation on semaphore 0 was undone, but the operation on semaphore 1 was not undone.

Limitations of SEM_UNDO

We conclude by noting that the SEM_UNDO flag is less useful than it first appears, for two reasons. One is that because modifying a semaphore typically corresponds to acquiring or releasing some shared resource, the use of SEM_UNDO on its own may be insufficient to allow a multiprocess application to recover in the event that a process unexpectedly terminates. Unless process termination also automatically returns the shared resource state to a consistent state (unlikely in many scenarios), undoing a semaphore operation is probably insufficient to allow the application to recover.

The second factor limiting the utility of SEM_UNDO is that, in some cases, it is not possible to perform semaphore adjustments when a process terminates. Consider the following scenario, applied to a semaphore whose initial value is 0:

1. Process A increases the value of a semaphore by 2, specifying the SEM_UNDO flag for the operation.
2. Process B decreases the value of the semaphore by 1, so that it has the value 1.
3. Process A terminates.

At this point, it is impossible to completely undo the effect of process A's operation in step 1, since the value of the semaphore is too low. There are three possible ways to resolve this situation:

*   Force the process to block until the semaphore adjustment is possible.
*   Decrease the semaphore value as far as possible (i.e., to 0) and exit.
*   Exit without performing any semaphore adjustment.

The first solution is infeasible since it might force a terminating process to block forever. Linux adopts the second solution. Some other UNIX implementations adopt the third solution. SUSv3 is silent on what an implementation should do in this situation.

> An undo operation that attempts to raise a semaphore's value above its permitted maximum value of 32,767 (the SEMVMX limit, described Section 47.10) also causes anomalous behavior. In this case, the kernel always performs the adjustment, thus (illegitimately) raising the semaphore's value above SEMVMX.

47.9 Implementing a Binary Semaphores Protocol

The API for System V semaphores is complex, both because semaphore values can be adjusted by arbitrary amounts, and because semaphores are allocated and operated upon in sets. Both of these features provide more functionality than is typically needed within applications, and so it is useful to implement some simpler protocols (APIs) on top of System V semaphores.

One commonly used protocol is binary semaphores. A binary semaphore has two values: *available* (free) and *reserved* (in use). Two operations are defined for binary semaphores:

*   *Reserve*: Attempt to reserve this semaphore for exclusive use. If the semaphore is already reserved by another process, then block until the semaphore is released.

- *Release*: Free a currently reserved semaphore, so that it can be reserved by another process.

> In academic computer science, these two operations often go by the names *P* and *V*, the first letters of the Dutch terms for these operations. This nomenclature was coined by the late Dutch computer scientist Edsger Dijkstra, who produced much of the early theoretical work on semaphores. The terms *down* (decrement the semaphore) and *up* (increment the semaphore) are also used. POSIX terms the two operations *wait* and *post*.

A third operation is also sometimes defined:

- *Reserve conditionally*: Make a nonblocking attempt to reserve this semaphore for exclusive use. If the semaphore is already reserved, then immediately return a status indicating that the semaphore is unavailable.

In implementing binary semaphores, we must choose how to represent the *available* and *reserved* states, and how to implement the above operations. A moment's reflection leads us to realize that the best way to represent the states is to use the value 1 for *free* and the value 0 for *reserved*, with the *reserve* and *release* operations decrementing and incrementing the semaphore value by one.

Listing 47-9 and Listing 47-10 provide an implementation of binary semaphores using System V semaphores. As well as providing the prototypes of the functions in the implementation, the header file in Listing 47-9 declares two global Boolean variables exposed by the implementation. The *bsUseSemUndo* variable controls whether the implementation uses the SEM_UNDO flag in *semop()* calls. The *bsRetryOnEintr* variable controls whether the implementation restarts *semop()* calls that are interrupted by signals.

Listing 47-9: Header file for `binary_sems.c`

—————————————————————————————————————— **svsem/binary_sems.h**
```
#ifndef BINARY_SEMS_H          /* Prevent accidental double inclusion */
#define BINARY_SEMS_H

#include "tlpi_hdr.h"

/* Variables controlling operation of functions below */

extern Boolean bsUseSemUndo;        /* Use SEM_UNDO during semop()? */
extern Boolean bsRetryOnEintr;      /* Retry if semop() interrupted by
                                       signal handler? */

int initSemAvailable(int semId, int semNum);

int initSemInUse(int semId, int semNum);

int reserveSem(int semId, int semNum);

int releaseSem(int semId, int semNum);

#endif
```
—————————————————————————————————————— **svsem/binary_sems.h**

Listing 47-10 shows the implementation of the binary semaphore functions. Each function in this implementation takes two arguments, which identify a semaphore set and the number of a semaphore within that set. (These functions don't deal with the creation and deletion of semaphore sets; nor do they handle the race condition described in Section 47.5.) We employ these functions in the example programs shown in Section 48.4.

Listing 47-10: Implementing binary semaphores using System V semaphores

———————————————————————————————————— svsem/binary_sems.c
```c
#include <sys/types.h>
#include <sys/sem.h>
#include "semun.h"                      /* Definition of semun union */
#include "binary_sems.h"

Boolean bsUseSemUndo = FALSE;
Boolean bsRetryOnEintr = TRUE;

int                      /* Initialize semaphore to 1 (i.e., "available") */
initSemAvailable(int semId, int semNum)
{
    union semun arg;

    arg.val = 1;
    return semctl(semId, semNum, SETVAL, arg);
}

int                      /* Initialize semaphore to 0 (i.e., "in use") */
initSemInUse(int semId, int semNum)
{
    union semun arg;

    arg.val = 0;
    return semctl(semId, semNum, SETVAL, arg);
}

/* Reserve semaphore (blocking), return 0 on success, or -1 with 'errno'
   set to EINTR if operation was interrupted by a signal handler */

int                      /* Reserve semaphore - decrement it by 1 */
reserveSem(int semId, int semNum)
{
    struct sembuf sops;

    sops.sem_num = semNum;
    sops.sem_op = -1;
    sops.sem_flg = bsUseSemUndo ? SEM_UNDO : 0;

    while (semop(semId, &sops, 1) == -1)
        if (errno != EINTR || !bsRetryOnEintr)
            return -1;

    return 0;
}
```

```
int                      /* Release semaphore - increment it by 1 */
releaseSem(int semId, int semNum)
{
    struct sembuf sops;

    sops.sem_num = semNum;
    sops.sem_op = 1;
    sops.sem_flg = bsUseSemUndo ? SEM_UNDO : 0;

    return semop(semId, &sops, 1);
}
```
—— svsem/binary_sems.c

47.10 Semaphore Limits

Most UNIX implementations impose various limits on the operation of System V
semaphores. The following is a list of the Linux semaphore limits. The system call
affected by the limit and the error that results if the limit is reached are noted in
parentheses.

SEMAEM

> This is the maximum value that can be recorded in a *semadj* total. SEMAEM is
> defined to have the same value as SEMVMX (described below). (*semop()*, ERANGE)

SEMMNI

> This is a system-wide limit on the number of semaphore identifiers (in
> other words, semaphore sets) that can be created. (*semget()*, ENOSPC)

SEMMSL

> This is the maximum number of semaphores that can be allocated in a
> semaphore set. (*semget()*, EINVAL)

SEMMNS

> This is a system-wide limit on the number of semaphores in all semaphore
> sets. The number of semaphores on the system is also limited by SEMMNI and
> SEMMSL; in fact, the default value for SEMMNS is the product of the defaults for
> these two limits. (*semget()*, ENOSPC)

SEMOPM

> This is the maximum number of operations per *semop()* call. (*semop()*, E2BIG)

SEMVMX

> This is the maximum value for a semaphore. (*semop()*, ERANGE)

The limits above appear on most UNIX implementations. Some UNIX implementations (but not Linux) impose the following additional limits relating to semaphore
undo operations (Section 47.8):

SEMMNU

> This is a system-wide limit on the total number of semaphore undo structures.
> Undo structures are allocated to store *semadj* values.

SEMUME

> This is the maximum number of undo entries per semaphore undo structure.

At system startup, the semaphore limits are set to default values. These defaults may vary across kernel versions. (Some distributors' kernels set different defaults from those provided by vanilla kernels.) Some of these limits can be modified by changing the values stored in the Linux-specific /proc/sys/kernel/sem file. This file contains four space-delimited numbers defining, in order, the limits SEMMSL, SEMMNS, SEMOPM, and SEMMNI. (The SEMVMX and SEMAEM limits can't be changed; both are fixed at 32,767.) As an example, here are the default limits that we see for Linux 2.6.31 on one x86-32 system:

```
$ cd /proc/sys/kernel
$ cat sem
250     32000   32      128
```

> The formats employed in the Linux /proc file system are inconsistent for the three System V IPC mechanisms. For message queues and shared memory, each configurable limit is controlled by a separate file. For semaphores, one file holds all configurable limits. This is a historical accident that occurred during the development of these APIs and is difficult to rectify for compatibility reasons.

Table 47-1 shows the maximum value to which each limit can be raised on the x86-32 architecture. Note the following supplementary information to this table:

- It is possible to raise SEMMSL to values larger than 65,536, and create semaphore sets up to that larger size. However, it isn't possible to use *semop()* to adjust semaphores in the set beyond the 65,536th element.

  > Because of certain limitations in the current implementation, the practical recommended upper limit on the size of a semaphore set is around 8000.

- The practical ceiling for the SEMMNS limit is governed by the amount of RAM available on the system.
- The ceiling value for the SEMOPM limit is determined by memory allocation primitives used within the kernel. The recommended maximum is 1000. In practical usage, it is rarely useful to perform more than a few operations in a single *semop()* call.

Table 47-1: System V semaphore limits

Limit	Ceiling value (x86-32)
SEMMNI	32768 (IPCMNI)
SEMMSL	65536
SEMMNS	2147483647 (INT_MAX)
SEMOPM	See text

The Linux-specific *semctl()* IPC_INFO operation retrieves a structure of type *seminfo*, which contains the values of the various semaphore limits:

```
union semun arg;
struct seminfo buf;

arg.__buf = &buf;
semctl(0, 0, IPC_INFO, arg);
```

A related Linux-specific operation, SEM_INFO, retrieves a *seminfo* structure that contains information about actual resources used for semaphore objects. An example of the use of SEM_INFO is provided in the file svsem/svsem_info.c in the source code distribution for this book.

Details about IPC_INFO, SEM_INFO, and the *seminfo* structure can be found in the *semctl(2)* manual page.

47.11 Disadvantages of System V Semaphores

System V semaphores have many of the same disadvantages as message queues (Section 46.9), including the following:

- Semaphores are referred to by identifiers, rather than the file descriptors used by most other UNIX I/O and IPC mechanisms. This makes it difficult to perform operations such as simultaneously waiting both on a semaphore and on input from a file descriptor. (It is possible to resolve this difficulty by creating a child process or thread that operates on the semaphore and writes messages to a pipe monitored, along with other file descriptors, using one of the methods described in Chapter 63.)

- The use of keys, rather than filenames, to identify semaphores results in additional programming complexity.

- The use of separate system calls for creating and initializing semaphores means that, in some cases, we must do extra programming work to avoid race conditions when initializing a semaphore.

- The kernel doesn't maintain a count of the number of processes referring to a semaphore set. This complicates the decision about when it is appropriate to delete a semaphore set and makes it difficult to ensure that an unused set is deleted.

- The programming interface provided by System V semaphores is overly complex. In the common case, a program operates on a single semaphore. The ability to simultaneously operate on multiple semaphores in a set is unnecessary.

- There are various limits on the operation of semaphores. These limits are configurable, but if an application operates outside the range of the default limits, this nevertheless requires extra work when installing the application.

However, unlike the situation with message queues, there are fewer alternatives to System V semaphores, and consequently there are more situations in which we may choose to employ them. One alternative to the use of semaphores is record locking, which we describe in Chapter 55. Also, from kernel 2.6 onward, Linux supports the use of POSIX semaphores for process synchronization. We describe POSIX semaphores in Chapter 53.

47.12 Summary

System V semaphores allow processes to synchronize their actions. This is useful when a process must gain exclusive access to some shared resource, such as a region of shared memory.

Semaphores are created and operated upon in sets containing one or more semaphores. Each semaphore within a set is an integer whose value is always greater than or equal to 0. The *semop()* system call allows the caller to add an integer to a semaphore, subtract an integer from a semaphore, or wait for a semaphore to equal 0. The last two of these operations may cause the caller to block.

A semaphore implementation is not required to initialize the members of a new semaphore set, so an application must initialize the set after creating it. When any of a number of peer processes may try to create and initialize the semaphore, special care must be taken to avoid the race condition that results from the fact that these two steps are performed via separate system calls.

Where multiple processes are trying to decrease a semaphore by the same amount, it is indeterminate which process will actually be permitted to perform the operation first. However, where different processes are trying to decrease a semaphore by different amounts, the operations complete in the order in which they become possible, and we may need to take care to avoid scenarios where a process is starved because the semaphore value never reaches a level that would allow the process's operation to proceed.

The SEM_UNDO flag allows a process's semaphore operations to be automatically undone on process termination. This can be useful to avoid scenarios where a process accidentally terminates, leaving a semaphore in a state that causes other processes to block indefinitely waiting for the semaphore's value to be changed by the terminated process.

System V semaphores are allocated and operated upon in sets, and can be increased and decreased by arbitrary amounts. This provides more functionality than is needed by most applications. A common requirement is for individual binary semaphores, which take on only the values 0 and 1. We showed how to implement binary semaphores on top of System V semaphores.

Further information

[Bovet & Cesati, 2005] and [Maxwell, 1999] provide some background on the implementation of semaphores on Linux. [Dijkstra, 1968] is a classic early paper on semaphore theory.

47.13 Exercises

47-1. Experiment with the program in Listing 47-8 (svsem_op.c) to confirm your understanding of the *semop()* system call.

47-2. Modify the program in Listing 24-6 (fork_sig_sync.c, on page 528) to use semaphores instead of signals to synchronize the parent and child processes.

47-3. Experiment with the program in Listing 47-8 (svsem_op.c) and the other semaphore programs provided in this chapter to see what happens to the *sempid* value if an exiting process performs a SEM_UNDO adjustment to a semaphore.

47-4. Add a *reserveSemNB()* function to the code in Listing 47-10 (binary_sems.c) to implement the *reserve conditionally* operation, using the IPC_NOWAIT flag.

47-5. For the VMS operating system, Digital provided a synchronization method similar to a binary semaphore, called an *event flag*. An event flag has two possible values, *clear* and *set*, and the following four operations can be performed: *setEventFlag*, to set the flag; *clearEventFlag*, to clear the flag; *waitForEventFlag*, to block until the flag is set; and *getFlagState*, to obtain the current state of the flag. Devise an implementation of event flags using System V semaphores. This implementation will require two arguments for each of the functions above: a semaphore identifier and a semaphore number. (Consideration of the *waitForEventFlag* operation will lead you to realize that the values chosen for *clear* and *set* are not the obvious choices.)

47-6. Implement a binary semaphores protocol using named pipes. Provide functions to reserve, release, and conditionally reserve the semaphore.

47-7. Write a program, analogous to the program in Listing 46-6 (svmsg_ls.c, on page 953), that uses the *semctl()* SEM_INFO and SEM_STAT operations to obtain and display a list of all semaphore sets on the system.

48

SYSTEM V SHARED MEMORY

This chapter describes System V shared memory. Shared memory allows two or more processes to share the same region (usually referred to as a *segment*) of physical memory. Since a shared memory segment becomes part of a process's user-space memory, no kernel intervention is required for IPC. All that is required is that one process copies data into the shared memory; that data is immediately available to all other processes sharing the same segment. This provides fast IPC by comparison with techniques such as pipes or message queues, where the sending process copies data from a buffer in user space into kernel memory and the receiving process copies in the reverse direction. (Each process also incurs the overhead of a system call to perform the copy operation.)

On the other hand, the fact that IPC using shared memory is not mediated by the kernel means that, typically, some method of synchronization is required so that processes don't simultaneously access the shared memory (e.g., two processes performing simultaneous updates, or one process fetching data from the shared memory while another process is in the middle of updating it). System V semaphores are a natural method for such synchronization. Other methods, such as POSIX semaphores (Chapter 53) and file locks (Chapter 55), are also possible.

> In *mmap()* terminology, a memory region is *mapped* at an address, while in System V terminology, a shared memory segment is *attached* at an address. These terms are equivalent; the terminology differences are a consequence of the separate origins of these two APIs.

48.1 Overview

In order to use a shared memory segment, we typically perform the following steps:

- Call *shmget()* to create a new shared memory segment or obtain the identifier of an existing segment (i.e., one created by another process). This call returns a shared memory identifier for use in later calls.

- Use *shmat()* to *attach* the shared memory segment; that is, make the segment part of the virtual memory of the calling process.

- At this point, the shared memory segment can be treated just like any other memory available to the program. In order to refer to the shared memory, the program uses the *addr* value returned by the *shmat()* call, which is a pointer to the start of the shared memory segment in the process's virtual address space.

- Call *shmdt()* to detach the shared memory segment. After this call, the process can no longer refer to the shared memory. This step is optional, and happens automatically on process termination.

- Call *shmctl()* to delete the shared memory segment. The segment will be destroyed only after all currently attached processes have detached it. Only one process needs to perform this step.

48.2 Creating or Opening a Shared Memory Segment

The *shmget()* system call creates a new shared memory segment or obtains the identifier of an existing segment. The contents of a newly created shared memory segment are initialized to 0.

```
#include <sys/types.h>        /* For portability */
#include <sys/shm.h>

int shmget(key_t key, size_t size, int shmflg);
```
                    Returns shared memory segment identifier on success, or –1 on error

The *key* argument is a key generated using one of the methods described in Section 45.2 (i.e., usually the value IPC_PRIVATE or a key returned by *ftok()*).

When we use *shmget()* to create a new shared memory segment, *size* specifies a positive integer that indicates the desired size of the segment, in bytes. The kernel allocates shared memory in multiples of the system page size, so *size* is effectively rounded up to the next multiple of the system page size. If we are using *shmget()* to obtain the identifier of an existing segment, then *size* has no effect on the segment, but it must be less than or equal to the size of the segment.

The *shmflg* argument performs the same task as for the other IPC *get* calls, specifying the permissions (Table 15-4, on page 295) to be placed on a new shared memory segment or checked against an existing segment. In addition, zero or more of the following flags can be ORed (|) in *shmflg* to control the operation of *shmget()*:

IPC_CREAT
        If no segment with the specified *key* exists, create a new segment.

IPC_EXCL

        If `IPC_CREAT` was also specified, and a segment with the specified *key* already exists, fail with the error EEXIST.

The above flags are described in more detail in Section 45.1. In addition, Linux permits the following nonstandard flags:

SHM_HUGETLB (since Linux 2.6)

        A privileged (`CAP_IPC_LOCK`) process can use this flag to create a shared memory segment that uses *huge pages*. Huge pages are a feature provided by many modern hardware architectures to manage memory using very large page sizes. (For example, x86-32 allows 4-MB pages as an alternative to 4-kB pages.) On systems that have large amounts of memory, and where applications require large blocks of memory, using huge pages reduces the number of entries required in the hardware memory management unit's translation look-aside buffer (TLB). This is beneficial because entries in the TLB are usually a scarce resource. See the kernel source file `Documentation/vm/hugetlbpage.txt` for further information.

SHM_NORESERVE (since Linux 2.6.15)

        This flag serves the same purpose for *shmget()* as the `MAP_NORESERVE` flag serves for *mmap()*. See Section 49.9.

On success, *shmget()* returns the identifier for the new or existing shared memory segment.

48.3 Using Shared Memory

The *shmat()* system call attaches the shared memory segment identified by *shmid* to the calling process's virtual address space.

```
#include <sys/types.h>        /* For portability */
#include <sys/shm.h>

void *shmat(int shmid, const void *shmaddr, int shmflg);
```
                  Returns address at which shared memory is attached on success,
                                         or *(void *)* −1 on error

The *shmaddr* argument and the setting of the SHM_RND bit in the *shmflg* bit-mask argument control how the segment is attached:

- If *shmaddr* is NULL, then the segment is attached at a suitable address selected by the kernel. This is the preferred method of attaching a segment.

- If *shmaddr* is not NULL, and SHM_RND is not set, then the segment is attached at the address specified by *shmaddr*, which must be a multiple of the system page size (or the error EINVAL results).

- If *shmaddr* is not NULL, and SHM_RND is set, then the segment is mapped at the address provided in *shmaddr*, rounded down to the nearest multiple of the constant SHMLBA (*shared memory low boundary address*). This constant is equal to some multiple of the system page size. Attaching a segment at an address that is a multiple of SHMLBA is necessary on some architectures in order to improve CPU cache performance and to prevent the possibility that different attaches of the same segment have inconsistent views within the CPU cache.

> On the x86 architectures, SHMLBA is the same as the system page size, reflecting the fact that such caching inconsistencies can't arise on those architectures.

Specifying a non-NULL value for *shmaddr* (i.e., either the second or third option listed above) is not recommended, for the following reasons:

- It reduces the portability of an application. An address valid on one UNIX implementation may be invalid on another.
- An attempt to attach a shared memory segment at a particular address will fail if that address is already in use. This could happen if, for example, the application (perhaps inside a library function) had already attached another segment or created a memory mapping at that address.

As its function result, *shmat()* returns the address at which the shared memory segment is attached. This value can be treated like a normal C pointer; the segment looks just like any other part of the process's virtual memory. Typically, we assign the return value from *shmat()* to a pointer to some programmer-defined structure, in order to impose that structure on the segment (see, for example, Listing 48-2).

To attach a shared memory segment for read-only access, we specify the flag SHM_RDONLY in *shmflg*. Attempts to update the contents of a read-only segment result in a segmentation fault (the SIGSEGV signal). If SHM_RDONLY is not specified, the memory can be both read and modified.

To attach a shared memory segment, a process requires read and write permissions on the segment, unless SHM_RDONLY is specified, in which case only read permission is required.

> It is possible to attach the same shared memory segment multiple times within a process, and even to make one attach read-only while another is read-write. The contents of the memory at each attachment point are the same, since the different entries of the process virtual memory page tables are referring to the same physical pages of memory.

One final value that may be specified in *shmflg* is SHM_REMAP. In this case, *shmaddr* must be non-NULL. This flag requests that the *shmat()* call replace any existing shared memory attachment or memory mapping in the range starting at *shmaddr* and continuing for the length of the shared memory segment. Normally, if we try to attach a shared memory segment at an address range that is already in use, the error EINVAL results. SHM_REMAP is a nonstandard Linux extension.

Table 48-1 summarizes the constants that can be ORed in the *shmflg* argument of *shmat()*.

When a process no longer needs to access a shared memory segment, it can call *shmdt()* to detach the segment from its virtual address space. The *shmaddr* argument identifies the segment to be detached. It should be a value returned by a previous call to *shmat()*.

```
#include <sys/types.h>          /* For portability */
#include <sys/shm.h>

int shmdt(const void *shmaddr);
```

Returns 0 on success, or –1 on error

Detaching a shared memory segment is not the same as deleting it. Deletion is performed using the *shmctl()* IPC_RMID operation, as described in Section 48.7.

A child created by *fork()* inherits its parent's attached shared memory segments. Thus, shared memory provides an easy method of IPC between parent and child.

During an *exec()*, all attached shared memory segments are detached. Shared memory segments are also automatically detached on process termination.

Table 48-1: *shmflg* bit-mask values for *shmat()*

Value	Description
SHM_RDONLY	Attach segment read-only
SHM_REMAP	Replace any existing mapping at *shmaddr*
SHM_RND	Round *shmaddr* down to multiple of SHMLBA bytes

48.4 Example: Transferring Data via Shared Memory

We now look at an example application that uses System V shared memory and semaphores. The application consists of two programs: the *writer* and the *reader*. The writer reads blocks of data from standard input and copies ("writes") them into a shared memory segment. The reader copies ("reads") blocks of data from the shared memory segment to standard output. In effect, the programs treat the shared memory somewhat like a pipe.

The two programs employ a pair of System V semaphores in a binary semaphore protocol (the *initSemAvailable()*, *initSemInUse()*, *reserveSem()*, and *releaseSem()* functions defined in Section 47.9) to ensure that:

- only one process accesses the shared memory segment at a time; and

- the processes alternate in accessing the segment (i.e., the writer writes some data, then the reader reads the data, then the writer writes again, and so on).

Figure 48-1 provides an overview of the use of these two semaphores. Note that the writer initializes the two semaphores so that it is the first of the two programs to be able to access the shared memory segment; that is, the writer's semaphore is initially available, and the reader's semaphore is initially in use.

The source code for the application consists of three files. The first of these, Listing 48-1, is a header file shared by the reader and writer programs. This header defines the *shmseg* structure that we use to declare pointers to the shared memory segment. Doing this allows us to impose a structure on the bytes of the shared memory segment.

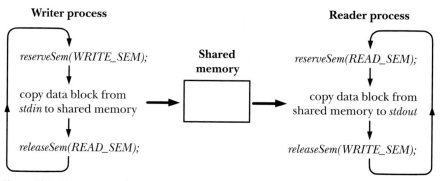

Figure 48-1: Using semaphores to ensure exclusive, alternating access to shared memory

Listing 48-1: Header file for svshm_xfr_writer.c and svshm_xfr_reader.c

── **svshm/svshm_xfr.h**

```
#include <sys/types.h>
#include <sys/stat.h>
#include <sys/sem.h>
#include <sys/shm.h>
#include "binary_sems.h"      /* Declares our binary semaphore functions */
#include "tlpi_hdr.h"

#define SHM_KEY 0x1234        /* Key for shared memory segment */
#define SEM_KEY 0x5678        /* Key for semaphore set */

#define OBJ_PERMS (S_IRUSR | S_IWUSR | S_IRGRP | S_IWGRP)
                             /* Permissions for our IPC objects */

#define WRITE_SEM 0           /* Writer has access to shared memory */
#define READ_SEM 1            /* Reader has access to shared memory */

#ifndef BUF_SIZE              /* Allow "cc -D" to override definition */
#define BUF_SIZE 1024         /* Size of transfer buffer */
#endif

struct shmseg {               /* Defines structure of shared memory segment */
    int cnt;                  /* Number of bytes used in 'buf' */
    char buf[BUF_SIZE];       /* Data being transferred */
};
```

── **svshm/svshm_xfr.h**

Listing 48-2 is the writer program. This program performs the following steps:

- Create a set containing the two semaphores that are used by the writer and reader program to ensure that they alternate in accessing the shared memory segment ①. The semaphores are initialized so that the writer has first access to the shared memory segment. Since the writer creates the semaphore set, it must be started before the reader.

- Create the shared memory segment and attach it to the writer's virtual address space at an address chosen by the system ②.
- Enter a loop that transfers data from standard input to the shared memory segment ③. The following steps are performed in each loop iteration:
  - Reserve (decrement) the writer semaphore ④.
  - Read data from standard input into the shared memory segment ⑤.
  - Release (increment) the reader semaphore ⑥.
- The loop terminates when no further data is available from standard input ⑦. On the last pass through the loop, the writer indicates to the reader that there is no more data by passing a block of data of length 0 (*shmp->cnt* is 0).
- Upon exiting the loop, the writer once more reserves its semaphore, so that it knows that the reader has completed the final access to the shared memory ⑧. The writer then removes the shared memory segment and semaphore set ⑨.

Listing 48-3 is the reader program. It transfers blocks of data from the shared memory segment to standard output. The reader performs the following steps:

- Obtain the IDs of the semaphore set and shared memory segment that were created by the writer program ①.
- Attach the shared memory segment for read-only access ②.
- Enter a loop that transfers data from the shared memory segment ③. The following steps are performed in each loop iteration:
  - Reserve (decrement) the reader semaphore ④.
  - Check whether *shmp->cnt* is 0; if so, exit this loop ⑤.
  - Write the block of data in the shared memory segment to standard output ⑥.
  - Release (increment) the writer semaphore ⑦.
- After exiting the loop, detach the shared memory segment ⑧ and releases the writer semaphore ⑨, so that the writer program can remove the IPC objects.

Listing 48-2: Transfer blocks of data from *stdin* to a System V shared memory segment

─── svshm/svshm_xfr_writer.c

```
#include "semun.h"              /* Definition of semun union */
#include "svshm_xfr.h"

int
main(int argc, char *argv[])
{
    int semid, shmid, bytes, xfrs;
    struct shmseg *shmp;
    union semun dummy;

①  semid = semget(SEM_KEY, 2, IPC_CREAT | OBJ_PERMS);
    if (semid == -1)
        errExit("semget");
```

```
        if (initSemAvailable(semid, WRITE_SEM) == -1)
            errExit("initSemAvailable");
        if (initSemInUse(semid, READ_SEM) == -1)
            errExit("initSemInUse");

②      shmid = shmget(SHM_KEY, sizeof(struct shmseg), IPC_CREAT | OBJ_PERMS);
        if (shmid == -1)
            errExit("shmget");

        shmp = shmat(shmid, NULL, 0);
        if (shmp == (void *) -1)
            errExit("shmat");

        /* Transfer blocks of data from stdin to shared memory */

③      for (xfrs = 0, bytes = 0; ; xfrs++, bytes += shmp->cnt) {
④          if (reserveSem(semid, WRITE_SEM) == -1)          /* Wait for our turn */
                errExit("reserveSem");

⑤          shmp->cnt = read(STDIN_FILENO, shmp->buf, BUF_SIZE);
            if (shmp->cnt == -1)
                errExit("read");

⑥          if (releaseSem(semid, READ_SEM) == -1)          /* Give reader a turn */
                errExit("releaseSem");

            /* Have we reached EOF? We test this after giving the reader
               a turn so that it can see the 0 value in shmp->cnt. */

⑦          if (shmp->cnt == 0)
                break;
        }

        /* Wait until reader has let us have one more turn. We then know
           reader has finished, and so we can delete the IPC objects. */

⑧      if (reserveSem(semid, WRITE_SEM) == -1)
            errExit("reserveSem");

⑨      if (semctl(semid, 0, IPC_RMID, dummy) == -1)
            errExit("semctl");
        if (shmdt(shmp) == -1)
            errExit("shmdt");
        if (shmctl(shmid, IPC_RMID, 0) == -1)
            errExit("shmctl");

        fprintf(stderr, "Sent %d bytes (%d xfrs)\n", bytes, xfrs);
        exit(EXIT_SUCCESS);
    }
```

—————————————————————————————————— **svshm/svshm_xfr_writer.c**

Listing 48-3: Transfer blocks of data from a System V shared memory segment to *stdout*

```c
#include "svshm_xfr.h"

int
main(int argc, char *argv[])
{
    int semid, shmid, xfrs, bytes;
    struct shmseg *shmp;

    /* Get IDs for semaphore set and shared memory created by writer */

①  semid = semget(SEM_KEY, 0, 0);
    if (semid == -1)
        errExit("semget");

    shmid  = shmget(SHM_KEY, 0, 0);
    if (shmid == -1)
        errExit("shmget");

②  shmp = shmat(shmid, NULL, SHM_RDONLY);
    if (shmp == (void *) -1)
        errExit("shmat");

    /* Transfer blocks of data from shared memory to stdout */

③  for (xfrs = 0, bytes = 0; ; xfrs++) {
④      if (reserveSem(semid, READ_SEM) == -1)          /* Wait for our turn */
            errExit("reserveSem");

⑤      if (shmp->cnt == 0)                    /* Writer encountered EOF */
            break;
        bytes += shmp->cnt;

⑥      if (write(STDOUT_FILENO, shmp->buf, shmp->cnt) != shmp->cnt)
            fatal("partial/failed write");

⑦      if (releaseSem(semid, WRITE_SEM) == -1)          /* Give writer a turn */
            errExit("releaseSem");
    }

⑧  if (shmdt(shmp) == -1)
        errExit("shmdt");

    /* Give writer one more turn, so it can clean up */

⑨  if (releaseSem(semid, WRITE_SEM) == -1)
        errExit("releaseSem");

    fprintf(stderr, "Received %d bytes (%d xfrs)\n", bytes, xfrs);
    exit(EXIT_SUCCESS);
}
```

The following shell session demonstrates the use of the programs in Listing 48-2 and Listing 48-3. We invoke the writer, using the file /etc/services as input, and then invoke the reader, directing its output to another file:

```
$ wc -c /etc/services                              Display size of test file
764360 /etc/services
$ ./svshm_xfr_writer < /etc/services &
[1] 9403
$ ./svshm_xfr_reader > out.txt
Received 764360 bytes (747 xfrs)                    Message from reader
Sent 764360 bytes (747 xfrs)                        Message from writer
[1]+  Done                ./svshm_xfr_writer < /etc/services
$ diff /etc/services out.txt
$
```

The *diff* command produced no output, indicating that the output file produced by the reader has the same content as the input file used by the writer.

48.5 Location of Shared Memory in Virtual Memory

In Section 6.3, we considered the layout of the various parts of a process in virtual memory. It is useful to revisit this topic in the context of attaching System V shared memory segments. If we follow the recommended approach of allowing the kernel to choose where to attach a shared memory segment, then (on the x86-32 architecture) the memory layout appears as shown in Figure 48-2, with the segment being attached in the unallocated space between the upwardly growing heap and the downwardly growing stack. To allow space for heap and stack growth, shared memory segments are attached starting at the virtual address 0x40000000. Mapped mappings (Chapter 49) and shared libraries (Chapters 41 and 42) are also placed in this area. (There is some variation in the default location at which shared memory mappings and memory segments are placed, depending on the kernel version and the setting of the process's RLIMIT_STACK resource limit.)

> The address 0x40000000 is defined as the kernel constant TASK_UNMAPPED_BASE. It is possible to change this address by defining this constant with a different value and rebuilding the kernel.
>
> A shared memory segment (or memory mapping) can be placed at an address below TASK_UNMAPPED_BASE, if we employ the unrecommended approach of explicitly specifying an address when calling *shmat()* (or *mmap()*).

Using the Linux-specific /proc/*PID*/maps file, we can see the location of the shared memory segments and shared libraries mapped by a program, as we demonstrate in the shell session below.

> Starting with kernel 2.6.14, Linux also provides the /proc/*PID*/smaps file, which exposes more information about the memory consumption of each of a process's mappings. For further details, see the *proc(5)* manual page.

Virtual memory address
(hexadecimal)

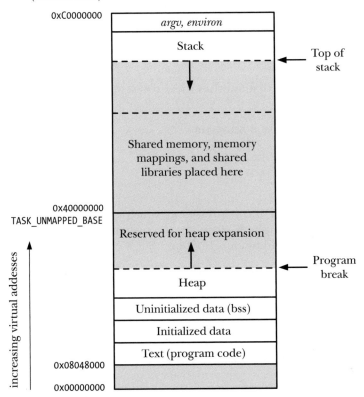

Figure 48-2: Locations of shared memory, memory mappings, and shared libraries (x86-32)

In the shell session below, we employ three programs that are not shown in this chapter, but are provided in the svshm subdirectory in the source code distribution for this book. These programs perform the following tasks:

- The svshm_create.c program creates a shared memory segment. This program takes the same command-line options as the corresponding programs that we provide for message queues (Listing 46-1, on page 938) and semaphores, but includes an additional argument that specifies the size of the segment.

- The svshm_attach.c program attaches the shared memory segments identified by its command-line arguments. Each of these arguments is a colon-separated pair of numbers consisting of a shared memory identifier and an attach address. Specifying 0 for the attach address means that the system should choose the address. The program displays the address at which the memory is actually attached. For informational purposes, the program also displays the value of the SHMLBA constant and the process ID of the process running the program.

- The svshm_rm.c program deletes the shared memory segments identified by its command-line arguments.

We begin the shell session by creating two shared memory segments (100 kB and 3200 kB in size):

```
$ ./svshm_create -p 102400
9633796
$ ./svshm_create -p 3276800
9666565
```

We then start a program that attaches these two segments at addresses chosen by the kernel:

```
$ ./svshm_attach 9633796:0 9666565:0
SHMLBA = 4096 (0x1000), PID = 9903
1: 9633796:0 ==> 0xb7f0d000
2: 9666565:0 ==> 0xb7bed000
Sleeping 5 seconds
```

The output above shows the addresses at which the segments were attached. Before the program completes sleeping, we suspend it, and then examine the contents of the corresponding /proc/*PID*/maps file:

```
Type Control-Z to suspend program
[1]+  Stopped                 ./svshm_attach 9633796:0 9666565:0
$ cat /proc/9903/maps
```

The output produced by the *cat* command is shown in Listing 48-4.

Listing 48-4: Example of contents of /proc/*PID*/maps

```
$ cat /proc/9903/maps
①  08048000-0804a000 r-xp 00000000 08:05 5526989   /home/mtk/svshm_attach
   0804a000-0804b000 r--p 00001000 08:05 5526989   /home/mtk/svshm_attach
   0804b000-0804c000 rw-p 00002000 08:05 5526989   /home/mtk/svshm_attach
②  b7bed000-b7f0d000 rw-s 00000000 00:09 9666565   /SYSV00000000 (deleted)
   b7f0d000-b7f26000 rw-s 00000000 00:09 9633796   /SYSV00000000 (deleted)
   b7f26000-b7f27000 rw-p b7f26000 00:00 0
③  b7f27000-b8064000 r-xp 00000000 08:06 122031    /lib/libc-2.8.so
   b8064000-b8066000 r--p 0013d000 08:06 122031    /lib/libc-2.8.so
   b8066000-b8067000 rw-p 0013f000 08:06 122031    /lib/libc-2.8.so
   b8067000-b806b000 rw-p b8067000 00:00 0
   b8082000-b8083000 rw-p b8082000 00:00 0
④  b8083000-b809e000 r-xp 00000000 08:06 122125    /lib/ld-2.8.so
   b809e000-b809f000 r--p 0001a000 08:06 122125    /lib/ld-2.8.so
   b809f000-b80a0000 rw-p 0001b000 08:06 122125    /lib/ld-2.8.so
⑤  bfd8a000-bfda0000 rw-p bffea000 00:00 0         [stack]
⑥  ffffe000-fffff000 r-xp 00000000 00:00 0         [vdso]
```

In the output from /proc/*PID*/maps shown in Listing 48-4, we can see the following:

- Three lines for the main program, *shm_attach*. These correspond to the text and data segments of the program ①. The second of these lines is for a read-only page holding the string constants used by the program.

- Two lines for the attached System V shared memory segments ②.

- Lines corresponding to the segments for two shared libraries. One of these is the standard C library (libc-*version*.so) ③. The other is the dynamic linker (ld-*version*.so), which we describe in Section 41.4.3 ④.

- A line labeled [stack]. This corresponds to the process stack ⑤.

- A line containing the tag [vdso] ⑥. This is an entry for the *linux-gate* virtual dynamic shared object (DSO). This entry appears only in kernels since 2.6.12. See *http://www.trilithium.com/johan/2005/08/linux-gate/* for further information about this entry.

The following columns are shown in each line of /proc/*PID*/maps, in order from left to right:

1. A pair of hyphen-separated numbers indicating the virtual address range (in hexadecimal) at which the memory segment is mapped. The second of these numbers is the address of the next byte *after* the end of the segment.

2. Protection and flags for this memory segment. The first three letters indicate the protection of the segment: read (r), write (w), and execute (x). A hyphen (-) in place of any of these letters indicates that the corresponding protection is disabled. The final letter indicates the mapping flag for the memory segment; it is either private (p) or shared (s). For an explanation of these flags, see the description of the MAP_PRIVATE and MAP_SHARED flags in Section 49.2. (A System V shared memory segment is always marked shared.)

3. The hexadecimal offset (in bytes) of the segment within the corresponding mapped file. The meanings of this and the following two columns will become clearer when we describe the *mmap()* system call in Chapter 49. For a System V shared memory segment, the offset is always 0.

4. The device number (major and minor IDs) of the device on which the corresponding mapped file is located.

5. The i-node number of the mapped file, or, for System V shared memory segments, the identifier for the segment.

6. The filename or other identifying tag associated with this memory segment. For a System V shared memory segment, this consists of the string SYSV concatenated with the *shmget()* key of the segment (expressed in hexadecimal). In this example, SYSV is followed by zeros because we created the segments using the key IPC_PRIVATE (which has the value 0). The string (deleted) that appears after the SYSV field for a System V shared memory segment is an artifact of the implementation of shared memory segments. Such segments are created as mapped files in an invisible *tmpfs* file system (Section 14.10), and then later unlinked. Shared anonymous memory mappings are implemented in the same manner. (We describe mapped files and shared anonymous memory mappings in Chapter 49.)

48.6 Storing Pointers in Shared Memory

Each process may employ different shared libraries and memory mappings, and may attach different sets of shared memory segments. Therefore, if we follow the recommended practice of letting the kernel choose where to attach a shared memory segment, the segment may be attached at a different address in each process. For this reason, when storing references inside a shared memory segment that point to other addresses within the segment, we should use (relative) offsets, rather than (absolute) pointers.

For example, suppose we have a shared memory segment whose starting address is pointed to by *baseaddr* (i.e., *baseaddr* is the value returned by *shmat()*). Furthermore, at the location pointed to by *p*, we want to store a pointer to the same location as is pointed to by *target*, as shown in Figure 48-3. This sort of operation would be typical if we were building a linked list or a binary tree within the segment. The usual C idiom for setting **p* would be the following:

```
*p = target;                 /* Place pointer in *p (WRONG!) */
```

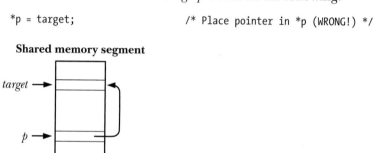

Figure 48-3: Using pointers in a shared memory segment

The problem with this code is that the location pointed to by *target* may reside at a different virtual address when the shared memory segment is attached in another process, which means that the value stored at **p* is meaningless in that process. The correct approach is to store an offset at **p*, as in the following:

```
*p = target - baseaddr;      /* Place offset in *p */
```

When dereferencing such pointers, we reverse the above step:

```
target = baseaddr + *p;      /* Interpret offset */
```

Here, we assume that in each process, *baseaddr* points to the start of the shared memory segment (i.e., it is the value returned by *shmat()* in each process). Given this assumption, an offset value is correctly interpreted, no matter where the shared memory segment is attached in a process's virtual address space.

Alternatively, if we are linking together a set of fixed-size structures, we can cast the shared memory segment (or a part thereof) as an array, and then use index numbers as the "pointers" referring from one structure to another.

48.7 Shared Memory Control Operations

The *shmctl()* system call performs a range of control operations on the shared memory segment identified by *shmid*.

```
#include <sys/types.h>          /* For portability */
#include <sys/shm.h>

int shmctl(int shmid, int cmd, struct shmid_ds *buf);
```
                                           Returns 0 on success, or −1 on error

The *cmd* argument specifies the control operation to be performed. The *buf* argument is required by the IPC_STAT and IPC_SET operations (described below), and should be specified as NULL for the remaining operations.

In the remainder of this section, we describe the various operations that can be specified for *cmd*.

Generic control operations

The following operations are the same as for other types of System V IPC objects. Further details about these operations, including the privileges and permissions required by the calling process, are described in Section 45.3.

IPC_RMID
  Mark the shared memory segment and its associated *shmid_ds* data structure for deletion. If no processes currently have the segment attached, deletion is immediate; otherwise, the segment is removed after all processes have detached from it (i.e., when the value of the *shm_nattch* field in the *shmid_ds* data structure falls to 0). In some applications, we can make sure that a shared memory segment is tidily cleared away on application termination by marking it for deletion immediately after all processes have attached it to their virtual address space with *shmat()*. This is analogous to unlinking a file once we've opened it.

  > On Linux, if a shared segment has been marked for deletion using IPC_RMID, but has not yet been removed because some process still has it attached, then it is possible for another process to attach that segment. However, this behavior is not portable: most UNIX implementations prevent new attaches to a segment marked for deletion. (SUSv3 is silent on what behavior should occur in this scenario.) A few Linux applications have come to depend on this behavior, which is why Linux has not been changed to match other UNIX implementations.

IPC_STAT
  Place a copy of the *shmid_ds* data structure associated with this shared memory segment in the buffer pointed to by *buf*. (We describe this data structure in Section 48.8.)

IPC_SET
  Update selected fields of the *shmid_ds* data structure associated with this shared memory segment using values in the buffer pointed to by *buf*.

Locking and unlocking shared memory

A shared memory segment can be locked into RAM, so that it is never swapped out. This provides a performance benefit, since, once each page of the segment is memory-resident, an application is guaranteed never to be delayed by a page fault when it accesses the page. There are two *shmctl()* locking operations:

- The SHM_LOCK operation locks a shared memory segment into memory.
- The SHM_UNLOCK operation unlocks the shared memory segment, allowing it to be swapped out.

These operations are not specified by SUSv3, and they are not provided on all UNIX implementations.

In versions of Linux before 2.6.10, only privileged (CAP_IPC_LOCK) processes can lock a shared memory segment into memory. Since Linux 2.6.10, an unprivileged process can lock and unlock a shared memory segment if its effective user ID matches either the owner or the creator user ID of the segment and (in the case of SHM_LOCK) the process has a sufficiently high RLIMIT_MEMLOCK resource limit. See Section 50.2 for details.

Locking a shared memory segment does not guarantee that all of the pages of the segment are memory-resident at the completion of the *shmctl()* call. Rather, nonresident pages are individually locked in only as they are faulted into memory by subsequent references by processes that have attached the shared memory segment. Once faulted in, the pages stay resident until subsequently unlocked, even if all processes detach the segment. (In other words, the SHM_LOCK operation sets a property of the shared memory segment, rather than a property of the calling process.)

> By *faulted into memory*, we mean that when the process references the nonresident page, a page fault occurs. At this point, if the page is in the swap area, then it is reloaded into memory. If the page is being referenced for the first time, no corresponding page exists in the swap file. Therefore, the kernel allocates a new page of physical memory and adjusts the process's page tables and the bookkeeping data structures for the shared memory segment.

An alternative method of locking memory, with slightly different semantics, is the use of *mlock()*, which we describe in Section 50.2.

48.8 Shared Memory Associated Data Structure

Each shared memory segment has an associated *shmid_ds* data structure of the following form:

```
struct shmid_ds {
    struct ipc_perm shm_perm;     /* Ownership and permissions */
    size_t   shm_segsz;           /* Size of segment in bytes */
    time_t   shm_atime;           /* Time of last shmat() */
    time_t   shm_dtime;           /* Time of last shmdt() */
    time_t   shm_ctime;           /* Time of last change */
    pid_t    shm_cpid;            /* PID of creator */
    pid_t    shm_lpid;            /* PID of last shmat() / shmdt() */
    shmatt_t shm_nattch;          /* Number of currently attached processes */
};
```

SUSv3 requires all of the fields shown here. Some other UNIX implementations include additional nonstandard fields in the *shmid_ds* structure.

The fields of the *shmid_ds* structure are implicitly updated by various shared memory system calls, and certain subfields of the *shm_perm* field can be explicitly updated using the *shmctl()* IPC_SET operation. The details are as follows:

shm_perm

When the shared memory segment is created, the fields of this substructure are initialized as described in Section 45.3. The *uid*, *gid*, and (the lower 9 bits of the) *mode* subfields can be updated via IPC_SET. As well as the usual permission bits, the *shm_perm.mode* field holds two read-only bit-mask flags. The first of these, SHM_DEST (destroy), indicates whether the segment is marked for deletion (via the *shmctl()* IPC_RMID operation) when all processes have detached it from their address space. The other flag, SHM_LOCKED, indicates whether the segment is locked into physical memory (via the *shmctl()* SHM_LOCK operation). Neither of these flags is standardized in SUSv3, and equivalents appear on only a few other UNIX implementations, in some cases with different names.

shm_segsz

On creation of the shared memory segment, this field is set to the requested size of the segment in bytes (i.e., to the value of the *size* argument specified in the call to *shmget()*). As noted in Section 48.2, shared memory is allocated in units of pages, so the actual size of the segment may be larger than this value.

shm_atime

This field is set to 0 when the shared memory segment is created, and set to the current time whenever a process attaches the segment (*shmat()*). This field and the other timestamp fields in the *shmid_ds* structure are typed as *time_t*, and store time in seconds since the Epoch.

shm_dtime

This field is set to 0 when the shared memory segment is created, and set to the current time whenever a process detaches the segment (*shmdt()*).

shm_ctime

This field is set to the current time when the segment is created, and on each successful IPC_SET operation.

shm_cpid

This field is set to the process ID of the process that created the segment using *shmget()*.

shm_lpid

This field is set to 0 when the shared memory segment is created, and then set to the process ID of the calling process on each successful *shmat()* or *shmdt()*.

shm_nattch

This field counts the number of processes that currently have the segment attached. It is initialized to 0 when the segment is created, and then incremented by each successful *shmat()* and decremented by each successful *shmdt()*. The *shmatt_t* data type used to define this field is an unsigned integer type that SUSv3 requires to be at least the size of *unsigned short*. (On Linux, this type is defined as *unsigned long*.)

48.9 Shared Memory Limits

Most UNIX implementations impose various limits on System V shared memory. Below is a list of the Linux shared memory limits. The system call affected by the limit and the error that results if the limit is reached are noted in parentheses.

SHMMNI

This is a system-wide limit on the number of shared memory identifiers (in other words, shared memory segments) that can be created. (*shmget()*, ENOSPC)

SHMMIN

This is the minimum size (in bytes) of a shared memory segment. This limit is defined with the value 1 (this can't be changed). However, the effective limit is the system page size. (*shmget()*, EINVAL)

SHMMAX

This is the maximum size (in bytes) of a shared memory segment. The practical upper limit for SHMMAX depends on available RAM and swap space. (*shmget()*, EINVAL)

SHMALL

This is a system-wide limit on the total number of pages of shared memory. Most other UNIX implementations don't provide this limit. The practical upper limit for SHMALL depends on available RAM and swap space. (*shmget()*, ENOSPC)

Some other UNIX implementations also impose the following limit (which is not implemented on Linux):

SHMSEG

This is a per-process limit on the number of attached shared memory segments.

At system startup, the shared memory limits are set to default values. (These defaults may vary across kernel versions, and some distributors' kernels set different defaults from those provided by vanilla kernels.) On Linux, some of the limits can be viewed or changed via files in the /proc file system. Table 48-2 lists the /proc file corresponding to each limit. As an example, here are the default limits that we see for Linux 2.6.31 on one x86-32 system:

```
$ cd /proc/sys/kernel
$ cat shmmni
4096
```

```
$ cat shmmax
33554432
$ cat shmall
2097152
```

The Linux-specific *shmctl()* IPC_INFO operation retrieves a structure of type *shminfo*, which contains the values of the various shared memory limits:

```
struct shminfo buf;

shmctl(0, IPC_INFO, (struct shmid_ds *) &buf);
```

A related Linux-specific operation, SHM_INFO, retrieves a structure of type *shm_info* that contains information about actual resources used for shared memory objects. An example of the use of SHM_INFO is provided in the file svshm/svshm_info.c in the source code distribution for this book.

Details about IPC_INFO, SHM_INFO, and the *shminfo* and *shm_info* structures can be found in the *shmctl(2)* manual page.

Table 48-2: System V shared memory limits

Limit	Ceiling value (x86-32)	Corresponding file in /proc/sys/kernel
SHMMNI	32768 (IPCMNI)	shmmni
SHMMAX	Depends on available memory	shmmax
SHMALL	Depends on available memory	shmall

48.10 Summary

Shared memory allows two or more processes to share the same pages of memory. No kernel intervention is required to exchange data via shared memory. Once a process has copied data into a shared memory segment, that data is immediately visible to other processes. Shared memory provides fast IPC, although this speed advantage is somewhat offset by the fact that normally we must use some type of synchronization technique, such as a System V semaphore, to synchronize access to the shared memory.

The recommended approach when attaching a shared memory segment is to allow the kernel to choose the address at which the segment is attached in the process's virtual address space. This means that the segment may reside at different virtual addresses in different processes. For this reason, any references to addresses within the segment should be maintained as relative offsets, rather than as absolute pointers.

Further information

The Linux memory-management scheme and some details of the implementation of shared memory are described in [Bovet & Cesati, 2005].

48.11 Exercises

48-1. Replace the use of binary semaphores in Listing 48-2 (svshm_xfr_writer.c) and Listing 48-3 (svshm_xfr_reader.c) with the use of event flags (Exercise 47-5).

48-2. Explain why the program in Listing 48-3 incorrectly reports the number of bytes transferred if the for loop is modified as follows:

```
for (xfrs = 0, bytes = 0; shmp->cnt != 0; xfrs++, bytes += shmp->cnt) {
    reserveSem(semid, READ_SEM);              /* Wait for our turn */

    if (write(STDOUT_FILENO, shmp->buf, shmp->cnt) != shmp->cnt)
        fatal("write");

    releaseSem(semid, WRITE_SEM);             /* Give writer a turn */
}
```

48-3. Try compiling the programs in Listing 48-2 (svshm_xfr_writer.c) and Listing 48-3 (svshm_xfr_reader.c) with a range of different sizes (defined by the constant BUF_SIZE) for the buffer used to exchange data between the two programs. Time the execution of svshm_xfr_reader.c for each buffer size.

48-4. Write a program that displays the contents of the *shmid_ds* data structure (Section 48.8) associated with a shared memory segment. The identifier of the segment should be specified as a command-line argument. (See the program in Listing 47-3, on page 973, which performs the analogous task for System V semaphores.)

48-5. Write a directory service that uses a shared memory segment to publish name-value pairs. You will need to provide an API that allows callers to create a new name, modify an existing name, delete an existing name, and retrieve the value associated with a name. Use semaphores to ensure that a process performing an update to the shared memory segment has exclusive access to the segment.

48-6. Write a program (analogous to program in Listing 46-6, on page 953) that uses the *shmctl()* SHM_INFO and SHM_STAT operations to obtain and display a list of all shared memory segments on the system.

49

MEMORY MAPPINGS

This chapter discusses the use of the *mmap()* system call to create memory mappings. Memory mappings can be used for IPC, as well as a range of other purposes. We begin with an overview of some fundamental concepts before considering *mmap()* in depth.

49.1 Overview

The *mmap()* system call creates a new *memory mapping* in the calling process's virtual address space. A mapping can be of two types:

- *File mapping*: A file mapping maps a region of a file directly into the calling process's virtual memory. Once a file is mapped, its contents can be accessed by operations on the bytes in the corresponding memory region. The pages of the mapping are (automatically) loaded from the file as required. This type of mapping is also known as a *file-based mapping* or *memory-mapped file*.

- *Anonymous mapping*: An anonymous mapping doesn't have a corresponding file. Instead, the pages of the mapping are initialized to 0.

  > Another way of thinking of an anonymous mapping (and one that is close to the truth) is that it is a mapping of a virtual file whose contents are always initialized with zeros.

The memory in one process's mapping may be shared with mappings in other processes (i.e., the page-table entries of each process point to the same pages of RAM). This can occur in two ways:

- When two processes map the same region of a file, they share the same pages of physical memory.

- A child process created by *fork()* inherits copies of its parent's mappings, and these mappings refer to the same pages of physical memory as the corresponding mappings in the parent.

When two or more processes share the same pages, each process can potentially see the changes to the page contents made by other processes, depending on whether the mapping is *private* or *shared*:

- *Private mapping* (MAP_PRIVATE): Modifications to the contents of the mapping are not visible to other processes and, for a file mapping, are not carried through to the underlying file. Although the pages of a private mapping are initially shared in the circumstances described above, changes to the contents of the mapping are nevertheless private to each process. The kernel accomplishes this using the copy-on-write technique (Section 24.2.2). This means that whenever a process attempts to modify the contents of a page, the kernel first creates a new, separate copy of that page for the process (and adjusts the process's page tables). For this reason, a MAP_PRIVATE mapping is sometimes referred to as a *private, copy-on-write mapping*.

- *Shared mapping* (MAP_SHARED): Modifications to the contents of the mapping are visible to other processes that share the same mapping and, for a file mapping, are carried through to the underlying file.

The two mapping attributes described above (file versus anonymous and private versus shared) can be combined in four different ways, as summarized in Table 49-1.

Table 49-1: Purposes of various types of memory mappings

Visibility of modifications	Mapping type	
	File	Anonymous
Private	Initializing memory from contents of file	Memory allocation
Shared	Memory-mapped I/O; sharing memory between processes (IPC)	Sharing memory between processes (IPC)

The four different types of memory mappings are created and used as follows:

- *Private file mapping*: The contents of the mapping are initialized from a file region. Multiple processes mapping the same file initially share the same physical pages of memory, but the copy-on-write technique is employed, so that changes to the mapping by one process are invisible to other processes. The main use of this type of mapping is to initialize a region of memory from the contents of a file. Some common examples are initializing a process's text and initialized data segments from the corresponding parts of a binary executable file or a shared library file.

- *Private anonymous mapping*: Each call to *mmap()* to create a private anonymous mapping yields a new mapping that is distinct from (i.e., does not share physical pages with) other anonymous mappings created by the same (or a different) process. Although a child process inherits its parent's mappings, copy-on-write semantics ensure that, after the *fork()*, the parent and child don't see changes made to the mapping by the other process. The primary purpose of private anonymous mappings is to allocate new (zero-filled) memory for a process (e.g., *malloc()* employs *mmap()* for this purpose when allocating large blocks of memory).

- *Shared file mapping*: All processes mapping the same region of a file share the same physical pages of memory, which are initialized from a file region. Modifications to the contents of the mapping are carried through to the file. This type of mapping serves two purposes. First, it permits *memory-mapped I/O*. By this, we mean that a file is loaded into a region of the process's virtual memory, and modifications to that memory are automatically written to the file. Thus, memory-mapped I/O provides an alternative to using *read()* and *write()* for performing file I/O. A second purpose of this type of mapping is to allow unrelated processes to share a region of memory in order to perform (fast) IPC in a manner similar to System V shared memory segments (Chapter 48).

- *Shared anonymous mapping*: As with a private anonymous mapping, each call to *mmap()* to create a shared anonymous mapping creates a new, distinct mapping that doesn't share pages with any other mapping. The difference is that the pages of the mapping are not copied-on-write. This means that when a child inherits the mapping after a *fork()*, the parent and child share the same pages of RAM, and changes made to the contents of the mapping by one process are visible to the other process. Shared anonymous mappings allow IPC in a manner similar to System V shared memory segments, but only between related processes.

We consider each of these types of mapping in more detail in the remainder of this chapter.

Mappings are lost when a process performs an *exec()*, but are inherited by the child of a *fork()*. The mapping type (MAP_PRIVATE or MAP_SHARED) is also inherited.

Information about all of a process's mappings is visible in the Linux-specific /proc/*PID*/maps file, which we described in Section 48.5.

> One further use of *mmap()* is with POSIX shared memory objects, which allow a region of memory to be shared between unrelated processes without having to create an associated disk file (as is required for a shared file mapping). We describe POSIX shared memory objects in Chapter 54.

49.2 Creating a Mapping: *mmap()*

The *mmap()* system call creates a new mapping in the calling process's virtual address space.

```
#include <sys/mman.h>

void *mmap(void *addr, size_t length, int prot, int flags, int fd, off_t offset);
```
                    Returns starting address of mapping on success, or MAP_FAILED on error

The *addr* argument indicates the virtual address at which the mapping is to be located. If we specify *addr* as NULL, the kernel chooses a suitable address for the mapping. This is the preferred way of creating a mapping. Alternatively, we can specify a non-NULL value in *addr*, which the kernel takes as a hint about the address at which the mapping should be placed. In practice, the kernel will at the very least round the address to a nearby page boundary. In either case, the kernel will choose an address that doesn't conflict with any existing mapping. (If the value MAP_FIXED is included in *flags*, then *addr* must be page-aligned. We describe this flag in Section 49.10.)

On success, *mmap()* returns the starting address of the new mapping. On error, *mmap()* returns MAP_FAILED.

> On Linux (and on most other UNIX implementations), the MAP_FAILED constant equates to *((void *) −1)*. However, SUSv3 specifies this constant because the C standards can't guarantee that *((void *) −1)* is distinct from a successful *mmap()* return value.

The *length* argument specifies the size of the mapping in bytes. Although *length* doesn't need to be a multiple of the system page size (as returned by *sysconf(_SC_PAGESIZE)*), the kernel creates mappings in units of this size, so that *length* is, in effect, rounded up to the next multiple of the page size.

The *prot* argument is a bit mask specifying the protection to be placed on the mapping. It can be either PROT_NONE or a combination (ORing) of any of the other three flags listed in Table 49-2.

Table 49-2: Memory protection values

Value	Description
PROT_NONE	The region may not be accessed
PROT_READ	The contents of the region can be read
PROT_WRITE	The contents of the region can be modified
PROT_EXEC	The contents of the region can be executed

The *flags* argument is a bit mask of options controlling various aspects of the mapping operation. Exactly one of the following values must be included in this mask:

MAP_PRIVATE

> Create a private mapping. Modifications to the contents of the region are not visible to other processes employing the same mapping, and, in the case of a file mapping, are not carried through to the underlying file.

MAP_SHARED

> Create a shared mapping. Modifications to the contents of the region are visible to other processes mapping the same region with the MAP_SHARED attribute and, in the case of a file mapping, are carried through to the underlying file. Updates to the file are not guaranteed to be immediate; see the discussion of the *msync()* system call in Section 49.5.

Aside from MAP_PRIVATE and MAP_SHARED, other flag values can optionally be ORed in *flags*. We discuss these flags in Sections 49.6 and 49.10.

The remaining arguments, *fd* and *offset*, are used with file mappings (they are ignored for anonymous mappings). The *fd* argument is a file descriptor identifying the file to be mapped. The *offset* argument specifies the starting point of the mapping in the file, and must be a multiple of the system page size. To map the entire file, we would specify *offset* as 0 and *length* as the size of the file. We say more about file mappings in Section 49.4.

Memory protection in more detail

As noted above, the *mmap() prot* argument specifies the protection on a new memory mapping. It can contain the value PROT_NONE, or a mask of one or more of the flags PROT_READ, PROT_WRITE, and PROT_EXEC. If a process attempts to access a memory region in a way that violates the protection on the region, then the kernel delivers the SIGSEGV signal to a process.

> Although SUSv3 specifies that SIGSEGV should be used to signal memory protection violations, on some implementations, SIGBUS is used instead.

One use of pages of memory marked PROT_NONE is as guard pages at the start or end of a region of memory that a process has allocated. If the process accidentally steps into one of the pages marked PROT_NONE, the kernel informs it of that fact by generating a SIGSEGV signal.

Memory protections reside in process-private virtual memory tables. Thus, different processes may map the same memory region with different protections.

Memory protection can be changed using the *mprotect()* system call (Section 50.1).

On some UNIX implementations, the actual protections placed on the pages of a mapping may not be exactly those specified in *prot*. In particular, limitations of the protection granularity of the underlying hardware (e.g., older x86-32 architectures) mean that, on many UNIX implementations, PROT_READ implies PROT_EXEC and vice versa, and on some implementations, specifying PROT_WRITE implies PROT_READ. However, applications should not rely on such behavior; *prot* should always specify exactly the memory protections that are required.

Modern x86-32 architectures provide hardware support for marking pages tables as *NX* (no execute), and, since kernel 2.6.8, Linux makes use of this feature to properly separate PROT_READ and PROT_EXEC permissions on Linux/x86-32.

Alignment restrictions specified in standards for *offset* and *addr*

SUSv3 specifies that the *offset* argument of *mmap()* must be page-aligned, and that the *addr* argument must also be page-aligned if MAP_FIXED is specified. Linux conforms to these requirements. However, it was later noted that the SUSv3 requirements differed from earlier standards, which imposed looser requirements on these arguments. The consequence of the SUSv3 wording was to (unnecessarily) render some formerly standards-conformant implementations nonconforming. SUSv4 returns to the looser requirements:

- An implementation may require that *offset* be a multiple of the system page size.
- If MAP_FIXED is specified, then an implementation may require that *addr* be page-aligned.
- If MAP_FIXED is specified, and *addr* is nonzero, then *addr* and *offset* shall have the same remainder modulo the system page size.

> A similar situation arose for the *addr* argument of *mprotect()*, *msync()*, and *munmap()*. SUSv3 specified that this argument must be page-aligned. SUSv4 says that an implementation may require this argument to be page-aligned.

Example program

Listing 49-1 demonstrates the use of *mmap()* to create a private file mapping. This program is a simple version of *cat(1)*. It maps the (entire) file named in its command-line argument, and then writes the contents of the mapping to standard output.

Listing 49-1: Using *mmap()* to create a private file mapping

─── mmap/mmcat.c

```
#include <sys/mman.h>
#include <sys/stat.h>
#include <fcntl.h>
#include "tlpi_hdr.h"

int
main(int argc, char *argv[])
{
    char *addr;
    int fd;
    struct stat sb;

    if (argc != 2 || strcmp(argv[1], "--help") == 0)
        usageErr("%s file\n", argv[0]);

    fd = open(argv[1], O_RDONLY);
    if (fd == -1)
        errExit("open");
```

```
    /* Obtain the size of the file and use it to specify the size of
       the mapping and the size of the buffer to be written */

    if (fstat(fd, &sb) == -1)
        errExit("fstat");

    addr = mmap(NULL, sb.st_size, PROT_READ, MAP_PRIVATE, fd, 0);
    if (addr == MAP_FAILED)
        errExit("mmap");

    if (write(STDOUT_FILENO, addr, sb.st_size) != sb.st_size)
        fatal("partial/failed write");
    exit(EXIT_SUCCESS);
}
```
_____ mmap/mmcat.c

49.3 Unmapping a Mapped Region: *munmap()*

The *munmap()* system call performs the converse of *mmap()*, removing a mapping
from the calling process's virtual address space.

```
#include <sys/mman.h>

int munmap(void *addr, size_t length);
```
                                    Returns 0 on success, or –1 on error

The *addr* argument is the starting address of the address range to be unmapped. It
must be aligned to a page boundary. (SUSv3 specified that *addr must* be page-aligned.
SUSv4 says that an implementation *may* require this argument to be page-aligned.)

The *length* argument is a nonnegative integer specifying the size (in bytes) of
the region to be unmapped. The address range up to the next multiple of the system
page size will be unmapped.

Commonly, we unmap an entire mapping. Thus, we specify *addr* as the address
returned by a previous call to *mmap()*, and specify the same *length* value as was used
in the *mmap()* call. Here's an example:

```
    addr = mmap(NULL, length, PROT_READ | PROT_WRITE, MAP_PRIVATE, fd, 0);
    if (addr == MAP_FAILED)
        errExit("mmap");

    /* Code for working with mapped region */

    if (munmap(addr, length) == -1)
        errExit("munmap");
```

Alternatively, we can unmap part of a mapping, in which case the mapping either
shrinks or is cut in two, depending on where the unmapping occurs. It is also possible
to specify an address range spanning several mappings, in which case all of the
mappings are unmapped.

If there are no mappings in the address range specified by *addr* and *length*, then *munmap()* has no effect, and returns 0 (for success).

During unmapping, the kernel removes any memory locks that the process holds for the specified address range. (Memory locks are established using *mlock()* or *mlockall()*, as described in Section 50.2.)

All of a process's mappings are automatically unmapped when it terminates or performs an *exec()*.

To ensure that the contents of a shared file mapping are written to the underlying file, a call to *msync()* (Section 49.5) should be made before unmapping a mapping with *munmap()*.

49.4   File Mappings

To create a file mapping, we perform the following steps:

1. Obtain a descriptor for the file, typically via a call to *open()*.
2. Pass that file descriptor as the *fd* argument in a call to *mmap()*.

As a result of these steps, *mmap()* maps the contents of the open file into the address space of the calling process. Once *mmap()* has been called, we can close the file descriptor without affecting the mapping. However, in some cases it may be useful to keep this file descriptor open—see, for example, Listing 49-1 and also Chapter 54.

> As well as normal disk files, it is possible to use *mmap()* to map the contents of various real and virtual devices, such as hard disks, optical disks, and /dev/mem.

The file referred to by the descriptor *fd* must have been opened with permissions appropriate for the values specified in *prot* and *flags*. In particular, the file must always be opened for reading, and, if PROT_WRITE and MAP_SHARED are specified in *flags*, then the file must be opened for both reading and writing.

The *offset* argument specifies the starting byte of the region to be mapped from the file, and must be a multiple of the system page size. Specifying *offset* as 0 causes the file to be mapped from the beginning. The *length* argument specifies the number of bytes to be mapped. Together, the *offset* and *length* arguments determine which region of the file is to be mapped into memory, as shown in Figure 49-1.

> On Linux, the pages of a file mapping are mapped in on the first access. This means that if changes are made to a file region after the *mmap()* call, but before the corresponding part (i.e., page) of the mapping is accessed, then the changes may be visible to the process, if the page has not otherwise already been loaded into memory. This behavior is implementation-dependent; portable applications should avoid relying on a particular kernel behavior in this scenario.

49.4.1   Private File Mappings

The two most common uses of private file mappings are the following:

- To allow multiple processes executing the same program or using the same shared library to share the same (read-only) text segment, which is mapped from the corresponding part of the underlying executable or library file.

Although the executable text segment is normally protected to allow only read and execute access (PROT_READ | PROT_EXEC), it is mapped using MAP_PRIVATE rather than MAP_SHARED, because a debugger or a self-modifying program can modify the program text (after first changing the protection on the memory), and such changes should not be carried through to the underlying file or affect other processes.

- To map the initialized data segment of an executable or shared library. Such mappings are made private so that modifications to the contents of the mapped data segment are not carried through to the underlying file.

Both of these uses of *mmap()* are normally invisible to a program, because these mappings are created by the program loader and dynamic linker. Examples of both kinds of mappings can be seen in the /proc/*PID*/maps output shown in Section 48.5.

One other, less frequent, use of a private file mapping is to simplify the file-input logic of a program. This is similar to the use of shared file mappings for memory-mapped I/O (described in the next section), but allows only for file input.

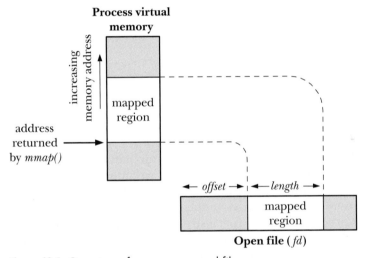

Figure 49-1: Overview of memory-mapped file

49.4.2 Shared File Mappings

When multiple processes create shared mappings of the same file region, they all share the same physical pages of memory. In addition, modifications to the contents of the mapping are carried through to the file. In effect, the file is being treated as the paging store for this region of memory, as shown in Figure 49-2. (We simplify things in this diagram by omitting to show that the mapped pages are typically not contiguous in physical memory.)

Shared file mappings serve two purposes: memory-mapped I/O and IPC. We consider each of these uses below.

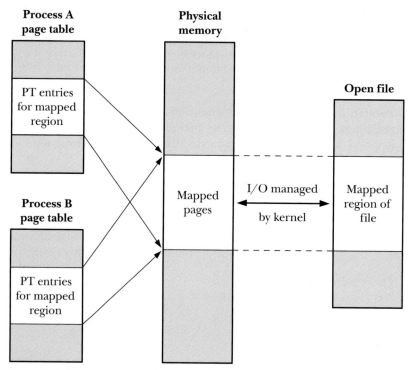

Figure 49-2: Two processes with a shared mapping of the same region of a file

Memory-mapped I/O

Since the contents of the shared file mapping are initialized from the file, and any modifications to the contents of the mapping are automatically carried through to the file, we can perform file I/O simply by accessing bytes of memory, relying on the kernel to ensure that the changes to memory are propagated to the mapped file. (Typically, a program would define a structured data type that corresponds to the contents of the disk file, and then use that data type to cast the contents of the mapping.) This technique is referred to as *memory-mapped I/O*, and is an alternative to using *read()* and *write()* to access the contents of a file.

Memory-mapped I/O has two potential advantages:

- By replacing *read()* and *write()* system calls with memory accesses, it can simplify the logic of some applications.
- It can, in some circumstances, provide better performance than file I/O carried out using the conventional I/O system calls.

The reasons that memory-mapped I/O can provide performance benefits are as follows:

- A normal *read()* or *write()* involves two transfers: one between the file and the kernel buffer cache, and the other between the buffer cache and a user-space buffer. Using *mmap()* eliminates the second of these transfers. For input, the data is available to the user process as soon as the kernel has mapped the corresponding file blocks into memory. For output, the user process merely needs to modify the contents of the memory, and can then rely on the kernel memory manager to automatically update the underlying file.

- In addition to saving a transfer between kernel space and user space, *mmap()* can also improve performance by lowering memory requirements. When using *read()* or *write()*, the data is maintained in two buffers: one in user space and the other in kernel space. When using *mmap()*, a single buffer is shared between the kernel space and user space. Furthermore, if multiple processes are performing I/O on the same file, then, using *mmap()*, they can all share the same kernel buffer, resulting in an additional memory saving.

Performance benefits from memory-mapped I/O are most likely to be realized when performing repeated random accesses in a large file. If we are performing sequential access of a file, then *mmap()* will probably provide little or no gain over *read()* and *write()*, assuming that we perform I/O using buffer sizes big enough to avoid making a large number of I/O system calls. The reason that there is little performance benefit is that, regardless of which technique we use, the entire contents of the file will be transferred between disk and memory exactly once, and the efficiency gains of eliminating a data transfer between user space and kernel space and reducing memory usage are typically negligible compared to the time required for disk I/O.

Memory-mapped I/O can also have disadvantages. For small I/Os, the cost of memory-mapped I/O (i.e., mapping, page faulting, unmapping, and updating the hardware memory management unit's translation look-aside buffer) can actually be higher than for a simple *read()* or *write()*. In addition, it can sometimes be difficult for the kernel to efficiently handle write-back for writable mappings (the use of *msync()* or *sync_file_range()* can help improve efficiency in this case).

IPC using a shared file mapping

Since all processes with a shared mapping of the same file region share the same physical pages of memory, the second use of a shared file mapping is as a method of (fast) IPC. The feature that distinguishes this type of shared memory region from a System V shared memory object (Chapter 48) is that modifications to the contents of the region are carried through to the underlying mapped file. This feature is useful in an application that requires the shared memory contents to persist across application or system restarts.

Example program

Listing 49-2 provides a simple example of the use of *mmap()* to create a shared file mapping. This program begins by mapping the file named in its first command-line argument. It then prints the value of the string lying at the start of the mapped region. Finally, if a second command-line argument is supplied, that string is copied into the shared memory region.

The following shell session log demonstrates the use of this program. We begin by creating a 1024-byte file that is populated with zeros:

```
$ dd if=/dev/zero of=s.txt bs=1 count=1024
1024+0 records in
1024+0 records out
```

We then use our program to map the file and copy a string into the mapped region:

```
$ ./t_mmap s.txt hello
Current string=
Copied "hello" to shared memory
```

The program displayed nothing for the current string because the initial value of the mapped files began with a null byte (i.e., zero-length string).

Next, we use our program to again map the file and copy a new string into the mapped region:

```
$ ./t_mmap s.txt goodbye
Current string=hello
Copied "goodbye" to shared memory
```

Finally, we dump the contents of the file, 8 characters per line, to verify its contents:

```
$ od -c -w8 s.txt
0000000   g   o   o   d   b   y   e nul
0000010 nul nul nul nul nul nul nul nul
*
0002000
```

Our trivial program doesn't use any mechanism to synchronize access by multiple processes to the mapped file. However, real-world applications typically need to synchronize access to shared mappings. This can be done using a variety of techniques, including semaphores (Chapters 47 and 53) and file locking (Chapter 55).

We explain the *msync()* system call used in Listing 49-2 in Section 49.5.

Listing 49-2: Using *mmap()* to create a shared file mapping

―― mmap/t_mmap.c
```c
#include <sys/mman.h>
#include <fcntl.h>
#include "tlpi_hdr.h"

#define MEM_SIZE 10

int
main(int argc, char *argv[])
{
    char *addr;
    int fd;

    if (argc < 2 || strcmp(argv[1], "--help") == 0)
        usageErr("%s file [new-value]\n", argv[0]);

    fd = open(argv[1], O_RDWR);
    if (fd == -1)
        errExit("open");
```

```
    addr = mmap(NULL, MEM_SIZE, PROT_READ | PROT_WRITE, MAP_SHARED, fd, 0);
    if (addr == MAP_FAILED)
        errExit("mmap");

    if (close(fd) == -1)                        /* No longer need 'fd' */
        errExit("close");

    printf("Current string=%.*s\n", MEM_SIZE, addr);
                /* Secure practice: output at most MEM_SIZE bytes */

    if (argc > 2) {                             /* Update contents of region */
        if (strlen(argv[2]) >= MEM_SIZE)
            cmdLineErr("'new-value' too large\n");

        memset(addr, 0, MEM_SIZE);          /* Zero out region */
        strncpy(addr, argv[2], MEM_SIZE - 1);
        if (msync(addr, MEM_SIZE, MS_SYNC) == -1)
            errExit("msync");

        printf("Copied \"%s\" to shared memory\n", argv[2]);
    }

    exit(EXIT_SUCCESS);
}
```
——— mmap/t_mmap.c

49.4.3 Boundary Cases

In many cases, the size of a mapping is a multiple of the system page size, and the mapping falls entirely within the bounds of the mapped file. However, this is not necessarily so, and we now look at what happens when these conditions don't hold.

Figure 49-3 portrays the case where the mapping falls entirely within the bounds of the mapped file, but the size of the region is not a multiple of the system page size (which we assume is 4096 bytes for the purposes of this discussion).

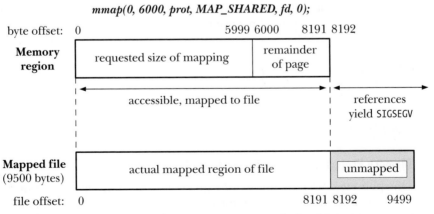

Figure 49-3: Memory mapping whose *length* is not a multiple of the system page size

Since the size of the mapping is not a multiple of the system page size, it is rounded up to the next multiple of the system page size. Because the file is larger than this rounded-up size, the corresponding bytes of the file are mapped as shown in Figure 49-3.

Attempts to access bytes beyond the end of the mapping result in the generation of a SIGSEGV signal (assuming that there is no other mapping at that location). The default action for this signal is to terminate the process with a core dump.

When the mapping extends beyond the end of the underlying file (see Figure 49-4), the situation is more complex. As before, because the size of the mapping is not a multiple of the system page size, it is rounded up. However, in this case, while the bytes in the rounded-up region (i.e., bytes 2200 to 4095 in the diagram) are accessible, they are not mapped to the underlying file (since no corresponding bytes exist in the file). Instead, they are initialized to 0 (SUSv3 requires this). These bytes will nevertheless be shared with other processes mapping the file, if they specify a sufficiently large *length* argument. Changes to these bytes are not written to the file.

If the mapping includes pages beyond the rounded-up region (i.e., bytes 4096 and beyond in Figure 49-4), then attempts to access addresses in these pages result in the generation of a SIGBUS signal, which warns the process that there is no region of the file corresponding to these addresses. As before, attempts to access addresses beyond the end of the mapping result in the generation of a SIGSEGV signal.

From the above description, it may appear pointless to create a mapping whose size exceeds that of the underlying file. However, by extending the size of the file (e.g., using *ftruncate()* or *write()*), we can render previously inaccessible parts of such a mapping usable.

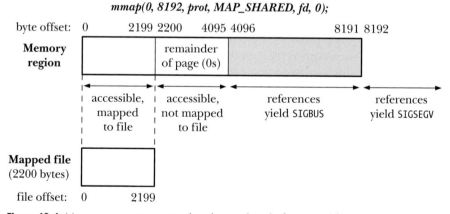

Figure 49-4: Memory mapping extending beyond end of mapped file

49.4.4 Memory Protection and File Access Mode Interactions

One point that we have not so far explained in detail is the interaction between the memory protection specified in the *mmap()* *prot* argument and the mode in which the mapped file is opened. As a general principle, we can say that the PROT_READ and PROT_EXEC protections require that the mapped file is opened O_RDONLY or O_RDWR, and that the PROT_WRITE protection requires that the mapped file is opened O_WRONLY or O_RDWR.

However, the situation is complicated by the limited granularity of memory protections provided by some hardware architectures (Section 49.2). For such architectures, we make the following observations:

- All combinations of memory protection are compatible with opening the file with the O_RDWR flag.

- No combination of memory protections—not even just PROT_WRITE—is compatible with a file opened O_WRONLY (the error EACCES results). This is consistent with the fact that some hardware architectures don't allow us write-only access to a page. As noted in Section 49.2, PROT_WRITE implies PROT_READ on those architectures, which means that if the page can be written, then it can also be read. A read operation is incompatible with O_WRONLY, which must not reveal the original contents of the file.

- The results when a file is opened with the O_RDONLY flag depend on whether we specify MAP_PRIVATE or MAP_SHARED when calling *mmap()*. For a MAP_PRIVATE mapping, we can specify any combination of memory protection in *mmap()*—because modifications to the contents of a MAP_PRIVATE page are never written to the file, the inability to write to the file is not a problem. For a MAP_SHARED mapping, the only memory protections that are compatible with O_RDONLY are PROT_READ and (PROT_READ | PROT_EXEC). This is logical, since a PROT_WRITE, MAP_SHARED mapping allows updates to the mapped file.

49.5 Synchronizing a Mapped Region: *msync()*

The kernel automatically carries modifications of the contents of a MAP_SHARED mapping through to the underlying file, but, by default, provides no guarantees about when such synchronization will occur. (SUSv3 doesn't require an implementation to provide such guarantees.)

The *msync()* system call gives an application explicit control over when a shared mapping is synchronized with the mapped file. Synchronizing a mapping with the underlying file is useful in various scenarios. For example, to ensure data integrity, a database application may call *msync()* to force data to be written to the disk. Calling *msync()* also allows an application to ensure that updates to a writable mapping are visible to some other process that performs a *read()* on the file.

```
#include <sys/mman.h>

int msync(void *addr, size_t length, int flags);
```
                                    Returns 0 on success, or –1 on error

The *addr* and *length* arguments to *msync()* specify the starting address and size of the memory region to be synchronized. The address specified in *addr* must be page-aligned, and *length* is rounded up to the next multiple of the system page size. (SUSv3 specified that *addr must* be page-aligned. SUSv4 says that an implementation *may* require this argument to be page-aligned.)

Possible values for the *flags* argument include one of the following:

MS_SYNC
> Perform a synchronous file write. The call blocks until all modified pages of the memory region have been written to the disk.

MS_ASYNC
> Perform an asynchronous file write. The modified pages of the memory region are written to the disk at some later point and are immediately made visible to other processes performing a *read()* on the corresponding file region.

Another way of distinguishing these two values is to say that after an MS_SYNC operation, the memory region is synchronized with the disk, while after an MS_ASYNC operation, the memory region is merely synchronized with the kernel buffer cache.

> If we take no further action after an MS_ASYNC operation, then the modified pages in the memory region will eventually be flushed as part of the automatic buffer flushing performed by the *pdflush* kernel thread (*kupdated* in Linux 2.4 and earlier). On Linux, there are two (nonstandard) methods of initiating the output sooner. We can follow the call to *msync()* with a call to *fsync()* (or *fdatasync()*) on the file descriptor corresponding to the mapping. This call will block until the buffer cache is synchronized with the disk. Alternatively, we can initiate asynchronous write out of the pages using the *posix_fadvise()* POSIX_FADV_DONTNEED operation. (The Linux-specific details in these two cases are not specified by SUSv3.)

One other value can additionally be specified for *flags*:

MS_INVALIDATE
> Invalidate cached copies of mapped data. After any modified pages in the memory region have been synchronized with the file, all pages of the memory region that are inconsistent with the underlying file data are marked as invalid. When next referenced, the contents of the pages will be copied from the corresponding locations in the file. As a consequence, any updates that have been made to the file by another process are made visible in the memory region.

Like many other modern UNIX implementations, Linux provides a so-called *unified virtual memory* system. This means that, where possible, memory mappings and blocks of the buffer cache share the same pages of physical memory. Thus, the views of a file obtained via a mapping and via I/O system calls (*read()*, *write()*, and so on) are always consistent, and the only use of *msync()* is to force the contents of a mapped region to be flushed to disk.

However, a unified virtual memory system is not required by SUSv3 and is not employed on all UNIX implementations. On such systems, a call to *msync()* is required to make changes to the contents of a mapping visible to other processes that *read()* the file, and the MS_INVALIDATE flag is required to perform the converse action of making writes to the file by another process visible in the mapped region. Multiprocess applications that employ both *mmap()* and I/O system calls to operate on the same file should be designed to make appropriate use of *msync()* if they are to be portable to systems that don't have a unified virtual memory system.

49.6 Additional *mmap()* Flags

In addition to `MAP_PRIVATE` and `MAP_SHARED`, Linux allows a number of other values to be included (ORed) in the *mmap() flags* argument. Table 49-3 summarizes these values. Other than `MAP_PRIVATE` and `MAP_SHARED`, only the `MAP_FIXED` flag is specified in SUSv3.

Table 49-3: Bit-mask values for the *mmap() flags* argument

Value	Description	SUSv3
`MAP_ANONYMOUS`	Create an anonymous mapping	
`MAP_FIXED`	Interpret *addr* argument exactly (Section 49.10)	•
`MAP_LOCKED`	Lock mapped pages into memory (since Linux 2.6)	
`MAP_HUGETLB`	Create a mapping that uses huge pages (since Linux 2.6.32)	
`MAP_NORESERVE`	Control reservation of swap space (Section 49.9)	
`MAP_PRIVATE`	Modifications to mapped data are private	•
`MAP_POPULATE`	Populate the pages of a mapping (since Linux 2.6)	
`MAP_SHARED`	Modifications to mapped data are visible to other processes and propagated to underlying file (converse of MAP_PRIVATE)	•
`MAP_UNINITIALIZED`	Don't clear an anonymous mapping (since Linux 2.6.33)	

The following list provides further details on the *flags* values listed in Table 49-3 (other than `MAP_PRIVATE` and `MAP_SHARED`, which have already been discussed):

`MAP_ANONYMOUS`
> Create an anonymous mapping—that is, a mapping that is not backed by a file. We describe this flag further in Section 49.7.

`MAP_FIXED`
> We describe this flag in Section 49.10.

`MAP_HUGETLB` (since Linux 2.6.32)
> This flag serves the same purpose for *mmap()* as the `SHM_HUGETLB` flag serves for System V shared memory segments. See Section 48.2.

`MAP_LOCKED` (since Linux 2.6)
> Preload and lock the mapped pages into memory in the manner of *mlock()*. We describe the privileges required to use this flag and the limits governing its operation in Section 50.2.

`MAP_NORESERVE`
> This flag is used to control whether reservation of swap space for the mapping is performed in advance. See Section 49.9 for details.

`MAP_POPULATE` (since Linux 2.6)
> Populate the pages of a mapping. For a file mapping, this will perform read-ahead on the file. This means that later accesses of the contents of the mapping won't be blocked by page faults (assuming that memory pressure has not in the meantime caused the pages to be swapped out).

`MAP_UNINITIALIZED` (since Linux 2.6.33)

Specifying this flag prevents the pages of an anonymous mapping from being zeroed. It provides a performance benefit, but carries a security risk, because the allocated pages may contain sensitive information left by a previous process. This flag is thus only intended for use on embedded systems, where performance may be critical, and the entire system is under the control of the embedded application(s). This flag is only honored if the kernel was configured with the `CONFIG_MMAP_ALLOW_UNINITIALIZED` option.

49.7 Anonymous Mappings

An *anonymous mapping* is one that doesn't have a corresponding file. In this section, we show how to create anonymous mappings, and look at the purposes served by private and shared anonymous mappings.

`MAP_ANONYMOUS` and `/dev/zero`

On Linux, there are two different, equivalent methods of creating an anonymous mapping with *mmap()*:

- Specify `MAP_ANONYMOUS` in *flags* and specify *fd* as −1. (On Linux, the value of *fd* is ignored when `MAP_ANONYMOUS` is specified. However, some UNIX implementations require *fd* to be −1 when employing `MAP_ANONYMOUS`, and portable applications should ensure that they do this.)

    We must define either the `_BSD_SOURCE` or the `_SVID_SOURCE` feature test macros to get the definition of `MAP_ANONYMOUS` from `<sys/mman.h>`. Linux provides the constant `MAP_ANON` as a synonym for `MAP_ANONYMOUS` for compatibility with some other UNIX implementations using this alternative name.

- Open the `/dev/zero` device file and pass the resulting file descriptor to *mmap()*.

    `/dev/zero` is a virtual device that always returns zeros when we read from it. Writes to this device are always discarded. A common use of `/dev/zero` is to populate a file with zeros (e.g., using the *dd(1)* command).

With both the `MAP_ANONYMOUS` and the `/dev/zero` techniques, the bytes of the resulting mapping are initialized to 0. For both techniques, the *offset* argument is ignored (since there is no underlying file in which to specify an offset). We show examples of each technique shortly.

    The `MAP_ANONYMOUS` and `/dev/zero` techniques are not specified in SUSv3, although most UNIX implementations support one or both of them. The reason for the existence of two different techniques with the same semantics is that one (`MAP_ANONYMOUS`) derives from BSD, while the other (`/dev/zero`) derives from System V.

MAP_PRIVATE anonymous mappings

MAP_PRIVATE anonymous mappings are used to allocate blocks of process-private memory initialized to 0. We can use the /dev/zero technique to create a MAP_PRIVATE anonymous mapping as follows:

```
fd = open("/dev/zero", O_RDWR);
if (fd == -1)
    errExit("open");
addr = mmap(NULL, length, PROT_READ | PROT_WRITE, MAP_PRIVATE, fd, 0);
if (addr == MAP_FAILED)
    errExit("mmap");
```

> The *glibc* implementation of *malloc()* uses MAP_PRIVATE anonymous mappings to allocate blocks of memory larger than MMAP_THRESHOLD bytes. This makes it possible to efficiently deallocate such blocks (via *munmap()*) if they are later given to *free()*. (It also reduces the possibility of memory fragmentation when repeatedly allocating and deallocating large blocks of memory.) MMAP_THRESHOLD is 128 kB by default, but this parameter is adjustable via the *mallopt()* library function.

MAP_SHARED anonymous mappings

A MAP_SHARED anonymous mapping allows related processes (e.g., parent and child) to share a region of memory without needing a corresponding mapped file.

> MAP_SHARED anonymous mappings are available only with Linux 2.4 and later.

We can use the MAP_ANONYMOUS technique to create a MAP_SHARED anonymous mapping as follows:

```
addr = mmap(NULL, length, PROT_READ | PROT_WRITE,
            MAP_SHARED | MAP_ANONYMOUS, -1, 0);
if (addr == MAP_FAILED)
    errExit("mmap");
```

If the above code is followed by a call to *fork()*, then, because the child produced by *fork()* inherits the mapping, both processes share the memory region.

Example program

The program in Listing 49-3 demonstrates the use of either MAP_ANONYMOUS or /dev/zero to share a mapped region between parent and child processes. The choice of technique is determined by whether USE_MAP_ANON is defined when compiling the program. The parent initializes an integer in the shared region to 1 prior to calling *fork()*. The child then increments the shared integer and exits, while the parent waits for the child to exit and then prints the value of the integer. When we run this program, we see the following:

```
$ ./anon_mmap
Child started, value = 1
In parent, value = 2
```

Listing 49-3: Sharing an anonymous mapping between parent and child processes

```c
#ifdef USE_MAP_ANON
#define _BSD_SOURCE                 /* Get MAP_ANONYMOUS definition */
#endif
#include <sys/wait.h>
#include <sys/mman.h>
#include <fcntl.h>
#include "tlpi_hdr.h"

int
main(int argc, char *argv[])
{
    int *addr;                      /* Pointer to shared memory region */

#ifdef USE_MAP_ANON                 /* Use MAP_ANONYMOUS */
    addr = mmap(NULL, sizeof(int), PROT_READ | PROT_WRITE,
                MAP_SHARED | MAP_ANONYMOUS, -1, 0);
    if (addr == MAP_FAILED)
        errExit("mmap");

#else                               /* Map /dev/zero */
    int fd;

    fd = open("/dev/zero", O_RDWR);
    if (fd == -1)
        errExit("open");

    addr = mmap(NULL, sizeof(int), PROT_READ | PROT_WRITE, MAP_SHARED, fd, 0);
    if (addr == MAP_FAILED)
        errExit("mmap");

    if (close(fd) == -1)            /* No longer needed */
        errExit("close");
#endif

    *addr = 1;                      /* Initialize integer in mapped region */

    switch (fork()) {               /* Parent and child share mapping */
    case -1:
        errExit("fork");

    case 0:                         /* Child: increment shared integer and exit */
        printf("Child started, value = %d\n", *addr);
        (*addr)++;

        if (munmap(addr, sizeof(int)) == -1)
            errExit("munmap");
        exit(EXIT_SUCCESS);

    default:                        /* Parent: wait for child to terminate */
        if (wait(NULL) == -1)
            errExit("wait");
        printf("In parent, value = %d\n", *addr);
```

```
        if (munmap(addr, sizeof(int)) == -1)
            errExit("munmap");
        exit(EXIT_SUCCESS);
    }
}
```

49.8 Remapping a Mapped Region: *mremap()*

On most UNIX implementations, once a mapping has been created, its location
and size can't be changed. However, Linux provides the (nonportable) *mremap()*
system call, which permits such changes.

```
#define _GNU_SOURCE
#include <sys/mman.h>

void *mremap(void *old_address, size_t old_size, size_t new_size, int flags, ...);
```
                    Returns starting address of remapped region on success,
                                              or MAP_FAILED on error

The *old_address* and *old_size* arguments specify the location and size of an existing
mapping that we wish to expand or shrink. The address specified in *old_address*
must be page-aligned, and is normally a value returned by a previous call to *mmap()*.
The desired new size of the mapping is specified in *new_size*. The values specified in
old_size and *new_size* are both rounded up to the next multiple of the system page size.

   While carrying out the remapping, the kernel may relocate the mapping within
the process's virtual address space. Whether or not this is permitted is controlled
by the *flags* argument, which is a bit mask that may either be 0 or include the following values:

MREMAP_MAYMOVE
          If this flag is specified, then, as space requirements dictate, the kernel may
          relocate the mapping within the process's virtual address space. If this flag
          is not specified, and there is insufficient space to expand the mapping at
          the current location, then the error ENOMEM results.

MREMAP_FIXED (since Linux 2.4)
          This flag can be used only in conjunction with MREMAP_MAYMOVE. It serves a
          purpose for *mremap()* that is analogous to that served by MAP_FIXED for *mmap()*
          (Section 49.10). If this flag is specified, then *mremap()* takes an additional
          argument, *void *new_address*, that specifies a page-aligned address to which
          the mapping should be moved. Any previous mapping in the address
          range specified by *new_address* and *new_size* is unmapped.

On success, *mremap()* returns the starting address of the mapping. Since (if the
MREMAP_MAYMOVE flag is specified) this address may be different from the previous
starting address, pointers into the region may cease to be valid. Therefore, applications that use *mremap()* should use only offsets (not absolute pointers) when referring to addresses in the mapped region (see Section 48.6).

On Linux, the *realloc()* function uses *mremap()* to efficiently reallocate large blocks of memory that *malloc()* previously allocated using *mmap()* MAP_ANONYMOUS. (We mentioned this feature of the *glibc malloc()* implementation in Section 49.7.) Using *mremap()* for this task makes it possible to avoid copying of bytes during the reallocation.

49.9 MAP_NORESERVE and Swap Space Overcommitting

Some applications create large (usually private anonymous) mappings, but use only a small part of the mapped region. For example, certain types of scientific applications allocate a very large array, but operate on only a few widely separated elements of the array (a so-called *sparse array*).

If the kernel always allocated (or reserved) enough swap space for the whole of such mappings, then a lot of swap space would potentially be wasted. Instead, the kernel can reserve swap space for the pages of a mapping only as they are actually required (i.e., when the application accesses a page). This approach is called *lazy swap reservation*, and has the advantage that the total virtual memory used by applications can exceed the total size of RAM plus swap space.

To put things another way, lazy swap reservation allows swap space to be overcommitted. This works fine, as long as all processes don't attempt to access the entire range of their mappings. However, if all applications *do* attempt to access the full range of their mappings, RAM and swap space will be exhausted. In this situation, the kernel reduces memory pressure by killing one or more of the processes on the system. Ideally, the kernel attempts to select the process causing the memory problems (see the discussion of the *OOM killer* below), but this isn't guaranteed. For this reason, we may choose to prevent lazy swap reservation, instead forcing the system to allocate all of the necessary swap space when the mapping is created.

How the kernel handles reservation of swap space is controlled by the use of the MAP_NORESERVE flag when calling *mmap()*, and via /proc interfaces that affect the system-wide operation of swap space overcommitting. These factors are summarized in Table 49-4.

Table 49-4: Handling of swap space reservation during *mmap()*

overcommit_memory value	MAP_NORESERVE specified in *mmap()* call?	
	No	Yes
0	Deny obvious overcommits	Allow overcommits
1	Allow overcommits	Allow overcommits
2 (since Linux 2.6)	Strict overcommitting	

The Linux-specific /proc/sys/vm/overcommit_memory file contains an integer value that controls the kernel's handling of swap space overcommits. Linux versions before 2.6 differentiated only two values in this file: 0, meaning deny obvious overcommits (subject to the use of the MAP_NORESERVE flag), and greater than 0, meaning that overcommits should be permitted in all cases.

Denying obvious overcommits means that new mappings whose size doesn't exceed the amount of currently available free memory are permitted. Existing allocations may be overcommitted (since they may not be using all of the pages that they mapped).

Since Linux 2.6, a value of 1 has the same meaning as a positive value in earlier kernels, but the value 2 (or greater) causes *strict overcommitting* to be employed. In this case, the kernel performs strict accounting on all *mmap()* allocations and limits the system-wide total of all such allocations to be less than or equal to:

```
[swap size] + [RAM size] * overcommit_ratio / 100
```

The overcommit_ratio value is an integer—expressing a percentage—contained in the Linux-specific /proc/sys/vm/overcommit_ratio file. The default value contained in this file is 50, meaning that the kernel can overallocate up to 50% of the size of the system's RAM, and this will be successful, as long as not all processes try to use their full allocation.

Note that overcommit monitoring comes into play only for the following types of mappings:

- private writable mappings (both file and anonymous mappings), for which the swap "cost" of the mapping is equal to the size of the mapping for each process that employs the mapping; and
- shared anonymous mappings, for which the swap "cost" of the mapping is the size of the mapping (since all processes share that mapping).

Reserving swap space for a read-only private mapping is unnecessary: since the contents of the mapping can't be modified, there is no need to employ swap space. Swap space is also not required for shared file mappings, because the mapped file itself acts as the swap space for the mapping.

When a child process inherits a mapping across a *fork()*, it inherits the MAP_NORESERVE setting for the mapping. The MAP_NORESERVE flag is not specified in SUSv3, but it is supported on a few other UNIX implementations.

> In this section, we have discussed how a call to *mmap()* may fail to increase the address space of a process because of the system limitations on RAM and swap space. A call to *mmap()* can also fail because it encounters the per-process RLIMIT_AS resource limit (described in Section 36.3), which places an upper limit on the size of the address space of the calling process.

The OOM killer

Above, we noted that when we employ lazy swap reservation, memory may become exhausted if applications attempt to employ the entire range of their mappings. In this case, the kernel relieves memory exhaustion by killing processes.

The kernel code dedicated to selecting a process to kill when memory is exhausted is commonly known as the out-of-memory (OOM) killer. The OOM killer tries to choose the best process to kill in order to relieve the memory exhaustion, where "best" is determined by a range of factors. For example, the more memory a process is consuming, the more likely it will be a candidate for the OOM killer. Other factors that increase a process's likelihood of selection are forking to create many child processes and having a low priority (i.e., a nice value that is greater than 0). The kernel disfavors killing the following:

- processes that are privileged, since they are probably performing important tasks;
- processes that are performing raw device access, since killing them may leave the device in an unusable state; and
- processes that have been running for a long time or have consumed a lot of CPU, since killing them would result in a lot of lost "work."

To kill the selected process, the OOM killer delivers a SIGKILL signal.

The Linux-specific /proc/*PID*/oom_score file, available since kernel 2.6.11, shows the weighting that the kernel gives to a process if it is necessary to invoke the OOM killer. The greater the value in this file, the more likely the process is to be selected, if necessary, by the OOM killer. The Linux-specific /proc/*PID*/oom_adj file, also available since kernel 2.6.11, can be used to influence the oom_score of a process. This file can be set to any value in the range −16 to +15, where negative values decrease the oom_score and positive values increase it. The special value −17 removes the process altogether as a candidate for selection by the OOM killer. For further details, see the *proc(5)* manual page.

49.10 The MAP_FIXED Flag

Specifying MAP_FIXED in the *mmap()* *flags* argument forces the kernel to interpret the address in *addr* exactly, rather than take it as a hint. If we specify MAP_FIXED, *addr* must be page-aligned.

Generally, a portable application should omit the use of MAP_FIXED, and specify *addr* as NULL, which allows the system to choose the address at which to place the mapping. The reasons for this are the same as those that we outlined in Section 48.3 when explaining why it is usually preferable to specify *shmaddr* as NULL when attaching a System V shared memory segment using *shmat()*.

There is, however, one situation where a portable application might use MAP_FIXED. If MAP_FIXED is specified when calling *mmap()*, and the memory region beginning at *addr* and running for *length* bytes overlaps the pages of any previous mapping, then the overlapped pages are replaced by the new mapping. We can use this feature to portably map multiple parts of a file (or files) into a contiguous region of memory, as follows:

1. Use *mmap()* to create an anonymous mapping (Section 49.7). In the *mmap()* call, we specify *addr* as NULL and don't specify the MAP_FIXED flag. This allows the kernel to choose an address for the mapping.
2. Use a series of *mmap()* calls specifying MAP_FIXED to map (i.e., overlay) file regions into different parts of the mapping created in the preceding step.

Although we could skip the first step, and use a series of *mmap()* MAP_FIXED operations to create a set of contiguous mappings at an address range selected by the application, this approach is less portable than performing both steps. As noted above, a portable application should avoid trying to create a new mapping at a fixed address. The first step avoids the portability problem, because we let the kernel select a contiguous address range, and then create new mappings within that address range.

From Linux 2.6 onward, the *remap_file_pages()* system call, which we describe in the next section, can also be used to achieve the same effect. However, the use of MAP_FIXED is more portable than *remap_file_pages()*, which is Linux-specific.

49.11 Nonlinear Mappings: *remap_file_pages()*

File mappings created with *mmap()* are linear: there is a sequential, one-to-one correspondence between the pages of the mapped file and the pages of the memory region. For most applications, a linear mapping suffices. However, some applications need to create large numbers of nonlinear mappings—mappings where the pages of the file appear in a different order within contiguous memory. We show an example of a nonlinear mapping in Figure 49-5.

We described one way of creating nonlinear mappings in the previous section: using multiple calls to *mmap()* with the MAP_FIXED flag. However, this approach doesn't scale well. The problem is that each of these *mmap()* calls creates a separate kernel virtual memory area (VMA) data structure. Each VMA takes time to set up and consumes some nonswappable kernel memory. Furthermore, the presence of a large number of VMAs can degrade the performance of the virtual memory manager; in particular, the time taken to process each page fault can significantly increase when there are tens of thousands of VMAs. (This was a problem for some large database management systems that maintain multiple different views in a database file.)

> Each line in the /proc/*PID*/maps file (Section 48.5) represents one VMA.

From kernel 2.6 onward, Linux provides the *remap_file_pages()* system call to create nonlinear mappings without creating multiple VMAs. We do this as follows:

1. Create a mapping with *mmap()*.
2. Use one or more calls to *remap_file_pages()* to rearrange the correspondence between the pages of memory and the pages of the file. (All that *remap_file_pages()* is doing is manipulating process page tables.)

> It is possible to use *remap_file_pages()* to map the same page of a file into multiple locations within the mapped region.

```
#define _GNU_SOURCE
#include <sys/mman.h>

int remap_file_pages(void *addr, size_t size, int prot, size_t pgoff, int flags);
```
Returns 0 on success, or −1 on error

The *pgoff* and *size* arguments identify a file region whose position in memory is to be changed. The *pgoff* argument specifies the start of the file region in units of the system page size (as returned by *sysconf(_SC_PAGESIZE)*). The *size* argument specifies the length of the file region, in bytes. The *addr* argument serves two purposes:

- It identifies the existing mapping whose pages we want to rearrange. In other words, *addr* must be an address that falls somewhere within a region that was previously mapped with *mmap()*.

- It specifies the memory address at which the file pages identified by *pgoff* and *size* are to be located.

Both *addr* and *size* should be specified as multiples of the system page size. If they are not, they are rounded down to the nearest multiple of the page size.

Suppose that we use the following call to *mmap()* to map three pages of the open file referred to by the descriptor *fd*, and that the call assigns the returned address 0x4001a000 to *addr*:

```
ps = sysconf(_SC_PAGESIZE);                /* Obtain system page size */
addr = mmap(0, 3 * ps, PROT_READ | PROT_WRITE, MAP_SHARED, fd, 0);
```

The following calls would then create the nonlinear mapping shown in Figure 49-5:

```
remap_file_pages(addr, ps, 0, 2, 0);
                            /* Maps page 2 of file into page 0 of region */
remap_file_pages(addr + 2 * ps, ps, 0, 0, 0);
                            /* Maps page 0 of file into page 2 of region */
```

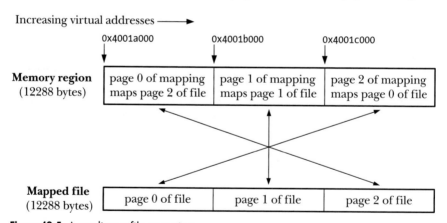

Figure 49-5: A nonlinear file mapping

There are two other arguments to *remap_file_pages()* that we haven't yet described:

- The *prot* argument is ignored, and must be specified as 0. In the future, it may be possible to use this argument to change the protection of the memory region affected by *remap_file_pages()*. In the current implementation, the protection remains the same as that on the entire VMA.

> Virtual machines and garbage collectors are other applications that employ multiple VMAs. Some of these applications need to be able to write-protect individual pages. It was intended that *remap_file_pages()* would allow permis-

sions on individual pages within a VMA to be changed, but this facility has not so far been implemented.

- The *flags* argument is currently unused.

As currently implemented, *remap_file_pages()* can be applied only to shared (MAP_SHARED) mappings.

The *remap_file_pages()* system call is Linux-specific; it is not specified in SUSv3 and is not available on other UNIX implementations.

49.12 Summary

The *mmap()* system call creates a new memory mapping in the calling process's virtual address space. The *munmap()* system call performs the converse operation, removing a mapping from a process's address space.

A mapping may be of two types: file-based or anonymous. A file mapping maps the contents of a file region into the process's virtual address space. An anonymous mapping (created by using the MAP_ANONYMOUS flag or by mapping /dev/zero) doesn't have a corresponding file region; the bytes of the mapping are initialized to 0.

Mappings can be either private (MAP_PRIVATE) or shared (MAP_SHARED). This distinction determines the visibility of changes made to the shared memory, and, in the case of file mappings, determines whether the kernel propagates changes to the contents of the mapping to the underlying file. When a process maps a file with the MAP_PRIVATE flag, any changes it makes to the contents of the mapping are not visible to other processes and are not carried through to the mapped file. A MAP_SHARED file mapping is the converse—changes to the mapping are visible to other processes and are carried through to the mapped file.

Although the kernel automatically propagates changes to the contents of a MAP_SHARED mapping to the underlying file, it doesn't provide any guarantees about when this is done. An application can use the *msync()* system call to explicitly control when the contents of a mapping are synchronized with the mapped file.

Memory mappings serve a variety of uses, including:

- allocating process-private memory (private anonymous mappings);
- initializing the contents of the text and initialized data segments of a process (private file mappings);
- sharing memory between processes related via *fork()* (shared anonymous mappings); and
- performing memory-mapped I/O, optionally combined with memory sharing between unrelated processes (shared file mappings).

Two signals may come into play when accessing the contents of a mapping. SIGSEGV is generated if we attempt access in a manner that violates the protections on the mapping (or if we access any currently unmapped address). SIGBUS is generated for file-based mappings if we access a part of the mapping for which no corresponding region exists in the file (i.e., the mapping is larger than the underlying file).

Swap space overcommitting allows the system to allocate more memory to processes than is actually available in RAM and swap space. Overcommitting is possible because, typically, each process does not make full use of its allocation. Overcommitting can be controlled on a per-*mmap()* basis using the MAP_NORESERVE flag, and on a system-wide basis using /proc files.

The *mremap()* system call allows an existing mapping to be resized. The *remap_file_pages()* system call allows the creation of nonlinear file mappings.

Further information

Information about the implementation of *mmap()* on Linux can be found in [Bovet & Cesati, 2005]. Information about the implementation of *mmap()* on other UNIX systems can be found in [McKusick et al., 1996] (BSD), [Goodheart & Cox, 1994] (System V Release 4), and [Vahalia, 1996] (System V Release 4).

49.13 Exercises

49-1. Write a program, analogous to *cp(1)*, that uses *mmap()* and *memcpy()* calls (instead of *read()* or *write()*) to copy a source file to a destination file. (Use *fstat()* to obtain the size of the input file, which can then be used to size the required memory mappings, and use *ftruncate()* to set the size of the output file.)

49-2. Rewrite the programs in Listing 48-2 (svshm_xfr_writer.c, page 1003) and Listing 48-3 (svshm_xfr_reader.c, page 1005) to use a shared memory mapping instead of System V shared memory.

49-3. Write programs to verify that the SIGBUS and SIGSEGV signals are delivered in the circumstances described in Section 49.4.3.

49-4. Write a program that uses the MAP_FIXED technique described in Section 49.10 to create a nonlinear mapping similar to that shown in Figure 49-5.

50

VIRTUAL MEMORY OPERATIONS

This chapter looks at various system calls that perform operations on a process's virtual address space:

- The *mprotect()* system call changes the protection on a region of virtual memory.
- The *mlock()* and *mlockall()* system calls lock a region of virtual memory into physical memory, thus preventing it from being swapped out.
- The *mincore()* system call allows a process to determine whether the pages in a region of virtual memory are resident in physical memory.
- The *madvise()* system call allows a process to advise the kernel about its future patterns of usage of a virtual memory region.

Some of these system calls find particular use in conjunction with shared memory regions (Chapters 48, 49, and 54), but they can be applied to any region of a process's virtual memory.

> The techniques described in this chapter are not in fact about IPC at all, but we include them in this part of the book because they are sometimes used with shared memory.

50.1 Changing Memory Protection: *mprotect()*

The *mprotect()* system call changes the protection on the virtual memory pages in the range starting at *addr* and continuing for *length* bytes.

```
#include <sys/mman.h>

int mprotect(void *addr, size_t length, int prot);
```
                                        Returns 0 on success, or −1 on error

The value given in *addr* must be a multiple of the system page size (as returned by *sysconf(_SC_PAGESIZE)*). (SUSv3 specified that *addr* must be page-aligned. SUSv4 says that an implementation *may* require this argument to be page-aligned.) Because protections are set on whole pages, *length* is, in effect, rounded up to the next multiple of the system page size.

The *prot* argument is a bit mask specifying the new protection for this region of memory. It must be specified as either PROT_NONE or a combination created by ORing together one or more of PROT_READ, PROT_WRITE, and PROT_EXEC. All of these values have the same meaning as for *mmap()* (Table 49-2, on page 1020).

If a process attempts to access a region of memory in a manner that violates the memory protection, the kernel generates a SIGSEGV signal for the process.

One use of *mprotect()* is to change the protection of a region of mapped memory originally set in a call to *mmap()*, as shown in Listing 50-1. This program creates an anonymous mapping that initially has all access denied (PROT_NONE). The program then changes the protection on the region to read plus write. Before and after making the change, the program uses the *system()* function to execute a shell command that displays the line from the /proc/*PID*/maps file corresponding to the mapped region, so that we can see the change in memory protection. (We could have obtained the mapping information by directly parsing /proc/self/maps, but we used the call to *system()* because it results in a shorter program.) When we run this program, we see the following:

```
$ ./t_mprotect
Before mprotect()
b7cde000-b7dde000 ---s 00000000 00:04 18258     /dev/zero (deleted)
After mprotect()
b7cde000-b7dde000 rw-s 00000000 00:04 18258     /dev/zero (deleted)
```

From the last line of output, we can see that *mprotect()* has changed the permissions of the memory region to PROT_READ | PROT_WRITE. (For an explanation of the (deleted) string that appears after /dev/zero in the shell output, refer to Section 48.5.)

Listing 50-1: Changing memory protection with *mprotect()*

── vmem/t_mprotect.c
```
#define _BSD_SOURCE          /* Get MAP_ANONYMOUS definition from <sys/mman.h> */
#include <sys/mman.h>
#include "tlpi_hdr.h"

#define LEN (1024 * 1024)

#define SHELL_FMT "cat /proc/%ld/maps | grep zero"
#define CMD_SIZE (sizeof(SHELL_FMT) + 20)
                        /* Allow extra space for integer string */
```

```
int
main(int argc, char *argv[])
{
    char cmd[CMD_SIZE];
    char *addr;

    /* Create an anonymous mapping with all access denied */

    addr = mmap(NULL, LEN, PROT_NONE, MAP_SHARED | MAP_ANONYMOUS, -1, 0);
    if (addr == MAP_FAILED)
        errExit("mmap");

    /* Display line from /proc/self/maps corresponding to mapping */

    printf("Before mprotect()\n");
    snprintf(cmd, CMD_SIZE, SHELL_FMT, (long) getpid());
    system(cmd);

    /* Change protection on memory to allow read and write access */

    if (mprotect(addr, LEN, PROT_READ | PROT_WRITE) == -1)
        errExit("mprotect");

    printf("After mprotect()\n");
    system(cmd);                    /* Review protection via /proc/self/maps */

    exit(EXIT_SUCCESS);
}
```
——————————————————————————————————————— vmem/t_mprotect.c

50.2 Memory Locking: *mlock()* **and** *mlockall()*

In some applications, it is useful to lock part or all of a process's virtual memory so that it is guaranteed to always be in physical memory. One reason for doing this is to improve performance. Accesses to locked pages are guaranteed never to be delayed by a page fault. This is useful for applications that must ensure rapid response times.

Another reason for locking memory is security. If a virtual memory page containing sensitive data is never swapped out, then no copy of the page is ever written to the disk. If the page was written to the disk, it could, in theory, be read directly from the disk device at some later time. (An attacker could deliberately engineer this situation by running a program that consumes a large amount of memory, thus forcing the memory of other processes to be swapped out to disk.) Reading information from the swap space could even be done after the process has terminated, since the kernel makes no guarantees about zeroing out the data held in swap space. (Normally, only privileged processes would be able to read from the swap device.)

> The suspend mode on laptop computers, as well some desktop systems, saves a copy of a system's RAM to disk, regardless of memory locks.

In this section, we look at the system calls used for locking and unlocking part or all of a process's virtual memory. However, before doing this, we first look at a resource limit that governs memory locking.

The RLIMIT_MEMLOCK resource limit

In Section 36.3, we briefly described the RLIMIT_MEMLOCK limit, which defines a limit on the number of bytes that a process can lock into memory. We now consider this limit in more detail.

In Linux kernels before 2.6.9, only privileged processes (CAP_IPC_LOCK) can lock memory, and the RLIMIT_MEMLOCK soft resource limit places an upper limit on the number of bytes that a privileged process can lock.

Starting with Linux 2.6.9, changes to the memory locking model allow unprivileged processes to lock small amounts of memory. This is useful for an application that needs to place a small piece of sensitive information in locked memory in order to ensure that it is never written to the swap space on disk; for example, *gpg* does this with pass phrases. As a result of these changes:

- no limits are placed on the amount of memory that a privileged process can lock (i.e., RLIMIT_MEMLOCK is ignored); and

- an unprivileged process is now able to lock memory up to the soft limit defined by RLIMIT_MEMLOCK.

The default value for both the soft and hard RLIMIT_MEMLOCK limits is 8 pages (i.e., 32,768 bytes on x86-32).

The RLIMIT_MEMLOCK limit affects:

- *mlock()* and *mlockall()*;
- the *mmap()* MAP_LOCKED flag, which is used to lock a memory mapping when it is created, as described in Section 49.6; and
- the *shmctl()* SHM_LOCK operation, which is used to lock System V shared memory segments, as described in Section 48.7.

Since virtual memory is managed in units of pages, memory locks apply to complete pages. When performing limit checks, the RLIMIT_MEMLOCK limit is rounded *down* to the nearest multiple of the system page size.

Although this resource limit has a single (soft) value, in effect, it defines two separate limits:

- For *mlock()*, *mlockall()*, and the *mmap()* MAP_LOCKED operation, RLIMIT_MEMLOCK defines a per-process limit on the number of bytes of its virtual address space that a process may lock.

- For the *shmctl()* SHM_LOCK operation, RLIMIT_MEMLOCK defines a per-user limit on the number of bytes in shared memory segments that may be locked by the real user ID of this process. When a process performs a *shmctl()* SHM_LOCK operation, the kernel checks the total number of bytes of System V shared memory that are already recorded as being locked by the real user ID of the calling process. If the size of the to-be-locked segment would not push that total over the process's RLIMIT_MEMLOCK limit, the operation succeeds.

The reason RLIMIT_MEMLOCK has different semantics for System V shared memory is that a shared memory segment can continue to exist even when it is not attached by any process. (It is removed only after an explicit *shmctl()* IPC_RMID operation, and then only after all processes have detached it from their address space.)

Locking and unlocking memory regions

A process can use *mlock()* and *munlock()* to lock and unlock regions of memory.

```
#include <sys/mman.h>

int mlock(void *addr, size_t length);
int munlock(void *addr, size_t length);
```
Both return 0 on success, or −1 on error

The *mlock()* system call locks all of the pages of the calling process's virtual address range starting at *addr* and continuing for *length* bytes. Unlike the corresponding argument passed to several other memory-related system calls, *addr* does not need to be page-aligned: the kernel locks pages starting at the next page boundary below *addr*. However, SUSv3 optionally allows an implementation to require that *addr* be a multiple of the system page size, and portable applications should ensure that this is so when calling *mlock()* and *munlock()*.

Because locking is done in units of whole pages, the end of the locked region is the next page boundary greater than *length* plus *addr*. For example, on a system where the page size is 4096 bytes, the call *mlock(2000, 4000)* will lock bytes 0 through to 8191.

> We can find out how much memory a process currently has locked by inspecting the VmLck entry of the Linux-specific /proc/*PID*/status file.

After a successful *mlock()* call, all of the pages in the specified range are guaranteed to be locked and resident in physical memory. The *mlock()* system call fails if there is insufficient physical memory to lock all of the requested pages or if the request violates the RLIMIT_MEMLOCK soft resource limit.

We show an example of the use of *mlock()* in Listing 50-2.

The *munlock()* system call performs the converse of *mlock()*, removing a memory lock previously established by the calling process. The *addr* and *length* arguments are interpreted in the same way as for *mlock()*. Unlocking a set of pages doesn't guarantee that they cease to be memory-resident: pages are removed from RAM only in response to memory demands by other processes.

Aside from the explicit use of *munlock()*, memory locks are automatically removed in the following circumstances:

- on process termination;
- if the locked pages are unmapped via *munmap()*; or
- if the locked pages are overlaid using the *mmap()* MAP_FIXED flag.

Details of the semantics of memory locking

In the following paragraphs, we note some details of the semantics of memory locks.

Memory locks are not inherited by a child created via *fork()*, and are not preserved across an *exec()*.

Where multiple processes share a set of pages (e.g., a MAP_SHARED mapping), these pages remain locked in memory as long as at least one of the processes holds a memory lock on the pages.

Memory locks don't nest for a single process. If a process repeatedly calls *mlock()* on a certain virtual address range, only one lock is established, and this lock will be removed by a single call to *munlock()*. On the other hand, if we use *mmap()* to map the same set of pages (i.e., the same file) at several different locations within a single process, and then lock each of these mappings, the pages remain locked in RAM until all of the mappings have been unlocked.

The fact that memory locks are performed in units of pages and can't be nested means that it isn't logically correct to independently apply *mlock()* and *munlock()* calls to different data structures on the same virtual page. For example, suppose we have two data structures within the same virtual memory page pointed to by pointers *p1* and *p2*, and we make the following calls:

```
mlock(p1, len1);
mlock(p2, len2);          /* Actually has no effect */
munlock(p1, len1);
```

All of the above calls will succeed, but at the end of this sequence, the entire page is unlocked; that is, the data structure pointed to by *p2* is not locked into memory.

Note that the semantics of the *shmctl()* SHM_LOCK operation (Section 48.7) differ from those of *mlock()* and *mlockall()*, as follows:

- After a SHM_LOCK operation, pages are locked into memory only as they are faulted in by subsequent references. By contrast, *mlock()* and *mlockall()* fault all of the locked pages into memory before the call returns.

- The SHM_LOCK operation sets a property of the shared memory segment, rather than the process. (For this reason, the value in the /proc/*PID*/status VmLck field doesn't include the size of any attached System V shared memory segments that have been locked using SHM_LOCK.) This means that, once faulted into memory, the pages remain resident even if all processes detach the shared memory segment. By contrast, a region locked into memory using *mlock()* (or *mlockall()*) remains locked only as long as at least one process holds a lock on the region.

Locking and unlocking all of a process's memory

A process can use *mlockall()* and *munlockall()* to lock and unlock all of its memory.

```
#include <sys/mman.h>

int mlockall(int flags);
int munlockall(void);
```
                                    Both return 0 on success, or −1 on error

The *mlockall()* system call locks all of the currently mapped pages in a process's virtual address space, all of the pages mapped in the future, or both, according to the *flags* bit mask, which is specified by ORing together one or both of the following constants:

MCL_CURRENT

Lock all pages that are currently mapped into the calling process's virtual address space. This includes all pages currently allocated for the program text, data segments, memory mappings, and the stack. After a successful call specifying the MCL_CURRENT flag, all of the pages of the calling process are guaranteed to be memory-resident. This flag doesn't affect pages that are subsequently allocated in the process's virtual address space; for this, we must use MCL_FUTURE.

MCL_FUTURE

Lock all pages subsequently mapped into the calling process's virtual address space. Such pages may, for example, be part of a shared memory region mapped via *mmap()* or *shmat()*, or part of the upwardly growing heap or downwardly growing stack. As a consequence of specifying the MCL_FUTURE flag, a later memory allocation operation (e.g., *mmap()*, *sbrk()*, or *malloc()*) may fail, or stack growth may yield a SIGSEGV signal, if the system runs out of RAM to allocate to the process or the RLIMIT_MEMLOCK soft resource limit is encountered.

The same rules regarding the constraints, lifetime, and inheritance of memory locks created with *mlock()* also apply for memory locks created via *mlockall()*.

The *munlockall()* system call unlocks all of the pages of the calling process and undoes the effect of any previous *mlockall(MCL_FUTURE)* call. As with *munlock()*, unlocked pages are not guaranteed to be removed from RAM by this call.

> Before Linux 2.6.9, privilege (CAP_IPC_LOCK) was required to call *munlockall()* (inconsistently, privilege was not required for *munlock()*). Since Linux 2.6.9, privilege is no longer required.

50.3 Determining Memory Residence: *mincore()*

The *mincore()* system call is the complement of the memory locking system calls. It reports which pages in a virtual address range are currently resident in RAM, and thus won't cause a page fault if accessed.

SUSv3 doesn't specify *mincore()*. It is available on many, but not all, UNIX implementations. On Linux, *mincore()* has been available since kernel 2.4.

```
#define _BSD_SOURCE          /* Or: #define _SVID_SOURCE */
#include <sys/mman.h>

int mincore(void *addr, size_t length, unsigned char *vec);
                                    Returns 0 on success, or −1 on error
```

The *mincore()* system call returns memory-residence information about pages in the virtual address range starting at *addr* and running for *length* bytes. The address supplied in *addr* must be page-aligned, and, since information is returned about whole pages, *length* is effectively rounded up to the next multiple of the system page size.

Information about memory residency is returned in *vec*, which must be an array of *(length + PAGE_SIZE − 1) / PAGE_SIZE* bytes. (On Linux, *vec* has the type *unsigned char **; on some other UNIX implementations, *vec* has the type *char **.) The least significant bit of each byte is set if the corresponding page is memory-resident. The setting of the other bits is undefined on some UNIX implementations, so portable applications should test only this bit.

The information returned by *mincore()* can change between the time the call is made and the time the elements of *vec* are checked. The only pages guaranteed to remain memory-resident are those locked with *mlock()* or *mlockall()*.

> Prior to Linux 2.6.21, various implementation problems meant that *mincore()* did not correctly report memory-residence information for MAP_PRIVATE mappings or for nonlinear mappings (established using *remap_file_pages()*).

Listing 50-2 demonstrates the use of *mlock()* and *mincore()*. After allocating and mapping a region of memory using *mmap()*, this program uses *mlock()* to lock either the entire region or otherwise groups of pages at regular intervals. (Each of the command-line arguments to the program is expressed in terms of pages; the program converts these to bytes, as required for the calls to *mmap()*, *mlock()*, and *mincore()*.) Before and after the *mlock()* call, the program uses *mincore()* to retrieve information about the memory residency of pages in the region and displays this information graphically.

Listing 50-2: Using *mlock()* and *mincore()*

── vmem/memlock.c
```
#define _BSD_SOURCE      /* Get mincore() declaration and MAP_ANONYMOUS
                            definition from <sys/mman.h> */
#include <sys/mman.h>
#include "tlpi_hdr.h"

/* Display residency of pages in range [addr .. (addr + length - 1)] */

static void
displayMincore(char *addr, size_t length)
{
    unsigned char *vec;
    long pageSize, numPages, j;

    pageSize = sysconf(_SC_PAGESIZE);

    numPages = (length + pageSize - 1) / pageSize;
    vec = malloc(numPages);
    if (vec == NULL)
        errExit("malloc");
```

```
        if (mincore(addr, length, vec) == -1)
            errExit("mincore");

        for (j = 0; j < numPages; j++) {
            if (j % 64 == 0)
                printf("%s%10p: ", (j == 0) ? "" : "\n", addr + (j * pageSize));
            printf("%c", (vec[j] & 1) ? '*' : '.');
        }
        printf("\n");

        free(vec);
}

int
main(int argc, char *argv[])
{
        char *addr;
        size_t len, lockLen;
        long pageSize, stepSize, j;

        if (argc != 4 || strcmp(argv[1], "--help") == 0)
            usageErr("%s num-pages lock-page-step lock-page-len\n", argv[0]);

        pageSize = sysconf(_SC_PAGESIZE);
        if (pageSize == -1)
            errExit("sysconf(_SC_PAGESIZE)");

        len =      getInt(argv[1], GN_GT_0, "num-pages") * pageSize;
        stepSize = getInt(argv[2], GN_GT_0, "lock-page-step") * pageSize;
        lockLen =  getInt(argv[3], GN_GT_0, "lock-page-len") * pageSize;

        addr = mmap(NULL, len, PROT_READ, MAP_SHARED | MAP_ANONYMOUS, -1, 0);
        if (addr == MAP_FAILED)
            errExit("mmap");

        printf("Allocated %ld (%#lx) bytes starting at %p\n",
                (long) len, (unsigned long) len, addr);

        printf("Before mlock:\n");
        displayMincore(addr, len);

        /* Lock pages specified by command line arguments into memory */

        for (j = 0; j + lockLen <= len; j += stepSize)
            if (mlock(addr + j, lockLen) == -1)
                errExit("mlock");

        printf("After mlock:\n");
        displayMincore(addr, len);

        exit(EXIT_SUCCESS);
}
```

—— vmem/memlock.c

The following shell session shows a sample run of the program in Listing 50-2. In this example, we allocate 32 pages, and in each group of 8 pages, we lock 3 consecutive pages:

```
$ su                                         Assume privilege
Password:
# ./memlock 32 8 3
Allocated 131072 (0x20000) bytes starting at 0x4014a000
Before mlock:
0x4014a000: ..............................
After mlock:
0x4014a000: ***.....***.....***.....***.....
```

In the program output, dots represent pages that are not resident in memory, and asterisks represent pages that are resident in memory. As we can see from the final line of output, 3 out of each group of 8 pages are memory-resident.

In this example, we assumed superuser privilege so that the program can use *mlock()*. This is not necessary in Linux 2.6.9 and later if the amount of memory to be locked falls within the RLIMIT_MEMLOCK soft resource limit.

50.4 Advising Future Memory Usage Patterns: *madvise()*

The *madvise()* system call is used to improve the performance of an application by informing the kernel about the calling process's likely usage of the pages in the range starting at *addr* and continuing for *length* bytes. The kernel may use this information to improve the efficiency of I/O performed on the file mapping that underlies the pages. (See Section 49.4 for a discussion of file mappings.) On Linux, *madvise()* has been available since kernel 2.4.

```
#define _BSD_SOURCE
#include <sys/mman.h>

int madvise(void *addr, size_t length, int advice);
```
                                        Returns 0 on success, or −1 on error

The value specified in *addr* must be page-aligned, and *length* is effectively rounded up to the next multiple of the system page size. The *advice* argument is one of the following:

MADV_NORMAL

This is the default behavior. Pages are transferred in clusters (a small multiple of the system page size). This results in some read-ahead and read-behind.

MADV_RANDOM

Pages in this region will be accessed randomly, so read-ahead will yield no benefit. Thus, the kernel should fetch the minimum amount of data on each read.

MADV_SEQUENTIAL

> Pages in this range will be accessed once, sequentially. Thus, the kernel can aggressively read ahead, and pages can be quickly freed after they have been accessed.

MADV_WILLNEED

> Read pages in this region ahead, in preparation for future access. The MADV_WILLNEED operation has an effect similar to the Linux-specific *readahead()* system call and the *posix_fadvise()* POSIX_FADV_WILLNEED operation.

MADV_DONTNEED

> The calling process no longer requires the pages in this region to be memory-resident. The precise effect of this flag varies across UNIX implementations. We first note the behavior on Linux. For a MAP_PRIVATE region, the mapped pages are explicitly discarded, which means that modifications to the pages are lost. The virtual memory address range remains accessible, but the next access of each page will result in a page fault reinitializing the page, either with the contents of the file from which it is mapped or with zeros in the case of an anonymous mapping. This can be used as a means of explicitly reinitializing the contents of a MAP_PRIVATE region. For a MAP_SHARED region, the kernel *may* discard modified pages in some circumstances, depending on the architecture (this behavior doesn't occur on x86). Some other UNIX implementations also behave in the same way as Linux. However, on some UNIX implementations, MADV_DONTNEED simply informs the kernel that the specified pages can be swapped out if necessary. Portable applications should not rely on the Linux's destructive semantics for MADV_DONTNEED.

> > Linux 2.6.16 added three new nonstandard *advice* values: MADV_DONTFORK, MADV_DOFORK, and MADV_REMOVE. Linux 2.6.32 and 2.6.33 added another four nonstandard *advice* values: MADV_HWPOISON, MADV_SOFT_OFFLINE, MADV_MERGEABLE, and MADV_UNMERGEABLE. These values are used in special circumstances and are described in the *madvise(2)* manual page.

Most UNIX implementations provide a version of *madvise()*, typically allowing at least the *advice* constants described above. However, SUSv3 standardizes this API under a different name, *posix_madvise()*, and prefixes the corresponding *advice* constants with the string POSIX_. Thus, the constants are POSIX_MADV_NORMAL, POSIX_MADV_RANDOM, POSIX_MADV_SEQUENTIAL, POSIX_MADV_WILLNEED, and POSIX_MADV_DONTNEED. This alternative interface is implemented in *glibc* (version 2.2 and later) by calls to *madvise()*, but it is not available on all UNIX implementations.

> SUSv3 says that *posix_madvise()* should not affect the semantics of a program. However, in *glibc* versions before 2.6, the POSIX_MADV_DONTNEED operation is implemented using *madvise()* MADV_DONTNEED, which does affect the semantics of a program, as described earlier. Since *glibc* 2.6, the *posix_madvise()* wrapper implements POSIX_MADV_DONTNEED to do nothing, so that it does not affect the semantics of a program.

50.5 Summary

In this chapter, we considered various operations that can be performed on a process's virtual memory:

- The *mprotect()* system call changes the protection on a region of virtual memory.
- The *mlock()* and *mlockall()* system calls lock part or all of a process's virtual address space, respectively, into physical memory.
- The *mincore()* system call reports which pages in a virtual memory region are currently resident in physical memory.
- The *madvise()* system call and the *posix_madvise()* function allow a process to advise the kernel about the process's expected patterns of memory use.

50.6 Exercises

50-1. Verify the effect of the RLIMIT_MEMLOCK resource limit by writing a program that sets a value for this limit and then attempts to lock more memory than the limit.

50-2. Write a program to verify the operation of the *madvise()* MADV_DONTNEED operation for a writable MAP_PRIVATE mapping.

51

INTRODUCTION TO POSIX IPC

The POSIX.1b realtime extensions defined a set of IPC mechanisms that are analogous to the System V IPC mechanisms described in Chapters 45 to 48. (One of the POSIX.1b developers' aims was to devise a set of IPC mechanisms that did not suffer the deficiencies of the System V IPC facilities.) These IPC mechanisms are collectively referred to as POSIX IPC. The three POSIX IPC mechanisms are the following:

- *Message queues* can be used to pass messages between processes. As with System V message queues, message boundaries are preserved, so that readers and writers communicate in units of messages (as opposed to the undelimited byte stream provided by a pipe). POSIX message queues permit each message to be assigned a priority, which allows high-priority messages to be queued ahead of low-priority messages. This provides some of the same functionality that is available via the type field of System V messages.

- *Semaphores* permit multiple processes to synchronize their actions. As with System V semaphores, a POSIX semaphore is a kernel-maintained integer whose value is never permitted to go below 0. POSIX semaphores are simpler to use than System V semaphores: they are allocated individually (as opposed to System V semaphore *sets*), and they are operated on individually using two operations that increase and decrease a semaphore's value by one (as opposed to the ability of the *semop()* system call to atomically add or subtract arbitrary values from multiple semaphores in a System V semaphore set).

- *Shared memory* enables multiple processes to share the same region of memory. As with System V shared memory, POSIX shared memory provides fast IPC. Once one process has updated the shared memory, the change is immediately visible to other processes sharing the same region.

This chapter provides an overview of the POSIX IPC facilities, focusing on their common features.

51.1 API Overview

The three POSIX IPC mechanisms have a number of common features. Table 51-1 summarizes their APIs, and we go into the details of their common features in the next few pages.

> Except for a mention in Table 51-1, in the remainder of this chapter, we'll overlook the fact that POSIX semaphores come in two flavors: named semaphores and unnamed semaphores. Named semaphores are like the other POSIX IPC mechanisms that we describe in this chapter: they are identified by a name, and are accessible by any process that has suitable permissions on the object. An unnamed semaphore doesn't have an associated identifier; instead, it is placed in an area of memory that is shared by a group of processes or by the threads of a single process. We go into the details of both types of semaphores in Chapter 53.

Table 51-1: Summary of programming interfaces for POSIX IPC objects

Interface	Message queues	Semaphores	Shared memory
Header file	<mqueue.h>	<semaphore.h>	<sys/mman.h>
Object handle	*mqd_t*	*sem_t **	*int* (file descriptor)
Create/open	*mq_open()*	*sem_open()*	*shm_open() + mmap()*
Close	*mq_close()*	*sem_close()*	*munmap()*
Unlink	*mq_unlink()*	*sem_unlink()*	*shm_unlink()*
Perform IPC	*mq_send()*, *mq_receive()*	*sem_post()*, *sem_wait()*, *sem_getvalue()*	operate on locations in shared region
Miscellaneous operations	*mq_setattr()*—set attributes	*sem_init()*—initialize unnamed semaphore	(none)
	mq_getattr()—get attributes	*sem_destroy()*—destroy unnamed semaphore	
	mq_notify()—request notification		

IPC object names

To access a POSIX IPC object, we must have some means of identifying it. The only portable means that SUSv3 specifies to identify a POSIX IPC object is via a name consisting of an initial slash, followed by one or more nonslash characters; for example, /myobject. Linux and some other implementations (e.g., Solaris) permit this type of portable naming for IPC objects.

On Linux, names for POSIX shared memory and message queue objects are limited to NAME_MAX (255) characters. For semaphores, the limit is 4 characters less, since the implementation prepends the string *sem.* to the semaphore name.

SUSv3 doesn't prohibit names of a form other than /myobject, but says that the semantics of such names are implementation-defined. The rules for creating IPC object names on some systems are different. For example, on Tru64 5.1, IPC object names are created as names within the standard file system, and the name is interpreted as an absolute or relative pathname. If the caller doesn't have permission to create a file in that directory, then the IPC *open* call fails. This means that unprivileged programs can't create names of the form /myobject on Tru64, since unprivileged users normally can't create files in the root directory (/). Some other implementations have similar implementation-specific rules for the construction of the names given to IPC *open* calls. Therefore, in portable applications, we should isolate the generation of IPC object names into a separate function or header file that can be tailored to the target implementation.

Creating or opening an IPC object

Each IPC mechanism has an associated *open* call (*mq_open()*, *sem_open()*, or *shm_open()*), which is analogous to the traditional UNIX *open()* system call used for files. Given an IPC object name, the IPC *open* call either:

- creates a new object with the given name, opens that object, and returns a handle for it; or
- opens an existing object and returns a handle for that object.

The handle returned by the IPC *open* call is analogous to the file descriptor returned by the traditional *open()* system call—it is used in subsequent calls to refer to the object.

The type of handle returned by the IPC *open* call depends on the type of object. For message queues, it is a message queue descriptor, a value of type *mqd_t*. For semaphores, it is a pointer of type *sem_t **. For shared memory, it is a file descriptor.

All of the IPC *open* calls permit at least three arguments—*name*, *oflag*, and *mode*—as exemplified by the following *shm_open()* call:

```
fd = shm_open("/mymem", O_CREAT | O_RDWR, S_IRUSR | S_IWUSR);
```

These arguments are analogous to the arguments of the traditional UNIX *open()* system call. The *name* argument identifies the object to be created or opened. The *oflag* argument is a bit mask that can include at least the following flags:

O_CREAT
> Create the object if it doesn't already exist. If this flag is not specified and the object doesn't exist, an error results (ENOENT).

O_EXCL
> If O_CREAT is also specified and the object already exists, an error results (EEXIST). The two steps—check for existence and creation—are performed atomically (Section 5.1). This flag has no effect if O_CREAT is not specified.

Depending on the type of object, *oflag* may also include one of the values O_RDONLY, O_WRONLY, or O_RDWR, with meanings similar to *open()*. Additional flags are allowed for some IPC mechanisms.

The remaining argument, *mode*, is a bit mask specifying the permissions to be placed on a new object, if one is created by the call (i.e., O_CREAT was specified and the object did not already exist). The values that may be specified for *mode* are the same as for files (Table 15-4, on page 295). As with the *open()* system call, the permissions mask in *mode* is masked against the process umask (Section 15.4.6). The ownership and group ownership of a new IPC object are taken from the effective user and group IDs of the process making the IPC *open* call. (To be strictly accurate, on Linux, the ownership of a new POSIX IPC object is determined by the process's file-system IDs, which normally have the same value as the corresponding effective IDs. Refer to Section 9.5.)

> On systems where IPC objects appear in the standard file system, SUSv3 permits an implementation to set the group ID of a new IPC object to the group ID of the parent directory.

Closing an IPC object

For POSIX message queues and semaphores, there is an IPC *close* call that indicates that the calling process has finished using the object and the system may deallocate any resources that were associated with the object for this process. A POSIX shared memory object is closed by unmapping it with *munmap()*.

IPC objects are automatically closed if the process terminates or performs an *exec()*.

IPC object permissions

IPC objects have a permissions mask that is the same as for files. Permissions for accessing an IPC object are similar to those for accessing files (Section 15.4.3), except that execute permission has no meaning for POSIX IPC objects.

Since kernel 2.6.19, Linux supports the use of access control lists (ACLs) for setting the permissions on POSIX shared memory objects and named semaphores. Currently, ACLs are not supported for POSIX message queues.

IPC object deletion and object persistence

As with open files, POSIX IPC objects are *reference counted*—the kernel maintains a count of the number of open references to the object. By comparison with System V IPC objects, this makes it easier for applications to determine when the object can be safely deleted.

Each IPC object has a corresponding *unlink* call whose operation is analogous to the traditional *unlink()* system call for files. The *unlink* call immediately removes the object's name, and then destroys the object once all processes cease using it (i.e., when the reference count falls to zero). For message queues and semaphores, this means that the object is destroyed after all processes have closed the object; for shared memory, destruction occurs after all processes have unmapped the object using *munmap()*.

After an object is unlinked, IPC *open* calls specifying the same object name will refer to a new object (or fail, if O_CREAT was not specified).

As with System V IPC, POSIX IPC objects have kernel persistence. Once created, an object continues to exist until it is unlinked or the system is shut down. This allows a process to create an object, modify its state, and then exit, leaving the object to be accessed by some process that is started at a later time.

Listing and removing POSIX IPC objects via the command line

System V IPC provides two commands, *ipcs* and *ipcrm*, for listing and deleting IPC objects. No standard commands are provided to perform the analogous tasks for POSIX IPC objects. However, on many systems, including Linux, IPC objects are implemented within a real or virtual file system, mounted somewhere under the root directory (/), and the standard *ls* and *rm* commands can be used to list and remove IPC objects. (SUSv3 doesn't specify the use of *ls* and *rm* for these tasks.) The main problem with using these commands is the nonstandard nature of POSIX IPC object names and their location in the file system.

On Linux, POSIX IPC objects are contained in virtual file systems mounted under directories that have the sticky bit set. This bit is the restricted deletion flag (Section 15.4.5); setting it means that an unprivileged process can unlink only the POSIX IPC objects that it owns.

Compiling programs that use POSIX IPC on Linux

On Linux, programs employing POSIX message queues and shared memory must be linked with the realtime library, *librt*, using the *cc -lrt* option. Programs employing POSIX semaphores must be compiled using the *cc -pthread* option.

51.2 Comparison of System V IPC and POSIX IPC

As we look at the POSIX IPC mechanisms in the following chapters, we'll compare each mechanism against its System V counterpart. Here, we consider a few general comparisons for these two types of IPC.

POSIX IPC has the following general advantages when compared to System V IPC:

- The POSIX IPC interface is simpler than the System V IPC interface.
- The POSIX IPC model—the use of names instead of keys, and the *open*, *close*, and *unlink* functions—is more consistent with the traditional UNIX file model.
- POSIX IPC objects are reference counted. This simplifies object deletion, because we can unlink a POSIX IPC object, knowing that it will be destroyed only when all processes have closed it.

However, there is one notable advantage in favor of System V IPC: portability. POSIX IPC is less portable than System V IPC in the following respects:

- System V IPC is specified in SUSv3 and supported on nearly every UNIX implementation. By contrast, each of the POSIX IPC mechanisms is an optional component in SUSv3. Some UNIX implementations don't support (all of) the POSIX IPC mechanisms. This situation is reflected in microcosm on

Linux: POSIX shared memory is supported only since kernel 2.4; a full implementation of POSIX semaphores is available only since kernel 2.6; and POSIX message queues are supported only since kernel 2.6.6.

- Despite the SUSv3 specification for POSIX IPC object names, the various implementations follow different conventions for naming IPC objects. These differences require us to do (a little) extra work to write portable applications.

- Various details of POSIX IPC are not specified in SUSv3. In particular, no commands are specified for displaying and deleting the IPC objects that exist on a system. (In many implementations, standard file-system commands are used, but the details of the pathnames used to identify IPC objects vary.)

51.3 Summary

POSIX IPC is the general name given to three IPC mechanisms—message queues, semaphores, and shared memory—that were devised by POSIX.1b as alternatives to the analogous System V IPC mechanisms.

The POSIX IPC interface is more consistent with the traditional UNIX file model. IPC objects are identified by names, and managed using *open*, *close*, and *unlink* calls that operate in a manner similar to the analogous file-related system calls.

POSIX IPC provides an interface that is superior in many respects to the System V IPC interface. However, POSIX IPC is somewhat less portable than System V IPC.

52

POSIX MESSAGE QUEUES

This chapter describes POSIX message queues, which allow processes to exchange data in the form of messages. POSIX message queues are similar to their System V counterparts, in that data is exchanged in units of whole messages. However, there are also some notable differences:

- POSIX message queues are reference counted. A queue that is marked for deletion is removed only after it is closed by all processes that are currently using it.
- Each System V message has an integer type, and messages can be selected in a variety of ways using *msgrcv()*. By contrast, POSIX messages have an associated priority, and messages are always strictly queued (and thus received) in priority order.
- POSIX message queues provide a feature that allows a process to be asynchronously notified when a message is available on a queue.

POSIX message queues are a relatively recent addition to Linux. The required implementation support was added in kernel 2.6.6 (in addition, *glibc* 2.3.4 or later is required).

> POSIX message queue support is an optional kernel component that is configured via the CONFIG_POSIX_MQUEUE option.

52.1 Overview

The main functions in the POSIX message queue API are the following:

- The *mq_open()* function creates a new message queue or opens an existing queue, returning a message queue descriptor for use in later calls.
- The *mq_send()* function writes a message to a queue.
- The *mq_receive()* function reads a message from a queue.
- The *mq_close()* function closes a message queue that the process previously opened.
- The *mq_unlink()* function removes a message queue name and marks the queue for deletion when all processes have closed it.

The above functions all serve fairly obvious purposes. In addition, a couple of features are peculiar to the POSIX message queue API:

- Each message queue has an associated set of attributes. Some of these attributes can be set when the queue is created or opened using *mq_open()*. Two functions are provided to retrieve and change queue attributes: *mq_getattr()* and *mq_setattr()*.
- The *mq_notify()* function allows a process to register for message notification from a queue. After registering, the process is notified of the availability of a message by delivery of a signal or by the invocation of a function in a separate thread.

52.2 Opening, Closing, and Unlinking a Message Queue

In this section, we look at the functions used to open, close, and remove message queues.

Opening a message queue

The *mq_open()* function creates a new message queue or opens an existing queue.

```
#include <fcntl.h>          /* Defines O_* constants */
#include <sys/stat.h>       /* Defines mode constants */
#include <mqueue.h>

mqd_t mq_open(const char *name, int oflag, ...
              /* mode_t mode, struct mq_attr *attr */);
              Returns a message queue descriptor on success, or (mqd_t) -1 on error
```

The *name* argument identifies the message queue, and is specified according to the rules given in Section 51.1.

The *oflag* argument is a bit mask that controls various aspects of the operation of *mq_open()*. The values that can be included in this mask are summarized in Table 52-1.

Table 52-1: Bit values for the *mq_open()* *oflag* argument

Flag	Description
O_CREAT	Create queue if it doesn't already exist
O_EXCL	With O_CREAT, create queue exclusively
O_RDONLY	Open for reading only
O_WRONLY	Open for writing only
O_RDWR	Open for reading and writing
O_NONBLOCK	Open in nonblocking mode

One of the purposes of the *oflag* argument is to determine whether we are opening an existing queue or creating and opening a new queue. If *oflag* doesn't include O_CREAT, we are opening an existing queue. If *oflag* includes O_CREAT, a new, empty queue is created if one with the given *name* doesn't already exist. If *oflag* specifies both O_CREAT and O_EXCL, and a queue with the given *name* already exists, then *mq_open()* fails.

The *oflag* argument also indicates the kind of access that the calling process will make to the message queue, by specifying exactly one of the values O_RDONLY, O_WRONLY, or O_RDWR.

The remaining flag value, O_NONBLOCK, causes the queue to be opened in non-blocking mode. If a subsequent call to *mq_receive()* or *mq_send()* can't be performed without blocking, the call will fail immediately with the error EAGAIN.

If *mq_open()* is being used to open an existing message queue, the call requires only two arguments. However, if O_CREAT is specified in *flags*, two further arguments are required: *mode* and *attr*. (If the queue specified by *name* already exists, these two arguments are ignored.) These arguments are used as follows:

- The *mode* argument is a bit mask that specifies the permissions to be placed on the new message queue. The bit values that may be specified are the same as for files (Table 15-4, on page 295), and, as with *open()*, the value in *mode* is masked against the process umask (Section 15.4.6). To read from a queue (*mq_receive()*), read permission must be granted to the corresponding class of user; to write to a queue (*mq_send()*), write permission is required.

- The *attr* argument is an *mq_attr* structure that specifies attributes for the new message queue. If *attr* is NULL, the queue is created with implementation-defined default attributes. We describe the *mq_attr* structure in Section 52.4.

Upon successful completion, *mq_open()* returns a *message queue descriptor*, a value of type *mqd_t*, which is used in subsequent calls to refer to this open message queue. The only stipulation that SUSv3 makes about this data type is that it may not be an array; that is, it is guaranteed to be a type that can be used in an assignment statement or passed by value as a function argument. (On Linux, *mqd_t* is an *int*, but, for example, on Solaris it is defined as *void **.)

An example of the use of *mq_open()* is provided in Listing 52-2.

Effect of *fork()*, *exec()*, and process termination on message queue descriptors

During a *fork()*, the child process receives copies of its parent's message queue descriptors, and these descriptors refer to the same open message queue descriptions.

(We explain message queue descriptions in Section 52.3.) The child doesn't inherit any of its parent's message notification registrations.

When a process performs an *exec()* or terminates, all of its open message queue descriptors are closed. As a consequence of closing its message queue descriptors, all of the process's message notification registrations on the corresponding queues are deregistered.

Closing a message queue

The *mq_close()* function closes the message queue descriptor *mqdes*.

```
#include <mqueue.h>

int mq_close(mqd_t mqdes);
```
$$\text{Returns 0 on success, or } -1 \text{ on error}$$

If the calling process has registered via *mqdes* for message notification from the queue (Section 52.6), then the notification registration is automatically removed, and another process can subsequently register for message notification from the queue.

A message queue descriptor is automatically closed when a process terminates or calls *exec()*. As with file descriptors, we should explicitly close message queue descriptors that are no longer required, in order to prevent the process from running out of message queue descriptors.

As with *close()* for files, closing a message queue doesn't delete it. For that purpose, we need *mq_unlink()*, which is the message queue analog of *unlink()*.

Removing a message queue

The *mq_unlink()* function removes the message queue identified by *name*, and marks the queue to be destroyed once all processes cease using it (this may mean immediately, if all processes that had the queue open have already closed it).

```
#include <mqueue.h>

int mq_unlink(const char *name);
```
$$\text{Returns 0 on success, or } -1 \text{ on error}$$

Listing 52-1 demonstrates the use of *mq_unlink()*.

Listing 52-1: Using *mq_unlink()* to unlink a POSIX message queue

――――――――――――――――――――――――――――――――― **pmsg/pmsg_unlink.c**
```c
#include <mqueue.h>
#include "tlpi_hdr.h"

int
main(int argc, char *argv[])
{
```

```
        if (argc != 2 || strcmp(argv[1], "--help") == 0)
            usageErr("%s mq-name\n", argv[0]);

        if (mq_unlink(argv[1]) == -1)
            errExit("mq_unlink");
        exit(EXIT_SUCCESS);
    }
```

—— **pmsg/pmsg_unlink.c**

52.3 Relationship Between Descriptors and Message Queues

The relationship between a message queue descriptor and an open message queue
is analogous to the relationship between a file descriptor and an open file (Figure 5-2,
on page 95). A message queue descriptor is a per-process handle that refers to an
entry in the system-wide table of open message queue descriptions, and this entry in
turn refers to a message queue object. This relationship is illustrated in Figure 52-1.

> On Linux, POSIX message queues are implemented as i-nodes in a virtual file
> system, and message queue descriptors and open message queue descriptions
> are implemented as file descriptors and open file descriptions, respectively.
> However, these are implementation details that are not required by SUSv3 and
> don't hold true on some other UNIX implementations. Nevertheless, we
> return to this point in Section 52.7, because Linux provides some nonstandard
> features that are made possible by this implementation.

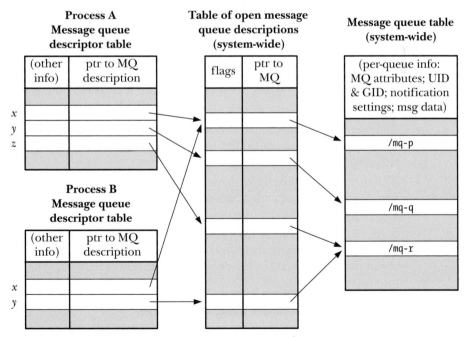

Figure 52-1: Relationship between kernel data structures for POSIX message queues

Figure 52-1 helps clarify a number of details of the use of message queue descriptors (all of which are analogous to the use of file descriptors):

- An open message queue description has an associated set of flags. SUSv3 specifies only one such flag, O_NONBLOCK, which determines whether I/O is nonblocking.

- Two processes can hold message queue descriptors (descriptor *x* in the diagram) that refer to the same open message queue description. This can occur because a process opens a message queue and then calls *fork()*. These descriptors share the state of the O_NONBLOCK flag.

- Two processes can hold open message queue descriptors that refer to different message queue descriptions that refer to the same message queue (e.g., descriptor *z* in process A and descriptor *y* in process B both refer to /mq-r). This occurs because the two processes each used *mq_open()* to open the same queue.

52.4 Message Queue Attributes

The *mq_open()*, *mq_getattr()*, and *mq_setattr()* functions all permit an argument that is a pointer to an *mq_attr* structure. This structure is defined in <mqueue.h> as follows:

```
struct mq_attr {
    long mq_flags;      /* Message queue description flags: 0 or
                           O_NONBLOCK [mq_getattr(), mq_setattr()] */
    long mq_maxmsg;     /* Maximum number of messages on queue
                           [mq_open(), mq_getattr()] */
    long mq_msgsize;    /* Maximum message size (in bytes)
                           [mq_open(), mq_getattr()] */
    long mq_curmsgs;    /* Number of messages currently in queue
                           [mq_getattr()] */
};
```

Before we look at the *mq_attr* structure in detail, it is worth noting the following points:

- Only some of the fields are used by each of the three functions. The fields used by each function are indicated in the comments accompanying the structure definition above.

- The structure contains information about the open message queue description (*mq_flags*) associated with a message queue descriptor and information about the queue referred to by that descriptor (*mq_maxmsg*, *mq_msgsize*, *mq_curmsgs*).

- Some of the fields contain information that is fixed at the time the queue is created with *mq_open()* (*mq_maxmsg* and *mq_msgsize*); the others return information about the current state of the message queue description (*mq_flags*) or message queue (*mq_curmsgs*).

Setting message queue attributes during queue creation

When we create a message queue with *mq_open()*, the following *mq_attr* fields determine the attributes of the queue:

- The *mq_maxmsg* field defines the limit on the number of messages that can be placed on the queue using *mq_send()*. This value must be greater than 0.

- The *mq_msgsize* field defines the upper limit on the size of each message that may be placed on the queue. This value must be greater than 0.

Together, these two values allow the kernel to determine the maximum amount of memory that this message queue may require.

The *mq_maxmsg* and *mq_msgsize* attributes are fixed when a message queue is created; they can't subsequently be changed. In Section 52.8, we describe two /proc files that place system-wide limits on the values that can be specified for the *mq_maxmsg* and *mq_msgsize* attributes.

The program in Listing 52-2 provides a command-line interface to the *mq_open()* function and shows how the *mq_attr* structure is used with *mq_open()*.

Two command-line options allow message queue attributes to be specified: *−m* for *mq_maxmsg* and *−s* for *mq_msgsize*. If either of these options is supplied, a non-NULL *attrp* argument is passed to *mq_open()*. Some default values are assigned to the fields of the *mq_attr* structure to which *attrp* points, in case only one of the *−m* and *−s* options is specified on the command line. If neither of these options is supplied, *attrp* is specified as NULL when calling *mq_open()*, which causes the queue to be created with the implementation-defined defaults for the queue attributes.

Listing 52-2: Creating a POSIX message queue

── **pmsg/pmsg_create.c**

```
#include <mqueue.h>
#include <sys/stat.h>
#include <fcntl.h>
#include "tlpi_hdr.h"

static void
usageError(const char *progName)
{
    fprintf(stderr, "Usage: %s [-cx] [-m maxmsg] [-s msgsize] mq-name "
            "[octal-perms]\n", progName);
    fprintf(stderr, "    -c          Create queue (O_CREAT)\n");
    fprintf(stderr, "    -m maxmsg   Set maximum # of messages\n");
    fprintf(stderr, "    -s msgsize  Set maximum message size\n");
    fprintf(stderr, "    -x          Create exclusively (O_EXCL)\n");
    exit(EXIT_FAILURE);
}

int
main(int argc, char *argv[])
{
    int flags, opt;
    mode_t perms;
    mqd_t mqd;
    struct mq_attr attr, *attrp;

    attrp = NULL;
    attr.mq_maxmsg = 10;
    attr.mq_msgsize = 2048;
    flags = O_RDWR;
```

```
            /* Parse command-line options */

        while ((opt = getopt(argc, argv, "cm:s:x")) != -1) {
            switch (opt) {
            case 'c':
                flags |= O_CREAT;
                break;

            case 'm':
                attr.mq_maxmsg = atoi(optarg);
                attrp = &attr;
                break;

            case 's':
                attr.mq_msgsize = atoi(optarg);
                attrp = &attr;
                break;

            case 'x':
                flags |= O_EXCL;
                break;

            default:
                usageError(argv[0]);
            }
        }

        if (optind >= argc)
            usageError(argv[0]);

        perms = (argc <= optind + 1) ? (S_IRUSR | S_IWUSR) :
                    getInt(argv[optind + 1], GN_BASE_8, "octal-perms");

        mqd = mq_open(argv[optind], flags, perms, attrp);
        if (mqd == (mqd_t) -1)
            errExit("mq_open");

        exit(EXIT_SUCCESS);
    }
```

—— pmsg/pmsg_create.c

Retrieving message queue attributes

The *mq_getattr()* function returns an *mq_attr* structure containing information
about the message queue description and the message queue associated with the
descriptor *mqdes*.

```
#include <mqueue.h>

int mq_getattr(mqd_t mqdes, struct mq_attr *attr);
```
                                            Returns 0 on success, or −1 on error

In addition to the *mq_maxmsg* and *mq_msgsize* fields, which we have already described, the following fields are returned in the structure pointed to by *attr*:

mq_flags

These are flags for the open message queue description associated with the descriptor *mqdes*. Only one such flag is specified: O_NONBLOCK. This flag is initialized from the *oflag* argument of *mq_open()*, and can be changed using *mq_setattr()*.

mq_curmsgs

This is the number of messages that are currently in the queue. This information may already have changed by the time *mq_getattr()* returns, if other processes are reading messages from the queue or writing messages to it.

The program in Listing 52-3 employs *mq_getattr()* to retrieve the attributes for the message queue specified in its command-line argument, and then displays those attributes on standard output.

Listing 52-3: Retrieving POSIX message queue attributes

─── pmsg/pmsg_getattr.c
```
#include <mqueue.h>
#include "tlpi_hdr.h"

int
main(int argc, char *argv[])
{
    mqd_t mqd;
    struct mq_attr attr;

    if (argc != 2 || strcmp(argv[1], "--help") == 0)
        usageErr("%s mq-name\n", argv[0]);

    mqd = mq_open(argv[1], O_RDONLY);
    if (mqd == (mqd_t) -1)
        errExit("mq_open");

    if (mq_getattr(mqd, &attr) == -1)
        errExit("mq_getattr");

    printf("Maximum # of messages on queue:  %ld\n", attr.mq_maxmsg);
    printf("Maximum message size:            %ld\n", attr.mq_msgsize);
    printf("# of messages currently on queue: %ld\n", attr.mq_curmsgs);
    exit(EXIT_SUCCESS);
}
```
─── pmsg/pmsg_getattr.c

In the following shell session, we use the program in Listing 52-2 to create a message queue with implementation-defined default attributes (i.e., the final argument to *mq_open()* is NULL), and then use the program in Listing 52-3 to display the queue attributes so that we can see the default settings on Linux.

```
$ ./pmsg_create -cx /mq
$ ./pmsg_getattr /mq
Maximum # of messages on queue:    10
Maximum message size:              8192
# of messages currently on queue: 0
$ ./pmsg_unlink /mq                          Remove message queue
```

From the above output, we see that the Linux default values for *mq_maxmsg* and *mq_msgsize* are 10 and 8192, respectively.

There is a wide variation in the implementation-defined defaults for *mq_maxmsg* and *mq_msgsize*. Portable applications generally need to choose explicit values for these attributes, rather than relying on the defaults.

Modifying message queue attributes

The *mq_setattr()* function sets attributes of the message queue description associated with the message queue descriptor *mqdes*, and optionally returns information about the message queue.

```
#include <mqueue.h>

int mq_setattr(mqd_t mqdes, const struct mq_attr *newattr,
               struct mq_attr *oldattr);
```
                                        Returns 0 on success, or −1 on error

The *mq_setattr()* function performs the following tasks:

- It uses the *mq_flags* field in the *mq_attr* structure pointed to by *newattr* to change the flags of the message queue description associated with the descriptor *mqdes*.

- If *oldattr* is non-NULL, it returns an *mq_attr* structure containing the previous message queue description flags and message queue attributes (i.e., the same task as is performed by *mq_getattr()*).

The only attribute that SUSv3 specifies that can be changed using *mq_setattr()* is the state of the O_NONBLOCK flag.

Allowing for the possibility that a particular implementation may define other modifiable flags, or that SUSv3 may add new flags in the future, a portable application should change the state of the O_NONBLOCK flag by using *mq_getattr()* to retrieve the *mq_flags* value, modifying the O_NONBLOCK bit, and calling *mq_setattr()* to change the *mq_flags* settings. For example, to enable O_NONBLOCK, we would do the following:

```
if (mq_getattr(mqd, &attr) == -1)
    errExit("mq_getattr");
attr.mq_flags |= O_NONBLOCK;
if (mq_setattr(mqd, &attr, NULL) == -1)
    errExit("mq_setattr");
```

52.5 Exchanging Messages

In this section, we look at the functions that are used to send messages to and receive messages from a queue.

52.5.1 Sending Messages

The *mq_send()* function adds the message in the buffer pointed to by *msg_ptr* to the message queue referred to by the descriptor *mqdes*.

```
#include <mqueue.h>

int mq_send(mqd_t mqdes, const char *msg_ptr, size_t msg_len,
            unsigned int msg_prio);
```
Returns 0 on success, or −1 on error

The *msg_len* argument specifies the length of the message pointed to by *msg_ptr*. This value must be less than or equal to the *mq_msgsize* attribute of the queue; otherwise, *mq_send()* fails with the error EMSGSIZE. Zero-length messages are permitted.

Each message has a nonnegative integer priority, specified by the *msg_prio* argument. Messages are ordered within the queue in descending order of priority (i.e., 0 is the lowest priority). When a new message is added to the queue, it is placed after any other messages of the same priority. If an application doesn't need to use message priorities, it is sufficient to always specify *msg_prio* as 0.

> As noted at the beginning of this chapter, the type attribute of System V messages provides different functionality. System V messages are always queued in FIFO order, but *msgrcv()* allows us to select messages in various ways: in FIFO order, by exact type, or by highest type less than or equal to some value.

SUSv3 allows an implementation to advertise its upper limit for message priorities, either by defining the constant MQ_PRIO_MAX or via the return from *sysconf(_SC_MQ_PRIO_MAX)*. SUSv3 requires this limit to be at least 32 (_POSIX_MQ_PRIO_MAX); that is, priorities at least in the range 0 to 31 are available. However, the actual range on implementations is highly variable. For example, on Linux, this constant has the value 32,768; on Solaris, it is 32; and on Tru64, it is 256.

If the message queue is already full (i.e., the *mq_maxmsg* limit for the queue has been reached), then a further *mq_send()* either blocks until space becomes available in the queue, or, if the O_NONBLOCK flag is in effect, fails immediately with the error EAGAIN.

The program in Listing 52-4 provides a command-line interface to the *mq_send()* function. We demonstrate the use of this program in the next section.

Listing 52-4: Writing a message to a POSIX message queue

———————————————————————————— pmsg/pmsg_send.c

```c
#include <mqueue.h>
#include <fcntl.h>                    /* For definition of O_NONBLOCK */
#include "tlpi_hdr.h"

static void
usageError(const char *progName)
{
    fprintf(stderr, "Usage: %s [-n] name msg [prio]\n", progName);
    fprintf(stderr, "    -n          Use O_NONBLOCK flag\n");
    exit(EXIT_FAILURE);
}

int
main(int argc, char *argv[])
{
    int flags, opt;
    mqd_t mqd;
    unsigned int prio;

    flags = O_WRONLY;
    while ((opt = getopt(argc, argv, "n")) != -1) {
        switch (opt) {
        case 'n':   flags |= O_NONBLOCK;         break;
        default:    usageError(argv[0]);
        }
    }

    if (optind + 1 >= argc)
        usageError(argv[0]);

    mqd = mq_open(argv[optind], flags);
    if (mqd == (mqd_t) -1)
        errExit("mq_open");

    prio = (argc > optind + 2) ? atoi(argv[optind + 2]) : 0;

    if (mq_send(mqd, argv[optind + 1], strlen(argv[optind + 1]), prio) == -1)
        errExit("mq_send");
    exit(EXIT_SUCCESS);
}
```

———————————————————————————— pmsg/pmsg_send.c

52.5.2 Receiving Messages

The *mq_receive()* function removes the oldest message with the highest priority from the message queue referred to by *mqdes* and returns that message in the buffer pointed to by *msg_ptr*.

```
#include <mqueue.h>

ssize_t mq_receive(mqd_t mqdes, char *msg_ptr, size_t msg_len,
                   unsigned int *msg_prio);
```
              Returns number of bytes in received message on success, or –1 on error

The *msg_len* argument is used by the caller to specify the number of bytes of space available in the buffer pointed to by *msg_ptr*.

Regardless of the actual size of the message, *msg_len* (and thus the size of the buffer pointed to by *msg_ptr*) must be greater than or equal to the *mq_msgsize* attribute of the queue; otherwise, *mq_receive()* fails with the error EMSGSIZE. If we don't know the value of the *mq_msgsize* attribute of a queue, we can obtain it using *mq_getattr()*. (In an application consisting of cooperating processes, the use of *mq_getattr()* can usually be dispensed with, because the application can typically decide on a queue's *mq_msgsize* setting in advance.)

If *msg_prio* is not NULL, then the priority of the received message is copied into the location pointed to by *msg_prio*.

If the message queue is currently empty, then *mq_receive()* either blocks until a message becomes available, or, if the O_NONBLOCK flag is in effect, fails immediately with the error EAGAIN. (There is no equivalent of the pipe behavior where a reader sees end-of-file if there are no writers.)

The program in Listing 52-5 provides a command-line interface to the *mq_receive()* function. The command format for this program is shown in the *usageError()* function.

The following shell session demonstrates the use of the programs in Listing 52-4 and Listing 52-5. We begin by creating a message queue and sending a few messages with different priorities:

```
$ ./pmsg_create -cx /mq
$ ./pmsg_send /mq msg-a 5
$ ./pmsg_send /mq msg-b 0
$ ./pmsg_send /mq msg-c 10
```

We then execute a series of commands to retrieve messages from the queue:

```
$ ./pmsg_receive /mq
Read 5 bytes; priority = 10
msg-c
$ ./pmsg_receive /mq
Read 5 bytes; priority = 5
msg-a
$ ./pmsg_receive /mq
Read 5 bytes; priority = 0
msg-b
```

As we can see from the above output, the messages were retrieved in order of priority.

At this point, the queue is now empty. When we perform another blocking receive, the operation blocks:

```
$ ./pmsg_receive /mq
```
Blocks; we type Control-C to terminate the program

On the other hand, if we perform a nonblocking receive, the call returns immediately with a failure status:

```
$ ./pmsg_receive -n /mq
ERROR [EAGAIN/EWOULDBLOCK Resource temporarily unavailable] mq_receive
```

Listing 52-5: Reading a message from a POSIX message queue

—— pmsg/pmsg_receive.c
```c
#include <mqueue.h>
#include <fcntl.h>              /* For definition of O_NONBLOCK */
#include "tlpi_hdr.h"

static void
usageError(const char *progName)
{
    fprintf(stderr, "Usage: %s [-n] name\n", progName);
    fprintf(stderr, "    -n          Use O_NONBLOCK flag\n");
    exit(EXIT_FAILURE);
}

int
main(int argc, char *argv[])
{
    int flags, opt;
    mqd_t mqd;
    unsigned int prio;
    void *buffer;
    struct mq_attr attr;
    ssize_t numRead;

    flags = O_RDONLY;
    while ((opt = getopt(argc, argv, "n")) != -1) {
        switch (opt) {
        case 'n':   flags |= O_NONBLOCK;        break;
        default:    usageError(argv[0]);
        }
    }

    if (optind >= argc)
        usageError(argv[0]);

    mqd = mq_open(argv[optind], flags);
    if (mqd == (mqd_t) -1)
        errExit("mq_open");

    if (mq_getattr(mqd, &attr) == -1)
        errExit("mq_getattr");

    buffer = malloc(attr.mq_msgsize);
    if (buffer == NULL)
        errExit("malloc");
```

```
    numRead = mq_receive(mqd, buffer, attr.mq_msgsize, &prio);
    if (numRead == -1)
        errExit("mq_receive");

    printf("Read %ld bytes; priority = %u\n", (long) numRead, prio);
    if (write(STDOUT_FILENO, buffer, numRead) == -1)
        errExit("write");
    write(STDOUT_FILENO, "\n", 1);

    exit(EXIT_SUCCESS);
}
```
_____ **pmsg/pmsg_receive.c**

52.5.3   Sending and Receiving Messages with a Timeout

The *mq_timedsend()* and *mq_timedreceive()* functions are exactly like *mq_send()* and *mq_receive()*, except that if the operation can't be performed immediately, and the O_NONBLOCK flag is not in effect for the message queue description, then the *abs_timeout* argument specifies a limit on the time for which the call will block.

```
#include <mqueue.h>
#include <time.h>

int mq_timedsend(mqd_t mqdes, const char *msg_ptr, size_t msg_len,
                 unsigned int msg_prio, const struct timespec *abs_timeout);
```
                                              Returns 0 on success, or −1 on error
```
ssize_t mq_timedreceive(mqd_t mqdes, char *msg_ptr, size_t msg_len,
                 unsigned int *msg_prio, const struct timespec *abs_timeout);
```
              Returns number of bytes in received message on success, or −1 on error

---

The *abs_timeout* argument is a *timespec* structure (Section 23.4.2) that specifies the timeout as an absolute value in seconds and nanoseconds since the Epoch. To perform a relative timeout, we can fetch the current value of the CLOCK_REALTIME clock using *clock_gettime()* and add the required amount to that value to produce a suitably initialized *timespec* structure.

If a call to *mq_timedsend()* or *mq_timedreceive()* times out without being able to complete its operation, then the call fails with the error ETIMEDOUT.

On Linux, specifying *abs_timeout* as NULL means an infinite timeout. However, this behavior is not specified in SUSv3, and portable applications can't rely on it.

The *mq_timedsend()* and *mq_timedreceive()* functions originally derive from POSIX.1d (1999) and are not available on all UNIX implementations.

52.6   Message Notification

A feature that distinguishes POSIX message queues from their System V counterparts is the ability to receive asynchronous notification of the availability of a message on a previously empty queue (i.e., when the queue transitions from being empty to nonempty). This feature means that instead of making a blocking *mq_receive()* call or marking the message queue descriptor nonblocking and performing periodic *mq_receive()* calls ("polls") on the queue, a process can request a notification of message arrival and then perform other tasks until it is notified. A process can choose to be notified either via a signal or via invocation of a function in a separate thread.

> The notification feature of POSIX message queues is similar to the notification facility that we described for POSIX timers in Section 23.6. (Both of these APIs originated in POSIX.1b.)

The *mq_notify()* function registers the calling process to receive a notification when a message arrives on the empty queue referred to by the descriptor *mqdes*.

```
#include <mqueue.h>

int mq_notify(mqd_t mqdes, const struct sigevent *notification);
```
                                         Returns 0 on success, or –1 on error

The *notification* argument specifies the mechanism by which the process is to be notified. Before going into the details of the *notification* argument, we note a few points about message notification:

- At any time, only one process ("the registered process") can be registered to receive a notification from a particular message queue. If there is already a process registered for a message queue, further attempts to register for that queue fail (*mq_notify()* fails with the error EBUSY).
- The registered process is notified only when a new message arrives on a queue that was previously empty. If a queue already contains messages at the time of the registration, a notification will occur only after the queue is emptied and a new message arrives.
- After one notification is sent to the registered process, the registration is removed, and any process can then register itself for notification. In other words, as long as a process wishes to keep receiving notifications, it must reregister itself after each notification by once again calling *mq_notify()*.
- The registered process is notified only if some other process is not currently blocked in a call to *mq_receive()* for the queue. If some other process is blocked in *mq_receive()*, that process will read the message, and the registered process will remain registered.
- A process can explicitly deregister itself as the target for message notification by calling *mq_notify()* with a *notification* argument of NULL.

We already showed the *sigevent* structure that is used to type the *notification* argument in Section 23.6.1. Here, we present the structure in simplified form, showing just those fields relevant to the discussion of *mq_notify()*:

```
union sigval {
    int     sival_int;          /* Integer value for accompanying data */
    void   *sival_ptr;          /* Pointer value for accompanying data */
};
```

```
struct sigevent {
    int     sigev_notify;       /* Notification method */
    int     sigev_signo;        /* Notification signal for SIGEV_SIGNAL */
    union sigval sigev_value;   /* Value passed to signal handler or
                                   thread function */
    void (*sigev_notify_function) (union sigval);
                                /* Thread notification function */
    void *sigev_notify_attributes;   /* Really 'pthread_attr_t *' */
};
```

The *sigev_notify* field of this structure is set to one of the following values:

SIGEV_NONE

> Register this process for notification, but when a message arrives on the previously empty queue, don't actually notify the process. As usual, the registration is removed when a new message arrives on an empty queue.

SIGEV_SIGNAL

> Notify the process by generating the signal specified in the *sigev_signo* field. The *sigev_value* field specifies data to accompany the signal (Section 22.8.1). This data can be retrieved via the *si_value* field of the *siginfo_t* structure that is passed to the signal handler or returned by a call to *sigwaitinfo()* or *sigtimedwait()*. The following fields in the *siginfo_t* structure are also filled in: *si_code*, with the value SI_MESGQ; *si_signo*, with the signal number; *si_pid*, with the process ID of the process that sent the message; and *si_uid*, with the real user ID of the process that sent the message. (The *si_pid* and *si_uid* fields are not set on most other implementations.)

SIGEV_THREAD

> Notify the process by calling the function specified in *sigev_notify_function* as if it were the start function in a new thread. The *sigev_notify_attributes* field can be specified as NULL or as a pointer to a *pthread_attr_t* structure that defines attributes for the thread (Section 29.8). The union *sigval* value specified in *sigev_value* is passed as the argument of this function.

52.6.1 Receiving Notification via a Signal

Listing 52-6 provides an example of message notification using signals. This program performs the following steps:

1. Open the message queue named on the command line in nonblocking mode ①, determine the *mq_msgsize* attribute for the queue ②, and allocate a buffer of that size for receiving messages ③.

2. Block the notification signal (SIGUSR1) and establish a handler for it ④.

3. Make an initial call to *mq_notify()* to register the process to receive message notification ⑤.

4. Execute an infinite loop that performs the following steps:

    a) Call *sigsuspend()*, which unblocks the notification signal and waits until the signal is caught ⑥. Return from this system call indicates that a message

notification has occurred. At this point, the process will have been deregistered for message notification.

b) Call *mq_notify()* to reregister this process to receive message notification ⑦.

c) Execute a while loop that drains the queue by reading as many messages as possible ⑧.

Listing 52-6: Receiving message notification via a signal

—————————————————————————————————— pmsg/mq_notify_sig.c
```c
#include <signal.h>
#include <mqueue.h>
#include <fcntl.h>                    /* For definition of O_NONBLOCK */
#include "tlpi_hdr.h"

#define NOTIFY_SIG SIGUSR1

static void
handler(int sig)
{
    /* Just interrupt sigsuspend() */
}

int
main(int argc, char *argv[])
{
    struct sigevent sev;
    mqd_t mqd;
    struct mq_attr attr;
    void *buffer;
    ssize_t numRead;
    sigset_t blockMask, emptyMask;
    struct sigaction sa;

    if (argc != 2 || strcmp(argv[1], "--help") == 0)
        usageErr("%s mq-name\n", argv[0]);

①  mqd = mq_open(argv[1], O_RDONLY | O_NONBLOCK);
    if (mqd == (mqd_t) -1)
        errExit("mq_open");

②  if (mq_getattr(mqd, &attr) == -1)
        errExit("mq_getattr");

③  buffer = malloc(attr.mq_msgsize);
    if (buffer == NULL)
        errExit("malloc");

④  sigemptyset(&blockMask);
    sigaddset(&blockMask, NOTIFY_SIG);
    if (sigprocmask(SIG_BLOCK, &blockMask, NULL) == -1)
        errExit("sigprocmask");
```

```
        sigemptyset(&sa.sa_mask);
        sa.sa_flags = 0;
        sa.sa_handler = handler;
        if (sigaction(NOTIFY_SIG, &sa, NULL) == -1)
            errExit("sigaction");

⑤       sev.sigev_notify = SIGEV_SIGNAL;
        sev.sigev_signo = NOTIFY_SIG;
        if (mq_notify(mqd, &sev) == -1)
            errExit("mq_notify");

        sigemptyset(&emptyMask);

        for (;;) {
⑥          sigsuspend(&emptyMask);            /* Wait for notification signal */

⑦          if (mq_notify(mqd, &sev) == -1)
                errExit("mq_notify");

⑧          while ((numRead = mq_receive(mqd, buffer, attr.mq_msgsize, NULL)) >= 0)
                printf("Read %ld bytes\n", (long) numRead);

            if (errno != EAGAIN)               /* Unexpected error */
                errExit("mq_receive");
        }
    }
```
── **pmsg/mq_notify_sig.c**

Various aspects of the program in Listing 52-6 merit further comment:

- We block the notification signal and use *sigsuspend()* to wait for it, rather than *pause()*, to prevent the possibility of missing a signal that is delivered while the program is executing elsewhere (i.e., is not blocked waiting for signals) in the for loop. If this occurred, and we were using *pause()* to wait for signals, then the next call to *pause()* would block, even though a signal had already been delivered.

- We open the queue in nonblocking mode, and, whenever a notification occurs, we use a while loop to read all messages from the queue. Emptying the queue in this way ensures that a further notification is generated when a new message arrives. Employing nonblocking mode means that the while loop will terminate (*mq_receive()* will fail with the error EAGAIN) when we have emptied the queue. (This approach is analogous to the use of nonblocking I/O with edge-triggered I/O notification, which we describe in Section 63.1.1, and is employed for similar reasons.)

- Within the for loop, it is important that we reregister for message notification *before* reading all messages from the queue. If we reversed these steps, the following sequence could occur: all messages are read from the queue, and the while loop terminates; another message is placed on the queue; *mq_notify()* is called to reregister for message notification. At this point, no further notification signal would be generated, because the queue is already nonempty. Consequently, the program would remain permanently blocked in its next call to *sigsuspend()*.

52.6.2 Receiving Notification via a Thread

Listing 52-7 provides an example of message notification using threads. This program shares a number of design features with the program in Listing 52-6:

- When message notification occurs, the program reenables notification before draining the queue ②.

- Nonblocking mode is employed so that, after receiving a notification, we can completely drain the queue without blocking ⑤.

Listing 52-7: Receiving message notification via a thread

————————————————————————————————— **pmsg/mq_notify_thread.c**

```
#include <pthread.h>
#include <mqueue.h>
#include <signal.h>
#include <fcntl.h>                    /* For definition of O_NONBLOCK */
#include "tlpi_hdr.h"

static void notifySetup(mqd_t *mqdp);

static void                          /* Thread notification function */
① threadFunc(union sigval sv)
{
    ssize_t numRead;
    mqd_t *mqdp;
    void *buffer;
    struct mq_attr attr;

    mqdp = sv.sival_ptr;

    if (mq_getattr(*mqdp, &attr) == -1)
        errExit("mq_getattr");

    buffer = malloc(attr.mq_msgsize);
    if (buffer == NULL)
        errExit("malloc");

②     notifySetup(mqdp);

    while ((numRead = mq_receive(*mqdp, buffer, attr.mq_msgsize, NULL)) >= 0)
        printf("Read %ld bytes\n", (long) numRead);

    if (errno != EAGAIN)                          /* Unexpected error */
        errExit("mq_receive");

    free(buffer);
}

static void
notifySetup(mqd_t *mqdp)
{
    struct sigevent sev;
```

```
③      sev.sigev_notify = SIGEV_THREAD;            /* Notify via thread */
       sev.sigev_notify_function = threadFunc;
       sev.sigev_notify_attributes = NULL;
               /* Could be pointer to pthread_attr_t structure */
④      sev.sigev_value.sival_ptr = mqdp;          /* Argument to threadFunc() */

       if (mq_notify(*mqdp, &sev) == -1)
           errExit("mq_notify");
   }

   int
   main(int argc, char *argv[])
   {
       mqd_t mqd;

       if (argc != 2 || strcmp(argv[1], "--help") == 0)
           usageErr("%s mq-name\n", argv[0]);

⑤      mqd = mq_open(argv[1], O_RDONLY | O_NONBLOCK);
       if (mqd == (mqd_t) -1)
           errExit("mq_open");

⑥      notifySetup(&mqd);
       pause();                       /* Wait for notifications via thread function */
   }
```

——— **pmsg/mq_notify_thread.c**

Note the following further points regarding the design of the program in Listing 52-7:

- The program requests notification via a thread, by specifying SIGEV_THREAD in the *sigev_notify* field of the *sigevent* structure passed to *mq_notify()*. The thread's start function, *threadFunc()*, is specified in the *sigev_notify_function* field ③.

- After enabling message notification, the main program pauses indefinitely ⑥; message notifications are delivered by invocations of *threadFunc()* in a separate thread ①.

- We could have made the message queue descriptor, *mqd*, visible in *threadFunc()* by making it a global variable. However, we adopted a different approach to illustrate the alternative: we place the address of the message queue descriptor in the *sigev_value.sival_ptr* field that is passed to *mq_notify()* ④. When *threadFunc()* is later invoked, this address is passed as its argument.

> We must assign a pointer to the message queue descriptor to *sigev_value.sival_ptr*, rather than (some cast version of) the descriptor itself because, other than the stipulation that it is not an array type, SUSv3 makes no guarantee about the nature or size of the type used to represent the *mqd_t* data type.

52.7 Linux-Specific Features

The Linux implementation of POSIX message queues provides a number of features that are unstandardized but nevertheless useful.

Displaying and deleting message queue objects via the command line

In Chapter 51, we mentioned that POSIX IPC objects are implemented as files in virtual file systems, and that these files can be listed and removed with *ls* and *rm*. In order to do this with POSIX message queues, we must mount the message queue file system using a command of the following form:

```
# mount -t mqueue source target
```

The *source* can be any name at all (specifying the string *none* is typical). Its only significance is that it appears in /proc/mounts and is displayed by the *mount* and *df* commands. The *target* is the mount point for the message queue file system.

The following shell session shows how to mount the message queue file system and display its contents. We begin by creating a mount point for the file system and mounting it:

```
$ su                                    Privilege is required for mount
Password:
# mkdir /dev/mqueue
# mount -t mqueue none /dev/mqueue
# exit                                  Terminate root shell session
```

Next, we display the record in /proc/mounts for the new mount, and then display the permissions for the mount directory:

```
$ cat /proc/mounts | grep mqueue
none /dev/mqueue mqueue rw 0 0
$ ls -ld /dev/mqueue
drwxrwxrwt  2 root root 40 Jul 26 12:09 /dev/mqueue
```

One point to note from the output of the *ls* command is that the message queue file system is automatically mounted with the sticky bit set for the mount directory. (We see this from the fact that there is a *t* in the other-execute permission field displayed by *ls*.) This means that an unprivileged process can unlink only message queues that it owns.

Next, we create a message queue, use *ls* to show that it is visible in the file system, and then delete the message queue:

```
$ ./pmsg_create -c /newq
$ ls /dev/mqueue
newq
$ rm /dev/mqueue/newq
```

Obtaining information about a message queue

We can display the contents of the files in the message queue file system. Each of these virtual files contains information about the associated message queue:

```
$ ./pmsg_create -c /mq                  Create a queue
$ ./pmsg_send /mq abcdefg               Write 7 bytes to the queue
$ cat /dev/mqueue/mq
QSIZE:7      NOTIFY:0   SIGNO:0    NOTIFY_PID:0
```

The QSIZE field is a count of the total number of bytes of data in the queue. The remaining fields relate to message notification. If NOTIFY_PID is nonzero, then the process with the specified process ID has registered for message notification from this queue, and the remaining fields provide information about the kind of notification:

- NOTIFY is a value corresponding to one of the *sigev_notify* constants: 0 for SIGEV_SIGNAL, 1 for SIGEV_NONE, or 2 for SIGEV_THREAD.

- If the notification method is SIGEV_SIGNAL, the SIGNO field indicates which signal is delivered for message notification.

The following shell session illustrates the information that appears in these fields:

```
$ ./mq_notify_sig /mq &              Notify using SIGUSR1 (signal 10 on x86)
[1] 18158
$ cat /dev/mqueue/mq
QSIZE:7       NOTIFY:0    SIGNO:10   NOTIFY_PID:18158
$ kill %1
[1]   Terminated   ./mq_notify_sig /mq
$ ./mq_notify_thread /mq &           Notify using a thread
[2] 18160
$ cat /dev/mqueue/mq
QSIZE:7       NOTIFY:2    SIGNO:0    NOTIFY_PID:18160
```

Using message queues with alternative I/O models

In the Linux implementation, a message queue descriptor is really a file descriptor. We can monitor this file descriptor using I/O multiplexing system calls (*select()* and *poll()*) or the *epoll* API. (See Chapter 63 for further details of these APIs.) This allows us to avoid the difficulty that we encounter with System V messages queues when trying to wait for input on both a message queue and a file descriptor (refer to Section 46.9). However, this feature is nonstandard; SUSv3 doesn't require that message queue descriptors are implemented as file descriptors.

52.8 Message Queue Limits

SUSv3 defines two limits for POSIX message queues:

MQ_PRIO_MAX

> We described this limit, which defines the maximum priority for a message, in Section 52.5.1.

MQ_OPEN_MAX

> An implementation can define this limit to indicate the maximum number of message queues that a process can hold open. SUSv3 requires this limit to be at least _POSIX_MQ_OPEN_MAX (8). Linux doesn't define this limit. Instead, because Linux implements message queue descriptors as file descriptors (Section 52.7), the applicable limits are those that apply to file descriptors. (In other words, on Linux, the per-process and system-wide limits on the number of file descriptors actually apply to the sum of file descriptors and message queue descriptors.) For further details on the applicable limits, see the discussion of the RLIMIT_NOFILE resource limit in Section 36.3.

As well as the above SUSv3-specified limits, Linux provides a number of /proc files for viewing and (with privilege) changing limits that control the use of POSIX message queues. The following three files reside in the directory /proc/sys/fs/mqueue:

msg_max

> This limit specifies a ceiling for the *mq_maxmsg* attribute of new message queues (i.e., a ceiling for *attr.mq_maxmsg* when creating a queue with *mq_open()*). The default value for this limit is 10. The minimum value is 1 (10 in kernels before Linux 2.6.28). The maximum value is defined by the kernel constant HARD_MSGMAX. The value for this constant is calculated as (131,072 / *sizeof(void *)*), which evaluates to 32,768 on Linux/x86-32. When a privileged process (CAP_SYS_RESOURCE) calls *mq_open()*, the msg_max limit is ignored, but HARD_MSGMAX still acts as a ceiling for *attr.mq_maxmsg*.

msgsize_max

> This limit specifies a ceiling for the *mq_msgsize* attribute of new message queues created by unprivileged processes (i.e., a ceiling for *attr.mq_msgsize* when creating a queue with *mq_open()*). The default value for this limit is 8192. The minimum value is 128 (8192 in kernels before Linux 2.6.28). The maximum value is 1,048,576 (INT_MAX in kernels before 2.6.28). This limit is ignored when a privileged process (CAP_SYS_RESOURCE) calls *mq_open()*.

queues_max

> This is a system-wide limit on the number of message queues that may be created. Once this limit is reached, only a privileged process (CAP_SYS_RESOURCE) can create new queues. The default value for this limit is 256. It can be changed to any value in the range 0 to INT_MAX.

Linux also provides the RLIMIT_MSGQUEUE resource limit, which can be used to place a ceiling on the amount of space that can be consumed by all of the message queues belonging to the real user ID of the calling process. See Section 36.3 for details.

52.9 Comparison of POSIX and System V Message Queues

Section 51.2 listed various advantages of the POSIX IPC interface over the System V IPC interface: the POSIX IPC interface is simpler and more consistent with the traditional UNIX file model, and POSIX IPC objects are reference counted, which simplifies the task of determining when to delete an object. These general advantages also apply to POSIX message queues.

POSIX message queues also have the following specific advantages over System V message queues:

- The message notification feature allows a (single) process to be asynchronously notified via a signal or the instantiation of a thread when a message arrives on a previously empty queue.

- On Linux (but not other UNIX implementations), POSIX message queues can be monitored using *poll()*, *select()*, and *epoll*. System V message queues don't provide this feature.

However, POSIX message queues also have some disadvantages compared to System V message queues:

- POSIX message queues are less portable. This problem applies even across Linux systems, since message queue support is available only since kernel 2.6.6.

- The facility to select System V messages by type provides slightly greater flexibility than the strict priority ordering of POSIX messages.

> There is a wide variation in the manner in which POSIX message queues are implemented on UNIX systems. Some systems provide implementations in user space, and on at least one such implementation (Solaris 10), the *mq_open()* manual page explicitly notes that the implementation can't be considered secure. On Linux, one of the motives for selecting a kernel implementation of message queues was that it was deemed not possible to provide a secure user-space implementation.

52.10 Summary

POSIX message queues allow processes to exchange data in the form of messages. Each message has an associated integer priority, and messages are queued (and thus received) in order of priority.

POSIX message queues have some advantages over System V message queues, notably that they are reference counted and that a process can be asynchronously notified of the arrival of a message on an empty queue. However, POSIX message queues are less portable than System V message queues.

Further information

[Stevens, 1999] provides an alternative presentation of POSIX message queues and shows a user-space implementation using memory-mapped files. POSIX message queues are also described in some detail in [Gallmeister, 1995].

52.11 Exercises

52-1. Modify the program in Listing 52-5 (pmsg_receive.c) to accept a timeout (a relative number of seconds) on the command line, and use *mq_timedreceive()* instead of *mq_receive()*.

52-2. Recode the sequence-number client-server application of Section 44.8 to use POSIX message queues.

52-3. Rewrite the file-server application of Section 46.8 to use POSIX message queues instead of System V message queues.

52-4. Write a simple chat program (similar to *talk(1)*, but without the *curses* interface) using POSIX messages queues.

52-5. Modify the program in Listing 52-6 (mq_notify_sig.c) to demonstrate that message notification established by *mq_notify()* occurs just once. This can be done by removing the *mq_notify()* call inside the for loop.

52-6. Replace the use of a signal handler in Listing 52-6 (`mq_notify_sig.c`) with the use of *sigwaitinfo()*. Upon return from *sigwaitinfo()*, display the values in the returned *siginfo_t* structure. How could the program obtain the message queue descriptor in the *siginfo_t* structure returned by *sigwaitinfo()*?

52-7. In Listing 52-7, could *buffer* be made a global variable and its memory allocated just once (in the main program)? Explain your answer.

53

POSIX SEMAPHORES

This chapter describes POSIX semaphores, which allow processes and threads to synchronize access to shared resources. In Chapter 47, we described System V semaphores, and we'll assume that the reader is familiar with the general semaphore concepts and rationale for using semaphores that were presented at the start of that chapter. During the course of this chapter, we'll make comparisons between POSIX semaphores and System V semaphores to clarify the ways in which these two semaphore APIs are the same and the ways in which they differ.

53.1 Overview

SUSv3 specifies two types of POSIX semaphores:

- *Named semaphores*: This type of semaphore has a name. By calling *sem_open()* with the same name, unrelated processes can access the same semaphore.

- *Unnamed semaphores*: This type of semaphore doesn't have a name; instead, it resides at an agreed-upon location in memory. Unnamed semaphores can be shared between processes or between a group of threads. When shared between processes, the semaphore must reside in a region of (System V, POSIX, or *mmap()*) shared memory. When shared between threads, the semaphore may reside in an area of memory shared by the threads (e.g., on the heap or in a global variable).

POSIX semaphores operate in a manner similar to System V semaphores; that is, a POSIX semaphore is an integer whose value is not permitted to fall below 0. If a process attempts to decrease the value of a semaphore below 0, then, depending on the function used, the call either blocks or fails with an error indicating that the operation was not currently possible.

Some systems don't provide a full implementation of POSIX semaphores. A typical restriction is that only unnamed thread-shared semaphores are supported. That was the situation on Linux 2.4; with Linux 2.6 and a *glibc* that provides NPTL, a full implementation of POSIX semaphores is available.

> On Linux 2.6 with NPTL, semaphore operations (increment and decrement) are implemented using the *futex(2)* system call.

53.2 Named Semaphores

To work with a named semaphore, we employ the following functions:

- The *sem_open()* function opens or creates a semaphore, initializes the semaphore if it is created by the call, and returns a handle for use in later calls.

- The *sem_post()* and *sem_wait()* functions respectively increment and decrement a semaphore's value.

- The *sem_getvalue()* function retrieves a semaphore's current value.

- The *sem_close()* function removes the calling process's association with a semaphore that it previously opened.

- The *sem_unlink()* function removes a semaphore name and marks the semaphore for deletion when all processes have closed it.

SUSv3 doesn't specify how named semaphores are to be implemented. Some UNIX implementations create them as files in a special location in the standard file system. On Linux, they are created as small POSIX shared memory objects with names of the form sem.*name*, in a dedicated *tmpfs* file system (Section 14.10) mounted under the directory /dev/shm (/run/shm on some systems). This file system has kernel persistence—the semaphore objects that it contains will persist, even if no process currently has them open, but they will be lost if the system is shut down.

Named semaphores are supported on Linux since kernel 2.6.

53.2.1 Opening a Named Semaphore

The *sem_open()* function creates and opens a new named semaphore or opens an existing semaphore.

```
#include <fcntl.h>          /* Defines O_* constants */
#include <sys/stat.h>       /* Defines mode constants */
#include <semaphore.h>

sem_t *sem_open(const char *name, int oflag, ...
                /* mode_t mode, unsigned int value */ );
```
            Returns pointer to semaphore on success, or SEM_FAILED on error

The *name* argument identifies the semaphore. It is specified according to the rules given in Section 51.1.

The *oflag* argument is a bit mask that determines whether we are opening an existing semaphore or creating and opening a new semaphore. If *oflag* is 0, we are accessing an existing semaphore. If O_CREAT is specified in *oflag*, then a new semaphore is created if one with the given *name* doesn't already exist. If *oflag* specifies both O_CREAT and O_EXCL, and a semaphore with the given *name* already exists, then *sem_open()* fails.

If *sem_open()* is being used to open an existing semaphore, the call requires only two arguments. However, if O_CREAT is specified in *oflag*, then two further arguments are required: *mode* and *value*. (If the semaphore specified by *name* already exists, then these two arguments are ignored.) These arguments are as follows:

- The *mode* argument is a bit mask that specifies the permissions to be placed on the new semaphore. The bit values are the same as for files (Table 15-4, on page 295), and, as with *open()*, the value in *mode* is masked against the process umask (Section 15.4.6). SUSv3 doesn't specify any access mode flags (O_RDONLY, O_WRONLY, and O_RDWR) for *oflag*. Many implementations, including Linux, assume an access mode of O_RDWR when opening a semaphore, since most applications using semaphores must employ both *sem_post()* and *sem_wait()*, which involve reading and modifying a semaphore's value. This means that we should ensure that both read and write permissions are granted to each category of user—owner, group, and other—that needs to access the semaphore.

- The *value* argument is an unsigned integer that specifies the initial value to be assigned to the new semaphore. The creation and initialization of the semaphore are performed atomically. This avoids the complexities required for the initialization of System V semaphores (Section 47.5).

Regardless of whether we are creating a new semaphore or opening an existing semaphore, *sem_open()* returns a pointer to a *sem_t* value, and we employ this pointer in subsequent calls to functions that operate on the semaphore. On error, *sem_open()* returns the value SEM_FAILED. (On most implementations, SEM_FAILED is defined as either *((sem_t *) 0)* or *((sem_t *) −1)*; Linux defines it as the former.)

SUSv3 states that the results are undefined if we attempt to perform operations (*sem_post()*, *sem_wait()*, and so on) on a *copy* of the *sem_t* variable pointed to by the return value of *sem_open()*. In other words, the following use of *sem2* is not permissible:

```
sem_t *sp, sem2
sp = sem_open(...);
sem2 = *sp;
sem_wait(&sem2);
```

When a child is created via *fork()*, it inherits references to all of the named semaphores that are open in its parent. After the *fork()*, the parent and child can use these semaphores to synchronize their actions.

Example program

The program in Listing 53-1 provides a simple command-line interface to the *sem_open()* function. The command format for this program is shown in the *usageError()* function.

The following shell session log demonstrates the use of this program. We first use the *umask* command to deny all permissions to users in the class other. We then exclusively create a semaphore and examine the contents of the Linux-specific virtual directory that contains named semaphores.

```
$ umask 007
$ ./psem_create -cx /demo 666          666 means read+write for all users
$ ls -l /dev/shm/sem.*
-rw-rw---- 1 mtk users 16 Jul 6 12:09 /dev/shm/sem.demo
```

The output of the *ls* command shows that the process umask overrode the specified permissions of read plus write for the user class other.

If we try once more to exclusively create a semaphore with the same name, the operation fails, because the name already exists.

```
$ ./psem_create -cx /demo 666
ERROR [EEXIST File exists] sem_open          Failed because of O_EXCL
```

Listing 53-1: Using *sem_open()* to open or create a POSIX named semaphore

── **psem/psem_create.c**

```c
#include <semaphore.h>
#include <sys/stat.h>
#include <fcntl.h>
#include "tlpi_hdr.h"

static void
usageError(const char *progName)
{
    fprintf(stderr, "Usage: %s [-cx] name [octal-perms [value]]\n", progName);
    fprintf(stderr, "    -c    Create semaphore (O_CREAT)\n");
    fprintf(stderr, "    -x    Create exclusively (O_EXCL)\n");
    exit(EXIT_FAILURE);
}

int
main(int argc, char *argv[])
{
    int flags, opt;
    mode_t perms;
    unsigned int value;
    sem_t *sem;

    flags = 0;
    while ((opt = getopt(argc, argv, "cx")) != -1) {
        switch (opt) {
        case 'c':   flags |= O_CREAT;          break;
        case 'x':   flags |= O_EXCL;           break;
        default:    usageError(argv[0]);
        }
    }
```

```
        if (optind >= argc)
            usageError(argv[0]);

        /* Default permissions are rw-------; default semaphore initialization
           value is 0 */

        perms = (argc <= optind + 1) ? (S_IRUSR | S_IWUSR) :
                    getInt(argv[optind + 1], GN_BASE_8, "octal-perms");
        value = (argc <= optind + 2) ? 0 : getInt(argv[optind + 2], 0, "value");

        sem = sem_open(argv[optind], flags, perms, value);
        if (sem == SEM_FAILED)
            errExit("sem_open");

        exit(EXIT_SUCCESS);
    }
```
—————————————————————————————————————— *psem/psem_create.c*

53.2.2 Closing a Semaphore

When a process opens a named semaphore, the system records the association
between the process and the semaphore. The *sem_close()* function terminates this
association (i.e., closes the semaphore), releases any resources that the system has
associated with the semaphore for this process, and decreases the count of processes referencing the semaphore.

```
#include <semaphore.h>

int sem_close(sem_t *sem);
```
                                        Returns 0 on success, or −1 on error

---

Open named semaphores are also automatically closed on process termination or
if the process performs an *exec()*.

Closing a semaphore does not delete it. For that purpose, we need to use
sem_unlink().

53.2.3 Removing a Named Semaphore

The *sem_unlink()* function removes the semaphore identified by *name* and marks
the semaphore to be destroyed once all processes cease using it (this may mean
immediately, if all processes that had the semaphore open have already closed it).

```
#include <semaphore.h>

int sem_unlink(const char *name);
```
                                        Returns 0 on success, or −1 on error

---

Listing 53-2 demonstrates the use of *sem_unlink()*.

Listing 53-2: Using *sem_unlink()* to unlink a POSIX named semaphore

—————————————————————————————————————— `psem/psem_unlink.c`

```
#include <semaphore.h>
#include "tlpi_hdr.h"

int
main(int argc, char *argv[])
{
    if (argc != 2 || strcmp(argv[1], "--help") == 0)
        usageErr("%s sem-name\n", argv[0]);

    if (sem_unlink(argv[1]) == -1)
        errExit("sem_unlink");
    exit(EXIT_SUCCESS);
}
```

—————————————————————————————————————— `psem/psem_unlink.c`

53.3 Semaphore Operations

As with a System V semaphore, a POSIX semaphore is an integer that the system never allows to go below 0. However, POSIX semaphore operations differ from their System V counterparts in the following respects:

- The functions for changing a semaphore's value—*sem_post()* and *sem_wait()*—operate on just one semaphore at a time. By contrast, the System V *semop()* system call can operate on multiple semaphores in a set.

- The *sem_post()* and *sem_wait()* functions increment and decrement a semaphore's value by exactly one. By contrast, *semop()* can add and subtract arbitrary values.

- There is no equivalent of the wait-for-zero operation provided by System V semaphores (a *semop()* call where the *sops.sem_op* field is specified as 0).

From this list, it may seem that POSIX semaphores are less powerful than System V semaphores. However, this is not the case—anything that we can do with System V semaphores can also be done with POSIX semaphores. In a few cases, a bit more programming effort may be required, but, for typical scenarios, using POSIX semaphores actually requires less programming effort. (The System V semaphore API is rather more complicated than is required for most applications.)

53.3.1 Waiting on a Semaphore

The *sem_wait()* function decrements (decreases by 1) the value of the semaphore referred to by *sem*.

```
#include <semaphore.h>

int sem_wait(sem_t *sem);
```
                                                    Returns 0 on success, or −1 on error

If the semaphore currently has a value greater than 0, *sem_wait()* returns immediately. If the value of the semaphore is currently 0, *sem_wait()* blocks until the semaphore value rises above 0; at that time, the semaphore is then decremented and *sem_wait()* returns.

If a blocked *sem_wait()* call is interrupted by a signal handler, then it fails with the error EINTR, regardless of whether the SA_RESTART flag was used when establishing the signal handler with *sigaction()*. (On some other UNIX implementations, SA_RESTART does cause *sem_wait()* to automatically restart.)

The program in Listing 53-3 provides a command-line interface to the *sem_wait()* function. We demonstrate the use of this program shortly.

Listing 53-3: Using *sem_wait()* to decrement a POSIX semaphore

—————————————————————————————————— psem/psem_wait.c
```c
#include <semaphore.h>
#include "tlpi_hdr.h"

int
main(int argc, char *argv[])
{
    sem_t *sem;

    if (argc < 2 || strcmp(argv[1], "--help") == 0)
        usageErr("%s sem-name\n", argv[0]);

    sem = sem_open(argv[1], 0);
    if (sem == SEM_FAILED)
        errExit("sem_open");

    if (sem_wait(sem) == -1)
        errExit("sem_wait");

    printf("%ld sem_wait() succeeded\n", (long) getpid());
    exit(EXIT_SUCCESS);
}
```
—————————————————————————————————— psem/psem_wait.c

The *sem_trywait()* function is a nonblocking version of *sem_wait()*.

```c
#include <semaphore.h>

int sem_trywait(sem_t *sem);
```
                                        Returns 0 on success, or −1 on error

If the decrement operation can't be performed immediately, *sem_trywait()* fails with the error EAGAIN.

The *sem_timedwait()* function is another variation on *sem_wait()*. It allows the caller to specify a limit on the time for which the call will block.

```
#include <semaphore.h>

int sem_timedwait(sem_t *sem, const struct timespec *abs_timeout);
```
                                              Returns 0 on success, or −1 on error

If a *sem_timedwait()* call times out without being able to decrement the semaphore, then the call fails with the error ETIMEDOUT.

The *abs_timeout* argument is a *timespec* structure (Section 23.4.2) that specifies the timeout as an absolute value in seconds and nanoseconds since the Epoch. If we want to perform a relative timeout, then we must fetch the current value of the CLOCK_REALTIME clock using *clock_gettime()* and add the required amount to that value to produce a *timespec* structure suitable for use with *sem_timedwait()*.

The *sem_timedwait()* function was originally specified in POSIX.1d (1999) and is not available on all UNIX implementations.

53.3.2 Posting a Semaphore

The *sem_post()* function increments (increases by 1) the value of the semaphore referred to by *sem*.

```
#include <semaphore.h>

int sem_post(sem_t *sem);
```
                                              Returns 0 on success, or −1 on error

If the value of the semaphore was 0 before the *sem_post()* call, and some other process (or thread) is blocked waiting to decrement the semaphore, then that process is awoken, and its *sem_wait()* call proceeds to decrement the semaphore. If multiple processes (or threads) are blocked in *sem_wait()*, then, if the processes are being scheduled under the default round-robin time-sharing policy, it is indeterminate which one will be awoken and allowed to decrement the semaphore. (Like their System V counterparts, POSIX semaphores are only a synchronization mechanism, not a queuing mechanism.)

> SUSv3 specifies that if processes or threads are being executed under a real-time scheduling policy, then the process or thread that will be awoken is the one with the highest priority that has been waiting the longest.

As with System V semaphores, incrementing a POSIX semaphore corresponds to releasing some shared resource for use by another process or thread.

The program in Listing 53-4 provides a command-line interface to the *sem_post()* function. We demonstrate the use of this program shortly.

Listing 53-4: Using *sem_post()* to increment a POSIX semaphore

—————————————————————————————— **psem/psem_post.c**

```c
#include <semaphore.h>
#include "tlpi_hdr.h"

int
main(int argc, char *argv[])
{
    sem_t *sem;

    if (argc != 2)
        usageErr("%s sem-name\n", argv[0]);

    sem = sem_open(argv[1], 0);
    if (sem == SEM_FAILED)
        errExit("sem_open");

    if (sem_post(sem) == -1)
        errExit("sem_post");
    exit(EXIT_SUCCESS);
}
```

—————————————————————————————— **psem/psem_post.c**

53.3.3 Retrieving the Current Value of a Semaphore

The *sem_getvalue()* function returns the current value of the semaphore referred to by *sem* in the *int* pointed to by *sval*.

```c
#include <semaphore.h>

int sem_getvalue(sem_t *sem, int *sval);
```

Returns 0 on success, or −1 on error

If one or more processes (or threads) are currently blocked waiting to decrement the semaphore's value, then the value returned in *sval* depends on the implementation. SUSv3 permits two possibilities: 0 or a negative number whose absolute value is the number of waiters blocked in *sem_wait()*. Linux and several other implementations adopt the former behavior; a few other implementations adopt the latter behavior.

> Although returning a negative *sval* if there are blocked waiters can be useful, especially for debugging purposes, SUSv3 doesn't require this behavior because the techniques that some systems use to efficiently implement POSIX semaphores don't (in fact, can't) record counts of blocked waiters.

Note that by the time *sem_getvalue()* returns, the value returned in *sval* may already be out of date. A program that depends on the information returned by *sem_getvalue()* being unchanged by the time of a subsequent operation will be subject to time-of-check, time-of-use race conditions (Section 38.6).

The program in Listing 53-5 uses *sem_getvalue()* to retrieve the value of the semaphore named in its command-line argument, and then displays that value on standard output.

Listing 53-5: Using *sem_getvalue()* to retrieve the value of a POSIX semaphore

―――――――――――――――――――――――――――――――――――― psem/psem_getvalue.c
```c
#include <semaphore.h>
#include "tlpi_hdr.h"

int
main(int argc, char *argv[])
{
    int value;
    sem_t *sem;

    if (argc != 2)
        usageErr("%s sem-name\n", argv[0]);

    sem = sem_open(argv[1], 0);
    if (sem == SEM_FAILED)
        errExit("sem_open");

    if (sem_getvalue(sem, &value) == -1)
        errExit("sem_getvalue");

    printf("%d\n", value);
    exit(EXIT_SUCCESS);
}
```
―――――――――――――――――――――――――――――――――――― psem/psem_getvalue.c

Example

The following shell session log demonstrates the use of the programs we have shown so far in this chapter. We begin by creating a semaphore whose initial value is zero, and then start a program in the background that attempts to decrement the semaphore:

```
$ ./psem_create -c /demo 600 0
$ ./psem_wait /demo &
[1] 31208
```

The background command blocks, because the semaphore value is currently 0 and therefore can't be decreased.

We then retrieve the semaphore value:

```
$ ./psem_getvalue /demo
0
```

We see the value 0 above. On some other implementations, we might see the value −1, indicating that one process is waiting on the semaphore.

We then execute a command that increments the semaphore. This causes the blocked *sem_wait()* in the background program to complete:

```
$ ./psem_post /demo
$ 31208 sem_wait() succeeded
```

(The last line of output above shows the shell prompt mixed with the output of the background job.)

We press *Enter* to see the next shell prompt, which also causes the shell to report on the terminated background job, and then perform further operations on the semaphore:

```
Press Enter
[1]- Done              ./psem_wait /demo
$ ./psem_post /demo                          Increment semaphore
$ ./psem_getvalue /demo                       Retrieve semaphore value
1
$ ./psem_unlink /demo                         We're done with this semaphore
```

53.4 Unnamed Semaphores

Unnamed semaphores (also known as *memory-based semaphores*) are variables of type *sem_t* that are stored in memory allocated by the application. The semaphore is made available to the processes or threads that use it by placing it in an area of memory that they share.

Operations on unnamed semaphores use the same functions (*sem_wait()*, *sem_post()*, *sem_getvalue()*, and so on) that are used to operate on named semaphores. In addition, two further functions are required:

- The *sem_init()* function initializes a semaphore and informs the system of whether the semaphore will be shared between processes or between the threads of a single process.
- The *sem_destroy()* function destroys a semaphore.

These functions should not be used with named semaphores.

Unnamed versus named semaphores

Using an unnamed semaphore allows us to avoid the work of creating a name for a semaphore. This can be useful in the following cases:

- A semaphore that is shared between threads doesn't need a name. Making an unnamed semaphore a shared (global or heap) variable automatically makes it accessible to all threads.
- A semaphore that is being shared between related processes doesn't need a name. If a parent process allocates an unnamed semaphore in a region of shared memory (e.g., a shared anonymous mapping), then a child automatically inherits the mapping and thus the semaphore as part of the operation of *fork()*.

- If we are building a dynamic data structure (e.g., a binary tree), each of whose items requires an associated semaphore, then the simplest approach is to allocate an unnamed semaphore within each item. Opening a named semaphore for each item would require us to design a convention for generating a (unique) semaphore name for each item and to manage those names (e.g., unlinking them when they are no longer required).

53.4.1 Initializing an Unnamed Semaphore

The *sem_init()* function initializes the unnamed semaphore pointed to by *sem* to the value specified by *value*.

```
#include <semaphore.h>

int sem_init(sem_t *sem, int pshared, unsigned int value);
```
                                         Returns 0 on success, or −1 on error

The *pshared* argument indicates whether the semaphore is to be shared between threads or between processes.

- If *pshared* is 0, then the semaphore is to be shared between the threads of the calling process. In this case, *sem* is typically specified as the address of either a global variable or a variable allocated on the heap. A thread-shared semaphore has process persistence; it is destroyed when the process terminates.

- If *pshared* is nonzero, then the semaphore is to be shared between processes. In this case, *sem* must be the address of a location in a region of shared memory (a POSIX shared memory object, a shared mapping created using *mmap()*, or a System V shared memory segment). The semaphore persists as long as the shared memory in which it resides. (The shared memory regions created by most of these techniques have kernel persistence. The exception is shared anonymous mappings, which persist only as long as at least one process maintains the mapping.) Since a child produced via *fork()* inherits its parent's memory mappings, process-shared semaphores are inherited by the child of a *fork()*, and the parent and child can use these semaphores to synchronize their actions.

The *pshared* argument is necessary for the following reasons:

- Some implementations don't support process-shared semaphores. On these systems, specifying a nonzero value for *pshared* causes *sem_init()* to return an error. Linux did not support unnamed process-shared semaphores until kernel 2.6 and the advent of the NPTL threading implementation. (The older LinuxThreads implementation of *sem_init()* fails with the error ENOSYS if a nonzero value is specified for *pshared*.)

- On implementations that support both process-shared and thread-shared semaphores, specifying which kind of sharing is required may be necessary because the system must take special actions to support the requested sharing. Providing this information may also permit the system to perform optimizations depending on the type of sharing.

The initial NPTL *sem_init()* implementation ignored *pshared*. However, since *glibc* version 2.7, this argument must be set appropriately so that the implementation provides correct behavior.

> The SUSv3 specification for *sem_init()* defines a failure return of −1, but makes no statement about the return value on success. Nevertheless, the manual pages on most modern UNIX implementations document a 0 return on success. (One notable exception is Solaris, where the description of the return value is similar to the SUSv3 specification. However, inspecting the OpenSolaris source code shows that, on that implementation, *sem_init()* does return 0 on success.) SUSv4 rectifies the situation, specifying that *sem_init()* shall return 0 on success.

There are no permission settings associated with an unnamed semaphore (i.e., *sem_init()* has no analog of the *mode* argument of *sem_open()*). Access to an unnamed semaphore is governed by the permissions that are granted to the process for the underlying shared memory region.

SUSv3 specifies that initializing an already initialized unnamed semaphore results in undefined behavior. In other words, we must design our applications so that just one process or thread calls *sem_init()* to initialize a semaphore.

As with named semaphores, SUSv3 says that the results are undefined if we attempt to perform operations on a *copy* of the *sem_t* variable whose address is passed as the *sem* argument of *sem_init()*. Operations should always be performed only on the "original" semaphore.

Example program

In Section 30.1.2, we presented a program (Listing 30-2) that used mutexes to protect a critical section in which two threads accessed the same global variable. The program in Listing 53-6 solves the same problem using an unnamed thread-shared semaphore.

Listing 53-6: Using a POSIX unnamed semaphore to protect access to a global variable

—————————————————————————————————— `psem/thread_incr_psem.c`

```c
#include <semaphore.h>
#include <pthread.h>
#include "tlpi_hdr.h"

static int glob = 0;
static sem_t sem;

static void *                       /* Loop 'arg' times incrementing 'glob' */
threadFunc(void *arg)
{
    int loops = *((int *) arg);
    int loc, j;

    for (j = 0; j < loops; j++) {
        if (sem_wait(&sem) == -1)
            errExit("sem_wait");
```

```
            loc = glob;
            loc++;
            glob = loc;

            if (sem_post(&sem) == -1)
                errExit("sem_post");
        }

    return NULL;
}

int
main(int argc, char *argv[])
{
    pthread_t t1, t2;
    int loops, s;

    loops = (argc > 1) ? getInt(argv[1], GN_GT_0, "num-loops") : 10000000;

    /* Initialize a semaphore with the value 1 */

    if (sem_init(&sem, 0, 1) == -1)
        errExit("sem_init");

    /* Create two threads that increment 'glob' */

    s = pthread_create(&t1, NULL, threadFunc, &loops);
    if (s != 0)
        errExitEN(s, "pthread_create");
    s = pthread_create(&t2, NULL, threadFunc, &loops);
    if (s != 0)
        errExitEN(s, "pthread_create");

    /* Wait for threads to terminate */

    s = pthread_join(t1, NULL);
    if (s != 0)
        errExitEN(s, "pthread_join");
    s = pthread_join(t2, NULL);
    if (s != 0)
        errExitEN(s, "pthread_join");

    printf("glob = %d\n", glob);
    exit(EXIT_SUCCESS);
}
```

———————————————————————————————————— psem/thread_incr_psem.c

53.4.2 Destroying an Unnamed Semaphore

The *sem_destroy()* function destroys the semaphore *sem*, which must be an unnamed semaphore that was previously initialized using *sem_init()*. It is safe to destroy a semaphore only if no processes or threads are waiting on it.

```
#include <semaphore.h>

int sem_destroy(sem_t *sem);
```

                                          Returns 0 on success, or −1 on error

After an unnamed semaphore segment has been destroyed with *sem_destroy()*, it can
be reinitialized with *sem_init()*.

An unnamed semaphore should be destroyed before its underlying memory is
deallocated. For example, if the semaphore is an automatically allocated variable, it
should be destroyed before its host function returns. If the semaphore resides in a
POSIX shared memory region, then it should be destroyed after all processes have
ceased using the semaphore and before the last process unmaps the region.

On some implementations, omitting calls to *sem_destroy()* doesn't cause problems. However, on other implementations, failing to call *sem_destroy()* can result in
resource leaks. Portable applications should call *sem_destroy()* to avoid such problems.

53.5 Comparisons with Other Synchronization Techniques

In this section, we compare POSIX semaphores with two other synchronization
techniques: System V semaphores and mutexes.

POSIX semaphores versus System V semaphores

POSIX semaphores and System V semaphores can both be used to synchronize the
actions of processes. Section 51.2 listed various advantages of POSIX IPC over
System V IPC: the POSIX IPC interface is simpler and more consistent with the traditional UNIX file model, and POSIX IPC objects are reference counted, which
simplifies the task of determining when to delete an IPC object. These general
advantages also apply to the specific case of POSIX (named) semaphores versus
System V semaphores.

POSIX semaphores have the following further advantages over System V
semaphores:

- The POSIX semaphore interface is much simpler than the System V semaphore interface. This simplicity is achieved without loss of functional power.

- POSIX named semaphores eliminate the initialization problem associated with
  System V semaphores (Section 47.5).

- It is easier to associate a POSIX unnamed semaphore with a dynamically allocated memory object: the semaphore can simply be embedded inside the object.

- In scenarios where there is a high degree of contention for a semaphore (i.e.,
  operations on the semaphore are frequently blocked because another process
  has set the semaphore to a value that prevents the operation proceeding immediately), then the performance of POSIX semaphores and System V semaphores is similar. However, in cases where there is low contention for a
  semaphore (i.e., the semaphore's value is such that operations can normally
  proceed without blocking), then POSIX semaphores perform considerably bet-

ter than System V semaphores. (On the systems tested by the author, the difference in performance is more than an order of magnitude; see Exercise 53-4.) POSIX semaphores perform so much better in this case because the way in which they are implemented only requires a system call when contention occurs, whereas System V semaphore operations always require a system call, regardless of contention.

However, POSIX semaphores also have the following disadvantages compared to System V semaphores:

- POSIX semaphores are somewhat less portable. (On Linux, named semaphores have been supported only since kernel 2.6.)

- POSIX semaphores don't provide an equivalent of the System V semaphore undo feature. (However, as we noted in Section 47.8, this feature may not be useful in some circumstances.)

POSIX semaphores versus Pthreads mutexes

POSIX semaphores and Pthreads mutexes can both be used to synchronize the actions of threads within the same process, and their performance is similar. However, mutexes are usually preferable, because the ownership property of mutexes enforces good structuring of code (only the thread that locks a mutex can unlock it). By contrast, one thread can increment a semaphore that was decremented by another thread. This flexibility can lead to poorly structured synchronization designs. (For this reason, semaphores are sometimes referred to as the "gotos" of concurrent programming.)

There is one circumstance in which mutexes can't be used in a multithreaded application and semaphores may therefore be preferable. Because it is async-signal-safe (see Table 21-1, on page 426), the *sem_post()* function can be used from within a signal handler to synchronize with another thread. This is not possible with mutexes, because the Pthreads functions for operating on mutexes are not async-signal-safe. However, because it is usually preferable to deal with asynchronous signals by accepting them using *sigwaitinfo()* (or similar), rather than using signal handlers (see Section 33.2.4), this advantage of semaphores over mutexes is seldom required.

53.6 Semaphore Limits

SUSv3 defines two limits applying to semaphores:

SEM_NSEMS_MAX
> This is the maximum number of POSIX semaphores that a process may have. SUSv3 requires that this limit be at least 256. On Linux, the number of POSIX semaphores is effectively limited only by available memory.

SEM_VALUE_MAX

> This is the maximum value that a POSIX semaphore may reach. Semaphores may assume any value from 0 up to this limit. SUSv3 requires this limit to be at least 32,767; the Linux implementation allows values up to INT_MAX (2,147,483,647).

53.7 Summary

POSIX semaphores allow processes or threads to synchronize their actions. POSIX semaphores come in two types: named and unnamed. A named semaphore is identified by a name, and can be shared by any processes that have permission to open the semaphore. An unnamed semaphore has no name, but processes or threads can share the same semaphore by placing it in a region of memory that they share (e.g., in a POSIX shared memory object for process sharing, or in a global variable for thread sharing).

The POSIX semaphore interface is simpler than the System V semaphore interface. Semaphores are allocated and operated on individually, and the wait and post operations adjust a semaphore's value by one.

POSIX semaphores have a number of advantages over System V semaphores, but they are somewhat less portable. For synchronization within multithreaded applications, mutexes are generally preferred over semaphores.

Further information

[Stevens, 1999] provides an alternative presentation of POSIX semaphores and shows user-space implementations using various other IPC mechanisms (FIFOs, memory-mapped files, and System V semaphores). [Butenhof, 1996] describes the use of POSIX semaphores in multithreaded applications.

53.8 Exercises

53-1. Rewrite the programs in Listing 48-2 and Listing 48-3 (Section 48.4) as a threaded application, with the two threads passing data to each other via a global buffer, and using POSIX semaphores for synchronization.

53-2. Modify the program in Listing 53-3 (psem_wait.c) to use *sem_timedwait()* instead of *sem_wait()*. The program should take an additional command-line argument that specifies a (relative) number of seconds to be used as the timeout for the *sem_timedwait()* call.

53-3. Devise an implementation of POSIX semaphores using System V semaphores.

53-4. In Section 53.5, we noted that POSIX semaphores perform much better than System V semaphores in the case where the semaphore is uncontended. Write two programs (one for each semaphore type) to verify this. Each program should simply increment and decrement a semaphore a specified number of times. Compare the times required for the two programs.

54

POSIX SHARED MEMORY

In previous chapters, we looked at two techniques that allow unrelated processes to share memory regions in order to perform IPC: System V shared memory (Chapter 48) and shared file mappings (Section 49.4.2). Both of these techniques have potential drawbacks:

- The System V shared memory model, which uses keys and identifiers, is not consistent with the standard UNIX I/O model, which uses filenames and descriptors. This difference means that we require an entirely new set of system calls and commands for working with System V shared memory segments.

- Using a shared file mapping for IPC requires the creation of a disk file, even if we are not interested in having a persistent backing store for the shared region. Aside from the inconvenience of needing to create the file, this technique incurs some file I/O overhead.

Because of these drawbacks, POSIX.1b defined a new shared memory API: POSIX shared memory, which is the subject of this chapter.

> POSIX talks about shared memory *objects*, while System V talks about shared memory *segments*. These differences in terminology are historical—both terms are used for referring to regions of memory shared between processes.

54.1 Overview

POSIX shared memory allows us to share a mapped region between unrelated processes without needing to create a corresponding mapped file. POSIX shared memory is supported on Linux since kernel 2.4.

SUSv3 doesn't specify any of the details of how POSIX shared memory is to be implemented. In particular, there is no requirement for the use of a (real or virtual) file system to identify shared memory objects, although many UNIX implementations do employ a file system for this purpose. Some UNIX implementations create the names for shared memory objects as files in a special location in the standard file system. Linux uses a dedicated *tmpfs* file system (Section 14.10) mounted under the directory /dev/shm (/run/shm on some systems). This file system has kernel persistence—the shared memory objects that it contains will persist even if no process currently has them open, but they will be lost if the system is shut down.

> The total amount of memory in all POSIX shared memory regions on the system is limited by the size of the underlying *tmpfs* file system. This file system is typically mounted at boot time with some default size (e.g., 256 MB). If necessary, the superuser can change the size of the file system by remounting it using the command *mount -o remount,size=<num-bytes>*.

To use a POSIX shared memory object, we perform two steps:

1. Use the *shm_open()* function to open an object with a specified name. (We described the rules governing the naming of POSIX shared memory objects in Section 51.1.) The *shm_open()* function is analogous to the *open()* system call. It either creates a new shared memory object or opens an existing object. As its function result, *shm_open()* returns a file descriptor referring to the object.

2. Pass the file descriptor obtained in the previous step in a call to *mmap()* that specifies MAP_SHARED in the *flags* argument. This maps the shared memory object into the process's virtual address space. As with other uses of *mmap()*, once we have mapped the object, we can close the file descriptor without affecting the mapping. However, we may need to keep the file descriptor open for subsequent use in calls to *fstat()* and *ftruncate()* (see Section 54.2).

> The relationship between *shm_open()* and *mmap()* for POSIX shared memory is analogous to that between *shmget()* and *shmat()* for System V shared memory. The origin of the two-step process (*shm_open()* plus *mmap()*) for using POSIX shared memory objects instead of the use of a single function that performs both tasks is historical. When the POSIX committee added this feature, the *mmap()* call already existed ([Stevens, 1999]). In effect, all that we are doing is replacing calls to *open()* with calls to *shm_open()*, with the difference that using *shm_open()* doesn't require the creation of a file in a disk-based file system.

Since a shared memory object is referred to using a file descriptor, we can usefully employ various file descriptor system calls already defined in the UNIX system (e.g., *ftruncate()*), rather than needing new special-purpose system calls (as is required for System V shared memory).

54.2 Creating Shared Memory Objects

The *shm_open()* function creates and opens a new shared memory object or opens an existing object. The arguments to *shm_open()* are analogous to those for *open()*.

```
#include <fcntl.h>          /* Defines O_* constants */
#include <sys/stat.h>       /* Defines mode constants */
#include <sys/mman.h>

int shm_open(const char *name, int oflag, mode_t mode);
```
> Returns file descriptor on success, or −1 on error

The *name* argument identifies the shared memory object to be created or opened. The *oflag* argument is a mask of bits that modify the behavior of the call. The values that can be included in this mask are summarized in Table 54-1.

Table 54-1: Bit values for the *shm_open()* oflag argument

Flag	Description
O_CREAT	Create object if it doesn't already exist
O_EXCL	With O_CREAT, create object exclusively
O_RDONLY	Open for read-only access
O_RDWR	Open for read-write access
O_TRUNC	Truncate object to zero length

One of the purposes of the *oflag* argument is to determine whether we are opening an existing shared memory object or creating and opening a new object. If *oflag* doesn't include O_CREAT, we are opening an existing object. If O_CREAT is specified, then the object is created if it doesn't already exist. Specifying O_EXCL in conjunction with O_CREAT is a request to ensure that the caller is the creator of the object; if the object already exists, an error results (EEXIST).

The *oflag* argument also indicates the kind of access that the calling process will make to the shared memory object, by specifying exactly one of the values O_RDONLY or O_RDWR.

The remaining flag value, O_TRUNC, causes a successful open of an existing shared memory object to truncate the object to a length of zero.

> On Linux, truncation occurs even on a read-only open. However, SUSv3 says that the result of using O_TRUNC with a read-only open is undefined, so we can't portably rely on a specific behavior in this case.

When a new shared memory object is created, its ownership and group ownership are taken from the effective user and group IDs of the process calling *shm_open()*, and the object permissions are set according to the value supplied in the *mode* bit-mask argument. The bit values for *mode* are the same as for files (Table 15-4, on page 295). As with the *open()* system call, the permissions mask in *mode* is masked against the process umask (Section 15.4.6). Unlike *open()*, the *mode* argument is always required for a call to *shm_open()*; if we are not creating a new object, this argument should be specified as 0.

The close-on-exec flag (FD_CLOEXEC, Section 27.4) is set on the file descriptor returned by *shm_open()*, so that the file descriptor is automatically closed if the process performs an *exec()*. (This is consistent with the fact that mappings are unmapped when an *exec()* is performed.)

When a new shared memory object is created, it initially has zero length. This means that, after creating a new shared memory object, we normally call *ftruncate()* (Section 5.8) to set the size of the object before calling *mmap()*. Following the *mmap()* call, we may also use *ftruncate()* to expand or shrink the shared memory object as desired, bearing in mind the points discussed in Section 49.4.3.

When a shared memory object is extended, the newly added bytes are automatically initialized to 0.

At any point, we can apply *fstat()* (Section 15.1) to the file descriptor returned by *shm_open()* in order to obtain a *stat* structure whose fields contain information about the shared memory object, including its size (*st_size*), permissions (*st_mode*), owner (*st_uid*), and group (*st_gid*). (These are the only fields that SUSv3 requires *fstat()* to set in the *stat* structure, although Linux also returns meaningful information in the time fields, as well as various other less useful information in the remaining fields.)

The permissions and ownership of a shared memory object can be changed using *fchmod()* and *fchown()*, respectively.

Example program

Listing 54-1 provides a simple example of the use of *shm_open()*, *ftruncate()*, and *mmap()*. This program creates a shared memory object whose size is specified by a command-line argument, and maps the object into the process's virtual address space. (The mapping step is redundant, since we don't actually do anything with the shared memory, but it serves to demonstrate the use of *mmap()*.) The program permits the use of command-line options to select flags (O_CREAT and O_EXCL) for the *shm_open()* call.

In the following example, we use this program to create a 10,000-byte shared memory object, and then use *ls* to show this object in /dev/shm:

```
$ ./pshm_create -c /demo_shm 10000
$ ls -l /dev/shm
total 0
-rw-------   1 mtk      users        10000 Jun 20 11:31 demo_shm
```

Listing 54-1: Creating a POSIX shared memory object

―――――――――――――――――――――――――――――――――――― pshm/pshm_create.c

```c
#include <sys/stat.h>
#include <fcntl.h>
#include <sys/mman.h>
#include "tlpi_hdr.h"
```

```
static void
usageError(const char *progName)
{
    fprintf(stderr, "Usage: %s [-cx] name size [octal-perms]\n", progName);
    fprintf(stderr, "    -c   Create shared memory (O_CREAT)\n");
    fprintf(stderr, "    -x   Create exclusively (O_EXCL)\n");
    exit(EXIT_FAILURE);
}

int
main(int argc, char *argv[])
{
    int flags, opt, fd;
    mode_t perms;
    size_t size;
    void *addr;

    flags = O_RDWR;
    while ((opt = getopt(argc, argv, "cx")) != -1) {
        switch (opt) {
        case 'c':   flags |= O_CREAT;           break;
        case 'x':   flags |= O_EXCL;            break;
        default:    usageError(argv[0]);
        }
    }

    if (optind + 1 >= argc)
        usageError(argv[0]);

    size = getLong(argv[optind + 1], GN_ANY_BASE, "size");
    perms = (argc <= optind + 2) ? (S_IRUSR | S_IWUSR) :
                getLong(argv[optind + 2], GN_BASE_8, "octal-perms");

    /* Create shared memory object and set its size */

    fd = shm_open(argv[optind], flags, perms);
    if (fd == -1)
        errExit("shm_open");

    if (ftruncate(fd, size) == -1)
        errExit("ftruncate");

    /* Map shared memory object */

    addr = mmap(NULL, size, PROT_READ | PROT_WRITE, MAP_SHARED, fd, 0);
    if (addr == MAP_FAILED)
        errExit("mmap");

    exit(EXIT_SUCCESS);
}
```
—— **pshm/pshm_create.c**

54.3 Using Shared Memory Objects

Listing 54-2 and Listing 54-3 demonstrate the use of a shared memory object to transfer data from one process to another. The program in Listing 54-2 copies the string contained in its second command-line argument into the existing shared memory object named in its first command-line argument. Before mapping the object and performing the copy, the program uses *ftruncate()* to resize the shared memory object to be the same length as the string that is to be copied.

Listing 54-2: Copying data into a POSIX shared memory object

—— pshm/pshm_write.c

```
#include <fcntl.h>
#include <sys/mman.h>
#include "tlpi_hdr.h"

int
main(int argc, char *argv[])
{
    int fd;
    size_t len;                     /* Size of shared memory object */
    char *addr;

    if (argc != 3 || strcmp(argv[1], "--help") == 0)
        usageErr("%s shm-name string\n", argv[0]);

    fd = shm_open(argv[1], O_RDWR, 0);      /* Open existing object */
    if (fd == -1)
        errExit("shm_open");

    len = strlen(argv[2]);
    if (ftruncate(fd, len) == -1)           /* Resize object to hold string */
        errExit("ftruncate");
    printf("Resized to %ld bytes\n", (long) len);

    addr = mmap(NULL, len, PROT_READ | PROT_WRITE, MAP_SHARED, fd, 0);
    if (addr == MAP_FAILED)
        errExit("mmap");

    if (close(fd) == -1)                    /* 'fd' is no longer needed */
        errExit("close");

    printf("copying %ld bytes\n", (long) len);
    memcpy(addr, argv[2], len);             /* Copy string to shared memory */
    exit(EXIT_SUCCESS);
}
```

—— pshm/pshm_write.c

The program in Listing 54-3 displays the string in the existing shared memory object named in its command-line argument on standard output. After calling *shm_open()*, the program uses *fstat()* to determine the size of the shared memory and uses that size in the call to *mmap()* that maps the object and in the *write()* call that prints the string.

Listing 54-3: Copying data from a POSIX shared memory object

—— **pshm/pshm_read.c**

```
#include <fcntl.h>
#include <sys/mman.h>
#include <sys/stat.h>
#include "tlpi_hdr.h"

int
main(int argc, char *argv[])
{
    int fd;
    char *addr;
    struct stat sb;

    if (argc != 2 || strcmp(argv[1], "--help") == 0)
        usageErr("%s shm-name\n", argv[0]);

    fd = shm_open(argv[1], O_RDONLY, 0);      /* Open existing object */
    if (fd == -1)
        errExit("shm_open");

    /* Use shared memory object size as length argument for mmap()
       and as number of bytes to write() */

    if (fstat(fd, &sb) == -1)
        errExit("fstat");

    addr = mmap(NULL, sb.st_size, PROT_READ, MAP_SHARED, fd, 0);
    if (addr == MAP_FAILED)
        errExit("mmap");

    if (close(fd) == -1);                       /* 'fd' is no longer needed */
                        errExit("close");

    write(STDOUT_FILENO, addr, sb.st_size);
    write(STDOUT_FILENO, "\n", 1);
    exit(EXIT_SUCCESS);
}
```

—— **pshm/pshm_read.c**

The following shell session demonstrates the use of the programs in Listing 54-2 and Listing 54-3. We first create a zero-length shared memory object using the program in Listing 54-1.

```
$ ./pshm_create -c /demo_shm 0
$ ls -l /dev/shm                        Check the size of object
total 4
-rw-------    1 mtk    users    0 Jun 21 13:33 demo_shm
```

We then use the program in Listing 54-2 to copy a string into the shared memory object:

```
$ ./pshm_write /demo_shm 'hello'
$ ls -l /dev/shm                        Check that object has changed in size
total 4
```

POSIX Shared Memory   **1113**

```
-rw-------   1 mtk    users    5 Jun 21 13:33 demo_shm
```

From the output, we can see that the program resized the shared memory object so that it is large enough to hold the specified string.

Finally, we use the program in Listing 54-3 to display the string in the shared memory object:

```
$ ./pshm_read /demo_shm
hello
```

Applications must typically use some synchronization technique to allow processes to coordinate their access to shared memory. In the example shell session shown here, the coordination was provided by the user running the programs one after the other. Typically, applications would instead use a synchronization primitive (e.g., semaphores) to coordinate access to a shared memory object.

54.4 Removing Shared Memory Objects

SUSv3 requires that POSIX shared memory objects have at least kernel persistence; that is, they continue to exist until they are explicitly removed or the system is rebooted. When a shared memory object is no longer required, it should be removed using *shm_unlink()*.

```
#include <sys/mman.h>

int shm_unlink(const char *name);
```
                                        Returns 0 on success, or –1 on error

The *shm_unlink()* function removes the shared memory object specified by *name*. Removing a shared memory object doesn't affect existing mappings of the object (which will remain in effect until the corresponding processes call *munmap()* or terminate), but prevents further *shm_open()* calls from opening the object. Once all processes have unmapped the object, the object is removed, and its contents are lost.

The program in Listing 54-4 uses *shm_unlink()* to remove the shared memory object specified in the program's command-line argument.

Listing 54-4: Using *shm_unlink()* to unlink a POSIX shared memory object

———————————————————————————————————— pshm/pshm_unlink.c
```
#include <fcntl.h>
#include <sys/mman.h>
#include "tlpi_hdr.h"

int
main(int argc, char *argv[])
{
    if (argc != 2 || strcmp(argv[1], "--help") == 0)
        usageErr("%s shm-name\n", argv[0]);
    if (shm_unlink(argv[1]) == -1)
        errExit("shm_unlink");
    exit(EXIT_SUCCESS);
```

```
        }
```

54.5 Comparisons Between Shared Memory APIs

By now, we have considered a number of different techniques for sharing memory regions between unrelated processes:

- System V shared memory (Chapter 48);
- shared file mappings (Section 49.4.2); and
- POSIX shared memory objects (the subject of this chapter).

> Many of the points that we make in this section are also relevant for shared anonymous mappings (Section 49.7), which are used for sharing memory between processes that are related via *fork()*.

A number of points apply to all of these techniques:

- They provide fast IPC, and applications typically must use a semaphore (or other synchronization primitive) to synchronize access to the shared region.
- Once the shared memory region has been mapped into the process's virtual address space, it looks just like any other part of the process's memory space.
- The system places the shared memory regions within the process virtual address space in a similar manner. We outlined this placement while describing System V shared memory in Section 48.5. The Linux-specific /proc/*PID*/maps file lists information about all types of shared memory regions.
- Assuming that we don't attempt to map a shared memory region at a fixed address, we should ensure that all references to locations in the region are calculated as offsets (rather than pointers), since the region may be located at different virtual addresses within different processes (Section 48.6).
- The functions described in Chapter 50 that operate on regions of virtual memory can be applied to shared memory regions created using any of these techniques.

There are also a few notable differences between the techniques for shared memory:

- The fact that the contents of a shared file mapping are synchronized with the underlying mapped file means that the data stored in a shared memory region can persist across system restarts.
- System V and POSIX shared memory use different mechanisms to identify and refer to a shared memory object. System V uses its own scheme of keys and identifiers, which doesn't fit with the standard UNIX I/O model and requires separate system calls (e.g., *shmctl()*) and commands (*ipcs* and *ipcrm*). By contrast, POSIX shared memory employs names and file descriptors, and consequently shared memory objects can be examined and manipulated using a variety of existing UNIX system calls (e.g., *fstat()* and *fchmod()*).

- The size of a System V shared memory segment is fixed at the time of creation (via *shmget()*). By contrast, for a mapping backed by a file or by a POSIX shared memory object, we can use *ftruncate()* to adjust the size of the underlying object, and then re-create the mapping using *munmap()* and *mmap()* (or the Linux-specific *mremap()*).

- Historically, System V shared memory was more widely available than *mmap()* and POSIX shared memory, although most UNIX implementations now provide all of these techniques.

With the exception of the final point regarding portability, the differences listed above are advantages in favor of shared file mappings and POSIX shared memory objects. Thus, in new applications, one of these interfaces may be preferable to System V shared memory. Which one we choose depends on whether or not we require a persistent backing store. Shared file mappings provide such a store; POSIX shared memory objects allow us to avoid the overhead of using a disk file when a backing store is not required.

54.6 Summary

A POSIX shared memory object is used to share a region of memory between unrelated processes without creating an underlying disk file. To do this, we replace the call to *open()* that normally precedes *mmap()* with a call to *shm_open()*. The *shm_open()* call creates a file in a memory-based file system, and we can employ traditional file descriptor system calls to perform various operations on this virtual file. In particular, *ftruncate()* must be used to set the size of the shared memory object, since initially it has a length of zero.

We have now described three techniques for sharing memory regions between unrelated processes: System V shared memory, shared file mappings, and POSIX shared memory objects. There are several similarities between the three techniques. There are also some important differences, and, except for the issue of portability, these differences favor shared file mappings and POSIX shared memory objects.

54.7 Exercise

54-1. Rewrite the programs in Listing 48-2 (svshm_xfr_writer.c) and Listing 48-3 (svshm_xfr_reader.c) to use POSIX shared memory objects instead of System V shared memory.

55

FILE LOCKING

Previous chapters have covered various techniques that processes can use to synchronize their actions, including signals (Chapters 20 to 22) and semaphores (Chapters 47 and 53). In this chapter, we look at further synchronization techniques designed specifically for use with files.

55.1 Overview

A frequent application requirement is to read data from a file, make some change to that data, and then write it back to the file. As long as just one process at a time ever uses a file in this way, then there are no problems. However, problems can arise if multiple processes are simultaneously updating a file. Suppose, for example, that each process performs the following steps to update a file containing a sequence number:

1. Read the sequence number from the file.
2. Use the sequence number for some application-defined purpose.
3. Increment the sequence number and write it back to the file.

The problem here is that, in the absence of any synchronization technique, two processes could perform the above steps at the same time with (for example) the consequences shown in Figure 55-1 (here, we assume that the initial value of the sequence number is 1000).

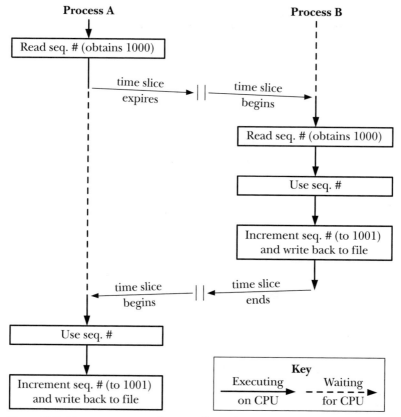

Figure 55-1: Two processes updating a file at the same time without synchronization

The problem is clear: at the end of these steps, the file contains the value 1001, when it should contain the value 1002. (This is an example of a race condition.) To prevent such possibilities, we need some form of interprocess synchronization.

Although we could use (say) semaphores to perform the required synchronization, using file locks is usually preferable, because the kernel automatically associates locks with files.

> [Stevens & Rago, 2005] dates the first UNIX file locking implementation to 1980, and notes that *fcntl()* locking, upon which we primarily focus in this chapter, appeared in System V Release 2 in 1984.

In this chapter, we describe two different APIs for placing file locks:

- *flock()*, which places locks on entire files; and
- *fcntl()*, which places locks on regions of a file.

The *flock()* system call originated on BSD; *fcntl()* originated on System V.

The general method of using *flock()* and *fcntl()* is as follows:

1. Place a lock on the file.
2. Perform file I/O.
3. Unlock the file so that another process can lock it.

Although file locking is normally used in conjunction with file I/O, we can also use it as a more general synchronization technique. Cooperating processes can follow a convention that locking all or part of a file indicates access by a process to some shared resource other than the file itself (e.g., a shared memory region).

Mixing locking and *stdio* functions

Because of the user-space buffering performed by the *stdio* library, we should be cautious when using *stdio* functions with the locking techniques described in this chapter. The problem is that an input buffer might be filled before a lock is placed, or an output buffer may be flushed after a lock is removed. There are a few ways to avoid these problems:

- Perform file I/O using *read()* and *write()* (and related system calls) instead of the *stdio* library.

- Flush the *stdio* stream immediately after placing a lock on the file, and flush it once more immediately before releasing the lock.

- Perhaps at the cost of some efficiency, disable *stdio* buffering altogether using *setbuf()* (or similar).

Advisory and mandatory locking

In the remainder of this chapter, we'll distinguish locks as being either advisory or mandatory. By default, file locks are *advisory*. This means that a process can simply ignore a lock placed by another process. In order for an advisory locking scheme to be workable, each process accessing the file must cooperate, by placing a lock before performing file I/O. By contrast, a *mandatory* locking system forces a process performing I/O to abide by the locks held by other processes. We say more about this distinction in Section 55.4.

55.2 File Locking with *flock()*

Although *fcntl()* provides a superset of the functionality provided by *flock()*, we nevertheless describe *flock()* because it is still used in some applications, and because it differs from *fcntl()* in some of the semantics of inheritance and release of locks.

```
#include <sys/file.h>

int flock(int fd, int operation);
```
                                                    Returns 0 on success, or −1 on error

The *flock()* system call places a single lock on an entire file. The file to be locked is specified via an open file descriptor passed in *fd*. The *operation* argument specifies one of the values LOCK_SH, LOCK_EX, or LOCK_UN, which are described in Table 55-1.

By default, *flock()* blocks if another process already holds an incompatible lock on a file. If we want to prevent this, we can OR (|) the value LOCK_NB into *operation*. In this case, if another process already holds an incompatible lock on the file, *flock()* doesn't block, but instead returns −1, with *errno* set to EWOULDBLOCK.

Table 55-1: Values for the *operation* argument of *flock()*

Value	Description
LOCK_SH	Place a *shared* lock on the file referred to by *fd*
LOCK_EX	Place an *exclusive* lock on the file referred to by *fd*
LOCK_UN	Unlock the file referred to by *fd*
LOCK_NB	Make a nonblocking lock request

Any number of processes may simultaneously hold a shared lock on a file. However, only one process at a time can hold an exclusive lock on a file. (In other words, exclusive locks deny both exclusive and shared locks by other processes.) Table 55-2 summarizes the compatibility rules for *flock()* locks. Here, we assume that process A is the first to place the lock, and the table indicates whether process B can then place a lock.

Table 55-2: Compatibility of *flock()* locking types

Process A	Process B	
	LOCK_SH	LOCK_EX
LOCK_SH	Yes	No
LOCK_EX	No	No

A process can place a shared or exclusive lock regardless of the access mode (read, write, or read-write) of the file.

An existing shared lock can be converted to an exclusive lock (and vice versa) by making another call to *flock()* specifying the appropriate value for *operation*. Converting a shared lock to an exclusive lock will block if another process holds a shared lock on the file, unless LOCK_NB was also specified.

A lock conversion is *not* guaranteed to be atomic. During conversion, the existing lock is first removed, and then a new lock is established. Between these two steps, another process's pending request for an incompatible lock may be granted. If this occurs, then the conversion will block, or, if LOCK_NB was specified, the conversion will fail and the process will lose its original lock. (This behavior occurred in the original BSD *flock()* implementation and also occurs on many other UNIX implementations.)

> Although it is not part of SUSv3, *flock()* appears on most UNIX implementations. Some implementations require the inclusion of either <fcntl.h> or <sys/fcntl.h> instead of <sys/file.h>. Because *flock()* originates on BSD, the locks that it places are sometimes known as *BSD file locks*.

Listing 55-1 demonstrates the use of *flock()*. This program locks a file, sleeps for a specified number of seconds, and then unlocks the file. The program takes up to three command-line arguments. The first of these is the file to lock. The second specifies the lock type (shared or exclusive) and whether or not to include the LOCK_NB (nonblocking) flag. The third argument specifies the number of seconds to sleep between acquiring and releasing the lock; this argument is optional and defaults to 10 seconds.

Listing 55-1: Using *flock()*

```c
#include <sys/file.h>
#include <fcntl.h>
#include "curr_time.h"                  /* Declaration of currTime() */
#include "tlpi_hdr.h"

int
main(int argc, char *argv[])
{
    int fd, lock;
    const char *lname;

    if (argc < 3 || strcmp(argv[1], "--help") == 0 ||
            strchr("sx", argv[2][0]) == NULL)
        usageErr("%s file lock [sleep-time]\n"
                "    'lock' is 's' (shared) or 'x' (exclusive)\n"
                "        optionally followed by 'n' (nonblocking)\n"
                "    'sleep-time' specifies time to hold lock\n", argv[0]);

    lock = (argv[2][0] == 's') ? LOCK_SH : LOCK_EX;
    if (argv[2][1] == 'n')
        lock |= LOCK_NB;

    fd = open(argv[1], O_RDONLY);                /* Open file to be locked */
    if (fd == -1)
        errExit("open");

    lname = (lock & LOCK_SH) ? "LOCK_SH" : "LOCK_EX";

    printf("PID %ld: requesting %s at %s\n", (long) getpid(), lname,
            currTime("%T"));

    if (flock(fd, lock) == -1) {
        if (errno == EWOULDBLOCK)
            fatal("PID %ld: already locked - bye!", (long) getpid());
        else
            errExit("flock (PID=%ld)", (long) getpid());
    }

    printf("PID %ld: granted    %s at %s\n", (long) getpid(), lname,
            currTime("%T"));

    sleep((argc > 3) ? getInt(argv[3], GN_NONNEG, "sleep-time") : 10);

    printf("PID %ld: releasing  %s at %s\n", (long) getpid(), lname,
            currTime("%T"));
    if (flock(fd, LOCK_UN) == -1)
        errExit("flock");

    exit(EXIT_SUCCESS);
}
```

Using the program in Listing 55-1, we can conduct a number of experiments to explore the behavior of *flock()*. Some examples are shown in the following shell session. We begin by creating a file, and then start an instance of our program that sits in the background and holds a shared lock for 60 seconds:

```
$ touch tfile
$ ./t_flock tfile s 60 &
[1] 9777
PID 9777: requesting LOCK_SH at 21:19:37
PID 9777: granted   LOCK_SH at 21:19:37
```

Next, we start another instance of the program that successfully requests a shared lock and then releases it:

```
$ ./t_flock tfile s 2
PID 9778: requesting LOCK_SH at 21:19:49
PID 9778: granted   LOCK_SH at 21:19:49
PID 9778: releasing LOCK_SH at 21:19:51
```

However, when we start another instance of the program that makes a nonblocking requests for an exclusive lock, the request immediately fails:

```
$ ./t_flock tfile xn
PID 9779: requesting LOCK_EX at 21:20:03
PID 9779: already locked - bye!
```

When we start another instance of the program that makes a blocking request for an exclusive lock, the program blocks. When the background process that was holding a shared lock for 60 seconds releases its lock, the blocked request is granted:

```
$ ./t_flock tfile x
PID 9780: requesting LOCK_EX at 21:20:21
PID 9777: releasing LOCK_SH at 21:20:37
PID 9780: granted   LOCK_EX at 21:20:37
PID 9780: releasing LOCK_EX at 21:20:47
```

55.2.1 Semantics of Lock Inheritance and Release

As shown in Table 55-1, we can release a file lock via an *flock()* call that specifies *operation* as LOCK_UN. In addition, locks are automatically released when the corresponding file descriptor is closed. However, the story is more complicated than this. A file lock obtained via *flock()* is associated with the open file description (Section 5.4), rather than the file descriptor or the file (i-node) itself. This means that when a file descriptor is duplicated (via *dup()*, *dup2()*, or an *fcntl()* F_DUPFD operation), the new file descriptor refers to the same file lock. For example, if we have obtained a lock on the file referred to by *fd*, then the following code (which omits error checking) releases that lock:

```
flock(fd, LOCK_EX);        /* Gain lock via 'fd' */
newfd = dup(fd);           /* 'newfd' refers to same lock as 'fd' */
flock(newfd, LOCK_UN);     /* Frees lock acquired via 'fd' */
```

If we have acquired a lock via a particular file descriptor, and we create one or more duplicates of that descriptor, then—if we don't explicitly perform an unlock operation—the lock is released only when all of the duplicate descriptors have been closed.

However, if we use *open()* to obtain a second file descriptor (and associated open file description) referring to the same file, this second descriptor is treated independently by *flock()*. For example, a process executing the following code will block on the second *flock()* call:

```
fd1 = open("a.txt", O_RDWR);
fd2 = open("a.txt", O_RDWR);
flock(fd1, LOCK_EX);
flock(fd2, LOCK_EX);              /* Locked out by lock on 'fd1' */
```

Thus, a process can lock itself out of a file using *flock()*. As we'll see later, this can't happen with record locks obtained by *fcntl()*.

When we create a child process using *fork()*, that child obtains duplicates of its parent's file descriptors, and, as with descriptors duplicated via *dup()* and so on, these descriptors refer to the same open file descriptions and thus to the same locks. For example, the following code causes a child to remove a parent's lock:

```
flock(fd, LOCK_EX);              /* Parent obtains lock */
if (fork() == 0)                 /* If child... */
    flock(fd, LOCK_UN);          /* Release lock shared with parent */
```

These semantics can sometimes be usefully exploited to (atomically) transfer a file lock from a parent process to a child process: after the *fork()*, the parent closes its file descriptor, and the lock is under sole control of the child process. As we'll see later, this isn't possible using record locks obtained by *fcntl()*.

Locks created by *flock()* are preserved across an *exec()* (unless the close-on-exec flag was set for the file descriptor and that file descriptor was the last one referencing the underlying open file description).

The Linux semantics described above conform to the classical BSD implementation of *flock()*. On some UNIX implementations, *flock()* is implemented using *fcntl()*, and we'll see later that the inheritance and release semantics of *fcntl()* locks differ from those of *flock()* locks. Because the interactions between locks created by *flock()* and *fcntl()* are undefined, an application should use only one of these locking methods on a file.

55.2.2 Limitations of *flock()*

Placing locks with *flock()* suffers from a number of limitations:

- Only whole files can be locked. Such coarse locking limits the potential for concurrency among cooperating processes. If, for example, we have multiple processes, each of which would like to simultaneously access different parts of the same file, then locking via *flock()* would needlessly prevent these processes from operating concurrently.

- We can place only advisory locks with *flock()*.

- Many NFS implementations don't recognize locks granted by *flock()*.

All of these limitations are addressed by the locking scheme implemented by *fcntl()*, which we describe in the next section.

Historically, the Linux NFS server did not support *flock()* locks. Since kernel 2.6.12, the Linux NFS server supports *flock()* locks by implementing them as an *fcntl()* lock on the entire file. This can cause some strange effects when mixing BSD locks on the server and BSD locks on the client: the clients usually won't see the server's locks, and vice versa.

55.3 Record Locking with *fcntl()*

Using *fcntl()* (Section 5.2), we can place a lock on any part of a file, ranging from a single byte to the entire file. This form of file locking is usually called *record locking*. However, this term is a misnomer, because files on the UNIX system are byte sequences, with no concept of record boundaries. Any notion of records within a file is defined purely within an application.

Typically, *fcntl()* is used to lock byte ranges corresponding to the application-defined record boundaries within the file; hence the origin of the term *record locking*. The terms *byte range*, *file region*, and *file segment* are less commonly used, but more accurate, descriptions of this type of lock. (Because this is the only kind of locking specified in the original POSIX.1 standard and in SUSv3, it is sometimes also called POSIX file locking.)

> SUSv3 requires record locking to be supported for regular files, and permits it to be supported for other file types. Although it generally makes sense to apply record locks only to regular files (since, for most other file types, it isn't meaningful to talk about byte ranges for the data contained in the file), on Linux, it is possible to apply a record lock to any type of file descriptor.

Figure 55-2 shows how record locking might be used to synchronize access by two processes to the same region of a file. (In this diagram, we assume that all lock requests are blocking, so that they will wait if a lock is held by another process.)

The general form of the *fcntl()* call used to create or remove a file lock is as follows:

```
struct flock flockstr;

/* Set fields of 'flockstr' to describe lock to be placed or removed */

fcntl(fd, cmd, &flockstr);          /* Place lock defined by 'flockstr' */
```

The *fd* argument is an open file descriptor referring to the file on which we wish to place a lock.

Before discussing the *cmd* argument, we first describe the *flock* structure.

The *flock* structure

The *flock* structure defines the lock that we wish to acquire or remove. It is defined as follows:

```
struct flock {
    short l_type;       /* Lock type: F_RDLCK, F_WRLCK, F_UNLCK */
    short l_whence;     /* How to interpret 'l_start': SEEK_SET,
                           SEEK_CUR, SEEK_END */
```

```
    off_t l_start;      /* Offset where the lock begins */
    off_t l_len;        /* Number of bytes to lock; 0 means "until EOF" */
    pid_t l_pid;        /* Process preventing our lock (F_GETLK only) */
};
```

The *l_type* field indicates the type of lock we want to place. It is specified as one of the values in Table 55-3.

Semantically, read (F_RDLCK) and write (F_WRLCK) locks correspond to the shared and exclusive locks applied by *flock()*, and they follow the same compatibility rules (Table 55-2): any number of processes can hold read locks on a file region, but only one process can hold a write lock, and that lock excludes read and write locks by other processes. Specifying *l_type* as F_UNLCK is analogous to the *flock()* LOCK_UN operation.

Table 55-3: Lock types for *fcntl()* locking

Lock type	Description
F_RDLCK	Place a read lock
F_WRLCK	Place a write lock
F_UNLCK	Remove an existing lock

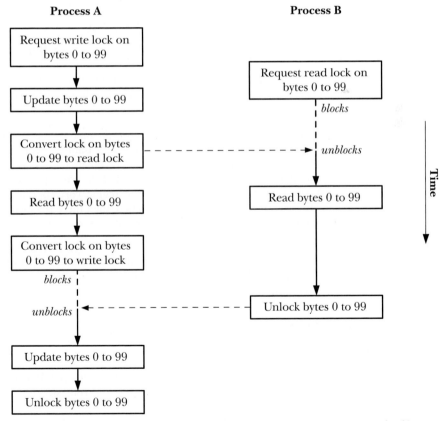

Figure 55-2: Using record locks to synchronize access to the same region of a file

In order to place a read lock on a file, the file must be open for reading. Similarly, to place a write lock, the file must be open for writing. To place both types of locks, we open the file read-write (O_RDWR). Attempting to place a lock that is incompatible with the file access mode results in the error EBADF.

The *l_whence*, *l_start*, and *l_len* fields together specify the range of bytes to be locked. The first two of these fields are analogous to the *whence* and *offset* arguments to *lseek()* (Section 4.7). The *l_start* field specifies an offset within the file that is interpreted with respect to one of the following:

- the start of the file, if *l_whence* is SEEK_SET;
- the current file offset, if *l_whence* is SEEK_CUR; or
- the end of the file, if *l_whence* is SEEK_END.

In the last two cases, *l_start* can be a negative number, as long as the resulting file position doesn't lie before the start of the file (byte 0).

The *l_len* field contains an integer specifying the number of bytes to lock, starting from the position defined by *l_whence* and *l_start*. It is possible to lock nonexistent bytes past the end of the file, but it is not possible to lock bytes before the start of the file.

Since kernel 2.4.21, Linux allows a negative value to be supplied in *l_len*. This is a request to lock the *l_len* bytes preceding the position specified by *l_whence* and *l_start* (i.e., bytes in the range *(l_start − abs(l_len))* through to *(l_start − 1)*). SUSv3 permits, but doesn't require, this feature. Several other UNIX implementations also provide it.

In general, applications should lock the minimum range of bytes necessary. This allows greater concurrency for other processes simultaneously trying to lock different regions of the same file.

> The term *minimum range* needs qualification in some circumstances. Mixing record locks and calls to *mmap()* can have unpleasant consequences on network file systems such as NFS and CIFS. The problem occurs because *mmap()* maps files in units of the system page size. If a file lock is page-aligned, then all is well, since the lock will cover the entire region corresponding to a dirty page. However, if the lock is not page-aligned, then there is a race condition—the kernel may write into the area that is not covered by the lock if any part of the mapped page has been modified.

Specifying 0 in *l_len* has the special meaning "lock all bytes from the point specified by *l_start* and *l_whence* through to the end of the file, no matter how large the file grows." This is convenient if we don't know in advance how many bytes we are going to add to a file. To lock the entire file, we can specify *l_whence* as SEEK_SET and both *l_start* and *l_len* as 0.

The *cmd* argument

When working with file locks, three possible values may be specified for the *cmd* argument of *fcntl()*. The first two are used for acquiring and releasing locks:

F_SETLK

Acquire (*l_type* is F_RDLCK or F_WRLCK) or release (*l_type* is F_UNLCK) a lock on the bytes specified by *flockstr*. If an incompatible lock is held by another process on any part of the region to be locked, *fcntl()* fails with the error EAGAIN. On some UNIX implementations, *fcntl()* fails with the error EACCES in this case. SUSv3 permits either possibility, and a portable application should test for both values.

F_SETLKW

This is the same as F_SETLK, except that if another process holds an incompatible lock on any part of the region to be locked, then the call blocks until the lock can be granted. If we are handling signals and have not specified SA_RESTART (Section 21.5), then an F_SETLKW operation may be interrupted (i.e., fail with the error EINTR). We can take advantage of this behavior to use *alarm()* or *setitimer()* to set a timeout on the lock request.

Note that *fcntl()* locks either the entire region specified or nothing at all. There is no notion of locking just those bytes of the requested region that are currently unlocked.

The remaining *fcntl()* operation is used to determine whether we can place a lock on a given region:

F_GETLK

Check if it would be possible to acquire the lock specified in *flockstr*, but don't actually acquire it. The *l_type* field must be F_RDLCK or F_WRLCK. The *flockstr* structure is treated as a value-result argument; on return, it contains information informing us whether or not the specified lock could be placed. If the lock would be permitted (i.e., no incompatible locks exist on the specified file region), then F_UNLCK is returned in the *l_type* field, and the remaining fields are left unchanged. If one or more incompatible locks exist on the region, then *flockstr* returns information about *one* of those locks (it is indeterminate which), including its type (*l_type*), range of bytes (*l_start* and *l_len*; *l_whence* is always returned as SEEK_SET), and the process ID of the process holding the lock (*l_pid*).

Note that there are potential race conditions when combining the use of F_GETLK with a subsequent F_SETLK or F_SETLKW. By the time we perform the latter operation, the information returned by F_GETLK may already be out of date. Thus, F_GETLK is less useful than it first appears. Even if F_GETLK says that it is possible to place a lock, we must still be prepared for an error return from F_SETLK or for F_SETLKW to block.

> The GNU C library also implements the function *lockf()*, which is just a simplified interface layered on top of *fcntl()*. (SUSv3 specifies *lockf()*, but doesn't specify the relationship between *lockf()* and *fcntl()*. However, most UNIX systems implement *lockf()* on top of *fcntl()*.) A call of the form *lockf(fd, operation, size)* is equivalent to a call to *fcntl()* with *l_whence* set to SEEK_CUR, *l_start* set to 0, and *l_len* set to *size*; that is, *lockf()* locks a sequence of bytes starting at the current file offset. The *operation* argument to *lockf()* is analogous to the *cmd* argument to *fcntl()*, but different constants are used for acquiring, releasing, and testing for the presence of locks. The *lockf()* function places only exclusive (i.e., write) locks. See the *lockf(3)* manual page for further details.

Details of lock acquisition and release

Note the following points regarding the acquisition and release of locks created with *fcntl()*:

- Unlocking a file region always immediately succeeds. It is not an error to unlock a region on which we don't currently hold a lock.

- At any time, a process can hold just one type of lock on a particular region of a file. Placing a new lock on a region we have already locked either results in no change (if the lock type is the same as the existing lock) or atomically converts the existing lock to the new mode. In the latter case, when converting a read lock to a write lock, we need to be prepared for the possibility that the call will yield an error (F_SETLK) or block (F_SETLKW). (This differs from *flock()*, whose lock conversions are not atomic.)

- A process can never lock itself out of a file region, even when placing locks via multiple file descriptors referring to the same file. (This contrasts with *flock()*, and we say more on this point in Section 55.3.5.)

- Placing a lock of a different mode in the middle of a lock we already hold results in three locks: two smaller locks in the previous mode are created on either side of the new lock (see Figure 55-3). Conversely, acquiring a second lock adjacent to or overlapping an existing lock in the same mode results in a single coalesced lock covering the combined area of the two locks. Other permutations are possible. For example, unlocking a region in the middle of a larger existing lock leaves two smaller locked regions on either side of the unlocked region. If a new lock overlaps an existing lock with a different mode, then the existing lock is shrunk, because the overlapping bytes are incorporated into the new lock.

- Closing a file descriptor has some unusual semantics with respect to file region locks. We describe these semantics in Section 55.3.5.

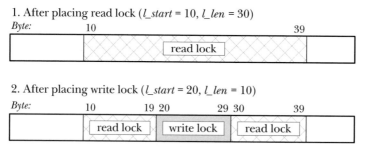

Figure 55-3: Splitting of an existing read lock by a write lock by the same process

55.3.1 Deadlock

When using F_SETLKW, we need to be aware of the type of scenario illustrated in Figure 55-4. In this scenario, each process's second lock request is blocked by a lock held by the other process. Such a scenario is referred to as a *deadlock*. If unchecked by the kernel, this would leave both processes blocked forever. To prevent this possibility, the kernel checks each new lock request made via F_SETLKW to see if it would result in a deadlock situation. If it would, then the kernel selects one of the blocked processes and causes its *fcntl()* call to unblock and fail with the error EDEADLK. (On Linux, the process making the most recent *fcntl()* call is selected, but this is not required by SUSv3, and may not hold true on future versions of Linux or on other UNIX implementations. Any process using F_SETLKW must be prepared to handle an EDEADLK error.)

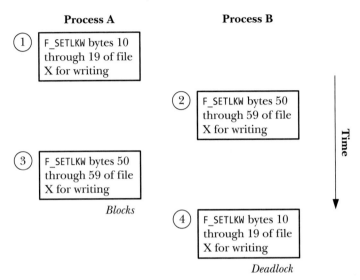

Figure 55-4: Deadlock when two processes deny each other's lock requests

Deadlock situations are detected even when placing locks on multiple different files, as are circular deadlocks involving multiple processes. (By *circular deadlock*, we mean, for example, process A waiting to acquire a lock on a region locked by process B, process B waiting on a lock held by process C, and process C waiting on a lock held by process A.)

55.3.2 Example: An Interactive Locking Program

The program shown in Listing 55-2 allows us to interactively experiment with record locking. This program takes a single command-line argument: the name of a file on which we wish to place locks. Using this program, we can verify many of our previous statements regarding the operation of record locking. The program is designed to be used interactively and accepts commands of this form:

---

cmd lock start length [*whence*]

For *cmd*, we can specify *g* to perform an F_GETLK, *s* to perform an F_SETLK, or *w* to perform an F_SETLKW. The remaining arguments are used to initialize the *flock* structure passed to *fcntl()*. The *lock* argument specifies the value for the *l_type* field and is *r* for F_RDLCK, *w* for F_WRLCK, or *u* for F_UNLCK. The *start* and *length* arguments are integers specifying the values for the *l_start* and *l_len* fields. Finally, the optional *whence* argument specifies the value for the *l_whence* field, and may be *s* for SEEK_SET (the default), *c* for SEEK_CUR, or *e* for SEEK_END. (For an explanation of why we cast the *l_start* and *l_len* fields to *long long* in the *printf()* call in Listing 55-2, see Section 5.10.)

Listing 55-2: Experimenting with record locking

—————————————————————————————— **filelock/i_fcntl_locking.c**

```c
#include <sys/stat.h>
#include <fcntl.h>
#include "tlpi_hdr.h"

#define MAX_LINE 100

static void
displayCmdFmt(void)
{
    printf("\n    Format: cmd lock start length [whence]\n\n");
    printf("    'cmd' is 'g' (GETLK), 's' (SETLK), or 'w' (SETLKW)\n");
    printf("    'lock' is 'r' (READ), 'w' (WRITE), or 'u' (UNLOCK)\n");
    printf("    'start' and 'length' specify byte range to lock\n");
    printf("    'whence' is 's' (SEEK_SET, default), 'c' (SEEK_CUR), "
            "or 'e' (SEEK_END)\n\n");
}

int
main(int argc, char *argv[])
{
    int fd, numRead, cmd, status;
    char lock, cmdCh, whence, line[MAX_LINE];
    struct flock fl;
    long long len, st;

    if (argc != 2 || strcmp(argv[1], "--help") == 0)
        usageErr("%s file\n", argv[0]);

    fd = open(argv[1], O_RDWR);
    if (fd == -1)
        errExit("open (%s)", argv[1]);

    printf("Enter ? for help\n");

    for (;;) {                    /* Prompt for locking command and carry it out */
        printf("PID=%ld> ", (long) getpid());
        fflush(stdout);

        if (fgets(line, MAX_LINE, stdin) == NULL)      /* EOF */
            exit(EXIT_SUCCESS);
        line[strlen(line) - 1] = '\0';                 /* Remove trailing '\n' */

        if (*line == '\0')
            continue;                                  /* Skip blank lines */

        if (line[0] == '?') {
            displayCmdFmt();
            continue;
        }

        whence = 's';                  /* In case not otherwise filled in */
```

```
            numRead = sscanf(line, "%c %c %lld %lld %c", &cmdCh, &lock,
                        &st, &len, &whence);
        fl.l_start = st;
        fl.l_len = len;

        if (numRead < 4 || strchr("gsw", cmdCh) == NULL ||
                strchr("rwu", lock) == NULL || strchr("sce", whence) == NULL) {
            printf("Invalid command!\n");
            continue;
        }

        cmd = (cmdCh == 'g') ? F_GETLK : (cmdCh == 's') ? F_SETLK : F_SETLKW;
        fl.l_type = (lock == 'r') ? F_RDLCK : (lock == 'w') ? F_WRLCK : F_UNLCK;
        fl.l_whence = (whence == 'c') ? SEEK_CUR :
                    (whence == 'e') ? SEEK_END : SEEK_SET;

        status = fcntl(fd, cmd, &fl);          /* Perform request... */

        if (cmd == F_GETLK) {                  /* ... and see what happened */
            if (status == -1) {
                errMsg("fcntl - F_GETLK");
            } else {
                if (fl.l_type == F_UNLCK)
                    printf("[PID=%ld] Lock can be placed\n", (long) getpid());
                else                           /* Locked out by someone else */
                    printf("[PID=%ld] Denied by %s lock on %lld:%lld "
                            "(held by PID %ld)\n", (long) getpid(),
                            (fl.l_type == F_RDLCK) ? "READ" : "WRITE",
                            (long long) fl.l_start,
                            (long long) fl.l_len, (long) fl.l_pid);
            }
        } else {                  /* F_SETLK, F_SETLKW */
            if (status == 0)
                printf("[PID=%ld] %s\n", (long) getpid(),
                        (lock == 'u') ? "unlocked" : "got lock");
            else if (errno == EAGAIN || errno == EACCES)          /* F_SETLK */
                printf("[PID=%ld] failed (incompatible lock)\n",
                        (long) getpid());
            else if (errno == EDEADLK)                        /* F_SETLKW */
                printf("[PID=%ld] failed (deadlock)\n", (long) getpid());
            else
                errMsg("fcntl - F_SETLK(W)");
        }
    }
}
```

————————————————————————————————— **filelock/i_fcntl_locking.c**

In the following shell session logs, we demonstrate the use of the program in Listing 55-2 by running two instances to place locks on the same 100-byte file (tfile).
Figure 55-5 shows the state of granted and queued lock requests at various points
during this shell session log, as noted in the commentary below.

We start a first instance (process A) of the program in Listing 55-2, placing a read lock on bytes 0 to 39 of the file:

```
Terminal window 1
$ ls -l tfile
-rw-r--r--    1 mtk       users        100 Apr 18 12:19 tfile
$ ./i_fcntl_locking tfile
Enter ? for help
PID=790> s r 0 40
[PID=790] got lock
```

Then we start a second instance of the program (process B), placing a read lock on a bytes 70 through to the end of the file:

```
Terminal window 2
$ ./i_fcntl_locking tfile
Enter ? for help
PID=800> s r -30 0 e
[PID=800] got lock
```

At this point, things appear as shown in part *a* of Figure 55-5, where process A (process ID 790) and process B (process ID 800) hold locks on different parts of the file.

Now we return to process A, where we try to place a write lock on the entire file. We first employ F_GETLK to test whether the lock can be placed and are informed that there is a conflicting lock. Then we try placing the lock with F_SETLK, which also fails. Finally, we try placing the lock with F_SETLKW, which blocks.

```
PID=790> g w 0 0
[PID=790] Denied by READ lock on 70:0 (held by PID 800)
PID=790> s w 0 0
[PID=790] failed (incompatible lock)
PID=790> w w 0 0
```

At this point, things appear as shown in part *b* of Figure 55-5, where process A and process B each hold a lock on different parts of the file, and process A has a queued lock request on the whole file.

We continue in process B, by trying to place a write lock on the entire file. We first test whether the lock can be placed using F_GETLK, which informs us that there is a conflicting lock. We then try placing the lock using F_SETLKW.

```
PID=800> g w 0 0
[PID=800] Denied by READ lock on 0:40
(held by PID 790)
PID=800> w w 0 0
[PID=800] failed (deadlock)
```

Part *c* of Figure 55-5 shows what happened when process B made a blocking request to place a write lock on the entire file: a deadlock. At this point, the kernel selected one of the lock requests to fail—in this case, the request by process B, which then receives the EDEADLK error from its *fcntl()* call.

We continue in process B, by removing all of its locks on the file:

```
PID=800> s u 0 0
[PID=800] unlocked
```

```
[PID=790] got lock
```

As we see from the last line of output, this allowed process A's blocked lock request to be granted.

It is important to realize that even though process B's deadlocked request was canceled, it still held its other lock, and so process A's queued lock request remained blocked. Process A's lock request is granted only when process B removes its other lock, bringing about the situation shown in part *d* of Figure 55-5.

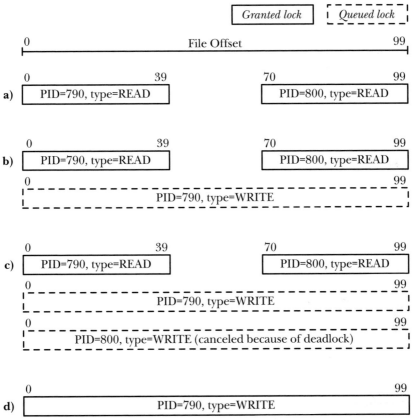

Figure 55-5: State of granted and queued lock requests while running i_fcntl_locking.c

55.3.3 Example: A Library of Locking Functions

Listing 55-3 provides a set of locking functions that we can use in other programs. These functions are as follows:

- The *lockRegion()* function uses F_SETLK to place a lock on the open file referred to by the file descriptor *fd*. The *type* argument specifies the lock type (F_RDLCK or F_WRLCK). The *whence*, *start*, and *len* arguments specify the range of bytes to lock. These arguments provide the values for the similarly named fields of the *flock* structure that is used to place the lock.

- The *lockRegionWait()* function is like *lockRegion()*, but makes a blocking lock request; that is, it uses F_SETLKW, rather than F_SETLK.

- The *regionIsLocked()* function tests whether a lock can be placed on a file. The arguments of this function are as for *lockRegion()*. This function returns 0 (false) if no process holds a lock that conflicts with the lock specified in the call. If one or more processes hold conflicting locks, then this function returns a nonzero value (i.e., true)—the process ID of one of the processes holding a conflicting lock.

Listing 55-3: File region locking functions

———————————————————————————————— `filelock/region_locking.c`

```
#include <fcntl.h>
#include "region_locking.h"          /* Declares functions defined here */

/* Lock a file region (private; public interfaces below) */

static int
lockReg(int fd, int cmd, int type, int whence, int start, off_t len)
{
    struct flock fl;

    fl.l_type = type;
    fl.l_whence = whence;
    fl.l_start = start;
    fl.l_len = len;

    return fcntl(fd, cmd, &fl);
}

int                     /* Lock a file region using nonblocking F_SETLK */
lockRegion(int fd, int type, int whence, int start, int len)
{
    return lockReg(fd, F_SETLK, type, whence, start, len);
}

int                     /* Lock a file region using blocking F_SETLKW */
lockRegionWait(int fd, int type, int whence, int start, int len)
{
    return lockReg(fd, F_SETLKW, type, whence, start, len);
}

/* Test if a file region is lockable. Return 0 if lockable, or
   PID of process holding incompatible lock, or -1 on error. */

pid_t
regionIsLocked(int fd, int type, int whence, int start, int len)
{
    struct flock fl;

    fl.l_type = type;
    fl.l_whence = whence;
    fl.l_start = start;
    fl.l_len = len;
```

```
if (fcntl(fd, F_GETLK, &fl) == -1)
    return -1;

return (fl.l_type == F_UNLCK) ? 0 : fl.l_pid;
}
```

`filelock/region_locking.c`

55.3.4 Lock Limits and Performance

SUSv3 allows an implementation to place fixed, system-wide upper limits on the number of record locks that can be acquired. When this limit is reached, *fcntl()* fails with the error ENOLCK. Linux doesn't set a fixed upper limit on the number of record locks that may be acquired; we are merely limited by availability of memory. (Many other UNIX implementations are similar.)

How quickly can record locks be acquired and released? There is no fixed answer to this question, since the speed of these operations is a function of the kernel data structure used to maintain record locks and the location of a particular lock within that data structure. We look at this structure in a moment, but first we consider some requirements that influence its design:

- The kernel needs to be able to merge a new lock with any existing locks (held by the same process) of the same mode that may lie on either side of the new lock.

- A new lock may completely replace one or more existing locks held by the calling process. The kernel needs to be able to easily locate all of these locks.

- When creating a new lock with a different mode in the middle of an existing lock, the job of splitting the existing lock (Figure 55-3) should be simple.

The kernel data structure used to maintain information about locks is designed to satisfy these requirements. Each open file has an associated linked list of locks held against that file. Locks within the list are ordered, first by process ID, and then by starting offset. An example of such a list is shown in Figure 55-6.

> The kernel also maintains *flock()* locks and file leases in the linked list of locks associated with an open file. (We briefly describe file leases when discussing the /proc/locks file in Section 55.5.) However, these types of locks are typically far fewer in number and therefore less likely to impact performance, so we ignore them in our discussion.

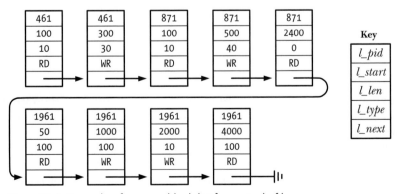

Figure 55-6: Example of a record lock list for a single file

Whenever a new lock is added to this data structure, the kernel must check for conflicts with any existing lock on the file. This search is carried out sequentially, starting at the head of the list.

Assuming a large number of locks distributed randomly among many processes, we can say that the time required to add or remove a lock increases roughly linearly with the number of locks already held on the file.

55.3.5 Semantics of Lock Inheritance and Release

The semantics of *fcntl()* record lock inheritance and release differ substantially from those for locks created using *flock()*. Note the following points:

- Record locks are not inherited across a *fork()* by a child process. This contrasts with *flock()*, where the child inherits a reference to the *same* lock and can release this lock, with the consequence that the parent also loses the lock.

- Record locks are preserved across an *exec()*. (However, note the effect of the close-on-exec flag, described below.)

- All of the threads in a process share the same set of record locks.

- Record locks are associated with both a process and an i-node (refer to Section 5.4). An unsurprising consequence of this association is that when a process terminates, all of its record locks are released. Less expected is that whenever a process closes a file descriptor, *all* locks held by the process on the corresponding file are released, regardless of the file descriptor(s) through which the locks were obtained. For example, in the following code, the *close(fd2)* call releases the lock held by the calling process on testfile, even though the lock was obtained via the file descriptor *fd1*:

```
struct flock fl;

fl.l_type = F_WRLCK;
fl.l_whence = SEEK_SET;
fl.l_start = 0;
fl.l_len = 0;

fd1 = open("testfile", O_RDWR);
fd2 = open("testfile", O_RDWR);

if (fcntl(fd1, cmd, &fl) == -1)
    errExit("fcntl");

close(fd2);
```

The semantics described in the last point apply no matter how the various descriptors referring to the same file were obtained and no matter how the descriptor is closed. For example, *dup()*, *dup2()*, and *fcntl()* can all be used to obtain duplicates of an open file descriptor. And, as well as performing an explicit *close()*, a descriptor can be closed by an *exec()* call if the close-on-exec flag was set, or via a *dup2()* call, which closes its second file descriptor argument if that descriptor is already open.

The semantics of *fcntl()* lock inheritance and release are an architectural blemish. For example, they make the use of record locks from library packages problematic, since a library function can't prevent the possibility that its caller will close a file descriptor referring to a locked file and thus remove a lock obtained by the library code. An alternative implementation scheme would have been to associate a lock with a file descriptor rather than with an i-node. However, the current semantics are the historical and now standardized behavior of record locks. Unfortunately, these semantics greatly limit the utility of *fcntl()* locking.

> With *flock()*, a lock is associated only with an open file description, and remains in effect until either any process holding a reference to the lock explicitly releases the lock or all file descriptors referring to the open file description are closed.

55.3.6 Lock Starvation and Priority of Queued Lock Requests

When multiple processes must wait in order to place a lock on a currently locked region, a couple of questions arise.

Can a process waiting to place a write lock be starved by a series of processes placing read locks on the same region? On Linux (as on many other UNIX implementations), a series of read locks can indeed starve a blocked write lock, possibly indefinitely.

When two or more processes are waiting to place a lock, are there any rules that determine which process obtains the lock when it becomes available? For example, are lock requests satisfied in FIFO order? And do the rules depend on the types of locks being requested by each process (i.e., does a process requesting a read lock have priority over one requesting a write lock or vice versa, or neither)? On Linux, the rules are as follows:

- The order in which queued lock requests are granted is indeterminate. If multiple processes are waiting to place locks, then the order in which they are satisfied depends on how the processes are scheduled.

- Writers don't have priority over readers, and vice versa.

Such statements don't necessarily hold true on other systems. On some UNIX implementations, lock requests are served in FIFO order, and readers have priority over writers.

55.4 Mandatory Locking

The kinds of locks we have described so far are *advisory*. This means that a process is free to ignore the use of *fcntl()* (or *flock()*) and simply perform I/O on the file. The kernel doesn't prevent this. When using advisory locking, it is up to the application designer to:

- set appropriate ownership (or group ownership) and permissions for the file, so as to prevent noncooperating process from performing file I/O; and

- ensure that the processes composing the application cooperate by obtaining the appropriate lock on the file before performing I/O.

Linux, like many other UNIX implementations, also allows *fcntl()* record locks to be *mandatory*. This means that every file I/O operation is checked to see whether it is compatible with any locks held by other processes on the region of the file on which I/O is being performed.

> Advisory mode locking is sometimes referred to as *discretionary locking*, while mandatory locking is sometimes referred to as *enforcement-mode locking*. SUSv3 doesn't specify mandatory locking, but it is available (with some variation in the details) on most modern UNIX implementations.

In order to use mandatory locking on Linux, we must enable it on the file system containing the files we wish to lock and on each file to be locked. We enable mandatory locking on a file system by mounting it with the (Linux-specific) *-o mand* option:

```
# mount -o mand /dev/sda10 /testfs
```

From a program, we can achieve the same result by specifying the MS_MANDLOCK flag when calling *mount(2)* (Section 14.8.1).

We can check whether a mounted file system has mandatory locking enabled by looking at the output of the *mount(8)* command with no options:

```
# mount | grep sda10
/dev/sda10 on /testfs type ext3 (rw,mand)
```

Mandatory locking is enabled on a file by the combination of having the set-group-ID permission bit turned on and the group-execute permission turned off. This combination of permission bits was otherwise meaningless and unused in earlier UNIX implementations. In this way, later UNIX systems added mandatory locking without needing to change existing programs or add new system calls. From the shell, we can enable mandatory locking on a file as follows:

```
$ chmod g+s,g-x /testfs/file
```

From a program, we can enable mandatory locking for a file by setting permissions appropriately using *chmod()* or *fchmod()* (Section 15.4.7).

When displaying permissions for a file whose permission bits are set for mandatory locking, *ls(1)* displays an S in the group-execute permission column:

```
$ ls -l /testfs/file
-rw-r-Sr--    1 mtk      users        0 Apr 22 14:11 /testfs/file
```

Mandatory locking is supported for all native Linux and UNIX file systems, but may not be supported on some network file systems or on non-UNIX file systems. For example, Microsoft's VFAT file system has no set-group-ID permission bit, so mandatory locking can't be used on VFAT file systems.

Effect of mandatory locking on file I/O operations

If mandatory locking is enabled for a file, what happens when a system call that performs data transfer (e.g., *read()* or *write()*) encounters a lock conflict (i.e., an attempt is made to write to a region that is currently read or write locked, or to read from a region that is currently write locked)? The answer depends on whether the file has been opened in blocking or nonblocking mode. If the file was opened in blocking mode, the system call blocks. If the file was opened with the O_NONBLOCK flag, the system call immediately fails with the error EAGAIN. Similar rules apply for *truncate()* and *ftruncate()*, if the bytes they are attempting to add or remove from the file overlap a region currently locked (for reading or writing) by another process.

If we have opened a file in blocking mode (i.e., O_NONBLOCK is not specified in the *open()* call), then I/O system calls can be involved in deadlock situations. Consider the example shown in Figure 55-7, involving two processes that open the same file for blocking I/O, obtain write locks on different parts of the file, and then each attempt to write to the region locked by the other process. The kernel resolves this situation in the same way that deadlock between two *fcntl()* calls is resolved (Section 55.3.1): it selects one of the processes involved in the deadlock and causes its *write()* system call to fail with the error EDEADLK.

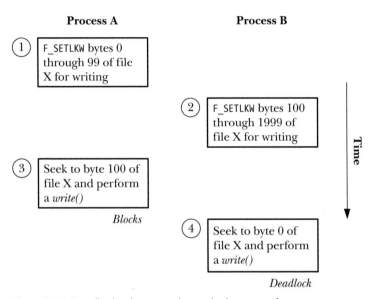

Figure 55-7: Deadlock when mandatory locking is in force

Attempts to *open()* a file with the O_TRUNC flag always fail immediately (with the error EAGAIN) if any other process holds a read or write lock on any part of the file.

It is not possible to create a shared memory mapping (i.e., *mmap()* with the MAP_SHARED flag) on a file if any other process holds a mandatory read or write lock on *any* part of the file. Conversely, it is not possible to place a mandatory lock on *any* part of a file that is currently involved in a shared memory mapping. In both cases, the relevant system call fails immediately with the error EAGAIN. The reason for these restrictions becomes clear when we consider the implementation of memory mappings. In Section 49.4.2, we saw that a shared file mapping both reads from and writes to a file (and the latter operation, in particular, conflicts with any type of lock on the file). Furthermore, this file I/O is performed by the memory-management subsystem, which has no knowledge of the location of any file locks in the system. Thus, to prevent a mapping from updating a file on which a mandatory lock is held, the kernel performs a simple check—testing at the time of the *mmap()* call whether there are locks anywhere in the file to be mapped (and vice versa for *fcntl()*).

Mandatory locking caveats

Mandatory locks do less for us than we might at first expect, and have some potential shortcomings and problems:

- Holding a mandatory lock on a file doesn't prevent another process from deleting it, since all that is required to unlink a file is suitable permissions on the parent directory.

- Careful consideration should be applied before enabling mandatory locks on a publicly accessible file, since not even privileged processes can override a mandatory lock. A malicious user could continuously hold a lock on the file in order to create a denial-of-service attack. (While in most cases, we could make the file accessible once more by turning off the set-group-ID bit, this may not be possible if, for example, the mandatory file lock is causing the system to hang.)

- There is a performance cost associated with the use of mandatory locking. For each I/O system call made on a file with mandatory locking enabled, the kernel must check for lock conflicts on the file. If the file has a large number of locks, this check can slow I/O system calls significantly.

- Mandatory locking also incurs a cost in application design. We need to handle the possibility that each I/O system call can return EAGAIN (for nonblocking I/O) or EDEADLK (for blocking I/O).

- As a consequence of some kernel race conditions in the current Linux implementation, there are circumstances in which system calls that perform I/O operations can succeed despite the presence of mandatory locks that should deny those operations.

In summary, the use of mandatory locks is best avoided.

55.5 The /proc/locks File

We can view the set of locks currently held in the system by examining the contents of the Linux-specific /proc/locks file. Here is an example of the information we can see in this file (in this case, for four locks):

```
$ cat /proc/locks
1: POSIX  ADVISORY  WRITE 458 03:07:133880 0 EOF
2: FLOCK  ADVISORY  WRITE 404 03:07:133875 0 EOF
3: POSIX  ADVISORY  WRITE 312 03:07:133853 0 EOF
4: FLOCK  ADVISORY  WRITE 274 03:07:81908 0 EOF
```

The /proc/locks file displays information about locks created by both *flock()* and *fcntl()*. The eight fields shown for each lock are as follows (from left to right):

1. The ordinal number of the lock within the set of all locks shown in this file. (Refer to Section 55.3.4.)

2. The type of lock. Here, FLOCK indicates a lock created by *flock()*, and POSIX indicates a lock created by *fcntl()*.

3. The mode of the lock, either ADVISORY or MANDATORY.

4. The type of lock, either READ or WRITE (corresponding to shared and exclusive locks for *flock()*).

5. The process ID of the process holding the lock.

6. Three colon-separated numbers that identify the file on which the lock is held. These numbers are the major and minor device numbers of the file system on which the file resides, followed by the i-node number of the file.

7. The starting byte of the lock. This is always 0 for *flock()* locks.

8. The ending byte of the lock. Here, EOF indicates that the lock runs to the end of the file (i.e., *l_len* was specified as 0 for a lock created by *fcntl()*). For *flock()* locks, this column is always EOF.

> In Linux 2.4 and earlier, each line of /proc/locks includes five additional hexadecimal values. These are pointer addresses used by the kernel to record locks in various lists. These values are not useful in application programs.

Using the information in /proc/locks, we can find out which process is holding a lock, and on what file. The following shell session shows how to do this for lock number 3 in the list above. This lock is held by process ID 312, on the i-node 133853 on the device with major ID 3 and minor ID 7. We begin by using *ps(1)* to list information about the process with process ID 312:

```
$ ps -p 312
  PID TTY          TIME CMD
  312 ?        00:00:00 atd
```

The above output shows that the program holding the lock is *atd*, the daemon that executes scheduled batch jobs.

In order to find the locked file, we first search the files in the /dev directory, and thus determine that the device with ID 3:7 is /dev/sda7:

```
$ ls -li /dev | awk '$6 == "3," && $7 == 7'
1311 brw-rw----   1 root     disk      3,  7 May 12  2006 /dev/sda7
```

We then determine the mount point for the device /dev/sda7 and search that part of the file system for the file whose i-node number is 133853:

```
$ mount | grep sda7
/dev/sda7 on / type reiserfs (rw)        Device is mounted on /
$ su                                     So we can search all directories
Password:
# find / -mount -inum 133853             Search for i-node 133853
/var/run/atd.pid
```

The *find −mount* option prevents *find* from descending into subdirectories under / that are mount points for other file systems.

Finally, we display the contents of the locked file:

```
# cat /var/run/atd.pid
312
```

Thus, we see that the *atd* daemon is holding a lock on the file /var/run/atd.pid, and that the content of this file is the process ID of the process running *atd*. This daemon is employing a technique to ensure that only one instance of the daemon is running at a time. We describe this technique in Section 55.6.

We can also use /proc/locks to obtain information about blocked lock requests, as demonstrated in the following output:

```
$ cat /proc/locks
1: POSIX  ADVISORY  WRITE 11073 03:07:436283 100 109
1: -> POSIX  ADVISORY  WRITE 11152 03:07:436283 100 109
2: POSIX  MANDATORY WRITE 11014 03:07:436283 0 9
2: -> POSIX  MANDATORY WRITE 11024 03:07:436283 0 9
2: -> POSIX  MANDATORY READ  11122 03:07:436283 0 19
3: FLOCK  ADVISORY  WRITE 10802 03:07:134447 0 EOF
3: -> FLOCK  ADVISORY  WRITE 10840 03:07:134447 0 EOF
```

Lines shown with the characters -> immediately after a lock number represent lock requests blocked by the corresponding lock number. Thus, we see one request blocked on lock 1 (an advisory lock created with *fcntl()*), two requests blocked on lock 2 (a mandatory lock created with *fcntl()*), and one request blocked on lock 3 (a lock created with *flock()*).

> The /proc/locks file also displays information about any file leases that are held by processes on the system. File leases are a Linux-specific mechanism available in Linux 2.4 and later. If a process takes out a lease on a file, then it is notified (by delivery of a signal) if another process tries to *open()* or *truncate()* that file. (The inclusion of *truncate()* is necessary because it is the only system call that can be used to change the contents of a file without first opening it.) File leases are provided in order to allow Samba to support the *opportunistic locks (oplocks)* functionality of the Microsoft SMB protocol and to allow NFS version 4 to support *delegations* (which are similar to SMB oplocks). Further details about file leases can be found under the description of the F_SETLEASE operation in the *fcntl(2)* manual page.

55.6 Running Just One Instance of a Program

Some programs—in particular, many daemons—need to ensure that only one instance of the program is running on the system at a time. A common method of doing this is to have the daemon create a file in a standard directory and place a write lock on it. The daemon holds the file lock for the duration of its execution and deletes the file just before terminating. If another instance of the daemon is started, it will fail to obtain a write lock on the file. Consequently, it will realize that another instance of the daemon must already be running, and terminate.

> Many network servers use an alternative convention of assuming that a server instance is already running if the well-known socket port to which the server binds is already in use (Section 61.10).

The /var/run directory is the usual location for such lock files. Alternatively, the location of the file may be specified by a line in the daemon's configuration file.

Conventionally, a daemon writes its own process ID into the lock file, and hence the file is often named with an extension .pid (for example, *syslogd* creates the file /var/run/syslogd.pid). This is useful if some application needs to find the process ID of the daemon. It also allows an extra sanity check—we can verify whether that process ID exists using *kill(pid, 0)*, as described in Section 20.6. (In older UNIX implementations that did not provide file locking, this was used as an imperfect, but usually practicable, way of assessing whether an instance of the daemon really was still running, or whether an earlier instance had simply failed to delete the file before terminating.)

There are many minor variations in the code used to create and lock a process ID lock file. Listing 55-4 is based on ideas presented in [Stevens, 1999] and provides a function, *createPidFile()*, that encapsulates the steps described above. We would typically call this function with a line such as the following:

```
if (createPidFile("mydaemon", "/var/run/mydaemon.pid", 0) == -1)
    errExit("createPidFile");
```

One subtlety in the *createPidFile()* function is the use of *ftruncate()* to erase any previous string in the lock file. This is done because the last instance of the daemon may have failed to delete the file, perhaps because of a system crash. In this case, if the process ID of the new daemon instance is small, we might otherwise not completely overwrite the previous contents of the file. For example, if our process ID is 789, then we would write just 789\n to the file, but a previous daemon instance might have written 12345\n. If we did not truncate the file, then the resulting content would be 789\n5\n. Erasing any existing string may not be strictly necessary, but it is tidier and removes any potential for confusion.

The *flags* argument can specify the constant CPF_CLOEXEC, which causes *createPidFile()* to set the close-on-exec flag (Section 27.4) for the file descriptor. This is useful for servers that restart themselves by calling *exec()*. If the file descriptor was not closed during the *exec()*, then the restarted server would think that a duplicate instance of the server is already running.

Listing 55-4: Creating a PID lock file to ensure just one instance of a program is started

––– **filelock/create_pid_file.c**
```
#include <sys/stat.h>
#include <fcntl.h>
#include "region_locking.h"        /* For lockRegion() */
#include "create_pid_file.h"       /* Declares createPidFile() and
                                       defines CPF_CLOEXEC */
#include "tlpi_hdr.h"

#define BUF_SIZE 100            /* Large enough to hold maximum PID as string */

/* Open/create the file named in 'pidFile', lock it, optionally set the
   close-on-exec flag for the file descriptor, write our PID into the file,
   and (in case the caller is interested) return the file descriptor
   referring to the locked file. The caller is responsible for deleting
   'pidFile' file (just) before process termination. 'progName' should be the
   name of the calling program (i.e., argv[0] or similar), and is used only for
   diagnostic messages. If we can't open 'pidFile', or we encounter some other
   error, then we print an appropriate diagnostic and terminate. */
```

```
int
createPidFile(const char *progName, const char *pidFile, int flags)
{
    int fd;
    char buf[BUF_SIZE];

    fd = open(pidFile, O_RDWR | O_CREAT, S_IRUSR | S_IWUSR);
    if (fd == -1)
        errExit("Could not open PID file %s", pidFile);

    if (flags & CPF_CLOEXEC) {

        /* Set the close-on-exec file descriptor flag */

        flags = fcntl(fd, F_GETFD);                    /* Fetch flags */
        if (flags == -1)
            errExit("Could not get flags for PID file %s", pidFile);

        flags |= FD_CLOEXEC;                           /* Turn on FD_CLOEXEC */

        if (fcntl(fd, F_SETFD, flags) == -1)           /* Update flags */
            errExit("Could not set flags for PID file %s", pidFile);
    }

    if (lockRegion(fd, F_WRLCK, SEEK_SET, 0, 0) == -1) {
        if (errno == EAGAIN || errno == EACCES)
            fatal("PID file '%s' is locked; probably "
                    "'%s' is already running", pidFile, progName);
        else
            errExit("Unable to lock PID file '%s'", pidFile);
    }

    if (ftruncate(fd, 0) == -1)
        errExit("Could not truncate PID file '%s'", pidFile);

    snprintf(buf, BUF_SIZE, "%ld\n", (long) getpid());
    if (write(fd, buf, strlen(buf)) != strlen(buf))
        fatal("Writing to PID file '%s'", pidFile);

    return fd;
}
```
—————————————————————————————————— filelock/create_pid_file.c

55.7 Older Locking Techniques

In older UNIX implementations that lacked file locking, a number of *ad hoc* locking techniques were employed. Although all of these have been superseded by *fcntl()* record locking, we describe them here since they still appear in some older programs. All of these techniques are advisory in nature.

open(file, O_CREAT | O_EXCL,...) plus unlink(file)

SUSv3 requires that an *open()* call with the flags O_CREAT and O_EXCL perform the steps of checking for the existence of a file and creating it atomically (Section 5.1). This means that if two processes attempt to create a file specifying these flags, it is guaranteed that only one of them will succeed. (The other process will receive the error EEXIST from *open()*.) Used in conjunction with the *unlink()* system call, this provides the basis for a locking mechanism. Acquiring the lock is performed by successfully opening the file with the O_CREAT and O_EXCL flags, followed by an immediate *close()*. Releasing the lock is performed using *unlink()*. Although workable, this technique has several limitations:

- If the *open()* fails, indicating that some other process has the lock, then we must retry the *open()* in some kind of loop, either polling continuously (which wastes CPU time) or with a delay between each attempt (which means that there may be some delay between the time the lock becomes available and when we actually acquire it). With *fcntl()*, we can use F_SETLKW to block until the lock becomes free.

- Acquiring and releasing locks using *open()* and *unlink()* involves file-system operations that are rather slower than the use of record locks. (On one of the author's x86-32 systems running Linux 2.6.31, acquiring and releasing 1 million locks on an *ext3* file using the technique described here required 44 seconds. Acquiring and releasing 1 million record locks on the same byte of a file required 2.5 seconds.)

- If a process accidentally exits without deleting the lock file, the lock is not released. There are *ad hoc* techniques for handling this problem, including checking the last modification time of the file and having the lock holder write its process ID to the file so that we can check if the process still exists, but none of these techniques is foolproof. By comparison, record locks are released automatically when a process terminates.

- If we are placing multiple locks (i.e., using multiple lock files), deadlocks are not detected. If a deadlock arises, the processes involved in the deadlock will remain blocked indefinitely. (Each process will be spinning, checking to see if it can obtain the lock it requires.) By contrast, the kernel provides deadlock detection for *fcntl()* record locks.

- NFS version 2 doesn't support O_EXCL semantics. Linux 2.4 NFS clients also fail to implement O_EXCL correctly, even for NFS version 3 and later.

link(file, lockfile) plus unlink(lockfile)

The fact that the *link()* system call fails if the new link already exists has also been used as a locking mechanism, again employing *unlink()* to perform the unlock function. The usual approach is to have each process that needs to acquire the lock create a unique temporary filename, typically one including the process ID (and possibly the hostname, if the lock file is created on a network file system). To acquire the lock, this temporary file is linked to some agreed-upon standard pathname. (The semantics of hard links require that the two pathnames reside in the same file system.)

If the *link()* call succeeds, we have obtained the lock. If it fails (EEXIST), then another process has the lock and we must try again later. This technique suffers the same limitations as the *open(file, O_CREAT | O_EXCL,...)* technique described above.

open(file, O_CREAT | O_TRUNC | O_WRONLY, 0) plus unlink(file)

The fact that calling *open()* on an existing file fails if O_TRUNC is specified and write permission is denied on the file can be used as the basis of a locking technique. To obtain a lock, we use the following code (which omits error checking) to create a new file:

```
fd = open(file, O_CREAT | O_TRUNC | O_WRONLY, (mode_t) 0);
close(fd);
```

> For an explanation of why we use the *(mode_t)* cast in the *open()* call above, see Appendix C.

If the *open()* call succeeds (i.e., the file didn't previously exist), we have the lock. If it fails with EACCES (i.e., the file exists and has no permissions for anyone), then another process has the lock, and we must try again later. This technique suffers the same limitations as the previous techniques, with the added caveat that we can't employ it in a program with superuser privileges, since the *open()* call will always succeed, regardless of the permissions that are set on the file.

55.8 Summary

File locks allow processes to synchronize access to a file. Linux provides two file locking system calls: the BSD-derived *flock()* and the System V–derived *fcntl()*. Although both system calls are available on most UNIX implementations, only *fcntl()* locking is standardized in SUSv3.

The *flock()* system call locks an entire file. Two types of locks may be placed: shared locks, which are compatible with shared locks held by other processes, and exclusive locks, which prevent other processes from placing any type of lock.

The *fcntl()* system call places locks ("record locks") on any region of a file, ranging from a single byte to the entire file. Two types of locks may be placed: read locks and write locks, which have similar compatibility semantics to the shared and exclusive locks placed via *flock()*. If a blocking (F_SETLKW) lock request would bring about a deadlock situation, then the kernel causes *fcntl()* to fail (with the error EDEADLK) in one of the affected processes.

Locks placed using *flock()* and *fcntl()* are invisible to one another (except on systems that implement *flock()* using *fcntl()*). The locks placed via *flock()* and *fcntl()* have different semantics with respect to inheritance across *fork()* and release when file descriptors are closed.

The Linux-specific /proc/locks file displays the file locks currently held by all processes on the system.

Further information

An extensive discussion of *fcntl()* record locking can be found in [Stevens & Rago, 2005] and [Stevens, 1999]. Some details of the implementation of *flock()* and *fcntl()*

locking on Linux are provided in [Bovet & Cesati, 2005]. [Tanenbaum, 2007] and [Deitel et al., 2004] describe deadlocking concepts in general, including coverage of deadlock detection, avoidance, and prevention.

55.9 Exercises

55-1. Experiment by running multiple instances of the program in Listing 55-1 (t_flock.c) to determine the following points about the operation of *flock()*:

   a) Can a series of processes acquiring shared locks on a file starve a process attempting to place an exclusive lock on the file?

   b) Suppose that a file is locked exclusively, and other processes are waiting to place both shared and exclusive locks on the file. When the first lock is released, are there any rules determining which process is next granted a lock? For example, do shared locks have priority over exclusive locks or vice versa? Are locks granted in FIFO order?

   c) If you have access to some other UNIX implementation that provides *flock()*, try to determine the rules on that implementation.

55-2. Write a program to determine whether *flock()* detects deadlock situations when being used to lock two different files in two processes.

55-3. Write a program to verify the statements made in Section 55.2.1 regarding the semantics of inheritance and release of *flock()* locks.

55-4. Experiment by running the programs in Listing 55-1 (t_flock.c) and Listing 55-2 (i_fcntl_locking.c) to see whether locks granted by *flock()* and *fcntl()* have any effect on one another. If you have access to other UNIX implementations, try the same experiment on those implementations.

55-5. In Section 55.3.4, we noted that, on Linux, the time required to add or check for the existence of a lock is a function of the position of the lock in the list of all locks on the file. Write two programs to verify this:

   a) The first program should acquire (say) 40,001 write locks on a file. These locks are placed on alternating bytes of the file; that is, locks are placed on bytes 0, 2, 4, 6, and so on through to (say) byte 80,000. Having acquired these locks, the process then goes to sleep.

   b) While the first program is sleeping, the second program loops (say) 10,000 times, using F_SETLK to try to lock one of the bytes locked by the previous program (these lock attempts always fail). In any particular execution, the program always tries to lock byte $N * 2$ of the file.

   Using the shell built-in *time* command, measure the time required by the second program for N equals 0, 10,000, 20,000, 30,000, and 40,000. Do the results match the expected linear behavior?

55-6. Experiment with the program in Listing 55-2 (i_fcntl_locking.c) to verify the statements made in Section 55.3.6 regarding lock starvation and priority for *fcntl()* record locks.

55-7. If you have access to other UNIX implementations, use the program in Listing 55-2 (i_fcntl_locking.c) to see if you can establish any rules for *fcntl()* record locking regarding starvation of writers and regarding the order in which multiple queued lock requests are granted.

55-8. Use the program in Listing 55-2 (i_fcntl_locking.c) to demonstrate that the kernel detects circular deadlocks involving three (or more) processes locking the same file.

55-9. Write a pair of programs (or a single program that uses a child process) to bring about the deadlock situation with mandatory locks described in Section 55.4.

55-10. Read the manual page of the *lockfile(1)* utility that is supplied with *procmail*. Write a simple version of this program.

56

SOCKETS: INTRODUCTION

Sockets are a method of IPC that allow data to be exchanged between applications, either on the same host (computer) or on different hosts connected by a network. The first widespread implementation of the sockets API appeared with 4.2BSD in 1983, and this API has been ported to virtually every UNIX implementation, as well as most other operating systems.

> The sockets API is formally specified in POSIX.1g, which was ratified in 2000 after spending about a decade as a draft standard. This standard has been superseded by SUSv3.

This chapter and the following chapters describe the use of sockets, as follows:

- This chapter provides a general introduction to the sockets API. The following chapters assume an understanding of the general concepts presented here. We don't present any example code in this chapter. Code examples in the UNIX and Internet domains are presented in the following chapters.
- Chapter 57 describes UNIX domain sockets, which allow communication between applications on the same host system.
- Chapter 58 introduces various computer networking concepts and describes key features of the TCP/IP networking protocols. It provides background needed for the next chapters.
- Chapter 59 describes Internet domain sockets, which allow applications on different hosts to communicate via a TCP/IP network.

- Chapter 60 discusses the design of servers that use sockets.
- Chapter 61 covers a range of advanced topics, including additional features for socket I/O, a more detailed look at the TCP protocol, and the use of socket options to retrieve and modify various attributes of sockets.

These chapters merely aim to give the reader a good grounding in the use of sockets. Sockets programming, especially for network communication, is an enormous topic in its own right, and forms the subject of entire books. Sources of further information are listed in Section 59.15.

56.1 Overview

In a typical client-server scenario, applications communicate using sockets as follows:

- Each application creates a socket. A socket is the "apparatus" that allows communication, and both applications require one.
- The server binds its socket to a well-known address (name) so that clients can locate it.

A socket is created using the *socket()* system call, which returns a file descriptor used to refer to the socket in subsequent system calls:

```
fd = socket(domain, type, protocol);
```

We describe socket domains and types in the following paragraphs. For all applications described in this book, *protocol* is always specified as 0.

Communication domains

Sockets exist in a *communication domain*, which determines:

- the method of identifying a socket (i.e., the format of a socket "address"); and
- the range of communication (i.e., either between applications on the same host or between applications on different hosts connected via a network).

Modern operating systems support at least the following domains:

- The *UNIX* (AF_UNIX) domain allows communication between applications on the same host. (POSIX.1g used the name AF_LOCAL as a synonym for AF_UNIX, but this name is not used in SUSv3.)
- The *IPv4* (AF_INET) domain allows communication between applications running on hosts connected via an Internet Protocol version 4 (IPv4) network.
- The *IPv6* (AF_INET6) domain allows communication between applications running on hosts connected via an Internet Protocol version 6 (IPv6) network. Although IPv6 is designed as the successor to IPv4, the latter protocol is currently still the most widely used.

Table 56-1 summarizes the characteristics of these socket domains.

In some code, we may see constants with names such as PF_UNIX instead of AF_UNIX. In this context, AF stands for "address family" and PF stands for "protocol family." Initially, it was conceived that a single protocol family might support multiple address families. In practice, no protocol family supporting multiple address families has ever been defined, and all existing implementations define the PF_ constants to be synonymous with the corresponding AF_ constants. (SUSv3 specifies the AF_ constants, but not the PF_ constants.) In this book, we always use the AF_ constants. Further information about the history of these constants can be found in Section 4.2 of [Stevens et al., 2004].

Table 56-1: Socket domains

Domain	Communication performed	Communication between applications	Address format	Address structure
AF_UNIX	within kernel	on same host	pathname	*sockaddr_un*
AF_INET	via IPv4	on hosts connected via an IPv4 network	32-bit IPv4 address + 16-bit port number	*sockaddr_in*
AF_INET6	via IPv6	on hosts connected via an IPv6 network	128-bit IPv6 address + 16-bit port number	*sockaddr_in6*

Socket types

Every sockets implementation provides at least two types of sockets: stream and datagram. These socket types are supported in both the UNIX and the Internet domains. Table 56-2 summarizes the properties of these socket types.

Table 56-2: Socket types and their properties

Property	Socket type	
	Stream	Datagram
Reliable delivery?	Y	N
Message boundaries preserved?	N	Y
Connection-oriented?	Y	N

Stream sockets (SOCK_STREAM) provide a reliable, bidirectional, byte-stream communication channel. By the terms in this description, we mean the following:

- *Reliable* means that we are guaranteed that either the transmitted data will arrive intact at the receiving application, exactly as it was transmitted by the sender (assuming that neither the network link nor the receiver crashes), or that we'll receive notification of a probable failure in transmission.

- *Bidirectional* means that data may be transmitted in either direction between two sockets.

- *Byte-stream* means that, as with pipes, there is no concept of message boundaries (refer to Section 44.1).

A stream socket is similar to using a pair of pipes to allow bidirectional communication between two applications, with the difference that (Internet domain) sockets permit communication over a network.

Stream sockets operate in connected pairs. For this reason, stream sockets are described as *connection-oriented*. The term *peer socket* refers to the socket at the other end of a connection; *peer address* denotes the address of that socket; and *peer application* denotes the application utilizing the peer socket. Sometimes, the term *remote* (or *foreign*) is used synonymously with *peer*. Analogously, sometimes the term *local* is used to refer to the application, socket, or address for this end of the connection. A stream socket can be connected to only one peer.

Datagram sockets (SOCK_DGRAM) allow data to be exchanged in the form of messages called *datagrams*. With datagram sockets, message boundaries are preserved, but data transmission is not reliable. Messages may arrive out of order, be duplicated, or not arrive at all.

Datagram sockets are an example of the more generic concept of a *connectionless* socket. Unlike a stream socket, a datagram socket doesn't need to be connected to another socket in order to be used. (In Section 56.6.2, we'll see that datagram sockets may be connected with one another, but this has somewhat different semantics from connected stream sockets.)

In the Internet domain, datagram sockets employ the User Datagram Protocol (UDP), and stream sockets (usually) employ the Transmission Control Protocol (TCP). Instead of using the terms *Internet domain datagram socket* and *Internet domain stream socket*, we'll often just use the terms *UDP socket* and *TCP socket*, respectively.

Socket system calls

The key socket system calls are the following:

- The *socket()* system call creates a new socket.

- The *bind()* system call binds a socket to an address. Usually, a server employs this call to bind its socket to a well-known address so that clients can locate the socket.

- The *listen()* system call allows a stream socket to accept incoming connections from other sockets.

- The *accept()* system call accepts a connection from a peer application on a listening stream socket, and optionally returns the address of the peer socket.

- The *connect()* system call establishes a connection with another socket.

> On most Linux architectures (the exceptions include Alpha and IA-64), all of the sockets system calls are actually implemented as library functions multiplexed through a single system call, *socketcall()*. (This is an artifact of the original development of the Linux sockets implementation as a separate project.) Nevertheless, we refer to all of these functions as system calls in this book, since this is what they were in the original BSD implementation, as well as in many other contemporary UNIX implementations.

Socket I/O can be performed using the conventional *read()* and *write()* system calls, or using a range of socket-specific system calls (e.g., *send()*, *recv()*, *sendto()*, and *recvfrom()*). By default, these system calls block if the I/O operation can't be completed immediately. Nonblocking I/O is also possible, by using the *fcntl()* F_SETFL operation (Section 5.3) to enable the O_NONBLOCK open file status flag.

> On Linux, we can call *ioctl(fd, FIONREAD, &cnt)* to obtain the number of unread bytes available on the stream socket referred to by the file descriptor *fd*. For a datagram socket, this operation returns the number of bytes in the next unread datagram (which may be zero if the next datagram is of zero length), or zero if there are no pending datagrams. This feature is not specified in SUSv3.

56.2 Creating a Socket: *socket()*

The *socket()* system call creates a new socket.

```
#include <sys/socket.h>

int socket(int domain, int type, int protocol);
```
                              Returns file descriptor on success, or −1 on error

The *domain* argument specifies the communication domain for the socket. The *type* argument specifies the socket type. This argument is usually specified as either SOCK_STREAM, to create a stream socket, or SOCK_DGRAM, to create a datagram socket.

The *protocol* argument is always specified as 0 for the socket types we describe in this book. Nonzero *protocol* values are used with some socket types that we don't describe. For example, *protocol* is specified as IPPROTO_RAW for raw sockets (SOCK_RAW).

On success, *socket()* returns a file descriptor used to refer to the newly created socket in later system calls.

> Starting with kernel 2.6.27, Linux provides a second use for the *type* argument, by allowing two nonstandard flags to be ORed with the socket type. The SOCK_CLOEXEC flag causes the kernel to enable the close-on-exec flag (FD_CLOEXEC) for the new file descriptor. This flag is useful for the same reasons as the *open()* O_CLOEXEC flag described in Section 4.3.1. The SOCK_NONBLOCK flag causes the kernel to set the O_NONBLOCK flag on the underlying open file description, so that future I/O operations on the socket will be nonblocking. This saves additional calls to *fcntl()* to achieve the same result.

56.3 Binding a Socket to an Address: *bind()*

The *bind()* system call binds a socket to an address.

```
#include <sys/socket.h>

int bind(int sockfd, const struct sockaddr *addr, socklen_t addrlen);
```
                              Returns 0 on success, or −1 on error

The *sockfd* argument is a file descriptor obtained from a previous call to *socket()*. The *addr* argument is a pointer to a structure specifying the address to which this socket is to be bound. The type of structure passed in this argument depends on the socket domain. The *addrlen* argument specifies the size of the address structure. The *socklen_t* data type used for the *addrlen* argument is an integer type specified by SUSv3.

Typically, we bind a server's socket to a well-known address—that is, a fixed address that is known in advance to client applications that need to communicate with that server.

> There are other possibilities than binding a server's socket to a well-known address. For example, for an Internet domain socket, the server could omit the call to *bind()* and simply call *listen()*, which causes the kernel to choose an ephemeral port for that socket. (We describe ephemeral ports in Section 58.6.1.) Afterward, the server can use *getsockname()* (Section 61.5) to retrieve the address of its socket. In this scenario, the server must then publish that address so that clients know how to locate the server's socket. Such publication could be done by registering the server's address with a centralized directory service application that clients then contact in order to obtain the address. (For example, Sun RPC solves this problem using its *portmapper* server.) Of course, the directory service application's socket must reside at a well-known address.

56.4 Generic Socket Address Structures: *struct sockaddr*

The *addr* and *addrlen* arguments to *bind()* require some further explanation. Looking at Table 56-1, we see that each socket domain uses a different address format. For example, UNIX domain sockets use pathnames, while Internet domain sockets use the combination of an IP address plus a port number. For each socket domain, a different structure type is defined to store a socket address. However, because system calls such as *bind()* are generic to all socket domains, they must be able to accept address structures of any type. In order to permit this, the sockets API defines a generic address structure, *struct sockaddr*. The only purpose for this type is to cast the various domain-specific address structures to a single type for use as arguments in the socket system calls. The *sockaddr* structure is typically defined as follows:

```
struct sockaddr {
    sa_family_t sa_family;      /* Address family (AF_* constant) */
    char        sa_data[14];    /* Socket address (size varies
                                   according to socket domain) */
};
```

This structure serves as a template for all of the domain-specific address structures. Each of these address structures begins with a *family* field corresponding to the *sa_family* field of the *sockaddr* structure. (The *sa_family_t* data type is an integer type specified in SUSv3.) The value in the *family* field is sufficient to determine the size and format of the address stored in the remainder of the structure.

> Some UNIX implementations also define an additional field in the *sockaddr* structure, *sa_len*, that specifies the total size of the structure. SUSv3 doesn't require this field, and it is not present in the Linux implementation of the sockets API.

If we define the _GNU_SOURCE feature test macro, then *glibc* prototypes the various socket system calls in <sys/socket.h> using a *gcc* extension that eliminates the need for the *(struct sockaddr *)* cast. However, reliance on this feature is nonportable (it will result in compilation warnings on other systems).

56.5 Stream Sockets

The operation of stream sockets can be explained by analogy with the telephone system:

1. The *socket()* system call, which creates a socket, is the equivalent of installing a telephone. In order for two applications to communicate, each of them must create a socket.

2. Communication via a stream socket is analogous to a telephone call. One application must connect its socket to another application's socket before communication can take place. Two sockets are connected as follows:

   a) One application calls *bind()* in order to bind the socket to a well-known address, and then calls *listen()* to notify the kernel of its willingness to accept incoming connections. This step is analogous to having a known telephone number and ensuring that our telephone is turned on so that people can call us.

   b) The other application establishes the connection by calling *connect()*, specifying the address of the socket to which the connection is to be made. This is analogous to dialing someone's telephone number.

   c) The application that called *listen()* then accepts the connection using *accept()*. This is analogous to picking up the telephone when it rings. If the *accept()* is performed before the peer application calls *connect()*, then the *accept()* blocks ("waiting by the telephone").

3. Once a connection has been established, data can be transmitted in both directions between the applications (analogous to a two-way telephone conversation) until one of them closes the connection using *close()*. Communication is performed using the conventional *read()* and *write()* system calls or via a number of socket-specific system calls (such as *send()* and *recv()*) that provide additional functionality.

Figure 56-1 illustrates the use of the system calls used with stream sockets.

Active and passive sockets

Stream sockets are often distinguished as being either active or passive:

- By default, a socket that has been created using *socket()* is *active*. An active socket can be used in a *connect()* call to establish a connection to a passive socket. This is referred to as performing an *active open*.

- A *passive* socket (also called a *listening* socket) is one that has been marked to allow incoming connections by calling *listen()*. Accepting an incoming connection is referred to as performing a *passive open*.

In most applications that employ stream sockets, the server performs the passive open, and the client performs the active open. We presume this scenario in subsequent sections, so that instead of saying "the application that performs the active socket open," we'll often just say "the client." Similarly, we'll equate "the server" with "the application that performs the passive socket open."

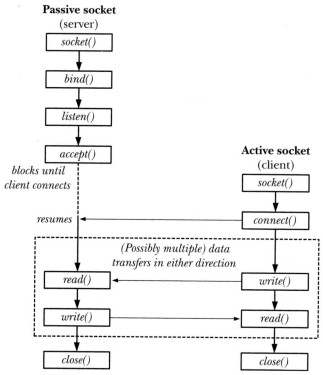

Figure 56-1: Overview of system calls used with stream sockets

56.5.1 Listening for Incoming Connections: *listen()*

The *listen()* system call marks the stream socket referred to by the file descriptor *sockfd* as *passive*. The socket will subsequently be used to accept connections from other (active) sockets.

```
#include <sys/socket.h>

int listen(int sockfd, int backlog);
```
                                        Returns 0 on success, or –1 on error

We can't apply *listen()* to a connected socket—that is, a socket on which a *connect()* has been successfully performed or a socket returned by a call to *accept()*.

To understand the purpose of the *backlog* argument, we first observe that the client may call *connect()* before the server calls *accept()*. This could happen, for example, because the server is busy handling some other client(s). This results in a *pending connection*, as illustrated in Figure 56-2.

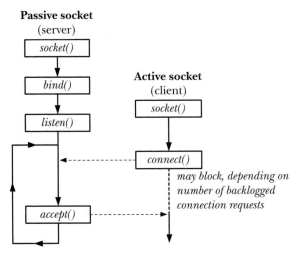

Passive socket
(server)

Active socket
(client)

*may block, depending on
number of backlogged
connection requests*

Figure 56-2: A pending socket connection

The kernel must record some information about each pending connection request so that a subsequent *accept()* can be processed. The *backlog* argument allows us to limit the number of such pending connections. Connection requests up to this limit succeed immediately. (For TCP sockets, the story is a little more complicated, as we'll see in Section 61.6.4.) Further connection requests block until a pending connection is accepted (via *accept()*), and thus removed from the queue of pending connections.

SUSv3 allows an implementation to place an upper limit on the value that can be specified for *backlog*, and permits an implementation to silently round *backlog* values down to this limit. SUSv3 specifies that the implementation should advertise this limit by defining the constant SOMAXCONN in <sys/socket.h>. On Linux, this constant is defined with the value 128. However, since kernel 2.4.25, Linux allows this limit to be adjusted at run time via the Linux-specific /proc/sys/net/core/somaxconn file. (In earlier kernel versions, the SOMAXCONN limit is immutable.)

> In the original BSD sockets implementation, the upper limit for *backlog* was 5, and we may see this number specified in older code. All modern implementations allow higher values of *backlog*, which are necessary for network servers employing TCP sockets to serve large numbers of clients.

56.5.2 Accepting a Connection: *accept()*

The *accept()* system call accepts an incoming connection on the listening stream socket referred to by the file descriptor *sockfd*. If there are no pending connections when *accept()* is called, the call blocks until a connection request arrives.

```
#include <sys/socket.h>

int accept(int sockfd, struct sockaddr *addr, socklen_t *addrlen);
```
                              Returns file descriptor on success, or −1 on error

The key point to understand about *accept()* is that it creates a *new* socket, and it is this new socket that is connected to the peer socket that performed the *connect()*. A file descriptor for the connected socket is returned as the function result of the *accept()* call. The listening socket (*sockfd*) remains open, and can be used to accept further connections. A typical server application creates one listening socket, binds it to a well-known address, and then handles all client requests by accepting connections via that socket.

The remaining arguments to *accept()* return the address of the peer socket. The *addr* argument points to a structure that is used to return the socket address. The type of this argument depends on the socket domain (as for *bind()*).

The *addrlen* argument is a value-result argument. It points to an integer that, prior to the call, must be initialized to the size of the buffer pointed to by *addr*, so that the kernel knows how much space is available to return the socket address. Upon return from *accept()*, this integer is set to indicate the number of bytes of data actually copied into the buffer.

If we are not interested in the address of the peer socket, then *addr* and *addrlen* should both be specified as NULL. (If desired, we can retrieve the peer's address later using the *getpeername()* system call, as described in Section 61.5.)

> Starting with kernel 2.6.28, Linux supports a new, nonstandard system call, *accept4()*. This system call performs the same task as *accept()*, but supports an additional argument, *flags*, that can be used to modify the behavior of the system call. Two flags are supported: SOCK_CLOEXEC and SOCK_NONBLOCK. The SOCK_CLOEXEC flag causes the kernel to enable the close-on-exec flag (FD_CLOEXEC) for the new file descriptor returned by the call. This flag is useful for the same reasons as the *open()* O_CLOEXEC flag described in Section 4.3.1. The SOCK_NONBLOCK flag causes the kernel to enable the O_NONBLOCK flag on the underlying open file description, so that future I/O operations on the socket will be nonblocking. This saves additional calls to *fcntl()* to achieve the same result.

56.5.3 Connecting to a Peer Socket: *connect()*

The *connect()* system call connects the active socket referred to by the file descriptor *sockfd* to the listening socket whose address is specified by *addr* and *addrlen*.

```
#include <sys/socket.h>

int connect(int sockfd, const struct sockaddr *addr, socklen_t addrlen);
```
                                        Returns 0 on success, or –1 on error

The *addr* and *addrlen* arguments are specified in the same way as the corresponding arguments to *bind()*.

If *connect()* fails and we wish to reattempt the connection, then SUSv3 specifies that the portable method of doing so is to close the socket, create a new socket, and reattempt the connection with the new socket.

56.5.4 I/O on Stream Sockets

A pair of connected stream sockets provides a bidirectional communication channel between the two endpoints. Figure 56-3 shows what this looks like in the UNIX domain.

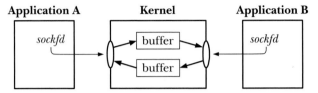

Figure 56-3: UNIX domain stream sockets provide a bidirectional communication channel

The semantics of I/O on connected stream sockets are similar to those for pipes:

- To perform I/O, we use the *read()* and *write()* system calls (or the socket-specific *send()* and *recv()*, which we describe in Section 61.3). Since sockets are bidirectional, both calls may be used on each end of the connection.

- A socket may be closed using the *close()* system call or as a consequence of the application terminating. Afterward, when the peer application attempts to read from the other end of the connection, it receives end-of-file (once all buffered data has been read). If the peer application attempts to write to its socket, it receives a SIGPIPE signal, and the system call fails with the error EPIPE. As we noted in Section 44.2, the usual way of dealing with this possibility is to ignore the SIGPIPE signal and find out about the closed connection via the EPIPE error.

56.5.5 Connection Termination: *close()*

The usual way of terminating a stream socket connection is to call *close()*. If multiple file descriptors refer to the same socket, then the connection is terminated when all of the descriptors are closed.

Suppose that, after we close a connection, the peer application crashes or otherwise fails to read or correctly process the data that we previously sent to it. In this case, we have no way of knowing that an error occurred. If we need to ensure that the data was successfully read and processed, then we must build some type of acknowledgement protocol into our application. This normally consists of an explicit acknowledgement message passed back to us from the peer.

In Section 61.2, we describe the *shutdown()* system call, which provides finer control of how a stream socket connection is closed.

56.6 Datagram Sockets

The operation of datagram sockets can be explained by analogy with the postal system:

1. The *socket()* system call is the equivalent of setting up a mailbox. (Here, we assume a system like the rural postal service in some countries, which both picks up letters from and delivers letters to the mailbox.) Each application that wants to send or receive datagrams creates a datagram socket using *socket()*.

2. In order to allow another application to send it datagrams (letters), an application uses *bind()* to bind its socket to a well-known address. Typically, a server binds its socket to a well-known address, and a client initiates communication by sending a datagram to that address. (In some domains—notably the UNIX domain—the client may also need to use *bind()* to assign an address to its socket if it wants to receive datagrams sent by the server.)

3. To send a datagram, an application calls *sendto()*, which takes as one of its arguments the address of the socket to which the datagram is to be sent. This is analogous to putting the recipient's address on a letter and posting it.

4. In order to receive a datagram, an application calls *recvfrom()*, which may block if no datagram has yet arrived. Because *recvfrom()* allows us to obtain the address of the sender, we can send a reply if desired. (This is useful if the sender's socket is bound to an address that is not well known, which is typical of a client.) Here, we stretch the analogy a little, since there is no requirement that a posted letter is marked with the sender's address.

5. When the socket is no longer needed, the application closes it using *close()*.

Just as with the postal system, when multiple datagrams (letters) are sent from one address to another, there is no guarantee that they will arrive in the order they were sent, or even arrive at all. Datagrams add one further possibility not present in the postal system: since the underlying networking protocols may sometimes retransmit a data packet, the same datagram could arrive more than once.

Figure 56-4 illustrates the use of the system calls employed with datagram sockets.

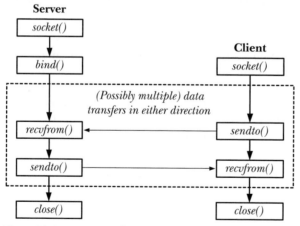

Figure 56-4: Overview of system calls used with datagram sockets

56.6.1 Exchanging Datagrams: *recvfrom()* and *sendto()*

The *recvfrom()* and *sendto()* system calls receive and send datagrams on a datagram socket.

```
#include <sys/socket.h>

ssize_t recvfrom(int sockfd, void *buffer, size_t length, int flags,
            struct sockaddr *src_addr, socklen_t *addrlen);
```
> Returns number of bytes received, 0 on EOF, or −1 on error

```
ssize_t sendto(int sockfd, const void *buffer, size_t length, int flags,
            const struct sockaddr *dest_addr, socklen_t addrlen);
```
> Returns number of bytes sent, or −1 on error

The return value and the first three arguments to these system calls are the same as for *read()* and *write()*.

The fourth argument, *flags*, is a bit mask controlling socket-specific I/O features. We cover these features when we describe the *recv()* and *send()* system calls in Section 61.3. If we don't require any of these features, we can specify *flags* as 0.

The remaining arguments are used to obtain or specify the address of the peer socket with which we are communicating.

For *recvfrom()*, the *src_addr* and *addrlen* arguments return the address of the remote socket used to send the datagram. (These arguments are analogous to the *addr* and *addrlen* arguments of *accept()*, which return the address of a connecting peer socket.) The *src_addr* argument is a pointer to an address structure appropriate to the communication domain. As with *accept()*, *addrlen* is a value-result argument. Prior to the call, *addrlen* should be initialized to the size of the structure pointed to by *src_addr*; upon return, it contains the number of bytes actually written to this structure.

If we are not interested in the address of the sender, then we specify both *src_addr* and *addrlen* as NULL. In this case, *recvfrom()* is equivalent to using *recv()* to receive a datagram. We can also use *read()* to read a datagram, which is equivalent to using *recv()* with a *flags* argument of 0.

Regardless of the value specified for *length*, *recvfrom()* retrieves exactly one message from a datagram socket. If the size of that message exceeds *length* bytes, the message is silently truncated to *length* bytes.

> If we employ the *recvmsg()* system call (Section 61.13.2), then it is possible to find out about a truncated datagram via the MSG_TRUNC flag returned in the *msg_flags* field of the returned *msghdr* structure. See the *recvmsg(2)* manual page for details.

For *sendto()*, the *dest_addr* and *addrlen* arguments specify the socket to which the datagram is to be sent. These arguments are employed in the same manner as the corresponding arguments to *connect()*. The *dest_addr* argument is an address structure suitable for this communication domain. It is initialized with the address of the destination socket. The *addrlen* argument specifies the size of *dest_addr*.

> On Linux, it is possible to use *sendto()* to send datagrams of length 0. However, not all UNIX implementations permit this.

56.6.2 Using *connect()* with Datagram Sockets

Even though datagram sockets are connectionless, the *connect()* system call serves a purpose when applied to datagram sockets. Calling *connect()* on a datagram socket causes the kernel to record a particular address as this socket's peer. The term *connected datagram socket* is applied to such a socket. The term *unconnected datagram socket* is applied to a datagram socket on which *connect()* has not been called (i.e., the default for a new datagram socket).

After a datagram socket has been connected:

* Datagrams can be sent through the socket using *write()* (or *send()*) and are automatically sent to the same peer socket. As with *sendto()*, each *write()* call results in a separate datagram.

* Only datagrams sent by the peer socket may be read on the socket.

Note that the effect of *connect()* is asymmetric for datagram sockets. The above statements apply only to the socket on which *connect()* has been called, not to the remote socket to which it is connected (unless the peer application also calls *connect()* on its socket).

We can change the peer of a connected datagram socket by issuing a further *connect()* call. It is also possible to dissolve the peer association altogether by specifying an address structure in which the address family (e.g., the *sun_family* field in the UNIX domain) is specified as AF_UNSPEC. Note, however, that many other UNIX implementations don't support the use of AF_UNSPEC for this purpose.

> SUSv3 was somewhat vague about dissolving peer associations, stating that a connection can be reset by making a *connect()* call that specifies a "null address," without defining that term. SUSv4 explicitly specifies the use of AF_UNSPEC.

The obvious advantage of setting the peer for a datagram socket is that we can use simpler I/O system calls when transmitting data on the socket. We no longer need to use *sendto()* with *dest_addr* and *addrlen* arguments, but can instead use *write()*. Setting the peer is useful primarily in an application that needs to send multiple datagrams to a single peer (which is typical of some datagram clients).

> On some TCP/IP implementations, connecting a datagram socket to a peer yields a performance improvement ([Stevens et al., 2004]). On Linux, connecting a datagram socket makes little difference to performance.

56.7 Summary

Sockets allow communication between applications on the same host or on different hosts connected via a network.

A socket exists within a communication domain, which determines the range of communication and the address format used to identify the socket. SUSv3 specifies the UNIX (AF_UNIX), IPv4 (AF_INET), and IPv6 (AF_INET6) communication domains.

Most applications use one of two socket types: stream or datagram. Stream sockets (SOCK_STREAM) provide a reliable, bidirectional, byte-stream communication channel between two endpoints. Datagram sockets (SOCK_DGRAM) provide unreliable, connectionless, message-oriented communication.

A typical stream socket server creates its socket using *socket()*, and then binds the socket to a well-known address using *bind()*. The server then calls *listen()* to allow connections to be received on the socket. Each client connection is then accepted on the listening socket using *accept()*, which returns a file descriptor for a new socket that is connected to the client's socket. A typical stream socket client creates a socket using *socket()*, and then establishes a connection by calling *connect()*, specifying the server's well-known address. After two stream sockets are connected, data can be transferred in either direction using *read()* and *write()*. Once all processes with a file descriptor referring to a stream socket endpoint have performed an implicit or explicit *close()*, the connection is terminated.

A typical datagram socket server creates a socket using *socket()*, and then binds it to a well-known address using *bind()*. Because datagram sockets are connectionless, the server's socket can be used to receive datagrams from any client. Datagrams can be received using *read()* or using the socket-specific *recvfrom()* system call, which returns the address of the sending socket. A datagram socket client creates a socket using *socket()*, and then uses *sendto()* to send a datagram to a specified (i.e., the server's) address. The *connect()* system call can be used with a datagram socket to set a peer address for the socket. After doing this, it is no longer necessary to specify the destination address for outgoing datagrams; a *write()* call can be used to send a datagram.

Further information

Refer to the sources of further information listed in Section 59.15.

57

SOCKETS: UNIX DOMAIN

This chapter looks at the use of UNIX domain sockets, which allow communication between processes on the same host system. We discuss the use of both stream and datagram sockets in the UNIX domain. We also describe the use of file permissions to control access to UNIX domain sockets, the use of *socketpair()* to create a pair of connected UNIX domain sockets, and the Linux abstract socket namespace.

57.1 UNIX Domain Socket Addresses: *struct sockaddr_un*

In the UNIX domain, a socket address takes the form of a pathname, and the domain-specific socket address structure is defined as follows:

```
struct sockaddr_un {
    sa_family_t sun_family;        /* Always AF_UNIX */
    char sun_path[108];            /* Null-terminated socket pathname */
};
```

> The prefix *sun_* in the fields of the *sockaddr_un* structure has nothing to do with Sun Microsystems; rather, it derives from *socket unix*.

SUSv3 doesn't specify the size of the *sun_path* field. Early BSD implementations used 108 and 104 bytes, and one contemporary implementation (HP-UX 11) uses 92 bytes. Portable applications should code to this lower value, and use *snprintf()* or *strncpy()* to avoid buffer overruns when writing into this field.

In order to bind a UNIX domain socket to an address, we initialize a *sockaddr_un* structure, and then pass a (cast) pointer to this structure as the *addr* argument to *bind()*, and specify *addrlen* as the size of the structure, as shown in Listing 57-1.

Listing 57-1: Binding a UNIX domain socket

```
const char *SOCKNAME = "/tmp/mysock";
int sfd;
struct sockaddr_un addr;

sfd = socket(AF_UNIX, SOCK_STREAM, 0);              /* Create socket */
if (sfd == -1)
    errExit("socket");

memset(&addr, 0, sizeof(struct sockaddr_un));       /* Clear structure */
addr.sun_family = AF_UNIX;                          /* UNIX domain address */
strncpy(addr.sun_path, SOCKNAME, sizeof(addr.sun_path) - 1);

if (bind(sfd, (struct sockaddr *) &addr, sizeof(struct sockaddr_un)) == -1)
    errExit("bind");
```

The use of the *memset()* call in Listing 57-1 ensures that all of the structure fields have the value 0. (The subsequent *strncpy()* call takes advantage of this by specifying its final argument as one less than the size of the *sun_path* field, to ensure that this field always has a terminating null byte.) Using *memset()* to zero out the entire structure, rather than initializing individual fields, ensures that any nonstandard fields that are provided by some implementations are also initialized to 0.

> The BSD-derived function *bzero()* is an alternative to *memset()* for zeroing the contents of a structure. SUSv3 specifies *bzero()* and the related *bcopy()* (which is similar to *memmove()*), but marks both functions LEGACY, noting that *memset()* and *memmove()* are preferred. SUSv4 removes the specifications of *bzero()* and *bcopy()*.

When used to bind a UNIX domain socket, *bind()* creates an entry in the file system. (Thus, a directory specified as part of the socket pathname needs to be accessible and writable.) The ownership of the file is determined according to the usual rules for file creation (Section 15.3.1). The file is marked as a socket. When *stat()* is applied to this pathname, it returns the value S_IFSOCK in the file-type component of the *st_mode* field of the *stat* structure (Section 15.1). When listed with *ls –l*, a UNIX domain socket is shown with the type *s* in the first column, and *ls –F* appends an equal sign (=) to the socket pathname.

> Although UNIX domain sockets are identified by pathnames, I/O on these sockets doesn't involve operations on the underlying device.

The following points are worth noting about binding a UNIX domain socket:

- We can't bind a socket to an existing pathname (*bind()* fails with the error EADDRINUSE).

- It is usual to bind a socket to an absolute pathname, so that the socket resides at a fixed address in the file system. Using a relative pathname is possible, but unusual, because it requires an application that wants to *connect()* to this socket to know the current working directory of the application that performs the *bind()*.

- A socket may be bound to only one pathname; conversely, a pathname can be bound to only one socket.

- We can't use *open()* to open a socket.

- When the socket is no longer required, its pathname entry can (and generally should) be removed using *unlink()* (or *remove()*).

In most of our example programs, we bind UNIX domain sockets to pathnames in the /tmp directory, because this directory is normally present and writable on every system. This makes it easy for the reader to run these programs without needing to first edit the socket pathnames. Be aware, however, that this is generally not a good design technique. As pointed out in Section 38.7, creating files in publicly writable directories such as /tmp can lead to various security vulnerabilities. For example, by creating a pathname in /tmp with the same name as that used by the application socket, we can create a simple denial-of-service attack. Real-world applications should *bind()* UNIX domain sockets to absolute pathnames in suitably secured directories.

57.2 Stream Sockets in the UNIX Domain

We now present a simple client-server application that uses stream sockets in the UNIX domain. The client program (Listing 57-4) connects to the server, and uses the connection to transfer data from its standard input to the server. The server program (Listing 57-3) accepts client connections, and transfers all data sent on the connection by the client to standard output. The server is a simple example of an *iterative* server—a server that handles one client at a time before proceeding to the next client. (We consider server design in more detail in Chapter 60.)

Listing 57-2 is the header file used by both of these programs.

Listing 57-2: Header file for us_xfr_sv.c and us_xfr_cl.c

———————————————————————————————————— sockets/us_xfr.h

```
#include <sys/un.h>
#include <sys/socket.h>
#include "tlpi_hdr.h"

#define SV_SOCK_PATH "/tmp/us_xfr"

#define BUF_SIZE 100
```
———————————————————————————————————— sockets/us_xfr.h

In the following pages, we first present the source code of the server and client, and then discuss the details of these programs and show an example of their use.

Listing 57-3: A simple UNIX domain stream socket server

```c
#include "us_xfr.h"
#define BACKLOG 5

int
main(int argc, char *argv[])
{
    struct sockaddr_un addr;
    int sfd, cfd;
    ssize_t numRead;
    char buf[BUF_SIZE];

    sfd = socket(AF_UNIX, SOCK_STREAM, 0);
    if (sfd == -1)
        errExit("socket");

    /* Construct server socket address, bind socket to it,
       and make this a listening socket */

    if (strlen(SV_SOCK_PATH) > sizeof(addr.sun_path) - 1)
        fatal("Server socket path too long: %s", SV_SOCK_PATH);

    if (remove(SV_SOCK_PATH) == -1 && errno != ENOENT)
        errExit("remove-%s", SV_SOCK_PATH);

    memset(&addr, 0, sizeof(struct sockaddr_un));
    addr.sun_family = AF_UNIX;
    strncpy(addr.sun_path, SV_SOCK_PATH, sizeof(addr.sun_path) - 1);

    if (bind(sfd, (struct sockaddr *) &addr, sizeof(struct sockaddr_un)) == -1)
        errExit("bind");

    if (listen(sfd, BACKLOG) == -1)
        errExit("listen");

    for (;;) {          /* Handle client connections iteratively */

        /* Accept a connection. The connection is returned on a new
           socket, 'cfd'; the listening socket ('sfd') remains open
           and can be used to accept further connections. */

        cfd = accept(sfd, NULL, NULL);
        if (cfd == -1)
            errExit("accept");

        /* Transfer data from connected socket to stdout until EOF */

        while ((numRead = read(cfd, buf, BUF_SIZE)) > 0)
            if (write(STDOUT_FILENO, buf, numRead) != numRead)
                fatal("partial/failed write");

        if (numRead == -1)
            errExit("read");
```

```
        if (close(cfd) == -1)
            errMsg("close");
    }
}
```

Listing 57-4: A simple UNIX domain stream socket client

```c
#include "us_xfr.h"

int
main(int argc, char *argv[])
{
    struct sockaddr_un addr;
    int sfd;
    ssize_t numRead;
    char buf[BUF_SIZE];

    sfd = socket(AF_UNIX, SOCK_STREAM, 0);        /* Create client socket */
    if (sfd == -1)
        errExit("socket");

    /* Construct server address, and make the connection */

    memset(&addr, 0, sizeof(struct sockaddr_un));
    addr.sun_family = AF_UNIX;
    strncpy(addr.sun_path, SV_SOCK_PATH, sizeof(addr.sun_path) - 1);

    if (connect(sfd, (struct sockaddr *) &addr,
                sizeof(struct sockaddr_un)) == -1)
        errExit("connect");

    /* Copy stdin to socket */

    while ((numRead = read(STDIN_FILENO, buf, BUF_SIZE)) > 0)
        if (write(sfd, buf, numRead) != numRead)
            fatal("partial/failed write");

    if (numRead == -1)
        errExit("read");

    exit(EXIT_SUCCESS);           /* Closes our socket; server sees EOF */
}
```

The server program is shown in Listing 57-3. The server performs the following steps:

- Create a socket.
- Remove any existing file with the same pathname as that to which we want to bind the socket.

- Construct an address structure for the server's socket, bind the socket to that address, and mark the socket as a listening socket.

- Execute an infinite loop to handle incoming client requests. Each loop iteration performs the following steps:

  - Accept a connection, obtaining a new socket, *cfd*, for the connection.
  - Read all of the data from the connected socket and write it to standard output.
  - Close the connected socket *cfd*.

The server must be terminated manually (e.g., by sending it a signal).

The client program (Listing 57-4) performs the following steps:

- Create a socket.

- Construct the address structure for the server's socket and connect to the socket at that address.

- Execute a loop that copies its standard input to the socket connection. Upon encountering end-of-file in its standard input, the client terminates, with the result that its socket is closed and the server sees end-of-file when reading from the socket on the other end of the connection.

The following shell session log demonstrates the use of these programs. We begin by running the server in the background:

```
$ ./us_xfr_sv > b &
[1] 9866
$ ls -lF /tmp/us_xfr                Examine socket file with ls
srwxr-xr-x    1 mtk      users       0 Jul 18 10:48 /tmp/us_xfr=
```

We then create a test file to be used as input for the client, and run the client:

```
$ cat *.c > a
$ ./us_xfr_cl < a                   Client takes input from test file
```

At this point, the client has completed. Now we terminate the server as well, and check that the server's output matches the client's input:

```
$ kill %1                            Terminate server
 [1]+  Terminated    ./us_xfr_sv >b  Shell sees server's termination
$ diff a b
$
```

The *diff* command produces no output, indicating that the input and output files are identical.

Note that after the server terminates, the socket pathname continues to exist. This is why the server uses *remove()* to remove any existing instance of the socket pathname before calling *bind()*. (Assuming we have appropriate permissions, this *remove()* call would remove any type of file with this pathname, even if it wasn't a socket.) If we did not do this, then the *bind()* call would fail if a previous invocation of the server had already created this socket pathname.

57.3 Datagram Sockets in the UNIX Domain

In the generic description of datagram sockets that we provided in Section 56.6, we stated that communication using datagram sockets is unreliable. This is the case for datagrams transferred over a network. However, for UNIX domain sockets, datagram transmission is carried out within the kernel, and is reliable. All messages are delivered in order and unduplicated.

Maximum datagram size for UNIX domain datagram sockets

SUSv3 doesn't specify a maximum size for datagrams sent via a UNIX domain socket. On Linux, we can send quite large datagrams. The limits are controlled via the SO_SNDBUF socket option and various /proc files, as described in the *socket(7)* manual page. However, some other UNIX implementations impose lower limits, such as 2048 bytes. Portable applications employing UNIX domain datagram sockets should consider imposing a low upper limit on the size of datagrams used.

Example program

Listing 57-6 and Listing 57-7 show a simple client-server application using UNIX domain datagram sockets. Both of these programs make use of the header file shown in Listing 57-5.

Listing 57-5: Header file used by ud_ucase_sv.c and ud_ucase_cl.c

―― sockets/ud_ucase.h

```
#include <sys/un.h>
#include <sys/socket.h>
#include <ctype.h>
#include "tlpi_hdr.h"

#define BUF_SIZE 10             /* Maximum size of messages exchanged
                                   between client and server */

#define SV_SOCK_PATH "/tmp/ud_ucase"
```
―― sockets/ud_ucase.h

The server program (Listing 57-6) first creates a socket and binds it to a well-known address. (Beforehand, the server unlinks the pathname matching that address, in case the pathname already exists.) The server then enters an infinite loop, using *recvfrom()* to receive datagrams from clients, converting the received text to upper-case, and returning the converted text to the client using the address obtained via *recvfrom()*.

The client program (Listing 57-7) creates a socket and binds the socket to an address, so that the server can send its reply. The client address is made unique by including the client's process ID in the pathname. The client then loops, sending each of its command-line arguments as a separate message to the server. After sending each message, the client reads the server response and displays it on standard output.

Listing 57-6: A simple UNIX domain datagram server

── **sockets/ud_ucase_sv.c**
```
#include "ud_ucase.h"

int
main(int argc, char *argv[])
{
    struct sockaddr_un svaddr, claddr;
    int sfd, j;
    ssize_t numBytes;
    socklen_t len;
    char buf[BUF_SIZE];

    sfd = socket(AF_UNIX, SOCK_DGRAM, 0);        /* Create server socket */
    if (sfd == -1)
        errExit("socket");

    /* Construct well-known address and bind server socket to it */

    if (strlen(SV_SOCK_PATH) > sizeof(svaddr.sun_path) - 1)
        fatal("Server socket path too long: %s", SV_SOCK_PATH);

    if (remove(SV_SOCK_PATH) == -1 && errno != ENOENT)
        errExit("remove-%s", SV_SOCK_PATH);

    memset(&svaddr, 0, sizeof(struct sockaddr_un));
    svaddr.sun_family = AF_UNIX;
    strncpy(svaddr.sun_path, SV_SOCK_PATH, sizeof(svaddr.sun_path) - 1);

    if (bind(sfd, (struct sockaddr *) &svaddr, sizeof(struct sockaddr_un)) == -1)
        errExit("bind");

    /* Receive messages, convert to uppercase, and return to client */

    for (;;) {
        len = sizeof(struct sockaddr_un);
        numBytes = recvfrom(sfd, buf, BUF_SIZE, 0,
                            (struct sockaddr *) &claddr, &len);
        if (numBytes == -1)
            errExit("recvfrom");

        printf("Server received %ld bytes from %s\n", (long) numBytes,
                claddr.sun_path);

        for (j = 0; j < numBytes; j++)
            buf[j] = toupper((unsigned char) buf[j]);

        if (sendto(sfd, buf, numBytes, 0, (struct sockaddr *) &claddr, len) !=
                numBytes)
            fatal("sendto");
    }
}
```
── **sockets/ud_ucase_sv.c**

Listing 57-7: A simple UNIX domain datagram client

——————————————————————————————————————— **sockets/ud_ucase_cl.c**

```c
#include "ud_ucase.h"

int
main(int argc, char *argv[])
{
    struct sockaddr_un svaddr, claddr;
    int sfd, j;
    size_t msgLen;
    ssize_t numBytes;
    char resp[BUF_SIZE];

    if (argc < 2 || strcmp(argv[1], "--help") == 0)
        usageErr("%s msg...\n", argv[0]);

    /* Create client socket; bind to unique pathname (based on PID) */

    sfd = socket(AF_UNIX, SOCK_DGRAM, 0);
    if (sfd == -1)
        errExit("socket");

    memset(&claddr, 0, sizeof(struct sockaddr_un));
    claddr.sun_family = AF_UNIX;
    snprintf(claddr.sun_path, sizeof(claddr.sun_path),
            "/tmp/ud_ucase_cl.%ld", (long) getpid());

    if (bind(sfd, (struct sockaddr *) &claddr, sizeof(struct sockaddr_un)) == -1)
        errExit("bind");

    /* Construct address of server */

    memset(&svaddr, 0, sizeof(struct sockaddr_un));
    svaddr.sun_family = AF_UNIX;
    strncpy(svaddr.sun_path, SV_SOCK_PATH, sizeof(svaddr.sun_path) - 1);

    /* Send messages to server; echo responses on stdout */

    for (j = 1; j < argc; j++) {
        msgLen = strlen(argv[j]);           /* May be longer than BUF_SIZE */
        if (sendto(sfd, argv[j], msgLen, 0, (struct sockaddr *) &svaddr,
                sizeof(struct sockaddr_un)) != msgLen)
            fatal("sendto");

        numBytes = recvfrom(sfd, resp, BUF_SIZE, 0, NULL, NULL);
        if (numBytes == -1)
            errExit("recvfrom");
        printf("Response %d: %.*s\n", j, (int) numBytes, resp);
    }

    remove(claddr.sun_path);                /* Remove client socket pathname */
    exit(EXIT_SUCCESS);
}
```

——————————————————————————————————————— **sockets/ud_ucase_cl.c**

The following shell session log demonstrates the use of the server and client programs:

```
$ ./ud_ucase_sv &                                Send 2 messages to server
[1] 20113
$ ./ud_ucase_cl hello world
Server received 5 bytes from /tmp/ud_ucase_cl.20150
Response 1: HELLO
Server received 5 bytes from /tmp/ud_ucase_cl.20150
Response 2: WORLD
$ ./ud_ucase_cl 'long message'                   Send 1 longer message to server
Server received 10 bytes from /tmp/ud_ucase_cl.20151
Response 1: LONG MESSA
$ kill %1                                         Terminate server
```

The second invocation of the client program was designed to show that when a *recvfrom()* call specifies a *length* (BUF_SIZE, defined in Listing 57-5 with the value 10) that is shorter than the message size, the message is silently truncated. We can see that this truncation occurred, because the server prints a message saying it received just 10 bytes, while the message sent by the client consisted of 12 bytes.

57.4 UNIX Domain Socket Permissions

The ownership and permissions of the socket file determine which processes are able to communicate with that socket:

- To connect to a UNIX domain stream socket, write permission is required on the socket file.
- To send a datagram to a UNIX domain datagram socket, write permission is required on the socket file.

In addition, execute (search) permission is required on each of the directories in the socket pathname.

By default, a socket is created (by *bind()*) with all permissions granted to owner (user), group, and other. To change this, we can precede the call to *bind()* with a call to *umask()* to disable the permissions that we do not wish to grant.

Some systems ignore the permissions on the socket file (SUSv3 allows this). Thus, we can't portably use socket file permissions to control access to the socket, although we can portably use permissions on the hosting directory for this purpose.

57.5 Creating a Connected Socket Pair: *socketpair()*

Sometimes, it is useful for a single process to create a pair of sockets and connect them together. This could be done using two calls to *socket()*, a call to *bind()*, and then either calls to *listen()*, *connect()*, and *accept()* (for stream sockets), or a call to *connect()* (for datagram sockets). The *socketpair()* system call provides a shorthand for this operation.

```
#include <sys/socket.h>

int socketpair(int domain, int type, int protocol, int sockfd[2]);
```
                                              Returns 0 on success, or −1 on error

This *socketpair()* system call can be used only in the UNIX domain; that is, *domain* must
be specified as AF_UNIX. (This restriction applies on most implementations, and is logical, since the socket pair is created on a single host system.) The socket *type* may be
specified as either SOCK_DGRAM or SOCK_STREAM. The *protocol* argument must be specified
as 0. The *sockfd* array returns the file descriptors referring to the two connected sockets.

Specifying *type* as SOCK_STREAM creates the equivalent of a bidirectional pipe (also
known as a *stream pipe*). Each socket can be used for both reading and writing, and
separate data channels flow in each direction between the two sockets. (On BSD-
derived implementations, *pipe()* is implemented as a call to *socketpair()*.)

Typically, a socket pair is used in a similar fashion to a pipe. After the
socketpair() call, the process then creates a child via *fork()*. The child inherits copies
of the parent's file descriptors, including the descriptors referring to the socket
pair. Thus, the parent and child can use the socket pair for IPC.

One way in which the use of *socketpair()* differs from creating a pair of connected sockets manually is that the sockets are not bound to any address. This can
help us avoid a whole class of security vulnerabilities, since the sockets are not
visible to any other process.

> Starting with kernel 2.6.27, Linux provides a second use for the *type* argument,
> by allowing two nonstandard flags to be ORed with the socket type. The
> SOCK_CLOEXEC flag causes the kernel to enable the close-on-exec flag (FD_CLOEXEC)
> for the two new file descriptors. This flag is useful for the same reasons as the
> *open()* O_CLOEXEC flag described in Section 4.3.1. The SOCK_NONBLOCK flag causes
> the kernel to set the O_NONBLOCK flag on both underlying open file descriptions,
> so that future I/O operations on the socket will be nonblocking. This saves
> additional calls to *fcntl()* to achieve the same result.

57.6 The Linux Abstract Socket Namespace

The so-called *abstract namespace* is a Linux-specific feature that allows us to bind a
UNIX domain socket to a name without that name being created in the file system.
This provides a few potential advantages:

*   We don't need to worry about possible collisions with existing names in the
    file system.
*   It is not necessary to unlink the socket pathname when we have finished using
    the socket. The abstract name is automatically removed when the socket is closed.
*   We don't need to create a file-system pathname for the socket. This may be
    useful in a *chroot* environment, or if we don't have write access to a file system.

To create an abstract binding, we specify the first byte of the *sun_path* field as a null byte (\0). This distinguishes abstract socket names from conventional UNIX domain socket pathnames, which consist of a string of one or more nonnull bytes terminated by a null byte. The name of the abstract socket is then defined by the remaining bytes (including any null bytes) in *sun_path* up to the length defined for the size of the address structure (i.e., *addrlen − sizeof(sa_family_t)*).

Listing 57-8 demonstrates the creation of an abstract socket binding.

Listing 57-8: Creating an abstract socket binding

────────────────────────────────── *from* **sockets/us_abstract_bind.c**
```
struct sockaddr_un addr;

memset(&addr, 0, sizeof(struct sockaddr_un));  /* Clear address structure */
addr.sun_family = AF_UNIX;                      /* UNIX domain address */

/* addr.sun_path[0] has already been set to 0 by memset() */

str = "xyz";          /* Abstract name is "\0xyz" */
strncpy(&addr.sun_path[1], str, strlen(str));

sockfd = socket(AF_UNIX, SOCK_STREAM, 0);
if (sockfd == -1)
    errExit("socket");

if (bind(sockfd, (struct sockaddr *) &addr,
        sizeof(sa_family_t) + strlen(str) + 1) == -1)
    errExit("bind");
```
────────────────────────────────── *from* **sockets/us_abstract_bind.c**

The fact that an initial null byte is used to distinguish an abstract socket name from a conventional socket name can have an unusual consequence. Suppose that the variable *name* happens to point to a zero-length string and that we attempt to bind a UNIX domain socket to a *sun_path* initialized as follows:

```
strncpy(addr.sun_path, name, sizeof(addr.sun_path) - 1);
```

On Linux, we'll inadvertently create an abstract socket binding. However, such a code sequence is probably unintentional (i.e., a bug). On other UNIX implementations, the subsequent *bind()* would fail.

57.7 Summary

UNIX domain sockets allow communication between applications on the same host. The UNIX domain supports both stream and datagram sockets.

A UNIX domain socket is identified by a pathname in the file system. File permissions can be used to control access to a UNIX domain socket.

The *socketpair()* system call creates a pair of connected UNIX domain sockets. This avoids the need for multiple system calls to create, bind, and connect the sockets. A socket pair is normally used in a similar fashion to a pipe: one process creates the socket pair and then forks to create a child that inherits descriptors referring to the sockets. The two processes can then communicate via the socket pair.

The Linux-specific abstract socket namespace allows us to bind a UNIX domain socket to a name that doesn't appear in the file system.

Further information

Refer to the sources of further information listed in Section 59.15.

57.8 Exercises

57-1. In Section 57.3, we noted that UNIX domain datagram sockets are reliable. Write programs to show that if a sender transmits datagrams to a UNIX domain datagram socket faster than the receiver reads them, then the sender is eventually blocked, and remains blocked until the receiver reads some of the pending datagrams.

57-2. Rewrite the programs in Listing 57-3 (us_xfr_sv.c) and Listing 57-4 (us_xfr_cl.c) to use the Linux-specific abstract socket namespace (Section 57.6).

57-3. Reimplement the sequence-number server and client of Section 44.8 using UNIX domain stream sockets.

57-4. Suppose that we create two UNIX domain datagram sockets bound to the paths /somepath/a and /somepath/b, and that we connect the socket /somepath/a to /somepath/b. What happens if we create a third datagram socket and try to send (*sendto()*) a datagram via that socket to /somepath/a? Write a program to determine the answer. If you have access to other UNIX systems, test the program on those systems to see if the answer differs.

58

SOCKETS: FUNDAMENTALS OF TCP/IP NETWORKS

This chapter provides an introduction to computer networking concepts and the TCP/IP networking protocols. An understanding of these topics is necessary to make effective use of Internet domain sockets, which are described in the next chapter.

Starting in this chapter, we begin mentioning various *Request for Comments* (RFC) documents. Each of the networking protocols discussed in this book is formally described in an RFC. We provide further information about RFCs, as well as a list of RFCs of particular relevance to the material covered in this book, in Section 58.7.

58.1 Internets

An *internetwork* or, more commonly, *internet* (with a lowercase *i*), connects different computer networks, allowing hosts on all of the networks to communicate with one another. In other words, an internet is a network of computer networks. The term *subnetwork*, or *subnet*, is used to refer to one of the networks composing an internet. An internet aims to hide the details of different physical networks in order to present a unified network architecture to all hosts on the connected networks. This means, for example, that a single address format is used to identify all hosts in the internet.

Although various internetworking protocols have been devised, TCP/IP has become the dominant protocol suite, supplanting even the proprietary networking protocols that were formerly common on local and wide area networks. The term *Internet* (with an uppercase *I*) is used to refer to the TCP/IP internet that connects millions of computers globally.

The first widespread implementation of TCP/IP appeared with 4.2BSD in 1983. Several implementations of TCP/IP are derived directly from the BSD code; other implementations, including the Linux implementation, are written from scratch, taking the operation of the BSD code as a reference standard defining the operation of TCP/IP.

> TCP/IP grew out of a project sponsored by the US Department of Defense Advanced Research Projects Agency (ARPA, later DARPA, with the *D* for Defense) to devise a computer networking architecture to be used in the ARPANET, an early wide area network. During the 1970s, a new family of protocols was designed for the ARPANET. Accurately, these protocols are known as the DARPA Internet protocol suite, but more usually they are known as the TCP/IP protocol suite, or simply TCP/IP.
>
> The web page *http://www.isoc.org/internet/history/brief.shtml* provides a brief history of the Internet and TCP/IP.

Figure 58-1 shows a simple internet. In this diagram, the machine tekapo is an example of a *router*, a computer whose function is to connect one subnetwork to another, transferring data between them. As well as understanding the internet protocol being used, a router must also understand the (possibly) different data-link-layer protocols used on each of the subnets that it connects.

A router has multiple network interfaces, one for each of the subnets to which it is connected. The more general term *multihomed host* is used for any host—not necessarily a router—with multiple network interfaces. (Another way of describing a router is to say that it is a multihomed host that forwards packets from one subnet to another.) A multihomed host has a different network address for each of its interfaces (i.e., a different address on each of the subnets to which it is connected).

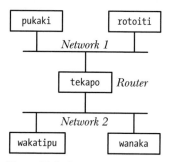

Figure 58-1: An internet using a router to connect two networks

58.2 Networking Protocols and Layers

A *networking protocol* is a set of rules defining how information is to be transmitted across a network. Networking protocols are generally organized as a series of *layers*, with each layer building on the layer below it to add features that are made available to higher layers.

The *TCP/IP protocol suite* is a layered networking protocol (Figure 58-2). It includes the *Internet Protocol* (IP) and various protocols layered above it. (The code that implements these various layers is commonly referred to as a *protocol stack*.) The name TCP/IP derives from the fact that the *Transmission Control Protocol* (TCP) is the most heavily used transport-layer protocol.

We have omitted a range of other TCP/IP protocols from Figure 58-2 because they are not relevant to this chapter. The *Address Resolution Protocol* (ARP) is concerned with mapping Internet addresses to hardware (e.g., Ethernet) addresses. The *Internet Control Message Protocol* (ICMP) is used to convey error and control information across the network. (ICMP is used by the *ping* program, which is frequently employed to check whether a particular host is alive and visible on a TCP/IP network, and by *traceroute*, which traces the path of an IP packet through the network.) The *Internet Group Management Protocol* (IGMP) is used by hosts and routers that support multicasting of IP datagrams.

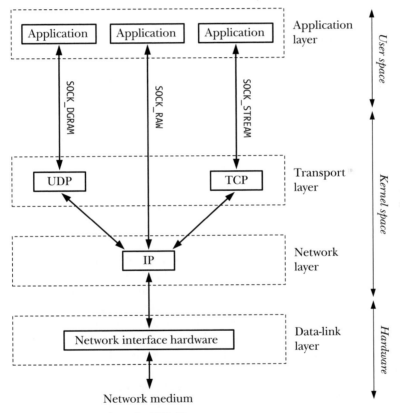

Figure 58-2: Protocols in the TCP/IP suite

One of the notions that lends great power and flexibility to protocol layering is *transparency*—each protocol layer shields higher layers from the operation and complexity of lower layers. Thus, for example, an application making use of TCP only needs to use the standard sockets API and to know that it is employing a reliable, byte-stream transport service. It doesn't need to understand the details of the operation of TCP. (When we look at socket options in Section 61.9, we'll see that this doesn't always strictly hold true; occasionally, an application does need to know some of the details of the operation of the underlying transport protocol.) Nor does the application need to know the details of the operation of IP or of the data-link layer. From the point of view of the applications, it is as though they are communicating directly with each other via the sockets API, as shown in Figure 58-3, where the dashed horizontal lines represent the virtual communication paths between corresponding application, TCP, and IP entities on the two hosts.

Encapsulation

Encapsulation is an important principle of a layered networking protocol. Figure 58-4 shows an example of encapsulation in the TCP/IP protocol layers. The key idea of encapsulation is that the information (e.g., application data, a TCP segment, or an IP datagram) passed from a higher layer to a lower layer is treated as opaque data by the lower layer. In other words, the lower layer makes no attempt to interpret information sent from the upper layer, but merely places that information inside whatever type of packet is used in the lower layer and adds its own layer-specific header before passing the packet down to the next lower layer. When data is passed up from a lower layer to a higher layer, a converse unpacking process takes place.

> We don't show it in Figure 58-4, but the concept of encapsulation also extends down into the data-link layer, where IP datagrams are encapsulated inside network frames. Encapsulation may also extend up into the application layer, where the application may perform its own packaging of data.

58.3 The Data-Link Layer

The lowest layer in Figure 58-2 is the *data-link layer*, which consists of the device driver and the hardware interface (network card) to the underlying physical medium (e.g., a telephone line, a coaxial cable, or a fiber-optic cable). The data-link layer is concerned with transferring data across a physical link in a network.

To transfer data, the data-link layer encapsulates datagrams from the network layer into units called *frames*. In addition to the data to be transmitted, each frame includes a header containing, for example, the destination address and frame size. The data-link layer transmits the frames across the physical link and handles acknowledgements from the receiver. (Not all data-link layers use acknowledgements.) This layer may perform error detection, retransmission, and flow control. Some data-link layers also split large network packets into multiple frames and reassemble them at the receiver.

From an application-programming point of view, we can generally ignore the data-link layer, since all communication details are handled in the driver and hardware.

One characteristic of the data-link layer that is important for our discussion of IP is the *maximum transmission unit* (MTU). A data-link layer's MTU is the upper limit that the layer places on the size of a frame. Different data-link layers have different MTUs.

> The command *netstat –i* displays a list of the system's network interfaces, along with their MTUs.

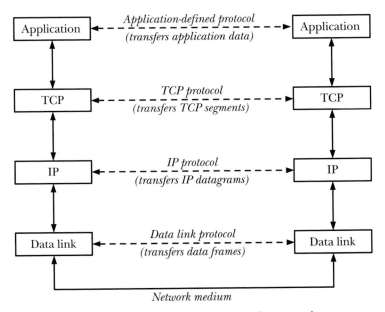

Figure 58-3: Layered communication via the TCP/IP protocols

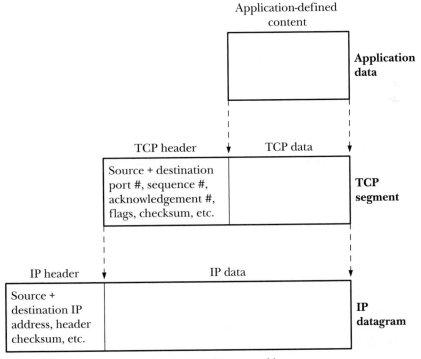

Figure 58-4: Encapsulation within the TCP/IP protocol layers

58.4 The Network Layer: IP

Above the data-link layer is the *network layer*, which is concerned with delivering packets (data) from the source host to the destination host. This layer performs a variety of tasks, including:

*   breaking data into fragments small enough for transmission via the data-link layer (if necessary);
*   routing data across the internet; and
*   providing services to the transport layer.

In the TCP/IP protocol suite, the principal protocol in the network layer is IP. The version of IP that appeared in the 4.2BSD implementation was IP version 4 (IPv4). In the early 1990s, a revised version of IP was devised: IP version 6 (IPv6). The most notable difference between the two versions is that IPv4 identifies subnets and hosts using 32-bit addresses, while IPv6 uses 128-bit addresses, thus providing a much larger range of addresses to be assigned to hosts. Although IPv4 is still the predominant version of IP in use on the Internet, in coming years, it should be supplanted by IPv6. Both IPv4 and IPv6 support the higher UDP and TCP transport-layer protocols (as well as many other protocols).

> Although a 32-bit address space theoretically permits billions of IPv4 network addresses to be assigned, the manner in which addresses were structured and allocated meant that the practical number of available addresses was far lower. The possible exhaustion of the IPv4 address space was one of the primary motivations for the creation of IPv6.
>
> A short history of IPv6 can be found at *http://www.laynetworks.com/ IPv6.htm*.
>
> The existence of IPv4 and IPv6 begs the question, "What about IPv5?" There never was an IPv5 as such. Each IP datagram header includes a 4-bit version number field (thus, IPv4 datagrams always have the number 4 in this field), and the version number 5 was assigned to an experimental protocol, *Internet Stream Protocol*. (Version 2 of this protocol, abbreviated as ST-II, is described in RFC 1819.) Initially conceived in the 1970s, this connection-oriented protocol was designed to support voice and video transmission, and distributed simulation. Since the IP datagram version number 5 was already assigned, the successor to IPv4 was assigned the version number 6.

Figure 58-2 shows a *raw* socket type (SOCK_RAW), which allows an application to communicate directly with the IP layer. We don't describe the use of raw sockets, since most applications employ sockets over one of the transport-layer protocols (TCP or UDP). Raw sockets are described in Chapter 28 of [Stevens et al., 2004]. One instructive example of the use of raw sockets is the *sendip* program (*http:// www.earth.li/projectpurple/progs/sendip.html*), which is a command-line-driven tool that allows the construction and transmission of IP datagrams with arbitrary contents (including options to construct UDP datagrams and TCP segments).

IP transmits datagrams

IP transmits data in the form of datagrams (packets). Each datagram sent between two hosts travels independently across the network, possibly taking a different route. An IP datagram includes a header, which ranges in size from 20 to 60 bytes. The header contains the address of the target host, so that the datagram can be routed through the network to its destination, and also includes the originating address of the packet, so that the receiving host knows the origin of the datagram.

> It is possible for a sending host to spoof the originating address of a packet, and this forms the basis of a TCP denial-of-service attack known as SYN-flooding. [Lemon, 2002] describes the details of this attack and the measures used by modern TCP implementations to deal with it.

An IP implementation may place an upper limit on the size of datagrams that it supports. All IP implementations must permit datagrams at least as large as the limit specified by IP's *minimum reassembly buffer size*. In IPv4, this limit is 576 bytes; in IPv6, it is 1500 bytes.

IP is connectionless and unreliable

IP is described as a *connectionless* protocol, since it doesn't provide the notion of a virtual circuit connecting two hosts. IP is also an *unreliable* protocol: it makes a "best effort" to transmit datagrams from the sender to the receiver, but doesn't guarantee that packets will arrive in the order they were transmitted, that they won't be duplicated, or even that they will arrive at all. Nor does IP provide error recovery (packets with header errors are silently discarded). Reliability must be provided either by using a reliable transport-layer protocol (e.g., TCP) or within the application itself.

> IPv4 provides a checksum for the IP header, which allows the detection of errors in the header, but doesn't provide any error detection for the data transmitted within the packet. IPv6 doesn't provide a checksum in the IP header, relying on higher-layer protocols to provide error checking and reliability as required. (UDP checksums are optional with IPv4, but generally enabled; UDP checksums are mandatory with IPv6. TCP checksums are mandatory with both IPv4 and IPv6.)
>
> Duplication of IP datagrams may occur because of techniques employed by some data-link layers to ensure reliability or when IP datagrams are tunneled through some non-TCP/IP network that employs retransmission.

IP may fragment datagrams

IPv4 datagrams can be up to 65,535 bytes. By default, IPv6 allows datagrams of up to 65,575 bytes (40 bytes for the header, 65,535 bytes for data), and provides an option for larger datagrams (so-called *jumbograms*).

We noted earlier that most data-link layers impose an upper limit (the MTU) on the size of data frames. For example, this upper limit is 1500 bytes on the commonly used Ethernet network architecture (i.e., much smaller than the maximum size of an IP datagram). IP also defines the notion of the *path MTU*. This is the minimum MTU on all of the data-link layers traversed on the route from the source to the destination. (In practice, the Ethernet MTU is often the minimum MTU in a path.)

When an IP datagram is larger than the MTU, IP fragments (breaks up) the datagram into suitably sized units for transmission across the network. These fragments are then reassembled at the final destination to re-create the original datagram.

(Each IP fragment is itself an IP datagram that contains an offset field giving the location of that fragment within the original datagram.)

IP fragmentation occurs transparently to higher protocol layers, but nevertheless is generally considered undesirable ([Kent & Mogul, 1987]). The problem is that, because IP doesn't perform retransmission, and a datagram can be reassembled at the destination only if all fragments arrive, the entire datagram is unusable if any fragment is lost or contains transmission errors. In some cases, this can lead to significant rates of data loss (for higher protocol layers that don't perform retransmission, such as UDP) or degraded transfer rates (for higher protocol layers that do perform retransmission, such as TCP). Modern TCP implementations employ algorithms (*path MTU discovery*) to determine the MTU of a path between hosts, and accordingly break up the data they pass to IP, so that IP is not asked to transmit datagrams that exceed this size. UDP provides no such mechanism, and we consider how UDP-based applications can deal with the possibility of IP fragmentation in Section 58.6.2.

58.5   IP Addresses

An IP address consists of two parts: a network ID, which specifies the network on which a host resides, and a host ID, which identifies the host within that network.

IPv4 addresses

An IPv4 address consists of 32 bits (Figure 58-5). When expressed in human-readable form, these addresses are normally written in *dotted-decimal notation*, with the 4 bytes of the address being written as decimal numbers separated by dots, as in 204.152.189.116.

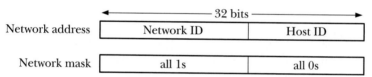

Figure 58-5: An IPv4 network address and corresponding network mask

When an organization applies for a range of IPv4 addresses for its hosts, it receives a 32-bit network address and a corresponding 32-bit *network mask*. In binary form, this mask consists of a sequence of 1s in the leftmost bits, followed by a sequence of 0s to fill out the remainder of the mask. The 1s indicate which part of the address contains the assigned network ID, while the 0s indicate which part of the address is available to the organization to assign as unique host IDs on its network. The size of the network ID part of the mask is determined when the address is assigned. Since the network ID component always occupies the leftmost part of the mask, the following notation is sufficient to specify the range of assigned addresses:

    204.152.189.0/24

The /24 indicates that the network ID part of the assigned address consists of the leftmost 24 bits, with the remaining 8 bits specifying the host ID. Alternatively, we could say that the network mask in this case is 255.255.255.0 in dotted-decimal notation.

An organization holding this address can assign 254 unique Internet addresses to its computers—204.152.189.1 through 204.152.189.254. Two addresses can't be assigned. One of these is the address whose host ID is all 0 bits, which is used to identify the network itself. The other is the address whose host ID is all 1 bits—204.152.189.255 in this example—which is the *subnet broadcast address*.

Certain IPv4 addresses have special meanings. The special address 127.0.0.1 is normally defined as the *loopback address*, and is conventionally assigned the host-name localhost. (Any address on the network 127.0.0.0/8 can be designated as the IPv4 loopback address, but 127.0.0.1 is the usual choice.) A datagram sent to this address never actually reaches the network, but instead automatically loops back to become input to the sending host. Using this address is convenient for testing client and server programs on the same host. For use in a C program, the integer constant INADDR_LOOPBACK is defined for this address.

The constant INADDR_ANY is the so-called IPv4 *wildcard address*. The wildcard IP address is useful for applications that bind Internet domain sockets on multi-homed hosts. If an application on a multihomed host binds a socket to just one of its host's IP addresses, then that socket can receive only UDP datagrams or TCP connection requests sent to that IP address. However, we normally want an application on a multihomed host to be able to receive datagrams or connection requests that specify any of the host's IP addresses, and binding the socket to the wildcard IP address makes this possible. SUSv3 doesn't specify any particular value for INADDR_ANY, but most implementations define it as 0.0.0.0 (all zeros).

Typically, IPv4 addresses are *subnetted*. Subnetting divides the host ID part of an IPv4 address into two parts: a subnet ID and a host ID (Figure 58-6). (The choice of how the bits of the host ID are divided is made by the local network administrator.) The rationale for subnetting is that an organization often doesn't attach all of its hosts to a single network. Instead, the organization may operate a set of sub-networks (an "internal internetwork"), with each subnetwork being identified by the combination of the network ID plus the subnet ID. This combination is usually referred to as the *extended network ID*. Within a subnet, the subnet mask serves the same role as described earlier for the network mask, and we can use a similar notation to indicate the range of addresses assigned to a particular subnet.

For example, suppose that our assigned network ID is 204.152.189.0/24, and we choose to subnet this address range by splitting the 8 bits of the host ID into a 4-bit subnet ID and a 4-bit host ID. Under this scheme, the subnet mask would consist of 28 leading ones, followed by 4 zeros, and the subnet with the ID of 1 would be designated as 204.152.189.16/28.

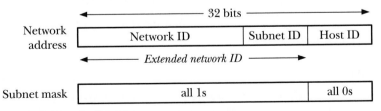

Figure 58-6: IPv4 subnetting

IPv6 addresses

The principles of IPv6 addresses are similar to IPv4 addresses. The key difference is that IPv6 addresses consist of 128 bits, and the first few bits of the address are a *format prefix*, indicating the address type. (We won't go into the details of these address types; see Appendix A of [Stevens et al., 2004] and RFC 3513 for details.)

IPv6 addresses are typically written as a series of 16-bit hexadecimal numbers separated by colons, as in the following:

    F000:0:0:0:0:0:A:1

IPv6 addresses often include a sequence of zeros and, as a notational convenience, two colons (::) can be employed to indicate such a sequence. Thus, the above address can be rewritten as:

    F000::A:1

Only one instance of the double-colon notation can appear in an IPv6 address; more than one instance would be ambiguous.

IPv6 also provides equivalents of the IPv4's loopback address (127 zeros, followed by a one, thus ::1) and wildcard address (all zeros, written as either 0::0 or ::).

In order to allow IPv6 applications to communicate with hosts supporting only IPv4, IPv6 provides so-called *IPv4-mapped IPv6 addresses*. The format of these addresses is shown in Figure 58-7.

all zeros	FFFF	IPv4 address
80 bits	16 bits	32 bits

Figure 58-7: Format of an IPv4-mapped IPv6 address

When writing an IPv4-mapped IPv6 address, the IPv4 part of the address (i.e., the last 4 bytes) is written in IPv4 dotted-decimal notation. Thus, the IPv4-mapped IPv6 address equivalent to 204.152.189.116 is ::FFFF:204.152.189.116.

58.6 The Transport Layer

There are two widely used transport-layer protocols in the TCP/IP suite:

* *User Datagram Protocol* (UDP) is the protocol used for datagram sockets.
* *Transmission Control Protocol* (TCP) is the protocol used for stream sockets.

Before considering these protocols, we first need to describe port numbers, a concept used by both protocols.

58.6.1 Port Numbers

The task of the transport protocol is to provide an end-to-end communication service to applications residing on different hosts (or sometimes on the same host). In order to do this, the transport layer requires a method of differentiating the applications on a host. In TCP and UDP, this differentiation is provided by a 16-bit *port number*.

Well-known, registered, and privileged ports

Some *well-known port numbers* are permanently assigned to specific applications (also known as *services*). For example, the *ssh* (secure shell) daemon uses the well-known port 22, and HTTP (the protocol used for communication between web servers and browsers) uses the well-known port 80. Well-known ports are assigned numbers in the range 0 to 1023 by a central authority, the Internet Assigned Numbers Authority (IANA, *http://www.iana.org/*). Assignment of a well-known port number is contingent on an approved network specification (typically in the form of an RFC).

IANA also records *registered ports*, which are allocated to application developers on a less stringent basis (which also means that an implementation doesn't need to guarantee the availability of these ports for their registered purpose). The range of IANA registered ports is 1024 to 49151. (Not all port numbers in this range are registered.)

The up-to-date list of IANA well-known and registered port assignments can be obtained online at *http://www.iana.org/assignments/port-numbers*.

In most TCP/IP implementations (including Linux), the port numbers in the range 0 to 1023 are also *privileged*, meaning that only privileged (CAP_NET_BIND_SERVICE) processes may bind to these ports. This prevents a normal user from implementing a malicious application that, for example, spoofs as *ssh* in order to obtain passwords. (Sometimes, privileged ports are referred to as *reserved* ports.)

Although TCP and UDP ports with the same number are distinct entities, the same well-known port number is usually assigned to a service under both TCP and UDP, even if, as is often the case, that service is available under only one of these protocols. This convention avoids confusion of port numbers across the two protocols.

Ephemeral ports

If an application doesn't select a particular port (i.e., in sockets terminology, it doesn't *bind()* its socket to a particular port), then TCP and UDP assign a unique *ephemeral port* (i.e., short-lived) number to the socket. In this case, the application—typically a client—doesn't care which port number it uses, but assigning a port is necessary so that the transport-layer protocols can identify the communication endpoints. It also has the result that the peer application at the other end of the communication channel knows how to communicate with this application. TCP and UDP also assign an ephemeral port number if we bind a socket to port 0.

IANA specifies the ports in the range 49152 to 65535 as *dynamic* or *private*, with the intention that these ports can be used by local applications and assigned as ephemeral ports. However, various implementations allocate ephemeral ports from different ranges. On Linux, the range is defined by (and can be modified via) two numbers contained in the file /proc/sys/net/ipv4/ip_local_port_range.

58.6.2 User Datagram Protocol (UDP)

UDP adds just two features to IP: port numbers and a data checksum to allow the detection of errors in the transmitted data.

Like IP, UDP is connectionless. Since it adds no reliability to IP, UDP is likewise unreliable. If an application layered on top of UDP requires reliability, then this must be implemented within the application. Despite this unreliability, we may sometimes prefer to use UDP instead of TCP, for the reasons detailed in Section 61.12.

The checksums used by both UDP and TCP are just 16 bits long, and are simple "add-up" checksums that can fail to detect certain classes of errors. Consequently, they do not provide extremely strong error detection. Busy Internet servers typically see an average of one undetected transmission error every few days ([Stone & Partridge, 2000]). Applications that need stronger assurances of data integrity can use the Secure Sockets Layer (SSL) protocol, which provides not only secure communication, but also much more rigorous detection of errors. Alternatively, an application could implement its own error-control scheme.

Selecting a UDP datagram size to avoid IP fragmentation

In Section 58.4, we described the IP fragmentation mechanism, and noted that it is usually best to avoid IP fragmentation. While TCP contains mechanisms for avoiding IP fragmentation, UDP does not. With UDP, we can easily cause IP fragmentation by transmitting a datagram that exceeds the MTU of the local data link.

A UDP-based application generally doesn't know the MTU of the path between the source and destination hosts. UDP-based applications that aim to avoid IP fragmentation typically adopt a conservative approach, which is to ensure that the transmitted IP datagram is less than the IPv4 minimum reassembly buffer size of 576 bytes. (This value is likely to be lower than the path MTU.) From these 576 bytes, 8 bytes are required by UDP's own header, and an additional minimum of 20 bytes are required for the IP header, leaving 548 bytes for the UDP datagram itself. In practice, many UDP-based applications opt for a still lower limit of 512 bytes for their datagrams ([Stevens, 1994]).

58.6.3 Transmission Control Protocol (TCP)

TCP provides a reliable, connection-oriented, bidirectional, byte-stream communication channel between two endpoints (i.e., applications), as shown in Figure 58-8. In order to provide these features, TCP must perform the tasks described in this section. (A detailed description of all of these features can be found in [Stevens, 1994].)

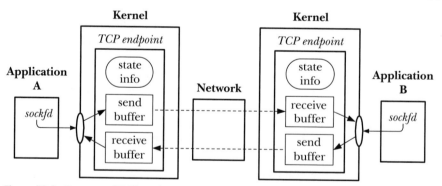

Figure 58-8: Connected TCP sockets

We use the term *TCP endpoint* to denote the information maintained by the kernel for one end of a TCP connection. (Often, we abbreviate this term further, for example, writing just "a TCP," to mean "a TCP endpoint," or "the client TCP" to mean "the TCP endpoint maintained for the client application.") This information includes the send and receive buffers for this end of the connection, as well as state information that is maintained in order to synchronize the operation of the two connected endpoints. (We describe this state information in further detail when we consider the TCP state transition diagram in Section 61.6.3.) In the remainder of this book, we use the terms *receiving TCP* and *sending TCP* to denote the TCP endpoints maintained for the receiving and sending applications on either end of a stream socket connection that is being used to transmit data in a particular direction.

Connection establishment

Before communication can commence, TCP establishes a communication channel between the two endpoints. During connection establishment, the sender and receiver can exchange options to advertise parameters for the connection.

Packaging of data in segments

Data is broken into segments, each of which contains a checksum to allow the detection of end-to-end transmission errors. Each segment is transmitted in a single IP datagram.

Acknowledgements, retransmissions, and timeouts

When a TCP segment arrives at its destination without errors, the receiving TCP sends a positive acknowledgement to the sender, informing it of the successfully delivered data. If a segment arrives with errors, then it is discarded, and no acknowledgement is sent. To handle the possibility of segments that never arrive or are discarded, the sender starts a timer when each segment is transmitted. If an acknowledgement is not received before the timer expires, the segment is retransmitted.

> Since the time taken to transmit a segment and receive its acknowledgement varies according to the range of the network and the current traffic loading, TCP employs an algorithm to dynamically adjust the size of the retransmission timeout (RTO).
>
> The receiving TCP may not send acknowledgements immediately, but instead wait for a fraction of a second to see if the acknowledgement can be piggybacked inside any response that the receiver may send straight back to the sender. (Every TCP segment includes an acknowledgement field, allowing for such piggybacking.) The aim of this technique, called *delayed ACK*, is to save sending a TCP segment, thus decreasing the number of packets in the network and decreasing the load on the sending and receiving hosts.

Sequencing

Each byte that is transmitted over a TCP connection is assigned a logical sequence number. This number indicates the position of that byte in the data stream for the connection. (Each of the two streams in the connection has its own sequence numbering.) When a TCP segment is transmitted, it includes a field containing the sequence number of the first byte in the segment.

Attaching sequence numbers to each segment serves a variety of purposes:

- The sequence number allows TCP segments to be assembled in the correct order at the destination, and then passed as a byte stream to the application layer. (At any moment, multiple TCP segments may be in transit between sender and receiver, and these segments may arrive out of order.)

- The acknowledgement message passed from the receiver back to the sender can use the sequence number to identify which TCP segment was received.

- The receiver can use the sequence number to eliminate duplicate segments. Such duplicates may occur either because of the duplication of IP datagrams or because of TCP's own retransmission algorithm, which could retransmit a successfully delivered segment if the acknowledgement for that segment was lost or was not received in a timely fashion.

The initial sequence number (ISN) for a stream doesn't start at 0. Instead, it is generated via an algorithm that increases the ISN assigned to successive TCP connections (to prevent the possibility of old segments from a previous incarnation of the connection being confused with segments for this connection). This algorithm is also designed to make guessing the ISN difficult. The sequence number is a 32-bit value that is wrapped around to 0 when the maximum value is reached.

Flow control

Flow control prevents a fast sender from overwhelming a slow receiver. To implement flow control, the receiving TCP maintains a buffer for incoming data. (Each TCP advertises the size of this buffer during connection establishment.) Data accumulates in this buffer as it is received from the sending TCP, and is removed as the application reads data. With each acknowledgement, the receiver advises the sender of how much space is available in its incoming data buffer (i.e., how many bytes the sender can transmit). The TCP flow-control algorithm employs a so-called *sliding window* algorithm, which allows unacknowledged segments containing a total of up to N (the offered window size) bytes to be in transit between the sender and receiver. If a receiving TCP's incoming data buffer fills completely, then the window is said to be closed, and the sending TCP stops transmitting.

> The receiver can override the default size for the incoming data buffer using the SO_RCVBUF socket option (see the *socket(7)* manual page).

Congestion control: slow-start and congestion-avoidance algorithms

TCP's congestion-control algorithms are designed to prevent a fast sender from overwhelming a network. If a sending TCP transmits packets faster than they can be relayed by an intervening router, that router will start dropping packets. This could lead to high rates of packet loss and, consequently, serious performance degradation, if the sending TCP kept retransmitting these dropped segments at the same rate. TCP's congestion-control algorithms are important in two circumstances:

- *After connection establishment*: At this time (or when transmission resumes on a connection that has been idle for some time), the sender could start by immediately injecting as many segments into the network as would be permitted by the window size advertised by the receiver. (In fact, this is what was done in early TCP implementations.) The problem here is that if the network can't handle this flood of segments, the sender risks overwhelming the network immediately.

- *When congestion is detected*: If the sending TCP detects that congestion is occurring, then it must reduce its transmission rate. TCP detects that congestion is occurring based on the assumption that segment loss because of transmission errors is very low; thus, if a packet is lost, the cause is assumed to be congestion.

TCP's congestion-control strategy employs two algorithms in combination: slow start and congestion avoidance.

The *slow-start* algorithm causes the sending TCP to initially transmit segments at a slow rate, but allows it to exponentially increase the rate as these segments are acknowledged by the receiving TCP. Slow start attempts to prevent a fast TCP sender from overwhelming a network. However, if unrestrained, slow start's exponential increase in the transmission rate could mean that the sender would soon overwhelm the network. TCP's *congestion-avoidance* algorithm prevents this, by placing a governor on the rate increase.

With congestion avoidance, at the beginning of a connection, the sending TCP starts with a small *congestion window*, which limits the amount of unacknowledged data that it can transmit. As the sender receives acknowledgements from the peer TCP, the congestion window initially grows exponentially. However, once the congestion window reaches a certain threshold believed to be close to the transmission capacity of the network, its growth becomes linear, rather than exponential. (An estimate of the capacity of the network is derived from a calculation based on the transmission rate that was in operation when congestion was detected, or is set at a fixed value after initial establishment of the connection.) At all times, the quantity of data that the sending TCP will transmit remains additionally constrained by the receiving TCP's advertised window and the local TCP's send buffer.

In combination, the slow-start and congestion-avoidance algorithms allow the sender to rapidly raise its transmission speed up to the available capacity of the network, without overshooting that capacity. The effect of these algorithms is to allow data transmission to quickly reach a state of equilibrium, where the sender transmits packets at the same rate as it receives acknowledgements from the receiver.

58.7 Requests for Comments (RFCs)

Each of the Internet protocols that we discuss in this book is defined in an RFC document—a formal protocol specification. RFCs are published by the *RFC Editor* (*http://www.rfc-editor.org/*), which is funded by the *Internet Society* (*http://www.isoc.org/*). RFCs that describe Internet standards are developed under the auspices of the *Internet Engineering Task Force* (IETF, *http://www.ietf.org/*), a community of network designers, operators, vendors, and researchers concerned with the evolution and smooth operation of the Internet. Membership of the IETF is open to any interested individual.

The following RFCs are of particular relevance to the material covered in this book:

- RFC 791, *Internet Protocol*. J. Postel (ed.), 1981.
- RFC 950, *Internet Standard Subnetting Procedure*. J. Mogul and J. Postel, 1985.

- RFC 793, *Transmission Control Protocol.* J. Postel (ed.), 1981.

- RFC 768, *User Datagram Protocol.* J. Postel (ed.), 1980.

- RFC 1122, *Requirements for Internet Hosts–Communication Layers.* R. Braden (ed.), 1989.

> RFC 1122 extends (and corrects) various earlier RFCs describing the TCP/IP protocols. It is one of a pair of RFCs that are often simply known as the *Host Requirements RFCs.* The other member of the pair is RFC 1123, which covers application-layer protocols such as *telnet*, FTP, and SMTP.

Among the RFCs that describe IPv6 are the following:

- RFC 2460, *Internet Protocol, Version 6.* S. Deering and R. Hinden, 1998.

- RFC 4291, *IP Version 6 Addressing Architecture.* R. Hinden and S. Deering, 2006.

- RFC 3493, *Basic Socket Interface Extensions for IPv6.* R. Gilligan, S. Thomson, J. Bound, J. McCann, and W. Stevens, 2003.

- RFC 3542, *Advanced Sockets API for IPv6.* W. Stevens, M. Thomas, E. Nordmark, and T. Jinmei, 2003.

A number of RFCs and papers provide improvements and extensions to the original TCP specification, including the following:

- *Congestion Avoidance and Control.* V. Jacobson, 1988. This was the initial paper describing the congestion-control and slow-start algorithms for TCP. Originally published in *Proceedings of SIGCOMM '88*, a slightly revised version is available at *ftp://ftp.ee.lbl.gov/papers/congavoid.ps.Z.* This paper is largely superseded by some of the following RFCs.

- RFC 1323, *TCP Extensions for High Performance.* V. Jacobson, R. Braden, and D. Borman, 1992.

- RFC 2018, *TCP Selective Acknowledgment Options.* M. Mathis, J. Mahdavi, S. Floyd, and A. Romanow, 1996.

- RFC 2581, *TCP Congestion Control.* M. Allman, V. Paxson, and W. Stevens, 1999.

- RFC 2861, *TCP Congestion Window Validation.* M. Handley, J. Padhye, and S. Floyd, 2000.

- RFC 2883, *An Extension to the Selective Acknowledgement (SACK) Option for TCP.* S. Floyd, J. Mahdavi, M. Mathis, and M. Podolsky, 2000.

- RFC 2988, *Computing TCP's Retransmission Timer.* V. Paxson and M. Allman, 2000.

- RFC 3168, *The Addition of Explicit Congestion Notification (ECN) to IP.* K. Ramakrishnan, S. Floyd, and D. Black, 2001.

- RFC 3390, *Increasing TCP's Initial Window.* M. Allman, S. Floyd, and C. Partridge, 2002.

58.8 Summary

TCP/IP is a layered networking protocol suite. At the bottom layer of the TCP/IP protocol stack is the IP network-layer protocol. IP transmits data in the form of datagrams. IP is connectionless, meaning that datagrams transmitted between source and destination hosts may take different routes across the network. IP is unreliable, in that it provides no guarantee that datagrams will arrive in order or unduplicated, or even arrive at all. If reliability is required, then it must be provided via the use of a reliable higher-layer protocol (e.g., TCP), or within an application.

The original version of IP is IPv4. In the early 1990s, a new version of IP, IPv6, was devised. The most notable difference between IPv4 and IPv6 is that IPv4 uses 32 bits to represent a host address, while IPv6 uses 128 bits, thus allowing for a much larger number of hosts on the world-wide Internet. Currently, IPv4 remains the most widely used version of IP, although in coming years, it is likely to be supplanted by IPv6.

Various transport-layer protocols are layered on top of IP, of which the most widely used are UDP and TCP. UDP is an unreliable datagram protocol. TCP is a reliable, connection-oriented, byte-stream protocol. TCP handles all of the details of connection establishment and termination. TCP also packages data into segments for transmission by IP, and provides sequence numbering for these segments so that they can be acknowledged and assembled in the correct order by the receiver. In addition, TCP provides flow control, to prevent a fast sender from overwhelming a slow receiver, and congestion control, to prevent a fast sender from overwhelming the network.

Further information

Refer to the sources of further information listed in Section 59.15.

59

SOCKETS: INTERNET DOMAINS

Having looked at generic sockets concepts and the TCP/IP protocol suite in previous chapters, we are now ready in this chapter to look at programming with sockets in the IPv4 (AF_INET) and IPv6 (AF_INET6) domains.

As noted in Chapter 58, Internet domain socket addresses consist of an IP address and a port number. Although computers use binary representations of IP addresses and port numbers, humans are much better at dealing with names than with numbers. Therefore, we describe the techniques used to identify host computers and ports using names. We also examine the use of library functions to obtain the IP address(es) for a particular hostname and the port number that corresponds to a particular service name. Our discussion of hostnames includes a description of the Domain Name System (DNS), which implements a distributed database that maps hostnames to IP addresses and vice versa.

59.1 Internet Domain Sockets

Internet domain stream sockets are implemented on top of TCP. They provide a reliable, bidirectional, byte-stream communication channel.

Internet domain datagram sockets are implemented on top of UDP. UDP sockets are similar to their UNIX domain counterparts, but note the following differences:

- UNIX domain datagram sockets are reliable, but UDP sockets are not—datagrams may be lost, duplicated, or arrive in a different order from that in which they were sent.

- Sending on a UNIX domain datagram socket will block if the queue of data for the receiving socket is full. By contrast, with UDP, if the incoming datagram would overflow the receiver's queue, then the datagram is silently dropped.

59.2 Network Byte Order

IP addresses and port numbers are integer values. One problem we encounter when passing these values across a network is that different hardware architectures store the bytes of a multibyte integer in different orders. As shown in Figure 59-1, architectures that store integers with the most significant byte first (i.e., at the lowest memory address) are termed *big endian*; those that store the least significant byte first are termed *little endian*. (The terms derive from Jonathan Swift's 1726 satirical novel *Gulliver's Travels*, in which the terms refer to opposing political factions who open their boiled eggs at opposite ends.) The most notable example of a little-endian architecture is x86. (Digital's VAX architecture was another historically important example, since BSD was widely used on that machine.) Most other architectures are big endian. A few hardware architectures are switchable between the two formats. The byte ordering used on a particular machine is called the *host byte order*.

	2-byte integer		**4-byte integer**			
	address N	address N + 1	address N	address N + 1	address N + 2	address N + 3
Big-endian byte order	1 (MSB)	0 (LSB)	3 (MSB)	2	1	0 (LSB)
	address N	address N + 1	address N	address N + 1	address N + 2	address N + 3
Little-endian byte order	0 (LSB)	1 (MSB)	0 (LSB)	1	2	3 (MSB)

MSB = Most Significant Byte, LSB = Least Significant Byte

Figure 59-1: Big-endian and little-endian byte order for 2-byte and 4-byte integers

Since port numbers and IP addresses must be transmitted between, and understood by, all hosts on a network, a standard ordering must be used. This ordering is called *network byte order*, and happens to be big endian.

Later in this chapter, we look at various functions that convert hostnames (e.g., www.kernel.org) and service names (e.g., *http*) into the corresponding numeric forms. These functions generally return integers in network byte order, and these integers can be copied directly into the relevant fields of a socket address structure.

However, we sometimes make direct use of integer constants for IP addresses and port numbers. For example, we may choose to hard-code a port number into our program, specify a port number as a command-line argument to a program, or use constants such as INADDR_ANY and INADDR_LOOPBACK when specifying an IPv4 address. These values are represented in C according to the conventions of the host machine, so they are in host byte order. We must convert these values to network byte order before storing them in socket address structures.

The *htons()*, *htonl()*, *ntohs()*, and *ntohl()* functions are defined (typically as macros) for converting integers in either direction between host and network byte order.

```
#include <arpa/inet.h>

uint16_t htons(uint16_t host_uint16);
```
> Returns *host_uint16* converted to network byte order
```
uint32_t htonl(uint32_t host_uint32);
```
> Returns *host_uint32* converted to network byte order
```
uint16_t ntohs(uint16_t net_uint16);
```
> Returns *net_uint16* converted to host byte order
```
uint32_t ntohl(uint32_t net_uint32);
```
> Returns *net_uint32* converted to host byte order

In earlier times, these functions had prototypes such as the following:

```
unsigned long htonl(unsigned long hostlong);
```

This reveals the origin of the function names—in this case, *host to network long*. On most early systems on which sockets were implemented, short integers were 16 bits, and long integers were 32 bits. This no longer holds true on modern systems (at least for long integers), so the prototypes given above provide a more exact definition of the types dealt with by these functions, although the names remain unchanged. The *uint16_t* and *uint32_t* data types are 16-bit and 32-bit unsigned integers.

Strictly speaking, the use of these four functions is necessary only on systems where the host byte order differs from network byte order. However, these functions should always be used, so that programs are portable to different hardware architectures. On systems where the host byte order is the same as network byte order, these functions simply return their arguments unchanged.

59.3 Data Representation

When writing network programs, we need to be aware of the fact that different computer architectures use different conventions for representing various data types. We have already noted that integer types can be stored in big-endian or little-endian form. There are also other possible differences. For example, the C *long* data type may be 32 bits on some systems and 64 bits on others. When we consider structures, the issue is further complicated by the fact that different implementations employ different rules for aligning the fields of a structure to address boundaries on the host system, leaving different numbers of padding bytes between the fields.

Because of these differences in data representation, applications that exchange data between heterogeneous systems over a network must adopt some common convention for encoding that data. The sender must encode data according to this convention, while the receiver decodes following the same convention. The process of putting data into a standard format for transmission across a network is referred to as *marshalling*. Various marshalling standards exist, such as XDR (External Data Representation, described in RFC 1014), ASN.1-BER (Abstract Syntax Notation 1, *http://www.asn1.org/*), CORBA, and XML. Typically, these standards define a fixed format for each data type (defining, for example, byte order and number of bits used). As well as being encoded in the required format, each data item is tagged with extra field(s) identifying its type (and, possibly, length).

However, a simpler approach than marshalling is often employed: encode all transmitted data in text form, with separate data items delimited by a designated character, typically a newline character. One advantage of this approach is that we can use *telnet* to debug an application. To do this, we use the following command:

```
$ telnet host port
```

We can then type lines of text to be transmitted to the application, and view the responses sent by the application. We demonstrate this technique in Section 59.11.

> The problems associated with differences in representation across heterogeneous systems apply not only to data transfer across a network, but also to any mechanism of data exchange between such systems. For example, we face the same problems when transferring files on disk or tape between heterogeneous systems. Network programming is simply the most common programming context in which we are nowadays likely to encounter this issue.

If we encode data transmitted on a stream socket as newline-delimited text, then it is convenient to define a function such as *readLine()*, shown in Listing 59-1.

```
#include "read_line.h"

ssize_t readLine(int fd, void *buffer, size_t n);
```
                    Returns number of bytes copied into *buffer* (excluding
                    terminating null byte), or 0 on end-of-file, or −1 on error

The *readLine()* function reads bytes from the file referred to by the file descriptor argument *fd* until a newline is encountered. The input byte sequence is returned in the location pointed to by *buffer*, which must point to a region of at least *n* bytes of memory. The returned string is always null-terminated; thus, at most *(n − 1)* bytes of actual data will be returned. On success, *readLine()* returns the number of bytes of data placed in *buffer*; the terminating null byte is not included in this count.

Listing 59-1: Reading data a line at a time

```c
#include <unistd.h>
#include <errno.h>
#include "read_line.h"                    /* Declaration of readLine() */

ssize_t
readLine(int fd, void *buffer, size_t n)
{
    ssize_t numRead;                      /* # of bytes fetched by last read() */
    size_t totRead;                       /* Total bytes read so far */
    char *buf;
    char ch;

    if (n <= 0 || buffer == NULL) {
        errno = EINVAL;
        return -1;
    }

    buf = buffer;                         /* No pointer arithmetic on "void *" */

    totRead = 0;
    for (;;) {
        numRead = read(fd, &ch, 1);

        if (numRead == -1) {
            if (errno == EINTR)           /* Interrupted --> restart read() */
                continue;
            else
                return -1;                /* Some other error */

        } else if (numRead == 0) {        /* EOF */
            if (totRead == 0)             /* No bytes read; return 0 */
                return 0;
            else                          /* Some bytes read; add '\0' */
                break;

        } else {                          /* 'numRead' must be 1 if we get here */
            if (totRead < n - 1) {        /* Discard > (n - 1) bytes */
                totRead++;
                *buf++ = ch;
            }

            if (ch == '\n')
                break;
        }
    }

    *buf = '\0';
    return totRead;
}
```

If the number of bytes read before a newline is encountered is greater than or equal to *(n − 1)*, then the *readLine()* function discards the excess bytes (including the newline). If a newline was read within the first *(n − 1)* bytes, then it is included in the returned string. (Thus, we can determine if bytes were discarded by checking if a newline precedes the terminating null byte in the returned *buffer*.) We take this approach so that application protocols that rely on handling input in units of lines don't end up processing a long line as though it were multiple lines. This would likely break the protocol, as the applications on either end would become desynchronized. An alternative approach would be to have *readLine()* read only sufficient bytes to fill the supplied buffer, leaving any remaining bytes up to the next newline for the next call to *readLine()*. In this case, the caller of *readLine()* would need to handle the possibility of a partial line being read.

We employ the *readLine()* function in the example programs presented in Section 59.11.

59.4 Internet Socket Addresses

There are two types of Internet domain socket addresses: IPv4 and IPv6.

IPv4 socket addresses: *struct sockaddr_in*

An IPv4 socket address is stored in a *sockaddr_in* structure, defined in <netinet/in.h> as follows:

```
struct in_addr {                            /* IPv4 4-byte address */
    in_addr_t s_addr;                       /* Unsigned 32-bit integer */
};

struct sockaddr_in {                        /* IPv4 socket address */
    sa_family_t    sin_family;              /* Address family (AF_INET) */
    in_port_t      sin_port;                /* Port number */
    struct in_addr sin_addr;                /* IPv4 address */
    unsigned char  __pad[X];                /* Pad to size of 'sockaddr'
                                               structure (16 bytes) */
};
```

In Section 56.4, we saw that the generic *sockaddr* structure commences with a field identifying the socket domain. This corresponds to the *sin_family* field in the *sockaddr_in* structure, which is always set to AF_INET. The *sin_port* and *sin_addr* fields are the port number and the IP address, both in network byte order. The *in_port_t* and *in_addr_t* data types are unsigned integer types, 16 and 32 bits in length, respectively.

IPv6 socket addresses: *struct sockaddr_in6*

Like an IPv4 address, an IPv6 socket address includes an IP address plus a port number. The difference is that an IPv6 address is 128 bits instead of 32 bits. An IPv6 socket address is stored in a *sockaddr_in6* structure, defined in <netinet/in.h> as follows:

```
struct in6_addr {                           /* IPv6 address structure */
    uint8_t s6_addr[16];                    /* 16 bytes == 128 bits */
};
```

```
struct sockaddr_in6 {                  /* IPv6 socket address */
    sa_family_t sin6_family;           /* Address family (AF_INET6) */
    in_port_t   sin6_port;             /* Port number */
    uint32_t    sin6_flowinfo;         /* IPv6 flow information */
    struct in6_addr sin6_addr;         /* IPv6 address */
    uint32_t    sin6_scope_id;         /* Scope ID (new in kernel 2.4) */
};
```

The *sin6_family* field is set to `AF_INET6`. The *sin6_port* and *sin6_addr* fields are the port number and the IP address. (The *uint8_t* data type, used to type the bytes of the *in6_addr* structure, is an 8-bit unsigned integer.) The remaining fields, *sin6_flowinfo* and *sin6_scope_id*, are beyond the scope of this book; for our purposes, they are always set to 0. All of the fields in the *sockaddr_in6* structure are in network byte order.

> IPv6 addresses are described in RFC 4291. Information about IPv6 flow control (*sin6_flowinfo*) can be found in Appendix A of [Stevens et al., 2004] and in RFCs 2460 and 3697. RFCs 3493 and 4007 provide information about *sin6_scope_id*.

IPv6 has equivalents of the IPv4 wildcard and loopback addresses. However, their use is complicated by the fact that an IPv6 address is stored in an array (rather than using a scalar type). We use the IPv6 wildcard address (`0::0`) to illustrate this point. The constant `IN6ADDR_ANY_INIT` is defined for this address as follows:

```
#define IN6ADDR_ANY_INIT { { 0,0,0,0,0,0,0,0,0,0,0,0,0,0,0,0 } }
```

> On Linux, some details in the header files differ from our description in this section. In particular, the *in6_addr* structure contains a union definition that divides the 128-bit IPv6 address into 16 bytes, eight 2-byte integers, or four 4-byte integers. Because of the presence of this definition, the *glibc* definition of the `IN6ADDR_ANY_INIT` constant actually includes one more set of nested braces than is shown in the main text.

We can use the `IN6ADDR_ANY_INIT` constant in the initializer that accompanies a variable declaration, but can't use it on the right-hand side of an assignment statement, since C syntax doesn't permit structured constants to be used in assignments. Instead, we must use a predefined variable, *in6addr_any*, which is initialized as follows by the C library:

```
const struct in6_addr in6addr_any = IN6ADDR_ANY_INIT;
```

Thus, we can initialize an IPv6 socket address structure using the wildcard address as follows:

```
struct sockaddr_in6 addr;

memset(&addr, 0, sizeof(struct sockaddr_in6));
addr.sin6_family = AF_INET6;
addr.sin6_addr = in6addr_any;
addr.sin6_port = htons(SOME_PORT_NUM);
```

The corresponding constant and variable for the IPv6 loopback address (`::1`) are `IN6ADDR_LOOPBACK_INIT` and *in6addr_loopback*.

Unlike their IPv4 counterparts, the IPv6 constant and variable initializers are in network byte order. But, as shown in the above code, we still must ensure that the port number is in network byte order.

If IPv4 and IPv6 coexist on a host, they share the same port-number space. This means that if, for example, an application binds an IPv6 socket to TCP port 2000 (using the IPv6 wildcard address), then an IPv4 TCP socket can't be bound to the same port. (The TCP/IP implementation ensures that sockets on other hosts are able to communicate with this socket, regardless of whether those hosts are running IPv4 or IPv6.)

The *sockaddr_storage* structure

With the IPv6 sockets API, the new generic *sockaddr_storage* structure was introduced. This structure is defined to be large enough to hold any type of socket address (i.e., any type of socket address structure can be cast and stored in it). In particular, this structure allows us to transparently store either an IPv4 or an IPv6 socket address, thus removing IP version dependencies from our code. The *sockaddr_storage* structure is defined on Linux as follows:

```
#define __ss_aligntype uint32_t         /* On 32-bit architectures */
struct sockaddr_storage {
    sa_family_t ss_family;
    __ss_aligntype __ss_align;          /* Force alignment */
    char __ss_padding[SS_PADSIZE];      /* Pad to 128 bytes */
};
```

59.5 Overview of Host and Service Conversion Functions

Computers represent IP addresses and port numbers in binary. However, humans find names easier to remember than numbers. Employing symbolic names also provides a useful level of indirection; users and programs can continue to use the same name even if the underlying numeric value changes.

A *hostname* is the symbolic identifier for a system that is connected to a network (possibly with multiple IP addresses). A *service name* is the symbolic representation of a port number.

The following methods are available for representing host addresses and ports:

- A host address can be represented as a binary value, as a symbolic hostname, or in presentation format (dotted-decimal for IPv4 or hex-string for IPv6).
- A port can be represented as a binary value or as a symbolic service name.

Various library functions are provided for converting between these formats. This section briefly summarizes these functions. The following sections describe the modern APIs (*inet_ntop()*, *inet_pton()*, *getaddrinfo()*, *getnameinfo()*, and so on) in detail. In Section 59.13, we briefly discuss the obsolete APIs (*inet_aton()*, *inet_ntoa()*, *gethostbyname()*, *getservbyname()*, and so on).

Converting IPv4 addresses between binary and human-readable forms

The *inet_aton()* and *inet_ntoa()* functions convert an IPv4 address in dotted-decimal notation to binary and vice versa. We describe these functions primarily because they appear in historical code. Nowadays, they are obsolete. Modern programs that need to do such conversions should use the functions that we describe next.

Converting IPv4 and IPv6 addresses between binary and human-readable forms

The *inet_pton()* and *inet_ntop()* functions are like *inet_aton()* and *inet_ntoa()*, but differ in that they also handle IPv6 addresses. They convert binary IPv4 and IPv6 addresses to and from *presentation* format—that is, either dotted-decimal or hex-string notation.

Since humans deal better with names than with numbers, we normally use these functions only occasionally in programs. One use of *inet_ntop()* is to produce a printable representation of an IP address for logging purposes. Sometimes, it is preferable to use this function instead of converting ("resolving") an IP address to a hostname, for the following reasons:

- Resolving an IP address to a hostname involves a possibly time-consuming request to a DNS server.

- In some circumstances, there may not be a DNS (PTR) record that maps the IP address to a corresponding hostname.

We describe these functions (in Section 59.6) before *getaddrinfo()* and *getnameinfo()*, which perform conversions between binary representations and the corresponding symbolic names, principally because they present a much simpler API. This allows us to quickly show some working examples of the use of Internet domain sockets.

Converting host and service names to and from binary form (obsolete)

The *gethostbyname()* function returns the binary IP address(es) corresponding to a hostname and the *getservbyname()* function returns the port number corresponding to a service name. The reverse conversions are performed by *gethostbyaddr()* and *getservbyport()*. We describe these functions because they are widely used in existing code. However, they are now obsolete. (SUSv3 marks these functions obsolete, and SUSv4 removes their specifications.) New code should use the *getaddrinfo()* and *getnameinfo()* functions (described next) for such conversions.

Converting host and service names to and from binary form (modern)

The *getaddrinfo()* function is the modern successor to both *gethostbyname()* and *getservbyname()*. Given a hostname and a service name, *getaddrinfo()* returns a set of structures containing the corresponding binary IP address(es) and port number. Unlike *gethostbyname()*, *getaddrinfo()* transparently handles both IPv4 and IPv6 addresses. Thus, we can use it to write programs that don't contain dependencies on the IP version being employed. All new code should use *getaddrinfo()* for converting hostnames and service names to binary representation.

The *getnameinfo()* function performs the reverse translation, converting an IP address and port number into the corresponding hostname and service name.

We can also use *getaddrinfo()* and *getnameinfo()* to convert binary IP addresses to and from presentation format.

The discussion of *getaddrinfo()* and *getnameinfo()*, in Section 59.10, requires an accompanying description of DNS (Section 59.8) and the /etc/services file (Section 59.9). DNS allows cooperating servers to maintain a distributed database that maps binary IP addresses to hostnames and vice versa. The existence of a system such as DNS is essential to the operation of the Internet, since centralized management of the enormous set of Internet hostnames would be impossible. The /etc/services file maps port numbers to symbolic service names.

59.6 The *inet_pton()* and *inet_ntop()* Functions

The *inet_pton()* and *inet_ntop()* functions allow conversion of both IPv4 and IPv6 addresses between binary form and dotted-decimal or hex-string notation.

```
#include <arpa/inet.h>

int inet_pton(int domain, const char *src_str, void *addrptr);
```

Returns 1 on successful conversion, 0 if *src_str* is not in presentation format, or −1 on error

```
const char *inet_ntop(int domain, const void *addrptr, char *dst_str, size_t len);
```

Returns pointer to *dst_str* on success, or NULL on error

The *p* in the names of these functions stands for "presentation," and the *n* stands for "network." The presentation form is a human-readable string, such as the following:

- 204.152.189.116 (IPv4 dotted-decimal address);
- ::1 (an IPv6 colon-separated hexadecimal address); or
- ::FFFF:204.152.189.116 (an IPv4-mapped IPv6 address).

The *inet_pton()* function converts the presentation string contained in *src_str* into a binary IP address in network byte order. The *domain* argument should be specified as either AF_INET or AF_INET6. The converted address is placed in the structure pointed to by *addrptr*, which should point to either an *in_addr* or an *in6_addr* structure, according to the value specified in *domain*.

The *inet_ntop()* function performs the reverse conversion. Again, *domain* should be specified as either AF_INET or AF_INET6, and *addrptr* should point to an *in_addr* or *in6_addr* structure that we wish to convert. The resulting null-terminated string is placed in the buffer pointed to by *dst_str*. The *len* argument must specify the size of this buffer. On success, *inet_ntop()* returns *dst_str*. If *len* is too small, then *inet_ntop()* returns NULL, with *errno* set to ENOSPC.

To correctly size the buffer pointed to by *dst_str*, we can employ two constants defined in <netinet/in.h>. These constants indicate the maximum lengths (including the terminating null byte) of the presentation strings for IPv4 and IPv6 addresses:

```
#define INET_ADDRSTRLEN  16     /* Maximum IPv4 dotted-decimal string */
#define INET6_ADDRSTRLEN 46     /* Maximum IPv6 hexadecimal string */
```

We provide examples of the use of *inet_pton()* and *inet_ntop()* in the next section.

59.7 Client-Server Example (Datagram Sockets)

In this section, we take the case-conversion server and client programs shown in Section 57.3 and modify them to use datagram sockets in the AF_INET6 domain. We present these programs with a minimum of commentary, since their structure is similar to the earlier programs. The main differences in the new programs lie in the declaration and initialization of the IPv6 socket address structure, which we described in Section 59.4.

The client and server both employ the header file shown in Listing 59-2. This header file defines the server's port number and the maximum size of messages that the client and server can exchange.

Listing 59-2: Header file used by i6d_ucase_sv.c and i6d_ucase_cl.c

———————————————————————————————— sockets/i6d_ucase.h

```
#include <netinet/in.h>
#include <arpa/inet.h>
#include <sys/socket.h>
#include <ctype.h>
#include "tlpi_hdr.h"

#define BUF_SIZE 10              /* Maximum size of messages exchanged
                                   between client and server */

#define PORT_NUM 50002          /* Server port number */
```
———————————————————————————————— sockets/i6d_ucase.h

Listing 59-3 shows the server program. The server uses the *inet_ntop()* function to convert the host address of the client (obtained via the *recvfrom()* call) to printable form.

The client program shown in Listing 59-4 contains two notable modifications from the earlier UNIX domain version (Listing 57-7, on page 1173). The first difference is that the client interprets its initial command-line argument as the IPv6 address of the server. (The remaining command-line arguments are passed as separate datagrams to the server.) The client converts the server address to binary form using *inet_pton()*. The other difference is that the client doesn't bind its socket to an address. As noted in Section 58.6.1, if an Internet domain socket is not bound to an address, the kernel binds the socket to an ephemeral port on the host system. We can observe this in the following shell session log, where we run the server and the client on the same host:

```
$ ./i6d_ucase_sv &
[1] 31047
$ ./i6d_ucase_cl ::1 ciao          Send to server on local host
Server received 4 bytes from (::1, 32770)
Response 1: CIAO
```

From the above output, we see that the server's *recvfrom()* call was able to obtain the address of the client's socket, including the ephemeral port number, despite the fact that the client did not do a *bind()*.

Listing 59-3: IPv6 case-conversion server using datagram sockets

—— **sockets/i6d_ucase_sv.c**

```c
#include "i6d_ucase.h"

int
main(int argc, char *argv[])
{
    struct sockaddr_in6 svaddr, claddr;
    int sfd, j;
    ssize_t numBytes;
    socklen_t len;
    char buf[BUF_SIZE];
    char claddrStr[INET6_ADDRSTRLEN];

    sfd = socket(AF_INET6, SOCK_DGRAM, 0);
    if (sfd == -1)
        errExit("socket");

    memset(&svaddr, 0, sizeof(struct sockaddr_in6));
    svaddr.sin6_family = AF_INET6;
    svaddr.sin6_addr = in6addr_any;                 /* Wildcard address */
    svaddr.sin6_port = htons(PORT_NUM);

    if (bind(sfd, (struct sockaddr *) &svaddr,
                sizeof(struct sockaddr_in6)) == -1)
        errExit("bind");

    /* Receive messages, convert to uppercase, and return to client */

    for (;;) {
        len = sizeof(struct sockaddr_in6);
        numBytes = recvfrom(sfd, buf, BUF_SIZE, 0,
                            (struct sockaddr *) &claddr, &len);
        if (numBytes == -1)
            errExit("recvfrom");

        if (inet_ntop(AF_INET6, &claddr.sin6_addr, claddrStr,
                    INET6_ADDRSTRLEN) == NULL)
            printf("Couldn't convert client address to string\n");
        else
            printf("Server received %ld bytes from (%s, %u)\n",
                    (long) numBytes, claddrStr, ntohs(claddr.sin6_port));

        for (j = 0; j < numBytes; j++)
            buf[j] = toupper((unsigned char) buf[j]);

        if (sendto(sfd, buf, numBytes, 0, (struct sockaddr *) &claddr, len) !=
                numBytes)
            fatal("sendto");
    }
}
```

—— **sockets/i6d_ucase_sv.c**

Listing 59-4: IPv6 case-conversion client using datagram sockets

—— **sockets/i6d_ucase_cl.c**

```c
#include "i6d_ucase.h"

int
main(int argc, char *argv[])
{
    struct sockaddr_in6 svaddr;
    int sfd, j;
    size_t msgLen;
    ssize_t numBytes;
    char resp[BUF_SIZE];

    if (argc < 3 || strcmp(argv[1], "--help") == 0)
        usageErr("%s host-address msg...\n", argv[0]);

    sfd = socket(AF_INET6, SOCK_DGRAM, 0);        /* Create client socket */
    if (sfd == -1)
        errExit("socket");

    memset(&svaddr, 0, sizeof(struct sockaddr_in6));
    svaddr.sin6_family = AF_INET6;
    svaddr.sin6_port = htons(PORT_NUM);
    if (inet_pton(AF_INET6, argv[1], &svaddr.sin6_addr) <= 0)
        fatal("inet_pton failed for address '%s'", argv[1]);

    /* Send messages to server; echo responses on stdout */

    for (j = 2; j < argc; j++) {
        msgLen = strlen(argv[j]);
        if (sendto(sfd, argv[j], msgLen, 0, (struct sockaddr *) &svaddr,
                    sizeof(struct sockaddr_in6)) != msgLen)
            fatal("sendto");

        numBytes = recvfrom(sfd, resp, BUF_SIZE, 0, NULL, NULL);
        if (numBytes == -1)
            errExit("recvfrom");

        printf("Response %d: %.*s\n", j - 1, (int) numBytes, resp);
    }

    exit(EXIT_SUCCESS);
}
```

—— **sockets/i6d_ucase_cl.c**

59.8 Domain Name System (DNS)

In Section 59.10, we describe *getaddrinfo()*, which obtains the IP address(es) corresponding to a hostname, and *getnameinfo()*, which performs the converse task. However, before looking at these functions, we explain how DNS is used to maintain the mappings between hostnames and IP addresses.

Before the advent of DNS, mappings between hostnames and IP addresses were defined in a manually maintained local file, /etc/hosts, containing records of the following form:

```
# IP-address    canonical hostname    [aliases]
127.0.0.1       localhost
```

The *gethostbyname()* function (the predecessor to *getaddrinfo()*) obtained an IP address by searching this file, looking for a match on either the canonical hostname (i.e., the official or primary name of the host) or one of the (optional, space-delimited) aliases.

However, the /etc/hosts scheme scales poorly, and then becomes impossible, as the number of hosts in the network increases (e.g., the Internet, with millions of hosts). DNS was devised to address this problem. The key ideas of DNS are the following:

- Hostnames are organized into a hierarchical namespace (Figure 59-2). Each *node* in the DNS hierarchy has a *label* (name), which may be up to 63 characters. At the root of the hierarchy is an unnamed node, the "anonymous root."

- A node's *domain name* consists of all of the names from that node up to the root concatenated together, with each name separated by a period (.). For example, google.com is the domain name for the node google.

- A *fully qualified domain name* (FQDN), such as www.kernel.org., identifies a host within the hierarchy. A fully qualified domain name is distinguished by being terminated by a period, although in many contexts the period may be omitted.

- No single organization or system manages the entire hierarchy. Instead, there is a hierarchy of DNS servers, each of which manages a branch (a *zone*) of the tree. Normally, each zone has a *primary master name server*, and one or more *slave name servers* (sometimes also known as *secondary master name servers*), which provide backup in the event that the primary master name server crashes. Zones may themselves be divided into separately managed smaller zones. When a host is added within a zone, or the mapping of a hostname to an IP address is changed, the administrator responsible for the corresponding local name server updates the name database on that server. (No manual changes are required on any other name-server databases in the hierarchy.)

  > The DNS server implementation employed on Linux is the widely used Berkeley Internet Name Domain (BIND) implementation, *named(8)*, maintained by the *Internet Systems Consortium (http://www.isc.org/)*. The operation of this daemon is controlled by the file /etc/named.conf (see the *named.conf(5)* manual page). The key reference on DNS and BIND is [Albitz & Liu, 2006]. Information about DNS can also be found in Chapter 14 of [Stevens, 1994], Chapter 11 of [Stevens et al., 2004], and Chapter 24 of [Comer, 2000].

- When a program calls *getaddrinfo()* to *resolve* (i.e., obtain the IP address for) a domain name, *getaddrinfo()* employs a suite of library functions (the *resolver library*) that communicate with the local DNS server. If this server can't supply the required information, then it communicates with other DNS servers within the hierarchy in order to obtain the information. Occasionally, this resolution process may take a noticeable amount of time, and DNS servers employ caching techniques to avoid unnecessary communication for frequently queried domain names.

Using the above approach allows DNS to cope with large namespaces, and does not require centralized management of names.

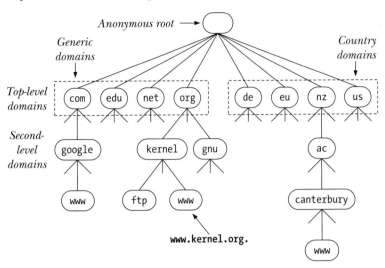

Figure 59-2: A subset of the DNS hierarchy

Recursive and iterative resolution requests

DNS resolution requests fall into two categories: *recursive* and *iterative*. In a recursive request, the requester asks the server to handle the entire task of resolution, including the task of communicating with any other DNS servers, if necessary. When an application on the local host calls *getaddrinfo()*, that function makes a recursive request to the local DNS server. If the local DNS server does not itself have the information to perform the resolution, it resolves the domain name iteratively.

We explain iterative resolution via an example. Suppose that the local DNS server is asked to resolve the name www.otago.ac.nz. To do this, it first communicates with one of a small set of *root name servers* that every DNS server is required to know about. (We can obtain a list of these servers using the command *dig . NS* or from the web page at *http://www.root-servers.org/*.) Given the name www.otago.ac.nz, the root name server refers the local DNS server to one of the nz DNS servers. The local DNS server then queries the nz server with the name www.otago.ac.nz, and receives a response referring it to the ac.nz server. The local DNS server then queries the ac.nz server with the name www.otago.ac.nz, and is referred to the otago.ac.nz server. Finally, the local DNS server queries the otago.ac.nz server with the name www.otago.ac.nz, and obtains the required IP address.

If we supply an incomplete domain name to *gethostbyname()*, the resolver will attempt to complete it before resolving it. The rules on how a domain name is completed are defined in /etc/resolv.conf (see the *resolv.conf(5)* manual page). By default, the resolver will at least try completion using the domain name of the local host. For example, if we are logged in on the machine oghma.otago.ac.nz and we type the command *ssh octavo*, the resulting DNS query will be for the name octavo.otago.ac.nz.

Top-level domains

The nodes immediately below the anonymous root form the so-called *top-level domains* (TLDs). (Below these are the *second-level domains*, and so on.) TLDs fall into two categories: *generic* and *country*.

Historically, there were seven *generic* TLDs, most of which can be considered international. We have shown four of the original generic TLDs in Figure 59-2. The other three are int, mil, and gov; the latter two are reserved for the United States. In more recent times, a number of new generic TLDs have been added (e.g., info, name, and museum).

Each nation has a corresponding *country* (or *geographical*) TLD (standardized as ISO 3166-1), with a 2-character name. In Figure 59-2, we have shown a few of these: de (Germany, *Deutschland*), eu (a supra-national geographical TLD for the European Union), nz (New Zealand), and us (United States of America). Several countries divide their TLD into a set of second-level domains in a manner similar to the generic domains. For example, New Zealand has ac.nz (academic institutions), co.nz (commercial), and govt.nz (government).

59.9 The /etc/services File

As noted in Section 58.6.1, well-known port numbers are centrally registered by IANA. Each of these ports has a corresponding *service name*. Because service numbers are centrally managed and are less volatile than IP addresses, an equivalent of the DNS server is usually not necessary. Instead, the port numbers and service names are recorded in the file /etc/services. The *getaddrinfo()* and *getnameinfo()* functions use the information in this file to convert service names to port numbers and vice versa.

The /etc/services file consists of lines containing three columns, as shown in the following examples:

```
# Service name  port/protocol  [aliases]
echo            7/tcp          Echo    # echo service
echo            7/udp          Echo
ssh             22/tcp                 # Secure Shell
ssh             22/udp
telnet          23/tcp                 # Telnet
telnet          23/udp
smtp            25/tcp                 # Simple Mail Transfer Protocol
smtp            25/udp
domain          53/tcp                 # Domain Name Server
domain          53/udp
http            80/tcp                 # Hypertext Transfer Protocol
http            80/udp
ntp             123/tcp                # Network Time Protocol
ntp             123/udp
login           513/tcp                # rlogin(1)
who             513/udp                # rwho(1)
shell           514/tcp                # rsh(1)
syslog          514/udp                # syslog
```

The *protocol* is typically either tcp or udp. The optional (space-delimited) *aliases* specify alternative names for the service. In addition to the above, lines may include comments starting with the # character.

As noted previously, a given port number refers to distinct entities for UDP and TCP, but IANA policy assigns both port numbers to a service, even if that service uses only one protocol. For example, *telnet*, *ssh*, HTTP, and SMTP all use TCP, but the corresponding UDP port is also assigned to these services. Conversely, NTP uses only UDP, but the TCP port 123 is also assigned to this service. In some cases, a service uses both UDP and TCP; DNS and *echo* are examples of such services. Finally, there are a very few cases where the UDP and TCP ports with the same number are assigned to different services; for example, *rsh* uses TCP port 514, while the *syslog* daemon (Section 37.5) uses UDP port 514. This is because these port numbers were assigned before the adoption of the present IANA policy.

> The /etc/services file is merely a record of name-to-number mappings. It is not a reservation mechanism: the appearance of a port number in /etc/services doesn't guarantee that it will actually be available for binding by a particular service.

59.10 Protocol-Independent Host and Service Conversion

The *getaddrinfo()* function converts host and service names to IP addresses and port numbers. It was defined in POSIX.1g as the (reentrant) successor to the obsolete *gethostbyname()* and *getservbyname()* functions. (Replacing the use of *gethostbyname()* with *getaddrinfo()* allows us to eliminate IPv4-versus-IPv6 dependencies from our programs.)

The *getnameinfo()* function is the converse of *getaddrinfo()*. It translates a socket address structure (either IPv4 or IPv6) to strings containing the corresponding host and service name. This function is the (reentrant) equivalent of the obsolete *gethostbyaddr()* and *getservbyport()* functions.

> Chapter 11 of [Stevens et al., 2004] describes *getaddrinfo()* and *getnameinfo()* in detail, and provides implementations of these functions. These functions are also described in RFC 3493.

59.10.1 The *getaddrinfo()* Function

Given a host name and a service name, *getaddrinfo()* returns a list of socket address structures, each of which contains an IP address and port number.

```
#include <sys/socket.h>
#include <netdb.h>

int getaddrinfo(const char *host, const char *service,
                const struct addrinfo *hints, struct addrinfo **result);
```
                                        Returns 0 on success, or nonzero on error

As input, *getaddrinfo()* takes the arguments *host*, *service*, and *hints*. The *host* argument contains either a hostname or a numeric address string, expressed in IPv4 dotted-decimal notation or IPv6 hex-string notation. (To be precise, *getaddrinfo()* accepts IPv4 numeric strings in the more general numbers-and-dots notation described in Section 59.13.1.) The *service* argument contains either a service name or a decimal port number. The *hints* argument points to an *addrinfo* structure that specifies further criteria for selecting the socket address structures returned via *result*. We describe the *hints* argument in more detail below.

As output, *getaddrinfo()* dynamically allocates a linked list of *addrinfo* structures and sets *result* pointing to the beginning of this list. Each of these *addrinfo* structures includes a pointer to a socket address structure corresponding to *host* and *service* (Figure 59-3). The *addrinfo* structure has the following form:

```
struct addrinfo {
    int       ai_flags;          /* Input flags (AI_* constants) */
    int       ai_family;         /* Address family */
    int       ai_socktype;       /* Type: SOCK_STREAM, SOCK_DGRAM */
    int       ai_protocol;       /* Socket protocol */
    socklen_t ai_addrlen;        /* Size of structure pointed to by ai_addr */
    char      *ai_canonname;     /* Canonical name of host */
    struct sockaddr *ai_addr;    /* Pointer to socket address structure */
    struct addrinfo *ai_next;    /* Next structure in linked list */
};
```

The *result* argument returns a list of structures, rather than a single structure, because there may be multiple combinations of host and service corresponding to the criteria specified in *host*, *service*, and *hints*. For example, multiple address structures could be returned for a host with more than one network interface. Furthermore, if *hints.ai_socktype* was specified as 0, then two structures could be returned—one for a SOCK_DGRAM socket, the other for a SOCK_STREAM socket—if the given *service* was available for both UDP and TCP.

The fields of each *addrinfo* structure returned via *result* describe properties of the associated socket address structure. The *ai_family* field is set to either AF_INET or AF_INET6, informing us of the type of the socket address structure. The *ai_socktype* field is set to either SOCK_STREAM or SOCK_DGRAM, indicating whether this address structure is for a TCP or a UDP service. The *ai_protocol* field returns a protocol value appropriate for the address family and socket type. (The three fields *ai_family*, *ai_socktype*, and *ai_protocol* supply the values required for the arguments used when calling *socket()* to create a socket for this address.) The *ai_addrlen* field gives the size (in bytes) of the socket address structure pointed to by *ai_addr*. The *ai_addr* field points to the socket address structure (a *sockaddr_in* structure for IPv4 or a *sockaddr_in6* structure for IPv6). The *ai_flags* field is unused (it is used for the *hints* argument). The *ai_canonname* field is used only in the first *addrinfo* structure, and only if the AI_CANONNAME flag is employed in *hints.ai_flags*, as described below.

As with *gethostbyname()*, *getaddrinfo()* may need to send a request to a DNS server, and this request may take some time to complete. The same applies for *getnameinfo()*, which we describe in Section 59.10.4.

We demonstrate the use of *getaddrinfo()* in Section 59.11.

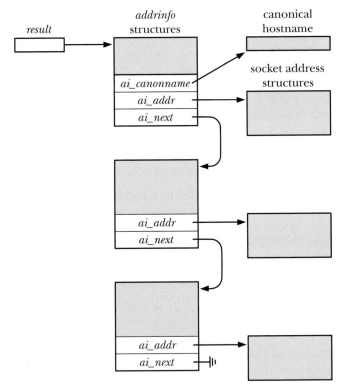

Figure 59-3: Structures allocated and returned by *getaddrinfo()*

The *hints* argument

The *hints* argument specifies further criteria for selecting the socket address structures returned by *getaddrinfo()*. When used as the *hints* argument, only the *ai_flags*, *ai_family*, *ai_socktype*, and *ai_protocol* fields of the *addrinfo* structure can be set. The other fields are unused, and should be initialized to 0 or NULL, as appropriate.

The *hints.ai_family* field selects the domain for the returned socket address structures. It may be specified as AF_INET or AF_INET6 (or some other AF_* constant, if the implementation supports it). If we are interested in getting back all types of socket address structures, we can specify the value AF_UNSPEC for this field.

The *hints.ai_socktype* field specifies the type of socket for which the returned address structure is to be used. If we specify this field as SOCK_DGRAM, then a lookup is performed for the UDP service, and a corresponding socket address structure is returned via *result*. If we specify SOCK_STREAM, a lookup for the TCP service is performed. If *hints.ai_socktype* is specified as 0, any socket type is acceptable.

The *hints.ai_protocol* field selects the socket protocol for the returned address structures. For our purposes, this field is always specified as 0, meaning that the caller will accept any protocol.

The *hints.ai_flags* field is a bit mask that modifies the behavior of *getaddrinfo()*. This field is formed by ORing together zero or more of the following values:

AI_ADDRCONFIG

> Return IPv4 addresses only if there is at least one IPv4 address configured for the local system (other than the IPv4 loopback address), and return IPv6 addresses only if there is at least one IPv6 address configured for the local system (other than the IPv6 loopback address).

AI_ALL

> See the description of AI_V4MAPPED below.

AI_CANONNAME

> If *host* is not NULL, return a pointer to a null-terminated string containing the canonical name of the host. This pointer is returned in a buffer pointed to by the *ai_canonname* field of the first of the *addrinfo* structures returned via *result*.

AI_NUMERICHOST

> Force interpretation of *host* as a numeric address string. This is used to prevent name resolution in cases where it is unnecessary, since name resolution can be time-consuming.

AI_NUMERICSERV

> Interpret *service* as a numeric port number. This flag prevents the invocation of any name-resolution service, which is not required if *service* is a numeric string.

AI_PASSIVE

> Return socket address structures suitable for a passive open (i.e., a listening socket). In this case, *host* should be NULL, and the IP address component of the socket address structure(s) returned by *result* will contain a wildcard IP address (i.e., INADDR_ANY or IN6ADDR_ANY_INIT). If this flag is not set, then the address structure(s) returned via *result* will be suitable for use with *connect()* and *sendto()*; if *host* is NULL, then the IP address in the returned socket address structures will be set to the loopback IP address (either INADDR_LOOPBACK or IN6ADDR_LOOPBACK_INIT, according to the domain).

AI_V4MAPPED

> If AF_INET6 was specified in the *ai_family* field of *hints*, then IPv4-mapped IPv6 address structures should be returned in *result* if no matching IPv6 address could be found. If AI_ALL is specified in conjunction with AI_V4MAPPED, then both IPv6 and IPv4 address structures are returned in *result*, with IPv4 addresses being returned as IPv4-mapped IPv6 address structures.

As noted above for AI_PASSIVE, *host* can be specified as NULL. It is also possible to specify *service* as NULL, in which case the port number in the returned address structures is set to 0 (i.e., we are just interested in resolving hostnames to addresses). It is not permitted, however, to specify both *host* and *service* as NULL.

If we don't need to specify any of the above selection criteria in hints, then *hints* may be specified as NULL, in which case *ai_socktype* and *ai_protocol* are assumed as 0, *ai_flags* is assumed as (AI_V4MAPPED | AI_ADDRCONFIG), and *ai_family* is assumed as AF_UNSPEC. (The *glibc* implementation deliberately deviates from SUSv3, which states that if *hints* is NULL, *ai_flags* is assumed as 0.)

59.10.2 Freeing *addrinfo* Lists: *freeaddrinfo()*

The *getaddrinfo()* function dynamically allocates memory for all of the structures referred to by *result* (Figure 59-3). Consequently, the caller must deallocate these structures when they are no longer needed. The *freeaddrinfo()* function is provided to conveniently perform this deallocation in a single step.

```
#include <sys/socket.h>
#include <netdb.h>

void freeaddrinfo(struct addrinfo *result);
```

If we want to preserve a copy of one of the *addrinfo* structures or its associated socket address structure, then we must duplicate the structure(s) before calling *freeaddrinfo()*.

59.10.3 Diagnosing Errors: *gai_strerror()*

On error, *getaddrinfo()* returns one of the nonzero error codes shown in Table 59-1.

Table 59-1: Error returns for *getaddrinfo()* and *getnameinfo()*

Error constant	Description
EAI_ADDRFAMILY	No addresses for *host* exist in *hints.ai_family* (not in SUSv3, but defined on most implementations; *getaddrinfo()* only)
EAI_AGAIN	Temporary failure in name resolution (try again later)
EAI_BADFLAGS	An invalid flag was specified in *hints.ai_flags*
EAI_FAIL	Unrecoverable failure while accessing name server
EAI_FAMILY	Address family specified in *hints.ai_family* is not supported
EAI_MEMORY	Memory allocation failure
EAI_NODATA	No address associated with *host* (not in SUSv3, but defined on most implementations; *getaddrinfo()* only)
EAI_NONAME	Unknown *host* or *service*, or both *host* and *service* were NULL, or AI_NUMERICSERV specified and *service* didn't point to numeric string
EAI_OVERFLOW	Argument buffer overflow
EAI_SERVICE	Specified *service* not supported for *hints.ai_socktype* (*getaddrinfo()* only)
EAI_SOCKTYPE	Specified *hints.ai_socktype* is not supported (*getaddrinfo()* only)
EAI_SYSTEM	System error returned in *errno*

Given one of the error codes in Table 59-1, the *gai_strerror()* function returns a string describing the error. (This string is typically briefer than the description shown in Table 59-1.)

```
#include <netdb.h>

const char *gai_strerror(int errcode);
```
                              Returns pointer to string containing error message

We can use the string returned by *gai_strerror()* as part of an error message displayed by an application.

59.10.4 The *getnameinfo()* Function

The *getnameinfo()* function is the converse of *getaddrinfo()*. Given a socket address structure (either IPv4 or IPv6), it returns strings containing the corresponding host and service name, or numeric equivalents if the names can't be resolved.

```
#include <sys/socket.h>
#include <netdb.h>

int getnameinfo(const struct sockaddr *addr, socklen_t addrlen, char *host,
                socklen_t hostlen, char *service, socklen_t servlen, int flags);
```
                              Returns 0 on success, or nonzero on error

The *addr* argument is a pointer to the socket address structure that is to be converted. The length of that structure is given in *addrlen*. Typically, the values for *addr* and *addrlen* are obtained from a call to *accept()*, *recvfrom()*, *getsockname()*, or *getpeername()*.

The resulting host and service names are returned as null-terminated strings in the buffers pointed to by *host* and *service*. These buffers must be allocated by the caller, and their sizes must be passed in *hostlen* and *servlen*. The <netdb.h> header file defines two constants to assist in sizing these buffers. NI_MAXHOST indicates the maximum size, in bytes, for a returned hostname string. It is defined as 1025. NI_MAXSERV indicates the maximum size, in bytes, for a returned service name string. It is defined as 32. These two constants are not specified in SUSv3, but they are defined on all UNIX implementations that provide *getnameinfo()*. (Since *glibc* 2.8, we must define one of the feature test macros _BSD_SOURCE, _SVID_SOURCE, or _GNU_SOURCE to obtain the definitions of NI_MAXHOST and NI_MAXSERV.)

If we are not interested in obtaining the hostname, we can specify *host* as NULL and *hostlen* as 0. Similarly, if we don't need the service name, we can specify *service* as NULL and *servlen* as 0. However, at least one of *host* and *service* must be non-NULL (and the corresponding length argument must be nonzero).

The final argument, *flags*, is a bit mask that controls the behavior of *getnameinfo()*. The following constants may be ORed together to form this bit mask:

NI_DGRAM

      By default, *getnameinfo()* returns the name corresponding to a *stream* socket (i.e., TCP) service. Normally, this doesn't matter, because, as noted in Section 59.9, the service names are usually the same for corresponding

TCP and UDP ports. However, in the few instances where the names differ, the NI_DGRAM flag forces the name of the datagram socket (i.e., UDP) service to be returned.

NI_NAMEREQD

By default, if the hostname can't be resolved, a numeric address string is returned in *host*. If the NI_NAMEREQD flag is specified, an error (EAI_NONAME) is returned instead.

NI_NOFQDN

By default, the fully qualified domain name for the host is returned. Specifying the NI_NOFQDN flag causes just the first (i.e., the hostname) part of the name to be returned, if this is a host on the local network.

NI_NUMERICHOST

Force a numeric address string to be returned in *host*. This is useful if we want to avoid a possibly time-consuming call to the DNS server.

NI_NUMERICSERV

Force a decimal port number string to be returned in *service*. This is useful in cases where we know that the port number doesn't correspond to a service name—for example, if it is an ephemeral port number assigned to the socket by the kernel—and we want to avoid the inefficiency of unnecessarily searching /etc/services.

On success, *getnameinfo()* returns 0. On error, it returns one of the nonzero error codes shown in Table 59-1.

59.11 Client-Server Example (Stream Sockets)

We now have enough information to look at a simple client-server application using TCP sockets. The task performed by this application is the same as that performed by the FIFO client-server application presented in Section 44.8: allocating unique sequence numbers (or ranges of sequence numbers) to clients.

In order to handle the possibility that integers may be represented in different formats on the server and client hosts, we encode all transmitted integers as strings terminated by a newline, and use our *readLine()* function (Listing 59-1) to read these strings.

Common header file

Both the server and the client include the header file shown in Listing 59-5. This file includes various other header files, and defines the TCP port number to be used by the application.

Server program

The server program shown in Listing 59-6 performs the following steps:

- Initialize the server's sequence number either to 0 or to the value supplied in the optional command-line argument ①.

- Ignore the SIGPIPE signal ②. This prevents the server from receiving the SIGPIPE signal if it tries to write to a socket whose peer has been closed; instead, the *write()* fails with the error EPIPE.

- Call *getaddrinfo()* ④ to obtain a set of socket address structures for a TCP socket that uses the port number PORT_NUM. (Instead of using a hard-coded port number, we would more typically use a service name.) We specify the AI_PASSIVE flag ③ so that the resulting socket will be bound to the wildcard address (Section 58.5). As a result, if the server is run on a multihomed host, it can accept connection requests sent to any of the host's network addresses.

- Enter a loop that iterates through the socket address structures returned by the previous step ⑤. The loop terminates when the program finds an address structure that can be used to successfully create and bind a socket ⑦.

- Set the SO_REUSEADDR option for the socket created in the previous step ⑥. We defer discussion of this option until Section 61.10, where we note that a TCP server should usually set this option on its listening socket.

- Mark the socket as a listening socket ⑧.

- Commence an infinite for loop ⑨ that services clients iteratively (Chapter 60). Each client's request is serviced before the next client's request is accepted. For each client, the server performs the following steps:

  - Accept a new connection ⑩. The server passes non-NULL pointers for the second and third arguments to *accept()*, in order to obtain the address of the client. The server displays the client's address (IP address plus port number) on standard output ⑪.

  - Read the client's message ⑫, which consists of a newline-terminated string specifying how many sequence numbers the client wants. The server converts this string to an integer and stores it in the variable *reqLen* ⑬.

  - Send the current value of the sequence number (*seqNum*) back to the client, encoding it as a newline-terminated string ⑭. The client can assume that it has been allocated all of the sequence numbers in the range *seqNum* to *(seqNum + reqLen − 1)*.

  - Update the value of the server's sequence number by adding *reqLen* to *seqNum* ⑮.

Listing 59-5: Header file used by is_seqnum_sv.c and is_seqnum_cl.c

── sockets/is_seqnum.h
```
#include <netinet/in.h>
#include <sys/socket.h>
#include <signal.h>
#include "read_line.h"        /* Declaration of readLine() */
#include "tlpi_hdr.h"

#define PORT_NUM "50000"       /* Port number for server */

#define INT_LEN 30             /* Size of string able to hold largest
                                  integer (including terminating '\n') */
```
── sockets/is_seqnum.h

Listing 59-6: An iterative server that uses a stream socket to communicate with clients

```c
#define _BSD_SOURCE           /* To get definitions of NI_MAXHOST and
                                 NI_MAXSERV from <netdb.h> */

#include <netdb.h>
#include "is_seqnum.h"

#define BACKLOG 50

int
main(int argc, char *argv[])
{
    uint32_t seqNum;
    char reqLenStr[INT_LEN];           /* Length of requested sequence */
    char seqNumStr[INT_LEN];           /* Start of granted sequence */
    struct sockaddr_storage claddr;
    int lfd, cfd, optval, reqLen;
    socklen_t addrlen;
    struct addrinfo hints;
    struct addrinfo *result, *rp;
#define ADDRSTRLEN (NI_MAXHOST + NI_MAXSERV + 10)
    char addrStr[ADDRSTRLEN];
    char host[NI_MAXHOST];
    char service[NI_MAXSERV];

    if (argc > 1 && strcmp(argv[1], "--help") == 0)
        usageErr("%s [init-seq-num]\n", argv[0]);

①  seqNum = (argc > 1) ? getInt(argv[1], 0, "init-seq-num") : 0;

②  if (signal(SIGPIPE, SIG_IGN) == SIG_ERR)
        errExit("signal");

    /* Call getaddrinfo() to obtain a list of addresses that
       we can try binding to */

    memset(&hints, 0, sizeof(struct addrinfo));
    hints.ai_canonname = NULL;
    hints.ai_addr = NULL;
    hints.ai_next = NULL;
    hints.ai_socktype = SOCK_STREAM;
    hints.ai_family = AF_UNSPEC;       /* Allows IPv4 or IPv6 */
③  hints.ai_flags = AI_PASSIVE | AI_NUMERICSERV;
                        /* Wildcard IP address; service name is numeric */
④  if (getaddrinfo(NULL, PORT_NUM, &hints, &result) != 0)
        errExit("getaddrinfo");

    /* Walk through returned list until we find an address structure
       that can be used to successfully create and bind a socket */

    optval = 1;
⑤  for (rp = result; rp != NULL; rp = rp->ai_next) {
        lfd = socket(rp->ai_family, rp->ai_socktype, rp->ai_protocol);
        if (lfd == -1)
            continue;                  /* On error, try next address */
```

Sockets: Internet Domains   **1221**

```
⑥          if (setsockopt(lfd, SOL_SOCKET, SO_REUSEADDR, &optval, sizeof(optval))
                    == -1)
                errExit("setsockopt");

⑦          if (bind(lfd, rp->ai_addr, rp->ai_addrlen) == 0)
                break;                          /* Success */

            /* bind() failed: close this socket and try next address */

            close(lfd);
        }

        if (rp == NULL)
            fatal("Could not bind socket to any address");

⑧      if (listen(lfd, BACKLOG) == -1)
            errExit("listen");

        freeaddrinfo(result);

⑨      for (;;) {                      /* Handle clients iteratively */

            /* Accept a client connection, obtaining client's address */

            addrlen = sizeof(struct sockaddr_storage);
⑩          cfd = accept(lfd, (struct sockaddr *) &claddr, &addrlen);
            if (cfd == -1) {
                errMsg("accept");
                continue;
            }

⑪          if (getnameinfo((struct sockaddr *) &claddr, addrlen,
                        host, NI_MAXHOST, service, NI_MAXSERV, 0) == 0)
                snprintf(addrStr, ADDRSTRLEN, "(%s, %s)", host, service);
            else
                snprintf(addrStr, ADDRSTRLEN, "(?UNKNOWN?)");
            printf("Connection from %s\n", addrStr);

            /* Read client request, send sequence number back */

⑫          if (readLine(cfd, reqLenStr, INT_LEN) <= 0) {
                close(cfd);
                continue;                       /* Failed read; skip request */
            }

⑬          reqLen = atoi(reqLenStr);
            if (reqLen <= 0) {                  /* Watch for misbehaving clients */
                close(cfd);
                continue;                       /* Bad request; skip it */
            }

⑭          snprintf(seqNumStr, INT_LEN, "%d\n", seqNum);
            if (write(cfd, seqNumStr, strlen(seqNumStr)) != strlen(seqNumStr))
                fprintf(stderr, "Error on write");
```

⑮   seqNum += reqLen;   /* Update sequence number */

         if (close(cfd) == -1)   /* Close connection */
             errMsg("close");
     }
}
                                                        ────── sockets/is_seqnum_sv.c

Client program

The client program is shown in Listing 59-7. This program accepts two arguments. The
first argument, which is the name of the host on which the server is running, is
mandatory. The optional second argument is the length of the sequence desired by
the client. The default length is 1. The client performs the following steps:

- Call *getaddrinfo()* to obtain a set of socket address structures suitable for connecting to a TCP server bound to the specified host ①. For the port number,
  the client specifies PORT_NUM.

- Enter a loop ② that iterates through the socket address structures returned by the
  previous step, until the client finds one that can be used to successfully create ③
  and connect ④ a socket to the server. Since the client has not bound its socket,
  the *connect()* call causes the kernel to assign an ephemeral port to the socket.

- Send an integer specifying the length of the client's desired sequence ⑤. This
  integer is sent as a newline-terminated string.

- Read the sequence number sent back by the server (which is likewise a newline-
  terminated string) ⑥ and print it on standard output ⑦.

When we run the server and the client on the same host, we see the following:

```
$ ./is_seqnum_sv &
[1] 4075
$ ./is_seqnum_cl localhost            Client 1: requests 1 sequence number
Connection from (localhost, 33273)    Server displays client address + port
Sequence number: 0                    Client displays returned sequence number
$ ./is_seqnum_cl localhost 10         Client 2: requests 10 sequence numbers
Connection from (localhost, 33274)
Sequence number: 1
$ ./is_seqnum_cl localhost            Client 3: requests 1 sequence number
Connection from (localhost, 33275)
Sequence number: 11
```

Next, we demonstrate the use of *telnet* for debugging this application:

```
$ telnet localhost 50000              Our server uses this port number
                                      Empty line printed by telnet
Trying 127.0.0.1...
Connection from (localhost, 33276)
Connected to localhost.
Escape character is '^]'.
1                                     Enter length of requested sequence
12                                    telnet displays sequence number and
Connection closed by foreign host.    detects that server closed connection
```

In the shell session log, we see that the kernel cycles sequentially through the ephemeral port numbers. (Other implementations exhibit similar behavior.) On Linux, this behavior is the result of an optimization to minimize hash lookups in the kernel's table of local socket bindings. When the upper limit for these numbers is reached, the kernel recommences allocating an available number starting at the low end of the range (defined by the Linux-specific /proc/sys/net/ipv4/ip_local_port_range file).

Listing 59-7: A client that uses stream sockets

―――――――――――――――――――――――――――――――――――――― sockets/is_seqnum_cl.c
```
#include <netdb.h>
#include "is_seqnum.h"

int
main(int argc, char *argv[])
{
    char *reqLenStr;                       /* Requested length of sequence */
    char seqNumStr[INT_LEN];               /* Start of granted sequence */
    int cfd;
    ssize_t numRead;
    struct addrinfo hints;
    struct addrinfo *result, *rp;

    if (argc < 2 || strcmp(argv[1], "--help") == 0)
        usageErr("%s server-host [sequence-len]\n", argv[0]);

    /* Call getaddrinfo() to obtain a list of addresses that
       we can try connecting to */

    memset(&hints, 0, sizeof(struct addrinfo));
    hints.ai_canonname = NULL;
    hints.ai_addr = NULL;
    hints.ai_next = NULL;
    hints.ai_family = AF_UNSPEC;                    /* Allows IPv4 or IPv6 */
    hints.ai_socktype = SOCK_STREAM;
    hints.ai_flags = AI_NUMERICSERV;
```
①
```
    if (getaddrinfo(argv[1], PORT_NUM, &hints, &result) != 0)
        errExit("getaddrinfo");

    /* Walk through returned list until we find an address structure
       that can be used to successfully connect a socket */
```
②
③
```
    for (rp = result; rp != NULL; rp = rp->ai_next) {
        cfd = socket(rp->ai_family, rp->ai_socktype, rp->ai_protocol);
        if (cfd == -1)
            continue;                              /* On error, try next address */
```
④
```
        if (connect(cfd, rp->ai_addr, rp->ai_addrlen) != -1)
            break;                                 /* Success */
```

```
              /* Connect failed: close this socket and try next address */

              close(cfd);
          }

          if (rp == NULL)
              fatal("Could not connect socket to any address");

          freeaddrinfo(result);

          /* Send requested sequence length, with terminating newline */

⑤         reqLenStr = (argc > 2) ? argv[2] : "1";
          if (write(cfd, reqLenStr, strlen(reqLenStr)) != strlen(reqLenStr))
              fatal("Partial/failed write (reqLenStr)");
          if (write(cfd, "\n", 1) != 1)
              fatal("Partial/failed write (newline)");

          /* Read and display sequence number returned by server */

⑥         numRead = readLine(cfd, seqNumStr, INT_LEN);
          if (numRead == -1)
              errExit("readLine");
          if (numRead == 0)
              fatal("Unexpected EOF from server");

⑦         printf("Sequence number: %s", seqNumStr);        /* Includes '\n' */

          exit(EXIT_SUCCESS);                               /* Closes 'cfd' */
      }
```
── sockets/is_seqnum_cl.c

59.12 An Internet Domain Sockets Library

In this section, we use the functions presented in Section 59.10 to implement a
library of functions to perform tasks commonly required for Internet domain sockets.
(This library abstracts many of the steps shown in the example programs presented
in Section 59.11.) Since these functions employ the protocol-independent
getaddrinfo() and *getnameinfo()* functions, they can be used with both IPv4 and IPv6.
Listing 59-8 shows the header file that declares these functions.

Many of the functions in this library have similar arguments:

- The *host* argument is a string containing either a hostname or a numeric
  address (in IPv4 dotted-decimal, or IPv6 hex-string notation). Alternatively,
  host can be specified as a NULL pointer to indicate that the loopback IP address is
  to be used.

- The *service* argument is either a service name or a port number specified as a
  decimal string.

- The *type* argument is a socket type, specified as either SOCK_STREAM or SOCK_DGRAM.

Listing 59-8: Header file for inet_sockets.c

—— **sockets/inet_sockets.h**

```
#ifndef INET_SOCKETS_H
#define INET_SOCKETS_H          /* Prevent accidental double inclusion */

#include <sys/socket.h>
#include <netdb.h>

int inetConnect(const char *host, const char *service, int type);

int inetListen(const char *service, int backlog, socklen_t *addrlen);

int inetBind(const char *service, int type, socklen_t *addrlen);

char *inetAddressStr(const struct sockaddr *addr, socklen_t addrlen,
            char *addrStr, int addrStrLen);

#define IS_ADDR_STR_LEN 4096
                    /* Suggested length for string buffer that caller
                       should pass to inetAddressStr(). Must be greater
                       than (NI_MAXHOST + NI_MAXSERV + 4) */
#endif
```

—— **sockets/inet_sockets.h**

The *inetConnect()* function creates a socket with the given socket *type*, and connects it to the address specified by *host* and *service*. This function is designed for TCP or UDP clients that need to connect their socket to a server socket.

```
#include "inet_sockets.h"

int inetConnect(const char *host, const char *service, int type);
```
                            Returns a file descriptor on success, or −1 on error

The file descriptor for the new socket is returned as the function result.

The *inetListen()* function creates a listening stream (SOCK_STREAM) socket bound to the wildcard IP address on the TCP port specified by *service*. This function is designed for use by TCP servers.

```
#include "inet_sockets.h"

int inetListen(const char *service, int backlog, socklen_t *addrlen);
```
                            Returns a file descriptor on success, or −1 on error

The file descriptor for the new socket is returned as the function result.

The *backlog* argument specifies the permitted backlog of pending connections (as for *listen()*).

If *addrlen* is specified as a non-NULL pointer, then the location it points to is used to return the size of the socket address structure corresponding to the returned file descriptor. This value allows us to allocate a socket address buffer of the appropriate size to be passed to a later *accept()* call if we want to obtain the address of a connecting client.

The *inetBind()* function creates a socket of the given *type*, bound to the wildcard IP address on the port specified by *service* and *type*. (The socket *type* indicates whether this is a TCP or UDP service.) This function is designed (primarily) for UDP servers and clients to create a socket bound to a specific address.

```
#include "inet_sockets.h"

int inetBind(const char *service, int type, socklen_t *addrlen);
```
                          Returns a file descriptor on success, or −1 on error

The file descriptor for the new socket is returned as the function result.

As with *inetListen()*, *inetBind()* returns the length of the associated socket address structure for this socket in the location pointed to by *addrlen*. This is useful if we want to allocate a buffer to pass to *recvfrom()* in order to obtain the address of the socket sending a datagram. (Many of the steps required for *inetListen()* and *inetBind()* are the same, and these steps are implemented within the library by a single function, *inetPassiveSocket().*)

The *inetAddressStr()* function converts an Internet socket address to printable form.

```
#include "inet_sockets.h"

char *inetAddressStr(const struct sockaddr *addr, socklen_t addrlen,
                     char *addrStr, int addrStrLen);
```
          Returns pointer to *addrStr*, a string containing host and service name

Given a socket address structure in *addr*, whose length is specified in *addrlen*, *inetAddressStr()* returns a null-terminated string containing the corresponding hostname and port number in the following form:

```
(hostname, port-number)
```

The string is returned in the buffer pointed to by *addrStr*. The caller must specify the size of this buffer in *addrStrLen*. If the returned string would exceed (*addrStrLen* − 1) bytes, it is truncated. The constant IS_ADDR_STR_LEN defines a suggested size for the *addrStr* buffer that should be large enough to handle all possible return strings. As its function result, *inetAddressStr()* returns *addrStr*.

The implementation of the functions described in this section is shown in Listing 59-9.

Listing 59-9: An Internet domain sockets library

—————————————————————————————————————— **sockets/inet_sockets.c**

```c
#define _BSD_SOURCE             /* To get NI_MAXHOST and NI_MAXSERV
                                   definitions from <netdb.h> */
#include <sys/socket.h>
#include <netinet/in.h>
#include <arpa/inet.h>
#include <netdb.h>
#include "inet_sockets.h"       /* Declares functions defined here */
#include "tlpi_hdr.h"

int
inetConnect(const char *host, const char *service, int type)
{
    struct addrinfo hints;
    struct addrinfo *result, *rp;
    int sfd, s;

    memset(&hints, 0, sizeof(struct addrinfo));
    hints.ai_canonname = NULL;
    hints.ai_addr = NULL;
    hints.ai_next = NULL;
    hints.ai_family = AF_UNSPEC;        /* Allows IPv4 or IPv6 */
    hints.ai_socktype = type;

    s = getaddrinfo(host, service, &hints, &result);
    if (s != 0) {
        errno = ENOSYS;
        return -1;
    }

    /* Walk through returned list until we find an address structure
       that can be used to successfully connect a socket */

    for (rp = result; rp != NULL; rp = rp->ai_next) {
        sfd = socket(rp->ai_family, rp->ai_socktype, rp->ai_protocol);
        if (sfd == -1)
            continue;                   /* On error, try next address */

        if (connect(sfd, rp->ai_addr, rp->ai_addrlen) != -1)
            break;                      /* Success */

        /* Connect failed: close this socket and try next address */

        close(sfd);
    }

    freeaddrinfo(result);

    return (rp == NULL) ? -1 : sfd;
}
```

```c
static int                  /* Public interfaces: inetBind() and inetListen() */
inetPassiveSocket(const char *service, int type, socklen_t *addrlen,
                  Boolean doListen, int backlog)
{
    struct addrinfo hints;
    struct addrinfo *result, *rp;
    int sfd, optval, s;

    memset(&hints, 0, sizeof(struct addrinfo));
    hints.ai_canonname = NULL;
    hints.ai_addr = NULL;
    hints.ai_next = NULL;
    hints.ai_socktype = type;
    hints.ai_family = AF_UNSPEC;        /* Allows IPv4 or IPv6 */
    hints.ai_flags = AI_PASSIVE;        /* Use wildcard IP address */

    s = getaddrinfo(NULL, service, &hints, &result);
    if (s != 0)
        return -1;

    /* Walk through returned list until we find an address structure
       that can be used to successfully create and bind a socket */

    optval = 1;
    for (rp = result; rp != NULL; rp = rp->ai_next) {
        sfd = socket(rp->ai_family, rp->ai_socktype, rp->ai_protocol);
        if (sfd == -1)
            continue;                   /* On error, try next address */

        if (doListen) {
            if (setsockopt(sfd, SOL_SOCKET, SO_REUSEADDR, &optval,
                    sizeof(optval)) == -1) {
                close(sfd);
                freeaddrinfo(result);
                return -1;
            }
        }

        if (bind(sfd, rp->ai_addr, rp->ai_addrlen) == 0)
            break;                      /* Success */

        /* bind() failed: close this socket and try next address */

        close(sfd);
    }

    if (rp != NULL && doListen) {
        if (listen(sfd, backlog) == -1) {
            freeaddrinfo(result);
            return -1;
        }
    }

    if (rp != NULL && addrlen != NULL)
        *addrlen = rp->ai_addrlen;      /* Return address structure size */
```

```
        freeaddrinfo(result);

        return (rp == NULL) ? -1 : sfd;
}

int
inetListen(const char *service, int backlog, socklen_t *addrlen)
{
        return inetPassiveSocket(service, SOCK_STREAM, addrlen, TRUE, backlog);
}

int
inetBind(const char *service, int type, socklen_t *addrlen)
{
        return inetPassiveSocket(service, type, addrlen, FALSE, 0);
}

char *
inetAddressStr(const struct sockaddr *addr, socklen_t addrlen,
               char *addrStr, int addrStrLen)
{
        char host[NI_MAXHOST], service[NI_MAXSERV];

        if (getnameinfo(addr, addrlen, host, NI_MAXHOST,
                        service, NI_MAXSERV, NI_NUMERICSERV) == 0)
            snprintf(addrStr, addrStrLen, "(%s, %s)", host, service);
        else
            snprintf(addrStr, addrStrLen, "(?UNKNOWN?)");

        return addrStr;
}
```

——————————————————————————————————— sockets/inet_sockets.c

59.13 Obsolete APIs for Host and Service Conversions

In the following sections, we describe the older, now obsolete functions for converting host names and service names to and from binary and presentation formats. Although new programs should perform these conversions using the modern functions described earlier in this chapter, a knowledge of the obsolete functions is useful because we may encounter them in older code.

59.13.1 The *inet_aton()* and *inet_ntoa()* Functions

The *inet_aton()* and *inet_ntoa()* functions convert IPv4 addresses between dotted-decimal notation and binary form (in network byte order). These functions are nowadays made obsolete by *inet_pton()* and *inet_ntop()*.

The *inet_aton()* ("ASCII to network") function converts the dotted-decimal string pointed to by *str* into an IPv4 address in network byte order, which is returned in the *in_addr* structure pointed to by *addr*.

```
#include <arpa/inet.h>

int inet_aton(const char *str, struct in_addr *addr);
```
                    Returns 1 (true) if *str* is a valid dotted-decimal address, or 0 (false) on error

The *inet_aton()* function returns 1 if the conversion was successful, or 0 if *str* was invalid.

The numeric components of the string given to *inet_aton()* need not be decimal. They can be octal (specified by a leading 0) or hexadecimal (specified by a leading 0x or 0X). Furthermore, *inet_aton()* supports shorthand forms that allow an address to be specified using fewer than four numeric components. (See the *inet(3)* manual page for details.) The term *numbers-and-dots notation* is used for the more general address strings that employ these features.

SUSv3 doesn't specify *inet_aton()*. Nevertheless, this function is available on most implementations. On Linux, we must define one of the feature test macros _BSD_SOURCE, _SVID_SOURCE, or _GNU_SOURCE in order to obtain the declaration of *inet_aton()* from <arpa/inet.h>.

The *inet_ntoa()* ("network to ASCII") function performs the converse of *inet_aton()*.

```
#include <arpa/inet.h>

char *inet_ntoa(struct in_addr addr);
```
                              Returns pointer to (statically allocated)
                              dotted-decimal string version of *addr*

Given an *in_addr* structure (a 32-bit IPv4 address in network byte order), *inet_ntoa()* returns a pointer to a (statically allocated) string containing the address in dotted-decimal notation.

Because the string returned by *inet_ntoa()* is statically allocated, it is overwritten by successive calls.

59.13.2 The *gethostbyname()* and *gethostbyaddr()* Functions

The *gethostbyname()* and *gethostbyaddr()* functions allow conversion between hostnames and IP addresses. These functions are nowadays made obsolete by *getaddrinfo()* and *getnameinfo()*.

```
#include <netdb.h>

extern int h_errno;

struct hostent *gethostbyname(const char *name);
struct hostent *gethostbyaddr(const void *addr, socklen_t len, int type);
```
                         Both return pointer to (statically allocated) *hostent* structure
                                            on success, or NULL on error

The *gethostbyname()* function resolves the hostname given in *name*, returning a pointer to a statically allocated *hostent* structure containing information about that hostname. This structure has the following form:

```
struct hostent {
    char  *h_name;              /* Official (canonical) name of host */
    char **h_aliases;          /* NULL-terminated array of pointers
                                  to alias strings */
    int    h_addrtype;         /* Address type (AF_INET or AF_INET6) */
    int    h_length;           /* Length (in bytes) of addresses pointed
                                  to by h_addr_list (4 bytes for AF_INET,
                                  16 bytes for AF_INET6) */
    char **h_addr_list;        /* NULL-terminated array of pointers to
                                  host IP addresses (in_addr or in6_addr
                                  structures) in network byte order */
};

#define h_addr  h_addr_list[0]
```

The *h_name* field returns the official name of the host, as a null-terminated string. The *h_aliases* fields points to an array of pointers to null-terminated strings containing aliases (alternative names) for this hostname.

The *h_addr_list* field is an array of pointers to IP address structures for this host. (A multihomed host has more than one address.) This list consists of either *in_addr* or *in6_addr* structures. We can determine the type of these structures from the *h_addrtype* field, which contains either AF_INET or AF_INET6, and their length from the *h_length* field. The *h_addr* definition is provided for backward compatibility with earlier implementations (e.g., 4.2BSD) that returned just one address in the *hostent* structure. Some existing code relies on this name (and thus is not multihomed-host aware).

With modern versions of *gethostbyname()*, *name* can also be specified as a numeric IP address string; that is, numbers-and-dots notation for IPv4 or hex-string notation for IPv6. In this case, no lookup is performed; instead, *name* is copied into the *h_name* field of the *hostent* structure, and *h_addr_list* is set to the binary equivalent of *name*.

The *gethostbyaddr()* function performs the converse of *gethostbyname()*. Given a binary IP address, it returns a *hostent* structure containing information about the host with that address.

On error (e.g., a name could not be resolved), both *gethostbyname()* and *gethostbyaddr()* return a NULL pointer and set the global variable *h_errno*. As the name suggests, this variable is analogous to *errno* (possible values placed in this variable are described in the *gethostbyname(3)* manual page), and the *herror()* and *hstrerror()* functions are analogous to *perror()* and *strerror()*.

The *herror()* function displays (on standard error) the string given in *str*, followed by a colon (:), and then a message for the current error in *h_errno*. Alternatively, we can use *hstrerror()* to obtain a pointer to a string corresponding to the error value specified in *err*.

```
#define _BSD_SOURCE              /* Or _SVID_SOURCE or _GNU_SOURCE */
#include <netdb.h>

void herror(const char *str);

const char *hstrerror(int err);
```

Returns pointer to *h_errno* error string corresponding to *err*

Listing 59-10 demonstrates the use of *gethostbyname()*. This program displays *hostent* information for each of the hosts named on its command line. The following shell session demonstrates the use of this program:

```
$ ./t_gethostbyname www.jambit.com
Canonical name: jamjam1.jambit.com
        alias(es):      www.jambit.com
        address type:   AF_INET
        address(es):    62.245.207.90
```

Listing 59-10: Using *gethostbyname()* to retrieve host information

─── **sockets/t_gethostbyname.c**
```
#define _BSD_SOURCE      /* To get hstrerror() declaration from <netdb.h> */
#include <netdb.h>
#include <netinet/in.h>
#include <arpa/inet.h>
#include "tlpi_hdr.h"

int
main(int argc, char *argv[])
{
    struct hostent *h;
    char **pp;
    char str[INET6_ADDRSTRLEN];

    for (argv++; *argv != NULL; argv++) {
        h = gethostbyname(*argv);
        if (h == NULL) {
            fprintf(stderr, "gethostbyname() failed for '%s': %s\n",
                    *argv, hstrerror(h_errno));
            continue;
        }

        printf("Canonical name: %s\n", h->h_name);

        printf("        alias(es):      ");
        for (pp = h->h_aliases; *pp != NULL; pp++)
            printf(" %s", *pp);
        printf("\n");
```

```
            printf("          address type:    %s\n",
                  (h->h_addrtype == AF_INET) ? "AF_INET" :
                  (h->h_addrtype == AF_INET6) ? "AF_INET6" : "???");

            if (h->h_addrtype == AF_INET || h->h_addrtype == AF_INET6) {
                printf("          address(es):    ");
                for (pp = h->h_addr_list; *pp != NULL; pp++)
                    printf(" %s", inet_ntop(h->h_addrtype, *pp,
                                               str, INET6_ADDRSTRLEN));
                printf("\n");
            }
        }

    exit(EXIT_SUCCESS);
}
```

─── *sockets/t_gethostbyname.c*

59.13.3   The *getservbyname()* and *getservbyport()* Functions

The *getservbyname()* and *getservbyport()* functions retrieve records from the /etc/services file (Section 59.9). These functions are nowadays made obsolete by *getaddrinfo()* and *getnameinfo()*.

```
#include <netdb.h>

struct servent *getservbyname(const char *name, const char *proto);
struct servent *getservbyport(int port, const char *proto);
```
               Both return pointer to a (statically allocated) *servent* structure
                            on success, or NULL on not found or error

The *getservbyname()* function looks up the record whose service name (or one of its aliases) matches *name* and whose protocol matches *proto*. The *proto* argument is a string such as *tcp* or *udp*, or it can be NULL. If *proto* is specified as NULL, any record whose service name matches *name* is returned. (This is usually sufficient since, where both UDP and TCP records with the same name exist in the /etc/services file, they normally have the same port number.) If a matching record is found, then *getservbyname()* returns a pointer to a statically allocated structure of the following type:

```
struct servent {
    char  *s_name;        /* Official service name */
    char **s_aliases;     /* Pointers to aliases (NULL-terminated) */
    int    s_port;        /* Port number (in network byte order) */
    char  *s_proto;       /* Protocol */
};
```

Typically, we call *getservbyname()* only in order to obtain the port number, which is returned in the *s_port* field.

The *getservbyport()* function performs the converse of *getservbyname()*. It returns a *servent* record containing information from the /etc/services record whose port number matches *port* and whose protocol matches *proto*. Again, we can specify *proto* as NULL, in which case the call will return any record whose port number matches the one specified in *port*. (This may not return the desired result in the few cases mentioned above where the same port number maps to different service names in UDP and TCP.)

> An example of the use of the *getservbyname()* function is provided in the file `sockets/t_getservbyname.c` in the source code distribution for this book.

59.14 UNIX Versus Internet Domain Sockets

When writing applications that communicate over a network, we must necessarily use Internet domain sockets. However, when using sockets to communicate between applications on the same system, we have the choice of using either Internet or UNIX domain sockets. In this case, which domain should we use and why?

Writing an application using just Internet domain sockets is often the simplest approach, since it will work on both a single host and across a network. However, there are some reasons why we may choose to use UNIX domain sockets:

- On some implementations, UNIX domain sockets are faster than Internet domain sockets.

- We can use directory (and, on Linux, file) permissions to control access to UNIX domain sockets, so that only applications with a specified user or group ID can connect to a listening stream socket or send a datagram to a datagram socket. This provides a simple method of authenticating clients. With Internet domain sockets, we need to do rather more work if we wish to authenticate clients.

- Using UNIX domain sockets, we can pass open file descriptors and sender credentials, as summarized in Section 61.13.3.

59.15 Further Information

There is a wealth of printed and online resources on TCP/IP and the sockets API:

- The key book on network programming with the sockets API is [Stevens at al., 2004]. [Snader, 2000] adds some useful guidelines on sockets programming.

- [Stevens, 1994] and [Wright & Stevens, 1995] describe TCP/IP in detail. [Comer, 2000], [Comer & Stevens, 1999], [Comer & Stevens, 2000], [Kozierok, 2005], and [Goralksi, 2009] also provide good coverage of the same material.

- [Tanenbaum, 2002] provides general background on computer networks.

- [Herbert, 2004] describes the details of the Linux 2.6 TCP/IP stack.

- The GNU C library manual (online at *http://www.gnu.org/*) has an extensive discussion of the sockets API.

- The IBM Redbook, *TCP/IP Tutorial and Technical Overview*, provides lengthy coverage of networking concepts, TCP/IP internals, the sockets API, and a host of related topics. It is freely downloadable from *http://www.redbooks.ibm.com/*.

- [Gont, 2008] and [Gont, 2009b] provide security assessments of IPv4 and TCP.

- The Usenet newsgroup *comp.protocols.tcp-ip* is dedicated to questions related to the TCP/IP networking protocols.

- [Sarolahti & Kuznetsov, 2002] describes congestion control and other details of the Linux TCP implementation.

- Linux-specific information can be found in the following manual pages: *socket(7)*, *ip(7)*, *raw(7)*, *tcp(7)*, *udp(7)*, and *packet(7)*.

- See also the RFC list in Section 58.7.

59.16 Summary

Internet domain sockets allow applications on different hosts to communicate via a TCP/IP network. An Internet domain socket address consists of an IP address and a port number. In IPv4, an IP address is a 32-bit number; in IPv6, it is a 128-bit number. Internet domain datagram sockets operate over UDP, providing connectionless, unreliable, message-oriented communication. Internet domain stream sockets operate over TCP, and provide a reliable, bidirectional, byte-stream communication channel between two connected applications.

Different computer architectures use different conventions for representing data types. For example, integers may be stored in little-endian or big-endian form, and different computers may use different numbers of bytes to represent numeric types such as *int* or *long*. These differences mean that we need to employ some architecture-independent representation when transferring data between heterogeneous machines connected via a network. We noted that various marshalling standards exist to deal with this problem, and also described a simple solution used by many applications: encoding all transmitted data in text form, with fields delimited by a designated character (usually a newline).

We looked at a range of functions that can be used to convert between (numeric) string representations of IP addresses (dotted-decimal for IPv4 and hex-string for IPv6) and their binary equivalents. However, it is generally preferable to use host and service names rather than numbers, since names are easier to remember and continue to be usable, even if the corresponding number is changed. We looked at various functions that convert host and service names to their numeric equivalents and vice versa. The modern function for translating host and service names into socket addresses is *getaddrinfo()*, but it is common to see the historical functions *gethostbyname()* and *getservbyname()* in existing code.

Consideration of hostname conversions led us into a discussion of DNS, which implements a distributed database for a hierarchical directory service. The advantage of DNS is that the management of the database is not centralized. Instead, local zone administrators update changes for the hierarchical component of the database for which they are responsible, and DNS servers communicate with one another in order to resolve a hostname.

59.17 Exercises

59-1. When reading large quantities of data, the *readLine()* function shown in Listing 59-1 is inefficient, since a system call is required to read each character. A more efficient interface would read a block of characters into a buffer and extract a line at a time from this buffer. Such an interface might consist of two functions. The first of these functions, which might be called *readLineBufInit(fd, &rlbuf)*, initializes the bookkeeping data structure pointed to by *rlbuf*. This structure includes space for a data buffer, the size of that buffer, and a pointer to the next "unread" character in that buffer. It also includes a copy of the file descriptor given in the argument *fd*. The second function, *readLineBuf(&rlbuf)*, returns the next line from the buffer associated with *rlbuf*. If required, this function reads a further block of data from the file descriptor saved in *rlbuf*. Implement these two functions. Modify the programs in Listing 59-6 (is_seqnum_sv.c) and Listing 59-7 (is_seqnum_cl.c) to use these functions.

59-2. Modify the programs in Listing 59-6 (is_seqnum_sv.c) and Listing 59-7 (is_seqnum_cl.c) to use the *inetListen()* and *inetConnect()* functions provided in Listing 59-9 (inet_sockets.c).

59-3. Write a UNIX domain sockets library with an API similar to the Internet domain sockets library shown in Section 59.12. Rewrite the programs in Listing 57-3 (us_xfr_sv.c, on page 1168) and Listing 57-4 (us_xfr_cl.c, on page 1169) to use this library.

59-4. Write a network server that stores name-value pairs. The server should allow names to be added, deleted, modified, and retrieved by clients. Write one or more client programs to test the server. Optionally, implement some kind of security mechanism that allows only the client that created the name to delete it or to modify the value associated with it.

59-5. Suppose that we create two Internet domain datagram sockets, bound to specific addresses, and connect the first socket to the second. What happens if we create a third datagram socket and try to send (*sendto()*) a datagram via that socket to the first socket? Write a program to determine the answer.

60

SOCKETS: SERVER DESIGN

This chapter discusses the fundamentals of designing iterative and concurrent servers and describes *inetd*, a special daemon designed to facilitate the creation of Internet servers.

60.1 Iterative and Concurrent Servers

Two common designs for network servers using sockets are the following:

- *Iterative*: The server handles one client at a time, processing that client's request(s) completely, before proceeding to the next client.
- *Concurrent*: The server is designed to handle multiple clients simultaneously.

We have already seen an example of an iterative server using FIFOs in Section 44.8 and an example of a concurrent server using System V message queues in Section 46.8.

Iterative servers are usually suitable only when client requests can be handled quickly, since each client must wait until all of the preceding clients have been serviced. A typical scenario for employing an iterative server is where the client and server exchange a single request and response.

Concurrent servers are suitable when a significant amount of processing time is required to handle each request, or where the client and server engage in an extended conversation, passing messages back and forth. In this chapter, we mainly focus on the traditional (and simplest) method of designing a concurrent server: creating a new child process for each new client. Each server child performs all tasks necessary to service a single client and then terminates. Since each of these processes can operate independently, multiple clients can be handled simultaneously. The principal task of the main server process (the parent) is to create a new child process for each new client. (A variation on this approach is to create a new thread for each client.)

In the following sections, we look at examples of an iterative and a concurrent server using Internet domain sockets. These two servers implement the *echo* service (RFC 862), a rudimentary service that returns a copy of whatever the client sends it.

60.2 An Iterative UDP *echo* Server

In this and the next section, we present servers for the *echo* service. The *echo* service operates on both UDP and TCP port 7. (Since this is a reserved port, the *echo* server must be run with superuser privileges.)

The UDP *echo* server continuously reads datagrams, returning a copy of each datagram to the sender. Since the server needs to handle only a single message at a time, an iterative server design suffices. The header file for the server (and the client that we discuss in a moment) is shown in Listing 60-1.

Listing 60-1: Header file for id_echo_sv.c and id_echo_cl.c

```
——————————————————————————————— sockets/id_echo.h
#include "inet_sockets.h"       /* Declares our socket functions */
#include "tlpi_hdr.h"

#define SERVICE "echo"          /* Name of UDP service */

#define BUF_SIZE 500            /* Maximum size of datagrams that can
                                   be read by client and server */
——————————————————————————————— sockets/id_echo.h
```

Listing 60-2 shows the implementation of the server. Note the following points regarding the server implementation:

- We use the *becomeDaemon()* function of Section 37.2 to turn the server into a daemon.

- To shorten this program, we employ the Internet domain sockets library developed in Section 59.12.

- If the server can't send a reply to the client, it logs a message using *syslog()*.

  > In a real-world application, we would probably apply some rate limit to the messages written with *syslog()*, both to prevent the possibility of an attacker filling the system log and because each call to *syslog()* is expensive, since (by default) *syslog()* in turn calls *fsync()*.

Listing 60-2: An iterative server that implements the UDP *echo* service

```c
#include <syslog.h>
#include "id_echo.h"
#include "become_daemon.h"

int
main(int argc, char *argv[])
{
    int sfd;
    ssize_t numRead;
    socklen_t len;
    struct sockaddr_storage claddr;
    char buf[BUF_SIZE];
    char addrStr[IS_ADDR_STR_LEN];

    if (becomeDaemon(0) == -1)
        errExit("becomeDaemon");

    sfd = inetBind(SERVICE, SOCK_DGRAM, NULL);
    if (sfd == -1) {
        syslog(LOG_ERR, "Could not create server socket (%s)", strerror(errno));
        exit(EXIT_FAILURE);
    }

    /* Receive datagrams and return copies to senders */

    for (;;) {
        len = sizeof(struct sockaddr_storage);
        numRead = recvfrom(sfd, buf, BUF_SIZE, 0,
                            (struct sockaddr *) &claddr, &len);
        if (numRead == -1)
            errExit("recvfrom");

        if (sendto(sfd, buf, numRead, 0, (struct sockaddr *) &claddr, len)
                    != numRead)
            syslog(LOG_WARNING, "Error echoing response to %s (%s)",
                    inetAddressStr((struct sockaddr *) &claddr, len,
                                    addrStr, IS_ADDR_STR_LEN),
                    strerror(errno));
    }
}
```

To test the server, we use the client program shown in Listing 60-3. This program also employs the Internet domain sockets library developed in Section 59.12. As its first command-line argument, the client program expects the name of the host on which the server resides. The client executes a loop in which it sends each of its remaining command-line arguments to the server as separate datagrams, and reads and prints each response datagram sent back by the server.

Listing 60-3: A client for the UDP *echo* service

─── **sockets/id_echo_cl.c**

```c
#include "id_echo.h"

int
main(int argc, char *argv[])
{
    int sfd, j;
    size_t len;
    ssize_t numRead;
    char buf[BUF_SIZE];

    if (argc < 2 || strcmp(argv[1], "--help") == 0)
        usageErr("%s host msg...\n", argv[0]);

    /* Construct server address from first command-line argument */

    sfd = inetConnect(argv[1], SERVICE, SOCK_DGRAM);
    if (sfd == -1)
        fatal("Could not connect to server socket");

    /* Send remaining command-line arguments to server as separate datagrams */

    for (j = 2; j < argc; j++) {
        len = strlen(argv[j]);
        if (write(sfd, argv[j], len) != len)
            fatal("partial/failed write");

        numRead = read(sfd, buf, BUF_SIZE);
        if (numRead == -1)
            errExit("read");

        printf("[%ld bytes] %.*s\n", (long) numRead, (int) numRead, buf);
    }

    exit(EXIT_SUCCESS);
}
```

─── **sockets/id_echo_cl.c**

Here is an example of what we see when we run the server and two instances of the client:

```
$ su                                    Need privilege to bind reserved port
Password:
# ./id_echo_sv                          Server places itself in background
# exit                                  Cease to be superuser
$ ./id_echo_cl localhost hello world    This client sends two datagrams
[5 bytes] hello                         Client prints responses from server
[5 bytes] world
$ ./id_echo_cl localhost goodbye        This client sends one datagram
[7 bytes] goodbye
```

60.3 A Concurrent TCP *echo* Server

The TCP *echo* service also operates on port 7. The TCP *echo* server accepts a connection and then loops continuously, reading all transmitted data and sending it back to the client on the same socket. The server continues reading until it detects end-of-file, at which point it closes its socket (so that the client sees end-of-file if it is still reading from its socket).

Since the client may send an indefinite amount of data to the server (and thus servicing the client may take an indefinite amount of time), a concurrent server design is appropriate, so that multiple clients can be simultaneously served. The server implementation is shown in Listing 60-4. (We show an implementation of a client for this service in Section 61.2.) Note the following points about the implementation:

- The server becomes a daemon by calling the *becomeDaemon()* function shown in Section 37.2.

- To shorten this program, we employ the Internet domain sockets library shown in Listing 59-9 (page 1228).

- Since the server creates a child process for each client connection, we must ensure that zombies are reaped. We do this within a SIGCHLD handler.

- The main body of the server consists of a for loop that accepts a client connection and then uses *fork()* to create a child process that invokes the *handleRequest()* function to handle that client. In the meantime, the parent continues around the for loop to accept the next client connection.

  > In a real-world application, we would probably include some code in our server to place an upper limit on the number of child processes that the server could create, in order to prevent an attacker from attempting a remote fork bomb by using the service to create so many processes on the system that it becomes unusable. We could impose this limit by adding extra code in the server to count the number of children currently executing (this count would be incremented after a successful *fork()* and decremented as each child was reaped in the SIGCHLD handler). If the limit on the number of children were reached, we could then temporarily stop accepting connections (or alternatively, accept connections and then immediately close them).

- After each *fork()*, the file descriptors for the listening and connected sockets are duplicated in the child (Section 24.2.1). This means that both the parent and the child could communicate with the client using the connected socket. However, only the child needs to perform such communication, and so the parent closes the file descriptor for the connected socket immediately after the *fork()*. (If the parent did not do this, then the socket would never actually be closed; furthermore, the parent would eventually run out of file descriptors.) Since the child doesn't accept new connections, it closes its duplicate of the file descriptor for the listening socket.

- Each child process terminates after handling a single client.

Listing 60-4: A concurrent server that implements the TCP *echo* service

─── **sockets/is_echo_sv.c**

```c
#include <signal.h>
#include <syslog.h>
#include <sys/wait.h>
#include "become_daemon.h"
#include "inet_sockets.h"        /* Declarations of inet*() socket functions */
#include "tlpi_hdr.h"

#define SERVICE "echo"           /* Name of TCP service */
#define BUF_SIZE 4096

static void                 /* SIGCHLD handler to reap dead child processes */
grimReaper(int sig)
{
    int savedErrno;             /* Save 'errno' in case changed here */

    savedErrno = errno;
    while (waitpid(-1, NULL, WNOHANG) > 0)
        continue;
    errno = savedErrno;
}

/* Handle a client request: copy socket input back to socket */

static void
handleRequest(int cfd)
{
    char buf[BUF_SIZE];
    ssize_t numRead;

    while ((numRead = read(cfd, buf, BUF_SIZE)) > 0) {
        if (write(cfd, buf, numRead) != numRead) {
            syslog(LOG_ERR, "write() failed: %s", strerror(errno));
            exit(EXIT_FAILURE);
        }
    }

    if (numRead == -1) {
        syslog(LOG_ERR, "Error from read(): %s", strerror(errno));
        exit(EXIT_FAILURE);
    }
}

int
main(int argc, char *argv[])
{
    int lfd, cfd;                   /* Listening and connected sockets */
    struct sigaction sa;

    if (becomeDaemon(0) == -1)
        errExit("becomeDaemon");
```

```c
    sigemptyset(&sa.sa_mask);
    sa.sa_flags = SA_RESTART;
    sa.sa_handler = grimReaper;
    if (sigaction(SIGCHLD, &sa, NULL) == -1) {
        syslog(LOG_ERR, "Error from sigaction(): %s", strerror(errno));
        exit(EXIT_FAILURE);
    }

    lfd = inetListen(SERVICE, 10, NULL);
    if (lfd == -1) {
        syslog(LOG_ERR, "Could not create server socket (%s)", strerror(errno));
        exit(EXIT_FAILURE);
    }

    for (;;) {
        cfd = accept(lfd, NULL, NULL);   /* Wait for connection */
        if (cfd == -1) {
            syslog(LOG_ERR, "Failure in accept(): %s", strerror(errno));
            exit(EXIT_FAILURE);
        }

        /* Handle each client request in a new child process */

        switch (fork()) {
        case -1:
            syslog(LOG_ERR, "Can't create child (%s)", strerror(errno));
            close(cfd);                 /* Give up on this client */
            break;                      /* May be temporary; try next client */

        case 0:                         /* Child */
            close(lfd);                 /* Unneeded copy of listening socket */
            handleRequest(cfd);
            _exit(EXIT_SUCCESS);

        default:                        /* Parent */
            close(cfd);                 /* Unneeded copy of connected socket */
            break;                      /* Loop to accept next connection */
        }
    }
}
```

———————————————————————————————————— `sockets/is_echo_sv.c`

60.4 Other Concurrent Server Designs

The traditional concurrent server model described in the previous section is adequate for many applications that need to simultaneously handle multiple clients via TCP connections. However, for very high-load servers (for example, web servers handling thousands of requests per minute), the cost of creating a new child (or even thread) for each client imposes a significant burden on the server (refer to Section 28.3), and alternative designs need to be employed. We briefly consider some of these alternatives.

Preforked and prethreaded servers

Preforked and prethreaded servers are described in some detail in Chapter 30 of [Stevens et al., 2004]. The key ideas are the following:

- Instead of creating a new child process (or thread) for each client, the server precreates a fixed number of child processes (or threads) immediately on startup (i.e., before any client requests are even received). These children constitute a so-called *server pool*.

- Each child in the server pool handles one client at a time, but instead of terminating after handling the client, the child fetches the next client to be serviced and services it, and so on.

Employing the above technique requires some careful management within the server application. The server pool should be large enough to ensure adequate response to client requests. This means that the server parent must monitor the number of unoccupied children, and, in times of peak load, increase the size of the pool so that there are always enough child processes available to immediately serve new clients. If the load decreases, then the size of the server pool should be reduced, since having excess processes on the system can degrade overall system performance.

In addition, the children in the server pool must follow some protocol to allow them to exclusively select individual client connections. On most UNIX implementations (including Linux), it is sufficient to have each child in the pool block in an *accept()* call on the listening descriptor. In other words, the server parent creates the listening socket before creating any children, and each of the children inherits a file descriptor for the socket during the *fork()*. When a new client connection arrives, only one of the children will complete the *accept()* call. However, because *accept()* is not an atomic system call on some older implementations, the call may need to be bracketed by some mutual-exclusion technique (e.g., a file lock) to ensure that only one child at a time performs the call ([Stevens et al., 2004]).

> There are alternatives to having all of the children in the server pool perform *accept()* calls. If the server pool consists of separate processes, the server parent can perform the *accept()* call, and then pass the file descriptor containing the new connection to one of the free processes in the pool, using a technique that we briefly describe in Section 61.13.3. If the server pool consists of threads, the main thread can perform the *accept()* call, and then inform one of the free server threads that a new client is available on the connected descriptor.

Handling multiple clients from a single process

In some cases, we can design a single server process to handle multiple clients. To do this, we must employ one of the I/O models (I/O multiplexing, signal-driven I/O, or *epoll*) that allow a single process to simultaneously monitor multiple file descriptors for I/O events. These models are described in Chapter 63.

In a single-server design, the server process must take on some of the scheduling tasks that are normally handled by the kernel. In a solution that involves one server process per client, we can rely on the kernel to ensure that each server process (and thus client) gets a fair share of access to the resources of the server host. But when we use a single server process to handle multiple clients, the server must do some work to ensure that one or a few clients don't monopolize access to the server while other clients are starved. We say a little more about this point in Section 63.4.6.

Using server farms

Other approaches to handling high client loads involve the use of multiple server systems—a *server farm*.

One of the simplest approaches to building a server farm (employed by some web servers) is *DNS round-robin load sharing* (or *load distribution*), where the authoritative name server for a zone maps the same domain name to several IP addresses (i.e., several servers share the same domain name). Successive requests to the DNS server to resolve the domain name return these IP addresses in round-robin order. Further information about DNS round-robin load sharing can be found in [Albitz & Liu, 2006].

Round-robin DNS has the advantage of being inexpensive and easy to set up. However, it does have some shortcomings. A DNS server performing iterative resolution may cache its results (see Section 59.8), with the result that future queries on the domain name return the same IP address, instead of the round-robin sequence generated by the authoritative DNS server. Also, round-robin DNS doesn't have any built-in mechanisms for ensuring good load balancing (different clients may place different loads on a server) or ensuring high availability (what if one of the servers dies or the server application that it is running crashes?). Another issue that we may need to consider—one that is faced by many designs that employ multiple server machines—is ensuring *server affinity*; that is, ensuring that a sequence of requests from the same client are all directed to the same server, so that any state information maintained by the server about the client remains accurate.

A more flexible, but also more complex, solution is *server load balancing*. In this scenario, a single load-balancing server routes incoming client requests to one of the members of the server farm. (To ensure high availability, there may be a backup server that takes over if the primary load-balancing server crashes.) This eliminates the problems associated with remote DNS caching, since the server farm presents a single IP address (that of the load-balancing server) to the outside world. The load-balancing server incorporates algorithms to measure or estimate server load (perhaps based on metrics supplied by the members of the server farm) and intelligently distribute the load across the members of the server farm. The load-balancing server also automatically detects failures in members of the server farm (and the addition of new servers, if demand requires it). Finally, a load-balancing server may also provide support for server affinity. Further information about server load balancing can be found in [Kopparapu, 2002].

60.5 The *inetd* (Internet Superserver) Daemon

If we look through the contents of /etc/services, we see literally hundreds of different services listed. This implies that a system could theoretically be running a large number of server processes. However, most of these servers would usually be doing nothing but waiting for infrequent connection requests or datagrams. All of these server processes would nevertheless occupy slots in the kernel process table, and consume some memory and swap space, thus placing a load on the system.

The *inetd* daemon is designed to eliminate the need to run large numbers of infrequently used servers. Using *inetd* provides two main benefits:

- Instead of running a separate daemon for each service, a single process—the *inetd* daemon—monitors a specified set of socket ports and starts other servers as required. Thus, the number of processes running on the system is reduced.

- The programming of the servers started by *inetd* is simplified, because *inetd* performs several of the steps that are commonly required by all network servers on startup.

Since it oversees a range of services, invoking other servers as required, *inetd* is sometimes known as the *Internet superserver*.

> An extended version of *inetd*, *xinetd*, is provided in some Linux distributions. Among other things, *xinetd* adds a number of security enhancements. Information about *xinetd* can be found at *http://www.xinetd.org/*.

Operation of the *inetd* daemon

The *inetd* daemon is normally started during system boot. After becoming a daemon process (Section 37.2), *inetd* performs the following steps:

1. For each of the services specified in its configuration file, /etc/inetd.conf, *inetd* creates a socket of the appropriate type (i.e., stream or datagram) and binds it to the specified port. Each TCP socket is additionally marked to permit incoming connections via a call to *listen()*.

2. Using the *select()* system call (Section 63.2.1), *inetd* monitors all of the sockets created in the preceding step for datagrams or incoming connection requests.

3. The *select()* call blocks until either a UDP socket has a datagram available to read or a connection request is received on a TCP socket. In the case of a TCP connection, *inetd* performs an *accept()* for the connection before proceeding to the next step.

4. To start the server specified for this socket, *inetd()* calls *fork()* to create a new process that then does an *exec()* to start the server program. Before performing the *exec()*, the child process performs the following steps:

   a) Close all of the file descriptors inherited from its parent, except the one for the socket on which the UDP datagram is available or the TCP connection has been accepted.

   b) Use the techniques described in Section 5.5 to duplicate the socket file descriptor on file descriptors 0, 1, and 2, and close the socket file descriptor itself (since it is no longer required). After this step, the execed server is able to communicate on the socket by using the three standard file descriptors.

   c) Optionally, set the user and group IDs for the execed server to values specified in /etc/inetd.conf.

5. If a connection was accepted on a TCP socket in step 3, *inetd* closes the connected socket (since it is needed only in the execed server).

6. The *inetd* server returns to step 2.

The /etc/inetd.conf file

The operation of the *inetd* daemon is controlled by a configuration file, normally /etc/inetd.conf. Each line in this file describes one of the services to be handled by *inetd*. Listing 60-5 shows some examples of entries in the /etc/inetd.conf file that comes with one Linux distribution.

Listing 60-5: Example lines from /etc/inetd.conf

```
# echo   stream  tcp  nowait  root    internal
# echo   dgram   udp  wait    root    internal
ftp      stream  tcp  nowait  root    /usr/sbin/tcpd    in.ftpd
telnet   stream  tcp  nowait  root    /usr/sbin/tcpd    in.telnetd
login    stream  tcp  nowait  root    /usr/sbin/tcpd    in.rlogind
```

The first two lines of Listing 60-5 are commented out by the initial # character; we show them now since we'll refer to the *echo* service shortly.

Each line of /etc/inetd.conf consists of the following fields, delimited by white space:

- *Service name*: This specifies the name of a service from the /etc/services file. In conjunction with the *protocol* field, this is used to look up /etc/services to determine which port number *inetd* should monitor for this service.

- *Socket type*: This specifies the type of socket used by this service—for example, stream or dgram.

- *Protocol*: This specifies the protocol to be used by this socket. This field can contain any of the Internet protocols listed in the file /etc/protocols (documented in the *protocols(5)* manual page), but almost every service specifies either tcp (for TCP) or udp (for UDP).

- *Flags*: This field contains either wait or nowait. This field specifies whether or not the server execed by *inetd* (temporarily) takes over management of the socket for this service. If the execed server manages the socket, then this field is specified as wait. This causes *inetd* to remove this socket from the file descriptor set that it monitors using *select()* until the execed server exits (*inetd* detects this via a handler for SIGCHLD). We say some more about this field below.

- *Login name*: This field consists of a username from /etc/passwd, optionally followed by a period (.) and a group name from /etc/group. These determine the user and group IDs under which the execed server is run. (Since *inetd* runs with an effective user ID of *root*, its children are also privileged and can thus use calls to *setuid()* and *setgid()* to change process credentials if desired.)

- *Server program*: This specifies the pathname of the server program to be execed.

- *Server program arguments*: This field specifies one or more arguments, separated by white space, to be used as the argument list when execing the server program. The first of these corresponds to *argv[0]* in the execed program and is thus usually the same as the basename part of the *server program* name. The next argument corresponds to *argv[1]*, and so on.

In the example lines shown in Listing 60-5 for the *ftp*, *telnet*, and *login* services, we see the server program and arguments are set up differently than just described. All three of these services cause *inetd* to invoke the same program, *tcpd(8)* (the TCP daemon wrapper), which performs some logging and access-control checks before in turn execing the appropriate program, based on the value specified as the first server program argument (which is available to *tcpd* via *argv[0]*). Further information about *tcpd* can be found in the *tcpd(8)* manual page and in [Mann & Mitchell, 2003].

Stream socket (TCP) servers invoked by *inetd* are normally designed to handle just a single client connection and then terminate, leaving *inetd* with the job of listening for further connections. For such servers, *flags* should be specified as nowait. (If, instead, the execed server is to accept connections, then wait should be specified, in which case *inetd* does not accept the connection, but instead passes the file descriptor for the *listening* socket to the execed server as descriptor 0.)

For most UDP servers, the *flags* field should be specified as wait. A UDP server invoked by *inetd* is normally designed to read and process all outstanding datagrams on the socket and then terminate. (This usually requires some sort of timeout when reading the socket, so that the server terminates when no new datagrams arrive within a specified interval.) By specifying wait, we prevent the *inetd* daemon from simultaneously trying to *select()* on the socket, which would have the unintended consequence that *inetd* would race the UDP server to check for datagrams and, if it won the race, start another instance of the UDP server.

Because the operation of *inetd* and the format of its configuration file are not specified by SUSv3, there are some (generally small) variations in the values that can be specified in the fields of /etc/inetd.conf. Most versions of *inetd* provide at least the syntax that we describe in the main text. For further details, see the *inetd.conf(8)* manual page.

As an efficiency measure, *inetd* implements a few simple services itself, instead of execing separate servers to perform the task. The UDP and TCP *echo* services are examples of services that *inetd* implements. For such services, the *server program* field of the corresponding /etc/inetd.conf record is specified as internal, and the *server program arguments* are omitted. (In the example lines in Listing 60-5, we saw that the *echo* service entries were commented out. To enable the *echo* service, we need to remove the # character at the start of these lines.)

Whenever we change the /etc/inetd.conf file, we need to send a SIGHUP signal to *inetd* to request it to reread the file:

```
# killall -HUP inetd
```

Example: invoking a TCP *echo* service via *inetd*

We noted earlier that *inetd* simplifies the programming of servers, especially concurrent (usually TCP) servers. It does this by carrying out the following steps on behalf of the servers it invokes:

1. Perform all socket-related initialization, calling *socket()*, *bind()*, and (for TCP servers) *listen()*.

2. For a TCP service, perform an *accept()* for the new connection.

3. Create a new process to handle the incoming UDP datagram or TCP connection. The process is automatically set up as a daemon. The *inetd* program handles all details of process creation via *fork()* and the reaping of dead children via a handler for SIGCHLD.

4. Duplicate the file descriptor of the UDP socket or the connected TCP socket on file descriptors 0, 1, and 2, and close all other file descriptors (since they are unused in the execed server).

5. Exec the server program.

(In the description of the above steps, we assume the usual cases that the *flags* field of the service entry in /etc/inetd.conf is specified as nowait for TCP services and wait for UDP services.)

As an example of how *inetd* simplifies the programming of a TCP service, in Listing 60-6, we show the *inetd*-invoked equivalent of the TCP *echo* server from Listing 60-4. Since *inetd* performs all of the above steps, all that remains of the server is the code executed by the child process to handle the client request, which can be read from file descriptor 0 (STDIN_FILENO).

If the server resides in the directory /bin (for example), then we would need to create the following entry in /etc/inetd.conf in order to have *inetd* invoke the server:

```
echo stream tcp nowait root /bin/is_echo_inetd_sv is_echo_inetd_sv
```

Listing 60-6: TCP *echo* server designed to be invoked via *inetd*

── sockets/is_echo_inetd_sv.c

```c
#include <syslog.h>
#include "tlpi_hdr.h"

#define BUF_SIZE 4096

int
main(int argc, char *argv[])
{
    char buf[BUF_SIZE];
    ssize_t numRead;

    while ((numRead = read(STDIN_FILENO, buf, BUF_SIZE)) > 0) {
        if (write(STDOUT_FILENO, buf, numRead) != numRead) {
            syslog(LOG_ERR, "write() failed: %s", strerror(errno));
            exit(EXIT_FAILURE);
        }
    }

    if (numRead == -1) {
        syslog(LOG_ERR, "Error from read(): %s", strerror(errno));
        exit(EXIT_FAILURE);
    }

    exit(EXIT_SUCCESS);
}
```

── sockets/is_echo_inetd_sv.c

60.6 Summary

An iterative server handles one client at a time, processing that client's request(s) completely, before proceeding to the next client. A concurrent server handles multiple clients simultaneously. In high-load scenarios, a traditional concurrent server design that creates a new child process (or thread) for each client may not perform well enough, and we outlined a range of other approaches for concurrently handling large numbers of clients.

The Internet superserver daemon, *inetd*, monitors multiple sockets and starts the appropriate servers in response to incoming UDP datagrams or TCP connections. Using *inetd* allows us to decrease system load by minimizing the number of network server processes on the system, and also simplifies the programming of server processes, since it performs most of the initialization steps required by a server.

Further information

Refer to the sources of further information listed in Section 59.15.

60.7 Exercises

60-1. Add code to the program in Listing 60-4 (is_echo_sv.c) to place a limit on the number of simultaneously executing children.

60-2. Sometimes, it may be necessary to write a socket server so that it can be invoked either directly from the command line or indirectly via *inetd*. In this case, a command-line option is used to distinguish the two cases. Modify the program in Listing 60-4 so that, if it is given a −*i* command-line option, it assumes that it is being invoked by *inetd* and handles a single client on the connected socket, which *inetd* supplies via STDIN_FILENO. If the −*i* option is not supplied, then the program can assume it is being invoked from the command line, and operate in the usual fashion. (This change requires only the addition of a few lines of code.) Modify /etc/inetd.conf to invoke this program for the *echo* service.

61

SOCKETS: ADVANCED TOPICS

This chapter considers a range of more advanced topics relating to sockets programming, including the following:

- the circumstances in which partial reads and writes can occur on stream sockets;

- the use of *shutdown()* to close one half of the bidirectional channel between two connected sockets;

- the *recv()* and *send()* I/O system calls, which provide socket-specific functionality not available with *read()* and *write()*;

- the *sendfile()* system call, which is used in certain circumstances to efficiently output data on a socket;

- details of the operation of the TCP protocol, with the aim of eliminating some common misunderstandings that lead to mistakes when writing programs that use TCP sockets;

- the use of the *netstat* and *tcpdump* commands for monitoring and debugging applications that use sockets; and

- the use of the *getsockopt()* and *setsockopt()* system calls to retrieve and modify options affecting the operation of a socket.

We also consider a number of other more minor topics, and conclude the chapter with a summary of some advanced sockets features.

61.1 Partial Reads and Writes on Stream Sockets

When we first introduced the *read()* and *write()* system calls in Chapter 4, we noted that, in some circumstances, they may transfer fewer bytes than requested. Such partial transfers can occur when performing I/O on stream sockets. We now consider why they can occur and show a pair of functions that transparently handle partial transfers.

A partial read may occur if there are fewer bytes available in the socket than were requested in the *read()* call. In this case, *read()* simply returns the number of bytes available. (This is the same behavior that we saw with pipes and FIFOs in Section 44.10.)

A partial write may occur if there is insufficient buffer space to transfer all of the requested bytes and one of the following is true:

- A signal handler interrupted the *write()* call (Section 21.5) after it transferred some of the requested bytes.

- The socket was operating in nonblocking mode (O_NONBLOCK), and it was possible to transfer only some of the requested bytes.

- An asynchronous error occurred after only some of the requested bytes had been transferred. By an *asynchronous error*, we mean an error that occurs asynchronously with respect to the application's use of calls in the sockets API. An asynchronous error can arise, for example, because of a problem with a TCP connection, perhaps resulting from a crash by the peer application.

In all of the above cases, assuming that there was space to transfer at least 1 byte, the *write()* is successful, and returns the number of bytes that were transferred to the output buffer.

If a partial I/O occurs—for example, if a *read()* returns fewer bytes than requested or a blocked *write()* is interrupted by a signal handler after transferring only part of the requested data—then it is sometimes useful to restart the system call to complete the transfer. In Listing 61-1, we provide two functions that do this: *readn()* and *writen()*. (The ideas for these functions are drawn from functions of the same name presented in [Stevens et al., 2004].)

```
#include "rdwrn.h"

ssize_t readn(int fd, void *buffer, size_t count);
```
                    Returns number of bytes read, 0 on EOF, or −1 on error
```
ssize_t writen(int fd, void *buffer, size_t count);
```
                    Returns number of bytes written, or −1 on error

The *readn()* and *writen()* functions take the same arguments as *read()* and *write()*. However, they use a loop to restart these system calls, thus ensuring that the requested number of bytes is always transferred (unless an error occurs or end-of-file is detected on a *read()*).

Listing 61-1: Implementation of *readn()* and *writen()*

```c
#include <unistd.h>
#include <errno.h>
#include "rdwrn.h"                      /* Declares readn() and writen() */

ssize_t
readn(int fd, void *buffer, size_t n)
{
    ssize_t numRead;                    /* # of bytes fetched by last read() */
    size_t totRead;                     /* Total # of bytes read so far */
    char *buf;

    buf = buffer;                       /* No pointer arithmetic on "void *" */
    for (totRead = 0; totRead < n; ) {
        numRead = read(fd, buf, n - totRead);

        if (numRead == 0)               /* EOF */
            return totRead;             /* May be 0 if this is first read() */
        if (numRead == -1) {
            if (errno == EINTR)
                continue;               /* Interrupted --> restart read() */
            else
                return -1;              /* Some other error */
        }
        totRead += numRead;
        buf += numRead;
    }
    return totRead;                     /* Must be 'n' bytes if we get here */
}

ssize_t
writen(int fd, const void *buffer, size_t n)
{
    ssize_t numWritten;                 /* # of bytes written by last write() */
    size_t totWritten;                  /* Total # of bytes written so far */
    const char *buf;

    buf = buffer;                       /* No pointer arithmetic on "void *" */
    for (totWritten = 0; totWritten < n; ) {
        numWritten = write(fd, buf, n - totWritten);

        if (numWritten <= 0) {
            if (numWritten == -1 && errno == EINTR)
                continue;               /* Interrupted --> restart write() */
            else
                return -1;              /* Some other error */
        }
        totWritten += numWritten;
        buf += numWritten;
    }
    return totWritten;                  /* Must be 'n' bytes if we get here */
}
```

61.2 The *shutdown()* System Call

Calling *close()* on a socket closes both halves of the bidirectional communication channel. Sometimes, it is useful to close one half of the connection, so that data can be transmitted in just one direction through the socket. The *shutdown()* system call provides this functionality.

```
#include <sys/socket.h>

int shutdown(int sockfd, int how);
```
                                    Returns 0 on success, or −1 on error

The *shutdown()* system call closes one or both channels of the socket *sockfd*, depending on the value of *how*, which is specified as one of the following:

SHUT_RD

> Close the reading half of the connection. Subsequent reads will return end-of-file (0). Data can still be written to the socket. After a SHUT_RD on a UNIX domain stream socket, the peer application receives a SIGPIPE signal and the EPIPE error if it makes further attempts to write to the peer socket. As discussed in Section 61.6.6, SHUT_RD can't be used meaningfully for TCP sockets.

SHUT_WR

> Close the writing half of the connection. Once the peer application has read all outstanding data, it will see end-of-file. Subsequent writes to the local socket yield the SIGPIPE signal and an EPIPE error. Data written by the peer can still be read from the socket. In other words, this operation allows us to signal end-of-file to the peer while still being able to read data that the peer sends back to us. The SHUT_WR operation is employed by programs such as *ssh* and *rsh* (refer to Section 18.5 of [Stevens, 1994]). The SHUT_WR operation is the most common use of *shutdown()*, and is sometimes referred to as a *socket half-close*.

SHUT_RDWR

> Close both the read and the write halves of the connection. This is the same as performing a SHUT_RD followed by a SHUT_WR.

Aside from the semantics of the *how* argument, *shutdown()* differs from *close()* in another important respect: it closes the socket channel(s) regardless of whether there are other file descriptors referring to the socket. (In other words, *shutdown()* is performing an operation on the open file description, rather than the file descriptor. See Figure 5-2, on page 95.) Suppose, for example, that *sockfd* refers to a connected stream socket. If we make the following calls, then the connection remains open, and we can still perform I/O on the connection via the file descriptor *fd2*:

```
fd2 = dup(sockfd);
close(sockfd);
```

However, if we make the following sequence of calls, then both channels of the connection are closed, and I/O can no longer be performed via *fd2*:

```
fd2 = dup(sockfd);
shutdown(sockfd, SHUT_RDWR);
```

A similar scenario holds if a file descriptor for a socket is duplicated during a *fork()*. If, after the *fork()*, one process does a SHUT_RDWR on its copy of the descriptor, then the other process also can no longer perform I/O on its descriptor.

Note that *shutdown()* doesn't close the file descriptor, even if *how* is specified as SHUT_RDWR. To close the file descriptor, we must additionally call *close()*.

Example program

Listing 61-2 demonstrates the use of the *shutdown()* SHUT_WR operation. This program is a TCP client for the *echo* service. (We presented a TCP server for the *echo* service in Section 60.3.) To shorten the implementation, we make use of functions in the Internet domain sockets library shown in Section 59.12.

> In some Linux distributions, the *echo* service is not enabled by default, and therefore we must enable it before running the program in Listing 61-2. Typically, this service is implemented internally by the *inetd(8)* daemon (Section 60.5), and, to enable the *echo* service, we must edit the file /etc/inetd.conf to uncomment the two lines corresponding to the UDP and TCP *echo* services (see Listing 60-5, on page 1249), and then send a SIGHUP signal to the *inetd* daemon.
>
> Many distributions supply the more modern *xinetd(8)* instead of *inetd(8)*. Consult the *xinetd* documentation for information about how to make the equivalent changes under *xinetd*.

As its single command-line argument, the program takes the name of the host on which the *echo* server is running. The client performs a *fork()*, yielding parent and child processes.

The client parent writes the contents of standard input to the socket, so that it can be read by the *echo* server. When the parent detects end-of-file on standard input, it uses *shutdown()* to close the writing half of its socket. This causes the *echo* server to see end-of-file, at which point it closes its socket (which causes the client child in turn to see end-of-file). The parent then terminates.

The client child reads the *echo* server's response from the socket and echoes the response on standard output. The child terminates when it sees end-of-file on the socket.

The following shows an example of what we see when running this program:

```
$ cat > tell-tale-heart.txt                         Create a file for testing
It is impossible to say how the idea entered my brain;
but once conceived, it haunted me day and night.
Type Control-D
$ ./is_echo_cl tekapo < tell-tale-heart.txt
It is impossible to say how the idea entered my brain;
but once conceived, it haunted me day and night.
```

Listing 61-2: A client for the *echo* service

── sockets/is_echo_cl.c

```c
#include "inet_sockets.h"
#include "tlpi_hdr.h"

#define BUF_SIZE 100

int
main(int argc, char *argv[])
{
    int sfd;
    ssize_t numRead;
    char buf[BUF_SIZE];

    if (argc != 2 || strcmp(argv[1], "--help") == 0)
        usageErr("%s host\n", argv[0]);

    sfd = inetConnect(argv[1], "echo", SOCK_STREAM);
    if (sfd == -1)
        errExit("inetConnect");

    switch (fork()) {
    case -1:
        errExit("fork");

    case 0:             /* Child: read server's response, echo on stdout */
        for (;;) {
            numRead = read(sfd, buf, BUF_SIZE);
            if (numRead <= 0)           /* Exit on EOF or error */
                break;
            printf("%.*s", (int) numRead, buf);
        }
        exit(EXIT_SUCCESS);

    default:            /* Parent: write contents of stdin to socket */
        for (;;) {
            numRead = read(STDIN_FILENO, buf, BUF_SIZE);
            if (numRead <= 0)           /* Exit loop on EOF or error */
                break;
            if (write(sfd, buf, numRead) != numRead)
                fatal("write() failed");
        }

        /* Close writing channel, so server sees EOF */

        if (shutdown(sfd, SHUT_WR) == -1)
            errExit("shutdown");
        exit(EXIT_SUCCESS);
    }
}
```

── sockets/is_echo_cl.c

61.3 Socket-Specific I/O System Calls: *recv()* and *send()*

The *recv()* and *send()* system calls perform I/O on connected sockets. They provide socket-specific functionality that is not available with the traditional *read()* and *write()* system calls.

```
#include <sys/socket.h>

ssize_t recv(int sockfd, void *buffer, size_t length, int flags);
                        Returns number of bytes received, 0 on EOF, or −1 on error
ssize_t send(int sockfd, const void *buffer, size_t length, int flags);
                                    Returns number of bytes sent, or −1 on error
```

The return value and the first three arguments to *recv()* and *send()* are the same as for *read()* and *write()*. The last argument, *flags*, is a bit mask that modifies the behavior of the I/O operation. For *recv()*, the bits that may be ORed in *flags* include the following:

MSG_DONTWAIT
> Perform a nonblocking *recv()*. If no data is available, then instead of blocking, return immediately with the error EAGAIN. We can obtain the same behavior by using *fcntl()* to set nonblocking mode (O_NONBLOCK) on the socket, with the difference that MSG_DONTWAIT allows us to control nonblocking behavior on a per-call basis.

MSG_OOB
> Receive out-of-band data on the socket. We briefly describe this feature in Section 61.13.1.

MSG_PEEK
> Retrieve a copy of the requested bytes from the socket buffer, but don't actually remove them from the buffer. The data can later be reread by another *recv()* or *read()* call.

MSG_WAITALL
> Normally, a *recv()* call returns the lesser of the number of bytes requested (*length*) and the number of bytes actually available in the socket. Specifying the MSG_WAITALL flag causes the system call to block until *length* bytes have been received. However, even when this flag is specified, the call may return fewer bytes than requested if: (a) a signal is caught; (b) the peer on a stream socket terminated the connection; (c) an out-of-band data byte (Section 61.13.1) was encountered; (d) the received message from a datagram socket is less than *length* bytes; or (e) an error occurs on the socket. (The MSG_WAITALL flag can replace the *readn()* function that we show in Listing 61-1, with the difference that our *readn()* function does restart itself if interrupted by a signal handler.)

All of the above flags are specified in SUSv3, except for MSG_DONTWAIT, which is nevertheless available on some other UNIX implementations. The MSG_WAITALL flag was a later addition to the sockets API, and is not present in some older implementations.

For *send()*, the bits that may be ORed in *flags* include the following:

MSG_DONTWAIT
> Perform a nonblocking *send()*. If the data can't be immediately transferred (because the socket send buffer is full), then, instead of blocking, fail with the error EAGAIN. As with *recv()*, the same effect can be achieved by setting the O_NONBLOCK flag for the socket.

MSG_MORE (since Linux 2.4.4)
> This flag is used with TCP sockets to achieve the same effect as the TCP_CORK socket option (Section 61.4), with the difference that it provides corking of data on a per-call basis. Since Linux 2.6, this flag can also be used with datagram sockets, where it has a different meaning. Data transmitted in successive *send()* or *sendto()* calls specifying MSG_MORE is packaged into a single datagram that is transmitted only when a further call is made that does not specify this flag. (Linux also provides an analogous UDP_CORK socket option that causes data from successive *send()* or *sendto()* calls to be accumulated into a single datagram that is transmitted when UDP_CORK is disabled.) The MSG_MORE flag has no effect for UNIX domain sockets.

MSG_NOSIGNAL
> When sending data on a connected stream socket, don't generate a SIGPIPE signal if the other end of the connection has been closed. Instead, the *send()* call fails with the error EPIPE. This is the same behavior as can be obtained by ignoring the SIGPIPE signal, with the difference that the MSG_NOSIGNAL flag controls the behavior on a per-call basis.

MSG_OOB
> Send out-of-band data on a stream socket. Refer to Section 61.13.1.

Of the above flags, only MSG_OOB is specified by SUSv3. SUSv4 adds a specification for MSG_NOSIGNAL. MSG_DONTWAIT is not standardized, but appears on a few other UNIX implementations. MSG_MORE is Linux-specific. The *send(2)* and *recv(2)* manual pages describe further flags that we don't cover here.

61.4 The *sendfile()* System Call

Applications such as web servers and file servers frequently need to transfer the unaltered contents of a disk file through a (connected) socket. One way to do this would be a loop of the following form:

```
while ((n = read(diskfilefd, buf, BUZ_SIZE)) > 0)
    write(sockfd, buf, n);
```

For many applications, such a loop is perfectly acceptable. However, if we frequently transfer large files via a socket, this technique is inefficient. In order to transmit the file, we must use two system calls (possibly multiple times within a loop): one to copy the file contents from the kernel buffer cache into user space, and the other to copy the user-space buffer back to kernel space in order to be transmitted via the socket. This scenario is shown on the left side of Figure 61-1. Such a two-step process is wasteful if the application doesn't perform any processing of the file contents before transmitting them. The *sendfile()* system call is designed to eliminate this inefficiency. When an application calls *sendfile()*, the file contents are transferred directly to the socket, without passing through user space, as shown on the right side of Figure 61-1. This is referred to as a *zero-copy transfer*.

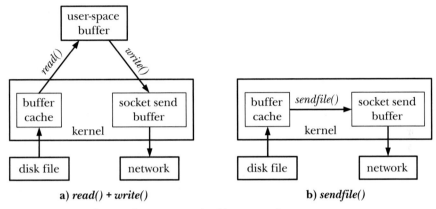

Figure 61-1: Transferring the contents of a file to a socket

```
#include <sys/sendfile.h>

ssize_t sendfile(int out_fd, int in_fd, off_t *offset, size_t count);
```
                              Returns number of bytes transferred, or −1 on error

The *sendfile()* system call transfers bytes from the file referred to by the descriptor *in_fd* to the file referred to by the descriptor *out_fd*. The *out_fd* descriptor must refer to a socket. The *in_fd* argument must refer to a file to which *mmap()* can be applied; in practice, this usually means a regular file. This somewhat restricts the use of *sendfile()*. We can use it to pass data from a file to a socket, but not vice versa. And we can't use *sendfile()* to pass data directly from one socket to another.

> Performance benefits could also be obtained if *sendfile()* could be used to transfer bytes between two regular files. On Linux 2.4 and earlier, *out_fd* could refer to a regular file. Some reworking of the underlying implementation meant that this possibility disappeared in the 2.6 kernel. Some later changes restored this feature in Linux 2.6.33.

If *offset* is not NULL, then it should point to an *off_t* value that specifies the starting file offset from which bytes should be transferred from *in_fd*. This is a value-result argument. On return, it contains the offset of the next byte following the last byte that was transferred from *in_fd*. In this case, *sendfile()* doesn't change the file offset for *in_fd*.

If *offset* is NULL, then bytes are transferred from *in_fd* starting at the current file offset, and the file offset is updated to reflect the number of bytes transferred.

The *count* argument specifies the number of bytes to be transferred. If end-of-file is encountered before *count* bytes are transferred, only the available bytes are transferred. On success, *sendfile()* returns the number of bytes actually transferred.

SUSv3 doesn't specify *sendfile()*. Versions of *sendfile()* are available on some other UNIX implementations, but the argument list is typically different from the version on Linux.

> Starting with kernel 2.6.17, Linux provides three new (nonstandard) system calls—*splice()*, *vmsplice()*, and *tee()*—that provide a superset of the functionality of *sendfile()*. See the manual pages for details.

The TCP_CORK socket option

To further improve the efficiency of TCP applications using *sendfile()*, it is sometimes useful to employ the Linux-specific TCP_CORK socket option. As an example, consider a web server delivering a page in response to a request by a web browser. The web server's response consists of two parts: HTTP headers, perhaps output using *write()*, followed by the page data, perhaps output using *sendfile()*. In this scenario, normally *two* TCP segments are transmitted: the headers are sent in the first (rather small) segment, and then the page data is sent in a second segment. This is an inefficient use of network bandwidth. It probably also creates unnecessary work for both the sending and the receiving TCP, since in many cases the HTTP headers and the page data would be small enough to fit inside a single TCP segment. The TCP_CORK option is designed to address this inefficiency.

When the TCP_CORK option is enabled on a TCP socket, all subsequent output is buffered into a single TCP segment until either the upper limit on the size of a segment is reached, the TCP_CORK option is disabled, the socket is closed, or a maximum of 200 milliseconds passes from the time that the first corked byte is written. (The timeout ensures that the corked data is transmitted if the application forgets to disable the TCP_CORK option.)

We enable and disable the TCP_CORK option using the *setsockopt()* system call (Section 61.9). The following code (which omits error checking) demonstrates the use of TCP_CORK for our hypothetical HTTP server example:

```
int optval;

/* Enable TCP_CORK option on 'sockfd' - subsequent TCP output is corked
   until this option is disabled. */

optval = 1;
setsockopt(sockfd, IPPROTO_TCP, TCP_CORK, &optval, sizeof(optval));

write(sockfd, ...);                     /* Write HTTP headers */
sendfile(sockfd, ...);                  /* Send page data */

/* Disable TCP_CORK option on 'sockfd' - corked output is now transmitted
   in a single TCP segment. */

optval = 0
setsockopt(sockfd, IPPROTO_TCP, TCP_CORK, &optval, sizeof(optval));
```

We could avoid the possibility of two segments being transmitted by building a single data buffer within our application, and then transmitting that buffer with a single *write()*. (Alternatively, we could use *writev()* to combine two distinct buffers in a single output operation.) However, if we want to combine the zero-copy efficiency of *sendfile()* with the ability to include a header as part of the first segment of transmitted file data, then we need to use TCP_CORK.

> In Section 61.3, we noted that the MSG_MORE flag provides similar functionality to TCP_CORK, but on a per-system-call basis. This is not necessarily an advantage. It is possible to set the TCP_CORK option on the socket, and then exec a program that performs output on the inherited file descriptor without being aware of the TCP_CORK option. By contrast, the use of MSG_MORE requires explicit changes to the source code of a program.
>
> FreeBSD provides an option similar to TCP_CORK in the form of TCP_NOPUSH.

61.5 Retrieving Socket Addresses

The *getsockname()* and *getpeername()* system calls return, respectively, the local address to which a socket is bound and the address of the peer socket to which the local socket is connected.

```
#include <sys/socket.h>

int getsockname(int sockfd, struct sockaddr *addr, socklen_t *addrlen);
int getpeername(int sockfd, struct sockaddr *addr, socklen_t *addrlen);
```
                                    Both return 0 on success, or −1 on error

For both calls, *sockfd* is a file descriptor referring to a socket, and *addr* is a pointer to a suitably sized buffer that is used to return a structure containing the socket address. The size and type of this structure depend on the socket domain. The *addrlen* argument is a value-result argument. Before the call, it should be initialized to the length of the buffer pointed to by *addr*; on return, it contains the number of bytes actually written to this buffer.

The *getsockname()* function returns a socket's address family and the address to which a socket is bound. This is useful if the socket was bound by another program (e.g., *inetd(8)*) and the socket file descriptor was then preserved across an *exec()*.

Calling *getsockname()* is also useful if we want to determine the ephemeral port number that the kernel assigned to a socket when performing an implicit bind of an Internet domain socket. The kernel performs an implicit bind in the following circumstances:

- after a *connect()* or a *listen()* call on a TCP socket that has not previously been bound to an address by *bind()*;
- on the first *sendto()* on a UDP socket that had not previously been bound to an address; or
- after a *bind()* call where the port number (*sin_port*) was specified as 0. In this case, the *bind()* specifies the IP address for the socket, but the kernel selects an ephemeral port number.

The *getpeername()* system call returns the address of the peer socket on a stream socket connection. This is useful primarily with TCP sockets, if the server wants to find out the address of the client that has made a connection. This information could also be obtained when the *accept()* call is performed; however, if the server was execed by the program that did the *accept()* (e.g., *inetd*), then it inherits the socket file descriptor, but the address information returned by *accept()* is no longer available.

Listing 61-3 demonstrates the use of *getsockname()* and *getpeername()*. This program employs the functions that we defined in Listing 59-9 (on page 1228), and performs the following steps:

1. Use our *inetListen()* function to create a listening socket, *listenFd*, bound to the wildcard IP address and the port specified in the program's sole command-line argument. (The port can be specified numerically or as a service name.) The *len* argument returns the length of the address structure for this socket's domain. This value is passed in a later call to *malloc()* to allocate a buffer that is used to return a socket address from calls to *getsockname()* and *getpeername()*.

2. Use our *inetConnect()* function to create a second socket, *connFd*, which is used to send a connection request to the socket created in step 1.

3. Call *accept()* on the listening socket in order to create a third socket, *acceptFd*, that is connected to the socket created in the previous step.

4. Use calls to *getsockname()* and *getpeername()* to obtain the local and peer addresses for the two connected sockets, *connFd* and *acceptFd*. After each of these calls, the program uses our *inetAddressStr()* function to convert the socket address into printable form.

5. Sleep for a few seconds so that we can run *netstat* in order to confirm the socket address information. (We describe *netstat* in Section 61.7.)

The following shell session log shows an example run of this program:

```
$ ./socknames 55555 &
getsockname(connFd):    (localhost, 32835)
getsockname(acceptFd):  (localhost, 55555)
getpeername(connFd):    (localhost, 55555)
getpeername(acceptFd):  (localhost, 32835)
[1] 8171
$ netstat -a | egrep '(Address|55555)'
Proto Recv-Q Send-Q Local Address      Foreign Address   State
tcp        0      0 *:55555            *:*               LISTEN
tcp        0      0 localhost:32835    localhost:55555   ESTABLISHED
tcp        0      0 localhost:55555    localhost:32835   ESTABLISHED
```

From the above output, we can see that the connected socket (*connFd*) was bound to the ephemeral port 32835. The *netstat* command shows us information about all three sockets created by the program, and allows us to confirm the port information for the two connected sockets, which are in the ESTABLISHED state (described in Section 61.6.3).

Listing 61-3: Using *getsockname()* and *getpeername()*

─── **sockets/socknames.c**

```c
#include "inet_sockets.h"          /* Declares our socket functions */
#include "tlpi_hdr.h"

int
main(int argc, char *argv[])
{
    int listenFd, acceptFd, connFd;
    socklen_t len;                  /* Size of socket address buffer */
    void *addr;                     /* Buffer for socket address */
    char addrStr[IS_ADDR_STR_LEN];

    if (argc != 2 || strcmp(argv[1], "--help") == 0)
        usageErr("%s service\n", argv[0]);

    listenFd = inetListen(argv[1], 5, &len);
    if (listenFd == -1)
        errExit("inetListen");

    connFd = inetConnect(NULL, argv[1], SOCK_STREAM);
    if (connFd == -1)
        errExit("inetConnect");

    acceptFd = accept(listenFd, NULL, NULL);
    if (acceptFd == -1)
        errExit("accept");

    addr = malloc(len);
    if (addr == NULL)
        errExit("malloc");

    if (getsockname(connFd, addr, &len) == -1)
        errExit("getsockname");
    printf("getsockname(connFd):   %s\n",
            inetAddressStr(addr, len, addrStr, IS_ADDR_STR_LEN));
    if (getsockname(acceptFd, addr, &len) == -1)
        errExit("getsockname");
    printf("getsockname(acceptFd): %s\n",
            inetAddressStr(addr, len, addrStr, IS_ADDR_STR_LEN));

    if (getpeername(connFd, addr, &len) == -1)
        errExit("getpeername");
    printf("getpeername(connFd):   %s\n",
            inetAddressStr(addr, len, addrStr, IS_ADDR_STR_LEN));
    if (getpeername(acceptFd, addr, &len) == -1)
        errExit("getpeername");
    printf("getpeername(acceptFd): %s\n",
            inetAddressStr(addr, len, addrStr, IS_ADDR_STR_LEN));

    sleep(30);                       /* Give us time to run netstat(8) */
    exit(EXIT_SUCCESS);
}
```

─── **sockets/socknames.c**

61.6　A Closer Look at TCP

Knowing some of the details of the operation of TCP helps us to debug applications that use TCP sockets, and, in some cases, to make such applications more efficient. In the following sections, we look at:

- the format of TCP segments;
- the TCP acknowledgement scheme;
- the TCP state machine;
- TCP connection establishment and termination; and
- the TCP TIME_WAIT state.

61.6.1　Format of a TCP Segment

Figure 61-2 shows the format of the TCP segments that are exchanged between the endpoints of a TCP connection. The meanings of these fields are as follows:

- *Source port number*: This is the port number of the sending TCP.
- *Destination port number*: This is the port number of the destination TCP.
- *Sequence number*: This is the sequence number for this segment. This is the offset of the first byte of data in this segment within the stream of data being transmitted in this direction over the connection, as described in Section 58.6.3.

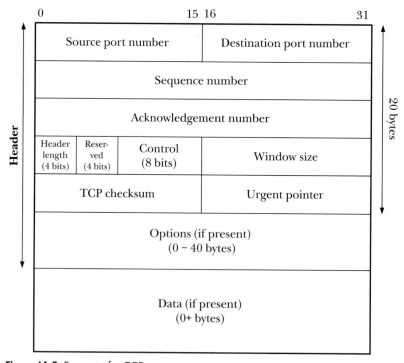

Figure 61-2: Format of a TCP segment

- *Acknowledgement number*: If the ACK bit (see below) is set, then this field contains the sequence number of the next byte of data that the receiver expects to receive from the sender.

- *Header length*: This is the length of the header, in units of 32-bit words. Since this is a 4-bit field, the total header length can be up to 60 bytes (15 words). This field enables the receiving TCP to determine the length of the variable-length *options* field and the starting point of the *data*.

- *Reserved*: This consists of 4 unused bits (must be set to 0).

- *Control bits*: This field consists of 8 bits that further specify the meaning of the segment:
  - *CWR*: the *congestion window reduced* flag.
  - *ECE*: the *explicit congestion notification echo* flag. The CWR and ECE flags are used as part of TCP/IP's Explicit Congestion Notification (ECN) algorithm. ECN is a relatively recent addition to TCP/IP and is described in RFC 3168 and in [Floyd, 1994]. ECN is implemented in Linux from kernel 2.4 onward, and enabled by placing a nonzero value in the Linux-specific /proc/sys/net/ipv4/tcp_ecn file.
  - *URG*: if set, then the *urgent pointer* field contains valid information.
  - *ACK*: if set, then the *acknowledgement number* field contains valid information (i.e., this segment acknowledges data previously sent by the peer).
  - *PSH*: push all received data to the receiving process. This flag is described in RFC 793 and in [Stevens, 1994].
  - *RST*: reset the connection. This is used to handle various error situations.
  - *SYN*: synchronize sequence numbers. Segments with this flag set are exchanged during connection establishment to allow the two TCPs to specify the initial sequence numbers to be used for transferring data in each direction.
  - *FIN*: used by a sender to indicate that it has finished sending data.

  Multiple control bits (or none at all) may be set in a segment, which allows a single segment to serve multiple purposes. For example, we'll see later that a segment with both the SYN and the ACK bits set is exchanged during TCP connection establishment.

- *Window size*: This field is used when a receiver sends an ACK to indicate the number of bytes of data that the receiver has space to accept. (This relates to the sliding window scheme briefly described in Section 58.6.3.)

- *Checksum*: This is a 16-bit checksum covering both the TCP header and the TCP data.

> The TCP checksum covers not just the TCP header and data, but also 12 bytes usually referred to as the TCP *pseudoheader*. The pseudoheader consists of the following: the source and destination IP address (4 bytes each); 2 bytes specifying the size of the TCP segment (this value is computed, but doesn't form part of either the IP or the TCP header); 1 byte containing the value 6, which is TCP's unique protocol number within the TCP/IP suite of protocols; and 1 padding byte containing 0 (so that the length of the pseudoheader is a multiple of 16 bits).

The purpose of including the pseudoheader in the checksum calculation is to allow the receiving TCP to double-check that an incoming segment has arrived at the correct destination (i.e., that IP has not wrongly accepted a datagram that was addressed to another host or passed TCP a packet that should have gone to another upper layer). UDP calculates the checksum in its packet headers in a similar manner and for similar reasons. See [Stevens, 1994] for further details on the pseudoheader.

- *Urgent pointer*: If the URG control bit is set, then this field indicates the location of so-called urgent data within the stream of data being transmitted from the sender to the receiver. We briefly discuss urgent data in Section 61.13.1.

- *Options*: This is a variable-length field containing options controlling the operation of the TCP connection.

- *Data*: This field contains the user data transmitted in this segment. This field may be of length 0 if this segment doesn't contain any data (e.g., if it is simply an ACK segment).

61.6.2 TCP Sequence Numbers and Acknowledgements

Each byte that is transmitted over a TCP connection is assigned a logical sequence number by TCP. (Each of the two streams in a connection has its own sequence numbering.) When a segment is transmitted, its *sequence number* field is set to the logical offset of the first byte of data in the segment within the stream of data being transmitted in this direction over the connection. This allows the receiving TCP to assemble the received segments in the correct order, and to indicate which data was received when sending an acknowledgement to the sender.

To implement reliable communication, TCP uses positive acknowledgements; that is, when a segment is successfully received, an acknowledgement message (i.e., a segment with the ACK bit set) is sent from the receiving TCP to the sending TCP, as shown in Figure 61-3. The *acknowledgement number* field of this message is set to indicate the logical sequence number of the next byte of data that the receiver expects to receive. (In other words, the value in the acknowledgement number field is the sequence number of the last byte in the segment that it acknowledges, plus 1.)

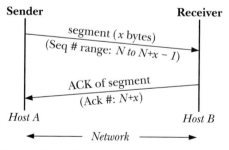

Figure 61-3: Acknowledgements in TCP

When the sending TCP transmits a segment, it sets a timer. If an acknowledgement is not received before the timer expires, the segment is retransmitted.

Figure 61-3 and later similar diagrams are intended to illustrate the exchange of TCP segments between two endpoints. An implicit time dimension is assumed when reading these diagrams from top to bottom.

61.6.3 TCP State Machine and State Transition Diagram

Maintaining a TCP connection requires the coordination of the TCPs at both ends of the connection. To reduce the complexity of this task, a TCP endpoint is modeled as a *state machine*. This means that the TCP can be in one of a fixed set of *states*, and it moves from one state to another in response to *events*, such as system calls by the application above the TCP or the arrival of TCP segments from the peer TCP. The TCP states are the following:

- LISTEN: The TCP is waiting for a connection request from a peer TCP.

- SYN_SENT: The TCP has sent a SYN on behalf of an application performing an active open and is waiting for a reply from the peer in order to complete the connection.

- SYN_RECV: The TCP, formerly in the LISTEN state, has received a SYN and has responded with a SYN/ACK (i.e., a TCP segment with both the SYN and ACK bits set), and is now waiting for an ACK from the peer TCP in order to complete the connection.

- ESTABLISHED: Establishment of the connection to the peer TCP has been completed. Data segments can now be exchanged in either direction between the two TCPs.

- FIN_WAIT1: The application has closed the connection. The TCP has sent a FIN to the peer TCP in order to terminate its side of the connection and is waiting for an ACK from the peer. This and the next three states are associated with an application performing an active close—that is, the first application to close its side of the connection.

- FIN_WAIT2: The TCP, formerly in the FIN_WAIT1 state, has now received an ACK from the peer TCP.

- CLOSING: The TCP, formerly awaiting an ACK in the FIN_WAIT1 state, instead received a FIN from its peer indicating that the peer simultaneously tried to perform an active close. (In other words, the two TCPs sent FIN segments at almost the same time. This is a rare scenario.)

- TIME_WAIT: Having done an active close, the TCP has received a FIN, indicating that the peer TCP has performed a passive close. This TCP now spends a fixed period of time in the TIME_WAIT state, in order to ensure reliable termination of the TCP connection and to ensure that any old duplicate segments expire in the network before a new incarnation of the same connection is created. (We explain the TIME_WAIT state in more detail in Section 61.6.7.) When this fixed time period expires, the connection is closed, and the associated kernel resources are freed.

- CLOSE_WAIT: The TCP has received a FIN from the peer TCP. This and the following state are associated with an application performing a passive close—that is, the second application to close the connection.

- LAST_ACK: The application performed a passive close, and the TCP, formerly in the CLOSE_WAIT state, sent a FIN to the peer TCP and is waiting for it to be acknowledged. When this ACK is received, the connection is closed, and the associated kernel resources are freed.

To the above states, RFC 793 adds one further, fictional state, CLOSED, representing the state when there is no connection (i.e., no kernel resources are allocated to describe a TCP connection).

> In the above list we use the spellings for the TCP states as defined in the Linux source code. These differ slightly from the spellings in RFC 793.

Figure 61-4 shows the *state transition diagram* for TCP. (This figure is based on diagrams in RFC 793 and [Stevens et al., 2004].) This diagram shows how a TCP endpoint moves from one state to another in response to various events. Each arrow indicates a possible transition and is labeled with the event that triggers the transition. This label is either an action by the application (in boldface) or the string *recv*, indicating the receipt of a segment from the peer TCP. As a TCP moves from one state to another, it may transmit a segment to the peer, and this is indicated by the *send* label on the transition. For example, the arrow for the transition from the ESTABLISHED to the FIN_WAIT1 state shows that the triggering event is a *close()* by the local application, and that, during the transition, the TCP sends a FIN segment to its peer.

In Figure 61-4, the usual transition path for a client TCP is shown with heavy solid arrows, and the usual transition path for a server TCP is shown with heavy dashed arrows. (Other arrows indicate paths less traveled.) Looking at the parenthetical numbering on the arrows in these paths, we can see that the segments sent and received by the two TCPs are mirror images of one another. (After the ESTABLISHED state, the paths traveled by the server TCP and the client TCP may be the opposite of those indicated, if it is the server that performs the active close.)

> Figure 61-4 doesn't show all possible transitions for the TCP state machine; it illustrates just those of principal interest. A more detailed TCP state transition diagram can be found at *http://www.cl.cam.ac.uk/~pes20/Netsem/poster.pdf*.

61.6.4 TCP Connection Establishment

At the sockets API level, two stream sockets are connected via the following steps (see Figure 56-1, on page 1156):

1. The server calls *listen()* to perform a passive open of a socket, and then calls *accept()*, which blocks until a connection is established.

2. The client calls *connect()* to perform an active open of a socket in order to establish a connection to the server's passive socket.

The steps performed by TCP to establish a connection are shown in Figure 61-5. These steps are often referred to as the *three-way handshake*, since three segments pass between the two TCPs. The steps are as follows:

1. The *connect()* causes the client TCP to send a SYN segment to the server TCP. This segment informs the server TCP of the client TCP's initial sequence number

(labeled *M* in the diagram). This information is necessary because sequence numbers don't begin at 0, as noted in Section 58.6.3.

2. The server TCP must both acknowledge the client TCP's SYN segment and inform the client TCP of its own initial sequence number (labeled *N* in the diagram). (Two sequence numbers are required because a stream socket is bidirectional.) The server TCP can perform both operations by returning a single segment with both the SYN and the ACK control bits set. (We say that the ACK is *piggybacked* on the SYN.)

3. The client TCP sends an ACK segment to acknowledge the server TCP's SYN segment.

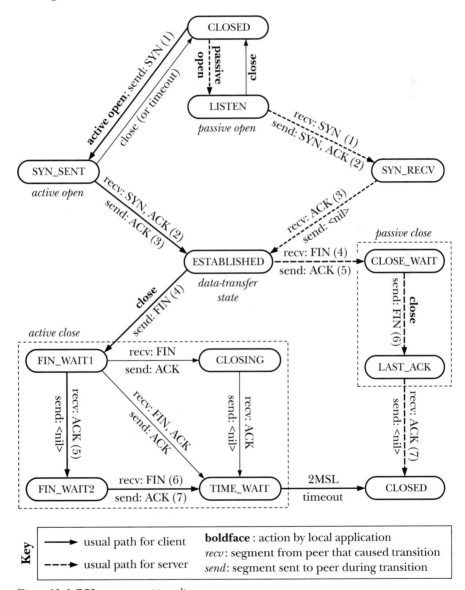

Figure 61-4: TCP state transition diagram

The SYN segments exchanged in the first two steps of the three-way handshake may contain information in the *options* field of the TCP header that is used to determine various parameters for the connection. See [Stevens et al., 2004], [Stevens, 1994], and [Wright & Stevens, 1995] for details.

The labels inside angle brackets (e.g., <LISTEN>) in Figure 61-5 indicate the states of the TCPs on either side of the connection.

The SYN flag consumes a byte of the sequence-number space for the connection. This is necessary so that this flag can be acknowledged unambiguously, since segments with this flag set may also contain data bytes. This is why we show the acknowledgement of the *SYN M* segment as *ACK M+1* in Figure 61-5.

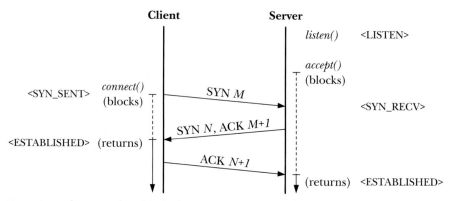

Figure 61-5: Three-way handshake for TCP connection establishment

61.6.5   TCP Connection Termination

Closing a TCP connection normally occurs in the following manner:

1. An application on one end of the connection performs a *close()*. (This is often, but not necessarily, the client.) We say that this application is performing an *active close*.

2. Later, the application on the other end of the connection (the server) also performs a *close()*. This is termed a *passive close*.

Figure 61-6 shows the corresponding steps performed by the underlying TCPs (here, we assume that it is the client that does the active close). These steps are as follows:

1. The client performs an active close, which causes the client TCP to send a FIN to the server TCP.

2. After receipt of the FIN, the server TCP responds with an ACK. Any subsequent attempt by the server to *read()* from the socket yields end-of-file (i.e., a 0 return).

3. When the server later closes its end of the connection, the server TCP sends a FIN to the client TCP.

4. The client TCP responds with an ACK to acknowledge the server's FIN.

As with the SYN flag, and for the same reasons, the FIN flag consumes a byte of the sequence-number space for the connection. This is why we show the acknowledgement of the *FIN M* segment as *ACK M+1* in Figure 61-6.

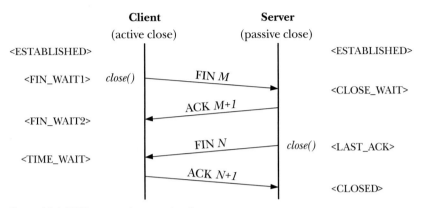

Figure 61-6: TCP connection termination

61.6.6 Calling *shutdown()* on a TCP Socket

The discussion in the preceding section assumed a full-duplex close; that is, an application closes both the sending and receiving channels of the TCP socket using *close()*. As noted in Section 61.2, we can use *shutdown()* to close just one channel of the connection (a half-duplex close). This section notes some specific details for *shutdown()* on a TCP socket.

Specifying *how* as SHUT_WR or SHUT_RDWR initiates the TCP connection termination sequence (i.e., the active close) described in Section 61.6.5, regardless of whether there are other file descriptors referring to the socket. Once this sequence has been initiated, the local TCP moves into the FIN_WAIT1 state, and then into the FIN_WAIT2 state, while the peer TCP moves into the CLOSE_WAIT state (Figure 61-6). If *how* is specified as SHUT_WR, then, since the socket file descriptor remains valid and the reading half of the connection remains open, the peer can continue to send data back to us.

The SHUT_RD operation can't be meaningfully used with TCP sockets. This is because most TCP implementations don't provide the expected behavior for SHUT_RD, and the effect of SHUT_RD varies across implementations. On Linux and a few other implementations, following a SHUT_RD (and after any outstanding data has been read), a *read()* returns end-of-file, as we expect from the description of SHUT_RD in Section 61.2. However, if the peer application subsequently writes data on its socket, then it is still possible to read that data on the local socket.

On some other implementations (e.g., the BSDs), SHUT_RD does indeed cause subsequent calls to *read()* to always return 0. However, on those implementations, if the peer continues to *write()* to the socket, then the data channel will eventually fill until the point where a further (blocking) call to *write()* by the peer will block. (With UNIX domain stream sockets, a peer would receive a SIGPIPE signal and the EPIPE error if it continued writing to its socket after a SHUT_RD had been performed on the local socket.)

In summary, the use of SHUT_RD should be avoided for portable TCP applications.

61.6.7 The TIME_WAIT State

The TCP TIME_WAIT state is a frequent source of confusion in network programming. Looking at Figure 61-4, we can see that a TCP performing an active close goes through this state. The TIME_WAIT state exists to serve two purposes:

- to implement reliable connection termination; and
- to allow expiration of old duplicate segments in the network so that they are not accepted by a new incarnation of the connection.

The TIME_WAIT state differs from the other states in that the event that causes a transition out of this state (to CLOSED) is a timeout. This timeout has a duration of twice the MSL (2MSL), where MSL (*maximum segment lifetime*) is the assumed maximum lifetime of a TCP segment in the network.

> An 8-bit time-to-live (TTL) field in the IP header ensures that all IP packets are eventually discarded if they don't reach their destination within a fixed number of hops (routers traversed) while traveling from the source to the destination host. The MSL is an estimate of the maximum time that an IP packet could take to exceed the TTL limit. Since it is represented using 8 bits, the TTL permits a maximum of 255 hops. Normally, an IP packet requires considerably fewer hops than this to complete its journey. A packet could encounter this limit because of certain types of router anomalies (e.g., a router configuration problem) that cause the packet to get caught in a network loop until it exceeds the TTL limit.

The BSD sockets implementation assumes a value of 30 seconds for the MSL, and Linux follows the BSD norm. Thus, the TIME_WAIT state has a lifetime of 60 seconds on Linux. However, RFC 1122 recommends a value of 2 minutes for the MSL, and, on implementations following this recommendation, the TIME_WAIT state can thus last 4 minutes.

We can understand the first purpose of the TIME_WAIT state—ensuring reliable connection termination—by looking at Figure 61-6. In this diagram, we can see that four segments are usually exchanged during the termination of a TCP connection. The last of these is an ACK sent from the TCP performing the active close to the TCP performing the passive close. Suppose that this ACK gets lost in the network. If this occurs, then the TCP performing the passive close will eventually retransmit its FIN. Having the TCP that performs the active close remain in the TIME_WAIT state for a fixed period ensures that it is available to resend the final ACK in this case. If the TCP that performs the active close did not still exist, then—since it wouldn't have any state information for the connection—the TCP protocol would respond to the resent FIN by sending an RST (reset) segment to the TCP performing the passive close, and this RST would be interpreted as an error. (This explains why the duration of the TIME_WAIT state is *twice* the MSL: one MSL for the final ACK to reach the peer TCP, plus a further MSL in case a further FIN must be sent.)

> An equivalent of the TIME_WAIT state is not required for the TCP performing the passive close, because it is the initiator of the final exchange in the connection termination. After sending the FIN, this TCP will wait for the ACK from its peer, and retransmit the FIN if its timer expires before the ACK is received.

To understand the second purpose of the TIME_WAIT state—ensuring the expiration of old duplicate segments in the network—we must remember that the retransmission algorithm used by TCP means that duplicate segments may be generated, and that, depending on routing decisions, these duplicates could arrive after the connection has been closed. For example, suppose that we have a TCP connection between two socket addresses, say, 204.152.189.116 port 21 (the FTP port) and 200.0.0.1 port 50,000. Suppose also that this connection is closed, and that later a new connection is established using exactly the same IP addresses and ports. This is referred to as a new incarnation of the connection. In this case, TCP must ensure that no old duplicate segments from the previous incarnation are accepted as valid data in the new incarnation. This is done by preventing a new incarnation from being established while there is an existing TCP in the TIME_WAIT state on one of the endpoints.

A frequent question posted to online forums is how to disable the TIME_WAIT state, since it can lead to the error EADDRINUSE ("Address already in use") when a restarted server tries to bind a socket to an address that has a TCP in the TIME_WAIT state. Although there are ways of doing this (see [Stevens et al., 2004]), and also ways of assassinating a TCP in this state (i.e., causing the TIME_WAIT state to terminate prematurely, see [Snader, 2000]), this should be avoided, since it would thwart the reliability guarantees that the TIME_WAIT state provides. In Section 61.10, we look at the use of the SO_REUSEADDR socket option, which can be used to avoid the usual causes of the EADDRINUSE error, while still allowing the TIME_WAIT to provide its reliability guarantees.

61.7 Monitoring Sockets: *netstat*

The *netstat* program displays the state of Internet and UNIX domain sockets on a system. It is a useful debugging tool when writing socket applications. Most UNIX implementations provide a version of *netstat*, although there is some variation in the syntax of its command-line arguments across implementations.

By default, when executed with no command-line options, *netstat* displays information for connected sockets in both the UNIX and Internet domains. We can use a number of command-line options to change the information displayed. Some of these options are listed in Table 61-1.

Table 61-1: Options for the *netstat* command

Option	Description
-a	Display information about all sockets, including listening sockets
-e	Display extended information (includes user ID of socket owner)
-c	Redisplay socket information continuously (each second)
-l	Display information only about listening sockets
-n	Display IP addresses, port numbers, and usernames in numerical form
-p	Show the process ID and name of program to which socket belongs
--inet	Display information for Internet domain sockets
--tcp	Display information for Internet domain TCP (stream) sockets
--udp	Display information for Internet domain UDP (datagram) sockets
--unix	Display information for UNIX domain sockets

Here is an abridged example of the output that we see when using *netstat* to list all Internet domain sockets on the system:

```
$ netstat -a --inet
Active Internet connections (servers and established)
Proto Recv-Q Send-Q Local Address      Foreign Address    State
tcp        0      0 *:50000            *:*                LISTEN
tcp        0      0 *:55000            *:*                LISTEN
tcp        0      0 localhost:smtp     *:*                LISTEN
tcp        0      0 localhost:32776    localhost:58000    TIME_WAIT
tcp    34767      0 localhost:55000    localhost:32773    ESTABLISHED
tcp        0 115680 localhost:32773    localhost:55000    ESTABLISHED
udp        0      0 localhost:61000    localhost:60000    ESTABLISHED
udp      684      0 *:60000            *:*
```

For each Internet domain socket, we see the following information:

- Proto: This is the socket protocol—for example, tcp or udp.
- Recv-Q: This is the number of bytes in the socket receive buffer that are as yet unread by the local application. For UDP sockets, this field counts not just data, but also bytes in UDP headers and other metadata.
- Send-Q: This is the number of bytes queued for transmission in the socket send buffer. As with the Recv-Q field, for UDP sockets, this field includes bytes in UDP headers and other metadata.
- Local Address: This is the address to which the socket is bound, expressed in the form *host-IP-address:port*. By default, both components of the address are displayed as names, unless the numeric values can't be resolved to corresponding host and service names. An asterisk (*) in the host part of the address means the wildcard IP address.
- Foreign Address: This is the address of the peer socket to which this socket is bound. The string *:* indicates no peer address.
- State: This is the current state of the socket. For a TCP socket, this state is one of those described in Section 61.6.3.

For further details, see the *netstat(8)* manual page.

Various Linux-specific files in the directory /proc/net allow a program to read much of the same information that is displayed by *netstat*. These files are named tcp, udp, tcp6, udp6, and unix, with the obvious purposes. For further details, see the *proc(5)* manual page.

61.8 Using *tcpdump* to Monitor TCP Traffic

The *tcpdump* program is a useful debugging tool that allows the superuser to monitor the Internet traffic on a live network, generating a real-time textual equivalent of diagrams such as Figure 61-3. Despite its name, *tcpdump* can be used to display traffic for all kinds of network packets (e.g., TCP segments, UDP datagrams, and ICMP packets). For each network packet, *tcpdump* displays information such as timestamps, the source and destination IP addresses, and further protocol-specific details. It is possible to select the packets to be monitored by protocol type, source and destination IP address and port number, and a range of other criteria. Full details are provided in the *tcpdump* manual page.

> The *wireshark* (formerly *ethereal*; *http://www.wireshark.org/*) program performs a similar task to *tcpdump*, but displays traffic information via a graphical interface.

For each TCP segment, *tcpdump* displays a line of the following form:

---

src > *dst*: *flags data-seqno ack window urg <options>*

These fields have the following meanings:

- *src*: This is the source IP address and port.
- *dst*: This is the destination IP address and port.
- *flags*: This field contains zero or more of the following letters, each of which corresponds to one of the TCP control bits described in Section 61.6.1: S (SYN), F (FIN), P (PSH), R (RST), E (ECE), and C (CWR).
- *data-seqno*: This is the range of the sequence-number space covered by the bytes in this packet.

  > By default, the sequence-number range is displayed relative to the first byte monitored for this direction of the data stream. The *tcpdump* −*S* option causes sequence numbers to be displayed in absolute format.

- *ack*: This is a string of the form "ack *num*" indicating the sequence number of the next byte expected from the other direction on this connection.
- *window*: This is a string of the form "win *num*" indicating the number of bytes of receive buffer space available for transmission in the opposite direction on this connection.
- *urg*: This is a string of the form "urg *num*" indicating that this segment contains urgent data at the specified offset within the segment.
- *options*: This string describes any TCP options contained in the segment.

The *src*, *dst*, and *flags* fields always appear. The remaining fields are displayed only if appropriate.

The shell session below shows how *tcpdump* can be used to monitor the traffic between a client (running on the host pukaki) and a server (running on tekapo). In this shell session, we use two *tcpdump* options that make the output less verbose. The −*t* option suppresses the display of timestamp information. The −*N* option causes hostnames to be displayed without a qualifying domain name. Furthermore, for brevity, and because we don't describe the details of TCP options, we have removed the *options* fields from the lines of *tcpdump* output.

The server operates on port 55555, so our *tcpdump* command selects traffic for that port. The output shows the three segments exchanged during connection establishment:

```
$ sudo tcpdump -t -N 'port 55555'
IP pukaki.60391 > tekapo.55555: S 3412991013:3412991013(0) win 5840
IP tekapo.55555 > pukaki.60391: S 1149562427:1149562427(0) ack 3412991014 win 5792
IP pukaki.60391 > tekapo.55555: . ack 1 win 5840
```

These three segments are the SYN, SYN/ACK, and ACK segments exchanged for the three-way handshake (see Figure 61-5).

In the following output, the client sends the server two messages, containing 16 and 32 bytes, respectively, and the server responds in each case with a 4-byte message:

```
IP pukaki.60391 > tekapo.55555: P 1:17(16) ack 1 win 5840
IP tekapo.55555 > pukaki.60391: . ack 17 win 1448
IP tekapo.55555 > pukaki.60391: P 1:5(4) ack 17 win 1448
IP pukaki.60391 > tekapo.55555: . ack 5 win 5840
IP pukaki.60391 > tekapo.55555: P 17:49(32) ack 5 win 5840
IP tekapo.55555 > pukaki.60391: . ack 49 win 1448
IP tekapo.55555 > pukaki.60391: P 5:9(4) ack 49 win 1448
IP pukaki.60391 > tekapo.55555: . ack 9 win 5840
```

For each of the data segments, we see an ACK sent in the opposite direction.

Lastly, we show the segments exchanged during connection termination (first, the client closes its end of the connection, and then the server closes the other end):

```
IP pukaki.60391 > tekapo.55555: F 49:49(0) ack 9 win 5840
IP tekapo.55555 > pukaki.60391: . ack 50 win 1448
IP tekapo.55555 > pukaki.60391: F 9:9(0) ack 50 win 1448
IP pukaki.60391 > tekapo.55555: . ack 10 win 5840
```

The above output shows the four segments exchanged during connection termination (see Figure 61-6).

61.9 Socket Options

Socket options affect various features of the operation of a socket. In this book, we describe just a couple of the many socket options that are available. An extensive discussion covering most standard socket options is provided in [Stevens et al., 2004]. See the *tcp(7)*, *udp(7)*, *ip(7)*, *socket(7)*, and *unix(7)* manual pages for additional Linux-specific details.

The *setsockopt()* and *getsockopt()* system calls set and retrieve socket options.

```
#include <sys/socket.h>

int getsockopt(int sockfd, int level, int optname, void *optval,
               socklen_t *optlen);
int setsockopt(int sockfd, int level, int optname, const void *optval,
               socklen_t optlen);
```
                                              Both return 0 on success, or −1 on error

For both *setsockopt()* and *getsockopt()*, *sockfd* is a file descriptor referring to a socket.

The *level* argument specifies the protocol level to which the socket option applies—for example, IP or TCP. For most of the socket options that we describe in this book, *level* is set to SOL_SOCKET, which indicates an option that applies at the sockets API level.

The *optname* argument identifies the option whose value we wish to set or retrieve. The *optval* argument is a pointer to a buffer used to specify or return the option value; this argument is a pointer to an integer or a structure, depending on the option.

The *optlen* argument specifies the size (in bytes) of the buffer pointed to by *optval*. For *setsockopt()*, this argument is passed by value. For *getsockopt()*, *optlen* is a value-result argument. Before the call, we initialize it to the size of the buffer pointed to by *optval*; upon return, it is set to the number of bytes actually written to that buffer.

As detailed in Section 61.11, the socket file descriptor returned by a call to *accept()* inherits the values of settable socket options from the listening socket.

Socket options are associated with an open file description (refer to Figure 5-2, on page 95). This means that file descriptors duplicated as a consequence of *dup()* (or similar) or *fork()* share the same set of socket options.

A simple example of a socket option is SO_TYPE, which can be used to find out the type of a socket, as follows:

```
int optval;
socklen_t optlen;

optlen = sizeof(optval);
if (getsockopt(sfd, SOL_SOCKET, SO_TYPE, &optval, &optlen) == -1)
    errExit("getsockopt");
```

After this call, *optval* contains the socket type—for example, SOCK_STREAM or SOCK_DGRAM. Using this call can be useful in a program that inherited a socket file descriptor across an *exec()*—for example, a program execed by *inetd*—since that program may not know which type of socket it inherited.

SO_TYPE is an example of a read-only socket option. It is not possible to use *setsockopt()* to change a socket's type.

61.10 The SO_REUSEADDR Socket Option

The SO_REUSEADDR socket option serves a number of purposes (see Chapter 7 of [Stevens et al., 2004] for details). We'll concern ourselves with only one common use: to avoid the EADDRINUSE ("Address already in use") error when a TCP server is restarted and tries to bind a socket to a port that currently has an associated TCP. There are two scenarios in which this usually occurs:

- A previous invocation of the server that was connected to a client performed an active close, either by calling *close()*, or by crashing (e.g., it was killed by a signal). This leaves a TCP endpoint that remains in the TIME_WAIT state until the 2MSL timeout expires.

- A previous invocation of the server created a child process to handle a connection to a client. Later, the server terminated, while the child continues to serve the client, and thus maintain a TCP endpoint using the server's well-known port.

In both of these scenarios, the outstanding TCP endpoint is unable to accept new connections. Nevertheless, in both cases, by default, most TCP implementations prevent a new listening socket from being bound to the server's well-known port.

> The EADDRINUSE error doesn't usually occur with clients, since they typically use an ephemeral port that won't be one of those ports currently in the TIME_WAIT state. However, if a client binds to a specific port number, then it also can encounter this error.

To understand the operation of the SO_REUSEADDR socket option, it can help to return to our earlier telephone analogy for stream sockets (Section 56.5). Like a telephone call (we ignore the notion of conference calls), a TCP socket connection is identifiable by the *combination* of a pair of connected endpoints. The operation of *accept()* is analogous to the task performed by a telephone operator on an internal company switchboard ("a server"). When an external telephone call arrives, the operator transfers it to some internal telephone ("a new socket") within the organization. From an outside perspective, there is no way of identifying that internal telephone. When multiple external calls are being handled by the switchboard, the only way of distinguishing them is via the combination of the external caller's number and the switchboard number. (The latter is necessary when we consider that there will be multiple company switchboards within the telephone network as a whole.) Analogously, each time we accept a socket connection on a listening socket, a new socket is created. All of these sockets are associated with the same local address as the listening socket. The only way of distinguishing them is via their connections to different peer sockets.

In other words, a connected TCP socket is identified by a 4-tuple (i.e., a combination of four values) of the following form:

```
{ local-IP-address, local-port, foreign-IP-address, foreign-port }
```

The TCP specification requires that each such tuple be unique; that is, only one corresponding connection incarnation ("telephone call") can exist. The problem is that most implementations (including Linux) enforce a stricter constraint: a local port can't be reused (i.e., specified in a call to *bind()*) if any TCP connection incarnation with a matching local port exists on the host. This rule is enforced even when the TCP could not accept new connections, as in the scenarios described at the start of this section.

Enabling the SO_REUSEADDR socket option relaxes this constraint, bringing it closer to the TCP requirement. By default, this option has the value 0, meaning that it is disabled. We enable the option by giving it a nonzero value before binding a socket, as shown in Listing 61-4.

Setting the SO_REUSEADDR option means that we can bind a socket to a local port even if another TCP is bound to the same port in either of the scenarios described at the start of this section. Most TCP servers should enable this option. We have already seen some examples of the use of this option in Listing 59-6 (page 1221) and Listing 59-9 (page 1228).

Listing 61-4: Setting the SO_REUSEADDR socket option

```
int sockfd, optval;

sockfd = socket(AF_INET, SOCK_STREAM, 0);
if (sockfd == -1)
    errExit("socket");

optval = 1;
if (setsockopt(sockfd, SOL_SOCKET, SO_REUSEADDR, &optval,
        sizeof(optval)) == -1)
    errExit("socket");

if (bind(sockfd, &addr, addrlen) == -1)
    errExit("bind");
if (listen(sockfd, backlog) == -1)
    errExit("listen");
```

61.11 Inheritance of Flags and Options Across *accept()*

Various flags and settings can be associated with open file descriptions and file descriptors (Section 5.4). Furthermore, as described in Section 61.9, various options can be set for a socket. If these flags and options are set on a listening socket, are they inherited by the new socket returned by *accept()*? We describe the details here.

On Linux, the following attributes are not inherited by the new file descriptor returned by *accept()*:

- The status flags associated with an open file description—the flags that can be altered using the *fcntl()* F_SETFL operation (Section 5.3). These include flags such as O_NONBLOCK and O_ASYNC.
- The file descriptor flags—the flags that can be altered using the *fcntl()* F_SETFD operation. The only such flag is the close-on-exec flag (FD_CLOEXEC, described in Section 27.4).
- The *fcntl()* F_SETOWN (owner process ID) and F_SETSIG (generated signal) file descriptor attributes associated with signal-driven I/O (Section 63.3).

On the other hand, the new descriptor returned by *accept()* inherits a copy of most of the socket options that can be set using *setsockopt()* (Section 61.9).

SUSv3 is silent on the details described here, and the inheritance rules for the new connected socket returned by *accept()* vary across UNIX implementations. Most notably, on some UNIX implementations, if open file status flags such as O_NONBLOCK and O_ASYNC are set on a listening socket, then they are inherited by the new socket returned by *accept()*. For portability, it may be necessary to explicitly reset these attributes on a socket returned by *accept()*.

61.12 TCP Versus UDP

Given that TCP provides reliable delivery of data, while UDP does not, an obvious question is, "Why use UDP at all?" The answer to this question is covered at some length in Chapter 22 of [Stevens et al., 2004]. Here, we summarize some of the points that may lead us to choose UDP over TCP:

- A UDP server can receive (and reply to) datagrams from multiple clients, without needing to create and terminate a connection for each client (i.e., transmission of single messages using UDP has a lower overhead than is required when using TCP).

- For simple request-response communications, UDP can be faster than TCP, since it doesn't require connection establishment and termination. Appendix A of [Stevens, 1996] notes that in the best-case scenario, the time using TCP is

    ```
    2 * RTT + SPT
    ```

    In this formula, RTT is the round-trip time (the time required to send a request and receive a response), and SPT is the time spent by the server processing the request. (On a wide area network, the SPT value may be small compared to the RTT.) For UDP, the best-case scenario for a single request-response communication is

    ```
    RTT + SPT
    ```

    This is one RTT less than the time required for TCP. Since the RTT between hosts separated by large (i.e., intercontinental) distances or many intervening routers is typically several tenths of a second, this difference can make UDP attractive for some types of request-response communication. DNS is a good example of an application that uses UDP for this reason—using UDP allows name lookup to be performed by transmitting a single packet in each direction between servers.

- UDP sockets permit broadcasting and multicasting. *Broadcasting* allows a sender to transmit a datagram to the same destination port on all of the hosts connected to a network. *Multicasting* is similar, but allows a datagram to be sent to a specified set of hosts. For further details see Chapters 21 and 22 of [Stevens et al., 2004].

- Certain types of applications (e.g., streaming video and audio transmission) can function acceptably without the reliability provided by TCP. On the other hand, the delay that may occur after TCP tries to recover from a lost segment may result in transmission delays that are unacceptably long. (A delay in streaming media transmission may be worse than a brief loss of the transmission stream.) Therefore, such applications may prefer UDP, and adopt application-specific recovery strategies to deal with occasional packet loss.

An application that uses UDP, but nevertheless requires reliability, must implement reliability features itself. Usually, this requires at least sequence numbers, acknowledgements, retransmission of lost packets, and duplicate detection. An example of how to do this is shown in [Stevens et al., 2004]. However, if more advanced features such as flow control and congestion control are also required, then it is probably best to use TCP instead. Trying to implement all of these features on top of UDP is complex, and, even when well implemented, the result is unlikely to perform better than TCP.

61.13 Advanced Features

UNIX and Internet domain sockets have many other features that we have not detailed in this book. We summarize a few of these features in this section. For full details, see [Stevens et al., 2004].

61.13.1 Out-of-Band Data

Out-of-band data is a feature of stream sockets that allows a sender to mark transmitted data as high priority; that is, the receiver can obtain notification of the availability of out-of-band data without needing to read all of the intervening data in the stream. This feature is used in programs such as *telnet*, *rlogin*, and *ftp* to make it possible to abort previously transmitted commands. Out-of-band data is sent and received using the MSG_OOB flag in calls to *send()* and *recv()*. When a socket receives notification of the availability of out-of-band data, the kernel generates the SIGURG signal for the socket owner (normally the process using the socket), as set by the *fcntl()* F_SETOWN operation.

When employed with TCP sockets, at most 1 byte of data may be marked as being out-of-band at any one time. If the sender transmits an additional byte of out-of-band data before the receiver has processed the previous byte, then the indication for the earlier out-of-band byte is lost.

> TCP's limitation of out-of-band data to a single byte is an artifact of the mismatch between the generic out-of-band model of the sockets API and its specific implementation using TCP's *urgent mode*. We touched on TCP's urgent mode when looking at the format of TCP segments in Section 61.6.1. TCP indicates the presence of urgent (out-of-band) data by setting the URG bit in the TCP header and setting the urgent pointer field to point to the urgent data. However, TCP has no way of indicating the length of an urgent data sequence, so the urgent data is considered to consist of a single byte.
>
> Further information about TCP urgent data can be found in RFC 793.

Under some UNIX implementations, out-of-band data is supported for UNIX domain stream sockets. Linux doesn't support this.

The use of out-of-band data is nowadays discouraged, and it may be unreliable in some circumstances (see [Gont & Yourtchenko, 2009]). An alternative is to maintain a pair of stream sockets for communication. One of these is used for normal communication, while the other is used for high-priority communication. An application can monitor both channels using one of the techniques described in Chapter 63. This approach allows multiple bytes of priority data to be transmitted. Furthermore, it can be employed with stream sockets in any communication domain (e.g., UNIX domain sockets).

61.13.2 The *sendmsg()* and *recvmsg()* System Calls

The *sendmsg()* and *recvmsg()* system calls are the most general purpose of the socket I/O system calls. The *sendmsg()* system call can do everything that is done by *write()*, *send()*, and *sendto()*; the *recvmsg()* system call can do everything that is done by *read()*, *recv()*, and *recvfrom()*. In addition, these calls allow the following:

- We can perform scatter-gather I/O, as with *readv()* and *writev()* (Section 5.7). When we use *sendmsg()* to perform gather output on a datagram socket (or *writev()* on a connected datagram socket), a single datagram is generated. Conversely, *recvmsg()* (and *readv()*) can be used to perform scatter input on a datagram socket, dispersing the bytes of a single datagram into multiple user-space buffers.

- We can transmit messages containing domain-specific *ancillary data* (also known as control information). Ancillary data can be passed via both stream and datagram sockets. We describe some examples of ancillary data below.

> Linux 2.6.33 adds a new system call, *recvmmsg()*. This system call is similar to *recvmsg()*, but allows multiple datagrams to be received in a single system call. This reduces the system-call overhead in applications that deal with high levels of network traffic. An analogous *sendmmsg()* system call is likely to be added in a future kernel version.

61.13.3 Passing File Descriptors

Using *sendmsg()* and *recvmsg()*, we can pass ancillary data containing a file descriptor from one process to another process on the same host via a UNIX domain socket. Any type of file descriptor can be passed in this manner—for example, one obtained from a call to *open()* or *pipe()*. An example that is more relevant to sockets is that a master server could accept a client connection on a TCP listening socket and pass that descriptor to one of the members of a pool of server child processes (Section 60.4), which would then respond to the client request.

Although this technique is commonly referred to as passing a file descriptor, what is really being passed between the two processes is a reference to the same open file description (Figure 5-2, on page 95). The file descriptor number employed in the receiving process would typically be different from the number employed in the sender.

> An example of passing file descriptors is provided in the files scm_rights_send.c and scm_rights_recv.c in the sockets subdirectory in the source code distribution for this book.

61.13.4 Receiving Sender Credentials

Another example of the use of ancillary data is for receiving sender credentials via a UNIX domain socket. These credentials consist of the user ID, the group ID, and the process ID of the sending process. The sender may specify its user and group IDs as the corresponding real, effective, or saved set IDs. This allows the receiving process to authenticate a sender on the same host. For further details, see the *socket(7)* and *unix(7)* manual pages.

Unlike passing file descriptors, passing sender credentials is not specified in SUSv3. Aside from Linux, this feature is implemented in some of the modern BSDs (where the credentials structure contains somewhat more information than on Linux), but is available on few other UNIX implementations. The details of credential passing on FreeBSD are described in [Stevens et al., 2004].

On Linux, a privileged process can fake the user ID, group ID, and process ID that are passed as credentials if it has, respectively, the CAP_SETUID, CAP_SETGID, and CAP_SYS_ADMIN capabilities.

> An example of passing credentials is provided in the files scm_cred_send.c and scm_cred_recv.c in the sockets subdirectory in the source code distribution for this book.

61.13.5 Sequenced-Packet Sockets

Sequenced-packet sockets combine features of both stream and datagram sockets:

- Like stream sockets, sequenced-packet sockets are connection-oriented. Connections are established in the same way as for stream sockets, using *bind()*, *listen()*, *accept()*, and *connect()*.

- Like datagram sockets, message boundaries are preserved. A *read()* from a sequenced-packet socket returns exactly one message (as written by the peer). If the message is longer than the buffer supplied by the caller, the excess bytes are discarded.

- Like stream sockets, and unlike datagram sockets, communication via sequenced-packet sockets is reliable. Messages are delivered to the peer application error-free, in order, and unduplicated, and they are guaranteed to arrive (assuming that there is not a system or application crash, or a network outage).

A sequenced-packet socket is created by calling *socket()* with the *type* argument specified as SOCK_SEQPACKET.

Historically, Linux, like most UNIX implementations, did not support sequenced-packet sockets in either the UNIX or the Internet domains. However, starting with kernel 2.6.4, Linux supports SOCK_SEQPACKET for UNIX domain sockets.

In the Internet domain, the UDP and TCP protocols do not support SOCK_SEQPACKET, but the SCTP protocol (described in the next section) does.

We don't show an example of the use of sequenced-packet sockets in this book, but, other than the preservation of message boundaries, their use is very similar to stream sockets.

61.13.6 SCTP and DCCP Transport-Layer Protocols

SCTP and DCCP are two newer transport-layer protocols that are likely to become increasingly common in the future.

The *Stream Control Transmission Protocol* (SCTP, *http://www.sctp.org/*) was designed to support telephony signaling in particular, but is also general purpose. Like TCP, SCTP provides reliable, bidirectional, connection-oriented transport. Unlike TCP, SCTP preserves message boundaries. One of the distinctive features of SCTP is multistream support, which allows multiple logical data streams to be employed over a single connection.

SCTP is described in [Stewart & Xie, 2001], [Stevens et al., 2004], and in RFCs 4960, 3257, and 3286.

SCTP is available on Linux since kernel 2.6. Further information about this implementation can be found at *http://lksctp.sourceforge.net/*.

Throughout the preceding chapters that describe the sockets API, we equated Internet domain stream sockets with TCP. However, SCTP provides an alternative protocol for implementing stream sockets, created using the following call:

```
socket(AF_INET, SOCK_STREAM, IPPROTO_SCTP);
```

Starting in kernel 2.6.14, Linux supports a new datagram protocol, the *Datagram Congestion Control Protocol* (DCCP). Like TCP, DCCP provides congestion control (removing the need to implement congestion control at the application level) to prevent a fast transmitter from overwhelming the network. (We explained congestion control when describing TCP in Section 58.6.3.) However, unlike TCP (but like UDP), DCCP doesn't provide guarantees about reliable or in-order delivery, and thus allows applications that don't need these features to avoid the delays that they can incur. Information about DCCP can be found at *http://www.read.cs.ucla.edu/dccp/* and RFCs 4336 and 4340.

61.14 Summary

In various circumstances, partial reads and writes can occur when performing I/O on stream sockets. We showed the implementation of two functions, *readn()* and *writen()*, that can be used to ensure a complete buffer of data is read or written.

The *shutdown()* system call provides more precise control over connection termination. Using *shutdown()*, we can forcibly shut down either or both halves of a bidirectional communication stream, regardless of whether there are other open file descriptors referring to the socket.

Like *read()* and *write()*, *recv()* and *send()* can be used to perform I/O on a socket, but calls provide an extra argument, *flags*, that controls socket-specific I/O functionality.

The *sendfile()* system call allows us to efficiently copy the contents of a file to a socket. This efficiency is gained because we don't need to copy the file data to and from user memory, as would be required with calls to *read()* and *write()*.

The *getsockname()* and *getpeername()* system calls retrieve, respectively, the local address to which a socket is bound and the address of the peer to which that socket is connected.

We considered some details of the operation of TCP, including TCP states and the TCP state transition diagram, and TCP connection establishment and termination. As part of this discussion, we saw why the TIME_WAIT state is an important part of TCP's reliability guarantee. Although this state can lead to the "Address already in use" error when restarting a server, we later saw that the SO_REUSEADDR socket option can be used to avoid this error, while nevertheless allowing the TIME_WAIT state to serve its intended purpose.

The *netstat* and *tcpdump* commands are useful tools for monitoring and debugging applications that use sockets.

The *getsockopt()* and *setsockopt()* system calls retrieve and modify options affecting the operation of a socket.

On Linux, when a new socket is created by *accept()*, it does not inherit the listening sockets open file status flags, file descriptor flags, or file descriptor attributes related to signal-driven I/O. However, it does inherit the settings of socket options. We noted that SUSv3 is silent on these details, which vary across implementations.

Although UDP doesn't provide the reliability guarantees of TCP, we saw that there are nevertheless reasons why UDP can be preferable for some applications.

Finally, we outlined a few advanced features of sockets programming that we don't describe in detail in this book.

Further information

Refer to the sources of further information listed in Section 59.15.

61.15 Exercises

61-1. Suppose that the program in Listing 61-2 (is_echo_cl.c) was modified so that, instead of using *fork()* to create two processes that operate concurrently, it instead used just one process that first copies its standard input to the socket and then reads the server's response. What problem might occur when running this client? (Look at Figure 58-8, on page 1190.)

61-2. Implement *pipe()* in terms of *socketpair()*. Use *shutdown()* to ensure that the resulting pipe is unidirectional.

61-3. Implement a replacement for *sendfile()* using *read()*, *write()*, and *lseek()*.

61-4. Write a program that uses *getsockname()* to show that, if we call *listen()* on a TCP socket without first calling *bind()*, the socket is assigned an ephemeral port number.

61-5. Write a client and a server that permit the client to execute arbitrary shell commands on the server host. (If you don't implement any security mechanism in this application, you should ensure that the server is operating under a user account where it can do no damage if invoked by malicious users.) The client should be executed with two command-line arguments:

```
$ ./is_shell_cl server-host 'some-shell-command'
```

After connecting to the server, the client sends the given command to the server, and then closes its writing half of the socket using *shutdown()*, so that the server sees end-of-file. The server should handle each incoming connection in a separate child process (i.e., a concurrent design). For each incoming connection, the server should read the command from the socket (until end-of-file), and then exec a shell to perform the command. Here are a couple hints:

- See the implementation of *system()* in Section 27.7 for an example of how to execute a shell command.
- By using *dup2()* to duplicate the socket on standard output and standard error, the execed command will automatically write to the socket.

61-6. Section 61.13.1 noted that an alternative to out-of-band data would be to create two socket connections between the client and server: one for normal data and one for priority data. Write client and server programs that implement this framework. Here are a few hints:

- The server needs some way of knowing which two sockets belong to the same client. One way to do this is to have the client first create a listening socket using an ephemeral port (i.e., binding to port 0). After obtaining the ephemeral port number of its listening socket (using *getsockname()*), the client connects its "normal" socket to the server's listening socket and sends a message containing the port number of the client's listening socket. The client then waits for the server to use the client's listening socket to make a connection in the opposite direction for the "priority" socket. (The server can obtain the client's IP address during the *accept()* of the normal connection.)

- Implement some type of security mechanism to prevent a rogue process from trying to connect to the client's listening socket. To do this, the client could send a cookie (i.e., some type of unique message) to the server using the normal socket. The server would then return this cookie via the priority socket so that the client could verify it.

- In order to experiment with transmitting normal and priority data from the client to the server, you will need to code the server to multiplex the input from the two sockets using *select()* or *poll()* (described in Section 63.2).

62

TERMINALS

Historically, users accessed a UNIX system using a terminal connected via a serial line (an RS-232 connection). Terminals were cathode ray tubes (CRTs) capable of displaying characters and, in some cases, primitive graphics. Typically, CRTs provided a monochrome display of 24 lines by 80 columns. By today's standards, these CRTs were small and expensive. In even earlier times, terminals were sometimes hard-copy teletype devices. Serial lines were also used to connect other devices, such as printers and modems, to a computer or to connect one computer to another.

> On early UNIX systems, the terminal lines connected to the system were represented by character devices with names of the form /dev/ttyn. (On Linux, the /dev/ttyn devices are the virtual consoles on the system.) It is common to see the abbreviation *tty* (derived from teletype) as a shorthand for *terminal*.

Especially during the early years of UNIX, terminal devices were not standardized, which meant that different character sequences were required to perform operations such as moving the cursor to the beginning of the line or the top of the screen. (Eventually, some vendor implementations of such *escape sequences*—for example, Digital's VT-100—became de facto and, ultimately, ANSI standards, but a wide variety of terminal types continued to exist.) This lack of standardization meant that it was difficult to write portable programs that used terminal features. The *vi* editor was an early example of a program with such requirements. The *termcap* and *terminfo* databases (described in [Strang et al., 1988]), which tabulate how to perform various screen-control operations for a wide variety of terminal types, and the *curses* library ([Strang, 1986]) were developed in response to this lack of standardization.

It is no longer common to see a conventional terminal. The usual interface to modern UNIX systems is an X Window System window manager on a high-performance bit-mapped graphical monitor. (An old-style terminal provided functionality roughly equivalent to a single terminal window—an *xterm* or similar—in an X Window System. The fact that the user of such a terminal had only a single "window" to the system was the driving force behind the development of the job-control facilities described in Section 34.7.) Similarly, many devices (e.g., printers) that were once connected directly to a computer are now often intelligent devices connected via a network.

All of the above is a preamble to saying that the need to program terminal devices is less frequent than it used to be. Therefore, this chapter focuses on the aspects of terminal programming that are particularly relevant to software terminal emulators (i.e., *xterm* and similar). It gives only brief coverage to serial lines; references for further information about serial programming are provided at the end of this chapter.

62.1 Overview

Both a conventional terminal and a terminal emulator have an associated terminal driver that handles input and output on the device. (In the case of a terminal emulator, the device is a pseudoterminal. We describe pseudoterminals in Chapter 64.) Various aspects of the operation of the terminal driver can be controlled using the functions described in this chapter.

When performing input, the driver is capable of operating in either of the following modes:

- *Canonical mode*: In this mode, terminal input is processed line by line, and line editing is enabled. Lines are terminated by a newline character, generated when the user presses the *Enter* key. A *read()* from the terminal returns only when a complete line of input is available, and returns at most one line. (If the *read()* requests fewer bytes than are available in the current line, then the remaining bytes are available for the next *read()*.) This is the default input mode.

- *Noncanonical mode*: Terminal input is not gathered into lines. Programs such as *vi*, *more*, and *less* place the terminal in noncanonical mode so that they can read single characters without the user needing to press the *Enter* key.

The terminal driver also interprets a range of special characters, such as the *interrupt* character (normally *Control-C*) and the *end-of-file* character (normally *Control-D*). Such interpretation may result in a signal being generated for the foreground process group or some type of input condition occurring for a program reading from the terminal. Programs that place the terminal in noncanonical mode typically also disable processing of some or all of these special characters.

A terminal driver operates two queues (Figure 62-1): one for input characters transmitted from the terminal device to the reading process(es) and the other for output characters transmitted from processes to the terminal. If terminal echoing is enabled, then the terminal driver automatically appends a copy of any input character to the end of the output queue, so that input characters are also output on the terminal.

> SUSv3 specifies the limit MAX_INPUT, which an implementation can use to indicate the maximum length of the terminal's input queue. A related limit, MAX_CANON, defines the maximum number of bytes in a line of input in canonical mode. On Linux, *pathconf()* returns the value 255 for both of these limits. However, neither of these limits is actually employed by the kernel, which simply imposes a limit of 4096 bytes on the input queue. A corresponding limit on the size of the output queue also exists. However, applications don't need to be concerned with this, since, if a process produces output faster than the terminal driver can handle it, the kernel suspends execution of the writing process until space is once more available in the output queue.
>
> On Linux, we can call *ioctl(fd, FIONREAD, &cnt)* to obtain the number of unread bytes in the input queue of the terminal referred to by the file descriptor *fd*. This feature is not specified in SUSv3.

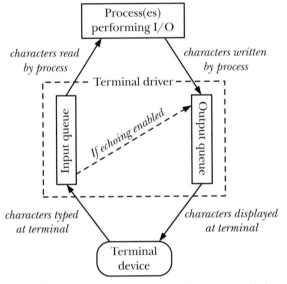

Figure 62-1: Input and output queues for a terminal device

62.2 Retrieving and Modifying Terminal Attributes

The *tcgetattr()* and *tcsetattr()* functions retrieve and modify the attributes of a terminal.

```
#include <termios.h>

int tcgetattr(int fd, struct termios *termios_p);
int tcsetattr(int fd, int optional_actions, const struct termios *termios_p);
```
                                            Both return 0 on success, or −1 on error

The *fd* argument is a file descriptor that refers to a terminal. (If *fd* doesn't refer to a terminal, these functions fail with the error ENOTTY.)

The *termios_p* argument is a pointer to a *termios* structure, which records terminal attributes:

```
struct termios {
    tcflag_t c_iflag;          /* Input flags */
    tcflag_t c_oflag;          /* Output flags */
    tcflag_t c_cflag;          /* Control flags */
    tcflag_t c_lflag;          /* Local modes */
    cc_t     c_line;           /* Line discipline (nonstandard)*/
    cc_t     c_cc[NCCS];       /* Terminal special characters */
    speed_t  c_ispeed;         /* Input speed (nonstandard; unused) */
    speed_t  c_ospeed;         /* Output speed (nonstandard; unused) */
};
```

The first four fields of the *termios* structure are bit masks (the *tcflag_t* data type is an integer type of suitable size) containing flags that control various aspects of the terminal driver's operation:

- *c_iflag* contains flags controlling terminal input;
- *c_oflag* contains flags controlling terminal output;
- *c_cflag* contains flags relating to hardware control of the terminal line; and
- *c_lflag* contains flags controlling the user interface for terminal input.

All of the flags used in the above fields are listed in Table 62-2 (on page 1302).

The *c_line* field specifies the line discipline for this terminal. For the purposes of programming terminal emulators, the line discipline will always be set to N_TTY, the so-called *new* discipline, a component of the kernel terminal-handling code that implements canonical mode I/O processing. Setting the line discipline can be relevant when programming serial lines.

The *c_cc* array contains the terminal special characters (*interrupt*, *suspend*, and so on) as well as fields controlling the operation of noncanonical mode input. The *cc_t* data type is an unsigned integer type suitable for holding these values, and the NCCS constant specifies the number of elements in this array. We describe the terminal special characters in Section 62.4.

The *c_ispeed* and *c_ospeed* fields are unused on Linux (and are not specified in SUSv3). We explain how Linux stores terminal line speeds in Section 62.7.

> The Seventh Edition and early BSD terminal driver (known as the *tty* driver) had grown over time so that it used no less than four different data structures to represent the information equivalent to the *termios* structure. System V replaced this baroque arrangement with a single structure called *termio*. The initial POSIX committee selected the System V API almost as is, in the process renaming it to *termios*.

When changing terminal attributes with *tcsetattr()*, the *optional_actions* argument determines when the change takes effect. This argument is specified as one of the following values:

TCSANOW

> The change is carried out immediately.

TCSADRAIN

> The change takes effect after all currently queued output has been transmitted to the terminal. Normally, this flag should be specified when making changes that affect terminal output, so that we don't affect output that has already been queued but not yet displayed.

TCSAFLUSH

> The change takes effect as for TCSADRAIN, but, in addition, any input that is still pending at the time the change takes effect is discarded. This is useful, for example, when reading a password, where we wish to disable terminal echoing and prevent user type-ahead.

The usual (and recommended) way to change terminal attributes is to use *tcgetattr()* to retrieve a *termios* structure containing a copy of the current settings, change the desired attributes, and then use *tcsetattr()* to push the updated structure back to the driver. (This approach ensures that we pass a fully initialized structure to *tcsetattr()*.) For example, we can use the following sequence to turn terminal echoing off:

```
struct termios tp;

if (tcgetattr(STDIN_FILENO, &tp) == -1)
    errExit("tcgetattr");
tp.c_lflag &= ~ECHO;
if (tcsetattr(STDIN_FILENO, TCSAFLUSH, &tp) == -1)
    errExit("tcsetattr");
```

The *tcsetattr()* function returns successfully if *any* of the requested changes to terminal attributes could be performed; it fails only if *none* of the requested changes could be made. This means that, when making multiple attribute changes, it may sometimes be necessary to make a further call to *tcgetattr()* to retrieve the new terminal attributes and compare them against the requested changes.

> In Section 34.7.2, we noted that if *tcsetattr()* is called from a process in a background process group, then the terminal driver suspends the process group by delivering a SIGTTOU signal, and that, if called from an orphaned process group, *tcsetattr()* fails with the error EIO. The same statements apply for various other functions described in this chapter, including *tcflush()*, *tcflow()*, *tcsendbreak()*, and *tcdrain()*.
>
> In earlier UNIX implementations, terminal attributes were accessed using *ioctl()* calls. Like several other functions described in this chapter, the *tcgetattr()* and *tcsetattr()* functions are POSIX inventions designed to address the problem that type checking of the third argument of *ioctl()* isn't possible. On Linux, as in many other UNIX implementations, these are library functions layered on top of *ioctl()*.

62.3 The *stty* Command

The *stty* command is the command-line analog of the *tcgetattr()* and *tcsetattr()* functions, allowing us to view and change terminal attributes from the shell. This is useful when trying to monitor, debug, or undo the effects of programs that modify terminal attributes.

We can view the current settings of all terminal attributes using the following command (here carried out on a virtual console):

```
$ stty -a
speed 38400 baud; rows 25; columns 80; line = 0;
intr = ^C; quit = ^\; erase = ^?; kill = ^U; eof = ^D; eol = <undef>;
eol2 = <undef>; start = ^Q; stop = ^S; susp = ^Z; rprnt = ^R;
werase = ^W; lnext = ^V; flush = ^O; min = 1; time = 0;
-parenb -parodd cs8 hupcl -cstopb cread -clocal -crtscts
-ignbrk brkint -ignpar -parmrk -inpck -istrip -inlcr -igncr icrnl ixon -ixoff
-iuclc -ixany imaxbel -iutf8
opost -olcuc -ocrnl onlcr -onocr -onlret -ofill -ofdel nl0 cr0 tab0 bs0 vt0 ff0
isig icanon iexten echo echoe echok -echonl -noflsh -xcase -tostop -echoprt
echoctl echoke
```

The first line of the above output shows the terminal line speed (bits per second), the terminal window size, and the line discipline in numeric form (0 corresponds to N_TTY, the new line discipline).

The next three lines show the settings of the various terminal special characters. The notation ^C denotes *Control-C*, and so on. The string <undef> means that the corresponding terminal special character is not currently defined. The *min* and *time* values relate to noncanonical mode input, and are described in Section 62.6.2.

The remaining lines show the settings of the various flags from (in order) the *c_cflag*, *c_iflag*, *c_oflag*, and *c_lflag* fields of the *termios* structure. Where a flag name is preceded by a hyphen (-), the flag is currently disabled; otherwise, it is currently enabled.

When entered without command-line arguments, *stty* shows just the terminal line speed, the line discipline, and any of the other settings that deviate from sane values.

We can change the settings of terminal special characters using commands such as the following:

```
$ stty intr ^L                    Make the interrupt character Control-L
```

When specifying a control character as the final argument, we can do so in a variety of ways:

- as a 2-character sequence consisting of a caret (^) followed by the corresponding character (as shown above);
- as an octal or hexadecimal number (thus: 014 or 0xC); or
- by typing the actual character itself.

If we employ the final option, and the character in question is one interpreted specially by the shell or the terminal driver, then we must precede it with the *literal next* character (usually *Control-V*):

```
$ stty intr Control-V Control-L
```

(Although, for readability, a space is shown between the *Control-V* and the *Control-L* in the above example, no white-space characters should be typed between the *Control-V* and the desired character.)

It is possible, though unusual, to define terminal special characters to be something other than control characters:

```
$ stty intr q          Make the interrupt character q
```

Of course, when we do this, we can no longer use the *q* key for its usual purpose (i.e., generating the letter *q*).

To change terminal flags, such as the TOSTOP flag, we can use commands such as the following:

```
$ stty tostop          Enable the TOSTOP flag
$ stty -tostop         Disable the TOSTOP flag
```

Sometimes, when developing programs that modify terminal attributes, a program may crash, leaving the terminal in a state that renders it all but unusable. On a terminal emulator, we have the luxury of simply closing the terminal window and starting another. Alternatively, we can type in the following character sequence to restore the terminal flags and special characters to a reasonable state:

```
Control-J stty sane Control-J
```

The *Control-J* character is the real newline character (ASCII 10 decimal). We use this character because, in some modes, the terminal driver may no longer map the *Enter* key (ASCII 13 decimal) into a newline character. We type an initial *Control-J* to ensure that we have a fresh command line with no preceding characters. This may not be easy to verify if, for example, terminal echoing has been disabled.

The *stty* command operates on the terminal referred to by standard input. Using the *−F* option, we can (subject to permission checks) monitor and set the attributes of a terminal other than the one on which the *stty* command is run:

```
$ su                          Need privilege to access another user's terminal
Password:
# stty -a -F /dev/tty3        Fetch attributes for terminal /dev/tty3
Output omitted for brevity
```

The *−F* option is a Linux-specific extension to the *stty* command. On many other UNIX implementations, *stty* always acts on the terminal referred to by standard input, and we must use the following alternative form (which can also be used on Linux):

```
# stty -a < /dev/tty3
```

62.4 Terminal Special Characters

Table 62-1 lists the special characters recognized by the Linux terminal driver. The first two columns show the name of the character and the corresponding constant that can be used as a subscript in the *c_cc* array. (As can be seen, these constants simply prefix the letter *V* in front of the character name.) The CR and NL characters don't have corresponding *c_cc* subscripts, because the values of these characters can't be changed.

The *Default setting* column of the table shows the usual default value for the special character. As well as being able to set a terminal special character to a specific value, it is also possible to disable the character by setting it to the value returned by the call *fpathconf(fd, _PC_VDISABLE)*, where *fd* is a file descriptor referring to a terminal. (On most UNIX implementations, this call returns the value 0.)

The operation of each of the special characters is subject to the setting of various flags in the *termios* bit-mask fields (described in Section 62.5), as shown in the penultimate column of the table.

The final column indicates which of these characters are specified by SUSv3. Regardless of the SUSv3 specification, most of these characters are supported on all UNIX implementations.

Table 62-1: Terminal special characters

Character	c_cc subscript	Description	Default setting	Relevant bit-mask flags	SUSv3
CR	(none)	Carriage return	^M	ICANON, IGNCR, ICRNL, OPOST, OCRNL, ONOCR	•
DISCARD	VDISCARD	Discard output	^O	(not implemented)	
EOF	VEOF	End-of-file	^D	ICANON	•
EOL	VEOL	End-of-line		ICANON	•
EOL2	VEOL2	Alternate end-of-line		ICANON, IEXTEN	
ERASE	VERASE	Erase character	^?	ICANON	•
INTR	VINTR	Interrupt (SIGINT)	^C	ISIG	•
KILL	VKILL	Erase line	^U	ICANON	•
LNEXT	VLNEXT	Literal next	^V	ICANON, IEXTEN	
NL	(none)	Newline	^J	ICANON, INLCR, ECHONL, OPOST, ONLCR, ONLRET	•
QUIT	VQUIT	Quit (SIGQUIT)	^\	ISIG	•
REPRINT	VREPRINT	Reprint input line	^R	ICANON, IEXTEN, ECHO	
START	VSTART	Start output	^Q	IXON, IXOFF	•
STOP	VSTOP	Stop output	^S	IXON, IXOFF	•
SUSP	VSUSP	Suspend (SIGTSTP)	^Z	ISIG	•
WERASE	VWERASE	Erase word	^W	ICANON, IEXTEN	

The following paragraphs provide more detailed explanations of the terminal special characters. Note that if the terminal driver performs its special input interpretation on one of these characters, then—with the exception of CR, EOL, EOL2, and NL—the character is discarded (i.e., it is not passed to any reading process).

CR

CR is the *carriage return* character. This character is passed to the reading process. In canonical mode (ICANON flag set) with the ICRNL (*map CR to NL on input*) flag set (the default), this character is first converted to a newline (ASCII 10 decimal, ^J) before being passed to the reading process. If the IGNCR (*ignore CR*) flag is set, then this character is ignored on input (in which case the true newline character must be used to terminate a line of input). An output CR character causes the terminal to move the cursor to the beginning of the line.

DISCARD

DISCARD is the *discard output* character. Although this character is defined within the *c_cc* array, it has no effect on Linux. On some other UNIX implementations, typing this character once causes program output to be discarded. This character is a toggle—typing it once more reenables the display of output. This is useful when a program is generating a large amount of output and we want to skip some of it. (This was much more useful on traditional terminals, where line speeds were slower and other "terminal windows" were unavailable.) This character is not passed to the reading process.

EOF

EOF is the canonical mode *end-of-file* character (usually *Control-D*). Entering this character at the beginning of a line causes an end-of-file condition to be detected by a process reading from the terminal (i.e., *read()* returns 0). If typed anywhere other than the initial character of a line, then this character simply causes *read()* to complete immediately, returning the characters so far input in the line. In both cases, the EOF character itself is not passed to the reading process.

EOL and EOL2

EOL and EOL2 are *additional line-delimiter* characters that operate like the standard newline (NL) character for canonical mode input, terminating a line of input and making it available to the reading process. By default, these characters are unde-fined. If they are defined, they are passed to the reading process. The EOL2 character is operational only if the IEXTEN (*extended input processing*) flag is set (the default).

These characters are rarely used. One application that does use them is *telnet*. By setting EOL or EOL2 to be the *telnet* escape character (usually *Control-]*, or, alternatively, the tilde character, ~, if operating in *rlogin* mode), *telnet* is able to immediately catch that character, even while reading input in canonical mode.

ERASE

In canonical mode, typing the ERASE character erases the previously input character on the current line. The erased character and the ERASE character itself are not passed to the reading process.

INTR

INTR is the *interrupt* character. If the ISIG (*enable signals*) flag is set (the default), typing this character causes an *interrupt* signal (SIGINT) to be sent to the terminal's foreground process group (Section 34.2). The INTR character itself is not passed to the reading process.

KILL

KILL is the *erase line* (also known as *kill line*) character. In canonical mode, typing this character causes the current line of input to be discarded (i.e., the characters typed so far, as well as the KILL character itself, are not passed to the reading process).

LNEXT

LNEXT is the *literal next* character. In some circumstances, we may wish to treat one of the terminal special characters as though it were a normal character for input to a reading process. Typing the literal next character (usually *Control-V*) causes the next character to be treated literally, voiding any special interpretation of the character that the terminal driver would normally perform. Thus, we could enter the 2-character sequence *Control-V Control-C* to supply a real *Control-C* character (ASCII 3) as input to the reading process. The LNEXT character itself is not passed to the reading process. This character is interpreted only in canonical mode with the IEXTEN (*extended input processing*) flag set (which is the default).

NL

NL is the *newline* character. In canonical mode, this character terminates an input line. The NL character itself is included in the line returned to the reading process. (The CR character is normally converted to NL in canonical mode.) An output NL character causes the terminal to move the cursor down one line. If the OPOST and ONLCR (*map NL to CR-NL*) flags are set (the default), then, on output, a newline character is mapped to the 2-character sequence CR plus NL. (The combination of the ICRNL and ONLCR flags means that an input CR is converted to a NL, and then echoed as CR plus NL.)

QUIT

If the ISIG flag is set (the default), typing the QUIT character causes a *quit* signal (SIGQUIT) to be sent to the terminal's foreground process group (Section 34.2). The QUIT character itself is not passed to the reading process.

REPRINT

REPRINT is the *reprint input* character. In canonical mode with the IEXTEN flag set (the default), typing this character causes the current (as yet incomplete) line of input to be redisplayed on the terminal. This is useful if some other program (e.g., *wall(1)* or *write(1)*) has written output that has messed up the terminal display. The REPRINT character itself is not passed to the reading process.

START and STOP

START and STOP are the *start output* and *stop output* characters, which operate if the IXON (*enable start/stop output control*) flag is enabled (the default). (The START and STOP characters are not honored by some terminal emulators.)

Typing the STOP character suspends terminal output. The STOP character itself is not passed to the reading process. If the IXOFF flag is set and the terminal input queue is full, then the terminal driver automatically sends a STOP character to throttle the input.

Typing the START character causes terminal output to resume after previously being stopped by the STOP character. The START character itself is not passed to the reading process. If the IXOFF (*enable start/stop input control*) flag is set (this flag is disabled by default) and the terminal driver had previously sent a STOP character because the input queue was full, the terminal driver automatically generates a START character when space once more becomes available in the input queue.

If the IXANY flag is set, then any character, not just START, may be typed in order to restart output (and that character is similarly not passed to the reading process).

The START and STOP characters are used for software flow control in either direction between the computer and the terminal device. One function of these characters is to allow users to stop and start terminal output. This is output flow control, as enabled by IXON. However, flow control in the other direction (i.e., control of input flow from the device to the computer, as enabled by IXOFF) is also important when, for example, the device in question is a modem or another computer. Input flow control makes sure that no data is lost if the application is slow to handle input and the kernel buffers fill up.

With the higher line speeds that are nowadays typical, software flow control has been superseded by hardware (RTS/CTS) flow control, whereby data flow is enabled and disabled using signals sent via separate wires on the serial port. (RTS stands for *Request To Send*, and CTS stands for *Clear To Send*.)

SUSP

SUSP is the *suspend* character. If the ISIG flag is set (the default), typing this character causes a *terminal suspend* signal (SIGTSTP) to be sent to the terminal's foreground process group (Section 34.2). The SUSP character itself is not passed to the reading process.

WERASE

WERASE is the *word erase* character. In canonical mode, with the IEXTEN flag set (the default), typing this character erases all characters back to the beginning of the previous word. A word is considered to be a sequence of letters, digits, and the underscore character. (On some UNIX implementations, a word is considered to be delimited by white space.)

Other terminal special characters

Other UNIX implementations provide terminal special characters in addition to those listed in Table 62-1.

BSD provides the DSUSP and STATUS characters. The DSUSP character (typically *Control-Y*) operates in a fashion similar to the SUSP character, but suspends the foreground process group only when it attempts to read the character (i.e., after all preceding input has been read). Several non-BSD-derived implementations also provide the DSUSP character.

The STATUS character (typically *Control-T*) causes the kernel to display status information on the terminal (including the state of the foreground process and how much CPU time it has consumed), and sends a SIGINFO signal to the foreground process group. If desired, processes can catch this signal and display further status information. (Linux provides a vaguely similar feature in the form of the *magic SysRq key*; see the kernel source file Documentation/sysrq.txt for details.)

System V derivatives provide the SWTCH character. This character is used to switch shells under *shell layers*, a System V predecessor to job control.

Example program

Listing 62-1 shows the use of *tcgetattr()* and *tcsetattr()* to change the terminal *interrupt* character. This program sets the *interrupt* character to be the character whose numeric value is supplied as the program's command-line argument, or disables the *interrupt* character if no command-line argument is supplied.

The following shell session demonstrates the use of this program. We begin by setting the *interrupt* character to *Control-L* (ASCII 12), and then verify the change with *stty*:

```
$ ./new_intr 12
$ stty
speed 38400 baud; line = 0;
intr = ^L;
```

We then start a process running *sleep(1)*. We find that typing *Control-C* no longer has its usual effect of terminating a process, but typing *Control-L* does terminate the process.

```
$ sleep 10
^C                                   Control-C has no effect; it is just echoed
Type Control-L to terminate sleep
```

We now display the value of the shell *$?* variable, which shows the termination status of the last command:

```
$ echo $?
130
```

We see that the termination status of the process was 130. This indicates that the process was killed by signal 130 − 128 = 2; signal number 2 is SIGINT.

Next, we use our program to disable the *interrupt* character.

```
$ ./new_intr
$ stty                               Verify the change
speed 38400 baud; line = 0;
intr = <undef>;
```

Now we find that neither *Control-C* nor *Control-L* generates a SIGINT signal, and we must instead use *Control-* to terminate a program:

```
$ sleep 10
^C^L                                 Control-C and Control-L are simply echoed
Type Control-\ to generate SIGQUIT
Quit
$ stty sane                          Return terminal to a sane state
```

Listing 62-1: Changing the terminal *interrupt* character

tty/new_intr.c

```
#include <termios.h>
#include <ctype.h>
#include "tlpi_hdr.h"

int
main(int argc, char *argv[])
{
    struct termios tp;
    int intrChar;

    if (argc > 1 && strcmp(argv[1], "--help") == 0)
        usageErr("%s [intr-char]\n", argv[0]);

    /* Determine new INTR setting from command line */

    if (argc == 1) {                                    /* Disable */
        intrChar = fpathconf(STDIN_FILENO, _PC_VDISABLE);
        if (intrChar == -1)
            errExit("Couldn't determine VDISABLE");
    } else if (isdigit((unsigned char) argv[1][0])) {
        intrChar = strtoul(argv[1], NULL, 0);           /* Allows hex, octal */
    } else {                                            /* Literal character */
        intrChar = argv[1][0];
    }

    /* Fetch current terminal settings, modify INTR character, and
       push changes back to the terminal driver */

    if (tcgetattr(STDIN_FILENO, &tp) == -1)
        errExit("tcgetattr");
    tp.c_cc[VINTR] = intrChar;
    if (tcsetattr(STDIN_FILENO, TCSAFLUSH, &tp) == -1)
        errExit("tcsetattr");

    exit(EXIT_SUCCESS);
}
```

tty/new_intr.c

62.5 Terminal Flags

Table 62-2 lists the settings controlled by each of the four flag fields of the *termios* structure. The constants listed in this table correspond to single bits, except those specifying the term *mask*, which are values spanning several bits; these may contain one of a range of values, shown in parentheses. The column labeled *SUSv3* indicates whether the flag is specified in SUSv3. The *Default* column shows the default settings for a virtual console login.

Many shells that provide command-line editing facilities perform their own manipulations of the flags listed in Table 62-2. This means that if we try using *stty(1)* to experiment with these settings, then the changes may not be effective when entering shell commands. To circumvent this behavior, we must disable command-line editing in the shell. For example, command-line editing can be disabled by specifying the command-line option *--noediting* when invoking *bash*.

Table 62-2: Terminal flags

Field/Flag	Description	Default	SUSv3
c_iflag			
BRKINT	Signal interrupt (SIGINT) on BREAK condition	on	•
ICRNL	Map CR to NL on input	on	•
IGNBRK	Ignore BREAK condition	off	•
IGNCR	Ignore CR on input	off	•
IGNPAR	Ignore characters with parity errors	off	•
IMAXBEL	Ring bell when terminal input queue is full (unused)	(on)	
INLCR	Map NL to CR on input	off	•
INPCK	Enable input parity checking	off	•
ISTRIP	Strip high bit (bit 8) from input characters	off	•
IUTF8	Input is UTF-8 (since Linux 2.6.4)	off	
IUCLC	Map uppercase to lowercase on input (if IEXTEN also set)	off	
IXANY	Allow any character to restart stopped output	off	•
IXOFF	Enable start/stop input flow control	off	•
IXON	Enable start/stop output flow control	on	•
PARMRK	Mark parity errors (with 2 prefix bytes: 0377 + 0)	off	•
c_oflag			
BSDLY	Backspace delay mask (BS0, BS1)	BS0	•
CRDLY	CR delay mask (CR0, CR1, CR2, CR3)	CR0	•
FFDLY	Form-feed delay mask (FF0, FF1)	FF0	•
NLDLY	Newline delay mask (NL0, NL1)	NL0	•
OCRNL	Map CR to NL on output (see also ONOCR)	off	•
OFDEL	Use DEL (0177) as fill character; otherwise NUL (0)	off	•
OFILL	Use fill characters for delay (rather than timed delay)	off	•
OLCUC	Map lowercase to uppercase on output	off	
ONLCR	Map NL to CR-NL on output	on	•
ONLRET	Assume NL performs CR function (move to start of line)	off	•
ONOCR	Don't output CR if already at column 0 (start of line)	off	•
OPOST	Perform output postprocessing	on	•
TABDLY	Horizontal-tab delay mask (TAB0, TAB1, TAB2, TAB3)	TAB0	•
VTDLY	Vertical-tab delay mask (VT0, VT1)	VT0	•
c_cflag			
CBAUD	Baud (bit rate) mask (B0, B2400, B9600, and so on)	B38400	
CBAUDEX	Extended baud (bit rate) mask (for rates > 38,400)	off	
CIBAUD	Input baud (bit rate), if different from output (unused)	(off)	
CLOCAL	Ignore modem status lines (don't check carrier signal)	off	•
CMSPAR	Use "stick" (mark/space) parity	off	

Table 62-2: Terminal flags (continued)

Field/Flag	Description	Default	SUSv3
CREAD	Allow input to be received	on	•
CRTSCTS	Enable RTS/CTS (hardware) flow control	off	
CSIZE	Character-size mask (5 to 8 bits: CS5, CS6, CS7, CS8)	CS8	•
CSTOPB	Use 2 stop bits per character; otherwise 1	off	•
HUPCL	Hang up (drop modem connection) on last close	on	•
PARENB	Parity enable	off	•
PARODD	Use odd parity; otherwise even	off	•
c_lflag			
ECHO	Echo input characters	on	•
ECHOCTL	Echo control characters visually (e.g., ^L)	on	
ECHOE	Perform ERASE visually	on	•
ECHOK	Echo KILL visually	on	•
ECHOKE	Don't output a newline after echoed KILL	on	
ECHONL	Echo NL (in canonical mode) even if echoing is disabled	off	•
ECHOPRT	Echo deleted characters backward (between \ and /)	off	
FLUSHO	Output is being flushed (unused)	-	
ICANON	Canonical mode (line-by-line) input	on	•
IEXTEN	Enable extended processing of input characters	on	•
ISIG	Enable signal-generating characters (INTR, QUIT, SUSP)	on	•
NOFLSH	Disable flushing on INTR, QUIT, and SUSP	off	•
PENDIN	Redisplay pending input at next read (not implemented)	(off)	
TOSTOP	Generate SIGTTOU for background output (Section 34.7.1)	off	•
XCASE	Canonical upper/lowercase presentation (unimplemented)	(off)	

Several of the flags listed in Table 62-2 were provided for historical terminals with limited capabilities, and these flags have little use on modern systems. For example, the IUCLC, OLCUC, and XCASE flags were used with terminals that were capable of displaying only uppercase letters. On many older UNIX systems, if a user tried logging in with an uppercase username, the *login* program assumed that the user was sitting at such a terminal and would set these flags, and then the following password prompt would appear:

    \PASSWORD:

From this point on, all lowercase characters were output in uppercase, and real uppercase characters were preceded by a backslash (\). Similarly, for input, a real uppercase character could be specified by a preceding backslash. The ECHOPRT flag was also designed for limited-capability terminals.

The various delay masks are also historical, allowing for terminals and printers that took longer to echo characters such as carriage return and form feed. The related OFILL and OFDEL flags specified how such a delay was to be performed. Most of these flags are unused on Linux. One exception is the TAB3 setting for the TABDLY mask, which causes tab characters to be output as (up to eight) spaces.

The following paragraphs provide more details about some of the *termios* flags.

BRKINT

If the `BRKINT` flag is set and the `IGNBRK` flag is not set, then a `SIGINT` signal is sent to the foreground process group when a BREAK condition occurs.

> Most conventional dumb terminals provided a *BREAK* key. Pressing this key doesn't actually generate a character, but instead causes a *BREAK condition*, whereby a series of 0 bits is sent to the terminal driver for a specified length of time, typically 0.25 or 0.5 seconds (i.e., longer than the time required to transmit a single byte). (Unless the `IGNBRK` flag has been set, the terminal driver consequently delivers a single 0 byte to the reading process.) On many UNIX systems, the BREAK condition acted as a signal to a remote host to change its line speed (baud) to something suitable for the terminal. Thus, the user would press the *BREAK* key until a valid login prompt appeared, indicating that the line speed was now suitable for this terminal.
>
> On a virtual console, we can generate a BREAK condition by pressing *Control-Break*.

ECHO

Setting the `ECHO` flag enables echoing of input characters. Disabling echoing is useful when reading passwords. Echoing is also disabled within the command mode of *vi*, where keyboard characters are interpreted as editing commands rather than text input. The `ECHO` flag is effective in both canonical and noncanonical modes.

ECHOCTL

If `ECHO` is set, then enabling the `ECHOCTL` flag causes control characters other than tab, newline, START, and STOP to be echoed in the form ^A (for *Control-A*), and so on. If `ECHOCTL` is disabled, control characters are not echoed.

> The control characters are those with ASCII codes less than 32, plus the DEL character (127 decimal). A control character, *x*, is echoed using a caret (^) followed by the character resulting from the expression *(x ^ 64)*. For all characters except DEL, the effect of the XOR (^) operator in this expression is to add 64 to the value of the character. Thus, *Control-A* (ASCII 1) is echoed as caret plus A (ASCII 65). For DEL, the expression has the effect of subtracting 64 from 127, yielding the value 63, the ASCII code for ?, so that DEL is echoed as ^?.

ECHOE

In canonical mode, setting the `ECHOE` flag causes ERASE to be performed visually, by outputting the sequence backspace-space-backspace to the terminal. If `ECHOE` is disabled, then the ERASE character is instead echoed (e.g., as ^?), but still performs its function of deleting a character.

ECHOK and ECHOKE

The `ECHOK` and `ECHOKE` flags control the visual display when using the KILL (erase line) character in canonical mode. In the default case (both flags enabled), a line is erased visually (see `ECHOE`). If either of these flags is disabled, then a visual erase is not performed (but the input line is still discarded), and the KILL character is echoed (e.g., as ^U). If `ECHOK` is set, but not `ECHOKE`, then a newline character is also output.

ICANON

Setting the ICANON flag enables canonical mode input. Input is gathered into lines, and special interpretation of the EOF, EOL, EOL2, ERASE, LNEXT, KILL, REPRINT, and WERASE characters is enabled (but note the effect of the IEXTEN flag described below).

IEXTEN

Setting the IEXTEN flag enables extended processing of input characters. This flag (as well as ICANON) must be set in order for the following characters to be interpreted: EOL2, LNEXT, REPRINT, and WERASE. The IEXTEN flag must also be set for the IUCLC flag to be effective. SUSv3 merely says that the IEXTEN flag enables extended (implementation-defined) functions; details may vary on other UNIX implementations.

IMAXBEL

On Linux, the setting of the IMAXBEL flag is ignored. On a console login, the bell is always rung when the input queue is full.

IUTF8

Setting the IUTF8 flag enables cooked mode (Section 62.6.3) to correctly handle UTF-8 input when performing line editing.

NOFLSH

By default, when a signal is generated by typing the INTR, QUIT, or SUSP character, any outstanding data in the terminal input and output queues is flushed (discarded). Setting the NOFLSH flag disables such flushing.

OPOST

Setting the OPOST flag enables output postprocessing. This flag must be set in order for any of the flags in the *c_oflag* field of the *termios* structure to be effective. (Put conversely, disabling the OPOST flag prevents all output postprocessing.)

PARENB, IGNPAR, INPCK, PARMRK, and PARODD

The PARENB, IGNPAR, INPCK, PARMRK, and PARODD flags are concerned with parity generation and checking.

The PARENB flag enables generation of parity check bits for output characters and parity checking for input characters. If we want to perform only output parity generation, then we can disable input parity checking by turning INPCK off. If the PARODD flag is set, then odd parity is used in both cases; otherwise, even parity is used.

The remaining flags specify how an input character with parity errors should be handled. If the IGNPAR flag is set, the character is discarded (not passed to the reading process). Otherwise, if the PARMRK flag is set, then the character is passed to the reading process, but is preceded by the 2-byte sequence 0377 + 0. (If the PARMRK flag is set and ISTRIP is clear, then a real 0377 character is doubled to become 0377 + 0377.) If PARMRK is not set, but INPCK is set, then the character is discarded, and a 0 byte is passed to the reading process instead. If none of IGNPAR, PARMRK, or INPCK is set, then the character is passed as is to the reading process.

Example program

Listing 62-2 demonstrates the use of *tcgetattr()* and *tcsetattr()* to turn off the ECHO flag, so that input characters are not echoed. Here is an example of what we see when running this program:

```
$ ./no_echo
Enter text:                          We type some text, which is not echoed,
Read: Knock, knock, Neo.            but was nevertheless read
```

Listing 62-2: Disabling terminal echoing

――――――――――――――――――――――――――――――――――― tty/no_echo.c
```c
#include <termios.h>
#include "tlpi_hdr.h"

#define BUF_SIZE 100

int
main(int argc, char *argv[])
{
    struct termios tp, save;
    char buf[BUF_SIZE];

    /* Retrieve current terminal settings, turn echoing off */

    if (tcgetattr(STDIN_FILENO, &tp) == -1)
        errExit("tcgetattr");
    save = tp;                      /* So we can restore settings later */
    tp.c_lflag &= ~ECHO;            /* ECHO off, other bits unchanged */
    if (tcsetattr(STDIN_FILENO, TCSAFLUSH, &tp) == -1)
        errExit("tcsetattr");

    /* Read some input and then display it back to the user */

    printf("Enter text: ");
    fflush(stdout);
    if (fgets(buf, BUF_SIZE, stdin) == NULL)
        printf("Got end-of-file/error on fgets()\n");
    else
        printf("\nRead: %s", buf);

    /* Restore original terminal settings */

    if (tcsetattr(STDIN_FILENO, TCSANOW, &save) == -1)
        errExit("tcsetattr");

    exit(EXIT_SUCCESS);
}
```
――――――――――――――――――――――――――――――――――― tty/no_echo.c

62.6 Terminal I/O Modes

We have already noted that the terminal driver is capable of handling input in either canonical or noncanonical mode, depending on the setting of the ICANON flag. We now describe these two modes in detail. We then describe three useful terminal modes—cooked, cbreak, and raw—that were available in Seventh Edition UNIX, and show how these modes are emulated on modern UNIX systems by setting appropriate values in the *termios* structure.

62.6.1 Canonical Mode

Canonical mode input is enabled by setting the ICANON flag. Terminal input in canonical mode is distinguished by the following features:

- Input is gathered into lines, terminated by one of the line-delimiter characters: NL, EOL, EOL2 (if the IEXTEN flag is set), EOF (at anything other than the initial position in the line), or CR (if the ICRNL flag is enabled). Except in the case of EOF, the line delimiter is passed back to the reading process (as the last character in the line).

- Line editing is enabled, so that the current line of input can be modified. Thus, the following characters are enabled: ERASE, KILL, and, if the IEXTEN flag is set, WERASE.

- If the IEXTEN flag is set, the REPRINT and LNEXT characters are also enabled.

In canonical mode, a terminal *read()* returns when a complete line of input is available. (The *read()* itself may fetch only part of that line if it requested fewer bytes; remaining bytes will be fetched by subsequent calls to *read()*.) A *read()* may also terminate if interrupted by a signal handler and restarting of system calls is not enabled for this signal (Section 21.5).

> While describing the NOFLSH flag in Section 62.5, we noted that the characters that generate signals also cause the terminal driver to flush the terminal input queue. This flushing occurs regardless of whether the signal is caught or ignored by an application. We can prevent such flushing by enabling the NOFLSH flag.

62.6.2 Noncanonical Mode

Some applications (e.g., *vi* and *less*) need to read characters from the terminal without the user supplying a line delimiter. Noncanonical mode is provided for this purpose. In noncanonical mode (ICANON unset), no special input processing is performed. In particular, input is no longer gathered into lines, but is instead available immediately.

In what circumstances does a noncanonical *read()* complete? We can specify that a noncanonical *read()* terminates after a certain time, after a certain number of bytes have been read, or both in combination. Two elements of the *termios c_cc* array determine the behavior: TIME and MIN. The TIME element (indexed using the constant VTIME) specifies a timeout value in tenths of a second. The MIN element (indexed using VMIN) specifies the minimum number of bytes to be read. (The MIN and TIME settings have no effect on canonical-mode terminal I/O.)

The precise operation and interaction of the MIN and TIME parameters depends on whether they each have nonzero values. The four possible cases are described below. Note that in all cases, if, at the time of a *read()*, sufficient bytes are already available to satisfy the requirements specified by MIN, *read()* returns immediately with the lesser of the number of bytes available and the number of bytes requested.

MIN == 0, TIME == 0 (polling read)

If data is available at the time of the call, then *read()* returns immediately with the lesser of the number of bytes available and the number of bytes requested. If no bytes are available, *read()* completes immediately, returning 0.

This case serves the usual requirements of polling, allowing the application to check if input is available without blocking if it is not. This mode is somewhat similar to setting the O_NONBLOCK flag (Section 5.9) for the terminal while in canonical mode. However, with O_NONBLOCK, if no bytes are available for reading, then *read()* returns −1 with the error EAGAIN.

MIN > 0, TIME == 0 (blocking read)

The *read()* blocks (possibly indefinitely) until MIN bytes are available, and returns up to the number of bytes requested.

Programs such as *less* typically set MIN to 1 and TIME to 0. This allows the program to wait for single key presses without needing to waste CPU time by polling in a busy loop.

If a terminal is placed in noncanonical mode with MIN set to 1 and TIME set to 0, then the techniques described in Chapter 63 can be used to check whether a single character (rather than a complete line) has been typed at the terminal.

MIN == 0, TIME > 0 (read with timeout)

A timer is started when *read()* is called. The call returns as soon as at least 1 byte is available, or when TIME tenths of a second have elapsed. In the latter case, *read()* returns 0.

This case is useful for programs talking to a serial device (e.g., a modem). The program can send data to the device and then wait for a response, using a timeout to avoid hanging forever in case the device doesn't respond.

MIN > 0, TIME > 0 (read with interbyte timeout)

After the initial byte of input becomes available, a timer is restarted as each further byte is received. The *read()* returns when either the lesser of MIN bytes and the number of bytes requested has been read, or when the time between receiving successive bytes exceeds TIME tenths of a second. Since the timer is started only after the initial byte becomes available, at least 1 byte is returned. (A *read()* can block indefinitely for this case.)

This case is useful for handling terminal keys that generate escape sequences. For example, on many terminals, the left-arrow key generates the 3-character sequence consisting of *Escape* followed by [D. These characters are transmitted in quick succession. Applications handling such sequences need to distinguish the pressing of such a key from the situation where the user slowly types each of the characters individually. This can be done by performing a *read()* with a small inter-byte timeout, say 0.2 seconds. Such a technique is used in the command mode of some versions of *vi*. (Depending on the length of the timeout, in such applications, we may be able to simulate a left-arrow key press by quickly typing the aforementioned 3-character sequence.)

Portably modifying and restoring MIN and TIME

For historical compatibility with some UNIX implementations, SUSv3 allows the values of the VMIN and VTIME constants to be the same as VEOF and VEOL, respectively, which means that these elements of the *termios c_cc* array may coincide. (On Linux, the values of these constants are distinct.) This is possible because VEOF and VEOL are unused in noncanonical mode. The fact that VMIN and VEOF may have the same value means that caution is needed in a program that enters noncanonical mode, sets MIN (typically to 1), and then later returns to canonical mode. On return to canonical mode, EOF will no longer have its usual value of ASCII 4 (*Control-D*). The portable way to deal with this problem is to save a copy of the *termios* settings prior to changing to noncanonical mode, and then use this saved structure to return to canonical mode.

62.6.3   Cooked, Cbreak, and Raw Modes

The terminal driver in Seventh Edition UNIX (as well as in early versions of BSD) was capable of handling input in three modes: *cooked*, *cbreak*, and *raw*. The differences between the three modes are summarized in Table 62-3.

Table 62-3: Differences between cooked, cbreak, and raw terminal modes

Feature	Mode		
	Cooked	**Cbreak**	**Raw**
Input available	line by line	char. by char.	char. by char.
Line-editing?	yes	no	no
Signal-generating characters interpreted?	yes	yes	no
START/STOP interpreted?	yes	yes	no
Other special characters interpreted?	yes	no	no
Other input processing performed?	yes	yes	no
Other output processing performed?	yes	yes	no
Input echoed?	yes	maybe	no

Cooked mode was essentially canonical mode with all of the default special character processing enabled (i.e., interpretation of CR, NL, and EOF; enabling of line editing; handling of signal-generating characters; ICRNL; OCRNL; and so on).

Raw mode was the converse: noncanonical mode, with all input and output processing, as well as echoing, switched off. (An application that needed to ensure that the terminal driver makes absolutely no changes to the data transferred across a serial line would use this mode.)

Cbreak mode was intermediate between cooked and raw modes. Input was noncanonical, but signal-generating characters were interpreted, and the various input and output transformations could still occur (depending on individual flag settings). Cbreak mode did not disable echoing, but applications employing this mode would usually disable echoing as well. Cbreak mode was useful in screen-handling applications (such as *less*) that permitted character-by-character input, but still needed to allow interpretation of characters such as INTR, QUIT, and SUSP.

Example: setting raw and cbreak mode

In the Seventh Edition and the original BSD terminal drivers, it was possible to switch to raw or cbreak mode by tweaking single bits (called RAW and CBREAK) in the terminal driver data structures. With the transition to the POSIX *termios* interface (now supported on all UNIX implementations), single bits for selecting raw and cbreak mode are no longer available, and applications emulating these modes must explicitly change the required fields of the *termios* structure. Listing 62-3 provides two functions, *ttySetCbreak()* and *ttySetRaw()*, that implement the equivalents of these terminal modes.

> Applications that use the *ncurses* library can call the functions *cbreak()* and *raw()*, which perform similar tasks to our functions in Listing 62-3.

Listing 62-3: Switching a terminal to cbreak and raw modes

──tty/tty_functions.c
```
#include <termios.h>
#include <unistd.h>
#include "tty_functions.h"            /* Declares functions defined here */

/* Place terminal referred to by 'fd' in cbreak mode (noncanonical mode
   with echoing turned off). This function assumes that the terminal is
   currently in cooked mode (i.e., we shouldn't call it if the terminal
   is currently in raw mode, since it does not undo all of the changes
   made by the ttySetRaw() function below). Return 0 on success, or -1
   on error. If 'prevTermios' is non-NULL, then use the buffer to which
   it points to return the previous terminal settings. */

int
ttySetCbreak(int fd, struct termios *prevTermios)
{
    struct termios t;

    if (tcgetattr(fd, &t) == -1)
        return -1;

    if (prevTermios != NULL)
        *prevTermios = t;

    t.c_lflag &= ~(ICANON | ECHO);
    t.c_lflag |= ISIG;

    t.c_iflag &= ~ICRNL;
```

```
        t.c_cc[VMIN] = 1;                    /* Character-at-a-time input */
        t.c_cc[VTIME] = 0;                   /* with blocking */

        if (tcsetattr(fd, TCSAFLUSH, &t) == -1)
            return -1;

        return 0;
    }

    /* Place terminal referred to by 'fd' in raw mode (noncanonical mode
       with all input and output processing disabled). Return 0 on success,
       or -1 on error. If 'prevTermios' is non-NULL, then use the buffer to
       which it points to return the previous terminal settings. */

    int
    ttySetRaw(int fd, struct termios *prevTermios)
    {
        struct termios t;

        if (tcgetattr(fd, &t) == -1)
            return -1;

        if (prevTermios != NULL)
            *prevTermios = t;

        t.c_lflag &= ~(ICANON | ISIG | IEXTEN | ECHO);
                            /* Noncanonical mode, disable signals, extended
                               input processing, and echoing */

        t.c_iflag &= ~(BRKINT | ICRNL | IGNBRK | IGNCR | INLCR |
                       INPCK | ISTRIP | IXON | PARMRK);
                            /* Disable special handling of CR, NL, and BREAK.
                               No 8th-bit stripping or parity error handling.
                               Disable START/STOP output flow control. */

        t.c_oflag &= ~OPOST;                 /* Disable all output processing */

        t.c_cc[VMIN] = 1;                    /* Character-at-a-time input */
        t.c_cc[VTIME] = 0;                   /* with blocking */

        if (tcsetattr(fd, TCSAFLUSH, &t) == -1)
            return -1;

        return 0;
    }
```
——tty/tty_functions.c

A program that places the terminal in raw or cbreak mode must be careful to
return the terminal to a usable mode when it terminates. Among other tasks, this
entails handling all of the signals that are likely to be sent to the program, so that

the program is not prematurely terminated. (Job-control signals can still be generated from the keyboard in cbreak mode.)

An example of how to do this is provided in Listing 62-4. This program performs the following steps:

- Set the terminal to either cbreak mode ⑨ or raw mode ⑫, depending on whether a command-line argument (any string) is supplied ⑧. The previous terminal settings are saved in the global variable *userTermios* ①.

- If the terminal was placed in cbreak mode, then signals can be generated from the terminal. These signals need to be handled so that terminating or suspending the program leaves the terminal in a state that the user expects. The program installs the same handler for SIGQUIT and SIGINT ⑩. The SIGTSTP signal requires special treatment, so a different handler is installed for that signal ⑪.

- Install a handler for the SIGTERM signal, in order to catch the default signal sent by the *kill* command ⑬.

- Execute a loop that reads characters one at a time from *stdin* and echoes them on standard output ⑭. The program treats various input characters specially before outputting them ⑮:

  - All letters are converted to lowercase before being output.

  - The newline (\n) and carriage return (\r) characters are echoed without change.

  - Control characters other than the newline and carriage return are echoed as a 2-character sequence: caret (^) plus the corresponding uppercase letter (e.g., *Control-A* echoes as ^A).

  - All other characters are echoed as asterisks (*).

  - The letter *q* causes the loop to terminate ⑯.

- On exit from the loop, restore the terminal to its state as last set by the user, and then terminate ⑰.

The program installs the same handler for SIGQUIT, SIGINT, and SIGTERM. This handler restores the terminal to its state as last set by the user and terminates the program ②.

The handler for the SIGTSTP signal ③ deals with the signal in the manner described in Section 34.7.3. Note the following additional details of the operation of this signal handler:

- Upon entry, the handler saves the current terminal settings (in *ourTermios*) ④, and then resets the terminal to the settings that were in effect (saved in *userTermios*) when the program was started ⑤, before once more raising SIGTSTP to actually stop the process.

- Upon resumption of execution after receipt of SIGCONT, the handler once more saves the current terminal settings in *userTermios* ⑥, since the user may have changed the settings while the program was stopped (using the *stty* command, for example). The handler then returns the terminal to the state (*ourTermios*) required by the program ⑦.

Listing 62-4: Demonstrating cbreak and raw modes

─────────────────────────────────────── **tty/test_tty_functions.c**

```
    #include <termios.h>
    #include <signal.h>
    #include <ctype.h>
    #include "tty_functions.h"              /* Declarations of ttySetCbreak()
                                               and ttySetRaw() */

    #include "tlpi_hdr.h"

①  static struct termios userTermios;
                        /* Terminal settings as defined by user */

    static void            /* General handler: restore tty settings and exit */
    handler(int sig)
    {
②      if (tcsetattr(STDIN_FILENO, TCSAFLUSH, &userTermios) == -1)
            errExit("tcsetattr");
        _exit(EXIT_SUCCESS);
    }

    static void            /* Handler for SIGTSTP */
③  tstpHandler(int sig)
    {
        struct termios ourTermios;         /* To save our tty settings */
        sigset_t tstpMask, prevMask;
        struct sigaction sa;
        int savedErrno;

        savedErrno = errno;                /* We might change 'errno' here */

        /* Save current terminal settings, restore terminal to
           state at time of program startup */

④      if (tcgetattr(STDIN_FILENO, &ourTermios) == -1)
            errExit("tcgetattr");
⑤      if (tcsetattr(STDIN_FILENO, TCSAFLUSH, &userTermios) == -1)
            errExit("tcsetattr");

        /* Set the disposition of SIGTSTP to the default, raise the signal
           once more, and then unblock it so that we actually stop */

        if (signal(SIGTSTP, SIG_DFL) == SIG_ERR)
            errExit("signal");
        raise(SIGTSTP);

        sigemptyset(&tstpMask);
        sigaddset(&tstpMask, SIGTSTP);
        if (sigprocmask(SIG_UNBLOCK, &tstpMask, &prevMask) == -1)
            errExit("sigprocmask");

        /* Execution resumes here after SIGCONT */

        if (sigprocmask(SIG_SETMASK, &prevMask, NULL) == -1)
            errExit("sigprocmask");         /* Reblock SIGTSTP */
```

```
        sigemptyset(&sa.sa_mask);            /* Reestablish handler */
        sa.sa_flags = SA_RESTART;
        sa.sa_handler = tstpHandler;
        if (sigaction(SIGTSTP, &sa, NULL) == -1)
            errExit("sigaction");

        /* The user may have changed the terminal settings while we were
           stopped; save the settings so we can restore them later */

⑥      if (tcgetattr(STDIN_FILENO, &userTermios) == -1)
            errExit("tcgetattr");

        /* Restore our terminal settings */

⑦      if (tcsetattr(STDIN_FILENO, TCSAFLUSH, &ourTermios) == -1)
            errExit("tcsetattr");

        errno = savedErrno;
    }

    int
    main(int argc, char *argv[])
    {
        char ch;
        struct sigaction sa, prev;
        ssize_t n;

        sigemptyset(&sa.sa_mask);
        sa.sa_flags = SA_RESTART;

⑧      if (argc > 1) {                      /* Use cbreak mode */
⑨          if (ttySetCbreak(STDIN_FILENO, &userTermios) == -1)
                errExit("ttySetCbreak");

            /* Terminal special characters can generate signals in cbreak
               mode. Catch them so that we can adjust the terminal mode.
               We establish handlers only if the signals are not being ignored. */

⑩          sa.sa_handler = handler;

            if (sigaction(SIGQUIT, NULL, &prev) == -1)
                errExit("sigaction");
            if (prev.sa_handler != SIG_IGN)
                if (sigaction(SIGQUIT, &sa, NULL) == -1)
                    errExit("sigaction");

            if (sigaction(SIGINT, NULL, &prev) == -1)
                errExit("sigaction");
            if (prev.sa_handler != SIG_IGN)
                if (sigaction(SIGINT, &sa, NULL) == -1)
                    errExit("sigaction");

⑪          sa.sa_handler = tstpHandler;
```

```
        if (sigaction(SIGTSTP, NULL, &prev) == -1)
            errExit("sigaction");
        if (prev.sa_handler != SIG_IGN)
            if (sigaction(SIGTSTP, &sa, NULL) == -1)
                errExit("sigaction");
    } else {                            /* Use raw mode */
⑫      if (ttySetRaw(STDIN_FILENO, &userTermios) == -1)
            errExit("ttySetRaw");
    }

⑬  sa.sa_handler = handler;
    if (sigaction(SIGTERM, &sa, NULL) == -1)
        errExit("sigaction");

    setbuf(stdout, NULL);              /* Disable stdout buffering */

⑭  for (;;) {                         /* Read and echo stdin */
        n = read(STDIN_FILENO, &ch, 1);
        if (n == -1) {
            errMsg("read");
            break;
        }

        if (n == 0)                    /* Can occur after terminal disconnect */
            break;

⑮      if (isalpha((unsigned char) ch))          /* Letters --> lowercase */
            putchar(tolower((unsigned char) ch));
        else if (ch == '\n' || ch == '\r')
            putchar(ch);
        else if (iscntrl((unsigned char) ch))
            printf("^%c", ch ^ 64);    /* Echo Control-A as ^A, etc. */
        else
            putchar('*');              /* All other chars as '*' */

⑯      if (ch == 'q')                 /* Quit loop */
            break;
    }

⑰  if (tcsetattr(STDIN_FILENO, TCSAFLUSH, &userTermios) == -1)
        errExit("tcsetattr");
    exit(EXIT_SUCCESS);
}
```

——————————————————————————————————————— tty/test_tty_functions.c

Here is an example of what we see when we ask the program in Listing 62-4 to use raw mode:

```
$ stty                              Initial terminal mode is sane (cooked)
speed 38400 baud; line = 0;
$ ./test_tty_functions
abc                                 Type abc, and Control-J
   def                              Type DEF, Control-J, and Enter
^C^Z                                Type Control-C, Control-Z, and Control-J
   q$                               Type q to exit
```

In the last line of the preceding shell session, we see that the shell printed its prompt on the same line as the *q* character that caused the program to terminate.

The following shows an example run using cbreak mode:

```
$ ./test_tty_functions x
XYZ                                        Type XYZ and Control-Z
[1]+  Stopped        ./test_tty_functions x
$ stty                                     Verify that terminal mode was restored
speed 38400 baud; line = 0;
$ fg                                       Resume in foreground
./test_tty_functions x
***                                        Type 123 and Control-J
    $                                      Type Control-C to terminate program
Press Enter to get next shell prompt
$ stty                                     Verify that terminal mode was restored
speed 38400 baud; line = 0;
```

62.7 Terminal Line Speed (Bit Rate)

Different terminals (and serial lines) are capable of transmitting and receiving at different speeds (bits per second). The *cfgetispeed()* and *cfsetispeed()* functions retrieve and modify the input line speed. The *cfgetospeed()* and *cfsetospeed()* functions retrieve and modify the output line speed.

> The term *baud* is commonly used as a synonym for the terminal line speed (in bits per second), although this usage is not technically correct. Precisely, baud is the per-second rate at which signal changes can occur on the line, which is not necessarily the same as the number of bits transmitted per second, since the latter depends on how bits are encoded into signals. Nevertheless, the term *baud* continues to be used synonymously with *bit rate* (bits per second). (The term *baud rate* is often also used synonymously with *baud*, but this is redundant; the baud is by definition a rate.) To avoid confusion, we'll generally use terms like *line speed* or *bit rate*.

```
#include <termios.h>

speed_t cfgetispeed(const struct termios *termios_p);
speed_t cfgetospeed(const struct termios *termios_p);
```
                    Both return a line speed from given *termios* structure
```
int cfsetospeed(struct termios *termios_p, speed_t speed);
int cfsetispeed(struct termios *termios_p, speed_t speed);
```
                    Both return 0 on success, or −1 on error

Each of these functions works on a *termios* structure that must be previously initialized by a call to *tcgetattr()*.

For example, to find out the current terminal output line speed, we would do the following:

```
struct termios tp;
speed_t rate;

if (tcgetattr(fd, &tp) == -1)
    errExit("tcgetattr");
rate = cfgetospeed(&tp);
if (rate == -1)
    errExit("cfgetospeed");
```

If we then wanted to change this line speed, we would continue as follows:

```
if (cfsetospeed(&tp, B38400) == -1)
    errExit("cfsetospeed");
if (tcsetattr(fd, TCSAFLUSH, &tp) == -1)
    errExit("tcsetattr");
```

The *speed_t* data type is used to store a line speed. Rather than directly assigning numeric values for line speeds, a set of symbolic constants (defined in <termios.h>) is used. These constants define a series of discrete values. Some examples of such constants are B300, B2400, B9600, and B38400, corresponding, respectively, to the line speeds 300, 2400, 9600, and 38,400 bits per second. The use of a set of discrete values reflects the fact that terminals are normally designed to work with a limited set of different (standardized) line speeds, derived from the division of some base rate (e.g., 115,200 is typical on PCs) by integral values (e.g., 115,200 / 12 = 9600).

SUSv3 specifies that the terminal line speeds are stored in the *termios* structure, but (deliberately) does not specify where. Many implementations, including Linux, maintain these values in the *c_cflag* field, using the CBAUD mask and the CBAUDEX flag. (In Section 62.2, we noted that the nonstandard *c_ispeed* and *c_ospeed* fields of the Linux *termios* structure are unused.)

Although the *cfsetispeed()* and *cfsetospeed()* functions allow separate input and output line speeds to be specified, on many terminals, these two speeds must be the same. Furthermore, Linux uses only a single field to store the line speed (i.e., the two rates are assumed to be always the same), which means that all of the input and output line-speed functions access the same *termios* field.

> Specifying *speed* as 0 in a call to *cfsetispeed()* means "set the input speed to whatever the output speed is when *tcsetattr()* is later called." This is useful on systems where the two line speeds are maintained as separate values.

62.8 Terminal Line Control

The *tcsendbreak()*, *tcdrain()*, *tcflush()*, and *tcflow()* functions perform tasks that are usually collectively grouped under the term *line control*. (These functions are POSIX inventions designed to replace various *ioctl()* operations.)

```
#include <termios.h>

int tcsendbreak(int fd, int duration);
int tcdrain(int fd);
int tcflush(int fd, int queue_selector);
int tcflow(int fd, int action);
```

                                        All return 0 on success, or −1 on error

In each function, *fd* is a file descriptor that refers to a terminal or other remote device on a serial line.

The *tcsendbreak()* function generates a BREAK condition, by transmitting a continuous stream of 0 bits. The *duration* argument specifies the length of the transmission. If *duration* is 0, 0 bits are transmitted for 0.25 seconds. (SUSv3 specifies at least 0.25 and not more than 0.5 seconds.) If *duration* is greater than 0, 0 bits are transmitted for *duration* milliseconds. SUSv3 leaves this case unspecified; the handling of a nonzero *duration* varies widely on other UNIX implementations (the details described here are for *glibc*).

The *tcdrain()* function blocks until all output has been transmitted (i.e., until the terminal output queue has been emptied).

The *tcflush()* function flushes (discards) the data in the terminal input queue, the terminal output queue, or both queues (see Figure 62-1). Flushing the input queue discards data that has been received by the terminal driver but not yet read by any process. For example, an application can use *tcflush()* to discard terminal type-ahead before prompting for a password. Flushing the output queue discards data that has been written (passed to the terminal driver) but not yet transmitted to the device. The *queue_selector* argument specifies one of the values shown in Table 62-4.

> Note that the term *flush* is used in a different sense with *tcflush()* than when talking about file I/O. For file I/O, *flushing* means forcing the output to be transferred either user-space memory to the buffer cache in the case of the *stdio fflush()*, or from the buffer cache to the disk, in the case of *fsync()*, *fdatasync()*, and *sync()*.

Table 62-4: Values for the *tcflush() queue_selector* argument

Value	Description
TCIFLUSH	Flush the input queue
TCOFLUSH	Flush the output queue
TCIOFLUSH	Flush both the input and the output queues

The *tcflow()* function controls the flow of data in either direction between the computer and the terminal (or other remote device). The *action* argument is one of the values shown in Table 62-5. The TCIOFF and TCION values are effective only if the terminal is capable of interpreting STOP and START characters, in which case these operations respectively cause the terminal to suspend and resume sending data to the computer, respectively.

Table 62-5: Values for the *tcflow() action* argument

Value	Description
TCOOFF	Suspend output to the terminal
TCOON	Resume output to the terminal
TCIOFF	Transmit a STOP character to the terminal
TCION	Transmit a START character to the terminal

62.9 Terminal Window Size

In a windowing environment, a screen-handling application needs to be able to monitor the size of a terminal window, so that the screen can be redrawn appropriately if the user modifies the window size. The kernel provides two pieces of support to allow this to happen:

- A SIGWINCH signal is sent to the foreground process group after a change in the terminal window size. By default, this signal is ignored.

- At any time—usually following the receipt of a SIGWINCH signal—a process can use the *ioctl()* TIOCGWINSZ operation to find out the current size of the terminal window.

The *ioctl()* TIOCGWINSZ operation is used as follows:

```
if (ioctl(fd, TIOCGWINSZ, &ws) == -1)
    errExit("ioctl");
```

The *fd* argument is a file descriptor referring to a terminal window. The final argument to *ioctl()* is a pointer to a *winsize* structure (defined in <sys/ioctl.h>), used to return the terminal window size:

```
struct winsize {
    unsigned short ws_row;      /* Number of rows (characters) */
    unsigned short ws_col;      /* Number of columns (characters) */
    unsigned short ws_xpixel;   /* Horizontal size (pixels) */
    unsigned short ws_ypixel;   /* Vertical size (pixels) */
};
```

Like many other implementations, Linux doesn't use the pixel-size fields of the *winsize* structure.

Listing 62-5 demonstrates the use of the SIGWINCH signal and the *ioctl()* TIOCGWINSZ operation. The following shows an example of the output produced when this program is run under a window manager and the terminal window size is changed three times:

```
$ ./demo_SIGWINCH
Caught SIGWINCH, new window size: 35 rows * 80 columns
Caught SIGWINCH, new window size: 35 rows * 73 columns
Caught SIGWINCH, new window size: 22 rows * 73 columns
```
Type Control-C to terminate program

Listing 62-5: Monitoring changes in the terminal window size

─── **tty/demo_SIGWINCH.c**

```c
#include <signal.h>
#include <termios.h>
#include <sys/ioctl.h>
#include "tlpi_hdr.h"

static void
sigwinchHandler(int sig)
{
}

int
main(int argc, char *argv[])
{
    struct winsize ws;
    struct sigaction sa;

    sigemptyset(&sa.sa_mask);
    sa.sa_flags = 0;
    sa.sa_handler = sigwinchHandler;
    if (sigaction(SIGWINCH, &sa, NULL) == -1)
        errExit("sigaction");

    for (;;) {
        pause();                        /* Wait for SIGWINCH signal */

        if (ioctl(STDIN_FILENO, TIOCGWINSZ, &ws) == -1)
            errExit("ioctl");
        printf("Caught SIGWINCH, new window size: "
                "%d rows * %d columns\n", ws.ws_row, ws.ws_col);
    }
}
```

─── **tty/demo_SIGWINCH.c**

It is also possible to change the terminal driver's notion of the window size by passing an initialized *winsize* structure in an *ioctl()* TIOCSWINSZ operation:

```c
ws.ws_row = 40;
ws.ws_col = 100;
if (ioctl(fd, TIOCSWINSZ, &ws) == -1)
    errExit("ioctl");
```

If the new values in the *winsize* structure differ from the terminal driver's current notion of the terminal window size, two things happen:

- The terminal driver data structures are updated using the values supplied in the *ws* argument.
- A SIGWINCH signal is sent to the foreground process group of the terminal.

Note, however, that these events on their own are insufficient to change the actual dimensions of the displayed window, which are controlled by software outside the kernel (such as a window manager or a terminal emulator program).

Although not standardized in SUSv3, most UNIX implementations provide access to the terminal window size using the *ioctl()* operations described in this section.

62.10 Terminal Identification

In Section 34.4, we described the *ctermid()* function, which returns the name of the controlling terminal for a process (usually /dev/tty on UNIX systems). The functions described in this section are also useful for identifying a terminal.

The *isatty()* function enables us to determine whether a file descriptor, *fd*, is associated with a terminal (as opposed to some other file type).

```
#include <unistd.h>

int isatty(int fd);
```
                     Returns true (1) if *fd* is associated with a terminal, otherwise false (0)

The *isatty()* function is useful in editors and other screen-handling programs that need to determine whether their standard input and output are directed to a terminal.

Given a file descriptor, the *ttyname()* function returns the name of the associated terminal device.

```
#include <unistd.h>

char *ttyname(int fd);
```
                     Returns pointer to (statically allocated) string containing
                     terminal name, or NULL on error

To find the name of the terminal, *ttyname()* uses the *opendir()* and *readdir()* functions described in Section 18.8 to walk through the directories holding terminal device names, looking at each directory entry until it finds one whose device ID (the *st_rdev* field of the *stat* structure) matches that of the device referred to by the file descriptor *fd*. Terminal device entries normally reside in two directories: /dev and /dev/pts. The /dev directory contains entries for virtual consoles (e.g., /dev/tty1) and BSD pseudoterminals. The /dev/pts directory contains entries for (System V-style) pseudoterminal slave devices. (We describe pseudoterminals in Chapter 64.)

> A reentrant version of *ttyname()* exists in the form of *ttyname_r()*.
>
> The *tty(1)* command, which displays the name of the terminal referred to by its standard input, is the command-line analog of *ttyname()*.

62.11 Summary

On early UNIX systems, terminals were real hardware devices connected to a computer via serial lines. Early terminals were not standardized, meaning that different escape sequences were required to program the terminals produced by different vendors. On modern workstations, such terminals have been superseded by bit-mapped monitors running the X Window System. However, the ability to program terminals is still required when dealing with virtual devices, such as virtual consoles and terminal emulators (which employ pseudoterminals), and real devices connected via serial lines.

Terminal settings (with the exception of the terminal window size) are maintained in a structure of type *termios*, which contains four bit-mask fields that control various terminal settings and an array that defines the various special characters interpreted by the terminal driver. The *tcgetattr()* and *tcsetattr()* functions allow a program to retrieve and modify the terminal settings.

When performing input, the terminal driver can operate in two different modes. In canonical mode, input is gathered into lines (terminated by one of the line-delimiter characters) and line editing is enabled. By contrast, noncanonical mode allows an application to read terminal input a character at a time, without needing to wait for the user to type a line-delimiter character. Line editing is disabled in noncanonical mode. Completion of a noncanonical mode read is controlled by the MIN and TIME fields of the *termios* structure, which determine the minimum number of characters to be read and a timeout to be applied to the read operation. We described four distinct cases for the operation of noncanonical reads.

Historically, the Seventh Edition and BSD terminal drivers provided three input modes—cooked, cbreak, and raw—which performed varying degrees of processing of terminal input and output. Cbreak and raw modes can be emulated by changing various fields within the *termios* structure.

A range of functions perform various other terminal operations. These include changing the terminal line speed and performing line-control operations (generating a break condition, pausing until output has been transmitted, flushing terminal input and output queues, and suspending or resuming transmission of data in either direction between the terminal and the computer). Other functions allow us to check if a given file descriptor refers to a terminal and to obtain the name of that terminal. The *ioctl()* system call can be used to retrieve and modify the terminal window size recorded by the kernel, and to perform a range of other terminal-related operations.

Further information

[Stevens, 1992] also describes terminal programming and goes into much more detail on programming serial ports. Several good online resources discuss terminal programming. Hosted at the LDP web site (*http://www.tldp.org*) are the *Serial HOWTO* and the *Text-terminal HOWTO*, both by David S. Lawyer. Another useful source of information is the *Serial Programming Guide for POSIX Operating Systems* by Michael R. Sweet, available online at *http://www.easysw.com/~mike/serial/*.

62.12 Exercises

62-1. Implement *isatty()*. (You may find it useful to read the description of *tcgetattr()* in Section 62.2.)

62-2. Implement *ttyname()*.

62-3. Implement the *getpass()* function described in Section 8.5. (The *getpass()* function can obtain a file descriptor for the controlling terminal by opening /dev/tty.)

62-4. Write a program that displays information indicating whether the terminal referred to by standard input is in canonical or noncanonical mode. If in noncanonical mode, then display the values of TIME and MIN.

63

ALTERNATIVE I/O MODELS

This chapter discusses three alternatives to the conventional file I/O model that we have employed in most programs shown in this book:

- I/O multiplexing (the *select()* and *poll()* system calls);
- signal-driven I/O; and
- the Linux-specific *epoll* API.

63.1 Overview

Most of the programs that we have presented so far in this book employ an I/O model under which a process performs I/O on just one file descriptor at a time, and each I/O system call blocks until the data is transferred. For example, when reading from a pipe, a *read()* call normally blocks if no data is currently present in the pipe, and a *write()* call blocks if there is insufficient space in the pipe to hold the data to be written. Similar behavior occurs when performing I/O on various other types of files, including FIFOs and sockets.

Disk files are a special case. As described in Chapter 13, the kernel employs the buffer cache to speed disk I/O requests. Thus, a *write()* to a disk returns as soon as the requested data has been transferred to the kernel buffer cache, rather than waiting until the data is written to disk (unless the O_SYNC flag was specified when opening the file). Correspondingly, a *read()* transfers data from the buffer cache to a user buffer, and if the required data is not in the buffer cache, then the kernel puts the process to sleep while a disk read is performed.

The traditional blocking I/O model is sufficient for many applications, but not all. In particular, some applications need to be able to do one or both of the following:

- Check whether I/O is possible on a file descriptor without blocking if it is not possible.
- Monitor multiple file descriptors to see if I/O is possible on any of them.

We have already encountered two techniques that can be used to partially address these needs: nonblocking I/O and the use of multiple processes or threads.

We described nonblocking I/O in some detail in Sections 5.9 and 44.9. If we place a file descriptor in nonblocking mode by enabling the O_NONBLOCK open file status flag, then an I/O system call that can't be immediately completed returns an error instead of blocking. Nonblocking I/O can be employed with pipes, FIFOs, sockets, terminals, pseudoterminals, and some other types of devices.

Nonblocking I/O allows us to periodically check ("poll") whether I/O is possible on a file descriptor. For example, we can make an input file descriptor nonblocking, and then periodically perform nonblocking reads. If we need to monitor multiple file descriptors, then we mark them all nonblocking, and poll each of them in turn. However, polling in this manner is usually undesirable. If polling is done only infrequently, then the latency before an application responds to an I/O event may be unacceptably long; on the other hand, polling in a tight loop wastes CPU time.

> In this chapter, we use the word *poll* in two distinct ways. One of these is as the name of the I/O multiplexing system call, *poll()*. In the other use, we mean "performing a nonblocking check on the status of a file descriptor."

If we don't want a process to block when performing I/O on a file descriptor, we can instead create a new process to perform the I/O. The parent process can then carry on to perform other tasks, while the child process blocks until the I/O is complete. If we need to handle I/O on multiple file descriptors, we can create one child for each descriptor. The problems with this approach are expense and complexity. Creating and maintaining processes places a load on the system, and, typically, the child processes will need to use some form of IPC to inform the parent about the status of I/O operations.

Using multiple threads instead of processes is less demanding of resources, but the threads will probably still need to communicate information to one another about the status of I/O operations, and the programming can be complex, especially if we are using thread pools to minimize the number of threads used to handle large numbers of simultaneous clients. (One place where threads can be particularly useful is if the application needs to call a third-party library that performs blocking I/O. An application can avoid blocking in this case by making the library call in a separate thread.)

Because of the limitations of both nonblocking I/O and the use of multiple threads or processes, one of the following alternatives is often preferable:

- *I/O multiplexing* allows a process to simultaneously monitor multiple file descriptors to find out whether I/O is possible on any of them. The *select()* and *poll()* system calls perform I/O multiplexing.

- *Signal-driven I/O* is a technique whereby a process requests that the kernel send it a signal when input is available or data can be written on a specified file descriptor. The process can then carry on performing other activities, and is notified when I/O becomes possible via receipt of the signal. When monitoring large numbers of file descriptors, signal-driven I/O provides significantly better performance than *select()* and *poll()*.

- The *epoll* API is a Linux-specific feature that first appeared in Linux 2.6. Like the I/O multiplexing APIs, the *epoll* API allows a process to monitor multiple file descriptors to see if I/O is possible on any of them. Like signal-driven I/O, the *epoll* API provides much better performance when monitoring large numbers of file descriptors.

> In the remainder of this chapter, we'll generally frame the discussion of the above techniques in terms of processes. However, these techniques can also be employed in multithreaded applications.

In effect, I/O multiplexing, signal-driven I/O, and *epoll* are all methods of achieving the same result—monitoring one or, commonly, several file descriptors simultaneously to see if they are *ready* to perform I/O (to be precise, to see whether an I/O system call could be performed without blocking). The transition of a file descriptor into a ready state is triggered by some type of I/O *event*, such as the arrival of input, the completion of a socket connection, or the availability of space in a previously full socket send buffer after TCP transmits queued data to the socket peer. Monitoring multiple file descriptors is useful in applications such as network servers that must simultaneously monitor multiple client sockets, or applications that must simultaneously monitor input from a terminal and a pipe or socket.

Note that none of these techniques performs I/O. They merely tell us that a file descriptor is ready. Some other system call must then be used to actually perform the I/O.

> One I/O model that we don't describe in this chapter is POSIX asynchronous I/O (AIO). POSIX AIO allows a process to queue an I/O operation to a file and then later be notified when the operation is complete. The advantage of POSIX AIO is that the initial I/O call returns immediately, so that the process is not tied up waiting for data to be transferred to the kernel or for the operation to complete. This allows the process to perform other tasks in parallel with the I/O (which may include queuing further I/O requests). For certain types of applications, POSIX AIO can provide useful performance benefits. Currently, Linux provides a threads-based implementation of POSIX AIO within *glibc*. At the time of writing, work is ongoing toward providing an in-kernel implementation of POSIX AIO, which should provide better scaling performance. POSIX AIO is described in [Gallmeister, 1995], [Robbins & Robbins, 2003], and the *aio(7)* manual page.

Which technique?

During the course of this chapter, we'll consider the reasons we may choose one of these techniques rather than another. In the meantime, we summarize a few points:

- The *select()* and *poll()* system calls are long-standing interfaces that have been present on UNIX systems for many years. Compared to the other techniques, their primary advantage is portability. Their main disadvantage is that they don't scale well when monitoring large numbers (hundreds or thousands) of file descriptors.

- The key advantage of the *epoll* API is that it allows an application to efficiently monitor large numbers of file descriptors. Its primary disadvantage is that it is a Linux-specific API.

    > Some other UNIX implementations provide (nonstandard) mechanisms similar to *epoll*. For example, Solaris provides the special /dev/poll file (described in the Solaris *poll(7d)* manual page), and some of the BSDs provide the *kqueue* API (which provides a more general-purpose monitoring facility than *epoll*). [Stevens et al., 2004] briefly describes these two mechanisms; a longer discussion of *kqueue* can be found in [Lemon, 2001].

- Like *epoll*, signal-driven I/O allows an application to efficiently monitor large numbers of file descriptors. However, *epoll* provides a number of advantages over signal-driven I/O:
    - We avoid the complexities of dealing with signals.
    - We can specify the kind of monitoring that we want to perform (e.g., ready for reading or ready for writing).
    - We can select either level-triggered or edge-triggered notification (described in Section 63.1.1).

    Furthermore, taking full advantage of signal-driven I/O requires the use of nonportable, Linux-specific features, and if we do this, signal-driven I/O is no more portable than *epoll*.

Because, on the one hand, *select()* and *poll()* are more portable, while signal-driven I/O and *epoll* deliver better performance, for some applications, it can be worthwhile writing an abstract software layer for monitoring file descriptor events. With such a layer, portable programs can employ *epoll* (or a similar API) on systems that provide it, and fall back to the use of *select()* or *poll()* on other systems.

> The *libevent* library is a software layer that provides an abstraction for monitoring file descriptor events. It has been ported to a number of UNIX systems. As its underlying mechanism, *libevent* can (transparently) employ any of the techniques described in this chapter: *select()*, *poll()*, signal-driven I/O, or *epoll*, as well as the Solaris specific /dev/poll interface or the BSD *kqueue* interface. (Thus, *libevent* also serves as an example of how to use each of these techniques.) Written by Niels Provos, *libevent* is available at *http://monkey.org/~provos/libevent/*.

63.1.1 Level-Triggered and Edge-Triggered Notification

Before discussing the various alternative I/O mechanisms in detail, we need to distinguish two models of readiness notification for a file descriptor:

- *Level-triggered notification*: A file descriptor is considered to be ready if it is possible to perform an I/O system call without blocking.
- *Edge-triggered notification*: Notification is provided if there is I/O activity (e.g., new input) on a file descriptor since it was last monitored.

Table 63-1 summarizes the notification models employed by I/O multiplexing, signal-driven I/O, and *epoll*. The *epoll* API differs from the other two I/O models in that it can employ both level-triggered notification (the default) and edge-triggered notification.

Table 63-1: Use of level-triggered and edge-triggered notification models

I/O model	Level-triggered?	Edge-triggered?
select(), *poll()*	•	
Signal-driven I/O		•
epoll	•	•

Details of the differences between these two notification models will become clearer during the course of the chapter. For now, we describe how the choice of notification model affects the way we design a program.

When we employ level-triggered notification, we can check the readiness of a file descriptor at any time. This means that when we determine that a file descriptor is ready (e.g., it has input available), we can perform some I/O on the descriptor, and then repeat the monitoring operation to check if the descriptor is still ready (e.g., it still has more input available), in which case we can perform more I/O, and so on. In other words, because the level-triggered model allows us to repeat the I/O monitoring operation at any time, it is not necessary to perform as much I/O as possible (e.g., read as many bytes as possible) on the file descriptor (or even perform any I/O at all) each time we are notified that a file descriptor is ready.

By contrast, when we employ edge-triggered notification, we receive notification only when an I/O event occurs. We don't receive any further notification until another I/O event occurs. Furthermore, when an I/O event is notified for a file descriptor, we usually don't know how much I/O is possible (e.g., how many bytes are available for reading). Therefore, programs that employ edge-triggered notification are usually designed according to the following rules:

- After notification of an I/O event, the program should—at some point—perform as much I/O as possible (e.g., read as many bytes as possible) on the corresponding file descriptor. If the program fails to do this, then it might miss the opportunity to perform some I/O, because it would not be aware of the need to operate on the file descriptor until another I/O event occurred. This could lead to spurious data loss or blockages in a program. We said "at some point," because sometimes it may not be desirable to perform all of the I/O immediately after we determine that the file descriptor is ready. The problem is that we may starve other file descriptors of attention if we perform a large amount of I/O on one file descriptor. We consider this point in more detail when we describe the edge-triggered notification model for *epoll* in Section 63.4.6.

- If the program employs a loop to perform as much I/O as possible on the file descriptor, and the descriptor is marked as blocking, then eventually an I/O system call will block when no more I/O is possible. For this reason, each monitored file descriptor is normally placed in nonblocking mode, and after notification of an I/O event, I/O operations are performed repeatedly until the relevant system call (e.g., *read()* or *write()*) fails with the error EAGAIN or EWOULDBLOCK.

63.1.2 Employing Nonblocking I/O with Alternative I/O Models

Nonblocking I/O (the O_NONBLOCK flag) is often used in conjunction with the I/O models described in this chapter. Some examples of why this can be useful are the following:

- As explained in the previous section, nonblocking I/O is usually employed in conjunction with I/O models that provide edge-triggered notification of I/O events.
- If multiple processes (or threads) are performing I/O on the same open file descriptions, then, from a particular process's point of view, a descriptor's readiness may change between the time the descriptor was notified as being ready and the time of the subsequent I/O call. Consequently, a blocking I/O call could block, thus preventing the process from monitoring other file descriptors. (This can occur for all of the I/O models that we describe in this chapter, regardless of whether they employ level-triggered or edge-triggered notification.)
- Even after a level-triggered API such as *select()* or *poll()* informs us that a file descriptor for a stream socket is ready for writing, if we write a large enough block of data in a single *write()* or *send()*, then the call will nevertheless block.
- In rare cases, level-triggered APIs such as *select()* and *poll()* can return spurious readiness notifications—they can falsely inform us that a file descriptor is ready. This could be caused by a kernel bug or be expected behavior in an uncommon scenario.

> Section 16.6 of [Stevens et al., 2004] describes one example of spurious readiness notifications on BSD systems for a listening socket. If a client connects to a server's listening socket and then resets the connection, a *select()* performed by the server between these two events will indicate the listening socket as being readable, but a subsequent *accept()* that is performed after the client's reset will block.

63.2 I/O Multiplexing

I/O multiplexing allows us to simultaneously monitor multiple file descriptors to see if I/O is possible on any of them. We can perform I/O multiplexing using either of two system calls with essentially the same functionality. The first of these, *select()*, appeared along with the sockets API in BSD. This was historically the more widespread of the two system calls. The other system call, *poll()*, appeared in System V. Both *select()* and *poll()* are nowadays required by SUSv3.

We can use *select()* and *poll()* to monitor file descriptors for regular files, terminals, pseudoterminals, pipes, FIFOs, sockets, and some types of character devices. Both system calls allow a process either to block indefinitely waiting for file descriptors to become ready or to specify a timeout on the call.

63.2.1 The *select()* System Call

The *select()* system call blocks until one or more of a set of file descriptors becomes ready.

```
#include <sys/time.h>          /* For portability */
#include <sys/select.h>

int select(int nfds, fd_set *readfds, fd_set *writefds, fd_set *exceptfds,
            struct timeval *timeout);
```
> Returns number of ready file descriptors, 0 on timeout, or −1 on error

The *nfds*, *readfds*, *writefds*, and *exceptfds* arguments specify the file descriptors that *select()* is to monitor. The *timeout* argument can be used to set an upper limit on the time for which *select()* will block. We describe each of these arguments in detail below.

> In the prototype for *select()* shown above, we include <sys/time.h> because that was the header specified in SUSv2, and some UNIX implementations require this header. (The <sys/time.h> header is present on Linux, and including it does no harm.)

File descriptor sets

The *readfds*, *writefds*, and *exceptfds* arguments are pointers to *file descriptor sets*, represented using the data type *fd_set*. These arguments are used as follows:

- *readfds* is the set of file descriptors to be tested to see if input is possible;
- *writefds* is the set of file descriptors to be tested to see if output is possible; and
- *exceptfds* is the set of file descriptors to be tested to see if an exceptional condition has occurred.

The term *exceptional condition* is often misunderstood to mean that some sort of error condition has arisen on the file descriptor. This is not the case. An exceptional condition occurs in only a few cases on Linux, including the following:

- A state change occurs on a pseudoterminal slave connected to a master that is in packet mode (Section 64.5).
- Out-of-band data is received on a stream socket (Section 61.13.1).

Typically, the *fd_set* data type is implemented as a bit mask. However, we don't need to know the details, since all manipulation of file descriptor sets is done via four macros: FD_ZERO(), FD_SET(), FD_CLR(), and FD_ISSET().

```
#include <sys/select.h>

void FD_ZERO(fd_set *fdset);
void FD_SET(int fd, fd_set *fdset);
void FD_CLR(int fd, fd_set *fdset);

int FD_ISSET(int fd, fd_set *fdset);
```
                    Returns true (1) if *fd* is in *fdset*, or false (0) otherwise

These macros operate as follows:

- FD_ZERO() initializes the set pointed to by *fdset* to be empty.

- FD_SET() adds the file descriptor *fd* to the set pointed to by *fdset*.

- FD_CLR() removes the file descriptor *fd* from the set pointed to by *fdset*.

- FD_ISSET() returns true if the file descriptor *fd* is a member of the set pointed to by *fdset*.

A file descriptor set has a maximum size, defined by the constant FD_SETSIZE. On Linux, this constant has the value 1024. (Other UNIX implementations have similar values for this limit.)

> Even though the FD_* macros are operating on user-space data structures, and the kernel implementation of *select()* can handle descriptor sets with larger sizes, *glibc* provides no simple way of modifying the definition of FD_SETSIZE. If we want to change this limit, we must modify the definition in the *glibc* header files. However, for reasons that we describe later in this chapter, if we need to monitor large numbers of descriptors, then using *epoll* is probably preferable to the use of *select()*.

The *readfds*, *writefds*, and *exceptfds* arguments are all value-result. Before the call to *select()*, the *fd_set* structures pointed to by these arguments must be initialized (using FD_ZERO() and FD_SET()) to contain the set of file descriptors of interest. The *select()* call modifies each of these structures so that, on return, they contain the set of file descriptors that are ready. (Since these structures are modified by the call, we must ensure that we reinitialize them if we are repeatedly calling *select()* from within a loop.) The structures can then be examined using FD_ISSET().

If we are not interested in a particular class of events, then the corresponding *fd_set* argument can be specified as NULL. We say more about the precise meaning of each of the three event types in Section 63.2.3.

The *nfds* argument must be set one greater than the highest file descriptor number included in any of the three file descriptor sets. This argument allows *select()* to be more efficient, since the kernel then knows not to check whether file descriptor numbers higher than this value are part of each file descriptor set.

The *timeout* argument

The *timeout* argument controls the blocking behavior of *select()*. It can be specified either as NULL, in which case *select()* blocks indefinitely, or as a pointer to a *timeval* structure:

```
struct timeval {
    time_t      tv_sec;         /* Seconds */
    suseconds_t tv_usec;        /* Microseconds (long int) */
};
```

If both fields of *timeout* are 0, then *select()* doesn't block; it simply polls the specified file descriptors to see which ones are ready and returns immediately. Otherwise, *timeout* specifies an upper limit on the time for which *select()* is to wait.

Although the *timeval* structure affords microsecond precision, the accuracy of the call is limited by the granularity of the software clock (Section 10.6). SUSv3 specifies that the timeout is rounded upward if it is not an exact multiple of this granularity.

> SUSv3 requires that the maximum permissible timeout interval be at least 31 days. Most UNIX implementations allow a considerably higher limit. Since Linux/ x86-32 uses a 32-bit integer for the *time_t* type, the upper limit is many years.

When *timeout* is NULL, or points to a structure containing nonzero fields, *select()* blocks until one of the following occurs:

- at least one of the file descriptors specified in *readfds*, *writefds*, or *exceptfds* becomes ready;
- the call is interrupted by a signal handler; or
- the amount of time specified by *timeout* has passed.

> In older UNIX implementations that lacked a sleep call with subsecond precision (e.g., *nanosleep()*), *select()* was used to emulate this functionality by specifying *nfds* as 0; *readfds*, *writefds*, and *exceptfds* as NULL; and the desired sleep interval in *timeout*.

On Linux, if *select()* returns because one or more file descriptors became ready, and if *timeout* was non-NULL, then *select()* updates the structure to which *timeout* points to indicate how much time remained until the call would have timed out. However, this behavior is implementation-specific. SUSv3 also allows the possibility that an implementation leaves the structure pointed to by *timeout* unchanged, and most other UNIX implementations *don't* modify this structure. Portable applications that employ *select()* within a loop should always ensure that the structure pointed to by *timeout* is initialized before each *select()* call, and should ignore the information returned in the structure after the call.

SUSv3 states that the structure pointed to by *timeout* may be modified only on a successful return from *select()*. However, on Linux, if *select()* is interrupted by a signal handler (so that it fails with the error EINTR), then the structure is modified to indicate the time remaining until a timeout would have occurred (i.e., like a successful return).

If we use the Linux-specific *personality()* system call to set a personality that includes the STICKY_TIMEOUTS personality bit, then *select()* doesn't modify the structure pointed to by *timeout*.

Return value from *select()*

As its function result, *select()* returns one of the following:

- A return value of −1 indicates that an error occurred. Possible errors include EBADF and EINTR. EBADF indicates that one of the file descriptors in *readfds*, *writefds*, or *exceptfds* is invalid (e.g., not currently open). EINTR, indicates that the call was interrupted by a signal handler. (As noted in Section 21.5, *select()* is never automatically restarted if interrupted by a signal handler.)
- A return value of 0 means that the call timed out before any file descriptor became ready. In this case, each of the returned file descriptor sets will be empty.
- A positive return value indicates that one or more file descriptors is ready. The return value is the number of ready descriptors. In this case, each of the returned file descriptor sets must be examined (using FD_ISSET()) in order to find out which I/O events occurred. If the same file descriptor is specified in more than one of *readfds*, *writefds*, and *exceptfds*, it is counted multiple times if it is ready for more than one event. In other words, *select()* returns the total number of file descriptors marked as ready in all three returned sets.

Example program

The program in Listing 63-1 demonstrates the use of *select()*. Using command-line arguments, we can specify the *timeout* and the file descriptors that we wish to monitor. The first command-line argument specifies the *timeout* for *select()*, in seconds. If a hyphen (-) is specified here, then *select()* is called with a timeout of NULL, meaning block indefinitely. Each of the remaining command-line arguments specifies the number of a file descriptor to be monitored, followed by letters indicating the operations for which the descriptor is to be checked. The letters we can specify here are *r* (ready for read) and *w* (ready for write).

Listing 63-1: Using *select()* to monitor multiple file descriptors

————————————————————————————————————— altio/t_select.c

```
#include <sys/time.h>
#include <sys/select.h>
#include "tlpi_hdr.h"

static void
usageError(const char *progName)
{
    fprintf(stderr, "Usage: %s {timeout|-} fd-num[rw]...\n", progName);
    fprintf(stderr, "    - means infinite timeout; \n");
    fprintf(stderr, "    r = monitor for read\n");
    fprintf(stderr, "    w = monitor for write\n\n");
    fprintf(stderr, "    e.g.: %s - 0rw 1w\n", progName);
    exit(EXIT_FAILURE);
}
```

```c
int
main(int argc, char *argv[])
{
    fd_set readfds, writefds;
    int ready, nfds, fd, numRead, j;
    struct timeval timeout;
    struct timeval *pto;
    char buf[10];                       /* Large enough to hold "rw\0" */

    if (argc < 2 || strcmp(argv[1], "--help") == 0)
        usageError(argv[0]);

    /* Timeout for select() is specified in argv[1] */

    if (strcmp(argv[1], "-") == 0) {
        pto = NULL;                     /* Infinite timeout */
    } else {
        pto = &timeout;
        timeout.tv_sec = getLong(argv[1], 0, "timeout");
        timeout.tv_usec = 0;            /* No microseconds */
    }

    /* Process remaining arguments to build file descriptor sets */

    nfds = 0;
    FD_ZERO(&readfds);
    FD_ZERO(&writefds);

    for (j = 2; j < argc; j++) {
        numRead = sscanf(argv[j], "%d%2[rw]", &fd, buf);
        if (numRead != 2)
            usageError(argv[0]);
        if (fd >= FD_SETSIZE)
            cmdLineErr("file descriptor exceeds limit (%d)\n", FD_SETSIZE);

        if (fd >= nfds)
            nfds = fd + 1;              /* Record maximum fd + 1 */
        if (strchr(buf, 'r') != NULL)
            FD_SET(fd, &readfds);
        if (strchr(buf, 'w') != NULL)
            FD_SET(fd, &writefds);
    }

    /* We've built all of the arguments; now call select() */

    ready = select(nfds, &readfds, &writefds, NULL, pto);
                                        /* Ignore exceptional events */
    if (ready == -1)
        errExit("select");

    /* Display results of select() */

    printf("ready = %d\n", ready);
```

```
    for (fd = 0; fd < nfds; fd++)
        printf("%d: %s%s\n", fd, FD_ISSET(fd, &readfds) ? "r" : "",
                FD_ISSET(fd, &writefds) ? "w" : "");

    if (pto != NULL)
        printf("timeout after select(): %ld.%03ld\n",
                (long) timeout.tv_sec, (long) timeout.tv_usec / 1000);
    exit(EXIT_SUCCESS);
}
```

—— altio/t_select.c

In the following shell session log, we demonstrate the use of the program in List-ing 63-1. In the first example, we make a request to monitor file descriptor 0 for input with a 10-second *timeout*:

```
$ ./t_select 10 0r
```
Press Enter, so that a line of input is available on file descriptor 0
```
ready = 1
0: r
timeout after select(): 8.003
$                                       Next shell prompt is displayed
```

The above output shows us that *select()* determined that one file descriptor was ready. This was file descriptor 0, which was ready for reading. We can also see that the *timeout* was modified. The final line of output, consisting of just the shell $ prompt, appeared because the *t_select* program didn't read the newline character that made file descriptor 0 ready, and so that character was read by the shell, which responded by printing another prompt.

In the next example, we again monitor file descriptor 0 for input, but this time with a *timeout* of 0 seconds:

```
$ ./t_select 0 0r
ready = 0
timeout after select(): 0.000
```

The *select()* call returned immediately, and found no file descriptor was ready.

In the next example, we monitor two file descriptors: descriptor 0, to see if input is available, and descriptor 1, to see if output is possible. In this case, we specify the *timeout* as NULL (the first command-line argument is a hyphen), meaning infinity:

```
$ ./t_select - 0r 1w
ready = 1
0:
1: w
```

The *select()* call returned immediately, informing us that output was possible on file descriptor 1.

63.2.2 The *poll()* System Call

The *poll()* system call performs a similar task to *select()*. The major difference between the two system calls lies in how we specify the file descriptors to be monitored. With *select()*, we provide three sets, each marked to indicate the file descriptors of interest. With *poll()*, we provide a list of file descriptors, each marked with the set of events of interest.

```
#include <poll.h>

int poll(struct pollfd fds[], nfds_t nfds, int timeout);
```
                  Returns number of ready file descriptors, 0 on timeout, or −1 on error

The *pollfd* array (*fds*) and the *nfds* argument specify the file descriptors that *poll()* is to monitor. The *timeout* argument can be used to set an upper limit on the time for which *poll()* will block. We describe each of these arguments in detail below.

The *pollfd* array

The *fds* argument lists the file descriptors to be monitored by *poll()*. This argument is an array of *pollfd* structures, defined as follows:

```
struct pollfd {
    int   fd;               /* File descriptor */
    short events;           /* Requested events bit mask */
    short revents;          /* Returned events bit mask */
};
```

The *nfds* arguments specifies the number of items in the *fds* array. The *nfds_t* data type used to type the *nfds* argument is an unsigned integer type.

The *events* and *revents* fields of the *pollfd* structure are bit masks. The caller initializes *events* to specify the events to be monitored for the file descriptor *fd*. Upon return from *poll()*, *revents* is set to indicate which of those events actually occurred for this file descriptor.

Table 63-2 lists the bits that may appear in the *events* and *revents* fields. The first group of bits in this table (POLLIN, POLLRDNORM, POLLRDBAND, POLLPRI, and POLLRDHUP) are concerned with input events. The next group of bits (POLLOUT, POLLWRNORM, and POLLWRBAND) are concerned with output events. The third group of bits (POLLERR, POLLHUP, and POLLNVAL) are set in the *revents* field to return additional information about the file descriptor. If specified in the *events* field, these three bits are ignored. The final bit (POLLMSG) is unused by *poll()* on Linux.

> On UNIX implementations providing STREAMS devices, POLLMSG indicates that a message containing a SIGPOLL signal has reached the head of the stream. POLLMSG is unused on Linux, because Linux doesn't implement STREAMS.

Table 63-2: Bit-mask values for *events* and *revents* fields of the *pollfd* structure

Bit	Input in *events?*	Returned in *revents?*	Description
POLLIN	•	•	Data other than high-priority data can be read
POLLRDNORM	•	•	Equivalent to POLLIN
POLLRDBAND	•	•	Priority data can be read (unused on Linux)
POLLPRI	•	•	High-priority data can be read
POLLRDHUP	•	•	Shutdown on peer socket
POLLOUT	•	•	Normal data can be written
POLLWRNORM	•	•	Equivalent to POLLOUT
POLLWRBAND	•	•	Priority data can be written
POLLERR		•	An error has occurred
POLLHUP		•	A hangup has occurred
POLLNVAL		•	File descriptor is not open
POLLMSG			Unused on Linux (and unspecified in SUSv3)

If *events* is specified as 0, the only bits that can be returned in *revents* are POLLERR, POLLHUP, and POLLNVAL.

Specifying a negative value for the *fd* field (e.g., negating its value if nonzero) causes the corresponding *events* field to be ignored and the *revents* field always to be returned as 0. This technique can be used to (perhaps temporarily) disable monitoring of a single file descriptor, without needing to rebuild the entire *fds* list.

Note the following further points regarding the Linux implementation of *poll()*:

- Although defined as separate bits, POLLIN and POLLRDNORM are synonymous.
- Although defined as separate bits, POLLOUT and POLLWRNORM are synonymous.
- POLLRDBAND is generally unused; that is, it is ignored in the *events* field and not set in *revents*.

> The only place where POLLRDBAND is set is in code implementing the (obsolete) DECnet networking protocol.

- Although set for sockets in certain circumstances, POLLWRBAND conveys no useful information. (There are no circumstances in which POLLWRBAND is set when POLLOUT and POLLWRNORM are not also set.)

> POLLRDBAND and POLLWRBAND are meaningful on implementations that provide System V STREAMS (which Linux does not). Under STREAMS, a message can be assigned a nonzero priority, and such messages are queued to the receiver in decreasing order of priority, in a band ahead of normal (priority 0) messages.

- The _XOPEN_SOURCE feature test macro must be defined in order to obtain the definitions of the constants POLLRDNORM, POLLRDBAND, POLLWRNORM, and POLLWRBAND from <poll.h>.

- POLLRDHUP is a Linux-specific flag available since kernel 2.6.17. In order to obtain this definition from `<poll.h>`, the `_GNU_SOURCE` feature test macro must be defined.

- POLLNVAL is returned if the specified file descriptor was closed at the time of the *poll()* call.

Summarizing the above points, the *poll()* flags of real interest are POLLIN, POLLOUT, POLLPRI, POLLRDHUP, POLLHUP, and POLLERR. We consider the meanings of these flags in greater detail in Section 63.2.3.

The *timeout* argument

The *timeout* argument determines the blocking behavior of *poll()* as follows:

- If *timeout* equals −1, block until one of the file descriptors listed in the *fds* array is ready (as defined by the corresponding *events* field) or a signal is caught.

- If *timeout* equals 0, do not block—just perform a check to see which file descriptors are ready.

- If *timeout* is greater than 0, block for up to *timeout* milliseconds, until one of the file descriptors in *fds* is ready, or until a signal is caught.

As with *select()*, the accuracy of *timeout* is limited by the granularity of the software clock (Section 10.6), and SUSv3 specifies that *timeout* is always rounded upward if it is not an exact multiple of the clock granularity.

Return value from *poll()*

As its function result, *poll()* returns one of the following:

- A return value of −1 indicates that an error occurred. One possible error is EINTR, indicating that the call was interrupted by a signal handler. (As noted in Section 21.5, *poll()* is never automatically restarted if interrupted by a signal handler.)

- A return of 0 means that the call timed out before any file descriptor became ready.

- A positive return value indicates that one or more file descriptors are ready. The returned value is the number of *pollfd* structures in the *fds* array that have a nonzero *revents* field.

> Note the slightly different meaning of a positive return value from *select()* and *poll()*. The *select()* system call counts a file descriptor multiple times if it occurs in more than one returned file descriptor set. The *poll()* system call returns a count of ready file descriptors, and a file descriptor is counted only once, even if multiple bits are set in the corresponding *revents* field.

Example program

Listing 63-2 provides a simple demonstration of the use of *poll()*. This program creates a number of pipes (each pipe uses a consecutive pair of file descriptors), writes bytes to the write ends of randomly selected pipes, and then performs a *poll()* to see which pipes have data available for reading.

The following shell session shows an example of what we see when running this program. The command-line arguments to the program specify that ten pipes should be created, and writes should be made to three randomly selected pipes.

```
$ ./poll_pipes 10 3
Writing to fd:    4 (read fd:    3)
Writing to fd:   14 (read fd:   13)
Writing to fd:   14 (read fd:   13)
poll() returned: 2
Readable:    3
Readable:   13
```

From the above output, we can see that *poll()* found two pipes had data available for reading.

Listing 63-2: Using *poll()* to monitor multiple file descriptors

——— altio/poll_pipes.c
```c
#include <time.h>
#include <poll.h>
#include "tlpi_hdr.h"

int
main(int argc, char *argv[])
{
    int numPipes, j, ready, randPipe, numWrites;
    int (*pfds)[2];                     /* File descriptors for all pipes */
    struct pollfd *pollFd;

    if (argc < 2 || strcmp(argv[1], "--help") == 0)
        usageErr("%s num-pipes [num-writes]\n", argv[0]);

    /* Allocate the arrays that we use. The arrays are sized according
       to the number of pipes specified on command line */

    numPipes = getInt(argv[1], GN_GT_0, "num-pipes");

    pfds = calloc(numPipes, sizeof(int [2]));
    if (pfds == NULL)
        errExit("calloc");
    pollFd = calloc(numPipes, sizeof(struct pollfd));
    if (pollFd == NULL)
        errExit("calloc");

    /* Create the number of pipes specified on command line */

    for (j = 0; j < numPipes; j++)
        if (pipe(pfds[j]) == -1)
            errExit("pipe %d", j);

    /* Perform specified number of writes to random pipes */

    numWrites = (argc > 2) ? getInt(argv[2], GN_GT_0, "num-writes") : 1;
```

```
        srandom((int) time(NULL));
        for (j = 0; j < numWrites; j++) {
            randPipe = random() % numPipes;
            printf("Writing to fd: %3d (read fd: %3d)\n",
                    pfds[randPipe][1], pfds[randPipe][0]);
            if (write(pfds[randPipe][1], "a", 1) == -1)
                errExit("write %d", pfds[randPipe][1]);
        }

        /* Build the file descriptor list to be supplied to poll(). This list
           is set to contain the file descriptors for the read ends of all of
           the pipes. */

        for (j = 0; j < numPipes; j++) {
            pollFd[j].fd = pfds[j][0];
            pollFd[j].events = POLLIN;
        }

        ready = poll(pollFd, numPipes, 0);
        if (ready == -1)
            errExit("poll");

        printf("poll() returned: %d\n", ready);

        /* Check which pipes have data available for reading */

        for (j = 0; j < numPipes; j++)
            if (pollFd[j].revents & POLLIN)
                printf("Readable: %3d\n", pollFd[j].fd);

        exit(EXIT_SUCCESS);
    }
```

—— **altio/poll_pipes.c**

63.2.3 When Is a File Descriptor Ready?

Correctly using *select()* and *poll()* requires an understanding of the conditions
under which a file descriptor indicates as being ready. SUSv3 says that a file
descriptor (with O_NONBLOCK clear) is considered to be ready if a call to an I/O function would not block, *regardless of whether the function would actually transfer data.*
The key point is italicized: *select()* and *poll()* tell us whether an I/O operation would
not block, rather than whether it would successfully transfer data. In this light, let
us consider how these system calls operate for different types of file descriptors.
We show this information in tables containing two columns:

- The *select()* column indicates whether a file descriptor is marked as readable (r),
  writable (w), or having an exceptional condition (x).

- The *poll()* column indicates the bit(s) returned in the *revents* field. In these
  tables, we omit mention of POLLRDNORM, POLLWRNORM, POLLRDBAND, and POLLWRBAND.
  Although some of these flags may be returned in *revents* in various circumstances (if they are specified in *events*), they convey no useful information
  beyond that provided by POLLIN, POLLOUT, POLLHUP, and POLLERR.

Regular files

File descriptors that refer to regular files are always marked as readable and writable by *select()*, and returned with POLLIN and POLLOUT set in *revents* for *poll()*, for the following reasons:

- A *read()* will always immediately return data, end-of-file, or an error (e.g., the file was not opened for reading).
- A *write()* will always immediately transfer data or fail with some error.

> SUSv3 says that *select()* should also mark a descriptor for a regular file as having an exceptional condition (though this has no obvious meaning for regular files). Only some implementations do this; Linux is one of those that do not.

Terminals and pseudoterminals

Table 63-3 summarizes the behavior of *select()* and *poll()* for terminals and pseudoterminals (Chapter 64).

When one half of a pseudoterminal pair is closed, the *revents* setting returned by *poll()* for the other half of the pair depends on the implementation. On Linux, at least the POLLHUP flag is set. However, other implementations return various flags to indicate this event—for example, POLLHUP, POLLERR, or POLLIN. Furthermore, on some implementations, the flags that are set depend on whether it is the master or the slave device that is being monitored.

Table 63-3: *select()* and *poll()* indications for terminals and pseudoterminals

Condition or event	*select()*	*poll()*
Input available	r	POLLIN
Output possible	w	POLLOUT
After *close()* by pseudoterminal peer	rw	See text
Pseudoterminal master in packet mode detects slave state change	x	POLLPRI

Pipes and FIFOs

Table 63-4 summarizes the details for the read end of a pipe or FIFO. The *Data in pipe?* column indicates whether the pipe has at least 1 byte of data available for reading. In this table, we assume that POLLIN was specified in the *events* field for *poll()*.

On some other UNIX implementations, if the write end of a pipe is closed, then, instead of returning with POLLHUP set, *poll()* returns with the POLLIN bit set (since a *read()* will return immediately with end-of-file). Portable applications should check to see if either bit is set in order to know if a *read()* will block.

Table 63-5 summarizes the details for the write end of a pipe or FIFO. In this table, we assume that POLLOUT was specified in the *events* field for *poll()*. The *Space for PIPE_BUF bytes?* column indicates whether the pipe has room to atomically write PIPE_BUF bytes without blocking. This is the criterion on which Linux considers a pipe ready for writing. Some other UNIX implementations use the same criterion; others consider a pipe writable if even a single byte can be written. (In Linux 2.6.10 and earlier, the capacity of a pipe is the same as PIPE_BUF. This means that a pipe is considered unwritable if it contains even a single byte of data.)

On some other UNIX implementations, if the read end of a pipe is closed, then, instead of returning with POLLERR set, *poll()* returns with either the POLLOUT bit or the POLLHUP bit set. Portable applications need to check to see if any of these bits is set to determine if a *write()* will block.

Table 63-4: *select()* and *poll()* indications for the read end of a pipe or FIFO

Condition or event		*select()*	*poll()*
Data in pipe?	Write end open?		
no	no	r	POLLHUP
yes	yes	r	POLLIN
yes	no	r	POLLIN | POLLHUP

Table 63-5: *select()* and *poll()* indications for the write end of a pipe or FIFO

Condition or event		*select()*	*poll()*
Space for PIPE_BUF bytes?	Read end open?		
no	no	w	POLLERR
yes	yes	w	POLLOUT
yes	no	w	POLLOUT | POLLERR

Sockets

Table 63-6 summarizes the behavior of *select()* and *poll()* for sockets. For the *poll()* column, we assume that *events* was specified as (POLLIN | POLLOUT | POLLPRI). For the *select()* column, we assume that the file descriptor is being tested to see if input is possible, output is possible, or an exceptional condition occurred (i.e., the file descriptor is specified in all three sets passed to *select()*). This table covers just the common cases, not all possible scenarios.

> The Linux *poll()* behavior for UNIX domain sockets after a peer *close()* differs from that shown in Table 63-6. As well as the other flags, *poll()* additionally returns POLLHUP in *revents*.

Table 63-6: *select()* and *poll()* indications for sockets

Condition or event	*select()*	*poll()*
Input available	r	POLLIN
Output possible	w	POLLOUT
Incoming connection established on listening socket	r	POLLIN
Out-of-band data received (TCP only)	x	POLLPRI
Stream socket peer closed connection	rw	POLLIN | POLLOUT | POLLRDHUP

The Linux-specific POLLRDHUP flag (available since Linux 2.6.17) needs a little further explanation. This flag—actually in the form of EPOLLRDHUP—is designed primarily for use with the edge-triggered mode of the *epoll* API (Section 63.4). It is returned when the remote end of a stream socket connection has shut down the writing half of the connection. The use of this flag allows an application that uses the *epoll* edge-triggered interface to employ simpler code to recognize a remote shutdown. (The alternative is for the application to note that the POLLIN flag is set and then perform a *read()*, which indicates the remote shutdown with a return of 0.)

63.2.4 Comparison of *select()* and *poll()*

In this section, we consider some similarities and differences between *select()* and *poll()*.

Implementation details

Within the Linux kernel, *select()* and *poll()* both employ the same set of kernel-internal *poll* routines. These *poll* routines are distinct from the *poll()* system call itself. Each routine returns information about the readiness of a single file descriptor. This readiness information takes the form of a bit mask whose values correspond to the bits returned in the *revents* field by the *poll()* system call (Table 63-2). The implementation of the *poll()* system call involves calling the kernel *poll* routine for each file descriptor and placing the resulting information in the corresponding *revents* field.

To implement *select()*, a set of macros is used to convert the information returned by the kernel *poll* routines into the corresponding event types returned by *select()*:

```
#define POLLIN_SET  (POLLRDNORM | POLLRDBAND | POLLIN | POLLHUP | POLLERR)
                                      /* Ready for reading */
#define POLLOUT_SET (POLLWRBAND | POLLWRNORM | POLLOUT | POLLERR)
                                      /* Ready for writing */
#define POLLEX_SET  (POLLPRI)         /* Exceptional condition */
```

These macro definitions reveal the semantic correspondence between the information returned by *select()* and *poll()*. (If we look at the *select()* and *poll()* columns in the tables in Section 63.2.3, we see that the indications provided by each system call are consistent with the above macros.) The only additional information we need to complete the picture is that *poll()* returns POLLNVAL in the *revents* field if one of the monitored file descriptors was closed at the time of the call, while *select()* returns −1 with *errno* set to EBADF.

API differences

The following are some differences between the *select()* and *poll()* APIs:

- The use of the *fd_set* data type places an upper limit (FD_SETSIZE) on the range of file descriptors that can be monitored by *select()*. By default, this limit is 1024 on Linux, and changing it requires recompiling the application. By contrast, *poll()* places no intrinsic limit on the range of file descriptors that can be monitored.

- Because the *fd_set* arguments of *select()* are value-result, we must reinitialize them if making repeated *select()* calls from within a loop. By using separate *events* (input) and *revents* (output) fields, *poll()* avoids this requirement.

- The *timeout* precision afforded by *select()* (microseconds) is greater than that afforded by *poll()* (milliseconds). (The accuracy of the timeouts of both of these system calls is nevertheless limited by the software clock granularity.)

- If one of the file descriptors being monitored was closed, then *poll()* informs us exactly which one, via the POLLNVAL bit in the corresponding *revents* field. By contrast, *select()* merely returns −1 with *errno* set to EBADF, leaving us to determine which file descriptor is closed by checking for an error when performing an I/O system call on the descriptor. However, this is typically not an important difference, since an application can usually keep track of which file descriptors it has closed.

Portability

Historically, *select()* was more widely available than *poll()*. Nowadays, both interfaces are standardized by SUSv3 and widely available on contemporary implementations. However, there is some variation in the behavior of *poll()* across implementations, as noted in Section 63.2.3.

Performance

The performance of *poll()* and *select()* is similar if either of the following is true:

- The range of file descriptors to be monitored is small (i.e., the maximum file descriptor number is low).

- A large number of file descriptors are being monitored, but they are densely packed (i.e., most or all of the file descriptors from 0 up to some limit are being monitored).

However, the performance of *select()* and *poll()* can differ noticeably if the set of file descriptors to be monitored is sparse; that is, the maximum file descriptor number, N, is large, but only one or a few descriptors in the range 0 to N are being monitored. In this case, *poll()* can perform better than *select()*. We can understand the reasons for this by considering the arguments passed to the two system calls. With *select()*, we pass one or more file descriptor sets and an integer, *nfds*, which is one greater than the maximum file descriptor to be examined in each set. The *nfds* argument has the same value, regardless of whether we are monitoring all file descriptors in the range 0 to *(nfds − 1)* or only the descriptor *(nfds − 1)*. In both cases, the kernel must examine *nfds* elements in each set in order to check exactly which file descriptors are to be monitored. By contrast, when using *poll()*, we specify only the file descriptors of interest to us, and the kernel checks only those descriptors.

> The difference in performance for *poll()* and *select()* with sparse descriptor sets was quite significant in Linux 2.4. Some optimizations in Linux 2.6 have narrowed the performance gap considerably.

We consider the performance of *select()* and *poll()* further in Section 63.4.5, where we compare the performance of these system calls against *epoll*.

63.2.5 Problems with *select()* and *poll()*

The *select()* and *poll()* system calls are the portable, long-standing, and widely used methods of monitoring multiple file descriptors for readiness. However, these APIs suffer some problems when monitoring a large number of file descriptors:

- On each call to *select()* or *poll()*, the kernel must check all of the specified file descriptors to see if they are ready. When monitoring a large number of file descriptors that are in a densely packed range, the time required for this operation greatly outweighs the time required for the next two operations.

- In each call to *select()* or *poll()*, the program must pass a data structure to the kernel describing all of the file descriptors to be monitored, and, after checking the descriptors, the kernel returns a modified version of this data structure to the program. (Furthermore, for *select()*, we must initialize the data structure before each call.) For *poll()*, the size of the data structure increases with the number of file descriptors being monitored, and the task of copying it from user to kernel space and back again consumes a noticeable amount of CPU time when monitoring many file descriptors. For *select()*, the size of the data structure is fixed by FD_SETSIZE, regardless of the number of file descriptors being monitored.

- After the call to *select()* or *poll()*, the program must inspect every element of the returned data structure to see which file descriptors are ready.

The consequence of the above points is that the CPU time required by *select()* and *poll()* increases with the number of file descriptors being monitored (see Section 63.4.5 for more details). This creates problems for programs that monitor large numbers of file descriptors.

The poor scaling performance of *select()* and *poll()* stems from a simple limitation of these APIs: typically, a program makes repeated calls to monitor the same set of file descriptors; however, the kernel doesn't remember the list of file descriptors to be monitored between successive calls.

Signal-driven I/O and *epoll*, which we examine in the following sections, are both mechanisms that allow the kernel to record a persistent list of file descriptors in which a process is interested. Doing this eliminates the performance scaling problems of *select()* and *poll()*, yielding solutions that scale according to the number of I/O events that occur, rather than according to the number of file descriptors being monitored. Consequently, signal-driven I/O and *epoll* provide superior performance when monitoring large numbers of file descriptors.

63.3 Signal-Driven I/O

With I/O multiplexing, a process makes a system call (*select()* or *poll()*) in order to check whether I/O is possible on a file descriptor. With signal-driven I/O, a process requests that the kernel send it a signal when I/O is possible on a file descriptor. The process can then perform any other activity until I/O is possible, at which time the signal is delivered to the process. To use signal-driven I/O, a program performs the following steps:

1. Establish a handler for the signal delivered by the signal-driven I/O mechanism. By default, this notification signal is SIGIO.

2. Set the *owner* of the file descriptor—that is, the process or process group that is to receive signals when I/O is possible on the file descriptor. Typically, we make the calling process the owner. The owner is set using an *fcntl()* F_SETOWN operation of the following form:

   ```
   fcntl(fd, F_SETOWN, pid);
   ```

3. Enable nonblocking I/O by setting the O_NONBLOCK open file status flag.

4. Enable signal-driven I/O by turning on the O_ASYNC open file status flag. This can be combined with the previous step, since they both require the use of the *fcntl()* F_SETFL operation (Section 5.3), as in the following example:

   ```
   flags = fcntl(fd, F_GETFL);                 /* Get current flags */
   fcntl(fd, F_SETFL, flags | O_ASYNC | O_NONBLOCK);
   ```

5. The calling process can now perform other tasks. When I/O becomes possible, the kernel generates a signal for the process and invokes the signal handler established in step 1.

6. Signal-driven I/O provides edge-triggered notification (Section 63.1.1). This means that once the process has been notified that I/O is possible, it should perform as much I/O (e.g., read as many bytes) as possible. Assuming a nonblocking file descriptor, this means executing a loop that performs I/O system calls until a call fails with the error EAGAIN or EWOULDBLOCK.

On Linux 2.4 and earlier, signal-driven I/O can be employed with file descriptors for sockets, terminals, pseudoterminals, and certain other types of devices. Linux 2.6 additionally allows signal-driven I/O to be employed with pipes and FIFOs. Since Linux 2.6.25, signal-driven I/O can also be used with *inotify* file descriptors.

In the following pages, we first present an example of the use of signal-driven I/O, and then explain some of the above steps in greater detail.

> Historically, signal-driven I/O was sometimes referred to as *asynchronous I/O*, and this is reflected in the name (O_ASYNC) of the associated open file status flag. However, nowadays, the term *asynchronous I/O* is used to refer to the type of functionality provided by the POSIX AIO specification. Using POSIX AIO, a process requests the kernel to perform an I/O operation, and the kernel *initiates* the operation, but immediately passes control back to the calling process; the process is then later notified when the I/O operation completes or an error occurs.
>
> O_ASYNC was specified in POSIX.1g, but was not included in SUSv3 because the specification of the required behavior for this flag was deemed insufficient.
>
> Several UNIX implementations, especially older ones, don't define the O_ASYNC constant for use with *fcntl()*. Instead, the constant is named FASYNC, and *glibc* defines this latter name as a synonym for O_ASYNC.

Example program

Listing 63-3 provides a simple example of the use of signal-driven I/O. This program performs the steps described above for enabling signal-driven I/O on standard input, and then places the terminal in cbreak mode (Section 62.6.3), so that input is available a character at a time. The program then enters an infinite loop, performing the "work" of incrementing a variable, *cnt*, while waiting for input to become available. Whenever input becomes available, the SIGIO handler sets a flag, *gotSigio*, that is monitored by the main program. When the main program sees that this flag is set, it reads all available input characters and prints them along with the current value of *cnt*. If a hash character (#) is read in the input, the program terminates.

Here is an example of what we see when we run this program and type the *x* character a number of times, followed by a hash (#) character:

```
$ ./demo_sigio
cnt=37; read x
cnt=100; read x
cnt=159; read x
cnt=223; read x
cnt=288; read x
cnt=333; read #
```

Listing 63-3: Using signal-driven I/O on a terminal

―― altio/demo_sigio.c
```c
#include <signal.h>
#include <ctype.h>
#include <fcntl.h>
#include <termios.h>
#include "tty_functions.h"        /* Declaration of ttySetCbreak() */
#include "tlpi_hdr.h"

static volatile sig_atomic_t gotSigio = 0;
                                /* Set nonzero on receipt of SIGIO */

static void
sigioHandler(int sig)
{
    gotSigio = 1;
}

int
main(int argc, char *argv[])
{
    int flags, j, cnt;
    struct termios origTermios;
    char ch;
    struct sigaction sa;
    Boolean done;
```

```c
        /* Establish handler for "I/O possible" signal */

        sigemptyset(&sa.sa_mask);
        sa.sa_flags = SA_RESTART;
        sa.sa_handler = sigioHandler;
        if (sigaction(SIGIO, &sa, NULL) == -1)
            errExit("sigaction");

        /* Set owner process that is to receive "I/O possible" signal */

        if (fcntl(STDIN_FILENO, F_SETOWN, getpid()) == -1)
            errExit("fcntl(F_SETOWN)");

        /* Enable "I/O possible" signaling and make I/O nonblocking
           for file descriptor */

        flags = fcntl(STDIN_FILENO, F_GETFL);
        if (fcntl(STDIN_FILENO, F_SETFL, flags | O_ASYNC | O_NONBLOCK) == -1)
            errExit("fcntl(F_SETFL)");

        /* Place terminal in cbreak mode */

        if (ttySetCbreak(STDIN_FILENO, &origTermios) == -1)
            errExit("ttySetCbreak");

        for (done = FALSE, cnt = 0; !done ; cnt++) {
            for (j = 0; j < 100000000; j++)
                continue;                   /* Slow main loop down a little */

            if (gotSigio) {                 /* Is input available? */
                gotSigio = 0;

                /* Read all available input until error (probably EAGAIN)
                   or EOF (not actually possible in cbreak mode) or a
                   hash (#) character is read */

                while (read(STDIN_FILENO, &ch, 1) > 0 && !done) {
                    printf("cnt=%d; read %c\n", cnt, ch);
                    done = ch == '#';
                }
            }
        }

        /* Restore original terminal settings */

        if (tcsetattr(STDIN_FILENO, TCSAFLUSH, &origTermios) == -1)
            errExit("tcsetattr");
        exit(EXIT_SUCCESS);
    }
```

—————————————————————————————————— **altio/demo_sigio.c**

Establish the signal handler before enabling signal-driven I/O

Because the default action of SIGIO is to terminate the process, we should enable the handler for SIGIO before enabling signal-driven I/O on a file descriptor. If we enable signal-driven I/O before establishing the SIGIO handler, then there is a time window during which, if I/O becomes possible, delivery of SIGIO will terminate the process.

> On some UNIX implementations, SIGIO is ignored by default.

Setting the file descriptor owner

We set the file descriptor owner using an *fcntl()* operation of the following form:

```
fcntl(fd, F_SETOWN, pid);
```

We may specify that either a single process or all of the processes in a process group are to be signaled when I/O is possible on the file descriptor. If *pid* is positive, it is interpreted as a process ID. If *pid* is negative, its absolute value specifies a process group ID.

> On older UNIX implementations, an *ioctl()* operation—either FIOSETOWN or SIOCSPGRP—was used to achieve the same effect as F_SETOWN. For compatibility, these *ioctl()* operations are also provided on Linux.

Typically, *pid* is specified as the process ID of the calling process (so that the signal is sent to the process that has the file descriptor open). However, it is possible to specify another process or a process group (e.g., the caller's process group), and signals will be sent to that target, subject to the permission checks described in Section 20.5, where the sending process is considered to be the process that does the F_SETOWN.

The *fcntl()* F_GETOWN operation returns the ID of the process or process group that is to receive signals when I/O is possible on a specified file descriptor:

```
id = fcntl(fd, F_GETOWN);
if (id == -1)
    errExit("fcntl");
```

A process group ID is returned as a negative number by this call.

> The *ioctl()* operation that corresponds to F_GETOWN on older UNIX implementations was FIOGETOWN or SIOCGPGRP. Both of these *ioctl()* operations are also provided on Linux.

A limitation in the system call convention employed on some Linux architectures (notably, x86) means that if a file descriptor is owned by a process group ID less than 4096, then, instead of returning that ID as a negative function result from the *fcntl()* F_GETOWN operation, *glibc* misinterprets it as a system call error. Consequently, the *fcntl()* wrapper function returns −1, and *errno* contains the (positive) process group ID. This is a consequence of the fact that the kernel system call interface indicates errors by returning a negative *errno* value as a function result, and there are a few cases where it is necessary to distinguish such results from a successful call that returns a valid negative value. To make this distinction, *glibc* interprets negative system call returns in the range −1 to −4095 as indicating an error, copies this (absolute) value into *errno*, and returns −1 as the function result for the application program. This technique is generally sufficient for dealing with the few system call service routines that can return a valid negative result; the *fcntl()* F_GETOWN operation is the only practical case where it fails. This limitation means that an application that uses process groups to receive "I/O possible" signals (which is unusual) can't reliably use F_GETOWN to discover which process group owns a file descriptor.

> Since *glibc* version 2.11, the *fcntl()* wrapper function fixes the problem of F_GETOWN with process group IDs less than 4096. It does this by implementing F_GETOWN in user space using the F_GETOWN_EX operation (Section 63.3.2), which is provided by Linux 2.6.32 and later.

63.3.1 When Is "I/O Possible" Signaled?

We now consider the details of when "I/O possible" is signaled for various file types.

Terminals and pseudoterminals

For terminals and pseudoterminals, a signal is generated whenever new input becomes available, even if previous input has not yet been read. "Input possible" is also signaled if an end-of-file condition occurs on a terminal (but not on a pseudoterminal).

There is no "output possible" signaling for terminals. A terminal disconnect is also not signaled.

Starting with kernel 2.4.19, Linux provides "output possible" signaling for the slave side of a pseudoterminal. This signal is generated whenever input is consumed on the master side of the pseudoterminal.

Pipes and FIFOs

For the read end of a pipe or FIFO, a signal is generated in these circumstances:

- Data is written to the pipe (even if there was already unread input available).
- The write end of the pipe is closed.

For the write end of a pipe or FIFO, a signal is generated in these circumstances:

- A read from the pipe increases the amount of free space in the pipe so that it is now possible to write PIPE_BUF bytes without blocking.
- The read end of the pipe is closed.

Sockets

Signal-driven I/O works for datagram sockets in both the UNIX and the Internet domains. A signal is generated in the following circumstances:

- An input datagram arrives on the socket (even if there were already unread datagrams waiting to be read).
- An asynchronous error occurs on the socket.

Signal-driven I/O works for stream sockets in both the UNIX and the Internet domains. A signal is generated in the following circumstances:

- A new connection is received on a listening socket.
- A TCP *connect()* request completes; that is, the active end of a TCP connection entered the ESTABLISHED state, as shown in Figure 61-5 (page 1272). The analogous condition is not signaled for UNIX domain sockets.
- New input is received on the socket (even if there was already unread input available).
- The peer closes its writing half of the connection using *shutdown()*, or closes its socket altogether using *close()*.
- Output is possible on the socket (e.g., space has become available in the socket send buffer).
- An asynchronous error occurs on the socket.

inotify file descriptors

A signal is generated when the *inotify* file descriptor becomes readable—that is, when an event occurs for one of the files monitored by the *inotify* file descriptor.

63.3.2 Refining the Use of Signal-Driven I/O

In applications that need to simultaneously monitor very large numbers (i.e., thousands) of file descriptors—for example, certain types of network servers—signal-driven I/O can provide significant performance advantages by comparison with *select()* and *poll()*. Signal-driven I/O offers superior performance because the kernel "remembers" the list of file descriptors to be monitored, and signals the program only when I/O events actually occur on those descriptors. As a result, the performance of a program employing signal-driven I/O scales according to the number of I/O events that occur, rather than the number of file descriptors being monitored.

To take full advantage of signal-driven I/O, we must perform two steps:

- Employ a Linux-specific *fcntl()* operation, F_SETSIG, to specify a realtime signal that should be delivered instead of SIGIO when I/O is possible on a file descriptor.
- Specify the SA_SIGINFO flag when using *sigaction()* to establish the handler for the realtime signal employed in the previous step (see Section 21.4).

The *fcntl()* F_SETSIG operation specifies an alternative signal that should be delivered instead of SIGIO when I/O is possible on a file descriptor:

```
if (fcntl(fd, F_SETSIG, sig) == -1)
    errExit("fcntl");
```

The F_GETSIG operation performs the converse of F_SETSIG, retrieving the signal currently set for a file descriptor:

```
sig = fcntl(fd, F_GETSIG);
if (sig == -1)
    errExit("fcntl");
```

(In order to obtain the definitions of the F_SETSIG and F_GETSIG constants from <fcntl.h>, we must define the _GNU_SOURCE feature test macro.)

Using F_SETSIG to change the signal used for "I/O possible" notification serves two purposes, both of which are needed if we are monitoring large numbers of I/O events on multiple file descriptors:

- The default "I/O possible" signal, SIGIO, is one of the standard, nonqueuing signals. If multiple I/O events are signaled while SIGIO is blocked—perhaps because the SIGIO handler is already invoked—all notifications except the first will be lost. If we use F_SETSIG to specify a realtime signal as the "I/O possible" signal, multiple notifications can be queued.

- If the handler for the signal is established using a *sigaction()* call in which the SA_SIGINFO flag is specified in the *sa.sa_flags* field, then a *siginfo_t* structure is passed as the second argument to the signal handler (Section 21.4). This structure contains fields identifying the file descriptor on which the event occurred, as well as the type of event.

Note that the use of *both* F_SETSIG and SA_SIGINFO is required in order for a valid *siginfo_t* structure to be passed to the signal handler.

If we perform an F_SETSIG operation specifying *sig* as 0, then we return to the default behavior: SIGIO is delivered, and a *siginfo_t* argument is not supplied to the handler.

For an "I/O possible" event, the fields of interest in the *siginfo_t* structure passed to the signal handler are as follows:

- *si_signo*: the number of the signal that caused the invocation of the handler. This value is the same as the first argument to the signal handler.

- *si_fd*: the file descriptor for which the I/O event occurred.

- *si_code*: a code indicating the type of event that occurred. The values that can appear in this field, along with their general descriptions, are shown in Table 63-7.

- *si_band*: a bit mask containing the same bits as are returned in the *revents* field by the *poll()* system call. The value set in *si_code* has a one-to-one correspondence with the bit-mask setting in *si_band*, as shown in Table 63-7.

Table 63-7: *si_code* and *si_band* values in the *siginfo_t* structure for "I/O possible" events

si_code	*si_band* mask value	Description
POLL_IN	POLLIN | POLLRDNORM	Input available; end-of-file condition
POLL_OUT	POLLOUT | POLLWRNORM | POLLWRBAND	Output possible
POLL_MSG	POLLIN | POLLRDNORM | POLLMSG	Input message available (unused)
POLL_ERR	POLLERR	I/O error
POLL_PRI	POLLPRI | POLLRDNORM	High-priority input available
POLL_HUP	POLLHUP | POLLERR	Hangup occurred

In an application that is purely input-driven, we can further refine the use of F_SETSIG. Instead of monitoring I/O events via a signal handler, we can block the nominated "I/O possible" signal, and then accept the queued signals via calls to *sigwaitinfo()* or *sigtimedwait()* (Section 22.10). These system calls return a *siginfo_t* structure that contains the same information as is passed to a signal handler established with SA_SIGINFO. Accepting signals in this manner returns us to a synchronous model of event processing, but with the advantage that we are much more efficiently notified about the file descriptors on which I/O events have occurred than if we use *select()* or *poll()*.

Handling signal-queue overflow

We saw in Section 22.8 that there is a limit on the number of realtime signals that may be queued. If this limit is reached, the kernel reverts to delivering the default SIGIO signal for "I/O possible" notifications. This informs the process that a signal-queue overflow occurred. When this happens, we lose information about which file descriptors have I/O events, because SIGIO is not queued. (Furthermore, the SIGIO handler doesn't receive a *siginfo_t* argument, which means that the signal handler can't determine the file descriptor that generated the signal.)

We can reduce the likelihood of signal-queue overflows by increasing the limit on the number of realtime signals that can be queued, as described in Section 22.8. However, this doesn't eliminate the need to handle the possibility of an overflow. A properly designed application using F_SETSIG to establish a realtime signal as the "I/O possible" notification mechanism must also establish a handler for SIGIO. If SIGIO is delivered, then the application can drain the queue of realtime signals using *sigwaitinfo()* and temporarily revert to the use of *select()* or *poll()* to obtain a complete list of file descriptors with outstanding I/O events.

Using signal-driven I/O with multithreaded applications

Starting with kernel 2.6.32, Linux provides two new, nonstandard *fcntl()* operations that can be used to set the target for "I/O possible" signals: F_SETOWN_EX and F_GETOWN_EX.

The F_SETOWN_EX operation is like F_SETOWN, but as well as allowing the target to be specified as a process or process group, it also permits a thread to be specified as the target for "I/O possible" signals. For this operation, the third argument of *fcntl()* is a pointer to a structure of the following form:

```
struct f_owner_ex {
    int    type;
    pid_t pid;
};
```

The *type* field defines the meaning of the *pid* field, and has one of the following values:

F_OWNER_PGRP
> The *pid* field specifies the ID of a process group that is to be the target of "I/O possible" signals. Unlike with F_SETOWN, a process group ID is specified as a positive value.

F_OWNER_PID
> The *pid* field specifies the ID of a process that is to be the target of "I/O possible" signals.

F_OWNER_TID

> The *pid* field specifies the ID of a thread that is to be the target of "I/O possible" signals. The ID specified in *pid* is a value returned by *clone()* or *gettid()*.

The F_GETOWN_EX operation is the converse of the F_SETOWN_EX operation. It uses the *f_owner_ex* structure pointed to by the third argument of *fcntl()* to return the settings defined by a previous F_SETOWN_EX operation.

> Because the F_SETOWN_EX and F_GETOWN_EX operations represent process group IDs as positive values, F_GETOWN_EX doesn't suffer the problem described earlier for F_GETOWN when using process group IDs less than 4096.

63.4 The *epoll* API

Like the I/O multiplexing system calls and signal-driven I/O, the Linux *epoll* (event poll) API is used to monitor multiple file descriptors to see if they are ready for I/O. The primary advantages of the *epoll* API are the following:

- The performance of *epoll* scales much better than *select()* and *poll()* when monitoring large numbers of file descriptors.
- The *epoll* API permits either level-triggered or edge-triggered notification. By contrast, *select()* and *poll()* provide only level-triggered notification, and signal-driven I/O provides only edge-triggered notification.

The performance of *epoll* and signal-driven I/O is similar. However, *epoll* has some advantages over signal-driven I/O:

- We avoid the complexities of signal handling (e.g., signal-queue overflow).
- We have greater flexibility in specifying what kind of monitoring we want to perform (e.g., checking to see if a file descriptor for a socket is ready for reading, writing, or both).

The *epoll* API is Linux-specific, and is new in Linux 2.6.

The central data structure of the *epoll* API is an *epoll instance*, which is referred to via an open file descriptor. This file descriptor is not used for I/O. Instead, it is a handle for kernel data structures that serve two purposes:

- recording a list of file descriptors that this process has declared an interest in monitoring—the *interest list*; and
- maintaining a list of file descriptors that are ready for I/O—the *ready list*.

The membership of the ready list is a subset of the interest list.

For each file descriptor monitored by *epoll*, we can specify a bit mask indicating events that we are interested in knowing about. These bit masks correspond closely to the bit masks used with *poll()*.

The *epoll* API consists of three system calls:

- The *epoll_create()* system call creates an *epoll* instance and returns a file descriptor referring to the instance.

- The *epoll_ctl()* system call manipulates the interest list associated with an *epoll* instance. Using *epoll_ctl()*, we can add a new file descriptor to the list, remove an existing descriptor from the list, and modify the mask that determines which events are to be monitored for a descriptor.

- The *epoll_wait()* system call returns items from the ready list associated with an *epoll* instance.

63.4.1 Creating an *epoll* Instance: *epoll_create()*

The *epoll_create()* system call creates a new *epoll* instance whose interest list is initially empty.

```
#include <sys/epoll.h>

int epoll_create(int size);
```
                    Returns file descriptor on success, or –1 on error

The *size* argument specifies the number of file descriptors that we expect to monitor via the *epoll* instance. This argument is not an upper limit, but rather a hint to the kernel about how to initially dimension internal data structures. (Since Linux 2.6.8, the *size* argument must be greater than zero but is otherwise ignored, because changes in the implementation meant that the information it provided is no longer required.)

As its function result, *epoll_create()* returns a file descriptor referring to the new *epoll* instance. This file descriptor is used to refer to the *epoll* instance in other *epoll* system calls. When the file descriptor is no longer required, it should be closed in the usual way, using *close()*. When all file descriptors referring to an *epoll* instance are closed, the instance is destroyed and its associated resources are released back to the system. (Multiple file descriptors may refer to the same *epoll* instance as a consequence of calls to *fork()* or descriptor duplication using *dup()* or similar.)

> Starting with kernel 2.6.27, Linux supports a new system call, *epoll_create1()*. This system call performs the same task as *epoll_create()*, but drops the obsolete *size* argument and adds a *flags* argument that can be used to modify the behavior of the system call. One flag is currently supported: EPOLL_CLOEXEC, which causes the kernel to enable the close-on-exec flag (FD_CLOEXEC) for the new file descriptor. This flag is useful for the same reasons as the *open()* O_CLOEXEC flag described in Section 4.3.1.

63.4.2 Modifying the *epoll* Interest List: *epoll_ctl()*

The *epoll_ctl()* system call modifies the interest list of the *epoll* instance referred to by the file descriptor *epfd*.

```
#include <sys/epoll.h>

int epoll_ctl(int epfd, int op, int fd, struct epoll_event *ev);
```
                    Returns 0 on success, or –1 on error

The *fd* argument identifies which of the file descriptors in the interest list is to have its settings modified. This argument can be a file descriptor for a pipe, FIFO, socket, POSIX message queue, *inotify* instance, terminal, device, or even another *epoll* descriptor (i.e., we can build a kind of hierarchy of monitored descriptors). However, *fd* can't be a file descriptor for a regular file or a directory (the error EPERM results).

The *op* argument specifies the operation to be performed, and has one of the following values:

EPOLL_CTL_ADD

> Add the file descriptor *fd* to the interest list for *epfd*. The set of events that we are interested in monitoring for *fd* is specified in the buffer pointed to by *ev*, as described below. If we attempt to add a file descriptor that is already in the interest list, *epoll_ctl()* fails with the error EEXIST.

EPOLL_CTL_MOD

> Modify the events setting for the file descriptor *fd*, using the information specified in the buffer pointed to by *ev*. If we attempt to modify the settings of a file descriptor that is not in the interest list for *epfd*, *epoll_ctl()* fails with the error ENOENT.

EPOLL_CTL_DEL

> Remove the file descriptor *fd* from the interest list for *epfd*. The *ev* argument is ignored for this operation. If we attempt to remove a file descriptor that is not in the interest list for *epfd*, *epoll_ctl()* fails with the error ENOENT. Closing a file descriptor automatically removes it from all of the *epoll* interest lists of which it is a member.

The *ev* argument is a pointer to a structure of type *epoll_event*, defined as follows:

```
struct epoll_event {
    uint32_t    events;        /* epoll events (bit mask) */
    epoll_data_t data;         /* User data */
};
```

The *data* field of the *epoll_event* structure is typed as follows:

```
typedef union epoll_data {
    void       *ptr;           /* Pointer to user-defined data */
    int         fd;            /* File descriptor */
    uint32_t    u32;           /* 32-bit integer */
    uint64_t    u64;           /* 64-bit integer */
} epoll_data_t;
```

The *ev* argument specifies settings for the file descriptor *fd*, as follows:

- The *events* subfield is a bit mask specifying the set of events that we are interested in monitoring for *fd*. We say more about the bit values that can be used in this field in the next section.

- The *data* subfield is a union, one of whose members can be used to specify information that is passed back to the calling process (via *epoll_wait()*) if *fd* later becomes ready.

Listing 63-4 shows an example of the use of *epoll_create()* and *epoll_ctl()*.

Listing 63-4: Using *epoll_create()* and *epoll_ctl()*

```
int epfd;
struct epoll_event ev;

epfd = epoll_create(5);
if (epfd == -1)
    errExit("epoll_create");

ev.data.fd = fd;
ev.events = EPOLLIN;
if (epoll_ctl(epfd, EPOLL_CTL_ADD, fd, &ev) == -1)
    errExit("epoll_ctl");
```

The max_user_watches limit

Because each file descriptor registered in an *epoll* interest list requires a small amount of nonswappable kernel memory, the kernel provides an interface that defines a limit on the total number of file descriptors that each user can register in all *epoll* interest lists. The value of this limit can be viewed and modified via max_user_watches, a Linux-specific file in the /proc/sys/fs/epoll directory. The default value of this limit is calculated based on available system memory (see the *epoll(7)* manual page).

63.4.3 Waiting for Events: *epoll_wait()*

The *epoll_wait()* system call returns information about ready file descriptors from the *epoll* instance referred to by the file descriptor *epfd*. A single *epoll_wait()* call can return information about multiple ready file descriptors.

```
#include <sys/epoll.h>

int epoll_wait(int epfd, struct epoll_event *evlist, int maxevents, int timeout);
```

Returns number of ready file descriptors, 0 on timeout, or −1 on error

The information about ready file descriptors is returned in the array of *epoll_event* structures pointed to by *evlist*. (The *epoll_event* structure was described in the previous section.) The *evlist* array is allocated by the caller, and the number of elements it contains is specified in *maxevents*.

Each item in the array *evlist* returns information about a single ready file descriptor. The *events* subfield returns a mask of the events that have occurred on this descriptor. The *data* subfield returns whatever value was specified in *ev.data* when we registered interest in this file descriptor using *epoll_ctl()*. Note that the *data* field provides the only mechanism for finding out the number of the file descriptor associated with this event. Thus, when we make the *epoll_ctl()* call that places a file descriptor in the interest list, we should either set *ev.data.fd* to the file descriptor number (as shown in Listing 63-4) or set *ev.data.ptr* to point to a structure that contains the file descriptor number.

The *timeout* argument determines the blocking behavior of *epoll_wait()*, as follows:

- If *timeout* equals −1, block until an event occurs for one of the file descriptors in the interest list for *epfd* or until a signal is caught.

- If *timeout* equals 0, perform a nonblocking check to see which events are currently available on the file descriptors in the interest list for *epfd*.

- If *timeout* is greater than 0, block for up to *timeout* milliseconds, until an event occurs on one of the file descriptors in the interest list for *epfd*, or until a signal is caught.

On success, *epoll_wait()* returns the number of items that have been placed in the array *evlist*, or 0 if no file descriptors were ready within the interval specified by *timeout*. On error, *epoll_wait()* returns −1, with *errno* set to indicate the error.

In a multithreaded program, it is possible for one thread to use *epoll_ctl()* to add file descriptors to the interest list of an *epoll* instance that is already being monitored by *epoll_wait()* in another thread. These changes to the interest list will be taken into account immediately, and the *epoll_wait()* call will return readiness information about the newly added file descriptors.

epoll events

The bit values that can be specified in *ev.events* when we call *epoll_ctl()* and that are placed in the *evlist[].events* fields returned by *epoll_wait()* are shown in Table 63-8. With the addition of an E prefix, most of these bits have names that are the same as the corresponding event bits used with *poll()*. (The exceptions are EPOLLET and EPOLLONESHOT, which we describe in more detail below.) The reason for this correspondence is that, when specified as input to *epoll_ctl()* or returned as output via *epoll_wait()*, these bits convey exactly the same meaning as the corresponding *poll()* event bits.

Table 63-8: Bit-mask values for the *epoll events* field

Bit	Input to *epoll_ctl()*?	Returned by *epoll_wait()*?	Description
EPOLLIN	•	•	Data other than high-priority data can be read
EPOLLPRI	•	•	High-priority data can be read
EPOLLRDHUP	•	•	Shutdown on peer socket (since Linux 2.6.17)
EPOLLOUT	•	•	Normal data can be written
EPOLLET	•		Employ edge-triggered event notification
EPOLLONESHOT	•		Disable monitoring after event notification
EPOLLERR		•	An error has occurred
EPOLLHUP		•	A hangup has occurred

The EPOLLONESHOT flag

By default, once a file descriptor is added to an *epoll* interest list using the *epoll_ctl()* EPOLL_CTL_ADD operation, it remains active (i.e., subsequent calls to *epoll_wait()* will inform us whenever the file descriptor is ready) until we explicitly remove it from the list using the *epoll_ctl()* EPOLL_CTL_DEL operation. If we want to be notified only once about a particular file descriptor, then we can specify the EPOLLONESHOT flag (available since Linux 2.6.2) in the *ev.events* value passed in *epoll_ctl()*. If this flag is specified, then, after the next *epoll_wait()* call that informs us that the corresponding file descriptor is ready, the file descriptor is marked inactive in the interest list, and we won't be informed about its state by future *epoll_wait()* calls. If desired, we can subsequently reenable monitoring of this file descriptor using the *epoll_ctl()* EPOLL_CTL_MOD operation. (We can't use the EPOLL_CTL_ADD operation for this purpose, because the inactive file descriptor is still part of the *epoll* interest list.)

Example program

Listing 63-5 demonstrates the use of the *epoll* API. As command-line arguments, this program expects the pathnames of one or more terminals or FIFOs. The program performs the following steps:

- Create an *epoll* instance ①.
- Open each of the files named on the command line for input ② and add the resulting file descriptor to the interest list of the *epoll* instance ③, specifying the set of events to be monitored as EPOLLIN.
- Execute a loop ④ that calls *epoll_wait()* ⑤ to monitor the interest list of the *epoll* instance and handles the returned events from each call. Note the following points about this loop:
  - After the *epoll_wait()* call, the program checks for an EINTR return ⑥, which may occur if the program was stopped by a signal in the middle of the *epoll_wait()* call and then resumed by SIGCONT. (Refer to Section 21.5.) If this occurs, the program restarts the *epoll_wait()* call.
  - If the *epoll_wait()* call was successful, the program uses a further loop to check each of the ready items in *evlist* ⑦. For each item in *evlist*, the program checks the *events* field for the presence of not just EPOLLIN ⑧, but also EPOLLHUP and EPOLLERR ⑨. These latter events can occur if the other end of a FIFO was closed or a terminal hangup occurred. If EPOLLIN was returned, then the program reads some input from the corresponding file descriptor and displays it on standard output. Otherwise, if either EPOLLHUP or EPOLLERR occurred, the program closes the corresponding file descriptor ⑩ and decrements the counter of open files (*numOpenFds*).
  - The loop terminates when all open file descriptors have been closed (i.e., when *numOpenFds* equals 0).

The following shell session logs demonstrate the use of the program in Listing 63-5. We use two terminal windows. In one window, we use the program in Listing 63-5 to monitor two FIFOs for input. (Each open of a FIFO for reading by this program will complete only after another process has opened the FIFO for writing, as described in Section 44.7.) In the other window, we run instances of *cat(1)* that write data to these FIFOs.

```
Terminal window 1                        Terminal window 2
$ mkfifo p q
$ ./epoll_input p q

                                         $ cat > p
Opened "p" on fd 4

                                         Type Control-Z to suspend cat
                                         [1]+  Stopped          cat >p
                                         $ cat > q
Opened "q" on fd 5
About to epoll_wait()
Type Control-Z to suspend the epoll_input program
[1]+  Stopped       ./epoll_input p q
```

Above, we suspended our monitoring program so that we can now generate input on both FIFOs, and close the write end of one of them:

```
                             qqq
                             Type Control-D to terminate "cat > q"
                             $ fg %1
                             cat >p
                             ppp
```

Now we resume our monitoring program by bringing it into the foreground, at which point *epoll_wait()* returns two events:

```
$ fg
./epoll_input p q
About to epoll_wait()
Ready: 2
  fd=4; events: EPOLLIN
    read 4 bytes: ppp

  fd=5; events: EPOLLIN EPOLLHUP
    read 4 bytes: qqq

About to epoll_wait()
Ready: 1
  fd=5; events: EPOLLHUP
    closing fd 5
About to epoll_wait()
```

The two blank lines in the above output are the newlines that were read by the instances of *cat*, written to the FIFOs, and then read and echoed by our program.

Now we type *Control-D* in the second terminal window in order to terminate the remaining instance of *cat*, which causes *epoll_wait()* to once more return, this time with a single event:

```
                             Type Control-D to terminate "cat >p"
Ready: 1
  fd=4; events: EPOLLHUP
    closing fd 4
All file descriptors closed; bye
```

Listing 63-5: Using the *epoll* API

———altio/epoll_input.c
```
#include <sys/epoll.h>
#include <fcntl.h>
#include "tlpi_hdr.h"

#define MAX_BUF      1000       /* Maximum bytes fetched by a single read() */
#define MAX_EVENTS   5          /* Maximum number of events to be returned from
                                   a single epoll_wait() call */

int
main(int argc, char *argv[])
{
    int epfd, ready, fd, s, j, numOpenFds;
    struct epoll_event ev;
    struct epoll_event evlist[MAX_EVENTS];
    char buf[MAX_BUF];

    if (argc < 2 || strcmp(argv[1], "--help") == 0)
        usageErr("%s file...\n", argv[0]);
```
①
```
    epfd = epoll_create(argc - 1);
    if (epfd == -1)
        errExit("epoll_create");

    /* Open each file on command line, and add it to the "interest
       list" for the epoll instance */
```
②
```
    for (j = 1; j < argc; j++) {
        fd = open(argv[j], O_RDONLY);
        if (fd == -1)
            errExit("open");
        printf("Opened \"%s\" on fd %d\n", argv[j], fd);

        ev.events = EPOLLIN;            /* Only interested in input events */
        ev.data.fd = fd;
```
③
```
        if (epoll_ctl(epfd, EPOLL_CTL_ADD, fd, &ev) == -1)
            errExit("epoll_ctl");
    }

    numOpenFds = argc - 1;
```
④
```
    while (numOpenFds > 0) {

        /* Fetch up to MAX_EVENTS items from the ready list */

        printf("About to epoll_wait()\n");
```
⑤
```
        ready = epoll_wait(epfd, evlist, MAX_EVENTS, -1);
        if (ready == -1) {
```
⑥
```
            if (errno == EINTR)
                continue;              /* Restart if interrupted by signal */
            else
                errExit("epoll_wait");
        }
```

```
            printf("Ready: %d\n", ready);

            /* Deal with returned list of events */

⑦          for (j = 0; j < ready; j++) {
                printf("  fd=%d; events: %s%s%s\n", evlist[j].data.fd,
                        (evlist[j].events & EPOLLIN)  ? "EPOLLIN "  : "",
                        (evlist[j].events & EPOLLHUP) ? "EPOLLHUP " : "",
                        (evlist[j].events & EPOLLERR) ? "EPOLLERR " : "");

⑧              if (evlist[j].events & EPOLLIN) {
                    s = read(evlist[j].data.fd, buf, MAX_BUF);
                    if (s == -1)
                        errExit("read");
                    printf("    read %d bytes: %.*s\n", s, s, buf);

⑨              } else if (evlist[j].events & (EPOLLHUP | EPOLLERR)) {

                    /* After the epoll_wait(), EPOLLIN and EPOLLHUP may both have
                       been set. But we'll only get here, and thus close the file
                       descriptor, if EPOLLIN was not set. This ensures that all
                       outstanding input (possibly more than MAX_BUF bytes) is
                       consumed (by further loop iterations) before the file
                       descriptor is closed. */

                    printf("    closing fd %d\n", evlist[j].data.fd);
⑩                  if (close(evlist[j].data.fd) == -1)
                        errExit("close");
                    numOpenFds--;
                }
            }
        }

        printf("All file descriptors closed; bye\n");
        exit(EXIT_SUCCESS);
    }
```

——**altio/epoll_input.c**

63.4.4   A Closer Look at *epoll* Semantics

We now look at some subtleties of the interaction of open files, file descriptors, and
epoll. For the purposes of this discussion, it is worth reviewing Figure 5-2 (page 95),
which shows the relationship between file descriptors, open file descriptions, and
the system-wide file i-node table.

When we create an *epoll* instance using *epoll_create()*, the kernel creates a new
in-memory i-node and open file description, and allocates a new file descriptor in
the calling process that refers to the open file description. The interest list for an
epoll instance is associated with the open file description, not with the *epoll* file
descriptor. This has the following consequences:

- If we duplicate an *epoll* file descriptor using *dup()* (or similar), then the duplicated descriptor refers to the same *epoll* interest and ready lists as the original
  descriptor. We may modify the interest list by specifying either file descriptor

as the *epfd* argument in a call to *epoll_ctl()*. Similarly, we can retrieve items from the ready list by specifying either file descriptor as the *epfd* argument in a call to *epoll_wait()*.

- The preceding point also applies after a call to *fork()*. The child inherits a duplicate of the parent's *epoll* file descriptor, and this duplicate descriptor refers to the same *epoll* data structures.

When we perform an *epoll_ctl()* EPOLL_CTL_ADD operation, the kernel adds an item to the *epoll* interest list that records both the number of the monitored file descriptor and a reference to the corresponding open file description. For the purpose of *epoll_wait()* calls, the kernel monitors the open file description. This means that we must refine our earlier statement that when a file descriptor is closed, it is automatically removed from any *epoll* interest lists of which it is a member. The refinement is this: an open file description is removed from the *epoll* interest list once all file descriptors that refer to it have been closed. This means that if we create duplicate descriptors referring to an open file—using *dup()* (or similar) or *fork()*—then the open file will be removed only after the original descriptor and all of the duplicates have been closed.

These semantics can lead to some behavior that at first appears surprising. Suppose that we execute the code shown in Listing 63-6. The *epoll_wait()* call in this code will tell us that the file descriptor *fd1* is ready (in other words, *evlist[0].data.fd* will be equal to *fd1*), even though *fd1* has been closed. This is because there is still one open file descriptor, *fd2*, referring to the open file description contained in the *epoll* interest list. A similar scenario occurs when two processes hold duplicate descriptors for the same open file description (typically, as a result of a *fork()*), and the process performing the *epoll_wait()* has closed its file descriptor, but the other process still holds the duplicate descriptor open.

Listing 63-6: Semantics of *epoll* with duplicate file descriptors

```
int epfd, fd1, fd2;
struct epoll_event ev;
struct epoll_event evlist[MAX_EVENTS];

/* Omitted: code to open 'fd1' and create epoll file descriptor 'epfd' ... */

ev.data.fd = fd1
ev.events = EPOLLIN;
if (epoll_ctl(epfd, EPOLL_CTL_ADD, fd1, ev) == -1)
    errExit("epoll_ctl");

/* Suppose that 'fd1' now happens to become ready for input */

fd2 = dup(fd1);
close(fd1);
ready = epoll_wait(epfd, evlist, MAX_EVENTS, -1);
if (ready == -1)
    errExit("epoll_wait");
```

63.4.5 Performance of *epoll* Versus I/O Multiplexing

Table 63-9 shows the results (on Linux 2.6.25) when we monitor N contiguous file descriptors in the range 0 to $N - 1$ using *poll()*, *select()*, and *epoll*. (The test was arranged such that during each monitoring operation, exactly one randomly selected file descriptor is ready.) From this table, we see that as the number of file descriptors to be monitored grows large, *poll()* and *select()* perform poorly. By contrast, the performance of *epoll* hardly declines as N grows large. (The small decline in performance as N increases is possibly a result of reaching CPU caching limits on the test system.)

> For the purposes of this test, FD_SETSIZE was changed to 16,384 in the *glibc* header files to allow the test program to monitor large numbers of file descriptors using *select()*.

Table 63-9: Times taken by *poll()*, *select()*, and *epoll* for 100,000 monitoring operations

Number of descriptors monitored (N)	*poll()* CPU time (seconds)	*select()* CPU time (seconds)	*epoll* CPU time (seconds)
10	0.61	0.73	0.41
100	2.9	3.0	0.42
1000	35	35	0.53
10000	990	930	0.66

In Section 63.2.5, we saw why *select()* and *poll()* perform poorly when monitoring large numbers of file descriptors. We now look at the reasons why *epoll* performs better:

- On each call to *select()* or *poll()*, the kernel must check all of the file descriptors specified in the call. By contrast, when we mark a descriptor to be monitored with *epoll_ctl()*, the kernel records this fact in a list associated with the underlying open file description, and whenever an I/O operation that makes the file descriptor ready is performed, the kernel adds an item to the ready list for the *epoll* descriptor. (An I/O event on a single open file description may cause multiple file descriptors associated with that description to become ready.) Subsequent *epoll_wait()* calls simply fetch items from the ready list.

- Each time we call *select()* or *poll()*, we pass a data structure to the kernel that identifies all of the file descriptors that are to be monitored, and, on return, the kernel passes back a data structure describing the readiness of all of these descriptors. By contrast, with *epoll*, we use *epoll_ctl()* to build up a data structure *in kernel space* that lists the set of file descriptors to be monitored. Once this data structure has been built, each later call to *epoll_wait()* doesn't need to pass any information about file descriptors to the kernel, and the call returns information about only those descriptors that are ready.

> In addition to the above points, for *select()*, we must initialize the input data structure prior to each call, and for both *select()* and *poll()*, we must inspect the returned data structure to find out which of the N file descriptors are ready. However, some testing showed that the time required for these other steps was

insignificant compared to the time required for the system call to monitor N descriptors. Table 63-9 doesn't include the times for the inspection step.

Very roughly, we can say that for large values of N (the number of file descriptors being monitored), the performance of *select()* and *poll()* scales linearly with N. We start to see this behavior for the $N = 100$ and $N = 1000$ cases in Table 63-9. By the time we reach $N = 10000$, the scaling has actually become worse than linear.

By contrast, *epoll* scales (linearly) according to the number of I/O events that occur. The *epoll* API is thus particularly efficient in a scenario that is common in servers that handle many simultaneous clients: of the many file descriptors being monitored, most are idle; only a few descriptors are ready.

63.4.6 Edge-Triggered Notification

By default, the *epoll* mechanism provides *level-triggered* notification. By this, we mean that *epoll* tells us whether an I/O operation can be performed on a file descriptor without blocking. This is the same type of notification as is provided by *poll()* and *select()*.

The *epoll* API also allows for *edge-triggered* notification—that is, a call to *epoll_wait()* tells us if there has been I/O activity on a file descriptor since the previous call to *epoll_wait()* (or since the descriptor was opened, if there was no previous call). Using *epoll* with edge-triggered notification is semantically similar to signal-driven I/O, except that if multiple I/O events occur, *epoll* coalesces them into a single notification returned via *epoll_wait()*; with signal-driven I/O, multiple signals may be generated.

To employ edge-triggered notification, we specify the EPOLLET flag in *ev.events* when calling *epoll_ctl()*:

```
struct epoll_event ev;

ev.data.fd = fd;
ev.events = EPOLLIN | EPOLLET;
if (epoll_ctl(epfd, EPOLL_CTL_ADD, fd, &ev) == -1)
    errExit("epoll_ctl");
```

We illustrate the difference between level-triggered and edge-triggered *epoll* notification using an example. Suppose that we are using *epoll* to monitor a socket for input (EPOLLIN), and the following steps occur:

1. Input arrives on the socket.
2. We perform an *epoll_wait()*. This call will tell us that the socket is ready, regardless of whether we are employing level-triggered or edge-triggered notification.
3. We perform a second call to *epoll_wait()*.

If we are employing level-triggered notification, then the second *epoll_wait()* call will inform us that the socket is ready. If we are employing edge-triggered notification, then the second call to *epoll_wait()* will block, because no new input has arrived since the previous call to *epoll_wait()*.

As we noted in Section 63.1.1, edge-triggered notification is usually employed in conjunction with nonblocking file descriptors. Thus, the general framework for using edge-triggered *epoll* notification is as follows:

1. Make all file descriptors that are to be monitored nonblocking.
2. Build the *epoll* interest list using *epoll_ctl()*.
3. Handle I/O events using the following loop:
    a) Retrieve a list of ready descriptors using *epoll_wait()*.
    b) For each file descriptor that is ready, process I/O until the relevant system call (e.g., *read()*, *write()*, *recv()*, *send()*, or *accept()*) returns with the error EAGAIN or EWOULDBLOCK.

Preventing file-descriptor starvation when using edge-triggered notification

Suppose that we are monitoring multiple file descriptors using edge-triggered notification, and that a ready file descriptor has a large amount (perhaps an endless stream) of input available. If, after detecting that this file descriptor is ready, we attempt to consume all of the input using nonblocking reads, then we risk starving the other file descriptors of attention (i.e., it may be a long time before we again check them for readiness and perform I/O on them). One solution to this problem is for the application to maintain a list of file descriptors that have been notified as being ready, and execute a loop that continuously performs the following actions:

1. Monitor the file descriptors using *epoll_wait()* and add ready descriptors to the application list. If any file descriptors are already registered as being ready in the application list, then the timeout for this monitoring step should be small or 0, so that if no new file descriptors are ready, the application can quickly proceed to the next step and service any file descriptors that are already known to be ready.
2. Perform a limited amount of I/O on those file descriptors registered as being ready in the application list (perhaps cycling through them in round-robin fashion, rather than always starting from the beginning of the list after each call to *epoll_wait()*). A file descriptor can be removed from the application list when the relevant nonblocking I/O system call fails with the EAGAIN or EWOULDBLOCK error.

Although it requires extra programming work, this approach offers other benefits in addition to preventing file-descriptor starvation. For example, we can include other steps in the above loop, such as handling timers and accepting signals with *sigwaitinfo()* (or similar).

Starvation considerations can also apply when using signal-driven I/O, since it also presents an edge-triggered notification mechanism. By contrast, starvation considerations don't necessarily apply in applications employing a level-triggered notification mechanism. This is because we can employ blocking file descriptors with level-triggered notification and use a loop that continuously checks descriptors for readiness, and then performs *some* I/O on the ready descriptors before once more checking for ready file descriptors.

63.5 Waiting on Signals and File Descriptors

Sometimes, a process needs to simultaneously wait for I/O to become possible on one of a set of file descriptors or for the delivery of a signal. We might attempt to perform such an operation using *select()*, as shown in Listing 63-7.

Listing 63-7: Incorrect method of unblocking signals and calling *select()*

```
sig_atomic_t gotSig = 0;

void
handler(int sig)
{
    gotSig = 1;
}

int
main(int argc, char *argv[])
{
    struct sigaction sa;
    ...

    sa.sa_handler = handler;
    sigemptyset(&sa.sa_mask);
    sa.sa_flags = 0;
    if (sigaction(SIGUSR1, &sa, NULL) == -1)
        errExit("sigaction");

    /* What if the signal is delivered now? */

    ready = select(nfds, &readfds, NULL, NULL, NULL);
    if (ready > 0) {
        printf("%d file descriptors ready\n", ready);
    } else if (ready == -1 && errno == EINTR) {
        if (gotSig)
            printf("Got signal\n");
    } else {
        /* Some other error */
    }

    ...
}
```

The problem with this code is that if the signal (SIGUSR1 in this example) arrives after establishing the handler but before *select()* is called, then the *select()* call will nevertheless block. (This is a form of race condition.) We now look at some solutions to this problem.

Since version 2.6.27, Linux provides a further technique that can be used to simultaneously wait on signals and file descriptors: the *signalfd* mechanism described in Section 22.11. Using this mechanism, we can receive signals via a file descriptor that is monitored (along with other file descriptors) using *select()*, *poll()*, or *epoll_wait()*.

63.5.1 The *pselect()* System Call

The *pselect()* system call performs a similar task to *select()*. The main semantic difference is an additional argument, *sigmask*, that specifies a set of signals to be unmasked while the call is blocked.

```
#include <sys/select.h>

int pselect(int nfds, fd_set *readfds, fd_set *writefds, fd_set *exceptfds,
            struct timespec *timeout, const sigset_t *sigmask);
```
                Returns number of ready file descriptors, 0 on timeout, or –1 on error

More precisely, suppose we have the following *pselect()* call:

```
ready = pselect(nfds, &readfds, &writefds, &exceptfds, timeout, &sigmask);
```

This call is equivalent to *atomically* performing the following steps:

```
sigset_t origmask;

pthread_sigmask(SIG_SETMASK, &sigmask, &origmask);
ready = select(nfds, &readfds, &writefds, &exceptfds, timeout);
pthread_sigmask(SIG_SETMASK, &origmask, NULL);    /* Restore signal mask */
```

Using *pselect()*, we can recode the first part of the body of our main program in Listing 63-7 as shown in Listing 63-8.

Aside from the *sigmask* argument, *select()* and *pselect()* differ in the following ways:

- The *timeout* argument to *pselect()* is a *timespec* structure (Section 23.4.2), which allows the timeout to be specified with nanosecond (instead of microsecond) precision.

- SUSv3 explicitly states that *pselect()* doesn't modify the *timeout* argument on return.

If we specify the *sigmask* argument of *pselect()* as NULL, then *pselect()* is equivalent to *select()* (i.e., it performs no manipulation of the process signal mask), except for the differences just noted.

The *pselect()* interface is an invention of POSIX.1g, and is nowadays incorporated in SUSv3. It is not available on all UNIX implementations, and was added to Linux only in kernel 2.6.16.

> Previously, a *pselect()* library function was provided by *glibc*, but this implementation didn't provide the atomicity guarantees that are required for the correct operation of the call. Such guarantees can be provided only by a kernel implementation of *pselect()*.

Listing 63-8: Using *pselect()*

```
sigset_t emptyset, blockset;
struct sigaction sa;

sigemptyset(&blockset);
sigaddset(&blockset, SIGUSR1);

if (sigprocmask(SIG_BLOCK, &blockset, NULL) == -1)
    errExit("sigprocmask");

sa.sa_handler = handler;
sigemptyset(&sa.sa_mask);
sa.sa_flags = SA_RESTART;
if (sigaction(SIGUSR1, &sa, NULL) == -1)
    errExit("sigaction");

sigemptyset(&emptyset);
ready = pselect(nfds, &readfds, NULL, NULL, NULL, &emptyset);
if (ready == -1)
    errExit("pselect");
```

The *ppoll()* and *epoll_pwait()* system calls

Linux 2.6.16 also added a new, nonstandard system call, *ppoll()*, whose relationship to *poll()* is analogous to the relationship of *pselect()* to *select()*. Similarly, starting with kernel 2.6.19, Linux also includes *epoll_pwait()*, providing an analogous extension to *epoll_wait()*. See the *ppoll(2)* and *epoll_pwait(2)* manual pages for details.

63.5.2 The Self-Pipe Trick

Since *pselect()* is not widely implemented, portable applications must employ other strategies to avoid race conditions when simultaneously waiting for signals and calling *select()* on a set of file descriptors. One common solution is the following:

1. Create a pipe, and mark its read and write ends as nonblocking.

2. As well as monitoring all of the other file descriptors that are of interest, include the read end of the pipe in the *readfds* set given to *select()*.

3. Install a handler for the signal that is of interest. When this signal handler is called, it writes a byte of data to the pipe. Note the following points about the signal handler:

    – The write end of the pipe was marked as nonblocking in the first step to prevent the possibility that signals arrive so rapidly that repeated invocations of the signal handler fill the pipe, with the result that the signal handler's *write()* (and thus the process itself) is blocked. (It doesn't matter if a write to a full pipe fails, since the previous writes will already have indicated the delivery of the signal.)

- The signal handler is installed after creating the pipe, in order to prevent the race condition that would occur if a signal was delivered before the pipe was created.
- It is safe to use *write()* inside the signal handler, because it is one of the async-signal-safe functions listed in Table 21-1, on page 426.

4. Place the *select()* call in a loop, so that it is restarted if interrupted by a signal handler. (Restarting in this fashion is not strictly necessary; it merely means that we can check for the arrival of a signal by inspecting *readfds*, rather than checking for an `EINTR` error return.)

5. On successful completion of the *select()* call, we can determine whether a signal arrived by checking if the file descriptor for the read end of the pipe is set in *readfds*.

6. Whenever a signal has arrived, read all bytes that are in the pipe. Since multiple signals may arrive, employ a loop that reads bytes until the (nonblocking) *read()* fails with the error `EAGAIN`. After draining the pipe, perform whatever actions must be taken in response to delivery of the signal.

This technique is commonly known as the *self-pipe trick*, and code demonstrating this technique is shown in Listing 63-9.

Variations on this technique can equally be employed with *poll()* and *epoll_wait()*.

Listing 63-9: Using the self-pipe trick

─── *from* `altio/self_pipe.c`

```
static int pfd[2];                      /* File descriptors for pipe */

static void
handler(int sig)
{
    int savedErrno;                     /* In case we change 'errno' */

    savedErrno = errno;
    if (write(pfd[1], "x", 1) == -1 && errno != EAGAIN)
        errExit("write");
    errno = savedErrno;
}

int
main(int argc, char *argv[])
{
    fd_set readfds;
    int ready, nfds, flags;
    struct timeval timeout;
    struct timeval *pto;
    struct sigaction sa;
    char ch;
```

```
        /* ... Initialize 'timeout', 'readfds', and 'nfds' for select() */

        if (pipe(pfd) == -1)
            errExit("pipe");

        FD_SET(pfd[0], &readfds);           /* Add read end of pipe to 'readfds' */
        nfds = max(nfds, pfd[0] + 1);       /* And adjust 'nfds' if required */

        flags = fcntl(pfd[0], F_GETFL);
        if (flags == -1)
            errExit("fcntl-F_GETFL");
        flags |= O_NONBLOCK;                /* Make read end nonblocking */
        if (fcntl(pfd[0], F_SETFL, flags) == -1)
            errExit("fcntl-F_SETFL");

        flags = fcntl(pfd[1], F_GETFL);
        if (flags == -1)
            errExit("fcntl-F_GETFL");
        flags |= O_NONBLOCK;                /* Make write end nonblocking */
        if (fcntl(pfd[1], F_SETFL, flags) == -1)
            errExit("fcntl-F_SETFL");

        sigemptyset(&sa.sa_mask);
        sa.sa_flags = SA_RESTART;           /* Restart interrupted read()s */
        sa.sa_handler = handler;
        if (sigaction(SIGINT, &sa, NULL) == -1)
            errExit("sigaction");

        while ((ready = select(nfds, &readfds, NULL, NULL, pto)) == -1 &&
                errno == EINTR)
            continue;                       /* Restart if interrupted by signal */
        if (ready == -1)                    /* Unexpected error */
            errExit("select");

        if (FD_ISSET(pfd[0], &readfds)) {   /* Handler was called */
            printf("A signal was caught\n");

            for (;;) {                      /* Consume bytes from pipe */
                if (read(pfd[0], &ch, 1) == -1) {
                    if (errno == EAGAIN)
                        break;              /* No more bytes */
                    else
                        errExit("read");    /* Some other error */
                }

                /* Perform any actions that should be taken in response to signal */
            }
        }

        /* Examine file descriptor sets returned by select() to see
           which other file descriptors are ready */

    }
```
── *from* **altio/self_pipe.c**

1372   Chapter 63

63.6 Summary

In this chapter, we explored various alternatives to the standard model for performing I/O: I/O multiplexing (*select()* and *poll()*), signal-driven I/O, and the Linux-specific *epoll* API. All of these mechanisms allow us to monitor multiple file descriptors to see if I/O is possible on any of them. None of these mechanisms actually performs I/O. Instead, once we have determined that a file descriptor is ready, we use the traditional I/O system calls to perform the I/O.

The *select()* and *poll()* I/O multiplexing calls simultaneously monitor multiple file descriptors to see if I/O is possible on any of the descriptors. With both system calls, we pass a complete list of to-be-checked file descriptors to the kernel on each system call, and the kernel returns a modified list indicating which descriptors are ready. The fact that complete file descriptor lists are passed and checked on each call means that *select()* and *poll()* perform poorly when monitoring large numbers of file descriptors.

Signal-driven I/O allows a process to receive a signal when I/O is possible on a file descriptor. To enable signal-driven I/O, we must establish a handler for the SIGIO signal, set the owner process that is to receive the signal, and enable signal generation by setting the O_ASYNC open file status flag. This mechanism offers significant performance benefits over I/O multiplexing when monitoring large numbers of file descriptors. Linux allows us to change the signal used for notification, and if we instead employ a realtime signal, then multiple notifications can be queued, and the signal handler can use its *siginfo_t* argument to determine the file descriptor and event type that generated the signal.

Like signal-driven I/O, *epoll* offers superior performance when monitoring large numbers of file descriptors. The performance advantage of *epoll* (and signal-driven I/O) derives from the fact that the kernel "remembers" the list of file descriptors that a process is monitoring (by contrast with *select()* and *poll()*, where each system call must again tell the kernel which file descriptors to check). The *epoll* API has some notable advantages over the use of signal-driven I/O: we avoid the complexities of dealing with signals and can specify which types of I/O events (e.g., input or output) are to be monitored.

In the course of this chapter, we drew a distinction between level-triggered and edge-triggered readiness notification. With a level-triggered notification model, we are informed whether I/O is currently possible on a file descriptor. By contrast, edge-triggered notification informs us whether I/O activity has occurred on a file descriptor since it was last monitored. The I/O multiplexing system calls offer a level-triggered notification model; signal-driven I/O approximates to an edge-triggered model; and *epoll* is capable of operating under either model (level-triggered is the default). Edge-triggered notification is usually employed in conjunction with nonblocking I/O.

We concluded the chapter by looking at a problem that sometimes faces programs that monitor multiple file descriptors: how to simultaneously also wait for the delivery of a signal. The usual solution to this problem is the so-called self-pipe trick, whereby a handler for the signal writes a byte to a pipe whose read end is included among the set of monitored file descriptors. SUSv3 specifies *pselect()*, a variation of *select()* that provides another solution to this problem. However, *pselect()* is not available on all UNIX implementations. Linux also provides the analogous (but nonstandard) *ppoll()* and *epoll_pwait()*.

Further information

[Stevens et al., 2004] describes I/O multiplexing and signal-driven I/O, with particular emphasis on the use of these mechanisms with sockets. [Gammo et al, 2004] is a paper comparing the performance of *select()*, *poll()*, and *epoll*.

A particularly interesting online resource is at *http://www.kegel.com/c10k.html*. Written by Dan Kegel, and entitled "The C10K problem," this web page explores the issues facing developers of web servers designed to simultaneously serve tens of thousands of clients. The web page includes a host of links to related information.

63.7 Exercises

63-1. Modify the program in Listing 63-2 (poll_pipes.c) to use *select()* instead of *poll()*.

63-2. Write an *echo* server (see Sections 60.2 and 60.3) that handles both TCP and UDP clients. To do this, the server must create both a listening TCP socket and a UDP socket, and then monitor both sockets using one of the techniques described in this chapter.

63-3. Section 63.5 noted that *select()* can't be used to wait on both signals and file descriptors, and described a solution using a signal handler and a pipe. A related problem exists when a program needs to wait for input on both a file descriptor and a System V message queue (since System V message queues don't use file descriptors). One solution is to fork a separate child process that copies each message from the queue to a pipe included among the file descriptors monitored by the parent. Write a program that uses this scheme with *select()* to monitor input from both the terminal and a message queue.

63-4. The last step of the description of the self-pipe technique in Section 63.5.2 stated that the program should first drain the pipe, and then perform any actions that should be taken in response to the signal. What might happen if these substeps were reversed?

63-5. Modify the program in Listing 63-9 (self_pipe.c) to use *poll()* instead of *select()*.

63-6. Write a program that uses *epoll_create()* to create an *epoll* instance and then immediately waits on the returned file descriptor using *epoll_wait()*. When, as in this case, *epoll_wait()* is given an *epoll* file descriptor with an empty interest list, what happens? Why might this be useful?

63-7. Suppose we have an *epoll* file descriptor that is monitoring multiple file descriptors, all of which are always ready. If we perform a series of *epoll_wait()* calls in which *maxevents* is much smaller than the number of ready file descriptors (e.g., *maxevents* is 1), without performing all possible I/O on the ready descriptors between calls, what descriptor(s) does *epoll_wait()* return in each call? Write a program to determine the answer. (For the purposes of this experiment, it suffices to perform no I/O between the *epoll_wait()* system calls.) Why might this behavior be useful?

63-8. Modify the program in Listing 63-3 (demo_sigio.c) to use a realtime signal instead of SIGIO. Modify the signal handler to accept a *siginfo_t* argument and display the values of the *si_fd* and *si_code* fields of this structure.

64

PSEUDOTERMINALS

A *pseudoterminal* is a virtual device that provides an IPC channel. On one end of the channel is a program that expects to be connected to a terminal device. On the other end is a program that drives the terminal-oriented program by using the channel to send it input and read its output.

This chapter describes the use of pseudoterminals, showing how they are employed in applications such as terminal emulators, the *script(1)* program, and programs such as *ssh*, which provide network login services.

64.1 Overview

Figure 64-1 illustrates one of the problems that pseudoterminals help us solve: how can we enable a user on one host to operate a terminal-oriented program (e.g., *vi*) on another host connected via a network?

As shown in the diagram, by permitting communication over a network, sockets provide part of the machinery needed to solve this problem. However, we can't connect the standard input, output, and error of a terminal-oriented program directly to a socket. This is because a terminal-oriented program expects to be connected to a terminal—to be able to perform the terminal-oriented operations described in Chapters 34 and 62. Such operations include placing the terminal in noncanonical mode, turning echoing on and off, and setting the terminal foreground process group. If a program tries to perform these operations on a socket, then the relevant system calls will fail.

Furthermore, a terminal-oriented program expects a terminal driver to perform certain kinds of processing of its input and output. For example, in canonical mode, when the terminal driver sees the end-of-file character (normally *Control-D*) at the start of a line, it causes the next *read()* to return no data.

Finally, a terminal-oriented program must have a controlling terminal. This allows the program to obtain a file descriptor for the controlling terminal by opening /dev/tty, and also makes it possible to generate job-control and terminal-related signals (e.g., SIGTSTP, SIGTTIN, and SIGINT) for the program.

From this description, it should be clear that the definition of a terminal-oriented program is quite broad. It encompasses a wide range of programs that we would normally run in an interactive terminal session.

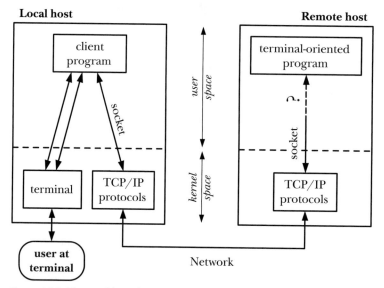

Figure 64-1: The problem: how to operate a terminal-oriented program over a network?

The pseudoterminal master and slave devices

A pseudoterminal provides the missing link for creating a network connection to a terminal-oriented program. A pseudoterminal is a pair of connected virtual devices: a *pseudoterminal master* and a *pseudoterminal slave*, sometimes jointly referred to as a *pseudoterminal pair*. A pseudoterminal pair provides an IPC channel somewhat like a bidirectional pipe—two processes can open the master and slave and then transfer data in either direction through the pseudoterminal.

The key point about a pseudoterminal is that the slave device appears just like a standard terminal. All of the operations that can be applied to a terminal device can also be applied to a pseudoterminal slave device. Some of these operations aren't meaningful for a pseudoterminal (e.g., setting the terminal line speed or parity), but that's okay, because the pseudoterminal slave silently ignores them.

How programs use pseudoterminals

Figure 64-2 shows how two programs typically employ a pseudoterminal. (The abbreviation *pty* in this diagram is a commonly used shorthand for *pseudoterminal*, and we employ this abbreviation in various diagrams and function names in this chapter.) The standard input, output, and error of the terminal-oriented program are connected to the pseudoterminal slave, which is also the controlling terminal for the program. On the other side of the pseudoterminal, a driver program acts as a proxy for the user, supplying input to the terminal-oriented program and reading that program's output.

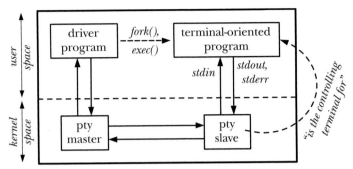

Figure 64-2: Two programs communicating via a pseudoterminal

Typically, the driver program is simultaneously reading from and writing to another I/O channel. It is acting as a relay, passing data in both directions between the pseudoterminal and another program. In order to do this, the driver program must simultaneously monitor input arriving from either direction. Typically, this is done using I/O multiplexing (*select()* or *poll()*), or using a pair of processes or threads to perform data transfer in each direction.

An application that uses a pseudoterminal typically does so as follows:

1. The driver program opens the pseudoterminal master device.

2. The driver program calls *fork()* to create a child process. The child performs the following steps:

    a) Call *setsid()* to start a new session, of which the child is the session leader (Section 34.3). This step also causes the child to lose its controlling terminal.

    b) Open the pseudoterminal slave device that corresponds to the master device. Since the child process is a session leader, and it doesn't have a controlling terminal, the pseudoterminal slave becomes the controlling terminal for the child process.

    c) Use *dup()* (or similar) to duplicate the file descriptor for the slave device on standard input, output, and error.

    d) Call *exec()* to start the terminal-oriented program that is to be connected to the pseudoterminal slave.

At this point, the two programs can now communicate via the pseudoterminal. Anything that the driver program writes to the master appears as input to the terminal-oriented program on the slave, and anything that the terminal-oriented program writes to the slave can be read by the driver program on the master. We consider further details of pseudoterminal I/O in Section 64.5.

Pseudoterminals can also be used to connect an arbitrary pair of processes (i.e., not necessarily a parent and child). All that is required is that the process that opens the pseudoterminal master informs the other process of the name of the corresponding slave device, perhaps by writing that name to a file or by transmitting it using some other IPC mechanism. (When we use *fork()* in the manner described above, the child automatically inherits sufficient information from the parent to enable it to determine the name of the slave.)

So far, our discussion of the use of pseudoterminals has been abstract. Figure 64-3 shows a specific example: the use of a pseudoterminal by *ssh*, an application that allows a user to securely run a login session on a remote system connected via a network. (In effect, this diagram combines the information from Figure 64-1 and Figure 64-2.) On the remote host, the driver program for the pseudoterminal master is the *ssh* server (*sshd*), and the terminal-oriented program connected to the pseudoterminal slave is the login shell. The *ssh* server is the glue that connects the pseudoterminal via a socket to the *ssh* client. Once all of the details of logging in have been completed, the primary purpose of the *ssh* server and client is to relay characters in either direction between the user's terminal on the local host and the shell on the remote host.

> We omit describing many details of the *ssh* client and server. For example, these programs encrypt the data transmitted in either direction across the network. We show a single *ssh* server process on the remote host, but, in fact, the *ssh* server is a concurrent network server. It becomes a daemon and creates a passive TCP socket to listen for incoming connections from *ssh* clients. For each connection, the master *ssh* server forks a child process that handles all of the details for a single client login session. (We refer to this child process as the *ssh* server in Figure 64-3.) Aside from the details of pseudoterminal setup described above, the *ssh* server child authenticates the user, updates the login accounting files on the remote host (as described in Chapter 40), and then execs the login shell.

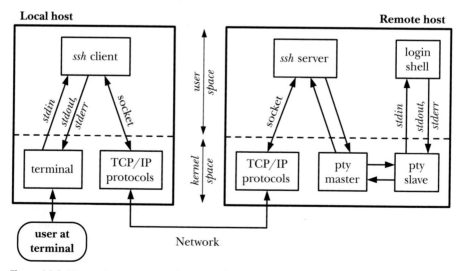

Figure 64-3: How *ssh* uses a pseudoterminal

In some cases, multiple processes may be connected to the slave side of the pseudoterminal. Our *ssh* example illustrates this point. The session leader for the slave is a shell, which creates process groups to execute the commands entered by the remote user. All of these processes have the pseudoterminal slave as their controlling terminal. As with a conventional terminal, one of these process groups can be the foreground process group for the pseudoterminal slave, and only this process group is allowed to read from the slave and (if the TOSTOP bit has been set) write to it.

Applications of pseudoterminals

Pseudoterminals are also used in many applications other than network services. Examples include the following:

- The *expect(1)* program uses a pseudoterminal to allow an interactive terminal-oriented program to be driven from a script file.

- Terminal emulators such as *xterm* employ pseudoterminals to provide the terminal-related functionality that goes with a terminal window.

- The *screen(1)* program uses pseudoterminals to multiplex a single physical terminal (or terminal window) between multiple processes (e.g., multiple shell sessions).

- Pseudoterminals are used in the *script(1)* program, which records all of the input and output that occurs during a shell session.

- Sometimes a pseudoterminal is useful to circumvent the default block buffering performed by the *stdio* functions when writing output to a disk file or pipe, as opposed to the line buffering used for terminal output. (We consider this point further in Exercise 64-7.)

System V (UNIX 98) and BSD pseudoterminals

BSD and System V provided different interfaces for finding and opening the two halves of a pseudoterminal pair. The BSD pseudoterminal implementation was historically the better known, since it was used with many sockets-based network applications. For compatibility reasons, many UNIX implementations eventually came to support both styles of pseudoterminals.

The System V interface is somewhat simpler to use than the BSD interface, and the SUSv3 specification of pseudoterminals is based on the System V interface. (A pseudoterminal specification first appeared in SUSv1.) For historical reasons, on Linux systems, this type of pseudoterminal is commonly referred to as a *UNIX 98* pseudoterminal, even though the UNIX 98 standard (i.e., SUSv2) required pseudoterminals to be STREAMS-based, and the Linux implementation of pseudoterminals is not. (SUSv3 doesn't require a STREAMS-based implementation.)

Early versions of Linux supported only BSD-style pseudoterminals, but, since kernel 2.2, Linux has supported both types of pseudoterminals. In this chapter, we focus on UNIX 98 pseudoterminals. We describe the differences for BSD pseudoterminals in Section 64.8.

64.2 UNIX 98 Pseudoterminals

Bit by bit, we'll work toward the development of a function, *ptyFork()*, that does most of the work to create the setup shown in Figure 64-2. We'll then use this function to implement the *script(1)* program. Before doing this though, we look at the various library functions used with UNIX 98 pseudoterminals:

- The *posix_openpt()* function opens an unused pseudoterminal master device, returning a file descriptor that is used to refer to the device in later calls.

- The *grantpt()* function changes the ownership and permissions of the slave device corresponding to a pseudoterminal master device.

- The *unlockpt()* function unlocks the slave device corresponding to a pseudoterminal master device, so that the slave device can be opened.

- The *ptsname()* function returns the name of the slave device corresponding to a pseudoterminal master device. The slave device can then be opened using *open()*.

64.2.1 Opening an Unused Master: *posix_openpt()*

The *posix_openpt()* function finds and opens an unused pseudoterminal master device, and returns a file descriptor that can later be used to refer to this device.

```
#define _XOPEN_SOURCE 600
#include <stdlib.h>
#include <fcntl.h>

int posix_openpt(int flags);
```
                              Returns file descriptor on success, or –1 on error

The *flags* argument is constructed by ORing zero or more of the following constants together:

O_RDWR

> Open the device for both reading and writing. Normally, we would always include this constant in *flags*.

O_NOCTTY

> Don't make this terminal the controlling terminal for the process. On Linux, a pseudoterminal master can't become a controlling terminal for a process, regardless of whether the O_NOCTTY flag is specified when calling *posix_openpt()*. (This makes sense because the pseudoterminal master isn't really a terminal; it is the other side of a terminal to which the slave is connected.) However, on some implementations, O_NOCTTY is required if we want to prevent a process from acquiring a controlling terminal as a consequence of opening a pseudoterminal master device.

Like *open()*, *posix_openpt()* uses the lowest available file descriptor to open the pseudoterminal master.

Calling *posix_openpt()* also results in the creation of a corresponding pseudoterminal slave device file in the /dev/pts directory. We say more about this file when we describe the *ptsname()* function below.

The *posix_openpt()* function is new in SUSv3, and was an invention of the POSIX committee. In the original System V pseudoterminal implementation, obtaining an available pseudoterminal master was accomplished by opening the *pseudoterminal master clone device*, /dev/ptmx. Opening this virtual device automatically locates and opens the next unused pseudoterminal master, and returns a file descriptor for it. This device is provided on Linux, where *posix_openpt()* is implemented as follows:

```
int
posix_openpt(int flags)
{
    return open("/dev/ptmx", flags);
}
```

Limits on the number of UNIX 98 pseudoterminals

Because each pseudoterminal pair in use consumes a small amount of nonswappable kernel memory, the kernel imposes a limit on the number of UNIX 98 pseudoterminal pairs on the system. In kernels up to 2.6.3, this limit is controlled by a kernel configuration option (CONFIG_UNIX98_PTYS). The default value for this option is 256, but we can change the limit to any value in the range 0 to 2048.

From Linux 2.6.4 onward, the CONFIG_UNIX98_PTYS kernel configuration option is discarded in favor of a more flexible approach. Instead, the limit on the number of pseudoterminals is defined by the value in the Linux-specific /proc/sys/kernel/pty/max file. The default value for this file is 4096, and it can be set to any value up to 1,048,576. A related read-only file, /proc/sys/kernel/pty/nr, shows how many UNIX 98 pseudoterminals are currently in use.

64.2.2   Changing Slave Ownership and Permissions: *grantpt()*

SUSv3 specifies the use of *grantpt()* to change the ownership and permissions of the slave device that corresponds to the pseudoterminal master referred to by the file descriptor *mfd*. On Linux, calling *grantpt()* is not actually necessary. However, the use of *grantpt()* is required on some implementations, and portable applications should call it after calling *posix_openpt()*.

```
#define _XOPEN_SOURCE
#include <stdlib.h>

int grantpt(int mfd);
```
                                     Returns 0 on success, or −1 on error

---

On systems where *grantpt()* is required, this function creates a child process that executes a set-user-ID-*root* program. This program, usually called *pt_chown*, performs the following operations on the pseudoterminal slave device:

- change the ownership of the slave to be the same as the real user ID of the calling process;
- change the group of the slave to *tty*; and

- change the permissions on the slave so that the owner has read and write permissions, and group has write permission.

The reason for changing the group of the terminal to *tty* and enabling group write permission is that the *wall(1)* and *write(1)* programs are set-group-ID programs owned by the *tty* group.

On Linux, a pseudoterminal slave is automatically configured in the above manner, which is why calling *grantpt()* isn't needed (but still should be done).

> Because it may create a child process, SUSv3 says that the behavior of *grantpt()* is unspecified if the calling program has installed a handler for SIGCHLD.

64.2.3 Unlocking the Slave: *unlockpt()*

The *unlockpt()* function removes an internal lock on the slave corresponding to the pseudoterminal master referred to by the file descriptor *mfd*. The purpose of this locking mechanism is to allow the calling process to perform whatever initialization is required for the pseudoterminal slave (e.g., calling *grantpt()*) before another process is allowed to open it.

```
#define _XOPEN_SOURCE
#include <stdlib.h>

int unlockpt(int mfd);
```
                                        Returns 0 on success, or –1 on error

An attempt to open a pseudoterminal slave before it has been unlocked with *unlockpt()* fails with the error EIO.

64.2.4 Obtaining the Name of the Slave: *ptsname()*

The *ptsname()* function returns the name of the pseudoterminal slave corresponding to the pseudoterminal master referred to by the file descriptor *mfd*.

```
#define _XOPEN_SOURCE
#include <stdlib.h>

char *ptsname(int mfd);
```
                  Returns pointer to (possibly statically allocated) string on success,
                                                          or NULL on error

On Linux (as on most implementations), *ptsname()* returns a name of the form /dev/pts/*nn*, where *nn* is replaced by a number that uniquely identifies this pseudoterminal slave.

The buffer used to return the slave name is normally statically allocated. It is thus overwritten by subsequent calls to *ptsname()*.

The GNU C library provides a reentrant analog of *ptsname()* in the form of *ptsname_r(mfd, strbuf, buflen)*. However, this function is nonstandard and is available on few other UNIX implementations. The `_GNU_SOURCE` feature test macro must be defined in order to obtain the declaration of *ptsname_r()* from `<stdlib.h>`.

Once we have unlocked the slave device with *unlockpt()*, we can open it by passing the name returned by *ptsname()* to the *open()* system call.

> On System V derivatives that employ STREAMS, it may be necessary to perform some further steps (pushing STREAMS modules onto the slave device after opening it). An example of how to perform these steps can be found in [Stevens & Rago, 2005].

64.3 Opening a Master: *ptyMasterOpen()*

We now present a function, *ptyMasterOpen()*, that employs the functions described in the previous sections to open a pseudoterminal master and obtain the name of the corresponding pseudoterminal slave. Our reasons for providing such a function are twofold:

- Most programs perform these steps in exactly the same way, so it is convenient to encapsulate them in a single function.
- Our *ptyMasterOpen()* function hides all of the details that are specific to UNIX 98 pseudoterminals. In Section 64.8, we present a reimplementation of this function that uses BSD-style pseudoterminals. All of the code that we present in the remainder of this chapter can work with either of these implementations.

```
#include "pty_master_open.h"

int ptyMasterOpen(char *slaveName, size_t snLen);
```
                            Returns file descriptor on success, or −1 on error

The *ptyMasterOpen()* function opens an unused pseudoterminal master, calls *grantpt()* and *unlockpt()* on it, and copies the name of the corresponding pseudoterminal slave into the buffer pointed to by *slaveName*. The caller must specify the amount of space available in this buffer in the argument *snLen*. We show the implementation of this function in Listing 64-1.

> It would be equally possible to omit the use of the *slaveName* and *snLen* arguments, and have the caller of *ptyMasterOpen()* call *ptsname()* directly in order to obtain the name of the pseudoterminal slave. However, we employ the *slaveName* and *snLen* arguments because BSD pseudoterminals don't provide an equivalent of the *ptsname()* function, and our implementation of the equivalent function for BSD-style pseudoterminals (Listing 64-4) encapsulates the BSD technique for obtaining the name of the slave.

Listing 64-1: Implementation of *ptyMasterOpen()*

———————————————————————————————— **pty/pty_master_open.c**

```c
#define _XOPEN_SOURCE 600
#include <stdlib.h>
#include <fcntl.h>
#include "pty_master_open.h"          /* Declares ptyMasterOpen() */
#include "tlpi_hdr.h"

int
ptyMasterOpen(char *slaveName, size_t snLen)
{
    int masterFd, savedErrno;
    char *p;

    masterFd = posix_openpt(O_RDWR | O_NOCTTY); /* Open pty master */
    if (masterFd == -1)
        return -1;

    if (grantpt(masterFd) == -1) {              /* Grant access to slave pty */
        savedErrno = errno;
        close(masterFd);                        /* Might change 'errno' */
        errno = savedErrno;
        return -1;
    }

    if (unlockpt(masterFd) == -1) {             /* Unlock slave pty */
        savedErrno = errno;
        close(masterFd);                        /* Might change 'errno' */
        errno = savedErrno;
        return -1;
    }

    p = ptsname(masterFd);                       /* Get slave pty name */
    if (p == NULL) {
        savedErrno = errno;
        close(masterFd);                        /* Might change 'errno' */
        errno = savedErrno;
        return -1;
    }

    if (strlen(p) < snLen) {
        strncpy(slaveName, p, snLen);
    } else {                        /* Return an error if buffer too small */
        close(masterFd);
        errno = EOVERFLOW;
        return -1;
    }

    return masterFd;
}
```

———————————————————————————————— **pty/pty_master_open.c**

64.4 Connecting Processes with a Pseudoterminal: *ptyFork()*

We are now ready to implement a function that does all of the work of setting up a connection between two processes using a pseudoterminal pair, as shown in Figure 64-2. The *ptyFork()* function creates a child process that is connected to the parent by a pseudoterminal pair.

```
#include "pty_fork.h"

pid_t ptyFork(int *masterFd, char *slaveName, size_t snLen,
            const struct termios *slaveTermios, const struct winsize *slaveWS);
```

In parent: returns process ID of child on success, or –1 on error;
in successfully created child: always returns 0

The implementation of *ptyFork()* is shown in Listing 64-2. This function performs the following steps:

- Open a pseudoterminal master using *ptyMasterOpen()* (Listing 64-1) ①.
- If the *slaveName* argument is not NULL, copy the name of the pseudoterminal slave into this buffer ②. (If *slaveName* is not NULL, then it must point to a buffer of at least *snLen* bytes.) The caller can use this name to update the login accounting files (Chapter 40), if appropriate. Updating the login accounting files would be appropriate for applications that provide login services—for example, *ssh*, *rlogin*, and *telnet*. On the other hand, programs such as *script(1)* (Section 64.6) do not update the login accounting files, because they don't provide login services.
- Call *fork()* to create a child process ③.
- All that the parent does after the *fork()* is to ensure that the file descriptor for the pseudoterminal master is returned to the caller in the integer pointed to by *masterFd* ④.
- After the *fork()*, the child performs the following steps:
  - Call *setsid()*, to create a new session (Section 34.3) ⑤. The child is the leader of the new session and loses its controlling terminal (if it had one).
  - Close the file descriptor for the pseudoterminal master, since it is not required in the child ⑥.
  - Open the pseudoterminal slave ⑦. Since the child lost its controlling terminal in the previous step, this step causes the pseudoterminal slave to become the controlling terminal for the child.
  - If the TIOCSCTTY macro is defined, perform a TIOCSCTTY *ioctl()* operation on the file descriptor for the pseudoterminal slave ⑧. This code allows our *ptyFork()* function to work on BSD platforms, where a controlling terminal can be acquired only as a consequence of an explicit TIOCSCTTY operation (refer to Section 34.4).
  - If the *slaveTermios* argument is non-NULL, call *tcsetattr()* to set the terminal attributes of the slave to the values in the *termios* structure pointed to by

this argument ⑨. Use of this argument is a convenience for certain interactive programs (e.g., *script(1)*) that use a pseudoterminal and need to set the attributes of the slave device to be the same as those of the terminal under which the program is run.

- If the *slaveWS* argument is non-NULL, perform an *ioctl()* TIOCSWINSZ operation to set the window size of the pseudoterminal slave to the values in the *winsize* structure pointed to by this argument ⑩. This step is performed for the same reason as the previous step.

- Use *dup2()* to duplicate the slave file descriptor to be the standard input, output, and error for the child ⑪. At this point, the child can now exec an arbitrary program, and that program can use the standard file descriptors to communicate with the pseudoterminal. The execed program can perform all of the usual terminal-oriented operations that can be performed by a program running on a conventional terminal.

As with *fork()*, *ptyFork()* returns the process ID of the child in the parent process, 0 in the child process, or –1 on error.

Eventually, the child process created by *ptyFork()* will terminate. If the parent doesn't terminate at the same time, then it must wait on the child to eliminate the resulting zombie. However, this step can often be eliminated, since applications that employ pseudoterminals are commonly designed so that the parent does terminate at the same time as the child.

> BSD derivatives provide two related, nonstandard functions for working with pseudoterminals. The first of these is *openpty()*, which opens a pseudoterminal pair, returns the file descriptors for the master and slave, optionally returns the name of the slave device, and optionally sets the terminal attributes and window size from arguments analogous to *slaveTermios* and *slaveWS*. The other function, *forkpty()*, is the same as our *ptyFork()*, except that it doesn't provide an analog of the *snLen* argument. On Linux, both of these functions are provided by *glibc* and are documented in the *openpty(3)* manual page.

Listing 64-2: Implementation of *ptyFork()*

─── pty/pty_fork.c
```
#include <fcntl.h>
#include <termios.h>
#include <sys/ioctl.h>
#include "pty_master_open.h"
#include "pty_fork.h"                    /* Declares ptyFork() */
#include "tlpi_hdr.h"

#define MAX_SNAME 1000

pid_t
ptyFork(int *masterFd, char *slaveName, size_t snLen,
        const struct termios *slaveTermios, const struct winsize *slaveWS)
{
    int mfd, slaveFd, savedErrno;
    pid_t childPid;
    char slname[MAX_SNAME];
```

```
①      mfd = ptyMasterOpen(slname, MAX_SNAME);
        if (mfd == -1)
            return -1;

②      if (slaveName != NULL) {               /* Return slave name to caller */
            if (strlen(slname) < snLen) {
                strncpy(slaveName, slname, snLen);

            } else {                          /* 'slaveName' was too small */
                close(mfd);
                errno = EOVERFLOW;
                return -1;
            }
        }

③      childPid = fork();

        if (childPid == -1) {                 /* fork() failed */
            savedErrno = errno;               /* close() might change 'errno' */
            close(mfd);                       /* Don't leak file descriptors */
            errno = savedErrno;
            return -1;
        }

④      if (childPid != 0) {                   /* Parent */
            *masterFd = mfd;                  /* Only parent gets master fd */
            return childPid;                  /* Like parent of fork() */
        }

        /* Child falls through to here */

⑤      if (setsid() == -1)                    /* Start a new session */
            err_exit("ptyFork:setsid");

⑥      close(mfd);                            /* Not needed in child */

⑦      slaveFd = open(slname, O_RDWR);        /* Becomes controlling tty */
        if (slaveFd == -1)
            err_exit("ptyFork:open-slave");

⑧  #ifdef TIOCSCTTY                           /* Acquire controlling tty on BSD */
        if (ioctl(slaveFd, TIOCSCTTY, 0) == -1)
            err_exit("ptyFork:ioctl-TIOCSCTTY");
    #endif

⑨      if (slaveTermios != NULL)              /* Set slave tty attributes */
            if (tcsetattr(slaveFd, TCSANOW, slaveTermios) == -1)
                err_exit("ptyFork:tcsetattr");

⑩      if (slaveWS != NULL)                   /* Set slave tty window size */
            if (ioctl(slaveFd, TIOCSWINSZ, slaveWS) == -1)
                err_exit("ptyFork:ioctl-TIOCSWINSZ");
```

```
                 /* Duplicate pty slave to be child's stdin, stdout, and stderr */

⑪      if (dup2(slaveFd, STDIN_FILENO) != STDIN_FILENO)
            err_exit("ptyFork:dup2-STDIN_FILENO");
        if (dup2(slaveFd, STDOUT_FILENO) != STDOUT_FILENO)
            err_exit("ptyFork:dup2-STDOUT_FILENO");
        if (dup2(slaveFd, STDERR_FILENO) != STDERR_FILENO)
            err_exit("ptyFork:dup2-STDERR_FILENO");

        if (slaveFd > STDERR_FILENO)          /* Safety check */
            close(slaveFd);                   /* No longer need this fd */

        return 0;                             /* Like child of fork() */
    }
```
─── pty/pty_fork.c

64.5 Pseudoterminal I/O

A pseudoterminal pair is similar to a bidirectional pipe. Anything that is written on the master appears as input on the slave, and anything that is written on the slave appears as input on the master.

The point that distinguishes a pseudoterminal pair from a bidirectional pipe is that the slave side operates like a terminal device. The slave interprets input in the same way as a normal controlling terminal would interpret keyboard input. For example, if we write a *Control-C* character (the usual terminal *interrupt* character) to the pseudoterminal master, the slave will generate a SIGINT signal for its foreground process group. Just as with a conventional terminal, when a pseudoterminal slave operates in canonical mode (the default), input is buffered line by line. In other words, the program reading from the pseudoterminal slave will see (a line of) input only when we write a newline character to the pseudoterminal master.

Like pipes, pseudoterminals have a limited capacity. If we exhaust this capacity, then further writes are blocked until the process on the other side of the pseudoterminal has consumed some bytes.

> On Linux, the pseudoterminal capacity is about 4 kB in each direction.

If we close all file descriptors referring to the pseudoterminal master, then:

- If the slave device has a controlling process, a SIGHUP signal is sent to that process (see Section 34.6).
- A *read()* from the slave device returns end-of-file (0).
- A *write()* to the slave device fails with the error EIO. (On some other UNIX implementations, *write()* fails with the error ENXIO in this case.)

If we close all file descriptors referring to the pseudoterminal slave, then:

- A *read()* from the master device fails with the error EIO. (On some other UNIX implementations, a *read()* returns end-of-file in this case.)

- A *write()* to the master device succeeds, unless the input queue of the slave device is full, in which case the *write()* blocks. If the slave device is subsequently reopened, these bytes can be read.

UNIX implementations vary widely in their behavior for the last case. On some UNIX implementations, *write()* fails with the error EIO. On other implementations, *write()* succeeds, but the output bytes are discarded (i.e., they can't be read if the slave is reopened). In general, these variations don't present a problem. Normally, the process on the master side detects that the slave has been closed because a *read()* from the master returns end-of-file or fails. At this point, the process performs no further writes to the master.

Packet mode

Packet mode is a mechanism that allows the process running above a pseudoterminal master to be informed when the following events related to software flow control occur on the pseudoterminal slave:

- the input or output queue is flushed;
- terminal output is stopped or started (*Control-S/Control-Q*); or
- flow control was enabled or disabled.

Packet mode helps with handling software flow control in certain pseudoterminal applications that provide network login services (e.g., *telnet* and *rlogin*).

Packet mode is enabled by applying the *ioctl()* TIOCPKT operation to the file descriptor referring to the pseudoterminal master:

```
int arg;

arg = 1;                    /* 1 == enable; 0 == disable */
if (ioctl(mfd, TIOCPKT, &arg) == -1)
    errExit("ioctl");
```

When packet mode is in operation, reads from the pseudoterminal master return either a single nonzero control byte, which is a bit mask indicating the state change(s) that occurred on the slave device, or a 0 byte followed by one or more bytes of data that were written on the pseudoterminal slave.

When a state change occurs on a pseudoterminal that is operating in packet mode, *select()* indicates that an exceptional condition (the *exceptfds* argument) has occurred on the master, and *poll()* returns POLLPRI in the *revents* field. (Refer to Chapter 63 for descriptions of *select()* and *poll()*.)

Packet mode is not standardized in SUSv3, and some details vary on other UNIX implementations. Further details of packet mode on Linux, including the bit-mask values used to indicate state changes, can be found in the *tty_ioctl(4)* manual page.

64.6 Implementing *script(1)*

We are now ready to implement a simple version of the standard *script(1)* program. This program starts a new shell session, and records all input and output from the session to a file. Most of the shell sessions shown in this book were recorded using *script*.

In a normal login session, the shell is connected directly to the user's terminal. When we run *script*, it places itself between the user's terminal and the shell, and uses a pseudoterminal pair to create a communication channel between itself and the shell (see Figure 64-4). The shell is connected to the pseudoterminal slave. The *script* process is connected to the pseudoterminal master. The *script* process acts as a proxy for the user, taking input entered at the terminal and writing it to the pseudoterminal master, and reading output from the pseudoterminal master and writing it to the user's terminal.

In addition, *script* produces an output file (named `typescript` by default) that contains a copy of all bytes that are output on the pseudoterminal master. This has the effect of recording not only the output produced by the shell session, but also the input that is supplied to it. The input is recorded because, just as with a conventional terminal device, the kernel echoes input characters by copying them to the terminal output queue (see Figure 62-1, on page 1291). However, when terminal echoing is disabled, as is done by programs that read passwords, the pseudoterminal slave input is not copied to the slave output queue, and thus is not copied to the script output file.

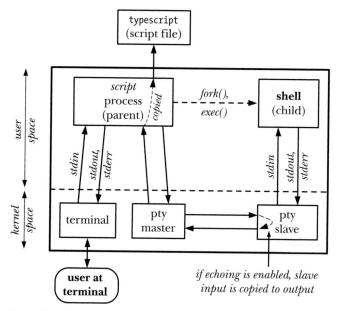

Figure 64-4: The *script* program

Our implementation of *script* is shown in Listing 64-3. This program performs the following steps:

- Retrieve the attributes and window size of the terminal under which the program is run ①. These are passed to the subsequent call to *ptyFork()*, which uses them to set the corresponding values for the pseudoterminal slave device.

- Call our *ptyFork()* function (Listing 64-2) to create a child process that is connected to the parent via a pseudoterminal pair ②.

- After the *ptyFork()* call, the child execs a shell ④. The choice of shell is determined by the setting of the SHELL environment variable ③. If the SHELL variable is not set or its value is an empty string, then the child execs /bin/sh.

- After the *ptyFork()* call, the parent performs the following steps:

    - Open the output script file ⑤. If a command-line argument is supplied, this is used as the name of the script file. If no command-line argument is supplied, the default name typescript is used.

    - Place the terminal in raw mode (using the *ttySetRaw()* function shown in Listing 62-3, on page 1310), so that all input characters are passed directly to the *script* program without being modified by the terminal driver ⑥. Characters output by the *script* program are likewise not modified by the terminal driver.

        > The fact that the terminal is in raw mode doesn't mean that raw, uninterpreted control characters will be transmitted to the shell, or whatever other process group is in the foreground for the pseudoterminal slave device, nor that output from that process group is passed raw to the user's terminal. Instead, interpretation of terminal special characters is taking place within the slave device (unless the slave was also explicitly placed in raw mode by an application). By placing the user's terminal in raw mode, we prevent a *second* round of interpretation of input and output characters from occurring.

    - Call *atexit()* to install an exit handler that resets the terminal to its original mode when the program terminates ⑦.

    - Execute a loop that transfers data in both directions between the terminal and the pseudoterminal master ⑧. In each loop iteration, the program first uses *select()* (Section 63.2.1) to monitor both the terminal and the pseudoterminal master for input ⑨. If the terminal has input available, then the program reads some of that input and writes it to the pseudoterminal master ⑩. Similarly, if the pseudoterminal master has input available, the program reads some of that input and writes it to the terminal and to the script file ⑪. The loop executes until end-of-file or an error is detected on one of the monitored file descriptors.

Listing 64-3: A simple implementation of *script(1)*

```
                                                               ─── pty/script.c
#include <sys/stat.h>
#include <fcntl.h>
#include <libgen.h>
#include <termios.h>
#include <sys/select.h>
#include "pty_fork.h"          /* Declaration of ptyFork() */
#include "tty_functions.h"     /* Declaration of ttySetRaw() */
#include "tlpi_hdr.h"

#define BUF_SIZE 256
#define MAX_SNAME 1000

struct termios ttyOrig;

static void                /* Reset terminal mode on program exit */
ttyReset(void)
{
    if (tcsetattr(STDIN_FILENO, TCSANOW, &ttyOrig) == -1)
        errExit("tcsetattr");
}

int
main(int argc, char *argv[])
{
    char slaveName[MAX_SNAME];
    char *shell;
    int masterFd, scriptFd;
    struct winsize ws;
    fd_set inFds;
    char buf[BUF_SIZE];
    ssize_t numRead;
    pid_t childPid;

①  if (tcgetattr(STDIN_FILENO, &ttyOrig) == -1)
        errExit("tcgetattr");
    if (ioctl(STDIN_FILENO, TIOCGWINSZ, &ws) < 0)
        errExit("ioctl-TIOCGWINSZ");

②  childPid = ptyFork(&masterFd, slaveName, MAX_SNAME, &ttyOrig, &ws);
    if (childPid == -1)
        errExit("ptyFork");

    if (childPid == 0) {          /* Child: execute a shell on pty slave */
③      shell = getenv("SHELL");
        if (shell == NULL || *shell == '\0')
            shell = "/bin/sh";

④      execlp(shell, shell, (char *) NULL);
        errExit("execlp");        /* If we get here, something went wrong */
    }
```

```
                /* Parent: relay data between terminal and pty master */

⑤        scriptFd = open((argc > 1) ? argv[1] : "typescript",
                                O_WRONLY | O_CREAT | O_TRUNC,
                                S_IRUSR | S_IWUSR | S_IRGRP | S_IWGRP |
                                        S_IROTH | S_IWOTH);
        if (scriptFd == -1)
            errExit("open typescript");

⑥        ttySetRaw(STDIN_FILENO, &ttyOrig);

⑦        if (atexit(ttyReset) != 0)
            errExit("atexit");

⑧        for (;;) {
            FD_ZERO(&inFds);
            FD_SET(STDIN_FILENO, &inFds);
            FD_SET(masterFd, &inFds);

⑨            if (select(masterFd + 1, &inFds, NULL, NULL, NULL) == -1)
                errExit("select");

⑩            if (FD_ISSET(STDIN_FILENO, &inFds)) {    /* stdin --> pty */
                numRead = read(STDIN_FILENO, buf, BUF_SIZE);
                if (numRead <= 0)
                    exit(EXIT_SUCCESS);

                if (write(masterFd, buf, numRead) != numRead)
                    fatal("partial/failed write (masterFd)");
            }

⑪            if (FD_ISSET(masterFd, &inFds)) {        /* pty --> stdout+file */
                numRead = read(masterFd, buf, BUF_SIZE);
                if (numRead <= 0)
                    exit(EXIT_SUCCESS);

                if (write(STDOUT_FILENO, buf, numRead) != numRead)
                    fatal("partial/failed write (STDOUT_FILENO)");
                if (write(scriptFd, buf, numRead) != numRead)
                    fatal("partial/failed write (scriptFd)");
            }
        }
    }
```
── **pty/script.c**

In the following shell session, we demonstrate the use of the program in Listing 64-3. We begin by displaying the name of the pseudoterminal used by the *xterm* on which the login shell is running and the process ID of the login shell. This information is useful later in the shell session.

```
$ tty
/dev/pts/1
$ echo $$
7979
```

We then start an instance of our *script* program, which invokes a subshell. Once more, we display the name of the terminal on which the shell is running and the process ID of the shell:

```
$ ./script
$ tty
/dev/pts/24                      Pseudoterminal slave opened by script
$ echo $$
29825                            PID of subshell process started by script
```

Now we use *ps(1)* to display information about the two shells and the process running *script*, and then terminate the shell started by *script*:

```
$ ps -p 7979 -p 29825 -C script -o "pid ppid sid tty cmd"
   PID   PPID   SID TT       CMD
  7979   7972  7979 pts/1    /bin/bash
 29824   7979  7979 pts/1    ./script
 29825  29824 29825 pts/24   /bin/bash
$ exit
```

The output of *ps(1)* shows the parent-child relationships between the login shell, the process running *script*, and the subshell started by *script*.

At this point, we have returned to the login shell. Displaying the contents of the file typescript shows a record of all input and output that was produced while *script* was running:

```
$ cat typescript
$ tty
/dev/pts/24
$ echo $$
29825
$ ps -p 7979 -p 29825 -C script -o "pid ppid sid tty cmd"
   PID   PPID   SID TT       CMD
  7979   7972  7979 pts/1    /bin/bash
 29824   7979  7979 pts/1    ./script
 29825  29824 29825 pts/24   /bin/bash
$ exit
```

64.7 Terminal Attributes and Window Size

The master and slave device share terminal attributes (*termios*) and window size (*winsize*) structures. (Both of these structures are described in Chapter 62.) This means that the program running above the pseudoterminal master can change these attributes for the pseudoterminal slave by applying *tcsetattr()* and *ioctl()* to the file descriptor of the master device.

One example of where changing terminal attributes can be useful is in the *script* program. Suppose we are running *script* in a terminal emulator window, and we change the size of the window. In this case, the terminal emulator program will inform the kernel of the change in the size of the corresponding terminal device, but this change is not reflected in the separate kernel record for the pseudoterminal slave (see Figure 64-4). As a consequence, screen-oriented programs (e.g., *vi*) running above the pseudoterminal slave will produce confusing output, since their understanding of the terminal window size differs from the actual size of the terminal. We can solve this problem as follows:

1. Install a handler for SIGWINCH in the *script* parent process, so that it is signaled when the size of the terminal window changes.

2. When the *script* parent receives a SIGWINCH signal, it uses an *ioctl()* TIOCGWINSZ operation to retrieve a *winsize* structure for the terminal window associated with its standard input. It then uses this structure in an *ioctl()* TIOCSWINSZ operation that sets the window size of the pseudoterminal master.

3. If the new pseudoterminal window size is different from the old size, then the kernel generates a SIGWINCH signal for the foreground process group of the pseudoterminal slave. Screen-handling programs such as *vi* are designed to catch this signal and perform an *ioctl()* TIOCGWINSZ operation to update their understanding of the terminal window size.

We described the details of terminal window sizes and the *ioctl()* TIOCGWINSZ and TIOCSWINSZ operations in Section 62.9.

64.8 BSD Pseudoterminals

For most of this chapter, we have focused on UNIX 98 pseudoterminals, since this is the style of pseudoterminal that is standardized in SUSv3 and thus should be used in all new programs. However, we may sometimes encounter BSD pseudoterminals in older applications or when porting programs to Linux from other UNIX implementations. Therefore, we now consider the details of BSD pseudoterminals.

> The use of BSD pseudoterminals is deprecated on Linux. From Linux 2.6.4 onward, BSD pseudoterminal support is an optional kernel component that can be configured via the CONFIG_LEGACY_PTYS option.

BSD pseudoterminals differ from their UNIX 98 counterparts only in the details of how pseudoterminal master and slave devices are found and opened. Once the master and slave have been opened, BSD pseudoterminals operate in the same way as UNIX 98 pseudoterminals.

With UNIX 98 pseudoterminals, we obtain an unused pseudoterminal master by calling *posix_openpt()*, which opens /dev/ptmx, the pseudoterminal master clone device. We then obtain the name of the corresponding pseudoterminal slave using *ptsname()*. By contrast, with BSD pseudoterminals, the master and slave device pairs are precreated entries in the /dev directory. Each master device has a name of the form /dev/pty*xy*, where *x* is replaced by a letter in the 16-letter range [p-za-e] and *y* is replaced by a letter in the 16-letter range [0-9a-f]. The slave corresponding to a particular pseudoterminal master has a name of the form /dev/tty*xy*. Thus, for example, the devices /dev/ptyp0 and /dev/ttyp0 constitute a BSD pseudoterminal pair.

> UNIX implementations vary in the number and names of BSD pseudoterminal pairs that they supply, with some supplying as few as 32 pairs by default. Most implementations provide at least the 32 master devices with names in the range /dev/pty[pq][0-9a-f], along with the corresponding slave devices.

To find an unused pseudoterminal pair, we execute a loop that attempts to open each master device in turn, until one of them is opened successfully. While executing this loop, there are two errors that we may encounter when calling *open()*:

- If a given master device name doesn't exist, *open()* fails with the error ENOENT. Typically, this means we've run through the complete set of pseudoterminal master names on the system without finding a free device (i.e., there was not the full range of devices listed above).

- If the master device is in use, *open()* fails with the error EIO. We can just ignore this error and try the next device.

> On HP-UX 11, *open()* fails with the error EBUSY on an attempt to open a BSD pseudoterminal master that is in use.

Once we have found an available master device, we can obtain the name of the corresponding slave by substituting tty for pty in the name of the master. We can then open the slave using *open()*.

> With BSD pseudoterminals, there is no equivalent of *grantpt()* to change the ownership and permissions of the pseudoterminal slave. If we need to do this, then we must make explicit calls to *chown()* (only possible in a privileged program) and *chmod()*, or write a set-user-ID program (like *pt_chown*) that performs this task for an unprivileged program.

Listing 64-4 shows a reimplementation of the *ptyMasterOpen()* function of Section 64.3 using BSD pseudoterminals. Substituting this implementation is all that is required to make our *script* program (Section 64.6) work with BSD pseudoterminals.

Listing 64-4: Implementation of *ptyMasterOpen()* using BSD pseudoterminals

──
                                                    —— pty/pty_master_open_bsd.c
```c
#include <fcntl.h>
#include "pty_master_open.h"            /* Declares ptyMasterOpen() */
#include "tlpi_hdr.h"

#define PTYM_PREFIX     "/dev/pty"
#define PTYS_PREFIX     "/dev/tty"
#define PTY_PREFIX_LEN  (sizeof(PTYM_PREFIX) - 1)
#define PTY_NAME_LEN    (PTY_PREFIX_LEN + sizeof("XY"))
#define X_RANGE         "pqrstuvwxyzabcde"
#define Y_RANGE         "0123456789abcdef"

int
ptyMasterOpen(char *slaveName, size_t snLen)
{
    int masterFd, n;
    char *x, *y;
    char masterName[PTY_NAME_LEN];

    if (PTY_NAME_LEN > snLen) {
        errno = EOVERFLOW;
        return -1;
    }
```

```
            memset(masterName, 0, PTY_NAME_LEN);
            strncpy(masterName, PTYM_PREFIX, PTY_PREFIX_LEN);

            for (x = X_RANGE; *x != '\0'; x++) {
                masterName[PTY_PREFIX_LEN] = *x;

                for (y = Y_RANGE; *y != '\0'; y++) {
                    masterName[PTY_PREFIX_LEN + 1] = *y;

                    masterFd = open(masterName, O_RDWR);

                    if (masterFd == -1) {
                        if (errno == ENOENT)      /* No such file */
                            return -1;            /* Probably no more pty devices */
                        else                      /* Other error (e.g., pty busy) */
                            continue;

                    } else {                /* Return slave name corresponding to master */
                        n = snprintf(slaveName, snLen, "%s%c%c", PTYS_PREFIX, *x, *y);
                        if (n >= snLen) {
                            errno = EOVERFLOW;
                            return -1;
                        } else if (n == -1) {
                            return -1;
                        }

                        return masterFd;
                    }
                }
            }

            return -1;                    /* Tried all ptys without success */
        }
```
── **pty/pty_master_open_bsd.c**

64.9 Summary

A pseudoterminal pair consists of a connected master device and slave device. Together, these two devices provide a bidirectional IPC channel. The benefit of a pseudoterminal is that, on the slave side of the pair, we can connect a terminal-oriented program that is driven by the program that has opened the master device. The pseudoterminal slave behaves just like a conventional terminal. All of the operations that can be applied to a conventional terminal can be applied to the slave, and input transmitted from the master to the slave is interpreted in the same manner as keyboard input is interpreted on a conventional terminal.

One common use of pseudoterminals is in applications that provide network login services. However, pseudoterminals are also used in many other programs, such as terminal emulators and the *script(1)* program.

Different pseudoterminals APIs arose on System V and BSD. Linux supports both APIs, but the System V API forms the basis for the pseudoterminal API that is standardized in SUSv3.

64.10 Exercises

64-1. In what order do the *script* parent process and the child shell process terminate when the user types the end-of-file character (usually *Control-D*) while running the program in Listing 64-3? Why?

64-2. Make the following modifications to the program in Listing 64-3 (`script.c`):

a) The standard *script(1)* program adds lines to the beginning and the end of the output file showing the time the script started and finished. Add this feature.

b) Add code to handle changes to the terminal window size as described in Section 64.7. You may find the program in Listing 62-5 (`demo_SIGWINCH.c`) useful for testing this feature.

64-3. Modify the program in Listing 64-3 (`script.c`) to replace the use of *select()* by a pair of processes: one to handle data transfer from the terminal to the pseudoterminal master, and the other to handle data transfer in the opposite direction.

64-4. Modify the program in Listing 64-3 (`script.c`) to add a time-stamped recording feature. Each time the program writes a string to the `typescript` file, it should also write a time-stamped string to a second file (say, `typescript.timed`). Records written to this second file might have the following general form:

```
<timestamp> <space> <string> <newline>
```

The *timestamp* should be recorded in text form as the number of milliseconds since the start of the script session. Recording the timestamp in text form has the advantage that the resulting file is human-readable. Within *string*, real newline characters will need to be escaped. One possibility is to record a newline as the 2-character sequence \n and a backslash as \\.

Write a second program, `script_replay.c`, that reads the time-stamped script file and displays its contents on standard output at the same rate at which they were originally written. Together, these two programs provide a simple recording and playback feature for shell session logs.

64-5. Implement client and server programs to provide a simple *telnet*-style remote login facility. Design the server to handle clients concurrently (Section 60.1). Figure 64-3 shows the setup that needs to be established for each client login. What isn't shown in that diagram is the parent server process, which handles incoming socket connections from clients and creates a server child to handle each connection. Note that all of the work of authenticating the user and starting a login shell can be dealt with in each server child by having the (grand)child created by *ptyFork()* go on to exec *login(1)*.

64-6. Add code to the program developed in the previous exercise to update the login accounting files at the start and end of the login session (Chapter 40).

64-7. Suppose we execute a long-running program that slowly generates output that is redirected to a file or pipe, as in this example:

```
$ longrunner | grep str
```

One problem with the above scenario is that, by default, the *stdio* package flushes standard output only when the *stdio* buffer is filled. This means that the output from the *longrunner* program will appear in bursts separated by long intervals of time. One way to circumvent this problem is to write a program that does the following:

a) Create a pseudoterminal.

b) Exec the program named in its command-line arguments with the standard file descriptors connected to the pseudoterminal slave.

c) Read output from the pseudoterminal master and write it immediately to standard output (STDOUT_FILENO, file descriptor 1), and, at the same time, read input from the terminal and write it to the pseudoterminal master, so that it can be read by the execed program.

Such a program, which we'll call *unbuffer*, would be used as follows:

```
$ ./unbuffer longrunner | grep str
```

Write the *unbuffer* program. (Much of the code for this program will be similar to that of Listing 64-3.)

64-8. Write a program that implements a scripting language that can be used to drive *vi* in a noninteractive mode. Since *vi* expects to be run from a terminal, the program will need to employ a pseudoterminal.

TRACING SYSTEM CALLS

The *strace* command allows us to trace the system calls made by a program. This is useful for debugging, or simply to find out what a program is doing. In its simplest form, we use *strace* as follows:

```
$ strace command arg...
```

This runs *command*, with the given command-line arguments, producing a trace of the system calls it makes. By default, *strace* writes its output to *stderr*, but we can change this using the *−o filename* option.

Examples of the type of output produced by *strace* include the following (taken from the output of the command *strace date*):

```
execve("/bin/date", ["date"], [/* 114 vars */]) = 0
access("/etc/ld.so.preload", R_OK)      = -1 ENOENT (No such file or directory)
open("/etc/ld.so.cache", O_RDONLY)      = 3
fstat64(3, {st_mode=S_IFREG|0644, st_size=111059, ...}) = 0
mmap2(NULL, 111059, PROT_READ, MAP_PRIVATE, 3, 0) = 0xb7f38000
close(3)                                = 0
open("/lib/libc.so.6", O_RDONLY)        = 3
fstat64(3, {st_mode=S_IFREG|0755, st_size=1491141, ...}) = 0
close(3)                                = 0
write(1, "Mon Jan 17 12:14:24 CET 2011\n", 29) = 29
exit_group(0)                           = ?
```

Each system call is displayed in the form of a function call, with both input and output arguments shown in parentheses. As can be seen from the above examples, arguments are printed in symbolic form:

- Bit masks are represented using the corresponding symbolic constants.
- Strings are printed in text form (up to a limit of 32 characters, but the *-s strsize* option can be used to change this limit).
- Structure fields are individually displayed (by default, only an abbreviated subset of large structures is displayed, but the *-v* option can be used to display the whole structure).

After the closing parenthesis of the traced call, *strace* prints an equal sign (=), followed by the return value of the system call. If the system call failed, the symbolic *errno* value is also displayed. Thus, we see ENOENT displayed for the failure of the *access()* call above.

Even for a simple program, the output produced by *strace* is made voluminous by the system calls executed by the C run-time startup code and the loading of shared libraries. For a complex program, the *strace* output can be extremely long. For these reasons, it is sometimes useful to selectively filter the output of *strace*. One way to do this is to use *grep*, like so:

```
$ strace date 2>&1 | grep open
```

Another method is to use the *-e* option to select the events to be traced. For example, we can use the following command to trace *open()* and *close()* system calls:

```
$ strace -e trace=open,close date
```

When using either of the above techniques, we need to be aware that, in a few cases, the true name of a system call differs from the name of its *glibc* wrapper. For example, though we refer to all of the *wait()*-type functions as system calls in Chapter 26, most of them (*wait()*, *waitpid()*, and *wait3()*) are wrappers that invoke the kernel's *wait4()* system call service routine. This latter name is displayed by *strace*, and we must specify that name in the *-e trace=* option. Similarly, all of the *exec* library functions (Section 27.2) invoke the *execve()* system call. Often, we can make a good guess about such transformations by looking at the *strace* output (or looking at the output produced by *strace -c*, described below), but, failing that, we may need to check the *glibc* source code to see what transformations may be occurring inside wrapper functions.

The *strace(1)* manual page documents a host of further options to *strace*, including the following:

- The *-p pid* option is used to trace an existing process, by specifying its process ID. Unprivileged users are restricted to tracing only processes that they own and that are not executing set-user-ID or set-group-ID programs (Section 9.3).
- The *-c* option causes *strace* to print a summary of all system calls made by the program. For each system call, the summary information includes the total number of calls, the number of calls that failed, and the total time spent executing the calls.

- The *-f* option causes children of this process also to be traced. If we are sending trace output to a file (*-o filename*), then the alternative *-ff* option causes each process to write its trace output to a file named *filename.PID*.

The *strace* command is Linux-specific, but most UNIX implementations provide their own equivalents (e.g., *truss* on Solaris and *ktrace* on the BSDs).

> The *ltrace* command performs an analogous task to *strace*, but for library functions. See the *ltrace(1)* manual page for details.

B

PARSING COMMAND-LINE OPTIONS

A typical UNIX command line has the following form:

---

command [*options*] *arguments*

An option takes the form of a hyphen (-) followed by a unique character identifying the option and a possible argument for the option. An option that takes an argument may optionally be separated from that argument by white space. Multiple options can be grouped after a single hyphen, and the last option in the group may be one that takes an argument. According to these rules, the following commands are all equivalent:

```
$ grep -l -i -f patterns *.c
$ grep -lif patterns *.c
$ grep -lifpatterns *.c
```

In the above commands, the *–l* and *–i* options don't have an argument, while the *–f* option takes the string *patterns* as its argument.

Since many programs (including some of the example programs in this book) need to parse options in the above format, the facility to do so is encapsulated in a standard library function, *getopt()*.

```
#include <unistd.h>

extern int optind, opterr, optopt;
extern char *optarg;

int getopt(int argc, char *const argv[], const char *optstring);
```

                              See main text for description of return value

The *getopt()* function parses the set of command-line arguments given in *argc* and *argv*, which would normally be taken from the arguments of the same name to *main()*. The *optstring* argument specifies the set of options that *getopt()* should look for in *argv*. This argument consists of a sequence of characters, each of which identifies an option. SUSv3 specifies that *getopt()* should permit at least the characters in the 62-character set [a-zA-Z0-9] as options. Most implementations allow other characters as well, with the exception of :, ?, and -, which have special meaning to *getopt()*. Each option character may be followed by a colon (:), indicating that this option expects an argument.

We parse a command line by calling *getopt()* repeatedly. Each call returns information about the next unprocessed option. If an option was found, the option character is returned as the function result. If the end of the option list was reached, *getopt()* returns −1. If an option has an argument, *getopt()* sets the global variable *optarg* to point to that argument.

Note that the function result of *getopt()* is *int*. We must not assign the result of *getopt()* to a variable of type *char*, because the comparison of the *char* variable with −1 won't work on systems where *char* is unsigned.

> If an option doesn't have an argument, then the *glibc getopt()* implementation (like most other implementations) sets *optarg* to NULL. However, SUSv3 doesn't specify this behavior, so applications can't portably rely on it (nor is it usually needed).
>
> SUSv3 specifies (and *glibc* implements) a related function, *getsubopt()*, that parses option arguments that consist of one or more comma-separated strings of the form *name[=value]*. See the *getsubopt(3)* manual page for details.

On each call to *getopt()*, the global variable *optind* is updated to contain the index of the next unprocessed element of *argv*. (When multiple options are grouped in a single word, *getopt()* does some internal bookkeeping to keep track of which part of the word is next to be processed.) The *optind* variable is automatically set to 1 before the first call to *getopt()*. There are two circumstances where we may make use of this variable:

• If *getopt()* returns −1, indicating that no more options are present and *optind* is less than *argc*, then *argv[optind]* is the location of the next nonoption word from the command line.

• If we are processing multiple command-line vectors or rescanning the same command line, then we must explicitly reset *optind* to 1.

The *getopt()* function returns −1, indicating the end of the option list, in the following circumstances:

- The end of the list described by *argc* plus *argv* was reached (i.e., *argv[optind]* is NULL).
- The next unprocessed word in *argv* does not start with an option delimiter (i.e., *argv[optind][0]* is not a hyphen).
- The next unprocessed word in *argv* consists of a single hyphen (i.e., *argv[optind]* is -). Some commands understand such a word as an argument with a special meaning, as described in Section 5.11.
- The next unprocessed word in *argv* consists of two hyphens (--). In this case, *getopt()* silently consumes the two hyphens and *optind* is adjusted to point to the next word after the double hyphen. This syntax enables a user to indicate the end of the options of a command, even when the next word on the command line (after the double hyphen) looks like an option (i.e., starts with a hyphen). For example, if we want to use *grep* to search for the string −k inside a file, then we would write *grep -- -k myfile*.

Two kinds of errors may occur as *getopt()* processes an option list. One error arises when an option that is not specified in *optstring* is encountered. The other error occurs when an argument is not supplied to an option that expects one (i.e., the option appears at the end of the command line). The rules about how *getopt()* handles and reports these errors are as follows:

- By default, *getopt()* prints an appropriate error message on standard error and returns the character ? as its function result. In this case, the global variable *optopt* returns the erroneous option character (i.e., the one that is unrecognized or whose argument is missing).
- The global variable *opterr* can be used to suppress the error messages printed by *getopt()*. By default, this variable is set to 1. If we set it to 0, then *getopt()* doesn't print error messages, but otherwise behaves as described in the preceding point. The program can detect the error via the ? function result and display a customized error message.
- Alternatively, we may suppress error messages by specifying a colon (:) as the first character in *optstring* (doing so overrides the effect of setting *opterr* to 0). In this case, an error is reported as with setting *opterr* to 0, except that an option with a missing argument is reported by returning : as the function result. This difference in return values allows us to distinguish the two types of errors (unrecognized option and missing option argument), if we need to do so.

The above error-reporting alternatives are summarized in Table B-1.

Table B-1: *getopt()* error-reporting behavior

Error-reporting method	*getopt()* displays error message?	Return for unrecognized option	Return for missing argument
default (*opterr == 1*)	Y	?	?
opterr == 0	N	?	?
: at start of *optstring*	N	?	:

Example program

Listing B-1 demonstrates the use of *getopt()* to parse the command line for two options: the *-x* option, which doesn't expect an argument, and the *-p* option which does expect an argument. This program suppresses error messages from *getopt()* by specifying a colon (:) as the first character in *optstring*.

To allow us to observe the operation of *getopt()*, we include some *printf()* calls to display the information returned by each *getopt()* call. On completion, the program prints some summary information about the specified options and also displays the next nonoption word on the command line, if there is one. The following shell session log shows the results when we run this program with different command-line arguments:

```
$ ./t_getopt -x -p hello world
opt =120 (x); optind = 2
opt =112 (p); optind = 4
-x was specified (count=1)
-p was specified with the value "hello"
First nonoption argument is "world" at argv[4]
$ ./t_getopt -p
opt = 58 (:); optind = 2; optopt =112 (p)
Missing argument (-p)
Usage: ./t_getopt [-p arg] [-x]
$ ./t_getopt -a
opt = 63 (?); optind = 2; optopt = 97 (a)
Unrecognized option (-a)
Usage: ./t_getopt [-p arg] [-x]
$ ./t_getopt -p str -- -x
opt =112 (p); optind = 3
-p was specified with the value "str"
First nonoption argument is "-x" at argv[4]
$ ./t_getopt -p -x
opt =112 (p); optind = 3
-p was specified with the value "-x"
```

Note that in the last example above, the string *-x* was interpreted as an argument to the *-p* option, rather than as an option.

Listing B-1: Using *getopt()*

─── getopt/t_getopt.c
```c
#include <ctype.h>
#include "tlpi_hdr.h"

#define printable(ch) (isprint((unsigned char) ch) ? ch : '#')

static void             /* Print "usage" message and exit */
usageError(char *progName, char *msg, int opt)
{
    if (msg != NULL && opt != 0)
        fprintf(stderr, "%s (-%c)\n", msg, printable(opt));
    fprintf(stderr, "Usage: %s [-p arg] [-x]\n", progName);
    exit(EXIT_FAILURE);
}
```

```
int
main(int argc, char *argv[])
{
    int opt, xfnd;
    char *pstr;

    xfnd = 0;
    pstr = NULL;

    while ((opt = getopt(argc, argv, ":p:x")) != -1) {
        printf("opt =%3d (%c); optind = %d", opt, printable(opt), optind);
        if (opt == '?' || opt == ':')
            printf("; optopt =%3d (%c)", optopt, printable(optopt));
        printf("\n");

        switch (opt) {
        case 'p': pstr = optarg;        break;
        case 'x': xfnd++;               break;
        case ':': usageError(argv[0], "Missing argument", optopt);
        case '?': usageError(argv[0], "Unrecognized option", optopt);
        default:  fatal("Unexpected case in switch()");
        }
    }

    if (xfnd != 0)
        printf("-x was specified (count=%d)\n", xfnd);
    if (pstr != NULL)
        printf("-p was specified with the value \"%s\"\n", pstr);
    if (optind < argc)
        printf("First nonoption argument is \"%s\" at argv[%d]\n",
                argv[optind], optind);
    exit(EXIT_SUCCESS);
}
```

———————————————————————————————————— getopt/t_getopt.c

GNU-specific behavior

By default, the *glibc* implementation of *getopt()* implements a nonstandard feature: it
allows options and nonoptions to be intermingled. Thus, for example, the following
are equivalent:

```
$ ls -l file
$ ls file -l
```

In processing command lines of the second form, *getopt()* permutes the contents of
argv so that all options are moved to the beginning of the array and all nonoptions
are moved to the end of the array. (If *argv* contains an element pointing to the
word --, then only the elements preceding that element are subject to permutation
and interpretation as options.) In other words, the const declaration of *argv* in the
getopt() prototype shown earlier is not actually true for *glibc*.

Permuting the contents of *argv* is not permitted by SUSv3 (or SUSv4). We can
force *getopt()* to provide standards-conformant behavior (i.e., to follow the rules

listed earlier for determining the end of the option list) by setting the environment variable POSIXLY_CORRECT to any value. This can be done in two ways:

- From within the program, we can call *putenv()* or *setenv()*. This has the advantage that the user is not required to do anything. It has the disadvantages that it requires modifications of the program source code and that it changes the behavior of only that program.
- We can define the variable from the shell before we execute the program:

```
$ export POSIXLY_CORRECT=y
```

This method has the advantage that it affects all programs that use *getopt()*. However, it also has some disadvantages. POSIXLY_CORRECT causes other changes in the behavior of various Linux tools. Furthermore, setting this variable requires explicit user intervention (most likely by setting the variable in a shell startup file).

An alternative method of preventing *getopt()* from permuting command-line arguments is to make the first character of *optstring* a plus sign (+). (If we want to also suppress *getopt()* error messages as described above, then the first two characters of *optstring* should be +:, in that order.) As with the use of *putenv()* or *setenv()*, this approach has the disadvantage that it requires changes to the program code. See the *getopt(3)* manual page for further details.

> A future technical corrigendum of SUSv4 is likely to add a specification for the use of the plus sign in *optstring* to prevent permutation of command-line arguments.

Note that the *glibc getopt()* permuting behavior affects how we write shell scripts. (This affects developers porting shell scripts from other systems to Linux.) Suppose we have a shell script that performs the following command on all of the files in a directory:

```
chmod 644 *
```

If one of these filenames starts with a hyphen, then the *glibc getopt()* permuting behavior would cause that filename to be interpreted as an option to *chmod*. This would not happen on other UNIX implementations, where the occurrence of the first nonoption (644) ensures that *getopt()* ceases looking for options in the remainder of the command line. For most commands, (if we don't set POSIXLY_CORRECT, then) the way of dealing with this possibility in shell scripts that must run on Linux is to place the string -- before the first nonoption argument. Thus, we would rewrite the above line as follows:

```
chmod -- 644 *
```

In this particular example, which employs filename generation, we could alternatively write this:

```
chmod 644 ./*
```

Although we have used the example of filename pattern matching (globbing) above, similar scenarios can also occur as a result of other shell processing (e.g., command substitution and parameter expansion), and they can be dealt with similarly, by using a -- string to separate options from arguments.

GNU extensions

The GNU C library provides a number of extensions to *getopt()*. We briefly note the following:

- The SUSv3 specification permits options to have only mandatory arguments. In the GNU version of *getopt()*, we can place two colons after an option character in *optstring* to indicate that its argument is optional. The argument to such an option must appear in the same word as the option itself (i.e., no spaces may appear between the option and its argument). If the argument is not present, then, on return from *getopt()*, *optarg* is set to NULL.

- Many GNU commands allow a form of long option syntax. A long option begins with two hyphens, and the option itself is identified using a word, rather than a single character, as in the following example:

```
$ gcc --version
```

The *glibc* function *getopt_long()* can be used to parse such options.

- The GNU C library provides an even more sophisticated (but nonportable) API for parsing the command-line, called *argp*. This API is described in the *glibc* manual.

CASTING THE NULL POINTER

Consider the following call to the variadic function *execl()*:

```
execl("ls", "ls", "-l", (char *) NULL);
```

> A *variadic function* is one that takes a variable number of arguments or arguments of varying types.

Whether the cast is required before the NULL in cases like this is the source of some confusion. While we can often get away without the cast, the C standards require it; failure to include it may lead an application to break on some systems.

NULL is typically defined as either 0 or as *(void *) 0*. (The C standards allow other definitions, but they are essentially equivalent to one of these two possibilities.) The main reason casts are needed is that NULL is allowed to be defined as 0, so this is the case we examine first.

The C preprocessor translates NULL to 0 before the source code is passed to the compiler. The C standards specify that the integer constant 0 may be used in any context where a pointer may be used, and the compiler will ensure that this value is treated as a null pointer. In most cases, everything is fine, and we don't need to worry about casts. We can, for example, write code such as the following:

```
int *p;

p = 0;                          /* Assign null pointer to 'p' */
p = NULL;                       /* Same as 'p = 0' */
```

The above assignments work because the compiler can determine that a pointer value is required on the right-hand side of the assignment, and it will convert the value 0 to a null pointer.

Similarly, for functions with prototypes specifying a fixed argument list, we can specify either 0 or NULL for a pointer argument, to indicate that a null pointer should be passed to the function:

```
sigaction(SIGINT, &sa, 0);
sigaction(SIGINT, &sa, NULL);            /* Equivalent to the preceding */
```

> If we are passing a null pointer to an old-style, nonprototyped C function, then all of the arguments given here about the need to appropriately cast 0 or NULL also apply, regardless of whether the argument is part of a variadic argument list.

Because casting is not required in any of the above examples, one might conclude that it is never required. But this is wrong. The need for casting arises when specifying a null pointer as one of the varying arguments in a call to a variadic function such as *execl()*. To realize why this is necessary, we need to be aware of the following:

- The compiler can't determine the expected types of the varying arguments of a variadic function.

- The C standards don't require that a null pointer is actually represented in the same way as the integer constant 0. (In theory, a null pointer could be represented by any bit pattern that wasn't the same as a valid pointer.) Nor do the standards even require that a null pointer is the same size as the integer constant 0. All that the standards require is that when the integer constant 0 is found in a context where a pointer is expected, the 0 should be interpreted as a null pointer.

Consequently, it is wrong to write either of the following:

```
execl(prog, arg, 0);
execl(prog, arg, NULL);
```

This is an error because the compiler will pass the integer constant 0 to *execl()*, and there is no guarantee that this is equivalent to a null pointer.

In practice, we can often get away without the cast, since, on many C implementations (e.g., Linux/x86-32), the representations of the integer (*int*) constant 0 and the null pointer are the same. However, there are implementations where they are not—for example, where the size of a null pointer is larger than the size of the integer constant 0—so that in the above examples, *execl()* is likely to receive some random bits adjacent to the integer 0, and the resulting value will be interpreted as a random (nonnull) pointer. Omitting the cast leads to programs breaking when ported to such implementations. (On some of the aforementioned implementations, NULL is defined as the *long* integer constant *0L*, and *long* and *void* * have the same size, which may save wrongly constructed programs that use the second of the *execl()* calls above.) Therefore, we should rewrite the above *execl()* calls in the following ways:

```
execl(prog, arg, (char *) 0);
execl(prog, arg, (char *) NULL);
```

Casting NULL in the manner of the last call above is generally required, even on implementations where NULL is defined as *(void *) 0*. This is because, although the C standards require that null pointers of different types should test true for comparisons on equality, they don't require that pointers of different types have the same internal representation (although on most implementations they do). And, as before, in a variadic function, the compiler can't cast *(void *) 0* to a null pointer of the appropriate type.

> The C standards make one exception to the rule that pointers of different types need not have the same representation: pointers of the types *char ** and *void ** are required to have the same internal representation. This means that passing *(void *) 0* instead of *(char *) 0* would not be a problem in the example case of *execl()*, but, in the general case, a cast is needed.

KERNEL CONFIGURATION

Many features of the Linux kernel are components that can be optionally configured. Before compiling the kernel, these components can be disabled, enabled, or, in many cases, enabled as loadable kernel modules. One reason to disable an unneeded component is to reduce the size of the kernel binary, and thus save memory, if the component is not required. Enabling a component as a loadable module means that it will be loaded into memory only if it is required at run time. This likewise can save memory.

Kernel configuration is done by executing one of a few different *make* commands in the root directory of the kernel source tree—for example, *make menuconfig*, which provides a *curses*-style configuration menu, or, more comfortably, *make xconfig*, which provides a graphical configuration menu. These commands produce a .config file in the root directory of the kernel source tree that is then used during kernel compilation. This file contains the settings of all configuration options.

The value of each option that is enabled is shown in the .config file in a line of the following form:

CONFIG_*NAME*=*value*

If an option is not set, then the file contains a line of this form:

CONFIG_*NAME* is not set

In the .config file, lines beginning with a # character are comments.

Throughout this book, when we describe kernel options, we won't describe precisely where in the *menuconfig* or *xconfig* menu the option can be found. There are a few reasons for this:

- The location can often be determined fairly intuitively by navigating through the menu hierarchy.

- The location of configuration options does change over time, as the menu hierarchy is restructured across kernel versions.

- If we can't find the location of a particular option within the menu hierarchy, then both *make menuconfig* and *make xconfig* provide search facilities. For example, we can search for the string CONFIG_INOTIFY to find the option for configuring support for the *inotify* API.

The configuration options that were used to build the currently running kernel are viewable via the /proc/config.gz virtual file, a compressed file whose contents are the same as the .config file that was used to build the kernel. This file can be viewed using *zcat(1)* and searched using *zgrep(1)*. The /proc/config.gz file is itself only available if the kernel was configured with the CONFIG_IKCONFIG and CONFIG_IKCONFIG_PROC configuration options enabled.

FURTHER SOURCES
OF INFORMATION

Aside from the material in this book, many other sources of information about Linux system programming are available. This appendix provides a short introduction to some of them.

Manual pages

Manual pages are accessible via the *man* command. (The command *man man* describes how to use *man* to read manual pages.) The manual pages are divided into numbered sections that categorize information as follows:

1. *Programs and shell commands*: commands executed by users at the shell prompt.
2. *System calls*: Linux system calls.
3. *Library functions*: standard C library functions (as well as many other library functions).
4. *Special files*: special files, such as device files.
5. *File formats*: formats of files such as the system password (/etc/passwd) and group (/etc/group) files.
6. *Games*: games.

7. *Overview, conventions, protocols, and miscellany*: overviews of various topics, and various pages on network protocols and sockets programming.

8. *System administration commands*: commands that are for use mainly by the superuser.

In some cases, there are manual pages in different sections with the same name. For example, there is a section 1 manual page for the *chmod* command and a section 2 manual page for the *chmod()* system call. To distinguish manual pages with the same name, we enclose the section number in parentheses after the name—for example, *chmod(1)* and *chmod(2)*. To display the manual page from a particular section, we can insert the section number into the *man* command:

```
$ man 2 chmod
```

The manual pages for system calls and library functions are divided into a number of parts, which usually include the following:

- *Name*: the name of the function, accompanied by a one-line description. The following command can be used to obtain a list of all manual pages whose one-line description contains the specified string:

```
$ man -k string
```

This is useful if we can't remember or don't know exactly which manual page we're looking for.

- *Synopsis*: the C prototype of the function. This identifies the type and order of the function's arguments, as well as the type of value returned by the function. In most cases, a list of header files precedes the function prototype. These header files define macros and C types needed for use with this function, as well as the function prototype itself, and should be included in a program using this function.

- *Description*: a description of what the function does.

- *Return value*: a description of the range of values returned by the function, including how the function informs the caller of an error.

- *Errors*: a list of the possible *errno* values that are returned in the event of an error.

- *Conforming to*: a description of the various UNIX standards to which the function conforms. This gives us an idea of how portable this function is to other UNIX implementations and also identifies Linux-specific aspects of the function.

- *Bugs*: a description of things that are broken or that don't work as they should.

> Although some of the later commercial UNIX implementations have preferred more marketable euphemisms, from early times, the UNIX manual pages called a bug a bug. Linux continues the tradition. Sometimes these "bugs" are philosophical, simply describing ways in which things could be improved, or warning about special or unexpected (but otherwise intended) behaviors.

- *Notes*: miscellaneous additional notes on the function.

- *See also*: a list of manual pages for related functions and commands.

The manual pages describing the kernel and *glibc* APIs are available online at *http://www.kernel.org/doc/man-pages/*.

GNU *info* documents

Rather than using the traditional manual page format, the GNU project documents much of its software using *info* documents, which are hyperlinked documents that can be browsed using the *info* command. A tutorial on the use of *info* can be obtained using the command *info info*.

Although in many cases the information in manual pages and corresponding *info* documents is the same, sometimes the *info* documentation for the C library contains additional information not found in the manual pages or vice versa.

> The reasons both manual pages and *info* documents exist, even though both may contain the same information, are somewhat religious. The GNU project prefers the *info* user interface, and so provides all documentation via *info*. However, users and programmers on UNIX systems have had a long history of using (and in many cases preferring) manual pages, so there is strong momentum in favor of upholding this format. The manual pages also tend to include more historical information (e.g., information about behavior changes across versions) than do the *info* documents.

The GNU C library (*glibc*) manual

The GNU C library includes a manual that describes the use of many of the functions in the library. The manual is available at *http://www.gnu.org/*. It is also provided with most distributions in both HTML format and *info* format (via the command *info libc*).

Books

An extensive bibliography can be found at the end of this book, but a few books deserve special mention.

At the top of the list are the books by the late W. Richard Stevens. *Advanced Programming in the UNIX Environment* ([Stevens, 1992]) provides detailed coverage of UNIX system programming, focusing on POSIX, System V, and BSD. A recent revision by Stephen Rago, [Stevens & Rago, 2005] updates the text for modern standards and implementations, and adds coverage of threads and a chapter on network programming. This book is a good place to look for an alternative viewpoint on many of the topics covered in this book. The two-volume *UNIX Network Programming* ([Stevens et al., 2004], [Stevens, 1999]) provides extremely detailed coverage of network programming and interprocess communication on UNIX systems.

> [Stevens et al., 2004] is a revision by Bill Fenner and Andrew Rudoff of [Stevens, 1998], the previous edition of Volume 1 of the *UNIX Network Programming*. While the revised edition covers several new areas, in most cases where we make reference to [Stevens et al., 2004], the same material can also be found in [Stevens, 1998], albeit under different chapter and section numbers.

Advanced UNIX Programming ([Rochkind, 1985]) was a good, brief, and sometimes humorous, introduction to UNIX (System V) programming. It is nowadays available in an updated and extended second edition ([Rochkind, 2004]).

The POSIX threading API is thoroughly described in *Programming with POSIX Threads* ([*Butenhof*, 1996]).

Linux and the Unix Philosophy ([Gancarz, 2003]) is a brief introduction to the philosophy of application design on Linux and UNIX systems.

Various books provide an introduction to reading and modifying the Linux kernel sources, including *Linux Kernel Development* ([Love, 2010]) and *Understanding the Linux Kernel* ([Bovet & Cesati, 2005]).

For more general background on UNIX kernels, *The Design of the UNIX Operating System* ([Bach, 1986]) remains very readable and contains material relevant to Linux. *UNIX Internals: The New Frontiers* ([Vahalia, 1996]) surveys kernel internals for more modern UNIX implementations.

For writing Linux device drivers, the essential reference is *Linux Device Drivers* ([Corbet et al., 2005]).

Operating Systems: Design and Implementation ([Tanenbaum & Woodhull, 2006]) describes operating system implementation using the example of Minix. (See also *http://www.minix3.org/*.)

Source code of existing applications

Looking at the source code of existing applications can often provide good examples of how to use particular system calls and library functions. On Linux distributions employing the RPM Package Manager, we can find the package that contains a particular program (such as *ls*) as follows:

```
$ which ls                        Find pathname of ls program
/bin/ls
$ rpm -qf /bin/ls                 Find out which package created the pathname /bin/ls
coreutils-5.0.75
```

The corresponding source code package will have a name similar to the above, but with the suffix .src.rpm. This package will be on the installation media for the distribution or be available for download from the distributor's web site. Once we obtain the package, we can install it using the *rpm* command, and then examine the source code, which is typically placed in some directory under /usr/src.

On systems using the Debian package manager, the process is similar. We can determine the package that created a pathname (for the *ls* program, in this example) using the following command:

```
$ dpkg -S /bin/ls
coreutils: /bin/ls
```

The Linux Documentation Project

The Linux Documentation Project (*http://www.tldp.org/*) produces freely available documentation on Linux, including HOWTO guides and FAQs (frequently asked questions and answers) on various system administration and programming topics. The site also offers more extensive electronic books on a range of topics.

The GNU project

The GNU project (*http://www.gnu.org/*) provides an enormous quantity of software source code and associated documentation.

Newsgroups

Usenet newsgroups can often be a good source of answers to specific programming questions. The following newsgroups are of particular interest:

- *comp.unix.programmer* addresses general UNIX programming questions.
- *comp.os.linux.development.apps* addresses questions relating to application development specifically on Linux.
- *comp.os.linux.development.system*, the Linux system development newsgroup, focuses on questions about modifying the kernel and developing device drivers and loadable modules.
- *comp.programming.threads* discusses programming with threads, especially POSIX threads.
- *comp.protocols.tcp-ip* discusses the TCP/IP networking protocol suite.

FAQs for many Usenet news groups can be found at *http://www.faqs.org/*.

> Before posting a question to a newsgroup, check the FAQ for the group (often posted regularly within the group itself) and to try a web search to find a solution to the question. The *http://groups.google.com/* web site provides a browser-based interface for searching old Usenet postings.

Linux kernel mailing list

The Linux kernel mailing list (LKML) is the principal broadcast communication medium for the Linux kernel developers. It provides an idea of what's going on in kernel development, and is a forum for submitting kernel bug reports and patches. (LKML is not a forum for system programming questions.) To subscribe to LKML, send an email message to *majordomo@vger.kernel.org* with the following message body as a single line:

```
subscribe linux-kernel
```

For information about the workings of the list server, send a message body containing just the word "help" to the same address.

To send a message to LKML, use the address *linux-kernel@vger.kernel.org*. The FAQ and pointers to some searchable archives for this mailing list are available at *http://www.kernel.org/*.

Web sites

The following web sites are of particular interest:

- *http://www.kernel.org/*, *The Linux Kernel Archives*, contains the source code for all versions of the Linux kernel, past and present.
- *http://www.lwn.net/*, *Linux Weekly News*, provides daily and weekly columns on various Linux-related topics. A weekly kernel-development column summarizes traffic through LKML.

- *http://www.kernelnewbies.org/, Linux Kernel Newbies,* is a starting point for programmers who want to learn about and modify the Linux kernel.
- *http://lxr.linux.no/linux/, Linux Cross-reference,* provides browser access to various versions of the Linux kernel source code. Each identifier in a source file is hyperlinked to make it easy to find the definition and uses of that identifier.

The kernel source code

If none of the preceding sources answer our questions, or if we want to confirm that documented information is true, then we can read the kernel source code. Although parts of the source code can be difficult to understand, reading the code of a particular system call in the Linux kernel source (or a library function in the GNU C library source) can often prove to be a surprisingly quick way to find the answer to a question.

If the Linux kernel source code has been installed on the system, it can usually be found in the directory /usr/src/linux. Table E-1 provides summary information about some of the subdirectories under this directory.

Table E-1: Subdirectories in the Linux kernel source tree

Directory	Contents
Documentation	Documentation of various aspects of the kernel
arch	Architecture-specific code, organized into subdirectories—for example, alpha, arm, ia64, sparc, and x86
drivers	Code for device drivers
fs	File system–specific code, organized into subdirectories—for example, btrfs, ext4, proc (the /proc file system), and vfat
include	Header files needed by kernel code
init	Initialization code for the kernel
ipc	Code for System V IPC and POSIX message queues
kernel	Code related to processes, program execution, kernel modules, signals, time, and timers
lib	General-purpose functions used by various parts of the kernel
mm	Memory-management code
net	Networking code (TCP/IP, UNIX and Internet domain sockets)
scripts	Scripts to configure and build the kernel

SOLUTIONS TO SELECTED EXERCISES

Chapter 5

5-3. A solution is provided in the file `fileio/atomic_append.c` in the source code distribution for this book. Here is an example of the results that we see when we run this program as suggested:

```
$ ls -l f1 f2
-rw-------    1 mtk      users      2000000 Jan  9 11:14 f1
-rw-------    1 mtk      users      1999962 Jan  9 11:14 f2
```

Because the combination of *lseek()* plus *write()* is not atomic, one instance of the program sometimes overwrote bytes written by the other instance. As a result, the file f2 contains less than 2 million bytes.

5-4. A call to *dup()* can be rewritten as:

```
fd = fcntl(oldfd, F_DUPFD, 0);
```

A call to *dup2()* can be rewritten as:

```
if (oldfd == newfd) {                          /* oldfd == newfd is a special case */
    if (fcntl(oldfd, F_GETFL) == -1) {                   /* Is oldfd valid? */
        errno = EBADF;
        fd = -1;
    } else {
        fd = oldfd;
    }
} else {
    close(newfd);
    fd = fcntl(oldfd, F_DUPFD, newfd);
}
```

5-6.   The first point to realize is that, since *fd2* is a duplicate of *fd1*, they both share a single open file description, and thus a single file offset. However, because *fd3* is created via a separate call to *open()*, it has a separate file offset.

- After the first *write()*, the file contents are Hello,.

- Since *fd2* shares a file offset with *fd1*, the second *write()* call appends to the existing text, yielding Hello, world.

- The *lseek()* call adjusts the single file offset shared by *fd1* and *fd2* to point to the start of the file, and thus the third *write()* call overwrites part of the existing text to yield HELLO, world.

- The file offset for *fd3* has not so far been modified, and so points to the start of the file. Therefore, the final *write()* call changes the file contents to Gidday world.

Run the program fileio/multi_descriptors.c in the source code distribution for this book to see these results.

Chapter 6

6-1.   Since the array *mbuf* is not initialized, it is part of the uninitialized data segment. Therefore, no disk space is required to hold this variable. Instead, it is allocated (and initialized to 0) when the program is loaded.

6-2.   A demonstration of the incorrect usage of *longjmp()* is provided in the file proc/bad_longjmp.c in the source code distribution for this book.

6-3.   Sample implementations of *setenv()* and *unsetenv()* are provided in the file proc/setenv.c in the source code distribution for this book.

Chapter 8

8-1.   The two *getpwuid()* calls are executed before the *printf()* output string is constructed, and—since *getpwuid()* returns its *pw_name* result in a statically allocated buffer—the second call overwrites the result returned by the first call.

Chapter 9

9-1. In considering the following, remember that changes to the effective user ID always also change the file-system user ID.

      a)   *real=2000, effective=2000, saved=2000, file-system=2000*

      b)   *real=1000, effective=2000, saved=2000, file-system=2000*

      c)   *real=1000, effective=2000, saved=0, file-system=2000*

      d)   *real=1000, effective=0, saved=0, file-system=2000*

      e)   *real=1000, effective=2000, saved=3000, file-system=2000*

9-2. Strictly speaking, such a process is unprivileged, since its effective user ID is nonzero. However, an unprivileged process can use the *setuid(), setreuid(), seteuid(),* or *setresuid()* calls to set its effective user ID to the same value as its real user ID or saved set-user-ID. Thus, this process could use one of these calls to regain privilege.

9-4. The following code shows the steps for each system call.

```
e = geteuid();      /* Save initial value of effective user ID */

setuid(getuid());                           /* Suspend privileges */
setuid(e);                                  /* Resume privileges */
/* Can't permanently drop the set-user-ID identity with setuid() */

seteuid(getuid());                          /* Suspend privileges */
seteuid(e);                                 /* Resume privileges */
/* Can't permanently drop the set-user-ID identity with seteuid() */

setreuid(-1, getuid());                     /* Temporarily drop privileges */
setreuid(-1, e);                            /* Resume privileges */
setreuid(getuid(), getuid());               /* Permanently drop privileges */

setresuid(-1, getuid(), -1);                /* Temporarily drop privileges */
setresuid(-1, e, -1);                       /* Resume privileges */
setresuid(getuid(), getuid(), getuid());    /* Permanently drop privileges */
```

9-5. With the exception of *setuid()*, the answers are the same as for the previous exercise, except that we can substitute the value 0 for the variable *e*. For *setuid()*, the following holds:

```
/* (a) Can't suspend and resume privileges with setuid() */

setuid(getuid());        /* (b) Permanently drop privileges */
```

Chapter 10

10-1. The maximum signed 32-bit integer value is 2,147,483,647. Divided by 100 clock ticks per second, this corresponds to somewhat more than 248 days. Divided by 1 million (CLOCKS_PER_SEC), this corresponds to 36 minutes and 47 seconds.

Chapter 12

12-1. A solution is provided in the file `sysinfo/procfs_user_exe.c` in the source code distribution for this book.

Chapter 13

13-3. This sequence of statements ensures that the data written to a *stdio* buffer is flushed to the disk. The *fflush()* call flushes the *stdio* buffer for *fp* to the kernel buffer cache. The argument given to the subsequent *fsync()* is the file descriptor underlying *fp*; thus, the call flushes the (recently filled) kernel buffer for that file descriptor to disk.

13-4. When standard output is sent to a terminal, it is line-buffered, so that the output of the *printf()* call appears immediately, and is followed by the output of *write()*. When standard output is sent to a disk file, it is block-buffered. Consequently, the output of the *printf()* is held in a *stdio* buffer and is flushed only when the program exits (i.e., after the *write()* call). (A complete program containing the code of this exercise is available in the file `filebuff/mix23_linebuff.c` in the source code distribution for this book.)

Chapter 15

15-2. The *stat()* system call doesn't change any file timestamps, since all it does is fetch information from the file i-node (and there is no *last i-node access* timestamp).

15-4. The GNU C library provides just such a function, named *euidaccess()*, in the library source file `sysdeps/posix/euidaccess.c`.

15-5. In order to do this, we must use two calls to *umask()*, as follows:

```
mode_t currUmask;

currUmask = umask(0);        /* Retrieve current umask, set umask to 0 */
umask(currUmask);            /* Restore umask to previous value */
```

Note, however, that this solution is not thread-safe, since threads share the process umask setting.

15-7. A solution is provided in the file `files/chiflag.c` in the source code distribution for this book.

Chapter 18

18-1. Using *ls -li* shows that the executable file has different i-node numbers after each compilation. What happens is that the compiler removes (unlinks) any existing file with the same name as its target executable, and then creates a new file with the same name. It is permissible to unlink an executable file that is running. The name is removed immediately, but the file itself remains in existence until the process executing it terminates.

18-2. The file `myfile` is created in the subdirectory `test`. The *symlink()* call creates a relative link in the parent directory. Despite appearances, this is a dangling link, since it is interpreted relative to the location of the link file, and thus refers to a nonexistent file in the parent directory. Consequently, *chmod()* fails with the error ENOENT ("No such file or directory"). (A complete program containing the code of this exercise is available in the file dirs_links/bad_symlink.c in the source code distribution for this book.)

18-4. A solution is provided in the file dirs_links/list_files_readdir_r.c, which can be found in the source code distribution for this book.

18-7. A solution is provided in the file dirs_links/file_type_stats.c, which can be found in the source code distribution for this book.

18-9. Using *fchdir()* is more efficient. If we are performing the operation repeatedly within a loop, then with *fchdir()* we can perform one call to *open()* before executing the loop, and with *chdir()* we can place the *getcwd()* call outside the loop. Then we are measuring the difference between repeated calls to *fchdir(fd)* and *chdir(buf)*. Calls to *chdir()* are more expensive for two reasons: passing the *buf* argument to the kernel requires a larger data transfer between user space and kernel space, and the pathname in *buf* must be resolved to the corresponding directory i-node on each call. (Kernel caching of directory entry information reduces the work required for the second point, but some work must still be done.)

Chapter 20

20-2. A solution is provided in the file signals/ignore_pending_sig.c in the source code distribution for this book.

20-4. A solution is provided in the file signals/siginterrupt.c in the source code distribution for this book.

Chapter 22

22-2. As with most UNIX implementations, Linux delivers standard signals before realtime signals (SUSv3 doesn't require this). This makes sense, because some standard signals indicate critical conditions (e.g., hardware exceptions) that a program should deal with as soon as possible.

22-3. Replacing *sigsuspend()* plus a signal handler with *sigwaitinfo()* in this program provides a 25 to 40 percent speed improvement. (The exact figure varies somewhat across kernel versions.)

Chapter 23

23-2. A modified program using *clock_nanosleep()* is provided in the file timers/t_clock_nanosleep.c in the source code distribution for this book.

23-3. A solution is provided in the file timers/ptmr_null_evp.c in the source code distribution for this book.

Chapter 24

24-1. The first *fork()* call creates one new child. Both parent and child carry on to execute the second *fork()*, and thus each creates a further process, making a total of four processes. All four processes carry on to execute the next *fork()*, each creating a further child. Consequently, a total of seven new processes are created.

24-2. A solution is provided in the file procexec/vfork_fd_test.c in the source code distribution for this book.

24-3. If we call *fork()*, and then have the child call *raise()* to send itself a signal such as SIGABRT, this will yield a core dump file that closely mirrors the state of the parent at the time of the *fork()*. The *gdb gcore* command allows us to perform a similar task for a program, without needing to change the source code.

24-5. Add a converse *kill()* call in the parent:

```
if (kill(childPid, SIGUSR1) == -1)
    errExit("kill")
```

And in the child, add a converse *sigsuspend()* call:

```
sigsuspend(&origMask);          /* Unblock SIGUSR1, wait for signal */
```

Chapter 25

25-1. Assuming a two's complement architecture, where −1 is represented by a bit pattern with all bits on, then the parent will see an exit status of 255 (all bits on in the least significant 8 bits, which are all that is passed back to the parent when it calls *wait()*). (The presence of the call *exit(−1)* in a program is usually a programmer error resulting from confusion with the −1 return used to indicate failure of a system call.)

Chapter 26

26-1. A solution is provided in the file procexec/orphan.c in the source code distribution for this book.

Chapter 27

27-1. The *execvp()* function first fails to exec the file xyz in dir1, because execute permission is denied. It therefore continues its search in dir2, where it successfully execs xyz.

27-2. A solution is provided in the file procexec/execlp.c in the source code distribution of this book.

27-3. The script specifies the *cat* program as its interpreter. The *cat* program "interprets" a file by printing its contents—in this case with the *−n* (line numbering) option enabled (as though we had entered the command *cat −n ourscript*). Thus, we would see the following:

```
1  #!/bin/cat -n
2  Hello world
```

27-4. Two successive *fork()* calls yield a total of three processes related as parent, child, and grandchild. Having created the grandchild process, the child immediately exits, and is reaped by the *waitpid()* call in the parent. As a consequence of being orphaned, the grandchild is adopted by *init* (process ID of 1). The program doesn't need to perform a second *wait()* call, since *init* automatically reaps the zombie when the grandchild terminates. Therein lies a possible use for this code sequence: if we need to create a child for which we can't later wait, then this sequence can be used to ensure that no zombie results. One example of such a requirement is where the parent execs some program that is not guaranteed to perform a wait (and we don't want to rely on setting the disposition of SIGCHLD to SIG_IGN, since the disposition of an ignored SIGCHLD after an *exec()* is left unspecified by SUSv3).

27-5. The string given to *printf()* doesn't include a newline character, and therefore the output is not flushed before the *execlp()* call. The *execlp()* overwrites the existing program's data segments (as well as the heap and stack), which contain the *stdio* buffers, and thus the unflushed output is lost.

27-6. SIGCHLD is delivered to the parent. If the SIGCHLD handler attempts to do a *wait()*, then the call returns an error (ECHILD) indicating that there were no children whose status could be returned. (This assumes that the parent had no other terminated children. If it did, then the *wait()* would block; or if *waitpid()* was used with the WNOHANG flag, *waitpid()* would return 0.) This is exactly the situation that may arise if a program establishes a handler for SIGCHLD before calling *system()*.

Chapter 29

29-1. There are two possible outcomes (both permitted by SUSv3): the thread deadlocks, blocked while trying to join with itself, or the *pthread_join()* call fails, returning the error EDEADLK. On Linux, the latter behavior occurs. Given a thread ID in *tid*, we can prevent such an eventuality using the following code:

```
if (!pthread_equal(tid, pthread_self()))
    pthread_join(tid, NULL);
```

29-2. After the main thread terminates, *threadFunc()* will continue working with storage on the main thread's stack, with unpredictable results.

Chapter 31

31-1. A solution is provided in the file threads/one_time_init.c in the source code distribution for this book.

Chapter 33

33-2. The SIGCHLD signal that is generated on child termination is process-directed. It may be delivered to any thread (not necessarily the one that called *fork()*) that is not blocking the signal.

Chapter 34

34-1. Suppose that the program is part of a shell pipeline:

```
$ ./ourprog | grep 'some string'
```

The problem is that *grep* will be part of the same process group as *ourprog*, and therefore the *killpg()* call will also terminate the *grep* process. This is probably not desired, and is likely to confuse users. The solution is to use *setpgid()* to ensure that the child processes are placed in their own new group (the process ID of the first child could be used as the process group ID of the group), and then signal that process group. This also removes the need for the parent to make itself immune to the signal.

34-5. If the SIGTSTP signal is unblocked before raising it again, then there is a small window of time (between the calls to *sigprocmask()* and *raise()*) during which, if the user types a second suspend character (*Control-Z*), the process will be stopped while still in the handler. Consequently, two SIGCONT signals will be required to resume the process.

Chapter 35

35-3. A solution is provided in the file procpri/demo_sched_fifo.c in the source code distribution for this book.

Chapter 36

36-1. A solution is provided in the file procres/rusage_wait.c in the source code distribution for this book.

36-2. A solution is provided in the files rusage.c and print_rusage.c in the procres subdirectory in the source code distribution for this book.

Chapter 37

37-1. A solution is provided in the file daemons/t_syslog.c in the source code distribution for this book.

Chapter 38

38-1. Whenever a file is modified by an unprivileged user, the kernel clears the file's set-user-ID permission bit. The set-group-ID permission bit is similarly cleared if the group-execute permission bit is enabled. (As detailed in Section 55.4, the combination of having the set-group-ID bit on while the group-execute bit is *off* has nothing to do with set-group-ID programs; instead, it is used to enable mandatory locking, and for this reason modifications to such a file don't disable the set-group-ID bit.) Clearing these bits ensures that if the program file is writable by arbitrary users, then it can't be modified and still retain its ability to give privileges to users executing the file. A privileged (CAP_FSETID) process can modify a file without the kernel clearing these permission bits.

Chapter 44

44-1. A solution is provided in the file pipes/change_case.c in the source code distribution for this book.

44-5. It creates a race condition. Suppose that between the time the server sees end-of-file and the time it closes the file reading descriptor, a client opens the FIFO for writing (this will succeed without blocking), and then writes data to the FIFO *after* the server has closed the reading descriptor. At this point, the client will receive a SIGPIPE signal, since no process has the FIFO open for reading. Alternatively, the client might be able to both open the FIFO and write data to it before the server closes the reading descriptor. In this case, the client's data would be lost, and it wouldn't receive a response from the server. As a further exercise, you could try to demonstrate these behaviors by making the suggested modification to the server and creating a special-purpose client that repeatedly opens the server's FIFOs, sends a message to the server, closes the server's FIFO, and reads the server's response (if any).

44-6. One possible solution would be to set a timer on the *open()* of the client FIFO using *alarm()*, as described in Section 23.3. This solution suffers from the drawback that the server would still be delayed for the period of the timeout. Another possible solution would be to open the client FIFO using the O_NONBLOCK flag. If this fails, then the server can assume a misbehaving client. This latter solution also requires changes to the client, which needs to ensure that it opens its FIFO (also using the O_NONBLOCK flag) prior to sending a request to the server. For convenience, the client should then turn off the O_NONBLOCK flag for the FIFO file descriptor, so that the subsequent *read()* call blocks. Finally, it is possible to implement a concurrent server solution for this application, with the main server process creating a child to send the response message to each client. (This would represent a rather resource-expensive solution in the case of this simple application.)

Other conditions that are not handled by this server remain. For example, it doesn't handle the possibilities of the sequence number overflowing or a misbehaving client requesting large groups of sequence numbers in order to produce such overflows. The server also does not handle the possibility that the client specifies a negative value for the sequence length. Furthermore, a malicious client could create its reply FIFO, and then open the FIFO for reading and writing, and fill it with data before sending a request to the server; as a consequence, the server would be able to successfully open the reply FIFO, but would block when it tries to write the reply. As a further exercise, you could try to devise strategies for dealing with these possibilities.

In Section 44.8, we also noted another limitation that applies to the server in Listing 44-7: if a client sends a message that contains the wrong number of bytes, then the server will be out of step when reading all subsequent client messages. One simple way to deal with this problem is to discard the use of fixed-length messages in favor of the use of a delimiter character.

Chapter 45

45-2. A solution is provided in the file svipc/t_ftok.c in the source code distribution for this book.

Chapter 46

46-3. The value 0 is a valid message queue identifier, but 0 can't be used as a message type.

Chapter 47

47-5. A solution is provided in the file svsem/event_flags.c in the source code distribution for this book.

47-6. A reserve operation can be implemented by reading a byte from the FIFO. Conversely, a release operation can be implemented by writing a byte to the FIFO. A conditional reserve operation can be implemented as a nonblocking read of a byte from the FIFO.

Chapter 48

48-2. Since access to the *shmp->cnt* value in the for loop increment step is no longer protected by the semaphore, there is a race condition between the writer next updating this value and the reader fetching it.

48-4. A solution is provided in the file svshm/svshm_mon.c in the source code distribution for this book.

Chapter 49

49-1. A solution is provided in the file mmap/mmcopy.c in the source code distribution for this book.

Chapter 50

50-2. A solution is provided in the file vmem/madvise_dontneed.c in the source code distribution for this book.

Chapter 52

52-6. A solution is provided in the file pmsg/mq_notify_sigwaitinfo.c in the source code distribution for this book.

52-7. It would not be safe to make *buffer* global. Once message notification is reenabled in *threadFunc()*, there is a chance that a second notification would be generated while *threadFunc()* is still executing. This second notification could initiate a second thread that executes *threadFunc()* at the same time as the first thread. Both threads would attempt to use the same global *buffer*, with unpredictable results. Note that the behavior here is implementation-dependent. SUSv3 permits an implementation to sequentially deliver notifications to the same thread. However, it is also permissible to deliver notifications in separate threads that execute concurrently, and this is what Linux does.

Chapter 53

53-2. A solution is provided in the file psem/psem_timedwait.c in the source code distribution for this book.

Chapter 55

55-1. The following hold for *flock()* on Linux:

    a) A series of shared locks can starve a process waiting to place an exclusive lock.

    b) There are no rules regarding which process is granted the lock. Essentially, the lock is granted to the process that is next scheduled. If that process happens to be one that obtains a shared lock, then all other processes requesting shared locks will also be able to have their requests granted simultaneously.

55-2. The *flock()* system call doesn't detect deadlock. This is true of most *flock()* implementations, except those that implement *flock()* in terms of *fcntl()*.

55-4. In all except early (1.2 and earlier) Linux kernels, the two types of locking operate independently, and have no affect on one another.

Chapter 57

57-4. On Linux, the *sendto()* call fails with the error EPERM. On some other UNIX systems, a different error results. Some other UNIX implementations don't enforce this constraint, letting a connected UNIX domain datagram socket receive datagrams from a sender other than its peer.

Chapter 59

59-1. A solution is provided in the files read_line_buf.h and read_line_buf.c in the sockets subdirectory in the source code distribution for this book.

59-2. A solution is provided in the files is_seqnum_v2_sv.c, is_seqnum_v2_cl.c, and is_seqnum_v2.h in the sockets subdirectory in the source code distribution for this book.

59-3. A solution is provided in the files unix_sockets.h, unix_sockets.c, us_xfr_v2.h, us_xfr_v2_sv.c, and us_xfr_v2_cl.c in the sockets subdirectory in the source code distribution for this book.

59-5. In the Internet domain, datagrams from a nonpeer socket are silently discarded.

Chapter 60

60-2. A solution is provided in the file sockets/is_echo_v2_sv.c in the source code distribution for this book.

Chapter 61

61-1. Since the send and receive buffers for a TCP socket have a limited size, if the client sent a large quantity of data, then it might fill these buffers, at which point a further *write()* would (permanently) block the client before it read any of the server's response.

61-3. A solution is provided in the file sockets/sendfile.c in the source code distribution for this book.

Chapter 62

62-1. The *tcgetattr()* function fails if it is applied to a file descriptor that doesn't refer to a terminal.

62-2. A solution is provided in the file tty/ttyname.c in the source code distribution for this book.

Chapter 63

63-3. A solution is provided in the file altio/select_mq.c in the source code distribution for this book.

63-4. A race condition would result. Suppose the following sequence of events: (a) after *select()* has informed the program that the self-pipe has data, it performs the appropriate actions in response to the signal; (b) another signal arrives, and the handler writes a byte to the self-pipe and returns; and (c) the main program drains the self-pipe. As a consequence, the program misses the signal that was delivered in step (b).

63-6. The *epoll_wait()* call blocks, even when the interest list is empty. This can be useful in a multithreaded program, where one thread might add a descriptor to the *epoll* interest list, while another thread is blocked in an *epoll_wait()* call.

63-7. Successive *epoll_wait()* calls cycle through the list of ready file descriptors. This is useful because it helps prevent file-descriptor starvation, which could occur if *epoll_wait()* always (for example) returned the lowest-numbered ready file descriptor, and that file descriptor always had some input available.

Chapter 64

64-1. First, the child shell process terminates, followed by the *script* parent process. Since the terminal is operating in raw mode, the *Control-D* character is not interpreted by the terminal driver, but is instead passed as a literal character to the *script* parent process, which writes it to the pseudoterminal master. The pseudoterminal slave is operating in canonical mode, so this *Control-D* character is treated as an end-of-file, which causes the child shell's next *read()* to return 0, with the result that the shell terminates. The termination of the shell closes the only file descriptor referring to the pseudoterminal slave. As a consequence, the next *read()* by the parent *script* process fails with the error EIO (or end-of-file on some other UNIX implementations), and this process then terminates.

64-7. A solution is provided in the file pty/unbuffer.c in the source code distribution for this book.

BIBLIOGRAPHY

Aho, A.V., Kernighan, B.W., and Weinberger, P. J. 1988. *The AWK Programming Language*. Addison-Wesley, Reading, Massachusetts.

Albitz, P., and Liu, C. 2006. *DNS and BIND (5th edition)*. O'Reilly, Sebastopol, California.

Anley, C., Heasman, J., Lindner, F., and Richarte, G. 2007. *The Shellcoder's Handbook: Discovering and Exploiting Security Holes*. Wiley, Indianapolis, Indiana.

Bach, M. 1986. *The Design of the UNIX Operating System*. Prentice Hall, Englewood Cliffs, New Jersey.

Bhattiprolu, S., Biederman, E.W., Hallyn, S., and Lezcano, D. 2008. "Virtual Servers and Checkpoint/Restart in Mainstream Linux," *ACM SIGOPS Operating Systems Review*, Vol. 42, Issue 5, July 2008, pages 104–113.

    http://www.mnis.fr/fr/services/virtualisation/pdf/cr.pdf

Bishop, M. 2003. *Computer Security: Art and Science*. Addison-Wesley, Reading, Massachusetts.

Bishop, M. 2005. *Introduction to Computer Security*. Addison-Wesley, Reading, Massachusetts.

Borisov, N., Johnson, R., Sastry, N., and Wagner, D. 2005. "Fixing Races for Fun and Profit: How to abuse atime," *Proceedings of the 14th USENIX Security Symposium*.

http://www.cs.berkeley.edu/~nks/papers/races-usenix05.pdf

Bovet, D.P., and Cesati, M. 2005. *Understanding the Linux Kernel (3rd edition)*. O'Reilly, Sebastopol, California.

Butenhof, D.R. 1996. *Programming with POSIX Threads*. Addison-Wesley, Reading, Massachusetts.

Further information, as well as source code for the programs in this book, can be found at *http://homepage.mac.com/dbutenhof/Threads/Threads.html*.

Chen, H., Wagner, D., and Dean, D. 2002. "Setuid Demystified," *Proceedings of the 11th USENIX Security Symposium*.

http://www.cs.berkeley.edu/~daw/papers/setuid-usenix02.pdf

Comer, D.E. 2000. *Internetworking with TCP/IP Vol. I: Principles, Protocols, and Architecture (4th edition)*. Prentice Hall, Upper Saddle River, New Jersey.

Further information about the *Internetworking with TCP/IP* book series (including source code) can be found at *http://www.cs.purdue.edu/homes/dec/netbooks.html*.

Comer, D.E., and Stevens, D.L. 1999. *Internetworking with TCP/IP Vol. II: Design, Implementation, and Internals (3rd edition)*. Prentice Hall, Upper Saddle River, New Jersey.

Comer, D.E., and Stevens, D.L. 2000. *Internetworking with TCP/IP, Vol. III: Client-Server Programming and Applications, Linux/Posix Sockets Version*. Prentice Hall, Englewood Cliffs, New Jersey.

Corbet, J. 2002. "The Orlov block allocator." *Linux Weekly News*, 5 November 2002.

http://lwn.net/Articles/14633/

Corbet, J., Rubini, A., and Kroah-Hartman, G. 2005. *Linux Device Drivers (3rd edition)*. O'Reilly, Sebastopol, California.

http://lwn.net/Kernel/LDD3/

Crosby, S.A., and Wallach, D. S. 2003. "Denial of Service via Algorithmic Complexity Attacks," *Proceedings of the 12th USENIX Security Symposium*.

http://www.cs.rice.edu/~scrosby/hash/CrosbyWallach_UsenixSec2003.pdf

Deitel, H.M., Deitel, P. J., and Choffnes, D. R. 2004. *Operating Systems (3rd edition)*. Prentice Hall, Upper Saddle River, New Jersey.

Dijkstra, E.W. 1968. "Cooperating Sequential Processes," *Programming Languages*, ed. F. Genuys, Academic Press, New York.

Drepper, U. 2004 (a). "Futexes Are Tricky."

http://people.redhat.com/drepper/futex.pdf

Drepper, U. 2004 (b). "How to Write Shared Libraries."

http://people.redhat.com/drepper/dsohowto.pdf

Drepper, U. 2007. "What Every Programmer Should Know About Memory."

http://people.redhat.com/drepper/cpumemory.pdf

Drepper, U. 2009. "Defensive Programming for Red Hat Enterprise Linux."

http://people.redhat.com/drepper/defprogramming.pdf

Erickson, J.M. 2008. *Hacking: The Art of Exploitation (2nd edition).* No Starch Press, San Francisco, California.

Floyd, S. 1994. "TCP and Explicit Congestion Notification," *ACM Computer Communication Review,* Vol. 24, No. 5, October 1994, pages 10–23.

http://www.icir.org/floyd/papers/tcp_ecn.4.pdf

Franke, H., Russell, R., and Kirkwood, M. 2002. "Fuss, Futexes and Furwocks: Fast Userlevel Locking in Linux," *Proceedings of the Ottawa Linux Symposium 2002.*

http://www.kernel.org/doc/ols/2002/ols2002-pages-479-495.pdf

Frisch, A. 2002. *Essential System Administration (3rd edition).* O'Reilly, Sebastopol, California.

Gallmeister, B.O. 1995. *POSIX.4: Programming for the Real World.* O'Reilly, Sebastopol, California.

Gammo, L., Brecht, T., Shukla, A., and Pariag, D. 2004. "Comparing and Evaluating epoll, select, and poll Event Mechanisms," *Proceedings of the Ottawa Linux Symposium 2002.*

http://www.kernel.org/doc/ols/2004/ols2004v1-pages-215-226.pdf

Gancarz, M. 2003. *Linux and the Unix Philosophy.* Digital Press.

Garfinkel, S., Spafford, G., and Schwartz, A. 2003. *Practical Unix and Internet Security (3rd edition).* O'Reilly, Sebastopol, California.

Gont, F. 2008. *Security Assessment of the Internet Protocol.* UK Centre for the Protection of the National Infrastructure.

http://www.gont.com.ar/papers/InternetProtocol.pdf

Gont, F. 2009 (a). *Security Assessment of the Transmission Control Protocol (TCP).* CPNI Technical Note 3/2009. UK Centre for the Protection of the National Infrastructure.

http://www.gont.com.ar/papers/tn-03-09-security-assessment-TCP.pdf

Gont, F., and Yourtchenko, A. 2009 (b). "On the implementation of TCP urgent data." Internet draft, 20 May 2009.

http://www.gont.com.ar/drafts/urgent-data/

Goodheart, B., and Cox, J. 1994. *The Magic Garden Explained: The Internals of UNIX SVR4*. Prentice Hall, Englewood Cliffs, New Jersey.

Goralski, W. 2009. *The Illustrated Network: How TCP/IP Works in a Modern Network*. Morgan Kaufmann, Burlington, Massachusetts.

Gorman, M. 2004. *Understanding the Linux Virtual Memory Manager*. Prentice Hall, Upper Saddle River, New Jersey.

> Available online at *http://www.phptr.com/perens*.

Grünbacher, A. 2003. "POSIX Access Control Lists on Linux," *Proceedings of USENIX 2003/Freenix Track*, pages 259–272.

> *http://www.suse.de/~agruen/acl/linux-acls/online/*

Gutmann, P. 1996. "Secure Deletion of Data from Magnetic and Solid-State Memory," *Proceedings of the 6th USENIX Security Symposium*.

> *http://www.cs.auckland.ac.nz/~pgut001/pubs/secure_del.html*

Hallyn, S. 2007. "POSIX file capabilities: Parceling the power of root."

> *http://www.ibm.com/developerworks/library/l-posixcap/index.html*

Harbison, S., and Steele, G. 2002. *C: A Reference Manual (5th edition)*. Prentice Hall, Englewood Cliffs, New Jersey.

Herbert, T.F. 2004. *The Linux TCP/IP Stack: Networking for Embedded Systems*. Charles River Media, Hingham, Massachusetts.

Hubička, J. 2003. "Porting GCC to the AMD64 Architecture," *Proceedings of the First Annual GCC Developers' Summit*.

> *http://www.ucw.cz/~hubicka/papers/amd64/index.html*

Johnson, M.K., and Troan, E.W. 2005. *Linux Application Development (2nd edition)*. Addison-Wesley, Reading, Massachusetts.

Josey, A. (ed.). 2004. *The Single UNIX Specification, Authorized Guide to Version 3*. The Open Group.

> This guide can be found online at *http://www.unix.org/version3/theguide.html*. A newer version of this guide (published in 2010) for version 4 of the specification can be found at *http://www.unix.org/version4/theguide.html*.

Kent, A., and Mogul, J.C. 1987. "Fragmentation Considered Harmful," *ACM Computer Communication Review*, Vol. 17, No. 5, August 1987.

> *http://ccr.sigcomm.org/archive/1995/jan95/ccr-9501-mogulf1.html*

Kernighan, B.W., and Ritchie, D.M. 1988. *The C Programming Language (2nd edition)*. Prentice Hall, Englewood Cliffs, New Jersey.

Kopparapu, C. 2002. *Load Balancing Servers, Firewalls, and Caches*. John Wiley and Sons.

Kozierok, C.M. 2005. *The TCP/IP Guide*. No Starch Press, San Francisco, California.

> *http://www.tcpipguide.com/*

Kroah-Hartman, G. 2003. "udev—A Userspace Implementation of devfs," *Proceedings of the 2003 Linux Symposium*.

> *http://www.kroah.com/linux/talks/ols_2003_udev_paper/Reprint-Kroah-Hartman-OLS2003.pdf*

Kumar, A., Cao, M., Santos, J., and Dilger, A. 2008. "Ext4 block and inode allocator improvements," *Proceedings of the 2008 Linux Symposium*, Ottawa, Canada.

> *http://ols.fedoraproject.org/OLS/Reprints-2008/kumar-reprint.pdf*

Lemon, J. 2001. "Kqueue: A generic and scalable event notification facility," *Proceedings of USENIX 2001/Freenix Track*.

> *http://people.freebsd.org/~jlemon/papers/kqueue_freenix.pdf*

Lemon, J. 2002. "Resisting SYN flood DoS attacks with a SYN cache," *Proceedings of USENIX BSDCon 2002*.

> *http://people.freebsd.org/~jlemon/papers/syncache.pdf*

Levine, J. 2000. *Linkers and Loaders*. Morgan Kaufmann, San Francisco, California.

> *http://www.iecc.com/linker/*

Lewine, D. 1991. *POSIX Programmer's Guide*. O'Reilly, Sebastopol, California.

Liang, S. 1999. *The Java Native Interface: Programmer's Guide and Specification*. Addison-Wesley, Reading, Massachusetts.

> *http://java.sun.com/docs/books/jni/*

Libes, D., and Ressler, S. 1989. *Life with UNIX: A Guide for Everyone*. Prentice Hall, Englewood Cliffs, New Jersey.

Lions, J. 1996. *Lions' Commentary on UNIX 6th Edition with Source Code*. Peer-to-Peer Communications, San Jose, California.

> [Lions, 1996] was originally produced by an Australian academic, the late John Lions, in 1977 for use in an operating systems class that he taught. At that time, it could not be formally published because of licensing restrictions. Nevertheless, pirated photocopies became widely distributed within the UNIX community, and, in Dennis Ritchie's words, "educated a generation" of UNIX programmers.

Love, R. 2010. *Linux Kernel Development (3rd edition)*. Addison-Wesley, Reading, Massachusetts.

Lu, H.J. 1995. "ELF: From the Programmer's Perspective."

> This paper can be found online at a variety of locations.

Mann, S., and Mitchell, E.L. 2003. *Linux System Security (2nd edition)*. Prentice Hall, Englewood Cliffs, New Jersey.

Matloff, N. and Salzman, P.J. 2008. *The Art of Debugging with GDB, DDD, and Eclipse*. No Starch Press, San Francisco, California.

Maxwell, S. 1999. *Linux Core Kernel Commentary*. Coriolis, Scottsdale, Arizona.

> This book provides an annotated listing of selected parts of the Linux 2.2.5 kernel.

McKusick, M.K., Joy, W.N., Leffler, S.J., and Fabry, R.S. 1984. "A fast file system for UNIX," *ACM Transactions on Computer Systems*, Vol. 2, Issue 3 (August).

> This paper can be found online at a variety of locations.

McKusick, M.K. 1999. "Twenty years of Berkeley Unix," *Open Sources: Voices from the Open Source Revolution*, C. DiBona, S. Ockman, and M. Stone (eds.). O'Reilly, Sebastopol, California.

McKusick, M.K., Bostic, K., and Karels, M.J. 1996. *The Design and Implementation of the 4.4BSD Operating System*. Addison-Wesley, Reading, Massachusetts.

McKusick, M.K., and Neville-Neil, G.V. 2005. *The Design and Implementation of the FreeBSD Operating System*. Addison-Wesley, Reading, Massachusetts.

Mecklenburg, R. 2005. *Managing Projects with GNU Make (3rd edition)*. O'Reilly, Sebastopol, California.

Mills, D.L. 1992. "Network Time Protocol (Version 3) Specification, Implementation and Analysis," RFC 1305, March 1992.

> *http://www.rfc-editor.org/rfc/rfc1305.txt*

Mochel, P. 2005. "The sysfs Filesystem," *Proceedings of the Linux Symposium 2005*.

Mosberger, D., and Eranian, S. 2002. *IA-64 Linux Kernel: Design and Implementation*. Prentice Hall, Upper Saddle River, New Jersey.

Peek, J., Todino-Gonguet, G., and Strang, J. 2001. *Learning the UNIX Operating System (5th edition)*. O'Reilly, Sebastopol, California.

Peikari, C., and Chuvakin, A. 2004. *Security Warrior*. O'Reilly, Sebastopol, California.

Plauger, P.J. 1992. *The Standard C Library*. Prentice Hall, Englewood Cliffs, New Jersey.

Quarterman, J.S., and Wilhelm, S. 1993. *UNIX, Posix, and Open Systems: The Open Standards Puzzle*. Addison-Wesley, Reading, Massachusetts.

Ritchie, D.M. 1984. "The Evolution of the UNIX Time-sharing System," *AT&T Bell Laboratories Technical Journal*, 63, No. 6 Part 2 (October 1984), pages 1577–93.

> Dennis Ritchie's home page (*http://www.cs.bell-labs.com/who/dmr/index.html*) provides a pointer to an online version of this paper, as well as [Ritchie & Thompson, 1974], and has many other pieces of UNIX history.

Ritchie, D.M., and Thompson, K.L. 1974. "The Unix Time-Sharing System," *Communications of the ACM*, 17 (July 1974), pages 365–375.

Robbins, K.A., and Robbins, S. 2003. *UNIX Systems Programming: Communication, Concurrency, and Threads (2nd edition)*. Prentice Hall, Upper Saddle River, New Jersey.

Rochkind, M.J. 1985. *Advanced UNIX Programming*. Prentice Hall, Englewood Cliffs, New Jersey.

Rochkind, M.J. 2004. *Advanced UNIX Programming (2nd edition)*. Addison-Wesley, Reading, Massachusetts.

Rosen, L. 2005. *Open Source Licensing: Software Freedom and Intellectual Property Law*. Prentice Hall, Upper Saddle River, New Jersey.

St. Laurent, A.M. 2004. *Understanding Open Source and Free Software Licensing*. O'Reilly, Sebastopol, California.

Salus, P.H. 1994. *A Quarter Century of UNIX*. Addison-Wesley, Reading, Massachusetts.

Salus, P.H. 2008. *The Daemon, the Gnu, and the Penguin*. Addison-Wesley, Reading, Massachusetts.

> *http://www.groklaw.net/staticpages/index.php?page=20051013231901859*
> A short history of Linux, the BSDs, the HURD, and other free software projects.

Sarolahti, P., and Kuznetsov, A. 2002. "Congestion Control in Linux TCP," *Proceedings of USENIX 2002/Freenix Track*.

> *http://www.cs.helsinki.fi/research/iwtcp/papers/linuxtcp.pdf*

Schimmel, C. 1994. *UNIX Systems for Modern Architectures*. Addison-Wesley, Reading, Massachusetts.

Snader, J.C. 2000. *Effective TCP/IP Programming: 44 tips to improve your network programming*. Addison-Wesley, Reading, Massachusetts.

Stevens, W.R. 1992. *Advanced Programming in the UNIX Environment*. Addison-Wesley, Reading, Massachusetts.

> Further information about all of the books of the late W. Richard Stevens (including program source code, with some modified code versions for Linux submitted by readers) can be found at *http://www.kohala.com/start/*.

Stevens, W.R. 1998. *UNIX Network Programming, Volume 1 (2nd edition): Networking APIs: Sockets and XTI*. Prentice Hall, Upper Saddle River, New Jersey.

Stevens, W.R. 1999. *UNIX Network Programming, Volume 2 (2nd edition): Interprocess Communications*. Prentice Hall, Upper Saddle River, New Jersey.

Stevens, W.R. 1994. *TCP/IP Illustrated, Volume 1: The Protocols*. Addison-Wesley, Reading, Massachusetts.

Stevens, W.R. 1996. *TCP/IP Illustrated, Volume 3: TCP for Transactions, HTTP, NNTP, and the UNIX Domain Protocols*. Addison-Wesley, Reading, Massachusetts.

Stevens, W.R., Fenner, B., and Rudoff, A.M. 2004. *UNIX Network Programming, Volume 1 (3rd edition): The Sockets Networking API*. Addison-Wesley, Boston, Massachusetts.

> Source code for this edition is available at *http://www.unpbook.com/*.
> In most cases where we make reference to [Stevens et al., 2004] in this book, the same material can also found in [Stevens, 1998], the preceding edition of *UNIX Network Programming, Volume 1*.

Stevens, W.R., and Rago, S.A. 2005. *Advanced Programming in the UNIX Environment (2nd edition)*. Addison-Wesley, Boston, Massachusetts.

Stewart, R.R., and Xie, Q. 2001. *Stream Control Transmission Protocol (SCTP)*. Addison-Wesley, Reading, Massachusetts.

Stone, J., and Partridge, C. 2000. "When the CRC and the TCP Checksum Disagree," *Proceedings of SIGCOMM 2000*.

> *http://dl.acm.org/citation.cfm?doid=347059.347561*

Strang, J. 1986. *Programming with Curses*. O'Reilly, Sebastopol, California.

Strang, J., Mui, L., and O'Reilly, T. 1988. *Termcap & Terminfo (3rd edition)*. O'Reilly, Sebastopol, California.

Tanenbaum, A.S. 2007. *Modern Operating Systems (3rd edition)*. Prentice Hall, Upper Saddle River, New Jersey.

Tanenbaum, A.S. 2002. *Computer Networks (4th edition)*. Prentice Hall, Upper Saddle River, New Jersey.

Tanenbaum, A.S., and Woodhull, A.S. 2006. *Operating Systems: Design And Implementation (3rd edition)*. Prentice Hall, Upper Saddle River, New Jersey.

Torvalds, L.B., and Diamond, D. 2001. *Just for Fun: The Story of an Accidental Revolutionary*. HarperCollins, New York, New York.

Tsafrir, D., da Silva, D., and Wagner, D. "The Murky Issue of Changing Process Identity: Revising 'Setuid Demystified'," *;login: The USENIX Magazine*, June 2008.

> *http://www.usenix.org/publications/login/2008-06/pdfs/tsafrir.pdf*

Vahalia, U. 1996. *UNIX Internals: The New Frontiers*. Prentice Hall, Upper Saddle River, New Jersey.

van der Linden, P. 1994. *Expert C Programming–Deep C Secrets*. Prentice Hall, Englewood Cliffs, New Jersey.

Vaughan, G.V., Elliston, B., Tromey, T., and Taylor, I.L. 2000. *GNU Autoconf, Automake, and Libtool*. New Riders, Indianapolis, Indiana.

> *http://sources.redhat.com/autobook/*

Viega, J., and McGraw, G. 2002. *Building Secure Software*. Addison-Wesley, Reading, Massachusetts.

Viro, A. and Pai, R. 2006. "Shared-Subtree Concept, Implementation, and Applications in Linux," *Proceedings of the Ottawa Linux Symposium 2006*.

> *http://www.kernel.org/doc/ols/2006/ols2006v2-pages-209-222.pdf*

Watson, R.N.M. 2000. "Introducing Supporting Infrastructure for Trusted Operating System Support in FreeBSD," *Proceedings of BSDCon 2000*.

> *http://www.trustedbsd.org/trustedbsd-bsdcon-2000.pdf*

Williams, S. 2002. *Free as in Freedom: Richard Stallman's Crusade for Free Software*. O'Reilly, Sebastopol, California.

Wright, G.R., and Stevens, W.R. 1995. *TCP/IP Illustrated, Volume 2: The Implementation*. Addison-Wesley, Reading, Massachusetts.

INDEX

The following conventions are used in the index:

- Library function and system call prototypes are indexed with a subentry labeled *prototype*. Normally, you'll find the main discussion of a function or system call in the same location as the prototype.

- Definitions of C structures are indexed with subentries labeled *definition*. This is where you'll normally find the main discussion of a structure.

- Implementations of functions developed in the text are indexed with a subentry labeled *code of implementation*.

- Instructional or otherwise interesting examples of the use of functions, variables, signals, structures, macros, constants, and files in example programs are indexed with subentries labeled *example of use*. Not all instances of the use of each interface are indexed; instead, just a few examples that provide useful guidance are indexed.

- Diagrams are indexed with subentries labeled *diagram*.

- The names of example programs are indexed to make it easy to find an explanation of a program that is provided in the source code distribution for this book.

- Citations referring to the publications listed in the bibliography are indexed using the name of the first author and the year of publication, in an entry of the form *Name (Year)*—for example, Rochkind (1985).

- Items beginning with nonalphabetic characters (e.g., /dev/stdin, _BSD_SOURCE) are sorted before alphabetic items.

ANSI (American National Standards
Institute), 11
ANSI C, 11
Anzinger, G., xli
application binary interface, 118, 867
ar command, 834
archive, 834
ARG_MAX constant, 214
argc argument to *main()*, 31, 123
argv argument to *main()*, 31, 118, 123,
124, 214, 564, 567
diagram, 123
example of use, 123
ARP (Address Resolution Protocol), 1181
ARPA (Advanced Research Projects
Agency), 1180
ARPANET, 1180
asctime(), 16, 191, 657
diagram, 188
example of use, 192, 199
prototype, 191
asctime_r(), 191, 658
ASN.1, 1200
ASU constant, 298, 594, 928
async-cancel-safe function, 680
asynchronous I/O, POSIX, 613,
1327, 1347
async-signal-safe function, 425–428
AT_EACCESS constant, 365
AT_FDCWD constant, 290, 366
AT_REMOVEDIR constant, 365
AT_SYMLINK_FOLLOW constant, 365, 366
AT_SYMLINK_NOFOLLOW constant, 290, 365, 366
atexit(), 532, 534–535, 866
example of use, 537, 915, 960, 1393
prototype, 534
atomic_append.c, 1425
atomicity, 90–92, 465
when accessing shared variables, 631
Austin Common Standards Revision
Group, 13
Autoconf program, 219, 1444
automatic variables, 116, 122
A/UX, 5
awk program, 574, 1437
AXSIG constant, 594

B

B programming language, 2
Bach (1986), 250, 278, 521, 530, 919,
1422, 1437
Bach, M., 1437
background process group, 700, 708, 714
diagram, 701, 717
bad_exclusive_open.c, 90

bad_longjmp.c, 1426
bad_symlink.c, 1428, 1429
basename(), 370–372, 657
example of use, 371
prototype, 370
bash (Bourne again shell), 25
baud, 1316
bcopy(), 1166
BCPL programming language, 2
Becher, S., xli
become_daemon.c, 770
become_daemon.h, 770
becomeDaemon(), 769–771
code of implementation, 770–771
example of use, 774, 1241, 1244
prototype, 769
Bell Laboratories, 2
Benedyczak, K., xli
Berkeley Internet Name Domain (BIND),
1210, 1437
Berkeley Software Distribution, 4, 7–8
bg shell command, 715
diagram, 717
Bhattiprolu (2008), 608, 1437
Bhattiprolu, S., 1437
Biddle, R.L., xl
Biederman, E.W., 1437
big-endian byte order, 1198
diagram, 1198
binary semaphores, 988–991
binary_sems.c, 990
binary_sems.h, 989
BIND (Berkeley Internet Name Domain),
1210, 1437
bind mount, 272–274
bind(), 345, 426, 1152, 1153–1154, 1155
diagram, 1156, 1160
example of use, 1166, 1168, 1172, 1173,
1176, 1208, 1222, 1229
prototype, 1153
Bishop (2003), 795, 1437
Bishop (2005), 795, 1437
Bishop, M., 795, 1437
Black, D., 1194
Blaess, C., xxxvi
blkcnt_t data type, 64, 280
casting in *printf()* calls, 107
blksize_t data type, 64, 280
block device, 252, 282
block groups (*ext2* file system), 256
Boolean data type, 51
boot block, 256
BOOT_TIME constant, 820, 822
Borisov (2005), 300, 1438
Borisov, N., 1438

FUSE (Filesystem in Userspace), 255, 267
fuser command, 342
futex (fast user space mutex), 605, 607, 638, 1438, 1439
futex(), 638, 1090
   interrupted by signal, 444
   interrupted by stop signal, 445
FUTEX_WAIT constant, 444, 445
futimens(), 15, 286, 426
futimes(), 15, 286, 288–289, 426
   prototype, 289

G

gai_strerror(), 1217–1218
   prototype, 1218
Gallmeister (1995), 222, 512, 751, 1087, 1327, 1439
Gallmeister, B.O., 1439
Gamin, 375
Gammo (2004), 1374, 1439
Gammo, L., 1439
Gancarz (2003), 1422, 1439
Gancarz, M., 1439
Garfinkel (2003), 20, 795, 1439
Garfinkel, S., 1439
gather output, 102
gcore (*gdb*) command, 448, 1430
gcvt(), 656, 657
gdb program, 1442
General Public License (GPL), 5
get_current_dir_name(), 364
get_num.c, 59
get_num.h, 59
get_robust_list(), 801
get_thread_area(), 692
getaddrinfo(), 1205, 1213–1217
   diagram, 1215
   example of use, 1221, 1224, 1228, 1229
   prototype, 1213
GETALL constant, 971, 972
   example of use, 974
getc_unlocked(), 657
getchar_unlocked(), 657
getconf command, 215
getcontext(), 442
getcwd(), 363–364
   prototype, 363
getdate(), 196, 657
getdate_r(), 196
getdents(), 352
getdomainname(), 230
getdtablesize(), 215
getegid(), 172–173, 426
   prototype, 173

getenv(), 127–128, 657
   example of use, 1392
   prototype, 127
geteuid(), 172–173, 426
   prototype, 173
getfacl command, 325
getfattr command, 312
getfsent(), 263
getgid(), 172–173, 426
   prototype, 173
getgrent(), 161, 657
getgrgid(), 158–159, 657
   example of use, 160
   prototype, 158
getgrgid_r(), 158, 658
getgrnam(), 158–159, 657
   example of use, 160
   prototype, 158
getgrnam_r(), 158, 658
getgroups(), 179, 426
   example of use, 183
   prototype, 179
gethostbyaddr(), 16, 656, 657, 1205, 1231–1232
   prototype, 1231
gethostbyname(), 16, 656, 657, 1205, 1231–1232,
   example of use, 1233
   prototype, 1231
gethostbyname_r(), 658
gethostent(), 657
gethostname(), 230
getInt(), 58–59
   code of implementation, 60–61
   prototype, 58
getitimer(), 16, 481
   example of use, 483
   prototype, 481
getlogin(), 657, 825, 826
   prototype, 825
getlogin_r(), 658, 825
getLong(), 58–59
   code of implementation, 60
   prototype, 58
getmntent(), 263
getmsg(), 673
getnameinfo(), 1205, 1218–1219
   example of use, 1230
   prototype, 1218
GETNCNT constant, 972
   example of use, 974
getnetbyaddr(), 657
getnetbyname(), 657
getnetent(), 657